Fodor's 2000

W9-CTM-173

California

Fodor's Travel Publications, Inc. • New York, Toronto, London, Sydney, Auckland
www.fodors.com/california

CONTENTS

MAPS

Circled letters in text correspond to letters on the photographs. For more information on the sights pictured, turn
to the indicated page number Ⓐ⟩ on each photograph.

DESTINATION
CALIFORNIA

California is too big, too diverse, too full of charming surprises
to be a single state. You do not visit just one California. You choose
a particular California. If you are looking for natural beauty, the
Big Sur coastline isn't a bad place to start, but it's only one
gem on a long, long list. If you favor worldly pleasures, San Francisco and the Wine Country beckon. Sybarites needing a fix are
well advised to head to Palm Springs. Aficionados of the edgy
love L.A. Wherever you go in
the Golden State, there's plenty
to fall in love with: very few visitors go home unsmitten.

THE NORTH COAST

Ⓐ▷ 48 Ⓑ▷ 53

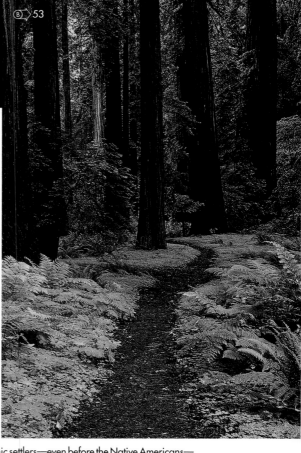

The shore running north from San Francisco to Oregon is a place for retreat—for restoring the soul. But although its pleasures are low-key, they are hardly unrefined. Elegant country inns, cozy Victorian B&Bs, and rustic lodges provide comfortable bases for touring. Many are destinations in themselves. Architecture hints at the area's history, as in Ⓐ**Mendocino** and other towns that dot the coast, which have a New England flavor. Some of their founders built out of nostalgia, bringing classic Americana to the continent's edge as a tonic for homesickness. But before them, before the missionaries and the Hispanic settlers—even before the Native Americans—there was the land and its beauty. Sample it at Ⓑ**Humboldt Redwoods State Park,** whose majestic trees inspire awe, even reverence, and at Stinson Beach

Ⓒ▷ 39

and Ⓒ**Point Reyes National Seashore.** All that beautiful coastline makes for excellent whale-watching, as well. If no Gold Rush had built San Francisco, if Los Angeles were still a bunch of orange groves in search of a freeway, this glory would still be worth the trip.

The earth's molten inner cauldron shaped this region, whose landscape is defined by reminders of ancient volcanic activity. Most notable is Ⓑ**Mount Shasta,** a dormant volcano that tops 14,000 feet. Eerie folklore surrounds the peak, mythology about its special powers. But its size and beauty are fantastical enough.

THE FAR NORTH

Tramping up it in summer and schussing down it in winter are two of the joys of being here. Anglers and boaters flock to Ⓐ**Lake Shasta** for its many watery diversions. Houseboating is popular. At Lassen Volcanic National Park, steam is the theme, especially along Ⓒ**Bumpass Hell Trail,** a paradise of hot springs, steam vents, and mud pots waiting to be discovered by hikers with a sense of wonder. Note that Mount Lassen is still active— it last went off in 1914—but if the Far North is your kind of place, you're probably not the kind of person to worry about a little magma under your feet.

Ⓑ 68

Ⓒ 67

(A) 92   (B) 92

THE WINE COUNTRY

(C) 87

America's answer to Tuscany, California's Wine Country—Napa and Sonoma counties—looks and feels like its Italian counterpart, with its rolling hills and soft Mediterranean climate. Wines made here have long won awards and have made the area a force in the industry and a vibrant destination for food-and-wine lovers. Don't think you need a cultivated palate to enjoy yourself here, however. Local wine makers such as (A)**Sebastiani Vineyards** happily educate the uninitiated during tours and in their tasting rooms. If you're lucky you might arrive in time to see the grape harvest at (D)**Domaine Chandon** or elsewhere. Whenever you visit, you will be greeted by row upon row of vines and wonderful food in scores of superb restaurants. No wonder the West Coast headquarters of the (E)**Culinary Institute of America** is located in St. Helena. You may not want to take its courses, but you can *order* a few courses at the institute's Wine Spectator Greystone Restaurant. The good life is also a hallmark of local inns and spas, including Rutherford's (C)**Auberge du Soleil**

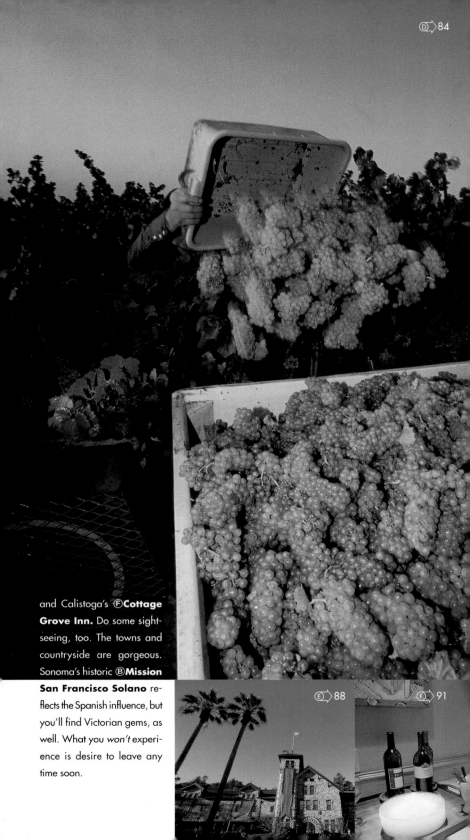

and Calistoga's Ⓕ**Cottage Grove Inn.** Do some sightseeing, too. The towns and countryside are gorgeous. Sonoma's historic Ⓑ**Mission San Francisco Solano** reflects the Spanish influence, but you'll find Victorian gems, as well. What you *won't* experience is desire to leave any time soon.

Ⓔ 88

Ⓕ 91

SAN
FRANCISCO

Ⓐ〉103

This is simply the most beautiful city in the United States, and one of the most beautiful in the world. It is to the urban landscape what Yosemite is to the natural one. As a visitor you can rub elbows with its lucky citizens in the Ⓐ**cable cars** that negotiate hilly Hyde Street with aplomb, and admire the rosy rococo Ⓑ**Palace of Fine Arts.** In sun or fog, drive or walk across the landmark Ⓒ**Golden Gate Bridge** and take in sweeping views of the city from atop Coit Tower. Just strolling

Ⓑ〉131

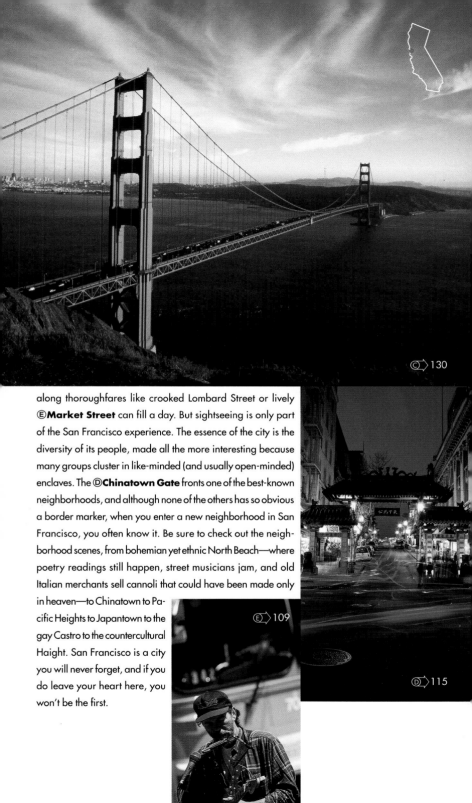

©> 130

along thoroughfares like crooked Lombard Street or lively
©**Market Street** can fill a day. But sightseeing is only part
of the San Francisco experience. The essence of the city is the
diversity of its people, made all the more interesting because
many groups cluster in like-minded (and usually open-minded)
enclaves. The ©**Chinatown Gate** fronts one of the best-known
neighborhoods, and although none of the others has so obvious
a border marker, when you enter a new neighborhood in San
Francisco, you often know it. Be sure to check out the neighborhood scenes, from bohemian yet ethnic North Beach—where
poetry readings still happen, street musicians jam, and old
Italian merchants sell cannoli that could have been made only
in heaven—to Chinatown to Pa-
cific Heights to Japantown to the
gay Castro to the countercultural
Haight. San Francisco is a city
you will never forget, and if you
do leave your heart here, you
won't be the first.

Ⓔ> 109

Ⓓ> 115

11

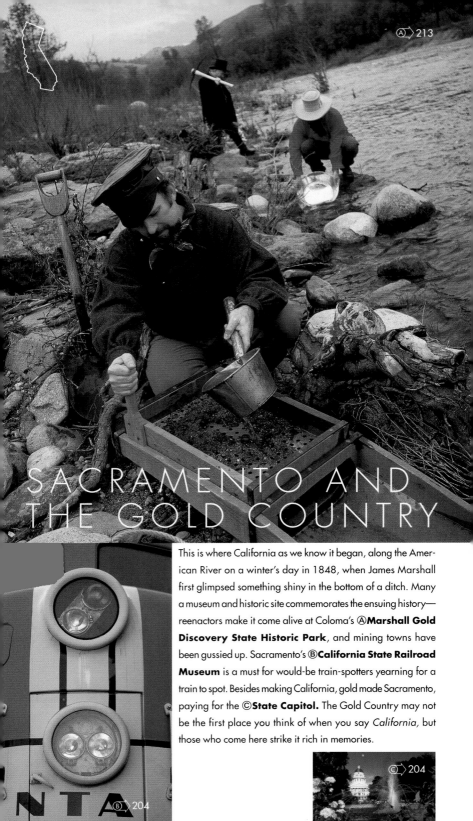

SACRAMENTO AND THE GOLD COUNTRY

This is where California as we know it began, along the American River on a winter's day in 1848, when James Marshall first glimpsed something shiny in the bottom of a ditch. Many a museum and historic site commemorates the ensuing history—reenactors make it come alive at Coloma's Ⓐ**Marshall Gold Discovery State Historic Park**, and mining towns have been gussied up. Sacramento's Ⓑ**California State Railroad Museum** is a must for would-be train-spotters yearning for a train to spot. Besides making California, gold made Sacramento, paying for the Ⓒ**State Capitol.** The Gold Country may not be the first place you think of when you say *California*, but those who come here strike it rich in memories.

Ⓑ ▷ 204

Ⓒ ▷ 204

LAKE TAHOE

Ⓐ 235

Ⓑ 235

Deep, clear, intensely blue-green, and surrounded by forests, this lake straddling the California–Nevada border is one of North America's prettiest alpine lakes. That strict environmental controls have kept it pristine is no small feat, considering its popularity. If you're staying on the California side you can golf, fish, hike or ski at Ⓒ**Squaw Valley, USA,** or pop in to see Ⓐ**Vikingsholm,** an authentic replica of a 1,200-year-old Viking castle, built in 1929 on the shore of jewel-like Ⓑ**Emerald Bay** by a woman of means. On the Nevada side, gambling is king and casinos abound, but once you leave the bright lights of the gaming tables, natural wonders surround you again.

Ⓒ 237

THE SIERRA NATIONAL PARKS

At Yosemite, Kings Canyon, and Sequoia national parks, nature has outdone itself, carving magnificent glacial valleys out of a landscape sized for titans. To appreciate the scale of Ⓐ**Yosemite Valley,** consider El Capitan, rising 3,593 feet above the valley, the cliff-sided giant known as Half Dome, and Yosemite Falls, North America's tallest cascade. Even the trees are Bunyanesque—every park has a sequoia grove. Not far from Yosemite are the ghost town of Bodie, Mammoth Mountain ski area, and Ⓑ**Mono Lake,** where tufa formations, resembling giants' fingers, seem borrowed from some other planet.

Ⓑ▷259

Ⓐ 292

Don't race through the San Joaquin Valley on your way to the national parks. California's farm country is a face of the state worth knowing, with attractions ranging from Victorian houses to rafting on the Ⓐ**Kern River.** Parts of the river test experts; others are forgiving enough for children to enjoy. To stoke up for the

Ⓑ 290

THE SAN JOAQUIN VALLEY

white water, munch on fresh strawberries and other fruit, sold up and down the Valley at roadside stands in Ⓑ**Bakersfield,** Fresno, and beyond. What you find in the produce aisles back home probably comes from here—asparagus, apples, grapes, oranges. The vast agricultural tracts of the Valley can be beautiful, and markets and festivals celebrating their bounty are numerous. Stop and linger, and you may well want to return.

For many the coast between Carmel and Santa Cruz presents California at its best. The many things that make the state so wonderful to visit converge here—from history, on view at the Ⓐ**Carmel Mission,** to

Ⓐ 318

natural splendor, unforgettable on 17-Mile Drive as it meanders along the Pacific past wind-bent cypress trees, to Ⓓ**Pebble Beach,** where golfing pilgrims come to perform their devotions. The coastal towns will charm you with great looks, great food, and occasional quirkiness. If the monarch butterflies clustered on the pine and eucalyptus trees in Ⓑ**Pacific Grove** every winter don't entice you, nothing will. John Steinbeck immortalized

MONTEREY BAY

Monterey's Cannery Row in his 1945 novel of the same name. Today the sardine canneries are gone, and the fantastic Ⓒ**Monterey Bay Aquarium,** re-creating the local marine habitat, stands on a street that Steinbeck would hardly recognize.

Ⓑ 312

Ⓒ 307

Ⓓ 317

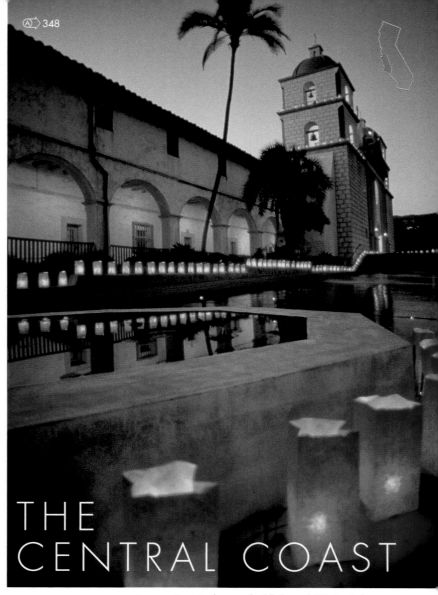

THE
CENTRAL COAST

Between Santa Barbara and wildly beautiful Big Sur is the staggeringly scenic Highway 1. The velvety Coastal Range rises from the pavement on the east; to the west the Pacific drops precipitously, spreading as far as the eye can see in stupendous vistas. Santa Barbara manages to blend sophistication and tranquillity, stimulation and repose, in perfect doses. Ⓐ**Mission Santa Barbara** is just one of the graceful sights, and newspaper baron William Randolph Hearst's Ⓑ**Hearst Castle** wows one and all.

Ⓑ 336

LOS ANGELES

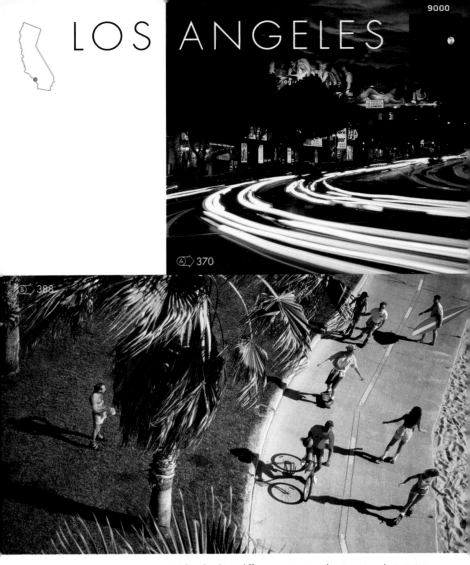

Ⓐ 370

Ⓑ 388

It's hard to be indifferent to Los Angeles. Love it or hate it, it is a city unlike any other. Start forming your own impressions along Ⓐ**Sunset Boulevard.** It'll take you through Hollywood all the way to the sea, through the city's multiple layers, including wealthy Bel-Air and Beverly Hills. The sheer length of the drive underscores the city's sprawl. When you get to the ocean you can experience the beach culture that's so integral to life here. Check out Ⓑ**Venice Boardwalk,** where Angelenos surf, skate, bodybuild, and stage some of the wackiest street theater in the galaxy. Most of it is fun and none of it is buttoned-down. Also pure L.A. are theme parks like

Ⓒ 390

Ⓒ**Universal Studios Hollywood,** where you can "live the movies," from *Jurassic Park* to *Back to the Future,* and Ⓓ **Mann's Chinese Theatre,** where celebrities press their hands and other body parts into cement for posterity. When you're ready for shopping (high-class or funky), nightlife (from alternative to swing), or dining (from *taquerías* to Asian-fusion innovators), you'll find it in L.A. Amid the freeways and smog, the city's numerous beauty spots sometimes come as a surprise—at the Richard Meier–designed Ⓔ**Getty Center,** or at sunset, when a cinematic glow bathes Ⓕ**Griffith Park Observatory** and ribbons of violet serve as backdrop for the twinkling town. Be here then, and you may think you're surveying a city of angels.

Ⓓ▷376

Ⓔ▷383

Ⓕ▷373

Ⓐ 480

ORANGE COUNTY

Ⓑ 467

©Disney Enterprises, Inc.

If Orange County issued its own license plates, they would have to read: "Quintessential Southern California." The glitz of L.A. drops off here, and what remains is an uncomplicated lifestyle with a serious focus on fun in the sun. The biggest draw for most visitors is Ⓑ**Disneyland,** the only one of Disney's magic kingdoms built while Walt was still alive. With its diminutive, idyllic Main Street and moss-hung New Orleans Square, it has an ineffable charm, a certain softness that you don't find in other Disney realms. For thrill rides, head for another vintage theme park nearby, Knott's Berry Farm, whose founder also created the boysenberry. Meanwhile, the Pacific exerts an irresistible pull. Some neighborhoods in Orange County's beach towns could be sisters to Beverly Hills and are well worth a gawk. Here and elsewhere on the coast, between ©**Laguna Beach** and Ⓐ**Huntington Beach,** beach life is thrilling. It's the perfect opportunity to work on your tan or learn to surf among masters.

© 485

SAN DIEGO

Ⓐ▷ 547

California's beautiful southernmost city is also its most laid-back, rendered deliciously mellow, almost like a small town, by near-perfect weather. The sun shines perpetually on lush Balboa Park, on Shamu's Sea World home, on Pacific-pounded strands like Ⓐ**Mission Beach** and pretty La Jolla's Black's Beach. Residents of the San Diego Zoo, one of the world's greats, love the weather, too. So do denizens of the zoo's Ⓑ**Wild Animal Park,** in nearby Escondido. Sunshine also blessed early California; historic sites such as Old Town and the ©**Mission San Diego de Alcalá,** Father Junípero Serra's first California outpost (1769), recall the days.

© ▷ 520

Ⓑ ▷ 561

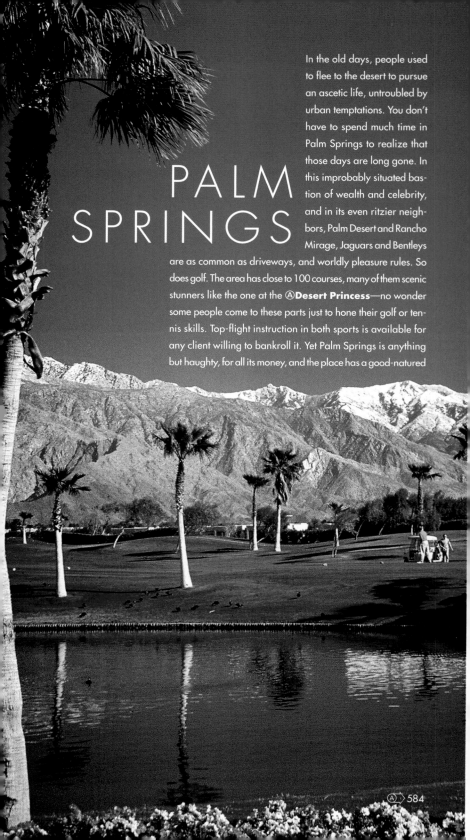

PALM
SPRINGS

In the old days, people used to flee to the desert to pursue an ascetic life, untroubled by urban temptations. You don't have to spend much time in Palm Springs to realize that those days are long gone. In this improbably situated bastion of wealth and celebrity, and in its even ritzier neighbors, Palm Desert and Rancho Mirage, Jaguars and Bentleys are as common as driveways, and worldly pleasure rules. So does golf. The area has close to 100 courses, many of them scenic stunners like the one at the Ⓐ**Desert Princess**—no wonder some people come to these parts just to hone their golf or tennis skills. Top-flight instruction in both sports is available for any client willing to bankroll it. Yet Palm Springs is anything but haughty, for all its money, and the place has a good-natured

Ⓐ⟩ 584

spirit that you'll sense at venues like the ⒟**Fabulous Palm Springs Follies,** a revue starring retired showgirls, singers, and other entertainers. Life here, or just vacation, can also be downright sybaritic, especially if you're staying at one of the many luxury resorts, where you can guiltlessly abandon yourself to total pampering. (If you don't, what's the point?) Understand that the pampering has a serious ob-

ⓐ 588

ⓒ 580

jective: to restore you physically, emotionally, and, yes, even spiritually. At ⒞**La Quinta,** for instance, you can receive sacred stone therapy, which uses techniques practiced originally by Native Americans. Connecting with the desert's wild beauty at ⒝**Joshua Tree National Park** can be restorative as well. The slanting late-afternoon or early morning light casts a tint (some say a spell) on the boulders and on the strange, towering trees that give the park its name, lending an otherworldly (some say supernatural) texture to the moment. Decide for yourself.

ⓓ 584

THE MOJAVE DESERT AND DEATH VALLEY

Ⓐ 600

A trip to Ⓐ**Death Valley** and the Mojave Desert may sound like the stuff of comedy routines, but discerning travelers who have experienced the great empty spaces of this stirring wilderness and heard the lore of the hardy late-19th-century mule teams at Furnace Creek know better. If you decide to join them, follow a few cardinal rules: Start at a visitor center and collect all the pamphlets. Read what they say and *follow the instructions*. Always have a full tank of gas. Bring water and keep drinking, even when you're not thirsty. Wear a hat. Don't expect to move too fast at mid-

Ⓒ 601

Ⓑ 604

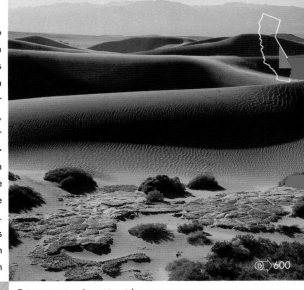

day. The desert, which so amply rewards the wise, can have serious consequences for the foolish. After your return to civilization, if you thirst for culture, visit Marta Becket, proprietress and performer at Ⓑ **Marta Becket's Amargosa Opera House** in Death Valley Junction. But do make reservations; she fills the house before she brings it down. Becket's oasis of the arts is no less improbable (which is to say, *extremely*) than

Ⓓ▷600

Ⓔ▷607

Ⓒ **Scotty's Castle,** a Moorish mansion built in 1924. See Ⓔ **Calico Ghost Town,** once a wealthy silver mining center. If it's vast scenery you're looking for, check out the sand dunes near Ⓓ **Stovepipe Wells Village,** or the Trona Pinnacles, the brilliantly colored Artists Palette, the magnificently panoramic Dante's View, or archetypal Red Rock Canyon State Park. To really get away from it all, take in the desolate salt flats at Ⓕ **Badwater,** 282 feet below sea level. On land in the Western Hemisphere, at least, you can't sink any lower than this. And, if you visit in the summer, you can't get much hotter.

Ⓕ▷603

GREAT ITINERARIES

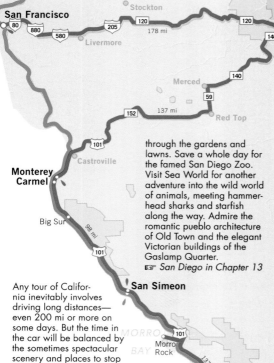

Sacramento
Stockton
San Francisco
80 880 580
205 120 178 mi 120
Livermore
Merced
140
59
152 137 mi
Red Top
101
Castroville
Monterey
Carmel
Big Sur 98 mi
101
San Simeon
MORRO
BAY 101
Morro
Rock
137 mi
247 mi
101
Santa Barbara
101
Yosemite
National Park
140
Santa
Monica
101 110 mi
1 90 mi Malibu
1
Anacapa
Island
Venice

through the gardens and lawns. Save a whole day for the famed San Diego Zoo. Visit Sea World for another adventure into the wild world of animals, meeting hammerhead sharks and starfish along the way. Admire the romantic pueblo architecture of Old Town and the elegant Victorian buildings of the Gaslamp Quarter.
☞ *San Diego in Chapter 13*

Any tour of California inevitably involves driving long distances—even 200 mi or more on some days. But the time in the car will be balanced by the sometimes spectacular scenery and places to stop along the way.

Highlights of California
11 days

California comprises so many different lands and people that to visit only one area would be to see only a single color in a rainbow. There is something tantalizing about life here that has as much to do with the silence of Yosemite as with the glitz of Hollywood. Tour some of the treasures of California, and you will soon understand why this is the Golden State.

SAN DIEGO
2 days. Start in Balboa Park, where you can visit more than a dozen museums and art galleries while strolling

ORANGE COUNTY
1 day. There is no place in the world quite like Disneyland. Step into Walt's fantasia for a day and experience the lightness of pure fun. As you continue to drive to Santa Barbara, you'll pass through Los Angeles.
☞ *Chapter 12*

Ⓐ 333

SANTA BARBARA
2 days. Framed by ocher mountains and a lapis ocean, Santa Barbara is a pleasant place to shop, eat, and wander along the beach. As you drive the Pacific Coast Highway northward you'll wind through grassy inland hills to the cool breezes of Morro Bay. Ancient and volcanic Morro Rock dominates the horizon here.
☞ *Santa Barbara in Chapter 10*

SAN SIMEON
1 day. Hearst Castle is nothing short of a fantasy. The main Casa Grande and its decadently named "cottages" (mansions in their own right) are decorated with museum-worthy art. Formal gardens, crystalline pools, and splendid terraces complete the grandeur.
☞ *San Simeon in Chapter 10*

MONTEREY AND CARMEL
3 days. As you drive the Pacific Coast Highway through Ⓐ Big Sur, delight in delicate waterfalls, dense redwood groves, and breathtaking coastal cliffs. This earthly beauty is a way of life in Carmel and Monterey, where the crashing ocean and twisted splendor of cypresses provide a backdrop for shops and restaurants. The 17-Mile Drive gives you a glimpse of the mansions and golf courses of Pebble Beach. Be prepared for the long drive from the coast to Yosemite.
☞ *Chapter 9*

YOSEMITE

2 days. The incomparable majesty of marvels like Half Dome and the sublime smell of sweet meadow air make Yosemite a world unto itself. Yosemite Valley is home to the park's most picturesque creations: gushing Yosemite Falls, proud and mighty El Capitan, and untamed Bridalveil Falls. The Mariposa Grove of Giant Sequoias is both humbling and inspiring. Sunrise and starlight from atop Glacier Point are sensational. From here, drive to San Francisco to end your trip.
☞ *Yosemite National Park in Chapter 7*

Beaches and Deserts
6 to 10 days

Southern California's beaches and deserts somehow produce a miracle of color and life. Black hills are striped with a rainbow of eroded earth; white sand is forever speckled with neon bikinis; and every spring, muted slopes of sage and shale give birth to a flurry of fuchsia and yellow flowers. Amid the kaleidoscope swirls a vibrant blend of surfers and starlets, jackrabbits and Joshua trees, and a nightly spectacle of city lights and starry skies. The horizon provides the most spectacular vision of all: Technicolor sunsets not even a postcard can capture. You may want to begin this tour in San Diego or end in Los Angeles.

PALM SPRINGS

2 or 3 days. Once a hideaway for Tinseltown stars, this oasis of green golf courses and extravagant homes stands alone in the midst of a subtle and delicate land. The view from the Tramway's 8,516-ft peak illuminates the startling contrast between Ⓑ Palm Springs and the slopes of the San Jacinto Mountains. Named after the biblical character for their prayer-like stances, the trees of Joshua Tree National Park are strikingly silhouetted against the open skies of this vast area.
☞ *Chapter 14*

BARSTOW

2 or 3 days. The Mojave Desert can look bleak from the road, but its subtle charms are entrancing. Go for a hike along one of the many trails to experience the musky smell of sage and mesquite and the tenacity of wildflowers rooted in crumbling soil. Death Valley National Park is the final frontier in unconventional beauty. Enjoy the area in the soft light of dawn or late afternoon to avoid intense temperatures. Consider spending a night at one of the campgrounds or hotels within the park; it's a fairly long drive back to Barstow.
☞ *Mojave Desert and Death Valley in Chapter 15*

Death Valley National Park

190

127

15

Barstow

157 mi

100 mi 40 Mojave Desert

15

114 mi

40 mi Joshua Tree National Park

Los Angeles
10 73 mi 62

26 mi 91 10

Knott's Berry Farm Disneyland Corona Palm Springs

ORANGE COUNTY 10

181 mi 15 86

5 93 mi 78 mi 78

79

8

San Diego

MEXICO

27

SANTA MONICA

1 or 2 days. The drive to Santa Monica Bay propels you out of the intensity of the desert toward the bright blue water. Sunbathe and swim on the white sands of Malibu. The boardwalk along Venice Beach is known for its daily parade of chain-saw jugglers and tattooed sun worshipers. Well-oiled bodybuilders pump iron at Venice's Muscle Beach, an open-air gym with Plexiglas walls that provide passersby a full view.
☞ *Santa Monica in Chapter 11*

SANTA BARBARA

1 or 2 days. Santa Barbara County offers a variety of coastal areas, the most popular and accessible of which is East Beach. The region's most captivating shorelines are within Channel Islands National Park and Marine Sanctuary, an expansive and undeveloped home to creatures including blue whales and endangered brown pelicans. For a day trip, take a cruise to Anacapa Island to admire lava tubes and sea caves and to watch seals basking at the base of 100-ft cliffs.
☞ *Santa Barbara in Chapter 10*

The Great Outdoors

9 to 12 days

If you've come to California looking for sun, sand, and surf, Northern California comes as a surprise. Towns here are remote and woodsy, colors are deep and intense rather than sun-washed. Residents of the northern coast and mountains have never disputed the image of California as a set of sunny beaches. They're happy to keep their emerald trees and sapphire seas a secret. San Francisco is the best city in which to begin and end this tour.

INVERNESS

2 days. Throughout Marin County, the California coast shows one of its most dramatic incarnations. Cliffs drop into secret coves. Waves spill over the horizon. Pelicans migrate from one volcanic sea stack to another. Stinson Beach is a placid stretch of white sand amid the chaos. Inland, the shade of Muir Woods National Monument offers ample room for contemplation. Point Reyes National Seashore is the undisputed jewel in the crown that is the Pacific Coast. Don't miss the black, white, and red sand beaches and beckoning lighthouse.
☞ *Southern Coastal Marin County in Chapter 1*

MENDOCINO

1 or 2 days.
North into Mendocino County, the coast is tamer but no less striking. Year-round blooms and Victorian buildings filled with shops, restaurants, and bed-and-breakfasts make Mendocino feel uniquely refined. If the weather is divine (which it can be at any time of year), take advantage of the local state parks' rugged and uncrowded shorelines.
☞ *Sonoma and Mendocino in Chapter 1*

NAPA

2 days. The hills of Napa and Sonoma counties offer wineries as varied and colorful as the vintages they produce. French castles and farmhouses mingle with long rows of grapevines. Vineyards offer distinctive wines in beautiful and friendly settings. Fine dining is a way of life.
☞ *The Napa Valley in Chapter 3*

SOUTH LAKE TAHOE

2 or 3 days. Although deep powdery snow is rightly the Lake Tahoe area's most famous commodity, outdoor adventure abounds year-round. From Crystal Bay you can bicycle, rock climb, and water-ski—or spend the day golfing. On the lake's southern shore, hike the steep trail

down to Vikingsholm for a tour of this elaborately decorated neo-Nordic mansion, then cool off in tropical-looking Emerald Bay. Even if you spend more time at the blackjack tables than outdoors, be sure to ride the Heavenly Tram for a panoramic view of the area, which is, well, heavenly.
☞ *South Lake Tahoe in Chapter 6*

YOSEMITE

2 or 3 days. Yosemite Valley offers the classic views immortalized by photographer Ansel Adams: Half Dome's glossy face, the stately grandeur of El Capitan, and Bridalveil and ©Yosemite Falls, whose only rivals for perfection are each other.
☞ *Yosemite National Park in Chapter 7*

Mendocino

128

118 mi

101

127 mi

12

1

NAPA COUNTY

SONOMA COUNTY

Napa

80

96 mi

Inverness

MARIN COUNTY

Point Reyes N S

34 mi

Muir Woods NM

Stinson Beach

1

San Francisco

80

880

580

280

San Jose

203 mi

17

Capitola

1

Castroville

Big Sur

©251

28

California with Kids

12 to 15 days

As a real-world land of make-believe, California seems to have been created just for children. Fantasy comes to life in castles, museums, and exotic animals. New fairy tales are created daily in the studios and streets of Hollywood. Check local newspapers for seasonal children's events.

SAN FRANCISCO

2 or 3 days. Seeing the city from a cable car is sure to thrill, and Coit Tower offers a scenic panorama. But high above the bay, the Golden Gate Bridge wins for best photo opportunity. Along the water, sample the chocolates that made Ghirardelli Square

Ⓓ⇨126

famous and bark back at the sea lions lounging at Pier 39. Ride a ferry to Ⓓ Alcatraz to see the island prison. Golden Gate Park's green pastures, woods, and water can offer a whole day of entertainment. If the weather doesn't cooperate, head inside to the Exploratorium or California Academy of Sciences for outrageous hands-on exhibits.
☞ *Chapter 4*

SAN SIMEON

2 or 3 days. Allow plenty of time to enjoy the Pacific Coast Highway's curves through temperate rain forests and salty seascapes as you drive south from San Francisco. While picnicking atop the craggy cliffs of Big Sur, keep your eyes peeled for otters, seals, and sea lions

surfing the waves below. Spend at least one afternoon daydreaming at Hearst Castle, a hilltop estate of unrivaled luxury. The drive to Los Angeles is long, so allow ample time.
☞ *San Simeon in Chapter 10*

LOS ANGELES

2 or 3 days. No visit is complete without a trip to Universal Studios for a behind-the-scenes look at the glamorous world of the movies. Night or day, stargaze for famous names along the Hollywood Walk of Fame. Haven't had your fill of celebrities yet? Seek out the rich and famous in Beverly Hills. Head to the Page Museum at La Brea Tar Pits and visit the onetime digs of woolly mammoths.
☞ *Chapter 11*

ORANGE COUNTY

2 days. Disneyland fulfills every kid's dreams. Knott's Berry Farm also offers diversion for the imagination, complete with international cuisine and lively shows recreating California history.
☞ *Chapter 12*

Ⓔ⇨492

SACRAMENTO

2 days. You won't strike it rich in the Gold Country, but you can catch the spirit of the Mother Lode at Marshall Gold Discovery State Historic Park. Along historic Highway 49, towns such as Sutter Creek maintain the charm of the area's colorful past. Save an afternoon to wander the streets of Old Sacramento. Ride a tugboat taxi and marvel at old locomotives in the California State Railroad Museum.
☞ *Chapter 5*

SAN DIEGO

2 days. In Ⓔ San Diego the first stop should be the San Diego Zoo. Wander the landscaped grounds and you're sure to find something you've never seen before, perhaps a two-headed corn snake or an East African bongo. Spend the next day at Sea World to see Shamu the killer whale and the world's largest collection of sharks.
☞ *Chapter 13*

Crystal Bay

Emerald Bay
Vikingsholm

Marshall
Gold Discovery
State Historic Park

Sacramento

Sutter Creek

Stockton

South Lake Tahoe

Yosemite National Park

San Simeon

To Los Angeles and San Diego

36 mi — 89
36 mi
28
207
49
164 mi
50
50
58 mi
395
114 mi
120
178 mi
205
120
120
120
247 mi

FODOR'S
CHOICE

Even with so many special places in California, Fodor's writer's and editors have their favorites. Here are a few that stand out.

BREATHTAKING SIGHTS

① **El Capitan and Half Dome, Yosemite.** El Capitan, the world's largest exposed granite monolith, and Half Dome, rising 4,733 ft above the valley floor with a 2,000-ft cliff on its fractured west side, are nothing short of mesmerizing. ☞ p. 254

Golden Gate Bridge Vista Point, Marin County. On a clear day San Francisco glistens from this vantage point at the bridge's north end. ☞ p. 130

Ⓗ **Highway 1, Big Sur to San Simeon.** This stretch of twisting coastal highway affords amazing ocean vistas. ☞ p. 333

Kings Canyon Highway. From late spring to early fall the stretch of Highway 180 in Kings Canyon National Park from Grant Grove to Cedar Grove is spectacular. Peer into the nation's deepest gorge and up to the High Sierra's gorgeous canyons. ☞ p. 269

La Jolla Cove at sunset. Always beautiful, it's never more splendid than when the setting sun gilds the cove and backlights the towering palms. ☞ p. 548

Mulholland Drive, Los Angeles. One of L.A.'s most famous thoroughfares winds through the Hollywood Hills, across the spine of the Santa Monica Mountains, almost to the Pacific. It's slow going, but the grand homes and the city and San Fernando Valley views are sensational. ☞ p. 390

17-Mile Drive, Pebble Beach. The wonders are both man-made and natural along this road between Pacific Grove and Carmel. Robert Louis Stevenson described the gnarled and twisted Monterey cypress en route as "ghosts fleeing before the wind." ☞ p. 317

Ⓒ **View from Emerald Bay Lookout, Lake Tahoe.** Massive glaciers carved this fjordlike bay millions of years ago. Famed for its jewel-like shape and colors, it surrounds Fannette, Tahoe's only island. Survey the glorious scene from the lookout. ☞ p. 235

HISTORIC BUILDINGS

Griffith Park Observatory and Planetarium, Los Angeles. One of the world's largest telescopes is open to the public for viewing every clear night. *Rebel Without a Cause* immortalized its planetarium. ☞ p. 373

Hearst Castle, San Simeon. This stunning pleasure palace towers over 127 acres at the heart of newspaper magnate William Randolph Hearst's 250,000-acre ranch. ☞ p. 336

Mann's Chinese Theatre, Hollywood. The former Grauman's Chinese is a fantasy of pagodas and temples. Check out the celebrity hand- and footprints in the courtyard pavement. ☞ p. 376

Ⓐ **Mission Santa Barbara.** Twin bell towers and Greco-Roman columns and statuary embellish the queen of the California missions. Established in 1786, it's still an active church. ☞ p. 348

Ⓕ **State Capitol, Sacramento.** With its lacy plasterwork, the rotunda of this 1869 structure is like a Fabergé egg. The 40-acre Capitol Park outside is one of the state's oldest gardens. ☞ p. 204

FLAVORS

Patina, Hollywood. Here, in one of L.A.'s best restaurants, the spare, elegant setting is as beguiling as Joachim Splichal's contemporary cuisine. $$$$ ☞ p. 405

Café Beaujolais, Mendocino. Peaceful, backwoods Mendocino charm pervades this cottage, and the cooking is great, to boot. The cross-cultural menu may include corn crepes filled with barbecued rock shrimp and served with avocado and blood-orange *pico de gallo*. $$$–$$$$ ☞ p. 49

Chez Panisse, Berkeley. The legendary Alice Waters still masterminds the culinary wizardry here. The prix-fixe menu in the formal restaurant changes daily; fare in the informal café is simpler and less expensive but no less exciting. $$–$$$$ ☞ p. 183

George's at the Cove, La Jolla. Come for the splendid love view in the elegant main dining room and for the wonderful fresh seafood. $$$ ☞ p. 527

Jardinière, San Francisco. One of the city's most talked-about restaurants is also the hot ticket before symphony, opera, and theater events. Chef Traci Des Jardins provides the creative touch. $$$ ☞ p. 142

Ⓑ **Montrio, Monterey.** If you like hearty fare with clean, strong flavors, don't miss this American bistro, all brick, rawhide, and wrought iron. $$–$$$ ☞ p. 308

RETREATS

Ⓔ **Château du Sureau, Oakhurst.** This fairy-tale castle is also home to Erna's Elderberry House restaurant, one of California's best. You may find it hard to tear yourself away to visit nearby Yosemite National Park. $$$$ ☞ p. 261

Ⓖ **Hotel Bel-Air, Bel-Air.** This ultra-luxurious escape in a secluded wooded canyon feels like a grand country home. To splurge, request a room with its own hot tub on the patio. $$$$ ☞ p. 427

Post Ranch Inn, Big Sur. In this indulgent hideaway, each room has its own hot tub, stereo, private deck, and massage table—in addition to dizzying Pacific or mountain views. $$$$ ☞ p. 334

Ⓓ **Ritz-Carlton, Laguna Niguel.** Hallmark Ritz-Carlton service and an unrivaled setting on the edge of the Pacific have made a star of this grand hotel with the feel of a Mediterranean country villa. $$$$ ☞ p. 488

Ⓙ **Hotel Monaco, San Francisco.** The whimsical postmodern Monaco stands out for its snappy public areas, comfortable rooms, and devotion to pampering its guests. $$$$ ☞ p. 158

1   THE NORTH COAST

From Muir Beach to Crescent City

Migrating whales and other sea mammals swim past the dramatic bluffs that make the 400 miles of shoreline north of San Francisco to the Oregon state line among the most photographed landscapes in the country. Along cypress- and redwood-studded Highway 1 you will find many small inns, uncrowded state beaches and parks, art galleries, and restaurants serving imaginative dishes that showcase locally produced ingredients.

By Marty
Olmstead

BETWEEN SAN FRANCISCO BAY and the Oregon state line lies the aptly named Redwood Empire, where national, state, and local parks welcome visitors year-round. The shoreline's natural attributes are self-evident, but the area is also rich in human history, having been the successive domain of Native American Miwoks and Pomos, Russian fur traders, Hispanic settlers, and more contemporary fishing folk and loggers. All have left visible legacies. Only a handful of towns in this sparsely populated region have more than 1,000 inhabitants.

Pleasures and Pastimes

Beaches
The waters of the Pacific Ocean along the North Coast are fine for seals, but most humans find the temperatures downright arctic. When it comes to spectacular cliffs and seascapes, though, the North Coast beaches are second to none. Explore tidal pools, watch for sea life, or dive for abalone. Don't worry about crowds: on many of these beaches you will have the sands largely to yourself.

Dining
Despite its small population, the North Coast lays claim to several well-regarded restaurants. Seafood is abundant, as are locally grown vegetables and herbs. In general, dining options are more varied near the coast than inland. Dress is usually informal, though dressy casual is the norm at some of the pricier establishments listed below.

CATEGORY	COST*
$$$$	over $50
$$$	$30–$50
$$	$20–$30
$	under $20

*per person for a three-course meal, excluding drinks, service, and 7¼% tax

Fishing
Depending on the season, you can fish for rockfish, salmon, and steelhead in the rivers. Charters leave from Fort Bragg, Eureka, and elsewhere for ocean fishing. There's particularly good abalone diving around Jenner, Fort Ross, Point Arena, Westport, and Trinidad.

Lodging
Restored Victorians, rustic lodges, country inns, and chic new hotels are among the accommodations available along the North Coast. In several towns there are only one or two places to spend the night; some of these lodgings are destinations in themselves. Make summer and weekend B&B reservations as far ahead as possible—rooms at the best inns often sell out months in advance.

CATEGORY	COST*
$$$$	over $175
$$$	$120–$175
$$	$80–$120
$	under $80

*All prices are for a standard double room, excluding 8%–10% tax.

Whale-Watching
From any number of excellent observation points along the coast, you can watch gray whales during their annual winter migration season or, in the summer and fall, blue or humpback whales. Another option

is a whale-watching cruise (☞ Contacts and Resources *in* the North Coast A to Z, *below*).

Exploring the North Coast

Exploring the northern California coast is easiest by car. Highway 1 is a beautiful, if sometimes slow and nerve-racking, drive. You'll want to stop frequently to appreciate the views, and there are many portions of the highway along which you won't drive faster than 20–40 mph. You can still have a fine trip even if you don't have much time, but be realistic and don't plan to drive too far in one day. The itineraries below proceed north from San Francisco.

Numbers in the text correspond to numbers in the margin and on the North Coast maps.

Great Itineraries

IF YOU HAVE 3 DAYS

Some of the finest redwoods in California are found less than 20 mi north of San Francisco in **Muir Woods National Monument** ①. After walking through the woods, stop for an early lunch in **Inverness** (on Sir Francis Drake Boulevard, northwest from Highway 1) or continue on Highway 1 to **Fort Ross State Historic Park** ⑦. Catch the sunset and stay the night in ⛺ **Gualala.** On day two, drive to ⛺ **Mendocino** ⑨. Spend the next day and a half browsing the many galleries, shops, historic sites, and beaches and parks of this cliffside enclave. Return to San Francisco via Highway 1, or the quicker (3½ hours, versus up to 5) and less winding route of Highway 128 east (off Highway 1 at the Navarro River, 10 mi south of Mendocino) to U.S. 101 south.

IF YOU HAVE 7 DAYS

Early on your first day, walk through **Muir Woods** ①. Then visit **Stinson Beach** ② for a walk on the shore and lunch. In springtime and early summer head north on Highway 1 to Bolinas Lagoon, where you can see bird nestings at **Audubon Canyon Ranch** ③. At other times of the year (or after you've visited the ranch) continue north on Highway 1. One-third of a mile beyond **Olema,** look for a sign marking the turnoff for the **Bear Valley Visitor Center** ⑤, the gateway to the **Point Reyes National Seashore.** Tour the reconstructed Miwok Indian village near the visitor center. Spend the night in nearby ⛺ **Inverness** or one of the other coastal Marin towns. The next day, stop at Goat Rock State Beach and **Fort Ross State Historic Park** ⑦ on the way to ⛺ **Mendocino** ⑨. On your third morning, head to **Fort Bragg** for a visit to the **Mendocino Coast Botanical Gardens** and possibly a trip on the *Skunk Train.* If you're in the mood to splurge, drive inland on Highway 1 to U.S. 101 north and spend the night at the Benbow Inn in ⛺ **Garberville.** Otherwise, linger in the Mendocino area and drive inland the next morning. On day four continue north through parts of **Humboldt Redwoods State Park** ⑪, including the Avenue of the Giants. Stop for the night in the Victorian village of ⛺ **Ferndale** ⑫ and visit the cemetery and the Ferndale Museum. On day five drive to ⛺ **Eureka** ⑬. Have lunch in Old Town, visit the shops, and get a feel for local marine life on a Humboldt Bay cruise. Begin day six with breakfast at the Samoa Cookhouse before driving to **Patrick's Point State Park** ⑮. Have a late lunch overlooking the harbor in **Trinidad** before returning to Eureka for the night. Return to San Francisco on day seven. The drive back takes six hours on U.S. 101; it's nearly twice as long if you take Highway 1.

When to Tour the North Coast

The North Coast is a year-round destination, though when you go determines what you will see. The migration of the Pacific gray whales

The North Coast (San Francisco to Fort Bragg)

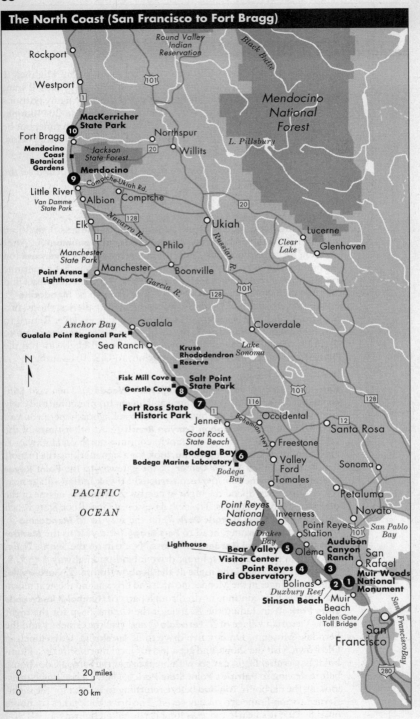

Rockport

Westport

Round Valley
Indian
Reservation

Black Butte

101

MacKerricher
State Park

10 Fort Bragg

Northspur

Mendocino
Coast
Botanical
Gardens

Jackson
State Forest

20

Willits

Mendocino
National
Forest

L. Pillsbury

9 Mendocino

Comptche-Ukiah Rd.

Little River

Van Damme
State Park

Albion

Comptche

Navarro R.

Elk

128

Philo

Ukiah

20

Clear
Lake

Lucerne

Glenhaven

Manchester
State Park

Point Arena
Lighthouse

Manchester

Boonville

Garcia R.

128

101

Russian R.

N

Anchor Bay

Gualala Point Regional Park

Gualala

Cloverdale

Sea Ranch

Kruse
Rhododendron
Reserve

Lake
Sonoma

Fisk Mill Cove

Gerstle Cove

Salt Point
State Park

8

7

Fort Ross State
Historic Park

116

101

128

Jenner

Occidental

12

Santa Rosa

Goat Rock
State Beach

Bohemian Hwy

Freestone

Bodega Bay

6

Bodega Marine Laboratory

Valley
Ford

Sonoma

Bodega
Bay

Tomales

Petaluma

PACIFIC

OCEAN

Point Reyes
National
Seashore

1

Inverness

Novato

San Pablo
Bay

Drakes
Bay

Point Reyes
Station

101

Lighthouse

Bear Valley
Visitor Center

5

Olema

Audubon
Canyon
Ranch

Point Reyes
Bird Observatory

4

3

San
Rafael

Bolinas

Muir Woods
National
Monument

Duxbury Reef

2

1

Stinson Beach

Muir
Beach

Golden Gate
Toll Bridge

San
Francisco

San
Francisco Bay

280

0   20 miles

0   30 km

The North Coast (Leggett to Crescent City)

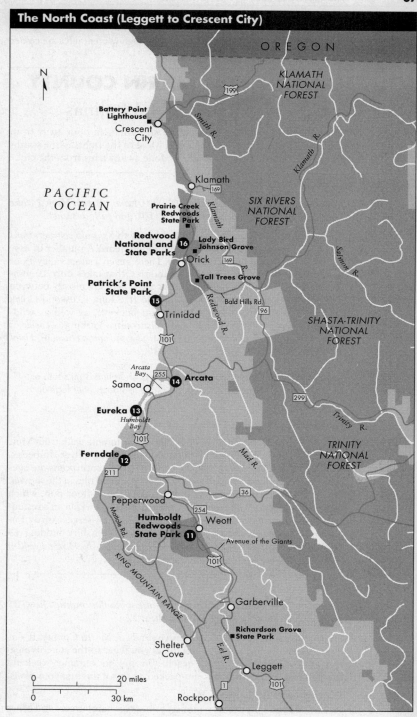

OREGON

KLAMATH NATIONAL FOREST

199

Smith R.

Battery Point Lighthouse
Crescent City

PACIFIC OCEAN

Klamath
169

SIX RIVERS NATIONAL FOREST

Klamath

Salmon R.

Prairie Creek Redwoods State Park

Redwood National and State Parks 16

Lady Bird Johnson Grove
Orick 169

Tall Trees Grove

Bald Hills Rd.
96

Redwood R.

SHASTA-TRINITY NATIONAL FOREST

Patrick's Point State Park 15
Trinidad

101

Arcata Bay
255
Samoa 14 Arcata

299

Eureka 13
Humboldt Bay

Trinity R.

Ferndale 12
211

101

TRINITY NATIONAL FOREST

Pepperwood

Mad R.

36

Humboldt Redwoods State Park 11
254
Weott

Avenue of the Giants

Mattole Rd.

101

KING MOUNTAIN RANGE

Garberville

Richardson Grove State Park

Shelter Cove

Eel R.

Leggett
101

0   20 miles
0   30 km

1

Rockport

is a wintertime phenomenon, roughly from mid-December to early April. In July and August, views are often obstructed by fog. The coastal climate is quite similar to San Francisco's, although winter nights are colder than in the city.

SOUTHERN COASTAL MARIN COUNTY
Muir Woods, Stinson Beach, and Bolinas

Much of the Marin County coastline is less than an hour away from San Francisco, but the pace is slower. Most of the sights in the southern coastal Marin area can easily be done as day trips from the city.

Muir Woods National Monument

★ ❶ *17 mi from San Francisco, north on U.S. 101 and west on Hwy. 1 (take Mill Valley/Stinson Beach exit off U.S. 101 and follow signs).*

The world's most popular grove of old-growth *Sequoia sempervirens* was one of the country's first national monuments. A number of easy hikes can be accomplished in an hour. There's even a short valley-floor trek, accessible to travelers with disabilities, that takes only 10 minutes to walk. The coast redwoods that grow here are mostly between 500 and 800 years old and as tall as 236 ft. Along Redwood Creek are other trees—live oak, madrone, and buckeye, as well as wildflowers (even in winter), ferns, and mushrooms. Parking is easier at Muir Woods before 10 AM and after 4 PM. ⊠ *Panoramic Hwy., off Hwy. 1,* ☎ *415/388–2595.* 🌫 *$2.* ☉ *Daily 8 AM–sunset.*

....
OFF THE   **MUIR BEACH –** Small but scenic, this patch of shoreline 3 mi south of
BEATEN PATH   Muir Woods off Highway 1 is a good place to stretch your legs and
                  gaze out at the Pacific.
....

Dining and Lodging

$$$–$$$$ ✕▥ **Pelican Inn.** This Tudor-style B&B is a five-minute walk from Muir
   ★   Beach. Rooms have Oriental rugs, English prints, velvet draperies, hanging tapestries, and half-tester beds. Even the bathrooms are special, with Victorian-style hardware and hand-painted tiles in the shower. Locals and tourists compete at darts in the ground-floor pub, which has a wide selection of brews, sherries, and ports. The Pelican's restaurant ($$–$$$; closed on Monday January–March) serves sturdy English fare, from fish-and-chips to prime rib and Yorkshire pudding. ⊠ *10 Pacific Way, at Hwy. 1, 94965,* ☎ *415/383–6000,* FAX *415/383–3424. 7 rooms. Restaurant, pub. Full breakfast. MC, V.*

Stinson Beach

❷ *8 mi from Muir Woods National Monument via Panoramic Hwy.; 25 mi from San Francisco, U.S. 101 to Hwy. 1.*

Stinson Beach has the most expansive sands in Marin County. It's as close (when the fog hasn't rolled in) as you'll get to the stereotypical feel of a southern California beach. On any hot summer weekend every road to Stinson Beach is jam-packed, so factor this into your plans.

Dining and Lodging

$–$$ ✕ **Sand Dollar.** This friendly, modest pub serves hamburgers and other sandwiches for lunch and decent seafood for dinner; there's an outdoor dining deck. ⊠ *Hwy. 1,* ☎ *415/868–0434. AE, D, MC, V.*

$-$$ ✕ **Stinson Beach Grill.** A great selection of beer and wine, art on the walls, and outdoor seating on a heated deck are among the draws here. The food is good, too. Seafood, including several types of oysters, is served at lunch and dinner. Pasta, lamb, chicken, and Southwestern specialties are on the evening menu. ⊠ *3465 Hwy. 1,* ☎ *415/868–2002. AE, MC, V.*

$$$–$$$$ ⬚ **Casa del Mar.** Extensive landscaping and white stucco gives this— one of Stinson's few inns—a decidedly Mediterranean ambience. Around the lobby fireplace and throughout the inn, the owner exhibits his large collection of works by local artists. Accommodations are on the small side, but light colors and the many windows create a feeling of spaciousness. ⊠ *37 Belvedere Ave., 94970,* ☎ *415/868–2124 or 800/ 552–2124. 6 rooms. AE, MC, V.*

Bolinas

❸   The **Audubon Canyon Ranch,** a 1,000-acre wildlife sanctuary along the Bolinas Lagoon, is open during courting and mating season, from mid-March to mid-July. Great blue herons and egrets are among the 60 species here. The egrets nest in the redwood trees in Schwarz Grove. Telescopes and bird-hide observation posts allow for easier viewing. A small museum surveys the geology and natural history of the region. ⊠ *4900 Hwy. 1, along Bolinas Lagoon,* ☎ *415/868–9244.* ⬚ *Donation requested.* ☉ *Mid-Mar.–mid-July, weekends 10–4.*

An unmarked road running west from Highway 1 about 2 mi beyond Audubon Canyon Ranch leads to the sleepy town of **Bolinas.** Don't expect a warm welcome: some residents of Bolinas are so wary of tourism that whenever the state tries to post road signs, they take them down.

Nightlife
Smiley's Schooner Saloon (41 Wharf Rd., ☎ 415/868–1311) hosts live music on Friday and Saturday.

POINT REYES NATIONAL SEASHORE
Duxbury Reef, Olema, and Inverness

The Point Reyes National Seashore, which borders the northern reaches of the Golden Gate National Recreation Area (☞ Chapter 4), is a great place for hiking to secluded beaches, viewing wildlife, and driving through rugged, rolling grasslands. Highlights include the ½-mi Earthquake Trail, which passes by what is believed to be the epicenter of the 1906 quake that destroyed much of San Francisco, and the late-19th-century Point Reyes Lighthouse, a good spot to watch for whales. Horses and mountain bikes are permitted on some trails. The towns of Olema, Point Reyes Station, and Inverness, all in or near the national seashore area, have dining, lodging, and recreational facilities.

Duxbury Reef Area

2 mi northwest of Bolinas off Mesa Rd.

❹   Birders love the **Point Reyes Bird Observatory,** a sanctuary and research center within the Point Reyes National Seashore but more easily accessible from Bolinas. The area harbors nearly 225 bird species. Banding (for identification purposes) occurs, weather permitting, Wednesday, Saturday, and Sunday. As you hike the trails, you're likely to see biologists banding the birds or measuring them. Trails pass waterfalls and a lake and lead to the national seashore. ⊠ *West on Mesa Rd. off Olema–*

Bolinas Rd., ☎ 415/868–0655. ▣ Free. ☉ Visitor center daily sunrise–sunset.

Mile-long **Duxbury Reef,** a nature preserve, is the largest shale intertidal reef in North America. Check a tide table if you plan to explore the reef, which is accessible only at low tide. Look for starfish, barnacles, sea anemones, purple urchins, limpets, sea mussels, and the occasional red and black abalone. ⊠ From Bolinas, take Mesa Rd. off Olema–Bolinas Rd.; turn left on Overlook Dr. and right on Elm Ave. to beach parking lot.

Olema

9 mi from Bolinas on Hwy. 1.

★ ❺ The Point Reyes National Seashore's **Bear Valley Visitor Center** has exhibits of park wildlife. The rangers here dispense advice about beaches, the Point Reyes Lighthouse, whale-watching, hiking trails, and camping. A reconstructed Miwok Indian village, a short walk from the visitor center, provides insight into the daily lives of the region's first human inhabitants. ⊠ Bear Valley Rd. west of Hwy. 1, ☎ 415/663–1092. ▣ Free. ☉ Weekdays 9–5, weekends 8–5.

Outdoor Activities and Sports

Many of the beaches in Point Reyes National Seashore are accessible off Bear Valley Road. **Limantour Beach** (⊠ End of Limantour Beach Rd.) is one of the most beautiful of Point Reyes sands; trails lead to other beaches north and south of here. **Trailhead Rentals** (⊠ 88 Bear Valley Rd., at Hwy. 1, ☎ 415/663–1958) supplies bicycles and binoculars. **Five Brooks Stables** (⊠ 8001 Hwy. 1, ☎ 415/663–1570) rents horses and equipment; from the stables, horseback trails wind through the Point Reyes woods and along the beaches.

Point Reyes Station

2 mi north of Olema on Hwy. 1.

The best place to find out what's going on in Point Reyes Station, a stop on the North Pacific Coast Narrow-Gauge Railroad until 1933, is Toby's Feed Barn. Toby's sells offbeat gifts (many festooned with cows) to tourists and locals and feed and grain to local farmers. There's a market on Main Street for picking up picnic supplies.

Lodging

$ 🏠 **Point Reyes Hostel.** These dorm-style lodgings in an old clapboard ranch house are a good deal for budget travelers. The family room is limited to families with children five and under and must be reserved well in advance. ⊠ Off Limantour Rd., Box 247, 94956, ☎ 415/663–8811. Shared kitchen. MC, V.

Shopping

Gallery Route One (⊠ 11101 Hwy. 1, ☎ 415/663–1347), a nonprofit cooperative, shows the works of area artists.

Inverness

4 mi from Point Reyes Station on Sir Francis Drake Blvd., northwest from Hwy. 1.

Inverness boomed after the 1906 earthquake when wealthy San Franciscans built summer homes in its hills. Today many of the structures serve as full-time residences or small inns. A deli, a grocery store, restaurants, and shops are along Sir Francis Drake Boulevard.

★ The **Point Reyes Lighthouse Visitors Center** is a 45-minute drive from Inverness, across rolling hills that resemble Scottish heath. Parking near the lighthouse is difficult on weekends during summer. The view alone persuades most people to make the effort of walking down—and then back up—the hundreds of steps from the cliff tops to the lighthouse below. ⊠ *Western end of Sir Francis Drake Blvd.,* ☎ *415/669–1534.* ☉ *Thurs.–Sun. 10–5 (steps close at 4:30).*

Dining and Lodging

$ ✕ **Grey Whale.** This casual place is a good stop for pizza, salad, pastries, and espresso. ⊠ *12781 Sir Francis Drake Blvd.,* ☎ *415/669–1244. MC, V.*

$$$–$$$$ ✕⊞ **Manka's.** Rustic wood-panel dining rooms glowing with candle-
★ light and piano music provide the setting for creative American cuisine. Specialties include line-caught fish, game such as caribou and pheasant that are grilled in the fireplace, and homemade desserts. Two of the four smallish guest rooms above the restaurant have private decks that look onto Tomales Bay. Rooms in the redwood annex and two cabins are also available. The restaurant, open for dinner only, is closed on Tuesday and Wednesday year-round and from Sunday through Thursday in January, February, and March. ⊠ *30 Calendar Way, 94937,* ☎ *415/669–1034. 14 rooms. Restaurant. Full breakfast. MC, V.*

$$$–$$$$ ⊞ **Blackthorne Inn.** There's no other inn quite like the Blackthorne, a combination of whimsy and sophistication in a woodsy setting. This imaginative structure has as its centerpiece a 3,500-square-ft deck with stairways to higher decks. The solarium was made with timbers from San Francisco wharves; the outer walls are salvaged doors from a railway station. A glass-sheathed octagonal tower called the Eagle's Nest crowns the inn. ⊠ *266 Vallejo Ave., Box 712, Inverness Park 94937,* ☎ *415/663–8621. 5 rooms, 2 with shared bath. Hot tub. Full breakfast. MC, V.*

$$$–$$$$ ⊞ **Ten Inverness Way.** This is the kind of place where guests sit around after breakfast and share tips for hiking the nearby Point Reyes National Seashore. The living room of this low-key inn has a stone fireplace and a player piano. The cozy rooms contain homespun touches like patchwork quilts, lived-in-looking antiques, and dormer ceilings with skylights. ⊠ *Inverness Way, Box 63, 94937,* ☎ *415/669–1648,* ℻ *415/669–7403. 5 rooms. Hot tub. Full breakfast. MC, V.*

Shopping

Shaker Shops West (⊠ 5 Inverness Way, ☎ 415/669–7256) carries fine reproduction Shaker furniture and gift items.

Valley Ford

23 mi north of Point Reyes Station on Hwy. 1.

Bird-watching is a favorite pastime in Valley Ford, where blue herons, egrets, hawks, and owls nest.

Lodging

$–$$ ⊞ **Inn at Valley Ford.** The rooms at this B&B, a Victorian farmhouse built in the late 1860s, are named after literary figures, characters, or periods. Books commemorating each chamber's theme grace the inn's bookshelves. The breakfast comes with old-fashioned cream scones. ⊠ *14395 Hwy. 1, Box 439, 94972,* ☎ *707/876–3182. 4 rooms with 2 shared baths, 1 cottage suite with private bath. Full breakfast. DC, MC, V.*

SONOMA AND MENDOCINO
Occidental and Bodega Bay to Fort Bragg

The gently rolling countryside of coastal Marin gives way to more dramatic scenery north of Bodega Bay. Cattle cling for their lives (or so it seems) to steep inclines alongside the increasingly curvy highway, now traveling right along the coast. Past Jenner, the road twists and turns. By the time it reaches Sea Ranch, hairpin curves and stunning vistas compete for drivers' attention.

Occidental

10 mi from Valley Ford, north on Hwy. 1, east on Hwy. 12 (Bodega Hwy.), and north on Bohemian Hwy.

A village in a clearing that's surrounded by the redwood forests, orchards, and vineyards of western Sonoma County, Occidental is so small that you might drive right through the town and barely take notice. A 19th-century logging hub with a present-day bohemian feel, Occidental has a top-notch B&B, good eats, and a handful of art galleries and crafts and clothing boutiques, all of which make the town an ideal base for day trips to Sonoma Coast beaches, Bodega Bay, Armstrong Redwoods Reserve, and Point Reyes National Seashore.

Dining and Lodging

$–$$ ✕ **Bohemian Café.** The name says it all. This is California free-to-be-you-and-me at its best. Colorful murals hang on the walls, and the crowd is mostly young and clad in tie-dyed togs. The main lunch and dinner staple is pizza with a decidedly unconventional twist: the Mediterranean has rock shrimp, spinach, roasted peppers, and apricots; the Bustelo is an even more outré combination of tomato, bell pepper, onion, chorizo, cumin, pineapple, hot sauce, honey, and Parmesan cheese. Rounding out the menu are unusual salads (one with strawberries, spinach, and walnuts), plus some more mainstream pastas and entrées. Breakfast is served daily. ✉ *3688 Bohemian Hwy.,* ☎ *707/874–3931. Reservations not accepted. MC, V.*

$$$–$$$$ 🏠 **The Inn at Occidental.** Jack Bullard had to open an inn to have a
  ★   place to show off his collections. Every room here showcases a collection of one sort or another. Antique English and Irish cut-glass jars decorate the Cut Glass room, which has its own sunny garden and outdoor whirlpool tub. Antiques, quilts, and original artwork fill the rooms. A fireplace, fine Asian rugs, and antique clocks create a cozy but dignified mood in the ground-floor living room. Homemade granola and fresh-squeezed orange juice are served for breakfast, along with entrées like eggs Florentine or orange pancakes with Vermont maple syrup. ✉ *3657 Church St., Box 857, 95465,* ☎ *707/874–1047 or 800/ 522–6324,* ℻ *707/874–1078. 5 rooms, 3 suites. Full breakfast. AE, D, MC, V.*

OFF THE
BEATEN PATH
OSMOSIS ENZYME BATHS – The tiny town of Freestone, 3 mi south of Occidental and 7½ mi east of Bodega Bay off Highway 12 (Bodega Highway), is famous regionally as the home of the unique Osmosis Enzyme Baths. This spa, in a two-story clapboard house on extensive grounds, specializes in several treatments, including a detoxifying "dry" bath in a blend of enzymes and fragrant wood shavings. After 20 minutes in the tub, opt for a 75-minute massage in one of the freestanding Japanese-style pagodas near the creek that runs through the property. ✉ *209 Bohemian Hwy., Freestone,* ☎ *707/823–8231.*

Bodega Bay

⑥ *8 mi from Valley Ford on Hwy. 1; 65 mi north of San Francisco via U.S. 101 and Hwy. 1.*

Bodega Bay is one of the busiest harbors on the Sonoma County coast. Commercial boats pursue ocean fish as well as the famed Dungeness crabs. T-shirt shops and galleries line both sides of Highway 1; a short drive around the harbor leads to the Pacific. This is the last stop, town-wise, before Gualala, and a good spot for stretching your legs and taking in the salt air. For a closer look, visit the **Bodega Marine Laboratory** (☎ 707/875–2211 for directions), on a 326-acre reserve on nearby Bodega Head. The lab gives free one-hour tours and peeks at intertidal invertebrates, such as sea stars and sea anemones, on Friday from 2 to 3:45 PM.

Dining and Lodging

$$$$ 🏨 **Sonoma Coast Villa.** This secluded oasis in the coastal hills between Valley Ford and Bodega Bay is a most unusual inn. Founded as an Arabian horse ranch in 1976, the 60-acre property has a single-story row of accommodations beside a swimming pool. Red-tile roofs, a stucco exterior, Mediterranean-style landscaping, and two courtyards create a European ambience. Rooms have slate floors, French doors, beamed ceilings, and wood-burning fireplaces. The small restaurant ($$$) is open on weekends. ✉ 16702 Hwy. 1, Bodega 94922, ☎ 707/876–9818 or 888/404–2255, FAX 707/876–9856. 12 rooms. Restaurant, pool, hot tub, spa. AE, MC, V.

$$$–$$$$ ✕🏨 **Inn at the Tides.** The condominium-style buildings at this complex have spacious rooms with high ceilings and an uncluttered decor. All rooms have views of the harbor, and some have fireplaces. The inn's two restaurants ($$–$$$) serve both old-style and more adventurous seafood dishes. In season you can buy a slab of salmon or live or cooked crab at a seafood market across the highway and have the kitchen prepare it for you. ✉ 800 Hwy. 1, Box 640, 94923, ☎ 707/875–2751 or 800/541–7788, FAX 707/875–2669. 86 rooms. 2 restaurants, bar, refrigerators, room service, pool, hot tub, sauna, coin laundry. Continental breakfast. AE, MC, V.

Outdoor Activities and Sports

Bodega Bay Sportfishing (✉ Bay Flat Rd., ☎ 707/875–3344) charters ocean-fishing boats and rents equipment. The operators of the 700-acre **Chanslor Guest Ranch** (✉ 2660 Hwy. 1, ☎ 707/875–2721) lead guided horseback rides.

Shopping

The **Ren Brown Gallery** (✉ 1781 Hwy. 1, ☎ 707/875–2922) in the north end of town is renowned for its selection of Asian arts, crafts, furnishings, and design books. This two-floor gallery also represents a number of local artists worth checking out.

Jenner

10 mi north of Bodega Bay on Hwy. 1.

The Russian River empties into the Pacific Ocean at Jenner. The town has a couple of good restaurants and some shops. South of the river is windy **Goat Rock State Beach,** where a colony of sea lions (walk north from the parking lot) resides most of the year. The beach is open daily from 8 AM to sunset; there's no day-use fee.

Dining

$$–$$$ ✕ **River's End.** At the right time of year, diners at this rustic restaurant
★   can view sea lions lazing on the beach below. The creative fare is eclec-
tic/German, with seafood, venison, and duck dishes. ⊠ *Hwy. 1, north
end of Jenner,* ☎ *707/865–2484. MC, V. Closed weekdays Jan.–Feb.
and Tues.–Wed. Mar.–June.*

Fort Ross State Historic Park

❼ *9 mi north of Jenner on Hwy. 1.*

Fort Ross, completed in 1821, became Russia's major fur-trading outpost in California. The Russians brought Aleut sea-otter hunters down
from Alaska. By 1841 the area was depleted of seals and otters, and
the Russians sold their post to John Sutter, later of gold-rush fame. After
a local Anglo rebellion against the Mexicans, the land fell under U.S.
domain, becoming part of California in 1850. The state park service
has reconstructed Fort Ross, including its Russian Orthodox chapel,
a redwood stockade, the officers' barracks, and a blockhouse. The excellent museum here documents the history of the fort and some of the
North Coast. ⊠ *Hwy. 1,* ☎ *707/847–3286.* ☒ *$6 per vehicle (day use).*
☉ *Daily 10–4:30. No dogs allowed past parking lot.*

Lodging

$$$$ 🏨 **Timberhill Ranch.** Tucked away on a long and winding country
★   road and accessible to some 6,000 acres for hiking, Timberhill Ranch
is the very image of quiet and serenity. The 15 cabins are decorated
with quilts and fresh flowers. Each cabin has a fireplace and a private
patio where you can enjoy breakfast, perhaps sharing croissants with
the resident ducks and geese. Timberhill's inspired six-course dinners
(included, with breakfast, in the room rates) take place by candlelight.
⊠ *35755 Hauser Bridge Rd. (Timber Cove Post Office), 95421,* ☎
707/847–3258, 📠 *707/847–3342. 15 cottages. Dining room, minibars,
refrigerators, pool, outdoor hot tub, 2 tennis courts, hiking. MAP. AE,
MC, V.*

$$–$$$$ 🏨 **Fort Ross Lodge.** Conveniently located about 1½ mi north of the same-
named fort, this lodge has a wind-bitten feel to it. Some of the rooms
have views of the shoreline; others have private hot tubs. Six hill units
have saunas, hot tubs, and fireplaces. ⊠ *20705 Hwy. 1, 95450,* ☎ *707/
847–3333,* 📠 *707/847–3330. 22 rooms. Refrigerators. AE, MC, V.*

Salt Point State Park

❽ *11 mi north of Jenner on Hwy. 1.*

Salt Point State Park yields a glimpse of nature virtually untouched by
humans. At the 6,000-acre park's **Gerstle Cove** you'll probably catch
sight of seals sunning themselves on the beach's rocks and deer roam-
ing in the meadowlands. The unusual formations in the sandstone are
called tafoni and are the product of centuries of erosion. A very short
drive leads to Fisk Mill Cove. A five-minute walk uphill brings you to
a dramatic overview of Sentinel Rock and the pounding surf below.
⊠ *Hwy. 1,* ☎ *707/847–3221; 800/444–7275 for camping information.*
☒ *$5 per vehicle (day use). Camping $16. Fire rings, flush toilets, pic-
nic areas, water.* ☉ *Daily sunrise–sunset.*

Kruse Rhododendron Reserve, a peaceful, 317-acre forested park, has
thousands of rhododendrons that bloom in light shade in the late
spring. ⊠ *Hwy. 1, north of Fisk Mill Cove.* ☒ *Free.*

Lodging

$ ☷ **Stillwater Cove Ranch.** Seventeen miles north of Jenner, this former boys' school that overlooks Stillwater Cove has been transformed into a pleasant, if spartan, place to lodge. ✉ *22555 Hwy. 1, 95450,* ☎ *707/ 847–3227. 6 rooms. No credit cards.*

Sea Ranch

18 mi from Fort Ross on Hwy. 1.

Sea Ranch is a dramatically positioned development of stylish homes on 5,000 acres overlooking the Pacific. To appease critics the developers provided public beach–access trails off Highway 1 south of Gualala. Even some militant environmentalists deem the structures designed by William Turnbull and Charles Moore to be reasonably congruent with the surroundings; some folks find the weathered wood buildings beautiful.

Dining and Lodging

$$$–$$$$ ✕☷ **Sea Ranch Lodge.** High on a bluff with ocean views, the lodge is close to beaches, trails, and golf. Some rooms have fireplaces, and some have hot tubs. Handcrafted wood furnishings and quilts create an earthy, contemporary look. The restaurant ($$–$$$), which overlooks the Pacific, serves good seafood and homemade desserts. ✉ *60 Sea Walk Dr., Box 44, 95497,* ☎ *707/785–2371 or 800/732–7262,* FAX *707/785– 2243. 20 rooms, 2 suites. Restaurant. AE, MC, V.*

$$–$$$$ ☷ **Sea Ranch Escape.** The Sea Ranch houses, sparsely scattered on a grass meadow fronting a stretch of ocean, are a striking sight from Highway 1. Groups or families can rent fully furnished houses for two nights (minimum) or more. Linen, housekeeping, and catering services are available for a fee. You can dine at superb nearby restaurants or stock up on provisions from one of the markets in Gualala and make use of the full kitchens. All houses have TVs and VCRs; some have hot tubs; and some owners allow pets. The rates are most expensive for accommodations next to the surf. Prices drop with distance from the beach. ✉ *60 Sea Walk Dr., Box 238, 95497,* ☎ *707/785–2426 or 800/732–7262,* FAX *707/785–2124. 55 houses. In-room VCRs. MC, V.*

Gualala

11 mi north of Sea Ranch on Hwy. 1

This former lumber port remains a sleepy drive-through except for the several ocean-view motels that serve as headquarters for visitors exploring the coast. The town lies north of the Gualala River—a good place for fishing and the county line for Mendocino. On the river's Sonoma side, **Gualala Point Regional Park** (✉ Hwy. 1, ☎ 707/785–2377), open daily from 8 AM until sunset, is an excellent whale-watching spot. The park has picnicking ($3 day-use fee) and camping ($15 per night). Campsites are available on a first-come, first-served basis and have fire rings, flush toilets, showers, and water but no hookups.

Dining and Lodging

$–$$$$ ✕☷ **St. Orres.** Two onion-dome towers evoke the area's Russian connection at one of the North Coast's most eye-catching inns. The main house is further accented by balconies, stained-glass windows, and wood-inlaid towers. Two rooms overlook the sea, and the other six are set over the garden or forest. All rooms in the main house share baths. The tranquil woods behind the house hold 11 rustic cottages; eight have woodstoves or fireplaces. There's also a three-bedroom house. The inn's restaurant (closed on Wednesday in winter) serves dinner only, a fixed-price meal ($$$–$$$$) with a choice of five entrées (meat or fish) plus soup and salad. ☒ *Hwy. 1, 2 mi north of Gualala, Box 523, 95445,* ☎ *707/884–3303,* ℻ *707/884–3903. 8 rooms with shared baths, 11 cottages, 1 house. Restaurant, hot tub, sauna, beach. Full breakfast. MC, V.*

$$$–$$$$ ☷ **Whale Watch Inn.** The largest accommodations at this multistructure inn are in the main house, but all have their merits. Most of them do indeed have views (through cypress trees) down the coast, where whales often come close to shore on their northern migration in early spring. Year-round, the scent of pine and salt-sea air fills the rooms, all of which have fireplaces and small decks. Some rooms have whirlpool baths or kitchens. A 132-step stairway leads down to a small, virtually private beach. Set amid 2½ acres, the inn maintains well-kept gardens that bloom even in winter. Breakfast is served in your room. ☒ *35100 Hwy. 1, 95445,* ☎ *707/884–3667 or 800/942–5342,* ℻ *707/ 884–4815. 13 rooms, 5 suites. Full breakfast. AE, MC, V.*

$$–$$$$ ☷ **Old Milano Hotel.** Fronted by a greensward that sweeps down to
★   the ocean cliffs, the Old Milano, a 1905 mansion on the National Register of Historic Places, is one of California's premier B&Bs. Exceptional antiques decorate the rooms. Five of the upstairs rooms have ocean views; all the upstairs rooms share bathrooms. The downstairs master suite has a private sitting room and a picture window framing the sea. Those in search of something different might consider the caboose with a wood-burning stove or one of the new cottages that have fireplaces or whirlpool baths. Dinner, not included in the rates, is served on weekends and most weeknights. ☒ *38300 Hwy. 1, 95445,* ☎ *707/884–3256,* ℻ *707/884–4249. 13 rooms. Hot tub. MC, V. Full breakfast. No smoking.*

$ ☷ **Gualala Hotel.** Gualala's oldest hotel, which once housed timbermill workers, has small, no-nonsense rooms furnished with well-worn antiques. Most rooms share baths. Rooms in the front have ocean views (and some street noise). The intensely atmospheric first-floor saloon was an old Jack London haunt. ☒ *39301 Hwy. 1,* ☎ *707/884–3441,* ℻ *707/884–3908. 19 rooms, 5 with private bath. Restaurant, bar. AE, D, MC, V.*

En Route   For a dramatic view of the surf and, in winter, migrating whales, take the marked road off Highway 1 north of the fishing village of Point Arena to the **Point Arena Lighthouse** (☎ 707/882–2777). First constructed in 1870, the lighthouse was destroyed by the 1906 earthquake that also devastated San Francisco. Rebuilt in 1907, it towers 115 ft from its base 50 ft above the sea. The lighthouse is open for tours daily from 11 until 2:30, one hour later in summer and on some holidays; admission is $2.50. As you continue north on Highway 1 toward Mendocino there are several beaches, most notably the one at **Manchester State Park,** 3 mi north of Point Arena. If you're driving directly to Mendocino from points south and want to grab a quick lunch or a good cup of coffee, visit the café at the **Greenwood Pier Inn** (☒ 5928 Hwy. 1, ☎ 707/877–9997) in Elk.

Elk

39 mi north of Gualala on Hwy. 1.

Dining and Lodging

$$$$ ✕☷ **Harbor House.** Constructed in 1916 by a timber company, this redwood ranch-style house has a dining room with a view of the Pacific. Five of the six rooms in the main house have fireplaces, and some are furnished with antiques original to the house. There are also four smallish cottages with fireplaces and decks. The room rates include breakfast and dinner. The restaurant ($$; reservations essential), which

serves California cuisine on a prix fixe menu, is highly recommended; there's limited seating for those not spending the night. ✉ *5600 S. Hwy. 1, 95432,* ☎ *707/877–3203 or 800/720–7474. 10 rooms. Restaurant. MAP. No credit cards.*

$$–$$$$ ✕⌂ **Elk Cove Inn.** Innkeeper Elaine Bryant loves the look of surprise
★ on guests' faces when they see the rooms perched on a bluff above the surf that pounds on a virtually private beach. The plushest suites are in a stone and cedar shingle Arts and Crafts–style building separate from the main house. All rooms have wet bars, refrigerators, stereos, and fireplaces; some have wood-burning stoves. The older accommodations range from a viewless but smartly furnished small room to a huge ocean-view suite with a whirlpool tub. The breakfast is a massive buffet. The dining room ($–$$), open Tuesday and Wednesday, serves California cuisine ranging from roast chicken to Thai shrimp. The full bar is open daily. Ask about off-season discount packages. ✉ *6300 S. Hwy. 1, Box 367, 95432,* ☎ *707/877–3321 or 800/275–2967,* FAX *707/877–1808. 10 rooms, 4 suites. Restaurant, bar, beach. Full breakfast. AE, MC, V.*

Albion

4 mi north of Elk on Hwy. 1.

Dining and Lodging

$$–$$$ ✕ **Ledford House.** There's nothing between this bluff-top restaurant and the Pacific Ocean but a great view. Entrées at this wood-and-glass structure are divided into hearty bistro dishes, mainly stews and pastas, and equally large-portioned examples of California cuisine—ahi tuna, grilled meats, and the like. ✉ *3000 N. Hwy. 1,* ☎ *707/937–0282. AE, MC, V. Closed Mon. in summer, Mon.–Tues. in winter. No lunch.*

$$$–$$$$ ✕⌂ **Albion River Inn.** Contemporary New England–style cottages at this inn overlook the dramatic bridge and seascape where the Albion River empties into the Pacific. All but two have decks facing the ocean. Six have hot tubs with ocean views. The decor ranges from antique furnishings to wide-back willow chairs. In the glassed-in dining room ($$), which serves grilled dishes and fresh seafood, the views are as captivating as the food. ✉ *3790 N. Hwy. 1, Box 100, 95410,* ☎ *707/ 937–1919; 800/479–7944 from northern CA;* FAX *707/937–2604. 20 rooms. Restaurant. Full breakfast. AE, DC, MC, V.*

Little River

3 mi north of Albion on Hwy. 1.

Van Damme State Park is one of the coast's best spots for abalone diving. The visitor center here has interesting displays on ocean life and Native American history. ✉ *Hwy. 1,* ☎ *707/937–5804 for park, 707/ 937–4016 for visitor center.*

The nearby **Pygmy Forest** contains wizened trees, some more than a century old, that stand only 3 to 4 ft tall. Highly acidic soil and poor drainage combine to stunt the trees. To reach the forest by car, turn east on Little River Airport Road, ½ mi south of Van Damme State Park, and continue 3½ mi to the clearly marked parking area.

Dining and Lodging

$$–$$$ ✕ **Little River Inn Restaurant.** There are fewer than a dozen entrées on the inn's menu, but they're varied—loin of lamb, petrale sole, grilled polenta with vegetables. Main courses come with soup or salad. Less expensive appetizers, salads, and sandwiches are served in the ocean-view Ole's Whale Watch Bar. ✉ *7551 N. Hwy. 1,* ☎ *707/937–5942. AE, MC, V.*

$$–$$$$ ✕🏠 **Heritage House.** The cottages at this resort have stunning ocean views. All the rooms contain plush furnishings and period antiques, and many have private decks, fireplaces, and whirlpool tubs. The dining room ($$$), also with a Pacific panorama, serves breakfast, brunch, and dinner. Salmon, quail, sirloin, and elegant desserts are the standouts on the evening menu. ⊠ *Hwy. 1, 95456,* ☎ *707/937–5885,* FAX *707/937–0318. 72 rooms. Restaurant. MC, V. Closed Jan.–mid-Feb. and most of December.*

$$–$$$$ 🏠 **Glendeven Inn.** The New England–style main house of this tranquil
   ★ inn has five rooms, all with private baths, three with fireplaces. A converted barn holds an art gallery and a two-bedroom suite with a kitchen. The 1986 Stevenscroft building, whose four rooms have fireplaces, has a high gabled roof and weathered barnlike siding. ⊠ *8221 N. Hwy. 1, 95456,* ☎ *707/937–0083,* FAX *707/937–6108. 9 rooms, 1 suite. Full breakfast. AE, MC, V.*

Mendocino

   ★ ❾   *2 mi north of Little River on Hwy. 1; 153 mi from San Francisco, north on U.S. 101, west on Hwy. 128, and north on Hwy. 1.*

Logging created the first boom in the windswept town of Mendocino, which flourished for most of the second half of the 19th century. As the timber industry declined in the early 20th century many residents left, but the town's setting was too beautiful for it to remain neglected for long. Artists and craftspeople began flocking here in the 1950s, and in their wake came entrepreneurial types who opened restaurants, cafés, and inns. By the 1970s a full-scale revival was under way. A bit of the old town can be seen in dives like Dick's Place, a bar near the Mendocino Hotel, but the rest of the small downtown area is devoted almost exclusively to contemporary restaurants and shops.

Mendocino may look familiar to fans of *Murder, She Wrote;* the town played the role of Cabot Cove, Maine, in the television show. The subterfuge worked because so many of the original settlers had come here from the Northeast and built houses in the New England style. The Blair House at 45110 Little Lake Street was the home of Jessica Fletcher (Angela Lansbury's character) in the series. Mendocino has also played the part of a California town, most notably in the Elia Kazan film of John Steinbeck's novel *East of Eden.* The building on Main Street (at Kasten Street) that houses the astronomy-oriented Out of This World store was the Bay City Bank in the 1955 movie, which starred James Dean.

An 1861 structure holds the **Kelley House Museum,** whose artifacts include antique cameras, Victorian-era clothing, furniture, and historical photographs of Mendocino's logging days. ⊠ *45007 Albion St.,* ☎ *707/937–5791.* 🎟 *$1.* ☽ *June–Sept., daily 1–4; Oct.–May, Fri.– Mon. 1–4.*

The **Mendocino Art Center** (⊠ 45200 Little Lake St., ☎ 707/937–5818), which hosts exhibits and art classes and contains a gallery and a theater, is the nexus of Mendocino's flourishing art scene. The tiny green and red **Temple of Kwan Tai** (⊠ Albion St., west of Kasten St., ☎ 707/ 937–5123), the oldest Chinese temple on the North Coast, dates from 1852. It's open only by appointment, but you can peer in the window and see everything there is to see.

The restored **Ford House,** built in 1854, serves as the visitor center for Mendocino Headlands State Park. The house has a scale model of Mendocino as it looked in 1890, when the town had 34 water towers and a 12-seat outhouse. History walks leave from Ford House on Saturday afternoon at 1. The park itself consists of the cliffs that border the town; access is free. ⊠ *Main St., west of Lansing St.,* ☎ *707/937–5397.* 🎦 *Free.* ◷ *Daily 11–4, with possible midweek closings in winter.*

★ The **Mendocino Coast Botanical Gardens** offer something for nature lovers every season. Even in winter, heather and Japanese tulips bloom. Along 2 mi of coastal trails, with ocean views and observation points for whale-watching, is a splendid array of flowers. The rhododendrons are at their peak from April through June, and fuchsias and azaleas are resplendent. You can have lunch or dinner at the on-site Gardens Grill (☞ Dining, Lodging, and Camping *in* Fort Bragg, *below*). ⊠ *18220 N. Hwy. 1, between Mendocino and Fort Bragg,* ☎ *707/964–4352.* 🎦 *$5.* ◷ *Mar.–Oct., daily 9–5; Nov.–Feb., daily 9–4.*

Side Trip to the Anderson Valley

Mendocino's ocean breezes might seem too cool for grape growing, but summer days can be quite warm just over the hills in the Anderson Valley, where the cool nights permit a longer ripening period. Chardonnays and pinot noirs find the valley's climate particularly hospitable. Tasting here is a decidedly more laid-back affair than in the Napa and Sonoma valleys. Most tasting rooms are open from 11 to 5 daily and charge a nominal fee (usually deducted if you purchase any wines) to sample a few vintages. To get to the Anderson Valley from Mendocino take Highway 1 south to Highway 128 east.

Husch (⊠ 4400 Hwy. 128, Philo, ☎ 707/895–3216), one of the valley's oldest wineries, sells award-winning chardonnays and a superb gewürztraminer. At the elegant tasting room at **Roederer Estate** (⊠ 4501 Hwy. 128, Philo, ☎ 707/895–2288), you can taste (for $3, deductible from wine purchase) sparkling wines produced by the American affiliate of the famous French champagne maker. **Pacific Echo** (⊠ 8501 Hwy. 128, Philo, ☎ 800/824–7754) was the first Anderson Valley winery to produce award-winning sparkling wines. If you're not up for a trip to the valley, **Fetzer Vineyards** (⊠ Main St. between Lansing and Kasten Sts., Mendocino, ☎ 707/937–6191) has a tasting room next to the Mendocino Hotel.

Dining and Lodging

$$$–$$$$ ✕ **Cafe Beaujolais.** This famous restaurant is housed in a charming cottage that makes it all the more appealing. The ever-evolving menu is cross-cultural and includes such delicacies as Yucatecan Thai crab cakes and a barbecued rock-shrimp-filled corn crepe with avocado and blood-orange pico de gallo. Owner Margaret Fox runs the mail-order Cafe Beaujolais bakery—be sure to take home a package or two of her irresistible *panforte,* a dense cake made with almonds, hazelnuts, or macadamia nuts. ⊠ *961 Ukiah St.,* ☎ *707/937–5614. AE, V.*

$$ ✕ **955 Ukiah.** The interior of this smart restaurant is woodsy and the California cuisine creative. Specialties include fresh fish, duck cannelloni, peppercorn New York steak, and pastas topped with the house sauce. ⊠ *955 Ukiah St.,* ☎ *707/937–1955. MC, V. Closed Mon.–Tues. July–Nov., Mon.–Wed. Dec.–June. No lunch.*

$$$$ ✕🏨 **Stanford Inn by the Sea.** This warm, family-run property is spread among several buildings set back from the highway. The older rooms are wood-panel; the newer ones are quite chic, and suites have ocean-view decks, four-poster or sleigh beds, fireplaces or woodstoves, and paintings by local artists. The inn is the only one on the North Coast with an organic garden *and* resident llamas. The inn's dining room ($$–$$$) serves pizzas, salads, soups, pastas, and, for dinner only, gourmet vegetarian entrées. ⊠ *South of Mendocino, east on Comptche–Ukiah Rd. (off Hwy. 1), Box 487, 95460,* ☎ *707/937–5615 or 800/331–8884,*

FAX 707/937–0305. 23 rooms, 10 suites. Refrigerators, indoor pool, hot tub, sauna, bicycles. Full breakfast. AE, D, DC, MC, V.

$$–$$$$ ✕🏠 **MacCallum House.** With the most meticulously restored Victorian exterior in Mendocino, this 1882 inn, complete with gingerbread trim, transports patrons back to another era. Comfortable furnishings and antiques enhance the period feel. In addition to the main house, there are individual cottages and barn suites around a garden with a gazebo. The menu at the redwood-panel restaurant ($$–$$$; reservations essential) changes quarterly. The focus is on local seafood and organic and free-range meats. ✉ 45020 Albion St., Box 206, 95460, ☎ 707/937–0289 or 800/609–0492. 18 rooms. Restaurant, bar. MC, V.

$$–$$$$ ✕🏠 **Mendocino Hotel.** From the street, this hotel looks like something out of the Wild West, with a period facade and balcony that overhangs the raised sidewalk. Stained-glass lamps, Remington paintings, polished wood, and Persian carpets lend the hotel a swank 19th-century appeal. All but 14 of the rooms have private baths. Deluxe garden rooms have fireplaces and TVs. The wood-panel dining room ($$–$$$), fronted by a glassed-in solarium, serves fine fish entrées and the best deep-dish ollalieberry pies in California. ✉ 45080 Main St., Box 587, 95460, ☎ 707/937–0511 or 800/548–0513, FAX 707/937–0513. 51 rooms. Restaurant, bar, room service. AE, MC, V.

$$$–$$$$ 🏠 **Whitegate Inn.** With a white picket fence, a latticework gazebo, and
★   a romantic garden, the Whitegate is a picture-book Victorian. High ceilings, floral fabrics, and pastel walls define the public spaces and the luxurious rooms, some of which have fireplaces. Best of all, you can watch the ocean breakers from the deck out back. ✉ 499 Howard St., 95460, ☎ 707/937–4892 or 800/531–7282, FAX 707/937–1131. 7 rooms. Full breakfast. AE, D, DC, MC, V.

$$–$$$$ 🏠 **Agate Cove Inn.** Facing the Mendocino Headlands across a rocky cove, this inn is ideally situated for watching whales during the winter. Adirondack chairs are set on a small deck for just that purpose; borrow the inn's binoculars for a closer look. Each blue-and-white cottage unit is individually decorated, mostly in quilts, floral wallpaper, and canopy or four-poster beds. There are four single and four duplex cottages; two more rooms are in the 1860s farmhouse, where country breakfasts are prepared on an antique woodstove in a kitchen with a full view of the Pacific. ✉ 11201 N. Lansing St., 95460, ☎ 707/937–0551, FAX 707/937–0550. 11 rooms. MC, V.

$$$ 🏠 **C. O. Packard House.** One of four landmark homes on "Executive Row," this Carpenter's Gothic Victorian was opened in 1998 by a husband-and-wife team of interior decorators. Three oddly shaped rooms are dazzlingly sophisticated with custom wall finishings, jet massage baths, and a mix of French and English antiques. A garden cottage is large enough to accommodate four but is less elegant than the rooms in the main house. ✉ 45170 Little Lake St., 95460, ☎ 707/937–2677 or 888/453–2677. 4 rooms. Full breakfast. AE, D, V.

$$–$$$ 🏠 **Blackberry Inn.** Each single-story unit here has a false front, creating the image of a frontier town. There's a bank, a saloon, Belle's Place (of hospitality), and "offices" for doctors and sheriffs, as well as other themed accommodations. The rooms are cheery and spacious. Most have wood-burning stoves or fireplaces and at least partial ocean views. The inn is a short drive east of town down a quiet side street. Two rooms have kitchenettes. ✉ 44951 Larkin Rd., 95460, ☎ 707/937–5281 or 800/950–7806. 16 rooms. Continental breakfast. MC, V.

$$–$$$ 🏠 **Joshua Grindle Inn.** The original farmhouse of this B&B on a 2-acre hilltop has five guest rooms, a parlor, and a dining room. Two other buildings, the Watertower (an upper room has windows on all four sides) and the Cottage, hold five additional rooms. Furnishings throughout are simple but comfortable American antiques: Salem rockers, wing chairs, steamer-trunk tables, painted pine beds. ⊠ *44800 Little Lake Rd., 95460,* ☎ *707/937–4143. 10 rooms. Full breakfast. MC, V.*

Nightlife and the Arts

Mendocino Theatre Company (⊠ Mendocino Art Center, 45200 Little Lake St., ☎ 707/937–4477) has been around for more than two decades. The community theater's repertoire ranges from classics like *Uncle Vanya* to more recent plays like *Other People's Money.*

Patterson's Pub (⊠ 10485 Lansing St., ☎ 707/937–4782), an Irish-style watering hole, is a friendly gathering place day or night, though it does become boisterous as the evening wears on. Bands entertain on Friday night.

Outdoor Activities and Sports

Catch-a-Canoe and Bicycles Too (⊠ Stanford Inn by the Sea, Mendocino, ☎ 707/937–0273) rents regular and outrigger canoes and mountain and suspension bicycles.

Shopping

Many artists exhibit their wares in Mendocino, and the streets of this compact town are so easily walkable that you're sure to find a gallery with something that strikes your fancy. You might start at the **Mendocino Art Center** (☞ *above*). **Old Gold** (6 Albion St., ☎ 707/937–5005) is a good place to look for locally crafted jewelry.

Fort Bragg

10 mi north of Mendocino on Hwy. 1.

Fort Bragg has changed more than any other coastal town in the past few years. The decline in what was the top industry, timber, is being offset in part by a boom in charter-boat excursions and other tourist pursuits. The city is also attracting many artists, some lured from Mendocino, where the cost of living is higher. This basically blue-collar town is the commercial center of Mendocino County.

The *Skunk Train,* a remnant of the region's logging days, dates from 1885 and travels a route, through redwood forests inaccessible to automobiles, from Fort Bragg to the town of Willits, 40 mi inland. A fume-spewing self-propelled train car that shuttled passengers along the railroad got nicknamed the *Skunk Train,* and the entire line has been called that ever since. Excursions are now given on historic trains and replicas of the *Skunk Train* motorcar that smell less foul than the original. In summer you can go partway, to Northspur, a three-hour round-trip, or make the full seven-hour journey to Willits and back. ⊠ *Foot of Laurel St., Fort Bragg,* ☎ *707/964–6371 or 800/777–5865.* 🎫 *$35 for Fort Bragg–Willits, $27 for Fort Bragg–Northspur.* ⊙ *Fort Bragg–Northspur: departs early June–late Sept., daily 9:20 AM and 1:40 PM; Fort Bragg–Willits: late Sept.–mid-June 10 AM and 2 PM.*

★ ⑩ **MacKerricher State Park** includes 10 mi of sandy beach and several square miles of dunes. Fishing (at two freshwater lakes, one stocked with trout), canoeing, hiking, jogging, bicycling, camping (☞ *below*), and harbor-seal watching at Laguna Point are among the popular activities, many of which are accessible to travelers with disabilities. Whales can often be spotted from December to mid-April from the nearby headland. Rangers lead nature hikes throughout the year. ⊠ *Hwy. 1, 3 mi north of Fort Bragg,* ☎ *707/937–5804.* 🎫 *Free.*

Dining, Lodging, and Camping

$$ ✕ **The Restaurant.** The name may be generic, but this place isn't. California cuisine is served in a dining room that doubles as an art gallery. A jazz brunch takes place on Sunday. ⊠ *418 N. Main St.,* ☎ *707/964–9800. MC, V. Closed Wed. No lunch Mon., Tues., Sat.*

$–$$ ✕ **Gardens Grill.** The restaurant at the Mendocino Coast Botanical Gardens (☞ Mendocino, *above*) specializes in apple-wood-grilled steak, seafood, and vegetarian dishes. The view of the gardens from the outdoor deck is splendid. Brunch is served on Sunday. ⊠ *18218 N. Hwy. 1, at the south end of Fort Bragg,* ☎ *707/964–7474. MC, V. No dinner Sun.–Wed.*

$–$$ ✕ **Samraat Restaurant.** Soothing pastels and sitar music set the mood for good, inexpensive Indian dishes. Tandoori, curry, and seafood are specialties. ⊠ *546 S. Main St.,* ☎ *707/964–0386. AE, DC, MC, V.*

$ ✕ **Headlands Coffee House.** The coffeehouse acts as a cultural center and local gathering place. Musicians perform on most nights. ⊠ *120 E. Laurel St.,* ☎ *707/964–1987. No credit cards.*

$$$ ☗ **Weller House Inn.** This 1886 mansion was transformed into an inn in 1998. Guest accommodations on the first and second floors are decorated with Victorian-style wallpaper and furnishings; the baths have hand-painted tiles. The third floor features a 900-square-ft ballroom (now the breakfast room) paneled in rare California redwood. ⊠ *524 Stewart St., 95437,* ☎ *707/964–4415 or 800/877–8935,* FAX *707/964–4198. 7 rooms. Breakfast room. Full breakfast. AE, D, DC, MC, V.*

$–$$$ ☗ **Surf and Sand Lodge.** You have to go north of Fort Bragg to find lodgings with unimpeded ocean views, and they're just what you'll get at this souped-up motel. As its name implies, it's practically on the beach. Right out the door are pathways down to the rock-strewn shore. The six cheaper rooms don't have views, but all the bright and fresh accommodations come with enough amenities (including coffeemakers, hair dryers, and binoculars) to make you feel that you're staying somewhere grander than a motel. The fancier of the second-story rooms have hot tubs and fireplaces. ⊠ *1131 N. Main St., 95437,* ☎ *707/964–9383 or 800/964–0184,* FAX *707/964–0314. 30 rooms. Refrigerators, in-room VCRs. AE, D, DC, MC, V.*

△ **MacKerricher State Park.** The campsites at MacKerricher (☞ *above*) are in woodsy settings ¼ mi or so from the ocean. Reservations on summer weekends should be made as early as possible, although each day 25 sites are available on a first-come, first-served basis. ⊠ *Hwy. 1, 3 mi north of Fort Bragg,* ☎ *707/937–5804 for park; 800/444–7275 for campsite reservations, taken Apr.–mid-Oct.* ⊟ *$16. 143 sites. Disposal station, fire rings, flush toilets, hot showers, water.*

Nightlife

North Coast Brewing Company (⊠ 444 N. Main St., ☎ 707/964–3400) hosts jazz musicians on Saturday night and serves home-brewed beer and pub grub from Tuesday through Saturday.

Outdoor Activities and Sports

Ricochet Ridge Ranch (⊠ 24201 N. Hwy. 1, ☎ 707/964–7669) conducts guided trail rides to the Mendocino–Fort Bragg beaches. **Matlick's Tally Ho II** (⊠ 11845 N. Main St., ☎ 707/964–2079) operates whale-watching trips from December through April, as well as fishing excursions.

En Route North on Highway 1 from Fort Bragg past the mill town of Westport, the road cuts inland around the **King Range,** a stretch of mountain so rugged that it was impossible to build the intended major highway through it. Highway 1 joins U.S. 101 at the town of Leggett. **Richardson Grove State Park,** north of Leggett along U.S. 101, marks your first encounter with the truly giant redwoods, but there are even more magnificent stands farther north in Humboldt and Del Norte counties.

REDWOOD COUNTRY
Garberville to Crescent City

The majestic redwoods that grace California's coast become more plentiful as you head north. Their towering ancient presence defines the landscape.

Garberville

70 mi from Fort Bragg, north and east on Hwy. 1 and north on U.S. 101; 197 mi north of San Francisco on U.S. 101.

Although it's the largest town in the vicinity of Humboldt Redwoods State Park, Garberville hasn't changed a whole lot since timber was king. The town is a pleasant place to stop for lunch, pick up picnic provisions, or poke through arts-and-crafts stores. A few miles below Garberville is an elegant Tudor resort, the **Benbow Inn** (☞ *below*). Even if you are not staying at the Benbow, stop in for a drink or a meal and take a look at the architecture and gardens.

Dining and Lodging

$ ✕ **Woodrose Cafe.** This unpretentious eatery serves basic breakfast items on the weekends and healthy lunches every day. Dishes include chicken, pasta, and vegetarian specials. ⊠ *911 Redwood Dr.,* ☎ *707/923–3191. No credit cards. No dinner.*

$$–$$$$ ✕⌂ **Benbow Inn.** South of Garberville alongside the Eel River, this three-★ story Tudor-style manor resort is the equal of any in the region. The most luxurious of the antiques-filled rooms are on the terrace, with fine views of the Eel River; some rooms have fireplaces, and 18 have TVs with VCRs. Guests have canoeing, tennis, golf, and pool privileges at an adjacent property. The wood-panel dining room ($$–$$$) serves American cuisine, with the focus on fresh salmon and trout. ⊠ *445 Lake Benbow Dr., 95542,* ☎ *707/923–2124 or 800/355–3301. 55 rooms, 1 cottage. Restaurant, lobby lounge, refrigerators, lake. AE, D, MC, V. Closed early Jan.–mid-Mar.*

Humboldt Redwoods State Park

⓫ *15 mi north of Garberville on U.S. 101.*

The **Avenue of the Giants** (Highway 254) begins about 7 mi north of Garberville and winds north, more or less parallel to U.S. 101, toward Pepperwood. Some of the tallest trees on the planet tower over this stretch of two-lane blacktop. The Avenue follows the south fork of the Eel River and cuts through part of the more than 53,000-acre Humboldt Redwoods State Park.

At the **Humboldt Redwoods State Park Visitor Center** you can pick up information about the redwoods, waterways, and recreational opportunities. Brochures are available for a self-guided auto tour of the park. Stops on the auto tour include short and long hikes into redwood groves. ⊠ *Avenue of the Giants, 2 mi south of Weott,* ☎ *707/946–2409 for park; 707/946–2263 for visitor center.* ☞ *Free; $5 day-use fee for parking and facilities in Williams Grove and Women's Federation Grove.* ☉ *Park 24 hrs year-round. Visitor center Mar.–Oct., daily 9–5; Nov.–Feb., Thurs.–Sun. 10–4.*

Four miles north of the visitor center on the Avenue of the Giants is **Founders Grove,** reached via a ½-mi trail. One of the most impressive trees here—the 362-ft-long Dyerville Giant—fell to the ground in 1991; its root base points skyward 35 ft. Six miles north of the Visitor Center on Mattole Road is **Rockefeller Forest.** The largest remaining coast redwood forest, it contains 40 of the 100 tallest trees in the world.

Ferndale

⑫ *30 mi from Weott, north on U.S. 101 to Hwy. 211 west.*

The residents of the stately town of Ferndale maintain some of the most sumptuous Victorian homes in California, many of them built by 19th-century Scandinavian, Swiss, and Portuguese dairy farmers who were drawn to the mild climate. The queen of them all is the **Gingerbread Mansion** (☞ Lodging, *below*). A beautiful sloped graveyard sits on Ocean Avenue west of Main Street. Many shops carry a map with self-guided tours of this lovingly preserved town.

The main building of the **Ferndale Museum** hosts changing exhibitions of Victoriana and has an old-style barbershop and a display of Wiyot Indian baskets. In the annex are a horse-drawn buggy, a re-created blacksmith's shop, and antique farming, fishing, and dairy equipment. ⊠ *515 Shaw Ave.,* ☎ *707/786–4466.* ☜ *$1.* ☉ *June–Sept., Tues.–Sat. 11–4, Sun. 1–4; Oct.–Dec. and Feb.–May, Wed.–Sat. 11–4, Sun. 1–4. Closed Jan.*

Lodging

$$$–$$$$ ☒ **Gingerbread Mansion.** This photogenic Victorian B&B rivals San Francisco's "painted ladies" for dazzle. The mansion's carved friezes set off its gables, and turrets dazzle the eye. The comfortable parlors and spacious bedrooms are laid out in flowery Victorian splendor. Some rooms have views of the mansion's English garden, and one has side-by-side bathtubs. Ask about off-season discounts. ⊠ *400 Berding St., off Brown St., Box 40, 95536,* ☎ *707/786–4000. 10 rooms, 1 suite. Full breakfast. AE, MC, V.*

Outdoor Activities and Sports

Eel River Delta Tours (⊠ 285 Morgan Slough Rd., ☎ 707/786–4187) conducts a two-hour boat trip that emphasizes the wildlife and history of the Eel River's estuary and salt marsh.

Shopping

Ferndale's shops are lined up along Main Street. **Golden Gait Mercantile** (⊠ 421 Main St., ☎ 707/786–4891) seems to be lost in a time warp, what with Burma Shave products and old-fashioned long johns as well as penny candy. For gifts, you can't do better than **Withywindle** (⊠ 358 Main St., ☎ 707/786–4763), which sells local stoneware, porcelain, jewelry, and wearable art. The shop also specializes in gift baskets crammed with gourmet products.

Eureka

⑬ *10 mi north of Ferndale and 269 mi north of San Francisco on U.S. 101.*

Eureka, population 28,500, is the North Coast's largest city. It has gone through cycles of boom and bust, first with mining and later with timber and fishing. There are nearly 100 Victorian buildings here, many of them well preserved. The most splendid is the **Carson Mansion** (⊠ M and 2nd Sts.), built in 1885 for timber baron William Carson. A private men's club occupies the house. Across the street is another extravaganza popularly known as the **Pink Lady.**

For proof that contemporary architects have the skills to design lovely Victoriana, take a look at the **Carter House** (⊠ 3rd and L Sts.) B&B and keep in mind that it was built in the 1980s, not the 1880s.

At the **Chamber of Commerce** you can pick up maps with self-guided driving tours of Eureka's architecture, and find out about organized tours. ⊠ *2112 Broadway,* ☎ *707/442–3738 or 800/356–6381.* ⊙ *Weekdays 9–5.*

The **Clarke Memorial Museum** contains extraordinary northwestern California Native American basketry and artifacts of Eureka's Victorian, logging, and maritime eras. ⊠ *240 E St.,* ☎ *707/443–1947.* ⊠ *Donations accepted.* ⊙ *Feb.–Dec., Tues.–Sat. noon–4.*

The structure that gave **Fort Humboldt State Historic Park** its name once protected white settlers from the Indians. Ulysses S. Grant was posted here in 1854. The old fort is no longer around, but on its grounds are a museum, some ancient steam engines (operators rev them up on the third Saturday of the month), and a logger's cabin. The park is a good place for a picnic. ⊠ *3431 Fort Ave.,* ☎ *707/445–6567.* ⊠ *Free.* ⊙ *Daily 9–5.*

To explore the waters around Eureka, take a **Humboldt Bay Harbor Cruise.** You can observe some of the region's bird life while sailing past fishing boats, oyster beds, and decaying timber mills. ⊠ *Pier at C St.,* ☎ *707/445–1910 or 707/444–9440.* ⊠ *$9.50; cocktail-cruise fare $7.50.* ⊙ *Departs Mar.–Nov., daily 1, 2:30, and 4. Cocktail cruise departs Tues.–Sat. at 5.*

Dining and Lodging

$$–$$$ ✕ **Restaurant 301.** Mark and Christi Carter, owners of Eureka's fanciest hotels, also run the town's best restaurant. Most of the vegetables and herbs used here are grown at the hotel's greenhouse and nearby ranch. Try the sea scallops, roasted pork chop, spring rack of lamb, or local petrale sole, and don't skip the appetizers—especially if the vegetable ragouts or gnocchi are on the menu. The wine list is one of the finest in northern California. ⊠ *301 L St.,* ☎ *707/444–8062. AE, D, DC, MC, V. No lunch.*

$$ ✕ **Celestino's in Old Town.** Pastas and made-to-order pizzas dominate the menu of this large restaurant, which serves grilled meats and several vegetarian choices (as well as vegan dishes on request). The tasty appetizers include grilled eggplant rolls and fried calamari. ⊠ *421 3rd St.,* ☎ *707/444–8995. AE, MC, V. Closed Mon. No lunch Sat.*

$$ ✕ **Chemin de Fer.** The food here is fresh and elaborate: grilled duck, prawns with curry and pears, pork tenderloin, and nearly a dozen first courses. The dessert list is even longer. ⊠ *518 F St.,* ☎ *707/441–9292. AE, MC, V. Closed Mon. No lunch weekends.*

$–$$ ✕ **Cafe Waterfront.** This small eatery across from the marina has a long bar with a TV. Sandwiches and affordable seafood dishes are the menu mainstays. ⊠ *102 F St.,* ☎ *707/443–9190. MC, V.*

$ ✕ **Ramone's.** A casual bakery café, Ramone's serves light sandwiches. ⊠ *2223 Harrison Ave.,* ☎ *707/442–6082. No credit cards. No dinner.*

$ ✕ **Samoa Cookhouse.** The recommendation here is more for atmosphere,
★ of which there is plenty: this is a longtime loggers' hangout. The Samoa's cooks serve three substantial set meals family style at long wooden tables. Meat dishes predominate. Save room (if possible) for dessert. ⊠ *Cookhouse Rd. (from U.S. 101, cross Samoa Bridge, turn*

left onto Samoa Rd., then left 1 block later onto Cookhouse), ☎ 707/
442–1659. AE, D, MC, V.

$$$–$$$$ 🖬 **Carter House, Hotel Carter, and Cottages.** Whether you like small
★   inns, country hotels, or the charm of a cottage, the Carter family has
something to offer. The Carter House, built in 1982 following the floor
plan of a San Francisco mansion, has large rooms with heirloom fur-
niture. Two doors down, the three-room Victorian cottage is decorated
in contemporary Southwestern style. The three-story hotel, catercorner
to the Carter House, has an elegant lobby and suites. Breakfast is
served in the hotel's sunny corner dining room. ✉ *301 L St., 95501,*
☎ *707/444–8062,* FAX *707/445–8067. 32 rooms. Full breakfast. AE,
D, DC, MC, V.*

$$–$$$$ 🖬 **An Elegant Victorian Mansion.** This meticulously restored Eastlake
★   mansion in a residential neighborhood east of the Old Town lives up
to its name. Each room is completely decked out in period furnishings
and wall coverings, down to the carved-wood beds, fringed lamp
shades, and pull-chain commodes. The innkeepers may even greet you
in vintage clothing and entertain you with silent movies on tape, old
records played on the windup Victrola, croquet on the rose-encircled
lawn, and guided tours of local Victoriana in their antique automobile.
✉ *1406 C St., 95501,* ☎ *707/444–3144,* FAX *707/442–5594. 4 rooms
with 4 shared baths. Sauna, croquet, bicycles, laundry service. Full breakfast. MC, V.*

Nightlife

Lost Coast Brewery & Cafe (✉ 617 4th St., ☎ 707/445–4480), a
bustling microbrewery, is the best place in town to relax with a pint
of ale or porter. Soups, salads, and light meals are served for lunch and
dinner.

Outdoor Activities and Sports

Hum-Boats (✉ 2 F St., ☎ 707/443–5157) provides sailing rides, sail-
boat rentals, guided kayak tours, and sea kayak rentals and lessons.
The company also runs a water-taxi service on Humboldt Bay.

Shopping

Eureka has several art galleries in the district running from C to I streets
between 2nd and 3rd streets. Specialty shops in Old Town include the
original **Restoration Hardware** (✉ 417 2nd St., ☎ 707/443–3152), a
good place to find stylish yet functional home and garden accessories
and clever polishing and cleaning products. The **Irish Shop** (✉ 334 2nd
St., ☎ 707/443–8343) carries imports from the Emerald Isle, mostly
fine woolens.

Arcata

⑭ *9 mi north of Eureka on U.S. 101.*

The home of Humboldt State University is one of the few California
burgs to retain a town square. A farmers' market takes place in the
square on Saturday morning from May through November. For a self-
guided tour of Arcata that includes some of its restored Victorian
buildings, pick up a map from the **Chamber of Commerce** (✉ 1062 G
St., ☎ 707/822–3619), open weekdays from 10 to 4.

Dining and Lodging

$$ ✕ **Abruzzi.** Salads and hefty pasta dishes take up most of the menu at
this upscale Italian restaurant in the lower level of Jacoby's Storehouse,
off the town square. One specialty is linguine *pescara,* with a spicy
seafood-and-tomato sauce. ✉ *H and 8th Sts.,* ☎ *707/826–2345. AE,
D, MC, V. No lunch.*

$ ✕ **Crosswinds.** This restaurant serves Continental cuisine in a sunny Victorian setting, at prices that attract students from Humboldt State. ✉ *10th and I Sts.,* ☎ *707/826–2133. MC, V. Closed Mon. No dinner.*

$ 🛏 **Hotel Arcata.** Rooms are clean and modest, but flowered bedspreads and claw-foot bathtubs lend a bit of character to this historic landmark overlooking the town square. ✉ *708 9th St., 95521,* ☎ *707/826–0217 or 800/344–1221,* 🖷 *707/826–1737. 32 rooms. Restaurant. Continental breakfast (weekdays only). AE, D, DC, MC, V.*

Shopping

For its size, Arcata has an impressive selection of book, housewares, clothing, fabric, and other shops, especially near its town square. **Plaza Design** (✉ 808 G St., ☎ 707/822–7732) specializes in gifts, papers, and innovative furnishings.

Trinidad

14 mi north of Arcata on U.S. 101.

Trinidad got its name from the Spanish mariners who entered the bay on Trinity Sunday, June 9, 1775. The town became a principal trading post for the mining camps along the Klamath and Trinity rivers. As mining, and then whaling, faded, so did the luster of this former boomtown. Development has overlooked this scenic spot for now, making it one of the quietest towns that still has inns and dining spots. Picturesque Trinidad Bay's harbor cove and rock formations look both raw and tranquil.

Dining and Lodging

$–$$ ✕ **Larrupin' Cafe.** Considered by many locals to be one of the best places
★ to eat on the North Coast, this restaurant has earned widespread fame for its mesquite-grilled ribs and fresh fish dishes, served in a bright-yellow two-story house on a quiet country road 2 mi north of Trinidad. ✉ *1658 Patrick's Point Dr.,* ☎ *707/677–0230. Reservations essential. No credit cards. Closed Mon.–Tues. in winter, Tues. in summer. No lunch.*

$–$$ ✕ **Merryman's Dinner House.** Fresh fish and a romantic oceanfront setting make this a perfect spot for hungry romance lovers. ✉ *100 Moonstone Beach,* ☎ *707/677–3111. No credit cards. Closed weekdays Oct.– Mar. No lunch.*

$ ✕ **Seascape.** With its glassed-in main room and deck for alfresco dining, this casual spot is an ideal place to take in the scenery of Trinidad Bay. The breakfasts are great, the lunches are substantial, and the dinners showcase local seafood. ✉ *At pier,* ☎ *707/677–3762. MC, V.*

$$$ 🛏 **Trinidad Bay Bed and Breakfast.** This Cape Cod–style shingle house overlooks the harbor and the coastline to the south. The innkeepers provide a wealth of information about the nearby wilderness, beach, and fishing habitats. A crackling fire warms the living room in chilly weather. ✉ *560 Edwards St., Box 849, 95570,* ☎ *707/677–0840. 2 rooms and 2 suites (1 with fireplace). Full breakfast. D, MC, V. Closed Dec.–Jan.*

$$–$$$ 🛏 **Turtle Rocks Inn.** Unobstructed ocean views from most of the rooms make this inn a desirable choice for nature lovers. Named for some of the enormous formations within view offshore, this B&B has a two-tier "Whale Watch" deck where you can sit on rocking chairs or chaise longues and take catnaps or scan the horizon. Contemporary and antique furnishings decorate the rooms, all but one of which have decks. ✉ *3392 Patrick's Point Dr., 95570,* ☎ *707/677–3707. 6 rooms. Full breakfast. MC, V.*

Patrick's Point State Park

⑮ *5 mi north of Trinidad and 25 mi north of Eureka on U.S. 101.*

Patrick's Point is the ultimate California coastal park. On a forested plateau almost 200 ft above the surf, it has stunning views of the Pacific, great whale- and sea-lion-watching in season, picnic areas, bike paths, and hiking trails through old-growth forest. There are tidal pools at Agate Beach and a small museum with natural-history exhibits. The park's campsites have fire rings, flush toilets, showers, and water. ☎ 707/677–3570. ⊠ *May–Sept. $6 per vehicle (day use), camping $16 per vehicle; Oct.–Apr. $5 per vehicle (day use), camping $12 per vehicle.*

Redwood National and State Parks

⑯ *22 mi north (Orick entrance) of Trinidad on U.S. 101.*

After 115 years of intensive logging, this 106,000-acre parcel of tall trees came under government protection in 1968, marking the California environmentalists' greatest victory over the timber industry. **Redwood National and State Parks** (☎ 707/464–6101, ext. 5064) encompasses three state parks (Prairie Creek Redwoods, Del Norte Coast Redwoods, and Jedediah Smith Redwoods) and is more than 40 mi long. There is no admission fee to the national or state parks, but the state parks charge $5 to use facilities such as the beach or picnic areas. *Park Headquarters, 1111 2nd St., Crescent City,* ☎ *707/464–6101, ext. 5064.*

At the **Redwood Information Center** you can get brochures, advice, and a free permit to drive up the steep, 17-mi road (the last 6 mi are gravel) to reach the **Tall Trees Grove,** where a 3-mi round-trip hiking trail leads to the world's first-, third-, and fifth-tallest redwoods. Whale-watchers will find the deck of the visitor center an excellent observation point, and birders will enjoy the nearby Freshwater Lagoon, a popular layover for migrating waterfowl. *Off U.S. 101, Orick,* ☎ *707/464–6101, ext. 5265.*

Within **Lady Bird Johnson Grove,** off Bald Hills Road, is a short circular trail to resplendent redwoods. This section of the park was dedicated by, and named for, the former first lady. For additional views, take Davison Road to Fern Canyon. This gravel road winds through 4 mi of second-growth redwoods, then hugs a bluff 100 ft above the pounding Pacific surf for another 4 mi.

To reach the entrance to **Prairie Creek Redwoods State Park** (☎ 707/464–6101, ext. 5300) take the Prairie Parkway exit off the U.S. 101 bypass. Extra space has been paved alongside the parklands, providing fine vantage points from which to observe an imposing herd of Roosevelt elk grazing in the adjoining meadow. Revelation Trail in Prairie Creek is fully accessible to visitors with disabilities.

Lodging and Camping

$ ✕ **Hostelling International—Redwood National Park.** This century-old inn is a stone's throw from the ocean; hiking begins just beyond its doors. Lodging is dormitory style. ⊠ *14480 U.S. 101, at Wilson Creek Rd. (20 mi north of Orick), Klamath, 95548,* ☎ FAX *707/482–8265. No credit cards.*

⚠ **Freshwater Lagoon.** A strip of sand between the ocean and Freshwater Lagoon holds an unofficial, primitive campground with no water or hookups—but great views. ⊠ *West side of U.S. 101, 1½ mi south of Orick (¼ mi south of Redwood Information Center),* ☎ *707/464–6101, ext. 5265. Chemical toilets, fire rings, picnic tables.* ⊠ *$6.*

Crescent City

40 mi north of Orick on U.S. 101.

Del Norte County's largest town (population just under 5,000) is
named for the shape of its harbor; during the 1800s this was an important steamship stop. At the bottom of B Street at **Popeye's Landing** you can rent a crab pot, buy some bait, and try your luck at
crabbing. At low tide from April through September, you can walk from
the pier across the ocean floor to the oldest lighthouse on the North
Coast, **Battery Point Lighthouse** (☎ 707/464–3089). Tours ($2) of the
1856 structure are given from Wednesday through Sunday between 10
and 4 from May through October and by appointment the rest of the
year.

Dining and Lodging

$–$$ ✕ **Harbor View Grotto.** This glassed-in dining hall overlooking the Pa-
cific prides itself on its fresh fish entrées. The white two-story building is marked only by a neon sign that reads "Restaurant." ⊠ *155
Starcross Way,* ☎ *707/464-3815. MC, V.*

$ ▦ **Curly Redwood Lodge.** A single redwood tree produced the 57,000
board feet of lumber used to build this lodge. The room decor makes
the most of that tree, with paneling, platform beds, and dressers built
into the walls. ⊠ *701 U.S. 101 S, 95531,* ☎ *707/464–2137, FAX 707/
464-1655. 36 rooms. AE, DC, MC, V.*

En Route Travelers continuing north to the Smith River near the Oregon state
line will find fine trout and salmon fishing as well as a profusion of
flowers. Ninety percent of America's lily bulbs are grown in this area.

THE NORTH COAST A TO Z

Arriving and Departing

By Bus

Greyhound buses (☎ 800/231–2222) travel along U.S. 101 from San
Francisco to Seattle, with regular stops in Eureka and Crescent City.
Bus drivers will stop in other towns along the route if you specify your
destination when you board.

By Car

Highway 1 and U.S. 101 are the main north–south coastal routes. Highway 1 is often curvy and difficult all along the coast. Driving directly
to Mendocino from San Francisco is quicker if instead of driving up
the coast on Highway 1 you take U.S. 101 north to Highway 128 west
(from Cloverdale) to Highway 1 north. Once it gets into Humboldt
County, U.S. 101 itself becomes as twisting as Highway 1 as it continues on to the northernmost corner of the state. **Hertz** (☎ 800/654–
3131) rents cars at the Arcata/Eureka Airport (☞ *below*).

By Plane

Arcata/Eureka Airport (off U.S. 101, McKinleyville, ☎ 707/839–5401)
receives United Express (☎ 800/241–6522) flights from San Francisco to Arcata/Eureka.

Getting Around

By Bus

Redwood Transit System (☎ 707/443-0826) connects Eureka, Arcata,
Scotia, Fortuna, and Trinidad.

By Car

Although there are excellent services along Highway 1 and U.S. 101, the main routes through the North Coast, gas stations and mechanics are few and far between on the smaller roads. If you're running low on fuel and see a gas station, stop for a refill.

Contacts and Resources

Emergencies

Ambulance (☎ 911). **Fire** (☎ 911). **Police** (☎ 911).

Guided Tours

New Sea Angler and Jaws (✉ Bodega Bay, ☎ 707/875–3495) runs cruises and fishing charters daily from December through April. **Oceanic Society Expeditions** (☎ 415/474–3385) conducts whale-watching and other nature cruises north and west of San Francisco throughout much of the year.

Visitor Information

Eureka/Humboldt County Convention and Visitors Bureau (✉ 1034 2nd St., Eureka 95501, ☎ 800/346–3482 or 800/809–5908). **Fort Bragg–Mendocino Coast Chamber of Commerce** (✉ Box 1141, Fort Bragg 95437, ☎ 800/726–2780). **Redwood Empire Association** (✉ Cannery, 2801 Leavenworth St., San Francisco 94133, ☎ 415/543–8334). **Sonoma County Visitors and Convention Bureau** (✉ 10 4th St., Santa Rosa 95401, ☎ 707/586–8100). **West Marin Chamber of Commerce** (✉ Box 1045, Point Reyes Station 94956, ☎ 415/663–9232).

2 THE FAR NORTH

Including Mount Shasta, Lake Shasta, and Lassen Volcanic National Park

Soaring mountain peaks, wild rivers brimming with fish, and almost infinite recreational possibilities make the Far North a sports-lover's paradise. You won't find many hot nightspots and cultural enclaves, but you will find some of the best hiking, fishing, and hunting in the state. Some Bay Area families return to this region year after year. Many enjoy the outdoors from their own piece of paradise—a private houseboat.

THE FAR NORTH LANDSCAPE has been writ large by ancient volcanic activity. The scenery is best symbolized
by Mount Shasta, a 14,162-ft-high mountain that
can be seen for miles around. Less dramatic but more extensive is Lassen
Volcanic National Park at the southern end of the Cascade Range. The
10,457-ft Mount Lassen and 50 wilderness lakes are the park's cen-
terpieces.

By Marty
Olmstead

Updated by
Tim Lohnes

The Far North's natural and artificially created wonders include immense Shasta Dam and the sulfur vents and bubbling mud pots of Lassen
Volcanic National Park. Plentiful access to uncrowded wilderness is
the Far North's hallmark. There are few towns and fewer cities. Natural history dwarfs the footsteps of mankind in this grand gymnasium
for body and soul.

Pleasures and Pastimes

Dining

Redding, the urban center of the Far North, has the greatest selection
of restaurants. In the smaller towns, cafés and simple restaurants are
the rule, though trendy, innovative restaurants have been opening.
Dress is always informal in the Far North.

CATEGORY	COST*
$$$$	over $50
$$$	$30–$50
$$	$20–$30
$	under $20

per person for a three-course meal, excluding drinks, service, and 8¼% tax

Lodging

Aside from the large chain hotels and motels in the Redding area, most
accommodations in the Far North blend rusticity, simplicity, and co-
ziness. Many visitors to rural areas spend much of their time in the
outdoors and prefer informal campsites and motels. Wilderness resorts
close in fall and reopen after the snow season ends in May.

CATEGORY	COST*
$$$$	over $175
$$$	$120–$175
$$	$80–$120
$	under $80

All prices are for a standard double room, excluding 8% tax.

Outdoor Activities and Sports

Fishing, houseboating, and animal-pack trips are popular regional diversions. Cascading rivers, mammoth lakes, and bountiful streams
draw sportfishers. Hikers, backpackers, hunters, skiers, and other outdoor enthusiasts also flock to the Far North. Castle Crags State Park
and Lassen Volcanic National Park have abundant hiking and walking trails. In winter the challenging, uncrowded slopes of Mount Shasta
tempt skiers. For information about campgrounds, contact Lassen
Volcanic National Park or the Shasta Cascade Wonderland Association (☞ Contacts and Resources *in* The Far North A to Z, *below*).

Exploring the Far North

The Far North encompasses three vast counties—Tehama, Shasta, and
Trinity—and part of Butte County. The area stretches from the valleys

east of the Coast Range to the Nevada border and from the almond and olive orchards north of Sacramento to the Oregon border.

Numbers in the text correspond to numbers in the margin and on the Far North map.

Great Itineraries

IF YOU HAVE 3 DAYS

From I–5 north of Redding, head northeast on Highways 299 and 89 to **McArthur-Burney Falls Memorial State Park** ⑥. To appreciate the falls, take the short stroll to an overlook or hike down for a closer view. Continue north on Highway 89. Long before you arrive in the town of ⊞ **Mount Shasta** ⑦ you will spy the conical peak for which it is named. The central Mount Shasta exit east leads out of town along the **Everett Memorial Highway.** Take this scenic drive, which climbs to almost 8,000 ft. The views of the mountain and the valley below are extraordinary. Stay overnight in town. On the second day, head south on I–5 toward the **Lake Shasta Caverns** ⑧ and the **Shasta Dam** ⑨. **Lake Shasta** is visible on both sides of the highway as it crosses the water near the dam, which is on the west side of I–5. Spend the night either in ⊞ **Weaverville** ⑩, on Highway 299, or in ⊞ **Redding** ⑪, on I–5. Near Redding, Highway 299 leads west toward the **Whiskeytown-Shasta-Trinity National Recreation Area.** Wherever you stay, take in Weaverville—don't miss its **Joss House**—on your third day.

IF YOU HAVE 5 OR 6 DAYS

Get a glimpse of the Far North's heritage in **Red Bluff** ② before heading north on I–5 to the town of ⊞ **Mount Shasta** ⑦. On day two drop by the Forest Service Ranger Station to check on trail conditions on **Mount Shasta** and pick up maps. Pack a picnic lunch before taking the **Everett Memorial Highway** up the mountain. After exploring the mountain, head south on I–5 and spend the night in ⊞ **Dunsmuir** at the **Railroad Car Resort,** where all the accommodations are old cabooses. On your third day, take an early morning hike in nearby **Castle Crags State Park.** Continue south on I–5 and tour **Shasta Dam** ⑨. Spend the night camping in the area or in ⊞ **Redding** ⑪. On your fourth morning, head west on Highway 299 and visit the town of **Shasta.** Continue west on 299 to ⊞ **Weaverville** ⑩ and stay the night there or back in Redding. If you will be leaving the area on your fifth day but have a little time, zip north and visit **Lake Shasta Caverns** ⑧. If you're staying and it's between late May and early October, spend the next day and a half exploring **Lassen Volcanic National Park.** Highway 44 heads east from Redding into the park.

When to Tour the Far North

This region attracts the greatest number of tourists during the summer, which can be dry and scorching. The valley around Redding is mild in the winter, but cooler temperatures prevail at the higher elevations to the east and north. In winter Mount Shasta is a good downhill ski area. The remainder of the Far North is too cold for outdoor pleasures, and snow closes the roads to the region's most awesome sights, including much of Lassen Volcanic National Park, from October until late May. Many restaurants and museums here have limited hours and sometimes close for stretches of the off season.

FROM CHICO TO MOUNT SHASTA

The Far North's most spectacular scenery lies along the two-lane roads that crisscross the region, which is bisected by I–5. East of I–5 are dramatic mountain peaks. To the west you'll find heavily forested areas and interesting small towns.

The Far North

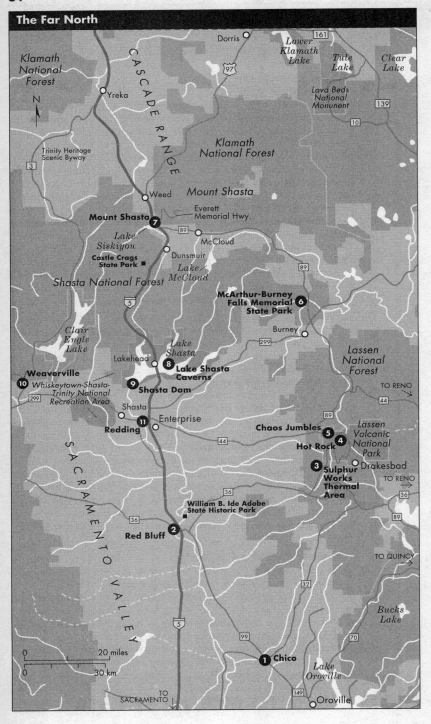

Klamath
National
Forest

CASCADE RANGE

Dorris

161

97

Lower
Klamath
Lake

Tule
Lake

Clear
Lake

Yreka

N

Lava Beds
National
Monument

139

10

Klamath
National
Forest

Trinity Heritage
Scenic Byway

3

Mount Shasta

Weed

Everett
Memorial Hwy.

Mount Shasta ⑦

89

Lake
Siskiyou

McCloud

**Castle Crags
State Park** ■

Dunsmuir

Lake
McCloud

89

Shasta National Forest

5

McArthur-Burney
Falls Memorial
State Park ⑥

Burney

299

Lassen
National
Forest

TO RENO

Clair
Engle
Lake

Lakehead

Lake
Shasta

⑧ **Lake Shasta
Caverns**

44

Weaverville
⑩ *Whiskeytown-Shasta-
Trinity National
Recreation Area*

299

⑨ **Shasta Dam**

Shasta

⑪

Enterprise

89

Chaos Jumbles ⑤ ④

Hot Rock

Lassen
Volcanic
National
Park

Redding

44

③ **Sulphur
Works
Thermal
Area**

Drakesbad

TO RENO

36

89

SACRAMENTO VALLEY

36

**William B. Ide Adobe
State Historic Park** ■

② **Red Bluff**

TO QUINCY

32

Bucks
Lake

5

99

149

70

① **Chico**

Lake
Oroville

Oroville

TO
SACRAMENTO

0   20 miles
0   30 km

Chico

❶ *180 mi from San Francisco, east on I–80, north on I–505 to I–5, and east on Hwy. 32; 86 mi north of Sacramento on Hwy. 99.*

The presence of California State University at Chico lends this city of 53,000 a distinct flavor—actually, two flavors: beer (locally made Sierra Nevada Pale Ale, of course) and coffee (at least a dozen coffee-houses keep the students awake). Chico is also an agricultural and arts center.

★ The 3,670-acre **Bidwell Park** (☎ 530/895–4972), which straddles Big Chico Creek, contains playgrounds, a golf course, swimming areas, and paved biking, hiking, and in-line skating trails. The second-largest city-run park in the nation starts as a sliver downtown and sprawls eastward toward the Sierra foothills.

Bidwell Mansion was built between 1865 and 1868 by General John Bidwell, who came west in 1841 with the first organized wagon train, worked in the gold mines, and then founded Chico. He and his wife settled into this 26-room mansion that was designed by Henry W. Cleaveland, architect of San Francisco's original Palace Hotel. The one-hour tour takes in the dining room, parlor, library, and a half-dozen bed-rooms, whose guests included President and Mrs. Rutherford B. Hayes, naturalist John Muir, and General William T. Sherman. ⊠ *Bidwell Mansion State Historic Park, 525 The Esplanade,* ☎ *530/895–6144.* 🎫 *$3.* ☉ *Weekdays noon–5, weekends 10–5; last tour daily at 4.*

★ The award-winning **Sierra Nevada Brewing Company,** one of the pioneers of the microbrewery movement, still has a hands-on approach to beer-making that makes touring its sparkling brewery a pleasure. You can enjoy a hearty lunch or dinner in the brew pub, which serves standard pub fare and interesting entrées. ⊠ *1075 E. 20th St.,* ☎ *530/345–2739.* 🎫 *Free.* ☉ *Tours Tues.–Fri. at 2:30 and Sat. noon–3 on the ½-hr.* ☉ *Closed Mon.*

Dining and Lodging

$–$$ ✕ **Kramore Inn.** Crepes—from ham and avocado to crab cannelloni—are the inn's specialty. The menu also includes salads, Asian dishes, and several pastas. Brunch is available on the weekends. ⊠ *1903 Park Ave.,* ☎ *530/343–3701. AE, D, MC, V.* ☉ *Open Tues.–Sun.*

$$–$$$ 🏨 **Johnson's Country Inn.** Two miles from downtown amid an almond orchard, this pink Victorian-style farmhouse complete with wraparound veranda is a welcome change from motel row. Johnson's, built in 1992, is full of Victorian charm and modern conveniences. ⊠ *3935 Morehead Ave., 95928,* ☎ FAX *530/345–7829. 4 rooms. Full breakfast. AE, MC, V.*

Shopping

There are numerous art galleries to visit in Chico. Shop and watch demonstrations of glass blowing at the **Satava Art Glass Studio** (⊠ 819 Wall St., ☎ 530/345–7985). **Made in Chico** (⊠ 232 Main St., ☎ 530/894–7009) carries locally made goods, including handwoven scarves, beautiful pottery, salad dressings, and mustards.

OFF THE BEATEN PATH

QUINCY – A two-hour drive from Chico, south on Highways 99 and 149 and east on Highway 70, leads through the scenic Feather River Canyon, ending at elevation 3,500 ft in quaint and highly strollable Quincy. Traditional Maidu baskets, woven by members of the local Native American community, are among the items on exhibit at the **Plumas County Museum** (⊠ 500 Jackson St., ☎ 530/283–6320). The museum (admission $1) is open weekdays year-round from 8 to 5 (and on weekends between May and September from 10 to 4). The cozy old **Feather Bed** (✉ 542 Jackson St., ☎ 530/283–0102) B&B has large rooms and bikes for guests to use. The **Morning Thunder Café** (✉ 557 Lawrence St., ☎ 530/283–1310), which serves breakfast until 2 PM, is always abuzz with espresso-heads. The most popular dinner spot is **Moon's** (✉ 497 Lawrence St., ☎ 530/283–0765), where daily specials augment a mostly Italian menu. You can sit on the patio in good weather. Quincy is a good base for forays into the **Plumas National Forest** (✉ Supervisor's Office, 159 Lawrence St., ☎ 530/283–2050), whose numerous waterfalls include the 640-ft-high Feather Falls. The supervisor's office has road and trail maps.

Red Bluff

2 *179 mi north of San Francisco, I–80 to I–505 to I–5.*

Named for the color of its soil and its location above the Sacramento River, Red Bluff was established in the mid-19th century, before Victorian architecture became the style of choice in the Far North. Historic structures of two types remain: restored Victorians line the streets west of Main Street; downtown looks like a stage set for a western movie.

The **Kelly-Griggs House Museum,** a beautifully restored 1880s home, holds an impressive collection of antique furniture, housewares, and clothing arranged as though a refined Victorian-era family were still in residence. An engraved silver tea server waits at the end table; a "Self Instructor in Penmanship" sits on a desk; and costumed mannequins seem frozen in conversation in the upstairs parlor. The museum's collection includes carved china cabinets and Native American basketry. *Persephone*, the painting over the fireplace, is by Sarah Brown, daughter of abolitionist John Brown, whose family settled in Red Bluff. ✉ *311 Washington St.,* ☎ *530/527–1129.* ▣ *Donation suggested.* ◷ *Thurs.–Sun. 1–4.*

The **William B. Ide Adobe State Historic Park** is a memorial to the first and only president of the short-lived California Republic of 1846. The Bear Flag Party proclaimed California a sovereign nation, no longer under the dominion of Mexico, and the republic existed for 25 days before it was occupied by the United States. The flag concocted for the republic has survived, with only minor refinements, as California's state flag. This adobe, thought to have been Abraham Dibble's, was built in the 1850s. Furnishings and artifacts of that era are on display. ✉ *21659 Adobe Rd.,* ☎ *530/529–8599.* ▣ *$3 donation requested per vehicle.* ◷ *Park and picnic facilities 8 AM–sunset year-round; home 11–4 in summer (in winter, look for ranger to unlock house).*

Dining and Lodging

$ ✕ **Snack Box.** Unabashedly corny pictures and knickknacks, all rural and many depicting cattle and sheep, decorate the renovated Victorian cottage that holds the Snack Box. The food need make no apologies, however. Soups, omelets, country-fried steaks, and even simple items such as grilled-cheese sandwiches are perfectly crafted. ✉ *257 Main St., 1 block from Kelly-Griggs House Museum,* ☎ *530/529–0227. MC, V. No dinner.*

$ ▥ **Lamplighter Lodge.** Simple rooms, some with refrigerators, are available. The pool area is a great place to relax on a sweltering summer day. ✉ *210 S. Main St. 96080,* ☎ *530/527–1150. 48 rooms, 2 suites. Pool. AE, D, DC, MC, V.*

Lassen Volcanic National Park

45 mi east of Redding on Hwy. 44; 48 mi east of Red Bluff on Hwy. 36.

Lassen Volcanic National Park provides a look at three sides of the world's largest plug volcano. Except for the Nordic ski area, the park is largely inaccessible from late October to late May because of heavy snow. The Lassen Park Road (the continuation of Highway 89 within the park) is closed to cars in winter but open to intrepid cross-country skiers, conditions permitting. Even in the best of weather, services are sparse. In the southwest corner of the park, a café and a gift shop are open during the summer. The *Lassen Park Guide,* available for a nominal fee at the visitor center and park entrance, details these and other facilities. ⊠ *Headquarters and visitor center: 38050 Hwy. 36 E, Mineral 96063,* ☎ *530/595–4444.* ☞ *$10 per vehicle, $5 on foot or bicycle; $8–$14 for campsites (reservations not accepted).* ☉ *Visitor center weekdays 8–4:30 year-round, summer weekends 8–4:30; hrs sometimes vary.*

In 1914 the 10,457-ft Mount Lassen began a series of 300 eruptions that continued for seven years. Molten rock overflowed the crater, and the mountain emitted clouds of smoke and hailstorms of rocks and volcanic cinders. Proof of the volcano's volatility becomes evident shortly ❸ after you enter the park at the **Sulphur Works Thermal Area.** Boardwalks take you over bubbling mud and hot springs and through the sulfur-emitting steam vents. ⊠ *Lassen Park Rd., south end of park.*

The **Lassen Peak Hike** winds 2½ mi—a good workout if you're in shape; you'll be huffing and puffing if you're not—to the mountaintop. At the peak you can take a peek into the rim and view the entire park (and much of the Far North). Bring sunscreen and water. ⊠ *Off Lassen Park Rd. at Mile Marker 22.*

Along **Bumpass Hell Trail,** a 3-mi round-trip hike to the park's most interesting thermal-spring area, you can view hot and boiling springs, steam vents, and mud pots up close. The trail climbs and descends several hundred feet. Stay on trails and boardwalks near the thermal areas. What appears to be firm ground may be only a thin crust over scalding mud. ⊠ *Off Lassen Park Rd., 5 mi north of Sulphur Works Thermal Area.*

❹ **Hot Rock,** a 400-ton boulder, tumbled down from the summit during the volcano's active period and was still hot to the touch when locals found it. Although cool now, it's still an impressive sight. ⊠ *Lassen Park Rd., north end of park.*

❺ **Chaos Jumbles** was created 300 years ago when an avalanche from the Chaos Crags lava domes spread hundreds of thousands of rocks 2 to 3 ft in diameter over a couple of square miles. ⊠ *Lassen Park Rd., north end of park.*

Dining, Lodging, and Camping

$$$$ ✕🏨 **Drakesbad Guest Ranch.** This century-old guest ranch, at elevation 5,700 ft near Lassen Volcanic National Park's southern border, is isolated from most of the rest of the park, which is one reason it is so popular. Rooms in the lodge, bungalows, and cabins don't have electricity; they're lighted by kerosene lamps. But the spartan accommodations are clean and comfortable and have furnace heat and either a half or full bath. Breakfast and lunch are simple affairs, but evening meals are rather elegant. Reservations should be made well ahead (the waiting list can be up to two years long). All meals are included. ⊠ *Chester–Warner Valley Rd., north from Hwy. 36 (booking office: 2150*

N. Main St., Suite 5, Red Bluff 96080), ☎ 530/529–9820, FAX 530/529–4511. 19 rooms. Dining room, pool, badminton, horseback riding, horseshoes, Ping-Pong, volleyball, fishing. FAP. D, MC, V. ☉ Early June.–early Oct.

$ ✕▥ **Lassen Mineral Lodge.** Reserve rooms at this motel-style property as far ahead as possible. You can rent cross-country skis, snowshoes, and snowboards at the lodge's ski shop. There's also a general store. ✉ Hwy. 36, Mineral 96063, ☎ 530/595–4422. 20 rooms. Restaurant, bar. AE, D, MC, V.

△ **Manzanita Lake Campground.** The largest of Lassen Volcanic National Park's seven campgrounds (reservations are not accepted at any of them) is near the northern entrance. A trail near the campground leads to Chaos Crags Lake. ✉ Off Lassen Park Rd. 2 mi east of junction of Hwys. 44 and 89, ☎ 530/595–4444. 179 sites. ▥ $14. Fire rings, flush toilets, showers, water, general store. ☉ Mid-May–mid-Oct.

McArthur-Burney Falls Memorial State Park

❻ 30 mi north of Lassen Volcanic National Park on Hwy. 89.

Just inside the southern boundary of this state park, Burney Creek wells up from the ground and divides into two cascades that fall over a 129-ft cliff and into a pool below. The thundering water creates a mist at the base of the falls, often highlighted by a rainbow. Countless ribbonlike falls stream from hidden moss-covered crevices—an ethereal backdrop to the main cascades. Each day 100 million gallons of water rush over these falls; Theodore Roosevelt proclaimed them "the eighth wonder of the world." A self-guided nature trail descends to the foot of the falls. There is a lake and beach for swimming. A campground, picnic sites, and other facilities are available. The camp store is open from Memorial Day to Labor Day. ✉ 24898 Hwy. 89, Burney 96013, ☎ 530/335–2777; 800/444–7275 for campground reservations (necessary in summer). ▥ $5 per vehicle (day use); $16 (campsites).

Mount Shasta

❼ 52 mi from McArthur-Burney Falls Memorial State Park on Hwy. 89; 61 mi north of Redding on I–5.

Mount Shasta—the mountain and the town—made headlines in 1987 when participants in the worldwide Harmonic Convergence descended on the region, believing the mountain held special powers. They weren't the first. Legends of eerie phenomena and mythical animals have been part of the mountain's folklore for decades.

The crowning jewel of the 2.5-million-acre Shasta–Trinity National Forest, Mount Shasta is popular with day hikers, especially in spring, when flowers like the fragrant Shasta lily adorn the rocky slopes. But few people make it to the perennially ice-packed summit of this 16-million-year-old dormant volcano. An automobile road travels only as high as the timberline, and the final 6,000 ft are a tough climb of rubble, ice, and snow.

The town of Mount Shasta is not so much a destination as a place to eat and sleep. Even on the main thoroughfare there isn't much to do or see.

Dining and Lodging

$–$$$ ✕ **Lily's.** This restaurant in a white clapboard home—complete with picket fence—serves everything from steaks and pastas to Mexican and vegetarian dishes. Among the unusual salads are a spicy shrimp-and-chicken dish and the Jalisco—steak and greens with tomatoes. ⊠ *1013 S. Mt. Shasta Blvd.*, ☎ *530/926–3372. AE, D, MC, V.*

$$ ✕ **Trinity Café.** This cozy little restaurant has gained popularity in the area with a menu that changes every week. Offerings range from a classic eggplant Parmesan to a more innovative fettuccine dish with sautéed mushrooms and a chive sauce. ⊠ *622 N. Mt. Shasta Blvd.*, ☎ *530/ 926–6200. MC, V.* ⊙ *Tues.–Sun.*

$–$$ ✕ **Michael's Restaurant.** Wood paneling, candlelight, and wildlife prints by local artists create an unpretentious setting for Italian specialties such as stuffed calamari, filet mignon scallopini, and linguine pesto. ⊠ *313 N. Mt. Shasta Blvd.*, ☎ *530/926–5288. AE, D, MC, V.* ⊙ *Tues.–Sat.*

$–$$ 🏠 **Best Western Tree House Motor Inn.** The clean, standard rooms at this motel less than a mile from downtown Mount Shasta are decorated with natural-wood furnishings. Some rooms have vaulted ceilings and mountain views. ⊠ *111 Morgan Way, at I–5 and Lake St., 96067*, ☎ *530/926–3101 or 800/545–7164,* FAX *530/926–3542. 94 rooms, 4 suites. Restaurant, refrigerators, indoor pool, hot tub. AE, D, DC, MC, V.*

Outdoor Activities and Sports

HIKING

The **Forest Service Ranger Station** (☎ 530/926–4511) keep tabs on trail conditions. The **Fifth Season Mountaineering Shop** (☎ 530/926–3606) operates a recorded 24-hour climber-skier report (☎ 530/926–5555).

MOUNTAIN CLIMBING

Fifth Season Mountaineering Shop (300 N. Mt. Shasta Blvd., ☎ 530/ 926–3606) rents skiing and climbing equipment. **Shasta Mountain Guides** (☎ 530/926–3117) leads hiking, climbing, and ski-touring groups to the summit of Mount Shasta.

SKIING

Mt. Shasta Board & Ski Park. On the southeast flank of Mount Shasta are three lifts on 425 skiable acres. The terrain is 20% beginner, 55% intermediate, and 25% advanced. Its vertical drop is 1,390 ft, with a top elevation of 6,600 ft. The longest run is 1¼ mi. You can ski until 10 PM from Wednesday through Saturday. A package for beginners, available through the ski school, includes a lift ticket, ski rental, and a lesson. The school also runs the SKIwee program for children ages four to seven. Within the base lodge are food and beverage facilities, a ski shop, and a ski-rental shop. ⊠ *Hwy. 89 exit east from I–5, south of Mt. Shasta*, ☎ *530/926–8610 or 800/SKI–SHASTA; 530/926–8686 for snow information.*

OFF THE
BEATEN PATH

LAVA BEDS NATIONAL MONUMENT – Much of the beauty at this rugged monument, the product of volcanic eruptions, is underground in 300-plus lava tube caves, some of which can be explored. Wear hard-sole boots, and pick up the necessary equipment (lights, "bump" hats, etc.) at the Indian Well Visitor Center, at the park's south end. Guided walks and cave tours, which take place between Memorial Day and Labor Day, depart from the visitor center. Campfire programs—the topic is determined by the ranger—are offered nightly in summer months. ⊠ *94 mi from the town of Mt. Shasta; head north on I–5, northeast on U.S. 97 at Weed, east on Hwy. 161 (3 mi north of Dorris), and south on Hill Rd. (from town of Burney head east on Hwy. 299 and north on Hwy. 139)*, ☎ *530/667–2282.* 🎫 *$4 per vehicle; $2 per visitor on foot or bicycle; $10 camping in summer and $6 in winter.* ⊙ *Park 24 hrs. Visitor center daily 8–5.*

Dunsmuir

10 mi south of Mt. Shasta on I–5.

Castle Crags State Park surrounds the town of Dunsmuir, which was named for a 19th-century coal baron. The town's other major attraction is the ✪ **Railroad Park Resort** (☞ *below*), where guests spend the night in restored railcars.

The 225-million-year-old granite crags at **Castle Crags State Park** tower over the Sacramento River at heights of up to 6,000 ft. There are excellent trails at lower altitudes in this 6,000-acre park, which also has picnic areas, rest rooms, showers, and plenty of campsites. ⊠ *Off I–5, 6 mi south of Dunsmuir,* ☎ *530/235–2684.* ☜ *$5 per vehicle (day use); $12 (campsites). Disposal station, fire rings, flush toilets, hot showers, water.*

Lodging

$ 🏨 **Dunsmuir Inn Bed and Breakfast.** It's not fancy, but this homey inn—a good deal considering that rates include a made-to-order breakfast—is comfortable and within easy walking distance of the historic downtown area. Rooms are decorated simply. ⊠ *5423 Dunsmuir Ave., 96025,* ☎ *530/235–4543. 5 rooms. Full breakfast. AE, D, MC, V.*

$ 🏨 **Railroad Park Resort.** The antique cabooses here have been converted into cozy, wood-panel motel rooms in honor of Dunsmuir's railroad legacy. The resort has a vaguely *Orient Express*–style dining room and a lounge fashioned from vintage railcars. The landscaped grounds contain a huge logging steam engine and a restored water tower. There's also an RV park. ⊠ *100 Railroad Park Rd., 96025,* ☎ *530/235–4440 or 800/974–7245,* 𝖥𝖠𝖷 *530/235–4470. 23 cabooses, 4 cabins. Restaurant (dinner only), pool, hot tub, camping. AE, D, MC, V.*

Lake Shasta Area

34 mi south of Mt. Shasta (to town of Lakehead) on I–5; 12 mi north of Redding on I–5.

The many Shastas—mountain, lake, river, town, dam, and forest—derive from the name of the Indians who inhabited parts of the region in the 19th century (variously, Shatasla and Sastise). The Indian pronunciation for the river was *tschasta.*

❽ Stalagmites, stalactites, odd flowstone deposits, and crystals entice visitors of all ages to the **Lake Shasta Caverns.** A two-hour tour includes a catamaran ride across the McCloud arm of Lake Shasta and a bus ride up Grey Rock Mountain to the cavern entrance. The caverns are 58°F year-round, making them an appealingly cool retreat on a hot summer day. The crowning jewel is the awe-inspiring cathedral room. The guides are friendly, enthusiastic, and knowledgeable. ⊠ *Shasta Caverns Rd. exit from I–5,* ☎ *530/238–2341 or 800/795–2283.* ☜ *$15.* ☉ *Daily 9–4; tours Memorial Day–Labor Day on the ½ hr, Sept., Apr., and May on the hr, Oct.–Mar. at 10, noon, and 2.*

★ Twenty-one varieties of fish inhabit **Lake Shasta.** You can rent fishing boats, ski boats, sailboats, canoes, paddleboats, Jet Skis, and windsurfing boards at one of the many marinas and resorts along the 370-mi shoreline. Lake Shasta is known as the houseboat capital of the world. *See* Outdoor Activities and Sports, *below,* for information about rentals.

★ ❾ **Shasta Dam** is the second-largest and the fourth-tallest concrete dam in the United States. At twilight the sight is magical, with Mount Shasta gleaming above the not-quite-dark water and deer frolicking on the hillside beside the dam. The dam is lit after dark, but there is no access from 10 PM to 6 AM. The visitor center has computerized photographic tours of the dam construction, video presentations, fact sheets, and historic displays. The friendly staff is very knowledgable about the area. ⊠ *16349 Shasta Dam Blvd.,* ☎ *530/275–4463.* ⊙ *Dam 6 AM–10 PM; visitor center 8:30–4:30; tours 9–4 on the hr in summer, winter weekdays 10, 11, 1, and 3, and winter weekends 9–4 on the hr.*

Dining

$$-$$$ ✕ **Tail O' the Whale.** This restaurant overlooking Lake Shasta is distinguished by its nautical decor. Seafood, pasta, prime rib, and poultry are the specialties. ⊠ *10300 Bridge Bay Rd., Bridge Bay exit from I–5,* ☎ *530/275–3021. D, MC, V.*

Outdoor Activities and Sports

FISHING

The Fishin' Hole (⊠ 3844 Shasta Dam Blvd., Central Valley, ☎ 530/275–4123) carries supplies and provides information about conditions, licenses, and fishing packages.

HOUSEBOATING

Houseboats come in all sizes except small. As a rule these moving homes come with cooking utensils, dishes, and most of the equipment you'll need. You supply food and linens. Renters are given a short course in how to maneuver the boats before they set out on cruises. It's not difficult, as the houseboats are slow moving. You can fish, swim, sunbathe on the flat roof, or sit on the deck and watch the world go by. The shoreline of Lake Shasta is beautifully ragged, with countless inlets; it's not hard to find privacy. Expect to spend a minimum of $200 a day for a craft that sleeps six. There is usually a three-night minimum in peak season. **Shasta Cascade Wonderland Association** (☞ Contacts and Resources *in* the Far North A to Z, *below*) has more information.

Shasta

6 mi west of Redding on Hwy. 299.

The ruins of the once prosperous gold-mining town of Shasta are now the 13-acre **Shasta State Historic Park.** Poke around the few restored buildings on the self-guided tour, and you'll get a sense of the lives of 19th-century prospectors. The eclectic holdings of the park's museum include California paintings, memorabilia, and a *Prairie Traveler* guidebook with advice on encounters with Indians. In the basement of the building, formerly the town's courthouse, are iron-bar jail cells; murderers were hanged from the scaffold outside. ⊠ *Hwy. 299,* ☎ *530/243–8194.* ▨ *$2.* ⊙ *Wed.–Sun. 10–5.*

Weaverville

➓ *40 mi west of Shasta on Hwy. 299 (called Main St. in town).*

This old mountain town with a population of 3,300 is one of the Far North's most charming. Although there are strips of car dealers and the like, the downtown blocks maintain their Gold-Rush ambience. Weaverville is a popular headquarters for family vacations and biking, hiking, fishing, hunting, and gold-panning excursions.

John Weaver was one of three men who built the first cabin, in 1850, in the town that would be named for him. By 1851 Weaverville was the Trinity County seat and included neighboring communities such as Frenchtown, Englishtown, Germantown, Irishtown, and a sizable Chinatown.

★ The most visible legacy of the Chinese presence is the **Weaverville Joss House,** a Taoist temple built in 1874. Called Won Lim Miao, the "Temple Amongst the Forest Beneath the Clouds," by Chinese miners, it attracts worshipers from around the world. With its golden altar, carved wooden canopies, and intriguing artifacts, the Joss House is a piece of California history that can best be appreciated in the company of a guide. The original temple building and many of its furnishings—some of which had come from China—were burned in 1873, but members of the local Chinese community soon rebuilt it. ⊠ *Oregon and Main Sts.,* ☎ *530/623–5284.* ⊠ *$2 for 40-min guided tours, on the hr 10–4.* ☉ *Summer daily 10–5, rest of yr Thurs.–Mon. 10–5.*

Fires destroyed many parts of Weaverville; surviving buildings are mostly brick. Since the upper floor of many old downtown buildings was often owned by a different person than the lower floor, outdoor spiral staircases were constructed to permit each owner a private entrance. Three such buildings remain visible in the downtown Historic District.

The **Trinity County Courthouse** (⊠ Court and Main Sts.), built in 1857 as a store, office building, and hotel, was converted to county use in 1865. The Apollo Saloon in the basement became the county jail.

Trinity County Historical Park is home to the Jake Jackson Memorial Museum, which has a blacksmith shop, a replica stamp mill, and the original jail cells of the Trinity County Courthouse. ⊠ *408 Main St.,* ☎ *530/623–5211.* ☉ *May–Oct., daily 10–5; Nov.–Apr., Tues. and Sat. noon–4.*

Dining and Lodging

$–$$ ✕ **La Grange Café.** This eatery is one of the few places in Weaverville open for lunch and dinner six days a week. Stick to basics like chicken and pasta. The kitchen is not as dependable when it comes to dishes like trout. On the plus side, La Grange serves plenty of vegetables and sells beer and wine. ⊠ *315 N. Main St.,* ☎ *530/623–5325. AE, D, MC, V. Closed Sun.*

$ ✕ **La Casita.** Here you'll find the standard regimen—all the quesadillas (including one with roasted chili peppers), tostadas, enchiladas, tacos, and tamales you could want, many of them available in a vegetarian version. This casual spot is open from late morning through early evening, so it's great for a mid-afternoon snack. ⊠ *254 Main St.,* ☎ *530/623–5797. No credit cards.*

$ 🏨 **Red Hill Motel.** Housekeeping cabins make this the best choice among Weaverville motels. A cozy cabin with a full kitchen is popular with families. ⊠ *Red Hill Rd., Box 234, 96093,* ☎ *530/623–4331. 14 rooms, 10 of them cabins with carports. AE, D, MC, V.*

Outdoor Activities and Sports

Below the Lewiston Dam, east of Weaverville on Highway 299, is the **Fly Stretch** of the Trinity River, a world-class fly-fishing area. The **Pine Cove Boat Ramp** provides quality fishing access for visitors with disabilities—decks here are built over prime trout-fishing water. Contact the **Weaverville Ranger Station** (☎ 530/623–2121) for maps and information about hiking trails in the Trinity Alps Wilderness.

Shopping

Hays Bookstore (⊠ 106 Main St., ☎ 530/623–2516) carries books on the natural history, attractions, and sights of the Far North. Check out the **Western Shop** (⊠ 226 Main St., ☎ 530/623–6494) for outdoor gear, bolo ties, cowboy hats, and much more.

OFF THE
BEATEN PATH
TRINITY HERITAGE SCENIC BYWAY – This road, shown on maps as Highway 3, runs north from Weaverville for 120 mi up to its intersection with I–5, south of Yreka. Natural attractions are visible all along this beautiful, forest-lined road, which is often closed during the winter months. A major portion of the route follows the path established by early miners and settlers as it climbs from 2,000 to 6,500 ft.

Redding

⑪ *218 mi from San Francisco on I–80 to I–505 to I–5 north; 12 mi south of Lake Shasta on I–5.*

With a population of more than 80,000, Redding is by far the largest city in the Far North. Though not of much interest, it serves as a useful headquarters for exploring the surrounding countryside.

Dining and Lodging

$–$$$ ✕ **Hatch Cover.** This establishment's dark-wood paneling and views of the adjacent Sacramento River give diners a shipboard feel. The menu emphasizes seafood, but you can also get steaks and combination plates. The appetizer menu is extensive, and there's an outside deck. ⊠ *202 Hemsted Dr. (from Cypress Ave. exit off I–5, turn left, then right on Hemsted Dr.),* ☎ *530/223–5606. AE, D, MC, V. No lunch weekends.*

$ ✕ **Jack's Grill.** Although it looks like a dive from the outside, this steak house and bar is immensely popular for its 16-ounce steaks. Be prepared to eat meat; it's your only choice here. The place is usually jam-packed and noisy. ⊠ *1743 California St.,* ☎ *530/241–9705. AE, D, MC, V. Closed Sun. No lunch.*

$–$$$ ✕🏠 **Doubletree Hotel.** Landscaped grounds and a large patio area with outdoor food service are the highlights here. Rooms are spacious and comfortable. Misty's, the lobby's fancy restaurant ($$–$$$), is popular among locals for its steak Diane. Pets are allowed with advance notice. ⊠ *1830 Hilltop Dr. (Hwy. 44/299 exit east from I–5), 96002,* ☎ *530/221–8700,* 🅵🅰🆇 *530/221–0324. 192 rooms, 2 suites. Restaurant, bar, coffee shop, room service, pool, wading pool, hot tub, exercise room. AE, D, DC, MC, V.*

$$$–$$$$ 🏠 **Brigadoon Castle Bed & Breakfast.** Fifteen winding miles from I–5 is an 83-acre estate crowned with an Elizabethan-style castle that opened as a B&B in 1996. Marble baths, antiques, and luxurious fabrics make the Brigadoon an elegant retreat. A separate cottage has a kitchen and a hot tub. From Friday through Sunday the rates include dinner. ⊠ *9036 Zogg Mine Rd., Igo 96047,* ☎ *530/396–2785 or 888/343–2836,* 🅵🅰🆇 *530/396–2784. 4 rooms, 1 cottage. Hot tub. Full breakfast. AE, D, MC, V.*

$ 🏠 **Howard Johnson Express.** Here's a budget option—doubles with queen-size beds go for around $50—off I–5's Cypress exit. ⊠ *2731 Bechelli La.,* ☎ *530/223–1935 or 800/354–5222,* 🅵🅰🆇 *530/223–1176. 75 rooms, 2 suites. Pool. AE, D, DC, MC, V.*

Outdoor Activities and Sports

The **Fly Shop** (⊠ 4140 Churn Creek Rd., ☎ 530/222–3555) sells fishing licenses and has information about guides, conditions, and fishing packages. **Park Marina Watersports** (⊠ 2210 Twin View Blvd., ☎ 530/246–8388) rents rafts and canoes from May through September.

THE FAR NORTH A TO Z

Arriving and Departing

By Bus
Greyhound Lines (☎ 800/231–2222) buses travel I–5, serving Chico, Red Bluff, Redding, Dunsmuir, and Mount Shasta. **Amtrak** (☎ 800/872–7245) also runs buses through Redding, Red Bluff, and Chico.

By Car
Interstate 5, an excellent four-lane divided highway, runs up the center of California through Red Bluff and Redding and continues north to Oregon. Chico is east of I–5 on Highway 32. Lassen Park can be reached by Highway 36 from Red Bluff or (except in winter) Highway 44 from Redding. Highway 299 leads from Redding to McArthur-Burney Falls Memorial State Park. Highways 36 and 299 are good two-lane roads that are kept open year-round. If you are traveling through this area in winter, however, always carry snow chains in your car.

By Plane
Chico Municipal Airport (⊠ 150 Airpark Blvd., off Cohasset Rd., ☎ 530/898–2359) and **Redding Municipal Airport** (⊠ Airport Rd., ☎ 530/224–4320) are served by United Express (☎ 800/241–6522). Horizon Air (☎ 800/547–9308) also uses the airport in Redding.

By Train
Amtrak (☎ 800/872–7245) has stations in Chico (⊠ W. 5th and Orange Sts.), Redding (⊠ 1620 Yuba St.) and Dunsmuir (⊠ 5750 Sacramento Ave.).

Getting Around

By Bus
Butte County Transit (☎ 530/342–0221 or 800/822–8145) serves Chico, Oroville, and elsewhere. **Chico Area Transit System** (CATS; ☎ 530/342–0221) provides bus service within Chico. The vehicles of the **Redding Area Bus Authority** (☎ 530/241–2877) operate daily except Sunday. **STAGE** (☎ 530/842–8295) buses travel from Montague to Dunsmuir, stopping in Mount Shasta and other towns, and provide service in Scott Valley.

By Car
An automobile is virtually essential to tour the Far North unless you arrive by bus, plane, or train and intend to travel the region by foot or bicycle.

Contacts and Resources

Car Rental
Avis (⊠ Redding Municipal Airport, ☎ 530/221–2855 or 800/331–1212). **Enterprise** (⊠ 357 E. Cypress Ave., Redding, ☎ 530/223–0700 or 800/325–8007). **Enterprise** (⊠ 570 Antelope Blvd., Red Bluff, ☎ 530/529–0177 or 800/325–8007). **Hertz** (⊠ Redding Municipal Airport, ☎ 530/221–4620 or 800/654–3131).

Emergencies
Ambulance (☎ 911). **Fire** (☎ 911). **Police** (☎ 911).

Visitor Information
Chico Chamber of Commerce (⊠ 300 Salem St., 95928, ☎ 530/891–5556 or 800/852–8570). **Shasta Cascade Wonderland Association** (⊠ 1699 Hwy. 273, Anderson 96007, ☎ 530/365–7500 or 800/326–6944).

3 THE WINE COUNTRY

You don't have to be a wine enthusiast to appreciate the mellow beauty of Napa and Sonoma counties, whose rolling hills and verdant vineyards resemble those of Tuscany and Provence. Here, among state-of-the-art wineries, fabulous restaurants, and luxury hotels where mud baths and massage are daily rituals, you just might discover that life need have no nobler purpose than enjoying the fruits of the earth.

Updated by
Marty
Olmstead

IN 1862, AFTER AN EXTENSIVE TOUR of the wine-pro-
ducing areas of Europe, Count Agoston Haraszthy de
Mokcsa reported a promising prognosis about his adopted
California: "Of all the countries through which I passed, not one pos-
sessed the same advantages that are to be found in California. . . . California can produce as noble and generous a wine as any in Europe;
more in quantity to the acre, and without repeated failures through
frosts, summer rains, hailstorms, or other causes."

The "dormant resources" that the father of California's viticulture saw
in the balmy days and cool nights of the temperate Napa and Sonoma
valleys are in full fruition today. The wines produced here are praised
and savored by connoisseurs throughout the world. The area also continues to be a proving ground for the latest techniques of grape growing and wine making.

In 1975 Napa Valley had no more than 20 wineries. Today there are
more than 240. In Sonoma County, there are well over 150 wineries,
and development is now claiming the cool Carneros region, at the head
of the San Francisco Bay, deemed ideal for growing the chardonnay
grape. Nowadays individual grape growers produce their own wines
instead of selling their grapes to larger wineries. As a result, smaller
"boutique" wineries harvest excellent, reasonably priced wines that have
caught the attention of connoisseurs and critics, while the larger wineries consolidate land and expand their varietals.

This state-of-the-art viticulture has also given rise to a gastronomic renaissance. Inspired by the creative spirit that produces the region's great
wines, esteemed chefs are opening restaurants in record numbers, making culinary history in the process.

You'll also find a wealth of California history here. Sonoma is filled
with remnants of Mexican California and the solid, ivy-covered, brick
wineries built by Haraszthy and his disciples. Calistoga is a virtual museum of Steamboat Gothic architecture, replete with the fretwork and
clapboard beloved of Gold Rush prospectors and late-19th-century spa
goers. St. Helena is home to a later architectural fantasy, the beautiful art nouveau mansion of the Beringer brothers.

Pleasures and Pastimes

Dining
Many star chefs from urban areas throughout the United States have
migrated to the Wine Country, drawn by the area's renowned produce
and world-class wines. Higher quality has, of course, meant higher prices.
However, those on a budget will also find appealing inexpensive eateries. High-end delis offer superb picnic fare, and brunch is a cost-ef-
fective strategy at expensive restaurants.

With few exceptions (which are noted in individual listings), dress is
informal. Where reservations are indicated as essential, you may need
to reserve a week or more ahead. During the summer and early fall
harvest seasons you may need to book several months ahead.

CATEGORY	COST*
$$$$	over $50
$$$	$30–$50
$$	$20–$30
$	under $20

*per person for a three-course meal, excluding drinks, service, and 8 ½%
sales tax

Hot-Air Ballooning

Day after day, colorful balloons fill the morning sky high above the valleys. Flights take place soon after sunrise. Prices depend on the duration of the flight, number of passengers, and services. Some companies provide such extras as pickup at your lodging or champagne brunch after the flight. Expect to spend about $175 per person.

Lodging

Ranging from quaint to utterly luxurious, the area's many inns, hotels, and spas are usually exquisitely appointed. Most local bed-and-breakfasts have historic Victorian and Spanish architecture and serve a full breakfast highlighting local produce. The newer hotels and spas are often state-of-the-art buildings offering such comforts as massage treatments or spring water–fed pools.

Not surprisingly, a stay in the Wine Country is expensive. Since Santa Rosa is the largest population center in the area, it has the largest selection of rooms, many at moderate rates. Try there if you've failed to reserve in advance or have a limited budget. Many B&Bs are fully booked long in advance of the summer season, and small children are often discouraged as guests. For all accommodations in the area, rates are lower on weeknights and about 20% less in the winter.

CATEGORY	COST*
$$$$	over $200
$$$	$120–$200
$$	$80–$120
$	under $80

All prices are for a standard double room, excluding 14% tax.

Spas and Mud Baths

Mineral water soaks, mud baths, and massage are rejuvenating local traditions. Calistoga is famous for its warm, spring water–fed mineral tubs and mud baths full of volcanic ash.

Wine Tasting

For those new to the wine tasting game, Robert Mondavi (☞ Oakville, *below*) and Korbel Champagne Cellars (☞ Healdsburg, *below*) give general tours geared toward teaching novices the basics on how wine and champagne are made and what to look for when you taste. Unless otherwise noted, the wineries in this chapter are open daily year-round and charge no fee for admission, tours, or tastings.

Exploring the Wine Country

Numbers in the text correspond to numbers in the margin and on the Wine Country map.

Great Itineraries

The Wine Country comprises two main areas: the Napa Valley and the Sonoma Valley. Five major paths cut through both valleys: U.S. 101 and Highways 12 and 121 through Sonoma County, and Highway 29 north from Napa. The 25-mi Silverado Trail, which runs parallel to Highway 29 north from Napa to Calistoga, is a more scenic, less crowded route with a number of distinguished wineries. Because the Wine Country is expansive, it's best to plan smaller, separate trips over the course of several days.

IF YOU HAVE 2 DAYS

Start at the **Buena Vista Carneros Winery** ㉙. From there, take Highway 12 north to the Oakville Grade to historic 🖼 **St. Helena.** After lunch in St. Helena, take the 30-minute tour of **Beringer Vineyards** ㉑. The next day drive to **Calistoga** for an early morning balloon ride, an

78

The Wine Country

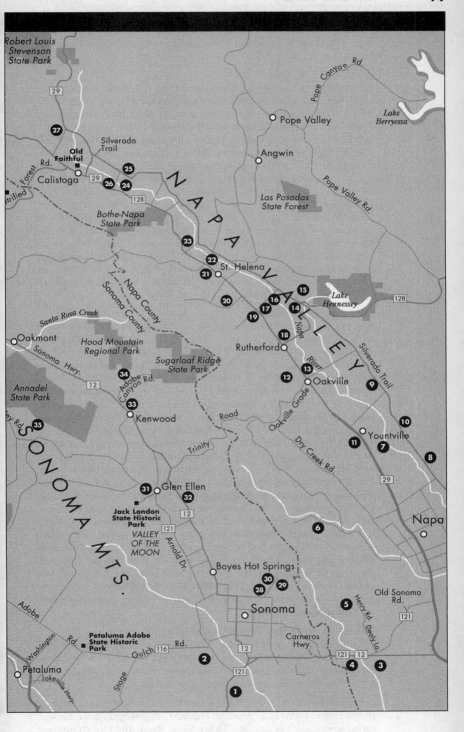

Robert Louis
Stevenson
State Park

29

Pope Canyon Rd.

Lake
Berryessa

Pope Valley

27

Silverado
Trail

Angwin

Old
Faithful

25

Rd.

Calistoga

29   26   24

128

NAPA

Las Posadas
State Forest

Pope Valley Rd.

Bothe-Napa
State Park

23

22

St. Helena

21

Napa County

20

Sonoma County

15

Lake
Hennessey

128

16   14

VALLEY

19   17

Oakmont

Santa Rosa Creek

Sonoma Hwy.

Hood Mountain
Regional Park

Sugarloaf Ridge
State Park

18

Rutherford

Napa River

Silverado Trail

Annadel
State Park

12

34

Adobe Canyon Rd.

33   Kenwood

Road

13

12   Oakville

9

Oakville Grade

Dry Creek Rd.

10

ley Rd.

35

Trinity

11   Yountville

7

SONOMA

31   Glen Ellen

8

Jack London
State Historic
Park

32

12

29

VALLEY
OF THE
MOON

121

6

Napa

MTS.

Arnold Dr.

Boyes Hot Springs

30   29

28

5

Old Sonoma
Rd.

Adobe

Sonoma

Henry Rd. Deahy La.

121

Washington   Rd.

Petaluma Adobe
State Historic
Park

Gulch   116   Rd.

12

Carneros
Hwy.

121   12

Petaluma

Stage

Lake ville Hwy.

2

121

4   3

1

afternoon trip to the mud baths, and a visit to **Clos Pegase** ㉖ before heading back to St. Helena for dinner at Greystone—the Culinary Institute of America's beautiful West Coast campus and highly acclaimed restaurant.

IF YOU HAVE 4 DAYS

Concentrate on the Napa Valley, starting at Yountville and traveling north to Calistoga. Make your first stop in **Oakville,** where the circa-1880s Oakville Grocery is the most popular place for lunch supplies. Enjoy the picnic grounds at **Robert Mondavi** ⑫ before touring the winery. If time permits, spend the night in the town of 🔯 **Rutherford** and visit either **Frog's Leap** ⑰ or the **Niebaum-Coppola Estate** ⑲, or continue north to 🔯 **St. Helena.** Take a look at the Silverado Museum and visit the shopping complex surrounding the **Freemark Abbey Winery** ㉓. On the third day drive to 🔯 **Calistoga** for a balloon ride before heading north to Old Faithful Geyser of California, then continue on to Robert Louis Stevenson State Park, which encompasses the summit of Mount St. Helena. On the fourth day take Highway 29 just north of Calistoga proper, head west on Petrified Forest Road and then south on Calistoga Road, which runs into Highway 12. Follow Highway 12 southeast to **Glen Ellen** for a taste of the Sonoma Valley. Visit Jack London State Historic Park, then loop back north on Bennett Valley Road to beautiful **Matanzas Creek Winery** ㉟ in Santa Rosa.

IF YOU HAVE 7 DAYS

Begin in the town of **Sonoma,** whose colorful plaza and mission evoke early California's Spanish past. Afterward, head north to 🔯 **Glen Ellen** and the Valley of the Moon. Picnic and explore the grounds at Jack London State Historic Park. Next morning visit **Kenwood Vineyards** ㉝ before heading north to 🔯 **Healdsburg** in Dry Creek Valley via Santa Rosa and U.S. 101. A host of wineries, including **Ferrari-Carano Winery** ㊴, lie nestled in the woods along the roads. Spend the night in **Healdsburg.** On the third day cross over into Napa Valley. Take Mark Springs Road east off U.S. 101's River Road exit and follow the signs on Porter Creek Road to Petrified Forest Road to Highway 29. Spend the day in the quaint town of 🔯 **Calistoga,** noted for its mud baths and mineral springs. Wake up early on the fourth day for a balloon ride. If you're feeling energetic, take to the Silverado Trail for a bike ride with stops at **Cuvaison** ㉕, **Stag's Leap Wine Cellars** ⑩, and **Clos du Val** ⑧. On day five, explore St. Helena before heading to the Oakville Grocery. Spend the night and visit the wineries in 🔯 **Rutherford.** On day six, explore nearby **Yountville,** stopping for lunch at one of its many acclaimed restaurants before heading up the hill to the **Hess Collection Winery and Vineyards** ⑥, on Mt. Veeder. On your last day return to the town of Sonoma via the Carneros Highway, stopping for a look at how brandies are made at the **RMS Brandy Distillery** ③, then moving on to the landmark **Buena Vista Carneros Winery** ㉙, or **Gloria Ferrer Champagne Caves** ②.

When to Tour the Wine Country

"Crush," the term used to indicate the season when grapes are picked and crushed, usually takes place in September or October, depending on the weather. From September until December the entire Wine Country celebrates its bounty with street fairs and festivals.

In season (April–October), Napa Valley draws crowds of tourists, and traffic along Highway 29 from St. Helena to Calistoga is often backed up on weekends. The Sonoma Valley, Santa Rosa, and Healdsburg are less crowded. Book lodging, restaurant, and winery reservations in advance. Many wineries give tours at specified times and require appointments.

To avoid crowds, visit the Wine Country during the week and get an early start (most wineries open around 10). Pack a sun hat, since summer is usually hot and dry, and autumn can be even hotter.

CARNEROS REGION

One of the most important viticultural areas in the Wine Country straddles southern Sonoma and Napa counties. The Carneros region has a long, cool growing season tempered by maritime breezes and lingering fogs off the San Pablo Bay—optimum slow-growing conditions for pinot noir and chardonnay grapes.

Southern Sonoma County

36 mi from San Francisco, north on U.S. 101, east on Hwy. 37, and north on Hwy. 121.

❶ Sam Sebastiani, of the famous Sebastiani family, decided to strike out on his own and with his wife, Vicki, opened **Viansa.** Reminiscent of a Tuscan villa, the winery's ocher-color building is surrounded by olive trees and overlooks the valley. The varietals produced here include muscat canelli and nebbiolo. ⊠ *25200 Arnold Dr., Sonoma County,* ☎ *707/935–4700.* ⊙ *Daily 10–5. Tours by appointment.*

❷ The array of sparkling and still wines at **Gloria Ferrer Champagne Caves** originated with a 700-year-old stock of Ferrer grapes. The method here is to age the wines in a "cava," or cellar, where several feet of earth maintain a constant temperature. ⊠ *23555 Carneros (Hwy. 121),* ☎ *707/996–7256.* 🎫 *Tasting fees vary.* ⊙ *Daily 10:30–5:30. Tours hourly 11–4.*

Southern Napa County

7 mi east of Hwy. 121/Hwy. 116 junction on Hwy. 121/12.

❸ Learn the history and folklore of rare alembic brandy at the **RMS Brandy Distillery.** Tours include an explanation of the double-distillation process, which eliminates all but the finest spirits for aging; a trip to the atmospheric oak barrel house; and a sensory evaluation of vintage brandies. ⊠ *1250 Cuttings Wharf Rd., Napa (from Domaine Carneros, head 1 mi east on Carneros Hwy.),* ☎ *707/253–9055,* FAX *707/253–0116.* ⊙ *Apr.–Oct., daily 10–5; Nov.–Mar., daily 10:30–4:30. Tours on the hr.*

❹ **Domaine Carneros** occupies a 138-acre estate dominated by a classic château inspired by Champagne Taittinger's historic Château de la Marquetterie in France. Carved into the hillside beneath the winery, Domaine Carneros's cellars produce sparkling wines reminiscent of the Taittinger style and using only Carneros grapes. ⊠ *1240 Duhig Rd., Napa,* ☎ *707/257–0101,* FAX *707/257–3020.* 🎫 *Tasting fees vary.* ⊙ *Mon.–Thurs. 10:30–5, Fri.–Sun. 10:30–6. Tours Mon.–Thurs. at 11, 1, and 3; Fri.–Sun. hourly 11–3.*

THE NAPA VALLEY

The Napa Valley is the undisputed capital of American wine production. Famed for its unrivaled climate and neat rows of vineyards, the area is made up of small, quirky towns.

Napa

*8 mi from Cuttings Wharf Rd. to downtown Napa, east on Hwy. 121/
12, north on Hwy. 29; 46 mi from San Francisco, east and north on
I–80 to Hwy. 37 west to Hwy. 29 north.*

The oldest town in the Napa Valley—established in 1848—Napa also
claims an advantageous location. Most destinations in both the Napa
and Sonoma valleys are easily accessible from here. For those seeking
an affordable alternative to the hotels and B&Bs in the heart of the
Wine Country, Napa is a good option. Choose lodgings on the north
side of town near Yountville. Parts of Napa are downright seedy.

⑤ Bunkered into a scenic Carneros hilltop, **Codorniu Napa** produces
California sparkling wines distinguished by a higher percentage of
chardonnay grapes than most sparklings (a 50–50 blend of chardonnay and pinot noir). ✉ *1345 Henry Rd., north off Old Sonoma Rd.
and Dealy La.,* ☎ *707/224–1668,* ℻ *707/224–1672.* ☽ *Daily 10–5.
Tours daily; times vary.*

★ ⑥ The **Hess Collection Winery and Vineyards** is a delightful discovery on
a hilltop 9 mi northwest of Napa (don't give up; the road leading to
the winery is long and winding). Within the simple, rustic limestone
structure, circa 1903, you'll find Swiss owner Donald Hess's personal
art collection. Cabernet sauvignon is the real strength here, though Hess
also produces some fine chardonnays. The winery and the art collection are open for self-guided tours. ✉ *4411 Redwood Rd., west off
Hwy. 29,* ☎ *707/255–1144,* ℻ *707/253–1682.* ☽ *Daily 10–4.*

⑦ The winery at **Trefethen Vineyards** was built in 1886. Today it's the
only wooden, gravity-powered winery in Napa. Trefethen is known
for its reserve cabernet as well as its 1993 merlot, available only on
the premises. ✉ *1160 Oak Knoll Ave., off Hwy. 29,* ☎ *707/255–7700.*
☽ *Daily 10–4:30. Tours by appointment.*

⑧ **Clos du Val,** founded by French owner Bernard Portet, produces a celebrated reserve cabernet. It also makes zinfandel, pinot noir, merlot,
sangiovese, and chardonnay. ✉ *5330 Silverado Trail,* ☎ *707/259–2200.*
🍷 *Tasting fee $5.* ☽ *Daily 10–5. Tours by appointment.*

⑨ Small **Pine Ridge** makes estate-bottled wines, including chardonnay,
cabernet, and merlot. Tours include barrel tastings in the winery's
caves. ✉ *5901 Silverado Trail,* ☎ *707/253–7500,* ℻ *707/253–1493.*
☽ *Daily 11–5. Tours by appointment at 10:15, 1, and 3.*

Dining and Lodging

$$$ ✕ **Silverado Country Club.** There are two restaurants and a bar and
grill at this large, famous resort. The elegant Vintner's Court, with Cal-
ifornia–Pacific Rim cuisine, serves dinner only; there is a seafood buf-
fet on Friday night and a champagne brunch on Sunday. Royal Oak
serves steak and seafood for dinner nightly. The bar and grill is open
for breakfast and lunch year-round. Summer lunch offerings include
an outdoor barbecue with chicken and hamburgers. ✉ *1600 Atlas Peak
Rd. (follow signs to Lake Berryessa),* ☎ *707/257–0200. Reservations
essential. AE, D, DC, MC, V. Vintner's Court closed Mon.–Tues. No
dinner Sun.*

$–$$ ✕ **Bistro Don Giovanni.** Even in winter, the valley views from the covered patio here are extraordinary. The wine list is as locally represen-
tative as their menu is eclectic. Don't miss the individual pizzas cooked
in a wood-burning oven and the handmade pastas. ✉ *4110 St. Helena Hwy. (Hwy. 29),* ☎ *707/224–3300. AE, D, MC, V.*

$-$$ ✕ **Celadon.** Dishes like flash-fried calamari with a chipotle chili and ginger glaze and a large crab cake laced with whole-seed mustard sauce make this an ideal place to sample contemporary cuisine accompanied by any of a dozen wines available by the glass. ⊠ *1040 Main St.,* ☎ *707/254–9690. AE, MC, V. Closed Sun.*

$$$–$$$$ 🏨 **Silverado Country Club and Resort.** This luxurious if somewhat staid 1,200-acre property in the hills east of Napa has cottages, kitchen apartments, and one- to three-bedroom efficiencies, many with fireplaces. With two golf courses, nine pools, and 23 tennis courts, it's a place for serious sports enthusiasts and anyone who enjoys the conveniences of a full-scale resort. ⊠ *1600 Atlas Peak Rd. (6 mi east of Napa via Hwy. 121), 94558,* ☎ *707/257–0200 or 800/532–0500,* FAX *707/257–2867. 277 condo units. 3 restaurants, bar, 9 pools, 2 18-hole golf courses, 23 tennis courts, bicycles. AE, D, DC, MC, V.*

$$ 🏨 **Chateau Hotel.** Despite the name, this is a pretty simple motel with only the barest nod to France. Clean rooms, a great location, Continental breakfast, facilities for travelers with disabilities, and discounts for senior citizens make up for its lack of charm. ⊠ *4195 Solano Ave. (west of Hwy. 29, exit at Trower Ave.), 94558,* ☎ *707/253–9300; 800/253–6272 in CA,* FAX *707/253–0906. 115 rooms. Refrigerators, pool, hot tub. AE, D, DC, MC, V.*

Outdoor Activities and Sports

FISHING

You can fish from the banks of the Napa River at **John F. Kennedy Park** (⊠ 2291 Streblow Dr., ☎ 707/257–9529). Call ahead for river conditions.

GOLF

The 18-hole **Chardonnay Club** (⊠ 2555 Jameson Canyon Rd., ☎ 707/257–8950) course is a favorite among Bay Area golfers. The greens fee, $65 weekdays and $85 weekends, includes a cart. The **Silverado Country Club** (⊠ 1600 Atlas Peak Rd., ☎ 707/257–0200) has two challenging 18-hole courses with a beautiful view at every hole. The greens fee is $120, including a cart; you must be a guest to play.

TENNIS

Vintage High School (⊠ 1375 Trower Ave.) maintains eight public tennis courts. **Napa High School** (⊠ 2474 Jefferson St.) maintains six tennis courts with coin-operated night lights. Call the Napa Valley School District (☎ 707/253–3715) for information.

Yountville

13 mi north of the town of Napa on Hwy. 29.

Yountville has become the valley's boomtown, with two new hotels and two new restaurants opening in 1998, plus a host of shops and wineries. Another attraction is **Vintage 1870** (⊠ 6525 Washington St., ☎ 707/944–2451), a 26-acre complex of boutiques, restaurants, and specialty food stores. The vine-covered brick buildings were built in 1870 and housed a winery, livery stable, and distillery. The original mansion of the property is now the popular Mexican-style **Compadres Bar and Grill;** nearby is the **Pacific Blues Café,** housed in the train depot Samuel Brannan built in 1868 for his privately owned Napa Valley Railroad. At **Yountville Park** there's a picnic area with tables, barbecue pits, and a view of grapevines.

At the intersection of Madison and Washington streets, Yountville's quaint and historic **Washington Square** was the town's original main square. Today it's a complex of boutiques and family-style restaurants. **Pioneer Cemetery,** the final resting place of the town's founder, George Yount, is across the street from Washington Square.

⑩ In 1995, the World Wine Championships gave **Stag's Leap Wine Cellars** a platinum award for its 1990 reserve chardonnay, designating it the highest-ranked premium chardonnay in the world. ⊠ *5766 Silverado Trail,* ☎ *707/944–2020.* 🍷 *Tasting fee $3.* ☉ *Daily 10–4. Tours by appointment.*

⑪ French-owned **Domaine Chandon** claims one of Yountville's prime pieces of real estate, on a knoll west of downtown. Tours of the sleek, modern facilities on the beautifully maintained property include sample flutes of the méthode champenoise sparkling wine. Champagne is $3.70–$6.75 per glass, hors d'oeuvres are complimentary, and an elegant restaurant beckons. ⊠ *California Dr., west of Hwy. 29,* ☎ *707/944–2280.* ☉ *Nov.–Feb., daily 11–6; Mar.–Oct., 11–8. Tours on the hr.*

Dining and Lodging

$$$$ ⨉ **French Laundry.** Napa Valley's most acclaimed restaurant can be found
★ inside an old converted brick building on a residential street corner. The prix fixe menus, which include four or five courses, always include two or three additional surprises—little bites—to start, such as a quail egg sandwiched between a crown of caviar and a base of brioche. Your meal thus launched, a full three hours will probably pass before you reach dessert. Chef Thomas Keller doesn't lack for admirers. Reservations are hard won and not accepted more than two months in advance, but lunch is a little easier to come by. ⊠ *6640 Washington St.,* ☎ *707/944–2380. Reservations essential. AE, MC, V. Closed 1st 2 wks in Jan.; lunch hrs and days vary with the season.*

$$$–$$$$ ⨉ **Domaine Chandon.** This large, formal dining room is decorated in shades of gray and green with gold accents, as if to match the oak trees outside. Wrought-iron grapevines twist through the railings that unobtrusively define spacious dining areas. Typical dishes, such as rack of lamb or Sonoma duck breast, blend Continental and California cuisines. The dining room looks out over acres of vineyards and native oaks. When the weather is good, try for a seat on the tree-shaded terrace. ⊠ *California Dr. (take Yountville exit off Hwy. 29 toward Veterans' Home),* ☎ *707/944–2892. Reservations essential. AE, D, DC, MC, V. No dinner Mon.–Tues. Apr.–Oct.*

$$$ ⨉ **Brix.** Overlooking vineyards and the Mayacamas Mountains, the spacious yellow-and-green dining room invites you to sit back and enjoy the East–West menu. Scallops are served with a Thai lime-butter sauce, and salmon is flavored with a light soy glaze. A wood-fired oven is used for cooking pizzas. ⊠ *7377 St. Helena Hwy.,* ☎ *707/944–2749. AE, D, DC, MC, V.*

$$–$$$ ⨉ **Bistro Jeanty.** In 1998 Philippe Jeanty, who put Domaine Chandon's restaurant on the map, opened his own restaurant with a menu inspired by the cooking of his French childhood. His traditional cassoulet will warm those nostalgic for bistro cooking, while classic coq au vin rises above the ordinary with the infusion of a spicy red wine sauce. The scene here is Gallic through and through with a small bar and a handful of tables in a crowded room. ⊠ *6510 Washington St.,* ☎ *707/944–0103. MC, V. Closed last wk of Jan., 1st wk of Feb.*

$$–$$$ ⨉ **Bouchon.** Thomas and Joseph Keller, flush with the success of their French Laundry, opened a second restaurant in the fall of 1998. And for the sake of everyone in their business (including fellow restaurant employees who work very late), they're keeping it open from 7 AM until 2 AM. On their French country menu, typical dishes include *steak*

frites, leg of lamb, and sole meunière. ⊠ *6534 Washington St.,* ☎ *707/ 944–8037. AE, MC, V.*

$$ ✕ **Mustards Grill.** Mustards attracts winemakers and other locals as
★   well as hungry tourists. Grilled fish, steak, local fresh produce, and an impressive wine list are the trademarks of this boisterous bistro with a black-and-white marble floor and upbeat artwork. The thin, crisp, golden onion rings are addictive. ⊠ *7399 St. Helena Hwy., 1 mi north of Yountville,* ☎ *707/944–2424,* FAX *707/944–0828. Reservations essential. D, DC, MC, V.*

$$$$ 🏨 **Napa Valley Lodge.** Balconies, covered walkways, and a red-tile roof imbue this lovely inn with the ambience of a hacienda. The large pool area is landscaped with lots of greenery. Many spacious second-floor rooms have vineyard views. Fresh brewed coffee, Continental breakfast, and the morning paper are complimentary. ⊠ *2230 Madison St., at Hwy. 29,* ☎ *707/944–2468 or 800/368–2468,* FAX *707/944–9362. 55 rooms. Refrigerators, pool, hot tub, sauna, exercise room. AE, D, DC, MC, V.*

$$$$ 🏨 **Vintage Inn.** Accommodations in this luxurious inn are arranged in two-story villas throughout the 3½-acre property. All the spacious rooms have fireplaces, whirlpool baths, refrigerators, and private verandas or patios. Guests are treated to a welcome bottle of wine, Continental breakfast with champagne, and afternoon tea. ⊠ *6541 Washington St., 94599,* ☎ *707/944–1112 or 800/351–1133,* FAX *707/ 944–1617. 80 rooms. Refrigerators, pool, hot tub, tennis court, bicycles. AE, D, DC, MC, V.*

$$$–$$$$ 🏨 **La Residence.** Even though it's within feet of the St. Helena Highway, "La Res" is secluded and romantic enough to make you feel as if you've flown to France, or at least New Orleans. The hotel is housed in two buildings: the Mansion, a renovated 1870s Gothic Revival manor house built by a riverboat captain from New Orleans; and Cabernet Hall, a French-style barn. Both buildings overlook a pool, a manicured garden, and towering oak trees that bathe the entire property in shade. The spacious rooms have period antiques, fireplaces, and double French doors opening onto verandas or patios. ⊠ *4066 St. Helena Hwy. (Hwy. 29), 4 mi south of Yountville,* ☎ *707/253–0337,* FAX *707/253–0382. 20 rooms. Dining room, pool, hot tub, business services. AE, DC, MC, V.*

$$$ 🏨 **Petit Logis.** Wall murals and 11-ft ceilings infuse each unique room at this small, charming one-story inn with elegance. Breakfast, included in the room rate, is offered at one of two nearby restaurants. ⊠ *6527 Yount St., 94599,* ☎ *707/944–2332. 5 rooms. MC, V.*

Hot-Air Ballooning
Balloons Above the Valley (⊠ Box 3838, Napa 94558, ☎ 707/253–2222; 800/464–6824 in CA) is a reliable organization. Also try **Napa Valley Balloons** (⊠ Box 2860, Yountville 94599, ☎ 707/944–0228; 800/253–2224 in CA).

Oakville

2 mi west of Yountville on Hwy. 29.

There are three reasons to visit the town of Oakville: its grocery store, its scenic mountain grade, and its magnificent, highly exclusive winery. The **Oakville Grocery** (⊠ 7856 St. Helena Hwy.), built in the late 1880s to serve as a grocery store and Wells Fargo Pony Express stop, carries gourmet foods and difficult-to-find wines. Custom-packed picnic baskets are a specialty. Along the mountain range that divides the Napa and Sonoma valleys, the **Oakville Grade** is a twisting half-hour route with breathtaking views of both valleys. Though the surface of the road is good, it can be difficult to negotiate at night, and trucks are advised not to attempt it at any time.

⑫ At **Robert Mondavi** visitors are encouraged to take the 60-minute production tour with complimentary tasting, before trying the reserve reds ($1–$5 per glass). In-depth three- to four-hour tours and lunch tours are also popular. ⊠ *7801 St. Helena Hwy., Oakville,* ☎ *707/259–9463.* ⊙ *Daily 9–5. Tours by appointment.*

⑬ **Opus One,** the combined venture of famed California wine maker Robert Mondavi and French baron Philippe Rothschild, is famed for its vast semicircular barrel cellar modeled on the Château Mouton Rothschild winery in France. The futuristic building is the work of the same architects who built San Francisco's Transamerica Pyramid. ⊠ *7900 St. Helena Hwy.,* ☎ *707/963–1979,* FAX *707/944–1753.* ☜ *Tasting fee $25.* ⊙ *Daily 10–3:30. Tours by appointment.*

Rutherford

1 mi northwest of Oakville on Hwy. 29.

From a fast-moving car, Rutherford is a quick blur of dark forest, a rustic barn or two, and maybe a country store. But don't speed by this tiny hamlet. With its singular microclimate and soil, this is an important viticultural center.

⑭ A joint venture of Mumm—the French champagne house—and Seagram, **Mumm Napa Valley** is considered one of California's premier sparkling-wine producers. Its Napa Brut Prestige and ultrapremium Vintage Reserve are the best known. The excellent tour and comfortable tasting room are two more good reasons to visit. An art gallery contains a permanent exhibit of photographs by Ansel Adams that record the wine-making process. ⊠ *8445 Silverado Trail,* ☎ *707/942–3434.* ☜ *Tasting fees vary.* ⊙ *May–Oct., daily 10:30–6; Nov.–Apr., daily 10–5. Tours daily 11–4.*

⑮ The wine at **Rutherford Hill Winery** is aged in French oak barrels stacked in more than 30,000 square ft of caves—one of the largest such facilities in the nation. Tours of the caves can be followed by a picnic in oak, olive, or madrone orchards. ⊠ *200 Rutherford Hill Rd., off the Silverado Trail,* ☎ *707/963–7194.* ☜ *Tasting fees vary.* ⊙ *Daily 10–5. Tour times vary seasonally; call ahead.*

⑯ **Caymus Vineyards** is run by wine master Chuck Wagner, who started making wine on the property in 1972. His family, however, had been farming the land since 1906. Today a cabernet sauvignon special selection is the winery's claim to fame. ⊠ *8700 Conn Creek Rd.,* ☎ *707/ 963–4204.* ⊙ *Daily 10–4:30. No tours.*

⑰ **Frog's Leap** is the perfect place for wine novices to begin their education. Owners John and Julie Williams maintain a sense of humor and a humble attitude that translates into an informative and satisfying experience. They also happen to produce some of the finest zinfandel, cabernet sauvignon, and sauvignon blanc in the Wine Country. Call ahead for directions. There is no tasting room. ⊠ *8815 Conn Creek Rd.,* ☎ *707/963–4704.* ⊙ *Tours by appointment.*

⑱ **Beaulieu Vineyard** utilizes the same wine-making process, from crush to bottle, as it did the day it opened in 1900. The winery's cabernet is a benchmark of the Napa Valley. The Georges du Latour Private Reserve (1994 and 1995 both received high scores from major wine publications) remains a collector's favorite. ⊠ *1960 St. Helena Hwy.*

(Hwy. 29), ☎ *707/963–2411.* 🍷 *Tasting fee $18 in Reserve Room.* ⊙ *Daily 10–5. Tours daily 11–4.*

In the 1970s, filmmaker Francis Ford Coppola bought the old Niebaum estate, a part of the then-world-famous Inglenook estate. He resurrected an early Inglenook-like quality red with his first bottle of Rubicon, re-
⑲ leased in 1985. Since then, **Niebaum-Coppola Estate** has consistently received high ratings, and in 1995 Coppola purchased the other half of the Inglenook estate, the ancient, ivy-covered château and an additional 95 acres of land. When you're through touring the winery, take a look at the Coppola movie memorabilia, which includes Don Corleone's desk and chair from *The Godfather.* ✉ *1991 St. Helena Hwy. (Hwy. 29),* ☎ *707/963–9099.* 🍷 *Tasting fee $7.50.* ⊙ *Daily 10–5. Tours daily; times vary.*

Dining and Lodging
$$$$ ✕🏨 **Auberge du Soleil.** This stunning property, terraced on a hill stud-
★ ded by olive trees, offers some of the valley's best views. The hotel's renowned restaurant has a frequently changing menu that emphasizes local produce and also includes such unusual specialties as roasted lobster sausage. Slow-roasted garlic with homemade pretzels and pan-seared salmon sandwiches are standouts on the moderately priced bar menu. Guest rooms, except for the most expensive ones, run a bit small. ✉ *180 Rutherford Hill Rd. (off Silverado Trail just north of Rte. 128), 94573,* ☎ *707/963–1211 or 800/348–5406,* 🖷 *707/963–8764. 50 rooms. Restaurant (reservations essential), pool, hot tub, massage, steam room, 3 tennis courts, exercise room. AE, D, DC, MC, V.*
$$$–$$$$ 🏨 **Rancho Caymus Inn.** California-Spanish in style, this cozy inn has well-maintained gardens and large suites with kitchens and whirlpool baths. Well-chosen details include beehive fireplaces, tile murals, stoneware basins, and llama-hair blankets. ✉ *1140 Rutherford Rd. (junction of Hwys. 29 and 128), 94573,* ☎ *707/963–1777 or 800/845–1777,* 🖷 *707/963–5387. 26 rooms. DC, MC, V. 2-night minimum Apr.–Nov.*

St. Helena

2 mi northwest of Oakville on Hwy. 29.

By the time Charles Krug planted grapes in St. Helena around 1860, quite a few vineyards already existed. Today the town beckons visitors with its abundant selection of wineries and restaurants, including Greystone on the West Coast campus of the Culinary Institute of America.

⑳ Known for its barrel-fermented chardonnay, the family-owned **Flora Springs** winery tasting room is housed in a lovely old stone building. The actual winery is a couple of miles away. ✉ *677 St. Helena Hwy. S. (Hwy. 29),* ☎ *707/967–8032.* 🍷 *Tasting fee $3.* ⊙ *Mon.–Sat. 10–4.*

Arguably the most beautiful winery in the Napa Valley, the 1876
㉑ **Beringer Vineyards** is also the oldest continuously operating one. In 1883 the Beringer brothers, Frederick and Jacob, built the Rhine House Mansion, where tastings are now held among Belgian art nouveau hand-carved oak and walnut furniture and stained-glass windows. Tours, given every 30 minutes, include a visit to underground wine tunnels made of volcanic ash that were dug by Chinese laborers during the 19th century. ✉ *2000 Main St.,* ☎ *707/963–4812.* ⊙ *Daily 9:30–4; summer hrs sometimes extend to 5. Tours daily every 30 mins.*

㉒ **Charles Krug Winery** opened in 1861 when Count Haraszthy loaned Krug a small cider press. Today, it is run by the Peter Mondavi family. The joint tasting and tour fee is $3. ⊠ *2800 N. Main St.,* ☎ *707/ 963–5057.* ☉ *Daily 10:30–5:30. Tours 11:30, 1:30, and 3:30.*

㉓ Freemark Abbey Winery, originally called the Tychson Winery after Josephine Tychson, the first woman to establish a winery in California, has long been known for its cabernets, whose grapes come from the fertile Rutherford Bench. ⊠ *3022 St. Helena Hwy. N,* ☎ *707/963– 9694.* ☉ *Daily 10–4:30. Tour daily at 2.*

The **Silverado Museum** houses Robert Louis Stevenson memorabilia, including first editions, manuscripts, and photographs. ⊠ *1490 Library La.,* ☎ *707/963–3757.* ☞ *Free.* ☉ *Tues.–Sun. noon–4.*

The **Culinary Institute of America** set up its West Coast headquarters in the century-old Greystone Winery, the former site of the Christian Brothers Winery and a national historic landmark. The CIA campus consists of 30 acres of herb and vegetable gardens, a 15-acre merlot vineyard, and a Mediterranean-inspired restaurant (☞ Wine Spectator Greystone Restaurant, *below*). Also on the property are a well-stocked culinary store, a quirky corkscrew and winepress museum, and a culinary library. ⊠ *2555 Main St.,* ☎ *800/333–9242,* ☏ *707/967–1113.*

Dining and Lodging

$$$–$$$$ ✕ **Terra.** A romantic restaurant housed in a century-old stone foundry, Terra is especially known for its exquisite Mediterranean-inspired dishes, many with Asian touches. Save room for dessert. ⊠ *1345 Railroad Ave.,* ☎ *707/963–8931. Reservations essential. MC, V. Closed Tues. No lunch.*

$$–$$$ ✕ **Showley's.** This local favorite is well worth a little detour from the beaten path. Garlic chicken and roasted monkfish with garlic mashed potatoes are among the recommended items on the changing menu here. ⊠ *1327 Railroad Ave.,* ☎ *707/963–1200. AE, D, MC, V. Closed Mon.*

$$–$$$ ✕ **Wine Spectator Greystone Restaurant.** This restaurant, housed in the handsome old Christian Brothers' winery, is run by the Culinary Institute of America. Century-old stone walls house a large and bustling restaurant, with cooking, baking, and grilling stations in full view. The menu has a Mediterranean spirit and emphasizes such small plates as bruschetta topped with wild mushrooms and *muhammara,* a spread of roasted red peppers and walnuts. ⊠ *2555 Main St.,* ☎ *707/967– 1010. AE, DC, MC, V.*

$$ ✕ **Brava Terrace.** Vegetables plucked straight from the restaurant's own garden are used to enliven chef Fred Halpert's trademark New American cuisine. Brava has a comfortably casual ambience with a full bar, a large stone fireplace, a romantic outdoor terrace overlooking a shady brook, and a heated deck with views of the valley floor and Howell Mountain. ⊠ *3010 St. Helena Hwy. (Hwy. 29), ½ mi north of downtown St. Helena,* ☎ *707/963–9300. Reservations essential. AE, D, DC, MC, V. Closed Wed. Nov.–Apr. and last 2 wks of Jan.*

$$ ✕ **Tra Vigne.** This Napa Valley fieldstone building has been transformed
★   into a striking trattoria with a huge wood bar, high ceilings, and plush banquettes. Homemade mozzarella, olive oil and vinegar, and house-cured pancetta and prosciutto contribute to a mouthwatering tour of Tuscan cuisine. In summer, the outdoor courtyard is a Mediterranean vision of striped umbrellas and awnings, crowded café tables, and rustic pots overflowing with flowers. On occasion, the kitchen has been maddeningly inconsistent. ⊠ *1050 Charter Oak Ave., off Hwy. 29,* ☎ *707/963–4444. Reservations essential. D, DC, MC, V.*

$$$$ ✕🏨 **Meadowood Resort.** Secluded at the end of a semiprivate road, this 256-acre resort has accommodations in a rambling country lodge and several bungalow suites. For the popular Sunday brunch, refined

French cuisine with a California twist is served à la carte or as part of a prix fixe menu indoors or out. The Grill serves a lighter menu of pizzas and spa food for breakfast and lunch (and early dinners on Friday and Saturday). ⊠ *900 Meadowood La., 94574,* ☎ *707/963–3646 or 800/458–8080,* FAX *707/963–5863. 40 rooms, 45 suites. 2 restaurants (reservations essential), bar, room service, 2 pools, hot tub, massage, sauna, steam room, 9-hole golf course, 7 tennis courts, croquet, health club. AE, D, DC, MC, V.*

$$$–$$$$ 🏠 **Harvest Inn.** The larger-than-average rooms at this Tudor-esque inn are on the dark side, but the lushly landscaped grounds are lovely. Most rooms have wet bars, refrigerators, antique furnishings, and fireplaces. Pets are allowed in certain rooms for a $20 fee. Complimentary breakfast is included. ⊠ *1 Main St., 94574,* ☎ *707/963–9463 or 800/ 950–8466,* FAX *707/963–4402. 55 rooms. Refrigerators, 2 pools, hot tub. AE, D, DC, MC, V.*

$$$–$$$$ 🏠 **Wine Country Inn.** Surrounded by a pastoral landscape of hills, old
★   barns, and stone bridges, this is a peaceful New England–style retreat. Rural antiques fill all the rooms, most of which overlook the vineyards with either a balcony, patio, or deck. Most rooms have fireplaces, and some have private hot tubs. A hearty country breakfast is served, and wine tastings are scheduled in the afternoon. ⊠ *1152 Lodi La. (off Hwy. 29), 94574,* ☎ *707/963–7077,* FAX *707/963–9018. 24 rooms. Pool, hot tubs. MC, V.*

Shopping

Handcrafted candles made on the premises are for sale at the **Hurd Beeswax Candle Factory** (⊠ 3020 St. Helena Hwy. N, ☎ 707/963–7211). Bargain hunters will delight in the many designer labels for sale at the **Village Outlet Stores** complex on St. Helena Highway, across the street from Freemark Abbey Winery.

At **I. Wolk Gallery** (⊠ 1235 Main St., ☎ 707/963–8800) you'll find works by established and emerging artists from New York, Chicago, Los Angeles, and Santa Fe. The **Gallery on Main Street** (⊠ 1359 Main St., ☎ 707/963–3350) features oils, watercolors, ceramics, and etchings by northern California artists. **Dean and Deluca** (⊠ 607 St. Helena Hwy., ☎ 707/967–9980) is crammed with everything you need in the kitchen.

Calistoga

3 mi northwest of St. Helena on Hwy. 29.

In addition to its wineries, Calistoga is noted for its mineral water, hot mineral springs, mud baths, steam baths, and massages. The Calistoga Hot Springs Resort was founded in 1859 by maverick entrepreneur Sam Brannan, whose ambition was to found "the Saratoga of California." He tripped up the pronunciation of the phrase at a formal banquet—it came out "Calistoga"—and the name stuck.

The **Sharpsteen Museum** has a magnificent diorama of the Calistoga Hot Springs Resort in its heyday. Other exhibits document Robert Louis Stevenson's time in the area and the career of museum founder Ben Sharpsteen, an animator at the Walt Disney studio. ⊠ *1311 Washington St.,* ☎ *707/942–5911.* 🎫 *Free.* 🕐 *May–Oct., daily 10–4; Nov.–Apr., daily noon–4.*

Indian Springs, an old-timey spa, has been pumping out 212-degree water from its three geysers for more than a century. The place offers some of the best bargains on mud bathing and short massages. The spa has 16 cottages with studio or one-bedroom units and a larger structure with three bedrooms. ⊠ *1712 Lincoln Ave.,* ☏ *707/942–4913.* ⊙ *Daily 9–7. Reservations recommended for spa treatments.*

㉔ **Sterling Vineyards** sits on a hilltop to the east of Calistoga, its pristine white Mediterranean-style buildings reached by an enclosed gondola from the valley floor. The view from the tasting room is superb. ⊠ *1111 Dunaweal La.,* ☏ *707/942–3300.* ⊡ *Tram $6.* ⊙ *Daily 10:30–4:30.*

㉕ **Cuvaison** specializes in chardonnay, merlot, and cabernet sauvignon for the export market. Two small picnic areas on the grounds look out over Napa Valley. ⊠ *4550 Silverado Trail,* ☏ *707/942–6266.* ⊡ *Tasting fees vary.* ⊙ *Daily 10–5. Tours by appointment.*

★ ㉖ Designed by postmodern architect Michael Graves, **Clos Pegase** is a one-of-a-kind structure packed with unusual art objects from the collection of art book publisher and owner Jan Shrem. Works of art even appear in the underground wine tunnels. ⊠ *1060 Dunaweal La.,* ☏ *707/942–4981.* ⊙ *Daily 10:30–5. Tours at 11 and 2.*

㉗ **Château Montelena** is a vine-covered stone French château constructed circa 1882 and set amid Chinese-inspired gardens, complete with a man-made lake with gliding swans and islands crowned by Chinese pavilions. Château Montelena produces award-winning chardonnays and cabernet sauvignons. ⊠ *1429 Tubbs La.,* ☏ *707/942–5105; 800/222–7288 outside the Bay Area.* ⊡ *Tasting fees vary.* ⊙ *Daily 10–4. Tours by reservation at 11 and 2.*

🅒 Many families bring children to Calistoga to see **Old Faithful Geyser of California** blast its 60-ft tower of steam and vapor about every 40 minutes. One of just three regularly erupting geysers in the world, it is fed by an underground river that heats to 350°F. ⊠ *1299 Tubbs La., 1 mi north of Calistoga,* ☏ *707/942–6463.* ⊡ *$6.* ⊙ *During daylight savings time, daily 9–6; winter, daily 9–5.*

🅒 The **Petrified Forest** contains the remains of the volcanic eruptions of Mount St. Helena 3.4 million years ago. The force of the explosion uprooted the gigantic redwoods, covered them with volcanic ash, and infiltrated the trees with silica and minerals, causing petrifaction. ⊠ *4100 Petrified Forest Rd., 5 mi west of Calistoga,* ☏ *707/942–6667.* ⊡ *$4.* ⊙ *Daily 10–5 (until 6 in summer).*

🅒 **Robert Louis Stevenson State Park,** on Highway 29, 3 mi northeast of Calistoga, encompasses the summit of Mount St. Helena. It was here, in the summer of 1880, in an abandoned bunkhouse of the Silverado Mine, that Stevenson and his bride, Fanny Osbourne, spent their honeymoon. The stay inspired Stevenson's "The Silverado Squatters," and Spyglass Hill in *Treasure Island* is thought to be a portrait of Mount St. Helena. The park's 3,000 acres are mostly undeveloped except for a fire trail leading to the site of the bunkhouse and to the summit beyond.

Dining and Lodging

$$–$$$ ✕ **All Seasons Café.** Bistro cuisine takes a California spin in this sun-filled setting with marble tables and a black-and-white checkerboard floor. The seasonal menu includes organic greens, local game birds, and house-smoked beef, as well as homemade breads, desserts, and ice cream. The café shares space with a well-stocked wine shop. ⊠ *1400 Lincoln Ave.,* ☏ *707/942–9111. MC, V. No lunch Wed.*

$$–$$$ ✕ **Catahoula Restaurant and Saloon.** This sleek restaurant, named after
★ Louisiana's state dog, is the brainchild of chef Jan Birnbaum, whose credentials include stints at the Quilted Giraffe in New York and Campton Place in San Francisco. Using a large wood-burning oven, Birnbaum turns out such dishes as spicy gumbo with andouille sausage

and chocolate s'mores cooked over a wood fire. ✉ *Mount View Hotel, 1457 Lincoln Ave.,* ☎ *707/942–2275. Reservations essential. MC, V. Closed Tues. and Jan.*

$$–$$$ ✕ **Wappo Bar and Bistro.** This colorful restaurant is an adventure in international dining with a menu ranging from Asian noodles to Thai shrimp curry to chiles rellenos. ✉ *1226 S. Washington St.,* ☎ *707/942– 4712. AE, MC, V.*

$$ ✕ **Calistoga Inn.** Grilled meat and fish for dinner, and soups, salads, and sandwiches for lunch are prepared with flair at this microbrewery with a tree-shaded outdoor patio. ✉ *1250 Lincoln Ave.,* ☎ *707/ 942–4101. AE, MC, V.*

$$$$ ▦ **Cottage Grove Inn.** These 16 elegant and contemporary cottages are shaded by elm trees. Fireplaces, CD players, two-person hot tubs, and front porches with wicker rocking chairs add to the coziness. Rates include Continental breakfast and afternoon wine and cheese. ✉ *1711 Lincoln Ave., 94515,* ☎ *707/942–8400 or 800/799–2284,* FAX *707/942– 2653. 16 rooms. Breakfast room, refrigerators, in-room VCRs. AE, D, DC, MC, V.*

$$$–$$$$ ▦ **Mount View Hotel.** The Mount View is one of the valley's most historic resorts. A full-service spa offers state-of-the-art pampering, and three cottages are each equipped with a private redwood deck, Jacuzzi, and wet bar. ✉ *1457 Lincoln Ave., 94515,* ☎ *707/942–6877,* FAX *707/ 942–6904. 33 rooms, 3 cottages. Restaurant, pool, spa. AE, MC, V.*

$$$ ▦ **Brannan Cottage Inn.** This pristine Victorian cottage is the only one of Sam Brannan's 1860 resort cottages still standing on its original site. Rooms have private entrances, and elegant stenciled friezes of stylized wildflowers cover the walls. A full breakfast is included. ✉ *109 Wapoo Ave., 94515,* ☎ *707/942–4200. 6 rooms. Breakfast room. MC, V.*

$$$ ▦ **Meadowlark Country House.** The ambience is decidedly laid-back and sophisticated at this inn surrounded by 20 hillside acres just north of downtown Calistoga. Innkeeper Kurt Stevens prides himself on being helpful but not intrusive. The main house, built in 1886, and a newer building down a gravel path hold unfussy but country-stylish rooms. Rates include a full breakfast. ✉ *601 Petrified Forest Rd.,* ☎ *707/942–5651 or 800/942–5651,* FAX *707/942–5023. 7 rooms. Breakfast room, pool, hot tub, sauna. MC, V.*

$–$$$ ▦ **Calistoga Spa Hot Springs.** The spa's no-nonsense rooms have kitchenettes stocked with utensils and coffeemakers, which makes them popular with families and budget travelers. The on-premises spa includes mineral baths, mud baths, three pools, and a hot tub. There's a two-night minimum on weekends (three nights on holiday weekends). ✉ *1006 Washington St., 94515,* ☎ *707/942–6269,* FAX *707/942–4214. 57 rooms. Snack bar, kitchenettes, 2 pools, wading pool, hot tub, spa, meeting room. MC, V.*

Outdoor Activities and Sports

BIKING

Getaway Adventures and Bike Shop (✉ 1117 Lincoln Ave., ☎ 707/ 942–0332) rents bikes and conducts winery and other bike tours.

HOT-AIR BALLOONING

The **Calistoga Balloon Adventures** (☎ 707/942–2282 or 800/333– 4359) charters early morning flights out of Calistoga or, depending on weather conditions, St. Helena, Oakville, or Rutherford. The company's deluxe balloon flight ($165 per person) includes a catered brunch finale at the Marriott in Napa or the Cafe Sarifornia in Calistoga.

Shopping

For connoisseurs seeking extraordinary values, the **All Seasons Café Wine Shop** (✉ 1400 Lincoln Ave., ☎ 707/942–6828) is a true find. A wine shop inside the **Calistoga Depot** (✉ 1458 Lincoln Ave., ☎ 707/942–5556), California's second-oldest existing train depot, carries 500 vintages.

SONOMA COUNTY

While the Napa Valley is upscale and elegant, Sonoma Valley is rustic and unpretentious. Other Sonoma County valleys, such as Alexander, Dry Creek, and Russian River, are equally haunting in their beauty and just as prolific in their production of award-winning wines. Here, family-run wineries treat visitors like friends, and tastings are usually free. Cool marine air from the Russian River helps vintners grow their vines because it allows for more sun while leaving the soil rockier. This agricultural mix forces the vines to root deeper, producing intensely flavored grapes that translate into especially complex reds.

Sonoma

14 mi west of Napa on Hwy. 12; 45 mi from San Francisco, north on U.S. 101, east on Hwy. 37, and north on Hwy. 121-12.

Sonoma is the oldest town in the Wine Country. Its historic town plaza is the site of the last and the northernmost of the 21 missions established by the Franciscan order of Father Junípero Serra. The central plaza also includes the largest group of old adobes north of Monterey. The **Mission San Francisco Solano,** whose chapel and school were used to bring Christianity to the Native Americans, is now a museum with a fine collection of 19th-century watercolors. ✉ *114 Spain St. E,* ☎ *707/938–1519.* ⌨ *$2, includes the Sonoma Barracks on the central plaza and General Vallejo's home, Lachryma Montis (☞ below).* ☉ *Daily 10–5.*

Originally planted by Franciscans of the Sonoma Mission in 1825, the
28 **Sebastiani Vineyards** were bought by Samuele Sebastiani in 1904. Red wines are king here. To complement them, Sylvia Sebastiani has recorded her good Italian home cooking in a family recipe book, *Mangiamo.* ✉ *389 4th St. E,* ☎ *707/938–5532.* ☉ *Daily 10–5. Tours 10–4:30.*

29 **Buena Vista Carneros Winery** (follow signs from the plaza) is the oldest continually operating winery in California. It was here, in 1857, that Count Agoston Haraszthy de Mokcsa laid the basis for modern California wine making, bucking the conventional wisdom that vines should be planted on well-watered ground by instead planting on well-drained hillsides. Chinese laborers dug tunnels 100 ft into the hillside, and the limestone they extracted was used to build the main house. The winery, which is surrounded by redwood and eucalyptus trees, has a specialty food shop, an art gallery, and picnic areas. ✉ *18000 Old Winery Rd., off Napa Rd.,* ☎ *707/938–1266.* ☉ *Daily 10:30–4:30. Tour daily at 2.*

30 **Ravenswood** is literally dug into the mountains like a bunker and famous for its legendary zinfandel. The merlot should be tasted as well. From late May through Labor Day the winery serves barbecued chicken and ribs ($5–$10) in the vineyards to complement its hearty wines. ✉ *18701 Gehricke Rd., off E. Spain St.,* ☎ *707/938–1960.* ☉ *Daily 10–4:30. Tours by appointment at 10:30.*

A tree-lined driveway leads to **Lachryma Montis,** which General Mariano G. Vallejo, the last Mexican governor of California, built for his large family in 1851; the state purchased the home in 1933. The Victorian Gothic house is secluded in the midst of beautiful gardens. Opulent Victorian furnishings, including a white-marble fireplace in every room, are particularly noteworthy. ⊠ *W. Spain St., near 3rd St. E,* ☎ *707/938–1519.* 🖾 *$2.* ☉ *Daily 10–5. Tours by appointment.*

Dining and Lodging

$$–$$$ ✕ **Babette's.** Chef Daniel Patterson serves memorable six-course, prix
★   fixe dinners just six months of the year in an intimate formal dining room on one of Sonoma's charming paseos. His menus offer three choices for each course, including such tantalizing combinations as quail breast on a bed of watercress and quinoa, or raw scallops dressed simply with olive oil and lemon juice. The café menu, which is served every day year-round in an adjoining room, features cassoulet with house-made sausage and other rustic fare. Call ahead for hours. ⊠ *464 1st St.,* ☎ *707/939–8921. MC, V. Restaurant closed Sun.–Mon. and Dec.–Apr.*

$$–$$$ ✕ **Freestyle.** This offbeat restaurant has a field day with local fish and produce. The appetizer taste of the day showcases a single ingredient prepared three distinctive ways—prawns, for example, in gumbo, grilled and served with salsa, and deep-fried tempura-style. Main courses such as steak with grilled Portobello mushrooms are often hearty, as are the desserts. ⊠ *522 Broadway,* ☎ *707/996–9916. AE, DC, MC, V. Closed Tues. No lunch Mon.*

$$ ✕ **La Salette.** Chef-owner Manny Azevedo, born in the Azores and raised in Sonoma, found culinary inspiration in his wide-ranging travels. The flavors of his dishes, such as salt cod baked with white onions, stand strong while complementing one another. Sophisticated paintings and sculpture enliven the off-white walls in this restaurant, which has patio seating. ⊠ *18625 Hwy. 12,* ☎ *707/938–1927. MC, V.*

$$ ✕ **Ristorante Piatti.** A beautiful room opens onto one of the finest patios in the valley at this, the first in a minichain of California trattorias. Try the pizza from the wood-burning oven and northern Italian specials such as ravioli with lemon cream. ⊠ *El Dorado Hotel, 405 1st St. W,* ☎ *707/996–2351. AE, MC, V.*

$$$–$$$$ ✕🏨 **Sonoma Mission Inn & Spa.** This 1920s resort blends Mediterranean and old-style California architecture for a look that's early Hollywood. Guests come from afar to use the hotel's extensive spa facilities and treatments—including a pool that's heated by warm mineral water pumped from underground wells—and also for the gourmet and classic spa food served at the Grille and at the less formal Café. Thirty suites in a secluded, tree-shaded area have verandas or patios, whirlpools, and fireplaces. At press time, an extensive renovation was under way. ⊠ *18140 Hwy. 12 (2 mi north of Sonoma at Boyes Blvd.), Box 1447, 95476,* ☎ *707/938–9000; 800/358–9022; 800/862–4945 in CA;* FAX *707/996–5358. 198 rooms, 30 suites. 2 restaurants, 2 bars, coffee shop, 2 pools, hot tub, spa. AE, DC, MC, V.*

$$$–$$$$ 🏨 **Thistle Dew Inn.** The public rooms of this turn-of-the-century Victorian home a half block from Sonoma Plaza are filled with collector's-quality Arts and Crafts furnishings. Owners Larry and Norma Barnett live on the premises, and Larry prepares creative, sumptuous breakfasts and hors d'oeuvres in the evening. Four of the six rooms have private entrances and decks, and all have queen-size beds with antique quilts, private baths, and air-conditioning. Some rooms have fireplaces or whirlpools. ⊠ *171 W. Spain St., 95476,* ☎ *707/938–2909; 800/382–7895 in CA. 6 rooms. Breakfast room, hot tub, bicycles. AE, MC, V.*

$$ 🏨 **Vineyard Inn.** Built as a roadside motor court in 1941, this inn with red-tile roofs brings a touch of Mexican village charm to an otherwise lackluster and somewhat noisy location at the junction of two main highways. Rooms have queen-size beds, and Continental breakfast is included. ⊠ *23000 Arnold Dr. (at junction of Hwys. 116 and 121),*

95476, ☎ 707/938–2350 or 800/359–4667, ꜰᴀx 707/938–2353. *9 rooms, 4 suites. Breakfast room. AE, MC, V.*

Nightlife and the Arts

The **Sebastiani Theatre** (☎ 707/996–2020) schedules first-run movies. Every Sunday in August and September **Shakespeare at Buena Vista** (☎ 707/938–1266) brings the Bard to Sonoma. Performances are best enjoyed with a picnic lunch and a bottle of wine.

Shopping

Several shops in the four-block **Sonoma Plaza** attract food lovers from miles around. Serious picnickers stop at the **Sonoma French Bakery** (✉ Sonoma Plaza, 466 1st St. E, ☎ 707/996–2691), famous for its sourdough bread and cream puffs. **The Sonoma Cheese Factory** (✉ Sonoma Plaza, 2 Spain St., ☎ 707/996–1000), run by the same family for four generations, makes Sonoma Jack cheese and the tangy Sonoma Teleme.

Glen Ellen

7 mi north of Sonoma on Hwy. 12.

Jack London lived in the Sonoma Valley for many years. The creek-bisected town of Glen Ellen commemorates him with place names and nostalgic establishments. **Jack London Village** (✉ 14301 Arnold Dr., ☎ 707/935–1240) has many interesting shops like **The Ranch Store** (☎ 707/935–2311), which carries garden art, handmade quilts, and rustic furnishings. The **Jack London Bookstore** (✉ 14300 Arnold Dr., ☎ 707/996–2888) carries many of London's books.

In the hills above Glen Ellen—known as the Valley of the Moon—lies **Jack London State Historic Park.** London's collection of South Seas and other artifacts are on view at the House of Happy Walls, a museum of London's effects. The ruins of Wolf House, which London designed and which mysteriously burned down just before he was to move in, are close to the House of Happy Walls. London is buried on the property. ✉ *2400 London Ranch Rd.,* ☎ *707/938–5216.* ☞ *Parking $6.* ⊘ *Park, daily 9:30–5; museum, daily 10–5.*

③① One of the best-known local wineries is **Benziger Family Winery,** which specializes in premium estate and Sonoma County wines. Benziger's Imagery Series is a low-volume release of unusual red and white wines distributed in bottles with art labels by well-known artists from all over the world. Free, educational tram tours through the vineyards depart several times a day, weather permitting. ✉ *1883 London Ranch Rd.,* ☎ *707/935–3000.* ☞ *Tasting fees vary.* ⊘ *Daily 10–4:30. Tours every ½ hr, Mar.–Sept., 9:30–5; Oct.–Feb., 9:30–4.*

③② Wine makers and critics are quite familiar with the excellent hand-crafted wines produced at **Arrowood Vineyards.** The feel is more New England farmhouse than California wine estate. The winery's harmonious architecture overlooking the Valley of the Moon earned it an award from the Sonoma Historic Preservation League. ✉ *14347 Sonoma Hwy.,* ☎ *707/938–5170.* ⊘ *Daily 10–4:30. Tours by appointment.*

Dining and Lodging

$$ ✕ **The Girl & the Fig.** Mustard-yellow walls, mismatched yellow chairs, and changing art exhibits set a bohemian tone here. The food, which may include apricot-glazed poussin, is almost overshadowed by a unique wine list focusing largely on regional Rhône-style varietals. ✉ *13690 Arnold Dr.,* ☎ *707/938–3634. AE, MC, V.*

$$$–$$$$ ▥ **Beltane Ranch.** On a slope of the Mayacamas range on the eastern side of the Sonoma Valley lies this 100-year-old house built by a retired San Francisco madam. Beltane Ranch, surrounded by miles of trails through oak-studded hills, is part of a working cattle and grape-growing ranch. The rooms, all with private baths and antique furniture, open onto the building's wraparound porch. The cottage apartment has a sitting room. ⊠ *11775 Sonoma Hwy. (Hwy. 12), 95442,* ☎ *707/996–6501. 5 rooms. Tennis court, hiking, horseshoes. No credit cards.*

$$$–$$$$ ⊞ **Gaige House Inn.** Built in the 19th century as a personal residence, the Gaige House was bought in 1996 by owners who have added chic, contemporary rooms to the mix of older, more traditional accommodations on the two main floors. A large pool surrounded by a green lawn, white umbrellas, and magnolias conjures up glamour in the middle of rustic Glen Ellen. The first-rate country breakfast is served in a bright dining room downstairs or on the terrace. ⊠ *13540 Arnold Dr., 95442,* ☎ *707/935–0237 or 800/935–0237,* FAX *707/935–6411. 13 rooms. Breakfast room, pool, outdoor hot tub. AE, D, MC, V.*

$$–$$$ ⊞ **Glenelly Inn.** Just outside the hamlet of Glen Ellen, this sunny little establishment, built as an inn in 1916, offers all the comforts of home—including a hot tub in the garden. Innkeeper Kristi Hallamore serves breakfast in front of the common room's cobblestone fireplace and provides local delicacies in the afternoon. ⊠ *5131 Warm Springs Rd., 95442,* ☎ *707/996–6720,* FAX *707/996–5227. 8 rooms. Breakfast room, outdoor hot tub. MC, V.*

Kenwood

3 mi north of Glen Ellen on Hwy. 12.

Kenwood has an historic train depot and several restaurants and shops that specialize in locally produced goods. Its inns, restaurants, and winding roads nestle in soothing bucolic landscapes.

㉝ The beautifully rustic grounds at **Kenwood Vineyards** complement the attractive tasting room and artistic bottle labels. The winery is best known for its Jack London Vineyard reds—pinot noir, zinfandel, merlot, and a unique Artist Series cabernet. ⊠ *9592 Sonoma Hwy., Kenwood,* ☎ *707/833–5891.* ⊙ *Daily 10–4:30. No tours.*

㉞ **Landmark Vineyards.** The landscaping and design of this boutique winery, established by the heirs of John Deere, are as classical as its winemaking methods. Landmark's Damaris Reserve and Overlook chardonnays have been particularly well received. The winery's first claret was introduced in 1998. ⊠ *101 Adobe Canyon Rd., off Sonoma Hwy.,* ☎ *707/833–1144 or 800/452–6365.* ⊙ *Daily 10–4:30. No tours.*

Dining

$$–$$$ ✕ **Kenwood Restaurant & Bar.** One of the enduring favorites in an area
  ★ known for fine dining, this is where Napa and Sonoma chefs eat on their nights off. Indulge in California country cuisine in the sunny, South of France–style dining room or head through the French doors to the patio for a memorable view of the vineyards. ⊠ *9900 Hwy. 12,* ☎ *707/833–6326. MC, V. Closed Mon.*

$ ✕ **Café Citti.** The aroma of garlic envelops the neighborhood whenever the Italian chef-owner is roasting chickens at this homey roadside café. The variety of deli items, hot pastas, and soups makes this a good budget stop. ⊠ *9049 Hwy. 12,* ☎ *707/833–2690. MC, V.*

Santa Rosa

8 mi northwest of Kenwood on Hwy. 12.

Santa Rosa is the Wine Country's largest city and a good bet for moderately priced hotel rooms, especially for those who have not reserved in advance.

The **Luther Burbank Home and Gardens** commemorates the great botanist who lived and worked on these grounds for 50 years, single-handedly developing the modern techniques of hybridization. The Santa Rosa plum, Shasta daisy, and lily of the Nile agapanthus are among the 800 or so plants he developed or improved. In the music room of his house, a Webster's Dictionary of 1946 lies open to a page on which the verb "burbank" is defined as "to modify and improve plant life." ⊠ *Santa Rosa and Sonoma Aves.,* ☎ *707/524–5445.* 🎫 *Gardens free; guided tours of house and greenhouse $2.* ☉ *Gardens Nov.–Mar., daily 8–5; Apr.–Oct., daily 8–7. Tours Apr.–Oct., Wed.–Sun. 10–4.*

★ ㉟ **Matanzas Creek Winery** specializes in three varietals—sauvignon blanc, merlot, and chardonnay. All three have won glowing reviews from various magazines. Huge windows in the visitor center overlook a field of 3,100 tiered and fragrant lavender plants. Acres and acres of gardens planted with unusual grasses and plants from all over the world have caught the attention of horticulturists. After you taste the wines, ask to see the self-guided garden tour book before taking a stroll. ⊠ *6097 Bennett Valley Rd.,* ☎ *707/528–6464.* ☉ *Daily 10–4:30. Tours by appointment.*

Dining and Lodging

$$$ ✕ **John Ash & Co.** The first Wine Country restaurant to tout locally grown ingredients in the 1980s, John Ash has maintained its status despite the departure of its namesake chef in 1991. With patio seating outside and a cozy fireplace indoors, the slightly formal restaurant looks like a Spanish villa amid the vineyards. A café menu offers delicious bites between meals. ⊠ *4330 Barnes Rd. (River Rd. exit west from Hwy. 101),* ☎ *707/527–7687. Weekend reservations essential. AE, MC, V. No lunch Mon.*

$$–$$$ ✕ **Cafe Lolo.** This casual but sophisticated spot is the territory of chef and co-owner Michael Quigley, who has single-handedly made downtown Santa Rosa a culinary destination. Don't pass up the chocolate kiss, an individual cake with a wonderfully soft, rich center. ⊠ *620 5th St.,* ☎ *707/576–7822. AE, MC, V. Closed Sun. No lunch Sat.*

$–$$$ ✕ **Mistral.** As Mediterranean as the wind for which it's named, Mistral is a warm and gracious restaurant that tries to make everybody happy. The extensive menu ranges from braised mahimahi to grilled pork tenderloin and offers a wide-ranging wine list to match. ⊠ *1229 N. Dutton Ave.,* ☎ *707/578–4511. AE, D, DC, MC, V. No lunch weekends.*

$ ✕ **Mixx.** Great service and an eclectic mix of dishes define this small restaurant with large windows, booth and table seating, high ceilings, and Italian blown-glass chandeliers. House-made ravioli and grilled Cajun prawns are among the favorites of the many regular customers. ⊠ *135 4th St., at Davis (behind the mall on Railroad Sq.),* ☎ *707/ 573–1344. AE, MC, V. No lunch weekends.*

$$$–$$$$ 🏨 **Vintner's Inn.** Set on 50 acres of vineyards, this French provincial inn has large rooms, many with wood-burning fireplaces, and a trellised sundeck. Breakfast is complimentary. Guests receive discount passes to an affiliated health club. ⊠ *4350 Barnes Rd. (River Rd. exit west from U.S. 101), 95403,* ☎ *707/575–7350 or 800/421–2584,* ℻ *707/575–1426. 44 rooms. Restaurant, hot tub. AE, DC, MC, V.*

$$$ 🏨 **Fountaingrove Inn.** A redwood sculpture and a wall of cascading ★ water distinguish the lobby at this elegant, comfortable inn. A buffet breakfast is complimentary, and there's also an elegant restaurant with a piano player. Guests have access to a nearby 18-hole golf course, a tennis court, and a health club, all for an additional fee. ⊠ *101 Fountaingrove Pkwy. (near U.S. 101), 95403,* ☎ *707/578–6101 or 800/222–*

6101, FAX *707/544–3126. 126 rooms. Restaurant, in-room data ports,
room service, pool, hot tub, meeting rooms. AE, D, DC, MC, V.*

$$ 🖫 **Los Robles Lodge.** This pleasant, relaxed motel overlooks a pool that's
set into a grassy landscape. Pets are allowed, except in executive rooms.
Some rooms have whirlpools. ✉ *1985 Cleveland Ave. (Steele La. exit
west from Hwy. 101), 95401,* ☎ *707/545–6330 or 800/255–6330,* FAX
*707/575–5826. 100 rooms. Restaurant, coffee shop, lobby lounge, pool,
outdoor hot tub, coin laundry. AE, DC, MC, V.*

Nightlife and the Arts

The **Luther Burbank Performing Arts Center** (✉ 50 Mark West Springs
Rd., ☎ 707/546–3600) presents performances by locally and inter-
nationally known artists. For symphony, ballet, and other live theater
performances, call the **Spreckels Performing Arts Center** (☎ 707/584–
1700 or 707/588–3434) in Rohnert Park. **SRT** (Summer Repertory
Theatre; ✉ 1501 Mendocino Ave., ☎ 707/527–4307) presents clas-
sic and contemporary plays.

Outdoor Activities and Sports

GOLF

The **Fountaingrove Country Club** (✉ 1525 Fountaingrove Pkwy., ☎
707/579–4653) has an 18-hole course. The greens fee, which includes
a mandatory cart, runs $35–$70 depending on time of day and day of
week. **Oakmont Golf Club** (✉ west course: 7025 Oakmont Dr., ☎ 707/
539–0415; ✉ east course: 565 Oak Vista Ct., ☎ 707/538–2454) has
two 18-hole courses. The greens fee is $24–$32, plus $20 for an op-
tional cart.

HOT-AIR BALLOONING

For views of the ocean coast, the Russian River, and San Francisco on
a clear day, **Sonoma Thunder Wine Country Balloon Safaris** (☎ 707/
538–7359 or 800/759–5638) operates out of Santa Rosa, although many
flights actually originate outside Healdsburg. The cost is $175 per per-
son, including a champagne brunch at a hilltop winery.

Healdsburg

17 mi north of Santa Rosa on U.S. 101.

The countryside around Dry Creek Valley and Healdsburg is a fantasy
of pastoral bliss, beautifully overgrown and in constant repose. Along-
side the relatively untrafficked roads, country stores offer just-plucked
fruits and vine-ripened tomatoes. Wineries here are barely visible,
tucked behind groves of eucalyptus or hidden high on fog-shrouded
hills.

Healdsburg is centered by a plaza surrounded by shade trees, appeal-
ing antiques shops, and restaurants. For a free map of the area, con-
tact **Russian River Wine Road** (✉ Box 46, Healdsburg 95448, ☎ 707/
433–6782).

㊱ **Dry Creek Vineyard,** whose fumé blanc is an industry landmark, is also
earning notice for its reds, especially zinfandels and cabernets. ✉ *3770
Lambert Bridge Rd.,* ☎ *707/433–1000.* ☉ *Daily 10:30–4:30. Tours
by appointment.*

㊲ **Quivira** produces some of the most interesting wines in Dry Creek Val-
ley. Though it is known for its exquisitely balanced and fruity zinfan-
del, it also makes a superb blend of red varietals called Dry Creek Cuvée.
✉ *4900 W. Dry Creek Rd.,* ☎ *707/431–8333.* ☉ *Daily 10–4:30.
Tours by appointment.*

38 The boutique winery **A. Rafanelli,** owned by third-generation vintner Dave Rafanelli and his wife Patty, has been in operation since 1906. Zinfandel and cabernet are the only wines produced here; the 1995 zinfandel won high marks from *The Wine Spectator.* ✉ *4685 Dry Creek Rd.,* ☎ *707/433–1385.* ⊙ *Daily 10–4. Tours by appointment.*

39 Noted for its beautiful Italian villa–style winery and visitor center, **Ferrari-Carano Winery** produces chardonnays, fumé blancs, and merlots. Tours take you between the rows of grape vines right into the vineyards themselves. ✉ *8761 Dry Creek Rd.,* ☎ *707/433–6700.* ⊙ *Daily 10–5. Tours by appointment.*

40 **Simi Winery.** Giuseppe and Pietro Simi began growing grapes in Sonoma in 1876. Though the winery's operations are high-tech these days, its tree-studded entrance area and stone buildings recall a more genteel era. ✉ *16275 Healdsburg Ave. (take Dry Creek Rd. exit off U.S. 101),* ☎ *707/433–6981.* ⊙ *Daily 10–4:30. Tours at 11, 1, and 3.*

OFF THE BEATEN PATH **CLOS DU BOIS –** Ten mi north of Healdsburg on Highway 116, these vineyards produce the fine estate chardonnays of the Alexander and Dry Creek valleys that have been mistaken for great French wines. ✉ 19410 Geyserville Ave., Geyserville, ☎ 707/857–3100 or 800/222–3189. ⊙ Daily 10–4:30. No tours.

Dining and Lodging

$$ ✕ **Bistro Ralph.** In a town where good restaurants rarely seem to last, Ralph Tingle has sustained success with his California home-style cuisine, serving up a small menu that changes weekly. The stark industrial setting includes a stunning wine rack of graceful curves fashioned in metal and wood. ✉ *109 Plaza St., off Healdsburg Ave.,* ☎ *707/433–1380. Reservations essential. MC, V. No lunch weekends.*

$$$–$$$$ ▦ **Healdsburg Inn on the Plaza.** This 1900 brick building on the town plaza has a bright solarium and a roof garden. The rooms, most with fireplaces, are spacious, with quilts and pillows piled high on antique beds. In the bathrooms claw-foot tubs are outfitted with rubber ducks. Full breakfast, afternoon coffee and cookies, and early evening wine and popcorn are included. ✉ *110 Matheson St., Box 1196, 95448,* ☎ *707/433–6991. 10 rooms. Breakfast room. MC, V.*

$$$–$$$$ ▦ **The Honor Mansion.** This photogenic 1883 Italianate Victorian opened in 1994 to rave reviews for its interior decor. Antiques, feather beds, and fancy water bottles add a luxurious ambience to the rooms. A full breakfast is included. ✉ *14891 Grove St., 95448,* ☎ *707/433–4277 or 800/554–4667,* FAX *707/431–7173. 8 rooms. Breakfast room, pool, hot tub. D, MC, V.*

$$$–$$$$ ▦ **Madrona Manor.** The oldest continuously operating inn in the area, this 1881 Victorian mansion, surrounded by 8 acres of wooded and landscaped grounds, provides a storybook setting. Sleep either in the splendid three-story mansion, the carriage house, or one of two separate cottages. Mansion rooms are recommended: all nine have fireplaces, and five contain the antique furniture of the original owner. ✉ *1001 Westside Rd. (take central Healdsburg exit from U.S. 101, turn left on Mill St.), Box 818, 95448,* ☎ *707/433–4231 or 800/258–4003,* FAX *707/433–0703. 21 rooms. Restaurant, pool. AE, D, DC, MC, V.*

OFF THE BEATEN PATH **KORBEL CHAMPAGNE CELLARS –** To be called champagne, a wine must be made in the French region of Champagne or technically it's just like any other bubbly—a sparkler. But despite the objections of the French, champagne has entered the lexicon of California wine makers. Whatever you call it, Korbel produces a tasty, reasonably priced wine. The tour, one of the best in Sonoma County, clearly explains the process of making sparkling wine. The winery's 19th-century buildings and gorgeous rose gardens are a delight. ⊠ *13250 River Rd., Guerneville,* ☎ *707/887–2294.* ☉ *Oct.–Apr., daily 9–4:30; May–Sept., daily 9–5. Tours on the hr 10–3.*

Shopping
Oakville Grocery (⊠ 124 Matheson St., ☎ 707/433–3200) has a bustling Healdsburg branch filled with wine, produce, and deli items. Head to **Salami Tree** (⊠ 304 Center St., ☎ no phone) for picnic supplies. **Tip Top Liquor Warehouse** (⊠ 90 Dry Creek Rd., ☎ 707/431–0841) has a large selection of local wines, including some hard-to-find labels.

Every Saturday morning from early May through October, Healdsburg locals gather at the open-air **Farmers' Market** (⊠ North Plaza parking lot, North and Vine Sts., ☎ 707/431–1956) to pick up supplies from local producers of vegetables, fruits, flowers, cheeses, and olive oils.

THE WINE COUNTRY A TO Z

Arriving and Departing

By Bus
Greyhound (☎ 800/231–2222) runs buses from the Transbay Terminal at 1st and Mission streets in San Francisco to Sonoma and Santa Rosa.

By Car
From San Francisco, cross the Golden Gate Bridge, go north on U.S. 101, east on Highway 37, and north and east on Highway 121. For Sonoma wineries, head north at Highway 12; for Napa's, turn left (to the northwest) when Highway 121 runs into Highway 29. From Berkeley and other East Bay towns, take I–80 north to Highway 37 west to Highway 29 north. From points north of the Wine Country, take U.S. 101 south to Geyserville and follow Highway 128 southeast into the Napa Valley.

Getting Around

By Bus
Sonoma County Area Transit (☎ 707/585–7516) and **Napa Valley Transit** (☎ 707/255–7631) both provide transportation between towns in their respective Wine Country counties.

By Car
Although traffic on the two-lane country roads can be heavy, the best way to get around the sprawling Wine Country is by car. Rentals are available at the airports and in San Francisco, Oakland, Sonoma, Santa Rosa, and Napa.

Contacts and Resources

B&B Reservation Agencies
Bed & Breakfast Exchange (⊠ 1407 Main St., Suite 102, St. Helena, ☎ 707/942–5900). The **Bed & Breakfast Association of Sonoma** (⊠ 3250 Trinity Rd., Glen Ellen, ☎ 800/969–4667). **The Wine Country Bed & Breakfast Inns of Sonoma County** (☎ 707/433–4667; 800/354–4743 for brochure). **Wine Country Reservations** (☎ 707/257–7757).

Emergencies
Ambulance (☎ 911). **Police** (☎ 911).

Guided Tours

Full-day guided tours of the Wine Country usually include lunch and cost about $50. Reservations are usually required.

Gray Line (⊠ 350 8th St., San Francisco 94103, ☎ 415/558–9400) has bright red double-decker buses that tour the Wine Country. **Great Pacific Tour Co.** (⊠ 518 Octavia St., San Francisco 94102, ☎ 415/626–4499) operates full-day tours of Napa and Sonoma, including a summer picnic lunch and a winter restaurant lunch, in passenger vans that seat 14. **HMS Travel Group** (⊠ 707 4th St., Santa Rosa 95404, ☎ 707/526–2922 or 800/367–5348) offers customized tours of the Wine Country for six or more people, by appointment only. The **Napa Valley Wine Train** (⊠ 1275 McKinstry St., Napa 94559, ☎ 707/253–2111 or 800/427–4124) allows you to enjoy lunch, dinner, or weekend brunch on one of several restored 1915 Pullman railroad cars that run between Napa and St. Helena. Dinner costs $70, lunch $65, brunch $57; per-person prices include train fare, meals, tax, and service. On weekend brunch trips and weekday lunch trips you can ride a special "Deli" car for $27.50. In winter service is sometimes limited to Thursday through Sunday; call ahead.

Visitor Information

Napa Valley Conference and Visitors Bureau (⊠ 1310 Napa Town Center, Napa 94559, ☎ 707/226–7459). The **Redwood Empire Association** (⊠ The Cannery, 2801 Leavenworth St., 2nd floor, San Francisco 94133, ☎ 415/543–8334). **Sonoma County Tourism Program** (⊠ 401 College Ave., Santa Rosa 95401, ☎ 707/524–5789). **Sonoma Valley Visitors Bureau** (⊠ 453 First St., Sonoma 95476, ☎ 707/996–1090).

4 SAN FRANCISCO

With Side Trips to Marin County, the East Bay, the Inland Peninsula, and the South Bay

San Francisco is a sophisticated city with world-class hotels and the greatest concentration of excellent restaurants in the state. The town has an undeserved reputation as the kook capital of the United States, yet it's the country's number-one tourist destination. Why? To use the vernacular, the vibe here is cool, from North Beach coffeehouses to Chinatown tea emporiums, Golden Gate Park, and Haight Street's head shops (yes, they're still around).

I N ITS FIRST LIFE, SAN FRANCISCO was little more than a small, well-situated settlement. Founded by Spaniards in 1776, it was prized for its natural harbor. The 1848 discovery of gold at John Sutter's sawmill in the nearby Sierra foothills transformed the sleepy village into a city of 30,000 by the early 1850s. As millions of dollars' worth of gold was panned and blasted out of the hills, a "western Wall Street" sprang up. Just when gold production began to taper off, prospectors turned up a rich vein of silver in and around Virginia City, Nevada. San Francisco, the nearest financial center, prospered again. The city remains a financial hub, though nowadays its attentions are as much transoceanic as transcontinental. San Francisco prides itself on its role as a Pacific Rim capital, and overseas investment has become a vital part of its economic life.

Loose, tolerant, and even licentious are words that are used to describe San Francisco. Bohemian communities thrive here. As early as the 1860s, the "Barbary Coast"—a collection of taverns, whorehouses, and gambling joints on or near Pacific Avenue close to the waterfront— was infamous. North Beach, the city's Little Italy, became the home of the beat movement in the 1950s. The Haight-Ashbury district became synonymous with hippiedom, giving rise to legendary bands like Jefferson Airplane and the Grateful Dead in the 1960s. And, as most of the world knows, lesbians and gay men have found the town hospitable.

Technically speaking, San Francisco is only California's fourth-largest city, behind Los Angeles, San Diego, and nearby San Jose. But that statistic is misleading: the Bay Area, which stretches from the bedroom communities north of Oakland and Berkeley south through Silicon Valley and San Jose, is really one continuous megacity, with San Francisco as its heart.

EXPLORING SAN FRANCISCO

Revised by
Daniel Mangin

San Francisco is a relatively small city. About 750,000 residents live on a 46.6-square-mi tip of land between San Francisco Bay and the Pacific Ocean. San Franciscans cherish the city's colorful past. Many older buildings have been spared from demolition and nostalgically converted into modern offices and shops. Bernard Maybeck, Julia Morgan, Willis Polk, and Arthur Brown Jr. are among the noteworthy architects whose designs remain.

The neighborhoods of San Francisco retain strong cultural, political, and ethnic identities. Experiencing San Francisco means visiting the neighborhoods: the colorful Mission District, the gay Castro, countercultural Haight Street, swank Pacific Heights, exotic Chinatown, and still-bohemian North Beach.

Exploring involves navigating a maze of one-way streets and restricted parking zones. San Francisco's famed 40-plus hills can be a problem for drivers who are new to the terrain. Cable cars, buses, and trolleys can take you to or near many attractions.

Union Square Area

Much of San Francisco may feel like a collection of small towns strung together, but the Union Square area bristles with big-city bravado. The city's finest department stores do business here, along with exclusive emporiums like Tiffany & Co. and big-name franchises like Niketown, Borders Books and Music, and the Virgin Megastore. Several dozen hotels within a three-block walk of the square cater to visitors. The downtown theater district and many fine arts galleries are nearby.

Numbers in the text correspond to numbers in the margin and on the Downtown San Francisco map.

A Good Walk

Begin three blocks south of Union Square at the **San Francisco Visitors Information Center** ①, on the lower level of Hallidie Plaza at Powell and Market streets. Up the escalators on the east side of the plaza, where Powell dead-ends into Market, lies the **cable car terminus** ② for two of the city's three lines. Head north on Powell from the terminus to Geary Street, make a left, and walk west 1½ blocks into the theater district for a peek at the **Geary Theater** ③. Backtrack on the north side of Geary Street, where the **Westin St. Francis Hotel** ④ dominates Powell between Geary and Post streets. **Union Square** ⑤ is across Powell from the hotel's main entrance. You can pick up discount and full-price event tickets at the **TIX Bay Area** ⑥ booth in the square.

From the square head south on Stockton Street to O'Farrell Street and take a spin through **F. A. O. Schwarz** ⑦ (also on Stockton are Planet Hollywood and the Virgin Megastore). Walk back toward Union Square past Geary Street and make a right on **Maiden Lane** ⑧, a two-block alley directly across Stockton from Union Square that runs east parallel to Geary. When the lane ends at Kearny Street, turn left, walk 1½ blocks to Sutter Street, make a right, and walk a half block to the **Hallidie Building** ⑨. After viewing this historic building, reverse direction and head west 1½ blocks up Sutter to the fanciful **Hammersmith Building** ⑩, on the southwest corner of Sutter Street and Grant Avenue. In the middle of the next block of Sutter stands a glorious Art Deco building at **450 Sutter Street** ⑪. From here, backtrack a half block east to Stockton Street and take a right. In front of the the Grand Hyatt hotel sits **Ruth Asawa's Fantasy Fountain** ⑫.

TIMING

Allow two hours to see everything around Union Square. Stepping into the massive Macy's department store or browsing boutiques can eat up countless hours. If you're a shopper, give yourself extra time.

Sights to See

② **Cable car terminus.** San Francisco's cable cars were declared National Landmarks (the only ones that move) in 1964. Two of the three operating lines begin and end their runs here. The Powell–Mason line climbs up Nob Hill, then winds through North Beach to Fisherman's Wharf. The Powell–Hyde line also crosses Nob Hill but then continues up Russian Hill and down Hyde Street to Victorian Park, across from the Buena Vista Cafe and near Ghirardelli Square. Buy your ticket ($2 one-way) on board, at nearby hotels, or at the police/information booth near the turnaround. ⊠ *Powell and Market Sts.*

⑦ **F. A. O. Schwarz.** The prices are not Toys 'R Us, but it's worth stopping by this three-floor playland to look at the 6-ft-tall stuffed animals and elaborate fairy-tale sculptures. ⊠ *48 Stockton St.,* ☎ *415/394–8700.* ⊙ *Mon.–Sat. 10–7, Sun. 11–6.*

⑪ **450 Sutter Street.** Handsome Mayan-inspired designs adorn the exterior and interior surfaces of this 1928 Art Deco skyscraper, a masterpiece of terra-cotta and other detailing. ⊠ *Between Stockton and Powell Sts.*

③ **Geary Theater.** The American Conservatory Theater (ACT), one of North America's leading repertory companies, uses the 1,035-seat Geary as its main venue. Built in 1910, the Geary has a serious neoclassic de-

Marina Park
Fort Mason
Fisherman's Wharf
NORTHERN WATERFRONT

San Francisco Bay

Downtown

TO BERKELEY

Palace of Fine Arts
MARINA
Bay St.
NORTH BEACH
Hyde St.
Columbus Ave.
Grant Ave.
Larkin St.
Polk St.
RUSSIAN HILL
Lombard St.
101
Divisadero St.
Broadway
Washington St.
PACIFIC HEIGHTS
Sacramento St.
California St.
[tunnel]
CHINA-TOWN
FINANCIAL DISTRICT
The Embarcadero
San Francisco-Oakland Bay Bridge
80

Pine St.
Bush St.
JAPAN-TOWN
Laguna St.
Van Ness
Gough St.
Post St.
Geary St.
NOB HILL
UNION SQUARE
Powell St.
1st St.
2nd St.

Presidio
Ave.
Geary
Blvd.
Steiner St.
Franklin St.
Turk St.
Market St.
Mission St.
6th St.
5th St.
4th St.
3rd St.
Yerba Buena Center

Market St.
Masonic Ave.
St.
HAIGHT-ASHBURY
Golden
Gate
Ave.
Fulton St.
HAYES VALLEY
CIVIC CENTER
SOMA
Folsom
Harrison
Bryant
Brannan St.
Townsend St.
King St.
Berry St.

Clayton St.
Fell St.
WESTERN ADDITION
Duboce Ave.
Castro St.
Central Fwy.
9th St.
10th St.
8th St.
7th St.
280

Buena Vista Park
Market St.
17th St.
Dolores Park
MISSION
Potrero Ave.
Harrison St.
South Van Ness Ave.
Mariposa St.
POTRERO
Indiana St.
Pennsylvania Ave.
3rd St.
Central Basin

CASTRO
20th St.
Dolores St.
Guerrero St.
Mission St.
San Francisco General Hospital
India Basin

Twin Peaks
NOE VALLEY
Diamond St.
25th St.
Cesar Chavez St.
Islais Cr. Channel

BERNAL HEIGHTS
Oakdale Ave.
280

Bosworth St.
Monterey Blvd.
Fwy.
Silver Ave.
Felton St.
GLEN PARK
101
3rd St.
Quesada Ave.
Hunters Point

Southern
Balboa Park
San Jose Ave.
Alemany Blvd.
Excelsior Ave.
Persia St.
Moscow St.
Mission St.
France Ave.
Geneva Ave.
Cow Palace
John McLaren Park
Mansell St.
Gilman Ave.
Jamestown Ave.
South Basin
3 Com Park at Candlestick Point

Downtown San Francisco

San Francisco Bay

sign lightened by colorful carved terra-cotta columns depicting a cornucopia of fruits. Damaged heavily in the 1989 earthquake, the Geary has been completely restored to highlight its historic splendor. ⊠ *415 Geary St. (box office at 405 Geary St.),* ☎ *415/749–2228.*

❾ Hallidie Building. Named for cable car inventor Andrew S. Hallidie, this 1918 structure is best viewed from across the street. Willis Polk's revolutionary glass-curtain wall—believed to be the world's first such facade—hangs a foot beyond the reinforced concrete of the frame. The reflecting glass, decorative exterior fire escapes that appear to be metal balconies, and Venetian Gothic cornice are worth noting. ⊠ *130 Sutter St., between Kearny and Montgomery Sts.*

❿ Hammersmith Building. Glass walls and a colorful design distinguish this four-story beaux arts–style structure, built in 1907. ⊠ *301 Sutter St.*

❽ Maiden Lane. Known as Morton Street in the raffish Barbary Coast era (☞ The Heart of the Barbary Coast, *below*), this former red-light district reported at least one murder a week during the late 19th century. After the 1906 fire destroyed the brothels, the street emerged as Maiden Lane, and it has since become a semi-chic pedestrian mall stretching two blocks, between Stockton and Kearny streets. Traffic is prohibited most days between 11 and 5, when the lane becomes a patchwork of umbrella-shaded tables.

With its circular interior ramp and skylights, the handsome brick 1948 structure at **140 Maiden Lane,** the only Frank Lloyd Wright building in San Francisco, is said to have been his model for the Guggenheim Museum in New York. The **Folk Art International/Boretti Amber/Xanadu** (☎ 415/392–9999) galleries, showcases for Baltic, Latin American, and African folk art, occupy the space. ⊠ *Between Stockton and Kearny Sts.*

⓬ Ruth Asawa's Fantasy Fountain. Local artist Ruth Asawa's sculpture, a wonderland of real and mythical creatures, honors the city's hills, bridges, and architecture. Children and friends helped Asawa shape the hundreds of tiny figures from baker's clay. These were assembled on 41 large panels from which molds were made for the bronze casting. ⊠ *In front of Grand Hyatt at 345 Stockton St.*

❶ San Francisco Visitors Information Center. A multilingual staff operates this facility below the cable car terminus. Staff members answer questions and provide maps and pamphlets. You can also pick up discount coupons and hotel brochures here. ⊠ *Hallidie Plaza, lower level, Powell and Market Sts.,* ☎ *415/391–2000.* ☉ *Weekdays 9–5:30, Sat. 9–3, Sun. 10–2.*

❻ TIX Bay Area. This excellent service provides half-price day-of-performance tickets (cash or traveler's checks only) to all types of performing arts events, as well as regular full-price box office services for concerts, clubs, and sporting events (credit cards accepted). Telephone reservations are not accepted for half-price tickets. Half-price tickets for Sunday and Monday events are sold on Saturday. Also sold at the booth is the **Golden Gate Park Explorer Pass** ($14; good for discount admission to the main attractions in Golden Gate Park) and Muni Passports and adult Fast Passes for use on the transit system. ⊠ *Union Square,* ☎ *415/433–7827.* ☉ *Tues.–Thurs. 11–6, Fri.–Sat. 11–7.*

❺ Union Square. The heart of San Francisco's downtown since 1850, the 2.6-acre square takes its name from the violent pro-union demonstrations staged here prior to the Civil War. At center stage, the *Victory Monument,* by Robert Ingersoll Aitken, commemorates Commodore

George Dewey's victory over the Spanish fleet at Manila in 1898. The 97-ft Corinthian column, topped by a bronze figure symbolizing naval conquest, was dedicated by Theodore Roosevelt in 1903 and withstood the 1906 earthquake. After the earthquake and fire of 1906, the square was dubbed "Little St. Francis" because of the temporary shelter erected for residents of the St. Francis Hotel. Once the jewel of downtown, the square looks rather dowdy in the late 20th century, but it is scheduled for a makeover during 2000, so you may find portions of it closed. ⊠ *Between Powell, Stockton, Post, and Geary Sts.*

❹ **Westin St. Francis Hotel.** The second-oldest hotel in the city, established in 1904, was conceived by railroad baron and financier Charles Crocker and his associates as a hostelry for their millionaire friends. Swift service and sumptuous surroundings have always been hallmarks of the property. After the hotel was ravaged by the 1906 fire, a larger Italian Renaissance–style residence was opened in 1907 to attract loyal clients from among the world's rich and powerful. The hotel's checkered past includes the ill-fated 1921 bash in the suite of the silent-film comedian Fatty Arbuckle, at which a woman became ill and later died. In 1975 Sara Jane Moore, standing among a crowd outside the hotel, attempted to shoot then-president Gerald R. Ford. No plaques commemorate these events, but the ever-helpful staff will direct you to tea (daily from 3 to 5) or champagne and caviar in the **Compass Rose** (☎ 415/774–0167) lounge. ⊠ *335 Powell St., at Geary St.,* ☎ *415/397–7000.*

South of Market (SoMa) and the Embarcadero

The vast tract of downtown land south of Market Street along the waterfront and west to the Mission District—also known by the acronym SoMa—is the center of a burgeoning arts scene.

Numbers in the text correspond to numbers in the margin and on the Downtown San Francisco map.

A Good Walk

The **San Francisco Museum of Modern Art** ⑬ dominates a half block of 3rd Street between Howard and Mission streets. Use the crosswalk near SFMOMA's entrance to head across 3rd Street into Yerba Buena Gardens. To your right after you've walked a few steps, a sidewalk leads to the main entrance of the **Center for the Arts** ⑭. Straight ahead is the East Garden of Yerba Buena Gardens and beyond that, on the 4th Street side of the block, is the **Metreon** ⑮ entertainment, retail, and restaurant complex. A second-level walkway in the southern portion of the East Garden, above the Martin Luther King Jr. waterfall, arches over Howard Street, leading to the main (south) entrance to **Moscone Convention Center** ⑯ and the **Rooftop@Yerba Buena Gardens** ⑰ facilities. Exit the rooftop near Folsom Street, cross 4th Street, turn right, and head back toward Howard Street. In the middle of the block, across from the rooftop, is the **Ansel Adams Center for Photography** ⑱. Continue north up 4th Street to Mission Street; a half block west on Mission is the **Cartoon Art Museum** ⑲. From here backtrack east on Mission (toward SFMOMA) past the monolithic San Francisco Marriott. Cross 3rd Street and continue a third of a block to the headquarters of the **California Historical Society** ⑳.

Backtrack a few steps on Mission to 3rd Street, where you can walk north and cross over Market Street to where 3rd, Market, Kearny, and Geary streets converge. In the traffic triangle here stands historic **Lotta's Fountain**—if it's not, never fear, it may be under refurbishment. Walk back to the south side of Market Street from the fountain and head east (left, toward the waterfront) to the **Palace Hotel** ㉑. Enter via the

Market Street entrance, checking out the Pied Piper Bar, Garden Court restaurant, and main lobby. Exit via the lobby and make a left, which will bring you back up to Market Street. Toward the end of Market a three-tier pedestrian mall connects the five buildings of the **Embarcadero Center** ㉒ office-retail complex. Embarcadero 5, at the very end of Market Street, houses the **Hyatt Regency Hotel** ㉓. On the waterfront side of the hotel is Justin Herman Plaza.

Across the busy Embarcadero roadway from the plaza stands the port's trademark, the **Ferry Building** ㉔. Head west on Mission Street and cross Steuart Street. In the middle of the block is the entrance to the historic sections of **Rincon Center** ㉕. Continue south within the center to its newer portions and make a left as you exit through the doors near Chalkers Billiards. Across Steuart Street you'll see the Jewish Community Federation Building, which houses **The Jewish Museum** ㉖.

TIMING

The walk above takes a good two hours, more if you visit the museums and galleries. SFMOMA merits about two hours, the Center for the Arts, the Cartoon Art Museum, and the Ansel Adams Center 45 minutes each.

Sights to See

⑱ **Ansel Adams Center for Photography.** Ansel Adams created this center in Carmel in 1967, and some of his work is always on display. Recent exhibits have included works by contemporary Native American photographers and images of a World War II–era Japanese internment camp shot by Adams, Dorothea Lange, and Toyo Miyataki. ✉ *250 4th St.,* ☎ *415/495–7000.* ▦ *$5.* ☉ *Daily 11–5, 1st Thurs. of month 11–8.*

⑳ **California Historical Society.** The society, founded in 1871, administers a vast repository of Californiana—500,000 photographs, 150,000 manuscripts, thousands of books, periodicals, and paintings as well as gold-rush paraphernalia. ✉ *678 Mission St.,* ☎ *415/357–1848.* ▦ *$2 (free 1st Tues. of month).* ☉ *Tues.–Sat. 11–5 (galleries close between exhibitions).*

⑲ **Cartoon Art Museum.** Krazy Kat, Zippy the Pinhead, Batman, and other colorful cartoon icons greet you as you walk in the door here. In addition to a 12,000-piece permanent collection, a 3,000-volume library, and a CD-ROM gallery, changing exhibits examine everything from the impact of underground comics to the output of women and African-American cartoonists. ✉ *814 Mission St., 2nd floor,* ☎ *415/227–8666.* ▦ *$5 (pay what you wish 1st Wed. of month).* ☉ *Wed.–Fri. 11–5, Sat. 10–5, Sun. 1–5.*

⑭ **Center for the Arts.** The dance, music, theater, visual arts, films, and videos presented at this facility in Yerba Buena Gardens range from the community-based to the international. ✉ *701 Mission St.,* ☎ *415/ 978–2787.* ▦ *Galleries $5; free 1st Thurs. of month 6 PM–8 PM.* ☉ *Galleries and box office: Tues.–Sun. 11–6 (until 8 PM 1st Thurs. of month).*

㉒ **Embarcadero Center.** John Portman designed this five-block complex built during the 1970s and early 1980s. Shops and restaurants abound on the first three levels; there's ample office space on the floors above. Louise Nevelson's 54-ft-high black-steel sculpture, *Sky Tree,* stands guard over Building 3 and is among 20-plus artworks throughout the center. The indoor-outdoor SkyDeck atop Embarcadero 1 (buy tickets on the ground floor and take the mezzanine-level elevator) provides an enticing 360-degree view of the city and interactive multimedia presentations about San Francisco history and culture. Tickets ($6) to the deck, which is open daily 9:30–9, sometimes sell out days in advance for certain hours. Call the hot line for information. ⊠ *Clay St. between Battery St. (Embarcadero 1) and the Embarcadero (Embarcadero 5),* ☎ *800/733–6318 for Embarcadero Center information; 888/737–5933 for SkyDeck hot line; 415/772–0591 for SkyDeck ticket booth.*

㉔ Ferry Building. The beacon of the port area, erected in 1896, has a 230-ft clock tower modeled after the campanile of the cathedral in Seville, Spain. On April 18, 1906, the four great clock faces on the tower, powered by the swinging of a 14-ft pendulum, stopped at 5:17—the moment the great earthquake struck—and stayed still for 12 months. The Ferry Building contains the offices of the Port Commission and the World Trade Center, though plans surface periodically for more high-profile uses of this prime real estate. Ferries behind the building sail to Sausalito, Larkspur, Tiburon, and the East Bay. ⊠ *The Embarcadero at the foot of Market St.*

㉓ Hyatt Regency Hotel. John Portman designed this hotel noted for its 17-story hanging garden. Christmas is the best time to see it, when strands of tiny white lights hang down above the lobby starting at the 12th floor. The Hyatt played a starring role in the 1970s disaster movie *The Towering Inferno.* ⊠ *Embarcadero 5,* ☎ *415/778–1234.*

㉖ The Jewish Museum. The exhibits at this small museum survey Jewish art, history, and culture. The museum was open only sporadically in 1999, but its operators expect to resume regular hours in 2000. ⊠ *121 Steuart St.,* ☎ *415/543–8880.* 🎫 *$5; free 1st Mon. of month.* ☉ *Mon.–Wed. noon–6, Thurs. noon–8, Sun. 11–6. Hrs may vary.*

Lotta's Fountain. San Franciscans gather each April 18, the anniversary of the 1906 earthquake, at this quirky monument, given in 1875 to the city by entertainer Lotta Crabtree. The exploits of this Madonna prototype so enthralled San Francisco's early population of miners that they were known to shower her with gold nuggets and silver dollars after her performances. The fountain, whose peculiar and a bit clunky design she had a hand in, was her way of saying thanks to her fans. The fountain was being restored in 1999, but it should be reinstalled by 2000. ⊠ *Traffic triangle at intersection of 3rd, Market, Kearny, and Geary Sts.*

☙ ⑮ Metreon. Kid-play meets the 21st century at this Sony entertainment center with interactive play areas based on books like Maurice Sendak's *Where the Wild Things Are* and a three-screen, three-dimensional installation that illustrates principles discussed in architect David Macauley's *The Way Things Work.* There's also a 15-screen multiplex, an IMAX theater, retail shops, and restaurants. ⊠ *4th St. between Mission and Howard Sts.,* ☎ *800/METREON (800/638–7366).*

⑯ Moscone Convention Center. The site of the 1984 Democratic convention, Moscone is distinguished by a contemporary glass-and-girder lobby at street level (all convention exhibit space is underground) and a column-free interior. ⊠ *Howard St. between 3rd and 4th Sts.*

㉑ Palace Hotel. The city's oldest hotel opened in 1875. Fire destroyed the original Palace following the 1906 earthquake despite the hotel's 28,000-gallon reservoir fed by four artesian wells; the current building dates from 1909. President Warren Harding died at the Palace while still in office in 1923, and the body of King Kalakaua of Hawaii spent a night chilling here after he died in San Francisco in 1891. The managers play up this ghoulish past with talk of a haunted guest room. Free guided tours (☎ 415/557–4266) take in the glass-dome Garden

Court restaurant, mosaic-tile floors in Oriental-rug designs, and Max-field Parrish's wall-size painting, *The Pied Piper.* ⊠ *2 New Montgomery St.,* ☎ *415/512–1111.* ⊙ *Tours Tues. and Sat. 10:30 AM, Thurs. 2 PM.*

㉕ Rincon Center. A five-story column of water resembling a minirainstorm stands out as the centerpiece of the indoor arcade at this office-retail complex. The lobby of the Streamline Moderne–style former post of-fice on the Mission Street side contains a Works Project Administra-tion **mural by Anton Refregier.** The 27 panels depict California life from the days when Native Americans were the state's sole inhabitants through World War I. A permanent exhibit below the murals contains photographs and artifacts of life in the Rincon area in the 1800s. ⊠ *Between Steuart, Spear, Mission, and Howard Sts.*

★ ☚ ⑰ Rooftop@Yerba Buena Gardens. Fun is the order of the day among these brightly colored concrete and corrugated-metal buildings atop Moscone Convention Center South. An historic **Looff carousel** ($1 per ride) twirls from Wednesday through Sunday between noon and 6. South of the carousel is **Zeum** (☎ 415/777–2800), a high-tech interactive arts and technology center ($7 adults, $5 kids ages 5–18) geared to children 8 and over. Zeum is open from Wednesday through Friday between noon and 6 and on weekends between 11 and 5. Also part of the rooftop complex are gardens, an ice-skating rink, and a bowling alley. ⊠ *4th St. between Mission and Howard Sts.*

★ ⑬ San Francisco Museum of Modern Art (SFMOMA). Mario Botta designed the striking SFMOMA facility, which consists of a sienna brick facade and a central tower of alternating bands of black and white stone. In-side, natural light from the tower floods the central atrium and some of the museum's galleries. Works by Matisse, Picasso, O'Keeffe, Kahlo, Pollock, and Warhol form the heart of SFMOMA's diverse permanent collection. The adventurous programming includes traveling exhibits and multimedia installations. The café, accessible from the street, pro-vides a comfortable, reasonably priced refuge for drinks and light meals. ⊠ *151 3rd St.,* ☎ *415/357–4000.* ⌗ *$8; free 1st Tues. of each month; ½-price entry Thurs. 6–9.* ⊙ *Memorial Day–Labor Day, Fri.–Tues. 10–6, Thurs. 10–9; Labor Day–Memorial Day, Fri.–Tues. 11–6, Thurs. 11–9.*

★ Yerba Buena Gardens. The centerpiece of the SoMa redevelopment area is the two blocks that encompass the Center for the Arts, Moscone Cen-ter, Metreon, and the Rooftop@Yerba Buena Gardens. A circular walk-way lined with benches and sculptures surrounds the East Garden, a large patch of green amid this visually stunning complex. The water-fall memorial to Martin Luther King Jr. is the focal point of the East Garden. Powerful streams of water surge over large, jagged stone columns, mirroring the enduring force of King's words that are carved on the stone walls and on glass blocks behind the waterfall. ⊠ *Between 3rd, 4th, Mission, and Folsom Sts.* ⊙ *Sunrise–10 PM.*

The Heart of the Barbary Coast

When San Francisco was a brawling, boozing, extravagant upstart of a town in the latter half of the 19th century, Jackson Square and the Financial District were at the heart of the action. The Gold Rush brought streams of people from across America and Europe, transforming the onetime frontier town into a cosmopolitan city almost overnight. The population of San Francisco jumped from a mere 800 in 1848 to more than 25,000 in 1850, and to nearly 150,000 in 1870. Along with the prospectors came many other fortune seekers. Saloon keepers, gamblers, and prostitutes all flocked to the so-called Barbary Coast (now

Jackson Square and the Financial District). Underground dance halls, casinos, bordellos, and palatial homes sprung up. Along with the quick money came a wave of violence. In 1852 the city suffered an average of two murders and one major fire each day.

By 1917 the excesses of the Barbary Coast had fallen victim to the Red-Light Abatement Act and the ire of church leaders. The wild era was over, and the young city was forced to grow up. Since then the red-light establishments have edged upward to the Broadway strip of North Beach, and Jackson Square evolved into a sedate district of re-furbished brick buildings decades ago. But below Montgomery Street between California Street and Broadway, underlying many building foundations along the former waterfront area (long since filled in), are at least 100 ships abandoned by frantic crews and passengers caught up in gold fever.

Numbers in the text correspond to numbers in the margin and on the Downtown San Francisco map.

A Good Walk

Bronze sidewalk plaques mark the street corners along the 50-site, 3.8-mi-long Barbary Coast Trail. The trail begins at the Old Mint, at 5th and Mission streets, and runs north through downtown, Chinatown, Jackson Square, North Beach, and Fisherman's Wharf, ending at Aquatic Park. For information about the sites on the trail, pick up a brochure at the San Francisco Visitors Information Center.

To catch the highlights of the Barbary Coast Trail and a glimpse of a few important Financial District structures, start at Montgomery and Market streets. Walk east on Market Street toward the Ferry Building to Sansome Street and turn left. At 155 Sansome Street is the Stock Exchange Tower. Around the corner (to the left) on Pine Street is the **Pacific Stock Exchange** ㉗ building. Continue north on Sansome. Turn left on California and right on Montgomery Street. Between California and Sacramento streets is the **Wells Fargo Bank History Museum** ㉘.

Two blocks north on Montgomery from the Wells Fargo museum stands the **Transamerica Pyramid** ㉙, between Clay and Washington streets. A tranquil redwood grove graces the east side of the pyramid. Walk through it, and you'll exit on Washington Street, across which you can see Hotaling Place to your left. Walk west (left) to the corner, cross Washington Street, and walk back to Hotaling. This historic alley is your entrance to **Jackson Square** ㉚, the heart of the Barbary Coast. Walk north on Jackson and make a left on Montgomery. Continue south on Montgomery to Washington Street, make a right, and cross Columbus Avenue. Head north (to the right) up Columbus to the **San Francisco Brewing Company** ㉛, the last standing saloon of the Barbary Coast era.

TIMING

Two hours should be enough time to see everything on this tour—unless you plan to try all the homemade beers at the San Francisco Brewing Company. The Wells Fargo Museum (open only on weekdays) deserves a half hour.

Sights to See

㉚ **Jackson Square.** Here was the heart of the Barbary Coast of the Gay '90s. Though most of the red-light district was destroyed in the 1906 fire, old redbrick buildings and narrow alleys recall the romance and rowdiness of the early days. Some of the city's earliest business buildings, survivors of the 1906 quake, still stand in Jackson Square, between Montgomery and Sansome streets.

By the end of World War II most of the 19th-century brick structures had fallen on hard times. But in 1951 a group of preservation-minded designers and furniture wholesale dealers selected the area for their showrooms, turning Jackson Square into the interior design center of the West. In 1972 the city officially designated the area San Francisco's first historic district. When property values soared, many of the fabric and furniture outlets fled to Potrero Hill. Advertising agencies, attorneys, and antiques dealers now occupy the Jackson Square area structures.

㉗ Pacific Stock Exchange. Ralph Stackpole's monumental 1930 granite sculptural groups, *Earth's Fruitfulness* and *Man's Inventive Genius,* flank this imposing structure, which dates from 1915. The Stock Exchange Tower, around the corner at 155 Sansome Street, is a 1930 modern classic by architects Miller and Pfleuger, with an Art Deco gold ceiling and a black marble wall entry. ⊠ *301 Pine St. (tower around corner at 155 Sansome St.).*

㉛ San Francisco Brewing Company. Built in 1907, this pub looks like a museum piece from the Barbary Coast days. Take a seat at the mahogany bar and look down at the white-tile spittoon. In an adjacent room look for the handmade copper brewing kettle used to produce a dozen beers. ⊠ *155 Columbus Ave.,* ☎ *415/434–3344.*

㉙ Transamerica Pyramid. The city's most photographed high-rise is the 853-ft Transamerica Pyramid. Designed by William Pereira and Associates in 1972, the initially controversial icon has become more acceptable to most locals over time. A fragrant redwood grove along the east side of the building, replete with benches and a cheerful fountain, is a placid patch in which to unwind. ⊠ *600 Montgomery St.*

㉘ Wells Fargo Bank History Museum. There were no formal banks in San Francisco during the early years of the Gold Rush, and miners often entrusted their gold dust to saloon keepers. In 1852 Wells Fargo opened its first bank in the city, and the company established banking offices in the mother-lode camps, using stagecoaches and pony express riders to service the burgeoning state. The museum displays samples of nuggets and gold dust from mines, a mural-size map of the Mother Lode, mementos of the poet bandit Black Bart, and an old telegraph machine on which you can practice sending codes. The showpiece is the red Concord stagecoach, the likes of which carried passengers from St. Joseph, Missouri, to San Francisco in three weeks during the 1850s. ⊠ *420 Montgomery St.,* ☎ *415/396–2619.* ⌨ *Free.* ☉ *Weekdays 9–5.*

OFF THE
BEATEN PATH

BANK OF AMERICA BUILDING – This 52-story polished red granite-and-marble building takes up nearly an entire downtown block. A massive, abstract black-granite sculpture designed by the Japanese artist Masayuki commands the corner of the complex at Kearny and California streets. On top of the building is the **Carnelian Room** (☎ 415/433–7500), a chic cocktail lounge and restaurant—open daily from 3 to 11 and for Sunday brunch from 10 to 1:30—with a view of the city and the bay. ⊠ *Between California, Pine, Montgomery, and Kearny Sts.*

Chinatown

Bordered roughly by Bush, Kearny, and Powell streets and Broadway, Chinatown is home to one of the largest Chinese communities outside Asia. The area is tightly packed, mostly because housing discrimination in the past kept residents from moving outside Chinatown. There was nowhere to go but up and down. The two main drags of Chinatown are Grant Avenue, jammed with kitschy tourist shops, and Stockton Street, where the locals do their business. Park outside the area, as a spot here is extremely hard to find and traffic is impossible.

Numbers in the text correspond to numbers in the margin and on the Downtown San Francisco map.

A Good Walk

Visitors usually enter Chinatown through the green-tile **Chinatown Gate** ㉜, at Bush Street and Grant Avenue. **Old St. Mary's Cathedral** ㉝ towers over the corner of Grant Avenue and California Street. Continue on Grant to Clay Street and turn right. A half block down on your left is **Portsmouth Square** ㉞. A walkway on the eastern edge of the park leads over Kearny Street to the third floor of the Holiday Inn, where you'll find the **Chinese Culture Center** ㉟.

Backtrack on the walkway to Portsmouth Square and head west up Washington Street a half block to the **Old Chinese Telephone Exchange** ㊱ (now the Bank of Canton), and continue west on Washington Street. Cross Grant Avenue and look for Waverly Place a half block up on the left. One of the best examples of this alley's traditional architecture is the **Tin How Temple** ㊲. After visiting Waverly Place and Tin How, walk back to Washington Street.

Across Washington Street from Superior is Ross Alley. Head north on Ross toward Jackson Street, stopping along the way to watch the bakers at the **Golden Gate Fortune Cookies Co.** ㊳. Turn right on Jackson. When you get to Grant Avenue, don't cross it. Head west (up the hill) on Pacific Avenue to Stockton Street, turn left, and walk south past Stockton Street's markets. At Clay Street make a right and head halfway up the hill to the **Chinatown YWCA** ㊴. Return to Stockton Street and make a right; a few doors down is the **Kong Chow Temple** ㊵.

TIMING

Allow at least two hours to see Chinatown. Brief stops will suffice at the cultural center and temples.

Sights to See

㉜ **Chinatown Gate.** Stone lions flank the base of this pagoda-top gate, the official entrance to Chinatown and a symbolic and literal transition from the generic downtown atmosphere to what sometimes seems like another country altogether. ⊠ *Bush St. and Grant Ave.*

㉟ **Chinatown YWCA.** Julia Morgan, the architect known for Hearst Castle, designed this handsome redbrick building, which originally served as a meeting place and residence for Chinese women in need of social services. The YWCA building will be closed for several years for seismic retrofitting and other structural repairs. ⊠ *965 Clay St.*

㉟ **Chinese Culture Center.** The San Francisco Redevelopment Commission agreed to let Holiday Inn build in Chinatown if the chain provided room for a Chinese culture center. Inside the center are the works of Chinese and Chinese-American artists as well as traveling exhibits relating to Chinese culture. Walking tours ($15; make reservations one week ahead) of historic points in Chinatown take place on most days at 10:30 AM and on Saturday at 2 PM. ⊠ *Holiday Inn, 750 Kearny St., 3rd floor,* ☎ *415/986–1822.* ⊠ *Free.* ☉ *Tues.–Sun. 10–4.*

㊳ **Golden Gate Fortune Cookies Co.** The workers at this small factory sit at motorized griddles. A dollop of batter drops onto a tiny metal plate, which rotates into an oven. A few moments later out comes a cookie that's pliable and ready for folding. It's easy to peek in for a moment here. ⊠ *56 Ross Alley (north of and parallel to Grant St. between Washington and Jackson Sts.),* ☎ *415/781–3956.* ☉ *Daily 10–7.*

④⓪ **Kong Chow Temple.** The god to whom the members of this temple pray represents honesty and trust. Your party can show its respect by placing a dollar or two in the donation box. Amid the statuary, flowers, orange offerings, and richly colored altars are a couple of plaques announcing that MRS. HARRY S. TRUMAN CAME TO THIS TEMPLE IN JUNE 1948 FOR A PREDICTION ON THE OUTCOME OF THE ELECTION. . . . THIS FORTUNE CAME TRUE. ⊠ *855 Stockton St.,* ☎ *415/434–2513.* ▧ *Free.* ☉ *Mon.– Sat. 9–4.*

③⑥ **Old Chinese Telephone Exchange.** Most of Chinatown burned down after the 1906 earthquake, and this was the first building to set the style for the new Chinatown. The intricate three-tier pagoda was built in 1909. The exchange's operators were renowned for their prodigious memories—they knew all their callers by name rather than number. ⊠ *Bank of Canton, 743 Washington St.*

③③ **Old St. Mary's Cathedral.** This building, whose structure includes granite quarried in China, was dedicated in 1854 and served as the city's Catholic cathedral until 1891. The cathedral hosts Noontime Concert, a notable chamber-music series on Tuesday and Thursday at 12:30. Across California Street from the cathedral in **St. Mary's Park** the late local sculptor Beniamino (Benny) Bufano's 12-ft-tall stainless-steel and rose-color granite statue of Sun Yat-sen towers over the site of the Chinese leader's favorite reading spot during his years in San Francisco. ⊠ *Grant Ave. and California St.,* ☎ *415/288–3840 (concert line).* ▧ *$3 suggested donation for concert series.*

③④ **Portsmouth Square.** Captain John B. Montgomery raised the American flag here in 1846, claiming the area from Mexico. The square—a former potato patch—was the plaza for Yerba Buena, the Mexican settlement that was renamed San Francisco. Robert Louis Stevenson lived on the edge of Chinatown in the late 19th century and often visited this site, chatting up the sailors who hung out here. Bruce Porter designed the bronze galleon that sits on top of a 9-ft granite shaft in the northwestern corner of the square in the writer's memory. With its pagoda-shape structures, Portsmouth Square is a favorite spot for morning tai chi. Children scamper about two playgrounds within the square, which has rest room facilities. ⊠ *Bordered by Walter Lum Pl. and Kearny, Washington, and Clay Sts.*

★ ③⑦ **Tin How Temple.** Day Ju, one of the first three Chinese to arrive in San Francisco, dedicated this temple to the Queen of the Heavens and the Goddess of the Seven Seas in 1852. Climb three flights of stairs to the temple's entryway, where elderly ladies can often be seen preparing "money" to be burned as offerings to various Buddhist gods or as funds for ancestors to use in the afterlife. Red-and-gold lanterns adorn the ceiling—the larger the lamp the larger its donor's contribution to the temple—and the smell of incense is usually thick. Oranges and other offerings rest on altars to various gods. A statue of Tin How sits in the middle of the back of the temple, flanked on one side by a red lesser god and the right by a green one. Photography is not permitted, and visitors are asked not to step onto the balcony. ⊠ *125 Waverly Pl.,* ☎ *no phone.* ▧ *Free (donations accepted).* ☉ *Daily 10–4.*

North Beach and Telegraph Hill

Novelist and resident Herbert Gold calls North Beach "the longest-running, most glorious American bohemian operetta outside Greenwich Village." Indeed, to anyone who's spent some time in its eccentric old bars and cafés or wandered the neighborhood, North Beach evokes everything from the Barbary Coast days to the no-less-sedate beatnik era. Italian bakeries appear frozen in time, homages to Jack Kerouac and Allen Ginsberg pop up everywhere, and the modern equivalent of the Barbary Coast's "houses of ill-repute," strip joints, do business on Broadway.

Numbers in the text correspond to numbers in the margin and on the Downtown San Francisco map.

A Good Walk

Stand on the northwest corner of Broadway and Columbus Avenue to get your bearings. To the southwest is Chinatown. The Financial District skyscrapers loom overhead to the south of the intersection of Columbus and Broadway. East across Columbus is the Condor, where in 1964 local celeb Carol Doda became the nation's first dancer at a nightclub to go topless. (These days the Condor is a sports bar.) Around the same time, North Beach was a nexus of comedy. Bill Cosby, Phyllis Diller, and other talents cut their teeth at clubs like the hungry i and the Purple Onion. To the north of Broadway and Columbus is the heart of Italian North Beach.

Walk south on Broadway across Columbus to **City Lights Bookstore** ㊶, where you can pick up a book by one of the beat writers or just soak up the ambience. Head up the east side of Columbus Avenue past Grant Avenue. On the northeast corner of Columbus and Vallejo Street is the Victorian-era **St. Francis of Assisi Church** ㊷. Head east on Vallejo Street to Grant Avenue and make another left. Check out the the eclectic shops and old-time bars and cafés between Vallejo and Union streets.

Turn left at Union Street and head west to **Washington Square** ㊸. On the north side stands the double-turreted **Saints Peter and Paul Catholic Church** ㊹. After getting your fill of North Beach, head up **Telegraph Hill** ㊺ from Washington Square. Atop the hill is **Coit Tower** ㊻. People in poor health will not want to attempt the walk up the steep hill; Coit Tower can be reached by car (though parking is very tight) or public transportation—board Muni Bus 39-Coit at Washington Square. To walk, head east up Filbert Street at the park. Turn left at Grant Avenue and go one block north, then right at Greenwich Street and ascend the steps on your right. Cross the street at the top of the first set of stairs and continue up the curving stone steps to Coit Tower.

On the other side of Coit Tower, the Greenwich steps take you down the east side of Telegraph Hill, with stunning views of the bay en route. At Montgomery Street, perched on the side of the hill, is **Julius' Castle** ㊼ restaurant. A block to the right at **1360 Montgomery Street,** where the Filbert steps intersect, is a brilliant Art Deco apartment building. Descend the Filbert steps amid roses, fuchsias, irises, and trumpet flowers. At the foot of the hill is the serene **Levi Strauss headquarters** ㊽.

TIMING

It takes a little more than an hour to walk the tour, but the point in both North Beach and Telegraph Hill is to linger—set aside at least a few hours.

Sights to See

★ ㊶ **City Lights Bookstore.** The hangout of beat-era writers—Allen Ginsberg and Lawrence Ferlinghetti among them—remains a vital part of San Francisco's literary scene. ✉ *261 Columbus Ave.,* ☎ *415/362–8193.*

★ ㊻ **Coit Tower.** The 210-ft-tall Coit Tower stands as a monument to the city's volunteer firefighters. During the Gold Rush, Lillie Hitchcock Coit was said to have deserted a wedding party and chased down the street after her favorite engine, Knickerbocker Number 5, while clad in her bridesmaid finery. She was soon made an honorary member of the Knickerbocker Company. Lillie died in 1929 at the age of 86, leaving the city $125,000 to "expend in an appropriate manner. . . to the beauty of San Francisco." Inside the tower, 19 Depression-era murals depict economic and political life in California. Ride the elevator to the top of the tower to enjoy the sweeping views. ⊠ *Telegraph Hill Blvd., at Greenwich St. or Lombard St.,* ☎ *415/362–0808.* 🎫 *$3.75.* ☉ *Daily 10–6.*

47 **Julius' Castle.** This contemporary Italian restaurant commands a regal view of the bay from its perch high up Telegraph Hill. An official historic landmark, whose founder, Julius Roz, had his craftsmen use materials left over from the 1915 Panama–Pacific International Exposition, the restaurant has a dark-paneled Victorian interior that befits the elegant setting. ⊠ *1541 Montgomery St.,* ☎ *415/392–2222.* ☉ *Daily 5 PM–10 PM.*

48 **Levi Strauss headquarters.** This carefully landscaped complex appears so collegiate it is affectionately known as LSU (Levi Strauss University). ⊠ *Levi's Plaza, 1155 Battery St.*

42 **St. Francis of Assisi Church.** This 1860 building stands on the site of the frame parish church that served the Catholic community during the Gold Rush. Its solid terra-cotta facade complements the many brightly colored restaurants and cafés nearby. ⊠ *610 Vallejo St.,* ☎ *415/983–0405.* ☉ *Daily 11–5.*

44 **Saints Peter and Paul Catholic Church.** Completed in 1924, the cathedral has Disney-esque stone-white towers that are local landmarks. On the first Sunday of October a mass followed by a parade to Fisherman's Wharf celebrates the Blessing of the Fleet. ⊠ *666 Filbert St., at Washington Square.*

45 **Telegraph Hill.** Telegraph Hill residents command some of the best views in the city, as well as the most difficult ascents to their aeries (the flower-lined steps flanking the hill make the climb more than tolerable for visitors, though). The Hill rises from the east end of Lombard Street to a height of 284 ft and is capped by Coit Tower. ⊠ *Between Lombard, Filbert, Kearny, and Sansome Sts.*

43 **Washington Square.** Once the daytime social heart of Little Italy, this grassy patch has changed character numerous times over the years. The beats hung out in the 1950s, hippies camped out (sometimes literally) in the 1960s and early 1970s, and nowadays you're just as likely to see kids from Southeast Asia tossing a Frisbee as Italian men or women chatting about their children and the old country. In the morning elderly Asians perform the motions of tai chi, but by mid-morning groups of conservatively dressed Italian men in their 70s and 80s begin to arrive. ⊠ *Bordered by Columbus Ave. and Stockton, Filbert, and Union Sts.*

Nob Hill and Russian Hill

Once called the Hill of Golden Promise, the slope above Union Square was officially dubbed Nob Hill during the 1870s, when San Francisco's "the Big Four" financiers—Charles Crocker, Leland Stanford, Mark Hopkins, and Collis Huntington—built their hilltop estates. Nob Hill is still home to many of the city's elite, as well as several of San Francisco's finest hotels. During the 1890s, a group of bohemian artists and writers that included Charles Norris, George Sterling, and Maynard Dixon lived on Russian Hill.

Numbers in the text correspond to numbers in the margin and on the Downtown San Francisco map.

A Good Walk

Begin on California and Taylor streets at the **Masonic Auditorium** ㊾. Across California Street is the majestic **Grace Cathedral** ㊿. From the cathedral walk east (toward Mason Street) on California to the **Pacific Union Club** ㊿. Across Mason Street from the Pacific Union Club is the lush **Fairmont Hotel** ㊿. Directly across California Street from the Fairmont is the **Mark Hopkins Inter-Continental Hotel** ㊿. Head east down the hill to Powell Street. Walk north three blocks to Washington Street and then west one block to Mason Street to the **Cable Car Museum** ㊿.

From the Cable Car Museum continue four blocks north on Mason Street to Vallejo Street, turn west, and start climbing the steps that lead to the multilevel **Ina Coolbrith Park** ㊻. At the top, you can see the **Vallejo steps area** across Taylor Street from the park. The Flag House, one of several brown-shingle prequake buildings in this area, is to your left at Taylor Street. Cross Taylor Street and ascend the Vallejo steps; the view east takes in downtown and the Bay Bridge. Continue west from the top of the Vallejo steps to two secluded Russian Hill alleys. Down and to your left is Florence Place, an enclave of 1920s stucco homes, and down a bit farther on your right is Russian Hill Place, with a row of 1915 Mediterranean town houses designed by Willis Polk. After reemerging on Vallejo Street from the alleys, walk north (right) on Jones Street one short block to Green Street. Head west (left) halfway down the block to the octagonal **Feusier House** ㊽. Backtrack to Jones Street, and head north to **Macondray Lane** ㊾. Walk west (to the left) on Macondray and follow it to Leavenworth Street. Head north (to the right) on Leavenworth to the bottom of **Lombard Street** ㊿, the "crookedest street in the world." Continue north one block on Leavenworth and then east on Chestnut Street to the **San Francisco Art Institute** ㊿.

TIMING

This tour covers a lot of ground, much of it steep. If you're in reasonably good shape you can complete this walk in 3½ to 4 hours, including 30-minute stops at Grace Cathedral and the Cable Car Museum.

Sights to See

★ ㊿ **Cable Car Museum.** On exhibit are photographs, old cable cars, signposts, ticketing machines, and other memorabilia dating from 1873. The massive powerhouse wheels that move the entire cable car system steal the show. You can also go downstairs to the sheave room and check out the innards of the system. ⊠ *1201 Mason St., at Washington St.,* ☎ *415/474–1887.* ☞ *Free.* ☉ *Oct.–Mar., daily 10–5; Apr.–Sept., daily 10–6.*

㊿ **Fairmont Hotel.** The Fairmont's dazzling opening was delayed a year by the 1906 quake, but since then the marble palace has hosted presidents, royalty, movie stars, and local nabobs. Things have changed since its early days. On the eve of World War I you could get a room for as low as $2.50 per night, meals included. Nowadays, prices go as high as $8,000, which buys a night in the eight-room, Persian art–filled penthouse suite. On Friday and Saturday from 3 to 6 and on Sunday from 1 to 6, afternoon tea is served in the plush lobby, all done up with flamboyant rose-floral carpeting, lush red-velvet chairs, gold faux-marble columns, and gilt ceilings. Don't miss an evening cocktail in the kitschy **Tonga Room,** complete with tiki huts, a sporadic tropical rainstorm, and a floating bandstand. ⊠ *950 Mason St.,* ☎ *415/772–5000.*

㊽ **Feusier House.** Octagonal houses were once thought to make the best use of space and enhance the physical and mental well-being of their occupants. A brief mid-19th-century craze inspired the construction of several in San Francisco. Only the Feusier House, built in 1857 and now a private residence surrounded by lush gardens, and the Octagon House (☞ Pacific Heights, *below*), remain standing. ⊠ *1067 Green St.*

⑤⓪ Grace Cathedral. The seat of the Episcopal Church in San Francisco, this soaring Gothic structure, erected on the site of Charles Crocker's mansion, took 53 years to build. The gilded bronze doors at the east entrance were taken from casts of Ghiberti's Gates of Paradise, which are on the baptistery in Florence, Italy. A black-and-bronze stone sculpture of St. Francis by Beniamino Bufano greets visitors as they enter.

The 35-ft-wide Labyrinth, a large, purplish rug, is a replica of the 13th-century stone labyrinth on the floor of the Chartres Cathedral. All are encouraged to walk the ¼-mi-long labyrinth, a ritual based on the tradition of meditative walking. There's also a terrazzo outdoor labyrinth on the church's north side. The AIDS Interfaith Chapel, to the right as you enter Grace, contains a sculpture by the late artist Keith Haring and panels from the AIDS Memorial Quilt. ⊠ *1100 California St., at Taylor St.,* ☎ *415/749–6300.* ☉ *Sun.–Fri. 7–6, Sat. 8–6.*

⑤⑤ Ina Coolbrith Park. This attractive park is composed of a series of terraces up a very steep hill. A poet and Oakland librarian whose uncle was the Mormon prophet Joseph Smith, Ina Coolbrith (1842–1928) introduced Jack London and Isadora Duncan to the world of books. In 1915 she was named poet laureate of California. ⊠ *Vallejo St. between Mason and Taylor Sts.*

★ ⑤⑧ Lombard Street. The block-long "Crookedest Street in the World" makes eight switchbacks down the east face of Russian Hill between Hyde and Leavenworth streets. Join the line of cars waiting to drive down the steep hill, or walk down the steps on either side of Lombard. ⊠ *Lombard St. between Hyde and Leavenworth Sts.*

⑤⑦ Macondray Lane. Enter this "secret garden" under a lovely wooden trellis and walk down a quiet cobbled pedestrian street lined with Edwardian cottages and flowering plants and trees. A flight of steep wooden stairs at the end of the lane leads down to Taylor Street—on the way down you can't miss the bay views. If you've read any of Armistead Maupin's *Tales of the City* or sequels, you may find the lane vaguely familiar; it's the thinly disguised setting for part of the series' action. ⊠ *Jones St. between Union and Green Sts.*

⑤③ Mark Hopkins Inter-Continental Hotel. A combination of French château and Spanish Renaissance architecture, with noteworthy terra-cotta detailing, this hotel has hosted statesmen, royalty, and Hollywood celebrities. The 11-room penthouse was turned into a glass-walled cocktail lounge in 1939: the **Top of the Mark** is remembered fondly by thousands of World War II veterans who jammed the lounge before leaving for overseas duty. Wives and sweethearts watching the ships depart gave the room's northwest nook its name—Weepers' Corner. ⊠ *1 Nob Hill, at California and Mason Sts.,* ☎ *415/392–3434.*

④⑨ Masonic Auditorium. Formally called the California Masonic Memorial Temple, this building was erected by Freemasons in 1957. The impressive lobby mosaic, done mainly in rich greens and yellows, depicts the Masonic fraternity's role in California history and industry. There's also an intricate model of King Solomon's Temple in the lobby. ⊠ *1111 California St.,* ☎ *415/776–4917.* ☉ *Lobby weekdays 8–5.*

⑤① Pacific Union Club. The former home of silver baron James Flood cost a whopping $1.5 million in 1886, when even a stylish Victorian like the Haas-Lilienthal House (☞ Pacific Heights, *below*) cost less than $20,000. All that cash did buy some structural stability. The Flood residence (to be precise, its shell) was the only Nob Hill mansion to survive the 1906 earthquake and fire. The Pacific Union Club, a bastion of the wealthy and powerful, purchased the house in 1907 and commissioned Willis Polk to redesign it. ⊠ *1000 California St.*

59 **San Francisco Art Institute.** A Moorish-tile fountain in a tree-shaded courtyard immediately draws the eye as you enter the institute. The highlight of a visit is Mexican master Diego Rivera's *The Making of a Fresco Showing the Building of a City* (1931), in the student gallery to your immediate left once inside the entrance. ⊠ *800 Chestnut St.,* ☎ *415/771–7020.* 🎟 *Galleries free.* 🕓 *McBean Gallery Tues.–Sat. 10– 5 (Thurs. until 8), Sun. noon–5; student gallery daily 9–9.*

Vallejo steps area. Several Russian Hill buildings survived the 1906 earthquake and fire and remain standing. Alert firefighters saved what's come to be known as the **Flag House** (⊠ 1652–56 Taylor St.) when they spotted the American flag on the property and doused the flames with seltzer water and wet sand. The owner, a flag collector, fearing the house would burn to the ground, wanted it to go down in style, with "all flags flying."

The Flag House, at the southwest corner of Ina Coolbrith Park, is one of a number of California Shingle–style homes in its neighborhood, several of them designed by Willis Polk, who also laid out the Vallejo steps. These steps climb the steep ridge across Taylor Street from the Flag House. Polk designed the **Polk-Williams House** (⊠ 1013–19 Vallejo St.) and lived in one of its sections, and **1034–1036 Vallejo,** across the street. ⊠ *Taylor and Vallejo Sts. (steps lead up toward Jones St.).*

Pacific Heights

Some of the city's most expensive and dramatic real estate is in Pacific Heights. Grand Victorians line the streets, and from almost any point in this neighborhood you get a magnificent view.

Numbers in the text correspond to numbers in the margin and on the Downtown San Francisco map.

A Good Walk

The first stop is the **Octagon House** 60, at the corner of Gough and Union streets. Stroll west through the upscale shopping district of Union Street. The modest **Wedding Houses** sit on the north side of Union Street just before Buchanan Street. Continue one block farther to Webster Street and then one block north to Filbert Street. You can't miss the elaborate, schizophrenically styled **Vedanta Society** 61, on the southwest corner of Filbert and Webster streets.

Prepare for a steep climb as you head south up Webster Street. At the crest of the hill, four notable **Broadway and Webster Street estates** 62 stand within a block of each other. Two are on the north side of Broadway to the west of the intersection, one is on the same side to the east, and the last is south a half block on Webster Street. After viewing the estates, continue south on Webster to Pacific Avenue and turn right (west). The Italianate gem at 2475 Pacific Avenue sat on a 25-acre farm in the 1850s. Several Queen Anne homes stand tall on the south side of the 2500 block (between Steiner and Pierce streets); a three-story circular glass-walled staircase distinguishes the more modern home at Number 2510, on the north side. Continue west on Pacific to Scott Street, and walk south into **Alta Plaza Park** 63.

Catch your breath at the park, and then walk east on Jackson Street several blocks to the **Whittier Mansion** 64, on the corner of Jackson and Laguna streets. Make a right on Laguna and a left at the next block,

Washington Street. The patch of green that spreads east from here is **Lafayette Park** ⑥⑤. Walk on Washington along the edge of Lafayette Park past the formal French **Spreckels Mansion** ⑥⑥, at the corner of Octavia Street, and continue east two more blocks to Franklin Street. Turn left (north); halfway down the block stands the handsome **Haas-Lilienthal House** ⑥⑦. Head south on Franklin Street, stopping to view several **Franklin Street buildings** ⑥⑧. At California Street, turn right (west) to see more **noteworthy Victorians** ⑥⑨ on that street and Laguna Street.

TIMING

Set aside about two hours to see the sights mentioned here, not including the tours of the Haas-Lilienthal House and the Octagon House. Unless you're in great shape, it'll be a slow walk up extremely steep Webster Street from the Union Street sights. Although most of the attractions are walk-bys, you'll be covering a good bit of pavement.

Sights to See

⑥③ **Alta Plaza Park.** Landscape architect John McLaren, who also created Golden Gate Park, designed Alta Plaza in 1910, modeling its terracing on the Grand Casino in Monte Carlo, Monaco. From the top you can see Marin to the north, downtown to the east, Twin Peaks to the south, and Golden Gate Park to the west. ⊠ *Between Clay, Steiner, Jackson, and Scott Sts.*

⑥② **Broadway and Webster Street estates.** Broadway uptown, unlike its garish North Beach stretch, is home to some prestigious addresses. At **2222 Broadway** is a three-story palace with an intricately filigreed doorway built by Comstock silver mine heir James Flood and later donated to a religious order. The Convent of the Sacred Heart purchased the Grant House at **2220 Broadway**. These two buildings, along with a Flood property at **2120 Broadway**, are all used as school quarters. A gold mine heir, William Bourn II, commissioned Willis Polk to build the nearby mansion at **2550 Webster St.**

⑥⑧ **Franklin Street buildings.** Don't be fooled by the **Golden Gate Church** (⊠ 1901 Franklin St.)—what at first looks like a stone facade is actually redwood painted white. A Georgian-style residence built in the early 1900s for a coffee merchant sits at **1735 Franklin.** On the northeast corner of Franklin and California streets is a **Christian Science church**; built in the Tuscan Revival style, it's noteworthy for its terracotta detailing. The **Coleman House** (⊠ 1701 Franklin St.) is an impressive twin-turreted Queen Anne mansion built for a Gold Rush mining and lumber baron. Don't miss the large stained-glass window on the house's north side. ⊠ *Franklin St. between Washington and California Sts.*

⑥⑦ **Haas-Lilienthal House.** A small display of photographs on the bottom floor of this elaborate 1886 Queen Anne house, which cost a mere $18,500 to build, makes clear that it was modest compared with some of the giants that fell victim to the 1906 earthquake and fire. The carefully kept rooms here provide an intriguing glimpse into late 19th-century life. Volunteers conduct one-hour house tours two days a week and an informative two-hour tour of the eastern portion of Pacific Heights on Sunday afternoon. ⊠ *2007 Franklin St., between Washington and Jackson Sts.,* ☎ *415/441–3004.* ⊡ *$5.* ☉ *Wed. noon–4 (last tour at 3), Sun. 11–5 (last tour at 4). Pacific Heights tours ($5) leave the house Sun. at 12:30.*

⑥⑤ **Lafayette Park.** Clusters of trees dot this four-block-square oasis for sunbathers and dog-and-Frisbee teams. ⊠ *Between Laguna, Gough, Sacramento, and Washington Sts.*

⑤⑨ Noteworthy Victorians. Two **Italianate Victorians** (1818 and 1834 California St.) stand out on the 1800 block of California. A block farther is the Victorian-era **Atherton House** (⊠ 1990 California St.), whose mildly daffy design incorporates Queen Anne, Stick-Eastlake, and other architectural elements. The oft-photographed **Laguna Street Victorians**, on the west side of the 1800 block of Laguna Street, cost between $2,000 and $2,600 when they were built in the 1870s. ⊠ *California St. between Franklin and Octavia Sts.; ⊠ Laguna St. between Pine and Bush Sts.*

⑥⓪ Octagon House. This eight-sided home sits across the street from its original site on Gough Street. It's full of antique American furniture, decorative arts, and documents from the 18th and 19th centuries. White quoins accent each of the eight corners of the pretty blue-gray exterior. ⊠ *2645 Gough St.,* ☎ *415/441–7512.* ☜ *Free; donations encouraged.* ☉ *Feb.–Dec., 2nd Sun. and 2nd and 4th Thurs. of each month, noon–3; group tours weekdays by appointment.*

⑥⑥ Spreckels Mansion. This estate was built for sugar heir Adolph Spreckels and his wife, Alma. Mrs. Spreckels was so pleased with her house that she commissioned George Applegarth to design another building in a similar vein: the California Palace of the Legion of Honor. One of the city's great iconoclasts, Alma Spreckels was the model for the bronze figure atop the Victory Monument in Union Square. ⊠ *2080 Washington St., at Octavia St.*

⑥① Vedanta Society. A pastiche of Colonial, Queen Anne, Moorish, and Hindu opulence, with turrets battling onion domes and Victorian detailing everywhere, this 1905 structure was the first Hindu temple in the West. ⊠ *2963 Webster St.,* ☎ *415/922–2323.*

⑥④ Whittier Mansion. An anomaly in a town that lost most of its grand mansions to the 1906 earthquake, the Whittier Mansion was built so solidly that only a chimney toppled over during the disaster. ⊠ *2090 Jackson St.*

Japantown

In about 1860 a wave of Japanese immigrants arrived in San Francisco, which they called Soko. After the 1906 earthquake and fire, many of these newcomers settled in the Western Addition. By the 1930s they had opened shops, markets, meeting halls, and restaurants and established Shinto and Buddhist temples. Known as Japantown, this area was virtually deserted during World War II when many of its residents, including second- and third-generation Americans, were forced into so-called relocation camps. Today Japantown is centered on the southern slope of Pacific Heights, north of Geary Boulevard between Fillmore and Laguna streets.

Though Japantown is a relatively safe area, the Western Addition, which lies to the south of Geary Boulevard, can be dangerous; after dark also avoid straying too far west of Fillmore Street just north of Geary.

Numbers in the text correspond to numbers in the margin and on the Downtown San Francisco map.

A Good Walk

Several key components of San Francisco's history intersect at Geary Boulevard and Fillmore Street. The three-block **Japan Center** ⑦⓪ sits on a portion of the area settled by Japanese and Japanese Americans in the early 20th century. The stretch of Fillmore on either side of Geary Boulevard was a center of African-American culture during the mid-20th century.

Near the southwest corner of Geary and Fillmore is the entrance to the legendary Fillmore Auditorium, where 1960s bands like Jefferson Airplane and the Grateful Dead performed. Next door on Geary Street, the western portion of the U.S. Postal Service branch sits on the lot that formerly held the People's Temple (since demolished), the head-quarters of the cult run by the Reverend Jim Jones, whose flock par-ticipated in a mass suicide in Guyana in November 1978.

Kabuki Springs and Spa ⑦ is on the northeast corner of Geary and Fill-more. Head north on Fillmore to Post Street and make a right. Pass the entrance to the eight-screen AMC Kabuki theater and enter the Japan Center midblock, in the Kinokuniya Building. A second-level bridge spans Webster Street, connecting the Kinokuniya and Kintetsu build-ings. After exploring the area and exiting the Kintetsu Building, pop across Post Street to the open-air **Japan Center Mall** ⑦, a short block of shoji-screened buildings on Buchanan Street between Post and Sut-ter streets.

TIMING

The distance covered in the tour is extremely short. Not including a visit to Kabuki Springs and Spa, an hour will probably suffice.

Sights to See

⑦ **Japan Center.** Noted American architect Minoru Yamasaki created this 5-acre complex that opened in 1968. The development includes a hotel (the Radisson Miyako, at Laguna and Post streets); a public garage with discounted validated parking; shops selling Japanese fur-nishings, clothing, cameras, tapes and records, porcelain, pearls, and paintings; an excellent spa; and a multiplex cinema. ✉ *Bordered by Geary Blvd. and Fillmore, Post, and Laguna Sts.,* ☎ *415/922–6776.*

⑦ **Japan Center Mall.** The buildings lining this open-air mall are of the shoji school of architecture. Seating in this area can be found on local artist Ruth Asawa's twin origami-style fountains, which sit in the mid-dle of the mall. They're squat circular structures made of fieldstone, with three levels for sitting and a brick floor that is also a drain. ✉ *Buchanan St. between Post and Sutter Sts.*

★ ⑦ **Kabuki Springs and Spa.** Japantown's house of tranquility got a com-plete makeover in 1999. The feel is less Japanese than before. Balinese urns decorate the communal bath area, and you're just as likely to hear soothing flute or classical music as you are Kitaro. The massage palette has also expanded well beyond the traditional shiatsu technique. You can take your massage in a private room with a bath or in a curtained-off area. The communal baths ($10 before 5 PM, $15 after 5) contain hot and cold tubs, a large Japanese-style bath, a sauna, a steam room, and showers. The baths are open for men only on Monday, Tuesday, Thursday, and Saturday, and for women only on Wednesday, Friday, and Sunday. Men and women can reserve private rooms daily. A 90-minute massage-and-bath package with a private room costs $90. ✉ *1750 Geary Blvd.,* ☎ *415/922–6000.* ☼ *Daily 10–10.*

Civic Center

The Civic Center—the Beaux-Arts complex between McAllister and Grove streets and Franklin and Hyde streets that includes City Hall, the War Memorial Opera House, the Veterans' Building, and the old Public Library—is a product of the "City Beautiful" movement of the early 20th century. City Hall, completed in 1915, is the centerpiece. The new main library on Larkin Street between Fulton and Grove streets, completed in 1996, is a modern variation on the Civic Center's archi-tectural theme.

Numbers in the text correspond to numbers in the margin and on the Downtown San Francisco map.

A Good Walk

Start at **United Nations Plaza** ⑬, set on an angle between Hyde and Market streets. Walk west along the plaza toward Fulton Street, which dead-ends at Hyde Street, and cross Hyde. Towering over the block of Fulton between Hyde and Larkin streets is the Pioneers Monument. The new main branch of the **San Francisco Public Library** ⑭ is south of the monument. North of it is the old library. The patch of green west of the library is Civic Center Plaza, and beyond that is **City Hall** ⑮. Walk around it to the north—to the right as you're facing it—and make a left at McAllister. Looking south (to the left) across the street on Van Ness, you'll see three grand edifices, each of which takes up most of its block. On the southwestern corner of McAllister and Van Ness Avenue is the **Veterans Building** ⑯. A horseshoe-shape carriage entrance on its south side separates the building from the **War Memorial Opera House** ⑰. In the next block of Van Ness Avenue, across Grove Street from the opera house, is **Louise M. Davies Symphony Hall** ⑱. The Civic Center borders the Western Addition; it's best not to stray west of Laguna at night.

TIMING

Walking around the Civic Center shouldn't take more than about 45 minutes. Another half hour or more can be spent browsing the shops along Hayes Street. On Wednesday or Sunday allot some extra time to take in the farmers' market in United Nations Plaza.

Sights to See

⑮ **City Hall.** This masterpiece of granite and marble was modeled after St. Peter's cathedral in Rome. City Hall's bronze and gold-leaf dome, which is even higher than the U.S. Capitol's version, dominates the area. Arthur Brown Jr., who also designed Coit Tower and the War Memorial Opera House, was trained in Paris; his classical influences can be seen throughout the structure. If the building's open, inspect the palatial interior, full of grand arches and with a sweeping central staircase. Across Polk Street is **Civic Center Plaza.** ⊠ *Between Van Ness Ave., Polk, Grove, and McAllister Sts.*

⑱ **Louise M. Davies Symphony Hall.** Fascinating and still futuristic looking after two decades, this 2,750-seat hall is the home of the San Francisco Symphony, conducted by Michael Tilson Thomas. The glass wraparound lobby and pop-out balcony high on the southeast corner are visible from the outside. The hall's 59 adjustable Plexiglas acoustical disks cascade from the ceiling like hanging windshields. Scheduled tours take in Davies and the nearby opera house and Herbst Theatre. ⊠ *201 Van Ness Ave.,* ☎ *415/552–8338.* 🎟 *Tours $5.* ☉ *Tours Mon. (except holidays) hourly 10–2.*

⑭ **San Francisco Public Library.** The main library, which opened in 1996, is a modernized version of the old Beaux-Arts library that sits just across Fulton Street. The several specialty rooms include centers for the hearing and visually impaired, a gay and lesbian history center, and African-American and Asian centers. The San Francisco History Room and Archives contains historic photographs, maps, and other city memorabilia. At the library's core is a five-story atrium with a skylight, a grand staircase, and murals painted by local artists. Tours of the library are conducted daily at 2:30 PM. ⊠ *100 Larkin St. between Grove and Fulton Sts.,* ☎ *415/557–4400.* ☉ *Mon. 10–6, Tues.–Thurs. 9–8, Fri. 11–5, Sat. 9–5, Sun. noon–5.*

⑦ **United Nations Plaza.** Brick pillars listing various nations and the dates of their admittance into the U.N. line the plaza, and its floor is inscribed with the goals and philosophy of the U.N. charter, which was signed at the War Memorial Opera House in 1945. On Wednesday and Sunday a farmers' market fills the space with homegrown produce and plants. ⊠ *Fulton St. between Hyde and Market Sts.*

⑦ **Veterans Building.** Performing and visual arts organizations occupy much of this 1930s structure. **Herbst Theatre** (☎ 415/392–4400) hosts lectures and readings, classical ensembles, and dance performances, along with City Arts and Lectures events. Also in the building are two galleries that charge no admission. The street-level **San Francisco Arts Commission Gallery** (☎ 415/554–6080), open from Wednesday through Saturday between noon and 5, displays the works of Bay Area artists. ⊠ *401 Van Ness Ave.*

⑦ **War Memorial Opera House.** Opera in San Francisco didn't have a permanent home until the War Memorial Opera House was inaugurated in 1932 with a performance of *Tosca*. Modeled after its European counterparts, the building has a vaulted and coffered ceiling, marble foyer, two balconies, and a huge silver Art Deco chandelier that resembles a sunburst. The San Francisco Opera and the San Francisco Ballet perform here. ⊠ *301 Van Ness Ave.,* ☎ *415/621–6600.*

The Northern Waterfront

For the sights, sounds, and smells of the sea, hop the Powell–Hyde cable car from Union Square and take it to the end of the line. The views as you descend Hyde Street down to the bay are breathtaking—tiny sailboats bob in the whitecaps, Alcatraz hovers ominously in the distance, and the Marin Headlands form a rugged backdrop to the Golden Gate Bridge. Bring good walking shoes and a jacket or sweater for mid-afternoon breezes or foggy mists.

Numbers in the text correspond to numbers in the margin and on the Northern Waterfront/Marina and the Presidio map.

A Good Walk

Begin at Polk and Beach streets at the **National Maritime Museum** ①. Across Beach from the museum is **Ghirardelli Square** ②. Continue east on Beach to Hyde Street and make a left. At the end of Hyde is the **Hyde Street Pier** ③. South on Hyde a block and a half is the former Del Monte **Cannery** ④. Walk east from the Cannery on Jefferson Street to **Fisherman's Wharf** ⑤. A few blocks farther east is **Pier 39** ⑥.

TIMING

For the entire Northern Waterfront circuit, set aside three or four hours, not including boat tours, which will take from one to three hours or more. All the attractions here are open daily.

Sights to See

★ **Alcatraz Island.** The boat ride to the island is brief (15 minutes) but affords beautiful views of the city, Marin County, and the East Bay. The audio tour includes observations of guards and prisoners about life in one of America's most notorious penal colonies. A separate ranger-led tour surveys the island's ecology. Plan your schedule to allow at least three hours for the visit and boat rides combined. Reservations are recommended. ⊠ *Pier 41,* ☎ *415/773–1188 (boat schedules and information); 415/705–5555 or 800/426–8687 (credit-card ticket orders); 415/705–1042 (park information).* ⓔ *$11 or $7.75 without audio ($18.50 for evening tours, which includes audio); add $2 per ticket to charge by phone.* ☉ *Ferry departures Sept.–May 23, daily 9:30–2:15*

Northern Waterfront/Marina and the Presidio

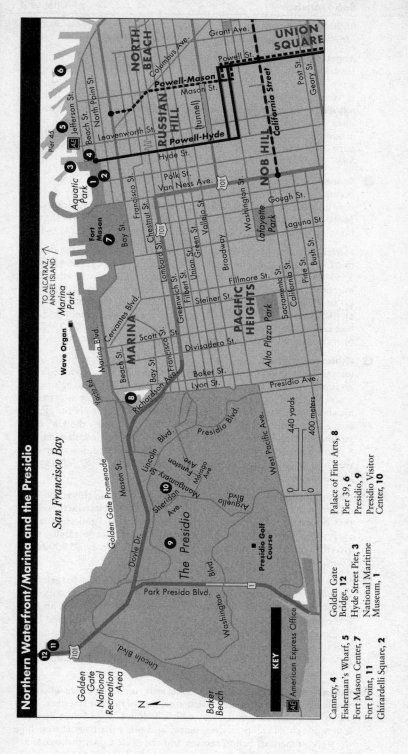

San Francisco Bay

UNION SQUARE

NORTH BEACH

Grant Ave.
Columbus Ave.
Powell St.
Powell-Mason
Mason St.

RUSSIAN HILL
(tunnel)
Powell-Hyde

NOB HILL

Post St.
Geary St.
California Street

Hyde St.
Leavenworth St.
Polk St.
Van Ness Ave.
Franklin St.
Gough St.
Octavia St.
Laguna St.
Webster St.
Fillmore St.
Steiner St.
Pierce St.
Scott St.
Divisadero St.
Broderick St.
Baker St.
Lyon St.
Presidio Ave.

Lafayette Park

PACIFIC HEIGHTS

Washington St.
Vallejo St.
Union St.
Green St.
Broadway
Filbert St.
Greenwich St.
Chestnut St.
Lombard St.
Francisco St.
Bay St.
Beach St.
North Point St.
Jefferson St.
Pier 45

Alta Plaza Park

Sacramento St.
California St.
Pine St.
Bush St.

MARINA

Cervantes Blvd.
Marina Blvd.
Scott St.
Beach St.
Bay St.
Richardson Ave.
San Francisco St.

Marina Park
Wave Organ

Fort Mason

TO ALCATRAZ, ANGEL ISLAND

Aquatic Park

Golden Gate Promenade

The Presidio

Golden Gate National Recreation Area

Baker Beach

Lincoln Blvd.
Doyle Dr.
Mason St.
Lincoln Blvd.
Montgomery St.
Sheridan Ave.
Funston Ave.
Moraga Ave.
Arguello Blvd.
West Pacific Ave.
Presidio Blvd.

Presidio Golf Course

Park Presidio Blvd.
Washington Blvd.

440 yards
400 meters

KEY

AE American Express Office

N

Cannery, **4**
Fisherman's Wharf, **5**
Fort Mason Center, **7**
Ghirardelli Square, **2**

Golden Gate Bridge, **12**
Hyde Street Pier, **3**
National Maritime Museum, **1**

Palace of Fine Arts, **8**
Pier 39, **6**
Presidio, **9**
Presidio Visitor Center, **10**

Fort Point, **11**

(4:20 for evening tour); May 24–Aug., daily 9:30–4:15 (6:30 and 7:30 for evening tour).

Angel Island. For an outdoorsy adventure, consider a day at Angel Island. Discovered by Spaniards in 1775 and declared a U.S. military reserve 75 years later, the island was used from 1910 until 1940 as a screening ground for Asian immigrants, who were often held for months, even years, before being granted entry. In 1963 the government designated Angel Island a state park. A scenic 5-mi path winds around the perimeter of the island. ⊠ *Pier 41,* ☎ *415/435–1915 for park information and ferry schedules; 415/705–5555 or 800/426–8687 for tickets.* ⊠ *$10.* ☽ *Call for schedule.*

❹ **Cannery.** This three-story structure was built in 1894 to house what became the Del Monte Fruit and Vegetable Cannery. Today the Cannery is home to shops, art galleries, and some unusual restaurants. The **Museum of the City of San Francisco** (☎ 415/928–0289), on the third floor, merits a brief stop. ⊠ *2801 Leavenworth St.,* ☎ *415/771–3112.*

Ferries. Alcatraz Island and Angel Island are just two of the destinations served by the **Blue and Gold Fleet** (⊠ Pier 41, ☎ 415/705–5555). Alcatraz is the best deal—all the fun of a bay cruise and a great tour of the prison. But the boats are also a fine way to day-trip to Sausalito and Tiburon. Blue and Gold also runs ferries to Oakland, Alameda, and Vallejo. The Vallejo boat docks near Six Flags Marine World. The **Red and White Fleet** (Pier 43½, ☎ 415/447–0591 or 800/229–2784) operates bay and other cruises.

☝ ❺ **Fisherman's Wharf.** The chaotic streets of the wharf are home to numerous seafood restaurants, among them sidewalk stands where shrimp and crab cocktails are sold. T-shirts and sweats, gold chains galore, redwood furniture, acres of artwork, and generally amusing street artists also beckon visitors. For an intriguing if mildly claustrophobic glimpse into life on a submarine during World War II, drop by the USS *Pampanito* (⊠ Pier 45, ☎ 415/775–1943). The sub, open daily from 9 to 6 (until 8 between Memorial Day and Labor Day), sank six Japanese warships and damaged four others. Admission is $7. ⊠ *Jefferson St. between Leavenworth St. and Pier 39.*

❷ **Ghirardelli Square.** Most of the redbrick buildings in this early 20th-century complex were part of the Ghirardelli chocolate factory. Now they house name-brand emporiums, restaurants, and galleries that sell everything from crafts and knickknacks to sports memorabilia. Placards throughout the square describe the factory's history. ⊠ *900 North Point,* ☎ *415/775–5500.*

❸ **Hyde Street Pier.** The pier, one of the wharf area's best bargains, always crackles with activity. The highlight of the pier is its collection of historic vessels, all of which can be boarded: the *Balclutha,* an 1886 full-rigged three-masted sailing vessel that sailed around Cape Horn 17 times; the *Eureka,* a side-wheel ferry; the *C. A. Thayer,* a three-masted schooner; and the *Hercules,* a steam-powered tugboat. ⊠ *Hyde and Jefferson Sts.,* ☎ *415/556–3002 or 415/556–0859.* ⊠ *$4.* ☽ *Daily 9:30–5; summer, daily 10–6.*

❶ **National Maritime Museum.** You'll feel as if you're out to sea when you step inside this sturdy, rounded structure. Part of the San Francisco Maritime National Historical Park, which includes Hyde Street Pier, the museum exhibits ship models, maps, and other artifacts chronicling the development of San Francisco and the West Coast through maritime history. ⊠ *Aquatic Park at the foot of Polk St.,* ☎ *415/556–3002.* ⊠ *Donation suggested.* ☽ *Daily 10–5.*

6 **Pier 39.** This shopping and entertainment complex is the most popular of San Francisco's waterfront attractions. Ongoing free entertainment, accessible validated parking, and nearby public transportation ensure crowds most days. Brilliant colors enliven the double-decker **Venetian Carousel,** often awhirl with happily howling children. The din on the northwest side of the pier comes courtesy of the hundreds of sea lions that bask and play on the docks. At **Underwater World** (☎ 415/623–5300 or 888/732–3483), moving walkways transport visitors through a space surrounded on three sides by water filled with indigenous San Francisco Bay marine life, from fish and plankton to sharks. Parking is at the Pier 39 Garage, off Powell Street at the Embarcadero. ✉ *Beach St. at the Embarcadero.*

The Marina and the Presidio

The Marina district was a coveted place to live until the 1989 earthquake, when the area's homes suffered the worst damage in the city—largely because the Marina is built on landfill. Many residents fled in search of more solid ground, but young professionals quickly replaced them. West of the Marina is the sprawling Presidio, a former military base with superb views and the best hiking and biking areas in San Francisco.

Numbers in the text correspond to numbers in the margin and on the Northern Waterfront/Marina and the Presidio map.

A Good Drive

Though you can visit the sights below using public transportation, this is the place to use your car if you have one. You might even consider renting one for a day to cover the area, as well as Lincoln Park, Golden Gate Park, and the western shoreline.

Start at **Fort Mason** ⑦, whose entrance for automobiles is off Marina Boulevard at Buchanan Street. If you're coming by bus, take the Bus 30-Stockton heading north (and later west). Get off at Chestnut and Laguna streets and walk north three blocks to the pedestrian entrance at Marina Boulevard and Laguna. To get from Fort Mason to the **Palace of Fine Arts** ⑧ by car, make a right on Marina Boulevard. The road curves past a small marina and the Marina Green. Turn left at Divisadero Street, right on North Point Street, left on Baker Street, and right on Bay Street, which passes the Palace's lagoon and dead-ends at the Lyon Street parking lot. Part of the Palace complex is the **Exploratorium,** a hands-on science museum. (If you're walking from Fort Mason to the Palace, follow Marina Boulevard to Scott Street. Cross to the south side of the street and continue past Divisadero Street to Baker Street, and turn left. You'll see the Palace's lagoon on your right. To take Muni, walk back to Chestnut and Laguna streets and take Bus 30-Stockton continuing west; get off at North Point and Broderick streets and walk west on North Point.)

The least confusing way to drive to the **Presidio** ⑨ from the Palace is to exit from the south end of the Lyon Street parking lot and head east (left) on Bay Street. Turn right (north) onto Baker Street, and right (west) on Francisco Street, taking it across Richardson Avenue to Lyon Street. Turn south (left) on Lyon and right (west) on Lombard Street, and go through the main gate to Presidio Boulevard. Turn right on Presidio, which becomes Lincoln Boulevard. Make a left at Montgomery Street. A half block up on the right is the **Presidio Visitor Center** ⑩. (To take the bus to the Presidio, walk north from the Palace to Lombard Street and catch Bus 28 heading west; it stops on Lincoln near the center.)

From the visitor center head north a half block to Sheridan Avenue, make a right, and make a left when Sheridan runs into Lincoln Boulevard. Lincoln winds through the Presidio past a large cemetery and some vista points. After a couple of miles you'll see a parking lot marked FORT POINT on the right. Park and follow the signs leading to **Fort Point** ⑪, walking downhill through a lightly wooded area. To walk the short distance to the **Golden Gate Bridge** ⑫, follow the signs from the Fort Point parking lot. To drive across the bridge, continue on Lincoln Boulevard a bit and watch for the turnoff on the right. Bus 28 serves stops fairly near these last two attractions.

TIMING

The time it takes to see this area will vary greatly depending on whether you'll be taking public transportation or driving. If you drive, plan to spend at least three hours, not including a walk across the Golden Gate Bridge or hikes along the shoreline. With or without kids, you could easily pass two hours at the Exploratorium.

Sights to See

★ ℭ **Exploratorium.** The curious of all ages flock to this fascinating "museum of science, art, and human perception" within the Palace of Fine Arts. The more than 650 exhibits focus on sea and insect life, computers, electricity, patterns and light, language, the weather, and much more. Reservations are required to crawl through the pitch-black, touchy-feely **Tactile Dome**, an adventure of 15 minutes. ⊠ *3601 Lyon St. at Marina Blvd.,* ☏ *415/561–0360 for general information; 415/ 561–0362 for Tactile Dome reservations.* ⊠ *$9; free 1st Wed. of month; Tactile Dome admission $3 extra.* ⊙ *Memorial Day–Labor Day, daily 10–6, Wed. 10–9; Labor Day–Memorial Day, Tues., Thurs.–Sun., and most Mon. holidays 10–5, Wed. 10–9.*

➐ **Fort Mason Center.** Originally a depot for the shipment of supplies to the Pacific during World War II, Fort Mason was converted into a cultural center in 1977. In business here are the popular vegetarian restaurant Greens and shops, galleries, and performance spaces, most of which are closed on Monday. Several worthwhile museums—including the Mexican Museum, Museo Italo-Americano, San Francisco African-American Historical and Cultural Society, and San Francisco Craft and Folk Art Museum—are housed here. Most of the museums and shops at Fort Mason close by 6 or 7. Museum admission fees range from pay-what-you-wish to $3. ⊠ *Buchanan St. and Marina Blvd.,* ☏ *415/979– 3010 for event information.*

⑪ **Fort Point.** Designed to mount 126 cannons with a range of up to 2 mi, Fort Point was constructed between 1853 and 1861 to protect San Francisco from sea attack during the Civil War—but it was never used for that purpose. It was, however, used as a coastal defense fortification post during World War II, when soldiers stood watch here. This National Historic Site is a museum filled with military memorabilia. On days when Fort Point is staffed, guided group tours and cannon drills take place. ⊠ *Marine Dr. off Lincoln Blvd.,* ☏ *415/556–1693.* ⊠ *Free.* ⊙ *Wed.–Sun. 10–5.*

★ ⑫ **Golden Gate Bridge.** San Francisco's connection to Marin County has long wowed sightseers with its rust-color beauty, 750-ft towers, and simple but powerful Art Deco design. At nearly 2 mi, the Golden Gate, completed in 1937 after four years of construction, was built to withstand winds of more than 100 mph. The east walkway yields a glimpse of the city skyline as well as the islands of the bay. A vista point on the Marin side affords a spectacular view of the city. Muni buses 28 and 29 make stops at the Golden Gate Bridge toll plaza, on the San Francisco side. ⊠ *Lincoln Blvd. near Doyle Dr. and Fort Point,* ☎ *415/ 921–5858.* ⊙ *Open daily, 24 hrs for cars and bikes, 5 AM–9 PM for pedestrians.*

★ ❽ **Palace of Fine Arts.** San Francisco's rosy rococo Palace of Fine Arts is at the western end of the Marina. The palace is the sole survivor of the many tinted plaster buildings built for the 1915 Panama-Pacific International Exposition, the world's fair that celebrated San Francisco's recovery from the 1906 earthquake and fire. Bernard Maybeck designed this faux Roman Classic beauty, which was reconstructed in concrete and reopened in 1967. ⊠ *Baker and Beach Sts.,* ☎ *415/561–0364 for palace tours.*

❾ **Presidio.** Part of the Golden Gate National Recreation Area, the Presidio was a military post for more than 200 years. Don Juan Bautista de Anza and a band of Spanish settlers first claimed the area in 1776. It became a Mexican garrison in 1822 when Mexico gained its independence from Spain; U.S. troops forcibly occupied the Presidio in 1846. The U.S. Sixth Army was stationed here until October 1994, when the coveted space was transferred into civilian hands. The more than 1,400 acres of rolling hills, majestic woods, and redbrick army barracks present an air of serenity on the edge of the city. There are two beaches, a golf course, a visitor center, and picnic sites. ⊠ *Between the Marina and Lincoln Park.*

❿ **Presidio Visitor Center.** National Park Service employees at what's officially the William P. Mott Jr. Visitor Center dispense maps, brochures, and schedules for guided walking and bicycle tours, along with information about the Presidio's past, present, and future. ⊠ *Montgomery St. between Lincoln Blvd. and Sheridan Ave.,* ☎ *415/561–4323.* ⊠ *Free.* ⊙ *Daily 9–5.*

Golden Gate Park

William Hammond Hall conceived one of the nation's great city parks and began in 1870 to put into action his plan for a natural reserve with no reminders of urban life. Hammond began work in the Panhandle and eastern portions of Golden Gate Park, but it took John McLaren the length of his tenure as park superintendent, from 1890 to 1943, to complete the transformation of 1,000 desolate brush- and sand-covered acres into a rolling, landscaped oasis. From May through October, **Friends of Recreation and Parks** (☎ 415/263–0991) conducts weekend walking tours. The fog can sweep into the park with amazing speed; always bring a sweatshirt or jacket.

The **Golden Gate Park Explorer Pass** ($14) grants admission to the M. H. de Young and Asian Art museums, plus the California Academy of Sciences and the Japanese Tea Garden. The passes can be purchased at the above sights except for the tea garden, or at TIX Bay Area in Union Square.

On weekends you can park all day for $3 at the University of California at San Francisco garage (enter at Irving Street and 2nd Avenue south of the park); from there a free shuttle leaves every 10 minutes for the park's museums. Muni also serves the park. The No. 5-Fulton bus stops along its northern edge, and the N-Judah light-rail car stops a block south of the park until 9th Avenue, two blocks the rest of the way west.

Numbers in the text correspond to numbers in the margin and on the Golden Gate Park map.

A Good Walk

Begin on the park's north side at Fulton Street and 6th Avenue. Walk south into the park at 6th Avenue. The road you'll come to is John F. Kennedy Drive. Turn left on the blacktop sidewalk and head east. Across the drive on your right is the Rhododendron Dell. Past the first stop sign you'll see the exterior gardens of the **Conservatory of Flowers** ① on your left. Explore the gardens, then walk south (back toward Kennedy Drive) from the conservatory entrance. Continue east on Kennedy Drive a short way to the three-way intersection and turn right (south) at Middle Drive East.

Less than a block away at the intersection of Middle Drive and Bowling Green drives you'll see a sign for the National AIDS Memorial Grove. Before you enter the grove, follow the curve of Bowling Green Drive to the left, past the **Bowling Green** ② to the **Children's Playground** ③. Reverse direction on Bowling Green Drive and enter the **National AIDS Memorial Grove** ④, a sunken meadow that stretches west along Middle Drive East. At the end of the wheelchair-access ramp make a left to view the Circle of Friends, then continue west along the graded paths to another circle with a poem by Thom Gunn. Exit north from this circle. As you're standing in the circle looking at the poem, the staircase to take is on your left. At the top of the staircase make a left and continue west on Middle Drive East. You'll come to the back entrance of the **California Academy of Sciences** ⑤.

At the end of Middle Drive East, turn right and follow the signs leading to the **Shakespeare Garden** ⑥. After touring the garden, exit via the path on which you entered and turn left (to the south). A hundred feet shy of the Ninth Avenue and Lincoln Way entrance to Golden Gate Park is the main entrance to **Strybing Arboretum & Botanical Gardens** ⑦.

Backtrack from the gardens to the path you started on and make a right. As the path continues to wind north and west, you'll see a large fountain off to the left. Just before you get to the fountain, make a right and head toward the duck pond. A wooden footbridge on the pond's left side crosses the water. Stay to the right on the path, heading toward the exit gate. Just before the gate, continue to the right to the Primitive Garden. Take the looped boardwalk past ferns, gingko, cycads, conifers, moss, and other plants. At the end of the loop, make a left and then a right, exiting via the Eugene L. Friend gate. Go straight ahead on the crosswalk to the blacktop path on the other side. Make a right, walk about 100 ft, and make a left on Tea Garden Drive. A few hundred feet east of here is the entrance to the **Japanese Tea Garden** ⑧.

Tour the Japanese Tea Garden, exiting near the gate you entered. Make a left, and you'll soon pass the **Asian Art Museum** ⑨ and **M. H. de Young Memorial Museum** ⑩. Near the main entrance to the de Young is a crosswalk that leads south to the Music Concourse, with its gnarled trees, century-old fountains and sculptures, and the Golden Gate Bandshell. Turn left at the closest of the fountains and head east toward the bronze sculpture of Francis Scott Key.

Turn left at the statue and proceed north through two underpasses. At the end of the second underpass, you'll have traveled about 2 mi. If you're ready to leave the park, take the short staircase to the left of the blue and green playground equipment. At the top of the staircase is the 10th Avenue and Fulton Street stop for the Bus 5-Fulton heading back downtown. If you're game for walking ½ mi more, make an immediate left as you exit the second underpass, cross 10th Avenue, and make a right on John F. Kennedy Drive. After ³⁄₁₀ mi you'll see the

Rose Garden on your right. Continue west to the first stop sign. To the left is a sign for **Stow Lake** ⑪. Follow the road past the log cabin to the boathouse.

From Stow Lake it's the equivalent of 30 long blocks on John F. Kennedy Drive to the western end of the park and the ocean. If you walk, you'll pass meadows, the Portals of the Past, the buffalo paddock, and a nine-hole golf course. You can skip most of this walk by proceeding west on John F. Kennedy Drive from the stop sign mentioned above, making the first right after you walk underneath Cross-Over Drive, and following the road as it winds left toward 25th Avenue and Fulton. On the northwest corner of Fulton Street and 25th Avenue, catch the Bus 5-Fulton heading west, get off at 46th Avenue, walk one block west to 47th Avenue, and make a left. Make a right on John F. Kennedy Drive.

By foot or vehicle, your goal is the **Dutch Windmill** ⑫ and adjoining garden. A block to the south is the **Beach Chalet** ⑬.

TIMING

You can easily spend a whole day in Golden Gate Park, especially if you walk the whole distance. Set aside at least an hour each for the Academy of Sciences, the Asian Art Museum, and the de Young Museum. Even if you plan to explore just the eastern end of the park (up to Stow Lake), allot at least four hours.

Sights to See

★ ⑨ **Asian Art Museum.** The museum's collection includes more than 12,000 sculptures, paintings, and ceramics from 40 countries, illustrating major periods of Asian art. On the first floor are special exhibitions as well as galleries dedicated to works from Korea and China. On the second floor are treasures from Iran, Turkey, Syria, India, Tibet, Nepal, Pakistan, India, Japan, Afghanistan, and Southeast Asia. ⊠ *Tea Garden Dr. off JFK Dr., near 10th Ave. and Fulton St.,* ☎ *415/668–8921 or 415/379–8801.* ⌑ *$7 ($2 off with Muni transfer), good also for same-day admission to the M. H. de Young Museum and the Legion of Honor Museum in Lincoln Park; free 1st Wed. of month.* ☉ *Tues.– Sun. 9:30–5, 1st Wed. of month until 8:45.*

⑬ **Beach Chalet.** This Spanish Colonial–style structure, Willis Polk's last design, was built in 1925 after his death. A wraparound federal works project mural by Lucien Labaudt depicts San Francisco in the 1930s. A three-dimensional model of Golden Gate Park, artifacts from the 1894 Mid-Winter Exposition and other park events, a visitor center, and a gift shop are on the first floor as well. On a clear day, the brew pub–restaurant upstairs has views past Ocean Beach to the Farallon Islands, about 30 mi offshore. ⊠ *1000 Great Hwy., at west end of John F. Kennedy Dr.*

★ ☙ ⑤ **California Academy of Sciences.** A three-in-one attraction, the nationally renowned academy houses an aquarium, numerous science and natural-history exhibits, and a planetarium. Leopard sharks, silver salmon, sea bass, and other fish loop around the mesmerizing Fish Roundabout, the big draw at **Steinhart Aquarium.** Feeding time is 2 PM. The multimedia earthquake exhibit in the Earth and Space Hall at the **Natural History Museum** simulates quakes, complete with special effects. Videos and displays in the Wild California Hall describe the state's wildlife, and there's a re-creation of the environment of the rocky Farallon Islands. There is an additional charge (up to $2.50) for **Morrison Planetarium** shows (☎ 415/750–7141 for schedule), which you enter through the Natural History Museum. Daily multimedia shows present the night sky through the ages under a 55-ft dome, complete with special effects and music. The **Laserium** presents evening laser-

Golden Gate Park

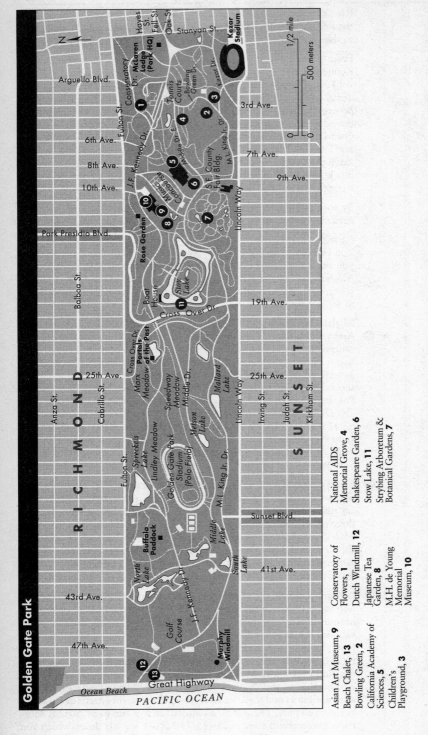

Asian Art Museum, **9**
Beach Chalet, **13**
Bowling Green, **2**
California Academy of
Sciences, **5**
Children's
Playground, **3**

Conservatory of
Flowers, **1**
Dutch Windmill, **12**
Japanese Tea
Garden, **8**
M.H. de Young
Memorial
Museum, **10**

National AIDS
Memorial Grove, **4**
Shakespeare Garden, **6**
Stow Lake, **11**
Strybing Arboretum &
Botanical Gardens, **7**

light shows (☎ 415/750–7138 for schedule and fees) at Morrison Planetarium; educational shows outline laser technology. A cafeteria is open daily until one hour before the museum closes. ⊠ *Music Concourse Dr. off South Dr., across from Asian Art and de Young museums,* ☎ *415/750–7145.* 🎟 *$8.50; $1 discount with Muni transfer; free 1st Wed. of month.* ☉ *Memorial Day–Labor Day, daily 9–6; Labor Day–Memorial Day, daily 10–5; first Wed. of month closes at 8:45 PM.*

☾ 🖐 ❸ **Children's Playground.** Kids have been coming here to cut loose since the 1880s. A menagerie of hand-crafted horses and other animals—among them cats, frogs, roosters, and a tiger—twirl on the 1912 Herschell-Spillman Carousel, inside a many-windowed circular structure. ⊠ *Bowling Green Dr., off Martin Luther King Jr. Dr.,* ☎ *415/831–2700.* 🎟 *Playground free, carousel $1.* ☉ *Playground open daily dawn–midnight; carousel June–Sept., daily 10–5, Oct.–May, Fri.–Sun. 10–4:30 (carousel hrs vary).*

❶ **Conservatory of Flowers.** The oldest building in the park and the last remaining wood-frame Victorian conservatory in the country, the Conservatory, which was built in the late 1870s, is a copy of the one in the Royal Botanical Gardens in Kew, England. Heavily damaged during a 1995 storm, the whitewashed facility is closed indefinitely but its architecture and gardens make it a worthy stop nonetheless. The gardens in front of the Conservatory are planted seasonally. ⊠ *John F. Kennedy Dr. at Conservatory Dr.*

❶❷ **Dutch Windmill.** The restored 1902 Dutch Windmill once pumped 20,000 gallons of well water per hour to the reservoir on Strawberry Hill. With its heavy cement bottom and wood-shingled arms and upper section the windmill cuts quite the sturdy figure. The structure overlooks the equally photogenic **Queen Wilhelmina Tulip Garden,** which bursts into full bloom in early spring and late summer. ⊠ *Between 47th Ave. and the Great Hwy.*

★ ❽ **Japanese Tea Garden.** A serene 4-acre landscape of small ponds, streams, waterfalls, stone bridges, Japanese sculptures, *mumsai* (planted bonsai) trees, perfect miniature pagodas, and some nearly vertical wooden "humpback" bridges, the tea garden was created for the 1894 Mid-Winter Exposition. The Tea House is a popular stop. ⊠ *Tea Garden Dr. off John F. Kennedy Dr.,* ☎ *415/752–4227 or 415/752–1171.* 🎟 *$3.50.* ☉ *Mar.–Sept., daily 9–6:30; Oct.–Feb., daily 8:30–6.*

❶⓪ **M. H. de Young Memorial Museum.** Works on display at the de Young include American paintings, sculpture, textiles, and decorative arts from Colonial times through the 20th century. The John D. Rockefeller III Collection of American Paintings contains more than 200 paintings of American masters such as John Singleton Copley, Thomas Eakins, George Caleb Bingham, and John Singer Sargent. The de Young also has collections of African and Native American art, including sculpture, baskets, and ceramics. The **Café de Young** has outdoor seating in the lovely Oakes Garden. ⊠ *Tea Garden Dr. off JFK Dr., near 10th Ave. and Fulton St.,* ☎ *415/863–3330.* 🎟 *$7, ($2 off with Muni transfer), good also for same-day admission to the Asian Art Museum and the Legion of Honor Museum in Lincoln Park; free 1st Wed. of month until 5.* ☉ *Tues.–Sun. 9:30–5, 1st Wed. of month until 8:45.*

❹ **National AIDS Memorial Grove.** This 15-acre grove, started in the early 1990s by people with AIDS and their families and friends, was conceived as a living memorial to those the disease has claimed. Coast live oaks, Monterey pines, coast redwoods, and other trees flank the grove, which is anchored at its east end by the stone Circle of Friends. ⊠ *Middle Dr. E., west of tennis courts.*

⑥ Shakespeare Garden. Two hundred flowers and herbs mentioned in the Bard's plays grow here; bronze-engraved passages contain relevant floral quotations. ⊠ *Middle Dr. E. at southwest corner of California Academy of Sciences.*

⑪ Stow Lake. One of the most picturesque spots in Golden Gate Park, this placid body of water surrounds Strawberry Hill. A couple of bridges allow you to cross over and ascend the hill. A waterfall cascades down from the top of the hill, and panoramic views make it worth the short hike up here. ⊠ *Off John F. Kennedy Dr. ½ mi west of 10th Ave.,* ☎ *415/752–0347.*

⑦ Strybing Arboretum & Botanical Gardens. The 55-acre arboretum specializes in plants from areas with climates similar to that of the Bay Area, such as the west coast of Australia, South Africa, and the Mediterranean. Among the highlights are the Biblical, fragrance, California native plants, succulents, and primitive gardens, the new and old world cloud forests, and the duck pond. ⊠ *9th Ave. at Lincoln Way,* ☎ *415/661–1316.* ⌻ *Free.* ☉ *Weekdays 8–4:30, weekends and holidays 10–5. Tours leave the bookstore weekdays at 1:30, weekends at 10:30.*

Lincoln Park and the Western Shoreline

From Land's End in Lincoln Park you'll have some of the best views of the Golden Gate (the name was originally given to the opening of San Francisco Bay long before the bridge was built) and the Marin Headlands. From the historic Cliff House south to the sprawling San Francisco Zoo, the Great Highway and Ocean Beach run along the western edge of the city. The wind is often strong along the shoreline, summer fog can blanket the ocean beaches, and the water is cold and usually rough. Carry a jacket and bring binoculars.

Numbers in the text correspond to numbers in the margin and on the Lincoln Park and the Western Shoreline map.

A Good Drive

A car is useful out here. There are plenty of hiking trails, and buses travel to all the sights mentioned, but the sights are far apart. Start at **Lincoln Park** ①. The park entrance is at 34th Avenue and Clement Street. Those without a car can take Bus 38-Geary—get off at 33rd Avenue and walk north (to the right) one block on 34th Avenue to the entrance. At the end of 34th Avenue is the **California Palace of the Legion of Honor** ②. From the museum, head back out to Clement Street and follow it west. At 45th Avenue Clement turns into Seal Rock Drive. When Seal Rock dead-ends at 48th Avenue, turn left on El Camino del Mar and right on Point Lobos Avenue. After a few hundred yards, you'll see parking lots for **Sutro Heights Park** ③ and the **Cliff House** ④. (To get from the Legion of Honor to Point Lobos Avenue by public transit, take Bus 18 from the Legion of Honor parking lot west to the corner of 48th and Point Lobos avenues.) Two large concrete lions near the southeast corner of 48th and Point Lobos guard the entrance to Sutro Heights Park. After taking a quick spin through the park, exit past the lions, cross Point Lobos, make a left, and walk down to the Cliff House. From the Cliff House it's a short walk farther downhill to **Ocean Beach** ⑤. The **San Francisco Zoo** ⑥ is a couple of miles south, at the intersection of the Great Highway and Sloat Boulevard.

TIMING

Set aside at least three hours for this tour—more if you don't have a car. An hour can easily be spent in the Palace of the Legion of Honor and 1½ hours at the zoo.

California
Palace of the
Legion of
Honor, **2**

Cliff House, **4**

Lincoln Park, **1**

Ocean Beach, **5**

San Francisco
Zoo, **6**

Sutro Heights
Park, **3**

Sights to See

★ ❷ **California Palace of the Legion of Honor.** Spectacularly situated on cliffs overlooking the ocean, the Golden Gate Bridge, and the Marin Headlands, this landmark building is a fine repository of European art. A pyramidal glass skylight in the entrance court illuminates the lower-level galleries, which exhibit prints and drawings, English and European porcelain, and ancient Assyrian, Greek, Roman, and Egyptian art. The 20-plus galleries on the upper level are devoted to the permanent collection of European art from the 14th through the 20th centuries. The noteworthy Rodin collection includes two galleries devoted to the master and a third with works by Rodin and other 19th-century sculptors. An original cast of Rodin's *The Thinker* welcomes you as you walk through the courtyard.

The **Legion Café,** on the lower level, has a garden terrace and a view of the Golden Gate Bridge. North of the museum (across Camino del Mar) is George Segal's *The Holocaust,* a sculpture that evokes life in concentration camps during World War II. ✉ *34th Ave. at Clement St.,* ☎ *415/863–3330 for 24-hr information.* 🎟 *$7 ($2 off with Muni transfer), good also for same-day admission to Asian Art and M. H. de Young museums, free 2nd Wed. of month.* ☉ *Tues.–Sun. 9:30–5; 1st Sat. of month until 8:45.*

❹ **Cliff House.** The original Cliff House, which dated from 1863 and was destroyed by fire on Christmas Day 1894, hosted several U.S. presidents and wealthy locals. The second Cliff House, the most beloved and resplendent of the three, was built in 1896; it rose eight stories with an observation tower 200 ft above sea level. The current building dates from 1909. The complex, which includes restaurants, a pub, and a gift shop, will remain open in 2000 while undergoing a gradual renovation to restore its early 20th-century look. The dining areas overlook Seal Rock (the barking marine mammals sunning themselves are actually sea lions).

The **Golden Gate National Recreation Area Visitors' Center** (☎ 415/ 556–8642) here contains fascinating historical photographs of the Cliff House and the glass-roof Sutro Baths. The Sutro complex, which comprised six enormous baths, 500 dressing rooms, and several restaurants, covered 3 acres north of the Cliff House. The baths were closed in 1952 and burned down in 1966. You can explore the ruins on your own or take ranger-led walks on weekends. The visitor center, open daily from 10 to 5 except major holidays, provides information about these and other trails. ⊠ *1090 Point Lobos Ave.,* ☎ *415/386–3330.* ⊙ *Weekdays 8 AM–10:30 PM, weekends 8 AM–11 PM; cocktails served nightly until 2 AM.*

❶ **Lincoln Park.** At one time most of the city's cemeteries were here, segregated by nationality. In 1900, the Board of Supervisors voted to ban burials within city limits (two exceptions are the cemetery at Mission Dolores and the one in the Presidio). Large Monterey cypresses line the fairways at Lincoln Park's 18-hole golf course. There are scenic walks throughout the 275-acre park, with postcard-perfect views from many spots. The trail out to **Land's End** starts outside the Palace of the Legion of Honor, at the end of El Camino del Mar. Be careful if you hike here; landslides are frequent. ⊠ *Entrance at 34th Ave. at Clement St.*

❺ **Ocean Beach.** Stretching 3 mi along the western side of the city, this is a good beach for walking, running, or lying in the sun—but not for swimming. Surfers here wear wet suits year-round as the water is extremely cold. Riptides are also very dangerous here. Paths on both sides of the Great Highway lead from Lincoln Way to Sloat Boulevard (near the zoo). ⊠ *Along the Great Hwy. from the Cliff House to Sloat Blvd. and beyond.*

👆 ❻ **San Francisco Zoo.** More than 1,000 birds and animals reside at the zoo. Among the more than 130 endangered species are the snow leopard, Sumatran tiger, jaguar, and Asian elephant. A favorite attraction is the greater one-horned rhinoceros, next to the African elephants. Another popular resident is Prince Charles, a rare white tiger. **Gorilla World** is one of the largest and most natural gorilla habitats of any zoo in the world. Magellanic penguins waddle about **Penguin Island,** splashing and frolicking in its 200-ft pool. Kangaroos and wallabies headline the **Walkabout** exhibit. The 7-acre **South American Gateway** re-creates habitats on that continent, replete with howler monkeys, tapirs, and a cloud forest. The **Feline Conservation Center** plays a key role in the zoo's efforts to encourage breeding among endangered felines. The **children's zoo** has a population of about 300 mammals, birds, and reptiles, plus an insect zoo, a baby-animal nursery, a deer park, a nature trail, a nature theater, and a restored 1921 Dentzel carousel. A ride astride one of the 52 hand-carved menagerie animals costs $1. ⊠ *Sloat Blvd. and the Great Hwy. (Muni L-Taraval streetcar from downtown),* ☎ *415/ 753–7080.* 🎟 *$9 ($1 off with Muni transfer); free 1st Wed. of month.* ⊙ *Daily 10–5; children's zoo weekdays 11–4, weekends 10:30–4:30.*

❸ **Sutro Heights Park.** Crows and other large birds battle the heady breezes at this cliff-top park on what were the grounds of the home of mining engineer and former San Francisco mayor Adolph Sutro. Monterey cypresses and Canary Island palms dot the park, and photos on placards depict what you would have seen before the house burned down in 1896. All that remains of the main house is its foundation. ⊠ *Point Lobos and 48th Aves.*

The Castro

Historians are still trying to discover what drew tens of thousands of gays and lesbians to the San Francisco area during the second half of the 20th century. Whatever the cause, San Francisco became the city of choice for lesbians and gay men, and in the 1970s Castro Street became its social, cultural, and political center.

Numbers in the text correspond to numbers in the margin and on the Castro and the Haight map.

A Good Walk

Begin at **Harvey Milk Plaza** ① on the southwest corner of 17th and Market streets. Across Castro Street from the plaza is the **Castro Theatre** ②. Many shops line Castro Street between 17th and 19th streets, 18th between Sanchez and Eureka streets, and Market Street heading east toward downtown. After exploring the shops on 18th and Castro streets, head west up 19th Street to Douglass Street and turn left. On the corner of Douglass and Caselli streets sprawls **Clarke's Mansion** ③. Continue north on Douglass Street to 18th Street and make a right. Cross Castro Street and make a left on Noe Street. Stay on the left (west) side of Noe. At the intersection of 16th, Market, and Noe streets, cross Market Street and turn left on the north side of the Market. At Number 2362 is the **Names Project** ④, the birthplace and continuing workshop for the AIDS Memorial Quilt.

TIMING

Allot an hour to an hour and a half to visit the Castro district.

Sights to See

★ ❷ **Castro Theatre.** The neon marquee is the neighborhood's great landmark, and the 1,500-seat theater, which opened in 1922, is the grandest of San Francisco's few remaining movie palaces. The Castro's elaborate Spanish baroque interior is fairly well preserved. Before many shows the theater's pipe organ rises from the orchestra pit and an organist plays pop and movie tunes, usually ending with the Jeanette McDonald standard "San Francisco." The crowd can be enthusiastic and vocal. ⊠ *429 Castro St.,* ☎ *415/621–6120.*

❸ **Clarke's Mansion.** Built for attorney Alfred "Nobby" Clarke, this off-white Baroque Queen Anne home completed in 1892 was dubbed Clarke's Folly when his wife refused to inhabit it because it was in an unfashionable part of town. At the time, everyone who was anyone lived on Nob Hill. ⊠ *250 Douglass St., between 18th and 19th Sts.*

❶ **Harvey Milk Plaza.** An 18-ft-long rainbow flag, a gay icon, flies above this plaza named for the man who electrified the city in 1977 by being elected to its Board of Supervisors as an openly gay candidate. The liberal Milk hadn't served a full year of his term before he and Mayor George Moscone, also a liberal, were shot in November 1978 at City Hall by conservative ex-supervisor Dan White, who had recently resigned his post and then become enraged when Moscone wouldn't reinstate him. Milk and White had often been at odds on the board, and White felt that Milk had been part of a cabal to keep him from returning to his post. Milk's assassination shocked the gay community, which became enraged when the famous "Twinkie defense"—that junk food had led to diminished mental capacity—resulted in a manslaughter verdict for White. During the White Night Riot of May 21, 1979, gays and their sympathizers stormed City Hall, torching its lobby and several police cars. ⊠ *Southwest corner of Castro and Market Sts.*

❹ **Names Project.** Open to anyone who wishes to work on a panel or view the work of those who have, the Names Project has created a gigan-

The Castro and the Haight

tic quilt made of more than 42,000 hand-sewn and -decorated panels, pieced together by loved ones to serve as a memorial to those who have died of AIDS. New additions to the quilt are always on display. ⊠ *2362 Market St.,* ☎ *415/863–1966.* ☉ *Mon.–Sat. noon–7, Sun. noon–6; quilting bee Wed. 7 PM–10 PM and 2nd Sat. of month 1–5.*

OFF THE BEATEN PATH — **THE MISSION** – The sunny Mission district was home to Italian and Irish communities in the early 20th century. But it has been heavily Latino since the late 1960s. Despite its distinctive Latino flavor, the Mission has in recent years seen an influx of Chinese, Vietnamese, Arabic, and other immigrants, along with a young bohemian crowd enticed by cheap rents and the burgeoning arts scene. The district is yet again in transition, as gentrification is leading to higher rents, forcing some longtime residents to move. The spiritual heart of the old Mission lies within the thick, white adobe walls of **Mission Dolores** (Dolores and 16th Sts., ☎ 415/621–8203). Completed in 1791, the small adobe building known as Mission San Francisco de Asís is the oldest standing structure in San Francisco and the sixth of the 21 California missions founded by Father Junípero Serra in the 18th and early 19th centuries.

The Haight

Once an enclave of large middle-class families of European immigrants, the Haight began to change during the late 1950s and early 1960s. Families were fleeing to the suburbs, and the big old Victorians were deteriorating or being chopped up into cheap housing. Young people found the neighborhood an affordable spot in which they could live according to new precepts. By 1966 the Haight had become a hot spot for rock bands like the Grateful Dead and Jefferson Airplane.

Numbers in the text correspond to numbers in the margin and on the Castro and the Haight map.

A Good Walk

Start your visit on the western edge of **Buena Vista Park** ⑤, at Haight Street and Buena Vista Avenue West. If you're up for a climb, walk a few blocks south on Buena Vista Avenue West along the edge of the park to **Spreckels Mansion** ⑥. From the mansion, backtrack on its side of the street to Central Avenue. Head down Central two blocks to Haight Street, and make a left. Continue west to the fabled **Haight-Ashbury intersection** ⑦. Despite the franchise operations, you won't need to close your eyes to conjure the 1960s. A motley contingent of folks attired in retro fashions and often sporting hippie-long hair hangs here. One block south of Haight and Ashbury is the **Grateful Dead house** ⑧.

TIMING

The distance covered here is only several blocks, and although there are shops aplenty and other amusements, an hour or so should be enough.

Sights to See

❺ **Buena Vista Park.** Great city views can be had from this eucalyptus-filled park. Although it's not exactly sedate (drug deals are common), it's a very pretty park, especially on a sunny day. Don't wander here after dark. ✉ *Haight St. between Lyon St. and Buena Vista Ave. W.*

❽ **Grateful Dead house.** Nothing unusual marks the house of legend. On the outside, it's just one more well-kept Victorian on a street that's full of them—but true fans of the Dead may find some inspiration here. The three-story house (closed to the public) is tastefully painted in sedate mauves, tans, and teals. ✉ *710 Ashbury St., just past Waller St.*

❼ **Haight/Ashbury intersection.** On October 6, 1967, hippies took over the intersection of Haight and Ashbury streets to proclaim the "Death of Hip." If they thought hip was dead then, they'd find absolute confirmation of it today, what with the Gap holding court on one quadrant of the famed corner. Among the folks who hung out in or near the Haight during the late 1960s were writers Allen Ginsberg and Ken Kesey; anarchist Abbie Hoffman; rock performers Jerry Garcia, Janis Joplin, and Grace Slick; LSD champion Timothy Leary; and filmmaker Kenneth Anger.

❻ **Spreckels Mansion.** Not to be confused with the Spreckels Mansion of Pacific Heights, this house was built for sugar baron Richard Spreckels in 1887. Later tenants included Jack London and Ambrose Bierce. The boxy, putty-color Victorian is in mint condition. ✉ *737 Buena Vista Ave. W.*

DINING

By Sharon Silva

Practically every ethnic cuisine is represented in San Francisco. Most upper-end establishments offer valet parking—worth considering in crowded neighborhoods like North Beach, Union Square, Nob Hill, and the Civic Center. There is often a nominal charge and a time-length restriction on validated parking.

CATEGORY	COST*
$$$$	over $50
$$$	$30–$50
$$	$20–$30
$	under $20

per person for a three-course meal, excluding drinks, service, and 8½% sales tax

The Castro

Contemporary

$$$ ✕ **Mecca.** This sleek bar and restaurant on the edge of the Castro is a mecca for both local Armani-clad cocktailers and Bay Area foodies. If clubbing is not your thing, reserve a seat in the dining area, away from the always crowded, velvet-curtained circular bar that anchors the cavernous space. In late 1998, Mike Fennelly took over the kitchen, delivering an American menu with strong Cajun and Asian accents. Choices include curried potato samosas with pineapple salsa, shrimp dumplings with a spicy tahini sauce, and lemon-mascarpone cheesecake. ⊠ 2029 Market St., ☎ 415/621–7000. AE, DC, MC, V. No lunch.

$$–$$$ ✕ **2223.** The smart, sophisticated 2223 attracts a loyal clientele. Thin-crust pizzas, earthy seasonal soups, pork loin with wilted escarole, and duck confit salad are among the kitchen's best dishes. For Saturday and Sunday brunch there might be French toast or eggs Benedict on a tasty herb scone. ⊠ 2223 Market St., ☎ 415/431–0692. MC, V. No lunch weekdays.

Chinatown

Chinese

$–$$ ✕ **Great Eastern.** Large tanks in the busy dining room are filled with Dungeness crabs, black bass, abalone, catfish, shrimp, rock cod, and other creatures of the sea. A wall-hung menu in both Chinese and English specifies the cost of selecting what can be pricey indulgences. Sea conch stir-fried with yellow chives, crab with vermicelli in a clay pot, and steamed fresh scallops with garlic sauce are among the chef's many specialties. ⊠ 649 Jackson St., ☎ 415/986–2550. AE, MC, V.

$–$$ ✕ **R&G Lounge.** Downstairs (entrance on Kearny Street) is a no-table-cloth dining room that is always packed at lunch and dinner. The classier upstairs space (entrance on Commercial Street) is a favorite stop for Chinese businessmen on expense accounts and anyone seeking exceptional Cantonese banquet fare. A menu with photographs helps diners decide among the many exotic dishes, from dried scallops with seasonal vegetables to deep-fried salt-and-pepper Dungeness crab. ⊠ 631 Kearny St., ☎ 415/982–7877 or 415/982–3811. AE, DC, MC, V.

Civic Center

Contemporary

$$$ ✕ **Jardinière.** One of the city's most talked-about restaurants is *the* place
★ to dine before a performance at the nearby Opera House and Davies Symphony Hall. The chef-owner is Traci Des Jardins, who made her name at the fashionable Rubicon. The sophisticated interior, with its eye-catching oval atrium and curving staircase, is the work of designer Pat Kuleto. First courses of rabbit rillettes, duck confit, and foie gras are pricey but memorable ways to launch any repast. Alas, not all the main courses reach the same culinary heights, but the finely honed service helps you to forget the few shortcomings. ⊠ 300 Grove St., ☎ 415/861–5555. Reservations essential. AE, DC, MC, V. No lunch.

$$$ ✕ **Stars.** It has been around for more than a decade, but this culinary
★ hot spot, the domain of superchef Jeremiah Tower, remains a must on every traveling gourmet's itinerary. The food ranges from grills to ragouts to sautés—some daringly creative and some classical. Those on a budget can order a stylish hamburger or thin-crust pizza at the counter, or slowly enjoy a flute of champagne at the mile-long bar. ⊠ 150 Redwood Alley, at Van Ness Ave., ☎ 415/861–7827. Reservations essential. AE, DC, MC, V. No lunch.

$$ ✗ **Carta.** The defining idea here is a difficult one to pull off: a different menu from a different country or region every month. Yet Carta makes it work beautifully. The talented chefs, alums of some of the city's toniest spots, travel to an assortment of destinations: Oaxaca, Turkey, Dordogne, Morocco, and New England, to name just a few. There are usually about 10 small plates, three main courses, and three desserts. Sunday brunch is a highlight. ⊠ *1772 Market St.,* ☎ *415/ 863–3516. AE, DC, MC, V. Closed Mon. No lunch Sat.*

Italian

$$$ ✗ **Vivande Ristorante.** Owner-chef Carlo Middione's spacious restaurant features the rustic flavors of southern Italy in dishes such as stuffed calamari, risotto laced with seafood, pasta tossed with a tangle of mushrooms, and a hearty osso buco. A late-supper menu lets music lovers grab a bite after performances. ⊠ *670 Golden Gate Ave.,* ☎ *415/673–9245. AE, MC, V.*

Mediterranean

$$$ ✗ **Zuni Café & Grill.** A spacious, window-filled balcony dining area over-
★ looks the large bar, where shellfish, one of the best oyster selections in town, and drinks are dispensed. A whole roast chicken and Tuscan bread salad for two is a popular order here, as are the grilled meats and vegetables. Don't miss the addictive shoestring potatoes. ⊠ *1658 Market St.,* ☎ *415/552–2522. Reservations essential. AE, MC, V. Closed Mon.*

Seafood

$$–$$$ ✗ **Hayes Street Grill.** Up to 15 different kinds of seafood are chalked on the blackboard each night at this extremely popular restaurant. The fish is simply grilled, with a choice of sauces ranging from tomato salsa to a spicy Sichuan peanut concoction to beurre blanc. Fresh crab slaw and superb crab cakes are regular appetizers, and the crème brûlée is legendary. ⊠ *320 Hayes St.,* ☎ *415/863–5545. Reservations essential. AE, D, DC, MC, V. No lunch weekends.*

Vegetarian

$$ ✗ **Millennium.** The "organic cuisine" label translates to a menu of low-fat, dairy-free dishes made with organic ingredients that keep vegans and their carnivore friends equally satisfied. The kitchen looks to the Mediterranean, with pastas and polenta among its most successful dishes. ⊠ *246 McAllister St.,* ☎ *415/487–9800. MC, V.*

Cow Hollow/Marina

American

$–$$ ✗ **Perry's.** The button-down singles set comes to this watering hole and meeting place for good, honest saloon food—London broil, corned beef hash, one of the best hamburgers in town, and a great breakfast. Brunch is served on weekends. ⊠ *1944 Union St.,* ☎ *415/922–9022. AE, MC, V.*

French

$–$$ ✗ **Bistro Aix.** This lively bistro is a comfortable space composed of light wood banquettes, paper-top tablecloths, and a heated patio. The friendly service and attractive prices draw diners from the surrounding neighborhood and beyond. On weekdays, an early bird two-course prix fixe dinner is available for not much more than the price of a movie ticket. Addictive cracker crust pizzas, superb steamed mussels, crisp-skinned roast chicken, and *steak frites* are additional draws. ⊠ *3340 Steiner St.,* ☎ *415/202–0100. MC, V. No lunch.*

$–$$ ✗ **Cassis Bistro.** This sunny yellow, postage stamp–size operation recalls the small bistros tucked away on side streets in French seaside towns. The food—onion tart, veal ragout, braised rabbit, tarte Tatin—

144

Downtown San Francisco Dining

The
Meetinghouse, **63**
Mifune, **89**
Millennium, **68**
Momo's, **60**
Moose's, **18**
One Market, **40**
Pane e Vino, **10**
Pastis, **25**
Perry's, **8**
Plouf, **55**
PlumpJack Café, **6**
Postrio, **47**
R&G Lounge, **38**
Ritz-Carlton Dining
Room and Terrace, **35**
Rose Pistola, **21**
Rubicon, **39**
Rumpus, **46**
San Tung No. 2, **81**
Sanppo, **90**
Scala's Bistro, **36**
Slanted Door, **75**
South Park Cafe, **51**
Stars, **66**
Straits Café, **87**
Tavolino, **23**
Thep Phanom, **79**
Thirstybear, **62**
Ton Kiang, **83**
2223, **72**
Vineria, **76**
Vivande Ristorante, **67**
Yank Sing, **34, 50**
Zarzuela, **12**
Zuni Café & Grill, **71**

is comfortingly home style and reasonably priced. ⊠ *2120 Greenwich St.,* ☎ *415/292–0770. No credit cards. Closed Sun.–Mon. No lunch.*

Italian

$$–$$$ ✕ **Pane e Vino.** A long table topped with prosciutto, a wheel of Parmi-giano-Reggiano, and various antipasti seduces everyone who enters this highly popular trattoria. Polenta with mushrooms, gnocchi with rab-bit, and thick veal chops are among the dishes regulars can't resist. ⊠ *3011 Steiner St.,* ☎ *415/346–2111. MC, V. No lunch Sun.*

Mediterranean

$$–$$$ ✕ **PlumpJack Café.** The regularly changing menu at this clubby din-
★ ing room spans the Mediterranean, with creamy risottos, an herbed chicken flanked by polenta, and crispy duck confit among the possi-bilities. The café is an offshoot of the nearby highly regarded wine shop of the same name, which stocks the racks that line the dining room with some of the most reasonably priced vintages in town. ⊠ *3127 Fillmore St.,* ☎ *415/463–4755. AE, MC, V. Closed Sun. No lunch Sat.*

Mexican

$–$$ ✕ **Café Marimba.** Fanciful folk art adorns the walls of this colorful Mex-ican café, where an open kitchen turns out contemporary renditions of regional specialties: silken *mole negro* (sauce of chilies and choco-late) from Oaxaca, served in tamales and other dishes; shrimp prepared with roasted onions and tomatoes in the style of Zihuatanejo; and chicken with a marinade from Yucatán stuffed into an excellent taco. ⊠ *2317 Chestnut St.,* ☎ *415/776–1506. AE, MC, V. No lunch Mon.*

Pan-Asian

$–$$ ✕ **Betelnut.** A pan-Asian menu and an adventurous drinks list draw a steady stream of hipsters for cuisine that is not always successful, yet always intriguing. Don't pass up a plate of the stir-fried dried anchovies, chilies, peanuts, garlic, and green onions. Sadly, service is often amateurish. ⊠ *2030 Union St.,* ☎ *415/929–8855. D, DC, MC, V.*

Steak

$$–$$$ ✕ **Izzy's Steak & Chop House.** Terrific steaks, chops, and seafood plus all the trimmings—such as cheesy scalloped potatoes and creamed spinach—are served here. There's validated parking at the Lombard garage. ⊠ *3345 Steiner St.,* ☎ *415/563–0487. AE, DC, MC, V. No lunch.*

Vegetarian

$$ ✕ **Greens.** Long popular with vegetarians and carnivores alike, this
★ beautiful restaurant with expansive bay views is owned and operated by the Green Gulch Zen Buddhist Center of Marin County. The din-ing room offers a creative spectrum of meatless cooking. Dinners are à la carte on weeknights, but only a five-course prix fixe dinner is served on Saturday. Sunday brunch is a good time to watch local sailboat own-ers take out their crafts. There's public parking at Fort Mason Center. ⊠ *Bldg. A, Fort Mason (enter across Marina Blvd. from Safeway),* ☎ *415/771–6222. MC, V. No lunch Mon., no dinner Sun.*

Embarcadero North

American

$$ ✕ **Fog City Diner.** The narrow dining room at Fog City Diner emulates a luxurious railroad car. The menu is both classic and contemporary, from burgers and fries, chili dogs, and hot fudge sundaes to crab cakes and salads of baby lettuce with candied walnuts. The shareable "small plates" are a fun way to go. ⊠ *1300 Battery St.,* ☎ *415/982–2000. D, DC, MC, V.*

$$ ✕ **MacArthur Park.** At happy hour, a sea of suits fills this handsomely renovated pre-earthquake brick warehouse. Much of the crowd stays on for the legendary baby back ribs, but the oak-wood smoker and mesquite grill also turn out a wide variety of other all-American dishes, from steaks to hamburgers to seafood. ⊠ *607 Front St.,* ☎ *415/398–5700. AE, DC, MC, V. No lunch weekends.*

Chinese

$$–$$$ ✕ **Harbor Village.** At lunchtime, businesspeople looking to impress their clients fill the dining room here, all of them enjoying the extraordinary array of dim sum offerings. At dinnertime, fresh seafood, crisp Peking duck, and various exotica are among the most popular requests from the loyal customers who regularly fill this opulent 400-seat branch of a Hong Kong establishment. There's validated parking at the Embarcadero Center Garage. ⊠ *4 Embarcadero Center,* ☎ *415/781–8833. AE, DC, MC, V.*

French

$$ ✕ **Pastis.** At lunchtime the sunny cement bar and sleek wooden banquettes in this exposed brick dining room are crowded with workers from nearby offices. They come to fuel up on steamed salmon with celery root or grilled prawns marinated in pastis (anise-flavored liqueur). The evening menu may include a dreamy seared foie gras with *verjuice* (sour grape juice) or lamb medallions on herby white beans. ⊠ *1015 Battery St.,* ☎ *415/391–2555. AE, MC, V. Closed Sun. No lunch Sat.*

Italian

$$–$$$ ✕ **Il Fornaio.** The draws at this handsome café, bakery, and upscale trattoria include outdoor seating and Tuscan specialties, among them pizzas from a wood-burning oven, house-made pastas and gnocchi, grilled poultry such as duck with a balsamic vinegar sauce, and meats like a veal chop with sage and rosemary. Anticipate a wait for a table. ⊠ *Levi's Plaza, 1265 Battery St.,* ☎ *415/986–0100. AE, DC, MC, V.*

Embarcadero South

Contemporary

$$$ ✕ **Boulevard.** Chef Nancy Oakes and designer Pat Kuleto are responsible for this highly successful eatery in one of the city's most magnificent buildings. The setting is the 1889 Audiffred Building, a Parisian look-alike that was one of the few downtown buildings to survive the 1906 earthquake and fire. Oakes's menu changes seasonally, but you can always count on her signature juxtaposition of delicacies such as foie gras with homey comfort foods like maple-cured pork loin and roasted chicken. Boulevard also offers a less formal weekday afternoon bistro service. ⊠ *1 Mission St.,* ☎ *415/543–6084. Reservations essential. AE, D, DC, MC, V. No lunch weekends.*

$$$ ✕ **One Market.** The bustling brasserie of Bradley Ogden and Michael Dellar seats 170, and a spacious bar-café serves snacks, including addictive wire-thin onion rings and oysters on the half shell, beginning at noon. The kitchen has had its ups and downs, however, due to a serious spate of executive chef turnover. ⊠ *1 Market St.,* ☎ *415/777–5577. Reservations essential. AE, DC, MC, V. Closed Sun. No lunch Sat.*

Financial District

American

$$–$$$ ✕ **Garden Court.** The Palace Hotel is the setting of this quintessential Old San Francisco restaurant. From breakfast until the early dinner hours, light splashes through the stunningly beautiful stained-glass

ceiling and against the towering Ionic columns and crystal chandeliers. Dinner here is not the strong suit. It is the extravagant Sunday buffet brunch, one of the city's great traditions, that draws accolades. ✉ *Market and New Montgomery Sts.,* ☎ *415/546–5011. Reservations essential. Jacket required. AE, DC, MC, V. No dinner Sun.*

Chinese

$ ✕ **Yank Sing.** The city's oldest teahouse, Yank Sing began in China-
★   town but moved to the Financial District several years ago. The kitchen offers five dozen or so varieties of dim sum on a rotating basis. The Battery Street location seats 300, while the older Stevenson Street site is far smaller, a cozy refuge for Market Street office workers who fuel up on steamed buns and parchment chicken at lunchtime. ✉ *427 Battery St.,* ☎ *415/362–1640;* ✉ *49 Stevenson St., at Market St.,* ☎ *415/ 541–4949. AE, DC, MC, V. Stevenson branch closed weekends. No dinner.*

Contemporary

$$$ ✕ **Cypress Club.** The contemporary American cooking here—roasted pumpkin soup, braised veal cheeks, hangar steak with bacon-potato tart—draws a loyal crowd, but the decor defies categorizing. It could be interpreted as anything from a parody of an ancient temple to a fu-turistic space bar, with stone mosaic floors, hammered copper arches, wall murals depicting scenes of northern California, yards of curved wood, imposing pillars, and overstuffed velvet upholstery. ✉ *500 Jackson St.,* ☎ *415/296–8555. AE, DC, MC, V. No lunch.*

$$$ ✕ **Rubicon.** With investors like Robin Williams, Robert De Niro, and Francis Ford Coppola, this sleek, cherry wood–lined restaurant, an off-shoot of New York's famed Drew Nierporent restaurant empire, was destined to be famous. Set in a stately 1908 stone building, Rubicon has the dignified air of a men's club in the downstairs dining room and a somewhat less appealing atmosphere in the more ascetic upstairs space. The excellent fare, primarily sophisticated renditions of seafood, meats, and poultry such as sea bass with leeks, lobster-crowned gnocchi, and grilled quail, is served on both floors to Hollywood big shots and San Francisco's glamorous set. ✉ *558 Sacramento St.,* ☎ *415/434–4100. AE, DC, MC, V. Closed Sun. No lunch Sat.*

$$–$$$ ✕ **Globe.** This smart spot with brick walls, slipcovered chairs, and terra-cotta floors seats less than four dozen diners, so book ahead. The so-phisticated food, which delivers a Californian punch with a thick Mediterranean accent, includes salad of frisée and lardons of pancetta topped with a poached egg, sea-fresh grilled sardines, and a T-bone steak with all the trimmings. ✉ *290 Pacific Ave.,* ☎ *415/391–4132. Reservations essential. AE, DC, MC, V. No lunch Sat. Closed Sun.*

$$–$$$ ✕ **Jack's.** Founded in 1864, Jack's is the oldest San Francisco restau-rant still in its original location. It reopened in late 1998, following a renovation that brought old-fashioned 22-karat gilding and a brand-new elevator to the four-floor building. The menu harkens back to the restaurant's early days, with lamb chops, mock turtle soup, and cel-ery Victor, but also looks ahead with gnocchi with a rabbit sauce and other contemporary plates. ✉ *615 Sacramento St.,* ☎ *415/421–7355. Reservations essential. AE, DC, MC, V. No lunch weekends.*

French

$–$$ ✕ **Plouf.** This sleek spot, handsomely turned out in chrome and the color of the sea, is a gold mine for mussel lovers, with seven gener-ously portioned, reasonably priced preparations from which to choose. Among them are *marinière* (garlic and parsley), apple cider, leeks and cream, and crayfish and tomato. Main courses run the gamut from steak frites to steamed sea bass. French vintages are well represented on the carefully selected wine list. ✉ *40 Belden Pl.,* ☎ *415/986–6491. MC, V. Closed Sun. No lunch Sat.*

$ ✕ **Café Claude.** This standout French bistro is on an alley near the Notre Dame des Victoires Catholic church and the French consulate. The interior design is comfortably French, with a zinc bar, old-fashioned banquettes, and cinema posters that once actually outfitted a bar in the City of Light's 11th arrondissement. Order a salade niçoise or simple daube from the French-speaking staff, and you might forget what country you're in. ✉ *7 Claude La.,* ☎ *415/392–3505. AE, DC, MC, V. Closed Sun.*

Japanese

$$–$$$$ ✕ **Kyo-ya.** The refined experience of dining in a fine Japanese restau-
★ rant has been introduced with extraordinary authenticity at this show-place within the Palace Hotel. In Japan a "kyo-ya" is a nonspecialized restaurant that serves a wide range of food. Here, the range is spectacular, encompassing tempuras, one-pot dishes, deep-fried and grilled meats, and three dozen sushi selections. The lunch menu is more limited than dinner but does include a *shokado,* a sampler of four dishes encased in a lacquered box. *Kaiseki* meals, multicourse seasonal dinners, are also offered, priced for an emperor. ✉ *Palace Hotel, 2 New Montgomery St., at Market St.,* ☎ *415/546–5000. AE, D, DC, MC, V. Closed Sun. No lunch Mon. and Sat.*

Seafood

$$$–$$$$ ✕ **Aqua.** This quietly elegant and ultrafashionable spot is among the
★ city's most lauded seafood restaurants. Chef-owner Michael Mina creates contemporary versions of French, Italian, and American classics. Mussel, crab, or lobster soufflé; chunks of lobster alongside lobster-stuffed ravioli; and the ultrarare ahi tuna paired with foie gras are especially good. Desserts are miniature museum pieces, and the wine list is superb. ✉ *252 California St.,* ☎ *415/956–9662. Reservations essential. Jacket and tie. AE, DC, MC, V. Closed Sun. No lunch Sat.*

The Haight

Contemporary

$$$ ✕ **Eos Restaurant & Wine Bar.** The culinary marriage of California cuisine and the Asian pantry is the specialty of chef-owner Arnold Wong, who serves an impressive East-West menu at this popular spot. Grilled skirt steak is marinated in a Thai red curry and served with mashed potatoes and bok choy, and rock shrimp cakes arrive with a gingery mayonnaise. The wine bar next door carries some 400 vintages, any of which is available at your table. ✉ *901 Cole St.,* ☎ *415/566–3063. Reservations essential. AE, MC, V. No lunch.*

Indian

$$–$$$ ✕ **Indian Oven.** One of the Lower Haight's most popular restaurants, this cozy Victorian storefront never lacks for customers. The tandoori specialties, *sag paneer* (spinach with Indian cheese), and *aloo gobhi* (potatoes and cauliflower with black mustard seeds and other spices) are excellent. ✉ *223 Fillmore St.,* ☎ *415/626–1628. AE, D, DC, MC, V. No lunch.*

Thai

$–$$ ✕ **Thep Phanom.** The fine Thai food and the lovely interior at this lower Haight institution keep local food critics and restaurant goers singing its praises. Duck is deliciously prepared in a variety of ways—in a fragrant curry, minced for salad, resting atop a bed of spinach. Other specialties are seafood, stuffed chicken wings, and fried quail. ✉ *400 Waller St.,* ☎ *415/431–2526. AE, D, DC, MC, V. No lunch.*

Japantown

Japanese

$–$$ ✕ **Sanppo.** This modestly priced, casual spot has an enormous selection of almost every type of Japanese food, including featherlight tempura and sushi. Seating is Western style. Ask for validated parking at the Japan Center garage. ✉ *1702 Post St.,* ☎ *415/346–3486. Reservations not accepted. MC, V.*

$ ✕ **Mifune.** Thin, brown soba and thick, white udon are the specialties at this outpost of an Osaka-based noodle empire. A line often snakes out the door, but the house-made noodles, served both hot and cold and with more than a score of toppings, are worth the wait. Seating is at rustic wooden tables. Validated parking is available at the Japan Center garage. ✉ *Japan Center, Kintetsu Building, 1737 Post St.,* ☎ *415/922–0337. Reservations not accepted. AE, D, DC, MC, V.*

Lower Pacific Heights

Contemporary

$$–$$$ ✕ **The Meetinghouse.** A small, regularly changing menu of modernized American dishes is served in this appealing room of creamy yellow walls, broad plank floors, and Shaker furniture. Among the most popular first courses are johnnycakes filled with rock shrimp and oyster stew with celery root; hominy-crusted catfish and roasted chicken on a savory bread pudding and greens are satisfying entrées. ✉ *1701 Octavia St.,* ☎ *415/922–6733. AE, MC, V. Closed Sun.–Mon. No lunch.*

Italian

$$–$$$ ✕ **Laghi.** For many years, Laghi was a much-loved trattoria in the Richmond District. In late 1998, chef-owner Gino Laghi moved his estimable operation to this much larger space. Old customers and new fans quickly flocked here to enjoy the pastas, including pumpkin-filled ravioli with butter and sage; creamy risottos with everything from fiddlehead ferns to porcini mushrooms to truffles; and roasted rabbit and other game. ✉ *2101 Sutter St.,* ☎ *415/931–3774. AE, DC, MC, V.*

The Mission District

Contemporary

$$–$$$ ✕ **42 Degrees.** Chef Jim Moffat is the culinary brains behind this sleek, industrial-style space with a curving metal staircase and a seductive view of the bay. The name refers to the latitude on which Provence, Tuscany, and northern Spain lie. The California menu, infused with Mediterranean touches, changes weekly. Nightly jazz keeps late-night patrons—mostly a younger crowd with bucks to spend—tapping their toes. ✉ *235 16th St.,* ☎ *415/777–5558. MC, V. Closed Sun. No dinner Mon. and Tues.*

Italian

$–$$ ✕ **Vineria.** The North Mission is home to a continually expanding population of eateries, but this is arguably the finest kitchen in the neigh-
★   borhood. The talented duo behind Vineria are the same women who run the highly successful L'Osteria del Forno in North Beach (☞ *below*), and many of the offerings are identical, including a full list of wonderful *panini* (Italian sandwiches). There are, however, more pastas at this slightly larger space. The wine list is small but superb. ✉ *3228 16th St.,* ☎ *415/552–3889. MC, V. Closed Mon.–Tues. No lunch.*

Mexican

$ ✕ **La Taqueria.** Although there are a number of taquerias in the Mission, this attractive spot, with its arched exterior and modest interior, is one of the oldest and finest. The tacos are superb: a pair of warm corn tortillas topped with your choice of meat—*carne asada* (grilled steak) and *carnitas* (slowly cooked pork) are favorites—and a spoonful of perfectly fresh salsa. ⊠ *2889 Mission St., ☎ 415/285–7117. No credit cards.*

Vietnamese

$$ ✕ **Slanted Door.** Behind the canted facade of this trendy north Mission restaurant, you'll find what owner Charles Phan describes as "real Vietnamese home cooking." Five-spice chicken, green papaya salad, and a special of steamed sea bass fillet are among the best dishes. The kitchen, alas, falters more than the crowded tables would have you believe. ⊠ *584 Valencia St., ☎ 415/861–8032. MC, V. Closed Mon.*

Nob Hill

French

$$$–$$$$ ✕ **Ritz-Carlton Dining Room and Terrace.** The Dining Room is formal
★ and elegant and has a harpist playing; it serves only three- to five-course dinners. The Terrace, a cheerful, informal spot with a large garden patio for outdoor dining, serves breakfast, lunch, dinner, and a Sunday jazz brunch, with piano music at lunchtime and a jazz trio at weekend dinners. In the Dining Room executive chef Sylvain Portay turns out an urbane seasonal French menu—squab with foie gras, lobster salad with caviar cream, a dreamy chocolate soufflé. ⊠ *600 Stockton St., ☎ 415/296–7465. AE, D, DC, MC, V. Closed Sun. No lunch.*

North Beach

Afghan

$–$$ ✕ **Helmand.** Don't be put off by its location on a scruffy block of Broadway—inside you'll find authentic Afghani cooking, elegant surroundings with white table linens and rich Afghan carpets, and amazingly low prices. Highlights include *aushak* (leek-filled ravioli served with yogurt and ground beef), pumpkin served with yogurt and garlic sauce, and any of the tender lamb dishes. There's free nighttime validated parking at 468 Broadway. ⊠ *430 Broadway, ☎ 415/362–0641. AE, MC, V. No lunch.*

American

$$$ ✕ **Bix.** Bix is reminiscent of a theater, with a bustling bar—memorable martinis and generous gin fizzes—and dining tables downstairs and banquettes on the balcony. Opt for the lower level; the acoustics upstairs are dreadful. The menu offers contemporary renditions of classic American fare, from Waldorf salad to bananas Foster. There's piano music in the evening. ⊠ *56 Gold St., ☎ 415/433–6300. AE, D, DC, MC, V. No lunch weekends.*

Contemporary

$$ ✕ **Enrico's Sidewalk Café.** For years this historic North Beach hangout was more a drinking spot than a dining destination, but a reliable kitchen has changed all that. Diners regularly tuck into the Caesar salad, thin-crust pizzas, grilled fish, and nicely done pastas, while gently swaying to first-rate live music. Grazers will be happy to find a slew of eclectic tapas, from smoked salmon bruschetta to fried oysters. ⊠ *504 Broadway, ☎ 415/982–6223. AE, DC, MC, V.*

French

$ ✕ **Des Alpes.** Opened in 1908, this spot has long been where the savvy diner finds a Basque meal at a rock-bottom price: soup, salad, two entrées, and ice cream are included in the budget tariff. Service is family style, and the *intime* bar that fronts the dining room is a delightful step back in time. ✉ *732 Broadway,* ☎ *415/788–9900. D, DC, MC, V. Closed Mon. No lunch.*

Italian

$$–$$$ ✕ **Rose Pistola.** The name honors one of North Beach's most revered
★   barkeeps, and the food celebrates the neighborhood's Ligurian roots. A wide assortment of small cold and hot antipasti and pizzas from the wood-burning oven are favorites, as is the classic San Francisco seafood stew called cioppino. A large and inviting bar area opens onto the sidewalk. ✉ *532 Columbus Ave.,* ☎ *415/399–0499. Reservations essential. AE, MC, V.*

$–$$ ✕ **Tavolino.** A snacker's paradise, this light, airy space celebrates the Venetian tradition of *cicchetti,* small plates usually consumed in a neighborhood bar with a glass of local wine. Some of the offerings fit right in with the classics, such as deep-fried anchovy-stuffed olives, fried calamari, and green beans dressed with olive oil. Other dishes are just shrunken versions of Italian *primi* or main dishes, such as squid ink risotto and a hearty lasagna. ✉ *401 Columbus Ave.,* ☎ *415/392–1472. AE, DC, MC, V.*

$ ✕ **Capp's Corner.** This is one of North Beach's last family-style trattorias, a pleasantly down-home spot where the men at the bar still roll dice for drinks and diners sit elbow to elbow at long oilcloth-covered tables. The fare is bountiful, well-prepared five-course dinners—not award winning, but priced well. For calorie counters or the budget-minded, a simpler option includes a tureen of minestrone, salad, and pasta. ✉ *1600 Powell St.,* ☎ *415/989–2589. AE, D, DC, MC, V.*

$ ✕ **L'Osteria del Forno.** An Italian-speaking staff, a small, unpretentious dining area, and irresistible aromas drifting from the open kitchen make customers who pass through the door of this modest storefront operation feel as if they've just stumbled into Italy. The kitchen produces small plates of simply cooked vegetables, a few baked pastas, a roast of the day, creamy polenta, and wonderful thin-crust pizzas. ✉ *519 Columbus Ave.,* ☎ *415/982–1124. Reservations not accepted. No credit cards. Closed Tues.*

Mediterranean

$$–$$$ ✕ **Moose's.** Restaurateur Ed Moose's latest venture was destined to become a celebrity hangout from the moment it opened in 1992, with politicians and media types following him from his former digs at Washington Square Bar & Grill. The Mediterranean menu has heavy French, Italian, and Californian accents. Among the popular dishes are the warm shiitake and buffalo mozzarella salad, risotto with wild mushrooms, and sturgeon wrapped in pancetta. The surroundings are classic and comfortable, with views of Washington Square and Russian Hill from a front café area; counter seats have a view of the open kitchen. There's live music at night and a fine Sunday brunch. ✉ *1652 Stockton St.,* ☎ *415/989–7800. Reservations essential. AE, DC, MC, V. No lunch Mon.–Wed.*

Middle Eastern

$$ ✕ **Maykadeh.** Although it sits in the middle of a decidedly Italian neighborhood, this authentic Persian restaurant serves a large following of faithful customers. Lamb dishes with rice are the specialties, served in a setting so elegant that the modest check comes as a surprise. The chicken, lamb, and beef kebabs and the *chelo* (Persian pilaf) are popular choices. ✉ *470 Green St.,* ☎ *415/362–8286. MC, V.*

Northern Waterfront

Seafood

$$ ✕ **McCormick & Kuleto's.** This seafood emporium in Ghirardelli Square is a visitor's dream come true: a fabulous view of the bay from every seat in the house; an Old San Francisco atmosphere; and dozens of varieties of fish and shellfish prepared in scores of globe-circling ways, from tacos, pot stickers, and fish cakes to grills, pastas, and stew. The food has its ups and downs—stick with the simplest preparations—but even on foggy days you can count on the view. Validated parking is available in the Ghirardelli Square garage. ⊠ *Ghirardelli Sq. at Beach and Larkin Sts.,* ☎ *415/929–1730. AE, D, DC, MC, V.*

Richmond District

Chinese

$$ ✕ **Hong Kong Flower Lounge.** This upmarket Cantonese restaurant was one of the first to serve San Franciscans the same plates that rich Hong Kong residents have long enjoyed. The kitchen is celebrated for its seafood, which is plucked straight from tanks. Chefs here keep up with whatever is hot in Hong Kong eateries, so check with the waiters to find out what's new. Ask about the prices before you order. Midday dim sum is available. ⊠ *5322 Geary Blvd.,* ☎ *415/668–8998. AE, D, DC, MC, V.*

$–$$ ✕ **Ton Kiang.** The lightly seasoned Hakka cuisine of southern China, rarely found in this country, was introduced to San Francisco at this restaurant, with such regional specialties as salt-baked chicken, braised stuffed bean curd, delicate fish and beef balls, and casseroles of meat and seafood cooked in clay pots. The dim sum is some of the finest in the city. ⊠ *5821 Geary Blvd.,* ☎ *415/387–8273. MC, V.*

$ ✕ **San Tung No. 2.** This modest but bright Shandong restaurant is a good introduction to the region's cuisine. Specialties include steamed dumplings and hand-pulled noodles either in soup or stir-fried. Typical accompaniments include a salad of jellyfish, seaweed, or cucumber and a plate of cold poached chicken marinated in Shaoxing wine. ⊠ *1031 Irving St.,* ☎ *415/242–0828. MC, V.*

Japanese

$$–$$$ ✕ **Kabuto Sushi.** For one of the most spectacular acts in town, head out Geary Boulevard past Japantown to tiny Kabuto. Here, behind the sushi counter, master chef Sachio Kojima has been flashing his knives for nearly two decades. In addition to exceptional sushi and sashimi, traditional Japanese dinners are served in the adjoining dining room. Be sure to consider the excellent selection of sakes, each one rated for dryness and labeled with its place of origin. ⊠ *5116 Geary Blvd.,* ☎ *415/752–5652. MC, V. Closed Mon. No lunch.*

Russian

$–$$ ✕ **Katia's.** This bright Richmond District gem offers Russian food with considerable flair at remarkably reasonable prices. Try the borscht, a dollop of sour cream topping a mélange of beets, cabbage, and other vegetables. Small plates of smoked salmon and blini, marinated mushrooms, and meat- or vegetable-filled piroshki are also wonderful ways to start a meal, and light chicken or potato cutlets or delicate *pelmeni* (small meat-filled dumplings in broth) are fine main courses. There is live Russian music on most evenings. The slow service may occasionally try your patience. ⊠ *600 5th Ave.,* ☎ *415/668–9292. AE, DC, MC, V. Closed Mon.*

Singaporean

$–$$ ✕ **Straits Café.** This highly popular restaurant serves the unique fare of Singapore, a cuisine that combines the culinary traditions of China, India, and the Malay archipelago. That exotic mix translates into complex curries, rice cooked in coconut milk, fragrant satays, and seafood noodle soups. The handsome dining room includes one wall that re-creates the old shop-house fronts of Singapore. ⊠ *3300 Geary Blvd.,* ☎ *415/668–1783. AE, MC, V.*

Vietnamese

$–$$ ✕ **Le Soleil.** The food of Vietnam is the specialty of this pastel, light-filled restaurant in the heart of Inner Richmond. An eye-catching painting of Saigon hangs on one wall, and a large aquarium of tropical fish adds to the tranquil mood. Try the excellent raw-beef salad; crisp, flavorful spring rolls; a simple stir-fry of chicken and aromatic fresh basil leaves; or large prawns simmered in a clay pot. ⊠ *133 Clement St.,* ☎ *415/668–4848. MC, V.*

Russian Hill

French

$$$$ ✕ **La Folie.** Long a favorite of dedicated Francophiles, this small, ter-
★   ribly Parisian establishment underwent a refurbishing in 1998, making the storefront café even lovelier. But the food is the true star here, especially the five-course discovery menu that allows a sample of such rarified mouthfuls as lobster salad with a mango vinaigrette and quail with white truffles. Much of the food is edible art—whimsical presentations in the form of savory terrines, *galettes* (flat, round cakes), and napoleons. The exquisite food and professional service come at a hefty price. ⊠ *2316 Polk St.,* ☎ *415/776–5577. Reservations essential. AE, D, DC, MC, V. Closed Sun. No lunch.*

Italian

$$$ ✕ **Acquerello.** This elegant restaurant is one of the most romantic spots in town. Both the service and the food are exemplary, and the menu covers the full range of Italian cuisine. Chef Suzette Gresham's fine creations include a first course of squab paired with greens and pine nuts, and a main of beef filet stuffed with prosciutto and Parmesan cheese. ⊠ *1722 Sacramento St.,* ☎ *415/567–5432. AE, D, DC, MC, V. Closed Sun.–Mon. No lunch.*

$$ ✕ **Antica Trattoria.** The dining room is stark, with off-white walls, dark wood, a partial view of the kitchen, and a strong sense of restraint. A small menu delivers classic plates such as fennel with blood oranges and red onions; whole wheat pasta tossed with Bolognese sauce; and venison medallions matched with wilted greens. The Italian wine list is fairly priced, and the genial service is polished but not overly formal. ⊠ *2400 Polk St.,* ☎ *415/928–5797. MC, V. Closed Mon. No lunch.*

Spanish

$$ ✕ **Zarzuela.** The small, crowded storefront serves nearly 40 different hot and cold tapas plus a dozen or so main courses. There is a tapa to suit every palate, from poached octopus atop new potatoes and hot garlic-flecked shrimp to slabs of Manchego cheese with paper-thin slices of serrano ham. ⊠ *2000 Hyde St.,* ☎ *415/346–0800. D, MC, V. Reservations not accepted. Closed Sun.*

Steak

$$$ ✕ **Harris'.** Ann Harris knows her beef. She grew up on a Texas cattle ranch
★   and was married to the late Jack Harris of Harris Ranch fame. In her own large, New York–style restaurant she serves some of the best dry-aged steaks in town. Be sure to include a side of the fine creamed spinach. ⊠ *2100 Van Ness Ave.,* ☎ *415/673–1888. AE, D, DC, MC, V. No lunch.*

South of Market

American

$$$ ✕ **Momo's.** Baseball fans spilling out of the new San Francisco Giants ballpark slated to open in April 2000 will want to stop at this former

printing plant, now a serious drinking and dining hangout. A shiny stainless steel exhibition kitchen delivers smoky-sweet baby back ribs, crisp onion rings, chopped salad, thick steaks, and thin pizzas to crowds in the Craftsman-appointed dining room with its big banquettes and high ceilings. The large patio and long, wood-lined bar are gathering places. ⊠ *760 Second St., ☎ 415/227–8660, AE, MC, V.*

Contemporary

$$$ ✕ **Hawthorne Lane.** In 1995 Anne and David Gingrass, of Postrio fame,
★ joined the booming bevy of SoMa eateries with this instantly popular establishment on a quiet alley a block or so from the Moscone Center and the Museum of Modern Art. In the large, high-ceiling bar there's a selection of irresistible small plates—Thai-style squid, skewers of grilled chicken, and tempura-battered green beans with mustard sauce. Patrons in the light-flooded dining room engage in more serious eating, from perfectly seared foie gras to grilled quail on scalloped potatoes. ⊠ *22 Hawthorne St., ☎ 415/777–9779. Reservations essential. D, DC, MC, V. No lunch weekends.*

French

$$–$$$ ✕ **Bizou.** Chef Loretta Keller, who once cooked alongside Jeremiah Tower at Stars, has developed her own distinctive French country menu here. Partisans of her rustic cooking cite the thin, crisp pizza topped with caramelized onions, fried snap beans with aioli or fig sauce, and pan-fried skate in brown butter as evidence of her talents. Although service can sometimes be uneven, Keller's faithful following doesn't seem to mind. ⊠ *598 4th St., ☎ 415/543–2222. AE, MC, V. Closed Sun. No lunch Sat.*

$$–$$$ ✕ **Fringale.** The bright yellow paint on this dazzling bistro stands out
★ like a beacon on an otherwise bleak industrial street, attracting a well-dressed clientele. They come for the reasonably priced French Basque–inspired creations of Biarritz-born chef Gerald Hirigoyen, whose classic steak frites, steamed mussels, and flaky apple tart are hallmarks. Small tables covered with cloths and white paper, a sensible wine list, and a crew of waiters sporting Gallic accents will have you practicing your French. ⊠ *570 4th St., ☎ 415/543–0573. Reservations essential. AE, MC, V. Closed Sun. No lunch Sat.*

$–$$ ✕ **South Park Café.** This utterly Parisian spot is open from early morning for your *café latte* to late at night for a wedge of fruit tart or a flute of champagne. No place in the City of Light itself serves a more authentic steak frites than this warm, sometimes clamorous spot overlooking a grassy square. ⊠ *108 South Park, at Bryant St., ☎ 415/495–7275. MC, V. Closed Sun. No lunch Sat.*

Latin

$$ ✕ **Thirstybear.** Just around the corner from the cathedral-like San Francisco Museum of Modern Art, Thirstybear is a combination brew pub and tapas outpost. The cavernous interior of concrete floors, rustic brick walls, and shiny tanks holding homemade brews is cool and utilitarian, but the small plates of garlic-and-sherry-infused fish cheeks, steamed mussels, grilled garlic-studded shrimp, and white beans with sausage and aioli will warm you right up. ⊠ *661 Howard St., ☎ 415/974–0905. MC, V. No lunch Sun.*

Mediterranean

$$–$$$ ✕ **LuLu.** Since its opening day in 1993, a seat at this boisterous restau-
★ rant has been one of the hottest tickets in town, although the throngs have faded somewhat since founding chef Reed Hearon divorced himself from the operation in 1996. The food, under the watchful eye of executive chef Jody Denton, has remained satisfyingly uncomplicated and delectable. Under the high barrel-vaulted ceiling, beside a large open

kitchen, diners feast on sizzling mussels roasted in an iron skillet, plus pizzas, pastas, and wood-roasted poultry, meats, and shellfish. The café serves food from morning until late at night. ⊠ *816 Folsom St.,* ☎ *415/495–5775. Reservations essential. AE, DC, MC, V.*

Sunset District
Contemporary
$$ ✕ **Beach Chalet.** In an historic colonnaded building with handsome Works Project Administration–produced murals, the Beach Chalet is the place to watch the sun set over the Pacific. The microbrewery beers run the gamut from a light pilsner to Playland pale ale, named for a now-gone nearby amusement park that entertained generations of San Franciscans. The food is an eclectic mix of steamed mussels and pizzette, buttermilk-dipped onion rings and house-made chorizo, thick burgers, and seafood gumbo. It's a 40-minute ride on the N Judah streetcar from downtown—and well worth the trip. ⊠ *1000 Great Hwy.,* ☎ *415/386–8439. MC, V.*

Union Square
Contemporary
$$$$ ✕ **Campton Place.** This elegant, ultrasophisticated small hotel put new
★ American cooking on the local culinary map with famed opening chef Bradley Ogden, who was followed by the nearly equally celebrated Jan Birnbaum, and later by yet another favorite, Todd Humphries, who left in early 1999. The kitchen continues to offer a refined American table that relies on the freshest local ingredients and handsome presentation. Brunch and breakfast are major events. ⊠ *340 Stockton St.,* ☎ *415/955–5555. Reservations essential. AE, D, DC, MC, V.*

$$$–$$$$ ✕ **Postrio.** There's always a chance to catch a glimpse of some celebrity here, including Postrio's owner, Wolfgang Puck, who periodically makes an appearance in the restaurant's open kitchen. A stunning three-level bar and dining area is highlighted by palm trees and museum-quality contemporary paintings. Attire is formal. The food is Puckish Californian with Mediterranean and Asian overtones: Chinese roast duck with mango sauce, house-cured salmon on a giant blini, and irresistible pastries. Substantial breakfast and bar menus (with great pizza) can be found here as well. Although ripples of dissatisfaction with the fare have been heard from some quarters, reservations are still tough to come by. ⊠ *545 Post St.,* ☎ *415/776–7825. Reservations essential. AE, D, DC, MC, V.*

$$–$$$ ✕ **Rumpus.** With Caesar salad, burgers, and club sandwiches at lunchtime, this casual bistro has a true American menu with a wallet-friendly price list. But there is also a handful of wonderful Mediterranean-inspired dishes, such as the onion tart with black olives and ravioli plump with crabmeat. Tucked at the end of an old-time alley, this convivial eatery has an insider's feel. ⊠ *1 Tillman Pl., at Grant Ave.,* ☎ *415/421–2300. AE, MC, V. No lunch Sun.*

French
$$$$ ✕ **Fleur de Lys.** The creative cooking of French chef-partner Hubert Keller has brought every conceivable culinary award to this romantic spot, which some consider the best French restaurant in town. The menu changes constantly, but such dishes as seared foie gras, truffled vichyssoise, and venison medallions with tender braised greens are Keller hallmarks. Perfectly smooth service adds to the overall enjoyment of eating here. There are tasting menus for both omnivores and vegetarians, and the elaborately canopied dining room is reminiscent of a sheikh's tent.

⊠ *777 Sutter St.,* ☎ *415/673–7779. Reservations essential. Jacket required. AE, DC, MC, V. Closed Sun. No lunch.*

$$$$ ✗ **Masa's.** Julian Serrano headed up the kitchen at this pretty, flower-
★ filled dining spot in the Vintage Court hotel for more than a dozen years, carrying on the tradition of the restaurant's late founder, Masa Kobayashi. In 1998, the torch was passed to Chad Callahan, who had served as the number two chef for several years. Time will tell if Callahan can develop his own style in this celebrated food temple, but regulars have generally been pleased with the silky smooth transition. Dinners are prix fixe, with two menus offered, a four-course menu du jour and a five-course menu, both laced with truffles and foie gras and both priced at a king's ransom. ⊠ *648 Bush St.,* ☎ *415/989–7154. Reservations essential. Jacket and tie required. AE, D, DC, MC, V. Closed Sun.–Mon. and 1st 2 wks of Jan. No lunch.*

Italian

$$–$$$ ✗ **Scala's Bistro.** Smart leather-and-wood booths, an extravagant mural along one wall, and an appealing menu of Italian plates make this one of downtown's most attractive destinations. Grilled Portobello mushrooms and a tower of fried calamari or zucchini are among the favorite antipasti, and the pastas and grilled meats are satisfying. ⊠ *432 Powell St.,* ☎ *415/395–8555. AE, D, DC, MC, V.*

Seafood

$$$ ✗ **Farallon.** Outfitted with sculpted purple-and-pink jellyfish lamps,
★ kelp-covered columns, sea urchin chandeliers, and seashell-covered walls, this swanky Pat Kuleto–designed restaurant is loaded with style *and* customers. Chef Mark Franz cooks up exquisite seafood that draws serious diners from coast to coast. Such showy concoctions as spot prawns, scallops, and lobster suspended in a pyramid of aspic are regular fare here. ⊠ *450 Post St.,* ☎ *415/956–6969. AE, DC, MC, V. No lunch Sun.*

Vietnamese

$$–$$$ ✗ **Le Colonial.** Until the mid-'90s, Trader Vic's, a well-known Polynesian-inspired haunt of the city's social elite, occupied this restaurant. In 1998, Le Colonial refurbished the space—stamped-tin ceiling, period photographs, slow-moving fans, tropical plants—creating a 1920s French colonial setting in which to serve its upscale Vietnamese food. The space still draws the local blue bloods, this time for its spring rolls, creamy coconut soup, steamed sea bass, coconut curry prawns, and sticky rice in a lotus leaf. Upstairs, a suave lounge with couches is the ideal place to sip a cocktail before dinner or polish off a nightcap at the end of the evening. ⊠ *20 Cosmo Pl.,* ☎ *415/931–3600. AE, MC, V. Closed Sun. No lunch Sat.*

LODGING

Updated by
Andy Moore

The hotels listed below are on or close to public transportation lines. A few properties on Lombard Street and in the Civic Center area have free parking, while hotels in the Union Square and Nob Hill areas almost invariably charge $17–$26 a day for a spot in their garage. Reservations are always advised, especially during the peak seasons (May–October and December). Weekend rates for double rooms downtown and at the wharf start at about $130 and average over $100 per night citywide (slightly less on weekdays and off-season). Adding to the expense is the city's 14% transient occupancy tax, which can significantly boost the cost of a lengthy stay. For those in search of true budget accommodations (under $60), try the **Adelaide Inn** (☞ Union

Square/Downtown, *below*) or the **YMCA Central Branch** (⊠ 220 Golden Gate Ave., ☎ 415/885–0460).

An alternative to hotels and motels is staying in private homes and apartments, available through **American Family Inn/Bed & Breakfast San Francisco** (⊠ Box 420009, San Francisco 94142, ☎ 415/931–3083, FAX 415/921–2273), **Bed & Breakfast California** (⊠ 205 Park Rd., Suite 209, Burlingame 94010, ☎ 650/696–1690 or 800/872–4500, FAX 650/696–1699), and **American Property Exchange** (⊠ 2800 Van Ness Ave., San Francisco 94109, ☎ 415/447–2040, FAX 415/447–2058).

CATEGORY	COST*
$$$$	over $200
$$$	$120–$200
$$	$80–$120
$	under $80
All prices are for a standard double room, excluding 14% tax.	

Union Square/Downtown

$$$$ ⊡ **Campton Place.** Behind a simple brownstone facade with a white
★ awning, quiet reigns. Highly attentive personal service—from unpacking assistance to nightly turndown—begins the moment uniformed doormen greet guests outside the marble-floor lobby. Rooms, though a little smaller than those at other luxury hotels, are supremely elegant, decorated with Asian touches in light, subtle tones. The Campton Place Restaurant, listed as one of San Francisco's best by *Gourmet* magazine in 1998, is famed for its breakfasts. ⊠ *340 Stockton St., 94108,* ☎ *415/781–5555 or 800/235–4300,* FAX *415/955–5536. 107 rooms, 10 suites. Restaurant, bar, in-room safes, minibars, no-smoking rooms, room service, dry cleaning, concierge, meeting rooms, parking (fee). AE, DC, MC, V.*

$$$$ ⊡ **The Clift.** Towering over San Francisco's theater district is the venerable Clift. In the lobby, dark paneling and enormous chandeliers lend a note of grandeur. Rooms—some rich with dark woods and burgundies, others refreshingly pastel—all have large writing desks. Be sure to sample a cocktail in the dramatic art deco Redwood Room lounge, complete with chandeliers and a sweeping redwood bar. ⊠ *495 Geary St., 94102,* ☎ *415/775–4700 or 800/652–5438,* FAX *415/441–4621. 218 rooms, 108 suites. Restaurant, bar, in-room data ports, minibars, no-smoking floor, room service, exercise room, laundry service and dry cleaning, concierge, meeting rooms, parking (fee). AE, DC, MC, V.*

$$$$ ⊡ **Hotel Monaco.** With its yellow beaux arts facade, the Monaco
★ stands in stark contrast to its more stately neighbor, the Clift. Though small, the rooms are comfortable and inviting, with Chinese-inspired armoires and high-back upholstered chairs. Though the riot of stripes and colors may strike some guests as a bit outré, it's all been done so tastefully you can't help but appreciate the flair. ⊠ *501 Geary St., 94102,* ☎ *415/292–0100 or 800/214–4220,* FAX *415/292–0111. 177 rooms, 24 suites. Restaurant, bar, in-room data ports, in-room safes, minibars, no-smoking rooms, room service, spa, laundry service and dry cleaning, business services, parking (fee). AE, D, DC, MC, V.*

$$$$ ⊡ **Pan Pacific Hotel.** Exotic flower arrangements and elegant Asian touches set this business hotel apart from others. A graceful sculpture, *Joie de Dance,* encircles the fountain in the lobby, where two fireplaces add to the refined atmosphere. Guest rooms feature such business amenities as in-room fax machines and modem lines. Complimentary personal valet service and the hotel's fleet of luxury cars serving as shuttles for guests add to a pampering experience. ⊠ *500 Post St., 94102,* ☎ *415/771–8600 or 800/327–8585,* FAX *415/398–0267. 311 rooms,*

19 suites. Restaurant, bar, lobby lounge, in-room data ports, in-room safes, minibars, no-smoking floors, refrigerators, room service, exercise room, piano, laundry service and dry cleaning, concierge, business services, meeting rooms, parking (fee). AE, D, DC, MC, V.

$$$$ ⚷ **Prescott Hotel.** A gourmet's delight might be the best way to describe
★ this plush hotel, thanks to its partnership with Wolfgang Puck's Postrio. Cuisine-conscious guests can order room service from the restaurant or dine at tables reserved for hotel guests. The Prescott's rooms are traditional in style and decorated in a rich hunter green. ⊠ *545 Post St., 94102,* ☎ *415/563–0303 or 800/283–7322,* 𝖥𝖠𝖷 *415/563–6831. 134 rooms, 30 suites. Restaurant, bar, lobby lounge, in-room data ports, minibars, no-smoking floors, room service, concierge, business services, meeting rooms, parking (fee). AE, D, DC, MC, V.*

$$$$ ⚷ **Westin St. Francis.** With an imposing facade, black-marble lobby, and gold-top columns, the St. Francis looks more like a great public building than a hotel. The effect is softened by the columns and exquisite woodwork of the Compass Rose bar and restaurant, a romantic retreat from the bustle of Union Square. Many rooms in the original building are small by modern standards, but all retain their original Victorian-style moldings and are decorated with Empire-style furnishings. Rooms in the modern tower are larger, with Oriental-style lacquered furniture; ask for a room above the 15th floor for a spectacular view of the city. ⊠ *335 Powell St., 94102,* ☎ *415/397–7000,* 𝖥𝖠𝖷 *415/774–0124. 1,108 rooms, 84 suites. 3 restaurants, 2 bars, in-room data ports, in-room safes, no-smoking floors, room service, exercise room, nightclub, laundry service and dry cleaning, concierge, business services, meeting rooms, travel services, parking (fee). AE, D, DC, MC, V.*

$$$–$$$$ ⚷ **Galleria Park.** A few blocks east of Union Square, this hotel with
★ a black-marble facade is close to the Chinatown Gate and the Crocker Galleria, one of San Francisco's most elegant shopping areas. The staff is remarkably pleasant and helpful. The comfortable rooms all have floral bedspreads, stylish striped wallpaper, and white furniture that includes a writing desk. The third floor rooftop Cityscape Park features an outdoor jogging track. ⊠ *191 Sutter St., 94104,* ☎ *415/781– 3060 or 800/792–9639, 800/792–9855 in CA,* 𝖥𝖠𝖷 *415/433–4409. 162 rooms, 15 suites. 2 restaurants, in-room data ports, minibars, no-smoking floors, room service, exercise room, jogging, laundry and dry cleaning, concierge, business services, meeting rooms, parking (fee). AE, D, DC, MC, V.*

$$$–$$$$ ⚷ **Hotel Rex.** Literary and artistic creativity are celebrated at the stylish
★ Hotel Rex, where thousands of books, largely antiquarian, line the 1920s-style lobby. Original artwork adorns the walls, and the proprietors even host book readings and roundtable discussions in the common areas, which are decorated in warm, rich tones. Striped bedspreads and carpets and restored period furnishings evoke the spirit of 1920s salon society, but rooms also have modern amenities like voice mail and CD players. ⊠ *562 Sutter St., 94102,* ☎ *415/433–4434 or 800/433–4434,* 𝖥𝖠𝖷 *415/433–3695. 92 rooms, 2 suites. Bar, lobby lounge, in-room data ports, minibars, no-smoking rooms, laundry service and dry cleaning, concierge, parking (fee). AE, D, DC, MC, V.*

$$$–$$$$ ⚷ **Hotel Triton.** The hotel caters to fashion, entertainment, music, and film-industry types, who seem to appreciate the iridescent multicolor rooms with S-curve chairs, curly-neck lamps, and oddball light fixtures. On the downside, rooms are uncommonly small; if you care about space, try a king room or junior suite. The trendy newsstand–coffeehouse–dining room Café de la Presse, which serves as a gathering place for foreign visitors to the city, is attached to the hotel. ⊠ *342 Grant Ave., 94108,* ☎ *415/394–0500 or 888/364–2622,* 𝖥𝖠𝖷 *415/394–0555. 133*

160

Downtown San Francisco Lodging

The Abigail, **17**
Adelaide Inn, **21**
The Andrews, **20**
The Archbishop's
Mansion, **15**
The Argent, **55**
Bed and Breakfast
Inn, **5**
Bijou, **48**
Campton Place, **41**
Chancellor Hotel, **39**

The Clift, **34**
Commodore
International, **22**
Coventry Motor
Inn, **12**
Galleria Park, **44**
Golden Gate Hotel, **29**
Grant Plaza Hotel, **45**
Harbor Court, **52**
Hotel Bohème, **49**

Hotel del Sol, **3**
Hotel Diva, **33**
Hotel Majestic, **14**
Hotel Monaco, **35**
Hotel Rex, **30**
Hotel Triton, **53**
The Huntington, **25**
Hyatt at Fisherman's
Wharf, **8**
Hyatt Regency, **47**

Inn at the Opera, **16**
Inn at Union
Square, **38**
King George, **37**
Mandarin Oriental, **50**
The Mansions, **6**
Mark Hopkins
Inter–Continental, **26**
Marriott at
Fisherman's Wharf, **7**

KEY

AE American Express Office

San Francisco Bay

Chestnut St.
Lombard St.
Greenwich St.
Filbert St.
Union St.

TELEGRAPH HILL

NORTH BEACH

Columbus Ave.
Grant Ave.
Front St.
Embarcadero
Davis St.
Drumm St.

Mason St.
Taylor St.
Powell St.
Stockton St.
Kearny St.
Montgomery St.
Sansome St.
Battery St.
Front St.
Davis St.

NOB HILL

CHINATOWN

Halleck St.

NOB HILL

Stewart St.
Spear St.
Main St.
Beale St.
Fremont St.
1st St.
2nd St.

Maiden Ln.

UNION SQUARE

New Montgomery St.
Hawthorne St.
3rd St.

Market St.

Moscone Convention Center

Mission St.
6th St.
5th St.
4th St.
Howard St.
7th St.

TO AIRPORT

80

N

0   440 yards
0   400 meters

Nob Hill Lambourne, **46**
Palace Hotel, **43**
Pan Pacific Hotel, **32**
Park Hyatt, **51**
Petite Auberge, **23**
Phoenix Hotel, **18**
Prescott Hotel, **31**
Radisson Miyako Hotel, **13**

The Ritz–Carlton, San Francisco, **28**
San Francisco Residence Club, **27**
San Remo, **11**
Shannon Court Hotel, **36**
Sherman House, **2**
Sir Francis Drake Hotel, **40**

Town House Motel, **4**
Travelodge Hotel at Fisherman's Wharf, **10**
Tuscan Inn, **9**
Union Street Inn, **1**
W San Francisco, **54**
Westin St. Francis, **42**
White Swan Inn, **24**
York Hotel, **19**

rooms, 7 suites. In-room data ports, minibars, no-smoking floors, exercise room, laundry service and dry cleaning, business services, meeting rooms, parking (fee). AE, D, MC, V.

$$$–$$$$ 🏨 **Inn at Union Square.** With its tiny but captivating lobby with trompe l'oeil bookshelves painted on the walls, this inn feels like someone's home. Comfortable rooms with sumptuous goose-down pillows promote indolence. Guests like to lounge in front of the wood-burning fireplaces found in each floor's tiny sitting area, and with good reason: by the time the staff clears away the afternoon tea and pastries, they're already setting out the complimentary evening wine and hors d'oeuvres. Tips are not accepted, and the hotel is completely no-smoking. ✉ 440 Post St., 94102, ☎ 415/397–3510 or 800/288–4346, FAX 415/989–0529. 30 rooms. In-room data ports, parking (fee). AE, DC, MC, V.

$$$–$$$$ 🏨 **Sir Francis Drake Hotel.** Beefeater-costumed doormen welcome you into the regal lobby, which has wrought-iron balustrades, chandeliers, and Italian marble. The guest rooms have a simpler decor with California-style furnishings and floral-print fabrics. On the top floor, Harry Denton's Starlight Room has been all the rage since its opening in 1995. ✉ 450 Powell St., 94102, ☎ 415/392–7755 or 800/227–5480, FAX 415/395–8559. 394 rooms. 23 suites. 2 restaurants, in-room data ports, minibars, no-smoking rooms, exercise room, nightclub, concierge, meeting rooms, parking (fee). AE, D, DC, MC, V.

$$$–$$$$ 🏨 **York Hotel.** Hitchcock fans may recognize the exterior of this reasonably priced, family-owned hotel four blocks west of Union Square. It's the building where Kim Novak as Judy Barton stayed in Vertigo. Inside, the peach-stone facade and ornate, high-ceiling lobby give the hotel a touch of elegance. The moderate-size rooms are a tasteful mix of Mediterranean styles, with a terra-cotta, burgundy, and forest green color scheme. Continental breakfast is included. ✉ 940 Sutter St., 94109, ☎ 415/885–6800 or 800/808–9675, FAX 415/885–2115. 91 rooms, 5 suites. Bar, in-room data ports, in-room safes, minibars, no-smoking floors, exercise room, nightclub, laundry service, concierge, business services, parking (fee). AE, D, DC, MC, V.

$$$ 🏨 **Chancellor Hotel.** Although not as grand as some of its neighbors, this busy hotel is one of the best buys on Union Square. The moderate-size Edwardian-style rooms have high ceilings and peach and green color schemes; deep bathtubs are a treat. Connecting rooms are available for families, and the Chancellor Café is a handy place for meals. ✉ 433 Powell St., 94102, ☎ 415/362–2004 or 800/428–4748, FAX 415/362–1403. 135 rooms, 2 suites. Restaurant, bar, no-smoking floors, room service, laundry service, concierge, car rental, parking (fee). AE, D, DC, MC, V.

$$$ 🏨 **Hotel Diva.** A gray awning and burnished silver facade give this reasonably priced hotel a slick, high-tech look that sets it apart from others in San Francisco. Although the Diva's proximity to the Curran Theater attracts actors, musicians, and others of an artistic bent, the hotel is also popular with business travelers, who have free access to the tiny business center, and families, who enjoy the in-room Nintendo and VCRs. A complimentary Continental breakfast is delivered to guests' rooms. ✉ 440 Geary St., 94102, ☎ 415/885–0200 or 800/553–1900, FAX 415/346–6613. 79 rooms, 32 suites. Restaurant, in-room data ports, in-room safes, minibars, no-smoking floors, room service, in-room VCRs, exercise room, laundry service and dry cleaning, concierge, business services, meeting room, parking (fee). AE, D, DC, MC, V.

$$$ 🏨 **Shannon Court Hotel.** Passing through the wrought-iron and glass entrance into the marble-tiled lobby of the Shannon Court evokes the old world charm of early 1900s San Francisco. This hotel has some of the most spacious standard rooms in the Union Square area; many have

sofa beds for families. ⊠ *550 Geary St., 94102,* ☎ *415/775–5000 or 800/228–8830,* FAX *415/928–6813. 172 rooms, 4 suites. Restaurant, bar, lobby lounge, no-smoking floor, refrigerators, laundry service and dry cleaning, concierge, parking (fee). AE, D, DC, MC, V.*

$$$ ⊞ **White Swan Inn.** The White Swan has all the comforts of home—personal front-door keys, complimentary soft drinks, and free copies of the *San Francisco Chronicle.* Rooms are large, with dark wood furniture and an English country theme. Each room has a fireplace. The breakfasts (included in the room rate) here are famous. The entire inn is no-smoking. ⊠ *845 Bush St., 94108,* ☎ *415/775–1755 or 800/999–9570,* FAX *415/775–5717. 23 rooms, 3 suites. Breakfast room, in-room data ports, concierge, meeting rooms, parking (fee). AE, MC, V.*

$$–$$$ ⊞ **The Andrews.** Two blocks west of Union Square, this Queen Anne–style abode with a gold and buff facade began its life in 1905 as the Sultan Turkish Baths. Today Victorian antique reproductions, old-fashioned flower curtains with lace sheers, iron bedsteads, and large closets more than make up for the diminutive size of guest rooms (the scrupulously clean bathrooms are even smaller). The buffet-style Continental breakfast is complimentary. ⊠ *624 Post St., 94109,* ☎ *415/ 563–6877 or 800/926–3739,* FAX *415/928–6919. 48 rooms. Restaurant, no-smoking floors, concierge, parking (fee). AE, DC, MC, V.*

$$–$$$ ⊞ **Bijou.** With plush velvet upholstery and rich detailing, this hotel is decorated as a nostalgic tribute to 1930s cinema. The mini lobby theater, Le Petit Theatre Bijou, shows movies from the hotel's collection of 65 San Francisco–themed films to guests. The smallish rooms are named after these films and decorated with black-and-white prints from them. The staff is friendly, but the service is definitely no-frills. ⊠ *111 Mason St., at Eddy St., 94102,* ☎ *415/771–1200 or 800/771–1022,* FAX *415/346–3196. 65 rooms. No-smoking rooms, laundry service, concierge, parking (fee). AE, D, DC, MC, V.*

$$–$$$ ⊞ **Commodore International.** Entering the lobby is like stepping onto the main deck of an ocean liner of yore. Neo-deco chairs look like the backdrop for a film about transatlantic crossings. Steps away is the Titanic Café, where goldfish bowls and bathysphere-inspired lights add to the sea-cruise mood. The fairly large rooms with monster closets are painted in soft yellows and golds. ⊠ *825 Sutter St., 94109,* ☎ *415/ 923–6800 or 800/338–6848,* FAX *415/923–6804. 113 rooms. Restaurant, in-room data ports, no-smoking rooms, nightclub, laundry service and dry cleaning, concierge, parking (fee). AE, D, MC, V.*

$$–$$$ ⊞ **King George.** The staff at the King George has prided itself on service and hospitality since the hotel's opening in 1914, when guest rooms started at $1 a night. Prices have remained relatively low compared with other hotels in the neighborhood. The front desk and concierge staff are adept at catering to their guests' every whim. High tea at the Windsor Tearoom is an authentic English treat. ⊠ *334 Mason St., 94102,* ☎ *415/781–5050 or 800/288–6005,* FAX *415/391–6976. 141 rooms, 2 suites. Tea shop, in-room data ports, safes, no-smoking floors, laundry service and dry cleaning, concierge, business services, meeting rooms, parking (fee). AE, D, DC, MC, V.*

$$–$$$ ⊞ **Petite Auberge.** The dozens of teddy bears in the reception area may seem a bit precious, but the rooms in this re-creation of a French country inn never stray past the mark. Rooms are small, but each has a teddy bear, bright flowered wallpaper, an old-fashioned writing desk, and a much-needed armoire. Most rooms have working fireplaces; the suite has a whirlpool tub. A full breakfast is included. The entire inn is no-smoking. ⊠ *863 Bush St., 94108,* ☎ *415/928–6000 or 800/365–3004,* FAX *415/775–5717. 25 rooms, 1 suite. Breakfast room, parking (fee). AE, DC, MC, V.*

$–$$ 🏨 **Golden Gate Hotel.** Captain Nemo, a 25-pound cat, serves as the unofficial doorman for this homey, family-run B&B three blocks northwest of Union Square. The four-story Edwardian has a yellow and cream facade with black trim, and bay windows front and back. Fourteen rooms have private baths, some with claw-foot tubs. Continental breakfast and afternoon tea and cookies are served in the cozy parlor by a fire. ✉ 775 Bush St., 94108, ☎ 415/392–3702 or 800/835–1118, FAX 415/392–6202. 25 rooms. Lobby lounge, no-smoking floor, parking (fee). AE, DC, MC, V.

$–$$ 🏨 **Grant Plaza Hotel.** Amazingly low rates for this part of town make the Grant Plaza a find for budget travelers wanting to look out their window at the exotic architecture and fascinating street life of Chinatown. The smallish rooms, all with private baths, are very clean and modern. All rooms have electronic locks, voice mail, and satellite TV. ✉ 465 Grant Ave., 94108, ☎ 415/434–3883 or 800/472–6899, FAX 415/434–3886. 72 rooms, 1 suite. Concierge, parking (fee). AE, DC, MC, V.

$ 🏨 **Adelaide Inn.** The bedspreads at this quiet retreat may not match the drapes or carpets, and the floors may creak, but the rooms are sunny, clean, and remarkably cheap. The funky European-style pension hosts many guests from Germany, France, and Italy, making it fun to chat over complimentary coffee and rolls downstairs in the mornings. Baths are shared. ✉ 5 Isadora Duncan Ct., at Taylor St. between Geary and Post Sts., 94102, ☎ 415/441–2474 or 415/441–2261, FAX 415/441–0161. 18 rooms. Breakfast room, refrigerators. AE, MC, V.

Financial District

$$$$ 🏨 **Hyatt Regency.** The gray bunkerlike exterior of the Hyatt Regency, at the foot of Market Street, is an unlikely introduction to the spectacular 17-story atrium lobby within. In addition to a plethora of meeting spaces, it has the Embarcadero Center, with more than 125 shops and restaurants, as its neighbor. The Equinox, San Francisco's only revolving rooftop restaurant, sits atop the hotel. ✉ 5 Embarcadero Center, 94111, ☎ 415/788–1234 or 800/233–1234, FAX 415/398–2567. 745 rooms, 60 suites. 2 restaurants, bar, lobby lounge, no-smoking floors, room service, exercise room, concierge, parking (fee). AE, D, DC, MC, V.

$$$$ 🏨 **Mandarin Oriental.** The Mandarin comprises the top 11 floors (38
★ to 48) of San Francisco's third-tallest building—the First California Center. All rooms provide panoramic vistas of the city and beyond. Rooms are decorated in light creamy yellow with black accents; those in the front tower fill up quickly because of their dramatic ocean views. The Mandarin Rooms in each tower have bathtubs flanked by windows; enjoy a decadent bathing experience with loofah sponges, plush robes, and silk slippers. ✉ 222 Sansome St., 94104, ☎ 415/276–9888 or 800/622–0404, FAX 415/433–0289. 154 rooms, 4 suites. Lobby lounge, in-room data ports, minibars, no-smoking floors, room service, health club, laundry service and dry cleaning, concierge, business services, meeting rooms, parking (fee). AE, D, DC, MC, V.

$$$$ 🏨 **Palace Hotel.** This landmark hotel—former guests include Woodrow Wilson and Amelia Earhart—was the epitome of luxury when it opened in 1875. Today its historic splendor is best seen in the stunning entryway and the belle epoque Garden Court restaurant, with its graceful chandeliers and lead-glass ceiling. After the lavish public spaces, the rooms seem uninspired. ✉ 2 New Montgomery St., 94105, ☎ 415/512–1111, FAX 415/543–0671. 517 rooms, 33 suites. 3 restaurants, bar, room service, health club, laundry service, parking (fee). AE, D, DC, MC, V.

$$$$ ☎ **Park Hyatt.** Contemporary in design meets Old World style at this well-managed property convenient to the waterfront, downtown, and the South of Market area. The good-size rooms are decorated with Australian lacewood, polished granite, stylish furniture, and fresh flowers. Amenities include voice mail and Neutrogena toiletries. Complimentary car service is offered within downtown San Francisco. ✉ *333 Battery St., 94111,* ☎ *415/392–1234 or 800/492–8822,* FAX *415/421–2433. 322 rooms, 38 suites. Restaurant, 2 bars, in-room data ports, minibars, room service, laundry service, dry cleaning, business services, conference center, parking (fee). AE, D, DC, MC, V.*

$$$–$$$$ ☎ **Harbor Court.** This cozy hotel, formerly an Army/Navy YMCA, is
★   noted for the exemplary service of its warm, friendly staff. Some guest rooms overlook the bay. Guests have free access to YMCA facilities (including a 150-ft heated indoor pool). There's also complimentary limousine service to the Financial District. ✉ *165 Steuart St., 94105,* ☎ *415/882–1300 or 800/346–0555,* FAX *415/882–1313. 136 rooms. In-room data ports, minibars, no-smoking floors, room service, laundry service and dry cleaning, business services, parking (fee). AE, D, DC, MC, V.*

South of Market (SoMa)

$$$$ ☎ **W San Francisco.** The city's first newly built hotel in 10 years, the W San Francisco's 31-story tower opened in May 1999, nodding architecturally to two of its neighbors, the landmark Pacific Telephone Building and SFMOMA. Across the street from the Yerba Buena Center for the Arts and Moscone Convention Center, the W's gray facade is trimmed with black granite piping, and its octagonal 3-story glass entrance leads into a lobby decorated—like the entire hotel—in modern high style. Stone, corrugated metal, frosted glass, and other urban-industrial elements are offset by accents of polished mahogany, floor-to-ceiling yellow-green mohair drapes, and broad-striped carpeting. Each guest room has either a cozy corner sitting area or a padded window seat perch overlooking the city. The snugly beds have pillow-top mattresses, goose-down comforters and pillows, and 250-thread count linens. Cordless phones and Aveda bath products are added bonuses. ✉ *181 Third St., 94103,* ☎ *415/626–0777,* FAX *415/817–7848. 418 rooms, 5 suites. Restaurant, bar, café, in-room data ports, in-room safes, minibars, no-smoking floor, refrigerators, room service, in-room VCRs, indoor pool, hot tub, massage, exercise room, laundry service and dry cleaning, concierge, business services, meeting rooms, parking (fee). AE, D, DC, MC, V.*

$$$ ☎ **The Argent.** Rising 36 stories over one of the busiest intersections in the city, the Argent has a luxuriously appointed lobby. The bar and adjacent restaurant overlook a sunny outdoor garden. The guest rooms all feature floor-to-ceiling picture windows with dramatic views of the city. About half of the larger-than-average rooms face south and are especially sunny. They overlook the nearby Yerba Buena Center For The Arts, the Moscone Convention Center, the southeastern part of the city, and the Bay and hills in the distance. The equally scenic rooms on the north side peer through the various tall buildings of the Financial District, old and new, with some glimpsing fragments of the Bay and Alcatraz. ✉ *50 Third St., 94103,* ☎ *415/974–6400 or 877/222–6699,* FAX *415/543–8268. 643 rooms, 24 suites. Restaurant, bar, lobby lounge, in-room data ports, in-room safes, minibars, no-smoking floor, refrigerators, room service, massage, exercise room, piano, laundry service and dry cleaning, concierge, business services, meeting rooms, parking (fee). AE, D, DC, MC, V.*

Nob Hill

$$$$ 🏨 **The Huntington.** The family-owned Huntington provides an oasis of gracious personal service and understated luxury. Rooms and suites, many of which have great views of Grace Cathedral, the bay, or the city skyline, are large because they used to be residential apartments. Most rooms have wet bars, all have large antique desks, and some suites have kitchens. ⊠ *1075 California St., 94108,* ☎ *415/474–5400 or 800/ 227–4683; 800/652–1539 in CA;* FAX *415/474–6227. 101 rooms, 36 suites. Restaurant, bar, in-room data ports, in-room safes, no-smoking rooms, room service, laundry service and dry cleaning, concierge, meeting rooms, parking (fee). AE, D, DC, MC, V.*

$$$$ 🏨 **Mark Hopkins Inter-Continental.** Rooms at this landmark have dramatic neoclassic furnishings of gray, silver, and khaki and bold leaf-print bedspreads; Italian marble lines the bathrooms. (At press time, a renovation of rooms is scheduled, which will include changes in decor.) Rooms on high floors have views of either the Golden Gate Bridge or the downtown cityscape. Be sure to visit the vibrant Top of the Mark, *the* rooftop cocktail lounge in San Francisco since 1939. ⊠ *999 California St., 94108,* ☎ *415/392–3434 or 800/662–4455,* FAX *415/421– 3302. 361 rooms, 30 suites. Restaurant, 2 bars, room service, exercise room, laundry service and dry cleaning, concierge, business services, meeting rooms, car rental, parking (fee). AE, D, DC, MC, V.*

$$$$ 🏨 **The Ritz-Carlton, San Francisco.** Consistently rated one of the top
★ hotels in the world by *Condé Nast Traveler,* the Ritz-Carlton is a stunning tribute to beauty, splendor, and warm, sincere service. Beyond the neoclassic facade, crystal chandeliers illuminate an opulent lobby adorned with Georgian antiques and a collection of museum-quality 18th- and 19th-century paintings. Afternoon tea in the Lobby Lounge is a San Francisco institution. ⊠ *600 Stockton St., at California St., 94108,* ☎ *415/296–7465 or 800/241–3333,* FAX *415/296–8261. 276 rooms, 60 suites. 2 restaurants, bar, lobby lounge, health club, laundry service and dry cleaning, concierge, business services, meeting rooms, parking (fee). AE, D, DC, MC, V.*

$$$ 🏨 **Nob Hill Lambourne.** This urban retreat, designed with the travel-
★ ing executive in mind, takes pride in pampering business travelers with personal computers, fax machines, and personalized voice mail; an on-site spa with massages, body scrubs, manicures, and pedicures helps them relax. Rooms have queen-size beds with hand-sewn mattresses, silk-damask bedding, and contemporary furnishings in muted colors. All rooms have modern kitchenettes and stereos. A deluxe Continental breakfast and evening wine service are complimentary. ⊠ *725 Pine St., at Stockton St., 94108,* ☎ *415/433–2287 or 800/274– 8466,* FAX *415/433–0975. 14 rooms, 6 suites. Lobby lounge, in-room data ports, no-smoking floors, in-room VCRs, spa, business services, parking (fee). AE, D, DC, MC, V.*

$–$$$ 🏨 **San Francisco Residence Club.** In contrast to the neighboring showplace hotels, the Residence Club, once an apartment building, is a humble guest house with million-dollar views and a money-saving meal plan. Though it has a fancy Nob Hill address, the building has seen better days and most of the very modest rooms share baths. Many of the rooms have sweeping views of the city and the bay. A full American breakfast *and* dinner are included in the daily, weekly, or monthly room rate. ⊠ *851 Powell St., 94108,* ☎ *415/421–2220,* FAX *415/421–2335. 84 rooms. Dining room, lobby lounge, coin laundry. No credit cards; $100 advance deposit via check required.*

Fisherman's Wharf/North Beach

$$$–$$$$ 🏨 **Hyatt at Fisherman's Wharf.** Location is the key to this hotel's popularity: it's within walking distance of Ghirardelli Square, the Cannery, Pier 39, Aquatic Park, and docks for Alcatraz ferries and bay cruises. It's also across the street from a cable car turnaround. The moderate-size guest rooms have double-pane windows to keep out the often considerable street noise. ✉ *555 N. Point St., 94133,* ☎ *415/563–1234 or 800/233–1234,* FAX *415/563–2218. 305 rooms, 8 suites. Restaurant, sports bar, in-room data ports, no-smoking floors, room service, pool, outdoor hot tub, health club, coin laundry, meeting rooms, parking (fee). AE, D, DC, MC, V.*

$$$–$$$$ 🏨 **Marriott at Fisherman's Wharf.** Behind an unremarkable sand-color facade, the Marriott strikes a grand note in its lavish, low-ceiling lobby, with marble floors and English club–style furniture. With the Transamerica Pyramid downtown to its left and the Cannery nearby on its right, the hotel is well situated for business and pleasure. ✉ *1250 Columbus Ave., 94133,* ☎ *415/775–7555 or 800/228–9290,* FAX *415/ 474–2099. 273 rooms, 12 suites. Restaurant, bar, no-smoking floors, health club, meeting rooms, parking (fee). AE, D, DC, MC, V.*

$$$–$$$$ 🏨 **Tuscan Inn.** The condolike exterior of the inn—reddish brick with white concrete—gives little indication of the charm of the relatively small, Italian-influenced guest rooms, with their white-pine furniture and floral bedspreads and curtains. Room service is provided by Cafe Pescatore, the Italian seafood restaurant off the lobby. ✉ *425 N. Point St., at Mason St., 94133,* ☎ *415/561–1100 or 800/648–4626,* FAX *415/ 561–1199. 208 rooms, 12 suites. Restaurant, minibars, no-smoking rooms, room service, laundry service and dry cleaning, meeting rooms, parking (fee). AE, D, DC, MC, V.*

$$$ 🏨 **Travelodge Hotel at Fisherman's Wharf.** Occupying an entire city block, this is the only bay-front hotel at Fisherman's Wharf and is known for its reasonable rates: as low as $89 in the off-season. The higher-price rooms on the third and fourth floors have balconies that provide unobstructed views of Alcatraz and overlook a landscaped courtyard and pool. (At press time an extensive renovation was being undertaken; call hotel for updates.) ✉ *250 Beach St., 94133,* ☎ *415/392–6700 or 800/578–7878,* FAX *415/986–7853. 242 rooms, 8 suites. 3 restaurants, no-smoking rooms, pool, parking (fee). AE, D, DC, MC, V.*

$$–$$$ 🏨 **Hotel Bohème.** In the middle of historic North Beach, this little bargain gives guests a taste of the area's bohemian flair. The small rooms, decorated with European armoires, bistro tables, and memorabilia from the 1950s and '60s, recall the beat generation. ✉ *444 Columbus Ave., 94133,* ☎ *415/433–9111,* FAX *415/362–6292. 15 rooms. In-room data ports. AE, D, MC, V.*

$ 🏨 **San Remo.** This three-story, blue-and-white Italianate Victorian
★ just a few blocks from Fisherman's Wharf has reasonably priced rooms and a down-home, slightly faded elegance. The smallish rooms are crowded with furniture: vanities, pedestal sinks, ceiling fans, antique armoires, and brass, iron, or wooden beds. Guests share six black-and-white-tile shower rooms, one bathtub chamber, and six scrupulously clean toilets with brass pull chains and oak tanks. ✉ *2237 Mason St., 94133,* ☎ *415/776–8688 or 800/352–7366,* FAX *415/776–2811. 61 rooms, 1 suite. No-smoking rooms, coin laundry, parking (fee). AE, DC, MC, V.*

Pacific Heights, Cow Hollow, and the Marina

$$$$ 🏨 **Sherman House.** This Italianate mansion at the foot of residential
★ Pacific Heights is San Francisco's most luxurious small hotel. Rooms are individually decorated with Biedermeier, English Jacobean, or

French Second Empire antiques. The decadent mood is enhanced by
tapestrylike canopies over four-poster featherbeds, wood-burning fireplaces with marble mantels, and sumptuous bathrooms, some with whirlpool baths. Room rates include a full breakfast, as well as evening wine
and hors d'oeuvres in an upstairs sitting room. ✉ *2160 Green St., 94123,*
☎ *415/563–3600 or 800/424–5777,* 🖷 *415/563–1882. 8 rooms, 6
suites. Dining room, room service, in-room VCRs, piano, concierge,
airport shuttle. AE, DC, MC, V.*

$$$–$$$$ 🏨 **Union Street Inn.** This ivy-draped 1902 Edwardian is a delightful
★   B&B filled with antiques and unique artwork. Equipped with candles,
fresh flowers, and wine glasses, the rooms here are very popular with
honeymooners. The private Carriage House, which has its own whirl-
pool tub, is separated from the main house by an old-fashioned En-
glish garden complete with lemon trees. An elaborate complimentary
breakfast is served to guests in the parlor, in the garden, or in their rooms.
✉ *2229 Union St., 94123,* ☎ *415/346–0424,* 🖷 *415/922–8046. 6
rooms. Breakfast room, no-smoking rooms, parking (fee). AE, MC,
V.*

$$–$$$ 🏨 **Bed and Breakfast Inn.** This ivy-covered Victorian contains English
country–style rooms full of antiques, plants, and floral paintings.
Though the rooms with shared baths are quite small, they are inex-
pensive at $80 a night. The Mayfair, a private apartment above the
main house, comes complete with a living room, kitchenette, and spi-
ral staircase leading to a sleeping loft. The Garden Suite, a larger, more
deluxe apartment, has a cozy country kitchen, whirlpool bath, and plenty
of room for four guests. ✉ *4 Charlton Ct., at Union St., 94123,* ☎
*415/921–9784. 9 rooms, 5 with bath, 2 apartments. Breakfast room,
parking (fee). No credit cards.*

$$–$$$ 🏨 **Hotel Del Sol.** Once a typical '50s-style motor court, the Hotel Del
Sol has been converted into an anything-but-typical artistic statement
playfully celebrating California's vibrant (some might say wacky) cul-
ture. The sunny courtyard and yellow and blue three-story building
are candy for the eyes. Rooms face boldly striped patios, citrus trees,
and a heated swimming pool and hammock under towering palm
trees. ✉ *3100 Webster St., 94123,* ☎ *415/921–5520 or 877/433–5765,*
🖷 *415/931–4137. 47 rooms, 10 suites. In-room data ports, in-room
safes, no-smoking rooms, pool, sauna, laundry service, concierge, free
parking. AE, D, DC, MC, V.*

$$ 🏨 **Coventry Motor Inn.** Among the many motels on busy Lombard Street,
this is one of the better-built and one of the quietest, especially in the
rooms not facing Lombard. Its handsome oak-paneled lobby has
leather furniture and photographs of historic San Francisco. The unusually spacious rooms—decorated with floral wallpaper and plaid bedspreads—all have well-lit dining/working areas. Many rooms have
bay windows; some on the upper floors have partial views of the
Golden Gate Bridge. ✉ *1901 Lombard St., 94123,* ☎ *415/567–1200,*
🖷 *415/921–8745. 69 rooms. No-smoking floor, free parking. AE, DC,
MC, V.*

$–$$ 🏨 **Town House Motel.** What this family-oriented motel lacks in lux-
ury and ambience, it makes up for in value: the simple rooms, most
with refrigerators, are nicely furnished with a Southwestern pastel
color scheme and lacquered-wood furnishings. Continental breakfast
in the lobby is complimentary. ✉ *1650 Lombard St., 94123,* ☎ *415/
885–5163 or 800/255–1516,* 🖷 *415/771–9889. 24 rooms. No-smoking rooms, airport shuttle, free parking. AE, D, DC, MC, V.*

Civic Center/Van Ness

$$$–$$$$ 🏨 **The Archbishop's Mansion.** Everything at the Archbishop's Mansion
★   is extravagantly romantic, starting with the cavernous common areas,
where a chandelier used in the movie *Gone With the Wind* hangs
above a 1904 Bechstein grand piano once owned by Noël Coward. The
15 guest rooms are individually decorated with intricately carved an-
tiques; many have Jacuzzi tubs or fireplaces. Though not within easy
walking distance of many restaurants or attractions, its perch on the
corner of Alamo Square near the Painted Ladies—San Francisco's fa-
mous Victorian homes—makes for a scenic, relaxed stay. ✉ *1000 Ful-
ton St., 94117,* ☎ *415/563–7872 or 800/543–5820,* FAX *415/885–
3193. 10 rooms, 5 suites. Breakfast room, lobby lounge, no-smoking
rooms, in-room VCRs, piano, meeting room, limited free parking.
AE, MC, V.*

$$$–$$$$ 🏨 **The Mansions.** An arresting combination of funky elegance and ec-
centricity, the Mansions is a lavish place that will delight some, but
possibly annoy others with its gimmickry. Fresh flowers and antique
furniture decorate the rooms, which vary in theme from the suppos-
edly haunted Coit to the grander Presidential and Josephine suites.
Housed in a twin-turret 1887 Queen Anne, the hotel's minimuseums
display historic documents and—as an indulgence to resident ghost Clau-
dia's predilection for pigs—various "porkabilia." Rates include a full
breakfast and a campy magic show. ✉ *2220 Sacramento St., 94115,*
☎ *415/929–9444,* FAX *415/567–9391. 15 rooms, 6 suites. Breakfast
room, dining room, billiards, laundry service, parking (fee). AE, DC,
MC, V.*

$$$–$$$$ 🏨 **Radisson Miyako Hotel.** This pagoda-style hotel is popular with busi-
ness travelers. Some guest rooms are in the tower building; others are
in the garden wing, which has a traditional Japanese garden with a wa-
terfall. Japanese-style rooms have futon beds with tatami mats, while
Western rooms have traditional beds with mattresses—but all feature
gorgeous Asian furniture and original artwork. Most have their own
soaking rooms with a bucket and stool and a Japanese tub (1 ft deeper
than Western tubs), and in-room shiatsu massages are available. ✉ *1625
Post St., at Laguna St., 94115,* ☎ *415/922–3200 or 800/533–4567,*
FAX *415/921–0417. 209 rooms, 9 suites. Restaurant, bar, in-room data
ports, minibars, exercise room, laundry service and dry cleaning, busi-
ness services. AE, D, DC, MC, V.*

$$$ 🏨 **Hotel Majestic.** One of San Francisco's original grand hotels, this
five-story white 1902 Edwardian surrounds you with elegance. Most
of the romantic guest rooms have gas fireplaces, a mix of French and
English antiques, and either a large, hand-painted, four-poster canopied
bed or two-poster bonnet twin beds; some have original claw-foot bathtubs. ✉ *1500 Sutter St., 94109,* ☎ *415/441–1100 or 800/869–8966,*
FAX *415/673–7331. 51 rooms, 9 suites. Restaurant, bar, laundry service and dry cleaning, parking (fee). AE, DC, MC, V.*

$$$ 🏨 **Inn at the Opera.** Behind the marble-floor lobby are rooms of var-
★   ious sizes, decorated with creamy pastels and dark-wood furnishings.
The bureau drawers are lined with sheet music, and every room is out-
fitted with terry-cloth robes, a microwave oven, a minibar, and a bas-
ket of apples. All rooms have queen-size beds, though the standard rooms
are a bit cramped. Continental breakfast is included in the room rate.
✉ *333 Fulton St., 94102,* ☎ *415/863–8400 or 800/325–2708; 800/
423–9610 in CA;* FAX *415/861–0821. 30 rooms. Restaurant, lobby
lounge, room service, concierge, parking (fee). AE, DC, MC, V.*

$$ 🏨 **The Abigail.** This hotel, a former B&B, retains its distinctive atmosphere with an eclectic mix of faux-stone walls, a faux-marble front
desk, and an old-fashioned telephone booth in the lobby. Hissing

steam radiators, down comforters, and antiques complete the mood. ✉ *246 McAllister St., 94102,* ☎ *415/861–9728 or 800/243–6510,* FAX *415/861–5848. 60 rooms, 1 suite. Restaurant, laundry service and dry cleaning, parking (fee). AE, D, DC, MC, V.*

$$ ⛛ **Phoenix Hotel.** From the piped-in, poolside jungle music to the aquatic-themed ultrahip Backflip restaurant and lounge immersed in shimmering hues of blue and green, the Phoenix evokes the tropics—or at least a fun, kitschy version of it. Although probably not the place for a traveling executive seeking peace and quiet—or anyone put off by its location on the fringes of the seedy Tenderloin District—the Phoenix does boast a list of celebrity guests, including such big-name bands as R.E.M. and Pearl Jam. ✉ *601 Eddy St., 94109,* ☎ *415/776–1380 or 800/248–9466,* FAX *415/885–3109. 41 rooms, 3 suites. Restaurant, bar, room service, pool, massage, nightclub, laundry service, free parking. AE, D, DC, MC, V.*

The Airport

Because they cater primarily to midweek business travelers, airport hotels often cut weekend prices. Airport shuttle buses and a full complement of services are provided by all of the following hotels.

$$$$ ⛛ **Hotel Sofitel–San Francisco Bay** (✉ 223 Twin Dolphin Dr., Redwood City 94065, ☎ 650/598–9000 or 800/763–4835, FAX 650/598–0459). ⛛ **The Westin** (✉ 1 Old Bayshore Hwy., Millbrae 94030, ☎ 650/692–3500 or 800/228–3000, FAX 650/872–8111).

$$$–$$$$ ⛛ **Embassy Suites San Francisco Airport–Burlingame** (✉ 150 Anza Blvd., Burlingame 94010, ☎ 650/342–4600 or 800/362–2779, FAX 650/343–8137). ⛛ **Hyatt Regency San Francisco Airport** (✉ 1333 Bayshore Hwy., Burlingame 94010, ☎ 650/347–1234, FAX 650/696–2669).

$$–$$$ ⛛ **The Clarion** (✉ 401 E. Millbrae Ave., Millbrae 94030, ☎ 650/692–6363 or 800/223–7111, FAX 650/697–8556). ⛛ **La Quinta Motor Inn** (✉ 20 Airport Blvd., South San Francisco 94080, ☎ 650/583–2223 or 800/531–5900, FAX 650/589–6770).

$–$$ ⛛ **Red Roof Inn** (✉ 777 Airport Blvd., Burlingame 94010, ☎ 650/342–7772 or 800/843–7663, FAX 650/342–2635).

NIGHTLIFE AND THE ARTS

Updated by
Denise M. Leto

A spirit of playfulness has pervaded San Francisco's arts, entertainment, and nightlife scenes ever since its days as a rowdy sailors' port. Perhaps nothing is more purely San Franciscan than *Beach Blanket Babylon* at Club Fugazi, a hilarious cabaret that parodies local moods and mores. In addition, the San Francisco Opera, the San Francisco Symphony, and the San Francisco Ballet are all nationally renowned, while dozens of alternative groups represent everything from gay and lesbian performance art to family circus and mime.

Nightlife

For information on who is performing where, check out the *San Francisco Chronicle*'s pink "Datebook" insert—or consult the *San Francisco Bay Guardian,* free and available in racks around the city, listing neighborhood, avant-garde, and budget-priced events. The *S.F. Weekly* is also free and packed with information on arts events around town. For a phone update on musical and cultural events, call the **Convention and Visitors Bureau's Events Hotline** (☎ 415/391–2001).

Rock, Pop, Folk, and Blues

Bottom of the Hill (✉ 1233 17th St., at Texas St., ☎ 415/621–4455) showcases some of the city's best local alternative rock. **The Fillmore**

(✉ 1805 Geary Blvd., at Fillmore St., ☎ 415/346–6000), San Francisco's most famous rock music hall, serves up a varied menu of national and local acts: rock, reggae, grunge, jazz, folk, acid house, and more. **Freight and Salvage Coffee House** (✉ 1111 Addison St., Berkeley, ☎ 510/548–1761), one of the finest folk houses in the country, is worth a trip across the bay. **Great American Music Hall** (✉ 859 O'-Farrell St., between Polk and Larkin Sts., ☎ 415/885–0750) hosts top-drawer entertainment, with acts running the gamut from the best in blues, folk, and jazz to alternative rock. **Justice League** (✉ 628 Divisadero St., near Hayes St., ☎ 415/289–2038) offers live jazz, hip-hop, and world grooves, as well as DJ-driven dance nights. **Red Devil Lounge** (✉ 1695 Polk St., at Clay St., ☎ 415/921–1695) is a trendy supper club featuring local and up-and-coming live funk, rock, and jazz acts. **Slim's** (✉ 333 11th St., near Folsom St., ☎ 415/522–0333) specializes in national touring acts—mostly classic rock, blues, and jazz. **The Warfield** (✉ 982 Market St., at 6th St., ☎ 415/775–7722) is one of the city's largest rock-and-roll venues.

Jazz

Blue Bar (✉ 501 Broadway, ☎ 415/981–2233) finds thirty- and fortysomethings lounging in funky aqua armchairs around Formica tables. **Bruno's** (✉ 2389 Mission St., at 19th St., ☎ 415/550–7455) is a slice of retro heaven in the Mission District. Huge red booths provide a comfy place to order swanky cocktails and listen to jazz, swing, and retro bands. **Cafe du Nord** (✉ 2170 Market St., at Sanchez St., ☎ 415/861–5016) hosts some of the coolest jazz, blues, and alternative sounds in town. **Elbo Room** (✉ 647 Valencia St., between 17th and 18th Sts., ☎ 415/552–7788) is a convivial spot to hear up-and-coming jazz acts upstairs, or to relax in the dark, moody bar downstairs. **Enrico's** (✉ 504 Broadway, at Kearny St., ☎ 415/982–6223) was the city's hippest North Beach hangout after its 1958 opening. Today it's hip once again, with an indoor/outdoor café and mellow nightly jazz combos. **Jazz at Pearl's** (✉ 256 Columbus Ave., near Broadway, ☎ 415/291–8255) is one of the few reminders of North Beach's heady beatnik days. With mostly straight-ahead jazz acts and dim lighting, this club has a mellow feel.

Kimball's East (✉ 5800 Shellmound St., Emeryville, ☎ 510/658–2555), in an East Bay shopping complex just off Highway 80, hosts such talents as Jeffrey Osborne, Tito Puente, and Mose Allison. This supper club features an elegant interior and fine food. **Up and Down Club** (✉ 1151 Folsom St., between 7th and 8th Sts., ☎ 415/626–2388), a hip restaurant and club, books emerging jazz artists downstairs and offers dancing to a DJ upstairs every day except Sunday. **Yoshi's** (✉ 510 Embarcadero St., Oakland, ☎ 510/238–9200) is one of the area's best jazz venues.

Cabarets

Club Fugazi (✉ 678 Green St., at Powell St., ☎ 415/421–4222) is most famous for *Beach Blanket Babylon,* a wacky musical send-up of San Francisco moods and mores that has run since 1974. Although the choreography is colorful, the singers brassy, and the songs witty, the real stars are the comically exotic costumes and famous ceiling-high "hats." Order tickets as far in advance as possible.

The Marsh (✉ 1062 Valencia St., near 22nd St., ☎ 415/826–5750) books an eclectic mix of alternative and avant-garde theater, performance art, comedy, and the occasional musical acts. **New Orleans Room** (✉ 950 Mason St., at California St., ☎ 415/772–5259), in the Fairmont Hotel, has a somewhat tacky 1960s hotel-bar ambience. Still, it's a low-key place to enjoy a cocktail along with show tunes by the pianist. **Plush**

Room (✉ 940 Sutter St., ☎ 415/885–2800), in the York Hotel, began in the 1920s as a speakeasy. The luster may have faded a bit, but the 120-seat room still books some excellent talent.

Dance Clubs

DNA Lounge (✉ 375 11th St., near Harrison St., ☎ 415/626–1409), a longtime, two-floor SoMa haunt, headlines alternative rock, funk, and hip-hop, as well as weekly theme nights. **El Rio** (✉ 3158 Mission St., at Precita St., ☎ 415/282–3325) is a casual Mission District spot with salsa dancing on Sunday (from 4 PM), lounge music from around the world on Tuesday, Arab dance on Thursday, a global dance party on Friday, and live rock starting at 9 PM on weekends. **Hi-Ball Lounge** (✉ 473 Broadway, ☎ 415/397–9464), a small, unpretentious North Beach club, is the place where the swing set gathers to jump and twist to live bands. Patrons sip swanky cocktails and swing until they sweat every night. **Metronome Ballroom** (✉ 1830 17th St., at De Haro St., ☎ 415/252–9000) is at its most lively on weekend nights, when ballroom, Latin, and swing dancers come for lessons and revelry at this alcohol-free spot.

Piano Bars

Ovation (✉ 333 Fulton St., near Franklin St., ☎ 415/553–8100), in the Inn at the Opera Hotel, is a popular spot for a romantic fireside rendezvous. **Grand Views** (✉ 345 Stockton St., at Sutter St., ☎ 415/398–1234), on the top floor of the Grand Hyatt, offers piano music Monday through Saturday from 8 PM and a view of North Beach and the bay. **Redwood Room** (✉ 495 Geary St., near Taylor St., ☎ 415/775–4700), in the Clift Hotel, is an art deco lounge with a low-key but sensuous ambience. **Ritz-Carlton Hotel** (✉ 600 Stockton St., at Pine St., ☎ 415/296–7465) has a tastefully appointed lobby lounge where a harpist plays during high tea. At 5:30, the lounge shifts to piano or a jazz trio for cocktails until 11 PM weeknights and 1 AM on weekends.

Skyline Bars

Carnelian Room (✉ 555 California St., at Kearny St., ☎ 415/433–7500), on the 52nd floor of the Bank of America Building, has what is perhaps the loftiest view of San Francisco's magnificent skyline. Enjoy dinner or cocktails at 779 ft above the ground; reservations are a must for dinner. **Crown Room** (✉ 650 Mason St., at California St., ☎ 415/772–5131), the aptly named lounge on the 23rd floor of the Fairmont Hotel, is one of the most luxurious of the city's skyline bars. **Harry Denton's Starlight Room** (✉ 450 Powell St., ☎ 415/395–8595), on the 21st floor of the Sir Francis Drake Hotel, re-creates the 1950s high life with rose velvet booths, romantic lighting, and staff clad in tuxes or full-length gowns. **Top of the Mark** (✉ 999 California St., at Mason St., ☎ 415/392–3434), in the Mark Hopkins Hotel, was immortalized by a famous magazine photograph as a hot spot for World War II servicemen on leave or about to ship out.

Singles Bars

Balboa Cafe (✉ 3199 Fillmore St., at Greenwich St., ☎ 415/921–3944) is a jam-packed hangout for the young and upwardly mobile crowd. **Harry Denton's** (✉ 161 Steuart St., near the Embarcadero, ☎ 415/882–1333), one of San Francisco's liveliest, most upscale saloons, is packed with well-dressed young professionals. **Holding Company** (✉ 2 Embarcadero Center, at Front and Clay Sts., ☎ 415/986–0797), one of the most popular Financial District watering holes, is where scores of office workers gather to enjoy friendly libations—open weekdays only. **Perry's** (✉ 1944 Union St., at Laguna St., ☎ 415/922–9022), the most famous of San Francisco's singles bars, is usually jam-packed.

Wine Bars

Eos Restaurant and Wine Bar (✉ 901 Cole St., at Carl St., ☎ 415/566–3064) has hundreds of wines—many available by the glass. **Hayes and Vine** (✉ 377 Hayes St., at Gough St., ☎ 415/626–5301) is dominated by a stunning white-onyx bar, where patrons relax and taste a few of the 550 wines available by the bottle, or the 40 selections served by the glass.

San Francisco's Favorite Bars

Bix (✉ 56 Gold St., off Montgomery St., ☎ 415/433–6300), a North Beach institution, is yet another place credited with the invention of the martini. **Buena Vista Café** (✉ 2765 Hyde St., at Beach St., ☎ 415/474–5044), the wharf area's most popular bar, introduced Irish coffee to the New World—or so they say. **Cypress Club** (✉ 500 Jackson St., at Columbus Ave., ☎ 415/296–8555) is an eccentric restaurant-bar where sensual, '20s-style opulence clashes with Fellini/Dalì frivolity. **Specs'** (✉ 12 Saroyan Pl., off Columbus Ave., ☎ 415/421–4112), a hidden hangout for artists and poets, is worth looking for. **The Tonga Room** (✉ 950 Mason St., at California St., ☎ 415/772–5278), on the Fairmont Hotel's terrace level, has given San Francisco a beloved taste of high Polynesian kitsch for over 50 years. **Vesuvio Café** (✉ 255 Columbus Ave., at Broadway, ☎ 415/362–3370), near the legendary City Lights Bookstore, is little altered since its 1960s heyday.

Gay and Lesbian Nightlife

LESBIAN BARS

Blondies' Bar and No Grill (✉ 540 Valencia St., near 16th St., ☎ 415/864–2052) plays host to "Red," a diverse all-women's night every Sunday. **Club Q** (✉ 177 Townsend St., at 3rd St., ☎ 415/647–8258), a monthly (first Friday of every month) dance party is geared to "women and their friends." **CoCo Club** (✉ 139 8th St., entrance on Minna St., ☎ 415/626–2337) offers a a drag cabaret, a coed erotic cabaret, and a woman's speakeasy. Every other Friday is "In Bed with Fairy Butch," an all-women's dance night. **G Spot** (✉ 401 6th St., at Harrison St., ☎ 415/337–4962), at SoMa's End Up club, features Top 40, house, and R&B every Saturday from 9 PM. **Hollywood Billiards** (✉ 61 Golden Gate Ave., near Taylor St., ☎ 415/252–2419) has become the unlikely host of a smoldering lesbian scene every Wednesday during its ladies' night. **The Lexington Club** (✉ 3464 19th St., at Lexington St., ☎ 415/863–2052) is geared toward the younger lesbian set.

GAY MALE BARS

Alta Plaza Restaurant & Bar (✉ 2301 Fillmore St., at Clay St., ☎ 415/922–1444) caters to nattily dressed guppies (gay yuppies) and their admirers. **The Metro** (✉ 3600 16th St., at Market St., ☎ 415/703–9750) is a semi-upscale bar with a balcony overlooking the intersection of Noe, 16th, and Market streets. **Midnight Sun** (✉ 4067 18th St., at Castro St., ☎ 415/861–4186) has riotously programmed giant video screens. **N Touch** (✉ 1548 Polk St., at Sacramento St., ☎ 415/441–8413), a tiny dance bar, has long been popular with Asian–Pacific Islander gay men. **The Stud** (✉ 399 9th St., at Harrison St., ☎ 415/252–7883) is still going strong after more than 30 years. Its DJs mix up-to-the-minute music with carefully chosen highlights from the glory days of gay disco. **The Swallow** (✉ 1750 Polk St., at Clay St., ☎ 415/775–4152), for those tired of the young and the buff, is a quiet, posh bar that caters to an older clientele.

The Arts

Half-price, same-day tickets to many local and touring stage shows go on sale (cash only) at 11 AM from Tuesday through Saturday at the **TIX**

Bay Area (☎ 415/433–7827) booth, on the Stockton Street side of Union Square, between Geary and Post streets. TIX is also a full-service ticket agency for theater and music events around the Bay Area (open Tuesday, Wednesday, and Thursday from 11 AM until 6 PM and Friday and Saturday until 7 PM).

The city's charge-by-phone ticket service is **BASS** (☎ 415/776–1999 or 510/762–2277), with one of its centers in the TIX booth (☞ *above*) and another at Tower Records (✉ Bay St. at Columbus Ave., ☎ 415/885–0500), near Fisherman's Wharf. **City Box Office** (✉ 153 Kearny St., Suite 401, ☎ 415/392–4400) has a downtown charge-by-phone service for many concerts and lectures.

Theater

The most venerable commercial theater is the **Curran** (✉ 445 Geary St., ☎ 415/551–2000). The **Golden Gate** is a stylishly refurbished movie theater (✉ Golden Gate Ave. at Taylor St., ☎ 415/551–2000), now primarily a musical house. The gorgeously restored 2,500-seat **Orpheum** (✉ 1192 Market St., near the Civic Center, ☎ 415/551–2000) is used for the biggest touring shows. The city's major nonprofit theater company is the **American Conservatory Theater (ACT).** The ACT ticket office is at 405 Geary Street (☎ 415/749–2228). Next door to ACT is its home, the **Geary Theater.**

The leading producer of new plays is the **Magic Theatre** (✉ Bldg. D, Fort Mason Center, Laguna St. at Marina Blvd., ☎ 415/441–8822). **Marines Memorial Theatre** (✉ 609 Sutter St., at Mason St., ☎ 415/771–6900) offers touring shows plus some local performances. The **Lorraine Hansberry Theatre** (✉ 620 Sutter St., ☎ 415/474–8800) specializes in plays by black writers. The **Asian American Theatre Company** (✉ 1840 Sutter St., ☎ 415/440–5545) is dedicated to working with local actors. **Theatre Rhinoceros** (✉ 2926 16th St., ☎ 415/861–5079) showcases gay and lesbian performers. The **San Francisco Shakespeare Festival** (☎ 415/422–2222) offers free weekend performances from Labor Day through October in Golden Gate Park.

The major avant-garde presenting organizations are **Theatre Artaud** (✉ 450 Florida St., in the Mission District, ☎ 415/621–7797) and the **Yerba Buena Center for the Arts** (✉ 3rd and Howard Sts., ☎ 415/978–2787).The **Berkeley Repertory Theatre** (☎ 510/845–4700) performs an adventurous mix of classics and new plays from fall to spring in a modern, intimate theater at 2025 Addison Street. Tickets are available at the TIX booth in San Francisco's Union Square. **California Shakespeare Festival** (☎ 510/548–9666), the Bay Area's largest outdoor summer theater event, performs in an amphitheater east of Oakland on Gateway Boulevard, just off state Highway 24.

Music

The **San Francisco Symphony** (✉ Davies Symphony Hall, 201 Van Ness Ave., at Grove St., ☎ 415/864–6000) performs from September through May under the direction of Michael Tilson Thomas. The **Berkeley Symphony Orchestra** (✉ Zellerbach Hall, Telegraph Ave. and Bancroft Way, UC Berkeley campus, ☎ 510/841–2800) has risen to considerable prominence under artistic director Kent Nagano's baton. **Cal Performances** (✉ Zellerbach Hall, Bancroft Way and Telegraph Ave., Berkeley, ☎ 510/642–9988) runs from August through June, offering the Bay Area's most varied bill of internationally acclaimed artists in all disciplines. **Chanticleer,** (✉ ☎ 415/896–5866) an all-male a cappella ensemble, is a Bay Area treasure. **Stern Grove,** (✉ Sloat Blvd. at 19th Ave., ☎ 415/252–6252) the nation's oldest continual free summer music festival, hosts Sunday afternoon performances of symphony, opera, jazz, pop music, and dance.

Opera

The **San Francisco Opera** (✉ 301 Van Ness Ave., at Grove St., ☎ 415/864–3330) presents approximately 70 performances of 10 operas from September through December and June through July.

Dance

The **San Francisco Ballet** (✉ 301 Van Ness Ave., ☎ 415/865–2000) has regained much of its luster under artistic director Helgi Tomasson, and both classical and contemporary works have won admiring reviews. The company's primary season runs from February through May. The annual December presentation of the *Nutcracker* is spectacular.

OUTDOOR ACTIVITIES AND SPORTS

Beaches

Updated by
Denise M. Leto

Baker Beach is a local favorite, with gorgeous views of the Golden Gate Bridge, the Marin Headlands, and the bay. Its strong waves make swimming a dangerous prospect, but the mile-long shoreline is ideal for fishing, building sand castles, or watching sea lions. On warm days the entire beach is packed with bodies (some nude) taking in the sun. ✉ *In the Presidio, at the end of Gibson Rod., off Bowley St.*

China Beach was named for the poor Chinese fishermen who once camped here. From April through October the tiny strip of sand offers swimmers gentle waters as well as changing rooms and showers. ✉ *In the Seacliff district: take 25th Ave. north to Scenic Way west to Seacliff Ave.*

South of the Cliff House, **Ocean Beach** stretches along the western (ocean) side of San Francisco. It's wide and sandy, stretching for miles. Swimming is not recommended, though it's popular with surfers. ✉ *Great Hwy. south of Balboa St.*

Participant Sports

For a listing of running races, tennis tournaments, bicycle races, and other participant sports, check the monthly issues of *City Sports* magazine, available free at sporting goods stores, tennis centers, and other recreational sites. The most important running event of the year is the *San Francisco Examiner*'s **Bay-to-Breakers race** (☎ 415/512–5000, ext. 2222) on the third Sunday in May. The **San Francisco Marathon & 5K** (☎ 415/296–7111) is held annually on the second Sunday in July.

Bicycling

With its legendary hills, the city offers countless cycling challenges—but also plenty of level ground. A completely flat route, the **Embarcadero** gives you a clear view of open waters and the Bay Bridge on the pier side and sleek high rises on the other. **Golden Gate Park** has paths throughout.

Boating and Sailing

A Day on the Bay (☎ 415/922–0227) is in San Francisco's small craft marina, minutes from the Golden Gate Bridge and open waters. **Cass' Marina** (✉ 1702 Bridgeway, at Napa St., ☎ 415/332–6789), in Sausalito, has a variety of sailboats that can be rented as long as you have a qualified sailor in the group. **Stow Lake** (☎ 415/752–0347), in Golden Gate Park, has rowboat, pedal boat, and electric boat rentals.

Fishing

Fishing boats leave from San Francisco, Sausalito, Berkeley, Emeryville, and Point San Pablo. They go for salmon and halibut outside the bay or striped bass and giant sturgeon within the bay. Lines can be cast from San Francisco Municipal Pier, Fisherman's Wharf, Baker Beach, or Aquatic Park. Trout fishing is possible at Lake Merced. Rent rods and boats and buy bait at the **Lake Merced Boating and Fishing Company** (⊠ 1 Harding Rd., ☏ 415/753–1101). One-day **licenses,** good for ocean fishing only, are available for around $10 on the charters. Most depart daily from Fisherman's Wharf during the salmon-fishing season, which is from March through October. **Lovely Martha's Sportfishing** (⊠ Fisherman's Wharf, Berth 3, ☏ 650/871–1691) offers salmon-fishing excursions as well as bay tours. **Wacky Jacky** (⊠ Fisherman's Wharf, Pier 45, ☏ 415/586–9800) will take you salmon fishing in a sleek, fast, and comfortable 50-ft boat.

Fitness

The various branches of **24-Hour Fitness** (⊠ 1200 Van Ness Ave., ☏ 415/776–2200; ⊠ 350 Bay St., ☏ 415/395–9595; ⊠ 3741 Buchanan St., ☏ 415/563–3535; ⊠ 100 California St., ☏ 415/434–5080; ⊠ 303 2nd St., at Folsom St., ☏ 415/543–7808) are open to the public for a $15 drop-in fee. Most of the clubs have saunas, Jacuzzis, and steam rooms as well as aerobics classes and a complete line of fitness equipment. The **Embarcadero YMCA** (⊠ 169 Steuart St., ☏ 415/957–9622) has racquetball, a 25-m swimming pool, and aerobics classes. The $12 drop-in fee includes use of the sauna, steam room, and whirlpool.

Golf

Call the **golf information line** (☏ 415/750–4653) to get detailed directions to the city's public golf courses or to reserve a tee time ($1 per player) up to seven days in advance. **Harding and Fleming parks** (⊠ Harding Rd. and Skyline Blvd., ☏ 415/664–4690) have an 18-hole, par-72 course and a 9-hole executive course, respectively. **Lincoln Park** (⊠ 34th Ave. and Clement St., ☏ 415/221–9911) has an 18-hole, par-68 course. **Golden Gate** (⊠ 47th Ave. between Fulton St. and John F. Kennedy Dr., ☏ 415/751–8987) is a 9-hole, par-27 course in Golden Gate Park just above Ocean Beach. The **Presidio Golf Course** (⊠ 300 Finley Rd., near W. Pacific Ave. and Arguello Blvd., ☏ 415/561–4653) is an 18-hole, par-72 course managed by Arnold Palmer's company.

Tennis

The San Francisco Recreation and Park Department maintains 132 public tennis courts throughout the city. All courts are free except those in Golden Gate Park. At **Mission Dolores Park** (⊠ 18th and Dolores Sts.) six courts are available on a first-come, first-served basis. The 16 courts in **Golden Gate Park** (☏ 415/753–7001) are the only public ones for which you can make advance reservations. The fee for visitors is $6 for 90 minutes weekdays and $8 weekends; the resident fees are $4 and $6, respectively.

Spectator Sports

Baseball

The **San Francisco Giants** play at 3Com Park at Candlestick Point (⊠ U.S. 101 at 3Com Park exit, 3 mi south of downtown, ☏ 415/467–8000 or 800/734–4268). Pacific Bell Park, a new downtown bay-front stadium, is scheduled to open in April 2000. Game-day tickets are usually available at 3Com. City shuttle buses marked BALLPARK EXPRESS run from numerous bus stops throughout San Francisco; call **Muni** (☏ 415/673–6864) for the stop nearest you. The **Oakland A's** play at the Oakland Coliseum (⊠ Coliseum Way off I–880, ☏ 510/638–0500 or

510/762–2255). Same-day tickets can usually be purchased at the stadium. To reach the Oakland Coliseum, take a BART train to the Coliseum stop.

Basketball

The **Golden State Warriors** play NBA basketball at the Oakland Coliseum Arena (⊠ Coliseum Way off I–880) from November through April. Tickets are available through **BASS** (☎ 510/762–2277).

Football

The **San Francisco 49ers** play at 3Com Park (⊠ U.S. 101 at 3Com Park exit, 3 mi south of downtown), but the games are almost always sold out far in advance (☎ 415/468–2249). The **Oakland Raiders** play at the Oakland Coliseum (⊠ Coliseum Way off I–880). Tickets (☎ 510/762–2277) are usually available.

SHOPPING

Updated by
Denise M. Leto

From fringe fashions in the Haight to leather chaps in the Castro, San Francisco's many distinctive neighborhoods offer consumers a bit of everything. There are ginseng health potions in Chinatown, antiques in Jackson Square, and handmade kimonos in Japantown. For those who prefer the mainstream, Union Street's boutiques and Union Square's department stores beckon.

Major Shopping Districts

The Castro/Noe Valley

Often called the gay capital of the world, the Castro is filled with clothing boutiques, home accessory stores, and various specialty stores. **Under One Roof** (⊠ 2362-B Market St., ☎ 415/252–9430), housed in the same building as the Names Project, donates the profits from its home and garden items, gourmet foods, bath products, books, frames, and cards to northern California AIDS organizations.

Just south of the Castro on 24th Street, largely residential Noe Valley is an enclave of gourmet food stores, used record and CD shops, clothing boutiques, and specialty gift stores.

Chinatown

Racks of Chinese silks, toy trinkets, colorful pottery, baskets, and carved figurines are displayed chockablock on the sidewalks, alongside fragrant herb shops. The **Great China Herb Co.** (⊠ 857 Washington St., ☎ 415/982–2195), where they add up the bill on an abacus, is one of the biggest herb stores around.

Embarcadero Center

Five modern towers of shops, restaurants, offices, and a popular movie theater—plus the Hyatt Regency Hotel—make up the Embarcadero Center, downtown at the end of Market Street.

Fisherman's Wharf

Pier 39, the Anchorage, Ghirardelli Square, and the Cannery are all here, each with shops and restaurants, as well as outdoor entertainment—musicians, mimes, and magicians.

The Haight

Haight Street is a perennial attraction for visitors, if only to see the sign at Haight and Ashbury streets—the geographic center of the Flower Power movement during the 1960s. In addition to ubiquitous tie-dyed shirts, you'll find vintage clothing, funky jewelry, folk art from around the world, and reproductions of art deco accessories. Used-book stores and used-record stores are another specialty.

Hayes Valley

Hayes Valley, just west of the Civic Center, is packed with art galleries and unusual stores.

Jackson Square

Gentrified Jackson Square is home to a dozen or so of San Francisco's finest retail antiques dealers, many of which occupy elegant Victorian-era buildings.

Japantown

The 5-acre **Japan Center** (between Laguna and Fillmore Sts. and Geary Blvd. and Post St.) is under one roof. Especially worthwhile are the Kintetsu and Kinokuniya buildings, where shops and showrooms sell cameras, tapes and records, pearls, antique kimonos, *tansu* chests, paintings, and more.

The Marina District

Chestnut Street, one block north of Lombard Street and stretching from Fillmore to Broderick streets, caters to the shopping whims of Marina District residents, many of whom go for specialty foodstuffs.

The Mission

The diverse Mission District, home to large Latino and Asian populations, plus young artists and musicians of all nations, draws bargain hunters with its many used clothing, vintage furniture, and alternative book stores. Shoppers can unwind with a cup of *café con leche* at one of a dozen or so cafés.

North Beach

Sometimes compared to New York City's Greenwich Village, North Beach is only a fraction of the size, clustered tightly around Washington Square and Columbus Avenue. Most of its businesses are small eateries, cafés, and shops selling clothing, antiques, and vintage wares. Once the center of the beat movement, North Beach still has a bohemian spirit.

Pacific Heights

Pacific Heights residents head straight for Fillmore Street between Post Street and Pacific Avenue, and Sacramento Street between Lyon and Maple streets, where private residences alternate with good bookstores, fine clothing and gift shops, thrift stores, and art galleries.

South of Market

The gritty warehouse and semi-industrial zone south of Market, often called SoMa, has the lowest prices. Dozens of **discount outlets,** most open daily, have sprung up along the streets and alleyways bordered by 2nd, Townsend, Howard, and 10th streets. At the other end of the spectrum are the high-class gift shops of the **San Francisco Museum of Modern Art** and the **Center for the Arts Gift Shop** at Yerba Buena Gardens; both sell handmade jewelry and other great gift items.

Union Square

Serious shoppers head straight to Union Square, San Francisco's main shopping area and the site of most department stores, including Macy's, Neiman Marcus, and Saks Fifth Avenue. Also here are the Virgin Megastore, F. A. O. Schwarz, the Disney Store, and Borders Books and Music, along with the boutiques of Emporio Armani, Versace, Gucci, Louis Vuitton, and Cartier.

The **San Francisco Shopping Centre** (⊠ 865 Market St., ☎ 415/495–5656), across from the cable car turnaround at Powell and Market streets, is distinguished by spiral escalators that wind up through the sunlit atrium. Inside are more than 35 retailers, including Nordstrom.

Union Street

Out-of-towners sometimes confuse Union Street with Union Square. Nestled at the foot of a hill between Pacific Heights and the Marina District, the street is lined with high-end clothing, antiques, and jewelry shops, along with a few art galleries.

SIDE TRIPS FROM SAN FRANCISCO

Sausalito and Tiburon

Sausalito

Updated by
Chris Baty and
Sharon Silva

Like much of San Francisco, Sausalito had a raffish reputation before it went upscale. Discovered in 1775 by Spanish explorers and named Sausalito (Little Willow) for the trees growing around its springs, the town served as a port for whaling ships during the 19th century. By the mid-1800s wealthy San Franciscans were making Sausalito their getaway across the bay. They built lavish Victorian summer homes in the hills, many of which still stand today. Sausalito tilted bohemian in the 1950s and '60s. Since then Sausalito has also become a major yachting center, and restaurants attract visitors for fresh seafood as well as spectacular views. The town remains friendly and casual, although summer traffic jams can fray nerves. If possible, visit on a weekday—and take the ferry.

Snaking between the bay and the hills is **Bridgeway,** Sausalito's main thoroughfare, crowded with shops, restaurants, and people. South on Bridgeway, an esplanade along the water is lined with restaurants on piers, all with picture-perfect views of the bay.

The **Village Fair** (✉ 777 Bridgeway, ☎ 415/332–1902) is a four-story former warehouse that's been converted into a warren of clothing, crafts, and gifts boutiques.

The U.S. Army Corps of Engineers uses the **Bay Model,** a 400-square-ft replica of the entire San Francisco Bay and the San Joaquin–Sacramento River delta, to reproduce the rise and fall of tides, the flow of currents, and the other physical forces at work on the bay. The model is housed in a former World War II shipyard building. At the same site is the *Wapama,* a hulking World War I–era steam freighter being restored by volunteers. ✉ *2100 Bridgeway, at Marinship Way,* ☎ *415/ 332–3871.* ☞ *Free.* ☉ *Labor Day–Memorial Day, Tues.–Sat. 9–4; Memorial Day–Labor Day, Tues.–Fri. 9–4 and weekends 10–6.*

Some of the 400 **houseboats** that make up Sausalito's floating homes community line the shore of Richardson Bay. The sight of these colorful, quirky abodes is one of Marin County's most famous views. For a close-up view of the houseboats, head north on Bridgeway from downtown, turn right on Gate 6 Road, and park where it dead-ends at the public shore.

☺ The **Bay Area Discovery Museum** fills five former military buildings with entertaining and enlightening hands-on exhibits. From San Francisco take the Alexander Avenue exit from U.S. 101 and follow signs to East Fort Baker. ✉ *557 McReynolds Rd., at East Fort Baker,* ☎ *415/ 487–4398.* ☞ *$7.* ☉ *Summer, Tues.–Sun. 10–5; fall–spring, Tues.–Thurs. 9–4 and Fri.–Sun. 10–5.*

Dining and Lodging

$$$ ✕ **Mikayla at Casa Madrona.** Although the food at this longtime Sausalito hilltop dining room has followed a rocky course, the view is superb. The California menu is based on grilled fish and meats treated

The Bay Area

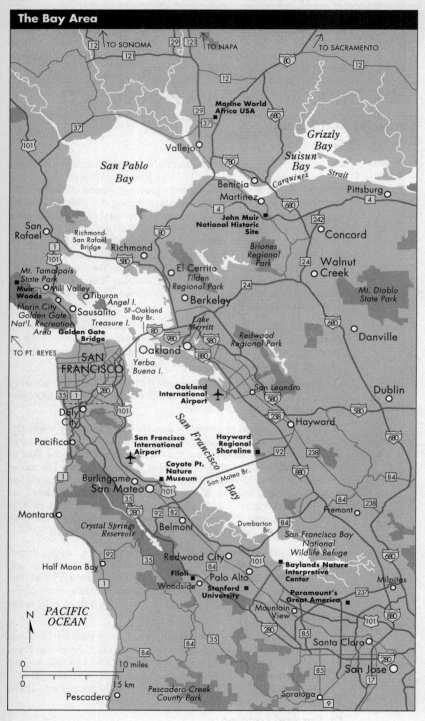

TO SONOMA

TO NAPA

TO SACRAMENTO

Marine World
Africa USA

Vallejo

San Pablo Bay

Grizzly Bay

Suisun Bay

Carquinez Strait

Benicia

Martinez

Pittsburg

Concord

John Muir
National Historic
Site

San
Rafael

Richmond-
San Rafael
Bridge

Richmond

El Cerrito

*Briones
Regional
Park*

Walnut
Creek

*Tilden
Regional Park*

*Mt. Tamalpais
State Park*

Muir
Woods

Mill Valley

Tiburon

Angel I.

Berkeley

*Mt. Diablo
State Park*

Marin City

Sausalito

Treasure I.

SF-Oakland
Bay Br.

*Golden Gate
Nat'l. Recreation
Area*

Golden Gate
Bridge

Lake
Merritt

*Redwood
Regional Park*

Danville

TO PT. REYES

SAN
FRANCISCO

*Yerba
Buena I.*

Oakland

Dublin

Daly
City

Oakland
International
Airport

San Leandro

Pacifica

San Francisco
International
Airport

Hayward
Regional
Shoreline

Hayward

San Francisco Bay

Montara

Coyote Pt.
Nature
Museum

Burlingame

San Mateo

San Mateo Br.

Belmont

Crystal Springs
Reservoir

Dumbarton
Br.

*San Francisco Bay
National
Wildlife Refuge*

Fremont

Half Moon Bay

Redwood City

Filoli

Palo Alto

Woodside

Stanford
University

Baylands Nature
Interpretive
Center

Milpitas

*PACIFIC
OCEAN*

Paramount's
Great America

N

Mountain
View

Santa Clara

San Jose

0   10 miles

0   15 km

Pescadero

*Pescadero Creek
County Park*

Saratoga

simply but elegantly. The Sunday buffet brunch is popular. ⊠ *801 Bridgeway,* ☎ *415/331–5888. Reservations essential weekends. AE, D, DC, MC, V. No lunch.*

$$ ✕ **Alta Mira.** This Sausalito landmark, in a Spanish-style hotel a block above Bridgeway, has spectacular views of the bay. It's a favored destination for Sunday brunch, lunch, or cocktails at sunset. The California-Continental cuisine is forgettable, but the view never fails. ⊠ *125 Bulkley Ave.,* ☎ *415/332–1350. AE, DC, MC, V.*

$$ ✕ **Spinnaker.** Spectacular bay views are the prime attraction in this contemporary building on a point beyond the harbor near the yacht club—but diners can fuel up on a passable menu of homemade pastas and various seafood specialties as they gaze out at the remarkable scene. ⊠ *100 Spinnaker Dr.,* ☎ *415/332–1500. AE, DC, MC, V.*

$–$$ ✕ **Christophe.** The early bird dinners at this charming French dining room are a penny pincher's delight. A four-course meal costs no more than two admissions to a first-run movie, and the choices include such irresistible plates as duck confit, lamb fillet with port wine sauce, and chocolate profiteroles. Prices rise reasonably as the night goes on. ⊠ *1919 Bridgeway,* ☎ *415/332–9244. MC, V. Closed Mon. No lunch.*

$ ✕ **Lighthouse Café.** This inexpensive coffee shop serves breakfast and lunch—omelets, sandwiches, and burgers—every day from 6:30 (7 on weekends). Most find the down-to-earth atmosphere and simple fare a welcome break from tourist traps and seafood extravaganzas. ⊠ *1311 Bridgeway,* ☎ *415/331–3034. Reservations not accepted. No credit cards.*

$$$ 🏨 **Hotel Sausalito.** Soft yellow, green, and orange tones create a warm, Mediterranean feel at this well-run inn decorated with handmade furniture and tasteful original art and reproductions. The rooms, some of which have harbor or park views, range from small ones that are good for budget-minded travelers to commodious suites. Continental breakfast is included. ⊠ *16 El Portal,* ☎ *415/332–0700 or 888/442-0700,* ℻ *415/332–8788. 14 rooms, 2 suites. In-room data ports, no-smoking rooms, concierge. 2-night minimum on weekends. AE, DC, MC, V.*

Tiburon

On a peninsula called Punta de Tiburon (Shark Point) by the Spanish explorers, this beautiful Marin County community maintains a villagelike atmosphere despite the ever-growing encroachment of commercial establishments concentrated in the downtown area. The harbor faces Angel Island across Raccoon Strait, and San Francisco is directly south, 6 mi across the bay. The ferry is the most relaxing way to visit and avoid traffic and parking problems.

Tiburon's **Main Street** is lined on the bay side with restaurants with outdoor decks that jut out over the harbor, giving diners a bird's-eye view of San Francisco. On the other side of the narrow street are shops and galleries.

At the end of the block, Main Street turns into **Ark Row,** a tree-shaded walk lined with antiques and specialty stores. **Windsor Vineyards** (⊠ 72 Main St., ☎ 415/435–3113) has free tastings in a converted 19th-century rooming house.

In a wildlife sanctuary on the route into Tiburon is the 1876 **Lyford House,** a Victorian fantasy complete with period decor and furniture. Visitors to the house should make a point of sticking around for the Audubon Society's program on area birds, held on the grounds; call in advance for specific times. ⊠ *376 Greenwood Beach Rd., off Tiburon Blvd.,* ☎ *415/388–2524.* 🎫 *Suggested $2 donation.* ☉ *Nov.-Apr., Sun. 1–4.*

Dining

$$–$$$ ✗ **Tutto Mare Ristorante.** With stunning views of the bay, Tutto Mare is a bustling outpost of Italian cuisine. A wood-burning oven ensures crisp-crust pizzas, and the kitchen turns out grilled fish, meats, and fowl, and house-made pastas. Although the food and service can be inconsistent, the view is guaranteed to satisfy. ✉ *9 Main St.,* ☎ *415/435–4747. AE, DC, MC, V.*

$$ ✗ **Guaymas.** This festive Mexican restaurant claims a knockout view of the bay, whitewashed adobe walls, tile floors, and a heated terrace bar. The large open kitchen churns out a long list of authentic Mexican dishes. Sunday brunch is popular, so reserve in advance. ✉ *5 Main St., at the ferry terminal,* ☎ *415/435–6300. DC, MC, V.*

$ ✗ **Sam's Anchor Cafe.** Sam's is a major draw for tourists and old salts who flock to its outside deck for bay views and beer. A college hangout since 1921, the informal restaurant has mahogany wainscoting and old photos on the walls. Burgers, sandwiches, soups, and salads are standards, but the food pales next to the atmosphere here. ✉ *27 Main St.,* ☎ *415/435–4527. AE, D, DC, MC, V.*

Sausalito and Tiburon Essentials

ARRIVING AND DEPARTING

By Bus: Golden Gate Transit buses (☎ 415/923–2000) travel to Sausalito and Tiburon from 1st and Mission streets and from other points in San Francisco. The trip takes 45 minutes one-way.

By Car: Take U.S. 101 north across the Golden Gate Bridge. For Sausalito, take the first exit, Alexander Avenue, just past Vista Point; follow signs to Sausalito and then go north on Bridgeway to the municipal parking lot near the center of town. For Tiburon, exit at Tiburon Boulevard. Both trips take from 30 to 45 minutes one-way, depending on traffic.

By Ferry: The **Golden Gate Ferry** (☎ 415/923–2000) crosses the bay to Sausalito from the south wing of the Ferry Building at Market Street and the Embarcadero; the trip takes 30 minutes. **Blue and Gold Fleet** ferries (☎ 415/705–5555) depart daily for Sausalito and Tiburon from Pier 41 at Fisherman's Wharf. Commuter ferries also depart to Tiburon weekdays only from the Ferry Building. The trip to Sausalito takes 30 minutes. Direct ferries travel to Tiburon in 20 minutes, but those making multiple stops can take up to an hour.

The East Bay

Berkeley

Although the **University of California** dominates Berkeley's history and contemporary life, the university and the town are not synonymous. The city of 100,000 facing San Francisco across the bay has other interesting attributes. More than fifty **cafés** surround the campus, without which the city might very well collapse. Students, faculty, and other Berkeley residents spend hours nursing coffee concoctions of various persuasions while they read, discuss, and debate.

Numbers in the text correspond to numbers in the margin and on the Berkeley map.

❶ The **U.C. Berkeley Art Museum** houses works spanning five centuries, with an emphasis on contemporary art. Changing exhibits line the spiral ramps and balcony galleries. Don't miss the series of vibrant paintings by abstract expressionist Hans Hofmann. On the ground floor, the **Pacific Film Archive** offers programs of historic and contemporary films. ✉ *2626 Bancroft Way,* ☎ *510/642–0808; 510/642–1124 for film-*

Lawrence Hall
of Science, **3**
Tilden Park, **4**
U.C. Berkeley
Art Museum, **1**
U.C. Botanical
Garden, **2**

program information. ☎ *$6.* ☉ *Wed. and Fri.–Sun. 11–5, Thurs. 11–
9.*

❷ More than 13,500 species of plants from all over the world flourish
in the 34-acre **U.C. Botanical Garden**—thanks to Berkeley's temperate
climate. Tours are given weekends at 1:30. ✉ *Centennial Dr.,* ☎ *510/
642-3343.* ☎ *$3.* ☉ *Daily 9–4:45.*

☪ ❸ The fortresslike **Lawrence Hall of Science,** a dazzling hands-on science
center, lets kids look at insects under microscopes, solve crimes using
chemical forensics, and explore the physics of baseball. On clear Saturday nights the museum sets up telescopes on its outdoor plaza for
the popular Saturday Night Stargazing from 8 to 11. ✉ *Centennial Dr.,*
☎ *510/642-5132.* ☎ *$6.* ☉ *Daily 10–5.*

❹ **Tilden Park** (☎ 510/562-7275), an oasis in the midst of the city, has
a botanical garden, an 18-hole golf course, and an environmental education center. You'll find paths and picnic sites on its 2,000 acres. Both
kids and kids at heart will love the park's miniature steam trains, pony
rides, and the vintage menagerie-style carousel. ✉ *Off Grizzly Peak
Blvd.*

Dining and Lodging

$$–$$$$ ✕ **Chez Panisse Café & Restaurant.** The famed Alice Waters remains
★ the mastermind behind the culinary wizardry at this legendary eatery.
In the downstairs restaurant, where formality and personal service cre-
ate the ambience of a private club, the daily-changing menu is prix fixe
and pricey. Upstairs in the café the atmosphere is informal, the crowd
livelier, the prices lower, and both an à la carte and a fixed menu are
in force. The food is simpler, too: penne with new potatoes, arugula,
and sheep's milk cheese; and grilled tuna with savoy cabbage. ✉ *1517
Shattuck Ave., north of University Ave.,* ☎ *510/548-5525 for restau-*

rant; 510/548–5049 for café. Reservations essential for restaurant. AE, D, DC, MC, V. Closed Sun.

$$ × **Lalime's.** The Mediterranean food served in this charming, flower-covered house is a favorite of Berkeleyites. Choices can range from grilled ahi tuna to creamy Italian risotto to seared duck foie gras. ⊠ *1329 Gilman St.,* ☎ *510/527–9838. Reservations essential. MC, V. No lunch.*

$$$$ 🛏 **Claremont Hotel.** Straddling the Oakland–Berkeley border, the Clare-
★   mont Hotel beckons like a gleaming white castle in the hills. Travel-ing executives come for the business amenities, including 40 rooms outfitted with computer terminals, T-1 Internet connections, and guest E-mail addresses. The Claremont also shines for leisure travelers with its luxurious suites, therapeutic massages, and personalized yoga work-outs at the on-site spa. ⊠ *41 Tunnel Road, at Ashby and Domingo Aves., 94705,* ☎ *510/843–3000 or 800/551–7266,* FAX *510/848–6200. 282 rooms. 3 restaurants, 2 bars, in-room data ports, no-smoking floors, in-room VCRs, 2 pools, spa, dry cleaning, concierge, meeting rooms, parking (fee). AE, D, DC, MC, V.*

$$$ 🛏 **Hotel Durant.** Long the mainstay of parents visiting their children at U.C. Berkeley, the Hotel Durant is a good option for those who want to be a short walk from campus and from the restaurants and shops of Telegraph Avenue. Rooms, accented with dark woods and stately plaids, are small without feeling cramped. ⊠ *2600 Durant Ave., 94704,* ☎ *510/845–8981,* FAX *510/486–8336. 140 rooms. Restaurant, bar, no-smoking rooms, room service, laundry service and dry cleaning, busi-ness services, meeting rooms, parking (fee). AE, D, DC, MC, V.*

Oakland

Oakland's allure lies in its amazing diversity. Only here can you find a Nigerian clothing store, a beautifully renovated Victorian home, a Buddhist meditation center, and a lively salsa club, all within the same block. Oakland's multifaceted nature reflects its colorful and often tu-multuous history. Once a cluster of Mediterranean-style homes and gar-dens that served as a bedroom community for San Francisco, the city became a hub of shipbuilding and industry almost overnight when the United States entered World War II. In the '60s and '70s this intense community pride gave rise to such militant groups as the Black Pan-ther Party and the Symbionese Liberation Army but was little match for the economic hardships and racial tensions that plagued Oakland. In many neighborhoods the reality was widespread poverty and gang violence.

Today Oakland is a mosaic of its past. Affluent types have once again flocked to the city's hillside homes, while a constant flow of new res-idents—many from Central America and Asia—ensures continued di-versity, vitality, and growing pains. Many neighborhoods to the west and south of downtown remain run-down, but a renovated downtown area and the thriving Jack London Square have injected new life into the city. Some areas, like Piedmont and Rockridge, are perfect places for browsing, eating, or just relaxing between sightseeing trips to Oak-land's architectural gems, rejuvenated waterfront, and numerous green spaces.

Numbers in the text correspond to numbers in the margin and on the Oakland map.

★ ❶ One of Oakland's top attractions, the **Oakland Museum of California** is an inviting series of landscaped buildings that display the state's art, history, and natural wonders. The museum is the best possible intro-duction to a tour of California. ⊠ *1000 Oak St., at 10th St.,* ☎ *510/ 238–3401.* 🎟 *$6.* ☉ *Wed.–Sat. 10–5, Sun. noon–5.*

❷ A proud reminder of the days when Oakland was a wealthy bedroom community, the **Camron-Stanford House** exudes dignity from its foundation up to its ornate widow's walk. Built in 1876, the Victorian served as the home of the Oakland Museum from 1910 to 1967, and a room containing documents and original artifacts chronicles the museum's history. Six painstakingly redecorated period rooms occupy the upper floor. ⊠ *1418 Lakeside Dr.,* ☎ *510/836–1976.* ⊒ *$4.* ☼ *Wed. 11–4 and Sun. 1–5.*

❸ **Lake Merritt** is a 155-acre oasis surrounded by parks, with several outdoor attractions on its north side. Joggers and power-walkers charge along the 3-mi path that encircles the lake.

❹ On the north shore of Lake Merritt, the **Rotary Nature Center and Waterfowl Refuge** is the nesting site of herons, egrets, geese, and ducks in the spring and summer. Migrating birds pass through from September through February, and visitors can watch the birds being fed daily at 3:30 year-round. ⊠ *Perkins St.,* ☎ *510/238–3739.* ☼ *Daily 10–5.*

★ **❺** The **Paramount Theatre** (⊠ 2025 Broadway, ☎ 510/465–6400), perhaps the most glorious example of Art Deco architecture in the city if not all the Bay Area, remains open and operating as a venue for concerts and performances of all kinds.

❻ **Preservation Park** is a surprisingly idyllic little business community made up of 14 restored Victorians with tidy, bright green lawns. Wooden benches surrounding a bubbling fountain provide an excellent place to enjoy the architecture and a brief respite from the busy city center.

❼ A former resident of Oakland, writer Jack London spent many a day boozing and brawling in the waterfront area now called **Jack London Square** (⊠ Embarcadero at Broadway, ☎ 510/814–6000), home to shops, restaurants, small museums, and historic sites. **Heinold's First**

and Last Chance Saloon (✉ 56 Jack London Sq., ☎ 510/839–6761) was one of London's old haunts.

The upscale neighborhood of **Rockridge** is one of Oakland's most desirable places to live. Explore the tree-lined streets that radiate out from College Avenue just north and south of the BART station for a look at California bungalow architecture at its finest. **College Avenue** is the main shopping strip here. The hub of College Avenue life is **Market Hall** (✉ 5655 College Ave., ☎ 510/652–4680), an airy European-style marketplace where eight specialty food shops offer everything from Napa Valley wines to organic produce.

East Bay Essentials

ARRIVING AND DEPARTING

By Car: Take I–80 east across the Bay Bridge. For Berkeley, take the University Avenue exit through downtown Berkeley to the campus or take the Ashby Avenue exit and turn left on Telegraph Avenue to the traditional campus entrance. For Oakland, take I–580 off the Bay Bridge to the Grand Avenue exit for Lake Merritt. To reach downtown and the waterfront, take I–980 from I–580 and exit at 12th Street. Both trips take about 30 minutes, longer during rush hour.

By Train: BART trains (☎ 415/992–2278) make stops in downtown Berkeley and in several parts of Oakland. Use the Lake Merritt station for the Oakland Museum and southern Lake Merritt, the Oakland City Center–12th Street station for downtown, and the 19th Street station for the Paramount Theater and the north side of Lake Merritt. From the Berkeley (not North Berkeley) station it's a five-minute walk on Center Street to the western edge of campus. Both trips take from 30 to 45 minutes one-way.

The Inland Peninsula

Palo Alto

Updated by
Amy
McConnell

Stanford University has its roots among the peninsula's estates. Originally the property was former California governor Leland Stanford's farm for breeding horses. Free one-hour **walking tours** leave daily at 11 and 3:15 from the Visitor Information Center (☎ 650/723–2560 or 650/723–2053) in front of Memorial Hall on Serra Street.

★ After a 10-year closure for structural repairs necessitated by the 1989 earthquake, the Stanford Museum, now named the **Iris and B. Gerald Cantor Center for Visual Arts** is bigger and better than ever. Works span the centuries as well as the globe, from pre-Columbian to modern, including the world's largest collection of Rodin sculptures outside of Paris, many of them displayed in the outdoor sculpture garden. Other highlights include a bronze Buddha from the Ming dynasty, wooden masks and carved figurines from 18th- and 19th-century Africa, paintings by Georgia O'Keeffe, and sculpture by Willem de Kooning. ✉ *Lomita Dr. and Museum Way, off Palm Dr. at Stanford University,* ☎ *650/723–4177.* ☞ *Free.* ☉ *Wed.–Sun. 11–5, Thurs. until 8. Rodin Sculpture Garden tours Sat. 11, Sun. 3.*

For a look at some less-traditional art, seek out the inconspicuous **Papua New Guinea Sculpture Garden,** tucked into a small, heavily wooded plot of land. The garden is filled with tall, ornately carved wooden poles, drums, and carved stones—all created on location by 10 artists from Papua New Guinea who spent six months here in 1994. ✉ *Santa Teresa St. and Lomita Dr.* ☞ *Free.*

Dining and Lodging

$$$-$$$$ ✕ **Spago.** The fare is inventive Californian and the service flawless at Wolfgang Puck's splashy, dashing Spago. Flat breads, bread sticks, whole wheat bread, and a loaf made of scallions and pine nuts will tide you over until the first course arrives. Dinner might include barbecued free-range squab with herbed risotto and caramelized fennel or tamarind-glazed rack of lamb. ✉ *265 Lytton Ave.,* ☎ *650/833–1000. Reservations essential. AE, D, DC, MC, V. No lunch weekends.*

$$$ ✕ **Zibibbo.** This lively restaurant's eclectic menu includes selections from
★   an oak-fired oven, rotisserie, grill, and oyster bar. Service is family-style, with large platters placed in the center of the table—all the better to taste just a bite of the skillet-roasted mussels, leg of lamb with chick-pea-and-tomato tagine, and more. The two-story Victorian house is full of nooks and crannies. ✉ *430 Kipling St.,* ☎ *650/328–6722. AE, DC, MC, V.*

$ ✕ **Pasta?** All the pastas here cost less than $7. What's more, it's very good food—nothing fancy, but made with fresh seasonal ingredients and presented with care. A handful of meat and fish entrées are priced well below $10. ✉ *326 University Ave.,* ☎ *650/328–4585. MC, V.*

$$$$ ☷ **Garden Court Hotel.** From the outside, this stylish boutique hotel
★   looks like an Italian villa, complete with columns and arches, a dormer roof, and balconies dressed up with bougainvillea. The tasteful, sun-light-filled rooms each have a two- or four-poster bed with comforter. Every room has a private terrace looking out on a beautiful central court-yard. ✉ *520 Cowper St., 94301,* ☎ *650/322–9000 or 800/824–9028,* FAX *650/324–3609. 62 rooms. Restaurant, bar, in-room data ports, room service, in-room VCRs, exercise room, laundry service, concierge, business services. AE, D, DC, MC, V.*

$$$-$$$$ ☷ **The Victorian on Lytton.** Only a block from downtown Palo Alto, this inn caters to business travelers who want comfort and amenities without teddy bears and lace. Breakfast is brought to your room in the morning. ✉ *555 Lytton Ave., 94301,* ☎ *650/322–8555,* FAX *650/ 322–7141. 10 rooms. No-smoking rooms. AE, MC, V.*

Woodside

One of the few great country houses in California that remains intact in its original setting is **Filoli,** in Woodside. Built between 1915 and 1917 for wealthy San Franciscan William B. Bourn II, it was designed by Willis Polk in a Georgian Revival style. The name is Bourn's acronym for "fight, love, live." As interesting to visitors as the house—once the setting of the television series *Dynasty*—are the 16 acres of formal gardens. The gardens rise south from the mansion to take advantage of the natural surroundings of the 700-acre estate and its vistas. Among the designs are a sunken garden. In the middle of it all is a charming teahouse de-signed in the Italian Renaissance style. From June through September Filoli hosts a monthly series of Sunday afternoon jazz concerts. ✉ *Cañada Rd. near Edgewood Rd.,* ☎ *650/364–2880.* ☎ *$10.* ☉ *Mid-Feb.–Oct., Tues.–Sat. for guided and self-guided tours. Reservations essential for guided tours.*

Inland Peninsula Essentials

ARRIVING AND DEPARTING

By Car: The most pleasant direct route down the peninsula is I–280, the Junipero Serra Freeway, which passes along Crystal Springs Reser-voir. For Stanford University, exit at Sand Hill Road and drive east. Turn right on Arboretum Drive, then right again on Palm Drive, which leads to the center of campus. U.S. 101, also known as the Bayshore Freeway, is more direct but also more congested; from there take Uni-versity Avenue or Embarcadero Road west to Stanford. For Woodside take the Woodside Road exit and drive west.

By Train: CalTrain (☎ 800/660–4287) runs from 4th and Townsend streets to Palo Alto ($4 each way); from there take the free **Marguerite shuttle bus** (☎ 650/723–9362) to the Stanford campus and the Palo Alto area. Buses run about every 15 minutes 6 AM–8 PM and are timed to connect with trains and public transit buses.

THE SOUTH BAY

Updated by
Lotus Abrams

The South Bay contains old-fashioned neighborhoods, abundant green hills, and the prestigious corporate corridors of Silicon Valley. The world's high-tech capital is wonderfully multifaceted, with some of the Bay Area's finest restaurants and shops. No longer a nondescript suburb of San Francisco, San Jose and its environs have grown up and blossomed into a lively metropolis.

San Jose

In the last few years San Jose's downtown has become a major destination for entertainment, arts, nightlife, and sports. At the same time, major technology-based companies have set up shop here. Strikingly modern architecture coexists with restored 19th-century Victorians and mission-style buildings. Downtown can be easily explored on foot, with side trips by light-rail, but you'll need a car to get to outlying communities and sights like the Egyptian Museum and the Winchester Mystery House.

Numbers in the text correspond to points of interest on the Downtown San Jose map.

❹ Cathedral Basilica of St. Joseph. The Renaissance-style cathedral, built in 1877, is completely restored and has extraordinary stained-glass windows and murals. The multidome cathedral occupies the site where a small adobe church served the first residents of the Pueblo of San Jose in 1803. ✉ *90 S. Market St.,* ☎ *408/283–8100.*

❶ Children's Discovery Museum. An angular purple building across the creek from the convention center at the rear of the Discovery Meadow park, the museum exhibits interactive installations on science, the humanities, and the arts. ✉ *180 Woz Way, at Auzerais St.,* ☎ *408/298–5437.* ▨ *$6.* ☽ *Tues.–Sat. 10–5, Sun. noon–5.*

★ Egyptian Museum and Planetarium. Owned by the Rosecrucian Order, the museum exhibits the West Coast's largest collection of Egyptian and Babylonian antiquities, including mummies and an underground replica of a rock tomb. The museum's entrance is a reproduction of the Avenue of Ram Sphinxes from the Temple at Karnak in Egypt. The planetarium offers programs like the popular "Celestial Nile," which describes the significant role astrology played in ancient Egyptian myths and religions. ✉ *1342 Naglee Ave., at Park Ave.,* ☎ *408/947–3636.* ▨ *$7 museum, $4 planetarium.* ☽ *Daily 10–5, planetarium weekdays only.*

❻ Fallon House. San Jose's seventh mayor, Thomas Fallon, built this Victorian mansion in 1855. The house's period-decorated rooms can be viewed on a 90-minute tour that includes the Peralta Adobe and a screening of a video about the two houses. Tickets are sold beside the Fallon House at the City Store gift shop. ✉ *175 W. St. John St.,* ☎ *408/993–8182.* ▨ *$6 (includes admission to Peralta Adobe).* ☽ *Guided tours Tues.–Sun. noon–5.*

❷ Guadalupe River Park. This downtown park includes the Arena Green, next to the sports arena, with a carousel, children's playground, and

Cathedral
Basilica of St.
Joseph, **4**
Children's
Discovery
Museum, **1**
Fallon
House, **6**
Guadalupe
River Park, **2**
Peralta
Adobe, **7**
San Jose
Museum of
Art, **3**
Tech Museum
of Innovation, **5**

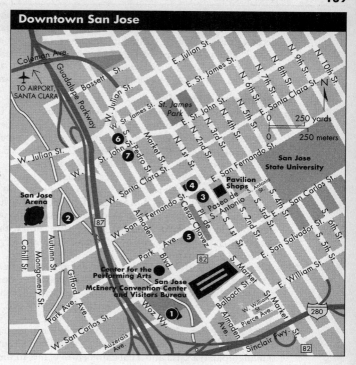

Downtown San Jose

artwork honoring five champion figure skaters from the area. The River Park path starts at the Children's Discovery Museum and runs north, ending at the Arena Green. ⊠ *W. Santa Clara St. and Woz Way.*

❼ **Peralta Adobe.** California pepper trees shade the circa-1797 last remaining structure from the pueblo that was once San Jose. The white-washed two-room home has been furnished to interpret life in the first Spanish civil settlement in California and during the Mexican rancho era. ⊠ *184 W. St. John St.,* ☎ *408/993–8182.* ☞ *$6 (includes admission to Fallon House).* ☉ *Guided tours Tues.–Sun. noon–5.*

❸ **San Jose Museum of Art.** In a four-part collaboration with New York's Whitney Museum, the San Jose Museum of Art is exploring the development of 20th-century American art with exhibits of pieces from the Whitney's permanent collection. The series will run through June of 2000, including works by American artists Georgia O'Keeffe, Edward Hopper, and John Marin. The museum's permanent collection includes paintings, large-scale multimedia installations, photographs, and sculptures. ⊠ *110 S. Market St.,* ☎ *408/294–2787.* ☞ *$7, free 1st Thurs. of month.* ☉ *Tues.–Wed. and Fri.–Sun. 10–5, Thurs. 10–8.*

☚ ★ **❺** **Tech Museum of Innovation.** The museum's high-tech and hands-on exhibits allow visitors to discover and demystify such disciplines as multimedia, communications, biotechnology, robotics, and space exploration. ⊠ *201 S. Market St., at Park Ave.,* ☎ *408/294–8324.* ☞ *$8 for museum or Imax, $13.50 for both.* ☉ *Tues.–Sun. 10–5 (until 6 PM Memorial Day–Labor Day, until 8 PM the 3rd Thurs. of each month).*

Winchester Mystery House. Convinced that spirits would harm her if construction ever stopped, firearms heiress Sarah Winchester constantly added to her house, now on the National Register of Historic Places. For 38 years, beginning in 1884, she kept hundreds of carpenters working around the clock, creating a bizarre 160-room Victorian labyrinth with stairs going nowhere and doors that open into walls. Explore the house on a 65-minute daytime tour or come on a Friday the 13th for an evening flashlight tour. ⊠ *525 S. Winchester Blvd., between Stevens Creek Blvd. and I–280,* ☎ *408/247–2101.* ⌘ *$13.95.* ⊙ *Guided tours Nov.–Feb., daily 9:30–4; Mar.–Oct., hrs vary, call ahead.*

Dining and Lodging

$$$–$$$$ ✕ **Emile's.** Swiss chef-owner Emile Mooser's menu is a blend of clas-
    ★   sical European and contemporary Californian influences. Specialties include house-cured gravlax, rack of lamb, fresh game, and Grand Marnier soufflé. ⊠ *545 S. 2nd St.,* ☎ *408/289–1960. AE, D, DC, MC, V. Closed Sun.–Mon. No lunch Tues.–Thurs. and Sat.*

$$$ ✕ **A. P. Stump's.** With its tin ceilings, dramatic lighting, and gold- and copper-toned walls, this restaurant's extravagant interior is well matched to the food. Chef-partner Jim Stump offers creative dishes on his frequently changing menu, which may include sesame ahi with bok choy and soba noodle cake or molasses-glazed pork chop with huckleberry sauce. ⊠ *163 W. Santa Clara St.,* ☎ *408/292–9928. AE, D, DC, MC, V. Closed Sun. No lunch Sat.*

$$–$$$ ✕ **Bella Mia.** Locals love this restaurant for its elegant interior and good Italian food. There are plenty of fresh pastas to choose from, like salmon ravioli in tomato dill sauce, as well as flat-bread pizzas and grilled entrées. ⊠ *58 S. First St.,* ☎ *408/280–1993. AE, D, DC, MC, V.*

$$ ✕ **71 Saint Peter.** This could easily be the best restaurant in San Jose. Each dish is prepared with care, from the grilled halibut served with a mango-papaya salsa and Thai chili beurre blanc, to the penne pasta with roasted chicken, Portobello mushrooms, and red peppers in a garlic-basil broth. ⊠ *71 N. San Pedro St.,* ☎ *408/971–8523,* ℻ *408/938–3440. AE, D, DC, MC, V. Closed Sun. No lunch Sat.*

$–$$ ✕ **Chez Sovan.** This Cambodian jewel is a wonderful addition to the South Bay dining scene. The original San Jose branch, which serves only lunch, stands in a rather homely stretch of town, but the Campbell location offers a pleasant setting in addition to its satisfying food. The spring rolls are delectable at both addresses, as are the noodle dishes, grilled meats, and flavorful curries. ⊠ *923 N. 13th St.,* ☎ *408/287–7619;* ⊠ *2425 S. Bascom Ave., Campbell,* ☎ *408/371–7711. AE, MC, V. No lunch Sun. at San Jose location.*

$ ✕ **Willow Street Wood-Fired Pizza.** What began as a quaint "secret" pizzeria in the Willow Glen neighborhood just south of downtown has become one of the best and trendiest spots in the South Bay. Order an individual wood-fired pizza with classic cheese or try something less mundane, such as artichoke and goat cheese. ⊠ *1072 Willow St.,* ☎ *408/971–7080;* ⊠ *1554 Saratoga Ave.,* ☎ *408/871–0400;* ⊠ *20 S. Santa Cruz Ave., Los Gatos,* ☎ *408/354–5566. AE, MC, V.*

$$$$ 🏨 **Fairmont Hotel.** Affiliated with the famous San Francisco hotel of the same name, this downtown gem offers the utmost in luxury and sophistication. Rooms have every imaginable comfort, from down pillows and custom-designed comforters to oversize bath towels changed twice a day. ⊠ *170 S. Market St., at Fairmont Pl., 95113,* ☎ *408/998–1900 or 800/527–4727,* ℻ *408/287–1648. 541 rooms. 3 restaurants, lobby lounge, no-smoking floors, room service, pool, health club, business services. AE, D, DC, MC, V.*

$$$$ 🏨 **Hotel De Anza.** Business travelers will appreciate the many amenities at this lushly appointed art deco hotel, including a full-service business center and personal voice-mail services. ⊠ *233 W. Santa Clara St., 95113,* ☎ *408/286–1000 or 800/843–3700,* ℻ *408/286–0500. 91* rooms, 9 suites. Restaurant, in-room data ports, minibars, in-room VCRs, exercise room, nightclub. AE, D, DC, MC, V.

$$–$$$ 🛏 **The Briar Rose Bed & Breakfast Inn.** This charming bed-and-breakfast is set on nearly half an acre of gardens in a restored 1875 Victorian farmhouse. There are plenty of thoughtful touches in the rooms, like antique furniture and feather mattresses. ⊠ 897 E. Jackson St., 95112, ☎ 408/279–5999, FAX 408/279–4534. 5 rooms, 1 suite. Breakfast room, in-room data ports. AE, DC, D, MC, V.

Nightlife and the Arts

NIGHTLIFE

Try **Big Lil's Barbary Coast Dinner Theater** (⊠ 157 W. San Fernando St., ☎ 408/295–7469) for a fresh take on the Old West; it serves up comedy, melodrama, and ribs on Friday and Saturday evenings. **Agenda** (⊠ 399 S. 1st St., ☎ 408/287–3991) is one of the most popular nightspots downtown, with a restaurant on the main floor, a bar upstairs, and a nightclub on the bottom floor. Pick up a pool cue at trendy **South First Billiards** (⊠ 420 S. 1st St., ☎ 408/294–7800). **Mirassou Vineyards** (⊠ 3000 Aborn Rd., ☎ 408/274–4000) organizes elegant eight-course candlelight dinners, accenting food and wine pairings ($95 per person). Dinners are offered every spring and fall; call for a schedule.

THE ARTS

BASS (☎ 408/998–2277) sells tickets to many arts events.

The **Center for Performing Arts** (⊠ 255 Almaden Blvd., ☎ 408/277–3900) is the city's main performance venue. **American Musical Theatre of San Jose** (☎ 408/453–7108), the **San Jose Symphony** (☎ 408/288–2828), and the **San Jose Cleveland Ballet** (☎ 408/288–2800) perform at the center.

The **San Jose Repertory Theatre** (⊠ 101 Paseo de San Antonio, ☎ 408/291–2255) occupies a contemporary four-story, 528-seat theater.

Sports

Known to area sports fans as the Shark Tank or, simply, the Tank, the 17,483-seat **San Jose Arena** (⊠ Santa Clara St. at Autumn St., ☎ 408/287–9200; 408/998–2277 for tickets) looks like a giant hothouse, with its glass entrance, shining metal armor, and skylight ceiling. In addition to hosting a national tennis tour, the Sybase Open in early February, basketball games, music concerts, ice-skating shows, and other events, the arena is home to the National Hockey League's **San Jose Sharks.** Call BASS (☎ 408/998–2277) for tickets.

The **San Jose Clash** (☎ 408/985–4625) play professional soccer at Spartan Stadium (⊠ 7th St. between E. Alma Ave. and E. Humboldt St.).

Santa Clara

Santa Clara University, founded in 1851 by Jesuits, was California's first college. The campus's **de Saisset Art Gallery and Museum** has a permanent collection that includes California mission artifacts and a full calendar of temporary exhibits. ⊠ 500 El Camino Real, ☎ 408/554–4528. 🎟 Free. ☉ Tues.–Sun. 11–4.

In the center of Santa Clara University's campus is the **Mission Santa Clara de Asis,** the eighth of 21 California missions founded under the direction of Father Junípero Serra and the first to honor a woman. ⊠ 500 El Camino Real, ☎ 408/554–4023. 🎟 Free. ☉ Daily 1 –sundown for self-guided tours.

Ⓒ Popular attractions at **Paramount's Great America** include the Drop Zone Stunt Tower, the tallest free-fall ride in North America; Xtreme

Skyflyer, which lifts you by harness more than 17 stories high and drops
you back to earth at 60 mph; and Nickelodeon Splat City, 3 acres of
obstacle courses designed for kids who love to get wet and dirty. ⊠
*Great America Pkwy. between U.S. 101 and Hwy. 237 (6 mi north of
San Jose),* ☎ *408/988–1776.* ☎ *$32.99; parking $6.* ☉ *Mid-Mar.–May
and Sept.–Oct., weekends; June–Aug., daily; opens 10* AM, *closing
times vary with season. AE, D, MC, V.*

Visitors to the **Intel Museum** can learn how computer chips are made
and follow the development of Intel Corporation's microprocessor, memory, and systems product lines. Guided tours are available by reservation. ⊠ *Robert Noyce Bldg., 2200 Mission College Blvd.,* ☎ *408/765–
0503.* ☎ *Free.* ☉ *Weekdays 8–5.*

Skylights cast natural light for viewing the exhibitions in the **Triton Museum of Art.** A permanent collection of 19th- and 20th-century sculpture by artists from the Bay Area is displayed in the garden, which you
can see through a curved-glass wall at the rear of the building. Inside
are rotating exhibits of contemporary works in a variety of media and
a permanent collection of 19th- and 20th-century American art. ⊠ *1505
Warburton Ave.,* ☎ *408/247–3754.* ☎ *$2 suggested donation.* ☉
Tues. 10–9, Wed.–Sun. 10–5.

South Bay Essentials
ARRIVING AND DEPARTING
By Car: The quickest route to San Jose from San Francisco is I–280.
From there take the Guadalupe Parkway (also known as Highway 87)
north, then the Santa Clara Street exit east for the most direct route
to downtown San Jose. To reach Santa Clara, take U.S. 101 and exit
south on San Tomas Expressway; turn left on El Camino Real (also
labeled Hwy. 82 on maps). Use Highway 280 during rush hours. From
I–280, just before the San Jose exit, take I–880 north to The Alameda,
which becomes El Camino Real (Hwy. 82); turn left off the exit ramp
and follow the signs to Santa Clara.

By Bus and Train: CalTrain (☎ 800/660–4287) runs from 4th and
Townsend streets in San Francisco to Santa Clara's Railroad and
Franklin streets stop near the university ($4.75 one-way) and to San
Jose's Rod Diridon station ($5.25 one-way). The trip to Santa Clara
takes approximately 1¼ hours; the trip to San Jose takes about 1½ hours.
A **shuttle** (☎ 408/321–2300) links downtown San Jose to the CalTrain
station, across from the Arena, every 20 minutes during morning and
evening commute hours.

By Plane: San Jose International Airport (⊠ 1661 Airport Blvd. off Hwy.
87, ☎ 408/277–4759) is served by most major airlines. **South & East
Bay Airport Shuttle** (☎ 408/559–9477) transports visitors to and from
the airport.

GETTING AROUND
In San Jose **light-rail trains** run 24 hours a day and serve most major
attractions, shopping malls, historic sites, and downtown. Trains run
every 10 minutes weekdays from 6 AM to 8 PM, and vary during weekends and late-night hours from every 15 minutes to once an hour. Tickets are valid for two hours; they cost $1.10 one-way or $2.50 for a
day pass. Historic trolleys operate in downtown San Jose from 10:30
to 5:30 during the summer and on some holidays throughout the year.
Buy tickets for both the light-rail and the trolleys at vending machines
in any transit station. For more information call or visit the **Downtown
Customer Service Center** (⊠ 2 N. 1st St., San Jose, ☎ 408/321–2300).

SAN FRANCISCO A TO Z

Arriving and Departing

By Bus

Greyhound (☎ 800/231–2222) serves San Francisco from the Transbay Terminal at 1st and Mission streets.

By Car

Interstate 80 finishes its westward journey from New York's George Washington Bridge at the San Francisco–Oakland Bay Bridge. U.S. 101 enters the city from the north at the Golden Gate Bridge and continues south down the peninsula, along the west side of the San Francisco Bay.

By Plane

San Francisco International Airport (⊠ U.S. 101, south of San Francisco, ☎ 650/761–0800) is the major gateway to San Francisco. **Oakland Airport** (⊠ 1 Airport Dr., off I–880, ☎ 510/577–4000) is across the bay. **San Jose International Airport** (☎ 408/277–4759) is 3 mi from downtown San Jose (☞ South Bay Essentials, *above*).

Carriers serving San Francisco include Alaska, America West, American, Continental, Delta, Midwest Express, Northwest, Reno Air, Southwest, TWA, United, and US Airways. Carriers flying into Oakland include America West, American, Delta, Southwest, and United. Carriers serving San Jose include Alaska, America West, American Continental, Delta, Northwest, TWA, and United. *See* Air Travel *in* Smart Travel Tips A to Z for airline phone numbers.

BETWEEN THE AIRPORT AND DOWNTOWN

From SFO: A taxi ride from SFO to downtown costs about $30. The **SFO Airporter** (☎ 415/495–8404) picks up passengers outside baggage claim (lower level) and stops at selected downtown hotels ($10). **SuperShuttle** (☎ 415/558–8500) stops at the upper-level traffic islands. The cost ranges from $10 to $13 depending on your destination within San Francisco. **Bayporter Express** (☎ 415/467–1800) shuttles to the East Bay (about $20) also depart from SFO's upper-level traffic islands. The cheapest way to get from the airport to San Francisco is via **SamTrans** (☎ 800/660–4287). Bus 7B (55 minutes; $2.20) and 7F (35 minutes; $3; only one small carry-on bag permitted) head to San Francisco; Bus 3X stops at the Colma BART station (☞ BART, Getting Around, *below*), where you can board a train headed downtown. Board the SamTrans buses on the upper (departures) level. If you have questions about the taxis, buses, and trains that serve the airport, you can talk to one of the staff members of the **Ground Transportation Hotline** (☎ 800/736–2008).

To drive to downtown San Francisco from the airport, take U.S. 101 north to the Civic Center (Ninth Street), Seventh Street, or Fourth Street exit. If you're headed to the Embarcadero or Fisherman's Wharf, take U.S. 101 north to just past 3Com Park and exit onto I–280 north, which you'll follow to the Fourth Street/King Street exit. King Street becomes the Embarcadero a few blocks east of the exit. The Embarcadero winds around the waterfront to Fisherman's Wharf.

From Oakland International: A taxi from Oakland's airport to downtown San Francisco costs between $30 and $35. **America's Shuttle** (☎ 515/841–0272 or 415/515–0273), Bayporter Express (☞ *above*), and other shuttles serve major hotels and provide door-to-door service to the East Bay and San Francisco; Bayporter Express also serves the Peninsula and the South Bay. The best way to get to San Francisco via public transit is to take the AIR BART bus ($2) to the Coliseum/Oakland International Airport BART station (BART fares vary depending on where you're going; the ride to San Francisco costs $2.75).

If you're driving to San Francisco from Oakland International Airport, take Hegenberger Road east to I–880 north and follow signs to I–80 west (eventually the San Francisco–Oakland Bay Bridge).

By Train

Amtrak (☎ 800/872–7245) trains—the *Zephyr,* from Chicago via Denver, and the *Coast Starlight,* traveling between Los Angeles and Seattle—stop in Emeryville (✉ 5885 Landregan St., Emeryville) and Oakland (✉ 245 2nd St., in Jack London Sq., Oakland). Shuttle buses connect the Emeryville station and San Francisco's Ferry Building (✉ 30 Embarcadero, at the foot of Market St.).

Getting Around

By Bus and Light Rail

San Francisco Municipal Railway System, or Muni (☎ 415/673–6864), includes buses, light-rail vehicles, and antique trolleys. There is 24-hour service; the fare is $1. The exact fare is always required; dollar bills or change are accepted. Transfers are issued free upon request at the time the fare is paid. They are valid for 90 minutes to two hours for two boardings of a bus or streetcar in any direction.

A $6 pass good for unlimited travel all day on all routes can be purchased from ticket machines at cable-car terminals and at the Visitor Information Center in Hallidie Plaza.

You can use **Bay Area Rapid Transit (BART)** (☎ 800/817–1717) trains to reach Oakland, Berkeley, Concord, Richmond, Fremont, Colma, and Martinez. Trains also travel south from San Francisco as far as Daly City. Fares run from $1.10 to $4.70, and a $3 excursion ticket buys a three-county tour.

By Cable Cars

Cable cars are popular, crowded, and an experience to ride: move toward one quickly as it pauses, wedge yourself into any available space, and hold on! The fare (for one direction) is $2. Exact change is preferred, but operators will make change up to $20. There are self-service ticket machines (which do make change) at a few major stops and at all the terminals. The one exception is the busy cable car terminal at Powell and Market streets; purchase tickets at the kiosk there.

The Powell-Mason line (No. 59) and the Powell-Hyde line (No. 60) begin at Powell and Market streets near Union Square and terminate at Fisherman's Wharf. The California Street line (No. 61), often less crowded than the other two, runs east and west from Market Street near the Embarcadero to Van Ness Avenue.

By Car

Driving in San Francisco can be a challenge because of the hills, the one-way streets, and the traffic. Curb your wheels when parking on hills, and use public transportation whenever possible. This is a great city for walking and a so-so city for parking. On certain streets, parking is forbidden during rush hours. Look for the warning signs. Illegally parked cars are towed.

The commercial parking lots downtown are often full and always expensive. The city-owned **Ellis-O'Farrell Garage** (✉ 123 O'Farrell St., at Stockton St., ☎ 415/986–4800), **5th and Mission Garage** (✉ 833

Mission St., at 5th St., ☎ 415/982–8522), and **Sutter-Stockton Garage** (✉ 444 Stockton St., at Sutter St., ☎ 415/982–7275) have the most reasonable rates in the downtown area. If you're going to North Beach and Chinatown, try the **766 Vallejo Garage** (✉ 766 Vallejo St., at Powell St., ☎ 415/989–4490) in North Beach. A few blocks south in Chinatown is the convenient, if expensive, **Portsmouth Square Garage** (✉ 733 Kearny St., at Clay St., ☎ 415/982–6353). The **Pier 39 Garage** (✉ 2550 Powell St., at the Embarcadero, ☎ 415/705–5418) and the **Wharf Garage** (✉ Fisherman's Wharf, 350 Beach St., at Taylor St., ☎ 415/921–0226) are two large garages along the Northern Waterfront.

Contacts and Resources

Doctors

Two hospitals with 24-hour emergency rooms are **San Francisco General Hospital** (✉ 1001 Potrero Ave., ☎ 415/206–8000) and the **Medical Center at the University of California, San Francisco** (✉ 500 Parnassus Ave., ☎ 415/476–1000). **Physician Access Medical Center** (✉ 26 California St., ☎ 415/397–2881) is a drop-in clinic in the Financial District, open weekdays 7:30 AM–4:30 PM. **Access Health Care** (☎ 415/565–6600) provides drop-in medical care at Davies Medical Center, Castro Street at Duboce Avenue, weekdays from 8 to 8.

Emergencies

Ambulance (☎ 911). **Fire** (☎ 911). **Police** (☎ 911).

Guided Tours

ORIENTATION TOURS

In addition to bus and van tours of the city, most tour companies run excursions to various Bay Area and northern California destinations such as Marin County and the Wine Country, as well as farther flung areas like Monterey and Yosemite. City tours generally last 3½ hours and cost between $25 and $30. It's wise to reserve space on tours at least a day ahead. Tour companies include **Golden Gate Tours** (☎ 415/788–5775), **Gray Line Tours** (☎ 415/558–9400), **Great Pacific Tour** (☎ 415/626–4499), and **Tower Tours** (☎ 415/434–8687).

WALKING TOURS

Trevor Hailey's 3¾-hour **Cruising the Castro** (☎ 415/550–8110) tour focuses on the history and development of the city's gay and lesbian community. The cost is $35, which includes brunch. Reservations are required. The **Chinatown with the "Wok Wiz"** (☎ 415/981–8989) tour by cookbook author Shirley Fong-Torres and her staff is a 3½-hour spin through Chinese markets, other businesses, and a fortune-cookie factory. The $37 fee includes lunch; the cost is $25 without lunch. Shorter group tours start at $15 per person. **Chinese Cultural Heritage Foundation** (☎ 415/986–1822) conducts two walking tours of Chinatown. The Heritage Walk leaves on Saturday at 2 PM and lasts about two hours; the cost is $15. The Culinary Walk, a three-hour stroll through the markets and food shops, plus a dim sum lunch, is given from Tuesday through Friday at 10:30 AM; the fee is $30. **City Guides** (☎ 415/557–4266), a free service sponsored by the Friends of the Library, tours Chinatown, North Beach, Coit Tower, Pacific Heights mansions, Japantown, the Haight-Ashbury, historic Market Street, the Palace Hotel, and downtown roof gardens and atriums. Schedules are available at the San Francisco Visitors Center at Powell and Market streets and at library branches.

Late-Night Pharmacies

Several **Walgreen Drug Stores** have 24-hour pharmacies (⊠ 135 Powell St., near Market St., ☎ 415/391–7222; ⊠ 3201 Divisadero St., at Lombard St., ☎ 415/931–6417).

Visitor Information

Redwood Empire Association Visitor Information Center (⊠ The Cannery, 2801 Leavenworth St., 2nd floor, 94133, ☎ 415/394–5991). **San Francisco Convention and Visitors Bureau** (⊠ 900 Market St., at Powell St., 94102, ☎ 415/391–2000).

5 SACRAMENTO AND THE GOLD COUNTRY

Including Highway 49 from Nevada City to Mariposa

The gold-mining region of the Sierra Nevada foothills is a less expensive, if less sophisticated, region of California but not without its pleasures, natural and man-made. Spring brings wildflowers, and in fall the hills are colored by bright-red berries and changing leaves. The hills are golden in the summer—and hot. The Gold Country has a mix of indoor and outdoor activities, one of the many reasons it's a great place to take the kids.

Updated by
Andy Moore

JAMES MARSHALL TURNED UP a gold nugget in the tailrace of a sawmill he was constructing along the American River and ushered in a whole new era for California. Before January 24, 1848, what would become the Golden State was a beautiful but sparsely populated land over which Mexico and the United States were still wrestling for ownership. With Marshall's discovery and its subsequent confirmation by President James Polk in his State of the Union speech on December 5, 1848, prospectors came to seek their fortunes in the Mother Lode.

As gold fever seized the nation, California's population of 15,000 swelled to 265,000 within three years—44,000 newcomers arrived by ship in San Francisco in the first 10 months alone, the majority of them men under 40, either unattached or with families back east. Most spent about two years in California before returning home, usually with empty pockets or having barely broken even. The consequences of the Gold Rush were more than monetary: '49ers—the term used to describe those who arrived in search of gold—who remained in California contributed to a freer culture that eschewed many of the constricting conventions of the eastern states.

Originally, the term Mother Lode denoted a gold-bearing quartz vein 120 mi long between Mariposa in the south and Auburn in the north. It ranged in width from 2 mi to only a few yards. By 1865 it had yielded more than $750 million in gold. As prospectors headed farther afield, the entire region came to be known as the Mother Lode. Neither Marshall, nor John Sutter, on whose property Marshall discovered gold, got rich from the discovery.

The boom brought on by the Gold Rush lasted scarcely 20 years, but it changed California forever. It produced 546 mining towns, of which fewer than 250 remain. The hills were alive, not only with prospecting and mining but also with business, the arts, gambling, and a fair share of crime. Opera houses went up alongside brothels, and the California State Capitol in Sacramento was built with the gold dug out of the hills. Some of the nation's most treasured writers—Mark Twain and Bret Harte among them—began their careers writing about the mining camps. Gold-Rush lore immortalized notorious bandits: when the law finally caught up with the debonair Black Bart, who targeted Wells Fargo stagecoaches and left behind poems (signed "Black Bart—PO-8") at his crime scenes, he turned out to be a well-known San Franciscan. Legend has it that Joaquin Murieta's crime spree—he robbed miners, then partied at local saloons—followed an assault on him and his family by Yankee prospectors.

Mexican miners weren't the only victims of the Yankee juggernaut. California's leaders in the mid-19th century engaged in a systematic plan to exterminate the local Indian population. Bounties were paid and private militias were hired to wipe out the Indians or sell them into slavery. A law in force from 1850 to 1863 prohibited nonwhites from appearing as witnesses in civil cases. Not surprisingly, verdicts and damage awards favored white plaintiffs and defendants.

The northern California cities of Sacramento, San Francisco, and Stockton grew quickly to meet the needs of the surrounding gold fields. Saloon keepers and canny merchants recognized that the real gold was to be made from the '49ers. Potatoes and onions sold for as much as $1 each, making entrepreneurs like storekeeper Samuel Brannan millionaires. Much important history was made in Sacramento, the key center of commerce during this period. Pony Express riders ended their nearly 2,000-mi journeys in the city in the 1860s. The transcontinental railroad, conceived here by the Big Four (Leland Stanford, Mark Hopkins, Collis P. Huntington, and Charles Crocker), was completed in 1869.

By the 1960s the scars mining had inflicted on the landscape had largely healed. To promote tourism, townspeople began restoring vintage structures, historians developed museums, and the state established parks and recreation areas to preserve this extraordinary episode in American history. Today visitors flock to Nevada City, Auburn, Coloma, Sutter Creek, and Columbia, not only to relive the past but also to explore museums and art galleries and to stay at inns.

Pleasures and Pastimes

Adventuring

Scenic and challenging Gold Country rivers, particularly the American and Tuolumne, lure white-water enthusiasts each spring and summer. Early morning hot-air balloon excursions float above treetops in deep canyons of the American River. Throughout the region weekend prospectors pan for gold, turning up nuggets frequently enough to inspire others to participate.

Dining

American, Italian, and Mexican fare are common in the Gold Country, but chefs also prepare ambitious Continental, French, and California cuisine. It's not difficult to find the makings for a good picnic in most towns.

CATEGORY	COST*
$$$$	over $50
$$$	$30–$50
$$	$20–$30
$	under $20

*per person for a three-course meal, excluding drinks, service, and 7¾% tax

Lodging

Full-service hotels, budget motels, small inns, and even a fine hostel can all be found in Sacramento. The main accommodations in the larger towns along Highway 49—among them Placerville, Nevada City, Auburn, and Mariposa—are chain motels and inns. Many Gold Country B&Bs occupy former mansions, miners' cabins, and other historic buildings.

For information about area B&Bs, contact: **Amador County Innkeepers Association** (☎ 209/267–1710 or 800/726–4667); **Gold Country Inns of Tuolumne County** (☎ 209/533–1845); or **Historic Bed & Breakfast Inns of Grass Valley & Nevada City** (☎ 530/477–6634 or 800/250–5808).

CATEGORY	COST*
$$$$	over $175
$$$	$120–$175
$$	$80–$120
$	under $80

*All prices are for a standard double room, excluding 7¼% tax (12% in Sacramento).

Shopping

Shoppers visit the Gold Country in search of antiques, collectibles, art, quilts, toys, tools, decorative items, and furnishings. Handmade quilts and crafts can be found in Sutter Creek, Jackson, and Amador City. Auburn and Nevada City support many gift boutiques.

Exploring Sacramento and the Gold Country

Visiting Old Sacramento's museums is a good way to steep yourself in history, but the Gold Country's heart lies along Highway 49, which winds the 325-mi north–south length of the historic mining area. The highway, often a twisting, hilly, two-lane road, begs for a convertible with the top down.

Numbers in the text correspond to numbers in the margin and on the Gold Country and Sacramento maps.

Great Itineraries

IF YOU HAVE 1 DAY

Drive east from Sacramento on I–80 to **Auburn** ⑰ for a tour of the **Placer County Courthouse** and its museum. Travel south on Highway 49 to the **Marshall Gold Discovery State Historic Park** ⑱ at Coloma. Head back to Sacramento for a drink at the bar on the *Delta King* and an evening stroll and dinner along the waterfront in **Old Sacramento.** The historical attractions will be closed, but you'll still get a feel for life here during the last half of the 19th century.

IF YOU HAVE 3 DAYS

Begin your tour on Highway 49 north of I–80. Walk deep into the recesses of the **Empire Mine** ⑯ near **Grass Valley,** and then drive 4 mi north on Highway 49 for a visit to the **Miners Foundry** in **Nevada City** ⑮. After lunch, travel south to 🍽 **Auburn** ⑰, where you can take in the **Placer County Courthouse** and museum, have dinner, and spend the night. Early the next morning head south to tour **Marshall Gold Discovery State Historic Park** ⑱ in Coloma. Continue south to 🍽 **Sutter Creek** ⑳ and spend the afternoon exploring the boutiques and antiques stores. If exploring a good vintage is more your game, take a detour to the **Shenandoah Valley,** southeast of **Placerville,** and taste some wine before continuing on to Sutter Creek. Either way, spend the night in Sutter Creek. Return early the next day to **Sacramento** to visit the **California State Railroad Museum** ① and **Sutter's Fort** ⑬.

IF YOU HAVE 5 DAYS

Visit the **Empire Mine** ⑯, **Nevada City** ⑮, and 🍽 **Auburn** ⑰ on day one. See Coloma's **Marshall Gold Discovery State Historic Park** ⑱ on the second day, and then continue on to 🍽 **Sutter Creek** ⑳. On your third morning, visit the **Amador County Museum** in **Jackson** ㉑ before heading south on Highway 49 and east on Highway 4 for lunch in **Murphys** ㉓. Back on Highway 49 still southward is 🍽 **Columbia State Historic Park** ㉔. You can relive the 1800s by dining and spending the night at the City Hotel. If you've been itching to pan for gold, do that in the morning in the state park, and then head back to 🍽 **Sacramento** (Highway 49 north to Highway 16 west) for a riverboat cruise. Visit the **California State Railroad Museum** ① and **Sutter's Fort** ⑬ on day five.

When to Tour the Gold Country

The Gold Country is the most pleasant in the spring, when the wildflowers are in bloom, and in the fall. Summers are beautiful but hot: temperatures near or above 100°F are common. Sacramento winters tend to be cold and foggy. Throughout the year Gold Country towns stage community and ethnic celebrations. In December many towns deck themselves out for Christmas. Sacramento hosts the annual Jazz Jubilee in May and the California State Fair in August. Flowers bloom on Daffodil Hill in March.

The Gold Country

Bullards Bar
Reservoir

Collins
Lake

Tahoe
National
Forest

TO
RENO

Grass Valley
15 Nevada City
**16 Empire Mine
State Historic Park**

N. Fork American

Olivehurst

Bear R.

Eldorado
National
Forest

Lincoln

Auburn 17

Cool

Pilot Hill

Coloma

**Hangtown's
Gold Bug Mine**

**18 Marshall Gold
Discovery State
Historic Park**

19
Placerville

TO LAKE
TAHOE

Folsom
Lake

Folsom

El Dorado

Fair Oaks

Shenandoah Valley

**Sacramento
1 — 14**

Cosumnes R.

Plymouth

Fiddletown

Daffodil
Hill

Drytown
Amador City

**Sutter Creek
20**

TO CALAVERAS
BIG TREES STATE PARK

Jackson 21

Mokelumne Hill

San Andreas

Lodi

**Murphys
23**

California
Caverns

**Columbia State
Historic Park**

Angels Camp 22

Moaning
Cavern

24

0   10 miles

0   15 km

Sonora 25

Stockton

Jamestown 26

TO OAKHURST

27 Mariposa

SACRAMENTO

The gateway to the Gold Country, the seat of California state government, and an agricultural hub, the city of Sacramento plays many important contemporary roles. One and a half million people live in the metropolitan area, and the continuing influx of newcomers seeking opportunity, sunshine, and lower housing costs than in coastal California have made it one of the nation's fastest-growing regions. Midtown's many new cafés and downtown's revived K Street Mall are testaments to Sacramento's growing sophistication.

Sacramento contains more than 2,000 acres of natural and developed parkland. This "city of a million trees" is planted with grand old evergreens, deciduous and fruit-bearing trees (some streets are littered with oranges in springtime), and even giant palms, giving it a shady, lush quality. Genteel Victorian edifices sit side-by-side with Art Deco and postmodern skyscrapers.

Old Sacramento and Downtown

87 mi northeast of San Francisco, I–80 to Hwy. 99.

Wooden sidewalks and horse-drawn carriages on cobblestone streets lend a 19th-century feel to Old Sacramento, a 28-acre district along the Sacramento River waterfront. The museums at the north end hold artifacts of state and national significance. Historic buildings house shops and restaurants. River cruises and train rides bring gold-rush history to life. Call the **Old Sacramento Events Hotline** (☎ 916/558–3912) for information about living-history re-creations and merchant hours.

A Good Tour

Old Sacramento, the Capitol and park surrounding it, and Sutter's Fort lie on an east–west axis that begins at the Sacramento River. The walk from Old Sacramento to the State Capitol is easy, passing through the Downtown Plaza shopping mall and pedestrians-only K Street. This area takes on a festive atmosphere during an outdoor market held on Thursday evening. A DASH (Downtown Area Shuttle) bus and the number 30 city bus both link Old Sacramento, K Street Mall, the Convention Center, downtown, midtown, and Sutter's Fort in a loop that travels eastward on J Street and westward on L Street. The fare is 50 cents within this area, and buses run every 15 minutes weekdays, every 20 minutes Saturdays, and every 30 minutes Sundays.

Park your car in the municipal garage under I–5 at 2nd Street (enter on I Street between 2nd and 3rd streets), and head to the superb **California State Railroad Museum** ①, then browse through the hardware and household items at the **Huntington, Hopkins & Co. Store** ②. Next door are the hands-on exhibits of the **Discovery Museum** ③.

To learn more about Sacramento's role in rail history walk a few paces south to the **Central Pacific Passenger Depot.** Across Front Street is the historic **Eagle Theater** ④. The **Central Pacific Freight Depot,** next to the Passenger Depot, houses a **Public Market** (closed on Monday), whose merchants sell food and gift items. The foot of K Street (at Front Street) is a great spot for viewing the Sacramento River wharf area and the restored stern-wheeler the *Delta King.*

At the corner of 2nd and J streets is the historic **B. F. Hastings Building** ⑤. The **Visitor Information Center** ⑥ is on 2nd Street in the same block as the **California Military Museum** ⑦. A must-see a few blocks south of Old Sacramento is the **Crocker Art Museum** ⑧, the oldest art museum in the American West. From here walk south on Front Street to the

Sacramento

(Map labels, from image)

Richards Blvd · Vine St. · American River · Sacramento River · N. 10th St. · N. B St. · 16th St. · 99 · 5 · 160 · Muir Park · Grant Park · N · OLD SACRAMENTO · Downtown Plaza · H St. · C St. · D St. · E St. · F St. · G St. · H St. · I St. · 25th St. · 27th St. · DOWNTOWN · J St. · K St. Mall · MIDTOWN · L St. · Front St. · Capitol Mall · N St. · Convention Center · K St. · L St. · AE · LAVENDER HEIGHTS · Leland Stanford Mansion · Capitol Ave. · P St. · 3rd St. · 5th St. · 8th St. · 10th St. · R St. · 160 · 160 · Fremont Park · N St. · O St. · P St. · Q St. · 29th St. · 30th St. · Alhambra Blvd · BUS 80 · South Side Park · O'Neil Field · TO SAN FRANCISCO · BUS 80 · 11th St. · 12th St. · 13th St. · 14th St. · 15th St. · 16th St. · 17th St. · 18th St. · 9th St. · 20th St. · 21st St. · 22nd St. · 23rd St. · S St. · T St. · U St. · 24th St. · 25th St. · 26th St. · 27th St. · 28th St. · V St. · W St. · 50 · Broadway · Regina Wy. · Land Park Dr. · 17th St. · X St. · 24th St. · 99 · Muir Wy. · 5th St.

KEY

AE American Express Office

B.F. Hastings Building, **5**

California Military Museum, **7**

California State Railroad Museum, **1**

Capitol, **10**

Crocker Art Museum, **8**

Discovery Museum, **3**

Eagle Theater, **4**

Golden State Museum, **11**

Governor's Mansion, **12**

Huntington, Hopkins & Co. Store, **2**

State Indian Museum, **14**

Sutter's Fort, **13**

Towe Auto Museum, **9**

Visitor Information Center, **6**

Towe Auto Museum ⑨. If you'd rather skip the automotive museum, walk up 3rd Street to the Capitol Mall, which leads to the **Capitol** ⑩. If you're still going strong, explore the **Golden State Museum** ⑪ at O and 10th streets, one block south of the Capitol, or walk north to H Street then east to **Governor's Mansion** ⑫. Otherwise, walk back to your car via J Street.

Though it requires a drive or a ride on the DASH or number 30 city bus, **Sutter's Fort** ⑬ is worth the trip. It was Sacramento's earliest settlement; evocative exhibits bring that era back to life. North of the fort is the **State Indian Museum** ⑭.

TIMING

This tour makes for a leisurely day. Most of the attractions are open daily, except for the Military Museum, the Eagle Theater, the Crocker Art Museum, and the Golden State Museum, which are closed on Monday.

Sights to See

❺ B. F. Hastings Building. A reconstruction of the first chambers of the California Supreme Court occupies the second floor of this 1853 building. On the first floor there's a Wells Fargo History Museum and an ATM. ⊠ *1000 2nd St.,* ☎ *916/440–4263.* ☉ *Daily 10–5.*

Cal Expo. The California State Fair, a celebration of the state's agricultural and other industries, takes place at the Cal Expo fairgrounds between mid-August and early September. Livestock and other animals are always on display, competing for ribbons in untold categories. Other events are also held here throughout the year. ⊠ *Exposition Blvd. (north of downtown, take Cal Expo exit off I–80 Business Loop),* ☎ *916/ 263–3247.*

❼ California Military Museum. A storefront entrance leads to three floors containing more than 30,000 artifacts—uniforms, weapons, photographs, documents, medals, and flags of all kinds—that trace Californians' roles in military and militia activities throughout U.S. history. An interesting display outlines the African-American experience; another includes Civil War–era medical equipment. ⊠ *1119 2nd St.,* ☎ *916/442–2883.* ⊡ *$3.* ☉ *Tues.–Sun. 10–4.*

★ ☾ **❶ California State Railroad Museum.** Near what was once the terminus of the transcontinental and Sacramento Valley railroads (the actual terminus was at Front and K streets), this 100,000-square-ft museum has 21 locomotives and railroad cars on display and 46 exhibits. You can walk through a post-office car and peer into cubbyholes and canvas bags of mail, enter a sleeping car that simulates the swaying on the roadbed and the flashing lights of a passing town at night, or glimpse the inside of the first-class dining car on the *Super Chief.* Allow at least two hours to enjoy the museum. ⊠ *125 I St.,* ☎ *916/445–6645.* ⊡ *$6.* ☉ *Daily 10–5.*

❿ Capitol. The Golden State's Capitol was built in 1869. The lacy plasterwork of the 120-ft-high rotunda has the complexity and color of a Fabergé egg. Underneath the gilded dome are marble floors, glittering chandeliers, monumental staircases, original artwork, replicas of 19th-century state offices, and legislative chambers decorated in the style of the 1890s. Hallway displays for each of California's counties reflect the state's diversity. Guides conduct tours of the building and the 40-acre Capitol Park, which contains a rose garden, an impressive display of camellias (Sacramento's city flower), and the California Vietnam Veterans Memorial. ⊠ *Capitol Mall and 10th St.,* ☎ *916/324–0333.* ⊡ *Free.* ☉ *Daily 9–4; tours hourly.*

Central Pacific Passenger Depot. At this reconstructed 1876 station there's rolling stock to admire, a typical waiting room, and a small restaurant. Rides on a steam-powered train depart from the freight depot, south of the passenger depot. The train makes a 40-minute loop along the Sacramento riverfront. ✉ *930 Front St.,* ☎ *916/445–6645.* 💲 *$6 (free with same-day ticket from California State Railroad Museum); train ride $5 additional.* ☉ *Depot daily 10–5. Train operates every weekend Apr.–Sept., 1st weekend of month Oct.–Dec.*

★ ❽ **Crocker Art Museum.** The oldest art museum in the American West has a collection of art from Europe, Asia, and California, including *Sunday Morning in the Mines* (1872), a large canvas by Charles Christian Nahl depicting the mining industry of the 1850s, and the magnificent *The Great Canyon of the Sierra, Yosemite* (1871) by Thomas Hill. The museum's lobby and ballroom retain the original 1870s woodwork, plaster moldings, and imported English tiles. ✉ *216 O St.,* ☎ *916/264–5423.* 💲 *$4.50.* ☉ *Tues.–Wed. and Fri.–Sun. 10–5, Thurs. 10–9.*

❸ **Discovery Museum.** The building that holds this kids-oriented museum is a replica of the 1854 City Hall and Waterworks. The emphasis is on interactive exhibits that combine history, science, and technology to examine the evolution of everyday life in the Sacramento area. You can sift for gold, examine an Indian thatched hut, or experience the goings-on in the print shop of the old *Sacramento Bee* newspaper. The Gold Gallery displays nuggets and veins. ✉ *101 I St.,* ☎ *916/264–7057.* 💲 *$4.* ☉ *Tues.–Sun. 10–5.*

❹ **Eagle Theater.** When the Eagle opened in 1849, audiences paid between $3 and $5 in gold coin or dust to sit on rough boards and watch professional actors. This replica was constructed with the tentlike canvas and ship's-timber walls of olden times, though now there's insulation and the bench seats are cushioned. The theater hosts programs that range from a 13-minute slide show to puppet, minstrel, and juggling acts. ✉ *925 Front St.,* ☎ *916/323–6343.* 💲 *Fees vary depending on the program.* ☉ *Spring–summer, Tues.–Fri. 10–4; fall–winter, Tues.–Thurs. 10–4.*

★ ⓫ **Golden State Museum.** Drawing from the vast collections of the California State Archives, this state-of-the-art museum vividly interprets the story of California's land, people, and politics. Exhibits utilize modern technology, but there are also scores of archival drawers that visitors can pull out to see the real artifacts of history and culture— from the California State Constitution to surfing magazines. Board a 1949 cross-country bus to view a video on immigration, visit a Chinese herb shop inhabited by a holographic proprietor, or stand on a gubernatorial balcony overlooking a sea of cameras and banners. Admission includes the use of an innovative personal audio guide—choose an adult or children's program and the level of detail you desire for each exhibit. There's also a café where you can take a break from the fun. ✉ *1020 O St.,* ☎ *916/653–7524.* 💲 *$6.50.* ☉ *Tues.–Sat. 10–5, Sun. noon–5.*

⓬ **Governor's Mansion.** This 15-room house was built in 1877 and used by the state's chief executives from the early 1900s until 1967, when Ronald Reagan vacated it in favor of a newly built home in the suburbs. Many of the Italianate mansion's interior decorative details were ordered from the Huntington, Hopkins & Co. hardware store, one of whose partners, Albert Gallatin, was the original occupant. Each of the seven marble fireplaces has a petticoat mirror that ladies strolled past to see if their slips were showing. The mansion is said to have been one of the first homes in California to have an indoor bathroom. ⊠ *1526 H St.,* ☏ *916/323–3047.* ⊡ *$3.* ☉ *Daily 10–4; tours hourly.*

❷ Huntington, Hopkins & Co. Store. This museum is a replica of the 1855 hardware store opened by Collis Huntington and Mark Hopkins, two of the Big Four businessmen who established the Central Pacific Railroad. Picks, shovels, gold pans, and other paraphernalia miners used during the Gold Rush are on display, along with typical household hardware and appliances from the 1880s. Some items, such as blue enamelware, wooden toys, and oil lamps, are for sale. ⊠ *113 I St.,* ☏ *916/323–7234.* ☉ *Hours vary.*

Leland Stanford Mansion. The home of Leland Stanford, a railroad baron, California governor, and U.S. senator, was built in 1856, with additions in 1862 and the early 1870s. This once-grand edifice is currently undergoing major renovations. Some of the floors of the mansion, which will operate as a museum and a site for official state receptions, may be open to the public by late 2000. ⊠ *802 N St.,* ☏ *916/324–0575.*

★ ☙ **⓮ State Indian Museum.** Among the interesting displays at this well-organized museum is one devoted to Ishi, the last Yahi Indian to emerge from the mountains, in 1911. Ishi provided scientists insight into the traditions and culture of this group of Native Americans. Arts-and-crafts exhibits, a demonstration village, and an evocative 10-minute video bring to life the multifaceted past and present of California's Indian peoples. ⊠ *2601 K St.,* ☏ *916/324–0971.* ⊡ *$3.* ☉ *Daily 10–5.*

★ ☙ **⓭ Sutter's Fort.** Sacramento's earliest settlement was founded by German-born Swiss immigrant John Augustus Sutter in 1839. Visitors walk a self-guided tour. Audio speakers at each stop explain exhibits that include a blacksmith's shop, a bakery, a prison, living quarters, and livestock areas. Costumed docents sometimes reenact fort life, demonstrating crafts, food preparation, and firearms maintenance. ⊠ *2701 L St.,* ☏ *916/445–4422.* ⊡ *$6 Memorial Day–Labor Day and on Living History Days; $3 rest of yr.* ☉ *Daily 10–5.*

☙ **❾ Towe Auto Museum.** With more than 150 vintage automobiles on display, and exhibits ranging from the Hall of Technology to Dreams of Speed and Dreams of Cool, this museum explores automotive history. Docents provide information about specific models, including a 1931 Chrysler, a 1960 Lotus, and a bullet-proof Cadillac limousine once used by the U.S. State Department. A 1920s roadside café and garage exhibit re-creates the early days of motoring. A gift shop sells vintage-car magazines, model kits, old license plates, and other car-related items. ⊠ *2200 Front St., one block off Broadway,* ☏ *916/442–6802.* ⊡ *$6.* ☉ *Daily 10–6.*

❻ Visitor Information Center. Obtain brochures about nearby attractions, arrange lodgings, check local restaurant menus, and get advice from the helpful staff here. ⊠ *1101 2nd St., at K St.,* ☏ *916/442–7644.* ☉ *Daily 9–5.*

Dining

$$$ ✕ **Restaurant 1201.** This softly lighted restaurant and cocktail lounge overlooks the promenade at the east end of the K Street Mall. Dramatic presentations on the menu, which changes monthly, might include Medusa crab cakes or baked leg of rabbit in thyme mousseline. Among the desserts are fresh berry tarts and the chocolate tulip cup with espresso ganache and caramel straws. Light jazz is performed weekend evenings. *1201 K St.,* ☏ *916/444–1015. AE, D, MC, V. No lunch weekends. No dinner Sun.–Mon.*

$$–$$$ ✕ **Biba.** Owner Biba Caggiano is an authority on Italian cuisine, au-
★ thor of several cookbooks, and the star of a national TV show on cooking. The Capitol crowd flocks here for homemade tortelloni, osso
buco, grilled pork loin, and a variety of veal and rabbit specials. ✉
2801 Capitol Ave., ☎ *916/455–2422. AE, DC, MC, V. Closed Sun.
No lunch Sat.*

$$–$$$ ✕ **City Treasure.** A curved wall of windows shows off the warm inte-
★ rior of this restaurant to its fashionable midtown neighbors. Burnished
copper tables and lamps, grapevine-pattern booths and banquettes, and
locally produced artwork create a delightful setting. The eclectic menu
changes seasonally. Smoked salmon croutons, jambalaya, grilled salmon,
and braised lamb shanks are among the past offerings. The triple-layer
chocolate cake is a must for dessert. From the list of more than 200
California wines, you can choose one of almost 50 by the glass, or have
a trio—a sampler of three 3-ounce pours. ✉ *1730 L St.,* ☎ *916/447–
7380. AE, D, DC, MC, V. No lunch Sat.*

$$–$$$ ✕ **Frank Fat's.** A longtime favorite of lawmakers and lobbyists, Frank
Fat's is renowned more for its watering-hole atmosphere than its so-
so Chinese food. The menu emphasizes Cantonese cuisine, but there
are items from other regions of China. Signature dishes include brandy-
fried chicken, stir-fried clams in black-bean sauce, plus a couple of American items: New York steak and banana cream pie. ✉ *806 L St.,* ☎
916/442–7092. AE, MC, V. No lunch weekends.

$$–$$$ ✕ **Moxie.** Despite its simple decor and banklike schedule—the place
is closed all holidays—Moxie has earned a reputation as one of the
best restaurants in Sacramento. Start with the pork short ribs glazed
with red wine and basil or grilled eggplant with feta and capers, and
then move on to entrées like spicy jambalaya, roasted duck in espresso–
red wine sauce, or prawns carbonara. *2028 H St.,* ☎ *916/443–7585.
AE, D, DC, MC, V. Closed Sun.–Mon. and Aug.*

$$–$$$ ✕ **Rio City Café.** Eclectic lunch and dinner menus and huge floor-to-
ceiling windows with views of an Old Sacramento wharf are the dual
attractions of this bright restaurant. Outdoor heaters allow you to enjoy
your meal at river's edge year-round. Rio City serves light and hearty
fare: calamari salad, duck enchiladas with tomatillo sauce, venison stew
in pinot noir sauce over spaetzle, fettuccine with sun-dried tomato pesto.
✉ *1110 Front St.,* ☎ *916/442–8226. AE, D, DC, MC, V.*

$$–$$$ ✕ **Twenty Eight.** An intimate space with smoked mirrors, a golden
crushed satin ceiling, richly upholstered furniture, and artful lighting,
Twenty Eight further charms with genteel and attentive service. The
food—appetizers like potato-leek soup with sage croutons and crème
fraîche and main courses that include sesame-crusted ahi tuna with crispy
noodles and grilled lamb loin with roasted artichokes—is as refined
as the decor. *2730 N St.,* ☎ *916/456–2800. AE, D, DC, MC, V. Closed
Sun. No lunch weekends.*

$–$$$ ✕ **California Fats.** The menu at this Old Sacramento spot combines in-
triguing flavors. Among the dishes are wok-fried seafood in a spicy bean
sauce, herb-roasted chicken from the wood-fired oven, and ginger-roasted
salmon with wild rice and potato cakes. ✉ *1015 Front St.,* ☎ *916/
441–7966. AE, MC, V. No lunch weekends.*

$–$$$ ✕ **Paragary's Bar and Oven.** Pastas and brick-oven pizzas are the spe-
cialties of this casual spot. You won't go hungry here—portions are
enormous. A waterfall flows near the back patio, which holds hundreds
of plants. ✉ *1401 28th St.,* ☎ *916/457–5737. AE, D, DC, MC, V. No
lunch weekends.*

$–$$ ✕ **Centro.** The motorcycle with a skeleton rider in the front window
denotes the vibrant wackiness that spices up this popular midtown Mexican eatery. Bright yellow booths and salsa music contribute to the ambience, but the food—tasty Mexican fare well outside the taco-burrito

realm—is the real attraction. Dishes include citrus-marinated rotisserie chicken with mango, mint, and salsa, and pork slow-roasted in banana leaves. The bar carries more than 60 Mexican tequilas. ⊠ *2730 J St.,* ☎ *916/442–2552. AE, DC, MC, V. No lunch weekends.*

Lodging

$$$–$$$$ ⊡ **Amber House Bed & Breakfast Inn.** Three separate homes compose
★ this B&B near the Capitol. The original house, the Poet's Refuge, is a Craftsman-style home with five bedrooms named for famous poets. Next door the 1913 Mediterranean-style Artist's Retreat has a French Impressionist motif. The third, an 1897 Dutch Colonial Revival home named Musician's Manor, has gardens where weddings occasionally take place. All rooms have private baths tiled with Italian marble. Several rooms have fireplaces and bathrooms with two-person hot tubs and skylights. ⊠ *1315 22nd St., 95816,* ☎ *916/444–8085 or 800/755–6526,* ℻ *916/552–6529. 14 rooms. Bicycles. Full breakfast. AE, D, DC, MC, V.*

$$$–$$$$ ⊡ **Hyatt Regency at Capitol Park.** With a marble-and-glass lobby and
★ luxurious rooms, this hotel across from the Capitol and adjacent to the convention center is arguably Sacramento's finest. The best rooms have Capitol Park views. The service and attention to detail are outstanding. ⊠ *1209 L St., 95814,* ☎ *916/443–1234 or 800/233–1234,* ℻ *916/321–6699. 500 rooms, 24 suites. 2 restaurants, bar, pool, hot tub, exercise room, meeting rooms, car rental. AE, D, DC, MC, V.*

$$$ ⊡ **Best Western Sutter House.** Many of the pleasant, modern rooms in this downtown hotel open onto a courtyard surrounding a pool. The stylish restaurant, Scorpio's, serves contemporary cuisine. ⊠ *1100 H St., 95814,* ☎ *916/441–1314; 800/830–1314 in CA,* ℻ *916/441–5961. 97 rooms, 1 suite. Restaurant, lounge, no-smoking floor, pool, laundry service, free parking, Continental breakfast. AE, D, DC, MC, V.*

$$$ ⊡ **Holiday Inn Capitol Plaza.** Despite its decided lack of charm, this hotel has modern rooms and the best location for visiting Old Sacramento and the Downtown Plaza. The Holiday Inn is within walking distance of the Capitol. ⊠ *300 J St., 95814,* ☎ *916/446–0100,* ℻ *916/446–0117. 358 rooms, 6 suites. Restaurant, bar, pool, 2 saunas, convention center. AE, DC, MC, V.*

$$–$$$ ⊡ **Abigail's Bed and Breakfast Inn.** Trees shade this 1912 Colonial Revival mansion near the Capitol, in the Boulevard Park neighborhood. The living room and parlor flank a grand staircase leading to guest rooms, some with four-poster or canopy feather beds. One room has a whirlpool tub. ⊠ *2120 G St., 95816,* ☎ *916/441–5007 or 800/858–1568,* ℻ *916/441–0621. 4 rooms. Outdoor hot tub. Full breakfast. AE, D, DC, MC, V.*

$$–$$$ ⊡ **Delta King.** This grand old riverboat, now permanently moored on Old Sacramento's waterfront, once transported passengers between Sacramento and San Francisco. Among many design elements of note are its main staircase, mahogany paneling, and brass fittings. The best of the 44 staterooms are on the river side toward the back of the boat. ⊠ *1000 Front St., 95814,* ☎ *916/444–5464 or 800/825–5464,* ℻ *916/447–5959. 44 rooms. Restaurant, bar, meeting rooms, parking (fee). Continental breakfast. AE, D, DC, MC, V.*

$$–$$$ ⊡ **Hartley House.** Innkeeper Randy Hartley's great-grandfather built Hartley House in 1906. The quiet midtown inn has the feel of a small European hotel. All the antiques-filled rooms, which are named after British cities, have stereos and satellite TV. Breakfast is cooked to order. Guests have access to a secluded courtyard hot tub. *700 22nd St., 95816,* ☎ *916/447–7829 or 800/831–5806,* ℻ *916/447–1820. 5 rooms. In-room data ports, hot tub. Full breakfast. AE, D, DC, MC, V.*

$$–$$$ 🏨 **Radisson Hotel Sacramento.** Mediterranean-style two-story buildings clustered around a large artificial lake on an 18-acre landscaped site contain good-size rooms, with Art Deco appointments and furnishings. Many have patios or balconies. More of a resort than other Sacramento-area hotels, the Radisson presents summer jazz concerts in a lakeside amphitheater and holds barbecues on warm evenings. ⊠ *500 Leisure La., 95815, ☎ 916/922–2020 or 800/333–3333, FAX 916/649–9463. 292 rooms, 22 suites. 2 restaurants, bar, room service, pool, outdoor hot tub, exercise room, jogging, boating, bicycles, meeting rooms. AE, D, DC, MC, V.*

$ 🏨 **Sacramento International Hostel.** This landmark 1885 Victorian mansion has a grand mahogany staircase, a stained-glass atrium, frescoed ceilings, and carved and tiled fireplaces. Dormitory rooms and bedrooms suitable for singles, couples, and families are available, as is a shared kitchen. ⊠ *900 H St., 95814, ☎ 916/443–1691 or 800/909–4776, ext. 40, FAX 916/443–4763. 70 beds. MC, V.*

Nightlife and the Arts

Downtown Events Line (☎ 916/442–2500) has recorded information about seasonal events in the downtown area.

The **Blue Cue** (⊠ 1004 28th St., ☎ 916/442–7208), upstairs from Centro restaurant, is a somewhat upscale yet eclectic billiard lounge that features a very large selection of single-malt Scotch whiskeys. The **Fox and Goose** (⊠ 1001 R St., ☎ 916/443–8825), a casual pub with live music (including open-mic Monday), has been rated the "best breakfast spot" by the *Sacramento Bee*. Traditional pub food (fish and chips, Cornish pasties) is served on weekday evenings from 5:30 to 9:30. **Harlow's** (⊠ 2708 J St., ☎ 916/441–4693) draws a young crowd to its Art Deco bar–nightclub for live music after 9.

Sacramento Community Center Theater (⊠ 13th and L Sts., ☎ 916/264–5181) hosts concerts, opera, and ballet. The **Sacramento Light Opera Association** (⊠ 1419 H St., ☎ 916/557–1999) presents Broadway shows at the Sacramento Community Center Theater and in the huge Music Circus tent during summer.

Outdoor Activities and Sports

The basement-level **California Family Health & Fitness** (⊠ 428 J St., at 5th St., ☎ 916/442–9090) has a workout area, weight machines, and a sauna. The drop-in fee for nonmembers is $10. **Jedediah Smith Memorial Bicycle Trail** runs for 23 mi from Old Sacramento to Beals Point in Folsom, mostly along the American River. The **Sacramento Kings** of the National Basketball Association play at the Arco Arena (⊠ 1 Sports Pkwy., ☎ 916/928–6900).

Shopping

Among the many T-shirt and frozen-yogurt emporiums in Old Sacramento are some interesting art galleries and bookstores. Top local artists and craftspeople exhibit their works at **Artists' Collaborative Gallery** (⊠ 1007 2nd St., ☎ 916/444–3764). **Bookmine** (⊠ 1015 2nd St., ☎ 916/441–4609) sells used and rare books. The **Elder Craftsman** (⊠ 130 J St., ☎ 916/264–7762) specializes in items made by local senior citizens.

Arden Fair Mall, northeast of downtown off I–80 in the North Area, is Sacramento's largest shopping center. **Downtown Plaza,** comprising the K Street Mall along with many neighboring shops and restaurants, has shopping and entertainment. There's a Thursday-night market, and an outdoor ice-skating rink is set up in winter. **Pavilions Mall** (⊠ Fair Oaks Blvd. and Howe Ave.) has many boutiques.

THE GOLD COUNTRY
Highway 49 from Nevada City to Mariposa

Highway 49 winds the length of the gold-mining area, linking the towns of Nevada City, Grass Valley, Auburn, Placerville, Sutter Creek, Sonora, and Mariposa. Most are gentrified versions of once-rowdy mining camps, vestiges of which remain in roadside museums, old mining structures, and historic inns.

Nevada City

⓯ *62 mi north of Sacramento, I–80 to Hwy. 49.*

Nevada City, once known as the Queen City of the Northern Mines, is the most appealing of the northern Mother Lode towns. The iron-shuttered brick buildings that line the narrow downtown streets contain antiques shops, galleries, a winery, bookstores, boutiques, B&Bs, and restaurants. Horse-drawn carriage tours add to the romance, as do gas-powered streetlights. At one point in the 1850s Nevada City had a population of nearly 10,000, enough to support much cultural activity. The **Nevada City Chamber of Commerce** (⊠ 132 Main St., ☎ 530/265–2692) has books about the area and a free walking-tour map.

With its gingerbread-trimmed bell tower, **Firehouse No. 1** is one of the Gold Country's most photographed buildings. A museum, it houses relics of the fateful Donner Party (victims of a severe Sierra Nevada snowstorm), Gold-Rush artifacts, and a Chinese joss house (temple). ⊠ *214 Main St.,* ☎ *530/265–5468.* ☉ *May–Oct., daily 11–4; Nov.–Apr., Thurs.–Sun. 11–4.*

The redbrick **Nevada Theatre,** constructed in 1865, is California's oldest theater building in continuous use. Mark Twain, Emma Nevada, and many other superstars of bygone times appeared on its stage. The Nevada, also the home of the **Foothill Theater Company** (☎ 530/265–8587 or 888/730–8587), screens films and hosts theatrical and musical events. ⊠ *401 Broad St.,* ☎ *530/265–6161.*

The **Miners Foundry,** erected in 1856, produced machines for gold mining and logging. The Pelton Water Wheel, a source of power for the mines (the wheel also jump-started the hydroelectric power industry), was invented here. A cavernous building, the foundry serves as a cultural center that presents plays, concerts, an antiques show, and other events. ⊠ *325 Spring St.,* ☎ *530/265–5040. Closed Mon.*

You can watch while you sip at the **Nevada City Winery,** where the tasting room overlooks the production area. ⊠ *Miners Foundry Garage, 321 Spring St.,* ☎ *530/265–9463.* ☉ *Tastings daily noon–5.*

Dining and Lodging

$$–$$$ ✕ **Country Rose Café.** The lengthy country-French menu at this antiques-laden café includes seafood, beef, lamb, chicken, and ratatouille. In the summer there is outdoor service on a verdant patio. ⊠ *300 Commercial St.,* ☎ *530/265–6248. AE, D, DC, MC, V.*

$$–$$$ ✕ **Friar Tuck's.** A guitar player performs nightly at this vaguely 1960s-retro gathering spot that feels like a wine cellar; sometimes patrons sing along. Rack of lamb, roast duck, fondue, Iowa beef, and Hawaiian fish specials are on the menu. There's an extensive wine and beer list as well as a full bar. ⊠ *111 N. Pine St.,* ☎ *530/265–9093. AE, MC, V. No lunch.*

$$–$$$ ✕ **Kirby's Creekside Restaurant & Bar.** This two-level restaurant/bar complex perches over the quieter side of Deer Creek. You can dine on the large outdoor deck in warm weather or sit by the fireplace on cooler days. Among the inventive Continental preparations is the pork loin stuffed with roasted peppers. In the Chef's Culinary Adventure, the chef designs a meal (of three to six courses) for you based on your food preferences. *101 Broad St.,* ☎ *530/265–3445. AE, MC, V.*

$–$$ ✕ **Cirino's.** American-Italian dishes—seafood, pasta, and veal—are served at this informal bar and grill. The restaurant's handsome Brunswick bar is of Gold-Rush vintage. ⊠ *309 Broad St.,* ☎ *530/265–2246. AE, D, MC, V.*

$$–$$$ ▥ **Deer Creek Inn.** The main veranda of this 1860 Queen Anne Victorian overlooks a huge lawn that rolls past a rose-covered arbor to the creek below. You can play croquet on the lawn or pan for gold from the creek. All rooms have king or queen beds. Some rooms have two-person tubs. *116 Nevada St., 95959,* ☎ *530/265–0363 or 800/655–0363,* ℻ *530/265–0980. 5 rooms. Full breakfast. AE, MC, V.*

$$–$$$ ▥ **Flume's End.** This homey and romantic inn was built at the end of a flume that once brought water into Nevada City's mines. Two rooms have hot tubs and most have creek views. The decor is eclectic Victorian. ⊠ *317 S. Pine St., 95959,* ☎ *530/265–9665 or 800/991–8118. 6 rooms. Full breakfast. MC, V.*

$$–$$$ ▥ **Red Castle Inn.** A state landmark, this 1857 Gothic Revival man-
★ sion stands on a forested hillside overlooking Nevada City. Its brick exterior is trimmed with white icicle woodwork. A steep private pathway leads down through the terraced gardens into town. Handsome antique furnishings and Oriental rugs decorate the rooms. Home-cooked recipes are featured at the opulent afternoon tea service and morning breakfast buffet. ⊠ *109 Prospect St., 95959,* ☎ *530/265–5135 or 800/761–4766. 7 rooms. Full breakfast. MC, V.*

$–$$ ▥ **Northern Queen Inn.** Most of the accommodations at this bright creek-side inn are typical motel units, but there are eight two-story chalets and eight rustic cottages with efficiency kitchens and gas log fireplaces in a secluded, wooded area. Guests ride free on the hotel's narrow-gauge railroad, which offers excursions through Maidu Indian homelands and a Chinese cemetery from Gold Rush days. ⊠ *400 Railroad Ave. (Sacramento St. exit off Hwy. 49), 95959,* ☎ *530/265–5824 or 800/226–3090,* ℻ *530/265–3720. 86 rooms. Restaurant, refrigerators, pool, hot tub, convention center. AE, DC, MC, V.*

Grass Valley

4 mi south of Nevada City on Hwy. 49.

More than half of California's total gold production was extracted from mines around Grass Valley. Unlike in neighboring Nevada City, urban sprawl surrounds Grass Valley's historic downtown. The Empire Mine and the North Star Power House and Pelton Wheel Exhibit are among the Gold Country's most fascinating exhibits.

A great source of local information, the **Grass Valley/Nevada County Chamber of Commerce** is in a reproduction of the home on this site that was owned by the notorious dancer Lola Montez. Lola, who arrived in Grass Valley in the early 1850s, was no great talent—her popularity among miners derived from her suggestive spider dance—but her loves, who reportedly included composer Franz Liszt, were legendary. According to one account, she arrived in California after having been "permanently retired from her job as Bavarian king Ludwig's mistress," literary muse, and political adviser. She seems to have pushed too hard for democracy, which contributed to his overthrow and her banishment as a witch—or so the story went. The memory of licentious Lola lingers in Grass Valley, as does her bathtub (in the front yard of the house). ✉ *248 Mill St.,* ☎ *916/273–4667.*

The landmark **Holbrooke Hotel,** built in 1851, hosted Lola Montez, Mark Twain, Ulysses S. Grant, and a stream of other U.S. presidents. Its restaurant/saloon is one of the oldest still operating west of the Mississippi. ✉ *212 W. Main St.,* ☎ *530/273–1353 or 800/933–7077.*

★ ⑯   The hard-rock gold mine at **Empire Mine State Historic Park** was one of California's richest. An estimated 5.8 million ounces were extracted from its 367 mi of underground passages between 1850 and 1956. On the 50-minute tours you can walk into a mine shaft, peer into the mine's deeper recesses, and view the owner's "cottage," whose woodwork is exquisite. The visitor center has mining exhibits, and a picnic area is nearby. ✉ *10791 E. Empire St. (exit south from Hwy. 49),* ☎ *530/ 273–8522.* ☐ *$3.* ◷ *June–Aug., daily 9–6; Sept.–Apr., daily 10–5; May, daily 9–6. Tours in summer on the hr 11–4; winter weekends only at 1 (cottage only) and 2 (mine yard only), weather permitting.*

☾   The **North Star Power House and Pelton Wheel Exhibit** stars a 32-ft-high Pelton enclosed waterwheel said to be the largest ever built. It was used to power mining operations and was a forerunner of the modern turbines that generate hydroelectricity. Hands-on displays are geared to children, and there's a picnic area. ✉ *Empire and McCourtney Sts. (Empire St. exit north from Hwy. 49),* ☎ *530/273–4255.* ☐ *Donation requested.* ◷ *May–mid-Oct., daily 10–5.*

Lodging

$$–$$$ ▥ **Murphy's Inn.** A gold baron built the main inn here as a wedding present for his bride. Both the 1866 inn, which revels in its Victorian opulence, and the historic Donation Day House across the street contain antiques, lace curtains, and floral print wallpaper. Half the guest rooms have their own fireplaces. ✉ *318 Neal St., 95945,* ☎ *530/273– 6873 or 800/895–2488. 8 rooms. Full breakfast. AE, MC, V.*

Auburn

⑰   *24 mi south of Grass Valley on Hwy. 49; 34 mi northeast of Sacramento on I–80.*

Auburn is the Gold Country town most accessible to travelers on the interstate. An important transportation center during the Gold Rush, Auburn has a small old-town district with narrow climbing streets, cobblestone lanes, wooden sidewalks, and many original buildings. A $1 trolley operated by the **Placer County Visitor Information Center** (☎ 530/887–2111 or 800/427–6463) loops through downtown and Old Town, with stops at some hotels and inns. Fresh produce, flowers, baked goods, and gifts are for sale at the farmers' market held each Saturday morning.

Auburn's standout structure is the **Placer County Courthouse.** The classic gold-dome building houses the Placer County Museum, which documents the area's history—Native American, railroad, agricultural, and mining—from the early 1700s to 1900. ✉ *101 Maple St.,* ☎ *530/889– 6500.* ☐ *Free.* ◷ *Tues.–Sun. 10–4.*

The **Bernhard Museum Complex,** whose centerpiece is the former Traveler's Rest Hotel, was built in 1851. A residence and adjacent winery buildings reflect family life in the late Victorian era; in the carriage house are period conveyances. ✉ *291 Auburn-Folsom Rd.,* ☎ *530/889–*

6500. 🔳 *$1 (includes entry to Gold Country Museum).* ⊙ *Tues.–Fri. 10:30–3, weekends noon–4.*

The **Gold Country Museum** surveys life in the mines. Exhibits include a walk-through mine tunnel, a gold-panning stream, and a replica saloon. ✉ *1273 High St., off Auburn-Folsom Rd.,* ☎ *530/889–6500.* 🔳 *$1 (includes entry to Bernhard Museum Complex).* ⊙ *Tues.–Fri. 10–3:30, weekends 11–4.*

Dining and Lodging

$–$$$ ✗ **Le Bilig French Café.** Simplicity and elegance of cuisine and decor are the goals of the chefs at this country-French café on the outskirts of Auburn. Escargots, coq au vin, and quiche are standard offerings; specials might include salmon in parchment paper. *11750 Atwood Rd., off Hwy. 49 near the Bel Air Mall,* ☎ *530/888–1491. MC, V. Closed Mon.–Tues. No lunch.*

$–$$ ✗ **Latitudes.** An 1870 Victorian is the setting for delicious multicul-
★   tural cuisine. The menu (with monthly specials from diverse geographical regions) includes seafood, chicken, beef and turkey entrées prepared with Mexican spices, curries, cheese, or teriyaki sauce. Sunday brunch is deservedly popular, as are evenings at the bar downstairs. ✉ *130 Maple St.,* ☎ *530/885–9535. AE, MC, V. No lunch Sat., no dinner Mon.–Tues.*

$ ✗ **Awful Annie's.** Big patio umbrellas (and outdoor heaters when necessary) allow patrons to sit inside or outside and take in the view of old-town Auburn from this popular spot for breakfast—one specialty is an omelet with chili—or lunch. ✉ *160 Sacramento St.,* ☎ *530/888–9857. AE, MC, V. No dinner.*

$$–$$$ 🏨 **Powers Mansion Inn.** This inn hints at the lavish lifestyle enjoyed by the gold-rush gentry. Two light-filled parlors have gleaming oak floors, Asian antiques, and ornate Victorian chairs and settees. A second-floor maze of narrow corridors leads to the guest rooms, which have brass and pencil-post beds with handmade quilts. ✉ *164 Cleveland Ave., 95603,* ☎ *530/885–1166,* 🆋 *530/885–1386. 13 rooms. Full breakfast. AE, MC, V.*

$$ 🏨 **Holiday Inn.** On a hill above the freeway across from Old Auburn, the hotel has an imposing columned entrance but a welcoming lobby. Rooms are chain-standard but attractively furnished. All have work areas and coffeemakers. Those nearest the parking lot can be noisy. ✉ *120 Grass Valley Hwy., 95603,* ☎ *530/887–8787 or 800/814–8787,* 🆋 *530/887–9824. 88 rooms, 8 suites. Restaurant, bar, in-room data ports, room service, pool, spa, exercise room, business services, convention center. AE, D, DC, MC, V.*

$ 🏨 **Auburn Inn.** The decor at this well-maintained property is contemporary, in teal and pastel colors. Though a short distance from the freeway, the inn is fairly quiet. ✉ *1875 Auburn Ravine Rd. (Forest Hill exit north from I–80), 95603,* ☎ *530/885–1800,* 🆋 *530/888–6424. 77 rooms, 2 suites. No-smoking floor, pool, spa, coin laundry, meeting rooms. Continental breakfast. AE, D, DC, MC, V.*

Coloma

18 mi south of Auburn on Hwy. 49.

The California gold rush started in Coloma. "My eye was caught with the glimpse of something shining in the bottom of the ditch," James Marshall recalled. Marshall himself never found any more "color," as gold came to be called.

★ ⑱   Most of Coloma lies within **Marshall Gold Discovery State Historic Park.** Though crowded with tourists in summer, Coloma hardly resembles the mob scene it was in 1849, when 2,000 prospectors staked out claims along the streambed. The town's population grew to 4,000, supporting seven hotels, three banks, and many stores and businesses. But when reserves of the precious metal dwindled, prospectors left as quickly as they had come. A working replica of John Sutter's mill lies near the spot where John Marshall first saw gold. A trail leads to a monument marking Marshall's discovery. The museum is not as interesting as the outdoor exhibits. ✉ *Hwy. 49*, ☎ *530/622–3470.* ☞ *$5 per vehicle (day use).* ☉ *Park daily 8 AM–sunset. Museum summer, daily 10–5; Labor Day–Memorial Day, daily 10–4:30.*

Lodging

$$–$$$ 🏨 **Coloma Country Inn.** Five of the rooms at this B&B on 5 acres in the State Historic Park are inside a restored 1852 Victorian; two suites, one with a kitchenette, are in the carriage house. Appointments include antique double and queen-size beds, handmade quilts, stenciled friezes, and fresh flowers. Balloon and white-water-rafting packages are available. ✉ *345 High St., 95613,* ☎ *530/622–6919,* 🖷 *530/622–1795. 5 rooms, 2 with shared bath; 2 suites. Full breakfast. No credit cards.*

Placerville

10 mi south of Coloma on Hwy. 49; 44 mi east of Sacramento on U.S. 50.

It's hard to imagine now, but in 1849 about 4,000 miners staked out every gully and hillside in Placerville, turning the town into a rip-roaring camp of log cabins, tents, and clapboard houses. The area was then known as Hangtown, a graphic allusion to the nature of frontier justice. It took on the name Placerville in 1854 and became an important supply center for the miners. Mark Hopkins, Philip Armour, and John Studebaker were among the industrialists who got their starts here.

★ ⑲   **Hangtown's Gold Bug Mine,** owned by the city of Placerville, has a fully lighted shaft and is open for self-guided touring. A shaded stream runs through the park, and there are picnic facilities. ✉ *1 mi off U.S. 50, north on Bedford Ave.,* ☎ *530/642–5238.* ☞ *$3.* ☉ *Mar.–mid-Apr., weekends noon–4; mid-Apr.–Oct., daily 10–4; Nov., weekends noon–4, weather permitting. Closed Dec.–Feb.*

OFF THE BEATEN PATH   **APPLE HILL –** Roadside stands sell fresh produce from more than 50 family farms in this area. During the fall harvest season (from September through December) members of the Apple Hill Growers Association (☎ 530/644–7692) open their orchards and vineyards for apple and berry picking, picnicking, and wine and cider tasting. Many sell baked items and picnic food. ✉ *About 5 mi east of Hwy. 49; take Camino exit from U.S. 50.*

Dining and Lodging

$$–$$$ ✕ **Zachary Jacques.** It's not easy to locate, so call for directions. But ★   finding this country-French restaurant is worth the effort. Appetizers on the seasonal menu might include escargots or mushrooms prepared in several ways, roasted garlic with olive oil served on toast, or spicy lamb sausage. Entrées such as roast rack of lamb, beef stew, and scallops and prawns in lime butter receive traditional preparation. The attached wine bar, open during the daytime, sells box lunches to go. ✉ *1821 Pleasant Valley Rd. (3 mi east of Diamond Springs),* ☎ *530/626–8045. AE, MC, V. Closed Mon.–Tues. No lunch.*

$–$$$ ✕ **Lil' Mama D. Carlo's Italian Kitchen.** This comfortable Italian restaurant with a pleasant wait staff serves large portions of homemade pasta, chicken, and some vegetarian dishes, heavy on the garlic, often in a red sauce. Local wines are available. ⊠ *482 Main St.,* ☎ *530/626–1612. MC, V. Closed Mon.–Tues. No lunch.*

$$ ✕ **Café Luna.** Tucked into the back of the Creekside Place shopping complex is a small restaurant with about 30 seats inside, plus outdoor tables overlooking a creek. The healthful entrées include grilled chicken breast with blueberry and pasilla salsa. ⊠ *451 Main St.,* ☎ *530/642–8669. AE, D, MC, V. Closed Sun. No dinner Mon.–Tues.*

$$–$$$ ▦ **The Seasons Bed & Breakfast.** One of the oldest historic homes in town has been transformed into a lovely and relaxing oasis. Decorated in an eclectic yet sophisticated manner, the main house, two garden cottages, and the wonderful gardens themselves are filled with original artwork. Privacy is treasured here; each guest room has its own entrance. A spacious suite with a sitting room and stained glass windows takes up the entire top floor of the main house. One cottage has a little white picket fence around its own minigarden; the other has a two-person shower. ⊠ *2934 Bedford Ave., 95667,* ☎ *530/626–4420. 3 rooms, 1 suite. No-smoking rooms. Full breakfast. MC, V.*

$$–$$$ ▦ **Shadowridge Ranch and Lodge.** In the wooded hills outside Placerville, you'll find a bit of rustic heaven in the form of a beautifully restored lodge complex. The immaculate hand-hewn log and stone cottages, most with wood-burning stoves, are filled with interesting artifacts of ranch and lodge life—including some dramatic taxidermy specimens—as well as many modern amenities. Each unit has its own patio. In the afternoon, guests are served complimentary local wines and a huge appetizer platter in the 19th-century stone wine cellar or on the patio off the main house. ⊠ *3500 Fort Jim Rd., 95667,* ☎ *530/295–1000 or 800/644–3498,* FAX *530/626–5613. 4 suites. No-smoking rooms, minibars, refrigerators, hiking. Full breakfast. AE, MC, V. Closed Jan.–Mar.*

$$ ▦ **Best Western Placerville Inn.** This motel's serviceable rooms are done in the chain's trademark pastels. The pool comes in handy during the hot summer months. ⊠ *6850 Greenleaf Dr., near U.S. 50's Missouri Flats exit, 95667,* ☎ *530/622–9100 or 800/854–9100,* FAX *530/622–9376. 105 rooms. Restaurant, pool, hot tub. AE, D, DC, MC, V.*

Shenandoah Valley

20 mi south of Placerville on Shenandoah Rd., east of Hwy. 49.

The most concentrated Gold Country wine-touring area lies in the rolling hills of the Shenandoah Valley, east of Plymouth. Robust zinfandel is the primary grape grown here, but vineyards also produce cabernet sauvignon, sauvignon blanc, and other varietals. Most wineries are open on weekend afternoons; several have shaded picnic areas, gift shops, and galleries or museums. Maps are available from the **Amador County Chamber of Commerce** (☞ Contacts and Resources *in* Sacramento and the Gold Country A to Z, *below*).

Sobon Estate (⊠ 14430 Shenandoah Rd., ☎ 209/245–6554) operates the Shenandoah Valley Museum, illustrating pioneer life and wine making in the valley. It's open daily from 10 to 5. **Charles Spinetta Winery** (⊠ 12557 Steiner Rd., ☎ 209/245–3384), which features a wildlife art gallery in addition to wine tasting, is open daily except Monday between 10 and 5. The gallery at **Shenandoah Vineyards** (⊠ 12300 Steiner Rd., ☎ 209/245–4455), open daily from 10 to 5, displays contemporary art.

Lodging

$$ ▦ **Amador Harvest Inn.** This B&B adjacent to Deaver Vineyards occupies a bucolic lakeside spot in the Shenandoah Valley. A contemporary Cape Cod–style structure has homey guest rooms with private baths.

Public areas include a living room with fireplace and a music room with a view of the lake. ⊠ *12455 Steiner Rd., 95669,* ☎ *209/245–5512. 4 rooms. Full breakfast. AE, MC, V.*

$$ ⊞ **Indian Creek Bed and Breakfast.** This log and stone lodge near Plymouth is a western movie buff's *and* a nature lover's dream. Built in 1932 by a Hollywood producer for parties with friends like John Wayne, the 10-acre spread includes a creek and frog pond and is a haven for birds of all kinds. The decor emphasizes a Hollywood version of the West. The two-story great room features a 28-ft-high stone fireplace. A big breakfast is served at the 14-ft oak table in the dining room. ⊠ *21950 Hwy. 49, 95669,* ☎ *209/245–4648,* FAX *209/245–3230. 4 rooms. Pool, outdoor hot tub. Full breakfast. D, MC, V.*

Amador City

6 mi south of Plymouth on Hwy. 49.

The history of tiny Amador City mirrors the boom-to-bust-to-boom cycle of many Gold Country towns. With an output of $42 million in gold, its Keystone Mine was one of the most productive in the Mother Lode. After all the gold was extracted, the miners cleared out and the area suffered. Amador City now derives its wealth from tourists, who come to browse its antiques and specialty shops, many of them on or off Highway 49.

Dining and Lodging

$$–$$$ ✕⊞ **Imperial Hotel.** The whimsically decorated rooms at this 1879 hotel
★ mock Victorian excesses in a modern way. Antique furnishings include iron and brass beds, gingerbread flourishes, and, in one room, Art Deco appointments. The two front rooms, which can be noisy, have balconies. The hotel's fine restaurant serves meals in a bright dining room and on the patio. The menu changes quarterly. The cuisine ranges from vegetarian to country-hearty to contemporary eclectic. ⊠ *Hwy. 49, 95601,* ☎ *209/267–9172 or 800/242–5594,* FAX *209/267–9249. 6 rooms. Restaurant, bar. Full breakfast. AE, D, DC, MC, V. 2-night minimum on weekends. No lunch.*

Sutter Creek

★ ⓴ *2 mi south of Amador City on Hwy. 49.*

Sutter Creek is a charming conglomeration of balconied buildings, Victorian homes, and neo–New England structures. The stores along Highway 49 (called Main Street in the town proper) are worth visiting for works by the many local artists and craftspeople.

OFF THE   **DAFFODIL HILL –** Each spring a 4-acre hillside east of Sutter Creek erupts
BEATEN PATH in a riot of yellow and gold as 300,000 daffodils burst into bloom. The garden is the work of members of the McLaughlin family, which has owned this site since 1887. Daffodil plantings began in the 1930s. The display usually takes place between mid-March and mid-April. ⊠ *From Main St. (Hwy. 49) in Sutter Creek take Shake Ridge Rd. east 13 mi,* ☎ *209/223–0350.* 🎫 *Free.* ☉ *Daily in season 9–5.*

Dining and Lodging

$$–$$$ ✕ **Zinfandel's.** Black-bean chili in an edible bread terrine and smoked mussels and bay shrimp with roasted garlic cloves are among the appetizers at this casual restaurant with an adventurous menu. Entrées might include filet mignon coated in a marinade of green onions and cumin. *51 Hanford St.,* ☎ *209/267–5008. AE, D, MC, V. Closed Mon.–Wed. No lunch.*

$ ✕ **Chatterbox Café.** This classic 1940s luncheonette has only 5 tables and 14 counter stools. Read a vintage newspaper or look around at the jazz instruments and Disney memorabilia on the shelves while you wait for your chicken-fried steak, burger, homemade pie, or hot fudge sundae. The menu is as big as the Chatterbox is small. ⊠ *39 Main St.,* ☎ *209/267–5935. AE, D, MC, V. Closed Thurs. No dinner.*

$ ✕ **Somewhere in Time.** Sip tea, sample a sinful dessert, or lunch on sandwiches and salads before or after browsing through the antiques shops in this complex that's part Victorian boutique, part dining room. The building, erected in 1860, was originally a miners' saloon run by Chinese immigrants. ⊠ *34 Main St.,* ☎ *209/267–5789. D, MC, V. No dinner.*

$$$–$$$$ ▣ **The Foxes Bed & Breakfast.** The rooms in this white 1857 clapboard
★ house are handsome, with high ceilings, antique beds, and lofty armoires. All have queen-size beds; five have wood-burning fireplaces or cable TV with VCRs. Breakfast is cooked to order and delivered on a silver service to your room or the gazebo in the garden. Innkeepers Min and Pete Fox have pampered guests here since 1980, and they are full of local wisdom. ⊠ *77 Main St., 95685,* ☎ *209/267–5882 or 800/987–3344,* ℻ *209/267–0712. 5 rooms, 2 suites. No-smoking rooms. Full breakfast. D, MC, V.*

$$–$$$ ▣ **Grey Gables Inn.** Charming yet modern, this inn brings a touch of the English countryside to the Gold Country. Each room, named after a British literary figure, has a gas-log fireplace. Afternoon tea and evening refreshments are served in the parlor. Birds flit about the wisteria in the terraced garden. *161 Hanford St., 95685,* ☎ *209/267–1039 or 800/ 473–9422,* ℻ *209/267–0998. 8 rooms. Full breakfast. MC, V.*

$$ ▣ **Picture Rock Inn.** Original redwood paneling, wainscoting, beams, and cabinets lend the Picture Rock a cozy feel, as do leaded- and stained-glass windows. Eclectic furnishings span eras from Victorian to Art Deco; a 1920s carousel horse is suspended mid-leap in the front room. Most rooms have views and gas-log fireplaces. ⊠ *55 Eureka St., 95685,* ☎ *209/267–5500 or 800/399–2389. 5 rooms. Full breakfast. AE, D, MC, V.*

$ ▣ **Aparicio's Hotel.** Budget-minded travelers will appreciate this clean hotel whose rooms contain two queen-size beds. ⊠ *271 Hanford St., 95685,* ☎ *209/267–9177,* ℻ *209/267–5303. 52 rooms. D, MC, V.*

Jackson

㉑ *8 mi south of Sutter Creek on Hwy. 49.*

Jackson once had the world's deepest and richest mines, the Kennedy and the Argonaut, which together produced $70 million in gold. These were deep-rock mines. Tunnels extended as much as a mile underground. Most of the miners who worked the lode were of Serbian or Italian origin, and they gave the town a European character that persists to this day. Jackson has aboveground pioneer cemeteries whose headstones tell the stories of local Serbian and Italian families. The terraced cemetery on the grounds of the handsome **St. Sava Serbian Orthodox Church** (⊠ 724 N. Main St.) is the most impressive.

Jackson wasn't the Gold Country's rowdiest town, but the party lasted longer here than most anywhere else: "Girls' dormitories" (brothels) and nickel slot machines flourished until the mid-1950s. The heart of Jackson's historic section is the **National Hotel** (⊠ 2 Water St.), which operates an old-time saloon in the lobby. The hotel is especially active on weekends, when people come from miles around to participate in the Saturday-night sing-alongs.

The **Amador County Museum,** built in the late 1850s as a private home, provides a colorful take on Gold-Rush life. Displays include a kitchen with a woodstove, the Amador County bicentennial quilt, and a classroom. A time line recounts the county's checkered past. The museum conducts hourly tours of large-scale working models of the nearby Kennedy Mine. ⊠ *225 Church St.,* ☎ *209/223–6386.* ☞ *Museum free, building with mine $1.* ⊘ *Wed.–Sun. 10–4.*

Dining and Lodging

$$–$$$ ✕ **Upstairs Restaurant.** Chef Layne McCollum takes a creative approach to contemporary American cuisine—fowl, fresh seafood, and meat—in his 12-table restaurant. The baked-Brie and roast-garlic appetizer and homemade soups are specialties. Local wines are reasonably priced. Downstairs there's a streetside bistro and wine bar. ⊠ *164 Main St.,* ☎ *209/223–3342. AE, D, MC, V. Closed Mon.*

$ ✕ **Rosebud's Classic Café.** Art Deco decor and music from the 1930s and 1940s set the mood at this homey café. Among the classic American dishes served are hot roast beef, turkey, and meat loaf with mashed potatoes smothered in gravy. Charbroiled burgers, freshly baked pies, and espresso or gourmet coffees round out the lunch menu. Omelets, hotcakes, and many other items are served for breakfast. ⊠ *26 Main St.,* ☎ *209/223–1035. MC, V. No dinner.*

$$–$$$ 🛏 **Court Street Inn.** This Victorian has tin ceilings and a redwood staircase. The cozy first-floor Angel Court room has a fireplace; the Crystal Court room has a large whirlpool and a Wedgewood stove. The Indian House, a two-bedroom cottage, has a large bathroom, a TV with VCR, and a stereo. A third building, Vintage Court, is decorated in wine colors and contains two guest rooms that share a parlor and deck. ⊠ *215 Court St., 95642,* ☎ *209/223–0416 or 800/200–0416,* FAX *209/223–5429. 5 rooms, 2 suites. Outdoor hot tub. Full breakfast. AE, D, MC, V.*

$–$$ 🛏 **Best Western Amador Inn.** Convenience and price are the main attractions of this two-story motel right on the highway. Rooms are nicely decorated; many have fireplaces. ⊠ *200 S. Hwy. 49, 95642,* ☎ *209/ 223–0211 or 800/543–5221,* FAX *209/223–4836. 118 rooms. Restaurant, pool, laundry service. AE, D, DC, MC, V.*

Angels Camp

㉒ *20 mi south of Jackson on Hwy. 49.*

Angels Camp is famed chiefly for its May jumping-frog contest, based on Mark Twain's "The Jumping Frog of Calaveras County." The writer reputedly heard the story of the jumping frog from Ross Coon, proprietor of Angels Hotel, which has been operating since 1856.

Angels Camp Museum has Gold-Rush relics—photos, rocks, petrified wood, old mining equipment, and a horse-drawn hearse. The huge Pelton Water Wheel exhibit explains how the apparatus supplied water power to the mines. The carriage house out back holds 25 carriages and an impressive display of mineral specimens. ⊠ *753 S. Main St.,* ☎ *209/736–2963.* ☞ *$1.* ⊘ *Jan.–Feb., weekends 10–3; Mar.–Nov., daily 10–3. Closed Dec.*

OFF THE BEATEN PATH **THE CALIFORNIA CAVERNS AND MOANING CAVERN –** A ½-mi subterranean trail at the California Caverns winds through large chambers and past underground streams and lakes. There aren't many steps to climb but it's a hefty walk, with some narrow passageways and steep spots. The caverns, at a constant 53°F, contain crystalline formations not found elsewhere; the 80-minute guided tour includes fascinating history and geology. A 235-step spiral staircase leads into the vast Moaning

Cavern. More adventurous sorts can rappel into the chamber—ropes and instruction are provided. Otherwise, the only way inside is via the 45-minute tour, during which you'll see giant (and still growing) stalactites and stalagmites and an archaeological site that holds some of the oldest human remains yet found in America (unlucky people have fallen into the cavern an average of once every 130 years starting 13,000 years ago). ⊠ *California Caverns: 9 mi east of San Andreas on Mountain Ranch Rd., then about 3 mi on Cave City Road (follow the signs),* ☏ *209/736–2708.* ⊒ *$8.* ⊘ *Usually May–Dec., but call ahead.* ⊠ *Moaning Cavern: Parrots Ferry Rd., 2 mi south of town of Vallecito, off Hwy. 4 east of Angels Camp,* ☏ *209/736–2708.* ⊒ *$7.75.* ⊘ *May–Oct., daily 9–6; Nov.–Apr., daily 10–5.*

Murphys

㉓ *10 mi east of Angels Camp on Hwy. 4.*

Murphys is a well-preserved town of white picket fences, Victorian houses, and interesting shops. Horatio Alger and Ulysses S. Grant are among the guests who have signed the register at **Murphys Historic Hotel and Lodge.** The men were among the 19th-century visitors to the giant sequoia groves in nearby Calaveras Big Trees State Park.

The **Kautz Ironstone Winery and Caverns** is worth a visit even if you don't drink wine. Tours take visitors into underground tunnels cooled by a waterfall from a natural spring; they include a performance of a huge automated pipe organ. The winery schedules concerts, art shows, and other events on weekends. On display is a 44-pound specimen of crystalline gold. A deli offers lunch items. ⊠ *1894 Six Mile Rd.,* ☏ *209/728–1251.* ⊘ *Daily 11–5.*

Dining and Lodging

$–$$ ✕ **Grounds.** Light Italian entrées, grilled vegetables, chicken, seafood, and steak are the specialties at this bistro and coffee shop. Sandwiches, salads, and homemade soups are served for lunch. The atmosphere is friendly and the service attentive. ⊠ *402 Main St.,* ☏ *209/728–8663. MC, V. Closed Tues. No dinner Wed.*

$$$–$$$$ 🏨 **Dunbar House 1880.** The oversize rooms in this elaborate Italianate-style home have brass beds, down comforters, gas-burning
★ stoves, and claw-foot tubs. Broad wraparound verandas encourage lounging, as do colorful gardens and shady elm trees. The Cedar Room's sunporch has a two-person whirlpool tub and a view of a white-flowering almond tree; in the Sequoia Room you can gaze at the garden while soaking in a bubble bath. Guests are served an appetizer and wine tray in their rooms in the afternoon, and breakfast is an extravagant affair. ⊠ *271 Jones St., 95247,* ☏ *209/728–2897 or 800/692–6006,* FAX *209/728–1451. 4 rooms. Refrigerators, in-room VCRs. Full breakfast. AE, MC, V.*

$$–$$$$ 🏨 **Redbud Inn.** Some rooms at this inn have double-sided fireplaces, cathedral ceilings, garden balconies, or Victorian claw-foot tubs. A room with brass beds and a tin ceiling replicates a miner's cabin. Wine and snacks are served in the parlor each evening. ⊠ *402 Main St., 95247,* ☏ *209/728–8533 or 800/827–8533,* FAX *209/728–9123. 13 rooms. Full breakfast. D, MC, V.*

$–$$ ✕🏨 **Murphys Historic Hotel and Lodge.** This 1855 stone hotel figured in Bret Harte's short story "A Night at Wingdam," and Mark Twain and the bandit Black Bart signed the register. Accommodations are in the hotel and a modern motel-style addition. The older rooms are furnished with antiques, many of them large and hand-carved. The hotel has a convivial old-time saloon, which can be noisy into the wee hours.

✉ 457 Main St., 95247, ☎ 209/728–3444 or 800/532–7684, FAX 209/728–1590. 29 rooms (9 historic rooms share baths). Restaurant, bar, meeting rooms. Continental breakfast. AE, D, DC, MC, V.

OFF THE
BEATEN PATH

CALAVERAS BIG TREES STATE PARK – This state park is home to hundreds of the largest and rarest living things on the planet—magnificent giant sequoia redwood trees. Some are almost 3,000 years old, 90 ft around at the base, and about 250 ft tall. The park's self-guided trails range from a 200-yard trail to 1-mi and 5-mi loops through the groves. There are campgrounds and picnic areas; swimming, wading, fishing, and sunbathing on the Stanislaus River are popular in summer. ✉ Off Hwy. 4, 15 mi northeast of Murphys (4 mi northeast of Arnold), ☎ 209/795–2334. 🖾 $5 per vehicle (day use); $16 for campsites. Disposal station, fire rings, flush toilets, hot showers, water. ☉ Park 8 AM–sunset (day use). Visitor center May–Oct., daily 10–4; Nov.–Apr., weekends 11–3.

Columbia State Historic Park

★ ㉔ 14 mi south of Angels Camp, Hwy. 49 to Parrots Ferry Rd.

🐣 Columbia State Historic Park, known as the Gem of the Southern Mines, comes as close to a Gold-Rush town in its heyday as any site in the Gold Country. You can ride a stagecoach, pan for gold, or watch a blacksmith working at his anvil. Street musicians perform in summer. Restored or reconstructed buildings include a Wells Fargo Express office, a Masonic temple, stores, saloons, two hotels, a firehouse, churches, a school, and a newspaper office. All are staffed to simulate a working 1850s town. ☎ 209/532–4301. 🖾 Free. ☉ Daily 8:30–5.

Dining and Lodging

$$ ✕🖾 **City Hotel.** The rooms in this restored 1856 hostelry are furnished with period antiques. Two have balconies overlooking Main Street, and six rooms open onto a second-floor parlor. All the accommodations have private half-baths with showers nearby; robes and slippers are provided. The restaurant ($$–$$$; closed Monday), one of the Gold Country's best, serves French-accented California cuisine complemented by a huge selection of wines from California. The What Cheer Saloon is right out of a western movie. ✉ Main St., Columbia 95310, ☎ 209/532–1479 or 800/532–1479, FAX 209/532–7027. 10 rooms. Restaurant, bar. Continental breakfast. AE, D, MC, V.

$–$$ 🖾 **Fallon Hotel.** The state of California restored this 1857 hotel. All rooms have antiques and a private half-bath; there are separate men's and women's showers. If you occupy one of the five balcony rooms, you can sit outside with your morning coffee and watch the town wake up. ✉ Washington St., Columbia 95310, ☎ 209/532–1470, FAX 209/532–7027. 14 rooms. Continental breakfast. AE, D, MC, V.

Nightlife and the Arts

Sierra Repertory Theater Company (☎ 209/532–4644), a local professional company, presents a full season of plays, comedies, and musicals at the Historic Fallon House Theater and another venue in East Sonora. The City Hotel (☞ above) offers combined lodging, dinner, and theater packages.

Sonora

㉕ 4 mi south of Columbia, Parrots Ferry Rd. to Hwy. 49.

Miners from Mexico founded Sonora and made it the biggest town in the Mother Lode. Following a period of racial and ethnic strife, the

Mexican settlers moved on. Yankees built the commercial city that is visible today. Sonora's downtown historic section sits atop the Big Bonanza Mine, one of the richest in the state. Another mine, on the site of nearby Sonora High School, yielded 990 pounds of gold in a single week in 1879. Reminders of the Gold Rush are everywhere in Sonora, in prim Victorian houses, typical Sierra-stone storefronts, and awning-shaded sidewalks. Reality intrudes beyond the town's historic heart with strip malls, shopping centers, and modern motels. If the countryside surrounding Sonora seems familiar, that's because much of it has appeared in western and other movies over the years. Scenes from *High Noon, For Whom the Bell Tolls, The Virginian, Back to the Future III*, and *Unforgiven* were filmed here.

The **Tuolumne County Museum and History Center** occupies a building that served as a jail until 1951. Restored to an earlier period, it houses a jail museum, vintage firearms and paraphernalia, a case with gold nuggets, and the libraries of an historical society and a genealogical society. ⊠ *158 W. Bradford St.,* ☎ *209/532–1317.* ☜ *Free.* ☉ *Sun.– Mon. 9–4, Tues.–Fri. 10–4, Sat. 10–3:30.*

Dining and Lodging

$$–$$$ ✕ **Josephine's California Trattoria.** Seared ahi tuna, duckling with polenta, Delta crayfish risotto, and angel-hair pasta with fresh seafood are among the dishes you might find on the seasonal menu. Single-portion pizzas are a staple. The reasonably priced wine list showcases Sierra foothill and Italian vintages. Musicians perform on some nights. ⊠ *Gunn House Hotel, 286 S. Washington St.,* ☎ *209/533–4111. Restaurant, bar. AE, D, MC, V. Closed Mon. No lunch.*

$–$$ ✕ **Banny's Cafe.** Its pleasant environment and hearty yet refined dishes make Banny's a quiet alternative to Sonora's eateries with live music. Try the grilled salmon fillet with spinach–red pepper aioli or eggplant grilled with shiitake mushrooms, leeks, roasted-tomato pesto, and mozzarella. ⊠ *83 S. Stewart St.,* ☎ *209/533–4709. D, MC, V.*

$ ✕ **Garcia's Taqueria.** This casual, inexpensive eatery serves Mexican and southwestern fare with an emphasis on seafood dishes. Murals of Yosemite and other California landscapes adorn the walls. The spicy roasted-garlic soup is popular. ⊠ *145 S. Washington St.,* ☎ *209/588– 1915. No credit cards. Closed Sun.*

$$–$$$ 🏠 **Ryan House 1855 Bed and Breakfast Inn.** Attentive innkeepers make this 1850s farmhouse a fine place to stay, and there's more privacy than might be expected at such a small inn. A suite in the attic has a large sitting area set into the gables, a pink and burgundy bathroom with a double soaking tub, and a brass-and-iron bed. Everyone has access to the four parlors and the sunny kitchen, where complimentary snacks and beverages are always available. In springtime the garden blooms with colorful flowers of all kinds, including some antique roses as old as the house itself. Lodging-and-theater packages are available. ⊠ *153 S. Shepherd St., 95370,* ☎ *209/533–3445 or 800/ 831–4897. 2 rooms, 1 suite. Full breakfast. AE, MC, V.*

$ 🏠 **Best Western Sonora Oaks Motor Hotel.** The standard motel-issue rooms at this East Sonora establishment are clean and roomy. The larger ones have outside sitting areas. Suites have fireplaces, whirlpool tubs, and tranquil hillside views. Because the motel is right off Highway 108, the front rooms can sometimes be noisy. ⊠ *19551 Hess Ave., 95370,* ☎ *209/533–4400 or 800/532–1944,* FAX *209/532–1964. 96 rooms, 4 suites. Restaurant, lounge, pool, meeting rooms. AE, D, DC, MC, V.*

Jamestown

㉖ *4 mi south of Sonora on Hwy. 49.*

Compact Jamestown supplies a touristy, superficial view of Gold-Rush-era life. Shops filling brightly colored buildings along Main Street sell antiques and gift items.

The California State Railroad Museum operates **Railtown 1897** at what were the headquarters and general shops of the Sierra Railway from 1897 to 1955. The railroad has appeared in more than 200 movies and television productions, including *Petticoat Junction, The Virginian, High Noon,* and *Unforgiven.* You can view the roundhouse, an air-operated 60-ft turntable, shop rooms, and old locomotives and coaches. Six-mile, 40-minute steam train rides through the countryside are operated on weekends during part of the year. ⊠ *5th Ave. and Reservoir Rd., off Hwy. 49,* ☎ *209/984–1600.* ☞ *$2 roundhouse tour; $6 train ride.* ◷ *Daily 9:30–4:30. Train rides Apr.–Oct., weekends 11–3; Nov., Sat. 11–3.*

Dining and Lodging

$$ ✕⊡ **National Hotel.** In business since 1859, the decor here is authentic—brass beds, patchwork quilts, and lace curtains—but not overly embellished. The saloon, which still has its original 19th-century redwood bar, is a great place to linger. The popular restaurant ($$–$$$) serves big lunches: hamburgers and fries, salads, and Italian entrées. More upscale Continental cuisine is prepared for dinner (reservations essential). Some rooms have no phone. ⊠ *77 Main St., 95327,* ☎ *209/984–3446; 800/894–3446 in CA,* ℻ *209/984–5620. 9 rooms. Restaurant, bar. Continental breakfast. AE, D, DC, MC, V.*

Mariposa

㉗ *50 mi south of Jamestown on Hwy. 49.*

Mariposa marks the southern end of the Mother Lode. Much of the land in this area was part of a 44,000-acre land grant Colonel John C. Fremont acquired from Mexico before gold was discovered and California became a state.

At the **California State Mining and Mineral Museum** a glittering, 13-pound chunk of crystallized gold makes it clear what the rush was about. Displays include a replica of a typical tunnel dug by hard-rock miners, a miniature stamp mill, and a panning and sluicing exhibit. ⊠ *Mariposa County Fairgrounds, Hwy. 49,* ☎ *209/742–7625.* ☞ *$3.50.* ◷ *May–Sept., Wed.–Mon. 10–6; Oct.–Apr., Wed.–Sun. 10–4.*

Dining and Lodging

$$–$$$ ✕ **Ocean Sierra Restaurant.** Deep in the woods about 14 mi southeast of Mariposa is this comfortable spot for seafood, meat, pasta, and vegetarian dishes. The owner-chef grows many of her own fresh ingredients, including the delicate crystallized rose petals atop some of the desserts. *3292 E. Westfall Rd. (from Hwy. 49 take Triangle Rd. 2 mi northeast),* ☎ *209/742–7050. D, MC, V. May–Sept., closed Mon.–Tues.; Oct.–Apr., closed Mon.–Thurs. No lunch.*

$ ✕ **Castillo's Mexican Food.** Tasty tacos, enchiladas, chili rellenos, and burrito combinations, plus chimichangas, fajitas, steak, and seafood, are served in a casual storefront setting. ⊠ *4995 5th St.,* ☎ *209/742–4413. MC, V.*

$$ ⊡ **Little Valley Inn.** Pine paneling, historical photos, and old mining tools recall Mariposa's heritage at this modern B&B with two charming guest bungalows. A suite that sleeps five people includes a full kitchen. All rooms have private entrances and decks. The large grounds include a creek where guests can pan for gold (a helpful dog stirs the creek bed). The enthusiastic innkeepers will also take guests to their offsite claim for prospecting. ⊠ *3483 Brooks Rd., off Hwy. 49, 95338,* ☎ *209/742– 6204 or 800/889–5444,* ℻ *209/742–5099. 2 rooms, 1 suite. Refrigerators, in-room VCRs, horseshoes. Full breakfast. AE, MC, V.*

$–$$ 🖭 **Comfort Inn of Mariposa.** This white three-story building with a broad veranda sits on a hill above Mariposa. Some of the comfortable rooms have sitting areas. ⊠ *4994 Bouillon St., 95338,* ☎ *209/966–4344,* ℻ *209/966–4655. 59 rooms, 2 suites. No-smoking rooms, pool, outdoor hot tub. Continental breakfast. AE, D, DC, MC, V.*

SACRAMENTO AND THE GOLD COUNTRY A TO Z

Arriving and Departing

By Bus
Greyhound (☎ 800/231–2222) serves Sacramento, Auburn, and Placerville. It's a two-hour trip from San Francisco's Transbay Terminal at 1st and Mission streets to the Sacramento station at 7th and L streets.

By Car
Sacramento lies at the junction of I–5 and I–80, about 90 mi northeast of San Francisco. The 406-mi drive north on I–5 from Los Angeles takes seven to eight hours. Interstate 80 continues northeast through the Gold Country toward Reno, about 163 mi (three hours or so) from Sacramento.

By Plane
Sacramento International Airport (⊠ 6900 Airport Blvd., 12 mi northwest of downtown off I–5, ☎ 916/874–0700) is served by Alaska, America West, American, Delta, Northwest, Southwest, and United airlines. *See* Air Travel *in* Smart Travel Tips A to Z for airline phone numbers.

By Train
Several trains operated by **Amtrak** (☎ 800/872–7245) stop in Sacramento. Trains making the 2½-hour trip from **Jack London Square** (⊠ 245 2nd St., Oakland) stop in Emeryville, Richmond, Martinez, and Davis; some stop in Berkeley and Suisun-Fairfield as well. Shuttle buses connect the **Emeryville station** (⊠ 5885 Landregan St.), across the bay from San Francisco, and the city's **Ferry Building** (⊠ 30 Embarcadero); other San Francisco pickup points are at the main entrance to Pier 39 and 835 Market Street at Powell Street, near Union Square.

Getting Around

By Bus
Sacramento Regional Transit (☎ 916/321–2877) buses and light-rail vehicles transport passengers in Sacramento. Most buses run from 6 AM to 10 PM, most trains from 5 AM to midnight. A DASH (Downtown Area Shuttle) bus and the number 30 city bus both link Old Sacramento, midtown, and Sutter's Fort in a loop that travels eastward on J Street and westward on L Street. The fare is 50 cents within this area.

By Car
Traveling by car is the most convenient way to see the Gold Country. From Sacramento three highways fan out toward the east, all intersecting with Highway 49: Interstate 80 heads 30 mi northeast to Auburn; U.S. 50 goes east 40 mi to Placerville; and Highway 16 angles southeast 45 mi to Plymouth. Highway 49 is an excellent two-lane

road that winds and climbs through the foothills and valleys, linking the principal Gold Country towns.

By Taxi and Water Taxi

A **water taxi** (☎ 916/448–4333) serves the Old Sacramento waterfront, stopping at points near restaurants and other sights. **Yellow Cab** (☎ 916/444–2208) serves all of Sacramento.

Contacts and Resources

Emergencies

Ambulance (☎ 911). **Fire** (☎ 911). **Police** (☎ 911).

Mercy Hospital of Sacramento (✉ 4001 J St., ☎ 916/453–4424). **Sutter General Hospital** (✉ 2801 L St., ☎ 916/733–8900). **Sutter Memorial Hospital** (✉ 52nd and F Sts., ☎ 916/733–1000).

Guided Tours

Channel Star Excursions (✉ 110 L St., Sacramento 95814, ☎ 916/552–2933 or 800/433–0263) operates the *Spirit of Sacramento*, a paddlewheel riverboat, which takes passengers on happy-hour, dinner, luncheon, and champagne brunch cruises in addition to one-hour narrated river tours. The **Coloma Country Inn** (☎ 530/622–6919) offers rafting excursions on the American River and balloon rides as part of B&B packages. **Gold Prospecting Expeditions** (☎ 209/984–4653 or 800/596–0009), based in Jamestown, arranges gold-panning trips. **Gray Line/Frontier Tours** (✉ 2600 North Ave., Sacramento 95838, ☎ 916/927–2877 or 800/356–9838) operates city tours for groups of 10 or more.

Visitor Information

Amador County Chamber of Commerce (✉ 125 Peek St., Jackson 95642, ☎ 209/223–0350). **El Dorado County Chamber of Commerce** (✉ 542 Main St., Placerville 95667, ☎ 530/621–5885 or 800/457–6279). **Grass Valley/Nevada County Chamber of Commerce** (✉ 248 Mill St., Grass Valley 95945, ☎ 530/273–4667 or 800/655–4667). **Mariposa County Visitors Bureau** (✉ 5158 Hwy. 140, Mariposa 95338, ☎ 209/966–2456 or 800/208–2434). **Placer County Tourism Authority** (✉ 13464 Lincoln Way, Auburn 95603, ☎ 530/887–2111 or 800/427–6463). **Sacramento Convention and Visitors Bureau** (✉ 1421 K St., Sacramento 95814, ☎ 916/264–7777). **Tuolumne County Visitors Bureau** (✉ Box 4020, 55 W. Stockton St., Sonora 95370, ☎ 209/533–4420 or 800/446–1333).

6 LAKE TAHOE

The California and Nevada Shores

The largest alpine lake in North America is famous for its clarity, deep blue water, and snowcapped peaks. Though Lake Tahoe possesses abundant natural beauty and accessible wilderness, nearby towns are highly developed and roads around the lake are often congested with traffic. Summertime is generally cooler here than in the Sierra Nevada foothills, and the clean mountain air is bracingly crisp. When it gets hot, the plentiful beaches and brisk water are only minutes away.

Updated by
Deke
Castleman

LAKE TAHOE lies 6,225 ft above sea level in the Sierra Nevada range, straddling the state line between California and Nevada. The border gives this popular resort region a split personality. About half the visitors here arrive intent on low-key sightseeing, hiking, fishing, camping, and boating. The rest head directly for the Nevada side, where bargain dining, big-name entertainment, and the lure of a jackpot draw them into the glittering casinos. Tahoe is also a popular wedding and honeymoon destination: couples can get married with no waiting period or blood tests at chapels all around the lake. On Valentine's Day the chapels become veritable assembly lines—four times as many ceremonies take place on that day than on any other. Incidentally, the legal marrying age in California and Nevada is 18 years, but one must be 21 to gamble or drink.

Summer's cool temperatures provide respite from the heat in the surrounding deserts and valleys. Swimming in Lake Tahoe is always brisk—68°F is about as warm as the water gets—and the lake's beaches are generally crowded at this time of year. Those who prefer solitude can escape to the many state parks, national forests, and protected tracts of wilderness that ring the 22-mi-long, 12-mi-wide lake. From mid-autumn to late spring, multitudes of skiers and winter-sports enthusiasts are attracted to Tahoe's downhill resorts and cross-country centers, North America's largest concentration of skiing facilities. Ski resorts try to open by Thanksgiving, if only with machine-made snow, and can operate through May or later. Most accommodations, restaurants, and even a handful of parks are open year-round.

The first white settler to find this spectacular region was Captain John C. Fremont in 1844, guided by famous scout Kit Carson. Not long afterward, silver was discovered in Nevada's Comstock Lode at Virginia City. As the bonanza hit, the Tahoe Basin's forests were leveled to provide lumber for mine-tunnel supports. By the early 1900s wealthy Californians were building lakeside estates here, some of which still stand. Improved roads brought the less affluent in the 1920s and 1930s, when modest bungalows began to appear. The first casinos opened in the 1940s. Ski resorts inspired another development boom in the 1950s and 1960s and turned the lake into a year-round destination.

Lake Tahoe's water is 99.7% pure, cleaner than drinking water in most U.S. cities. The water is so clear that you can see as deep as 75 ft. During the past few decades, however, road construction and other building projects have washed soil and minerals into the lake, leading to a growth of algae that threatens its clarity. The efforts of environmentalists during the 1970s resulted in a moratorium on shoreline construction, and a master plan was instituted to control development. Today Tahoe is one of the most strictly controlled environments in the country.

During some summer weekends it seems that absolutely every tourist—100,000 at peak periods—is in a car on the main road that circles the 72-mi shoreline. The crowds and congestion increase as the day wears on. But at a vantage point overlooking Emerald Bay early in the morning, on a trail in the national forests that ring the basin, or on a sunset cruise on the lake itself, you can forget the hordes and commercial development and absorb the grandeur.

Pleasures and Pastimes

Camping

Campgrounds abound in the Tahoe area, operated by the state's park department, the U.S. Forest Service, city utility districts, and private operators. Sites range from primitive and rustic to upscale and luxurious. Make reservations far ahead in summer, when sites are in high demand (☞ Contacts and Resources *in* Lake Tahoe A to Z, *below*).

Dining

On weekends and in high season expect a long wait in the more popular restaurants. During slower periods some places may close temporarily or limit their hours, so call ahead to make sure your choice is open.

Casinos use their restaurants to attract gaming customers. Marquees often tout "$5.99 prime rib dinners" or "$1.39 breakfast specials." Some of these meal deals, usually found in the coffee shops and buffets, may not be top quality. But the finer restaurants in casinos generally deliver good food, service, and atmosphere.

Unless otherwise noted, even the most expensive Tahoe restaurants welcome customers in casual clothes—not surprising in this year-round vacation mecca—but don't expect to be served in most places if you're barefoot, shirtless, or wearing a skimpy bathing suit.

CATEGORY	COST*
$$$$	over $50
$$$	$30–$50
$$	$20–$30
$	under $20

*per person for a three-course meal, excluding drinks, service, and 7%–7¼% tax

Gambling

Nevada's major casinos are also full-service hotels and resorts. They offer discounted lodging packages throughout the year. The casinos share an atmosphere of garish neon and noise, but air conditioning and no-smoking areas have eliminated the hazy pall of the past. Six casinos are clustered on a strip of U.S. 50 in Stateline—Caesars, Harrah's, Harvey's, Horizon, and Lakeside, plus Bill's, a lower-stakes "junior" casino (no lodging) that appeals to frugal gamblers. Five other casinos operate on the north shore: the Hyatt Regency, Cal-Neva, Tahoe Biltmore, Crystal Bay Club, and Jim Kelley's Nugget. Open 24 hours a day, 365 days a year, these gambling parlors have table games (craps, blackjack, roulette, baccarat, poker, keno, pai gow poker, bingo, and big six), race and sports books, and thousands of slot and video poker machines—1,750, for instance, at Harrah's. There is no charge to enter and there is no dress code.

The hotels attract potential players into their high-profit casinos with shows, celebrity entertainers, and restaurants and lounges that are open around the clock. All gamblers are offered complimentary beverages. Higher-stakes players can qualify for complimentary meals, rooms, room service, golf, even private yacht parties. Parking is plentiful in enclosed garages and open lots; valet parking is free, but a $1 or $2 tip is customary.

Golf

The Tahoe area is nearly as popular with golfers as it is with skiers. A half-dozen superb courses dot the mountains around the lake, with magnificent views, thick pines, fresh cool air, and lush fairways and greens.

Encountering wildlife is not uncommon if you have to search for your ball out-of-bounds.

Hiking

There are five national forests in the Tahoe Basin and a half-dozen state parks. The main areas for hiking include the Tahoe Rim Trail, a 150-mi path along the ridgelines above the lake; Desolation Wilderness, a vast 63,473-acre preserve of granite peaks, glacial valleys, subalpine forests, the Rubicon River, and more than 50 lakes; and the trail systems near Lake Tahoe Visitor Center and D. L. Bliss, Emerald Bay, Sugar Pine Point, and Lake Tahoe–Nevada state parks.

Lodging

Quiet inns on the water, motels in the heart of the casino area, rooms at the casinos themselves, and lodges close to ski runs are among the Tahoe options. During summer and ski season the lake is crowded; reserve space as far ahead as possible. Spring and fall give you a little more leeway and lower—sometimes significantly lower—rates. Price categories listed below reflect high-season rates.

CATEGORY	COST*
$$$$	over $175
$$$	$120–$175
$$	$80–$120
$	under $80

All prices are for a standard double room, excluding 9%–10% tax.

Skiing

The Lake Tahoe area is a Nordic skier's paradise. You can even cross-country ski on fresh snow right on the lakeshore beaches. Skinny skiing (slang for cross-country) at the resorts can be costly, but you get the benefits of machine grooming and trail preparation. If it's bargain Nordic you're after, take advantage of thousands of acres of public forest and parkland trails.

The mountains around Lake Tahoe are bombarded by blizzards throughout the winter (and sometimes the fall and spring); 10- to 12-ft bases are not uncommon. The profusion of downhill resorts guarantees a nearly infinite variety of terrains, conditions, and challenges. To save money, look for packages offered by lodges and resorts; some include interchangeable lift tickets that allow you to try different slopes. Midweek packages are usually cheaper, and most resorts offer family discounts. Free shuttle-bus service is available between most ski resorts and lodgings.

Sno-Park Areas

There are five public Sno-Park areas, where you can park your car and then snowmobile, cross-country ski, or sled. All are maintained by the California State Department of Parks and Recreation (☞ Contacts and Resources *in* Lake Tahoe A to Z, *below*). To use them you need to obtain a permit in advance.

Exploring Lake Tahoe

The most common way to explore the Lake Tahoe area is to drive the 72-mi road that follows the shore through wooded flatlands and past beaches, climbing to vistas on the rugged west side of the lake and descending to the busiest commercial developments and casinos on its northeastern and southeastern edges. Undeveloped Lake Tahoe–Nevada State Park occupies more than half of the Nevada side of Lake Tahoe, stretching north a few miles from Spooner Lake to just south of the upscale master-planned community of Incline Village. The California side, particularly South Lake Tahoe, is more developed, though much wilderness remains.

Great Itineraries

Although, or perhaps because, the distance around Lake Tahoe is relatively short, the desire to experience the whole area can be overwhelming. It takes only one day "to see it"—drive around the lake, stretch your legs at a few overlooks, take a nature walk, and wander among the casinos at Stateline. If you have more time, you can laze on a beach and swim, venture onto the lake or into the mountains, and sample Tahoe's finer restaurants. If you have five days, you may become so attached to Tahoe that you begin visiting real-estate agents.

Numbers in the text correspond to numbers in the margin and on the Lake Tahoe map.

IF YOU HAVE 3 DAYS

On your first day, stop in **South Lake Tahoe** ① and pick up provisions for a picnic lunch. Start with some morning beach fun at the **Pope-Baldwin Recreation Area** ③ and check out the area's **Tallac Historic Site.** Head west on Highway 89, stopping at the **Lake Tahoe Visitor Center** ④ and the **Emerald Bay** ⑤ lookout. Have lunch at the lookout, or hike down (the trip back up is steep) to **Vikingsholm,** a Viking castle replica. In the late afternoon explore the trails and mansions at **Sugar Pine Point State Park** ⑦, then backtrack on Highway 89 and U.S. 50 for dinner in **Stateline** ⑱. On your second day, cruise on the *Hornblower's Tahoe Queen* glass-bottom stern-wheeler out of South Lake Tahoe or the MS *Dixie II* stern-wheeler out of **Zephyr Cove** ⑰ in the morning, and then ride the **Heavenly Tram** ② at Heavenly Ski Resort. Have lunch high above the lake and (except in snow season) take a walk on one of Heavenly's nature trails. You'll have an hour or two to try your luck at the Stateline casinos before it's time for dinner. Start your third day by heading north on U.S. 50, stopping at **Cave Rock** ⑯ and (after turning north on Highway 28) at **Sand Harbor Beach** ⑮. If *Bonanza* looms large in your memory, drop by **Ponderosa Ranch** ⑭, or continue on to **Crystal Bay** ⑫ to hike the Stateline Lookout Trail above Crystal Bay. If you have the time, drive to **Tahoe City** ⑧ to see its Gatekeeper's Log Cabin Museum.

IF YOU HAVE 5 DAYS

On your first day, have a picnic at **Pope-Baldwin Recreation Area** ③. Then head west to **Lake Tahoe Visitor Center** ④ and the **Emerald Bay** ⑤ lookout. Hike to **Vikingsholm** or, if that seems too strenuous, proceed directly to **Sugar Pine Point State Park** ⑦. Have dinner in **Tahoe City** ⑧ or **South Lake Tahoe** ①. On your second day, cruise on the *Hornblower's Tahoe Queen* or MS *Dixie II* in the morning, then ride the **Heavenly Tram** ② and have lunch and possibly a hike. Spend the late afternoon or early evening at one of the **Stateline** ⑱ casinos. On the third day, visit **Cave Rock** ⑯ and the **Ponderosa Ranch** ⑭, and hike the Stateline Lookout Trail above **Crystal Bay** ⑫. Have lunch in Crystal Bay and spend the afternoon at the nearby **Kings Beach State Recreation Area** ⑨. On the fourth day, hang out at **Sand Harbor Beach** ⑮ or, if it's winter, on the ski slopes. On day five, rent a bike and ride from **D. L. Bliss State Park** ⑥ to **Tahoe City** ⑧ and explore the Gatekeeper's Log Cabin Museum.

When to Tour Lake Tahoe

Unless you want to ski, you'll find that Tahoe is most fun during the summer. The best strategy for avoiding crowds is to do as much as you can early in the day. The parking lots for the Lake Tahoe Visitor Center, Vikingsholm, and Gatekeeper's Log Cabin Museum can be jammed

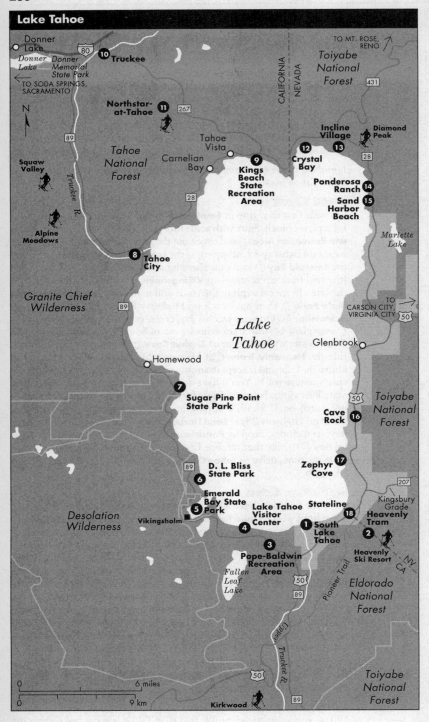

Lake Tahoe

at any time. Weekends are the most congested, but weekdays are busy as well.

September and October, when the throngs have dispersed but the weather is still pleasant, are among the most satisfying months to visit Lake Tahoe. During the winter ski season Tahoe's population swells on the weekends. If you're able to come midweek, you'll have the resorts and neighboring towns almost to yourself. Most of the visitor centers, mansions, state parks, and beaches are closed between November and May.

CALIFORNIA SIDE
South Lake Tahoe to Kings Beach

Lake Tahoe lends itself to a geopolitical division between the two states that share it. The California side is the more developed, both with commercial enterprises—restaurants, motels, lodges, resorts, residential subdivisions—and public-access facilities, such as historic sites, parks, campgrounds, and beaches.

South Lake Tahoe

❶ *50 mi south of Reno on U.S. 395 and U.S. 50; 198 mi northeast of San Francisco on I–80 to U.S. 50.*

South Lake Tahoe's raison d'être is tourism. The lake region's largest community feeds the casinos at Stateline; the ski slopes at Heavenly Valley; the beaches, docks, bike trails, and campgrounds of the south shore; and the backcountry of Eldorado National Forest and Desolation Wilderness. Motels, lodges, and restaurants line U.S. 50 heading northeast into town, but if you head to the northwest on Highway 89, which straddles the lakefront, commercial development gives way to national forests and state parks.

★ ℃ **❷** Whether you ski or not, you'll appreciate the impressive view of Lake Tahoe from the 50-passenger **Heavenly Tram,** which runs 2,000 ft up the slopes of Heavenly Ski Resort to 8,200 ft. When the weather's fine you can take one of three (successively more difficult) hikes around the mountaintop. Monument Peak Restaurant, open daily during tram hours, serves basic American food cafeteria style—lunch, dinner, and Sunday brunch in summer, and lunch only in winter. ☒ *Head north on Ski Run Blvd. off U.S. 50 and follow signs to parking lot,* ☎ *775/ 586–7000.* ☒ *$12.* ☉ *Tram runs June–Oct., daily 9–9; Nov.–May, daily 9–4.*

The 500-passenger **Hornblower's Tahoe Queen** (☒ Ski Run Marina, off U.S. 50, ☎ 530/541–3364 or 800/238–2463), a glass-bottom paddle wheeler, makes 1½-hour happy-hour cruises, 2¼-hour sightseeing cruises, and 3½-hour dinner-dance cruises year-round from South Lake Tahoe. Fares range from $17 to $42. In winter the boat becomes the only waterborne ski shuttle in the world: $105 covers hotel transfers, transportation across the lake to Squaw Valley, and a lift ticket.

Dining and Lodging

$$–$$$ ✕ **Nepheles.** A chalet on the road to Heavenly Ski Resort houses this cozy restaurant that serves creative California cuisine. Entrées range from ahi tuna in a pineapple vinaigrette to broiled elk with a sauce made from black currants and merlot. Appetizers include escargots, swordfish egg rolls, and seafood cheesecake. ☒ *1169 Ski Run Blvd.,* ☎ *530/ 544–8130. AE, D, DC, MC, V. No lunch.*

$$-$$$ ✕ **Swiss Chalet.** Swiss decor is carried out with great consistency at this Tahoe institution. The steep sloping roof, wrought-iron grillwork, Swiss clocks, and cowbells may make you feel as if you've been transported to the Alps. The Continental menu includes schnitzel, sauerbraten, fondue, steaks, and homemade pastries. ⊠ 2544 U.S. 50, ☎ 530/544–3304. AE, MC, V. Closed late Nov.–early Dec. No lunch.

$–$$ ✕ **Scusa!** This intimate Italian restaurant on the road to the Heavenly Ski Resort has a smart, modern decor. Capellini, linguine, fettuccine, penne, ravioli, and lasagna are on the menu, along with hearty calzones, exotic pizzas, steak, chicken, and fresh fish. The panfried calamari with red peppers and capers are a treat. Don't pass up the rosemary-flavored flat bread, baked fresh daily. ⊠ 1142 Ski Run Blvd., ☎ 530/542–0100. AE, MC, V. No lunch.

$ ✕ **Red Hut Waffle Shop.** A vintage Tahoe diner, all chrome and red plastic, the Red Hut is a tiny place with a dozen counter stools and a dozen booths. It's a traditional breakfast spot for locals and visitors in the know, all of whom appreciate the huge omelets, the banana, pecan, and coconut waffles, and other tasty vittles. ⊠ 2749 U.S. 50, ☎ 530/541–9024. Reservations not accepted. No credit cards. No dinner.

$$-$$$$ ✕⌂ **Christiania Inn.** An antiques-filled bed-and-breakfast across the street from the base of the Heavenly Tram, the Christiania is a local favorite. The American-Continental menu emphasizes fresh seafood, prime beef, and veal. Upstairs at the inn, two rooms and four suites come with king- or queen-size beds and private baths. Three of the suites are two-story affairs with wood-burning fireplaces and wet bars; two have saunas and one has a whirlpool tub. ⊠ 3819 Saddle Rd., 96151, ☎ 530/544–7337 or 530/541–5210, FAX 530/544–5342. 6 rooms. Restaurant, bar. Continental breakfast. MC, V.

$$$-$$$$ ⌂ **Embassy Suites.** In this opulent all-suites hotel, decorated Sierra-lodge style, fountains and waterwheels splash in the nine-story atriums, where complimentary breakfasts and evening cocktails are served daily. Glass elevators rise to guest suites, each with a living room, dining area, and separate bedroom. ⊠ 4130 Lake Tahoe Blvd., 96150, ☎ 530/544–5400 or 800/362–2779, FAX 530/544–4900. 400 suites. 4 restaurants, indoor pool, hot tub, sauna, exercise room, nightclub. Full breakfast. AE, D, DC, MC, V.

$$$-$$$$ ⌂ **Tahoe Seasons Resort.** Most rooms at this resort, which is set among pine trees on a mountain across from the Heavenly Ski Resort, are outfitted with fireplaces. Every room has a whirlpool and a small kitchen. The decor is contemporary, heavy on the teal. ⊠ 3901 Saddle Rd., 96157, ☎ 530/541–6700, 530/541–6010, or 800/540–4874, FAX 530/541–0653. 183 suites. Restaurant, refrigerators, pool, hot tub, 2 tennis courts, volleyball. AE, DC, MC, V.

$$-$$$$ ⌂ **Inn by the Lake.** Across the road from a beach, this luxury motel has spacious rooms furnished in contemporary style (blond oak and pale peach). All have balconies; some have lake views, wet bars, and in-room kitchens. The inn provides a free shuttle to the casinos. ⊠ 3300 Lake Tahoe Blvd., 96150, ☎ 530/542–0330 or 800/877–1466, FAX 530/541–6596. 87 rooms, 12 suites. Pool, hot tub, sauna, bicycles, coin laundry. Continental breakfast. AE, D, DC, MC, V.

$$-$$$$ ⌂ **Lakeland Village Beach and Ski Resort.** This complex with 1,000 ft of private beach has a range of accommodations: studios, suites, and town houses, all with kitchens, fireplaces, and private decks or balconies. Ask about ski packages. ⊠ 3535 Lake Tahoe Blvd., 96150, ☎ 530/544–1685 or 800/822–5969, FAX 530/544–0193. 210 units. 2 pools, wading pool, hot tub, sauna, 2 tennis courts, beach, boating, fishing, coin laundry. AE, MC, V.

$$–$$$ 🏨 **Best Western Station House Inn.** This inn has won design awards
★ for its exterior and interior. The rooms have king- and queen-size beds
and double-vanity bathrooms. The location is good, near a private beach
yet close to the casinos. An American breakfast is complimentary. ⊠
901 Park Ave., 96150, ☎ *530/542–1101 or 800/822–5953,* FAX *530/
542–1714. 100 rooms, 2 suites. Restaurant, pool, hot tub. AE, D, DC,
MC, V.*

$$–$$$ 🏨 **Forest Inn Suites.** The location is excellent—5½ acres bordering a
forest, a half block from Harrah's and Harvey's, and adjacent to a su-
permarket, cinema, and shops. Rooms are modern and pleasant. Ski
rentals are available, and free shuttles to Heavenly and Kirkwood ski
areas stop here. ⊠ *1101 Park Ave., 96150,* ☎ *530/541–6655 or 800/
822–5950,* FAX *530/544–3135. 17 rooms, 101 suites. Kitchenettes, 2
pools, 2 hot tubs, sauna, 5 putting greens, health club, volleyball, bicycles, coin laundry. AE, D, DC, MC, V.*

$$ 🏨 **Travelodge.** There are two members of the national chain in South
Lake Tahoe. Both are convenient to casinos, shopping, and recreation
and have some no-smoking rooms. Free local calls, cable TV, and in-
room coffee add to the budget appeal. ⊠ *3489 U.S. 50 at Bijou Cen-
ter, 96150,* ☎ *530/544–5266 or 800/982–1466,* FAX *530/544–6985.* ⊠
4003 U.S. 50, 96150, ☎ *530/541–5000 or 800/982–2466,* FAX *530/544–
6910. 59 rooms at Bijou Center, 66 rooms at 4003 U.S. 50. Pool at
each; Bijou Center has a restaurant. AE, D, DC, MC, V.*

$–$$ 🏨 **Lake Tahoe Inn.** Near Harrah's on 6 acres, with gardens and the
Heavenly Ski Resort directly behind it, this large motel has modern rooms
decorated in soothing colors. ⊠ *4110 Lake Tahoe Blvd., 96150,* ☎
530/541–2010 or 800/972–8557, FAX *530/542–1428. 392 rooms, 8 suites.
Restaurant, 2 pools, hot tub. Full breakfast. AE, D, DC, MC, V.*

$–$$ 🏨 **Royal Valhalla Motor Lodge.** Two- and three-bedroom suites with
complete kitchens make this motel attractive to families. Some of the
simple, modern rooms have private balconies with views of the mountains. ⊠ *4104 Lakeshore Blvd., 96157,* ☎ *530/544–2233 or 800/999–
4104,* FAX *530/544–1436. 80 suites. Pool, hot tub, coin laundry. Continental breakfast. AE, DC, MC, V.*

$ 🏨 **Best Tahoe West Inn.** The Tahoe West is three blocks from the beach
and casinos. The exterior is rustic, rooms are neatly furnished, and beds
are queen-size. Twelve rooms have kitchenettes. The inn provides a free
shuttle to the casinos and ski areas. ⊠ *4107 Pine Blvd., 96150,* ☎ *530/
544–6455, 800/522–1021, or 800/700–8246,* FAX *530/544–0508. 60
rooms. Pool, hot tub, sauna, beach. AE, D, DC, MC, V.*

Outdoor Activities and Sports

CROSS-COUNTRY SKIING

For the ultimate in groomed conditions head to the nation's largest cross-
country ski resort, **Royal Gorge** (⊠ follow signs from Soda Springs–
Norden exit off I–80, Box 1100, Soda Springs 95728, ☎ 530/426–3871),
which has 197 mi of 18-ft-wide track for all abilities, 88 trails on 9,172
acres, two ski schools, and 10 warming huts. Four cafés, two hotels,
and a hot tub and sauna are among the facilities. **Kirkwood Ski Resort**
(☞ *below*) has 50 mi of groomed-track skiing, with skating lanes, instruction, and rentals.

DOWNHILL SKIING

Heavenly Ski Resort. When first seen from the California side, Heavenly's mogul-choked slopes look impossibly difficult. But this vast resort—composed of nine peaks, two valleys, and three base-lodge
areas—has something for every skier. Beginners can choose wide, well-
groomed trails accessed via the Heavenly Tram, or short and gentle
runs in the Enchanted Forest area. The Sky Express high-speed quad
chair whisks intermediate and advanced skiers to the summit for wide

cruisers or steep tree skiing. Mott and Killebrew canyons draw expert skiers to the Nevada side for the steep chutes and thick-timbered slopes. For snowboarders there's the Airport Park near the Olympic lift. The ski school, like everything else at Heavenly, is large and offers everything from learn-to-ski packages for novices to canyon adventure tours for advanced skiers. Skiing lessons and day care are available for children age 4 and up. ⊠ *Ski Run Blvd. off Hwy. 89/U.S. 50 (mailing address: Box 2180, Stateline, NV 89449),* ☎ *775/586–7000 or 800/243–2836; 530/541–7544 snow phone. 82 trails on 4,800 acres, rated 20% beginner, 45% intermediate, 35% expert. Longest run 5½ mi, base 6,540′, summit 10,040′. Lifts: 26, including 1 aerial tram, 1 high-speed 6-passenger lift, and 3 high-speed quads.*

Kirkwood Ski Resort. Thirty-six miles south of Lake Tahoe in an alpine-village setting, Kirkwood is a destination resort with 120 condominiums, several shops and restaurants in the base village, overnight RV parking, and a shuttle bus to Lake Tahoe. Most of the runs off the top are rated expert-only, but intermediate and beginning skiers have their own vast bowl, where they can ski through trees or on wide, open trails. Snowboarding is permitted on all runs and in an exclusive terrain park. Skiing and snowboarding lessons and equipment rentals and sales are available. The children's ski school has programs for ages 4 to 12, and day care is available for children ages 2 to 6. Arrangements for younger children must be made in advance. For Nordic skiing, *see* Cross-Country Skiing, *above.* ⊠ *Hwy. 88 off Hwy. 89 (mailing address: Box 1, Kirkwood, CA 95646),* ☎ *209/258–6000; 209/258–7000 lodging information; 209/258–3000 snow phone. 65 trails on 2,300 acres, rated 15% beginner, 50% intermediate, 20% advanced, 15% expert. Longest run 2½ mi, base 7,800′, summit 9,800′. Lifts: 12.*

Shopping

There's some good shopping—Levi's, Van Heusen, Oneida—south of town at the **Factory Outlet Stores** (⊠ *U.S. 50 at Hwy. 89).*

Pope-Baldwin Recreation Area

❸ *5 mi west of South Lake Tahoe on Hwy. 89.*

George S. Pope, who made his money in shipping and lumber, hosted the business and cultural elite of 1920s America at his home, the **Pope House.** The magnificently restored 1894 mansion and two other estates—those of entrepreneur "Lucky" Baldwin (which holds a museum of Baldwin memorabilia and Washoe Indian artifacts) and Walter Heller (the Valhalla, used for community events)—form the heart of the Pope-Baldwin Recreation Area's **Tallac Historic Site.** The lakeside site, a pleasant place to take a stroll or have a picnic, hosts cultural activities (including a Renaissance festival) throughout the summer. Docents conduct tours of the Pope House during summer. ☎ *530/541–5227.* 🈺 *Pope House tour $2.* ☉ *Tallac Historic Site grounds dawn–sunset; house and museum hrs vary.*

❹ The U.S. Forest Service operates the **Lake Tahoe Visitor Center** on Taylor Creek. You can visit the site of a Washoe Indian settlement; walk self-guided trails through meadow, marsh, and forest; and inspect the Stream Profile Chamber, an underground underwater display with windows that afford views right into Taylor Creek. (In the fall you may see spawning salmon digging their nests). In summer Forest Service naturalists organize discovery walks and nighttime campfires, with singing and marshmallow roasts. *Hwy. 89,* ☎ *530/573–2674 (in season only).* ☉ *June–Sept., daily 8–5:30; Oct., weekends 8–5:30.*

Emerald Bay State Park

★ ❺ *4 mi west of Pope-Baldwin Recreation Area on Hwy. 9.*

Emerald Bay, a 3-mi-long and 1-mi-wide fjordlike bay, was carved by massive glaciers millions of years ago. Famed for its jewel-like shape and colors, it surrounds Fannette, Tahoe's only island. Highway 89 curves high above the lake through Emerald Bay State Park; from the Emerald Bay lookout, the centerpiece of the park, you can survey the whole scene.

A steep, 1-mi-long trail from the lookout leads down to **Vikingsholm,** a 38-room estate completed in 1929. The original owner, Lora Knight, had this precise replica of a 1,200-year-old Viking castle built out of materials native to the area. She furnished it with Scandinavian antiques and hired artisans to custom-build period reproductions. The sod roof sprouts wildflowers each spring. There are picnic tables nearby and a gray-sand beach for strolling. The hike back up is hard (especially if you're not yet acclimated to the elevation), but there are benches and stone culverts to rest on. At the 150-ft-high peak of Fannette Island are the remnants of a stone structure known as the Tea House, built in 1928 so that guests of Lora Knight could have a place to enjoy afternoon refreshments after a motorboat ride out to Fannette. The island is off-limits from February through June to protect nesting Canada geese. The rest of the year it's open for day use only. ☎ *530/525–7277.* ☒ *$2.* ☉ *Memorial Day–Labor Day, daily 10–4.*

D. L. Bliss State Park

❻ *3 mi north of Emerald Bay State Park on Hwy. 89.*

D. L. Bliss State Park takes its name from Duane LeRoy Bliss, a 19th-century lumber magnate. At one time Bliss owned nearly 75% of Tahoe's lakefront, along with local steamboats, railroads, and banks. The Bliss family donated these 1,200 acres to the state in the 1930s. The park now shares 6 mi of shoreline with Emerald Bay State Park. At the north end of Bliss is **Rubicon Point,** which overlooks one of the lake's deepest spots. Short trails lead to an old lighthouse and Balancing Rock, which weighs in at 250,000 pounds and balances on a fist of granite. Longer trails lead to remote beaches and all the way to Vikingsholm. ☎ *530/525–7277.* ☒ *$5 per vehicle (day use).* ☉ *Memorial Day–Sept., daily sunrise–sunset.*

Camping

⛺ **D. L. Bliss State Park Campground.** A wooded, hilly, quiet setting makes for blissful family camping near the lake. Reserve sites as far in advance as possible. ☒ *Off Hwy. 89,* ☎ *800/444–7275. 168 sites.* ☒ *$12–$21. Fire rings, flush toilets, disposal station, showers, water (no hookups).* ☉ *Memorial Day–Sept.*

Sugar Pine Point State Park

★ ❼ *8 mi north of D. L. Bliss State Park on Hwy. 89.*

The main attraction at Sugar Pine Point State Park is **Ehrman Mansion,** a stone-and-shingle 1903 summer home, furnished in period style, that in its day was the height of modernity: it had a refrigerator, an elevator, and an electric stove. Also in the park are a trapper's log cabin from the mid-19th century, a nature preserve with wildlife exhibits, a lighthouse, the start of the 10-mi-long biking trail to Tahoe City, and an extensive system of hiking and cross-country trails. ☎ *530/525–7232 year-round; 530/525–7982 in season.* ☒ *$5 per vehicle (day use).* ☉ *Memorial Day–Labor Day, daily 11–4.*

Camping

⚠ **General Creek Campground.** This homey campground on the mountain side of Highway 89 is one of the few public ones to remain open in winter, primarily for cross-country skiers. ⊠ *Hwy. 89,* ☎ *800/444–7275. 175 sites.* 🖃 *$12–$16. Fire rings, flush toilets, disposal station, showers, water (no hookups).* ⊙ *Year-round; facilities available Memorial Day–Labor Day.*

Tahoe City

❽ *10 mi north of Sugar Pine Point State Park on Hwy. 89; 14 mi south of Truckee on Hwy. 89.*

Tahoe City is home to many stores and restaurants within a compact area, and to the Outlet Gates, where water is spilled into the Truckee River to control the surface level of the lake. Giant trout, common before the severe drought of the late 1980s and early 1990s, have returned; look down and see them from Fanny Bridge, so called for the views of the backsides of visitors leaning over the railing. Here, Highway 89 turns north from the lake and leads to Squaw Valley, Donner Lake, and Truckee, and Highway 28 continues northeast around the lake toward Kings Beach and Nevada.

★ The **Gatekeeper's Log Cabin Museum** in Tahoe City preserves the area's past, displaying Washoe and Paiute artifacts as well as pioneer memorabilia. ⊠ *130 W. Lake Blvd.,* ☎ *530/583–1762.* 🖃 *Free.* ⊙ *May 15–Sept., daily 11–5.*

The **Watson Cabin Living Museum,** a 1909 log cabin built by Robert M. Watson and his son and filled with century-old furnishings, is in the middle of Tahoe City. Costumed docents act out the daily life of a typical pioneer family. ⊠ *560 N. Lake Blvd.,* ☎ *530/583–8717 or 530/583–1762.* 🖃 *Free.* ⊙ *June 15–Labor Day, daily noon–4.*

Dining and Lodging

$$–$$$ ✕ **Christy Hill.** Panoramic lake views and fireside dining distinguish this restaurant, which serves California cuisine including fresh seafood (such as Atlantic salmon with a ginger-pepper crust in a cabernet demiglace) and game (including broiled New Zealand venison). ⊠ *Lakehouse Mall, 115 Grove St.,* ☎ *530/583–8551. MC, V. Closed Mon. (spring and fall). No lunch.*

$$–$$$ ✕ **Wolfdale's.** An intimate restaurant inside a 100-year-old house,
★ Wolfdale's food has Japanese and Californian overtones. The menu, which changes weekly, showcases several imaginative entrées, such as grilled Southwestern-style chicken with celery-root potatoes, and braised lamb shank with tomatoes, rosemary, and parsnip puree. ⊠ *640 N. Lake Blvd.,* ☎ *530/583–5700. MC, V. No lunch.*

$–$$$ ✕ **Grazie! Ristorante & Bar.** The smell of garlic warms you as soon as you enter this northern Italian restaurant, as does the fire in the wide, double-sided fireplace. Hearty pasta dishes and pizzas are on the menu, but the stars are the antipasti and pasta salads. Chicken is cooked on a wood-burning rotisserie and rack of lamb on the grill. Both are served with homemade sauces. ⊠ *Roundhouse Mall, 700 N. Lake Blvd.,* ☎ *530/583–0233. AE, D, DC, MC, V.*

$–$$$ ✕ **Jake's on the Lake.** Handsome rooms of oak and glass provide a
★ suitably soothing waterfront setting for Continental food. The seafood bar here is extensive. The varied dinner menu includes meat and poultry but emphasizes fresh fish. ⊠ *Boatworks Mall, 780 N. Lake Blvd.,* ☎ *530/583–0188. AE, MC, V. No lunch weekdays in winter.*

$$–$$$$ ✕🏨 **Sunnyside Restaurant and Lodge.** This impressive lodge has a ma-
★   rina and an expansive lakefront deck with steps down to a narrow gravel beach. Rooms are decorated in a crisp nautical style. Prints of boats hang on the pinstripe wall coverings and sea chests act as coffee tables. Each room has its own deck with a lake or mountain view. Seafood is the specialty of the very fine American-Continental restaurant. Lunch is not served in the off-season. ✉ *1850 W. Lake Blvd., Box 5969, 96145,* ☎ *530/583–7200 or 800/822–2754,* Ⅸ *530/583–2551. 20 rooms, 2 suites. Restaurant, room service, beach. Continental breakfast. AE, D, MC, V.*

$$$$ 🏨 **Chinquapin Resort.** A deluxe development on 95 acres of forested
★   land 3 mi northeast of Tahoe City contains roomy one- to four-bedroom town houses and condos with great views of the lake and the mountains. Each unit has a fireplace, a fully equipped kitchen, and a washer and dryer. A one-week minimum stay is required in July, August, and late December. In winter the minimum is two nights. ✉ *3600 N. Lake Blvd., 96145,* ☎ *530/583–6991 or 800/732–6721,* Ⅸ *530/583–0937. 172 town houses and condos. Pool, saunas, 7 tennis courts, hiking, horseshoes, 2 beaches. MC, V.*

$$$$ 🏨 **Resort at Squaw Creek.** Nearly half the rooms are suites at this complex composed of a main lodge, an outdoor arcade of shops and boutiques, and a 404-room hotel. Some units have fireplaces and full kitchens, and all have original art, custom furnishings, and good views. Outside the hotel entrance is a triple chairlift to Squaw Valley's slopes. Dining options range from haute cuisine to pastries and coffee. ✉ *400 Squaw Creek Rd., Olympic Valley 96146,* ☎ *530/583–6300 or 800/327–3353,* Ⅸ *530/581–5407. 234 rooms, 170 suites. 5 restaurants, bar, 3 pools, 4 hot tubs, sauna, spa, 18-hole golf course, 2 tennis courts, health club, ice-skating. AE, D, DC, MC, V.*

$–$$ 🏨 **Peppertree Inn.** This skinny seven-story tower is within easy walking distance of the beaches, marina, shops, and restaurants of Tahoe City. Rooms are clean and comfortable, if not luxurious, and have great lake views. ✉ *645 N. Lake Blvd., 96145,* ☎ *530/583–3711 or 800/624–8590,* Ⅸ *530/583–6938. 45 rooms, 5 suites. Pool, hot tub. AE, D, DC, MC, V.*

Outdoor Activities and Sports

DOWNHILL SKIING

Alpine Meadows Ski Area. Alpine is an intermediate skier's paradise with two peaks. For snowboarders there's a terrain park with a halfpipe. The ski area has some of Tahoe's most reliable conditions; this is usually one of the first areas to open in November, and one of the last to close in May. There is a ski school for adults and children of all skill levels and for skiers with disabilities. There's also an area for overnight RV parking. ✉ *6 mi northwest of Tahoe City off Hwy. 89, 13 mi south of I–80 (mailing address: Box 5279, 96145),* ☎ *530/583–4232; 530/581–8374 snow phone; 800/441–4423 information. 100 trails on 2,000 acres, rated 25% easier, 40% more difficult, 35% most difficult. Longest run 2½ mi, base 6,835′, summit 8,637′. Lifts: 12, including 1 high-speed 6-passenger lift and 1 high-speed quad.*

Squaw Valley USA. Home to some of the toughest skiing in the Tahoe area, Squaw was the site of the 1960 Olympics. Although the immense resort has changed significantly since then, the skiing is still world-class, with steep chutes and cornices on six Sierra peaks. Expert skiers often head directly to the untamed terrain of the infamous KT-22 face, which has bumps, cliffs, and gulp-and-go chutes. Plenty of wide, groomed trails start near the beginner-designated High Camp lift and around the more challenging Snow King Peak. Snowboarders have the run of two terrain parks. You can ski until 9 PM, and lift tickets for skiers under

12 are only $5. Nonskiing recreational opportunities—bungee jumping, rock climbing, and ice skating—abound. The Village Mall has shops, eateries, and accommodations. ⊠ *Hwy. 89, 5 mi northwest of Tahoe City (mailing address: Box 2007, Olympic Valley, 96146),* ☎ *530/583–6985; 800/545–4350 reservations; 530/583–6955 snow phone. 100 trails on 4,300 acres, rated 25% beginner, 45% intermediate, 30% advanced. Longest run 3 mi, base 6,200', summit 9,050'. Lifts: 29, including a gondola, a cable car, and 5 high-speed quads.*

GOLF

Resort at Squaw Creek Golf Course (⊠ 400 Squaw Creek Rd., Olympic Valley, ☎ 530/583–6300), an 18-hole championship course, was designed by Robert Trent Jones Jr. The $85–$115 greens fee includes the use of a cart. Golfers use pull carts at the nine-hole **Tahoe City Golf Course** (⊠ Hwy. 28, Tahoe City, ☎ 530/583–1516). The greens fees are $26–$30 for 9 holes, $40–$50 for 18; a power cart is $8–12 additional.

Carnelian Bay to Kings Beach

5 to 10 mi northeast of Tahoe City on Hwy. 28.

The small lakeside commercial districts of Carnelian Bay and Tahoe Vista service the thousand or so locals who live in the area year-round and the thousands more who have summer residences or launch their boats here. Kings Beach, the last town heading east on Highway 28 before the Nevada border, is to Crystal Bay what South Lake Tahoe is to Stateline: a bustling California village full of motels and rental condos, restaurants and shops, used by the hordes of hopefuls who pass through on their way to the casinos.

☞ ❾ The 28-acre **Kings Beach State Recreation Area,** one of the largest such areas on the lake, is open year-round. Its long beach becomes crowded with people swimming, sunbathing, jet skiing, riding in paddleboats, and playing volleyball and Frisbee. There's a good playground here. ⊠ *North Lake Blvd., Kings Beach,* ☎ *530/546–7248.* ☜ *Free day use, parking $5 in summer, free in winter.*

Dining

$$–$$$ ✕ **Captain Jon's.** The dining room at Captain Jon's is cozy, with linen cloths and fresh flowers on the tables. On chilly evenings a fireplace with a brick hearth warms diners. The lengthy dinner menu is country French, with two dozen daily specials; the emphasis is on fish and hearty salads. The restaurant's lounge, which serves light meals, is on the water in a separate building with a pier where guests can tie up their boats. ⊠ *7220 N. Lake Blvd., Tahoe Vista,* ☎ *530/546–4819 or 775/831–4176. AE, DC, MC, V. No lunch during ski season.*

$–$$$ ✕ **Gar Woods Grill and Pier.** This stylish but casual lakeside restaurant recalls the area's past with boating photographs and a river-rock fireplace. Floor-to-ceiling picture windows overlook the lake. The menu includes dishes such as Thai chicken salad, prime rib, filet mignon, and pastas. There's an extensive wine list, and Sunday brunch is served. ⊠ *5000 N. Lake Blvd., Carnelian Bay,* ☎ *530/546–3366. AE, MC, V.*

$ ✕ **Log Cabin Caffe.** Almost always hopping, this Kings Beach eatery specializes in healthful, hearty breakfast and lunch entrées—pancakes, waffles, freshly baked pastries, sandwiches, and ice cream. It's a good place on the north shore for an espresso or cappuccino. Get here early on weekends; this is a popular spot for brunch. ⊠ *8692 N. Lake Blvd., Kings Beach,* ☎ *530/546–7109. MC, V.*

Outdoor Activities and Sports

SNOWMOBILING

Snowmobiling Unlimited (⊠ Hwys. 267 and 28, Kings Beach, ☎ 530/583–5858) conducts guided tours and rents equipment.

SWIMMING

The **North Tahoe Beach Center** has a 26-ft hot tub and a beach with an enclosed swimming area and four sand volleyball courts. The complex includes a barbecue and picnic area, a fitness center, windsurfing and nonmotorized boat rentals, a snack bar, and a clubhouse with games. ⊠ *7860 N. Lake Blvd., Kings Beach,* ☎ *530/546–2566.* ☞ *$7.*

Truckee

🔟 *13 mi northwest of Kings Beach on Hwy. 267; 14 mi north of Tahoe City on Hwy. 89.*

Old West facades line the main street of Truckee, a favorite stopover for people traveling from the Bay Area to the north shore of Lake Tahoe. Galleries and boutiques are plentiful, but you will also find low-key diners, discount skiwear, and an old-fashioned five-and-dime store. Stop by the **information booth** in the Amtrak depot (⊠ Railroad St. at Commercial Rd.) for a walking-tour map of historic Truckee.

Donner Memorial State Park commemorates the Donner Party, a group of 89 westward-bound pioneers who were trapped in the Sierra in the winter of 1846–47 in snow 22 ft deep. Only 47 survived, some by cannibalism and others by eating animal hides. The Immigrant Museum's hourly slide show details the Donner Party's plight. Other displays relate the history of other settlers and of railroad development through the Sierra. ⊠ *Off I–80, 2 mi west of Truckee,* ☎ *530/582–7892.* ☞ *$2.* ☉ *Daily 9–4.*

Northstar-at-Tahoe

⓫ *6 mi south of Truckee on Hwy. 267; 15 mi north of Tahoe City on Hwy. 28 to Hwy. 267.*

Dining and Lodging

$$$–$$$$ ✕🏨 **Northstar-at-Tahoe Resort.** This is the area's most complete destination resort. The center of action is the Village Mall, a concentration of restaurants, shops, recreation facilities, and accommodations—hotel rooms, condos, and private houses. The many sports activities make the resort especially popular with families. Summer rates are lower than winter rates. ⊠ *Off Hwy. 267, Box 129, 96160,* ☎ *530/562–1010 or 800/466–6784,* ⅀ *530/562–2215. 230 units. 4 restaurants, deli, 18-hole golf course, 10 tennis courts, horseback riding, bicycles, skiing, sleigh rides, snowmobiling, recreation room, baby-sitting. AE, D, MC, V.*

Outdoor Activities and Sports

CROSS-COUNTRY AND DOWNHILL SKIING

Northstar-at-Tahoe Resort. Two northeast-facing, wind-protected bowls provide some of the best powder skiing in the area, including steep chutes and long cruising runs. Top-to-bottom snowmaking and intense grooming assure good conditions for cross-country and downhill skiing. Northstar-at-Tahoe provides 40 mi of groomed, tracked trails, with a wide skating lane for Nordic skiers. For snowboarders there's a terrain park and trails with features like dragon tails and magic moguls, created especially for snowboarders. The ski school offers programs for skiers ages five and up, and day care is available for children older than two. ⊠ *Hwy. 267 between Truckee and Kings Beach (mailing ad-*

dress: Box 129, Truckee 96160), ☎ 530/562–1010, 530/562–1330 snow phone, ℻ 530/562–2215. 63 trails on 1,800 acres, rated 25% beginner, 50% intermediate, 25% advanced. Longest run 2.9 mi, base 6,400', summit 8,600'. Lifts: 12 lifts, including a gondola and 4 high-speed quads.

NEVADA SIDE

From Crystal Bay to Stateline

You don't need a roadside marker to know when you've crossed from California into Nevada. The lake's water and the pine trees may be identical, but the flashing lights and elaborate marquees of casinos announce legal gambling in garish hues.

Crystal Bay

⑫ *1 mi east of Kings Beach on Hwy. 28; 30 mi north of South Lake Tahoe on U.S. 50 to Hwy. 28.*

Right at the Nevada border, Crystal Bay holds a cluster of casinos. One, the **Cal-Neva Lodge** (☞ Dining and Lodging, *below*), is bisected by the state line. This joint opened in 1927 and has weathered nearly as many scandals—the largest involving one-time-owner Frank Sinatra (he lost his gaming license in the 1960s for alleged mob connections)—as it has blizzards. The **Tahoe Biltmore** has a popular $1.99 breakfast special served 24 hours a day. **Jim Kelley's Nugget** closes during the winter months—the only casino in Nevada that ever closes.

Dining and Lodging

$$–$$$ ✕ **Soule Domain.** A romantic 1927 pine-log cabin with a stone fireplace is the setting for some of Lake Tahoe's most creative and delicious dinners. Chef-owner Charles Edward Soule IV's specialties include curried cashew chicken, rock shrimp with sea scallops, and a vegan sauté. ⌧ *Cove St. across from Tahoe Biltmore,* ☎ 530/546–7529. *Reservations essential on weekends. AE, DC, MC, V. No lunch.*

$–$$$$ 🏨 **Cal-Neva Lodge.** All the rooms in this hotel-casino on Highway 28 at Crystal Bay have views of Lake Tahoe and the mountains. There is an arcade with video games for children, cabaret entertainment, and, in addition to rooms in the main hotel, seven two-bedroom chalets, and 12 cabins with living rooms. ⌧ *2 Stateline Rd., Box 368, 89402,* ☎ 775/832–4000 *or* 800/225–6382, ℻ 775/831–9007. *261 rooms, 20 suites, 19 cabins. Restaurant, coffee shop, pool, hot tub, sauna, tennis court, casino, 3 chapels. AE, D, DC, MC, V.*

Incline Village

⑬ *3 mi east of Crystal Bay on Hwy. 28.*

Incline Village, one of Nevada's few master-planned towns, dates back to the early 1960s. It's still privately owned. Check out **Lakeshore Drive** to see some of the most expensive real estate in Nevada. Incline is the only town on Lake Tahoe without a central commercial district, planned this way to prevent congestion and to preserve a natural feel. The town's **Recreation Center** (⌧ 980 Incline Way, ☎ 775/832–1300) has an eight-lane swimming pool and a fitness area, basketball court, game room, and snack bar.

OFF THE   **MOUNT ROSE** – If you want to ski some of the highest slopes in the Lake
BEATEN PATH   Tahoe region, Highway 431 leads north out of Incline Village to Mount Rose. Reno is another 30 mi farther. ☎ *775/849–0704.*

⑭ The 1960s television western *Bonanza* inspired the **Ponderosa Ranch** theme park. Attractions include the Cartwrights' ranch house, a western town, and a saloon. There's a self-guided nature trail, free pony rides for children, and, if you're here from 8 to 9:30 in the morning, a breakfast hayride. ⊠ *Hwy. 28, 2 mi south of Incline Village*, ☎ 775/831–0691. ⚏ *$9.50, hayride $2.* ⊙ *Mid-Apr.–Oct., daily 9:30–5.*

Dining and Lodging

$–$$$ ✕ **Stanley's Restaurant and Lounge.** With its intimate bar and pleasant dining room, this local favorite is a good bet any time for straightforward American fare on the hearty side (barbecued pork ribs, beef Stroganoff). Lighter bites, such as seafood Cobb salad, are also available, along with ample breakfasts. Try the eggs Benedict or a chili-cheese omelet. There's a deck for outdoor dining in summer. ⊠ *941 Tahoe Blvd.,* ☎ *775/831–9944. AE, D, MC, V.*

$–$$ ✕ **Azzara's.** A typical Italian trattoria with light, inviting decor, Azzara's serves a dozen pasta dishes and many pizzas, as well as chicken, lamb, veal, shrimp, and beef. Dinners include soup or salad, a vegetable, a pasta, and garlic bread. ⊠ *Incline Center Mall, 930 Tahoe Blvd.,* ☎ *775/831–0346. MC, V. Closed Mon.*

$$–$$$$ ✕▥ **Hyatt Lake Tahoe Resort Hotel/Casino.** Some of the rooms in this luxurious hotel on the lake have fireplaces, and all the accommodations are top-notch. The restaurants are the Lone Eagle Grille (fairly good Continental, with steak, seafood, pasta, and rotisserie dishes), Ciao Mein Trattoria (Asian-Italian), and the Sierra Café (open 24 hours). ⊠ *Lakeshore and Country Club Drs., 89450,* ☎ *775/831–1111 or 800/233–1234,* ⒻⒶⓍ *775/831–7508. 432 rooms, 28 suites. 3 restaurants, coffee shop, lobby lounge, room service, pool, 2 saunas, spa, 2 tennis courts, health club, beach, bicycles, casino, children's programs, laundry service. AE, D, DC, MC, V.*

Outdoor Activities and Sports

BOAT CRUISE

The **Sierra Cloud** (☎ 775/831–1111), a trimaran with a big trampoline lounging surface, cruises the north-shore area mornings and afternoons from the Hyatt Regency Hotel in Incline Village from May through October. Fares run between $35 and $50.

CROSS-COUNTRY AND DOWNHILL SKIING

Diamond Peak. A fun, family atmosphere prevails at Diamond Peak, which has many special programs and affordable rates. Snowmaking covers 80% of the mountain, and runs are groomed nightly. The ride up the 1-mi Crystal chair rewards you with the best views of the lake from any ski area. Diamond Peak is less crowded than some of the larger areas and provides free shuttles to lodging in nearby Incline Village. A first-timer's package, which includes rentals, a lesson, and a lift ticket, is $39. A parent-child ski package is $45, with each additional child's lift ticket $6. There is a half-pipe for snowboarders. **Diamond Peak Cross-Country** (⊠ off Hwy. 431, ☎ 775/832–1177) has 22 mi of groomed track with skating lanes. The trail system goes from 7,400 ft to 9,100 ft with endless wilderness to explore. ⊠ *1210 Ski Way, off Hwy. 28 to Country Club Dr., Incline Village, NV 89450,* ☎ *775/832–1177 or 800/468–2463. 29 trails on 655 acres, rated 18% beginner, 46% intermediate, 36% advanced. Longest run 2½ mi, base 6,700', summit 8,540'. Lifts: 6, including 2 high-speed quads.*

GOLF

Incline Championship (⊠ 955 Fairway Blvd., ☎ 775/832–1144) is an 18-hole, par-72 course with a driving range. The greens fee of $95 to $115 includes an optional power cart. **Incline Mountain** (⊠ 690 Wilson Way, ☎ 775/832–1150) is an easy 18-holer; par is 58. The greens fee—from $40 to $50—includes an optional power cart.

OFF THE
BEATEN PATH **CARSON CITY AND VIRGINIA CITY –** Nevada's capital, Carson City, is a 30-minute drive from Stateline. At Spooner Junction, where Highway 28 meets U.S. 50, head east on U.S. 50, away from the lake. In 10 mi you reach U.S. 395, where you turn left and go 1 mi north to Carson City. Most of its historic buildings and other attractions are along U.S. 395, the main street through town. At the south end of town is the **Carson City Chamber of Commerce** (✉ 1900 S. Carson St., ☎ 775/882–1565), which has visitor information. About a 30-minute drive northeast of Carson City, on Highway 342 off U.S. 50 East, is the fabled mining town of Virginia City, which has sights and activities of historical interest amid touristy diversions.

Sand Harbor Beach

★ ⑮ *4 mi south of Incline Village on Hwy. 28; 22 mi north of South Lake Tahoe on U.S. 50 to Hwy. 28.*

Sand Harbor Beach, within the Lake Tahoe–Nevada State Park, has a popular beach that is sometimes filled to capacity by 11 AM on summer weekends. A **pop-music festival** (☎ 775/832–1606 or 800/468–2463) is held here in July and a **Shakespeare festival** (☎ 775/832–1616) every August.

U.S. 50 from Spooner Junction to Zephyr Cove

13 mi south of Sand Harbor Beach (to Cave Rock), Hwy. 28 to U.S. 50.

★ ⑯ **Cave Rock,** 25 yards of solid stone at the southern end of Lake Tahoe–Nevada State Park, is the throat of an extinct volcano. This is the stuff of local lore: for the Washoe Indians this area is a sacred burial site. Tahoe Tessie, the lake's version of the Loch Ness monster, is reputed to live in a cavern below the impressive outcropping. Cave Rock towers over a parking lot, a lakefront picnic ground, and a boat launch. The rest area provides the best vantage point of this cliff. ✉ *U.S. 50, 3 mi south of Glenbrook.*

⑰ The largest settlement between Incline Village and Stateline is **Zephyr Cove,** which is still only a tiny resort. It has a beach, marina, campground, picnic area, coffee shop in an historic log lodge, rustic cabins for rent, and nearby riding stables. The 550-passenger **MS Dixie II** (☎ 775/588–3508), a stern-wheeler, sails year-round from Zephyr Cove Marina to Emerald Bay on lunch and dinner cruises. Fares range from $18 to $42. The **Woodwind** (☎ 775/588–3000), a glass-bottom trimaran, sails on regular and champagne cruises from April through October from Zephyr Cove Resort. Fares range from $18 to $40.

OFF THE
BEATEN PATH **KINGSBURY GRADE –** This road, also known as Route 207, is one of three roads that access Tahoe from the east. Originally a toll road used by wagon trains to get over the crest of the Sierra, it has sweeping views of the Carson Valley. Off Route 206, which intersects Route 207, is Genoa, the oldest settlement in Nevada. Along Main Street are interesting museums and the state's longest-standing saloon.

Stateline

⑱ *5 mi south of Zephyr Cove on U.S. 50.*

Stateline is a great border town in the Nevada tradition. Its four high-rise casinos are as vertical and contained as the commercial district of South Lake Tahoe on the California side is horizontal and sprawling. And Stateline is as relentlessly indoors-oriented as the rest of the lake is focused on the outdoors. This strip is where you'll find the most concentrated action at Lake Tahoe: restaurants (including the typically Nevadan buffets), showrooms with famous headliners and razzle-dazzle revues, luxury rooms and suites, and 24-hour casino gambling.

Dining and Lodging

$$$-$$$$ ✕ **Chart House.** It's worth the drive up the steep grade to see the view from here. Try to arrive for sunset. The American menu of steak and seafood is complemented by an abundant salad bar. The restaurant has a children's menu. ✉ *329 Kingsbury Grade,* ☎ *775/588–6276. AE, D, DC, MC, V. No lunch.*

$$-$$$ ✕ **Llewellyn's Restaurant.** Elegantly decorated in blond wood and
★ pastels, the restaurant atop Harvey's casino merits special mention. Almost every table has superb views of Lake Tahoe. Dinner entrées—seafood, meat, and poultry—are served with unusual accompaniments, such as sturgeon in potato crust with saffron sauce or veal with polenta, herbs, and pancetta. Lunches are reasonably priced, with gourmet selections as well as hamburgers. ✉ *Harvey's Resort, U.S. 50,* ☎ *775/588–2411 or 800/553–1022. AE, D, DC, MC, V.*

$$$-$$$$ ✕▥ **Harrah's Tahoe Hotel/Casino.** Luxurious guest rooms here have two full bathrooms, each with a television and telephone. All rooms have views of the lake and the mountains; higher floors have the least-obstructed vistas. Top-name entertainment is presented in the South Shore Room. Among the restaurants, the romantic 16th-floor Summit is a standout. The menu changes nightly and includes creatively presented salads; lamb, venison, or seafood entrées with delicate sauces; and sensuous desserts. Other restaurants serve Italian, deli, and traditional meat-and-potatoes cuisine. There's also a 24-hour café, a buffet with a view, and a candy store. ✉ *U.S. 50, Box 8, 89449,* ☎ *775/588–6611 or 800/427–7247,* ℻ *775/588–6607. 470 rooms, 62 suites. 5 restaurants, café, room service, indoor pool, barbershop, beauty salon, hot tubs, health club, casino, video games, laundry service, kennel. AE, D, DC, MC, V.*

$$$-$$$$ ✕▥ **Harvey's Resort Hotel/Casino.** Owner Harvey Gross played an im-
★ portant role in persuading the state to keep U.S. 50 open year-round, making Tahoe accessible in winter. His namesake hotel, which started as a cabin in 1944, is now the largest resort in Tahoe. Any description of the place runs to superlatives, from the 40-ft-tall crystal chandelier in the lobby to the 88,000-square-ft casino. Rooms have custom furnishings, oversize marble baths, and minibars. Use of the health club, spa, and pool is free to guests, a rarity for this area. ✉ *U.S. 50, Box 128, 89449,* ☎ *775/588–2411 or 800/648–3361,* ℻ *775/782–4889. 705 rooms, 38 suites. 8 restaurants, pool, barbershop, beauty salon, hot tub, spa, health club, casino, chapel. AE, D, DC, MC, V.*

$$-$$$$ ▥ **Caesars Tahoe.** Most of the rooms and suites at this 16-story hotel-casino have oversize tubs, king-size beds, two telephones, and a view of Lake Tahoe or the encircling mountains. The opulent casino encompasses 40,000 square ft. Top-name entertainers perform in the 1,600-seat Circus Maximus. Planet Hollywood is here, plus Chinese, Italian, and American restaurants, a 24-hour coffee shop that also houses the buffet, and a frozen-yogurt emporium. ✉ *55 U.S. 50, Box 5800, 89449,* ☎ *775/588–3515; 800/648–3353 reservations and show in-*

formation, FAX *775/586–2068. 328 rooms, 112 suites. 5 restaurants, indoor pool, hot tub, saunas, spa, 4 tennis courts, health club, showroom. AE, D, DC, MC, V.*

$–$$$$ 🏨 **Horizon Casino Resort.** Many of the guest rooms at this hotel-casino have lake views. The casino has a beaux arts decor, brightened by pale molded wood and mirrors. The Grande Lake Theatre, Golden Cabaret, and Aspen Lounge present shows, as well as up-and-coming and name entertainers. Le Grande Buffet has a nightly prime-rib special. ⊠ *U.S. 50, Box C, 89449,* ☎ *775/588–6211 or 800/322–7723,* FAX *775/588–1344. 516 rooms, 23 suites. 3 restaurants, pool, 3 hot tubs, exercise room, casino, meeting rooms. AE, D, DC, MC, V.*

$–$$$ 🏨 **Lakeside Inn and Casino.** The smallest of the Stateline casinos, the Lakeside has a rustic look. Guest rooms are in lodges, away from the casino area. ⊠ *U.S. 50 at Kingsbury Grade, Box 5640, 89449,* ☎ *775/588–7777 or 800/624–7980,* FAX *775/588–4092. 115 rooms, 8 suites. Restaurant, pool, casino. AE, D, DC, MC, V.*

Nightlife

The top entertainment venues are the Circus Maximus at Caesars Tahoe, the Emerald Theater at Harvey's, the South Shore Room at Harrah's, and Horizon's Grand Lake Theatre. Typical headliners include Jay Leno, David Copperfield, and Johnny Mathis. For Las Vegas–style production shows—fast-paced dancing, singing, and novelty acts—try Harrah's or the Horizon. The big showrooms occasionally present performances of musicals by touring Broadway companies or casts assembled for the casino. Reservations are almost always required for superstar shows. Depending on the act, cocktail shows usually cost from $12 to $40. Smaller casino cabarets sometimes have a cover charge or drink minimum.

Bars around the lake present pop and country-western singers and musicians, and in winter the ski resorts do the same. Summer alternatives are outdoor music events, from chamber quartets to rock performers, at Sand Harbor and the Lake Tahoe Visitors Center amphitheater.

Outdoor Activities and Sports

GOLF

Edgewood Tahoe (⊠ U.S. 50 and Lake Pkwy., behind Horizon Casino, Stateline, ☎ 775/588–3566) is an 18-hole, par-72 course with a driving range, and the only golf course with holes on the lakeshore. The $150 greens fee includes a cart (though you can walk if you wish); the course is open from 7 AM to 4 PM between May and October. The 18-hole, par-70 **Lake Tahoe Golf Course** (⊠ U.S. 50, between Lake Tahoe Airport and Meyers, ☎ 530/577–0788) has a driving range. The greens fee is $50; a cart (mandatory from Friday to Sunday) costs $20.

SCUBA DIVING

Sun Sports (⊠ 1018 Herbert Ave., No. 4, South Lake Tahoe, ☎ 530/541–6000) is a full-service PADI dive center with rentals and instruction.

LAKE TAHOE A TO Z

Arriving and Departing

By Bus

Greyhound Lines (☎ 800/231–2222) stops in Sacramento, Truckee, and Reno, Nevada.

By Car

Lake Tahoe is 198 mi northeast of San Francisco, a drive of less than four hours when traffic and the weather cooperate. Try to avoid the heavy traffic leaving the San Francisco area for Tahoe on Friday afternoon and returning on Sunday afternoon. The major route is I–80, which cuts through the Sierra Nevada about 14 mi north of the lake. From there Highway 89 and Highway 267 reach the west and north shores, respectively. U.S. 50 is the more direct highway to the south shore, taking about 2½ hours from Sacramento. From Reno you can get to the north shore by heading west on Highway 431 off U.S. 395, 8 mi south of town (a total of 35 mi). For the south shore, continue south on U.S. 395 through Carson City, and then head west on U.S. 50 (55 mi total).

By Plane

Reno–Tahoe International Airport (U.S. 395, Exit 65B, Reno, NV, ☎ 775/328–6400), 35 mi northeast of the closest point on the lake, is served by airlines that include Alaska, American, America West, Continental, Delta, Northwest, Reno Air, Skywest, Southwest, and United. *See* Air Travel *in* Smart Travel Tips A to Z for airline phone numbers. **Tahoe Casino Express** (☎ 775/785–2424 or 800/446–6128) has daily scheduled transportation from the airport in Reno to Stateline casinos from 6:15 AM to 12:30 AM, $17 one-way and $30 round-trip.

Lake Tahoe Airport (☎ 530/542–6180) on U.S. 50 is 3 mi south of the lake's shore. No commercial carriers operate scheduled service to this airport; for charters or sightseeing, contact **Alpine Lake Aviation** (☎ 530/544–4343).

Getting Around

By Bus

South Tahoe Area Ground Express (STAGE, ☎ 530/573–2080) runs along U.S. 50 and through the neighborhoods of South Lake Tahoe daily from 6 AM to 12:15 AM. **Tahoe Area Regional Transit** (TART, ☎ 530/581–6365 or 800/736–6365) operates buses along Lake Tahoe's northern and western shores between Tahoma (from Meeks Bay in summer) and Incline Village daily from 6:30 AM to 6:30 PM. Free shuttle buses run among the casinos, major ski resorts, and motels of South Lake Tahoe.

By Car

The scenic 72-mi highway around the lake is marked Highway 89 on the southwest and west, Highway 28 on the north and northeast shores, and U.S. 50 on the east and southeast. Sections of Highway 89 sometimes close during winter, making it impossible to complete the circular drive. Interstate 80, U.S. 50, and U.S. 395 are all-weather highways, but there may be delays as snow is cleared during major storms. Carry tire chains from October through May (car-rental agencies provide them with their vehicles). *See* Road Conditions, *below,* for hot line phone numbers.

By Taxi

Yellow Cab (☎ 530/544–5555) serves all of Tahoe Basin. **Ace Taxi** (☎ 530/544–2900) serves Tahoe's south shore. On the north shore try **Tahoe-Truckee Taxi** (☎ 530/582–8294).

Contacts and Resources

Emergencies

Ambulance (☎ 911). **Fire** (☎ 911). **California Highway Patrol** (☎ 530/587–3510). **Nevada Highway Patrol** (☎ 775/687–5300). **Police** (☎ 911).

Guided Tours

BY BOAT

Hornblower's Tahoe Queen (☞ South Lake Tahoe *in* California Side, *above*), the *Sierra Cloud* (☞ Incline Village *in* Nevada Side, *above*), and *MS Dixie II* and *Woodwind* (☞ U.S. 50 from Spooner Junction to Zephyr Cove *in* Nevada Side, *above*) all operate guided boat tours.

BY BUS OR CAR

Gray Line and Frontier Tours (☎ 775/331–1147 or 800/446–6128) runs daily tours to South Lake Tahoe, Carson City, and Virginia City. **Tahoe Lake Lapper** (☎ 530/542–5900) provides daily around-the-lake transportation in both directions: the Green Bus travels clockwise and the Blue Bus travels counterclockwise. Buses leave South Lake Tahoe at 7, 10, and 11 AM and 1, 2, 4, and 5 PM; a late Blue Bus leaves at 8 PM on Friday and Saturday. The fare is $5. **Lake Tahoe Adventures** (✉ 2286 Utah Ave., South Lake Tahoe 96150, ☎ 530/541–5875) operates a trek skirting the Desolation Wilderness on the Rubicon Trail in four-wheel-drive all-terrain vehicles.

BY HOT-AIR BALLOON

Lake Tahoe Balloons (☎ 530/544–1221) conducts excursions year-round over the lake or over the Carson Valley for $99 a person for half-hour flights and $165 for hour-long flights (champagne brunch included).

BY PLANE

CalVada Seaplanes Inc. (☎ 530/546–3984) provides rides over the lake for $55 to $90 per person, depending on the length of the trip. **High Country Soaring** (☎ 775/782–4944) glider rides over the lake and valley depart from the Douglas County Airport, Gardnerville.

Reservations Agencies

Park.net (☎ 800/444–7275 for campgrounds in California state parks). **Lake Tahoe Visitors Authority** (☎ 800/288–2463 for south-shore lodging). **North Lake Tahoe Resort Association** (☎ 800/824–6348 for north-shore lodging).

Road Conditions

California roads in Tahoe area (☎ 530/445–7623). **California roads approaching Tahoe** (☎ 800/427–7623). **Nevada roads** (☎ 775/793–1313).

Visitor Information

California State Department of Parks and Recreation (☎ 916/324–4442). **Lake Tahoe Hotline** (☎ 530/542–4636 for south-shore events; 530/546–5253 for north-shore events; 775/831–6677 for Nevada events). **Lake Tahoe Visitors Authority** (✉ 1156 Ski Run Blvd., South Lake Tahoe, CA 96150, ☎ 530/544–5050 or 800/288–2463). **North Lake Tahoe Resort Association** (✉ Box 5578, Tahoe City, CA 96145, ☎ 530/583–3494 or 800/824–6348, FAX 530/581–4081). **Ski Report Hotline** (☎ 415/864–6440). **U.S. Forest Service** backcountry recording (☎ 530/587–2158).

7 THE SIERRA NATIONAL PARKS

With Mono Lake and Mammoth Lakes

The highlight for many California travelers is a visit to one of the national parks in the Sierra Nevada range. Yosemite, the state's most famous park, is every bit as sublime as one expects. Its Yosemite-type or U-shape valleys were carved by glaciers during the Ice Age. Other glacial valleys are found about 150 miles southeast in Kings Canyon and Sequoia national parks, which are adjacent to each other and usually visited together. All the Sierra national parks contain groves of giant sequoia (*Sequoiadendron giganteum*) trees, nature's largest living things.

YOSEMITE, KINGS CANYON, AND SEQUOIA national parks are famous throughout the world for their granite peaks, towering waterfalls, and giant sequoias, among other natural wonders. Yosemite, especially, should be on your "don't miss" list. Unfortunately, it's on everyone else's as well (the park receives about 4 million visitors annually), so lodging reservations are essential. During a week's stay you can exit and reenter the parks as often as you wish by showing your pass.

Updated by
Clark Norton

Pleasures and Pastimes

Camping

One highlight of camping in the Sierra national parks is awakening to the sights of nearby meadows and streams and, in the distance, the unforgettable landscape of giant granite. Another is gazing up at an awe-inspiring number of constellations and spying a shooting star in the night sky. For reservations and other information *see* Contacts and Resources *in* Yosemite National Park A to Z *and* Kings Canyon and Sequoia National Parks A to Z, *below*).

Dining

Snack bars, coffee shops, and cafeterias in the parks are not expensive, but you may not want to waste precious time finding food, especially during the day. Stop at a grocery store and fill your ice chest with picnic supplies to enjoy under giant trees.

The three fanciest lodgings within Yosemite National Park are also the prime dining spots. If the roads are clear of traffic or snow, you may also want to drive out of the park to dine at restaurants in the border towns (☞ Outside Yosemite National Park, *below*). With few exceptions, which are noted, dress is casual at the restaurants listed below.

CATEGORY	COST*
$$$$	over $50
$$$	$30–$50
$$	$20–$30
$	under $20
per person for a three-course meal, excluding drinks, service, and 10% tax	

Hiking

Hiking is the primary outdoor sport in the Sierra national parks. Whether you walk the paved loops that pass by major attractions or head off the beaten path into the backcountry, a hike through groves, meadows, or alongside streams and waterfalls will allow you to see, smell, and feel nature up close. Some of the most popular trails are described briefly in this chapter; stop by the visitor centers for maps and advice from park rangers.

Lodging

Most accommodations inside Yosemite, Kings Canyon, and Sequoia national parks can best be described as "no frills." Some have no electricity or indoor plumbing. Other than the Ahwahnee and Wawona hotels in Yosemite, lodgings tend to be basic motels or rustic cabins. Except during the off-peak season, from November through March, rates in Yosemite are pricey given the general quality of the lodging. Reserve well ahead, especially during summer; you can reserve up to a year and a day in advance. *See* Contacts and Resources *in* Yosemite National Park A to Z, *below,* for the phone number of the park's reservations service.

Reservations are recommended for visits to Kings Canyon and Sequoia at any time of the year because it's a long way back to civilization if the lodgings there are full. All the park's lodges and cabins are open during the summer months, but in winter only some in Grant Grove remain open. Lodging rates are consistent throughout the year. The town of Three Rivers, on Highway 198 southwest of Sequoia, has some lodgings. *See* Contacts and Resources *in* Kings Canyon and Sequoia National Parks A to Z, *below,* for park lodging reservation numbers.

CATEGORY	COST*
$$$$	over $175
$$$	$120–$175
$$	$80–$120
$	under $80
All prices are for a standard double room, excluding 10% tax.	

Nature Lore

In Yosemite from early May to late September and during some holiday periods, actor Lee Stetson portrays naturalist John Muir, bringing to life Muir's wit, wisdom, and storytelling skill. You can also join park rangers on free, daily, 60- to 90-minute nature walks focusing on geology, wildlife, waterfalls, forest ecology, and other topics. Locations and times for both are listed in the *Yosemite Guide,* the newspaper handed to visitors upon entering the park.

Exploring the Sierra National Parks

For the full Sierra experience, stay in the parks themselves instead of the "gateway cities" in the foothills or the Central Valley. Save your time and energy for exploring, not driving to and from the parks. Yosemite Valley is the primary destination for many visitors. Because the valley is only 7 mi long and averages less than 1 mi in width, you can visit its attractions in whatever order you choose and return to your favorites at different times of the day. Famous for their hiking trails and giant sequoias, Kings Canyon and Sequoia provide a true wilderness experience, less interrupted by civilization and crowds.

Separate A to Z information listings follow the Yosemite National Park, Outside Yosemite National Park, Mammoth Lakes, and Kings Canyon and Sequoia National Parks sections, below.

Numbers in the text correspond to numbers in the margin and on the Yosemite and Kings Canyon and Sequoia national parks maps.

Great Itineraries

IF YOU HAVE 3 DAYS

If your time is limited, choose Yosemite National Park to explore. Enter the park via the Big Oak Flat Entrance, and head east on Big Oak Flat Road. As you enter the valley, traffic is diverted onto a one-way road. Continue east, following the signs to the **Valley Visitor Center** ①. Loop back west for a short hike near **Yosemite Falls** ②, the highest waterfall in North America. Continue west for a valley view of famous **El Capitan** ⑦ peak. This area is a good place for a picnic. Backtrack onto Southside Drive, stopping at misty **Bridalveil Fall** ③, then follow Highway 41/Wawona Road south 14 mi to the Chinquapin junction and make a left turn onto Glacier Point Road. From **Glacier Point** ⑨ (road closed in winter) you'll get a phenomenal bird's-eye view of the entire valley, including **Half Dome** ⑧, **Vernal Fall** ⑤, and **Nevada Fall** ⑥. If you want to avoid the busloads of tourists at Glacier Point, stop at **Sentinel Dome** ⑩ instead. After a mildly strenuous 1-mi hike you get a view similar to the one from Glacier Point except for the peek into the valley. Continue south on Highway 41 to the Wawona Hotel (closed weekdays much of winter), where you can have a relaxing drink on the veranda or in the cozy lobby bar.

On day two, visit the **Mariposa Grove of Big Trees** ⑫ and return to Wawona to tour the **Pioneer Yosemite History Center** ⑪. Head back to Yosemite Valley on Wawona Road for an early evening beverage at the Ahwahnee Hotel's bar (enjoy the patio view in good weather), and explore the hotel's lobby and other public areas. On the third day have breakfast near the Valley Visitor Center before hiking to **Vernal Fall** ⑤ or **Nevada Fall** ⑥.

IF YOU HAVE 5 DAYS

Spend your first day exploring the ⌸ **Yosemite Valley area** ①–⑩. On the second day, pack some food and drive to **Hetch Hetchy Reservoir** (closed in winter) via Big Oak Flat Road and Highway 120. Then continue east on Tioga Road to **Tuolumne Meadows,** the largest subalpine meadow in the Sierra. Time permitting, head east through 9,900-ft Tioga Pass to **Mono Lake** and, possibly, **Bodie Ghost Town** ⑬. (Tioga Road closes for several months after the first snow; if the road isn't open, on day two you can instead take a hike to **Vernal Fall** ⑤ or **Nevada Fall** ⑥.) Wake up early on day three and spend the morning visiting Wawona's **Pioneer Yosemite History Center** ⑪ and wandering beneath the giant sequoias at the nearby **Mariposa Grove of Big Trees** ⑫. Then head south to ⌸ **Kings Canyon National Park** (about a three- to four-hour drive), entering on Highway 180 at the Big Stump Entrance. Stop at **Grant Grove** ⑲. If you're camping, you'll need to get situated before sunset; if you're staying at one of the park's lodges, check in and have dinner. On the fifth day, pass briefly through **Lodgepole** ㉑ in **Sequoia National Park** and pick up tickets to **Crystal Cave** ㉔. Visit the **Giant Forest** ㉒ before stopping at the cave.

When to Tour the Sierra National Parks

Summer is the most crowded season for all the parks, though things never get as hectic at Kings Canyon and Sequoia as they do at Yosemite. During extremely busy periods—when snow closes high-country roads in late spring or on crowded summer weekends—Yosemite Valley may be closed to all vehicles unless their drivers have overnight reservations. Avoid these restrictions by visiting from mid-April through Memorial Day and from Labor Day to mid-October, when the parks are less busy and the weather is usually hospitable.

The falls at Yosemite are at their most spectacular in May and June. By the end of summer, some will have dried up. They begin flowing again in late fall with the first storms, and during winter they may be hung with ice, a dramatic sight. Snow on the floor of Yosemite Valley is never deep, so you can camp there even in winter (January highs are in the mid-40s, lows in the mid-20s). Tioga Road is usually closed from late October through May; unless you ski or snowshoe in, you can't see Tuolumne Meadows then. The road to Glacier Point beyond the turnoff for Badger Pass is not cleared in winter, but it is groomed for cross-country skiing. In parts of Kings Canyon and Sequoia snow may remain on the ground into June; the flowers in the Giant Forest meadows hit their peak in June or July.

YOSEMITE NATIONAL PARK
Yosemite Valley, Wawona, the High Country

Yosemite, with 1,169 square mi of parkland, is 94½% undeveloped wilderness, most of it accessible only to backpackers and horseback riders. The western boundary dips as low as 2,000 ft in the chaparral-covered foothills; the eastern boundary rises to 13,000 ft at points along the Sierra crest.

Yosemite is so large that it functions as five parks. **Yosemite Valley** and **Wawona** are open all year. **Hetch Hetchy** closes after the first main snow and reopens in May or June. The high country, **Tuolumne Meadows,** is open for summer hiking and camping; in winter, it's accessible only by cross-country ski or snowshoe. **Badger Pass Ski Area** is open in winter only. The fee to visit Yosemite National Park (good for seven days) is $20 per car, $10 per person if you don't arrive in a car.

Yosemite Valley Area

214 mi southeast of San Francisco, I–80 to I–580 to I–205 to Hwy. 120; 330 mi northeast of Los Angeles, I–5 to Hwy. 99 to Hwy. 41.

Yosemite Valley has been so extravagantly praised (John Muir described it as "a revelation in landscape affairs that enriches one's life forever") and so beautifully photographed (by Ansel Adams and others) that you may wonder if the reality can possibly measure up. For almost everyone it does. Yosemite is truly a reminder of what "breathtaking" and "marvelous" really mean. The Miwok people, the last of several Native American tribes who inhabited the Yosemite area, called the valley "Ahwahnee," which is said to mean "the place of the gaping mouth." Members of the tribe, who were forced out of the area by gold miners in 1851, called themselves the Ahwahneechee.

❶ You can get your bearings, pick up maps, and obtain information from park rangers at the **Valley Visitor Center,** which has exhibits on the natural and human history of Yosemite Valley. The adjacent **Yosemite Museum** has an Indian Cultural Exhibit with displays about the Miwok and Pauite people who lived in the region; there's a re-created **Ahwahneechee village** behind it. The nearby **Ansel Adams Gallery** shows works of the master Yosemite photographer. They're all part of **Yosemite Village,** which contains restaurants, stores, a post office, the Ahwahnee Hotel, Yosemite Lodge, a medical clinic, and other facilities. **A Changing Yosemite,** a 1-mi paved loop from the visitor center, traces the park's natural evolution. ✉ *Off Northside Dr.,* ☎ *209/372–0200.* ☉ *Daily 9–5; extended hrs in summer.*

The staff at the **Wilderness Center** provides trail-use reservations (recommended for popular trailheads on weekends or from May through September), permits ($3), maps, and advice to hikers heading into the backcountry. When the Wilderness Center is closed, you can make inquiries at the nearby Valley Visitor Center or other information stations. *See* Hiking *in* Outdoor Activities and Sports, *below,* for more information about backcountry permits. ✉ *Yosemite Village between post office and Ansel Adams Gallery (mailing address: Box 545, Yosemite 95389),* ☎ *209/372–0200 for information; 209/372–0740 for permit reservations.* ☉ *Apr.–Oct., daily 8–5.*

★ **❷** **Yosemite Falls** is the highest waterfall in North America and the fifth-highest in the world. The upper fall (1,430 ft), the middle cascades (675 ft), and the lower fall (320 ft) combine for a total of 2,425 ft and, when viewed from the valley, appear as a single waterfall. A ¼-mi trail leads from the parking lot to the base of the falls. The Upper Yosemite Fall Trail, a strenuous 3½-mi climb rising 2,700 ft, takes you above the top of the falls. It starts at Sunnyside Campground.

★ **❸** **Bridalveil Fall,** a filmy fall of 620 ft that is often diverted as much as 20 ft one way or the other by the breeze, is the first view of Yosemite Valley for those who arrive via the Wawona Road. Native Americans

252

Yosemite National Park

called the fall Pohono ("spirit of the puffing wind"). A ¼-mi trail leads from the parking lot off Wawona Road to the base of the falls.

④ At 1,612 ft, **Ribbon Fall** is the highest single fall in North America, but also the first valley waterfall to dry up in summer; the rainwater and melted snow that create the slender fall evaporate quickly at this height.

⑤ Fern-covered black rocks frame **Vernal Fall** (317 ft), and rainbows play in the spray at its base. The hike on a paved trail from the Happy Isles Nature Center to the bridge at the base of Vernal Fall is only moderately strenuous and less than 1 mi long. It's another steep (and often wet) ¾ mi up the Mist Trail—which is open only from late spring to early fall—to the top of Vernal Fall. Allow 2 to 4 hours for the 3-mi round-trip hike.

⑥ **Nevada Fall** (594 ft) is the first major fall as the Merced River plunges out of the high country toward the eastern end of Yosemite Valley. A strenuous 2-mi section of the Mist Trail leads from Vernal Fall to the top of Nevada Fall. Allow 6 to 8 hours for the full 7-mi round-trip hike.

The roads at the eastern fringes of the valley are closed to private cars, but a free shuttle bus runs frequently from the village. Both Vernal and Nevada falls can also be viewed from Glacier Point (☞ *below*). From about May through October the Happy Isles Nature Center, which contains ecology exhibits, is open daily between 9 and 5.

★ **⑦** **El Capitan,** rising 3,593 ft above the valley, is the largest exposed granite monolith in the world, almost twice the height of the Rock of Gibraltar.

★ **⑧** Astounding **Half Dome** rises 4,733 ft from the valley floor to a height 8,842 ft above sea level. The west side of the dome is fractured vertically and cut away to form a 2,000-ft cliff. The 16¾-mi round-trip, highly strenuous **John Muir Trail** (which incorporates the Mist Trail) leads from Yosemite Valley to the top of Half Dome. Allow 10 to 12 hours for this hike; start early in the morning and beware of afternoon thunderstorms.

★ **⑨** **Glacier Point** yields what may be the most spectacular vistas of the valley and the High Sierra—especially at sunset—that you can get without hiking. The Glacier Point Road leaves Wawona Road (Highway 41) about 23 mi southwest of the valley; then it's a 16-mi drive, with fine views into higher country. From the parking area walk a few hundred yards and you'll be able to see Nevada, Vernal, and Yosemite falls as well as Half Dome and other peaks; the valley lies 3,214 ft below. You can hike down to it via the Panorama or Four-Mile trails. To avoid a grueling round-trip, catch a ride to Glacier Point on one of the three daily hikers' buses ($10) that run from late spring through October (☎ 209/372–1240 for reservations). The road to Glacier Point is closed beyond the turnoff for the Badger Pass Ski Area in winter.

⑩ The view from **Sentinel Dome** is similar to that from Glacier Point, except for the vantage point of the valley floor. A 1.1-mi path begins at a parking lot on Glacier Point Road a few miles below Glacier Point. The trail is long and steep enough to keep the crowds and tour buses away, but not overly rugged.

OFF THE
BEATEN PATH   **HETCH HETCHY RESERVOIR AND TUOLUMNE MEADOWS –** The Hetch Hetchy Reservoir, which supplies water and hydroelectric power to San Francisco, is about 40 mi from Yosemite Valley via Big Oak Flat Road to Highway 120 to Evergreen Road to Hetch Hetchy Road. Some say John

Muir died of heartbreak when this valley was dammed and buried beneath 300 ft of water in 1913. Tioga Road (Highway 120) stays open until the first big snow of the year, usually about mid-October. The road is the scenic route to Tuolumne Meadows, altitude 8,575 ft, which is 55 mi from Yosemite Valley. The largest subalpine meadow in the Sierra and the trailhead for many backpack trips into the High Sierra, the area contains campgrounds, a gas station, a store (with limited and expensive provisions), stables, a lodge, and a visitor center that is open from late June until Labor Day from 8 AM to 7:30 PM.

Dining, Lodging, and Camping

$$–$$$ ✕ **Mountain Room Restaurant.** The food becomes secondary when you see Yosemite Falls through this dining room's window-wall. Almost every patron has a view of the falls. Gulf shrimp stuffed with crabmeat, steak, pasta, and several children's dishes are on the menu. ⌧ *Yosemite Lodge, off Northside Dr.,* ☎ *209/372–1281. D, DC, MC, V. No lunch. Closed weekdays from Thanksgiving–Easter except for holiday periods.*

$$$$ ✕⌧ **Ahwahnee Hotel & Dining Room.** This grand 1920s-era mountain ★ lodge is constructed of rocks and sugar-pine logs, with exposed timbers. The decorative style of the Great Lounge and Solarium is a tribute to the Miwok and Paiute Indians who inhabited the area; the motifs continue in the room decor. The Ahwahnee Dining Room ($$–$$$), with its 34-ft-tall trestle-beam ceiling, full-length windows, and wrought-iron chandeliers, is by far the most impressive and romantic eating establishment in the park. Jeans, shorts, and sneakers are banned at dinner, and jackets are requested for men. The classic American specialties include New York steak, broiled swordfish fillet, and prime rib, all competently prepared. ⌧ *Ahwahnee Rd. north of Northside Dr.,* ☎ *559/252–4848 for lodging reservations, 209/372–1489 for restaurant. 99 rooms, 24 cottages. Restaurant, lounge, pool, tennis. D, DC, MC, V.*

$$ ✕⌧ **Yosemite Lodge.** This lodge near Yosemite Falls has motel-style units with two double beds and a bathroom; the larger units also have dressing areas and patio or balcony. Although all rooms have phones, none have TVs or air-conditioning. Of the lodge's three eating places, the Mountain Room Restaurant (☞ *above*) is the most formal. The Garden Terrace Restaurant, open for dinner year-round, prepares an all-you-can-eat, serve-yourself buffet of salads, soups, pastas, and hot meats. A cafeteria serves three meals a day. ⌧ *Off Northside Dr.,* ☎ *559/252–4848 for lodging reservations. 245 rooms. 2 restaurants, cafeteria, bar, pool. D, DC, MC, V.*

$–$$ ⌧ **Curry Village.** These are plain accommodations: cabins with bath and without, and tent cabins with rough wood frames and canvas walls and roofs. It's a step up from camping (linens, blankets, and maid service are provided), but food and cooking are not allowed. Showers and toilets are centrally located, as they would be in a campground. ⌧ *South side of Southside Dr.,* ☎ *209/372–8333; 559/252–4848 for reservations. 183 cabins, 427 tent cabins, 18 motel rooms. Cafeteria, pizzeria, pool. D, DC, MC, V.*

$ ⌧ **Housekeeping Camp.** These rustic three-walled cabins with canvas roofs, set on a beach along the Merced River, may be rented up to seven nights but are difficult to get; reserving 366 days in advance is advised. You can cook here on gas stoves rented from the front desk. ⌧ *North side of Southside Dr. between Curry Village and chapel,* ☎ *209/372–8338; 559/252–4848 for reservations. 266 units without bath (maximum 4 per cabin). Toilet and shower in central shower house. D, DC, MC, V. Closed early Oct.–late May.*

Outdoor Activities and Sports

BICYCLING

Yosemite Lodge and Curry Village both have bicycle rentals (☎ 209/372–1208 for Yosemite Lodge or 209/372–8319 for Curry Village). Rentals at the lodge are year-round, weather permitting; Curry Village rents from April through October. Baby-jogger strollers and bikes with child trailers are also available. The eastern valley has 8 mi of bike paths, or you can ride on 196 mi of paved park roads.

CAMPING

For information about campground reservations, *see* Yosemite National Park A to Z, *below*.

HIKING

Yosemite's 840 mi of hiking trails range from short strolls to rugged, multiday treks. The park's visitor centers have trail maps and information and rangers will recommend easy trails to get you acclimated to the altitude. Overnight backpackers need wilderness permits, which can be obtained during the off-season at permit stations within the park. Reservations ($3 per person) are strongly advised during summer and can be made through the **Wilderness Center** in Yosemite Valley (Box 545, Yosemite, 95389, ☎ 209/372–0740).

HORSEBACK RIDING

Yosemite Valley Stables (☎ 209/372–8348) offers 2-hr guided trail rides.

ROCK CLIMBING

Yosemite Mountaineering (☎ 209/372–8344) conducts rock-climbing and backpacking classes.

WINTER SPORTS

Badger Pass Ski Area, off Yosemite's Glacier Point Road, has nine downhill runs, 90 mi of free, groomed cross-country trails, and two excellent ski schools. Its gentle slopes make **Yosemite Ski School** (☎ 209/372–8430) an ideal downhill beginners' area. The highlight of the **cross-country skiing center** is a 21-mi loop from Badger Pass to Glacier Point. The **outdoor ice-skating rink** (☎ 209/372–8341) at Curry Village in Yosemite Valley is open from Thanksgiving Day through April.

Wawona

25 mi south of Yosemite Valley on Hwy. 41; 16 mi north of Fish Camp on Hwy. 41.

⑪ The historic buildings in **Pioneer Yosemite History Center** were moved to Wawona from their original sites in the park. From Wednesday through Sunday in summer, costumed park employees re-create life in 19th-century Yosemite in a blacksmith's shop, a Wells Fargo office, a jail, and other structures. Ranger-led walks leave from the covered bridge on Saturday at 10 AM in summer. Near the center are a post office, the Wawona General Store, and a gas station. ⊠ *On Hwy. 41.* ◷ *Historic buildings open year-round (hrs vary).*

⑫ **Mariposa Grove of Big Trees,** Yosemite's largest grove of giant sequoias, can be visited on foot—trails all lead uphill—or, during the summer, on one-hour tram rides. The Grizzly Giant, the oldest tree here, is estimated to be 2,700 years old. If the road to the grove is closed (which happens when Yosemite is crowded) park in Wawona and take the free shuttle; passengers are picked up near the gas station. The access road to the grove may also be closed by snow for extended periods from November to mid-May. You can still usually walk, snowshoe, or ski in. ⊠ *Off Hwy. 41 near the Fish Camp entrance to Yosemite*

National Park. 🖼 *Grove: free; tram ride: $8.50.* 🕓 *Grove: 24 hrs; tram: May–Oct., daily 9–4; shuttle: Memorial Day–Labor Day, daily 9–5.*

Dining and Lodging

$$ ✕🖼 **Wawona Hotel and Dining Room.** This 1879 National Historic Landmark sits at the southern end of Yosemite National Park, near the Mariposa Grove of Big Trees. It's an old-fashioned Victorian estate of whitewashed buildings with wraparound verandas. The hotel has small but pleasant rooms, about half of which do not have private baths; none have TVs or phones. You can watch deer graze on the meadow while dining in the romantic, candlelighted dining room ($$–$$$; reservations essential for dinner in summer), which dates from the late 1800s. The American-style cuisine favors California ingredients and flavors. Trout is a menu staple. Sunday brunch is served. Neat casual dress is requested at dinner. ✉ *Hwy. 41, 95389,* ☎ *559/252-4848 (reservations), 209/375–6556 (front desk), 209/375–1425 (dining room),* FAX *559/456–0542. 78 rooms, 24 cottage rooms. Restaurant, lounge, pool, 9-hole golf course, tennis, horseback riding. D, DC, MC, V. Closed weekdays Nov.–Easter, except during holiday periods.*

Yosemite National Park A to Z

Arriving and Departing

BY BUS

Greyhound (☎ 800/231–2222) serves Fresno and Merced from many California cities. **Yosemite VIA** (✉ 710 W. 16th St., Merced, ☎ 209/384–1315 or 800/369–7275) runs three daily buses from Merced to Yosemite Valley; buses also depart daily from Mariposa. The 2½- to 4½-hour trip from Merced costs $38 per person round-trip, which includes admission to the park.

BY CAR

Yosemite is a four- to five-hour drive from San Francisco (take Interstate–80 to Interstate–580 to Interstate–205 to Highway 120) and a six-hour drive from Los Angeles (take Interstate–5 north to Highway 99 to Fresno, and Highway 41 north to Yosemite). Highways 41, 120, and 140 all intersect with Highway 99, which runs north–south through the Central Valley. Try to fill up your gas tank in one of the gateway towns near the park; there's no gas station in Yosemite Valley. Within the park, gas stations are in Crane Flat, Wawona, and, in summer only, Tuolumne Meadows.

Via Highway 41: If you're coming from the south, Highway 41—which passes through Fresno in the San Joaquin Valley and then climbs through hills to Oakhurst and past Bass Lake—is the most direct path to Yosemite. Called Wawona Road inside the park, it provides the most stunning entrance, via the Wawona Tunnel, into Yosemite Valley. The distance from Fresno is 105 mi, but the latter part of the trip can be quite slow; allow 2 ½ hours. If you're coming from Madera, 60 mi away, take Highway 145 to Highway 41, then go north.

Via Highway 140: Arch Rock Entrance is 75 mi northeast of Merced via Highway 140, the least mountainous route into the park. The highway is undergoing extensive widening and reconstruction that may continue for several years. Construction may be halted, however, during busy summer months and holiday periods.

Via Highway 120: Highway 120 is the northernmost route—the one that travels farthest and slowest through the foothills. You'll arrive at the park's Big Oak Flat Entrance, 88 mi east of Manteca. If you are coming from the east, you could cross the Sierra from Lee Vining on Highway 120 (Tioga Road). This route takes you over the Sierra crest and past Tuolumne Meadows. It's scenic, but the mountain driving may be stressful for some, and it's open only in summer.

Fresno Air Terminal (✉ 5175 Clinton Way, ☎ 559/498–4095), the nearest major airport, is served by Delta, American, United Express, US Airways, and several regional carriers. *See* Air Travel *in* Smart Travel Tips A to Z for airline phone numbers.

Getting Around
BY BUS
A free shuttle runs around the eastern end of Yosemite Valley (between 7 AM and 10 PM in the summer and early fall, from 9 AM to 10 PM the rest of the year). A free shuttle connects Wawona to the Mariposa Grove of Big Trees in summer only from 9 AM to 4:30 PM. The last return shuttle from the grove departs at 5 PM. Free shuttle buses from Yosemite Valley to Badger Pass operate in ski season.

BY CAR
Auto traffic in Yosemite National Park is sometimes restricted during peak periods. Check conditions before driving in. Large RVs and trailers are not allowed on some roads. Carry tire chains when you drive in the mountains from mid-October through April.

Contacts and Resources
CAMPING
Yosemite Campground Reservations (☎ 800/436–7275) handles bookings for the reservable campgrounds within the park (☞ *below*). Beginning on the 15th of each month you can reserve a site up to five months in advance. **Yosemite Concession Services** (☎ 559/252–4848) handles reservations for the tent-cabin and other sites in Yosemite Valley at Curry Village and at the camping shelters at Housekeeping Camp.

Most of Yosemite's 15 campgrounds are found in Yosemite Valley and along the Tioga Road. Glacier Point and Wawona have one each. None have water or electric hookups, but there are dump stations and shower facilities in Yosemite Valley year-round. The dump stations in Wawona and Tuolumne Meadows are open in summer only. Several campgrounds operate on a first-come, first-served basis. During summer, reservations are strongly recommended for the campgrounds at Tuolumne Meadows, Hodgdon Meadow, Lower Pines, North Pines, Upper Pines, Wawona, and Crane Flat; the rest of the year, some of these are first-come, first-served. With a total of 1,840 sites open in summer, it's sometimes possible to get a campsite upon arrival by stopping at the Campground Reservations Office in Yosemite Valley, but this is a risky strategy. Some 400 sites remain open year-round.

When you're at your site, use the metal food-storage boxes to prevent bears from pilfering your edibles. Move all food, coolers, and items with a scent (including toiletries and air fresheners) from your car to the metal storage box. (Canisters for backpackers can be rented for $3 a day in most park stores.) Keep an eye peeled for rattlesnakes, which live below 7,000 ft. Though rarely fatal, their bites require a doctor's attention. Marmots, small members of the squirrel family, enjoy getting under a vehicle and chewing on radiator hoses and car wiring. Always check under the hood before driving away. Don't drink water directly from streams and lakes, as intestinal disorders may result.

EMERGENCIES
Ambulance (☎ 911). **Fire** (☎ 911). **Police** (☎ 911).

GUIDED TOURS
California Parlor Car Tours (☎ 415/474–7500 or 800/227–4250) in San Francisco serves Yosemite. Lodging and some meals are included. **Yosemite Concession Services** (☎ 209/372–1240) operates daily guided bus tours of the Yosemite Valley floor year-round, plus seasonal tours of Glacier Point and the Mariposa Grove of Big Trees. The company's Grand Tour ($45.25), offered between Memorial Day and November, weather permitting, covers the park's highlights.

LODGING RESERVATIONS
Yosemite Concession Services Corporation (✉ Central Reservations, 5410 E. Home, Fresno 93727, ☎ 559/252–4848).

ROAD CONDITIONS
Yosemite Area Road and Weather Conditions (☎ 209/372–0200).

VISITOR INFORMATION
Yosemite Concession Services Corporation (☎ 209/372–1000). **Yosemite National Park** (✉ Information Office, Box 577, Yosemite National Park 95389, ☎ 209/372–0200 or 209/372–0264).

OUTSIDE YOSEMITE NATIONAL PARK

Mono Lake, Bodie, and the Gateway Cities

The area to the north and east of Yosemite National Park includes some ruggedly handsome terrain, most notably around Mono Lake. Bodie Ghost Town is north of the lake. Several gateway towns to the south and west of Yosemite National Park, most within an hour's drive of Yosemite Valley, have food, lodging, and other services.

Mono Lake

★ *20 mi east of Tuolumne Meadows, Hwy. 120 to U.S. 395; 30 mi north of Mammoth Lakes on U.S. 395.*

Eerie tufa towers—calcium carbonate formations that often resemble castle turrets—rise from impressive **Mono Lake.** Since the 1940s the city of Los Angeles has been diverting water from streams that feed the lake, lowering its water level and exposing the tufa. Court victories by environmentalists in the 1990s forced a reduction of the diversions, and the lake has since risen about 9 ft. Millions of migratory birds nest in and around Mono Lake.

The best place to view the tufa is at the south end of the lake along the mile-long **South Tufa Trail.** To reach it drive 5 mi south from Lee Vining on U.S. 395, then 5 mi east on Highway 120. Pay the $2 fee at the trail or at the **Scenic Area Visitor Center** (✉ U.S. 395, Lee Vining, ☎ 760/647–3044); the center is open daily from April through October, 9 to 5:30, and the rest of the year Thursday through Monday, 9 to 4. You can swim (or float) in the highly salty water at Navy Beach (near the South Tufa Trail) or take a kayak or canoe trip for close-up views of the tufa. Check with rangers for boating restrictions during bird-nesting season (April–August). Rangers and naturalists lead walking tours of the tufa daily in summer and on weekends only (sometimes on cross-country skis) in winter.

Bodie Ghost Town and State Historic Park

23 mi from Lee Vining, north on U.S. 395, east on Hwy. 270 (last 3 mi are unpaved). Snow may close Hwy. 270 in winter and early spring, but park stays open.

★ ⑬ Old shacks and shops, abandoned mine shafts, a Methodist church, the mining village of Rattlesnake Gulch, and the remains of a small Chinatown are among the sights at fascinating **Bodie Ghost Town,** elevation 8,200 ft. The town boomed from about 1878 to 1881 as gold prospectors, having worked the best of the western Sierra mines, headed to the high desert on the eastern slopes. Bodie had a nasty reputation—the booze flowed freely, shootings were commonplace, and licentiousness reigned. The big strikes were made during the boom years, and though some mining continued into the 1930s, the town had long since begun its decline. By the late 1940s, all the residents had departed. A state park was established in 1962, with a mandate to preserve but not restore the town. Evidence of Bodie's wild past survives at an excellent museum, and you can tour an old stamp mill (where ore was stamped into fine powder to extract gold and silver) and a ridge that contains many mine sites. No food, drink, or lodging is available in Bodie, and the nearest picnic area is ½ mi away. *Museum: Main and Green Sts.,* ☎ *760/647–6445.* ☞ *Park: $2 per person, $1 per dog; museum: free.* ☉ *Park: Memorial Day–mid-Sept., daily 8–7; rest of yr, daily 8–4; Museum: May–Oct., daily 10–5; open sporadically rest of yr.*

Bass Lake

18 mi south of Yosemite National Park's South Entrance, Hwy. 41 to Bass Valley Rd.

Dining

$$–$$$ ✕ **Ducey's on the Lake.** With a lakeside view and elaborate chandeliers sculpted from antlers, the lodge-style restaurant at Ducey's (part of the larger Pines Resort complex) attracts boaters, locals, and tourists with standard lamb, beef, seafood, and pasta dishes. Burgers, salads, tacos, and sandwiches are served at the upstairs Rudy's Bar & Grill. Sunday brunch is served from 10 AM to 2 PM. ⊠ *54432 Rd. 432,* ☎ *559/642–3121. Reservations essential for brunch. AE, D, DC, MC, V.*

Outdoor Activities and Sports

Pines Marina (⊠ Bass Lake Reservoir, ☎ 559/642–3565), open from April through October, rents ski boats, houseboats, and fishing boats.

El Portal

14 mi west of Yosemite Valley on Hwy. 140.

The gas station in this small community is a good place to fill up before entering the park. There's also a small convenience store and a post office.

Lodging

$$–$$$ 🏠 **Cedar Lodge.** The lobby of this complex in the pines is heavy on plaids and teddy bears. Rooms range from suites with kitchenettes to family units to romantic accommodations with whirlpool tubs for two. ⊠ *9966 Hwy. 140, 95318,* ☎ *209/379–2612,* fax *209/379–2712. 188 rooms, 22 suites, 2 apartments, 1 house. Restaurant, 2 pools, hot tub. AE, MC, V.*

$$–$$$ 🏠 **Yosemite View Lodge.** The back building at Yosemite View has rooms with balconies overlooking the boulder-strewn Merced River and majestic pines. Also in view is a picnic patio with hot tubs and heated pools. The pleasant facility is on the public bus route to Yosemite National Park and near fishing and river rafting. Many of the rooms have spa baths, fireplaces, and kitchenettes. ⊠ *11136 Hwy. 140, 95318,* ☎ *209/379–2681,* fax *209/379–2704. 276 rooms. Restaurant,*

bar, indoor pool, 2 outdoor pools, 4 hot tubs, coin laundry, meeting room. MC, V.

Fish Camp

37 mi south of Yosemite Valley floor on Hwy. 41; 4 mi south of Yosemite National Park's South Entrance on Hwy. 41.

In the small town of Fish Camp are a service station, a post office, a general store, and the **Yosemite Mountain Sugar Pine Railroad,** a 4-mi narrow-gauge train ride through the forest. The Saturday-evening Moonlight Special excursion (reservations advised) includes dinner and old-fashioned entertainment. ✉ *56001 Hwy. 41,* ☎ *559/683–7273.* 🎟 *$11; $32.50 for Moonlight Special.* ☉ *Mar.–Oct., daily.*

Dining and Lodging

$$$$ ✕🏨 **Tenaya Lodge.** One of the region's largest hotels is ideal for people who enjoy hiking in the wilderness but prefer returning at night to luxury. A Southwestern motif prevails in the ample regular rooms. The deluxe rooms have minibars and other extras, and the suites have balconies. The cozy Sierra Restaurant ($–$$$) offers Continental cuisine; the fare at the lodge's casual Jackalopes Bar and Grill includes burgers, salads, and sandwiches. Off-season room rates here run as low as $99. ✉ *1122 Hwy. 41, Box 159, 93623,* ☎ *559/683–6555; 800/635–5807 for lodging reservations and restaurant;* FAX *559/683–0249. 208 rooms, 36 suites. 2 restaurants, bar, deli, room service, indoor and outdoor pool, 2 hot tubs, health club, hiking, mountain bikes, cross-country skiing, children's programs, playground, laundry service, meeting rooms. AE, D, DC, MC, V.*

$$–$$$ ✕🏨 **Narrow Gauge Inn.** This eye-grabbing motel-style property is comfortably furnished, with old-fashioned decor and railroad memorabilia. The inn's lodgelike restaurant, which serves cuisine inspired by the California ranchero era of the late 1800s, is festooned with moose, bison, and other wildlife trophies. ✉ *48571 Hwy. 41, 93623,* ☎ *559/683–7720 or 888/644–9050,* FAX *559/683–2139. 24 rooms, 1 suite. Restaurant, bar, pool, hot tub. AE, D, MC, V. Closed Nov.–Mar.*

Oakhurst

50 mi south of Yosemite Valley on Hwy. 41; 23 mi south of Yosemite National Park's South Entrance on Hwy. 41.

Motels and restaurants line both sides of Highway 41 as it cuts through the town of Oakhurst. Two theaters in the Oakhurst mall show current movies, and you can stock up on major provisions at the grocery and general stores.

Dining and Lodging

$$$$ ✕ **Erna's Elderberry House.** The restaurant, operated by Vienna-born ★ Erna Kubin, owner of Château du Sureau (☞ *below*), is another expression of her passion for beauty, charm, and impeccable service. White walls and dark beams accent the dining room's high ceilings, and arched windows reflect the glow of many candles. A six-course, prix-fixe dinner in rhythm with the seasons is elegantly paced and accompanied by superb wines. This is a dining experience to remember. Brunch is served weekends. ✉ *48688 Victoria La.,* ☎ *559/683–6800. AE, MC, V. Closed 1st 3 wks in Jan. No lunch Mon.–Tues.*

$$$$ 🏨 **Château du Sureau.** This romantic inn, adjacent to Erna's Elder-★ berry House (☞ *above*), is like a fairy tale. From the moment regal gates open and you step out of your car (think mice-driven coach), you will be pampered until checkout. A winding staircase seems to carry you up to your room. You'll fall asleep in the glow of a crackling fire

amid goose-down pillows and a comforter that rivals Cloud Nine. When you raise the curtains the next morning, you'll breathe in the cool, fragrant air from the gardens and the mist-shrouded pines. After a hearty European breakfast in the dining room, plan your Sierra stay in the piano room, which has an exquisite ceiling mural. ⊠ 48688 *Victoria La., Box 577, 93464,* ☎ *559/683–6860,* FAX *559/683–0800. 10 rooms, 1 villa. Restaurant, pool. Full breakfast. AE, MC, V.*

$$$–$$$$ 🏨 **The Homestead.** Serenity is the order of the day at this secluded getaway in Ahwahnee, 6 mi west of Oakhurst. On 160 acres that once held a Miwok Indian village, the Homestead's cottages have fireplaces, living rooms, fully equipped kitchens, some antiques, and queen-size beds. Smoking and pets are not allowed on the premises. ⊠ *41110 Rd. 600, 2½ mi off Hwy. 49, Ahwahnee, 93601,* ☎ *559/683–0495,* FAX *559/ 683–8165. 4 cottages, 1 loft. AE, D, MC, V.*

$$ 🏨 **Shilo Inn.** The Shilo's spacious, sunny, pine-furnished rooms come with microwaves, refrigerators, and satellite TV. ⊠ *40644 Hwy. 41, 93644,* ☎ *559/683–3555,* FAX *559/683–3386. 80 rooms, 1 suite. Kitchenettes, pool, hot tub, sauna, steam room, exercise room, coin laundry. Continental breakfast. AE, D, DC, MC, V.*

Outside Yosemite National Park A to Z

Arriving and Departing

See Yosemite National Park A to Z, *above.*

Getting Around

The area surrounding Yosemite National Park is best visited by car. U.S. 395, the main north–south road on the eastern side of the Sierra Nevada, passes by the west edge of Mono Lake and west of Bodie Ghost Town. Highway 140 heads east from the San Joaquin Valley to El Portal. Highway 41 heads north from Fresno to Oakhurst and Fish Camp; Bass Lake is off Highway 41.

Visitor Information

Bodie State Historic Park (⊠ Box 515, Bridgeport 93517, ☎ 760/647– 6445). **Mono Lake** (⊠ Box 49, Lee Vining 93541, ☎ 760/647–3044). **Yosemite Sierra Visitors Bureau** (⊠ 41729 Hwy. 41, Box 1998, Oakhurst 93644, ☎ 559/683–4636).

MAMMOTH LAKES

A jewel in the eastern Sierra Nevada, resting amid glistening mountain peaks and glacier-carved alpine lakes, Mammoth Lakes provides California's finest skiing and snowboarding south of Lake Tahoe. At 11,053-ft-high Mammoth Mountain, skiers hit the slopes as late as June or even July. As soon as snows melt, Mammoth transforms itself into a warm-weather playground—fishing, mountain biking, hiking, and horseback riding are among the options. Nine deep-blue lakes form the Mammoth Lakes Basin, and another 100 lakes dot the surrounding countryside. Crater-pocked Mammoth Mountain hasn't had a major eruption for 50,000 years, but the region is alive with hot springs, mud pots, fumaroles, and steam vents.

Mammoth Lakes

30 mi south of Mono Lake on U.S. 395.

Much of the architecture in the hub town of Mammoth Lakes, elevation 7,800 ft, is in the faux-alpine category. You'll find basic services here, plus plenty of dining and lodging options.

Even if you don't ski, it makes sense to start at the aptly named land-mass in the middle of it all—Mammoth Mountain. **Gondolas** serve skiers in winter and mountain bikers and sightseers in summer. The high-speed 8-passenger Panorama Gondola opened in 1998 runs from the Mid-Chalet to the summit. The boarding area for the lower gondola is at the main lodge of the ski area. ☎ *760/934–2571, ext. 3850.* 🎫 *$10.* ✆ *July 4–Oct., daily 9:30–5; Nov.–July 3, daily 8:30–4.*

The sawtooth, glacial-carved spires of the Minarets, the remains of an ancient lava flow, are best viewed from the **Minaret Vista,** off Highway 203 west of Mammoth Lakes.

The **lakes of the Mammoth Lakes Basin,** reached by Lake Mary Road southwest of town, are popular for fishing and boating in summer. First comes **Twin Lakes**, at the far end of which is Twin Falls, where water cascades 300 ft over a shelf of volcanic rock. **Lake Mary** is the largest lake in the basin. Others include **Lake Mamie** and **Lake George**. Horse-shoe **Lake** is the only lake in which you can swim.

🖐 ⑭ An easy 10-minute walk from the ranger station at **Devil's Postpile National Monument** takes you to the base of Devil's Postpile, a geologic formation of smooth, vertical basalt columns sculpted by volcanic and glacial forces. A short but steep trail winds to the top of the 60-ft-high rocky cliff for a bird's-eye view of the columns. A 2-mi hike past the Postpile leads to the monument's second scenic wonder, **Rainbow Falls**, where a branch of the San Joaquin River plunges more than 100 ft over a lava ledge. When the water hits the pool below, mists rise to form a rainbow of color; walk down a bit from the top of the falls for the best viewing. During the daytime in summer the national monument is accessible only via a shuttle bus ($9) that begins operation as soon as the road is cleared of snow—usually in June, but sometimes as late as July. The shuttle departs from Mammoth Mountain Inn (☞ *below*) every 20 minutes from 7:30 AM to 5:30 PM. The shuttle stops running after Labor Day, but you can drive to the falls until snows come again, usually around the beginning of November. Scenic picnic spots dot the bank of the San Joaquin River. ✉ *Box 501; follow Minaret Rd. (Hwy. 203) 13 mi west from Mammoth Lakes 93546.* ☎ *760/934–2289 (summer), 559/565–3341 (winter); 760/934–0606 for shuttle bus information.* 🎫 *Free.* ✆ *Late June–late Oct., daily, weather permitting.*

The **June Lake Loop** (Hwy. 158 west from U.S. 395), a wonderfully scenic 17-mi drive that follows an old glacial canyon past Grant, June, Gull, and other alpine lakes, is especially colorful in fall.

OFF THE BEATEN PATH
HOT CREEK GEOLOGIC SITE/HOT CREEK FISH HATCHERY – Forged by an ancient volcanic eruption, the Hot Creek Geologic Site is a landscape of boiling hot springs, fumaroles, and occasional geysers about 10 mi southeast of the town of Mammoth Lakes. You can soak (at your own risk) in hot springs or walk along boardwalks through the canyon to view the steaming volcanic features. Fly-fishing for trout is popular upstream from the springs. En route to the geologic site is the Hot Creek Fish Hatchery, the breeding ponds for most of the 3 million to 5 million fish the state stocks annually in eastern Sierra lakes and rivers. ✉ *Hot Creek Hatchery Rd., east off U.S. 395,* ☎ *760/924–5500 for site; 760/934–2664 for hatchery.* 🎫 *Free.* ✆ *Site: daily sunrise–sunset; hatchery: daily 8–4, weather permitting.*

Dining and Lodging

$$–$$$ ✕ **Nevados.** In a restaurant scene known mostly for meat, potatoes, and pizza, Nevados serves contemporary cuisine in a bistro setting. The menu changes frequently but always includes creative soups and salads, fresh seafood, and grilled meats. Grilled eggplant lasagna, sesame-crusted ahi tuna, and orange-scented duckling are among the past entrées. Ask about the three-course prix fixe menu. ⊠ *Main St. and Minaret Rd.,* ☎ 760/934–4466. *Reservations essential on weekends and holidays. AE, D, DC, MC, V. No lunch. Closed 1 wk in early June and late Oct.–early Nov.*

$–$$$ ✕ **The Mogul.** This longtime steak house has a friendly, relaxed ambience. The charbroiled shrimp and the grilled beef or chicken come with a baked potato or rice pilaf and soup or salad. A children's menu is available. ⊠ *Mammoth Tavern Rd. off Old Mammoth Rd.,* ☎ 760/934–3039. *AE, D, MC, V. No lunch.*

$–$$ ✕ **Berger's.** Don't even think about coming to this bustling pine-panel restaurant unless you're hungry. Berger's is known, appropriately enough, for burgers and other generously sized sandwiches. Everything comes in big, even mountainous portions. For dinner try the beef ribs or the buffalo steak. ⊠ *Minaret Rd. near Canyon Blvd.,* ☎ 760/934–6622. *MC, V. Closed 4–6 wks in May and June and 4–6 wks in Oct. and Nov. (call ahead).*

$–$$ ✕ **Giovanni's Pizza.** Kids enjoy this casual restaurant that serves good pizza and standard Italian dinners (best bet: stick to the pizza). Don't come here for quiet conversation—it's a high-decibel atmosphere. ⊠ *Minaret Village Mall, Old Mammoth Rd. and Meridian St.,* ☎ 760/934–7563. *AE, MC, V. No lunch Sun.*

$ ✕ **Blondie's Kitchen and Waffle Shop.** A good place to stoke up before a morning on the slopes or trails (it opens at 5:30 AM), this comic-strip-theme diner serves up Belgian waffles, pancakes, omelets, and Dagwood "pig-out" plates. ⊠ *Main and Lupin Sts.,* ☎ 760/934–4048. *No credit cards. No dinner.*

$$–$$$$ ▨ **Mammoth Mountain Inn.** If you want to be within walking distance of the Mammoth Mountain ski area, this is the place to stay. You can check your skis with the concierge after a day on the slopes and pick them up in the morning and head directly to the lifts, right across the way. At breakfast, inn personnel will keep you apprised of snow and weather conditions. The accommodations, some of which are cramped, include standard hotel rooms and condo units; the latter have kitchenettes and many have lofts. The inn has licensed on-site child care. ⊠ *Minaret Rd. 4 mi west of Mammoth Lakes (Box 353), 93546,* ☎ *760/934–2581 or 800/228–4947,* FAX *760/934–0701. 124 rooms, 91 condo units. 2 restaurants, bar, 3 hot tubs, ski storage, video games, nursery, playground, meeting rooms. AE, MC, V.*

$$–$$$$ ▨ **Snowcreek Resort.** In a valley surrounded by mountain peaks, this 355-acre condominium community on the outskirts of Mammoth Lakes contains one- to four-bedroom units. All have kitchens, living and dining rooms, fireplaces, and TVs with VCRs; some have laundry facilities. There's an on-premises nursery, and guests have free use of the well-supplied athletic club. ⊠ *Old Mammoth Rd., Box 1647, 93546,* ☎ *760/934–3333 or 800/544–6007,* FAX *760/934–1619. 150 condo units. 2 pools, 5 hot tubs, sauna, 18-hole golf course, 9 tennis courts, health club, racquetball, nursery, meeting rooms. AE, MC, V.*

$–$$$$ ▨ **Tamarack Lodge Resort.** Nordic skiers (and, in summer, nature lovers) favor this lodge that overlooks Twin Lakes, about 3 mi west of town. Lodge rooms and housekeeping cabins occupy a quiet, woodsy setting, and cross-country ski trails loop past the cabins. In warm months, fishing, canoeing, hiking, and mountain biking are close by. The cozy cabins are modern, neat, and clean, with knotty-pine kitchens and private baths; some have fireplaces or wood-burning stoves. Alert the kids: there are no TVs. ✉ *Box 69; take Lake Mary Rd. off Hwy. 203, 93546,* ☎ *760/934–2442 or 800/237–6879 in CA and NV,* FAX *760/934–2281. 11 rooms, 25 cabins. Restaurant, cross-country skiing, ski shop. D, MC, V.*

$$–$$$ 🏨 **Sierra Lodge.** This motel on Main Street has spacious rooms. A covered parking garage with ski lockers is helpful in wintertime. Free shuttles take skiers to Mammoth Mountain. All rooms are no-smoking. ✉ *3540 Main St., 93546,* ☎ *760/934–8881; 800/356–5711 in southern CA,* FAX *760/934–7231. 35 rooms. Kitchenettes, hot tub, ski storage. Continental breakfast. MC, V.*

$–$$ 🏨 **Swiss Chalet.** One of the most reasonably priced motels in town, the Swiss Chalet has million-dollar views of the mountains. Among the amenities are an indoor sauna and hot tub, a fish-cleaning area, and a freezer to keep your summer catch fresh. ✉ *3776 Viewpoint Rd., Box 16, 93546,* ☎ *760/934–2403 or 800/937–9477,* FAX *760/934–2403. 21 rooms. Kitchenettes, hot tub, sauna. AE, D, MC, V.*

Nightlife and the Arts

The summertime jazz, country-western, rock, and reggae concerts of **Mammoth Mountain Music** (☎ 760/934–0606 or 800/228–4947) take place at Yodler Pavilion at the Mammoth Mountain ski area.

Goats Bar (Mono and Main Sts., ☎ 760/934–4629), a popular watering hole, has a pool table and a dartboard. Rock, country, and blues acts perform at **La Sierra's** (Main St. near Minaret Rd., ☎ 760/ 934–8083), which has Mammoth's largest dance floor. The bar at **Whiskey Creek** (Main St. and Minaret Rd., ☎ 760/934–2555) hosts bands or solo musicians on weekends year-round and on most nights in winter.

Outdoor Activities and Sports

BICYCLING

Mammoth Mountain Bike Park (☎ 760/934–0706), at the ski area, opens when the snows melt, usually by July, with 70-plus mi of single-track trails—from mellow to super-challenging. Chairlifts and shuttles provide trail access, and rentals are available.

DOGSLEDDING

Dog Sled Adventures (☎ 760/934–6270) operates 25-minute rides through the forest on dogsleds pulled by teams of 10 dogs.

FISHING

Crowley Lake is the top trout-fishing spot in the area; Convict Lake, June Lake, and the lakes of the Mammoth Basin are other prime spots. One of the best trout rivers is the San Joaquin near Devil's Postpile (☞ *above*). Hot Creek (☞ *above*), a designated Wild Trout Stream, is renowned for fly-fishing (catch and release only). The fishing season runs from the last Saturday in April until the end of October. **Kittredge Sports** (Main St. and Forest Trail, ☎ 760/934–7566) rents rods and reels and conducts guided trips.

HIKING

Trails wind around the Lakes Basin and through pristine alpine scenery. Stop at the U.S. Forest Service ranger station (☞ Visitor Information, *below*) for a trail map and permits for backpacking in wilderness areas.

HORSEBACK RIDING

Stables are typically open from June through September. Outfitters include **Mammoth Lakes Pack Outfit** (Box 61, along Lake Mary Rd., 93546, ☎ 760/934–2434); **McGee Creek Pack Station** (Box 162, Rte. 1, 93546,

☎ 760/935–4324 or 800/854–7407); and **Sierra Meadows Ranch** (Sherwin Creek Rd., ☎ 760/934–6161).

HOT-AIR BALLOONING

The balloons of **Mammoth Ballooning** (☎ 760/934–7188 or 800/484–6936, ext. 1122) glide over the countryside in the morning from spring until fall, weather permitting.

SKIING AND SNOWBOARDING

June Mountain Ski Area. This low-key resort 20 mi north of Mammoth Mountain is a favorite of snowboarders, who have a halfpipe all to themselves. Seven lifts service the area, which has a 2,590-ft vertical drop; the skiing ranges from beginner to expert. A rental and repair shop, a ski school, and a sport shop are all on the premises, and there's child care. ⊠ *Box 146, off June Lake Loop (Hwy. 158), June Lake 93529,* ☎ *760/648–7733 or 888/586–3668.*

Mammoth Mountain Ski Area. With 30 lifts and more than 3,500 acres of skiable terrain, Mammoth is one of the West's largest ski areas. The base elevation is 7,953 ft. When it's not too windy, you can ski off the top of the mountain (11,053 ft), for a 3,100-ft vertical drop. The terrain includes beginning-to-expert runs. Snowboarders are welcome on all slopes; the Unbound Snowboard Arena has a halfpipe and two freestyle terrain parks. Mammoth's season begins in November and often lingers until June or beyond. Night skiing is available on weekends and holidays, from Christmas to Easter. Lessons and rental equipment are available, and there's a kids' ski and snowboard school. ⊠ *Minaret Rd. west of Mammoth Lakes, Box 24, 93546,* ☎ *760/934–0745 or 888/462–6668.*

Trails at **Tamarack Cross Country Ski Center** (Lake Mary Rd. off Hwy. 203, ☎ 760/934–2442), adjacent to Tamarack Lodge (☞ *above*) meander around several lakes. Rentals are available.

Sandy's Ski & Sport (Main St., near Center St., ☎ 760/934–7518) rents and sells equipment.

SNOWMOBILING

Mammoth Snowmobile Adventures, at the Main Lodge at the Mammoth Mountain Ski Area (☎ 760/934–9645), conducts guided tours along wooded trails.

Mammoth Lakes A to Z

Arriving and Departing

BY CAR

In summer and early fall (or whenever snows aren't blocking Tioga Road) you can drive from San Francisco to Mammoth via Highway 120 (to U.S. 395 south) through the Yosemite high country, a distance of about 300 mi. The quickest route when Tioga Road is closed is Interstate–80 to U.S. 50 in the Lake Tahoe area; from the lake's Nevada side take the Kingsbury Grade (Route 207) east to U.S. 395 south to Highway 203 west. This trip is a total of 320 mi. From the Los Angeles area, the route is the same all year: Highway 14 and U.S. 395 north to Highway 203 west, a distance of about 310 mi. If you're coming from San Diego or Orange County, take Interstate–15 north to U.S. 395 and follow that north to 203; the trip from San Diego is about 375 mi.

BY PLANE

Mountain Air Express (☎ 562/595–1011 or 800/788–4247) operates flights to Mammoth Lakes from Long Beach. Flights land at Mammoth Lakes Airport, about 6 mi south of town.

Getting Around

BY CAR

Highway 203 heads west from U.S. 395, becoming Main Street as it passes through the town of Mammoth Lakes and later Minaret Road (which makes a right turn) as it continues west to the Mammoth Mountain ski area and Devil's Postpile National Monument. To get to the Lakes Basin, take Hwy. 203 (Main St.) to Lake Mary Road, going straight at the Minaret Road intersection.

BY SHUTTLE BUS

Mammoth Mountain runs four free **shuttle bus** (☎ 760/934–0687) routes around town to and from the ski area. Buses run from 7 AM to 5:30 PM daily in snow season, with limited night service from Christmas to Easter.

BY TAXI

Mammoth Shuttle (☎ 760/934–3030) provides airport and ski-lift transport.

Contacts and Resources

EMERGENCIES

Ambulance (☎ 911). **Fire** (☎ 911). **Police** (☎ 911).

VISITOR INFORMATION

Mammoth Lakes Visitors Bureau (Box 48; along Hwy. 203 (Main St.), near Sawmill Cutoff Rd. 93546, ☎ 760/934–2712 or 888/466–2666). **Snow Report** (☎ 760/934–7669 or 888/766–9778). **U.S. Forest Service ranger station** (along Hwy. 203 (Main St.), near Sawmill Cutoff Rd. 93546, ☎ 760/924–5500).

KINGS CANYON AND SEQUOIA NATIONAL PARKS

Grant Grove, Cedar Grove, and Lodgepole

General Grant and Sequoia national parks were established in 1890, along with Yosemite. Additions to General Grant National Park included the Redwood Canyon area and the drainages of the south and middle forks of the Kings River. The expanded region of General Grant Park was renamed Kings Canyon National Park in 1940. Though they're overshadowed by Yosemite, naturalist John Muir thought no less of these two parks. He declared that the beauty of Kings Canyon rivaled that of Yosemite and described the sequoia trees as "the most beautiful and majestic on Earth." *Sequoiadendron giganteum* trees are not as tall as the coast redwoods (*Sequoia sempervirens*), but on average they are older and more massive. Exhibits at the visitor centers explain the special relationship between these trees and fire (their thick, fibrous bark helps protect them from fire and insects) and their ability to live so long and grow so big.

A little more than 1.5 million people visit Kings Canyon and Sequoia annually, wandering trails through groves and meadows or tackling the rugged backcountry. The topography of the two parks runs the gamut from chaparral, at an elevation of 1,500 ft, to the giant sequoia belt, at 5,000 to 7,000 ft, to the towering peaks of the Great Western Divide and the Sierra Crest. Mount Whitney, the highest point in the contiguous United States at 14,494 ft, is the crown jewel of the eastern side.

Kings Canyon and Sequoia national parks share their administration and a main highway, called the Generals Highway, which connects High-

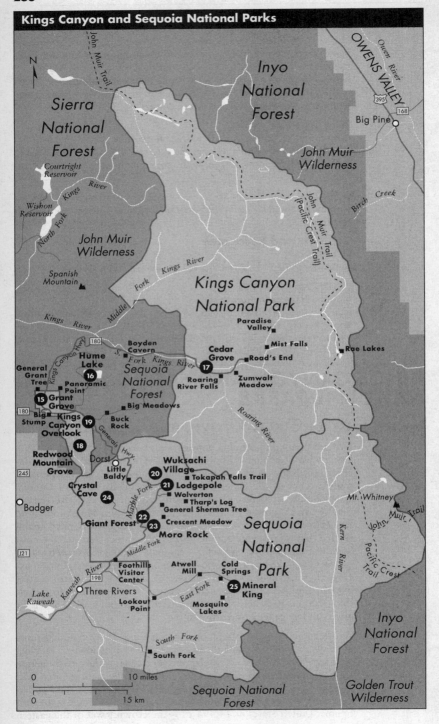

Kings Canyon and Sequoia National Parks

way 180 in Kings Canyon to Highway 198 in Sequoia. The entrance fee to Kings Canyon and Sequoia (good for admission to both on seven consecutive days) is $10 per vehicle, $5 for those who don't arrive by car. An information-packed quarterly newspaper and a map are handed out at the parks' entrances.

Grant Grove and Cedar Grove

100 mi southeast of Oakhurst, Hwy. 41 to Hwy. 180.

⑮   **Grant Grove** (✉ Kings Canyon Hwy./Hwy. 180, 1 mi from Big Stump Entrance), Kings Canyon's most highly developed area, is the original grove that was designated as General Grant National Park in 1890. A walk along the 1-mi **Big Stump Trail,** which starts near the park entrance, graphically demonstrates the toll heavy logging takes on the wilderness. An alternative ⅓-mi trail is fairly accessible to travelers with disabilities; there are some rough spots and rain can muddy up the trail. The **General Grant Tree Trail,** a paved ⅜-mi path through Grant Grove, winds past the **General Grant,** an enormous, estimated 2,000-year-old sequoia that's designated the nation's Christmas Tree. The **Gamlin Cabin,** an 1867 structure listed on the National Register of Historic Places, is a pioneer cabin. Also within Grant Grove is the **Centennial Stump,** the remains of a huge sequoia cut for display at the 1876 Philadelphia Centennial Exhibition.

Grant Grove Village has a visitor center (☎ 559/335–2856), a grocery store, a gift shop, campgrounds, a coffee shop, overnight lodging, a horse-rental concession, and a post office. The visitor center has exhibits on the sequoias and the area.

⑯   **Hume Lake** (✉ Hwy. 180 northeast 8 mi from Grant Grove off Hume Lake Rd.), a reservoir built in the early 1900s by loggers, is now the site of several church-affiliated camps, a gas station, and a public campground. This small lake outside Kings Canyon's borders has views of high mountains in the distance.

★ ⑰   The **Cedar Grove** area is a valley that snakes along the south fork of the Kings River. A spectacular 30-mi descent along Kings Canyon Highway takes about one hour from Grant Grove to the end of the road, where you can hike, camp, or turn right around for the drive back up. Built by convict labor in the 1930s, the road (usually closed from mid-October to April) clings to some dramatic cliffs along the way: watch out for falling rocks. The highway passes the scars where large groves of sequoias were logged at the beginning of the 20th century. It runs along the south fork and through dry foothills covered with yuccas that bloom in the summer. There are amazing views into the deepest gorge in the United States, at the confluence of the two forks, and up the canyons to the High Sierra.

Cedar Grove was named for the incense cedars that grow in the area. You can rent horses here, a good way to continue your explorations; campgrounds, lodgings, a small visitor center (☎ 559/565–3793), a snack bar, a restaurant, a convenience market, a gift shop, and a gas station round out the facilities.

Short trails circle **Zumwalt Meadow.** The trails from the meadow lead to the base of **Roaring River Falls.** Hikers can self-register for wilderness permits at **Road's End,** 6 mi east of Cedar Grove Village. Permits are free and some are given out on a first-come, first-served basis; from mid-May to late September. It's advisable to pay the $10 for a 21-day-advance reservation (☎ 559/565–3766).

Dining, Lodging, and Camping

$$ ✕🛏 **Cedar Grove Lodge.** Although accommodations are close to the road, Cedar Grove manages to retain a quiet atmosphere. Book way in advance—the motel-lodge has only 18 rooms. Each one is air-conditioned and carpeted and has a private shower and two queen-size beds. The fare for lunch and dinner at the self-serve restaurant is trout, hamburgers, hot dogs, and sandwiches. Breakfast is eggs, bacon, and toast. You can take food from the restaurant to picnic tables along the river's edge. ☎ 559/335–5500 for reservations. 18 rooms. MC, V. Closed mid-Oct.–mid-May.

$–$$ ✕🛏 **Grant Grove Lodge.** The nine carpeted cabins here have private baths, propane wall heaters, and double beds. Simpler cabins, heated by woodstoves and lit by battery lamps—as well as some even more rustic tent cabins—are near a central rest room and shower facility. Meadowview Fine Dining ($$–$$$) is the lodge's upscale eatery; the Grant Grove Restaurant, a family-style coffee shop, serves American standards for breakfast, lunch, and dinner. ☎ 559/335–5500 or 559/335–2354, FAX 559/335–2498. 54 cabins. Restaurant, coffee shop. MC, V.

$$$–$$$$ 🛏 **John Muir Lodge.** This new lodge, opened in May 1999, is about ¼ mile north of Grant Grove Village. The 30 rooms and six suites all have queen beds and private baths. There's a lobby with a fireplace, but no restaurant on the premises. ✉ ☎ 559/335–5500. 30 rooms, 6 suites. Meeting rooms. MC, V.

🏕 **Azalea Campground.** One of three campgrounds in the Grant Grove area (the other two are Sunset and Crystal Springs, both open May–September only), Azalea sits amid giant sequoias yet is close to restaurants, stores, and other facilities. Pay showers are available nearby. The 144 sites are allocated on a first-come, first-served basis. ✉ ☎ 559/565–3341, ext. 2. Flush toilets, disposal station (summer only), fire rings, water. 🚐 $12. ☉ Year-round.

Outdoor Activities and Sports

WINTER SPORTS

Grant Grove Village (☎ 559/335–2665) has a cross-country ski concession with marked trails; rentals are available.

YEAR-ROUND SPORTS

Montecito-Sequoia Lodge, in the Sequoia National Forest just south of Kings Canyon National Park, provides year-round family-oriented recreation. Lodging rates vary with the season but always include a breakfast buffet and dinner. Visitors not staying at the lodge are welcome to drop in for meals. Winter activities include cross-country skiing and lessons, snowshoeing, and snowboarding. Among the summer activities offered in a six-night Club Med–like package are canoeing, sailing, and water-skiing on the resort's private lake; horseback riding; tennis; archery; and nature hikes. Fewer activities are offered in spring and fall, but you can book shorter stays. ✉ Generals Hwy., 11 mi south of Grant Grove, ☎ 800/227–9900 for reservations, brochures, and information. 32 rooms, 14 cabins. AE, D, MC, V.

Along the Generals Highway

The **Generals Highway** begins south of Grant Grove, continuing through the lower portion of Kings Canyon National Park and through a grand section of the Sequoia National Forest before entering Sequoia National Park.

★ ⑱ The **Redwood Mountain Grove** is the largest grove of big trees in the world. As you exit Kings Canyon on the Generals Highway, several paved turnouts allow you to look out over the grove (and into the smog of the Central Valley). The grove itself is accessible only on foot or horse-back.

⑲ Kings Canyon Overlook, a large turnout on the north side of the Generals Highway less than 2 mi from Redwood Mountain Grove, has views across the canyon of mountain peaks and the backcountry. If you drive east on Highway 180 to Cedar Grove along the south fork, you will see these canyons at much closer range.

Wuksachi Village

⑳ *21 mi south of Grant Grove on the Generals Hwy.*

The new northern gateway to Sequoia National Park, **Wuksachi Village,** opened in May 1999. New dining and lodging facilities (☞ *below*) have been built here to replace the antiquated and now permanently closed facilities in the old Giant Forest Village. The buildings there were endangering the sequoias by interfering with their root systems. The onetime Giant Forest Market is being converted into a museum, scheduled to open in 2001.

Dining and Lodging

$$–$$$ ✕⌷ **Wuksachi Village.** The new main lodge has modern rooms with TVs and phones with modem hookups. The restaurant ($–$$$) serves standard American cuisine. ☎ *559/561–3314 or 888/252–5757. 102 rooms. Restaurant, bar, in-room data ports, hiking, meeting rooms. D, MC, V.*

Lodgepole

㉑ *5 mi south of Wuksachi Village on the Generals Hwy.*

Lodgepole sits in a canyon on the Marble Fork of the Kaweah River. Lodgepole pines, rather than sequoias, grow here because the U-shape canyon directs air down from the high country that is too cold for the big trees but is just right for lodgepoles. This developed area has a campground, a market and deli, a public laundry, a gift shop, and a post office. A pizza stand, an ice cream parlor, and showers are open in the summer only.

★ ☙ The **Lodgepole Visitor Center** has the best exhibits in Sequoia or Kings Canyon, a small theater that shows films about the parks, and a first aid center. You can buy tickets for the Crystal Cave (☞ *below*), get advice from park rangers, purchase maps and books, and pick up wilderness permits (except during summer, when they're available from 7 AM to 4 PM at the permit office next door). ☎ *559/565–3782.* ☉ *Mid-June–Labor Day, daily 8–6; rest of yr, daily 9–6.*

The **Tokopah Falls Trail** is an easy and rewarding 3½-mi round-trip hike from the Lodgepole Campground up the Marble Fork of the Kaweah River. The walk to the 1,200-ft falls, which flow down granite cliffs, is the closest you can get to the high country without putting substantial wear and tear on your hiking boots. Trail maps are available at the Lodgepole Visitor Center. Bring insect repellent during the summer; the mosquitoes can be ferocious.

Camping

⚠ **Lodgepole Campground.** The largest of the campgrounds in the Lodgepole area is also the noisiest, though things do quiet down at night. Pay showers are nearby. Lodgepole and Dorst (a mile or so to the west) are the two campgrounds within Sequoia where reservations are accepted (up to five months in advance for stays between mid-May and mid-October). ✉ *Off Generals Hwy.,* ☎ *559/565–3341, ext. 2, for camping information; 800/365–2267 for reservations for stays mid-*

May–Sept. Fire rings, flush toilets, disposal station (summer only), water. 📷 $12–$14. ⊘ Year-round.

Outdoor Activities and Sports

Wolverton (☎ 559/565–3435), near Lodgepole, has a cross-country ski center (rentals are available) and marked trails.

Giant Forest

㉒   *4 mi south of Lodgepole on the Generals Hwy.*

The Giant Forest is known for its trails through a series of sequoia groves. You can get the best views of the big trees from the park's meadows, where flowers are in full bloom by June or July. **Round Meadow,** which has a ⅓-mi, wheelchair-accessible "Trail for All People," is easiest to reach. John Muir called **Crescent Meadow** the "gem of the Sierra"— brilliant wildflowers bloom here by midsummer; a 1 ⁵⁄₁₀-mi trail loops around the meadow. A 1 ⁶⁄₁₀-mi round-trip trail that begins at Crescent Meadow leads to **Tharp's Log,** named for Hale Tharp, who built a pioneer cabin (still standing) out of a fire-hollowed sequoia.

The most famous sequoia in the area is the **General Sherman Tree,** off the Generals Highway 3 mi south of Lodgepole and about 1 mi north of the Giant Forest. Benches allow you to sit and contemplate the tree's immensity: weighing in at 2.7 million pounds, it has the greatest volume of any living thing in the world. The first major branch is 130 ft above the ground.

The paved **Congress Trail,** the area's most popular hike, starts at the General Sherman Tree and loops through the heart of the Giant Forest. Pick up a booklet (75¢) from one of the racks at the trailhead, where you'll find detailed information about the ecology of the groves.

The **Moro Rock–Crescent Meadow Road** is a 3-mi spur road (closed in winter) that begins just south of the old Giant Forest Village and leads to Crescent and Log meadows, passing several landmarks along the way. The Auto Log is a wide fallen tree that you can drive onto to pose for photographs. The road also passes through the Tunnel Log, which is exactly that. If your vehicle is too tall—7 ft, 9 inches and more—a bypass is provided.

★ **㉓**   **Moro Rock,** an immense, granite monolith, also lies along the road, rising 6,725 ft from the edge of the Giant Forest. Four hundred steps lead to the top; the trail often climbs along narrow ledges over steep drops. The view from the top is striking. To the southwest you look down the Kaweah River to Three Rivers, Lake Kaweah, and—on clear days— the Central Valley and the Coast Range. To the northeast are views of the High Sierra. Thousands of feet below lies the middle fork of the Kaweah River.

★ **㉔**   **Crystal Cave** is the best known of Sequoia's many caves. Its interior, which was formed from limestone that metamorphosed into marble, is decorated with stalactites and stalagmites of various shapes, sizes, and colors. To visit the cave, you must first stop at the Lodgepole Visitor Center (☞ *above*) or the Foothills Visitor Center at Ash Mountain (on the Generals Highway, 1 mi inside Sequoia National Park) to buy tickets—they're not sold at the cave. Drive to the end of a narrow, twisting, 7-mi road off the Generals Highway, 2.2 mi south of the old Giant Forest Village. From the parking area it is a 15-minute hike down a steep path to the cave's entrance. It's cool inside—48°F—so bring a sweater. ☎ 559/565–3759. 📷 $5. ⊘ Guided tours (45 min) mid-June–Labor Day, daily 10–3 on the half hr; mid-May–mid-June and Labor Day–Sept., Fri.–Mon. 10–3 on the hr; closed rest of yr.

Mineral King

 52 mi south of Lodgepole on the Generals Hwy. and Mineral King Rd.

The Mineral King area was incorporated into Sequoia National Park in 1978. It is accessible from Memorial Day weekend through October (weather permitting) by a narrow, twisting, steep road (trailers and RVs are prohibited) off Highway 198 several miles outside the park entrance. This is a tough but exciting 25-mi drive (budget 90 minutes each way) to an alpine valley. There are two campgrounds and a ranger station here. Facilities are limited, but some supplies are available. Many backpackers use this as a trailhead. Fine day-hiking trails lead from here as well.

Kings Canyon and Sequoia National Parks A to Z

Arriving and Departing

BY BUS

Greyhound (☎ 800/231–2222) serves Fresno and Visalia.

BY CAR

Under average conditions, it takes about six hours to reach Kings Canyon and Sequoia national parks from San Francisco and about five hours from Los Angeles. Two major routes, Highways 180 and 198, intersect with Highway 99, which runs north–south through the San Joaquin Valley.

From the north, enter Kings Canyon via Highway 180, 53 mi east of Fresno. From the south, enter Sequoia via Highway 198, 36 mi from Visalia. If you are coming from Los Angeles, take Highway 65 north from Bakersfield to Highway 198 east of Visalia.

BY PLANE

Fresno Air Terminal (✉ 5175 Clinton Way, ☎ 559/498–4095) is the nearest major airport to Kings Canyon and Sequoia national parks. *See* Arriving and Departing *in* Yosemite National Park, *above*, for more information.

Getting Around

BY BUS

Delaware North Park Services at Sequoia (☎ 559/565–3301) runs a free shuttle bus between major points in the Giant Forest and Lodgepole.

BY CAR

Try to fill up your gas tank before you arrive. Buying gas in the parks is difficult, though there are stations 10 mi from Grant Grove at Hume Lake Christian Camp and 15 mi from the Grove at King's Canyon Lodge. Emergency gas is sold at the park markets.

Most people take Highway 180 to Kings Canyon–Sequoia, coming into Kings Canyon National Park at the Big Stump Entrance. Highways 180 and 198 are connected by the Generals Highway, a paved two-lane road that is open year-round, though portions between Lodgepole and Grant Grove may be closed for weeks at a time following heavy snowstorms (carry chains in winter). Drivers of RVs over 22 ft in length and those who are not comfortable negotiating mountain roads should avoid the twisting, narrow, 16-mi southern stretch between the Potwisha Campground and the old Giant Forest Village. The rest of the Generals Highway is a well-graded two-lane road and a pleasure to drive in good weather.

Highway 180 (called Kings Canyon Highway inside the park) beyond Grant Grove to Cedar Grove is open late spring through October—

weather permitting—as is the road to Mineral King. Both roads can be challenging to inexperienced drivers. Large vehicles are discouraged, and trailers and RVs are not permitted on the Mineral King road.

Contacts and Resources

CAMPING

Campgrounds near each of the major tourist centers in Kings Canyon and Sequoia parks are equipped with tables, fire grills, garbage cans, and either flush or pit toilets. All the sites have drinking water, but you may want to bring your own water, especially during off-season when taps can freeze. Except for Lodgepole and Dorst in Sequoia, all sites in the two parks are assigned on a first-come, first-served basis; on weekends in July and August they are often filled by Friday afternoon. *See* Reservations, *below,* for contact numbers.

RVs and trailers are permitted in most of the campgrounds, though space is scarce at some. The length limit is 40 ft for RVs and 35 ft for trailers, but the park service recommends that trailers be no longer than 22 ft. Disposal stations are available in most of the main camping areas. Lodgepole, Potwisha, and Azalea campsites stay open all year, but Lodgepole is not plowed and camping is limited to snow tenting or recreational vehicles in plowed parking lots. Other campgrounds are open from whenever the snow melts until late September or early October. Use the bear-proof food-storage containers that are provided.

EMERGENCIES
Ambulance (☎ 911). **Fire** (☎ 911). **Police** (☎ 911).

GUIDED TOURS
From mid-May to mid-October **Sequoia–Kings Canyon Park Services Company** (☎ 559/335–5500) conducts an all-day van tour (about $70) of Grant Grove, Cedar Grove, and other sights.

RESERVATIONS
Lodgepole/Dorst campgrounds: (☎ 800/365–2267 or 559/565–3774). **Other campgrounds:** (☎ 559/565–3341).

Kings Canyon Lodging: (☎ 559/335–5500). **Sequoia Lodging:** (☎ 559/561–3314 or 888/252–5757).

ROAD CONDITIONS
Sequoia–Kings Canyon Road and Weather Information (☎ 559/565–3341).

Northern California Road Conditions (☎ 800/427–7623).

VISITOR INFORMATION
National Park Service (✉ Fort Mason, Bldg. 201, San Francisco 94123, ☎ 415/556–0560). **Sequoia and Kings Canyon National Parks** (✉ Three Rivers 93271, ☎ 559/565–3341 or 559/565–3134).

8 THE SAN JOAQUIN VALLEY

From Stockton to Bakersfield

The San Joaquin Valley, one of the world's most fertile agricultural zones, is California's heartland. This sun-baked region contains a wealth of rivers, lakes, and waterways. The water, in turn, nurtures vineyards, dairy farms, orchards, fields, and pastures that stretch to the horizon. Cities, mountains, and national parks are just beyond the Valley, but you'll find that the area possesses attractions of its own, beginning with the warmth of its land and people.

By Clark
Norton

Revised by
Andy Moore

Updated by
Herb Benham

UNTIL THE MID-19TH CENTURY the San Joaquin Valley was a desert waiting to bloom. Millions of acres of flat, often parched land lay in wait for workers and water. When settlers and irrigation techniques did arrive, the region was transformed into a miracle of cultivation. Gold discoveries, starting in the 1850s, sparked the birth of some towns; the coming of the railroads in the next few decades spurred the development of others. During the past century and a half the Valley's open lands and untapped resources have attracted a polyglot of pioneers, adventurers, farmers, ranchers, developers, railroad tycoons, gold prospectors, oil riggers, dairymen, sheepherders, and war refugees—including immigrants from places as diverse as Portugal, China, Mexico, Armenia, and Laos.

The mix has produced sometimes volatile labor relations—most prominently in Cesar Chavez's United Farm Workers Union's controversial grape boycotts of the 1960s and '70s—and social strife: early battles between railroad men and farmers, long-standing discrimination against Chinese and other Asians. But the region's diversity has also created a vibrant social fabric that has been chronicled by some of the country's finest writers. Fresno native and Pulitzer Prize winner William Saroyan, Stockton native Maxine Hong Kingston, 19th-century novelist Frank Norris, and *Grapes of Wrath* author John Steinbeck have all contributed to the Valley's literary heritage.

Though the Valley's agricultural riches remain, potential changes whirl like dust devils in the fields. Modesto, Fresno, and Bakersfield are among the fastest growing cities in the country, as big-city dwellers arrive in search of cheaper real estate, safer neighborhoods, and more space. With development has come unsightly sprawl, traffic jams, air pollution, and pressure on crucial water supplies, all of which threatens to overwhelm the Valley's traditional charms.

For most travelers the Valley is primarily a place to pass through en route to Yosemite, Sequoia, and Kings Canyon national parks or while driving between San Francisco and Los Angeles. But if you spend a few hours or days here, you'll discover historic mansions, abundant outdoor recreation, and friendly people proud of their local treasures.

Pleasures and Pastimes

Dining
Fast-food places and chain restaurants dominate Valley highways and major intersections, but off the main drag the possibilities increase. Armenian, Basque, and Vietnamese restaurants—along with more common Mexican, Chinese, and Italian eateries—reflect the Valley's ethnic mix. A few cutting-edge bistros serve the type of California cuisine found in San Francisco and Los Angeles. And why not? The Valley produces many of the ingredients used by big-city chefs.

CATEGORY	COST*
$$$$	over $50
$$$	$30–$50
$$	$20–$30
$	under $20

per person for a three-course meal, excluding drinks, service, and 7¼% tax

Festivals, Tours, and Tastings
Anyone who likes to eat can enjoy an agricultural theme trip through the San Joaquin Valley. Apple ranches, almond and pistachio orchards,

and cheese and chocolate factories are among the many options. Watch for seasonal farmers' markets. Some towns block off entire streets and turn the weekly markets into minifestivals. Official Valley festivals celebrate everything from the asparagus and raisin crops to residents' Chinese, Greek, Swedish, and Tahitian roots. Especially in the fall, call the local chamber of commerce (☞ Visitor Information *in* the San Joaquin Valley A to Z, *below*) for festival information.

Lodging

Chain motels and hotels are the norm in the San Joaquin Valley. Most are utilitarian but perfectly clean and comfortable, and prices tend to be considerably lower than those in more touristy destinations. A few Victorian-style bed-and-breakfasts, some of them great values, also operate here.

CATEGORY	COST*
$$$$	over $175
$$$	$120–$175
$$	$80–$120
$	under $80

All prices are for a standard double room, excluding 8% tax.

Outdoor Activities and Sports

Several cities and towns serve as convenient starting points for whitewater rafting trips on the Stanislaus, Merced, Kings, and Kern rivers. Fishing is another favored activity in the rivers and lakes; the lakes are also prime spots for boating and windsurfing. Stockton is a popular rental area for houseboating on the Sacramento Delta, and Bakersfield is a center for NASCAR racing. Wildlife refuges provide opportunities for watching birds and other animals.

Exploring the San Joaquin Valley

The 225-mi San Joaquin Valley cuts through San Joaquin, Stanislaus, Merced, Madera, Fresno, Kings, Tulare, and Kern counties, and is bounded by the mighty Sierra Nevada to the east and the smaller coastal ranges to the west. Besides the San Joaquin, other rivers include the Stanislaus, Tuolumne, Fresno, and Kern; an elaborate system of sloughs and canals also provides water to the countryside. Interstate 5 runs north–south through the Valley, as does Highway 99.

Numbers in the text correspond to numbers in the margin and on the San Joaquin Valley and Fresno Area maps.

Great Itineraries

IF YOU HAVE 1 DAY

Touring the Fresno area is a good strategy if you only have a day to spend in the Valley. Within the **Chaffee Zoological Gardens** in **Roeding Park** ⑦ is a striking tropical rain forest; **Playland** and **Storyland** are great stops if you have children. Don't miss the **Forestiere Underground Gardens** ⑥ on Shaw Avenue if it's open. In springtime take the self-guided **Blossom Trail** driving tour through orchards, vineyards, and fields. Along the trail in **Reedley** is the **Mennonite Quilt Center.** Depending on your mood and the weather, you can spend part of the afternoon at **Wild Water Adventures** or visit the **Fresno Metropolitan Museum** ⑧, whose highlights include an exhibit about author William Saroyan.

IF YOU HAVE 3 DAYS

On your first morning, visit the 🏛 **Stockton** area. Start at the **Micke Grove Park** ①, 10 mi north of the city off Highway 99. The art-filled **Haggin Museum** ② and the **World Wildlife Museum** are both in Stockton proper. The next morning, stop off at the **Castle Air Museum** ④ north

The San Joaquin Valley

CONTRA COSTA
TO SACRAMENTO
Stockton
Tracy
SAN JOAQUIN
ALAMEDA
Manteca
San Joaquin R.
SANTA CLARA
Modesto
McHenry Mansion 3
STANISLAUS
Turlock
Livingston
Atwater
MERCED
Merced
Hershey Chocolate Factory
Oakdale
Stanislaus R.
Knights Ferry Recreation Area
Castle Air Museum 4
Merced County Courthouse Museum 5
L. Yosemite
Chowchilla
Madera
MADERA
Fresno R.
Clovis
FRESNO
Fresno 6 – 8
San Joaquin R.
Reedley
Mennonite Quilt Center
Kingsburg
Hanford
Coalinga
San Joaquin R.
Visalia
Tulare
Kaweah Oaks Preserve
KINGS
Corcoran
Colonel Allensworth State Historic Park 9
Kern National Wildlife Refuge
Delano
TULARE
Porterville
Three Rivers
Bakersfield
California Living Museum 11
Kern County Museum and Lori Brock Children's Discovery Center 10
Kernville
Lake Isabella
Kern R.
KERN

1 Micke Grove Park
2 Haggin Museum

CALAVERAS

Stanislaus National Forest
TUOLUMNE

Yosemite National Park
Merced R.
MARIPOSA
Mariposa
Oakhurst

SAN BENITO

Sierra National Forest

Kings Canyon National Park

Sequoia National Park

Sequoia National Forest

SAN LUIS OBISPO

N

0   20 miles
0   30 km

of Merced in Atwater or proceed directly to ⊡ **Fresno** ⑥–⑧. In the evening take in a show at **Roger Rocka's** or the **Tower Theatre,** both in Fresno's Tower District. On the third morning, drive to **Hanford** via Highways 99 and 43 and stroll around **Courthouse Square** and **China Alley.** After lunch continue south on Highway 43 to **Colonel Allensworth State Historic Park** ⑨, which is on the site of a now deserted town founded by African Americans in 1908. Head south on Highway 43 and east on Highway 46 to return to Highway 99, which continues south to ⊡ **Bakersfield.** If you arrive before it closes, stop in for a quick visit to the **Kern County Museum** ⑩.

When to Visit the San Joaquin Valley

Spring, when wildflowers are in bloom and the scent of fruit blossoms is in the air, and fall, when leaves turn red and gold, are the prettiest times to visit. Many of the Valley's top festivals take place during these seasons. Summertime, when temperatures often top 100°F, can be oppressive. Wintertime can get cold and raw—thick, ground-hugging fog is a common driving hazard—and some attractions close.

NORTH SAN JOAQUIN VALLEY

The northern section of the Valley cuts through San Joaquin, Stanislaus, and Merced counties, from the edges of the Sacramento Delta and the fringes of the Gold Country south to the flat, almost featureless terrain between Modesto and Merced. If you're heading to Yosemite National Park from northern California, chances are you'll pass through (or very near) at least one of these gateway cities.

Stockton Area

80 mi from San Francisco, east on I–80 to I–580 to I–205 and north on I–5; 45 mi south of Sacramento on I–5 or Hwy. 99.

California's first inland port—connected since 1933 to San Francisco via a 60-mi-long deepwater channel—is wedged between I–5 and Highway 99, on the eastern end of the great Sacramento River Delta. Stockton, founded during the gold rush as a way station for miners traveling from San Francisco to the Mother Lode, and now a city of 250,000, helps distribute the Valley's agricultural products to the world. Its best-known natives include author Maxine Hong Kingston and rock singer Chris Isaak. If you're here in late April, don't miss the **Stockton Asparagus Festival** (℡ 209/943–1987).

⌘ ❶ Among the attractions at oak-shaded **Micke Grove Park,** halfway between Stockton and Lodi, are a zoo and an agricultural museum. *11793 N. Micke Grove Rd.; take Armstrong Rd. off Hwy. 99, 8 mi north of Stockton, then go ½ mi west to Micke Grove Rd., Lodi,* ℡ *209/331–7400.* ⊡ *Park entry fee $2 weekdays, $4 weekends and holidays.* ☉ *Park daily 8 AM–sunset.*

Ring-tailed lemurs and other endangered primates found only on the African island of Madagascar inhabit the An Island Lost in Time exhibit at the **Micke Grove Zoo.** Mountain lions have the run of Paseo Pantera, another highlight of this compact facility. *Micke Grove Park,* ℡ *209/331–7270.* ⊡ *$1.50.* ☉ *May–Aug., weekdays 10–5, weekends 10–7; Sept.–Apr., daily 10–5.*

The rides and other diversions at **Funderwoods** (Micke Grove Park, ℡ 209/369–5437), a family-oriented amusement park (days and hours vary), are geared to children under 10. Ride tickets cost $1 (10 for $8).

★ ❷ The **Haggin Museum** in pretty Victory Park has one of the San Joaquin Valley's finest art collections. Late-19th-century American and French paintings—landscapes by Albert Bierstadt and Thomas Moran, a still life by Paul Gauguin, and a Native American gallery—are among the highlights, supplemented by antiquities that include an Egyptian mummy. You can bone up on local history here, too. ✉ *1201 N. Pershing Ave.,* ☎ *209/462–4116.* 🎫 *Free; suggested donation $2.* ☉ *Tues.–Sun. 1:30–5.*

🐾 The **World Wildlife Museum,** which claims to have the largest collection of mounted zoological specimens—more than 2,000—is aimed primarily at school groups but is open to the public. Two cavernous rooms are a testament to taxidermy: displays include Alaska Yukon moose, Indian black bears, Russian wild boars, African bongos, and South American jaguars. At the Sheep Mountain Bighorns, you'll find ibexes, mountain goats, and rare argalis and golden takins. ✉ *1245 W. Weber Ave.,* ☎ *209/465–2834.* 🎫 *$4.* ☉ *Wed.–Sun. 9–5.*

Dining and Lodging

$$$–$$$$ ✕ **Le Bistro.** The dishes at one of the Valley's most upscale restaurants are fairly standard Continental fare—lamb tenderloin, fillet of sole, sautéed prawns, soufflé Grand Marnier—but you can count on high-quality ingredients and presentation with a flourish. ✉ *Marina Center Mall, 3121 W. Benjamin Holt Dr. (off I–5, behind Lyon's),* ☎ *209/951–0885. AE, D, DC, MC, V.*

$–$$ ✕ **On Lock Sam.** Run by the same family since 1898, this Stockton landmark is in a modern pagoda-style building, with framed Chinese prints on the walls, a garden outside one window, and a sparkling bar area. One touch of old-time Chinatown remains: a few booths have curtains that can be drawn for complete privacy. The Cantonese food would be ho-hum in San Francisco, but it's among the Valley's best. ✉ *333 S. Sutter St.,* ☎ *209/466–4561. AE, D, MC, V.*

$$ 🏨 **Best Western Stockton Inn.** Four miles from downtown, this good-size motel has a convenient location off Highway 99. The large central courtyard with a pool and lounge chairs is a big plus on hot days. Most rooms are spacious; free in-room movies are provided by satellite. ✉ *4219 Waterloo Rd., 95215,* ☎ *209/931–3131,* 𝖥𝖠𝖷 *209/931–0423. 141 rooms. Restaurant, bar, no-smoking rooms, pool, wading pool, hot tub, laundry service, meeting rooms. AE, D, DC, MC, V.*

$ 🏨 **City Center Days Inn.** If you want to stay near Stockton's waterfront, this is a good budget choice. Rooms are of decent size, and the rates include TV with free HBO. The motel is at a busy intersection; the smallish outdoor pool area can get noisy. ✉ *33 N. Center St., 95202,* ☎ *209/948–6151,* 𝖥𝖠𝖷 *209/948–1220. 93 rooms. No-smoking rooms, pool, meeting rooms. Continental breakfast. AE, D, MC, V.*

Outdoor Activities and Sports

Several companies rent houseboats (of various sizes, usually for three, four, or seven days) on the Delta waterways near Stockton. Call the **Delta Rental Houseboat Hotline** (☎ 209/477–1840), or try **Herman & Helen's** (✉ Venice Island Ferry, ☎ 209/951–4634), **King Island Resort** (✉ 11530 W. Eight Mile Rd., ☎ 209/951–2188), or **Paradise Point Marina** (✉ 8095 Rio Blanco Rd., ☎ 209/952–1000).

En Route Manteca, population 45,000, is the largest town between Stockton and Modesto. The top attraction is the **Manteca Waterslides at Oakwood Lake** (✉ 874 E. Woodward Ave., between I–5 and Hwy. 99, ☎ 209/239–2500). The park has a children's area, and the attached resort has a lake, a campground (open all year), and picnic grounds. The water park is open from May through September (daily from Memorial Day to Labor Day, weekends the rest of May and September); call for hours.

Modesto

29 mi south of Stockton on Hwy. 99.

Modesto, a gateway to Yosemite and the southern reaches of the Gold Country, was founded in 1870 to serve the Central Pacific Railroad. The frontier town was originally named Ralston, after a railroad baron, but as the story goes he modestly declined—thus "Modesto." The Stanislaus County seat, a tree-lined city of 190,000, is perhaps best known as the site of the annual Modesto Invitational Track Meet and Relays and birthplace of film producer-director George Lucas, creator of *Star Wars* and *American Graffiti.*

The **Modesto Arch** (⊠ 9th and I Sts.) bears Modesto's motto: "Water, Wealth, Contentment, Health." Modesto holds a well-attended **International Festival** (☎ 209/521–3852) in early October that celebrates the cultures, crafts, and cuisines of many nationalities. The **Blue Diamond Growers Store** (⊠ 4800 Sisk Rd., ☎ 209/545–3222) offers free samples, shows a film about almond-growing, and sells nuts in many flavors.

★ ❸ A wheat farmer and banker built the 1883 **McHenry Mansion,** the city's sole surviving original Victorian home. The Italianate-style mansion has been decorated to reflect Modesto life in the late 19th century. Oaks, elms, magnolias, redwoods, and palms shade the grounds. ⊠ *15th and I Sts.,* ☎ *209/577–5341.* ⚏ *Free.* ☉ *Jan.–mid-Nov. and Dec., Sun.–Thurs. 1–4, Fri. noon–3. Closed last 2 wks of Nov.*

The **McHenry Museum** is a jumbled repository of early Modesto and Stanislaus County memorabilia, including re-creations of an old-time barbershop, a doctor's office, a blacksmith's shop, and a general store—the latter stocked with goods from hair crimpers to corsets. ⊠ *1402 I St.,* ☎ *209/577–5366.* ⚏ *Free.* ☉ *Tues.–Sun. noon–4.*

Dining and Lodging

$–$$$ ✕ **Early Dawn Cattlemen's Steakhouse and Saloon.** The parking lots overflow at this local hangout, and so do the platters bearing barbecued steaks of two pounds and even heavier. The whiskey-marinated saloon steak is a house specialty; chicken and seafood are among the lighter choices. ⊠ *1000 Kansas Ave.,* ☎ *209/577–5833. AE, D, MC, V. No lunch Sat.*

$–$$ ✕ **Hazel's Elegant Dining.** Hazel's is *the* special-occasion restaurant in Modesto. The seven-course dinners include Continental entrées served with soup, salad, pasta, dessert, and beverage. Members of the Gallo family, who own much vineyard land in the San Joaquin Valley, eat here often, perhaps because the wine cellar is so comprehensive. *431 12th St.,* ☎ *209/578–3463. AE, D, DC, MC, V. Closed Sun.–Mon. No lunch Sat.*

$–$$ ✕ **St. Stan's.** This brew-pub–eatery is home to Modesto's most famous microbrewery, makers of St. Stan's beers. There are 14 beers; try the Whistle Stop Pale Ale. The restaurant is casual and serves up good corned beef sandwiches loaded with sauerkraut and a tasty beer sausage nibbler. ⊠ *821 L St.,* ☎ *209/524–4782. AE, D, MC, V.*

$–$$ ▦ **Best Western Mallard's Inn.** The duck decor is, thankfully, unobtrusive at this nicely landscaped motel off Highway 99. The comfortably furnished rooms are large and all have coffeemakers. Some rooms have microwaves and refrigerators stocked with milk and cookies. ⊠ *1720 Sisk Rd., 95350,* ☎ *209/577–3825 or 800/294–4040,* FAX *209/577–1717. 120 rooms, 6 suites. Restaurant, no-smoking rooms, room service, pool, hot tub, exercise room, laundry service, business services, meeting rooms. AE, D, DC, MC, V.*

$–$$ 🛏 **Doubletree Hotel.** Modesto's largest lodging towers 15 stories over downtown; the convention center is adjacent; and a good brew pub, St. Stan's, is across the street. The rooms have coffeemakers, irons, desks, and three phones. ⊠ *1150 9th St., 95354,* ☎ *209/526–6000,* FAX *209/ 526–6096. 258 rooms. Restaurant, café, bar, no-smoking rooms, room service, pool, hot tub, sauna, exercise room, nightclub, laundry service, meeting rooms, airport shuttle. AE, D, DC, MC, V.*

Oakdale

15 mi east of Modesto on Hwy. 108.

Oakdale, a bit off the beaten path from Modesto, has two year-round attractions of great interest to children. If you're here in mid-May, check out the **Oakdale Chocolate Festival** (☎ 209/847–2244).

🐾   The only **Hershey Chocolate Factory** in the country that allows the public to tour its production facilities plays Willy Wonka to a host of chocolate lovers. After the half-hour guided walking tours—which cover the chocolate-making process from cocoa bean to candy bar—everyone gets a sample. ⊠ *120 S. Sierra Ave.,* ☎ *209/848–8126.* 🎫 *Free.* ☉ *Tours weekdays 8:30–3, visitor center weekdays 8:30–5.*

★ 🐾   The featured attraction at the **Knights Ferry Recreation Area** is the 355-ft-long Knights Ferry covered bridge. The bridge is beautiful and haunting—a true must-see. Built in 1863, the bridge (closed to motor vehicles) crosses the Stanislaus River near the ruins of an old grist mill. The park has picnic and barbecue areas along the riverbanks. Fishing, hiking, rafting, and canoeing are among the activities here. ⊠ *Corps of Engineers Park, 18020 Sonora Rd., Knights Ferry; 12 mi east of Oakdale via Hwy. 108,* ☎ *209/881–3517.* 🎫 *Free.* ☉ *Weekdays 8–noon and 1–4; weekends 10–2.*

You can sample the wares at **Oakdale Cheese & Specialties** (⊠ 10040 Hwy. 120, ☎ 209/848–3139), which has tastings (try the aged gouda) and cheese-making tours. There's a picnic area next to a pond and a petting zoo.

Merced and Atwater

38 mi south of Modesto (to Merced) on Hwy. 99; 53 mi from Oakdale, west and then south on Hwy. 108 and south on Hwy. 99.

Merced, population 56,000, is a common stopover en route to Yosemite National Park. In 1995, the city was picked as the site for a new University of California branch. The town of Atwater is 6 mi north of Merced on Highway 99.

🐾 ❹   At the outdoor **Castle Air Museum,** adjacent to the former Castle Air Force Base (now Castle Aviation, an industrial park) you can stroll among fighter planes and other historic military aircraft. The 44 restored vintage war birds include the B-25 Mitchell medium-range bomber (best known for the "Jimmy Doolittle raid" on Tokyo following the attack on Pearl Harbor) and the speedy SR-71 Blackbird, used for reconnaissance over Vietnam and Libya. ⊠ *Santa Fe Dr. and Buhach Rd. (take the Buhach Rd. exit off Hwy. 99 in Atwater and follow signs), Atwater,* ☎ *209/723–2178.* 🎫 *$5.* ☉ *Memorial Day–Sept., daily 9– 5; Oct.–Memorial Day, daily 10–4.*

❺   Even if you don't go inside, be sure to swing by the **Merced County Courthouse Museum.** The three-story former courthouse, built in 1875, is a striking example of the Victorian Italianate style. The upper two floors are now a museum of early Merced history. Highlights include an 1870 Chinese temple with carved redwood altars, and an ornate restored courtroom. ⊠ *21st and N Sts., Merced,* ☎ *209/723–2401.* ☷ *Free.* ⊙ *Wed.–Sun. 1–4.*

The **Merced Multicultural Arts Center** displays paintings, sculpture, and photography. Threads: A Tapestry of Cultures, a festival that celebrates the area's ethnic diversity, is held here on a mid-October weekend. ⊠ *645 W. Main St., Merced,* ☎ *209/388–1090.* ☷ *Free.* ⊙ *Weekdays 9–5, Sat. 10–2.*

Dining and Lodging

$$–$$$ ✕ **DeAngelo's.** Not only the best restaurant in Merced, DeAngelo's is one of the best in the San Joaquin Valley. Chef Vincent DeAngelo brings his considerable skill to fresh fish, seafood, and locally grown produce. The delicious, crusty bread, from the Golden Sheath in Watsonville, is a meal in itself. ⊠ *350 W. Main St., Merced,* ☎ *209/383–3020. AE, D, DC, MC, V. Closed Sun., except Dec.–Feb.*

$ ✕ **Main Street Café.** This bright downtown café dishes up soups, pizza, salads, sandwiches, pastries, ice cream, and espresso. Sandwiches (try the chicken breast with pesto mayonnaise on Francesi bread) are served with tasty side salads. ⊠ *460 W. Main St.,* ☎ *209/725–1702. AE, MC, V. Closed Sun. No dinner.*

$ ☷ **Days Inn.** The compact rooms here manage to pack in an impressive array of amenities: writing table, refrigerator, microwave, radio, coffeemaker, bathroom phone, safe, and a 27-inch TV with cable and a VCR (tapes are for rent in the lobby). ⊠ *1199 Motel Dr., near the intersection of Hwys. 99 and 140, 95340,* ☎ *209/722–2726,* FAX *209/722–7083. 24 rooms. No-smoking rooms, refrigerators, in-room VCRs, pool. AE, D, DC, MC, V.*

Outdoor Activities and Sports

At **Lake Yosemite Regional Park** (⊠ N. Lake Rd., off Yosemite Ave., 5 mi northeast of Merced, ☎ 209/385–7426), you can boat, swim, windsurf, waterski, and fish on a 387-acre reservoir. Boat rentals and picnic areas are available.

MID–SAN JOAQUIN VALLEY

Fresno, Hanford, and Visalia

The mid–San Joaquin Valley extends over three counties—Fresno, Kings, and Tulare. From Fresno, Highway 41 leads north 95 mi to Yosemite and Highway 180 snakes east 55 mi to Kings Canyon (Sequoia National Park is 30 mi farther). From Visalia, Highway 198 winds east 35 mi to the Generals Highway, which leads into Sequoia and Kings Canyon. Historic Hanford, about 16 mi west of Visalia along Highway 198, is a gem of a town.

Fresno

50 mi south of Merced on Hwy. 99; 110 mi north of Bakersfield on Hwy. 99.

Sprawling Fresno, with more than 400,000 people, is the center of the richest agricultural county in America; grapes, cotton, oranges, and turkeys are among the major products. The city's most famous native, Pulitzer Prize–winning playwright and novelist William Saroyan (*The Time of Your Life, The Human Comedy*), was born here in 1908. The seemingly endless parade of strip malls and fast-food joints can be depressing, but local character does lurk beneath the commercialization. The Tower District, with its restaurants, theaters, and coffeehouses,

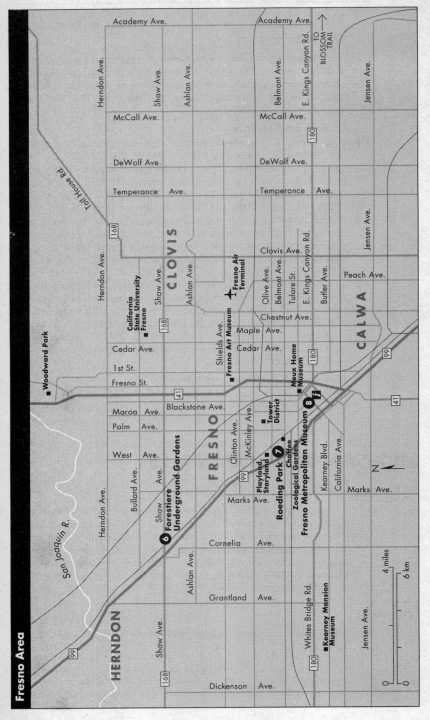

Fresno Area

Academy Ave.

Academy Ave.

TO
BLOSSOM
TRAIL

Herndon Ave.

Shaw Ave.

Ashlan Ave.

Belmont Ave.

Jensen Ave.

McCall Ave.

McCall Ave.

180

DeWolf Ave.

DeWolf Ave.

Temperance Ave.

Temperance Ave.

E. Kings Canyon Rd.

Jensen Ave.

Toll House Rd.

168

CLOVIS

Clovis Ave.

Herndon Ave.

Shaw Ave.

Ashlan Ave.

Fresno Air
Terminal

Olive Ave.

Belmont Ave.

Tulare St.

Peach Ave.

Butler Ave.

E. Kings Canyon Rd.

California
State University
Fresno

168

Shields Ave.

Fresno Art Museum

Chestnut Ave.

Maple Ave.

Woodward Park

Cedar Ave.

Cedar Ave.

180

CALWA

1st St.

Meux Home
Museum

99

Fresno St.

41

41

Maroa Ave.

Blackstone Ave.

Tower
District

8 i

Palm Ave.

McKinley Ave.

Clinton Ave.

Chaffee
Zoological Gardens

FRESNO

West Ave.

Forestiere Underground Gardens

7

Fresno Metropolitan Museum

Kearney Blvd.

N

Bullard Ave.

Shaw Ave.

Playland,
Storyland

Roeding Park

California Ave.

Marks Ave.

Herndon Ave.

99

Marks Ave.

6

Cornelia Ave.

San Joaquin R.

Jensen Ave.

4 miles

6 km

Ashlan Ave.

Grantland Ave.

Whites Bridge Rd.

Kearney Mansion
Museum

HERNDON

99

Shaw Ave.

180

168

Dickenson Ave.

offers a taste of San Francisco. The city is home to 75 ethnic communities (from Armenian to Vietnamese), a burgeoning arts scene, and several public parks.

Woodward Park, 300 acres of jogging trails, picnic areas, and playgrounds in the northern reaches of the city, is especially pretty in the spring—when plum and cherry trees, magnolias, and camellias bloom—and the fall, when leaves burst into riots of color. Big-band concerts take place in summer. Well worth a look is the **Shin Zen Japanese Friendship Garden,** which has a teahouse, a koi pond, arched bridges, a waterfall, and lakes. ⊠ *Audubon Dr. and Friant Rd.,* ☎ *559/498–1551.* ⊡ *Park $2 per car; garden $1 per person.* ⊙ *Mar.–Oct., daily 7 AM–10 PM; Nov.–Dec., daily 7–5, Jan.–Feb., daily 7–7.*

★ ☺ ❻ Sicilian immigrant Baldasare Forestiere spent four decades (1906–1946) carving out the **Forestiere Underground Gardens,** a subterranean realm of rooms, tunnels, grottoes, alcoves, and arched passageways that extends for more than 10 acres beneath busy, mall-pocked Shaw Avenue. Only a fraction of Forestiere's prodigious output is on view, but you can tour his underground living quarters, including bedrooms (one with a fireplace), the kitchen, the living room, the bath, a fish pond, and an aquarium. Skylights allow exotic, full-grown fruit trees—including one that through grafting is able to bear seven kinds of citrus—to flourish as far as 22 ft below ground. ⊠ *5021 W. Shaw Ave., 2 blocks east of Hwy. 99,* ☎ *559/271–0734.* ⊡ *$6. Reservations essential.* ⊙ *Memorial Day–Labor Day, Wed.–Sun. 10–4 (tours at 10, noon, 2, and 4); Easter–Memorial Day and Labor Day–Thanksgiving (weather permitting; tour hrs vary), weekends noon–3. Closed Dec.–Mar.*

★ ☺ ❼ Tree-shaded **Roeding Park,** Fresno's largest park, has picnic areas, playgrounds, tennis courts, and a zoo (☞ *below*). ⊠ *Olive and Belmont Aves.,* ☎ *559/498–4239.* ⊡ *Parking $1 (Feb.–Oct.).* ⊙ *Mar.–Oct., daily 7 AM–10 PM; Oct.–Mar., daily 7–7.*

The most striking exhibit at **Chaffee Zoological Gardens** is the tropical rain forest, where exotic birds often greet visitors along the paths and bridges. Elsewhere you'll find tigers, grizzly bears, sea lions, tule elk, camels, elephants, and hooting siamangs. Also here are a high-tech reptile house and a petting zoo. *Roeding Park,* ☎ *559/498–2671,* ⊡ *$4.95.* ⊙ *Mar.–Oct., daily 9–5; Nov.–Feb., daily 10–4.*

☺ A minitrain, a Ferris wheel, a small roller coaster, and a merry-go-round are among the amusements at **Playland** (Roeding Park, ☎ 559/486–2124), which is open (days and hours vary) between February and November. Kids can explore attractions with fairy-tale themes and at-
☺ tend puppet shows at **Storyland** (Roeding Park, ☎ 559/264–2235). Storyland is open between February and November. Admission is $2.75.

The drive along palm-lined Kearney Boulevard is one of the best reasons to visit the **Kearney Mansion Museum,** which stands in shaded 225-acre **Kearney Park,** 7 mi west of town. Guided 45-minute tours take you through the century-old home of M. Theo Kearney, Fresno's onetime "Raisin King." ⊠ *7160 W. Kearney Blvd.,* ☎ *559/441–0862.* ⊡ *$4 (park entrance $3, waived for museum visitors).* ⊙ *Museum Fri.–Sun., tours at 1, 2, and 3.*

The **Legion of Valor Museum,** the national museum for winners of the Medal of Honor and the Distinguished Service Cross, is a real jewel for military buffs of all ages. It has German bayonets and daggers, a Japanese Namby pistol, a full-size Gatlin gun, and an extensive collection of Japanese, German, and American uniforms. The staff is extremely enthusiastic. ⊠ *2425 Fresno St.,* ☎ *559/498–0510.* ☞ *Free.* ☼ *Mon.–Sat. 10–3.*

☜ ⑧ The **Fresno Metropolitan Museum** mounts art, history, and hands-on science exhibits, many of them quite innovative. The William Saroyan History Gallery presents a riveting introduction in words and pictures to the author's life and times. ⊠ *1555 Van Ness Ave.,* ☎ *559/441–1444.* ☞ *$5.* ☼ *Tues.–Sun. 11–5.*

The **Fresno Art Museum** exhibits American, Mexican, and French art; highlights of the permanent collection include pre-Columbian works and graphic art from the post-Impressionist period. The 152-seat Bonner Auditorium hosts lectures, films, and concerts. ⊠ *Radio Park, 2233 N. 1st St.,* ☎ *559/441–4220.* ☞ *$2; free Tues.* ☼ *Tues.–Fri. 10–5, weekends noon–5. Closed last 2 wks of Aug.*

The **Meux Home Museum,** inside a restored 1888 Victorian, displays furnishings and decor typical of early Fresno. Guided tours lead from the front parlor to the backyard carriage house. ⊠ *Tulare and R Sts.,* ☎ *559/233–8007.* ☞ *$4.* ☼ *Feb.–Dec., Fri.–Sun. noon–4.*

OFF THE BEATEN PATH

BLOSSOM TRAIL – This 62-mi self-guided driving tour takes in Fresno-area orchards, citrus groves, and vineyards during spring blossom season. Almond, plum, apple, orange, lemon, apricot, and peach blossoms shower the landscape with shades of white, pink, and red. (The most colorful and aromatic time to go is from late February to mid-March.) The route passes through several small towns and past rivers, lakes, and canals. The Fresno Convention & Visitors Bureau (⊠ 808 M St., 559/233–0836 or 800/788–0836) has route maps; directional and crop identification signs also mark the trail. Allow at least two to three hours for the tour.

Dining and Lodging

$$–$$$ ✕ **Giulia's Italian Trattoria.** The look here is light and airy, but the Abruzzi cuisine (from southern Italy's Adriatic coast) is hearty and intensely flavored. Bruschetta, steamed mussels, and polenta with grilled sausage are top choices. The adjoining b. b.'s Oyster Bar & Grill serves sandwiches and seafood appetizers; many patrons have cocktails at b. b.'s before dining at Giulia's. ⊠ *Winepress Shopping Center, 3050 W. Shaw Ave.,* ☎ *559/276–3573. AE, D, DC, MC, V. Closed Sun. No lunch weekends.*

$ ✕ **Armenian Cuisine.** Local Armenians flock to this small restaurant for tasty lamb, beef, and chicken kebabs, which come with pita bread, eggplant salad, and stuffed grape leaves. ⊠ *742 W. Bullard,* ☎ *559/435–4892. AE, DC, MC, V. Closed Sun.*

$ ✕ **Kim's Vietnamese Restaurant.** You'll find good food at bargain prices at Kim's: specialties include hot beef salad, sizzling chicken, and sautéed seafood with ginger. Complete lunches or dinners—from soup to dessert and tea, with salad, entrée, and rice in between—cost as little as $10. ⊠ *5048 N. Maroa St.,* ☎ *559/225–0406. MC, V. Closed Sun.*

$$ ▣ **Piccadilly Inn Shaw.** This two-story property is attractively landscaped, with a big central swimming pool on 7 ½ acres. The sizable rooms have king- and queen-size beds, full-size robes, ironing boards, fresh cookies, and coffeemakers; some rooms have refrigerators, microwaves, and fireplaces. ⊠ *2305 W. Shaw Ave., 93711,* ☎ *559/226–3850,* FAX *559/226–2448. 188 rooms, 6 suites. No-smoking rooms, pool, hot tub, exercise room, coin laundry, laundry service, business services, meeting rooms. AE, D, DC, MC, V.*

$ 🖵 **La Quinta Inn.** Rooms are of good size at this basic but decent three-story motel near downtown. Some rooms have king-size beds, microwaves, and refrigerators. ⊠ *2926 Tulare St., 93721,* ☎ *559/442–1110,* ﬞᴀˣ *559/237–0415. 130 rooms. No-smoking rooms, pool. Continental breakfast. AE, D, DC, MC, V.*

Nightlife and the Arts

The **Tower Theatre for the Performing Arts** (⊠ 815 E. Olive Ave., ☎ 559/485–9050), a onetime movie house that has given its name to the trendy Tower District of theaters, clubs, restaurants, and cafés, presents theatrical, ballet, classical, jazz, and other cultural events from spring to fall. **Roger Rocka's Music Hall** (⊠ 1226 N. Wishon Ave., ☎ 559/266–9494 or 800/371–4747), a dinner theater in the Tower District, stages six Broadway-style musicals or comedies a year. The **Fresno Philharmonic Orchestra** (☎ 559/261–0600) performs classical concerts (sometimes pops) on weekends, usually at the William Saroyan Theatre (⊠ 700 M St.), from September through June.

Outdoor Activities and Sports

Wild Water Adventures (⊠ 11413 E. Shaw Ave., Clovis, ☎ 559/299–9453 or 800/564–9453), a 50-acre water theme park about 10 mi east of Fresno, is open from late May to early September.

Shopping

Old Town Clovis (⊠ 5th and Pollasky Sts., Clovis) is an area of restored brick buildings and brick sidewalks, with numerous antiques shops and art galleries (along with restaurants and saloons). Head east on Fresno's Shaw Avenue about 10 mi to get to Clovis.

OFF THE
BEATEN PATH

MENNONITE QUILT CENTER – The colorful handiwork of local Mennonite quilters is on display here. Try to visit on Monday (except holidays), when two dozen or so quilters come in to stitch, patch, and chat over coffee. Prime viewing time—with the largest number of quilts—is in February and March, right before the center holds its early April auction. Ask a docent to take you to the locked upstairs room, where most of the quilts are hung; she'll explain the fine points of patterns such as the Log Cabin Romance, the Dahlia, and the Snowball-Star. ⊠ *1012 G St. (take Manning Ave. exit off Hwy. 99 and head east 12 mi), Reedley;* ☎ *559/638–3560.* 🖵 *Free.* ☉ *Weekdays 9:30–4:30, Sat. 10–2.*

Hanford

★ *35 mi from Fresno, south on Hwy. 99 and Hwy. 43.*

Founded in 1877 as a Southern Pacific Railroad stop, Hanford had one of California's largest Chinatowns—the Chinese came to help build the railroads and stayed to farm and open restaurants. You can take a self-guided walking tour or sign up in advance for guided tours ($2.50 per adult) arranged by the **Hanford Visitor Agency** (☎ 559/582–5024). One tour explores the restored historic buildings of Courthouse Square. Another heads to narrow China Alley, with stops at the town's Taoist Temple and other sights.

The **Hanford Carnegie Museum,** inside the former Carnegie Library, a Romanesque building dating from 1905, displays fashions, furnishings, toys, and military artifacts. ⊠ *109 E. 8th St.,* ☎ *559/584–1367.* 🖵 *$1.* ☉ *Tues.–Fri. noon–3, Sat. noon–4.*

If you have kids who are itching to get out their skateboards and perform ollies or kick flips, the **Hanford Skate Park** will let them blow off some steam. ⊠ *415 Ford St.,* ☎ *559/585–2525.* 🖵 *Free.*

A first-floor museum in the 1893 **Taoist Temple** displays photos, furnishings, and kitchenware from Hanford's once-bustling Chinatown. The second-floor temple, largely unchanged for a century, contains altars, carvings, and ceremonial staves. You can visit as part of a guided walking tour (☞ *above*) or by calling the temple directly and making an appointment two weeks in advance. ⊠ *12 China Alley,* ☎ *559/582–4508.* ⊟ *Free; donations welcome.* ⊙ *By appointment only.*

Dining and Lodging

$–$$$ ✕ **Imperial Dynasty.** Despite its name and elegant teak-and-porcelains Chinese decor, Imperial Dynasty serves primarily French cuisine. For a memorable meal, start with the garlicky escargots and continue with the veal sweetbreads or rack of lamb. Avoid the overcooked, over-sauced seafood. Its heyday was in the 1970s and '80s, but this spot is still one of the better restaurants in the Valley. The extensive wine list contains many prized vintages. ⊠ *China Alley (corner of 7th and Green Sts.),* ☎ *559/582–0196. AE, MC, V. Closed Mon. No lunch.*

$ ✕ **La Fiesta.** Mexican-American families, farmworkers, and farmers all eat here. La Fiesta features traditional Mexican dishes such as enchiladas and tacos. The Fiesta Special—for two or more—includes nachos, garlic shrimp, deviled-style shrimp, clams, and two pieces of top sirloin. ⊠ *106 N. Green St.,* ☎ *559/583–8775. AE, D, DC, MC, V.*

$$ ▦ **Irwin Street Inn.** This bed-and-breakfast inn is one of the few lodg-
★   ings in the Valley that warrants a detour. Four tree-shaded, restored Victorian homes have been converted into spacious, comfortable rooms and suites. Most have antique armoires, dark wood detailing, leaded-glass windows, and four-poster beds; bathrooms have old-fashioned tubs, brass fixtures, and marble basins. ⊠ *522 N. Irwin St., 93230,* ☎ *559/583–8000 or 888/583–8080,* FAX *559/583–8793. 30 rooms. Restaurant, pool. Continental breakfast. AE, D, DC, MC, V.*

Nightlife and the Arts

The 1,000-seat, restored Moorish-Castillian–style **Hanford Fox Theater** (⊠ 326 N. Irwin St., ☎ 559/584–7423), built as a movie palace in 1929, now periodically hosts country-western bands and other live performances.

Visalia

16 mi from Hanford, east on Hwy. 198; 40 mi from Fresno, south on Hwy. 99 and east on Hwy. 198.

A native of Visalia, Kentucky, founded Visalia, the Tulare County seat, in 1852. The center of one of the world's top milk-producing regions, the town, population 93,000, is also a major exporter of oranges, grapes, plums, peaches, and cotton. On a clear day the views of the Sierra Nevada peaks to the east are stunning. Visalia contains a number of historic homes; ask at the **visitor center** (⊠ 301 E. Acequia, 93921, ☎ 559/738–3435 or 800/524–0303) for a free guide detailing them.

The **Chinese Cultural Center,** housed in a pagoda-style building, mounts exhibits about Chinese art and culture. ⊠ *500 Akers Rd., at Hwy. 198,* ☎ *559/625–4545.* ⊟ *Free.* ⊙ *Wed.–Sun. 11–6.*

🌣 In oak-shaded **Mooney Grove Park** you can picnic alongside duck ponds, rent a boat in a lagoon, and view a replica of the famous **End of the Trail Statue.** The original, designed by James Earl Fraser for the 1915 Panama-Pacific International Exposition, is now in the Cowboy Hall of Fame in Oklahoma. *27000 S. Mooney Blvd., 5 mi south of downtown,* ☎ *559/733–6616.* ⊟ *$4 per car.* ⊙ *Daily 8 AM–sunset.*

The indoor-outdoor **Tulare County Museum** contains several re-created environments from the pioneer era and displays Yokuts tribal artifacts (basketry, arrowheads, clamshell-necklace currency). Also here are saddles and guns, Victorian-era dolls, and quilts and gowns. ⊠ *Mooney Grove Park, 27000 S. Mooney Blvd., 5 mi south of downtown,* ☎ *559/ 733–6616.* 🎫 *Free with admission to Mooney Grove Park.* ☉ *June–Aug., Mon. and Wed.–Fri. 10–4, weekends noon–6; Sept.–Oct., Thurs.–Mon. 10–4; Nov.–Feb., Mon., Thurs., Fri. 10–4, weekends 1–4; Mar.–May, Thurs.–Mon. 10–4.*

Trails at the 300-acre **Kaweah Oaks Preserve,** a wildlife sanctuary off the main road to Sequoia National Park and accessible only to hikers, lead past oak, sycamore, cottonwood, and willow trees. Among the 125 bird species you might spot are hawks, hummingbirds, and great blue herons. Lizards, coyotes, and cottontails also live here. ⊠ *Follow Hwy. 198 for 7 mi east of Visalia, turn north on Rd. 182, and proceed ½ mi to gate on left-hand side of road,* ☎ *559/738–0211.* 🎫 *Free.* ☉ *Daily sunrise–sunset.*

Dining and Lodging

$–$$ ✕ **The Vintage Press.** Built in 1966, the Vintage Press is the best restau-
★   rant in the San Joaquin Valley. Cut-glass doors and bar fixtures decorate the artfully designed rooms. The California-Continental cuisine includes dishes such as baby abalone in champagne butter sauce; wild mushrooms in puff pastry; and sturgeon in caviar butter. The chocolate Grand Marnier cake is a standout among the many wonderful homemade desserts and ice creams. The wine list has more than 900 choices. ⊠ *216 N. Willis St.,* ☎ *559/733–3033. AE, DC, MC, V.*

$ ✕ **Café 225.** Tall ceilings and warm yellow and blue walls help make this downtown restaurant a local favorite. The oak-rotisserie chicken is excellent alone or in a sandwich. The butcher-paper table coverings and crayons are kid-friendly. ⊠ *225 W. Main St.,* ☎ *559/733–2967. AE, D, DC, MC, V. Closed Sun.*

$$–$$$ 🏠 **The Spalding House.** This restored Colonial-Revival B&B—decked out with antiques, Oriental rugs, handcrafted woodwork, and glass doors—is one of several historic homes in the vicinity. The house, built in 1901, is in pristine condition. The three guest suites have separate sitting rooms and private baths, but no phones or TVs. ⊠ *631 N. Encina St., 93291,* ☎ *559/739–7877,* 𝔽𝔸𝕏 *559/625–0902. 3 suites. No-smoking rooms. Full breakfast. MC, V.*

$–$$ 🏠 **The Lamp Liter Inn.** Rooms here are of a decent size, and some have refrigerators. A large, partially tree-shaded pool beckons on hot days. Large common areas make this a good choice for family reunions. ⊠ *3300 W. Mineral King Ave., off Hwy. 198, 93291,* ☎ *559/732–4511,* 𝔽𝔸𝕏 *559/732–1840. 100 rooms. Restaurant, coffee shop, lounge, pool, meeting rooms. AE, D, DC, MC, V.*

Colonel Allensworth State Historic Park

★ ❾   *40 mi from Visalia, south on Hwy. 99, west on J22 (at town of Earlimart) and south on Hwy. 43.*

An ex-slave who rose to become the country's highest-ranking black officer of his time founded Allensworth—the only California town settled, governed, and financed by African-Americans—in 1908. After enjoying early prosperity, **Allensworth** became a ghost town. Its buildings have been rebuilt or restored to reflect the era when it thrived. Each October three days of festivities mark the town's rededication. ⊠ *4129 Palmer Ave.,* ☎ *661/849–3433.* 🎫 *$3 per car.* ☉ *Daily 10–4:30.*

OFF THE
BEATEN PATH
KERN NATIONAL WILDLIFE REFUGE – Ducks, snowy egrets, peregrine fal-
cons, warblers, and other birds inhabit the marshes and wetlands here
from November through April. Follow the 3½-mi radius tour route (pick
up maps at the entrance), which has several good viewing spots. ⊠
*10811 Corcoran Rd., 19 mi west of Delano on Hwy. 155 (Garces
Hwy.); from Allensworth take Hwy. 43 south to Hwy. 155 west,* ☎ *661/
725-2767.* 🎫 *Free.* ☉ *Feb.–Sept., daily sunrise–sunset; Oct.–Jan.,
Wed. and Sat. sunrise to sunset.*

SOUTHERN SAN JOAQUIN VALLEY
Bakersfield and Kernville

When gold was discovered in Kern County in the 1860s, settlers
flocked to the southern end of the San Joaquin Valley. Black gold—
oil—is now the area's most valuable commodity, but Kern is also the
country's third-largest agriculture-producing county. From the flat
plains around Bakersfield, the landscape graduates to rolling hills and
then mountains as it climbs east to Kernville, which lies in the Kern
River Valley.

Bakersfield

*80 mi from Visalia, west on Hwy. 198, south on Hwy. 99; 288 mi from
San Francisco, east on I–80 and I–580, south on I–5; 112 mi north of
Los Angeles, I–5 to Hwy. 99.*

Bakersfield's founder, Colonel Thomas Baker, arrived with the discovery
of gold in the nearby Kern River Valley in 1851. Now Kern County's
largest city (population 212,000), Bakersfield probably is best known
as "Nashville West," a country-music haven and hometown of performers Buck Owens and Merle Haggard. It's also home to a symphony
orchestra and two good museums.

★ ☺ ⑩ The **Kern County Museum and Lori Brock Children's Discovery Center**
form one of the San Joaquin Valley's top museum complexes. The indoor-outdoor Kern County Museum—whose centerpiece is an open-
air, walk-through historic village with more than 50 restored or
re-created buildings—pays homage to the era of the 1860s to 1940s.
The indoor part of the museum holds exhibits about Native Americans and the "Bakersfield Sound" in country music. The adjacent
Children's Discovery Center has permanent and changing hands-on displays and activities. ⊠ *3801 Chester Ave.,* ☎ *661/861–2132.* 🎫 *$5.*
☉ *Weekdays 8–5, Sat. 10–5, Sun. noon–5.*

★ ☺ ⑪ At the **California Living Museum** (CALM), a combination zoo, botanical garden, and natural-history museum—the emphasis is on zoo—
all animal and plant species displayed are native to the state. Within
CALM's reptile house lives every species of rattlesnake found in California. The landscaped grounds—nestled among the rolling hills about
a 20-minute drive northeast of Bakersfield—also shelter bald eagles,
tortoises, coyotes, mountain lions, black bears, and foxes. ⊠ *14000
Alfred Harrell Hwy. (Hwy. 178 east, then 3½ mi northwest on Alfred
Harrell Hwy.),* ☎ *661/872–2256.* 🎫 *$3.50.* ☉ *Tues.–Sun. 9–5.*

Dining and Lodging

$$ ✕ **Noriega Hotel.** Established in 1893, this family-style Basque restau-
rant still has the oldest boarding house in California, home to gener-
ations of sheepherders. The restaurant is known for its thick and
tender lamb chops, oxtail stew, prime rib, soup, pink beans, hors

d'oeuvres, vegetables, and potatoes—all served family-style. ✉ *525 Sumner St.*, ☎ *661/322–8419. No credit cards. Closed Mon.*

$–$$ ✗ **Uricchio's Trattoria.** This downtown restaurant draws everyone from office workers to oil barons—all attracted by the tasty food, trendy open kitchen, and indoor and outdoor seating. *Panini* (Italian sandwiches, served at lunch only), pasta, and Italian-style chicken dishes dominate the menu; the chicken piccata outsells all other offerings. ✉ *1400 17th St.*, ☎ *661/326–8870. AE, D, DC, MC, V. Closed Sun. No lunch Sat.*

$$ 🏨 **Doubletree Hotel.** The location is convenient, off Highways 99, 58, and 178. The spacious rooms have coffeemakers, irons, ironing boards, hair dryers, and balconies or patios. ✉ *3100 Camino Del Rio Ct., 93308,* ☎ *661/323–7111,* ℻ *661/323–0331. 248 rooms and 14 suites. Restaurant, bar, coffee shop, no-smoking rooms, room service, pool, hot tub, dry cleaning, business services, meeting rooms, free airport shuttle. AE, D, DC, MC, V.*

$ 🏨 **Quality Inn.** Near downtown in a relatively quiet location off Highway 99, this two-story motel offers good value. Most rooms have king- or queen-size beds, and all have free in-room movies. Some have refrigerators and a patio or a balcony looking out on the heated pool. Complimentary coffee and donuts are served. ✉ *1011 Oak St., 93304,* ☎ *661/325–0772,* ℻ *661/325–4646. 90 rooms. Pool, indoor hot tub, exercise room, coin laundry. AE, D, DC, MC, V.*

Nightlife and the Arts

The **Bakersfield Symphony Orchestra** (☎ 661/323–7928) performs classical music concerts at the Convention Center (✉ 1001 Truxton Ave.) on Sunday from October through May.

Buck Owens' Crystal Palace (✉ 2800 Buck Owens Blvd., ☎ 661/328–7560) is a combination nightclub, restaurant, and showcase of country-music memorabilia. Country-western singers—owner Buck Owens among them—perform. Buck Owens and the Buckaroos perform Fridays and Saturdays. A dance floor beckons customers who can still twirl after sampling the menu of steaks, burgers, nachos, and gooey desserts. Entertainment is free on most weeknights; Friday and Saturday nights bring a $6 cover charge, and some big-name acts require tickets.

Outdoor Activities and Sports

CAR RACING

At **Bakersfield Speedway** (✉ 304 Egret Ct., ☎ 661/393–3373), stock and sprint cars race around a ⅓-mi clay oval track. **Mesa Marin Raceway** (✉ 11000 Kern Canyon Rd., ☎ 661/366–5711) presents high-speed stock-car, super-truck, and NASCAR racing on a ½-mi paved oval course.

Shopping

Many antiques shops are on 18th and 19th streets between H and R streets, and H Street between Brundage Lane and California Avenue. **Central Park Antique Mall** (✉ 701 19th St., ☎ 661/633–1143), and the **Great American Antique Mall** (✉ 625 19th St., ☎ 661/322–1776) all have huge selections.

Dewar's Candy Shop (✉ 1120 Eye St., ☎ 661/322–0933) was founded in 1909 and has been owned by the Dewar family ever since. Try the hand-dipped chocolate cherries and the Dewar's Chews, a mouthwatering taffy concoction available in peanut butter, peppermint, caramel, and almond. There's also an old-fashioned soda fountain.

Kernville

50 mi from Bakersfield, northeast on Hwy. 178 and north on Hwy. 155.

The wild and scenic Kern River, which flows through Kernville en route from Mount Whitney to Bakersfield, delivers some of the most exciting white-water rafting in the state. Kernville (population 1,200) rests in a mountain valley on both banks of the river, and also at the northern tip of Lake Isabella (a dammed portion of the river used as a reservoir and for recreation). A center for rafting outfitters, Kernville has lodgings, restaurants, and antiques shops. The main streets are lined with Old West–style buildings, reflecting Kernville's heritage as a rough-and-tumble gold-mining town known as Whiskey Flat. (Present-day Kernville dates from the 1950s, when it was moved upriver to make room for Lake Isabella). The scenic road from Bakersfield winds between the rushing river on one side and sheer granite cliffs on the other.

Dining and Lodging

$ ✕ **Robin's River Restaurant.** This down-home restaurant serves up some of the best food in town. The hamburgers and fried chicken are the stars of the show—along with the colorful talk from the locals, who drop in for biscuits and gravy or meat loaf. Don't miss the freshly baked pastries, pies, and cobblers. ✉ *13423 Sierra Way,* ☎ *760/376–4663. DC, MC, V.*

$ ✕ **That's Italian.** For Northern Italian cuisine in a typical trattoria atmosphere, this is the spot. Try the chicken marsala stuffed with prosciutto and mozzarella or the pasta with clams, mussels, calamari, and white fish in a red or white clam sauce. ✉ *9 Big Blue Rd.,* ☎ *760/376–6020. AE, D, MC, V. No lunch Nov.–Apr.*

$$–$$$ 🛏 **Whispering Pines Lodge.** You can choose a cottage or a river-view bungalow here. Some accommodations have full kitchens, fireplaces, and whirlpool tubs; all have refrigerators, coffeemakers, and cable TV. ✉ *13745 Sierra Way, 93238,* ☎ *760/376–3733,* FAX *760/376–6513. 17 rooms. Pool. Full breakfast. AE, D, MC, V.*

$–$$ 🛏 **River View Lodge.** This rustic motel has knotty-pine walls and compact but clean rooms, some with microwaves and VCRs. And yes, many units do have river views. Picnic and barbecue facilities are in the tree-shaded yard. ✉ *2 Sirretta St., off Kernville Rd., 93238,* ☎ *760/376–6019,* FAX *760/376–4147. 10 rooms. No-smoking rooms, refrigerators. Continental breakfast. AE, DC, MC, V.*

Outdoor Activities and Sports

WHITE-WATER RAFTING

The three sections of the **Kern River**—known as the Lower Kern, Upper Kern, and the Forks—add up to nearly 50 mi of white water, ranging from Class I to Class V (easy to expert). The Lower and Upper Kern are the most popular and accessible sections. Organized trips can last from one hour (for as little as $15) to two days and more. Rafting season generally runs from late spring until the end of summer. Outfitters include **Chuck Richards Whitewater** (☎ 760/379–4444), **Kern River Tours** (☎ 760/379–4616), **Mountain & River Adventures** (☎ 760/376–6553 or 800/861–6553), and **Sierra South** (☎ 760/376–3745 or 800/457–2082).

BOATING, FISHING, AND WINDSURFING

The Lower Kern River, which extends from Lake Isabella to Bakersfield and beyond, is open for fishing year-round. Catches include rainbow trout, catfish, smallmouth bass, crappie, and bluegill. Lake Isabella is popular with anglers, water skiers, sailors, and windsurfers. Its shoreline marinas— **French Gulch Marina** (☎ 760/379–8774), **Red's**

Kern Valley Marina (☎ 760/379–1634 or 800/553–7337), and **Dean's North Fork Marina** (☎ 760/376–1812) —have boats for rent, bait and tackle, and moorings year-round.

THE SAN JOAQUIN VALLEY A TO Z

Arriving and Departing

By Bus

Greyhound Lines (☎ 800/231–2222) stops in Stockton, Modesto, Merced, Fresno, Visalia, and Bakersfield.

By Car

To drive to the San Joaquin Valley from San Francisco, take I–80 east to I–580, and I–580 east to I–5, which leads south into the Valley (several roads from I–5 head east to Highway 99); or continue east on I–580 to I–205, which leads to I–5 north to Stockton or (via Highway 120) east to Highway 99 at Manteca. To reach the Valley from Los Angeles, follow I–5 north; Highway 99 veers north about 15 mi after entering the Valley.

By Plane

Fresno Air Terminal (✉ 5175 E. Clinton Ave., ☎ 559/498–4095) is serviced by America West Express, American and American Eagle, Skywest, United Express, and US Airways Express. **Kern County Airport at Meadows Field** (✉ 1401 Skyway Dr., Bakersfield, ☎ 661/393–7990) is serviced by American and American Eagle, America West Express, Skywest-Delta, and United Express. United Express flies from San Francisco to **Modesto City Airport** (✉ 617 Airport Way, ☎ 209/577–5318) and **Visalia Municipal Airport** (✉ 9500 Airport Dr., ☎ 559/738–3201). *See* Air Travel *in* Smart Travel Tips A to Z for airline phone numbers.

By Train

Amtrak's (☎ 800/872–7245) daily *San Joaquin* trains travel between San Jose, Oakland, and Bakersfield, stopping in Stockton, Riverbank (near Modesto), Merced, Fresno, and Hanford. Amtrak Thruway bus service connects Bakersfield with Los Angeles.

Getting Around

By Bus

Greyhound (☎ 800/231–2222) provides service between major Valley cities. **Orange Belt Stages** (☎ 800/266–7433) provides bus service, including Amtrak connections, to many Valley locations, including Stockton, Merced, Madera, Fresno, Hanford, and Bakersfield.

By Car

Highway 99 is the main route between the Valley's major cities and towns. Interstate 5 runs roughly parallel to it to the west, but misses the major population centers; its main use is for quick access from San Francisco or Los Angeles. Major roads that connect I–5 with Highway 99 are Highways 120 (to Manteca), 132 (to Modesto), 140 (to Merced), 152 (to Chowchilla, via Los Banos), 198 (to Hanford and Visalia), and 58 (to Bakersfield).

Contacts and Resources

Car Rentals

All the major car rental agencies except Alamo have outlets in the San Joaquin Valley. *See* Car Rental *in* Smart Travel Tips A to Z for company phone numbers.

Emergencies
Ambulance (☎ 911). **Fire** (☎ 911). **Police** (☎ 911).

Guided Tours
Central Valley Tours (✉ 1869 E. Everglade, Fresno 93720, ☎ 559/323–5552) provides general and customized tours of the Fresno area and the Valley. **Kings River Expeditions** (✉ 211 N. Van Ness, Fresno, ☎ 559/233–4881 or 800/846–3674) arranges white-water rafting trips on the Kings River. Contact **River Journey** (✉ 14842 Orange Blossom Rd., Oakdale, ☎ 209/847–4671 or 800/292–2938) and **Sunshine River Adventures** (✉ Box 1445, Oakdale 95361, ☎ 209/848–4800 or 800/829–7238) to raft the Stanislaus River.

Visitor Information
Fresno City & County Convention and Visitors Bureau (✉ 808 M St., 93721, ☎ 559/233–0836 or 800/788–0836). **Greater Bakersfield Convention & Visitors Bureau** (✉ 1325 P St., 93301, ☎ 661/325–5051 or 800/325–6001). **Hanford Visitor Agency** (✉ 200 Santa Fe Ave., Suite D, 93230, ☎ 559/582–5024). **Kern County Board of Trade** (✉ 2101 Oak St., Bakersfield 93302, ☎ 661/861–2367 or 800/500–5376). **Merced Conference and Visitors Bureau** (✉ 690 W. 16th St., 95340, ☎ 209/384–3333 or 800/446–5353). **Modesto Convention and Visitors Bureau** (✉ 1114 J St., 95353, ☎ 209/571–6480). **Stockton/San Joaquin Convention and Visitors Bureau** (✉ 46 W. Fremont St., Stockton 95202, ☎ 209/943–1987 or 800/350–1987). **Visalia Convention and Visitors Bureau** (✉ 301 E. Acequia, 93291, ☎ 559/738–3435 or 800/524–0303).

9 MONTEREY BAY

From Santa Cruz to Carmel Valley

The Monterey Peninsula is steeped in history. The town of Monterey was California's first capital, the Carmel Mission headquarters for California's mission system. The peninsula also has a rich literary past. John Steinbeck's novels immortalized the area, and Robert Louis Stevenson strolled its streets, gathering inspiration for *Treasure Island*. The present is equally illustrious. Blessed with a natural splendor undiminished by time or commerce, the peninsula is home to high-tech marine habitats and luxurious resorts.

Updated by
Clark Norton

THE OHLONE INDIANS SETTLED IN THE MONTEREY AREA
about 2,500 years ago, the first Native American
people to build a community that centered on the region's maritime bounty. In 1542, Monterey Bay's white-sand beaches,
pine forests, and rugged coastline captivated explorer Juan Rodríguez
Cabrillo, who claimed it for Spain. Spanish missionaries, Mexican
rulers, and land developers would come and go, all of them, perhaps,
instinctively knowing not to destroy the peninsula's natural assets or
historical sites.

The region has never relied solely on its looks, however. You can't ig-
nore its deep green forests of Monterey cypress—oddly gnarled trees
that grow naturally nowhere else—its aquamarine waters, or the dance
of cloud shadows upon its rolling emerald hills and winsome meadows. Yet there are industrial, and a bit messy, claims to fame—whaling, sardines. And the meticulously preserved adobe houses and
missions, layers of a Spanish and Mexican past left remarkably undis-
turbed, create a terra-cotta skyline that testifies to the Monterey Peninsula's singular place in California history.

With the arrival of Father Junípero Serra and Commander Don Gas-
par de Portola from Spain in 1770, Monterey became the military and
ecclesiastical capital of Alta California (the Spanish-held territory north
of present-day Baja California, in Mexico). Portola established the first
of California's four Spanish presidios. Serra founded the second of 21
Franciscan missions, later moving it from Monterey to Carmel.

Century magazine, whose publisher was a major booster of California, printed in the 1890s the reflections of Brigida Briones, a Monterey
resident during the days of Spanish and Mexican rule. "The ladies of
Monterey in 1827," she wrote, "were rarely seen in the street, except
very early in the morning on their way to church. . . . The *rebozo*
(shawl) and the petticoat being black, always of cheap stuff. . . . All
classes wore the same; the padres told us that we must never forget
that all ranks of men and women were equal in the presence of the Creator." Briones writes elsewhere in the magazine about the participants
at a carnival ball held in 1829, "all on horseback and full of gaiety
and youthfulness such as only a race that lives outdoors in such a climate as California, and without cares or troubles, can show."

Modern historians might argue that equality for all was more theory
than practice for many in Briones's class. The ladies may have led a
carefree life at this time, but their husbands were caught up in the con-
flict between Mexico and the United States for control of California—
with both nations casting a wary eye on England, which was thought
to have designs on the state as well. Captain John Charles Fremont of
the United States wrote later that "the men who understood the future of our country . . . regarded the California coast as the boundary
fixed by nature to round off our national domain . . . it was naturally
separated from Mexico, and events pointed to its sure and near political separation."

The Mexican government, which was formed in 1822 when Mexico
revolted against Spain, disputed these notions about Alta California's
natural and political separation from the rest of Mexico, but between
the time of Mexican independence and the mid-1840s, Monterey had
changed. It had grown into a lively seaport that drew many Yankee
sea traders. By July 7, 1846, when Commodore John Sloat raised the
American flag over the Custom House and claimed California for the
United States, many Monterey-area residents supported the U.S. cause.

Economics was a major factor. The majority of Monterey's business-people felt that being under the Yankee umbrella would be far more profitable than being aligned with Mexico. Their hunch proved correct, at least for them. For the Ohlone Indian population, the transition was disastrous: state and federal laws passed during the first half-century of U.S. rule divested them of rights and property granted under Spanish and Mexican rule.

California's constitution was framed in Monterey's Colton Hall, but the town was all but forgotten once gold was discovered at Sutter's Mill on the American River. After the Gold Rush, the state capital moved to Sacramento, while Monterey became a sleepy backwater—though the whaling industry boomed in the last half of the 19th century and thrived until the early 1900s.

As the 20th century dawned, the Monterey Peninsula had begun to draw tourists with the opening of the Del Monte Hotel, the most palatial resort the West Coast had ever seen. Writers and artists such as John Steinbeck (1902–1968), Henry Miller (1891–1980), Robinson Jeffers (1887–1962), and Ansel Adams (1902–1984) also discovered the peninsula, adding their legacy to the region while capturing its magic on canvas, paper, and film. In the 1920s and 1930s Cannery Row's sardine industry took off, but by the late 1940s and early 1950s the fish had disappeared. The causes are still in dispute, though overfishing, water contamination, and a change in ocean currents that lowered the area's water temperature were the likely culprits. Sardines were packed again in 1995 in nearby Salinas for the first time since the 1950s. Visitors can buy them on Cannery Row, where activity has returned in the form of renovated buildings that house shops, restaurants, hotels, and the Monterey Bay Aquarium.

All aspects of the peninsula's diverse cultural and maritime heritage can be felt today, from Monterey's 19th-century buildings to its busy harbor and wharf. Modern-day attractions include the Monterey Jazz Festival and the Monterey Bay National Marine Sanctuary—the nation's largest undersea canyon, bigger and deeper than the Grand Canyon. The sanctuary supports a rich brew of marine life, from fat, barking sea lions to tiny plantlike anemones. Annual events and festivities such as Pacific Grove's Butterfly Parade, the Carmel Shakespeare Festival, and Monterey's Christmas in the Adobes pay tribute to old traditions and link the past with the present.

Pleasures and Pastimes

Dining

Monterey is the richest area for dining along the coast between San Francisco and Los Angeles. The surrounding waters abound with fish, wild game roams the foothills, and the inland valleys are the vegetable basket of California; nearby Castroville dubs itself the Artichoke Capital of the World. Except at beachside stands and the inexpensive eateries listed below, casual but attractive resort wear is the norm. The few places where more formal attire is required are noted.

CATEGORY	COST*
$$$$	over $50
$$$	$30–$50
$$	$20–$30
$	under $20

*per person for a three-course meal, excluding drinks, service, and 7 ¼%–8¼% tax

Golf

Since the opening of the Del Monte Golf Course in 1897, golf has been an integral part of the Monterey Peninsula's social and recreational scene. Pebble Beach's championship courses host prestigious tournaments, and though the greens fees at these courses can run well over $200, elsewhere on the peninsula you'll find less expensive—but still challenging and scenic—options. Many hotels will help with golf reservations or have golf packages; inquire when you make your room reservation.

Lodging

Monterey-area accommodations range from no-frills motels and historic hotels to upscale establishments that are a bit impersonal and clearly designed for conventions. Others pamper the individual traveler in grand style, especially some of the area's small inns and bed-and-breakfasts, many of which provide full breakfasts and afternoon or early evening wine and hors d'oeuvres. Pacific Grove has quietly turned itself into the region's B&B capital. Carmel also has fine B&Bs. Even more luxurious are the resorts in exclusive Pebble Beach and some of those in pastoral Carmel Valley. The rates below are for two people in the high season, from April through October. Rates during winter, especially at the larger hotels, may drop by 50% or more, and B&Bs often offer midweek specials in the off-season. If you book lodgings through Monterey's 800/555–9283 number, request an informational brochure and discount coupons that are good at restaurants, attractions, and shops.

CATEGORY	COST*
$$$$	over $175
$$$	$120–$175
$$	$80–$120
$	under $80

*All prices are for a standard double room, excluding 10%–10½% tax.

Whale-Watching

On their annual migration between the Bering Sea and Baja California, thousands of gray whales pass by not far off the Monterey coast. They are sometimes visible through binoculars from shore, but a whale-watching cruise is the best way to get a close look at these magnificent 45-ft mammals. The migration south takes place between December and March. January is prime viewing time. The migration north occurs between March and June. In addition, some 2,000 blue whales and 600 humpbacks pass the coast and are easily spotted in late summer and early fall. Smaller numbers of minke whales, orcas, sperm whales, and fin whales have been sighted in mid-August. Even if no whales surface, bay cruises almost always encounter some unforgettable marine life, including sea otters, sea lions, and porpoises.

Exploring Monterey Bay

The individual charms of the towns here complement Monterey Bay's natural beauty. Santa Cruz sits at the northern tip of the crescent formed by Monterey Bay; the Monterey Peninsula, including Monterey, Pacific Grove, and Carmel, occupies the southern end. In between, Highway 1 cruises along the coastline, passing windswept beaches piled high with sand dunes. Along the route are artichoke fields and the towns of Watsonville and Castroville.

Numbers in the text correspond to numbers in the margin and on the Monterey Bay, Monterey and Pacific Grove, and Carmel and 17-Mile Drive maps.

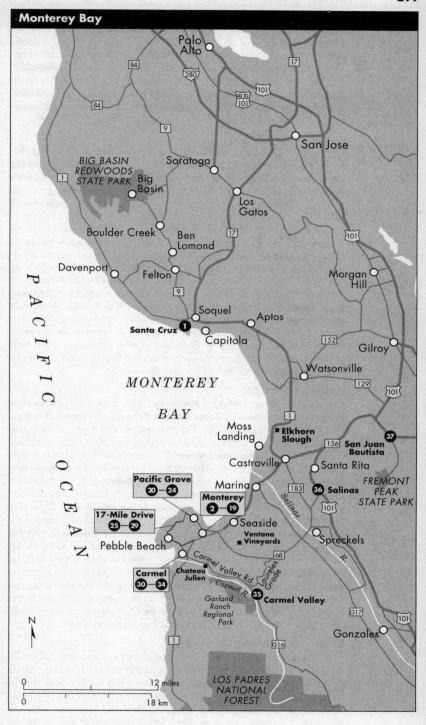

Palo Alto

84

280

17

BUS 101

101

9

San Jose

BIG BASIN REDWOODS STATE PARK

Big Basin

Saratoga

Los Gatos

101

Boulder Creek

Ben Lomond

17

Davenport

Felton

9

Morgan Hill

101

Soquel

Aptos

Santa Cruz ❶

Capitola

152

Gilroy

MONTEREY

Watsonville

129

101

BAY

Moss Landing

■ Elkhorn Slough

1

156

San Juan Bautista

37

Castroville

Santa Rita

FREMONT PEAK STATE PARK

Pacific Grove
20 — 24

Marina

Monterey
2 — 19

36 **Salinas**

183

17-Mile Drive
25 — 29

Seaside

Pebble Beach

Ventana Vineyards ■

Spreckels

101

P A C I F I C

O C E A N

Carmel Valley Rd.

68

Carmel
30 — 34

Chateau Julien ■

Carmel R.

35 **Carmel Valley**

Laureles Grade

Salinas R.

Garland Ranch Regional Park

G17

101

N

1

Gonzales

G16

0 ————— 12 miles
0 ————— 18 km

LOS PADRES NATIONAL FOREST

Great Itineraries

Despite its compact size, the Monterey Peninsula is packed with diversions. If you have an interest in California history and historic preservation, the place to start is Monterey, with its adobe buildings along the downtown Path of History. Fans of Victorian architecture will want to explore the many fine examples in Pacific Grove. In Carmel you can shop till you drop, and when summer and weekend hordes overwhelm the town's clothing boutiques, art galleries, housewares outlets, and gift shops, you can slip off to enjoy the coast.

IF YOU HAVE 3 DAYS

Start at the far end of Cannery Row in ⛺ **Monterey** ②–⑲ with a visit to the **Monterey Bay Aquarium** ⑲. Have lunch there or at one of the restaurants on Cannery Row. As you walk the Row, stop at **Steinbeck's Spirit of Monterey Wax Museum** ⑯ or the **Wing Chong Building** ⑰, then continue on foot via the oceanfront recreation trail to **Fisherman's Wharf** ⑬ to enjoy the sights and catch the sunset. If you're not up to the hubbub along the wharf, slip into the serene bar at the Monterey Plaza Hotel and Spa. On the following day, visit the **Larkin House** ⑥, **Cooper-Molera Adobe** ⑦, **Stevenson House** ⑧, and other historic Monterey buildings, stopping for lunch when the need hits. Then pick up some late-afternoon snacks and motor through **17-Mile Drive** ㉕–㉙. Linger for sunset views along 17-Mile Drive or at nearby **Point Lobos State Reserve** ㉞. On the third day, drive south to **Carmel** ㉚–㉞. Visit the **Carmel Mission** ㉛ and have lunch while browsing through the Ocean Avenue shopping area before stopping (if open) at **Tor House** ㉜, the residence of the late poet Robinson Jeffers. No matter what time of year you visit Monterey Bay, stroll over to Scenic Road and spend time on Carmel Beach before leaving the area.

IF YOU HAVE 5 DAYS

On your first three days, visit **Monterey** ②–⑲, stopping at the **Custom House** ②, **Larkin House** ⑥, **Cooper-Molera Adobe** ⑦, **Stevenson House** ⑧, and **Colton Hall** ⑨ on day one. On your second morning, get a visceral feel for Monterey Bay marine life by boarding a whale-watching or other cruise vessel at **Fisherman's Wharf** ⑬. Have lunch upon your return to the wharf, and then visit Cannery Row for **Steinbeck's Spirit of Monterey Wax Museum** ⑯ and the **Wing Chong Building** ⑰. On day three, tour the **Monterey Bay Aquarium** ⑲, have lunch along Cannery Row, and then spend the rest of the afternoon either enjoying the Monterey waterfront or tasting wine at Ventana Vineyards on the Monterey–Salinas Highway. On your fourth day, visit **Carmel Mission** ㉛ and **Tor House** ㉜ (if open) and have lunch while exploring the shops along Ocean Avenue in Carmel. Pick up some late-afternoon snacks for a spin on **17-Mile Drive** ㉕–㉙. Catch the sunset along 17-Mile Drive or at nearby **Point Lobos State Reserve** ㉞. On day five, explore the shoreline and Victorian houses of **Pacific Grove** ⑳–㉔ in the morning and lunch there. If you have time, visit **San Juan Bautista** �37, a classic mission village 35 mi from Monterey (take Highway 1 to Highway 156).

When to Tour Monterey Bay

Summer is peak season, with crowds everywhere and generally mild weather. A sweater or windbreaker is nearly always necessary along the coast, where a cool breeze usually blows and fog is on the way in or out. Inland, temperatures in Salinas or Carmel Valley can be a good 15 or 20 degrees warmer than those in Carmel and Monterey. Off-season, from November through April, fewer people visit and the mood is more introspective. Rains fall heaviest in January and February. Most of the sights in Monterey are open daily.

MONTEREY BAY
Santa Cruz to Carmel Valley

Set along 90 mi of arc-shaped coastline, like jewels in a tiara, the towns of Monterey Bay combine the somewhat funky, beachcomber aspects of California's culture with the state's more refined tendencies. Past and present merge gracefully here. As the city of Monterey's first mayor, Carmel Martin, described it early in the 20th century: "Monterey Bay is the one place where people can live without being disturbed by manufacturing and big factories. I am certain that the day is coming when this will be the most desirable place in the whole state of California."

Santa Cruz

❶ *74 mi south of San Francisco, I–280 to Hwy. 17 to Hwy. 1; 48 mi north of Monterey on Hwy. 1.*

The beach town of Santa Cruz is sheltered by the surrounding mountains to the north and south from the coastal fog and from the smoggy skies of the San Francisco Bay Area. The climate here is mild, and it is usually warmer and sunnier than elsewhere along the coast this far north. A haven for those opting out of the rat race and a bastion of 1960s-style counterculture values, Santa Cruz has been at the forefront of such very Californian trends as health food, recycling, and environmentalism. The heart of the downtown area is along Pacific Avenue, where you'll find shops, restaurants, and other establishments in **Pacific Garden Mall.** Although it remains less manicured than its upmarket neighbors to the south, Santa Cruz is more urban than the agricultural towns between it and the Monterey Peninsula. Nearby Capitola, Soquel, and Aptos are home to some quality restaurants, small inns, resorts, and antiques shops.

The town gets some of its youthful and unflagging spirit from the nearby **University of California at Santa Cruz.** The school's harmonious redwood buildings are perched on the forested hills above the town, and the campus is tailor-made for the contemplative life, with a juxtaposition of sylvan settings and sweeping vistas over open meadows onto the bay. ⊠ *Bay and High Sts.,* ☎ *831/459–0111.*

★ ⚲   Santa Cruz has been a seaside resort since the mid-19th century. The Looff carousel and classic wooden Giant Dipper roller coaster at the **Santa Cruz Beach Boardwalk** date from the early 1900s. Elsewhere along the boardwalk, the Casino Fun Center has its share of video-game technology, as does Neptune's Kingdom, whose highlights include a state-of-the-art miniature golf course with robotic and fiber-optic special effects. But this is still primarily a place for good old-fashioned fun, with rides and games appealing to toddlers, teens, and adults. ⊠ *Boardwalk: along Beach St. west from San Lorenzo River,* ☎ *831/423–5590 or 831/426–7433.* ⊡ *$19.95 (day pass for unlimited rides).* ☉ *Memorial Day–Labor Day, 11–11; rest of yr, weekends only, weather permitting (call for hrs).*

The **Santa Cruz Municipal Wharf,** just up the beach from the Boardwalk, is lined with restaurants, shops, and seafood takeout windows. The barking and baying of sea lions that lounge in communal heaps under the wharf's pilings enliven the area. Down the West Cliff Drive promontory at **Seal Rock,** pinnipeds hang out, sunbathe, and occasionally frolic.

The **Mark Abbott Memorial Lighthouse,** which is southwest of the wharf, has a surfing museum with artifacts that include the remains of a board a shark munched on. ☒ *W. Cliff Dr.,* ☎ *831/429–3429.* 🖾 *Free.* ☉ *Museum Wed.–Mon. noon–4.*

🐦 West of the lighthouse is secluded **Natural Bridges State Beach,** a stretch of soft sand with tidal pools and a natural rock bridge nearby. From October to early March a colony of monarch butterflies resides here. ☒ *2531 W. Cliff Dr.,* ☎ *831/423–4609.* 🖾 *$6 parking fee.* ☉ *Park 8* AM*–sunset. Visitor center Oct.–Feb., daily 10–4; Mar.–Sept., weekends 10–4.*

Dining and Lodging

$$–$$$ ✗ **Bittersweet Bistro.** An old tavern that was moved a few miles south
★   of Santa Cruz houses the popular bistro of chef-owner Thomas Vinolus. Start with a pizzetta or a mesclun salad; move on to a grilled vegetable platter, a seafood puttanesca with fettuccine, or grilled lamb tenderloins; then finish with any of the chocolate desserts. ☒ *787 Rio Del Mar Blvd., off Hwy. 1, Aptos,* ☎ *831/662–9799. AE, MC, V. Closed Mon. No lunch Sat.–Tues.*

$$–$$$ ✗ **Chez Renee.** The husband-and-wife team that owns this redwood-
★   shaded retreat cooks and serves French-inspired cuisine. Specialties include sweetbreads with marsala sauce, duck with home-preserved brandied cherries, and sea scallops garnished with smoked salmon and dill. Save room for the excellent dessert soufflés. ☒ *9051 Soquel Dr., Aptos,* ☎ *831/688–5566. MC, V. Closed Sun.–Mon. No lunch Tues. and Sat.*

$–$$$ ✗ **El Palomar.** The restaurant of the Palomar Hotel has vaulted ceilings, wood beams, and an atrium that opens up in warm weather. Among the best Tex-Mex dishes are ceviche tostadas, chili verde, and fish tacos. The attractive taco bar, off to one side, is open all day. ☒ *1336 Pacific Ave.,* ☎ *831/425–7575. Reservations not accepted for Fri.–Sat. dinner. AE, D, DC, MC, V.*

$–$$ ✗ **Dolphin Restaurant.** Occupying a scenic site at the end of the Municipal Wharf, this casual restaurant serves filling breakfasts—hotcakes, French toast, omelets—plus seafood lunches and dinners. For a quick bowl of chowder or plate of fish and chips, visit the adjacent takeout window. ☒ *At the end of Santa Cruz Municipal Wharf,* ☎ *831/426–5830. MC, V.*

$–$$ ✗ **Gabriella Cafe.** In a small brown stucco building, the Gabriella is intimate without being stuffy. The seasonal Italian menu highlights local organic produce. Watch for dishes like steamed mussels, braised lamb shank, and grilled Portobello mushrooms. ☒ *910 Cedar St.,* ☎ *831/ 457–1677. AE, D, DC, MC, V.*

$–$$ ✗ **India Joze.** Char-grilled meats and seafood with exotic marinades are the highlights at this local Pan-Asian favorite. Good bets include the curries, chicken or snapper in Javan pesto (fresh basil, ginger, and tamarind), and any of the grilled dishes with *panggang* (a ginger-lime marinade). ☒ *1001 Center St.,* ☎ *831/427–3554. AE, D, DC, MC, V.*

$–$$ ✗ **Positively Front Street.** Seafood chowder, steamed clams, grilled prawns, and oysters on the half shell are among the seafood entrées at this lively eatery near the wharf that also caters to the beach-and-boardwalk crowd with burgers and pizza. ☒ *44 Front St.,* ☎ *831/426–1944. AE, D, MC, V.*

$ ✗ **Zachary's.** With its potted plants, rough wooden floors, and mostly young clientele, this noisy café defines the funky essence of Santa Cruz. It also dishes up great breakfasts: omelets, sourdough pancakes, artichoke frittatas, and Mike's Mess—eggs scrambled with bacon, mushrooms, and home fries, topped with sour cream, melted cheese, and fresh tomatoes. ⊠ *819 Pacific Ave.,* ☎ *831/427–0646. MC, V.*

$$$$ 🖭 **Inn at Depot Hill.** This inventively designed B&B in a former rail depot sees itself as a link to the era of luxury train travel. Each double room or suite, complete with fireplace and feather beds, is inspired by a different destination—Portofino, Italy; the Côte d'Azur, France; Kyoto, Japan. One suite is decorated like a Pullman car for a railroad baron. Some accommodations have private patios with hot tubs. All are no-smoking. ⊠ *250 Monterey Ave. (Box 1934), Capitola-by-the-Sea 95010,* ☎ *831/462–3376 or 800/572–2632,* FAX *831/462–3697. 6 rooms, 6 suites. In-room data ports, in-room VCRs. Full breakfast. AE, MC, V.*

$$$$ 🖭 **Seascape Resort.** On a bluff overlooking Monterey Bay, with waves crashing on the beach below, Seascape is a place to unwind. The spacious all-suite units sleep from two to six people, and each has a kitchenette, a fireplace, and an ocean-view patio with a barbecue grill. The resort is about 9 mi south of Santa Cruz. ⊠ *1 Seascape Resort Dr., Aptos 95003,* ☎ *831/688–6800 or 800/929–7727,* FAX *831/685–2753. 285 suites. Restaurant, in-room data ports, room service, in-room VCRs, 3 pools, 3 hot tubs, spa, sauna, golf privileges, health club, beach, children's programs, laundry service, convention center, meeting rooms. AE, D, DC, MC, V.*

$$$$ 🖭 **WestCoast Santa Cruz Hotel.** Within a short stroll of the Beach Boardwalk and wharf, this resort opens right onto Cowell Beach. All rooms have private balconies or patios overlooking the Pacific. If it's too cold to swim in the ocean, you can head for the heated swimming pool and tub. Children under 12 stay free in their parents' room. ⊠ *175 W. Cliff Dr., 95060,* ☎ *831/426–4330 or 800/426–0670,* FAX *831/ 427–2025. 147 rooms, 16 suites. Restaurant, 2 bars, refrigerators, room service, in-room VCRs, pool, 2 hot tubs, laundry service. AE, D, DC, MC, V.*

$$$–$$$$ 🖭 **Inn at Manresa Beach.** Ansel Adams once occupied the 1867 mansion that Brian Denny and Susan Van Horn moved to a country setting about 10 mi south of Santa Cruz. The rooms in their comfortable B&B, which are all no-smoking and have nature-theme decor, contain gas fireplaces; most have whirlpool baths. Children are welcome. ⊠ *1258 San Andreas Rd., La Selva Beach 95076,* ☎ *831/728–1000 or 888/523–2244,* FAX *831/728–8294. 9 rooms. In-room VCRs, 2 tennis courts, volleyball. Full breakfast. AE, D, MC, V.*

$$–$$$$ 🖭 **Ocean Pacific Lodge.** By staying a few blocks from the beach, you can save money at this modern multistory motel that has a heated pool, two hot tubs, and in-room microwaves and VCRs. ⊠ *120 Washington St., 95060,* ☎ *831/457–1234 or 800/995–0289,* FAX *831/457– 0861. 44 rooms, 13 suites. Refrigerators, pool, 2 hot tubs, exercise room. Continental breakfast. AE, D, DC, MC, V.*

Nightlife and the Arts

Shakespeare Santa Cruz (⊠ Performing Arts Complex, University of California at Santa Cruz, ☎ 831/459–2121) stages a six-week Shakespeare festival in July and August that also may include one modern-day work. Most performances are outdoors in the striking Redwood Glen.

Outdoor Activities and Sports

BICYCLING
Bicycle Rental and Tour Center (⊠ 131 Center St., ☎ 831/426–8687).

BOATS AND CHARTERS
Chardonnay **Sailing Charters** (☎ 831/423–1213) accommodates 49 passengers for year-round cruises on Monterey Bay aboard the 70-ft

Chardonnay II, leaving from the yacht harbor in Santa Cruz. Reservations are essential. **Original Stagnaro Fishing Trips** (✉ Center of Santa Cruz Municipal Wharf, ☎ 831/423–2010) operates salmon and rock-cod fishing expeditions; the fees ($32–$45) include bait. The company also runs whale-watching cruises ($17–$20) between December and April.

SURFING

Manresa State Beach (✉ Manresa Dr., La Selva Beach, ☎ 831/761–1795), south of Santa Cruz, has premium surfing conditions, but the water can be treacherous. The surf at **New Brighton State Beach** (✉ 1500 State Park Dr., Capitola) is challenging; campsites are available. Surfers gather for the spectacular waves and sunsets at **Pleasure Point** (✉ East Cliff and Pleasure Point Drs.) **Steamer's Lane,** near the lighthouse on West Cliff Drive, has a decent break. The area plays host to several competitions in the summer.

Cowell's Beach 'n' Bikini Surf Shop (✉ 109 Beach St., ☎ 831/427–2355) rents surfboards and wet suits.

Monterey

48 mi south of Santa Cruz on Hwy. 1; 122 mi south of San Francisco on I–280 to Hwy. 17 to Hwy. 1; 334 mi north of Los Angeles on U.S. 101 to Hwy. 68 west from Salinas.

★ Much of Monterey's early history can be gleaned from the well-preserved adobe buildings of **Monterey State Historic Park** (☎ 831/649–7118). Far from being a hermetic period museum, the park facilities are an integral part of the day-to-day business life of the town—within some of the buildings are a store, a theater, and government offices. The 2-mi Path of History, marked by round gold tiles set into the sidewalk, passes by several landmark buildings. A $5 all-day park ticket gains you entrance to Casa Soberanes, the Cooper-Molera Adobe, the Larkin House, and the Stevenson House (☞ *below*) and includes a selection of guided walking tours.

❷ The **Custom House,** an adobe structure built by the Mexican government in 1827—now California's oldest standing public building—was the first stop for sea traders whose goods were subject to duties. An upper story was later added. At the beginning of the Mexican-American War in 1846, Commodore John Sloat raised the American flag over the building and claimed California for the United States. The house's lower floor displays typical cargo from a 19th-century trading ship. ✉ *1 Custom House Plaza, across from Fisherman's Wharf,* ☎ *831/649–2909.* 🎟 *Free.* ☉ *Daily 10–5.*

❸ The **Maritime Museum of Monterey** includes the private collection of maritime artifacts of Allen Knight, who was Carmel's mayor from 1950–52. Among the exhibits of ship models, scrimshaw items, and nautical prints, the highlight is the enormous multifaceted Fresnel lens from the Point Sur Light Station. ✉ *5 Custom House Plaza,* ☎ *831/375–2553.* 🎟 *$3.* ☉ *Daily 10–5.*

❹ The **Pacific House,** a former hotel and saloon, is a park visitor center and museum that surveys life in early California with gold-rush relics, photographs of old Monterey, and a costume gallery of fashions from various periods. The upper floor displays Native American artifacts. ✉ *10 Custom House Plaza,* ☎ *831/649–7118.* 🎟 *Free.* ☉ *Daily 10–5.*

❺ **Casa Soberanes,** a low-ceiling classic adobe structure built in 1842, was once a Custom House guard's residence. Exhibits at the house survey life in Monterey from the era of Mexican rule to the present.

Monterey and Pacific Grove

California's First Theatre, **10**
Casa Soberanes, **5**
Colton Hall, **9**
Cooper-Molera Adobe, **7**
Custom House, **2**

Dennis the Menace Playground, **12**
Fisherman's Wharf, **13**
Green Gables, **21**
La Mirada, **11**
Larkin House, **6**
Maritime Museum of Monterey, **3**

Monarch Grove Sanctuary, **23**
Monterey Bay Aquarium, **19**
Monterey Plaza Hotel and Spa, **14**
Pacific Biological Laboratories, **18**

Pacific Grove Museum of Natural History, **24**
Pacific House, **4**
Point Piños Lighthouse, **22**
Pryor House, **20**

651 Cannery Row, **15**
Steinbeck's Spirit of Monterey Wax Museum, **16**
Stevenson House, **8**
Wing Chong Building, **17**

There's a peaceful garden in back. ⊠ *336 Pacific St.,* ☎ *831/649–7118.* 🎟 *House $5, garden free.* ☉ *Guided tours daily; call for times. Garden daily 8–5.*

6 The **Larkin House** was built in 1835. A veranda encircles the second floor of this architecturally significant two-story adobe, whose design bears witness to the Mexican and New England influences on the Monterey style. The rooms are furnished with period antiques, many of them brought from New Hampshire by the Larkin family. ⊠ *510 Calle Principal, between Jefferson and Pacific Sts.,* ☎ *831/649–7118.* 🎟 *$5.* ☉ *Guided tours daily; call for times.*

7 The restored **Cooper-Molera Adobe,** a 2-acre complex, includes a house dating from the 1820s, a visitor center, and a large garden enclosed by a high adobe wall. The mostly Victorian-era antiques and memorabilia that fill the tile-roof house provide a glimpse into the life of a prosperous pioneer family. ⊠ *Polk and Munras Sts.,* ☎ *831/649–7118.* 🎟 *$5.* ☉ *Guided tours daily; call for times.*

8 The **Stevenson House** was named in honor of author Robert Louis Stevenson, who boarded here briefly in a tiny upstairs room. Items from his family's estate furnish Stevenson's room. Period-decorated chambers elsewhere in the house include a gallery of the author's memorabilia and a children's nursery stocked with Victorian toys and games. ⊠ *530 Houston St.,* ☎ *831/649–7118.* 🎟 *$5.* ☉ *Guided tours daily; call for times. Gardens daily 8–5.*

9 A convention of delegates met in 1849 to draft the first state constitution at **Colton Hall,** California's equivalent of Independence Hall. The white building, which has served as a school, a courthouse, and the county seat, is a museum furnished as it was during the constitutional convention. The extensive grounds outside the hall surround the Old Monterey Jail. ⊠ *500 block of Pacific St., between Madison and Jefferson Sts.,* ☎ *831/646–5640.* 🎟 *Free.* ☉ *Mar.–Oct., daily 10–noon and 1–5; Nov.–Feb., daily 10–noon and 1–4.*

10 **California's First Theatre** was constructed in the 1840s by Jack Swan, an English sailor who settled in Monterey, as a saloon with adjoining apartments. Soldiers from the New York Volunteers who were on assignment in Monterey put on plays in the building. Melodramas and other theatrical performances are still staged here (☞ Nightlife and the Arts, *below*). ⊠ *Scott and Pacific Sts.,* ☎ *831/649–7118 or 831/375–4916 (box office).* 🎟 *Free.* ☉ *Wed.–Sat. 1–5.*

The **Monterey Peninsula Museum of Art** displays the works of photographers Ansel Adams and Edward Weston and other artists who have spent time on the peninsula. Another focus is international folk art; the colorful collection ranges from Kentucky hearth brooms to Tibetan prayer wheels. ⊠ *559 Pacific St., across from Colton Hall,* ☎ *831/372–7591.* 🎟 *$3.* ☉ *Wed.–Sat. 11–5, Sun. 1–4.*

11 At **La Mirada,** Asian and European antiques fill a 19th-century adobe house. A newer 10,000-square-ft gallery space, designed by Charles Moore, houses Asian and Californian regional art and a large netsuke collection. Outdoors are magnificent rose and rhododendron gardens. ⊠ *720 Via Mirada, at Fremont St.,* ☎ *831/372–3689.* 🎟 *$3.* ☉ *Thurs.–Sat. 11–5, Sun. 1–4.*

★ ☪ **12** **Dennis the Menace Playground** (⊠ Pearl St. and Camino El Estero), in El Estero Park, is an imaginative play area designed by local resident and cartoonist Hank Ketcham. The equipment is on a grand scale and made for daredevils; there's a roller slide, a clanking suspension bridge, and a real Southern Pacific steam locomotive. You can rent a rowboat or a paddleboat to cruise about U-shape Lake El Estero, home to a varied assortment of ducks, mud hens, and geese.

The mournful barking of sea lions draws visitors to Monterey's waterfront. The whiskered marine mammals are best enjoyed while walking along **Fisherman's Wharf,** an aging pier across from Custom House Plaza that's lined with souvenir shops, fish markets, seafood restaurants, and popcorn stands. Although most commercial fishermen have moved to Wharf No. 2, a five-minute walk away, Fisherman's Wharf, a lively and entertaining place to bring children, is still the departure point for fishing, diving, and whale-watching trips. The shallow waters of **Monterey Municipal Beach,** east of Wharf No. 2, are usually warm and calm enough for wading.

Cannery Row has undergone several transformations since it was immortalized in John Steinbeck's 1945 novel of the same name. The street that Steinbeck described was crowded with sardine canneries processing, at their peak, nearly 200,000 tons of the smelly silver fish a year. During the mid-1940s, however, the sardines disappeared from the bay, eventually causing the canneries to close. Through the years the old tin-roof canneries have been converted into restaurants, art galleries, and minimalls with shops selling T-shirts, fudge, and plastic sea otters. Recent tourist development along the row has been more tasteful, however, including several stylish inns and hotels.

The **Monterey Plaza Hotel and Spa** (⊠ 400 Cannery Row), on the site of a historic estate, is a good place to relax over a drink and watch for sea otters. Though John Steinbeck would have trouble recognizing Cannery Row today, wisps of its colorful past can still be detected. Check out **651 Cannery Row.** Its tiled Chinese dragon roof dates from 1929.

Characters from the novel *Cannery Row* are depicted at **Steinbeck's Spirit of Monterey Wax Museum,** which presents an easy-to-digest 25-minute narration of 400 years of Monterey history, recorded by an actor playing John Steinbeck. ⊠ *700 Cannery Row,* ☎ *831/375–3770.* 🖃 *$5.95.* ☉ *Memorial Day–Labor Day, daily 9–9; rest of yr, Mon.–Thurs. noon–6, Fri. and Sun. 10–8, Sat. 10–10.*

The **Wing Chong Building** (⊠ 835 Cannery Row) is the former Wing Chong Market that Steinbeck called Lee Chong's Heavenly Flower Grocery in *Cannery Row.* A weathered wooden building at 800 Cannery Row was the **Pacific Biological Laboratories** where Edward F. Ricketts, the inspiration for Doc in *Cannery Row,* did much of his marine research.

The Outer Bay wing of the **Monterey Bay Aquarium** contains a million-gallon indoor ocean—observed through the largest window on Earth—that re-creates the sunlit blue water where Monterey Bay meets the open sea. In this habitat blue and soupfin sharks, barracuda, pelagic stingrays, ocean sunfish (which can weigh a ton or more), green sea turtles, and schools of fast-moving tuna swim together. The Outer Bay wing also houses a mesmerizing collection (the largest in the nation) of jellyfish. Expect long lines and sizable crowds at the aquarium on weekends, especially during the summer, but braving the masses is worth it. Don't miss the original wing's three-story Kelp Forest exhibit, the only one of its kind in the world, or the display of the sea creatures and vegetation found in Monterey Bay. Among other standouts are a bat-ray petting pool, where you can touch the flat velvetlike creatures as they swim by; a 55,000-gallon sea-otter tank; and an enormous outdoor artificial tidal pool that supports anemones, crabs, sea stars, and other colorful creatures. A special exhibit devoted to deep-sea life runs through 2001. ⊠ *886 Cannery Row,* ☎ *831/648–4888; 800/756–*

3737 in CA for advance tickets. 🎟 *$15.95.* ⊙ *Daily 10–6 (9:30–6 in summer and major holiday periods); ticket window closes at 5:30.*

A short drive from downtown Monterey leads to **Ventana Vineyards,** known for chardonnays and Johannisberg Rieslings. Ventana's knowledgeable and hospitable owners, Doug and LuAnn Meador, invite guests to bring lunch to eat while tasting wines on a patio and deck. ⊠ *2999 Monterey–Salinas Hwy. (Hwy. 68),* ☎ *831/372–7415.* ⊙ *Daily 11–5.*

<table>
<tr>
<td>OFF THE
BEATEN PATH</td>
<td>ELKHORN SLOUGH – A few miles north of Monterey, east of the tiny harbor town of Moss Landing, is one of only two federal research reserves in California, the Elkhorn Slough at the National Estuarine Research Reserve. Its 1,400 acres of tidal flats and salt marshes form a complex environment that supports more than 200 species of birds. A walk along the meandering waterways and wetlands can reveal hawks, white-tailed kites, owls, herons, and egrets. Wander at your leisure or, on weekends, take a guided walk (10 AM and 2 PM) to the heron rookery. ⊠ 1700 Elkhorn Rd., Moss Landing, ☎ 831/728–2822 for directions. 🎟 $2.50; free with any California hunting or fishing license. ⊙ Wed.–Sun. 9–5.</td>
</tr>
</table>

Dining and Lodging

$$$–$$$$ ✕ **Fresh Cream.** The views of the bay are as superb as the imaginative French cuisine at this outstanding restaurant in Heritage Harbor. The menu, which changes weekly, might include rack of lamb Dijonnaise, roast boned duck in black-currant sauce, or blackened ahi tuna with pineapple rum-butter sauce. ⊠ *99 Pacific St., Suite 100C,* ☎ *831/375–9798. AE, D, DC, MC, V. No lunch.*

$$$ ✕ **Duck Club.** The elegant and romantic dining room of the Monterey Plaza Hotel and Spa (☞ *below*) is built over the waterfront on Cannery Row, overlooking the bay. The seasonal dinner menu strongly emphasizes duck but also includes seafood, meat, and pasta. The Duck Club is open for breakfast. ⊠ *400 Cannery Row,* ☎ *831/646–1706. AE, D, DC, MC, V. No lunch.*

$$–$$$ ✕ **Domenico's.** Italian seafood preparations, mesquite-grilled meats, and homemade pastas are the specialties at Domenico's. The blue-and-white nautical decor keeps the place comfortably casual; white drapery lends an air of elegance other wharf restaurants lack. ⊠ *50 Fisherman's Wharf,* ☎ *831/372–3655. AE, D, DC, MC, V.*

$$–$$$ ✕ **Monterey's Fish House.** Casual yet stylish and a real find away from the hubbub of the wharf, this always-packed seafood restaurant attracts locals and frequent travelers to the city. If the dining room is full, you can wait at the bar and tide yourself over with deliciously plump oysters on the half shell. The bartenders and wait staff will gladly advise you on the perfect wine to go with your poached, blackened, or oakwood-grilled seafood. ⊠ *2114 Del Monte Ave.,* ☎ *831/373–4647. Reservations essential. AE, D, DC, MC, V. No lunch weekends.*

$$–$$$ ✕ **Montrio.** If your appetite for hearty cooking and clean, strong fla-
★   vors has been stimulated by a day of bracing Monterey Bay breezes, this European-inspired American bistro, a montage of brick, rawhide, and wrought iron inside Monterey's former firehouse, is the place to go. Grilled Portobello mushrooms with polenta and rotisserie chicken with garlic mashed potatoes are two of the menu highlights. ⊠ *414 Calle Principal,* ☎ *831/648–8880. Reservations essential on weekends. AE, D, MC, V.*

$$–$$$ ✕ **Stokes Adobe.** Brandon Miller's sunny restaurant may be inside an 1833 adobe, but his cooking is strictly cutting edge. Miller specializes in the cuisines of Provence, northern Italy, and Catalan Spain, turning

out imaginative pasta, seafood, and vegetarian dishes that change with the seasons. His creations have included seared ahi tuna with lentil tomato salad, rustic pasta tubes with fennel sausage and Manila clams, and chicken with garlic mashed potatoes. ⊠ *500 Hartnell St.*, ☎ *831/ 373–1110. AE, DC, MC, V.*

$$–$$$ ✕ **Whaling Station Prime Steaks and Seafood.** A pleasing mixture of
★ rough-hewn wood and sparkling white linen makes this restaurant above Cannery Row a festive yet comfortable place to enjoy seafood—try the sand dabs—and tender Kobe steaks. ⊠ *763 Wave St.*, ☎ *831/373–3778. AE, D, DC, MC, V. No lunch.*

$–$$$ ✕ **Abalonetti.** Squid reigns here: deep-fried, sautéed with wine and garlic, or baked with eggplant. Abalone is another specialty, and the fresh fish is broiled or blackened and served with beurre blanc or pesto. Next door, the Abalonetti Deli serves up antipasti and fried squid in casual surroundings. ⊠ *57 Fisherman's Wharf,* ☎ *831/373–1851. AE, D, DC, MC, V.*

$–$$$ ✕ **Cafe Fina.** Mesquite-grilled fish dishes and linguine in clam sauce with baby shrimp and tomatoes are among the highlights at this understated Italian restaurant on the wharf. The wine list is extensive. ⊠ *47 Fisherman's Wharf,* ☎ *831/372–5200. AE, D, DC, MC, V.*

$–$$$ ✕ **Paradiso Trattoria and Oyster Bar.** Follow the aroma of marinating olives, roasted garlic, and platters of focaccia to this bright Cannery Row establishment. Mediterranean specialties and pizzas from a wood-burning oven are the luncheon fare. Seafood is a good choice for dinner, served in a dining room overlooking a lighted beachfront and lapping surf or at the gleaming oyster bar. ⊠ *654 Cannery Row,* ☎ *831/375–4155. AE, D, DC, MC, V.*

$–$$$ ✕ **Tarpy's Roadhouse.** Fun, dressed-down roadhouse lunch and dinner are served in this renovated farmhouse built in the early 1900s. The kitchen cooks everything Mom used to make, only better. Eat indoors by a fireplace or outdoors in the courtyard. ⊠ *2999 Monterey– Salinas Hwy. (Hwy. 68), at Canyon Del Rey Rd.,* ☎ *831/647–1444. AE, D, MC, V.*

$–$$ ✕ **Consuelo's.** Meals at this Tex-Mex restaurant—housed somewhat incongruously in an 1886 Victorian—start with complimentary quesadillas, presented on a huge platter, then move on to fajitas, tostadas, enchiladas, marinated chicken, flautas, and other dishes. If the weather's nice, you can sit outside in the shade of a huge Indian pine tree. ⊠ *361 Lighthouse Ave.,* ☎ *831/372–8111. AE, D, DC, MC, V.*

$ ✕ **Old Monterey Cafe.** Breakfast here, which is served until closing time (2:30 PM), might include fresh-baked muffins and eggs Benedict. Soups, salads, and sandwiches appear on the lunch menu. This is also a good place to relax with a cappuccino after touring Monterey's historic adobes. ⊠ *489 Alvarado St.,* ☎ *831/646–1021. Reservations not accepted. D, MC, V. No dinner.*

$$$$ 🏨 **Hotel Pacific.** All the rooms at this modern adobe-style hotel are junior suites, handsomely appointed with featherbeds, hardwood floors, fireplaces, and balconies or patios. The rates include parking, breakfast, and afternoon snacks. ⊠ *300 Pacific St., 93940,* ☎ *831/373–5700 or 800/554–5542,* FAX *831/373–6921. 105 rooms. Refrigerators, minibars, 2 hot tubs, meeting rooms. Continental breakfast. AE, D, DC, MC, V.*

$$$$ 🏨 **Hyatt Regency Monterey.** Although its rooms and atmosphere are less glamorous than those at some other resorts in the region, the facilities here are excellent. ⊠ *1 Old Golf Course Rd., 93940,* ☎ *831/ 372–1234; 800/824–2196 in CA,* FAX *831/372–4277. 535 rooms, 40 suites. Restaurant, café, bar, 2 pools, 2 hot tubs, massage, 18-hole golf course, 6 tennis courts, exercise room, bicycles, children's programs. AE, D, DC, MC, V.*

$$$$ ⊡ **Monterey Bay Inn.** On Cannery Row and with breathtaking bay views from most rooms, this hotel takes full advantage of its location, even providing guests binoculars for viewing marine life. Rooms, decorated in peach and green tones, come with private balconies, TVs with VCRs, honor bars, and robes. ✉ *242 Cannery Row, 93940,* ☎ *831/373–6242 or 800/424–6242,* FAX *831/373–7603. 47 rooms. Refrigerators, in-room VCRs, 2 hot tubs, sauna, exercise room, meeting rooms, free parking. Continental breakfast. No smoking. AE, D, DC, MC, V.*

$$$$ ⊡ **Monterey Plaza Hotel and Spa.** This sophisticated full-service hotel
★   commands a waterfront location on Cannery Row, where frolicking sea otters can be observed from the wide outdoor patio and many room balconies. The architecture and decor blend early Californian and Mediterranean styles and retain elements of the old cannery design. Guests have use of a new rooftop spa facility. ✉ *400 Cannery Row, 93940,* ☎ *831/646–1700 or 800/631–1339; 800/334–3999 in CA,* FAX *831/646–0285. 285 rooms, 3 suites. 2 restaurants, minibars, room service, spa, exercise room, laundry service. AE, D, DC, MC, V.*

$$$$ ⊡ **Old Monterey Inn.** One of just two residential-area B&Bs in Mon-
★   terey, this inn conjures up both the past history and the present beauty of the Monterey Peninsula. The three-story English Tudor country manor was completed in 1929, replete with hand-carved window frames, balustrades, and Gothic archways. Loving restoration by proprietors Gene and Ann Swett included a rose garden surrounded by giant holly trees, gnarled oaks, and majestic redwoods. The innkeepers' legendary hospitality includes 20 different bathroom amenities, featherbeds with down comforters, a sumptuous breakfast, and solicitous service. ✉ *500 Martin St., 93940,* ☎ *831/375–8284 or 800/350–2344,* FAX *831/375–6730. 8 rooms, 2 suites. Concierge. Full breakfast. MC, V.*

$$$$ ⊡ **Spindrift Inn.** This small hotel on Cannery Row, under the same man-
★   agement as the Hotel Pacific and the Monterey Bay Inn, has beach access and a rooftop garden that overlooks Monterey Bay. Spacious rooms with sitting areas, hardwood floors, fireplaces, and down comforters are among the indoor pleasures. ✉ *652 Cannery Row, 93940,* ☎ *831/646–8900 or 800/841–1879,* FAX *831/646–5342. 42 rooms. Refrigerators. Continental breakfast. AE, D, DC, MC, V.*

$$$–$$$$ ⊡ **Embassy Suites.** As you drive into Monterey from the north on Highway 1, you can't miss the high-rise Embassy Suites, which towers over the town of Seaside just before the Monterey line. Two blocks from the beach, it overlooks Laguna Grande Lake and Monterey Bay. All accommodations here are smallish two-room suites with microwaves, refrigerators, and coffeemakers. ✉ *1441 Canyon Del Rey, Seaside 93955,* ☎ *831/393–1115,* FAX *831/393–1113. 225 suites. Restaurant, bar, kitchenettes, indoor pool, hot tub, sauna, exercise room, meeting room. Full breakfast. AE, D, DC, MC, V.*

$$–$$$$ ⊡ **Best Western Monterey Beach Hotel.** The rooms here may be nondescript, but this hotel has a great waterfront location about 2 mi north of town, with views of the bay and the Monterey skyline. The grounds are pleasantly landscaped, and there's a large pool with a sunbathing area. ✉ *2600 Sand Dunes Dr., 93940,* ☎ *831/394–3321 or 800/242–8627,* FAX *831/393–1912. 196 rooms. Restaurant, lounge, pool, hot tub, exercise room. AE, D, DC, MC, V.*

$$–$$$$ ⊡ **Monterey Hotel.** Standard rooms in this restored Victorian are small but contain well-chosen reproduction antique furniture; the master suites have fireplaces and sunken baths. The entire hotel is no-smoking. ✉ *406 Alvarado St., 93940,* ☎ *831/375–3184 or 800/727–0960,* FAX *831/373–2899. 39 rooms, 6 suites. Continental breakfast. AE, D, DC, MC, V.*

$$–$$$$ ▦ **Quality Inn Cannery Row.** Gas fireplaces are among the amenities at this small hotel on a street above Cannery Row. Some rooms have private balconies with bay views. ✉ *200 Foam St., 93940,* ☎ *831/649–8580 or 800/876–8580,* FAX *831/649–2566. 32 rooms. Refrigerators, hot tub. Continental breakfast. AE, D, MC, V.*

$–$$$$ ▦ **Quality Inn Monterey.** This stylish motel has a friendly, country-inn atmosphere. Breakfast is served in a blue-wallpapered lobby; in-room coffee is also complimentary. Rooms are light and airy, some with fireplaces and some with accessibility for visitors with disabilities. ✉ *1058 Munras Ave., 93940,* ☎ *831/372–3381,* FAX *831/372–4687. 55 rooms. Indoor pool, hot tub. Continental breakfast. AE, D, DC, MC, V.*

$$–$$$ ▦ **Monterey Bay Lodge.** Its location on the edge of Monterey's El Es-
★ tero Park gives this motel an edge over those along the busy Munras Avenue motel row. Indoor plants and a secluded courtyard with a heated pool are other pluses. ✉ *55 Camino Aguajito Rd., 93940,* ☎ *831/372–8057 or 800/558–1900,* FAX *831/655–2933. 45 rooms. Restaurant, pool. AE, D, DC, MC, V.*

$–$$ ▦ **Del Monte Beach Inn.** The rooms at this small, reasonably priced B&B are decorated the way rooms in your grandmother's home might have been. Check in or call before 8 PM, when the office closes. ✉ *1110 Del Monte Ave., 93940,* ☎ *831/649–4410,* FAX *831/375–3818. 16 rooms, 2 suites. Continental breakfast. AE, D, MC, V.*

Nightlife and the Arts

BARS, CLUBS

Doc's Nightclub (✉ 95 Prescott St., ☎ 831/649–4241), one block above Cannery Row, hosts bands—rock, blues, jazz, reggae, or folk—every night but Sunday. **Planet Gemini** (✉ 625 Cannery Row, ☎ 831/373–1449) presents comedy shows on most nights, followed by dancing to DJ or live music. **Sly McFlys** (✉ 700-A Cannery Row, ☎ 831/649–8050), a popular watering hole, has a publike atmosphere.

MUSIC FESTIVALS

Dixieland Monterey (✉ 177 Webster St., Suite A-206, ☎ 831/443–5260 or 888/349–6879), held on the first full weekend of March, presents Dixieland jazz bands in cabarets, restaurants, and hotel lounges on the Monterey waterfront. The **Monterey Bay Blues Festival** (☎ 831/394–2652 or 831/649–6544) draws blues fans to the Monterey Fairgrounds over a June weekend. The **Monterey Jazz Festival,** the world's oldest, (☎ 831/373–3366) attracts jazz and blues greats from around the world to the Monterey Fairgrounds on the third full weekend of September.

THEATER

California's First Theatre (✉ Scott and Pacific Sts., ☎ 831/375–4916) is home to the Troupers of the Gold Coast, who perform 19th-century melodramas year-round, mostly on weekends. **Monterey Bay Theatrefest** (☎ 831/622–0700) presents free outdoor performances at Custom House Plaza on weekend afternoons and evenings from late June to mid-July. The **Wharf Theater** (✉ Fisherman's Wharf, ☎ 831/649–2332) focuses on American musicals past and present.

Outdoor Activities and Sports

BICYCLING

For bicycle rentals try **Bay Sports** (✉ 640 Wave St., ☎ 831/646–9090) or **Adventures by the Sea Inc.** (✉ 299 Cannery Row, ☎ 831/372–1807).

CAR RACING

Five major races take place each year on the 2.2-mi, 11-turn **Laguna Seca Raceway** (✉ 1021 Monterey–Salinas Hwy., ☎ 831/648–5100 or 800/327–7322).

FISHING

For half- and full-day fishing trips, contact **Monterey Sport Fishing** (✉ 96 Fisherman's Wharf, ☎ 831/372–2203 or 800/200–2203), **Randy's Fishing Trips** (✉ 66 Fisherman's Wharf, ☎ 831/372–7440), or **Sam's Fishing Fleet** (✉ 84 Fisherman's Wharf, ☎ 831/372–0577).

GOLF

The greens fee at the 18-hole **Del Monte Golf Course** (✉ 1300 Sylvan Rd., ☎ 831/373–2700) is $75, plus $18 per person for an optional cart. The $15 twilight special (plus cart rental) begins two hours before sunset.

KAYAKING

Monterey Bay Kayaks (✉ 693 Del Monte Ave., ☎ 831/373–5357; 800/649–5357 in CA) rents equipment and conducts classes and natural-history tours.

ROLLERSKATING AND IN-LINE SKATING

Adventures by the Sea Inc. (✉ 299 Cannery Row, ☎ 408/372–1807) rents rollerblades. **Del Monte Gardens** (✉ 2020 Del Monte Ave., ☎ 831/375–3202) is an old-fashioned rink for rollerskating and in-line skating.

SCUBA DIVING

The staff at **Aquarius Dive Shops** (✉ 2040 Del Monte Ave., ☎ 831/375–1933; ✉ 32 Cannery Row, ☎ 831/375–6605) gives diving lessons and tours and rents equipment. The **scuba-diving conditions information line** (☎ 831/657–1020) is updated regularly.

WHALE-WATCHING

Monterey Sport Fishing (✉ 96 Fisherman's Wharf, ☎ 831/372–2203 or 800/200–2203), **Randy's Fishing Trips** (✉ 66 Fisherman's Wharf, ☎ 831/372–7440), and **Sam's Fishing Fleet** (✉ 84 Fisherman's Wharf, ☎ 831/372–0577) operate whale-watching expeditions.

Shopping

Alicia's Antiques (835 Cannery Row, ☎ 831/372–1423) occupies the back of the Wing Chong Building. Owner Alicia Harby-DeNoon, who knew John Steinbeck and Doc Ricketts, knows much about the old Cannery Row. **Old Monterey Book Co.** (✉ 136 Bonifacio Pl., off Alvarado St., ☎ 831/372–3111) specializes in rare old books and prints.

Pacific Grove

3 mi from Monterey south on Hwy. 1 and west on Hwy. 68; from Cannery Row, Wave St. heading west becomes Ocean View Blvd. at Monterey–Pacific Grove border.

If not for the dramatic strip of coastline in its backyard, Pacific Grove could easily pass for a typical small town in the Heartland. The town, which began as a summer retreat for church groups more than a century ago, recalls its prim and proper Victorian heritage in its host of tiny board-and-batten cottages and stately mansions.

Even before the church groups flocked here, Pacific Grove had been receiving thousands of annual guests in the form of bright orange-and-black monarch butterflies. Known as Butterfly Town USA, Pacific Grove is the winter home of monarchs that migrate south from Canada and the Pacific Northwest to take residence in pine and eucalyptus groves from October through March. The sight of a mass of butterflies hanging from the branches like a long, fluttering veil is unforgettable.

A prime way to enjoy Pacific Grove is to walk or bicycle along its 3 mi of city-owned shoreline, a cliff-top area following Ocean View Boulevard that is landscaped with succulents and native plants and has benches on which to sit and gaze at the sea. You can spot marine life and birds here, including colonies of cormorants drawn to the massive rocks rising out of the surf.

⓴ Among the Victorians of note is the **Pryor House** (⊠ 429 Ocean View Blvd.), a massive shingled structure with a leaded- and beveled-glass
㉑ doorway. **Green Gables** (⊠ 5th St. and Ocean View Blvd.), a romantic Swiss Gothic–style mansion with steeply peaked gables and stained-glass windows, is a B&B.

Ⓒ The view of the coast is gorgeous from **Lovers Point Park,** on Ocean View Boulevard midway along the waterfront. The park's sheltered beach has a children's pool and picnic area. Glass-bottom boat rides, which provide views of the plant and sea life below, are offered in summer.

★ Ⓒ ㉒ At the 1855-vintage **Point Piños Lighthouse,** the oldest continuously operating lighthouse on the West Coast, you can learn about the lighting and foghorn operations and wander through a small museum containing U.S. Coast Guard memorabilia. ⊠ *Lighthouse Ave. off Asilomar Blvd.,* ☎ *831/648–3116.* 🎫 *Free.* ☉ *Thurs.–Sun. 1–4.*

Monarchs sometimes vary their nesting sites from year to year, but the
㉓ **Monarch Grove Sanctuary** (⊠ 1073 Lighthouse Ave., at Ridge Rd.) is a fairly reliable spot for viewing the butterflies.

If you are in Pacific Grove when the monarch butterflies aren't, you
Ⓒ ㉔ can view the well-crafted butterfly tree exhibit at the **Pacific Grove Museum of Natural History.** The museum also displays 400 mounted birds and has a Touch Gallery for kids. ⊠ *165 Forest Ave.,* ☎ *831/ 648–3116.* 🎫 *Free.* ☉ *Tues.–Sun. 10–5.*

★ **Asilomar State Beach,** a beautiful coastal area, is on Sunset Drive between Point Piños and the Del Monte Forest in Pacific Grove. The 100 acres of dunes, tidal pools, and pocket-size beaches form one of the region's richest areas for marine life.

Dining and Lodging

$$$ ✕ **Cypress Grove.** Taking over a well-loved French restaurant (Melac's) in 1998, Chef Kurt Steeber and his wife, Rosemarie, are making their own mark with contemporary French cuisine that relies on regional, seasonal ingredients and light sauces. Foie gras, sweetbreads, lamb shanks, and sea bass are among the offerings. Brunch is served weekends. ⊠ *663 Lighthouse Ave.,* ☎ *831/375–1743. AE, MC, V. No dinner Mon.*

$$$ ✕ **Old Bath House.** A romantic, nostalgic atmosphere permeates this
★ converted bathhouse overlooking the water at Lovers Point. The classic regional menu makes the most of local seafood (such as Monterey Bay prawns) and produce. The restaurant has a less expensive menu for late-afternoon diners. ⊠ *620 Ocean View Blvd.,* ☎ *831/375– 5195. AE, D, DC, MC, V. No lunch.*

$$–$$$ ✕ **Fandango.** With its stone walls and country furniture, Fandango has the earthy feel of a southern European farmhouse. Complementing the ambience are the robust flavors of the cuisine, which ranges from southern France, Italy, Spain, and Greece to North Africa, from paella

and cannelloni to couscous. ⊠ *223 17th St.,* ☎ *831/372–3456. AE, D, DC, MC, V.*

$$–$$$ ✕ **Gernot's.** The ornate Victorian-era Hart Mansion is a delightful setting in which to dine on seafood and game served with light sauces. Austrian/Continental specialties include wild-boar bourguignonne, roast venison, and rack of lamb. ⊠ *649 Lighthouse Ave.,* ☎ *831/646–1477. AE, MC, V. Closed Mon. No lunch.*

$–$$$ ✕ **The Tinnery.** This family-oriented restaurant has an enviable location overlooking Lovers Point. The menu runs toward the tried-and-true: pancakes and omelets for breakfast, burgers and sandwiches for lunch. Broiled salmon with hollandaise sauce, mesquite-grilled meats, and fish-and-chips are dinner highlights. ⊠ *631 Ocean View Blvd.,* ☎ *831/646–1040. Reservations not accepted. AE, D, DC, MC, V.*

$–$$ ✕ **Crocodile Grill.** South American artwork and artifacts form the decor, and a Latin flavor permeates many of the Crocodile's adventurous concoctions, such as crispy squid with spicy orange-cilantro vinaigrette and black bean–goat cheese ravioli. Fresh fish is paired with a variety of creative sauces. Wines are an exceptional value here. ⊠ *701 Lighthouse Ave.,* ☎ *831/655–3311. AE, D, MC, V. Closed Tues. No lunch.*

$–$$ ✕ **Fishwife.** Fresh fish with a Latin accent makes this a favorite of locals for lunch or a casual dinner. ⊠ *1996½ Sunset Dr., at Asilomar Blvd.,* ☎ *831/375–7107. AE, D, MC, V. Closed Tues.*

$–$$ ✕ **Peppers Mexicali Cafe.** This cheerful white-walled restaurant serves fresh seafood and traditional dishes from Mexico and Latin America. The red and green salsas are excellent. ⊠ *170 Forest Ave.,* ☎ *831/373–6892. AE, D, DC, MC, V. Closed Tues. No lunch Sun.*

$–$$ ✕ **Toasties Cafe.** Three-egg omelets, burritos, pancakes, waffles, French toast, and other breakfast items are served at this crowded café until 3 PM. The lunch selections include burgers and other sandwiches. Toasties also serves dinner—fish and chips, seafood pasta—but it's best to stick to daytime meals. ⊠ *702 Lighthouse Ave.,* ☎ *831/373–7543. AE, MC, V.*

$$$–$$$$ ⊞ **Centrella Inn.** A handsome century-old Victorian mansion two
★   blocks from Lovers Point Beach, the Centrella fills its guest rooms and cottages with wicker and brass furnishings and claw-foot bathtubs. A buffet breakfast is served each morning, and a sideboard in the large parlor is later laden with cookies, wine, and hors d'oeuvres. ⊠ *612 Central Ave., 93950,* ☎ *831/372–3372 or 800/233–3372,* ℻ *831/372–2036. 17 rooms, 4 suites, 5 cottages. Concierge. Full breakfast. AE, D, MC, V. No smoking indoors. 2-night minimum weekends.*

$$$–$$$$ ⊞ **Martine Inn.** Most B&Bs in Pacific Grove are in Victorian houses;
★   this one is in a pink-stucco, Mediterranean-style villa overlooking the water. The many antiques include a mahogany suite exhibited at the 1893 Chicago World's Fair, movie costume designer Edith Head's bedroom suite, and an 1860 Chippendale Revival four-poster bed. The glassed-in parlor and several rooms have stunning ocean views. Lavish breakfasts are served on lace-clad tables set with china, crystal, and silver. ⊠ *255 Ocean View Blvd., 93950,* ☎ *831/373–3388 or 800/852–5588,* ℻ *831/373–3896. 25 rooms. Refrigerators. Full breakfast. AE, D, MC, V.*

$$$–$$$$ ⊞ **Seven Gables Inn.** Five yellow-gabled clapboard buildings share a corner lot and a great view of the ocean. The main house was built in 1886, the others between 1910 and 1940. European antiques of various periods—gold-leaf mirrors, crystal chandeliers, and marble statues—create a formal atmosphere. The gracious innkeeper, Susan Flatley, grew up in the house and shares her knowledge about it and the area.

⊠ *555 Ocean View Blvd., 93950,* ☎ *831/372–4341. 10 rooms, 4 cottages. Full breakfast. MC, V. No smoking indoors. 2-night minimum weekends.*

$$–$$$$ ⊞ **Green Gables Inn.** Stained-glass windows framing an ornate fireplace and other interior detail work compete with the spectacular
★   ocean views at this Queen Anne–style mansion built by a businessman for his mistress in 1888. Rooms in a carriage house perched on a hill out back are larger, have more modern amenities, and afford more privacy than rooms in the main house, but the latter have more charm. ⊠ *104 5th St., 93950,* ☎ *831/375–2095 or 800/722–1774,* FAX *831/ 375–5437. 10 rooms, 4 with shared bath; 1 suite. Bicycles. Full breakfast. AE, MC, V.*

$$–$$$$ ⊞ **Lighthouse Lodge and Suites.** On two sides of Lighthouse Avenue—the lodge is on one side, the all-suites facility on the other—this complex near the tip of the peninsula provides a woodsy alternative to downtown Pacific Grove's B&B scene. The suites have fireplaces, whirlpool tubs, and kitchenettes. Some of the lodge rooms could use remodeling, but they're decent in size and much less expensive than the suites. ⊠ *1150 and 1249 Lighthouse Ave., 93950,* ☎ *831/655– 2111 or 800/858–1249,* FAX *831/655–4922. 68 rooms, 31 suites. Pool, hot tub. Full breakfast. AE, D, DC, MC, V.*

$$–$$$ ⊞ **Gosby House Inn.** Though in the town center, this turreted yellow Queen Anne Victorian B&B has an informal, country air. The two most private rooms are in the rear carriage house; they have fireplaces, balconies, and whirlpool tubs. Buffet breakfast is served in the parlor or garden. ⊠ *643 Lighthouse Ave., 93950,* ☎ *831/375–1287 or 800/527– 8828,* FAX *831/655–9621. 22 rooms, 2 with shared bath. Full breakfast. AE, MC, V. No smoking indoors.*

$–$$$ ⊞ **Asilomar Conference Center.** A summer-camp atmosphere prevails at this assortment of 28 rustic but comfortable lodges in the middle of a woodsy 105-acre state park near the beach. Rooms are available when they're not booked for conferences. ⊠ *800 Asilomar Blvd., Box 537, 93950,* ☎ *831/372–8016,* FAX *831/372–7227. 314 rooms. Cafeteria, pool. Full breakfast. MC, V.*

Outdoor Activities and Sports

GOLF

The greens fee at the 18-hole **Pacific Grove Municipal Golf Links** (⊠ 77 Asilomar Blvd., ☎ 831/648–3177) runs between $30 and $35 (you can play nine holes for between $15 and $18), with an 18-hole twilight rate of $14. Optional carts cost $25. The course has spectacular ocean views on its back nine—and ice-plant-covered sand dunes that make keeping the ball on the fairway a must. Tee times may be reserved up to seven days in advance.

TENNIS

Pacific Grove Municipal Courts (⊠ 515 Junipero St., ☎ 831/648–3129) are available for public play.

Shopping

American Tin Cannery Outlet Center (⊠ 125 Ocean View Blvd., ☎ 831/ 372–3071) carries designer clothing, jewelry, accessories, and home decorating items at discounts between 25% and 65%. **Wooden Nickel** (⊠ Central and Fountain Aves., ☎ 831/646–8050) sells Victorian accent pieces for the home.

316

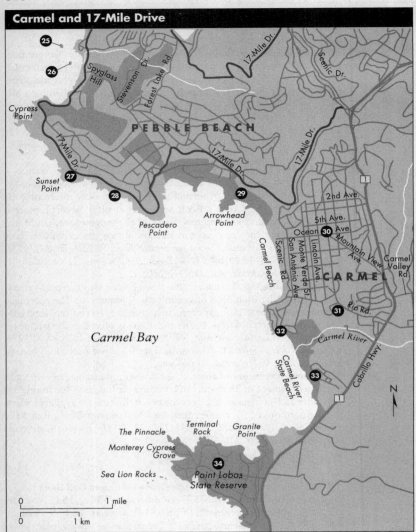

Bird Rock, **25**
Carmel Mission, **31**
Carmel Plaza, **30**
Carmel River State Beach, **33**
Crocker Marble Palace, **28**
Lone Cypress, **27**

Pebble Beach Golf Links, **29**
Point Lobos State Reserve, **34**
Seal Rock, **26**
Tor House, **32**

17-Mile Drive and Pebble Beach

Off Sunset Dr. in Pacific Grove or N. San Antonio Rd. in Carmel.

★ Primordial nature resides in quiet harmony with palatial estates along **17-Mile Drive,** which winds through an 8,400-acre microcosm of the Monterey coastal landscape. Dotting the drive are rare Monterey cypress, trees so gnarled and twisted that Robert Louis Stevenson once described them as "ghosts fleeing before the wind." Some sightseers balk at the $7.25-per-car fee collected at the gates—this is the only private toll road west of the Mississippi—but most find the drive well worth the price. (An alternative is to grab a bike; cyclists tour for free.)

㉕ **Bird Rock,** the largest of several islands at the southern end of the Monterey Country Club's golf course, teems with harbor seals, sea lions,
㉖ cormorants, and pelicans. Sea creatures and birds also make use of **Seal Rock,** the larger of a group of islands south of Bird Rock. The most
㉗ photographed tree along 17-Mile Drive is the weather-sculpted **Lone Cypress** that grows out of a precipitous outcropping above the waves. You can stop for a view of the Lone Cypress at a parking area, but you can't walk out to the tree.

Many of the stately homes along 17-Mile Drive reflect the classic Monterey or Spanish Mission style typical of the region. A standout
㉘ is the **Crocker Marble Palace,** a waterfront estate inspired by a Byzantine castle. This baroque mansion is easily identifiable by its dozens of marble arches.

㉙ The ocean plays a major role in the 18th hole of the famed **Pebble Beach Golf Links** (☞ Outdoor Activities and Sports, *below*). Each winter the course is the main site of the AT&T Pebble Beach Pro-Am, where show-business celebrities and pros team up for one of the nation's most glamorous golf tournaments. Views of the impeccable greens at two tournament golf courses can be enjoyed over a drink or lunch at the Lodge at Pebble Beach or the Inn at Spanish Bay, the pair of resorts located along the drive.

Dining and Lodging

$$$$ ✕🏠 **Inn at Spanish Bay.** This 269-room resort sprawls across a breath-
★ taking stretch of shoreline along 17-Mile Drive. Under the same management as the Lodge at Pebble Beach (☞ *below*), the inn has a slightly more casual feel, though its 600-square-ft rooms are no less luxurious. The inn has its own tennis courts and golf course, but guests also have privileges at all the Lodge facilities. The Bay Club restaurant ($$$; reservations essential), which serves haute Italian cuisine, overlooks the coastline and the golf links. Try Roy's Restaurant for more casual and innovative Euro-Asian fare. ⊠ *2700 17-Mile Dr., Box 1418, Pebble Beach 93953,* ☎ *831/647–7500 or 800/654–9300,* ℻ *831/644–7960. 252 rooms, 17 suites. 3 restaurants, bar, pool, massage, 8 tennis courts, health club, hiking, horseback riding. AE, DC, MC, V.*

$$$$ ✕🏠 **Lodge at Pebble Beach.** Luxurious rooms with fireplaces and
★ wonderful views set the tone at this renowned resort that was built in 1919. The golf course, tennis club, and equestrian center are highly regarded. Guests of the lodge have privileges at the Inn at Spanish Bay. Overlooking the 18th green, the very fine Club XIX restaurant is an intimate, café-style spot serving French cuisine prepared with a light touch. ⊠ *1700 17-Mile Dr., Box 1128, Pebble Beach 93953,* ☎ *831/ 624–3811 or 800/654–9300,* ℻ *831/644–7960. 142 rooms, 19 suites. 3 restaurants, bar, coffee shop, pool, hot tub, massage, sauna, spa, 18-hole golf course, 12 tennis courts, exercise room, health club, horseback riding, beach, bicycles. AE, DC, MC, V.*

Outdoor Activities and Sports

GOLF

The Links at Spanish Bay (⊠ 17-Mile Dr., north end, ☎ 831/624–3811 or 831/624–6611), which hugs a choice stretch of shoreline, is designed in the rugged manner of a traditional Scottish course, with sand dunes and coastal marshes interspersed among the greens. The greens fee is $185, plus $25 cart rental ($165 for resort guests, including cart); nonguests can reserve tee times two months in advance.

Pebble Beach Golf Links (⊠ 17-Mile Dr., ☎ 831/624–3811 or 831/624–6611) attracts golfers from around the world, despite a greens fee of $295, plus $25 for an optional cart ($255 with a complimentary cart for guests of the Pebble Beach or Spanish Bay resorts). Nonguests can reserve a tee time only one day in advance on a space-available basis (up to a year for groups); resort guests can reserve up to 18 months in advance.

Peter Hay (⊠ 17-Mile Dr., ☎ 831/624–3811 or 831/624–6611), a nine-hole par-three course, charges $15 per person, no reservations necessary.

Poppy Hills (⊠ 3200 Lopez Rd. at 17-Mile Dr., ☎ 831/625–2035), a splendid course designed in 1986 by Robert Trent Jones Jr., has a greens fee of $115 to $130; an optional cart costs $30. Individuals may reserve up to one month in advance, groups up to a year.

Spyglass Hill (⊠ Stevenson Dr. and Spyglass Hill Rd., ☎ 831/624–3811 or 831/624–6611) is among the most challenging Pebble Beach courses. With the first five holes bordering on the Pacific and the rest reaching deep into the Del Monte Forest, the views offer some consolation. The greens fee is $225; an optional cart costs $25 ($195 with complimentary cart for resort guests). Reservations are essential and may be made up to one month in advance (18 months for guests).

HORSEBACK RIDING

The **Pebble Beach Equestrian Center** (⊠ Portola Rd. and Alva La., ☎ 831/624–2756) offers guided trail rides along the beach and through the Del Monte Forest, which has 26 mi of bridle trails.

Carmel

5 mi south of Monterey on Hwy. 1 (or via 17-Mile Drive's Carmel Gate).

Although the community has grown quickly through the years and its population quadruples with tourists on weekends and during the summer, Carmel retains its identity as a quaint village. Buildings still have no street numbers, and live music is banned in the local watering holes. You can wander the side streets at your own pace, poking into hidden courtyards and stopping at cafés for tea and crumpets.

Downtown Carmel's chief lure is shopping. Its main street, **Ocean Avenue,** is a mishmash of ersatz English Tudor, Mediterranean, and other styles. **Carmel Plaza,** in the east end of the village proper at Ocean and Junipero avenues, holds more than 50 shops and restaurants.

Before it became an art colony in the early 20th century and long before it became a shopping and browsing mecca, Carmel was an important religious center during the establishment of Spanish California. That heritage is preserved in the Mission San Carlos Borromeo del Rio Carmelo, more commonly known as the **Carmel Mission.** Founded in 1770, it served as headquarters for the mission system in California under Father Junípero Serra. Adjoining the stone church are a tranquil garden planted with California poppies. Museum rooms at the mission include an early kitchen, Serra's spartan sleeping quarters, and the oldest college library in California. ⊠ *3080 Rio Rd. (at Lasuen Dr.),* ☎ *831/624–3600.* ⊞ *$2.* ⊘ *Sept.–May, Mon.–Sat. 9:30–4:30, Sun. 10:30–4:30; June–Aug., Mon.–Sat. 9:30–7:30, Sun. 10:30–7:30.*

Scattered throughout the pines in Carmel are the houses and cottages that were built for writers, artists, and photographers who discovered **❸❷** the area decades ago. Among the most impressive dwellings is **Tor House,** a stone cottage built in 1919 by the poet Robinson Jeffers on a craggy knoll overlooking the sea. Portraits, books, and unusual art objects fill the low-ceiling rooms. The highlight of the small estate is Hawk Tower, a detached edifice set with stones from the Carmel coastline as well as one from the Great Wall of China. The docents who lead tours (six persons maximum) are well informed about the poet's work and life. ⊠ *26304 Ocean View Ave.,* ☎ *831/624–1813 or 831/624–1840.* ⊞ *$7. No children under 12.* ⊘ *Tours Fri. and Sat. 10–3; reservations essential.*

Carmel's greatest beauty is its rugged coastline, with pine and cypress forests and countless inlets. **Carmel Beach,** an easy walk from downtown shops, has sparkling white sands and magnificent sunsets. ⊠ *End of Ocean Ave.*

❸❸ **Carmel River State Beach** stretches for 106 acres along Carmel Bay. On sunny days the waters appear nearly as turquoise as those of the Caribbean. The sugar-white beach is adjacent to a bird sanctuary where you might spot pelicans, kingfishers, hawks, and sandpipers. ⊠ *Off Scenic Rd., south of Carmel Beach,* ☎ *831/624–4909.* ⊘ *Daily 9 AM–sunset.*

★ **❸❹** **Point Lobos State Reserve,** a 350-acre headland harboring a wealth of marine life, lies a few miles south of Carmel. The best way to explore the reserve is to walk along one of its many trails. The Cypress Grove Trail leads through a forest of Monterey cypress (one of only two natural groves remaining), clinging to the rocks above an emerald-green cove. Sea Lion Point Trail is a good place to view sea lions. From those and other trails you may also spot otters, harbor seals, and (during winter and spring) migrating whales. An additional 750 acres of the reserve is an undersea marine park open to qualified scuba divers. Arrive early (or in late afternoon) to avoid crowds; the parking lots fill up. No pets are allowed. ⊠ *Hwy. 1,* ☎ *831/624–4909; 831/624–8413 for scuba-diving reservations.* ⊞ *$7 per vehicle.* ⊘ *May–Sept., daily 9–7; Oct.–Apr., daily 9–5.*

Dining and Lodging

$$$ ✕ **Kincaid's Bistro.** At chef-owner Robert Kincaid's French bistro, ★ dried sage and lavender hanging from exposed ceiling beams, ragpainted floors, and ochre-washed walls will make you feel as if you've stepped into an old farmhouse in Provence. Cassoulet made with white beans, duck confit, rabbit sausage, and garlic prawns is always on the stove and best enjoyed with a rustic red wine; lobster ravioli is another winner. Leave room for dessert, particularly the soufflé with lemon and orange zest or the chocolate bag with chocolate shake, a masterful invention. ⊠ *Crossroads Center, 217 Crossroads Blvd.,* ☎ *831/624–9626. AE, D, MC, V. No lunch weekends.*

$$–$$$ ✕ **Anton and Michel.** Expect superb European cuisine at this elegant restaurant in Carmel's shopping district. The tender lamb dishes are fantastic and well complemented by the wines. The ultimate treats, however, are the flaming desserts. You can dine in the outdoor courtyard in summer. ⊠ *Mission St. and 7th Ave.,* ☎ *831/624–2406. AE, D, DC, MC, V.*

$$–$$$ ✕ **Casanova.** Southern French and northern Italian cuisine come together at Casanova, one of the most romantic restaurants in Carmel. A heated outdoor garden and the more than 1,000 domestic and imported wines enhance the dining experience. The menu changes weekly; highlights include house-made pasta and desserts. All entrées come with an antipasto plate and choice of appetizers. ⊠ *5th Ave. between San Carlos and Mission Sts.,* ☎ *831/625–0501. MC, V.*

$$–$$$ ✕ **French Poodle.** Specialties on the traditional French menu at this intimate restaurant include the duck breast in port and the abalone. The floating island—a meringue and custard combo—for dessert is delicious. ⊠ *Junipero and 5th Aves.,* ☎ *831/624–8643. AE, DC, MC, V. Closed Sun. No lunch.*

$$–$$$ ✕ **Raffaello.** Sparkling Raffaello serves exceptional pasta, seafood, and meat dishes such as Monterey Bay prawns with garlic butter, local sole poached in champagne, and the specialty of the house, veal Piemontese. ⊠ *Mission St. between Ocean and 7th Aves.,* ☎ *831/624–1541. AE, DC, MC, V. Closed Tues. and 1st 2 wks in Jan. No lunch.*

$$–$$$ ✕ **Simpson's.** Warm service and dependable classic American dishes are the hallmarks of this family-run restaurant. An open dining room and tables with flowers and white tablecloths set the mood for grilled steak, fresh seafood, and roasted poultry. Soups, breads, salad dressings, and desserts are all made in-house. ⊠ *San Carlos St. and 5th Ave.,* ☎ *831/624–5755. AE, MC, V. Closed Sun.–Mon. No lunch.*

$–$$$ ✕ **Flaherty's Oyster Bar & Seafood Grill.** These bright and inviting side-by-side fish houses crank out steaming bowls of mussels, clams, cioppino, and crab chowder. Seafood pastas and daily fresh fish selections are also available. The Oyster Bar, with counter seating and a few tables, is the more casual and less expensive of the two restaurants. ⊠ *6th Ave. and San Carlos St.,* ☎ *831/624–0311 (Oyster Bar); 831/625–1500 (Seafood Grill). AE, D, DC, MC, V.*

$–$$$ ✕ **Hog's Breath Inn.** Although resting a bit on its Hollywood laurels, this eatery co-owned by actor and former Carmel mayor Clint Eastwood has a publike atmosphere, with roaring fireplaces and rustic decor. The food is no-nonsense: meat and seafood entrées with sautéed vegetables. Several items—Dirty Harry Burger, Sudden Impact (Polish sausage) sandwich, and so on—are named after Eastwood movies. Reservations are accepted only for parties of 7 or more. ⊠ *San Carlos St. and 5th Ave.,* ☎ *831/625–1044. AE, DC, MC, V.*

$–$$$ ✕ **Il Fornaio at the Pine Inn.** The Carmel branch of the upscale Il Fornaio chain dishes up tasty antipasti, pastas, mesquite-grilled fish, and steak Florentine. Il Fornaio also serves breakfast. All the fresh-baked breads are winners. ⊠ *Ocean Ave. and Monte Verde St.,* ☎ *831/622–5100. AE, D, DC, MC, V.*

$–$$$ ✕ **Lugano Swiss Bistro.** Fondue is the centerpiece here. The house specialty is an original version made with Gruyère, Emmental, and Appenzeller. Rosemary chicken, plum-basted duck, and fennel pork loin rotate on the rotisserie. Ask for a table in the back room, which contains a hand-painted street scene of Lugano. ⊠ *The Barnyard, Hwy. 1 and Carmel Valley Rd.,* ☎ *831/626–3779. AE, MC, V.*

$–$$$ ✕ **Rio Grill.** Don't let its shopping-center location fool you. The Rio
★ Grill is one of the Monterey Peninsula's most appealing restaurants. The best bets in this lively Santa Fe–style setting are the meat and seafood cooked over an oak-wood grill. The fire-roasted artichoke and the Monterey Bay squid are exceptional starters. ⊠ *Crossroads Center, 101 Crossroads Blvd., Hwy. 1 and Rio Rd.,* ☎ *831/625–5436. AE, D, DC, MC, V.*

$$ ✕ **La Bohème.** The chefs at campy La Bohème prepare one entrée each night, accompanied by soup and salad. You may find yourself bumping elbows with your neighbor in the faux-European-village courtyard, but the predominantly French cuisine is delicious, and the atmosphere is convivial. ⊠ *Dolores St. and 7th Ave.,* ☎ *831/624–7500. Reservations not accepted. MC, V. No lunch.*

$–$$ ✕ **Cafe Gringo.** The zesty variations on Mexican cuisine here include the fresh tamales with spinach, zucchini, and mushrooms and the quesadilla with Monterey Jack and manchego cheeses, bacon, and roasted *pasilla* chilies, topped with mango salsa. The bar serves margaritas, Mexican beers, and South American and local wines. Outdoor tables beckon in warm weather. ⊠ *Paseo San Carlos Courtyard, San Carlos St. between Ocean and 7th Aves.,* ☎ *831/626–8226. AE, MC, V.*

$–$$ ✕ **Caffé Napoli.** Redolent of garlic and olive oil, this small, atmospheric Italian restaurant is a favorite of locals, who come for the crisp-crusted pizzas, house-made pastas, and fresh seafood. Specialties include grilled artichokes, fresh salmon and grilled vegetable risotto, and fisherman's pasta. There's a good Italian wine list. ⊠ *Ocean Ave. and Lincoln Ave.,* ☎ *831/625–4033. Reservations essential on weekends. MC, V.*

$ ✕ **Friar Tuck's.** This busy wood-panel coffee shop serves huge omelets at breakfast and dishes up 16 different hamburgers at lunch. ⊠ *5th Ave. and Dolores St.,* ☎ *831/624–4274. Reservations not accepted. MC, V. No dinner.*

$$$$ ✕🏨 **Highlands Inn.** An unparalleled location south of Carmel on high ★ cliffs above the Pacific gives the Highlands views that stand out even in a region famous for them. Accommodations are in plush spa suites and condominium-style units with wood-burning fireplaces and ocean-view decks; some rooms have full kitchens. The contemporary French menu at the inn's excellent Pacific's Edge restaurant ($$$–$$$$) includes roasted rack of lamb with creamy polenta and ratatouille; grilled Atlantic salmon wrapped in pancetta on saffron-infused couscous; and a brick-roasted half chicken with grilled Portobello mushrooms. ⊠ *Hwy. 1, Box 1700, 93921,* ☎ *831/624–3801 or 800/682–4811; 831/622–5445 restaurant;* ℻ *831/626–1574. 102 suites, 40 rooms. 2 restaurants, lounge, refrigerators, pool, 3 hot tubs, bicycles, baby-sitting. AE, D, DC, MC, V.*

$$$$ 🏨 **Carriage House Inn.** This small inn with a wood-shingle exterior has spacious rooms with open-beam ceilings, fireplaces, down comforters, and, in most, whirlpool baths. Continental breakfast and afternoon wine and hors d'oeuvres are included. ⊠ *Junipero Ave. between 7th and 8th Aves., Box 1900, 93921,* ☎ *831/625–2585 or 800/422–4732,* ℻ *831/624–0974. 11 rooms, 2 suites. In-room safes, minibars, refrigerators. Continental breakfast. AE, D, MC, V.*

$$$$ 🏨 **Tickle Pink Inn.** Atop a towering cliff, this inn has views of the Big ★ Sur coastline, which you can contemplate from your private balcony. Fall asleep to the sound of surf crashing below and wake up to Continental breakfast and the morning paper in bed. If you prefer the company of fellow travelers, breakfast is also served buffet-style in the lounge, as are complimentary wine and cheese in the afternoon. Many rooms have wood-burning fireplaces, and there are four luxurious spa suites. ⊠ *155 Highlands Dr., 93923,* ☎ *831/624–1244 or 800/635–4774,* ℻ *831/626–9516. 24 rooms, 11 suites. Refrigerators, outdoor hot tub. Continental breakfast. AE, MC, V.*

$$$–$$$$ 🏨 **Best Western Carmel Mission Inn.** This modern inn on the edge of Carmel Valley has a lushly landscaped pool and hot tub area and is close to the Barnyard and Crossroads shopping centers. Rooms are large, some with spacious decks. ⊠ *3665 Rio Rd., at Hwy. 1, 93923,* ☎ *831/624–1841 or 800/348–9090,* ℻ *831/624–8684. 163 rooms, 2 suites. Restaurant, bar, refrigerators, pool, 2 hot tubs. AE, D, DC, MC, V.*

$$$–$$$$ 🏨 **La Playa Hotel.** Norwegian artist Christopher Jorgensen built this structure in 1902 for his bride, a member of the Ghirardelli chocolate clan. The Terrace Grill and central garden, riotous with color, have vistas of Carmel's magnificent coastline. The rooms are done in pale terracotta with green and blue accents and contain hand-carved furniture. Some accommodations have ocean views. You can also opt for a cottage; most have full kitchens and wood-burning fireplaces, and all have a patio or a terrace. ⊠ *Camino Real at 8th Ave., Box 900, 93921,* ☎ *831/624–6476 or 800/582–8900,* FAX *831/624–7966. 75 rooms, 5 cottages. Restaurant, bar, pool, laundry service. AE, DC, MC, V.*

$$–$$$$ 🏨 **Carmel River Inn.** Besides attracting those looking for a relative bargain in pricey Carmel, this half-century-old inn appeals to travelers who enjoy a bit of distance from the madding crowd—downtown Carmel in July, for instance. Yet the area's beaches are only 1½ mi away. The blue and white motel at the front of the property contains units with cable TV, small refrigerators, and coffeemakers. Cabins out back sleep up to six; some have fireplaces and kitchens. ⊠ *Hwy. 1 at Carmel River Bridge, Box 221609, 93922,* ☎ *831/624–1575 or 800/882–8142,* FAX *831/624–0290. 19 rooms, 24 cabins. Pool. MC, V.*

$$–$$$$ 🏨 **Cobblestone Inn.** Thick quilts and country antiques, stone fireplaces
★   in guest rooms and the sitting-room area, and a complimentary breakfast buffet and afternoon tea contribute to the homey feel at this English-style inn. ⊠ *8th and Junipero Aves., Box 3185, 93921,* ☎ *831/625–5222 or 800/833–8836,* FAX *831/625–0478. 22 rooms, 2 suites. Refrigerators. Full breakfast. AE, DC, MC, V. No smoking indoors.*

$$–$$$$ 🏨 **Cypress Inn.** When Doris Day became part owner of this inn in 1988, she added her own touches, such as posters from her many movies and photo albums of her favorite canines. (Pets are welcome in most rooms here.) In nice weather, you can enjoy the complimentary Continental breakfast in a garden courtyard surrounded by bougainvillea. ⊠ *Lincoln and 7th Aves., Box Y, 93921,* ☎ *831/624–3871 or 800/443–7443,* FAX *831/624–8216. 33 rooms, 1 suite. Refrigerators. Continental breakfast. AE, D, MC, V. 2-night minimum weekends.*

$$–$$$$ 🏨 **Lobos Lodge.** The white stucco units here are set amid cypress, oaks, and pines on the edge of the business district. All accommodations have fireplaces and some have private patios. ⊠ *Monte Verde St. and Ocean Ave., Box L–1, 93921,* ☎ *831/624–3874,* FAX *831/624–0135. 28 rooms, 2 suites. Refrigerators. Continental breakfast. AE, MC, V.*

$$–$$$$ 🏨 **Mission Ranch.** Sheep graze in the ocean-side pasture near the main 19th-century farmhouse at Mission Ranch. The six rooms in the main house are set around a Victorian parlor; other options include cottages, a hayloft, and a bunkhouse. Handmade quilts, stuffed mattresses, and carved wooden beds lend all of the accommodations a country ambience. ⊠ *26270 Dolores St., 93923,* ☎ *831/624–6436 or 800/538–8221,* FAX *831/626–4163. 31 rooms. Restaurant, piano bar, 6 tennis courts, exercise room, pro shop. MC, V.*

$$–$$$$ 🏨 **Pine Inn.** A favorite of generations of Carmel visitors, the Pine Inn
★   has Victorian-style decor, complete with grandfather clock, padded fabric wall panels, antique tapestries, and marble-topped furnishings. Only four blocks from the beach, the complex includes a brick courtyard of specialty shops and an Italian restaurant, Il Fornaio (*see above*). ⊠ *Ocean and Lincoln Aves., Box 250, 93921,* ☎ *831/624–3851 or 800/228–3851,* FAX *831/624–3030. 43 rooms, 6 suites. Restaurant. AE, D, DC, MC, V.*

$$–$$$$ 🏨 **Tally Ho Inn.** This inn with an English garden courtyard is one of the few in Carmel's center with good views of the ocean. The penthouse units have fireplaces. ⊠ *Monte Verde St. and 6th Ave., Box 3726, 93921,* ☎ *831/624–2232 or 800/624–2290,* FAX *831/624–2661. 12 rooms, 2 suites. Continental breakfast. AE, D, DC, MC, V.*

Nightlife and the Arts

MUSIC

Carmel Bach Festival (☎ 831/624–2046) has presented the works of Johann Sebastian Bach and his contemporaries in concerts and recitals since 1935. The festival runs for 23 days, starting in mid-July. **Monterey County Symphony** (☎ 831/624–8511) performs concerts—from classical to pop—from September through May in Salinas and Carmel.

THEATER

Pacific Repertory Theater (☎ 831/622–0700) specializes in contemporary comedy and drama. **Sunset Community Cultural Center** (⊠ San Carlos St. between 8th and 10th Aves., ☎ 831/624–3996), which presents concerts, lectures, and headline performers, is the Monterey Bay area's top venue for the performing arts.

Shopping

ART GALLERIES

Carmel Art Association (⊠ Dolores St. between 5th and 6th Aves., ☎ 831/624–6176) exhibits the paintings, sculpture, and prints of local artists. **Cottage Gallery** (⊠ Mission St. and 6th Ave., ☎ 831/624–7888) focuses on representational art, sculpture, and heirloom-quality collectible furniture. **Highlands Sculpture Gallery** (⊠ Dolores St. between 5th and 6th Aves., ☎ 831/624–0535) is devoted to indoor and outdoor sculpture, primarily works done in stone, bronze, wood, metal, and glass. **Masterpiece Gallery** (⊠ Dolores St. and 6th Ave., ☎ 831/624–2163) shows California Impressionist and Bay Area figurative art. **Photography West Gallery** (⊠ Ocean Ave. and Dolores St., ☎ 831/625–1587) exhibits photography by Ansel Adams and other 20th-century artists.

CHILDREN

Mischievous Rabbit (⊠ Lincoln Ave. between 7th and Ocean Aves., ☎ 831/624–6854) sells toys, nursery bedding, books, music boxes, china, and children's clothing, with a specialty in Beatrix Potter items.

CLOTHING AND ACCESSORIES

Madrigal (⊠ Carmel Plaza and Mission St., ☎ 831/624–3477) carries sportswear, sweaters, and accessories for women and men. **Pat Areias Sterling** (⊠ Lincoln Ave., between Ocean and 7th Aves., ☎ 831/626–8668) puts a respectfully modern spin on the Mexican tradition of silversmithing in its line of sterling silver belt buckles, jewelry, and accessories.

GARDEN

Shop in the Garden (⊠ Lincoln Ave. between Ocean and 7th Aves., ☎ 831/624–6047) is an indoor-outdoor sculpture garden where you can buy fountains or garden accoutrements. You'll hear the babble of its outdoor fountains and tinkle of its wind chimes before you see the courtyard establishment.

Carmel Valley

35 *5 to 10 mi east of Carmel, Hwy. 1 to Carmel Valley Rd.*

Carmel Valley Road, which turns inland at Highway 1 south of Carmel, is the main thoroughfare through the town of Carmel Valley, a secluded enclave of horse ranchers and other well-heeled residents who prefer the area's sunny climate to the fog and wind on the coast. Tiny Carmel Valley village holds several crafts shops and art galleries. **Garland Ranch Regional Park** (⊠ Carmel Valley Rd., 9 mi east of Carmel, ☎ 831/659–4488) has hiking trails and picnic tables.

The beautiful **Château Julien** winery, recognized internationally for its chardonnays and merlots, gives tours on weekdays at 10:30 and 2:30 and weekends at 12:30 and 2:30, all by appointment. The tasting room is open daily. ⊠ *8940 Carmel Valley Rd.,* ☎ *831/624–2600.* ☉ *Weekdays 8–5, weekends 11–5.*

Dining and Lodging

$

★ ✕ **Wagon Wheel Coffee Shop.** Grab a seat at the counter or wait for a table at this local hangout decorated with wood-beam ceilings, hanging wagon wheels, cowboy hats, and lassos. Then chow down on huge breakfasts of huevos rancheros, Italian sausage and eggs, or trout and eggs; this is also the place to stoke up on biscuits and gravy. For lunch choose among a dozen types of burgers or other sandwiches. ⊠ *Valley Hill Center, Carmel Valley Rd. next to Quail Lodge,* ☎ *831/624– 8878. No credit cards. No dinner.*

$$$$

★ ✕🏨 **Quail Lodge.** Guests at this resort on the grounds of a private country club have access to golf, tennis, and an 850-acre wildlife preserve frequented by deer and migratory fowl. Modern rooms with European decor are clustered in several low-rise buildings. Each room has a private deck or patio overlooking the golf course, gardens, or a lake. The Covey at Quail Lodge ($$$–$$$$; jacket required; no lunch) serves European cuisine in a romantic lakeside setting. The menu changes daily, but look for rack of lamb, mustard-crusted salmon, and mousseline of sole, all accompanied by fresh local produce. ⊠ *8205 Valley Greens Dr., 93923,* ☎ *831/624–1581 or 800/538–9516,* 🆝 *831/624–3726. 86 rooms, 14 suites. 2 restaurants, 2 bars, room service, 2 pools, hot tub, sauna, 18-hole golf course, putting greens, 4 tennis courts, hiking, bicycles, concierge. AE, DC, MC, V.*

$$$$

★ 🏨 **Carmel Valley Ranch Resort.** This all-suites resort, well off Carmel Valley Road on a hill overlooking the valley, is a stunning piece of contemporary California architecture. Down-home touches include handmade quilts, wood-burning fireplaces, and watercolors by local artists. Rooms have cathedral ceilings, oversize decks, and fully stocked wet bars. The greens fee for guests at the resort's 18-hole golf course is $145, including cart rental; special golf packages can reduce this rate considerably. ⊠ *1 Old Ranch Rd., 93923,* ☎ *831/625–9500 or 800/422– 7635,* 🆝 *831/624–2858. 100 suites. 2 restaurants, 2 pools, 2 hot tubs, sauna, 18-hole golf course, 13 tennis courts. AE, DC, MC, V.*

$$$$

🏨 **Stonepine Estate Resort.** The former estate of the Crocker banking family has been converted to an ultradeluxe inn nestled in 330 pastoral acres. The oak-paneled, antiques-laden main chateau holds eight elegantly furnished rooms and suites and a private dining room for guests only. The property's romantic cottages include one that is straight out of *Hansel and Gretel.* An equestrian center offers riding lessons. ⊠ *150 E. Carmel Valley Rd., Box 1543, 93924,* ☎ *831/659–2245,* 🆝 *831/ 659–5160. 8 rooms, 4 suites, 2 cottages. Dining room, minibars, room service, in-room VCRs, 2 pools, 2 tennis courts, archery, exercise room, hiking, horseback riding, mountain bikes, library. Full breakfast; MAP available. AE, MC, V.*

$$$–$$$$

🏨 **Carmel Valley Lodge.** In this small inn there are rooms surrounding a garden patio and separate one- and two-bedroom cottages with fireplaces and full kitchens. ⊠ *8 Ford Rd., at Carmel Valley Rd., Box 93, 93924,* ☎ *831/659–2261 or 800/641–4646,* 🆝 *831/659–4558. 19 rooms, 4 suites, 8 cottages. Pool, hot tub, sauna, exercise room. Continental breakfast. AE, MC, V.*

Outdoor Activities and Sports

GOLF

Golf Club at Quail Lodge (⊠ 8000 Valley Greens Dr., ☎ 831/624–2770) incorporates several lakes into its course. Depending on the season and day of the week, greens fees range from $105 to $125 for guests, and $125 to $165 for nonguests, including cart rental. **Rancho Cañada Golf Club** (⊠ 4860 Carmel Valley Rd., 1 mi east of Hwy. 1, ☎ 831/624–0111) is a public course with 36 holes, some of them overlooking the Carmel River. Fees range from $30 to $75, plus $32 cart rental, depending on course and tee time selected.

Salinas

36 *17 mi east of the Monterey Peninsula on Hwy. 68; from Carmel Valley Rd. take Laureles Grade north to Hwy. 68.*

Salinas is the population center of a rich agricultural valley where fertile soil, an ideal climate, and a good underground water supply produce optimum growing conditions for crops such as lettuce, broccoli, tomatoes, strawberries, flowers, and wine grapes. This unpretentious town may lack the sophistication and scenic splendors of the coast, but it will interest literary and architectural buffs. Turn-of-the-century buildings have been the focus of ongoing renovation, much of it centered on the original downtown area of South Main Street, with its handsome stone storefronts. The memory and literary legacy of Salinas native (and winner of the Pulitzer and Nobel prizes) John Steinbeck are well honored here.

The **National Steinbeck Center** is a museum and archive dedicated to the life and works of John Steinbeck. Many exhibits are interactive, bringing to life Steinbeck worlds such as Cannery Row, Hooverville (from *The Grapes of Wrath*), and the Mexican Plaza (from *The Pearl*). The library and archives contain Steinbeck first editions, notebooks, photographs, and audiotapes. Access to the archives is by appointment only. The center has information about Salinas' annual Steinbeck Festival in August and about tours of area landmarks mentioned in his novels. ⊠ *1 Main St.,* ☎ *831/796–3833.* ☞ *$7.* ☉ *Daily 10–5.*

The **Jose Eusebio Boronda Adobe** contains furniture and artifacts depicting the lifestyle of Spanish California in the 1840s. Call for directions. ⊠ *333 Boronda Rd.,* ☎ *831/757–8085.* ☞ *Free (donation requested).* ☉ *Weekdays 10–2, Sun. 1–4.*

Dining

$–$$ ✕ **Spado's.** One of several trendy new restaurants in Salinas, gleaming Spado's brings Monterey-style culinary sophistication to the valley. For lunch, visit the antipasto bar for fresh salads and Mediterranean morsels; the *panini* (Italian sandwiches) are also excellent. For dinner, try the pizza with chicken and sun-dried-tomato pesto, the angel-hair pasta and prawns, or the risotto of the day. ⊠ *66 W. Alisal St.,* ☎ *831/424–4139. AE, D, DC, MC, V. No lunch weekends.*

$ ✕ **Steinbeck House.** John Steinbeck's birthplace, a Victorian frame house, has been converted into a lunch-only (11:30 AM–2 PM) eatery run by the volunteer Valley Guild. The restaurant displays some Steinbeck memorabilia. The set menu incorporates locally grown produce. ⊠ *132 Central Ave.,* ☎ *831/424–2735. MC, V. Closed Sun. and 3 wks in late Dec. and early Jan.*

Outdoor Activities and Sports

The **California Rodeo** (☎ 831/757–2951), one of the oldest and most famous rodeos in the West, takes place in mid-July.

San Juan Bautista

❸ *18 mi north of Salinas on U.S. 101, then 2 mi east on Hwy. 156.*

Sleepy San Juan Bautista, protected from development since 1933, when much of it became ★**San Juan Bautista State Historic Park,** is about as close to early 19th-century California as you can get. On Living History Day, which takes place on the first Saturday of each month, costumed volunteers engage in quilting bees, tortilla making, butter churning, and other period activities. ✉ *2nd and Franklin Sts., off Hwy. 156,* ☎ *831/623–4881.* ▤ *$2.* ☉ *Daily 10–4:30.*

The centerpiece of San Juan Bautista is a wide, green plaza ringed by historic buildings: a restored blacksmith shop, a stable, a pioneer cabin, and a jailhouse. Running along one side of the square is **Mission San Juan Bautista,** a long, low, colonnaded structure founded by Father Fermin Lasuen in 1797. Adjoining it is Mission Cemetery, where more than 4,300 Native Americans who converted to Christianity are buried in unmarked graves. ✉ *408 S. 2nd St.,* ☎ *831/623–2127.* ▤ *$2.* ☉ *Mon.–Sat. 9:30–5, Sun. 10–5.*

After the mission era, San Juan Bautista became an important crossroads for stagecoach travel. The principal stop in town was the **Plaza Hotel,** a collection of adobe buildings with furnishings from the 1860s. The **Castro-Breen Adobe,** furnished with Spanish colonial antiques, presents a view of domestic life in the village. It is next to the Plaza Hotel.

Shopping
Small antiques shops and art galleries line San Juan Bautista's side streets.

MONTEREY BAY A TO Z

Arriving and Departing

By Bus
Greyhound Lines (☎ 800/231–2222) serves Monterey from San Francisco three times daily. The trip takes about 4½ hours.

By Car
The drive south from San Francisco to Monterey can be made comfortably in three hours or less. The most scenic way is to follow Highway 1 down the coast past flower, pumpkin, and artichoke fields and the seaside communities of Pacifica, Half Moon Bay, and Santa Cruz. Unless you drive on sunny weekends when locals are heading for the beach, the two-lane coast highway may take no longer than the freeway.

A sometimes faster route is I–280 south from San Francisco to Highway 17, south of San Jose. Highway 17 crosses the redwood-filled Santa Cruz mountains between San Jose and Santa Cruz, where it intersects with Highway 1. The traffic can crawl to a standstill, however, heading into Santa Cruz. Another option is to follow U.S. 101 south through San Jose to Salinas and then take Highway 68 west to Monterey; the latter part passes through rolling hills.

From Los Angeles, the drive to Monterey can be made in five to six hours by heading north on U.S. 101 to Salinas and then heading west on Highway 68. The spectacular but slow alternative is to take U.S. 101 to San Luis Obispo and then follow the hairpin turns of Highway 1 up the coast. Allow about three extra hours if you take this route.

By Plane
Monterey Peninsula Airport (⊠ 200 Fred Kane Dr., ☎ 831/648–7000) is 3 mi east of downtown Monterey—on Highway 68 to Olmsted Road—and is served by American Eagle, Skywest-Delta, United, United Express, and US Airways Express. *See* Air Travel *in* Smart Travel Tips A to Z for airline phone numbers.

By Train
The **Amtrak** (☎ 800/872–7245) *Coast Starlight,* which runs between Los Angeles, Oakland, and Seattle, stops in Salinas (⊠ 11 Station Pl.). Connecting Amtrak Thruway buses serve Monterey and Carmel.

Getting Around

By Bus
Monterey–Salinas Transit (☎ 831/424–7695) provides frequent service between the peninsula's towns and many major sightseeing spots and shopping areas. The base fare is $1.50, with an additional $1.50 for each zone you travel into. A day pass costs from $3 to $6, depending on how many zones you'll be traveling through. The transit company runs the **WAVE shuttle,** which links major attractions on the Monterey waterfront. The shuttle operates daily between Memorial Day and Labor Day from 9 AM to 6:30 PM. The fare is $1 per day for unlimited rides.

By Car
Highway 1 runs north–south, linking the towns of Santa Cruz, Monterey, and Carmel. Highway 68 runs northeast from Pacific Grove toward Salinas, which U.S. 101 bisects. North of Salinas, U.S. 101 links up with Highway 156 to San Juan Bautista. Parking is especially difficult in Carmel and in heavily touristed areas of Monterey.

Contacts and Resources

B & B Reservations Services
Monterey Peninsula Reservations (☎ 888/655–3424). **Santa Cruz County Bed and Breakfast Referral Service** (☎ 831/425–8212). **Time to Coast Reservations** (☎ 800/555–9283).

Doctors
Community Hospital of Monterey Peninsula (⊠ 23625 Holman Hwy., Monterey, ☎ 831/624–5311). **Monterey County Medical Society** (☎ 831/655–1019).

Emergencies
Ambulance (☎ 911). **Fire** (☎ 911). **Police** (☎ 911).

Guided Tours
California Parlor Car Tours (☎ 415/474–7500 or 800/227–4250) operates motor-coach tours from San Francisco to Los Angeles that include the Monterey Peninsula. **Rider's Guide** (⊠ 484 Lake Park Ave., Suite 255, Oakland 94610, ☎ 510/653–2553) produces a self-guided audiotape tour detailing the history, landmarks, and attractions of the Monterey Peninsula and Big Sur for $12.95 plus $2.50 postage and, for California residents, sales tax.

Pharmacy
The pharmacy at **Surf 'n' Sand** (⊠ 6th and Junipero Aves., Carmel, ☎ 831/624–1543) is open on weekdays from 9 to 7, Saturday and holidays from 9 to 2.

Visitor Information

Monterey Peninsula Visitors and Convention Bureau (✉ 380 Alvarado St., Monterey 93942, ☎ 831/649–1770). **Monterey County Vintners and Growers Association** (☎ 831/375–9400). **Salinas Valley Chamber of Commerce** (✉ 119 E. Alisal St., Salinas 93901, ☎ 831/424–7611). **Santa Cruz County Conference and Visitors Council** (✉ 701 Front St., Santa Cruz 95060, ☎ 831/425–1234 or 800/833–3494). **Santa Cruz Mountain Winegrowers Association** (☎ 831/479–9463).

10 THE CENTRAL COAST

From Big Sur to Santa Barbara

Highway 1 between Big Sur and Santa Barbara is a spectacular stretch of terrain. The curving road demands an unhurried pace, but even if it didn't, you'd find yourself stopping often to take in the scenery. Don't expect much in the way of dining, lodging, or even history until you arrive at Hearst Castle, publisher William Randolph Hearst's testament to his own fabulousness. Sunny, well-scrubbed Santa Barbara's Spanish-Mexican heritage is reflected in the architectural style of its courthouse and mission.

THE COASTLINE BETWEEN CARMEL and Santa Barbara, a distance of about 200 mi, is one of the most popular drives in California. Except for a few smallish cities—Ventura and Santa Barbara in the south and San Luis Obispo in the north—the area is sparsely populated. Grazing cattle dot the countryside, whose human inhabitants relish their isolation at the sharp edge of land and sea. Around Big Sur the Santa Lucia mountains drop down to the Pacific with dizzying grandeur, but as you move south, the shoreline gradually flattens into the long, sandy beaches of Santa Barbara and Ventura.

Updated by
Sasha
Abramsky

Artists create and sell their works in towns like Cambria and Ojai. The wineries of the Santa Ynez Valley are steadily building reputations for quality vintages. The Danish town of Solvang is an amusing stopover for hearty Scandinavian fare and an architectural change of pace. Santa Barbara, only 95 mi north of Los Angeles, is your introduction to the unhurried hospitality and easy living of southern California. Santa Barbara's setting, climate, and architecture produce a Mediterranean feel and pace.

Pleasures and Pastimes

Dining

The Central Coast from Big Sur to Solvang is far enough off the interstate to ensure that nearly every restaurant or café has its own personality—from chic to down-home and funky. There aren't many restaurants between Big Sur and Hearst Castle. Cambria's cooks, true to the town's British-Welsh origins, craft English dishes complete with peas and Yorkshire pudding but also serve Continental and contemporary fare.

The dishes of Santa Barbara's chefs rival those of their counterparts in the state's larger centers. Fresh seafood is plentiful, prepared old-style American in longtime wharf-side hangouts or with trendier accents at newer eateries. If you're after good, cheap food with an international flavor, follow the locals to Milpas Avenue on the eastern edge of Santa Barbara's downtown. Dining attire on the Central Coast is generally casual, though slightly dressy casual wear is the custom at the expensive to very expensive restaurants listed below.

CATEGORY	COST*
$$$$	over $40
$$$	$30–$40
$$	$20–$30
$	under $20

*per person for a three-course meal, excluding drinks, service, and 7¼%–7¾% sales tax

Lodging

Big Sur has only a few lodgings, but even its budget accommodations have character. Many moderately priced hotels and motels—some nicer than others, but most of them basic places to hang your hat—can be found between San Simeon and San Luis Obispo. Wherever you stay, make reservations for the summer well ahead of time.

CATEGORY	COST*
$$$$	over $200
$$$	$125–$200
$$	$75–$125
$	under $75

*All prices are for a standard double room, excluding 9%–10% tax.

Missions

Three important California missions established by Franciscan friars are within the Central Coast region. La Purisima is the most fully restored, Mission Santa Barbara is perhaps the most beautiful of the state's 21 missions, and Mission San Luis Obispo de Tolosa has a fine museum with many Chumash Indian artifacts.

Wineries

Centered in the Solvang area and spreading north toward San Luis Obispo and south toward Santa Barbara is a wine-making region with much of the variety but none of the glitz or crowds of northern California's Napa Valley. The many wineries in the rolling hills of the Santa Maria and Santa Ynez valleys tend to be small, but most have tasting rooms (some have tours), and you'll often meet the wine makers themselves. There are maps and brochures at the visitor centers in Solvang, San Luis Obispo, and Santa Barbara, or you can contact the wine associations of Paso Robles and Santa Barbara (☞ Contacts and Resources *in* The Central Coast A to Z, *below*).

Exploring the Central Coast

Numbers in the text correspond to numbers in the margin and on the Central Coast and Santa Barbara maps.

Great Itineraries

Driving is the easiest way to experience the Central Coast. The three-day itinerary below is arranged in two ways: as a loop from San Francisco or from Los Angeles. The seven-day trip is organized from north to south.

IF YOU HAVE 3 DAYS

Especially in the summertime, make reservations for a visit to Hearst Castle well before you depart for the coast. From Los Angeles maximize your time by taking U.S. 101 directly to **San Luis Obispo** ⑩. North of town, poke your head into the kitschy **Madonna Inn.** Continue on to **Mission San Luis Obispo de Tolosa** and the nearby **County Historical Museum.** Drive west on Highway 46 and north on Highway 1 and stay overnight in 🏨 **Cambria.** Take a morning tour of **Hearst Castle** ⑦, spend some time viewing the exhibits at the visitor center, and then drive up to **Nepenthe** ⑤ in **Big Sur,** for a late lunch. After lunch, head south on U.S. 101 to 🏨 **Santa Barbara** ⑮–㉙. Spend the late afternoon and early evening exploring **Stearns Wharf** ⑰ and other waterfront sights. The next morning, tour the **Santa Barbara County Courthouse** ㉔ and **Mission Santa Barbara** ㉘. In the afternoon, stroll **State Street** if you like to shop, or catch some rays at **East Beach** ⑲. From San Francisco, drive down the coast to **Big Sur.** Have lunch at **Nepenthe,** ⑤ and continue south to 🏨 **Cambria.** The next day, tour **Hearst Castle,** ⑦ drive through **Morro Bay** and **San Luis Obispo** ⑩ and on to **Santa Barbara** ⑮–㉙. Spend the night and explore town the next morning.

IF YOU HAVE 7 DAYS

Make 🏨 **Big Sur** your destination for the first day and most of the second. If you're in the area on a weekend, tour the **Point Sur Light Station** ②. Watch the waves break on **Pfeiffer Beach** ④, one of the few places where you can actually set foot on the shore. Observe the glories of **Los Padres National Forest** up close by hiking one of the many trails in the **Ventana Wilderness,** or stay along the shore and hunt for jade at **Jade Cove.** Plan to reach 🏨 **Cambria** by the evening of day two. Have dinner and explore the town's shops.

The Central Coast

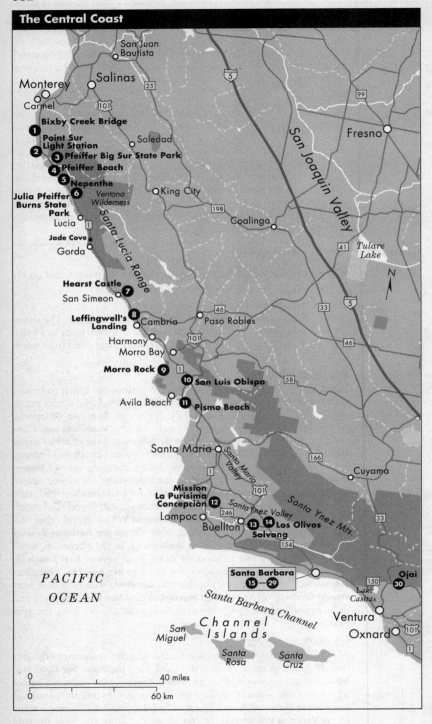

PACIFIC OCEAN

Monterey
Carmel

Salinas

San Juan Bautista

Soledad

① **Bixby Creek Bridge**

② **Point Sur Light Station**

③ **Pfeiffer Big Sur State Park**

④ **Pfeiffer Beach**

⑤ **Nepenthe**

⑥ **Julia Pfeiffer Burns State Park**

Ventana Wilderness

King City

Lucia

Gorda

Jade Cove

Santa Lucia Range

Coalinga

San Joaquin Valley

Fresno

Tulare Lake

⑦ **Hearst Castle**
San Simeon

⑧ **Leffingwell's Landing**
Cambria

Harmony

Morro Bay

⑨ **Morro Rock**

Paso Robles

⑩ **San Luis Obispo**

Avila Beach

⑪ **Pismo Beach**

Santa Maria

Santa Maria Valley

Cuyama

⑫ **Mission La Purisima Concepción**

Lompoc

Santa Ynez Valley

Buellton

⑬ **Los Olivos**

⑭ **Solvang**

Santa Ynez Mts.

Santa Barbara
⑮ — ㉙

Ojai
㉚

Lake Casitas

Ventura

Oxnard

Santa Barbara Channel

Channel Islands

San Miguel

Santa Rosa

Santa Cruz

N

0   40 miles
0   60 km

On day three, have a beachfront breakfast at **Morro Bay,** tour **Hearst Castle** ⑦, have lunch, and take U.S. 101 south to Highway 246 west to get to **Mission La Purisima Concepción** ⑫. Loop back east on Highway 246 to U.S. 101 and head south to 🏨 **Santa Barbara** ⑮–㉙. On day four, visit **Stearns Wharf** ⑰ and walk or bike to **East Beach** ⑲ and the **Andree Clark Bird Refuge** ⑳. Have dinner on **State Street** and check out the area's shops and clubs. On your fifth day, get a feel for the city's architecture, history, and vegetation at, respectively, the **Santa Barbara County Courthouse** ㉔, **Mission Santa Barbara** ㉘, and the **Santa Barbara Botanic Garden** ㉗. Have dinner in **Montecito** and explore the Coast Village Road shopping district. It's a short walk south from here to the shore to catch the sunset before or after you eat. On your sixth day, experience the area's marine life on a half-day cruise of the **Channel Islands.** On day seven, take U.S. 101 south to Highway 150 east to reach 🏨 **Ojai** ㉚.

When to Tour the Central Coast

The Central Coast is hospitable most of the year. Fog often rolls in north of Pismo Beach during the summer; you'll need a jacket, especially after sunset, close to the shore. The rains usually come between December and March. Santa Barbara is pleasant year-round. Hotel rooms fill up in the summer, but from April to early June and in the early fall the weather is almost as fine and it's less hectic. Most hotels offer considerable discounts during the winter.

HIGHWAY 1 TO SOLVANG

Big Sur, San Simeon, and San Luis Obispo

Big Sur

152 mi from San Francisco, south on I–280 and U.S. 101, west on Hwy. 68 and south on Hwy. 1; 27 mi south of Monterey on Hwy. 1.

Long a retreat of artists and writers, Big Sur contains ancient forests and a rugged coastline that residents have protected from overdevelopment. Much of the area lies within several state parks and the more than 165,000-acre **Ventana Wilderness,** itself part of the Los Padres National Forest. The counterculture spirit of Big Sur is evident today in tie-dyed clothing some locals wear and the presence of the Esalen Institute, a mecca of the human growth-potential movement. Established in 1910 as a haven with curative baths, Esalen exploded in the 1960s as a place to explore consciousness, environmental issues, and nude bathing.

❶ The graceful arc of **Bixby Creek Bridge** (✉ Hwy. 1, 13 mi south of Carmel) is a photographer's dream. From the parking area on the north side you can take a photo or begin a walk across the 550-ft span.

★ ❷ **Point Sur Light Station,** a century-old beacon, stands watch from atop a sandstone cliff. Four lighthouse keepers lived here with their families. Their homes and working spaces are open to the public on 2½- to 3-hour, ranger-led tours. Considerable walking is involved. ✉ *Point Sur State Historical Park, Hwy. 1, 19 mi south of Carmel,* ☎ *831/625–4419.* 🎟 *$5.* ⊙ *Tours generally Sat. 10 AM and 2 PM, Sun. 10 AM, plus Apr.–Oct., Wed. 10 and 2; call ahead to confirm.*

❸ A short hiking trail at **Pfeiffer Big Sur State Park** leads up a redwood-filled valley to a waterfall. You can go back the same (easier) way or continue on the trail and take a loop that leads you along the valley wall, with views of the tops of the redwood trees you were just walking among. Stop in at the **Big Sur Station**, west of the park entrance, for information about the entire area. ✉ *Hwy. 1, 8½ mi south of Point Sur Light Station,* ☎ *831/667–2315.* ✑ *$6 per vehicle (day use).* ☉ *Daily sunrise–sunset.*

❹ Through a hole in one of the big rocks at secluded **Pfeiffer Beach** you can watch the waves break first on the sea side and then again on the beach side. ✉ *Off Hwy. 1; the 2-mi road to beach is immediately past Big Sur Station.* ✑ *$6 per vehicle (day use).*

❺ **Nepenthe** (✉ Hwy. 1, 2½ mi south of Big Sur Station) overlooks lush meadows to the ocean below. The house was once owned by Orson Welles and Rita Hayworth, though one of his biographers writes that they spent little time here. Downstairs from the on-site restaurant and café is a crafts and gift shop displaying, among other items, the work of the acclaimed fabric designer Kaffe Fassett, who grew up at Nepenthe.

❻ **Julia Pfeiffer Burns State Park** has some fine hiking trails. Summertime crowds lessen the appeal of the big attraction here, the coastal **MyWay Falls**, but you'll still get an idea why the park's namesake, a pioneer woman whose father was among the first white settlers in the Big Sur area, liked to sit near the falls to contemplate nature. A ½-mi path leads to a bluff with marvelous ocean views; the 6-mi Ewoldsen Trail loop, a fairly strenuous hike, winds through a cross section of the region's plant life. *Hwy. 1, 12 mi south of Big Sur Station,* ☎ *831/667–2315.* ✑ *$6.* ☉ *Daily sunrise–sunset.*

Dining, Lodging, and Camping

$$$–$$$$ ✕ **Nepenthe.** You'll not find a grander coastal view between San Francisco and Los Angeles than the one from here. The American food—burgers, sandwiches, and salads at lunchtime—is overpriced. The superb location is the draw. Don't bother coming after dark. Nepenthe serves dinner, too; the outdoor Café Kevah serves breakfast and lunch. ✉ *Hwy. 1, south end of town,* ☎ *831/667–2345. AE, MC, V.*

$$ ✕ **Ragged Point Inn.** A good place to lunch on the way into or out of the area's parks, this restaurant perched over the southernmost end of Big Sur is not as fancy as the places farther north. But neither are the prices, and the food—sandwiches, salads, pastas, and fish and meat dishes—is tasty. ✉ *Hwy. 1, 16 mi north of San Simeon,* ☎ *805/927–5708. AE, D, MC, V.*

$$$$ ✕▥ **Post Ranch Inn.** This luxurious retreat is the ultimate in environ-
★ mentally conscious architecture. The redwood guest houses, all with dizzyingly splendid views of the Pacific Ocean or the mountains, blend unobtrusively into a wooded cliff 1,200 ft above the ocean. Each unit, done in a spare style, has its own spa tub, fireplace, stereo, private deck, and massage table. A refrigerator holds free snacks. On-site activities include everything from guided hikes to tarot-card readings. The inn's restaurant, which serves cutting-edge American food, is the best in the area. ✉ *Hwy. 1, Box 219, 93920,* ☎ *831/667–2200 or 800/527–2200,* 🅵🅰🆇 *831/667–2512 or 831/687–2824. 30 units. Restaurant, bar, 2 pools, spa, exercise room, library. Continental breakfast. AE, MC, V.*

$$$$ ✕▥ **Ventana Inn.** The activities at this quintessential California get-
★ away are purposely limited to sunning at poolside—there is a cloth-ing-optional deck—and walks in the hills nearby. Buildings that blend into the rugged surroundings are scattered in clusters on a wooded hill-side above the Pacific. Rooms have natural-wood walls and cool tile floors. Some of the more expensive ones have private hot tubs on their patios. The Ventana Restaurant serves contemporary California cuisine with Continental influences. For a real event, come here for week-end brunch on the terrace, with spectacular views over golden hills down

to the ocean. ⊠ *Hwy. 1, 93920,* ☎ *831/667–2331 or 800/628–6500,* ℻ *831/667–2419. 59 rooms, 3 houses. Restaurant, 2 pools, 2 Japanese baths, sauna, exercise room. Continental breakfast. AE, D, DC, MC, V. 2-night minimum stay on weekends and holidays.*

$–$$$ ✕▣ **Big Sur River Inn.** The Big Sur River flows past the forested grounds of this old wooden structure. Guests often sip afternoon drinks on the river's banks in the summer. Some rooms are merely functional, but others are quite nice. Ask for one of the upper-floor, gnarled-redwood–panel rooms. When there's a chill in the air, a fire roars in the stone fireplace in the inn's huge dining room ($–$$), which serves fresh fish entrées and specials like pasta Castroville (with artichokes and chicken in a pesto cream sauce). ⊠ *Hwy 1. at Pheneger Creek, 93920,* ☎ *831/667–2700,* ℻ *831/667–2743. 14 rooms, 6 suites. Restaurant, bar, general store. AE, D, MC, V.*

$–$$$ ✕▣ **Deetjen's Big Sur Inn.** This inn amid the redwoods has rustic charm, especially if you're not too attached to creature comforts. The room doors lock only from the inside, half the rooms have only wood-burning stoves to supply heat, and your neighbor can often be heard through the walls. Still, Deetjen's is a special place. The restaurant (reservations essential) in the main house serves stylish food that includes roasted half duck, steak, and lamb chops for dinner and wonderfully light and flavorful pancakes for breakfast. ⊠ *Hwy. 1, south end of town, 93920,* ☎ *831/667–2377 for inn; 831/667–2378 for restaurant.* ℻ *831/ 667–0466. 20 rooms, 15 with showers. Restaurant. MC, V.*

$$–$$$ ▣ **Big Sur Lodge.** The motel-style cottages of this property in Pfeiffer Big Sur State Park make it a good choice for families. The lodging area sits in a meadow surrounded by redwood and oak trees. Some accommodations have fireplaces, some have kitchens; none have TVs or phones. ⊠ *Hwy. 1, Box 190, 93920,* ☎ *831/667–3100 or 800/424– 4787,* ℻ *831/667–3110. 61 rooms. Restaurant, grocery, pool, shop. AE, MC, V.*

$$ ▣ **Glen Oaks Motel.** At this simple lodging in the heart of Big Sur you can choose between bland motel-style rooms and slightly more expensive log cabins in the woods. The cabins combine Laura Ashley flourishes with frontier style. ⊠ *Hwy. 1, 93920,* ☎ *831/667–2105. 15 rooms, 2 cottages. No credit cards.*

⚠ **Pfeiffer Big Sur State Park.** Redwood trees tower over this large campground that is often crowded in summer (so reserve a site as far ahead as possible) but still a wonderful place to camp. ⊠ *Hwy. 1, 8½ mi south of Point Sur Light Station,* ☎ *831/667–2315 for information; 800/444–7275 to reserve a site. 218 sites.* ▣ *$16–$23. Fire rings, flush toilets, showers, water.*

En Route Highway 1 snakes south along the coast from Big Sur toward San Simeon. Ten miles south of the town of Lucia is **Jade Cove,** a well-known jade-hunting spot. Rock hunting is allowed on the beach, but you may not remove anything from the walls of the cliffs.

San Simeon

57 mi south of Big Sur on Hwy. 1.

Whalers founded San Simeon in the 1850s but had virtually abandoned the town by the time Senator George Hearst reestablished it 20 years later. Hearst bought up most of the surrounding ranch land, built a 1,000-ft wharf, and turned San Simeon into a bustling port. His son, William Randolph, further developed the area during the construction of Hearst Castle. Today the town, which is 3 mi east of the road leading to the castle, is basically a row of gift shops, restaurants, and motels along Highway 1.

★ ❼ **Hearst Castle,** known officially as the Hearst San Simeon State Historical Monument, sits in solitary splendor atop La Cuesta Encantada (the Enchanted Hill). Its buildings and gardens are spread over the 127 acres that were the heart of newspaper magnate William Randolph Hearst's 250,000-acre ranch.

Buses from the visitor center at the bottom of the hill take visitors to the neoclassical extravaganza above. Hearst devoted nearly 30 years and about $10 million to building this elaborate estate. He commissioned renowned architect Julia Morgan—who was also responsible for buildings at the University of California at Berkeley—but was very much involved with the final product, a pastiche of Italian, Spanish, Moorish, and French styles. The art-filled main building and three guest "cottages" are connected by terraces and staircases and surrounded by pools, gardens, and statuary. In its heyday the castle was a playground for Hearst, Hollywood celebrities, and the rich and powerful from around the world.

Although construction began in 1919, the project was never officially completed. Work was halted in 1947 when Hearst had to leave San Simeon due to failing health. The Hearst family presented the property to the state of California in 1958.

Guides conduct four different daytime tours and (part of the year) one evening tour of various parts of the main house and grounds; if this is your first visit, Tour No. 1, the most basic, is recommended. Daytime tours take about two hours. Docents dress in period costume as Hearst's guests and staff for the slightly longer evening tour, which begins at sunset. All tours include a ½-mi walk and between 150 and 400 stairs. A 40-minute film shown at a giant-screen theater gives a sanitized version of Hearst's life and of the construction of the castle, but the shots of the scenery are dazzling. Reservations for the tours, which can be made up to eight weeks in advance, are necessary. ⊠ *San Simeon State Park, 750 Hearst Castle Rd.,* ☎ *805/927–2020 or 800/444–4445.* 🖳 *Day tour $14, evening tour (spring and fall) $25, film $6.* ⊙ *Tours daily 8:20–3:20 (later in summer); additional tours take place most Fri. and Sat. evenings Mar.–May and Sept.–Dec. MC, V.*

Dining and Lodging

$$ ✗ **Europa.** The menu here includes dishes from Germany, Hungary, and Italy—goulash with späetzle, stuffed pork roast with kielbasa, and homemade pasta. Steaks and fresh fish are also served. Crisp linen tablecloths brighten the small dining room. ⊠ *9240 Castillo Dr. (Hwy. 1),* ☎ *805/927–3087. MC, V. Closed Sun. No lunch.*

$$–$$$ ▥ **Best Western Cavalier.** Reasonable rates, an oceanfront location, and
★ well-equipped rooms—all with TVs with VCRs and some with wood-burning fireplaces and private patios—make this motel a good choice. ⊠ *9415 Hearst Dr., 93452,* ☎ *805/927–4688 or 800/826–8168,* ℻ *805/927–6472. 90 rooms. 2 restaurants, refrigerators, 2 outdoor pools, hot tub, exercise room, coin laundry. AE, D, DC, MC, V.*

Cambria

9 mi south of San Simeon on Hwy. 1.

Cambria, an artists' colony with many late-Victorian homes, is divided into the newer West Village and the original East Village. Each section has its own personality and B&Bs, restaurants, art galleries, and shops. You can still detect traces of the Welsh miners who settled in Cambria in the 1890s. Motels line Moonstone Beach Drive, which runs along the coast.

❽   **Leffingwell's Landing,** a state picnic ground, is a good place for examining tidal pools and watching otters as they frolic in the surf. Footpaths wind along the beach side of the the drive. ⊠ *Moonstone Beach Dr., northern end.*

Dining and Lodging

$$–$$$ ✕ **The Sea Chest.** By far the best seafood restaurant in town, this clifftop inn serves all kinds of fish, much of it locally caught. Oysters from the oyster bar are highly recommended. Come early to catch the sunset. ⊠ *6216 Moonstone Beach Dr.,* ☎ *805/927–4514. Reservations not accepted. No credit cards. No lunch.*

$–$$$ ✕ **Hamlet at Moonstone Gardens.** In the middle of 3 acres of luxuri-
★   ant gardens, this restaurant has an enchanting patio that's perfect for lunch. The views from the upstairs dining room are of the Pacific or the gardens. The fish of the day comes poached in white wine; other entrées range from hamburgers to rack of lamb. The output of more than 50 wineries is represented downstairs at the Pacific Wine Works. ⊠ *Hwy. 1 at Moonstone Beach Dr.,* ☎ *805/927–3535. MC, V.*

$–$$ ✕ **Robin's.** Multiethnic only begins to describe the dining possibilities at this antiques-filled restaurant amid Monterey pines. Tandoori prawns, quesadillas, a Thai red curry, an array of salads (more for lunch than dinner), numerous vegetarian entrées, hamburgers for the kids, and some truly fine desserts are all on Robin's menu. ⊠ *4095 Burton Dr.,* ☎ *805/927–5007. MC, V. No lunch Sun.*

$–$$ ✕ **The Greenwoods.** Ribs, filet mignon, and large New York steaks lure locals and tourists to the restaurant attached to the Cambria Pines Lodge. Bands in the lounge play light rock, jazz, and other music. ⊠ *2905 Burton Dr.,* ☎ *805/927–4200. AE, D, DC, MC, V.*

$$–$$$$ 🏨 **Blue Dolphin.** The luxurious beachfront rooms here look like they've been transported straight out of a middle-class home in Surrey circa 1910. Heavy on frills and pinks and pastels, they have hair dryers, TVs with VCRs, and superb ocean views. Five rooms have whirlpool tubs. ⊠ *6470 Moonstone Beach Dr., 93428,* ☎ *805/927–3300. 18 rooms. Refrigerators. Continental breakfast. AE, D, DC, MC, V.*

$$–$$$$ 🏨 **Pelican Suites.** The newest hotel in town, this beachfront abode offers great views and extremely comfortable rooms. The storied king-size beds, complete with steps leading up to the mattress, the large fireplaces, and the low-key wallpapering along with the hot tubs in some of the rooms make this a good romantic getaway. Ask for an ocean view. ⊠ *6316 Moonstone Beach Dr., 93428,* ☎ *805/927–1500,* 𝐅𝐀𝐗 *805/ 927–0218. 24 rooms. Refrigerators, pool, hot tubs, exercise room. AE, D, MC, V.*

$$–$$$ 🏨 **Cypress Cove Inn.** Like many hotels on the beach, this romantic getaway was designed in the Welsh style, with outside walls made of old stone and rooms on the upper floors crisscrossed by wood beams. Ask for a room facing the Pacific. ⊠ *6348 Moonstone Beach Dr., 93428,* ☎ *805/927–2600 or 800/568–8517. 21 rooms, 1 suite. No-smoking rooms, refrigerators, in-room VCRs, hot tub. AE, MC, V.*

$$–$$$ 🏨 **Fog Catcher Inn.** Its landscaped gardens and 10 thatched-roof buildings lend the Fog Catcher the feel of an English country village. Most rooms (among them 10 minisuites) have ocean views. All have fireplaces and are done in floral chintz with light-wood furniture. ⊠ *6400 Moonstone Beach Dr., 93428,* ☎ *805/927–1400 or 800/425–4121,* 𝐅𝐀𝐗 *805/ 927–0204. 50 rooms, 10 suites. Pool, hot tub. Full breakfast. AE, D, DC, MC, V.*

$$–$$$ 🏨 **Squibb House.** Owner Bruce Black restored this 1877 Gothic Revival–Italianate structure, and his craftsmen built many of the pine furnishings. The house radiates history, community, and pride of place. The rooms contain antiques but have modern conveniences such as reading lamps with ample light, and showers with sufficient water pressure. ⊠ *4063 Burton Dr., 93428,* ☎ *805/927–9600,* FAX *805/927–9606. 5 rooms. No-smoking rooms. Continental breakfast. MC, V.*

$–$$$ ⌂ **Best Western Fireside Inn.** This modern motel has spacious rooms with sofas, upholstered lounge chairs, refrigerators, and coffeemakers. Some rooms have whirlpools or ocean views, and all have fireplaces. The inn is across from a particularly striking rocky outcrop of the beach. ⊠ *6700 Moonstone Beach Dr., 93428,* ☎ *805/927–8661 or 888/910– 7100,* FAX *805/927–8584. 46 rooms. Pool, hot tub. Continental breakfast. AE, D, DC, MC, V.*

$–$$$ ⌂ **Bluebird Motel.** Rooms at this garden motel near Cambria's East Village include simply furnished doubles and nicer creekside suites with patios, fireplaces, refrigerators, and TVs with VCRs. The Bluebird isn't the fanciest place, but if you don't require beachside accommodations, it's a decent bargain. The wooded gardens are beautiful. ⊠ *1880 Main St., 93428,* ☎ *805/927–4634 or 800/552–5434,* FAX *805/ 927–5215. 37 rooms. AE, D, DC, MC, V.*

$$ ⌂ **San Simeon Pines Resort.** Amid 9 acres of pines and cypress, this motel-style resort has its own golf course and is directly across from Leffingwell's Landing. The accommodations include cottages with landscaped backyards. Rooms in parts of the complex are for adults only; others are reserved for families. ⊠ *7200 Moonstone Beach Dr. (mailing address: Box 117, San Simeon 93452,* ☎ *805/927–4648. 58 rooms. Pool, 9-hole golf course, croquet, shuffleboard, playground. AE, MC, V.*

Nightlife

Cambria doesn't have much of a nightlife, but if you're looking for a bar with music, cruise up Main Street until you hear some sounds that suit your fancy. A crowd of all ages hangs out at the pine-panel **Camozzi's Saloon** (⊠ 2262 Main St., ☎ 805/927–8941), where the atmosphere is old-time cowboy but the music is rock and R&B.

En Route   Seven miles south of Cambria on Highway 1 is the town of **Harmony,** population 18. The **Harmony Pottery Studio Gallery** (Hwy. 1, ☎ 805/ 927–4293) shows some fine work.

Morro Bay

20 mi south of Cambria on Hwy. 1.

Fishermen in the town of Morro Bay slog around the harbor in galoshes, and old-style ships teeter in its protected waters. Chumash Indians were the area's main inhabitants when Portuguese explorer Juan Rodríguez Cabrillo dropped anchor in 1542. The Spanish claimed the region in 1587, but Morro Bay remained a relatively quiet place until the second half of the 19th century, when an enterprising farmer built the town's wharf. Fishing was the main industry in the early 20th century, and it remains a vital part of the economy.

★ ❾ Except for the highly visible smokestacks of an electric power plant (and a restaurant scene that's completely au courant), the town retains a retro feel. The other big landmark is 576-ft-high **Morro Rock.** A short walk to the base of the rock—one of nine such small volcanic peaks, or "morros," in the area—leads to a breakwater, with the harbor on one side and the crashing waves of the Pacific on the other. Morro Bay is a wildlife preserve where endangered falcons and other birds nest. You can't climb on Morro Rock, but even from its base you'll be able to divine that the peak is alive with birds.

The center of the action on land is the **Embarcadero,** which holds restaurants, lodgings, and a few attractions. The town's well-designed aquarium is here, as is the outdoor Giant Chessboard, made up of nearly life-size hand-carved pieces.

Dining and Lodging

$$$–$$$$ ✕ **Hoppe's.** Morro Bay's most notable restaurant is the one place in town where you can get real caviar. On the second floor of a wooden seafront building, it is only open for dinner and Sunday brunch. The fish is always fresh and prepared with style. ⊠ *699 Embarcadero, No. 7,* ☎ *805/772–9012. AE, D, MC, V.*

$$–$$$ ✕ **The Great American Fish Company.** Opposite Morro Rock, this is a great spot to come and watch the seagulls and look out for frolicking otters. The only drawback is the power plant looming behind the restaurant. Shark steaks, filet mignon with scampi, squid burgers, and other entrées come in generous portions. ⊠ *1185 Embarcadero,* ☎ *805/ 772–4707. MC, V.*

$–$$$ ✕ **Dorn's.** This seafood café that overlooks the harbor resembles a Cape Cod cottage. It's open for breakfast, lunch, and dinner. Excellent fish and native abalone are on the dinner menu. ⊠ *801 Market Ave.,* ☎ *805/772–4415. AE, MC, V.*

$$–$$$$ ⌂ **Ascot Suites.** A hop and a skip away from the Embarcadero, this is the newest upscale hotel in Morro Bay. Rooms have all the modern conveniences. There are large hot tubs in most of the bathrooms, well-stocked wet bars, and gas fireplaces. ⊠ *260 Morro May Blvd, 93442,* ☎ *805/772–4437 or 800/887–6454,* FAX *805/772–8860. 31 suites. Restaurant, refrigerators, pool, hot tubs. AE, D, MC, V.*

$–$$$$ ⌂ **The Inn at Morro Bay.** Inside Morro Bay State Park and across from a heron rookery, this upscale hotel complex has romantic country French–style rooms. Some have fireplaces, whirlpool tubs, and bay views; others look out at extensive gardens. There's a golf course across the road, and mountain bikes are free for guests. Even if you're a bird lover, it's best not to book a room near the rookery. The morning din can be overwhelming. ⊠ *60 State Park Rd., 93442,* ☎ *805/772–5651 or 800/ 321–9566,* FAX *805/772–4779. 96 rooms. Restaurant, bar, room service, pool, meeting rooms. AE, D, DC, MC, V.*

$$–$$$ ⌂ **Embarcadero Inn.** A drab metallic-color wooden exterior hides a more welcoming interior of sparkling clean rooms, all of them with old maritime photographs on the walls and balconies that face the sea. ⊠ *456 Embarcadero, 93442,* ☎ *805/772–2700 or 800/292–7625,* FAX *805/ 772–1060. 28 rooms, 4 suites. Refrigerators, 2 hot tubs. AE, D, DC, MC, V.*

$–$$$ ⌂ **Adventure Inn.** Nautical murals decorate this small motel on the harbor and facing Morro Rock. Rooms are plain but comfortable. Amenities include coffeemakers and free HBO and local calls. ⊠ *1150 Embarcadero, 93442,* ☎ *805/772–5607; 800/799–5607 in CA,* FAX *805/ 772–8377. 16 rooms. Refrigerators, pool, hot tub. AE, MC, V.*

$$ ⌂ **Grays Inn and Gallery.** With only three rooms, you may have trouble getting a reservation at this tiny beachfront property. But make an effort, because the place is a hidden treasure whose cozy rooms have large glass walls facing the sea. ⊠ *561 Embarcadero, 93442,* ☎ *805/ 772–3911. 3 rooms. Kitchenettes. AE, MC, V.*

Outdoor Activities and Sports

Kayaks of Morro Bay (⊠ 699 Embarcadero, ☎ 805/772–1119) rents canoes and kayaks. **Sub-Sea Tours** (699 Embarcadero, ☎ 805/772–9463) operates fish-viewing boat rides in glass-bottom boats. **Virg's Sport Fishing** (⊠ 1215 Embarcadero, ☎ 805/772–1222 or 800/762–5263) conducts deep-sea fishing trips.

San Luis Obispo

⑩ *14 mi south of Morro Bay on Hwy. 1; 230 mi south of San Francisco on I–280 to U.S. 101; 112 mi north of Santa Barbara on U.S. 101.*

About halfway between San Francisco and Los Angeles, San Luis Obispo is an appealing urban center set among rolling hills and extinct volcanos. It is home to two decidedly different institutions: California Polytechnic State University, known as Cal Poly, and the exuberantly garish Madonna Inn. The town has restored its old railroad depot as well as several Victorian-era homes; the Chamber of Commerce (☞ Contacts and Resources *in* the Central Coast A to Z, *below*) has a list of self-guided historic walks. On Thursday from 6 AM to 9 PM a four-block-long farmers market takes place on Higuera Street.

★ **Mission San Luis Obispo de Tolosa,** established in 1772, overlooks San Luis Obispo Creek. The mission's museum exhibits artifacts of the Chumash Indians and early Spanish settlers. ⊠ *751 Palm St.,* ☎ *805/543–6850.* 🔁 *$2 suggested donation.* ☉ *Memorial Day weekend–Dec., daily 9–5; Jan.–late May, daily 9–4.*

★ Inside an old redbrick building across from the mission, the **County Historical Museum** holds a captivating hodgepodge of exhibits—Native American arrows, tiles from the original mission roof, and an intriguing late-19th-century hand organ. ⊠ *696 Monterey St.,* ☎ *805/543–0638.* 🔁 *$2.* ☉ *Daily 9–5.*

Dining and Lodging

$–$$$ ✕ **Beau's Russian Tea Room.** As the name suggests, Russian food dominates this elegant restaurant. From caviar to borscht to chicken Kiev—and vodka—it's all here. Desserts are excellent. Service can be slightly slow. ⊠ *699 Higuera St.,* ☎ *805/784–0174. AE, MC, V.*

$–$$ ✕ **Buona Tavola.** Homemade *agnolotti* (pasta) filled with scampi in a creamy saffron sauce and braised lamb shank with grilled polenta are among the northern Italian dishes served at this local favorite. In good weather you can dine on the flower-filled patio. ⊠ *1037 Monterey St.,* ☎ *805/545–8000. D, MC, V.*

$–$$ ✕ **Cafe Roma.** Authentic northern Italian cuisine is the specialty of this restaurant on Railroad Square. Under a large mural of sunny Tuscany, you can dine on squash-filled ravioli with sage and butter sauce or filet mignon glistening with port and Gorgonzola. ⊠ *1010 Railroad Ave.,* ☎ *805/541–6800. AE, D, DC, MC, V. Closed Mon. No lunch weekends.*

$ ✕ **Big Sky Café.** The menu here roams the world—the Mediterranean,
★ the Sun Belt, North Africa, and the Southwest—but many of the ingredients are local: organic fruits and vegetables, hormone-free chicken, and pork and chicken sausages produced right in town. Big Sky is a hip gathering spot for breakfast, lunch, and dinner. ⊠ *1121 Broad St.,* ☎ *805/545–5401. MC, V.*

$–$$$$ 🏨 **Apple Farm.** Decorated to the hilt with floral bedspreads, wallpa-
★ per, and watercolors by local artists, this is the most comfortable place to stay in town. Each room in the country-style hotel has a gas fireplace; some have canopy beds and cozy window seats. There's a working grist mill in the garden courtyard. An American restaurant and cluttered gift shop cater to guests. ⊠ *2015 Monterey St., 93401,* ☎ *805/544–2040; 800/374–3705 in CA;* 📠 *805/546–9495. 103 rooms. Restaurant, pool, hot tub. AE, D, MC, V.*

$$–$$$ 🏨 **Madonna Inn.** From its rococo bathrooms to its pink-on-pink, froufrou dining areas, the Madonna Inn is the ultimate in kitsch. Each room is unique, to say the least: Rock Bottom is all stone, even the bathroom; the Safari Room is decked out in animal skins. Humor value

aside, the Madonna is pretty much a duded-up motel, so don't expect much in the way of luxury. ⊠ *100 Madonna Rd., 93405,* ☎ *805/543–3000 or 800/543–9666,* FAX *805/543–1800. 87 rooms, 22 suites. Bar, coffee shop, dining room, shops. MC, V.*

$$ 🏨 **La Cuesta Inn.** The room decor at this adobe-style motel on the northern edge of town is understated, almost to the point of being generic. If you can forgo elegance, this is a good bet. ⊠ *2074 Monterey St., 93401,* ☎ *805/543–2777 or 800/543–2777,* FAX *805/544–0696. 72 rooms. Pool, hot tub. Continental breakfast. AE, D, DC, MC, V.*

$–$$ 🏨 **Adobe Inn.** The friendly owners of this establishment of cheerful motel-style rooms serve excellent breakfasts. They'll help you plan your stay in the area, even if you don't choose to go on one of their reasonably priced winery, bicycle-tour, or other packages. ⊠ *1473 Monterey St., 93401,* ☎ *805/549–0321 or 800/676–1588,* FAX *805/549–0383. 15 rooms. Kitchenettes. Full breakfast. AE, D, DC, MC, V.*

Nightlife and the Arts

The **San Luis Obispo Mozart Festival** (☎ 805/781–3008) takes place in late July and early August. Not all the music is Mozart; you'll hear Haydn and other composers. The **Festival Fringe** presents free concerts outdoors. The **Performing Arts Center** (1 Grand Ave., ☎ 805/756–7222) at Cal Poly hosts concerts and recitals.

The club scene in this college town is centered around Higuera Street off Monterey Street. The **Frog and Peach** is a decent spot to nurse a beer and listen to music (728 Higuera St., ☎ 805/595–3764). **Linnaea's Cafe** (110 Garden St., ☎ 805/541–5888), a mellow java joint, sometimes hosts poetry readings, blues and alternative rock performances, and other diversions. Bands playing music from swing to blues to rock perform at **Mother's Tavern** (725 Higuera St., ☎ 805/541–8733), which is something of a frat-party scene on the weekend.

En Route   Highway 1 and U.S. 101 become one road for a short stretch south of San Luis Obispo. San Luis Bay Drive loops off the highway to Avila Beach, a usually quiet town that comes alive on weekends, when Cal Poly students take over. As you continue south, 20 mi of sandy, southern California–style shoreline begins at the town of Pismo Beach, where the action centers on the shops and arcades near the pier. From here there are **two routes to Solvang.** The direct route is U.S. 101, past Arroyo Grande, Santa Maria, and rural countryside that is becoming increasingly less rural. At Buellton, head east on Highway 246 to Solvang. The other option is to take Highway 1, which twists along the coast (and inland a bit at times) past Guadalupe, Vandenberg Air Force Base, and Lompoc. Along the roads near Lompoc, also known as the Flower-Seed Capital of the World, vast fields of brightly colored flowers bloom from May through August. At Lompoc, Highway 246 travels east from Highway 1, past Mission La Purísima Concepción through Buellton to Solvang. Highway 1 continues south and east until it rejoins U.S. 101 at Las Cruces, 9 mi below Buellton.

Pismo Beach

⓫   *15 mi southwest of San Luis Obispo.*

Nestled about halfway between San Francisco and Los Angeles, and an easy drive from the hot towns of the Central Valley, Pismo Beach is optimistically nicknamed the "Bakersfield Riviera." The southern end runs along gorgeous beaches and sand dunes, some of which are open to drive on. The northern section sits perched above chalky cliffs.

For a town with a native population of less than 10,000, Pismo Beach has a large number of hotels and restaurants. Despite the neon signs that announce all accommodations and dining spots, the area doesn't feel inundated by tourists. Most of the best hotels and restaurants provide great views out over the Pacific Ocean. Good beachfront walks, top-quality clam chowder, a growing Dixieland jazz festival in February, and a colony of Monarch butterflies in the town's eucalyptus grove are some of the attractions.

From Pismo, take Highway 101 five miles north to **Avila Beach** and the neighboring **Port San Louis.** Both are funky old fishing villages, facing southward onto a cove and thus escaping the fog that rolls in off the water. The port is still functioning, with a vibrant fish market lining the pier. Unfortunately, the Diablo Canyon nuclear power plant is situated right next to the port.

Dining and Lodging

$$–$$$$ ✕ **Shore Cliff.** With probably the best seafood and clam chowder in town, this restaurant also has spectacular cliff-top views. The interior feels very airy, with glass windows drawing in oodles of light. ✉ *2555 Price St.,* ☎ *805/773–4671. AE, D, DC, MC, V.*

$$–$$$ ✕ **F. McLintocks.** A cross between a truck stop and a cowboy saloon, this place prides itself on enormous portions of Western cuisine. Before you even order your meal, you'll find a large bowl of onion rings in front of you. Every cut of steak you can imagine is here, along with piles of ribs, lobsters, and much more. ✉ *750 Mattie Rd.,* ☎ *805/773–1892. AE, D, MC, V.*

$$–$$$$ ▦ **The Cliffs at Shell Beach.** With a Spanish-modern exterior surrounded by manicured palm trees and marble-floored interiors, this spot offers everything you would expect in a beachfront resort. Many rooms have fine ocean views (make sure your room faces the beach) and all are decorated with modern furnishings. Suites have huge marble bathrooms and hot tubs. ✉ *2757 Shell Beach Rd., 93449,* ☎ *805/773–5000 or 800/826–7827,* FAX *805/773–0764. 142 rooms, 23 suites. Restaurant, bar, pool, spa, meeting rooms. AE, D, DC, MC, V.*

$$–$$$$ ▦ **Sea Venture Hotel.** The rooms here aren't high on atmosphere, but those with an ocean view are perched over a beautiful stretch of sand. The best amenity is the private hot tub on most of the rooms' balconies. ✉ *100 Ocean View Ave., 93449,* ☎ *805/773–4994 or 800/662–5545,* FAX *805/773–0924. 50 rooms, 43 with hot tubs. Restaurant, pool, hot tubs. Continental breakfast. AE, D, DC, MC, V.*

La Purisima Mission State Historic Park

58 mi south of San Luis Obispo, Hwy. 1 to Hwy. 246 east or U.S. 101 to Hwy. 246 west.

★ ⑫ **Mission La Purisima Concepción,** the most fully restored mission in the state, was founded in 1787. Its stark and still-remote setting powerfully evokes the lives of California's Spanish settlers. Displays illustrate the secular and religious activities at the mission, and once a month from March through September costumed docents demonstrate crafts. A corral near the parking area holds several farm animals, including sheep that are descendants of the original mission stock. ✉ *2295 Purisima Rd., off Mission Gate Rd.,* ☎ *805/733–3713; 805/733–1303 to schedule a tour.* ▣ *$5 per vehicle.* ☉ *Daily 9–5.*

Solvang

⑬ *23 mi east of Mission La Purisima Concepción on Hwy. 246; 3 mi east of U.S. 101 on Hwy. 246.*

You'll know when you've reached the Danish town of Solvang: the architecture suddenly turns to half-timbered buildings and windmills, with flags galore. Though the activities here are aimed squarely at tourists, the town has a genuine Danish heritage—more than two-thirds of the residents are of Danish descent. The 300 or so shops that sell Danish goods and knickknacks are all within easy walking distance; many are along Copenhagen Drive and Alisal Road. Solvang Bakery, at 460 Alisal Road, is one of a half-dozen aroma-filled bakeries. If Solvang seems too serene and orderly to be true, find a copy of William Castle's 1961 film *Homicidal*, which used the town as the backdrop for gender-bending murder and mayhem.

Dining and Lodging

$$–$$$ ✕ **The Hitching Post.** You'll find everything from grilled artichokes to ostrich at this casual eatery in Buellton, but most people come for what is said to be the best Santa Maria–style barbecue in the state. The oak used in the barbecue imparts a wonderfully smoky taste. ⊠ *406 E. Hwy. 246, Buellton,* ☎ *805/688–0676. AE, MC, V. No lunch.*

$–$$ ✕ **Bit O' Denmark.** Perhaps the most authentic Danish eatery in Solvang, this restaurant is in an old beamed building that was a church until 1929. The dishes have names like *Frikadeller* (heavy meatballs with pickled red cabbage, potatoes, and thick brown gravy) and *Medisterpolse* (Danish beef and pork sausage with cabbage). ⊠ *473 Alisal Rd.,* ☎ *805/688–5426. AE, D, MC, V.*

$–$$ ✕ **Restaurant Molle-Kroen.** Locals come to this cheerful upstairs dining room when they want a good Danish meal at a reasonable price. ⊠ *435 Alisal Rd.,* ☎ *805/688–4555. AE, D, DC, MC, V.*

$$$$ ✕▥ **Alisal Guest Ranch and Resort.** Sixteen hundred or so head of cattle graze the 10,000-acre grounds of Alisal Ranch, which opened to guests in 1946 and soon attracted the likes of Clark Gable and Doris Day. More recent guests have included Barbra Streisand and Kevin Costner. Rooms are plain, with appealing Western touches; all have refrigerators and wood-burning fireplaces. The land-based activities include golf, tennis, horseback riding, and nature-watching. Sailing, windsurfing, pedal boating, and fishing take place on the 90-acre lake. Hearty meals are served home-style in the rustic yet elegant Ranch Room if the weather isn't warm enough for an outdoor barbecue. Breakfast and dinner are included in the room rates, but many of the activities cost extra. ⊠ *1054 Alisal Rd., 93463,* ☎ *805/688–6411 or 800/425–4725,* FAX *805/688–2510. 36 rooms, 37 suites. Restaurant, bar, pool, 2 18-hole golf courses, 7 tennis courts, croquet, Ping-Pong, shuffleboard, volleyball, bike rentals, billiards. AE, D, MC, V.*

$$$ ▥ **Petersen Village Inn.** As with most of the buildings in Solvang, this
★ property is heavy on the wood. The overall effect is along the lines of a hunting lodge. The four-poster beds here are plush, the bathrooms small but sparkling. The inn welcomes children over age seven. ⊠ *1576 Mission Dr., 93463,* ☎ *805/688–3121 or 800/321–8985,* FAX *805/688–5732. 39 rooms, 1 suite. Café, bar. Full breakfast. AE, MC, V.*

$$–$$$ ▥ **Chimney Sweep Inn.** The regular rooms at this inn with a landscaped garden and pond are well maintained. The larger (and more expensive) cottages were inspired by the C. S. Lewis children's series, *The Chronicles of Narnia*. The six cottages have kitchens and fireplaces; five also have hot tubs. In a town of kitsch, this dwelling gives a good impersonation of authenticity. ⊠ *1564 Copenhagen Dr., 93463,* ☎ *805/688–2111 or 800/824–6444,* FAX *805/688–8824. 50 rooms, 6 cottages. Hot tub, spa. Continental breakfast. AE, D, MC, V.*

$$–$$$ ▥ **Story Book Inn.** Someone in Solvang had to do it: all the rooms at this B&B are named after Hans Christian Andersen stories. Some rooms are on the small side, but others are large and luxurious. All have a light, airy feel. The suites have four-poster beds and roomy marble whirlpool tubs. ⊠ *409 1st St., 93463,* ☎ *805/688–1703 or 800/786–7925,* FAX *805/688–0953. 7 rooms, 2 suites. Full breakfast. D, MC, V.*

$-$$ ⊞ **Best Western King Fredric.** Rooms at this comfortable and central motel are fairly spacious and come with TVs. If you're traveling with the kids and don't want to spend a fortune, this is a good bet. ⊠ *1617 Copenhagen Dr., 93463,* ☎ *805/688-5515,* FAX *805/688-2067. 39 rooms. Pool, hot tub. Continental breakfast. AE, D, DC, MC, V.*

Nightlife and the Arts
Pacific Conservatory of the Performing Arts (☎ 805/922-8313; 800/549-7272 in CA) presents contemporary and classic plays, along with a few musicals, in different theaters in Solvang and Santa Maria. Summer events in Solvang are held in the open-air Festival Theatre, on 2nd Street off Copenhagen Drive.

Outdoor Activities and Sports
Cachuma Lake (⊠ Hwy. 154, ☎ 805/688-4658), a jewel of an artificial lake 12 mi east of Solvang, has hiking, fishing, boating, and interpretive nature programs.

BICYCLING
Quadricycles, four-wheel carriages, and bicycles are available at **Breezy's Carriages** (⊠ 414 1st St., ☎ 805/688-0091) and **Surrey Cycle Rental** (⊠ 475 1st St., ☎ 805/688-0091).

GLIDER RIDES
The scenic rides operated by **Windhaven Glider** (⊠ Santa Ynez Airport, Hwy. 246 east of Solvang, ☎ 805/688-2517) cost between $65 and $135 and last up to 40 minutes.

Los Olivos
⑭ *5 mi north of Solvang on Alamo Pintado Rd.*

This pretty village in the Santa Ynez Valley was once on the Spanish-built El Camino Real and later on major stagecoach and rail routes. It's so sleepy today, though, that it was selected as the site for TV's *Return to Mayberry.* A row of art galleries, antiques stores, and country markets lines Grand Avenue. At **Los Olivos Tasting Room & Wine Shop** (⊠ 2905 Grand Ave., ☎ 805/688-7406) you can sample locally produced wines and pick up winery maps. **Sanone Gallery** (⊠ 2948 Nojoqui Ave., ☎ 805/693-9769) boasts the best artwork in town.

Dining and Lodging
$$$-$$$$ ✕⊞ **Fess Parker's Wine Country Inn and Spa.** Until 1998, this was known as the Los Olivos Grand Hotel. The rooms at this luxury inn—the only place you can spend the night in Los Olivos—are in a lawn-fronted house and an equally attractive residence across the street with a pool and a hot tub. The spacious accommodations have fireplaces, seating areas, and wet bars; six also have hot tubs. At the Vintage Room ($$-$$$), well-selected local wines complement entrées like oven-roasted salmon and grilled lamb T-bone. Unfortunately, the inn's service is not as special under the new ownership, and the restaurant's quality has slipped. ⊠ *2860 Grand Ave., 93441,* ☎ *805/688-7788 or 800/446-2455,* FAX *805/688-1942. 20 rooms, 1 suite. Restaurant, pool, hot tub, spa. AE, MC, V.*

OFF THE BEATEN PATH   **SAN MARCOS PASS** – Highway 154 winds its spectacular way south from Solvang (drive east on Highway 246 to 154) through the Los Padres National Forest. This former stagecoach route rejoins U.S. 101 north of Santa Barbara. The lively Cold Spring Tavern (☞ Santa Barbara Dining and Lodging, *below*) has been serving travelers since the stagecoach days.

SANTA BARBARA

45 mi south of Solvang on U.S. 101.

Santa Barbara has long been an oasis for Los Angeles residents in need of rest and recuperation. The attractions in Santa Barbara begin with the ocean and end in the foothills of the Santa Ynez Mountains. In the few miles between the beaches and the hills are downtown, then the old mission, and, a little higher up, the botanic gardens. A few miles farther up the coast, but still very much a part of Santa Barbara, is the exclusive residential district of Hope Ranch. To the east is the district called Montecito, whose Coast Village Road has shops and restaurants.

Santa Barbara is on a jog in the coastline, so the ocean is actually to the south. Directions can be confusing. "Up" the coast is west, "down" toward Los Angeles is actually east, and the mountains are north. A car is handy but not essential if you're planning to stay in town. The beaches and downtown are easily explored by bicycle or on foot, and the Santa Barbara Trolley (☞ Contacts and Resources in the Central Coast A to Z, *below*) takes visitors to most major hotels and sights, which can also be reached on the local buses.

The Waterfront

You'll hear locals refer to the waterfront as "the ocean," but by any name it's a beautiful area, with palm-studded promenades and plenty of sand.

A Good Tour

Start your tour at the **Santa Barbara Yacht Harbor** ⑮. Walk east on Cabrillo Boulevard, the main harbor-front drag, to **Stearns Wharf** ⑰, where the **Sea Center** ⑱ is a major attraction. Unless you're an inveterate walker, drive east along Cabrillo Boulevard to **East Beach** ⑲ and the nearby **Andree Clark Bird Refuge** ⑳. More creatures await at the **Santa Barbara Zoo** ㉑, which is adjacent to the refuge.

TIMING

You could make this an all-day excursion or devote only two or three hours to it if you drive and only stop briefly at the various attractions. A spin through the zoo takes about an hour.

Sights to See

⑳ **Andree Clark Bird Refuge.** This peaceful lagoon and gardens sits north of East Beach. Bike trails and footpaths, punctuated by signs identifying native and migratory birds, skirt the lagoon. ⊠ *1400 E. Cabrillo Blvd.* ☜ *Free.*

OFF THE BEATEN PATH **CHANNEL ISLANDS NATIONAL PARK AND NATIONAL MARINE SANCTUARY –** The five Channel Islands often appear in a haze on the Santa Barbara horizon. The most popular is Anacapa Island, 11 mi off the coast. The islands' remoteness and unpredictable seas protected them from development and now provide a nature-enthusiast's paradise. On a good day you'll be able to view seals, sea lions, and much bird life. Migrating whales can be seen close up from December through March. Tidal pools are often accessible. Divers can view fish, giant squid, and coral. Frenchy's Cove, on the west end of the island, has a swimming beach and fine snorkeling. The waters of the channel are often rough and can make for a rugged boat ride out to the islands (☞ Boats and Charters *in* Outdoor Activities and Sports, *below*, for information about group outings).

⑲ **East Beach.** The wide swath of sand at the east end of Cabrillo Boulevard is a great spot for people-watching. Sand volleyball courts, sum-

Santa Barbara

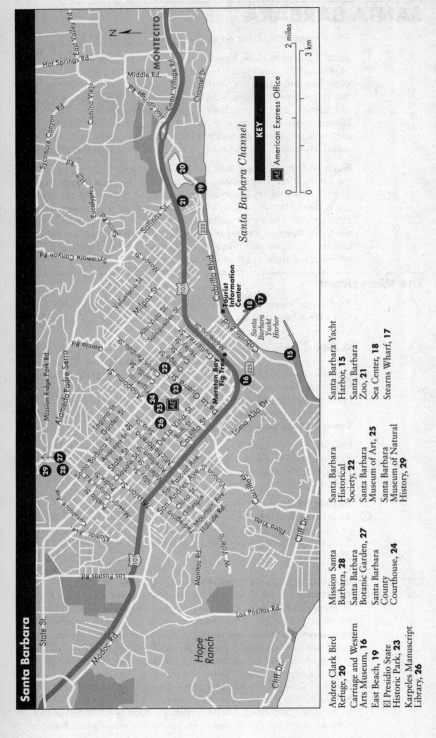

KEY

AE American Express Office

Santa Barbara Channel

MONTECITO

Hope Ranch

Andree Clark Bird
Refuge, **20**

Carriage and Western
Arts Museum, **16**

East Beach, **19**

El Presidio State
Historic Park, **23**

Karpeles Manuscript
Library, **26**

Mission Santa
Barbara, **28**

Santa Barbara
Botanic Garden, **27**

Santa Barbara
County
Courthouse, **24**

Santa Barbara
Historical
Society, **22**

Santa Barbara
Museum of Art, **25**

Santa Barbara
Museum of Natural
History, **29**

Santa Barbara Yacht
Harbor, **15**

Santa Barbara
Zoo, **21**

Sea Center, **18**

Stearns Wharf, **17**

mertime lifeguard and sports competitions, and arts-and-crafts shows on Sunday and holidays make for an often lively experience. Showers (no towels), lockers, and beach rentals—also a weight room—are provided at the **Cabrillo Pavilion Bathhouse** (⊠ 1118 Cabrillo Blvd., ☎ 805/965–0509). Next to the boathouse, there's an elaborate jungle-gym play area for children.

Moreton Bay Fig Tree. Planted in 1874 and transplanted to its present location in 1877, this tree is so huge it reputedly can provide shade for 10,000 people. ⊠ *Chapala St. at U.S. 101.*

⑮ **Santa Barbara Yacht Harbor.** A paved, man-made breakwater protects this harbor. You can take a ½-mi walk along the breakwater; check out the tackle and bait shops, or hire a boat. ⊠ *West end of Cabrillo Blvd.*

🐾 ㉑ **Santa Barbara Zoo.** The natural settings of the zoo shelter elephants, gorillas, exotic birds, and big cats such as the rare amur leopard, a thick-furred, high-altitude dweller from Asia. For the kids there's a scenic railroad and barnyard petting zoo. ⊠ *500 Niños Dr.,* ☎ *805/962–5339.* 🎟 *$6.* ⊘ *Daily 10–5.*

🐾 ⑱ **Sea Center.** A branch of the Santa Barbara Museum of Natural History, the Sea Center specializes in marine life. Aquariums, life-size models of whales and dolphins, undersea dioramas, interactive computer-video displays, and the remains of shipwrecks depict marine activity from the Santa Barbara coastline to the Channel Islands. At the Touch Tank you can handle invertebrates, fish, and plants collected from nearby waters. ⊠ *211 Stearns Wharf,* ☎ *805/962–0885.* 🎟 *$3.* ⊘ *Sea Center Oct.–May, weekdays noon–5, weekends 10–5; June–Sept., daily 10–5. Touch Tank exhibit weekdays noon–4, weekends noon–5.*

⑰ **Stearns Wharf.** Extending the length of three city blocks into the Pacific, the wharf has a view back toward Santa Barbara that gives visitors a good sense of the city's size and general layout. Although it's a nice walk from the Cabrillo Boulevard parking areas, you can also drive out and park (for a fee) on the pier and then wander through the shops or stop for a meal at one of the wharf's restaurants or the snack bar. ⊠ *Cabrillo Blvd. at the foot of State St.,* ☎ *805/564–5518.*

Downtown and the Foothills

A Good Tour

Begin at the **Santa Barbara County Courthouse** ㉔, at the corner of Anacapa and Anapamu streets. A block or so away at Anapamu and State streets, beyond the Spanish-style public library, is the **Santa Barbara Museum of Art** ㉕; across State on Anapamu is the **Karpeles Manuscript Library** ㉖. Backtrack on Anapamu to the courthouse and head south on Anacapa. You'll soon pass **El Paseo,** a handsome shopping arcade built around an old adobe home. Make a right at East Cañon Perdido Street to reach **El Presidio State Historic Park** ㉓. From the park, head south one block to De La Guerra Street and turn left (east) to reach the museum of the **Santa Barbara Historical Society** ㉒.

Hop in your car and take State Street north (away from the water) to Los Olivos Street. Turn right (east) and you'll soon see **Mission Santa Barbara** ㉘. From the mission you can walk the block north to the **Santa Barbara Museum of Natural History** ㉙. You'll probably want to drive the 1½ mi north to the **Santa Barbara Botanic Garden** ㉗.

TIMING

Set aside an hour each for the art and natural-history museums and for the botanic gardens. Add more time if you're a shopper. The stores and galleries along and near State Street may sidetrack you for hours.

Sights to See

🖐 ⑯ **Carriage and Western Arts Museum.** The country's largest collection of old horse-drawn vehicles—painstakingly renovated—is exhibited here. Everything from polished hearses to police transport buggies to old stagecoaches and circus vehicles are on display. In August the Old Spanish Days Fiesta borrows many of the vehicles for a jaunt about town. This is one of the city's true hidden gems, a wonderful example of history come alive. ⊠ *129 Castillo St.,* ☎ *805/982–2353.* 🎫 *Free.* ⊙ *Daily 10–4.*

㉓ **El Presidio State Historic Park.** Founded in 1782, the Presidio was one of four military strongholds established by the Spanish along the coast of California. The guardhouse, El Cuartel, one of the two original adobe structures that remain of the complex, is the oldest building owned by the state. ⊠ *123 E. Cañon Perdido St.,* ☎ *805/965–0093.* 🎫 *Free.* ⊙ *Daily 10:30–4:30.*

🖐 **Kids' World public playground.** Children and adults enjoy this complex maze of fantasy climbing structures, turrets, slides, and tunnels built by Santa Barbara parents. ⊠ *Santa Barbara St. near Micheltorena St.*

㉖ **Karpeles Manuscript Library.** Ancient political tracts and old Disney cartoons are among the varied holdings of this facility, which also houses one of the world's largest privately owned collections of rare manuscripts. Fifty cases contain a sampling of the archive's million-plus documents. ⊠ *21 W. Anapamu St.,* ☎ *805/962–5322.* 🎫 *Free.* ⊙ *Daily 10–4.*

OFF THE
BEATEN PATH

LOTUSLAND – Only a limited number of people are permitted to visit the 37-acre estate that once belonged to Polish opera singer Ganna Walska; the hours that Lotusland is open are limited, and one must take part in a 1½- to 2-hour guided group tour. It's worth trying to get a reservation to see the celebrated gardens. Many of the exotic trees and other subtropical flora were planted in 1882 by horticulturist R. Kinton Stevens; Madame Walska, who purchased the estate in 1941, further developed the grounds. Among the highlights are an outdoor theater, a topiary garden, a huge collection of rare bromeliads, and a lotus pond. ⊠ *Ganna Walska Lotusland, 695 Ashley Rd., Montecito,* ☎ *805/969–9990.* 🎫 *$10.* ⊙ *Tours mid-Feb.–mid-Nov., Wed.–Sun. 10:30* AM *and 1:30* PM.

★ ㉘ **Mission Santa Barbara.** The architecture and layout of this mission, which was established in 1786, evolved from adobe-brick buildings with thatched roofs to more permanent edifices as its population burgeoned. An earthquake in 1812 destroyed the third church built on the site. Its replacement, the present structure, is still a Catholic church, though during the post-Mission era it also served as a boys school and a seminary. Cacti, palms, and other succulents grow in the garden beside the mission. ⊠ *2201 Laguna St.,* ☎ *805/682–4713.* 🎫 *$3.* ⊙ *Daily 9–5.*

★ ㉗ **Santa Barbara Botanic Garden.** Five-plus miles of trails meander through the garden's 65 acres of native plants. The Mission Dam, built in 1806, stands just beyond the redwood grove and above the partially uncovered aqueduct that once carried water to Mission Santa Barbara. An ethnobotanical display contains replicas of the plants used by the Chumash Indians. ⊠ *1212 Mission Canyon Rd.,* ☎ *805/682–4726.* 🎫 *$3.* ⊙ *Mar.–Oct., weekdays 9–5, weekends 9–6; Nov.–Feb., weekdays 9–4, weekends 9–5. Guided tours Sun.–Tues. and Thurs.–Sat. at 2; additional tour at 10:30* AM *Thurs., Sat., and Sun.*

★ ㉔ **Santa Barbara County Courthouse.** Hand-painted tiles and a spiral stair-case infuse the courthouse with the grandeur of a Moorish palace. This magnificent building was completed in 1929, part of a rebuilding process after a 1925 earthquake destroyed many downtown structures. At the time Santa Barbara was also in the midst of a cultural awakening, and the trend was toward an architecture appropriate to the area's climate and history. The result is the harmonious Mediterranean-Spanish look of much of the downtown area, especially municipal buildings. An elevator rises to an arched observation area in the courthouse tower that provides a panoramic view of the city. The murals in the supervisors' ceremonial chambers on the courthouse's second floor were painted by an artist who did backdrops for some of Cecil B. DeMille's silent films. ⊠ *1100 block of Anacapa St.,* ☎ *805/962–6464.* ☉ *Daily 8:30–4:45. Free 1-hr guided tours Fri. 10:30 AM, Mon.–Sat. 2 PM.*

㉒ **Santa Barbara Historical Society.** The society's museum exhibits decorative and fine arts, furniture, costumes, and documents from the town's past. Adjacent is the Gledhill Library, a collection of books, photographs, maps, and manuscripts about the area. ⊠ *136 E. De La Guerra St.,* ☎ *805/966–1601.* ⊞ *Museum $3 (suggested donation), library $2 per hr up to $5 for research work.* ☉ *Museum Tues.–Sat. 10–5, Sun. noon–5; library Tues.–Fri. 10–4, 1st Sat. of month 10–1:30.*

㉕ **Santa Barbara Museum of Art.** The highlights of this museum's fine permanent collection include ancient sculpture, Asian art, French and Impressionist paintings, and American works in several media. ⊠ *1130 State St.,* ☎ *805/963–4364.* ⊞ *$5; free Thurs. and 1st Sun. of month.* ☉ *Tues.–Sat. 11–5 (until 9 Thurs.), Sun. noon–5. Guided tours Tues.–Sun. 1 PM.*

☚ ㉙ **Santa Barbara Museum of Natural History.** A full-size skeleton of a blue whale at the entrance serves as a landmark for this museum complex. The major draws include the planetarium and E. L. Wiegand Space Lab. A room of dioramas illustrates Chumash Indian history and culture. Startlingly lifelike stuffed specimens, complete with nests and eggs, roost in the bird diversity room. Many of the exhibits have interactive components. ⊠ *2559 Puesta del Sol Rd.,* ☎ *805/682–4711.* ⊞ *$5.* ☉ *Mon.– Sat. 9–5, Sun. 10–5.*

Dining and Lodging

$$$$ ✕ **Citronelle.** At this offspring of chef Michel Richard's Citrus in Los
★ Angeles, intriguing flavors animate dishes such as the lamb loin with couscous and cumin sauce and the seared ahi tuna with an Anaheim-chili sauce. The desserts are stupendous. The dining room's picture windows yield splendid, sweeping views. Try to arrive before sunset. ⊠ *901 E. Cabrillo Blvd.,* ☎ *805/963–0111. Reservations essential. AE, D, DC, MC, V.*

$$$$ ✕ **Emilio's.** Starters on the seasonal northern Italian menu at this harborside restaurant might include crispy roast duck on a risotto cake. The main courses of ravioli stuffed with butternut squash or potato gnocchi with rock shrimp are standouts. During the week a vegetarian tasting menu is available, as are two prix-fixe wine-tasting menus. ⊠ *324 W. Cabrillo Blvd.,* ☎ *805/966–4426. AE, D, MC, V. No lunch.*

$$$$ ✕ **The Stonehouse.** This atmospheric restaurant in a century-old granite farmhouse is part of the San Ysidro Ranch resort. The contemporary southern fare includes dry-aged New York steak with smoked tomato-horseradish sauce and clam hash, seared ahi tuna in an herb crust with sun-dried-tomato couscous, and excellent vegetarian options. Even better than the generally wonderful food is the pastoral setting. Have lunch—salads, pastas, and sandwiches—on the tree-house-like outdoor patio. At night the candlelighted interior is seriously roman-

tic. ✉ *900 San Ysidro La., Montecito,* ☎ *805/969–4100. Reservations essential. AE, DC, MC, V.*

$$$–$$$$ ✕ **Wine Cask.** Sautéed swordfish and Colorado lamb sirloin, each
★ prepared with a wine-based sauce, are among the most popular entrées
at this slick restaurant with a beautiful wood interior. In fine weather
the outdoor patio is one of the most romantic dining spots in Santa
Barbara. ✉ *813 Anacapa St.,* ☎ *805/966–9463. AE, DC, MC, V.*

$$–$$$$ ✕ **Arigato Sushi.** Sushi fans will appreciate the fresh seafood served in
this atmospheric Japanese restaurant and sushi bar. Innovation reigns,
with creations such as sushi pizza on seaweed and Hawaiian sashimi
salad. ✉ *11 W. Victoria St.,* ☎ *805/965–6074. Reservations not accepted. AE, MC, V. No lunch.*

$$–$$$ ✕ **Andria's Harborside.** The seafood entrées are decent enough at this
sprawling, nautical-style eatery, but most people come for the creamy
clam chowder or the fresh oysters—and the harbor views. Nightly entertainment at the piano bar adds to the bustling atmosphere. ✉ *336
W. Cabrillo Blvd.,* ☎ *805/966–3000. AE, D, DC, MC, V.*

$$–$$$ ✕ **Bouchon.** Santa Barbara's newest upscale restaurant exists as a
showcase for fine local wines. Food runs to the meaty: braised rabbit,
veal chops with asparagus. The atmosphere is intimate and the wine
selection huge. ✉ *11 West Victoria St.,* ☎ *805/730–1160. AE, MC,
V. No lunch.*

$$–$$$ ✕ **Brophy Bros.** The outdoor tables at this casual restaurant have perfect views of the harbor and fishing vessels. A fine place to lunch, Brophy Bros. serves enormous, exceptionally fresh seafood plates. Try the
seafood salad. ✉ *119 Harbor Way,* ☎ *805/966–4418. AE, MC, V.*

$$–$$$ ✕ **Harbor Restaurant.** This sparkling spot on the pier is where locals
take out-of-town guests for great views and standard American food.
The nautical-theme bar and grill upstairs serves sandwiches, large salads, and many appetizers; on a sunny day the outdoor terrace is a glorious spot for a sandwich or a beer. Downstairs you can dine on
seafood, prime rib, and steaks. ✉ *210 Stearns Wharf,* ☎ *805/963–3311.
AE, MC, V.*

$$–$$$ ✕ **Palace Grill.** The Palace has won acclaim for Cajun and Creole
dishes like blackened redfish and jambalaya with dirty rice. Caribbean
fare here includes delicious coconut shrimp. If the dishes aren't spicy
enough for you, each table has a bottle of hot sauce. Be prepared to
wait as long as 45 minutes on weekends. ✉ *8 E. Cota St.,* ☎ *805/963–
5000. AE, MC, V.*

$$–$$$ ✕ **Trattoria Mollie's.** Ethiopian-born chef-owner Mollie Ahlstrand
spent several years in Italy before ending up in California. Her seafood
pasta and plate of seafood and vegetables are among the many subtly
flavored entrées. Lush potted plants surround the tables at this chic,
popular trattoria. ✉ *1250 Coast Village Rd.,* ☎ *805/565–9381. Reservations essential on weekends. AE, MC, V. Closed Mon.*

$–$$$ ✕ **Brigitte's.** This lively State Street café serves California cuisine and
local wines at relatively low prices. The individual pizzas are always
worth trying, as are the pastas, grilled fresh fish, and roast lamb. ✉
1325–1327 State St., ☎ *805/966–9676. AE, D, DC, MC, V. No lunch
Sun.*

$$ ✕ **Pane & Vino.** This tiny trattoria with an equally small sidewalk dining terrace sits in a tree-shaded, flower-decked shopping center. The
cold antipasto is very good, as are the salads, pastas, and grilled meats
and fish. ✉ *1482 E. Valley Rd., Montecito,* ☎ *805/969–9274. Reservations essential. AE, MC, V. No lunch Sun.*

$–$$ ✕ **Café Buenos Aires.** Salads, sandwiches, pastas, and traditional Argentine empanadas (small turnovers filled with chicken, beef, or vegetables) are on the lunch menu at the elegant Buenos Aires. Dinner can
be fashioned from potato omelets, Spanish red sausage in beer sauce,

octopus stewed with tomato and onion, and other tapas. Pastas, fish, larger empanadas, or grilled rib-eye steak (the beef imported from Argentina) sautéed in sweet butter are among the entrées. ⊠ *1316 State St.,* ☎ *805/963–0242. Reservations essential for dinner Thurs.–Sun. AE, DC, MC, V.*

$–$$ ✕ **Cold Spring Tavern.** Well worth the drive out of town, this old road-
★ house, off Hwy. 154 near Cachuma Lake, is on the former stagecoach route through the San Marcos Pass. It's part Harley-biker hangout and part romantic country hideaway, a mix that works surprisingly well. Game dishes—rabbit, venison, quail—are the specialty, along with American standards like ribs, steak, and a great chili. It's a one-of-a-kind spot. ⊠ *5995 Stagecoach Rd., San Marcos Pass,* ☎ *805/967–0066. AE, MC, V.*

$–$$ ✕ **Montecito Café.** The ambience is upscale yet casual at this restau-
rant that serves contemporary cuisine—fresh fish, grilled chicken, steak, and pasta. The salads and lamb dishes are particularly inventive. ⊠ *1295 Coast Village Rd.,* ☎ *805/969–3392. AE, MC, V.*

$ ✕ **D'Angelo.** The bread served by many of the town's best restaurants comes from the ovens of this bakery, which has a few indoor and out-
door tables. Come for breakfast—the brioches are awesome—or for a sandwich or pastry break. D'Angelo is open weekdays from 7 to 6 and weekends from 7 to 3. ⊠ *25 W. Gutierrez St.,* ☎ *805/962–5466. MC, V. No dinner.*

$ ✕ **La Super-Rica.** Praised by Julia Child, this food stand with a patio
★ serves some of the spiciest Mexican dishes between Los Angeles and San Francisco. Fans drive for miles to fill up on the soft tacos and in-
credible beans. ⊠ *622 N. Milpas St., at Alphonse St.,* ☎ *805/963–4940. No credit cards.*

$ ✕ **Roy.** Owner-chef Leroy Gandy serves a $15 fixed-price dinner—a real bargain—that includes a small salad, fresh soup, and a tempting roster of Cal-Mediterranean main courses: shrimp ravioli, marinated leg of lamb with eggplant ratatouille, grilled salmon with pineapple-
orange-mango chutney and a mint-butter sauce. Expect a wait at this downtown storefront on weekends. ⊠ *7 W. Carrillo St.,* ☎ *805/966–5636. AE, D, DC, MC, V.*

$ ✕ **Your Place.** Tasty seafood (try the sea scallops garnished with crispy basil), curries, and vegetarian dishes keep this small restaurant packed for lunch and dinner. Your Place has consistently been named as the best Thai restaurant by local periodicals. ⊠ *22 N. Milpas St.,* ☎ *805/ 966–5151. AE, MC, V. Closed Mon.*

$$$$ ✕ ⬚ **Four Seasons Biltmore Hotel.** Santa Barbara's grande dame has
★ long been the favored spot for the town's high society and the visiting rich and famous to indulge in quiet California-style luxury. Muted pastels and bleached woods give the cabanas behind the main building an airy feel without sacrificing the hotel's reputation for understated el-
egance. Surrounded by lush (but always perfectly manicured) gardens and palms, the Biltmore is a bit more formal than other properties in town. Dining is indoors and formal at the hotel's La Marina Restau-
rant—the California-Continental menu changes monthly—and outdoors and more casual at The Patio. ⊠ *1260 Channel Dr., Montecito 93108,* ☎ *805/969–2261 or 800/332–3442,* 𝔽𝔸𝕏 *805/565–8329. 200 rooms, 17 suites. 2 restaurants, bar, pool, hot tub, spa, putting green, 3 tennis courts, health club, croquet, shuffleboard. AE, DC, MC, V.*

$$$$ ⬚ **San Ysidro Ranch.** At this luxury "ranch" you can feel at home in
★ jeans and cowboy boots, but be prepared to dress for dinner. A hang-
out for the Hollywood set, this romantic hideaway hosted John and Jackie Kennedy on their honeymoon. Guest cottages, all with down comforters and wood-burning stoves or fireplaces, are scattered among 14 acres of orange trees and flower beds. The Eucalyptus Cottage comes

with a private butler. Hiking trails crisscross 500 acres of open space surrounding the property. The Stonehouse Restaurant (☞ *above*) is a Santa Barbara institution. The hotel, which welcomes children and pets, provides personal beauty services and 24-hour room service. ⊠ *900 San Ysidro La., Montecito 93108,* ☎ *805/969–5046 or 800/368–6788,* FAX *805/565–1995. 21 cottages with total of 38 rooms. Restaurant, room service, pool, massage, spa, 2 tennis courts, boccie, exercise room, horseshoes. AE, DC, MC, V. 2-day minimum stay on weekends, 3 days on holidays.*

$$$–$$$$ 🏨 **Cheshire Cat Inn.** A five-minute walk from downtown, this B&B with an *Alice in Wonderland* motif is accessible yet quiet. The largest rooms hold king-size beds and sunken whirlpool tubs. The smaller rooms, dominated by the beds, come with low-lying armchairs and have a twee, Edwardian look. ⊠ *36 W. Valerio St., 93101,* ☎ *805/569–1610,* FAX *805/682–1876. 13 rooms, 4 suites. Full breakfast. AE, D, MC, V.*

$$$–$$$$ 🏨 **El Encanto Hotel.** Actress Hedy Lamarr and President Franklin D. Roosevelt are among the guests who have unwound at this woodsy property near Mission Santa Barbara. Mediterranean-style villas dot the lush 10-acre grounds, along with Craftsman cottages with pine beds and living rooms with old brick fireplaces. ⊠ *1900 Lasuen Rd., 93103,* ☎ *805/687–5000 or 800/346–7039,* FAX *805/687–3903. 83 rooms. Restaurant, bar, minibars, room service, pool, tennis court, conference rooms. AE, D, MC, V.*

$$$–$$$$ 🏨 **Montecito Inn.** Every room at this late-1920s marble palace is adorned with original posters from the films of Charlie Chaplin. The glass doors to the conference room are etched with the great man's image, and the video library contains his entire oeuvre. The rooms on the second floor lead onto a cloisterlike arched colonnade. The bathrooms are fairly basic, although some suites have large marble whirlpool tubs. The suites also have vast Romanesque-style marble fireplaces. ⊠ *1295 Coast Village Rd., 93108,* ☎ *805/969–7854 or 800/843–2017,* FAX *805/969–0623. 53 rooms, 7 suites. Restaurant, bar, refrigerators, in-room VCRs, pool, exercise room, bicycles. Continental breakfast. AE, D, DC, MC, V.*

$$$–$$$$ 🏨 **Simpson House Inn.** Traditional B&B fans will enjoy the beautifully ★ appointed Victorian main house of this inn on a quiet acre in the heart of town. Those seeking total privacy and sybaritic comfort should choose one of the exceptional cottages or century-old barn suites, each with a wood-burning fireplace, luxurious bedding, and state-of-the-art electronics, and several with a whirlpool bath. In-room spa services such as massage and body wraps are available. ⊠ *121 E. Arrellaga St., 93101,* ☎ *805/963–7067 or 800/676–1280,* FAX *805/564–4811. 7 rooms, 4 suites, 3 cottages. Full breakfast. AE, D, MC, V. 2-night minimum stay on weekends.*

$$–$$$$ 🏨 **Glenborough Inn.** One of the best B&Bs in Santa Barbara County, ★ this inn is composed of four buildings constructed around 1900. Several of the very private, themed rooms retain an old, dark-wood feel. If you stay in the Craftsman Room, you'll nearly be swallowed up by the vast bed. As with several of the accommodations in this romantic abode, a private hot tub perches on the patio outside the room. ⊠ *1327 Bath St., 93101,* ☎ *805/966–0589 or 800/962–0589,* FAX *805/564–8610. 7 rooms, 5 suites. Full breakfast. AE, D, DC, MC, V.*

$$–$$$$ 🏨 **Hotel Santa Barbara.** The central location of this hotel makes it one of the better bargains in town. You won't experience all the luxuries of Santa Barbara's pricier accommodations, but the rooms are clean and modern, if a tad charmless. The top-floor rooms have ocean views. Ask for a room in back, away from the noise of State Street. ⊠ *533 State St., 93101,* ☎ *888/259–7700. 72 rooms, 3 suites. Concierge. AE, D, MC, V.*

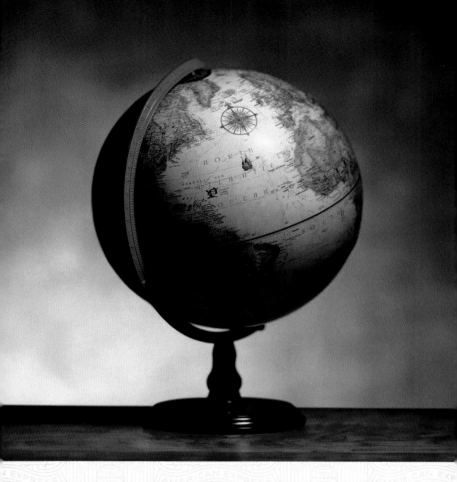

In case you want to see the world.

At American Express, we're here to make your journey a smooth one. So we have over 1,700 travel service locations in over 130 countries ready to help. What else would you expect from the world's largest travel agency?

do more AMERICAN EXPRESS

Travel

Call 1 800 AXP-3429 or visit
www.americanexpress.com/travel

In case you want to be welcomed there.

We're here to see that you're always welcomed at establishments everywhere. That's why millions of people carry the American Express® Card – for peace of mind, confidence, and security, around the world or just around the corner.

do more

Cards

In case you're running low.

We're here to help with more than 190,000 Express Cash locations around the world. In order to enroll, just call American Express at 1 800 CASH-NOW before you start your vacation.

do more

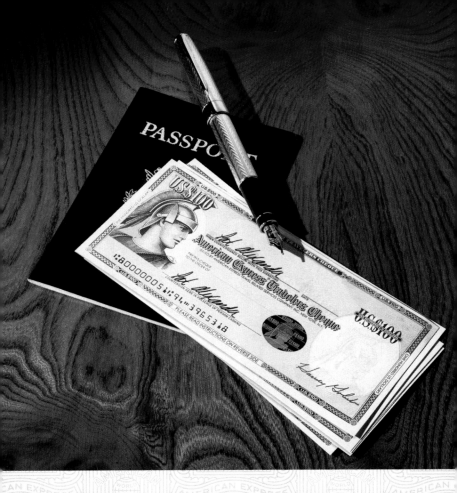

And in case you'd rather be safe than sorry.

We're here with American Express® Travelers Cheques. They're the safe way to carry money on your vacation, because if they're ever lost or stolen you can get a refund, practically anywhere or anytime. To find the nearest place to buy Travelers Cheques, call 1 800 495-1153. Another way we help you do more.

do more

Travelers Cheques

$$–$$$$ ⊞ Villa Rosa. The rooms and intimate lobby of this Spanish-style stucco-and-wood hotel one block from the beach are decorated in an informal Southwestern style. ⊠ *15 Chapala St., 93101,* ☎ *805/966–0851,* FAX *805/962–7159. 18 rooms. Pool, hot tub. Continental breakfast. AE, MC, V. 3-night minimum during holiday periods.*

$$–$$$ ⊞ Old Yacht Club Inn. Built in 1912 as a private home in the California Craftsman style, this inn near the beach was one of Santa Barbara's first B&Bs. The rooms have century-old furnishings and Oriental rugs. The adjacent Hitchcock House holds five rooms with private entrances. ⊠ *431 Corona del Mar Dr., 93103,* ☎ *805/962–1277 or 800/676–1676; 800/549–1676 in CA;* FAX *805/962–3989. 10 rooms, 2 suites. Full breakfast. No smoking. AE, MC, V.*

$$–$$$ ⊞ The Upham. This restored Victorian hotel amid an acre of gardens in the historic downtown area was established in 1871. Period furnishings and antiques adorn the rooms and cottages, some of which have fireplaces and private patios. The rooms vary in size from small to quite spacious. ⊠ *1404 De La Vina St., 93101,* ☎ *805/962–0058 or 800/727–0876,* FAX *805/963–2825. 46 rooms, 4 suites. Restaurant, meeting rooms. Continental breakfast. AE, D, DC, MC, V.*

Nightlife and the Arts

Most major hotels present entertainment nightly during the summer season and on weekends all year. State Street has a good jazz scene. Santa Barbara supports a professional symphony and a chamber orchestra. The proximity to the University of California at Santa Barbara assures an endless stream of visiting artists and performers. To see what's scheduled around town pick up a copy of the free weekly *Santa Barbara Independent* newspaper.

BARS AND CLUBS

Rich leather couches, a crackling fire in chilly weather, a cigar balcony, and pool tables draw a fancy Gen-X crowd to **Blue Agave** (⊠ 20 E. Cota St., ☎ 805/899–4694) for good food and designer martinis. **The James Joyce** (⊠ 513 State St., ☎ 805/962–2688), which sometimes hosts folk and rock performers, is a good place to while away an evening, beer in hand.

Old jazz photos and low lighting lend **Jazz Hall** (⊠ 29 E. Victoria. St.) an ambience that's about as close to the Greenwich Village experience as you're likely to get in these parts. Musicians perform on weekends. **Joe's Cafe** (⊠ 536 State St., ☎ 805/966–4638), where steins of beer accompany hearty bar food, is a fun, if occasionally rowdy, collegiate scene.

The bartenders at **Left at Albuquerque** (⊠ 803 State St., ☎ 805/564–5040) pour 141 tequilas, making the Southwestern-style bar one of your less sedate nightspots. The determinedly pretentious **Martini Madness Lounge** (⊠ 434 State St., ☎ 805/962–5516) hosts a chic crowd that sits on high stools and basks in fluorescent lighting (if you're not in the prime of youth, you'll look awful). The **Plow & Angel** (⊠ San Ysidro Ranch, 900 San Ysidro La., Montecito, ☎ 805/969–5046) books mellow jazz performers on Thursday and Friday. The bar is perfect for those seeking quiet conversation, even romance. **Soho** (⊠ 1221 State St., ☎ 805/962–7776), a hip restaurant and bar, presents weeknight jazz music; on weekends the mood livens with good blues and rock.

PERFORMING ARTS

Arlington Theater (⊠ 1317 State St., ☎ 805/963–4408), a Moorish-style movie palace, is home to the Santa Barbara Symphony. **Center Stage Theatre** (⊠ Paseo Nuevo, 700 block of State St., 2nd floor, ☎ 805/963–0408) presents plays and readings. **Ensemble Theatre Company**

(✉ 914 Santa Barbara St., ☎ 805/962–8606) stages plays by authors ranging from Priestley to Mamet.

The **Granada Theatre** (✉ 1216 State St., ☎ 805/966–2324), a restored movie palace, is the headquarters of the Santa Barbara Civic Light Opera. The **Lobero Theatre** (✉ 33 E. Cañon Perdido St., ☎ 805/963–0761), a state landmark, hosts community theater groups and touring professionals. The **Music Academy of the West** (✉ 1070 Fairway Rd., Montecito, ☎ 805/687–7820), showcases orchestral and operatic works.

Outdoor Activities and Sports

BEACHES

Santa Barbara's beaches don't have the big surf of the shoreline farther south, but they also don't have the crowds. Walk from the parking lot, and you'll usually find a solitary spot. Fog often hugs the coast until about noon in June and July.

The usually gentle surf at **Arroyo Burro County Beach** (✉ Cliff Dr. at Las Positas Rd.) makes it ideal for families with young children. **Goleta Beach Park** (✉ Ward Memorial Hwy.) is a favorite with college students from the nearby University of California campus. Successively west of Santa Barbara off U.S. 101 are **El Capitan, Refugio, and Gaviota state beaches,** each with campsites, picnic tables, and fire rings. East of the city is sheltered, sunny, often crowded **Carpinteria State Beach.**

BICYCLING

The level, two-lane, 3-mi Cabrillo Bike Lane passes the Santa Barbara Zoo, the Andree Clark Bird Refuge, beaches, and the harbor. There are restaurants along the way, or you can stop for a picnic along the palm-lined path looking out on the Pacific. **Beach Rentals** (✉ 22 State St., ☎ 805/966–6733) has bikes, quadricycles, and skates. **Cycles 4 Rent** (✉ Fess Parker's Doubletree Resort, 633 E. Cabrillo Blvd., ☎ 805/564–4333, ext. 444; ✉ 101 State St., ☎ 805/652–0462) has bikes and quadricycles.

BOATS AND CHARTERS

Adventure Outdoor Excursions (☎ 805/963–2248) arranges everything from kayak to mountain bike excursions. **Island Packers** (☎ 805/642–1393) conducts day trips and camping excursions (reservations essential in summer) to the five Channel Islands. **Santa Barbara Sailing Association** (✉ Santa Barbara Yacht Harbor launching ramp, ☎ 805/962–2826 or 800/350–9090) provides sailing instruction, rents and charters sailboats, and organizes dinner and sunset champagne cruises, island excursions, and whale-watching expeditions. **Sea Landing Aquatic Center** (✉ Cabrillo Blvd. at Bath St. and the breakwater, ☎ 805/963–3564) operates surface and deep-sea fishing charters year-round, plus dinner cruises and island and whale-watching excursions.

GOLF

Sandpiper Golf Course (✉ 7925 Hollister Ave., Goleta, ☎ 805/968–1541) is a challenging 18-hole, par-72 course. The greens fee ranges from $70 to $110; an optional cart costs $24. **Santa Barbara Golf Club** (✉ Las Positas Rd. and McCaw Ave., ☎ 805/687–7087) has an 18-hole, par-70 course. The greens fee is about $20; an optional cart costs $10.

HORSEBACK RIDING

The Circle Bar B Guest Ranch (✉ 1800 Refugio Rd., Goleta, ☎ 805/968–1113) operates trail rides.

TENNIS

Many hotels in Santa Barbara have courts. Day permits ($3) can be purchased for these excellent public courts: **Las Positas Municipal**

Courts (✉ 1002 Las Positas Rd.), **Municipal Courts** (✉ Near Salinas St. and U.S. 101). For permits, call ☎ 805/564–5418. For **Pershing Park** (✉ Castillo St. and Cabrillo Blvd.), call ☎ 805/564–5517.

Shopping

State Street, the commercial hub of Santa Barbara, is a joy to shop. Chic malls, quirky storefronts, antiques emporiums, elegant boutiques, and funky thrift shops are on or near the street, and they're all accessible on foot or by taking the battery-powered trolley (25¢) that runs between the waterfront and the 1300 block. Swank boutiques line Montecito's **Coast Village Road,** where members of the landed gentry pick up truffle oil, picture frames, and designer sweats.

SHOPPING AREAS

Shops, art galleries, and studios share the courtyard and gardens of **El Paseo** (✉ Cañon Perdido St. between State and Anacapa Sts.), an arcade rich in history. Lunch on the outdoor patio is a nice break during a downtown tour. Open-air **Paseo Nuevo** (✉ 700 and 800 blocks of State St.), home to chains such as the Eddie Bauer Home Store and Macy's, also contains cherished local institutions like Stampa Barbara (a rubber-stamp paradise) and the children's clothier This Little Piggy.

Antiques and gift shops are clustered in restored Victorian buildings on Brinkerhoff Avenue, two blocks west of State Street at West Cota Street. Serious antiques hunters head a few miles south of Santa Barbara to the beach town of Summerland, which is rife with shops and markets. For a map and guide to Santa Barbara antiques dealers, drop by 533 Brinkerhoff Avenue or call ☎ 805/962–4247 to have one mailed.

BOOKS

Barnes & Noble (✉ 829 State St., ☎ 805/962–8509) and **Borders** (✉ 900 State St., ☎ 805/899–3668) hold court on State Street. **Chaucer's Bookstore** (✉ Loreta Plaza, 3321 State St., ☎ 805/682–6787) is a well-stocked independent. **Sullivan Goss** (✉ 7 E. Anapamu St., ☎ 805/730–1460) stocks books on California history and art. **The Book Den** (✉ 11 E. Anapamu St., ☎ 805/962–3321) has the town's largest selection of used books.

CLOTHING

The complete line of **Big Dog Sportswear** (✉ 6 E. Yanonali St., ☎ 805/963–8728) is sold at the Santa Barbara–based company's flagship store. **Pacific Leisure** (✉ 929 State St., ☎ 805/962–8828) stocks the latest in casual wear, shoes, and beach towels. **Territory Ahead** (✉ 515 State St., ☎ 805/962–5558), a high-quality outdoorsy catalog company, sells fashionably rugged clothing for men and women. **Tienda Ho** (✉ 1105 State St., ☎ 805/564–7030) is a bohemian bazaar combining Indian, Moroccan, and Indonesian influences.

Wendy Foster–Pierre LaFond (✉ 833 State St., ☎ 805/966–2276), an upscale local clothier, captures the fluid California style of women's wear. There are two even tonier branches in Montecito (✉ 516 San Ysidro Rd., ☎ 805/565–1502; ✉ 1121 Coast Village Rd., ☎ 805/565–1599). The store on Coast Village Road goes by the name Angel.

OJAI

 40 mi southeast of Santa Barbara, U.S. 101 to Hwy. 150 to Hwy. 33.

The acres of orange and avocado groves in and around rural Ojai look like the postcard images of agricultural southern California from decades ago. Recent years have seen an influx of artists, showbiz types, and others who have opted for a life out of the fast lane. The Ojai Valley, which director Frank Capra used as a backdrop for his 1936 film *Lost Horizon,* sizzles in the summer, when temperatures routinely reach 90°F.

Compact Ojai can be easily explored on foot, or you can hop on **The Ojai Valley Trolley,** which takes riders on a one-hour loop (between 7:40 and 5:40 on weekdays, 9 and 5 on weekends). Tell the driver you're a visitor, and you'll get an informal guided tour.

The works of local artists can be seen in the Spanish-style shopping arcade along the main street. **The Art Center** (⊠ 113 S. Montgomery, ☎ 805/646–0117) exhibits artwork and presents theater and dance. **The Ojai Valley Museum** (⊠ 130 W. Ojai Ave., ☎ 805/640–1390) documents the valley's history and displays Native American artifacts.

Native oaks shelter the used titles at **Bart's Books** (⊠ 302 W. Matilija, ☎ 805/646–3755), an outdoor store. **Local Hero** (⊠ 254 E. Ojai Ave., ☎ 805/646–3165) sells books and hosts music, readings, and book signings on weekend evenings. There's also a café here.

Organic and specialty growers sell their produce on Sunday from 10 to 2 (9 to 1 in summer) at the **Farmers Market** behind the arcade. On Wednesday evening in summer the free all-American music played by the Ojai Band draws crowds to **Libbey Park** (⊠ Ojai Ave. in downtown Ojai).

The 9-mi **Ojai Valley Trail** is one of several paths in the hills surrounding town. **Ojai Valley Chamber of Commerce** (⊠ 150 W. Ojai Ave., ☎ 805/646–8126) publishes a regional trail map and runs a visitor center.

For more than five decades the **Ojai Festival** (☎ 805/646–2094) has attracted internationally known progressive and traditional musicians for outdoor concerts in Libbey Park on the weekend after Memorial Day.

Dining and Lodging

$$$ ✕ **The Ranch House.** The town's best eatery serves rich paté appetizers and main dishes like chicken soaked in vermouth and salmon poached in white wine. The verdant patio is a delight. ⊠ *S. Lomita Ave.,* ☎ *805/646–2360. AE, D, DC, MC, V.*

$$–$$$ ✕ **Go Fish California Sushi & Grill.** Sushi mingles with American and Mexican seafood dishes on the menu of this fun place. Entertainers perform on the patio on weekend nights. ⊠ *469 E. Ojai Ave.,* ☎ *805/ 640–1057. MC, V.*

$$–$$$ ✕ **L'Auberge.** Tasty French–Belgian food is paired with a terrific country setting here. When the weather's fine, those in the know reserve an early table on the patio so they can accompany their rack of lamb with a glorious sunset. ⊠ *314 El Paseo Rd.,* ☎ *805/646–2288. AE, MC, V. No lunch weekdays.*

$$–$$$ ✕ **Suzanne's Cuisine.** Peppered filet mignon, linguine with steamed clams, and salmon with sauerkraut in a dill beurre blanc are among the offerings at this European-style restaurant. Pastas and meat dishes dominate the dinner menu and salads and soups star at lunchtime. Most of the bread and all the desserts are made on the premises. ⊠ *502 W. Ojai Ave.,* ☎ *805/640–1961. MC, V. Closed Tues. and 1st 2 wks in Jan.*

$$$$ ✕▥ **Oaks at Ojai.** Comfortable but not luxurious, this spa has a fitness package that includes lodging, use of the spa facilities, 16 fitness classes, and three nutritionally balanced low-calorie meals. ⊠ *122 E. Ojai Ave., 93023,* ☎ *805/646–5573 or 800/753–6257,* ℻ *805/640–*

1504. *46 rooms. Dining room, pool, beauty salon, massage, hot tub, sauna, spa, exercise room. D, MC, V. 2-day minimum stay.*

$$$$ ⊞ **Ojai Valley Inn & Spa.** This outdoorsy golf-oriented resort is set on
★ landscaped grounds lush with flowers. The peaceful setting comes with hillside views in nearly all directions. Nearby is the inn's 800-acre ranch, where you can hike, mountain bike, ride horses, and bird-watch. Some of the nicest rooms are in the original adobe building. Families can make use of Camp Ojai, held in summer and on holidays for kids from age 3 to 12, and the remarkable collection of miniature animals in the petting farm. The spa has massage and treatment rooms, a cardiovascular floor, a beauty salon, and quiet rooms. The two restaurants tout "Ojai regional cuisine" that incorporates locally grown produce and locally made foods. ⊠ *905 Country Club Rd., 93023,* ☎ *805/646–5511 or 800/422–6524,* ᶠᴬˣ *805/646–7969. 207 units. 2 restaurants, bar, 2 pools, spa, 18-hole golf course, 8 tennis courts, hiking, horseback riding, mountain bikes. AE, D, DC, MC, V.*

$$–$$$ ⊞ **The Blue Iguana Inn.** Local artists run this Southwestern-style hotel west of downtown. Small and cozy, the inn is designed around a courtyard. The work of the artist-owners decorate the rooms. If you like a particular work, you can negotiate with the front desk to purchase it. The suites have kitchenettes. ⊠ *11794 N. Ventura Ave. (Hwy. 33), 93023.,* ☎ *805/646–5277. 4 rooms, 7 suites. Refrigerators, pool, hot tub. AE, D, DC, MC, V.*

$$ ⊞ **Best Western Casa Ojai.** This modern hotel sits on Ojai's main drag, across from Soule Park Golf Course. Rooms are simple and clean. ⊠ *1302 E. Ojai Ave., 93023,* ☎ *805/646–8175 or 800/255–8175,* ᶠᴬˣ *805/640–8247. 43 rooms, 2 suites. In-room modem lines, pool, hot tub. Continental breakfast. AE, D, DC, MC, V.*

THE CENTRAL COAST A TO Z

Arriving and Departing

By Bus
Greyhound Lines (☎ 800/231–2222) provides service from San Francisco and Los Angeles to San Luis Obispo and Santa Barbara.

By Car
U.S. 101 and Highway 1 are the main routes into the Central Coast from Los Angeles and San Francisco. Interstate 280 to U.S. 101 to San Luis Obispo is the quickest route from San Francisco to the southern portion of the Central Coast, but it's not the scenic route. Highway 46 heads west from the Central Valley to Paso Robles, where it becomes narrower as it continues to the coast, intersecting Highway 1 a few miles south of Cambria. Highway 33 heads south from the Central Valley to Ojai; about 60 mi north of Ojai, Highway 166 leaves Highway 33, traveling due west through the Sierra Madre Mountains. Highway 166 intersects with U.S. 101 north of Santa Maria, and then continues west to Highway 1.

By Plane
America West Express, American/American Eagle, Skywest/Delta, United/United Express, and US Airways Express fly into **Santa Barbara Municipal Airport** (⊠ 500 Fowler Rd., ☎ 805/683–4011), 8 mi from downtown. *See* Air Travel *in* Smart Travel Tips A to Z for airline phone numbers.

Santa Barbara Airbus (☎ 805/964–7759 or 800/733–6354) shuttles travelers between Santa Barbara and Los Angeles for $35 one-way and $65 round-trip (slight discount with 24-hour notice). The **Santa Bar-**

bara Metropolitan Transit District (☎ 805/683–3702) Bus 11 runs from the airport to the downtown transit center.

By Train

The **Amtrak** (☎ 800/872–7245) *Coast Starlight,* which runs between Los Angeles, Oakland, and Seattle, stops in Santa Barbara and San Luis Obispo. Several *San Diegan* trains operate daily between Santa Barbara, Los Angeles, and San Diego. Local numbers are, in Santa Barbara, ☎ 805/963–1015; in San Luis Obispo, ☎ 805/541–0505.

Getting Around

By Bus

From Monterey and Carmel, **Monterey–Salinas Transit** (☎ 831/899–2555) operates buses to Big Sur between May and September. From San Luis Obispo, **Central Coast Transit** (☎ 805/541–2228) runs buses around Santa Maria and out to the coast. **Santa Barbara Metropolitan Transit District** (☎ 805/683–3702 or 805/963–3364) provides local service. The **State Street and Waterfront shuttles** cover their respective sections of Santa Barbara during the day.

By Car

The best way to see the most dramatic section of the Central Coast, the 70 mi between Big Sur and San Simeon, is by car. Heading south on Highway 1, you'll be on the ocean side of the road and will get the best views. Don't expect to make good time along here. The road is narrow and twisting with a single lane in each direction, making it difficult to pass the many lumbering RVs. In fog or rain the drive can be downright nerve-racking. Once you start south from Carmel, there is no route east from Highway 1 until Highway 46 heads inland from Cambria to connect with U.S. 101.

Highway 1 and U.S. 101 run north–south and more or less parallel, with Highway 1 hugging the coast and U.S. 101 remaining a few to a few dozen miles inland. Along some stretches the two roads join and run together for a while. At Morro Bay, Highway 1 moves inland for 13 mi and connects with U.S. 101 at San Luis Obispo. From here south to Pismo Beach the two highways run concurrently. U.S. 101 is the quicker route to Santa Barbara; Highway 1 rejoins it north of town at Las Cruces.

Contacts and Resources

B&B Reservations Service

Bed and Breakfast Santa Barbara (☎ 805/898–1905 or 800/557–7898).

Doctors

Cottage Hospital (✉ Pueblo St. at Bath St., Santa Barbara, ☎ 805/682–7111; 805/569–7210 for emergency).

Emergencies

Ambulance (☎ 911). **Fire** (☎ 911). **Police** (☎ 911).

Guided Tours

Eagle- and wildlife-watching excursions take place on the *Osprey,* a 48-ft cruiser that plies Cachuma Lake, a 20-minute drive from Solvang and a 40-minute one from Santa Barbara. For additional information, contact the **Cachuma Lake Recreation Area,** Santa Barbara County Park Department (✉ Star Route, Santa Barbara 93105, ☎ 805/688–4658).

A motorized San Francisco–style cable car operated by **Santa Barbara Trolley Co.** (☎ 805/965–0353) makes 90-minute runs from 10 AM to

4 PM past major hotels, shopping areas, and attractions. Get off when you wish to, and pick up another trolley when you're ready to move on. The trolley departs from and returns to Stearns Wharf. The fare is $5.

Road Conditions

Caltrans (☎ 800/427–7623).

Visitor Information

Central Coast Tourism Council (⊠ Box 14011, San Luis Obispo, 93406, ☎ 805/544–0241). **Ojai Chamber of Commerce** (⊠ Box 1134, 150 W. Ojai Ave., 93024, ☎ 805/646–8126). **Paso Robles Chamber of Commerce** (⊠ 1225 Paso Robles, 93446, ☎ 805/238–0506). **Paso Robles Vintners and Growers Association** (⊠ 1940 Spring St., Paso Robles 93446, ☎ 805/239–8463). **Santa Barbara Conference and Visitors Bureau** (⊠ 12 E. Carrillo St., 93101, ☎ 805/966–9222 or 800/927–4688). **Santa Barbara County Vintners' Association** (⊠ Box 1558, Santa Ynez 93460, ☎ 805/688–0881 or 800/218–0881). **Solvang Visitors Center** (⊠ 1511 Mission Dr., 93434, ☎ 805/688–6144).

11 LOS ANGELES

In certain lights Los Angeles displays its
Spanish heritage, but even more evident is
its vibrancy as a Pacific Rim cultural and
economic center. Hollywood, the beaches,
and the valleys are all within an hour's
drive. There are also important examples of
20th-century domestic architecture, miles of
freeways, and glamorous enclaves like
Beverly Hills. Everything about Los Angeles
is grand—even overdone—which is part of
the city's charm. It's all for show, but the
show's usually a good one.

DON'T BELIEVE EVERYTHING YOU'VE HEARD about Los Angeles. Chances are it's an exaggeration, good or bad, and the truth is probably somewhere in between. Few places on this planet are as hard to categorize as L.A. It's too large and diverse. The city of 3.5 million sprawls across 476 square mi of desert basin, mountain canyons, and coastal beaches. Outside the city limits, another 6 million people live in 80 incorporated cities within Los Angeles County. Another 5 million reside in the four surrounding counties.

The largest population of Pacific Islanders in the nation lives here, as well as the world's third-largest Hispanic population (after Mexico City and Guadalajara). People from more than 100 countries call Los Angeles home. Signs in Spanish, Korean, Thai, Chinese, Japanese, Armenian, and Russian are as common in some areas of the city as English signs. What isn't so well known is that this diversity dates back to the city's beginnings: Indians, blacks, mestizos, and Spaniards were among the 44 settlers who first arrived from the Mexican provinces of Sonora and Sinaloa in September 1781.

Though its myriad cultures lend the city variety, life is not uniformly harmonious. There's ceaseless rankling about bilingual education in the schools, and bloody rioting has divided the city along racial lines more than once, most recently in 1992 when the acquittal of police officers accused of beating motorist Rodney King provoked the nation's worst civil unrest ever. That experience left a scar of misunderstanding and mistrust that has yet to heal completely.

But communities throughout the region pulled together after the devastating 1994 Northridge earthquake and two years later, when wildfires raged in Malibu. The cooperation of Los Angelenos in these times of crisis contradicts the stereotype of a self-indulgent populace concerned only about going to the gym and buying expensive gadgets.

If there's a universal symbol of Los Angeles, it's the automobile. As for the freeways—well, they're really not so bad. They're well-signed and for travel at times other than rush hour, they're the best route from one end of the city to the other. Here are a couple tips: most freeways are known by a name and a number; for example, the Hollywood (U.S. 101). Depending on the time of day you're traveling, distance in miles doesn't mean much. The 10 mi between the San Fernando Valley and downtown Los Angeles, for instance, might take an hour to travel during rush hour but only 20 minutes at other times.

EXPLORING LOS ANGELES

Revised and updated by Stephen Dolainski

Seeing Los Angeles requires covering a lot of territory, but that doesn't mean you have to spend all your time in a car. Getting out of your car is the only way to really get to know Los Angeles. The following tours, designed to cover the highlights, should give you a glimpse of what makes this city unique. We've divided the major sightseeing areas of Los Angeles into nine driving and walking tours:

Downtown, the historical and cultural heart of Los Angeles, has a vibrant, multicultural personality.

Hollywood still reigns as the entertainment capital of the world.

Museum Row and Farmers Market make for an entertaining day of novelties, such as a fossil-filled tar pit and a museum of miniatures, as well as high culture—all jump-started with coffee and pastries at L.A.'s most colorful marketplace.

Beverly Hills and Century City is the best place to go if you're looking for glamour and glitz.

Westside has become a hot destination with the arrival of the Getty Center.

Santa Monica, Venice, and Malibu are the coastall communities that give Los Angeles its sunny, surf-swept image.

The San Fernando Valley, home to Universal Studios, Warner Bros., and NBC, also has an historic mission.

Pasadena, famed for the town's annual Tournament of Roses parade, has a rich legacy of historic architecture, a top-notch museum, a botanic garden, a historic mission, and an old town with a lively street scene.

Palos Verdes, San Pedro, and Long Beach are South Bay communities with a working harbor, an historic luxury liner, and an aquarium as their main draws.

Orientation

Looking at a map of sprawling Los Angeles, first-time visitors are sometimes overwhelmed. Where to begin? What to see first? And what about all those freeways? Here's some advice: relax. Begin by setting your priorities—movie and television fans should first head to Hollywood, Universal Studios, and a taping of a television show. Beach lovers and outdoorsy types might start out in Santa Monica or Venice or Malibu, or spend an afternoon in Griffith Park, one of the largest city parks in the country. Those with a cultural bent will probably make a beeline for the new Getty Center in Brentwood (make parking reservations far in advance) or the reorganized Los Angeles County Museum of Art. Urban explorers might begin with downtown Los Angeles.

Downtown Los Angeles

Most visitors to Los Angeles who aren't staying at one of the big convention hotels downtown never make it to this part of the city. But downtown is the heart of this great city, its financial core, as well as its historical and cultural soul.

A Good Tour
Numbers in the text correspond to numbers in the margin and on the Downtown Los Angeles map.

A convenient and inexpensive minibus service—DASH, or Downtown Area Short Hop—has several routes that travel past most of the sights on this tour, stopping every two blocks or so. Each ride costs 25¢, so you can hop on and off without spending a fortune. Special routes operate on weekends. Call **DASH** (☎ from all Los Angeles area codes, 808–2273) for routes and hours of operation.

Begin a downtown tour by heading north on **Broadway** ① from 8th or 9th Street. At the southeast corner of Broadway and 3rd is the **Bradbury Building** ②. Across the street is the **Grand Central Market** ③. Once you've made your way through its tantalizing stalls you'll come out the opposite side onto Hill Street.

Cross Hill Street and climb aboard **Angels Flight Railway** ④, a funicular that sweeps you up a steep incline to a courtyard called Watercourt (it's surrounded by bubbling, cascading fountains). From here, walk toward the glass pyramidal skylight topping the **Museum of Contemporary Art** ⑤, visible a half block north on Grand Avenue.

You can now either retrace your steps to Watercourt for the Angels Flight descent to Hill Street, Grand Central Market, and your car; or walk two blocks south on Grand to 5th Street. There you'll find two of downtown's historical and architectural treasures: the **Regal Biltmore Hotel** ⑥ and the **Central Library** ⑦. Behind the library are the tranquil MacGuire Gardens. Across 5th Street are the **Bunker Hill Steps** ⑧.

Back in your car, continue north on Broadway to 1st Street. A right turn here will take you into **Little Tokyo** ⑨ and the expanded **Japanese American National Museum** ⑩. The **Geffen Contemporary** ⑪ art museum, an arm of MOCA, is just one block north on Central. For a tranquil respite, backtrack on Central to 2nd Street and head two blocks north to Los Angeles Street to get to the rooftop **Japanese Garden** ⑫ at the New Otani Hotel.

From Little Tokyo, turn left (north) from 1st onto Alameda Street. As you pass over the freeway, you'll come to the next stop, **Union Station** ⑬, on the right. Street parking is limited, so your best bet is to park in the pay lot at Union Station (about $5). After a look inside this grand railway terminal, cross Alameda to **Olvera Street** ⑭.

From Union Station, turn right on Alameda and then immediately left on Cesar Chavez Avenue for three blocks. At Broadway, turn right to **Chinatown** ⑮. If you have kids in tow, reverse your route on Broadway from Chinatown; cross back over the freeway, and at Temple Street make a left for the three-block drive to the **Los Angeles Children's Museum** ⑯ at the Los Angeles Mall. Look to the right as you drive down Temple to see the back of **Los Angeles City Hall** ⑰. A few blocks farther west at Grand Avenue is the **Music Center** ⑱.

TIMING
The weekend is the best time to explore downtown. There's less traffic, parking is easier to find on the streets (bring quarters for meters), and cheaper day rates prevail in the lots. Seeing everything mentioned on this tour would take at least a full day, if not two. Expect to spend at least an hour in Chinatown, Olvera Street, and Little Tokyo—longer if you stop to eat, watch a parade, or visit a museum. The **Los Angeles Conservancy** (☎ 213/623–2489) regularly conducts Saturday morning walking tours of downtown architectural landmarks and districts.

Sights to See

❹ **Angels Flight Railway.** This turn-of-the-century funicular was dubbed "the shortest in the world." Two original orange-and-black wooden cable railway cars take riders on a 70-second ride up a 298-ft incline from Hill Street (between 3rd and 4th streets) to the Watercourt at California Plaza. ☎ 213/626–1901. ⬛ 25¢ one-way. ☉ Daily 6:30 AM–10 PM.

★ ❷ **Bradbury Building.** Designed in 1893 by a novice architect who drew his inspiration from a science-fiction story and a conversation with his dead brother via a Ouija board, this building is a marvelous specimen of Victorian-era commercial architecture. Originally the site of turn-of-the-century sweatshops, it now houses somewhat more genteel firms. The interior atrium courtyard, with its glass skylight and open balconies and elevator, is frequently used as a movie locale (*Blade Runner* was filmed here). The building is open weekdays from 9 to 6 and on weekends until 5 for a peek, as long as you don't wander past the lobby. ⊠ 304 S. Broadway (southeast corner Broadway and 3rd St.), ☎ 213/626–1893.

Exploring Los Angeles *(Boxes Refer to Detail Maps)*

SAN FERNANDO

Foothill Fwy.

San Fernando Valley

BURBANK

GLENDALE

CANOGA PARK

RESEDA

Ventura

Sepulveda Dam Recreation Area

VAN NUYS

NORTH HOLLYWOOD

Fwy.

Golden State Fwy.

Mulholland Dr.

SHERMAN OAKS

Hollywood

Griffith Park

SANTA MONICA MTS.

Topanga State Park

WEST HOLLYWOOD

Hollywood Blvd.

Sunset Blvd

Beverly Hills and the Westside

BEVERLY HILLS

HOLLYWOOD

WESTWOOD

Museum Row and Farmers Market

DOWN TOWN

Sunset Blvd.

Santa

Monica Blvd.

Monica

Monica Fwy.

Downt Los An

MALIBU

PACIFIC PALISADES

Santa Monica, Venice, and Malibu

SANTA MONICA

Santa

San Diego Fwy.

CULVER CITY

Santa

Slauson Ave.

N

VENICE

MARINA DEL REY

INGLEWOOD

Los Angeles International Airport

EL SEGUNDO

Imperial Hwy.

Sepulveda

Hawthorne Blvd.

Western Ave.

Harbor Fwy.

MANHATTAN BEACH

HERMOSA BEACH

TORRANCE

San Diego

REDONDO BEACH

Pacific

Coast

Hwy.

PACIFIC OCEAN

PALOS VERDES ESTATES

RANCHO PALOS VERDES

SAN PEDRO

0   5 miles

0   5 km

Long Beach, San Pedro, and Palos Verdes

366

Downtown Los Angeles

Angels Flight
Railway, **4**

Bradbury
Building, **2**

Broadway, **1**

Bunker Hill Steps, **8**

Central Library, **7**

Chinatown, **15**

The Geffen
Contemporary at
MOCA, **11**

Grand Central
Market, **3**

Japanese American
National Museum, **10**

Japanese Garden, **12**

Little Tokyo, **9**

Los Angeles
Children's
Museum, **16**

Los Angeles City
Hall, **17**

The Museum of
Contemporary
Art at California
Plaza, **5**

Music Center, **18**

Olvera Street, **14**

Regal Biltmore
Hotel, **6**

Union Station, **13**

❶ **Broadway.** From the late 19th century to the 1950s Broadway was the main shopping and entertainment street downtown. Photos taken during those glory days show sidewalks crowded with shoppers and lights ablaze on movie marquees. About the only evidence of that period are the few movie palaces still in operation between 8th and 5th streets: look for the **Orpheum** (✉ 842 S. Broadway) and the **Million Dollar** (✉ 307 S. Broadway).

Much of the historical character of Broadway has suffered over the years, but the avenue today is as colorful, vibrant, and noisy as ever. Shops and businesses catering to a mostly Mexican and Central American immigrant clientele have moved into the old movie palaces between 1st and 9th streets.

❽ **Bunker Hill Steps.** A "stream" flows down the center of this monumental staircase into a small pool at its base. The stream originates at the top of the stairs where Robert Graham's nude female sculpture *Source Figure* stands atop a cylindrical base that mimics the shape of the trunks of the surrounding palm trees. ✉ *5th St., between Grand Ave. and Figueroa St.*

★ ☙ **California Science Center.** Interactive exhibits here illustrate the relevance of science to everyday life. Tess, the 50-ft Animatronic star of the exhibit "Body Works," demonstrates how the body's organs work together to maintain balance. You can also build a structure to see how it stands up to an earthquake, or ride a high-wire bicycle to learn about gravity. The IMAX theater, with 3-D capabilities and a seven-story movie screen, features science-related films. ✉ *700 State Dr., Exposition Park,* ☎ *323/724–3623; IMAX 213/744–2019.* ☑ *Free, except for IMAX (prices vary); parking $5.* ☉ *Daily 10–5.*

★ ❼ **Central Library.** Major fires in the 1980s closed the library for six years. Today, at twice its former size, it's the third-largest public library in the nation. The original building, designed by Bertram Goodhue, was completely restored to its 1926 condition, with the pyramid tower and its torch symbolizing the Light of Learning still crowning the building. ✉ *630 W. 5th St. (at Flower St.),* ☎ *213/228–7000.* ☑ *Free.* ☉ *Mon.–Thurs. 10–5:30, Fri.–Sat. 10–6, Sun. 1–5; docent tours weekdays at 12:30, Sat. at 11 and 2, Sun. at 2.*

⓯ **Chinatown.** Los Angeles's Chinatown is bordered by Yale, Bernard, Ord, and Alameda streets, but North Broadway is the heart. More than 15,000 Chinese and Southeast Asians live in the Chinatown area, but many thousands more regularly frequent the savory markets. Dim sum parlors are another big draw; **Empress Pavilion** (✉ 988 N. Hill St., ☎ 213/ 617–9898) is one of the best. Call the **Chinese Chamber of Commerce** (☎ 213/617–0396) for information about Chinese New Year and other events.

El Pueblo de Los Angeles Historical Monument. This site that commemorates Los Angeles's heritage encompasses many significant buildings, a park, and festive **Olvera Street** (☞ *below*). ✉ *Olvera and Temple Sts.*

⓫ **Geffen Contemporary at MOCA.** In 1982, Los Angeles architect Frank Gehry transformed a warehouse in Little Tokyo into a temporary space while the permanent home for the **Museum of Contemporary Art (MOCA)** (☞ *below*) was being built a mile away. The Temporary Contemporary, with its large, flexible space allowing for wacky installations and big multimedia projects, was such a hit that it remains part of the museum facility. The Geffen houses part of MOCA's permanent collection, which spans the years from the 1940s to the present, and usually one or two temporary exhibits. ⊠ *152 N. Central Ave.,* ☎ *213/626–6222.* ⊡ *$6, free with MOCA admission on same day; free Thurs. 5–8.* ◯ *Tues.–Sun. 11–5, Thurs. until 8.*

★ ❸ **Grand Central Market.** The city's largest and most active food market is also a testament to Los Angeles's diversity. This block-long marketplace of colorful and exotic produce, herbs, and meat draws a faithful clientele from the Latino community, senior citizens on a budget, and Westside matrons for whom money is no object. Even if you don't plan to buy anything, the market is a delightful place to browse. The butcher shops display everything from lambs' heads to pigs' tails; the produce stalls are piled high with locally grown avocados and very ripe, very red tomatoes. Several taco stands make for a tasty on-the-go meal. ⊠ *317 S. Broadway,* ☎ *213/624–2378.* ⊡ *Free.* ◯ *Mon.–Sat. 9–6; Sun. 10–6.*

★ ❿ **Japanese American National Museum.** What was it like to grow up on a coffee plantation in Hawaii? How was life for Japanese Americans interned in concentration camps during World War II? These questions are addressed by changing exhibits at this museum in Little Tokyo. Volunteer docents are on hand to share their own stories and experiences. ⊠ *369 E. 1st St., at Central Ave.,* ☎ *213/625–0414.* ⊡ *$6.* ◯ *Tues.–Thurs. and weekends 10–5, Fri. 11–8.*

⓬ **Japanese Garden.** Landscape architect Sentaru Iwaki modeled this rooftop oasis at the New Otani Hotel and Garden after a 400-year-old garden in Tokyo. ⊠ *New Otani Hotel and Garden, 120 S. Los Angeles St.,* ☎ *213/629–1200.* ⊡ *Free.*

❾ **Little Tokyo.** The original neighborhood of Los Angeles's Japanese community, this downtown area has been deserted by most of those immigrants, who have moved to suburban areas such as Gardena and West Los Angeles. Still, Little Tokyo remains a cultural focal point. Nisei Week ("nisei" is the name for second-generation Japanese) is celebrated here every August with traditional drums, dancing, a carnival, and a huge parade. Bounded by 1st, San Pedro, 3rd, and Central streets, Little Tokyo has dozens of sushi bars, tempura restaurants, and trinket shops. **The Japanese American Cultural and Community Center** (⊠ 244 S. San Pedro St., ☎ 213/628–2725) presents traditional and contemporary cultural events.

🦆 ⓰ **Los Angeles Children's Museum.** Hands-on exhibits allow kids to record a song, make a TV show, learn about recycling, create arts and crafts, build a city out of pillows, and practice being a firefighter. ⊠ *310 N. Main St.,* ☎ *213/687–8800.* ⊡ *$5.* ◯ *Weekends 10–5 (during summer vacation, daily 10–5).*

⓱ **Los Angeles City Hall.** This often-photographed, very recognizable building has made numerous appearances on *Superman, Dragnet,* and other popular television shows. Erected in the late 1920s with a pointy spire at the top, the 28-story Art Deco treasure is closed for seismic renovations, and won't be open again until probably after the turn of the century. ⊠ *200 N. Spring St.*

★ ❺ **The Museum of Contemporary Art at California Plaza.** The 5,000-piece permanent collection of MOCA is split between **Geffen Contemporary** (☞ *above*) and the galleries of this site, a red sandstone building designed by Japanese architect Arata Isozaki. The collection represents art from 1940 to the present, including works by Mark Rothko, Franz Kline, Susan Rothenberg, Diane Arbus, and Robert Frank. MOCA also sponsors at least 20 exhibitions a year by both established and new artists in all visual media. ⊠ *250 S. Grand Ave.,* ☎ *213/626–*

6222. ⬚ *$6; free on same day with Geffen Contemporary admission, and also Thurs. 5–8.*

⑱ **Music Center.** L.A.'s major performing arts center since its opening in 1969, the Music Center is home to the Los Angeles Philharmonic, the Los Angeles Opera (where Plácido Domingo will be artistic director in 2000), and the Center Theater Group. The Music Center has also been the site of the Academy Awards. The largest and grandest of the three theaters is the **Dorothy Chandler Pavilion,** named after the wife of former *Los Angeles Times* publisher Norman Chandler (she was instrumental in raising the money to build the complex). The round building in the middle, the **Mark Taper Forum,** is a smaller theater showing mainly experimental works, many on a pre-Broadway run. The **Ahmanson,** at the north end, is the venue for big musicals. The vast complex's cement plaza has a fountain and a Jacques Lipchitz sculpture. ⬚ *135 N. Grand Ave., at 1st St.,* ☎ *213/972–7211; 213/972–7483 tour information.* ⬚ *Free.* ⊙ *60-min tour year-round, but call for days and times.*

★ ⬚ **Natural History Museum of Los Angeles County.** The museum has a rich collection of prehistoric fossils and extensive bird, insect, and marine-life exhibits. A brilliant display of stones can be seen in the Gem and Mineral Hall. Exhibits typifying various cultural groups include pre-Columbian artifacts and a display of crafts from the South Pacific. The Times-Mirror Hall of Native American Cultures delves into the history of Los Angeles's earliest inhabitants. The Ralph M. Parsons Discovery Center for children has hands-on exhibits. ⬚ *900 Exposition Blvd.,* ☎ *213/763–3466.* ⬚ *$8; free 1st Tues. of month.* ⊙ *Weekdays 9:30–5, weekends and holidays 10–5.*

★ ⬚ ⑭ **Olvera Street.** Lively, one-block Olvera Street tantalizes with tile walkways, piñatas, mariachis, and authentic Mexican food. Restored as an open-air Mexican market in 1930, the street is the symbol of the city's beginnings when the original settlers built earthen and willow huts near the river. Vendors sell puppets, tooled leather goods, sandals, and other items from little stalls that line the center of the narrow street. On weekends the restaurants are packed, and there is usually music in the plaza and along the street. Two Mexican holidays, Cinco de Mayo (May 5) and Independence Day (September 16), draw huge crowds. To see Olvera Street at its quietest, visit late on a weekday afternoon. For information, stop by the **Olvera Street Visitors Center,** housed in the Sepulveda House (⬚ 622 N. Main St., ☎ 213/628–1274), a Victorian built in 1887 as a hotel and boardinghouse. The center is open from Monday through Saturday between 10 and 3.

Pelanconi House (⬚ W-17 Olvera St.), built in 1855, was the first brick building in Los Angeles and has been home to La Golondrina restaurant for 60 years.

Avila Adobe (⬚ E-10 Olvera St.), built in 1818, is considered the oldest building still standing in Los Angeles. This graceful, simple adobe with a traditional interior courtyard is furnished in the style of the 1840s. It is open daily from 9 to 5 (until 4 in winter).

The south wall of the **Italian Hall building** (⬚ 650 N. Main St.) bears a controversial mural. Mexican muralist David Alfaro Siqueiros shocked his patrons when, in the 1930s, he depicted the oppressed workers of Latin America held in check by a menacing American eagle. The anti-imperialist mural was promptly whitewashed into oblivion. The whitewash has since been removed and work is underway to shelter the mural and allow public viewing of it.

At the beginning of Olvera Street is **The Plaza,** a wonderful Mexican-style park shaded by a huge Moreton Bay fig tree. On weekends, mariachis and folkloric dance groups often perform. Two annual events particularly worth seeing are the Blessing of the Animals and Las Posadas. The blessing takes place on the Saturday before Easter. Residents bring their pets to be blessed by a priest. For Las Posadas (every night between December 16 and 24), merchants and visitors parade up and down the street, led by children dressed as angels, to commemorate Mary and Joseph's search for shelter on Christmas Eve.

The Old Firehouse, an 1884 building on the south side of the Plaza, contains early fire-fighting equipment and old photographs. Free 50-minute walking tours start from the docent office next door and take in the Merced Theater, Masonic Hall, Pico House, and Garnier Block—all ornate examples of the late-19th-century style. On request, the docent will show you the tunnel passageways under the buildings that were once used by Chinese immigrants. Tours leave on the hour, from 10 to 1, every day but Monday.

NEED A BREAK?	Dining choices on Olvera Street range from fast-food stands to comfortable, sit-down restaurants. The most authentic Mexican food is at **La Luz del Dia** (⊠ 107 Paseo de la Plaza, ☎ 213/628–7495). The handmade tortillas are patted out in a practiced rhythm by the women behind the counter.

⑥ Regal Biltmore Hotel. The beaux-arts Biltmore opened in 1923. The lobby has the feel of a Spanish palace, the indoor pool looks like a Roman bath, and the ornate Rendezvous Court is a civilized retreat for an afternoon cocktail. The Academy Awards were held here in the 1930s, and the hotel has also been used in many films, such as *The Fabulous Baker Boys* and *Independence Day.* ⊠ 506 S. Grand Ave., ☎ 213/624–1011.

★ ⑬ **Union Station.** This building is familiar to moviegoers the world over. It was built in 1939 in a Spanish Mission style that subtly combines Streamline Moderne and Moorish design elements. The waiting room alone is worth a look, its majestic scale evocative of movies past.

OFF THE BEATEN PATH	**WATTS TOWERS** – The jewel of rough South Central L.A. is the legacy of Simon Rodia, a tile setter who emigrated from Italy to California and erected one of the world's greatest folk-art structures. From 1921 until 1954, without any help, this eccentric man built the three main cement towers, using pipes, bed frames, and anything else he could find. He embellished them with bits of colored glass, broken pottery, and more than 70,000 seashells. The towers still stand preserved, now the centerpiece of a state historic park and cultural center. ⊠ *Watts Towers Arts Center, 1727 E. 107th St. (take I–110 to I–105 east; exit north at S. Central Ave., turn right onto 108th St., left onto Willowbrook Ave.).* ☎ *323/847–4646.* ☎ *Free; weekend tours (scheduled to resume summer 2000) $1.* ☉ *Tues.–Sat. 10–4, Sun. noon–4.*

Hollywood and Sunset Boulevard

For nine decades Hollywood has lured us with its carefully manufactured images promising glitz and glamour. As visitors, we just want a chance to come close enough to be able to say, "I was there!" Reality check: the magic of Hollywood takes place, for the most part, on sound stages that are not even in Hollywood anymore, and in nondescript film-processing labs and editing bays. Go to Beverly Hills and look at jewelry store windows if you want glitz. As for glamour, well,

Hollywood is really a working town. Granted, many of the people who work in Hollywood—actors, directors, writers, composers—are among the highest paid and most celebrated workers in the world. But most of them face the same workaday grind as the rest of us, commuting daily and working long hours every day. So much for glamour. But Hollywood is still the entertainment capital of the world. Here's a tour that will get you as close to some of that magic as possible.

A Good Tour

Numbers in the text correspond to numbers in the margin and on the Hollywood map.

Drive up into the Hollywood Hills on Beachwood Drive (off Franklin Avenue, just east of Gower Street) for an up-close look at one of the world's most familiar icons: the **HOLLYWOOD sign** ①. Follow the small sign pointing the way to the LAFD Helispot. Turn left onto Rodgerton Drive, which twists and turns higher into the hills. At Deronda Drive, turn right and drive to the end. The Hollywood sign looms off to the left. Turn around and retrace your route down the hill, back to Beachwood for the drive into Hollywood.

Make a right (west) at Franklin Avenue, and prepare to turn left at the next light at Gower Street. Stay on Gower, driving through the section of Sunset Boulevard known as **Gower Gulch**. At Gower and Santa Monica Boulevard, look for the entrance to **Hollywood Memorial Park Cemetery** ②, a half block east on Santa Monica. If you visit the park, retrace your route back to Gower Street and turn left to drive along the western edge of the cemetery flanking Gower. Abutting the cemetery's southern edge is **Paramount Pictures** ③. The famous gate Norma Desmond (Gloria Swanson in *Sunset Boulevard*) was driven through is no longer accessible to the public, but a replica marks the new entrance on Melrose Avenue: turn left from Gower Street to reach the gate.

Next, drive west (right off Gower) on Melrose for three blocks to Vine Street, turn right, and continue to **Hollywood** (Boulevard) **and Vine** ④— an intersection whose fame is worldwide. Across the street, the so-called "record stack" **Capitol Records Tower** ⑤ resembles a stack of 45s. A block west on **Ivar Street** ⑥ are the former homes of literary giants William Faulkner and Nathanael West.

Drive west along Hollywood Boulevard for a look at the bronze stars that make up the **Hollywood Walk of Fame** ⑦. If you want to stop along the way to visit the Lingerie Museum at the purple **Frederick's of Hollywood** ⑧ or the **Hollywood Wax Museum** ⑨—both shrines to Hollywood camp—metered parking is fairly easy to find.

At Hollywood Boulevard and Las Palmas Avenue is the **Egyptian Theatre** ⑭. Restored to its 1922 splendor, it now houses American Cinematheque, which screens classic and independent films. Continue west on Hollywood Boulevard. At the northwest corner of Hollywood and Highland is the new Hollywood & Highland retail-entertainment complex that contains the 3,300-seat theater that in 2001 becomes the new home of the annual Academy Awards broadcast. Also at Highland, just south of the boulevard, is the new **Hollywood History Museum** ⑬, housed in the old Max Factor building.

West of Highland, on the north side of the street is **Mann's Chinese Theatre** ⑩, a genuine, if kitschy, monument to Hollywood history. The elaborate pagoda-style movie palace is still the biggest draw along the boulevard. Also on the north side of the boulevard and west of the Chinese Theatre is the **Hollywood Entertainment Museum** ⑪. From the mu-

Hollywood

Capitol Records
Tower, **5**

Egyptian Theatre, **14**

Frederick's of
Hollywood, **8**

Hollywood
Bowl, **15**

Hollywood
Entertainment
Museum, **11**

Hollywood History
Museum, **13**

Hollywood
Memorial Park
Cemetery, **2**

Hollywood
Roosevelt Hotel, **12**

HOLLYWOOD Sign, **1**

Hollywood and
Vine, **4**

Hollywood Walk
of Fame, **7**

Hollywood Wax
Museum, **9**

Ivar Street, **6**

Mann's Chinese
Theatre, **10**

Paramount Pictures, **3**

seum, cross Hollywood Boulevard and loop back east along the boulevard past the historic **Hollywood Roosevelt Hotel** ⑫.

Several blocks north of the boulevard on Highland Avenue is the **Hollywood Bowl** ⑮, with its interesting museum.

From Hollywood Boulevard, travel south on Highland or La Brea Avenue and drive to the next major intersection, at Sunset Boulevard. Turn west on Sunset toward West Hollywood, for a swing along the fabled **Sunset Strip** nightclub district.

TIMING

Plan to spend the better part of a morning or afternoon taking in Hollywood and Sunset boulevards. A walking tour of Paramount Studios will add at least two and a half hours to your itinerary. Hollywood Boulevard attracts a sometimes-bizarre group of folks. Your best bet for a safe walk down the boulevard is during the day.

Sights to See

★ ❺ **Capitol Records Tower.** The romantic story about the origin of this symbol of '50s chic is that singer Nat King Cole and songwriter Johnny Mercer suggested that the record company's headquarters be shaped to look like a stack of 45s. Architect Welton Beckett claimed he just wanted to design a structure that economized space. On its south wall, artist Richard Wyatt's mural *Hollywood Jazz, 1945–1972,* immortalizes musical greats Duke Ellington, Billie Holiday, Ella Fitzgerald, and Miles Davis. ✉ *1750 N. Vine St.*

⑭ **Egyptian Theatre.** Hollywood's first movie palace, complete with hieroglyphics, was built by impresario Sid Grauman in 1922. That year *Robin Hood,* starring Douglas Fairbanks, premiered. Over the years films such as *The Ten Commandments* (1923) and *Funny Girl* (1968) premiered at the 1,200-seat theater. But, with a cast of various owners, the Egyptian slumped towards disrepair and closed in 1992. The historic theater was renovated and reopened in 1999 to house American Cinematheque, a nonprofit film-screening organization. Daytime visitors can watch a documentary about Hollywood history, have lunch in the restaurant, and visit the grand forecourt of the theater. Film screenings are held in the evening. Silent films, accompanied by live music from a 1922 Wurlitzer organ, are screened on Tuesday evenings. ✉ *6712 Hollywood Blvd.,* ☎ *323/466–3456.* ◪ *Free. Film screenings $7.*

❽ **Frederick's of Hollywood.** Though you can stock up on risqué lingerie here, the real reason to visit Frederick's is to view the undergarments of some of Hollywood's legends: in the **Lingerie Museum,** Madonna's bustier shares space with Cher's kinky underwear and Marilyn Monroe's merry widow from *Let's Make Love.* ✉ *6608 Hollywood Blvd.,* ☎ *323/466–8506.*

Griffith Park. With so much of Los Angeles paved in cement and asphalt, the 4,100-acre Griffith Park stands out as a special place. In the northwest corner of the city, it's the largest municipal park and urban wilderness area in the United States. Though most people come here simply to take in the tranquillity of open space, several attractions are worthwhile in their own right. The **Griffith Observatory and Planetarium** sits on a promontory overlooking Hollywood and downtown. This art deco landmark off Vermont Avenue was immortalized in *Rebel Without a Cause,* and *The Terminator* was also filmed here. Other attractions include the **Los Angeles Zoo,** the **Autry Museum of Western Heritage,** and the **Greek Theatre.** Kids love **Travel Town** and the **Griffith Park & Southern Railroad**; there are also pony rides and a vintage carousel. ⊠ *Los Feliz Blvd. at Western Canyon Rd., Vermont Ave., Crystal Springs Dr., and Riverside Dr.* ☎ *Observatory and planetarium 323/664–1191; laserium* ☎ *818/901–9405; zoo* ☎ *323/644– 6400; Autry museum* ☎ *323/667–2000; Greek theater* ☎ *323/665– 1927; Travel Town* ☎ *323/662–5874; railroad* ☎ *323/664–6903; pony rides* ☎ *323/664–3266; carousel* ☎ *323/665–3051.* ☞ *Observatory and Hall of Science free; planetarium $4; laserium $7–$8; zoo $8.25 (Safari Shuttle Tour $3.50); museum $7.50; Travel Town free, railroad $1.75; pony rides $1.50; carousel $1.* ⊙ *Observatory and planetarium daily 12:30 PM–10 PM in summer (Tues.–Fri. 2 PM–10 PM, weekends 12:30 PM–10 PM rest of yr); zoo daily, 10–5 (animals removed from view starting at 4:30); museum Tues.–Sun. 10–5; theater performances Apr.–Oct.; Travel Town weekdays 10–4, weekends and holidays 10– 5; railroad daily 10–4:30 (later in summer); carousel weekends only (daily in summer); pony rides Tues.–Sun. 10–4 (later in summer), weather permitting.*

OFF THE
BEATEN PATH

HOLLYHOCK HOUSE – The first of several houses Frank Lloyd Wright designed in Los Angeles, this 1921 manse is a perfect example of the pre-Columbian style that Wright was so fond of at that time. It contains original, Wright-designed furniture. ⊠ *4800 Hollywood Blvd.,* ☎ *323/ 913-4157.* ☞ *$2.* ⊙ *Tours Wed.–Sun., noon, 1, 2, and 3.*

⑮ Hollywood Bowl. Summer evening concerts have been a tradition since 1922 at this amphitheater cradled in the Hollywood Hills. The Bowl is the summer home of the Los Angeles Philharmonic, but musical fare also includes pop and jazz. The 17,000-plus seating capacity ranges from boxes to concrete bleachers in the rear. Come early for a picnic in the surrounding grounds. Before the concert, or during the day, visit the **Hollywood Bowl Museum** (☎ 323/850–2058) for a capsulized version of the Bowl's long history. ⊠ *2301 N. Highland Ave.,* ☎ *323/ 850–2000.* ⊙ *Museum, Tues.–Sat. 10–4:30, later in summer; grounds daily sunrise–sunset (call for performance schedule).*

⑪ Hollywood Entertainment Museum. A multimedia presentation in the main rotunda and interactive exhibits track the evolution of Hollywood, from the low-tech silent era to today's hyper-tech world of special effects. Highlights are the marvelously detailed miniature model of 1936 Hollywood, and sets from television shows such as the bar from TV's *Cheers.* ⊠ *7021 Hollywood Blvd.,* ☎ *323/465–7900.* ☞ *$7.50.* ⊙ *Tues.–Sun. 10–6.*

⑬ Hollywood History Museum. The legendary Max Factor building, once home to makeup czar Max Factor and his beauty empire, is a fitting place in which to present Hollywood's glamorous history. Opening in 1999 after a two-year restoration, the grand Art Deco building houses exhibits and displays about the film capital's most memorable eras: "Hollywood, a New Town and Infant Industry," "The Silent Era," and "Talkies and Color" cover Tinseltown's fledgling years. Other exhibits include "Hollywood's Golden Era," "The Musical Comedies," and "The Art of Advanced Technology." Adjoining the museum is Chasen's Hollywood Café, named after the legendary restaurant where stars used to gather. ⊠ *1660 N. Highland Ave.,* ☎ *323/464–7776.* ☞ *$8.* ⊙ *Daily 9–9; call to confirm.*

② Hollywood Memorial Park Cemetery. Rudolph Valentino, Tyrone Power, and Jayne Mansfield are among the celebrities buried here. Sadly, the cemetery has fallen into a state of neglect. You can pick up a map of the grounds in the office at the entrance. ⊠ *6000 Santa Monica Blvd.,* ☎ *323/469–1181.* ⊙ *Daily 8–5.*

⑫ **Hollywood Roosevelt Hotel.** The first Academy Awards banquet was held here in 1927. A display of vintage Hollywood photographs and other historical memorabilia occupies the hotel's mezzanine level. In the hotel is Cinegrill, a cabaret steeped in Hollywood history. Have a look at the pool out back: David Hockney was commissioned to paint the "mural" at the bottom (actually nothing more than a series of blue blotches). ⊠ *7000 Hollywood Blvd.*, ☎ *323/466–7000.*

★ ❶ **HOLLYWOOD Sign.** With letters 50 ft tall, Hollywood's trademark sign can be spotted from miles away. The sign, which originally spelled out "Hollywoodland," was erected in the Hollywood Hills in 1923 to promote a real-estate development. In 1949 the "land" portion of the sign was taken down. Over the years pranksters have altered it, albeit temporarily, to spell out "Hollyweed" (in the 1970s, to commemorate lenient marijuana laws) and "Go Navy" (before a Rose Bowl game). In 1994, a fence and surveillance equipment were installed to deter intruders.

❹ **Hollywood and Vine.** In the old days this was the hub of the radio and movie industry, and there was nothing unusual about film stars like Gable and Garbo hurrying in or out of office buildings at the intersection on their way to or from their agents' offices. These days, Hollywood and Vine is far from the action. The **Brown Derby** restaurant once stood a half-block south of the intersection (⊠ 1628 N. Vine St.). Nearby is the **Palace Theater** (⊠ 1735 N. Vine St.), where the 1950s TV show *This Is Your Life* was recorded; it's now a rental venue for rock shows. Within a block or two of the intersection, however, you can still see the **Capitol Records** building (☞ *above*) and the **Pantages Theater** (⊠ 6233 Hollywood Blvd.), a former opulent movie palace now used to house large-scale Broadway musicals on tour. The arrival of the Metro Rail Red Line subway in 1999 may revive some activity around the intersection.

★ ❼ **Hollywood Walk of Fame.** All along this mile-long stretch of Hollywood Boulevard sidewalk, entertainment legends' names are embossed in brass, each at the center of a pink star embedded in dark-gray terrazzo. The first eight stars were unveiled in 1960 at the northwest corner of Highland Avenue and Hollywood Boulevard. Since then, more than 2,000 others have been immortalized. The honor doesn't come cheaply. Upon selection by a special committee, the personality in question (or more likely his or her movie studio or record company) pays about $7,500 for the privilege. Here's a miniguide to a few of the more famous celebs' stars: Marlon Brando at 1765 Vine, Charlie Chaplin at 6751 Hollywood, W. C. Fields at 7004 Hollywood, Clark Gable at 1608 Vine, Marilyn Monroe at 6774 Hollywood (in front of McDonald's), Rudolph Valentino at 6164 Hollywood, Michael Jackson at 6927 Hollywood, and John Wayne at 1541 Vine. Call the **Hollywood Chamber of Commerce** (⊠ 7018 Hollywood Blvd., ☎ 213/469–8311) or the **Hollywood Visitor Information Center** (⊠ 6541 Hollywood Blvd., ☎ 213/236–2331 or 213/689–8822) to find out where your favorite celebrity's star can be found. Ask when the next sidewalk star installation ceremony is scheduled to take place. The honoree usually shows up for the event.

❾ **Hollywood Wax Museum.** Here you'll spot celebrities that real life can no longer provide (Mary Pickford, Elvis Presley, and Clark Gable) and a few that even real life never did (such as the *Star Trek* cast). A short film on Academy Award winners screens daily. ⊠ *6767 Hollywood Blvd.*, ☎ *323/462–8860.* ⊡ *$8.95.* ☉ *Sun.–Thurs. 10 AM–midnight, Fri.–Sat. 10 AM–1 AM.*

NEED A   **Musso & Frank Grill** (✉ 6667 Hollywood Blvd., ☎ 323/467–5123),
BREAK?   open since 1919, is the last remaining Old Hollywood watering hole.
            Wash down a plate of lamb chops, spinach, and sourdough bread with
            a martini, or just stop in for a Coke and soak up some atmosphere. Ex-
            pect high prices and some attitude.

⑥ Ivar Street. William Faulkner wrote *Absalom, Absalom!* while he lived
at the old **Knickerbocker Hotel** (✉ 1714 N. Ivar St.), and Nathanael
West wrote *The Day of the Locust* in his apartment at the **Parva Sed-
Apta** (✉ 1817 N. Ivar St.).

★ ⑩ **Mann's Chinese Theatre.** The former "Grauman's Chinese," a fantasy
of Chinese pagodas and temples, is a place only Hollywood could turn
out. You have to buy a movie ticket to appreciate the interior trappings,
but the courtyard is open to the public. Here you'll see those famous
cement hand- and footprints. This tradition is said to have begun at
the theater's opening in 1927, with the premiere of Cecil B. DeMille's
King of Kings, when actress Norma Talmadge accidentally stepped into
the wet cement. Now more than 160 celebrities have contributed imprints of their appendages for posterity, along with a few other odd-
ball imprints, like the one of Jimmy Durante's nose. ✉ *6925 Hollywood
Blvd.,* ☎ *323/464–8111.*

❸ Paramount Pictures. The last major studio still located in Hollywood
is the best place to see what a real Hollywood movie studio looks like.
Two-hour guided walking tours of the 86-year-old studio include historical narrative about Rudolph Valentino, Mae West, Mary Pickford,
Lucille Ball, and other stars who worked on the lot. Movies and TV
shows are still filmed here. If you're lucky, you might see a show being
produced. Tours are first-come, first-served and leave from the pedestrian walk-up gate on Melrose Street; park in the lot at Bronson and
Melrose avenues. Children under 10 are not admitted. ✉ *5555 Melrose Ave.,* ☎ *323/956–5575.* 💲 *$15.* 🕐 *2-hr walking tour weekdays
on the half hr, 9–2.*

Sunset Strip. For 60 years the Hollywood nighttime crowd has headed
for the 1¾-mi stretch of Sunset Boulevard between Crescent Heights
Boulevard on the east and Doheny Drive on the west, known as the
Sunset Strip. In the 1930s and '40s, stars like Tyrone Power, Errol Flynn,
Norma Shearer, and Rita Hayworth got themselves gussied up in tuxe-
dos and fancy gowns for wild evenings of dancing and drinking at nightclubs like Trocadero, Ciro's, and Mocambo. By the '60s and '70s, the
Strip had become the center of rock 'n' roll: the Doors, Elton John,
and Bruce Springsteen gave legendary performances on stages at clubs
like the **Whisky** (✉ 8901 Sunset Blvd., ☎ 310/652–4202) and **Roxy**
(✉ 9009 Sunset Blvd., ☎ 310/276–2222). Nowadays it's the **Viper Room**
(✉ 8852 Sunset Blvd., ☎ 310/358–1880), the **House of Blues** (✉ 8430
Sunset Blvd., ☎ 323/848–5100), and **The Key Club** (✉ 9039 Sunset
Blvd., ☎ 310/274–5800) that keep young Hollywood busy after dark.

Museum Row and Farmers Market

East of Fairfax Avenue in the Miracle Mile district is the three-block
stretch of Wilshire Boulevard known as Museum Row. A few blocks
away is the historic Farmers Market.

A Good Tour

*Numbers in the text correspond to numbers in the margin and on the
Museum Row and Farmers Market map.*

Start the day with coffee and fresh-baked pastries at **Farmers Market** ①,
a few blocks north of Wilshire Boulevard at 3rd Street and Fairfax Av-

Museum Row and Farmers Market

enue. Drive south on Fairfax Avenue to the **Miracle Mile** ② district of Wilshire Boulevard. The black-and-gold Art Deco building on the northeast corner is a former department store that's now called LACMA West and houses satellite exhibition galleries of the Los Angeles County Museum of Art (LACMA) and the **Southwest Museum at LACMA West.** Turn left onto Wilshire and proceed to Ogden Drive or a block farther to Spaulding Avenue, where you can park the car and explore the museums on foot.

The large complex of contemporary buildings surrounded by a park (on the corner of Wilshire and Ogden Drive) is **The Los Angeles County Museum of Art** ③. It's the largest museum west of Chicago and houses works spanning the history of art from ancient times to the present. Also occupying the park are the prehistoric **La Brea Tar Pits** ④, where many of the fossils displayed at the adjacent **Page Museum at the La Brea Tar Pits** ⑤ were found. Across Wilshire are the **Carole & Barry Kaye Museum of Miniatures** ⑥ and, back at the corner of Wilshire and Fairfax, the **Petersen Automotive Museum** ⑦, which surveys the history of the car in Los Angeles.

TIMING

The museums open between 10 and noon, so plan your tour around the opening time of the museum you wish to visit first. LACMA is closed Wednesday, and has extended hours into the evening, closing at 8 (9 on Friday). The other museums are closed on Monday (except the Page, which is open Mondays in the summer). Weekends bring the largest crowds to Farmers Market and the museums. On the second Tuesday of the month, admission to all but ticketed exhibits at LACMA is free. Set aside a good portion of the day to do this tour: an hour for the Farmers Market and four to five hours for the museums.

Sights to See

❻ Carole & Barry Kaye Museum of Miniatures. Besides scaled-down models of the Hollywood Bowl, the Vatican, and several famous European châteaux, the George Stuart Gallery of miniature historical figures is one of the highlights of this pint-sized world. There's also a tribute to America's First Ladies (as far back as Martha Washington), dolled up in their inaugural ball gowns. ⊠ *5900 Wilshire Blvd.,* ☎ *323/937–6464.* ⊡ *$7.50.* ⊙ *Tues.–Sat. 10–5, Sun. 11–5.*

★ ❶ Farmers Market. In July 1934, two entrepreneurs envisioned a European-style open-air market, to be built near the corner of 3rd Street and Fairfax, where farmers would sell their produce to local housewives. The idea was an instant success. Soon after the marketplace opened, Blanche Magee, a local restaurateur, drove by and saw a crowd of customers buying produce and flowers from the backs of the trucks. The next day she returned with a hamper full of sandwiches and soft drinks, which she sold to the farmers and customers. Soon afterwards, **Magee's Kitchen and Deli** became the Farmers Market's first restaurant. Today the market has more than 110 stalls and more than 20 restaurants. Close to CBS Television Studios, the market is a major hub for stars and stargazers, tourists and locals. It's one of the few community gathering points in the sprawling city. Parking is free. ⊠ *6333 W. 3rd St.,* ☎ *323/933–9211.* ⊙ *Mon.–Sat. 9–6:30, Sun. 10–5 (later in summer).*

NEED A
BREAK?
At Farmers Market, stop for a BLT on sourdough, a chicken chopped salad chock-full of veggies, or a slice of apple-ginger-buttermilk coffee cake and a mocha–French-roast malt at **Kokomo Café,** (☎ 213/933–0773), a favorite fueling station among celebs, black-clad hipsters, and people who like good food. At **Bob's Coffee & Donuts** (☎ 213/933–8929), Bob Tusquellas, a.k.a. "the Donut Man," churns out nearly 2,000 fresh-made jelly-filled, cinnamon-rolled, and glazed creations every day.

★ ❹ La Brea Tar Pits. About 40,000 years ago, deposits of oil rose to the earth's surface, collected in shallow pools, and coagulated into sticky asphalt. In the early 20th century, geologists discovered that the sticky goo contained the largest collection of Pleistocene, or Ice Age, fossils ever found at one location: more than 600 species of birds, mammals, plants, reptiles, and insects. More than 100 tons of fossil bones have been removed in excavations over the last seven decades. Statues of a family of mammoths in the big pit near the corner of Wilshire and Curson suggest how many of them were entombed: edging down to a pond of water to drink, animals were caught in the tar.

❸ Los Angeles County Museum of Art (LACMA). Still a young museum (it opened in 1966), LACMA has assembled an encyclopedic collection of more than 150,000 works from around the world. Its collection is widely considered the most comprehensive in the western United States. Islamic, South and Southeast Asian, Far Eastern, and American works are especially well represented. The museum's five buildings also house fine collections of modern and contemporary art, costumes and textiles, decorative arts, European paintings and sculpture, photography, drawings, and prints.

Galleries of Islamic art are arranged chronologically, emphasizing visual connections and recurrent themes. South and Southeast Asian galleries, which contain one of the finest collections outside Asia, contain several new acquisitions, including the *Hindu Saint Manikkavacakar,* an elegant 12th-century South Indian bronze statue, and *Buddha Calling the Earth to Witness,* a bronze image from 11th-century Tibet.

LACMA's collection of American art from the Colonial era to the early 20th century is one of the finest in the nation. A core of galleries presents these works together. In addition to furniture, silver, glass, ceramics, paintings, and sculpture of the same periods, there are landscape and genre paintings from the Federal period, frontier art, works from the Ash Can School, and regional developments such as California impressionism and surrealism. Masterworks such as George Bellows's *Cliff Dwellers,* Mary Cassatt's *Mother About to Wash Her Sleepy Child,* and Winslow Homer's *The Cotton Pickers* have been cleaned and restored. ☒ *5905 Wilshire Blvd.,* ☎ *323/857–6000; 323/857–0098 TDD.* ☒ *$7, free 2nd Tues. of month.* ☉ *Mon., Tues., and Fri. noon–9; Thurs. noon–8; weekends 11–8.*

❷ **Miracle Mile.** The strip of Wilshire Boulevard between La Brea and Fairfax avenues was vacant land in the 1920s, when a developer bought the parcel to develop into a shopping and business district. The auto age was just emerging and nobody thought the venture could be successful, so the strip became known as Miracle Mile. It was the world's first linear downtown, with building designs incorporating wide store windows to attract attention from passing automobiles. The area went into a decline in the '50s and '60s, but it's now enjoying a comeback, as Los Angeles's Art Deco architecture has come to be appreciated, preserved, and restored.

❺ **Page Museum at the La Brea Tar Pits.** At the La Brea Tar Pits, this member of the Natural History Museum family is set, bunkerlike, half underground. A bas-relief around four sides depicts life in the Pleistocene era, and the museum has more than 3 million Ice Age fossils. Exhibits include reconstructed, life-size skeletons of mammoths, wolves, sloths, eagles, and condors. A permanent installation shows a robotic saber-toothed cat attacking a huge ground sloth. A hologram magically puts flesh on 9,000-year-old "La Brea Woman," and an interactive tar mechanism shows just how hard it would be to free oneself from the sticky mess. ☒ *5801 Wilshire Blvd.,* ☎ *323/934–7243.* ☒ *$6, free 1st Tues. of month.* ☉ *Tues.–Sun. 10–5, summer daily 10–5.*

★ ❼ **Petersen Automotive Museum.** More than just a building full of antique or unique cars, the Petersen is highly entertaining and informative. Rotating exhibits may include Hollywood-celebrity and movie cars (for example, Fred's rockmobile from *The Flintstones*), "muscle" cars (like a 1969 Dodge Daytona 440 Magnum), motorcycles, and commemorative displays of the Ferrari. ☒ *6060 Wilshire Blvd.,* ☎ *323/930–2277.* ☒ *$7.* ☉ *Tues.–Sun. 10–6.*

Southwest Museum at LACMA West. L.A.'s oldest museum expanded in 1998 from its main Mt. Washington facility in Highland Park into this 8,000-square-ft satellite location. The additional space gives the museum a chance to present even more of its fine collection of Native American art and culture dating from 1800 to the present. Contrasting with the Art Deco exterior of the LACMA West structure, the design of the museum's galleries suggests an adobe structure awash in hues of cactus and red earth. A museum store sells contemporary Native American weavings, jewelry, toys, and books. ☒ *Northeast corner of Fairfax Ave. and Wilshire Blvd.,* ☎ *323/933–4510.* ☒ *$5.* ☉ *Daily 9–8.*

Beverly Hills and Century City

If you've got money to spend—lots of it—come to Beverly Hills. Rodeo Drive is the platinum vein of its commercial district (a.k.a. the Golden Triangle) and has been likened to Rome's Via Condotti and London's Bond Street. Beverly Hills means expensive retailers like Tiffany, Gucci, and Cartier; sky-high real estate prices; legendary hotels; high-powered restaurants; and—most of all—movie stars. Fable-making Hollywood and fabled Beverly Hills are inseparably linked in the popular imagination. Mary Pickford and Douglas Fairbanks Sr. led the way 80 years ago by setting up house in an old hunting lodge in Benedict Canyon, renovating it into what became known as Pickfair. Hollywood royalty followed suit, and pretty soon Beverly Hills, once a tract of bean patches known as Morocco Junction, was on its way to becoming hometown to Hollywood's royalty. The allure of Beverly Hills continues to draw armies of visitors on the lookout for a famous face and a glimpse of an opulent lifestyle.

A Good Tour

Numbers in the text correspond to numbers in the margin and on the Beverly Hills and the Westside map.

Begin a tour of Beverly Hills with a drive into the hills above Sunset Boulevard for a look at **Greystone Mansion** ① on Loma Vista Drive. Less than a mile west on Sunset is the landmark **Beverly Hills Hotel** ②. Behind the hotel, on Elden Way, is the **Virginia Robinson Gardens** ③, the oldest estate in Beverly Hills.

Across the street from the hotel is the little triangular park named for the cowboy-philosopher Will Rogers, who was once honorary mayor of Beverly Hills. Turn south here onto **Rodeo Drive** ④. You'll pass through a residential neighborhood before hitting the shopping stretch of Rodeo south of Santa Monica Boulevard. This is where you'll want to get out of the car and walk around. At Rodeo Drive and Dayton Way, the **Beverly Hills Trolley** ⑤ departs for 40-minute tours of the city (between May and December). Across Wilshire is the **Regent Beverly Wilshire Hotel** ⑥. The **Museum of Television & Radio** ⑦ stands a block east of Rodeo, on Beverly Drive at Little Santa Monica Boulevard. Adjacent to Beverly Hills on the west is the high-rise office-tower and shopping-center complex known as **Century City** ⑧.

TIMING

After a drive along Sunset Boulevard and a foray or two up into the hills for a look at the opulent homes, plan to arrive in the Golden Triangle of Beverly Hills at midday. Park the car in one of several municipal lots, and stroll along Rodeo Drive. There are plenty of reasonably priced cafés and restaurants for lunch. The major routes in and out of Beverly Hills—Wilshire and Santa Monica boulevards—get very congested during rush hours.

Sights to See

★ ② **Beverly Hills Hotel.** Built in 1912, the Pink Palace is steeped in Hollywood lore. Greta Garbo, Howard Hughes, and other movie-industry guests kept low profiles when staying at this pastel landmark, while other film luminaries, notably Cecil B. DeMille, cut very visible deals in the **Polo Lounge.** ⊠ *9641 Sunset Blvd., 1 mi west of Doheny Dr.,* ☎ *310/276–2251.*

⑤ **Beverly Hills Trolley.** The 40-minute "Sights and Scenes" or "Art and Architecture" tour swings into the residential area for a look at former homes of Hollywood celebrities. ⊠ *Dayton Way and Rodeo Dr.,*

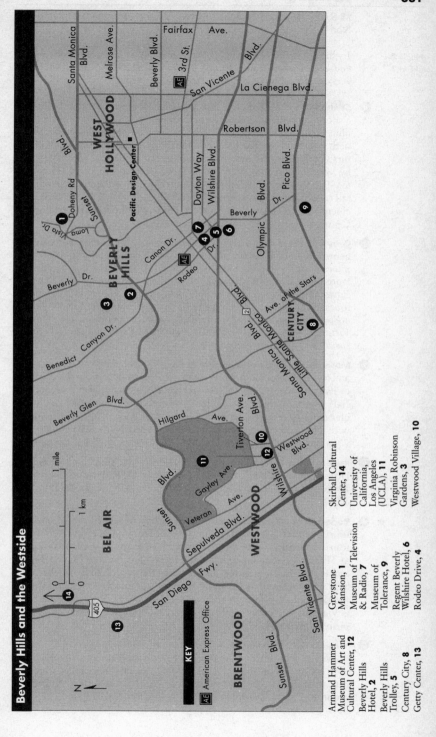

Beverly Hills and the Westside

Armand Hammer
Museum of Art and
Cultural Center, **12**

Beverly Hills
Hotel, **2**

Beverly Hills
Trolley, **5**

Century City, **8**

Getty Center, **13**

Greystone
Mansion, **1**

Museum of Television
& Radio, **7**

Museum of
Tolerance, **9**

Regent Beverly
Wilshire Hotel, **6**

Rodeo Drive, **4**

Skirball Cultural
Center, **14**

University of
California,
Los Angeles
(UCLA), **11**

Virginia Robinson
Gardens, **3**

Westwood Village, **10**

KEY

AE American Express Office

☎ *310/285–2438.* 🎟 *$5.* ⊙ *May–Dec., Sat. only on the hr noon–4;*
Nov.–Dec., call for additional tours.

NEED A   Try the courtyard of the unpretentious and not terribly expensive **Café**
BREAK?   **Rodeo** (⊠ Summit Hotel, 360 N. Rodeo Dr., ☎ 310/273–0300). Sand-
             wiches, salads, and pizzas are big enough to split.

❽ Century City. This 280-acre mixed-use development of office buildings,
a shopping center, hotels, an entertainment complex, and housing was
built in the '60s on what used to be the back lot of the film studio Twentieth Century Fox. The focal point is the pair of silvery triangular **Century City Towers** (⊠ Ave. of the Stars and Constellation Blvd.), designed
by Minoru Yamasaki, who also designed New York's World Trade Center. The **Century City Shopping Center** is one of the last open-air retail centers, with a festive, marketplacelike arrangement of eateries and
cinemas. At the cavernous **Shubert Theater** in the ABC Entertainment
Center, big Broadway musicals are performed.

❶ Greystone Mansion. Doheny Drive is named for oilman Edward Doheny, the original owner of this 1927 neo-Gothic mansion of 46,000-
plus square ft. Now owned by the city of Beverly Hills, it sits on 18½
landscaped acres and has been used in such films as *The Witches of
Eastwick* and *Indecent Proposal*. The gardens are open for self-guided
tours, and peeking (only) through the windows is permitted. Picnics
are permitted in specified areas during hours of operation. ⊠ *905 Loma
Vista Dr.,* ☎ *310/550–4796.* 🎟 *Free.* ⊙ *Fall and winter, daily 10–5;
spring and summer, daily 10–6.*

❼ Museum of Television & Radio. Search for your favorite commercials
and television and radio shows on easy-to-use computers, and then watch
or listen to them in an adjacent room. The museum also presents special exhibits of television- and radio-related art and costumes, and schedules daily screenings and listening series, as well as frequent seminars
with television and radio cast members. ⊠ *465 N. Beverly Dr.,* ☎ *310/
786–1000.* 🎟 *$6.* ⊙ *Wed. and Fri.–Sun. noon–5, Thurs. noon–9.*

❻ Regent Beverly Wilshire Hotel. Anchoring the south end of Rodeo
Drive at Wilshire Boulevard since opening in 1928, the hotel often hosts
visiting royalty and celebrities. ⊠ *9500 Wilshire Blvd.,* ☎ *310/275–
5200.*

★ **❹ Rodeo Drive.** Rodeo Drive is one of southern California's bona fide
tourist attractions. Just as if they were at Disneyland or in Hollywood,
tourists wander along this tony stretch of avenue, window-shopping
at Tiffany & Co., Gucci, Armani, Harry Winston, and Lladro. Fortunately the browsing is free, and strolling the section of Rodeo between
Santa Monica and Wilshire boulevards is a fun way to spend the afternoon. At the southern end of Rodeo Drive (at Wilshire Boulevard)
is **Via Rodeo,** a curvy cobblestone street designed to resemble a European shopping *via*.

❸ Virginia Robinson Gardens. The estate, the oldest in Beverly Hills, was
owned by department store heir Harry Robinson and his wife, Virginia,
who bequeathed it to the County of Los Angeles. The classic Mediterranean-style villa is surrounded by nearly 6 acres of lush planted
grounds. Call in advance to schedule a tour. ☎ *310/276–5367.* ⊙ *Tours
by appointment.*

The Westside

An informal and unscientific survey of Westside districts like West Los Angeles, Westwood, Bel-Air, Brentwood, and Pacific Palisades would probably reveal high concentrations of plastic surgeons and Land Rovers. The Westside, however, is also rich cultural territory, and the rewards of visiting UCLA's Westwood campus, the Museum of Tolerance, and the Getty Center in Brentwood are great.

A Good Tour

Numbers in the text correspond to numbers in the margin and on the Beverly Hills and the Westside map.

The major sights on the Westside are spread out, so the best strategy is to select one of the major attractions as a destination and plan your visit accordingly. A visit to the **Museum of Tolerance** ⑨ in the morning, for example, can be easily followed with lunch and shopping in Beverly Hills or Century City. Afterward, you might drive through **Westwood Village** ⑩, home of the **UCLA** ⑪ campus and the **Fowler Museum of Cultural History,** stopping at the **Armand Hammer Museum of Art and Cultural Center** ⑫. The vast **Getty Center** ⑬, fortresslike atop a hill in Brentwood, is currently L.A.'s most high-profile attraction. About 2 mi north on Sepulveda Boulevard is the **Skirball Cultural Center** ⑭ and its gallery exhibition of Jewish life.

For a less destination-oriented tour of the posh Westside, simply follow Wilshire Boulevard west out of low-rise Beverly Hills as it turns into a canyon of million-dollar condos. Once past the San Diego Freeway (I–405), detour to the right onto San Vicente Boulevard and the upscale urban-village center of **Brentwood.** At the Santa Monica city line, turn right on 26th Street and follow it as it turns into Allenford Avenue. The route will loop you around to Sunset Boulevard. A left turn here will take you to Pacific Palisades and the ocean. A right leads back toward Beverly Hills and West Hollywood.

TIMING

Advance reservations are required for visits to the Museum of Tolerance, closed Saturday, and the Getty Center, closed Monday. Each museum merits at least a half day. In the evening and on weekends, Westwood Village and Brentwood's commercial district on San Vicente Boulevard come alive with a busy restaurant, café, and street scene. The afternoon rush hour is congested along Wilshire and Sunset boulevards.

Sights to See

⑫ **Armand Hammer Museum of Art and Cultural Center.** The eclectic permanent collection here contains thousands of works, including some by Daumier, van Gogh, Gauguin, Degas, and Cassatt. In addition to works by Old Masters, French Impressionists, and Postimpressionists, there's an important collection of drawings by Michelangelo, Raphael, and Rembrandt. ✉ *10899 Wilshire Blvd.,* ☎ *310/443–7000.* ☞ *$4.50, free Thurs. 6–9; parking $2.75 with validation.* ⏰ *Tues.–Wed. and Fri.–Sat. 11–7, Thurs. 11–9, Sun. 11–5. Tours Sun. at 1.*

Brentwood. From the looks of it, Brentwood seems more like a posh urban village than the scene of such mysteries as the death of Marilyn Monroe and the murder of Nicole Brown Simpson. San Vicente Boulevard, the main drag, sports chic restaurants, cafés, and shops.

★ ⑬ **Getty Center.** Architect Richard Meier designed the white city on a hill to house the world's richest museum and its affiliated research, conservation, and philanthropic institutes. The crunch of visitors has subsided somewhat, and those essential parking reservations are available, though limited.

J. Paul Getty, the billionaire oil magnate and art collector, began collecting Greek and Roman antiquities and French decorative arts in the 1930s. He opened the J. Paul Getty Museum at his Malibu estate in 1954. In the 1970s, he built a re-creation of an ancient Roman villa to house his initial collection. When Getty died in 1976, the museum received an endowment of $700 million that has grown to a reported $4.2 billion. The Malibu villa closed in 1997, but it will reopen in 2001, to house only the antiquities.

All visitors arrive at the entrance pavilion at the bottom of the hill. Those with parking reservations are guaranteed entrance. Those who arrive by public bus (MTA #561 or Santa Monica Big Blue #14), cab, or private shuttle may encounter long lines before gaining entrance, or, depending on attendance, may be turned away. A tram transports visitors to the top of the hill. There, the principal destination for most visitors is the museum, a series of five pavilions built around a central courtyard and bridged by walkways. Outside, the structures are clad primarily in cleft-cut Italian travertine stone. In a ravine separating the museum and the Getty Research Institute, artist Robert Irwin created the **Central Garden**, whose focal point is an azalea maze in a pool. Inside the pavilions are the galleries featuring the permanent collections of European paintings, drawings, sculpture, illuminated manuscripts, and decorative arts, as well as American and European photographs. The Getty's renowned collection of French furniture and decorative arts is on view, including a paneled Régence salon from 1710 and a neoclassical salon from 1788. Notable among the paintings are Rembrandt's *Portrait of Marten Looten* and *The Abduction of Europa*, van Gogh's *Irises*, Monet's *Wheatstack, Snow Effects, Morning*, and James Ensor's *Christ's Entry Into Brussels*.

Interconnected pavilions around the courtyard allow you to choose various paths through the museum, so you may head straight for the pavilion that interests you most. The curators have also organized a quick tour that takes in 15 highlights of the collection. It's outlined in a brochure available in the entrance hall. There's an instructive audio tour ($2) with commentaries by art historians. The complex includes a restaurant (reservations required), a cafeteria, and an outdoor coffee bar. ✉ *1200 Getty Center Dr., ☎ 310/440–7300; TTY 310/440–7305. 🎟 Free, $5 parking. ☉ Tues.–Wed. 11–7, Thurs.–Fri. 11–9, weekends 10–6; call several months ahead for parking reservations.*

★ ⑨ **Museum of Tolerance.** Using state-of-the-art interactive technology, this important museum adjacent to the Simon Wiesenthal Center challenges visitors to confront bigotry and racism. One of the most affecting sections covers the Holocaust, with actual film footage of deportation scenes and simulated sets of concentration camps. Each visitor is issued a "passport" bearing the name of a child whose life was dramatically changed by the German Nazi rule and by World War II. Later, you learn the fate of that child. Anne Frank artifacts are part of the museum's permanent collection. To ensure a visit to the museum, make reservations in advance and plan to spend at least three hours there. ✉ *9786 W. Pico Blvd., ☎ 310/553–8403. 🎟 $8. ☉ Sun. 10:30–5, Mon.–Thurs. 10–4, Fri. 10–1.*

⑭ **Skirball Cultural Center.** The core exhibition here is "Visions and Values: Jewish Life from Antiquity to America," the story of the Jewish immigration experience. Highlights include a large collection of Judaica, a two-thirds-size replica of the torch of the Statue of Liberty, and a Hannukah menorah with each of the eight branches fashioned after the Statue of Liberty. Children can participate in an outdoor simulated archaeological dig at the interactive Discovery Center. ⊠ *2701 N. Sepulveda Blvd.,* ☎ *310/440–4500.* ☜ *$8.* ☉ *Tues.–Sat. noon–5, Sun. 11–5.*

⑪ University of California, Los Angeles (UCLA). The parklike UCLA campus makes for a fine stroll. In the heart of the north campus, the **Franklin Murphy Sculpture Garden** contains more than 70 works of artists such as Henry Moore and Gaston Lachaise. The **Mildred Mathias Botanic Garden** is in the southeast section of the campus and is accessible from Tiverton Avenue. West of the main campus bookstore, the **Morgan Center Hall of Fame** displays the sports memorabilia and trophies of the university's athletic departments. Many visitors head straight to the **UCLA Fowler Museum of Cultural History** (☎ 310/825–4361), which presents changing exhibits on the art and culture of past and present peoples of Latin America, Oceania, Africa, and Asia.

Campus maps and information are available at drive-by kiosks at major entrances seven days a week, and free 90-minute walking tours of the campus are given on weekdays at 10:15 and 2:15, and Saturdays at 10:15. Call 310/825–8764 for reservations several days in advance. The campus has indoor and outdoor cafés, plus bookstores selling UCLA Bruins paraphernalia. The main entrance gate is on Westwood Boulevard. Campus parking costs $5. ⊠ *Main entrance on Westwood Plaza; Le Conte, Hilgard, and Gayley Aves. and Sunset Blvd. border the campus.* ☜ *Campus free; Fowler Museum free.*

⑩ Westwood Village. Next to the Los Angeles campus of the University of California, Westwood Village is one of the busiest places in the city on weekend evenings. The lures are a concentration of first-run movie theaters, eateries, and a lively youth-oriented street scene that gets so busy during the summer that many streets are closed to car traffic and visitors must park at the **Federal Building** (⊠ Wilshire Blvd. and Veteran Ave.) and shuttle over. Behind one of the behemoth office buildings on Wilshire Boulevard is **Westwood Village Memorial Park** (⊠ 1218 Glendon Ave.). Marilyn Monroe is buried in a simply marked crypt on the north wall. Also buried here are Truman Capote and Natalie Wood.

Santa Monica, Venice, and Malibu

In Los Angeles all roads lead, eventually, to the beach and Santa Monica, Venice, and Malibu. These coastal communities hug the Santa Monica Bay, in an arc of diversity, from the rich-as-can-be Malibu to the bohemian-seedy mix of Venice. What they have in common, however, is cleaner coastal air and an emphasis on being out in the sunshine.

A Good Drive

Numbers in the text correspond to numbers in the margin and on the Santa Monica, Venice, and Malibu map.

Look for the arched neon sign at the foot of Colorado Avenue marking the entrance to the **Santa Monica Pier** ①, the city's number-one landmark, built in 1906. Park on the pier and take a turn through **Pacific Park** ②, a 2-acre amusement park. The wide swath of sand on the north side of the pier is Santa Monica Beach, on hot summer weekends one of the most crowded beaches in southern California. From the pier, walk to Ocean Avenue, where **Palisades Park** ③, a strip of lawn and palms above the cliffs, provides panoramic ocean views. Three blocks inland is **Third Street Promenade** ④, an active outdoor mall with shopping, dining, and entertainment.

Retrieve the car and drive two blocks inland on Colorado to Main Street. Turn right and continue to Ocean Park Boulevard. Look for a colorful mural on the side of the building on the southeast corner. On the southwest corner you'll find the **California Heritage Museum** ⑤. The next several blocks south along Main Street are great for browsing.

Next stop: **Venice Boardwalk** ⑥. Walk up Main Street through the trendy shopping district until you hit Rose Avenue. Ahead on the left you'll spot an enormous pair of binoculars, the front of the Frank Gehry–designed Chiat-Day Mojo building. Turn right toward the sea. The main attraction of this dead end is the boardwalk, where the classic California beach scene is in progress.

For the drive to **Malibu,** retrace your route along Main Street. At Pico Boulevard, turn west, toward the ocean, and then right on Ocean Avenue. When you pass the pier, prepare to turn left down the California Incline (the incline is at the end of Palisades Park at Wilshire Boulevard) to Pacific Coast Highway (Highway 1), also known as PCH. About 11 mi north, you'll enter Malibu. Unfortunately, Malibu Pier is closed indefinitely due to storm damage and a lack of funds to repair it. Park in the adjacent lot and take a walk on **Malibu Lagoon State Beach** ⑦, also known as Surfrider Beach. On the highway side of the beach is the Moorish-Spanish **Adamson House and Malibu Lagoon Museum** ⑧, a tiled beauty with a great Pacific view. From here, you can walk along the strand of beach that fronts the famed Malibu Colony, the exclusive residential enclave of film, television, and recording stars.

TIMING

If you've got the time, break your coastal visit into two excursions: Santa Monica and Venice in one, and Malibu in another. The best way to "do" L.A.'s coastal communities is to park the car, and walk, cycle, or skate along the 3-mi beachside bike path. Late morning is a good time to get started. Places like Santa Monica Pier, Main Street, and the Venice Boardwalk are more interesting to observe as the day progresses. Avoid the boardwalk at night, when the crowd becomes unsavory. You can park on the Santa Monica Pier and in small lots close to the beach in Venice (the smart thing to do, since break-ins are common in the area) and Malibu. Avoid driving to Malibu during rush hour, when traffic along the Pacific Coast Highway moves at a snail's pace— but do try to be there at sunset to watch the sun dip into the Pacific.

Sights to See

⑧ **Adamson House and Malibu Lagoon Museum.** The Rindge family, which owned much of the Malibu area in the early part of the 20th century, also originally owned this home. The Moorish Spanish–style structure was built in 1929. The house, covered with magnificent tile work from the now-defunct Malibu Potteries in rich blues, greens, yellows, and oranges, is right on the beach. Docent-led tours provide insights on family life here as well as the history of Malibu and its real estate. Signs posted around the grounds outside direct you on a self-guided tour as well. Park in the adjacent county lot, or in the lot at Pacific Coast Highway and Cross Creek Road. ⊠ *23200 Pacific Coast Hwy.,* ☎ *310/456–8432.* ☜ *House tours, $2.* ☉ *Wed.–Sat. 11–3.*

⑤ **California Heritage Museum.** Three rooms in this 1894 late-Victorian house have been fully restored: the dining room in the style of 1890–1910; the living room, 1910–1920; and the kitchen, 1920–1930. The second-floor galleries contain photography and historical exhibits as well as shows by contemporary California artists. ⊠ *2612 Main St.,* ☎ *310/392–8537.* ☜ *$3.* ☉ *Wed.–Sat. 11–4, Sun. 10–4.*

Santa Monica, Venice, and Malibu

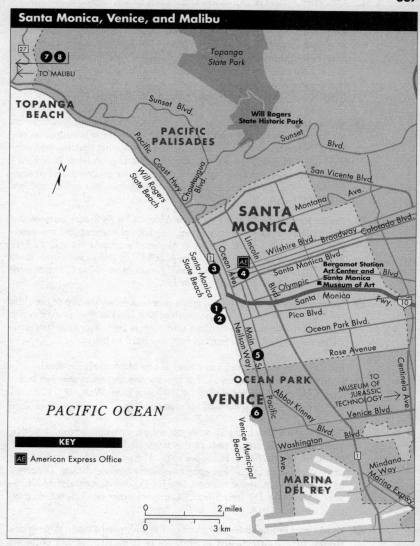

KEY

AE American Express Office

Adamson House and Malibu Lagoon Museum, **8**

California Heritage Museum, **5**

Malibu Lagoon State Beach, **7**

Pacific Park, **2**

Palisades Park, **3**

Santa Monica Pier, **1**

Third Street Promenade, **4**

Venice Boardwalk, **6**

MARINA DEL REY – A brilliant sight on a sunny day, this enormous man-made marina with moorings for 10,000 boats is just south of Venice. Stop by Burton Chace Park (at the foot of Mindanao Way) to watch the wind carry colorful sailboats out to sea. Small "Mother's Beach" (Marina Beach) has calm, protected waters ideal for young children. Call **Hornblower Dining Yachts** in Fisherman's Village (⊠ 13755 Fiji Way, ☎ 310/301–9900) to arrange marina and dining cruises.

⑦ Malibu Lagoon State Beach. Stay on the boardwalks at this 5-acre haven for native and migratory birds so that the egrets, blue herons, avocets, and gulls can enjoy the marshy area. The signs listing opening and closing hours refer only to the parking lot. The lagoon itself is open 24 hours and is particularly enjoyable in the early morning and at sunset. Street-side parking is available at those times, but not at midday. ⊠ 23200 Pacific Coast Hwy.

② Pacific Park. The 12 rides at Santa Monica Pier's 2-acre amusement facility include a giant Ferris wheel, a flying submarine, and a motion-simulated action ride. ⊠ 380 Santa Monica Pier, Santa Monica, ☎ 310/260–8747. 🎟 Rides $1–$4, all-day pass $15. ⊙ Entire park open daily May–Sept.; winter, selected rides and games Mon.–Thurs., entire park Fri. evening–Sun. evening; call for hrs.

③ Palisades Park. The ribbon of green that runs along the top of the cliffs from Colorado Avenue to just north of San Vicente Boulevard has flat walkways where casual strollers and joggers come to enjoy spectacular views of the Pacific. Sunsets here are hard to beat.

For a beach picnic you can buy food at one of the many fast-food stands that line the boardwalk. For a more relaxing meal, stand in line for a table at **Sidewalk Café** (⊠ 1401 Ocean Front Walk, ☎ 310/399–5547). It's worth the wait for a patio table.

★ ☝ ① Santa Monica Pier. Eateries, souvenir shops, a psychic adviser, arcades, and **Pacific Park** are all part of this truncated pier at the foot of Colorado Boulevard below Palisades Park. The pier's trademark 46-horse carousel, built in 1922, has appeared in many films, including *The Sting*. ⊠ Colorado Ave. and the ocean, ☎ 310/458–8900; carousel 310/458–8867. 🎟 Rides 25¢ and 50¢. ⊙ Carousel summer, daily 11–6; winter, weekends 10–5.

④ Third Street Promenade. Only foot traffic is allowed along a three-block stretch of 3rd Street, just a whiff away from the Pacific. Outdoor cafés, street vendors, several movie theaters, and a rich nightlife make this one of Santa Monica's main gathering spots. The mix of folks down here is great, from elderly couples out for a bite to skateboarders and street musicians. ⊠ 3rd St. between Wilshire Blvd. and Broadway.

★ ⑥ Venice Boardwalk. "Boardwalk" may be something of a misnomer—it's really a paved walkway—but this L.A. must-see delivers year-round action: bicyclists zip along and bikini-clad roller and in-line skaters attract crowds as they put on impromptu demonstrations, vying for attention with magicians, fortune tellers, a chain-saw juggler, and street artists. A local bodybuilding club works out on the adjacent "Muscle Beach." It's nearly impossible not to stop and ogle the strongmen's pecs. You can rent in-line skates, roller skates, and bicycles (some with baby seats) at the south end of the boardwalk (also known as Ocean Front Walk), along Washington Street, near the Venice Pier.

OFF THE
BEATEN PATH

WILL ROGERS STATE HISTORIC PARK – The late cowboy-humorist Will Rogers lived on this site in the 1920s and 1930s. The ranch-house museum features Rogers memorabilia. Rogers was a polo enthusiast, and in the 1930s, his front-yard polo field attracted such friends as Douglas Fairbanks, Sr., for weekend games. The tradition continues, with free weekend games scheduled April–October, weather permitting. The park is excellent for picnicking, and there's hiking on miles of trails. From Pacific Coast Highway, turn inland at Sunset Boulevard. Follow Sunset for about 5 mi to the park entrance. ⊠ *1501 Will Rogers State Park Rd., Pacific Palisades,* ☎ *310/454–8212.* ☜ *Free, parking $6.* ☉ *Park, daily 8–sunset daily; house tours, daily 10:30–4:30.*

The San Fernando Valley

There are other valleys in the Los Angeles area, but this is the one that people refer to simply as the Valley. Large portions of the Valley are bedroom communities of neat bungalows and shopping centers, but most of the major film and television studios, such as Warner Bros., NBC, and ABC, are also here. Universal City is a one-industry town, and that industry is Universal Studios. The studio has been at this site since 1915.

A Good Drive

Numbers in the text correspond to points of interest on the San Fernando Valley map.

On a clear day or evening, a drive along **Mulholland Drive** gives you a spectacular view of the sprawling San Fernando Valley below. Just over the hill from Hollywood via the Hollywood Freeway (U.S. 101, north) is Universal City, which has its own freeway off-ramp (Universal Center Drive). **Universal Studios Hollywood** ① is on a large hill overlooking the San Fernando Valley, a city-within-a-city. As you exit Universal, follow signs to Barham Boulevard. At Barham, turn left toward Burbank. After driving about a mile, the street curves around **Warner Bros. Studios** ②, whose outside wall is covered with billboards of current films and television shows. After the curve, you will be on West Olive Avenue. Keep to the right and look for the entrance to Gate No. 4 at Hollywood Way.

Just a minute away at the second big intersection, West Olive and Alameda avenues, is the main entrance to **NBC Television Studios** ③. Continue east on Alameda; on the next block to your right is **Disney Studios** ④, a very colorful bit of architecture. Drive south on Buena Vista and then turn left on Riverside to get a good look at the whimsical architecture.

To reach **Mission San Fernando Rey de España** ⑤, drive north on either the San Diego (I–405) or Golden State (I–5) freeway; Alameda Avenue will lead you to I–5, as will the Hollywood Freeway (Hwy. 170, north). Drive about 12 mi and exit at San Fernando Mission Boulevard. From I–405, drive east; from I–5, drive west. The mission is about ½ mi from either freeway on the north side of the street. (A scenic, but lengthy, route back to L.A. is via Mulholland Drive, whose exit is about 15 mi, or 20 minutes, from the mission off I–405.)

TIMING

The Valley is surrounded by mountains, and the major routes to and from it go through mountain passes. During rush hour, traffic jams on the Hollywood Freeway (U.S. 101/Hwy. 170), San Diego Freeway (I–405), and Ventura Freeway (U.S. 101/Hwy. 134) can be brutal. Expect to spend a full day at Universal Studios Hollywood and CityWalk. Studio tours at NBC and Warner Bros. last about two hours. A visit to the mission will eat up more time driving to and from it than touring the grounds.

Sights to See

❹ Disney Studios. Although tours of this animation and film studio are not available, a peek from Riverside Drive shows you that Disney's innovations go beyond the big and small screens to fanciful touches of architecture as well (note the little Mickey Mouse heads mounted on the surrounding fence). Disney's animation operation is housed in a Michael Graves–designed building, erected in 1995, that's made almost entirely of glass. It's clearly visible from the Ventura (Hwy. 134) Freeway. ⊠ *500 S. Buena Vista, Burbank.*

❺ Mission San Fernando Rey de España. An important member of a chain of 21 California missions established by Franciscan friars, Mission San Fernando was founded in 1797 and named in honor of King Ferdinand III of Spain. Fifty-six Native Americans joined the mission and made it a self-supporting community. In 1834, after Mexico extended its rule over California, a civil administrator was appointed for the mission and the priests were restricted to religious duties. The Native Americans began leaving, and what had been flourishing one year before became unproductive. Twelve years later the mission, along with its properties (those being the entire San Fernando Valley), was sold for $14,000. During the next 40 years, the mission buildings were neglected; settlers stripped roof tiles, and the adobe walls were ravaged by the weather. In 1923 a restoration program was initiated. Inside the mission, Native American designs and artifacts of Spanish craftsmanship depict the mission's 18th-century culture. Look for the small museum and gift shop. ⊠ *15151 San Fernando Mission Blvd., Mission Hills,* ☎ *818/361–0186.* ☜ *$4.* ☉ *Daily 9–4:30.*

Mulholland Drive. Driving the length of the hilltop road is slow and can be treacherous, but the rewards are sensational views of valley and city on each side and expensive homes along the way. From Hollywood reach Mulholland via Outpost Drive off Franklin Avenue or Cahuenga Boulevard West via Highland Avenue north.

❸ NBC Television Studios. Free tickets are available for tapings of the various NBC shows, and 70-minute walking tours of the studio are given on weekdays. ⊠ *3000 W. Alameda Ave., Burbank,* ☎ *818/840–3537.* ☜ *$7.* ☉ *Tour weekdays 9–3.*

★ ❶ Universal Studios Hollywood. Though you probably won't see anything that actually has to do with making a real film, visiting the theme park is an enlightening (if somewhat sensational) introduction to the principles of special effects. Seated aboard a comfortable tram (narrated, hour-long tours traverse the 420-acre complex all day), you can experience the parting of the Red Sea, an avalanche, and a flood; meet a 30-ft-tall version of King Kong; live through an encounter with a runaway train; be attacked by the ravenous killer shark of *Jaws* fame; endure a confrontation by aliens armed with death rays; and survive an all-too-real simulation of an earthquake that measured 8.3 on the Richter scale—complete with collapsing earth. The park's latest attraction is *Terminator 2–3D.* Based on the Arnold Schwarzenegger movies, it mixes 3-D with virtual reality and live action. *Jurassic Park—The Ride* is a tour through a jungle full of dinosaurs with an 84-ft water drop. Long lines form at *Back to the Future,* a flight simulator disguised as a DeLorean car that shows off state-of-the-art special effects. Within the slew of shops and restaurants known as **CityWalk,** the Wolfgang Puck Café is a poor man's version of Spago, Puck's star-studded Sun-

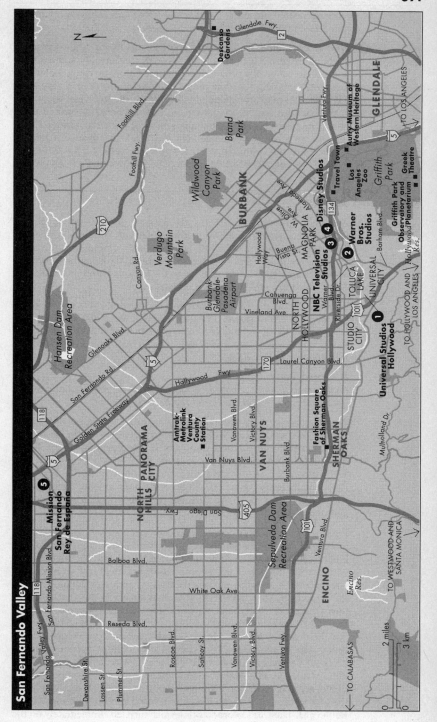

San Fernando Valley

Descanso Gardens

Glendale Fwy.

GLENDALE

TO LOS ANGELES

Foothill Blvd.

Foothill Fwy.

Ventura Fwy.

Brand
Park

Autry Museum of
Western Heritage

Wildwood
Canyon
Park

Disney Studios

Travel Town

BURBANK

Los
Angeles
Zoo

Greek
Theatre

Griffith
Park

210

Verdugo
Mountain
Park

Warner
Bros.
Studios

Griffith Park
Observatory and
Hollywood Planetarium

Canyon Rd.

Hollywood
Way

NBC Television
Studios

Barham Blvd.

Hansen Dam
Recreation Area

MAGNOLIA
PARK

Buena
Vista St.

Burbank-
Glendale-
Pasadena
Airport

TOLUCA
LAKE

UNIVERSAL
CITY

TO HOLLYWOOD AND
LOS ANGELES

Glenoaks Blvd.

Cahuenga
Blvd.

STUDIO
CITY

Universal Studios
Hollywood

5

Vineland Ave.

San Fernando Rd.

NORTH
HOLLYWOOD

Riverside Dr.

Laurel Canyon Blvd.

170

Mulholland Dr.

Hollywood Fwy.

118

Amtrak-
Metrolink
Ventura
County
Station

Vanowen Blvd.

Victory Blvd.

VAN NUYS

Fashion Square
of Sherman Oaks

SHERMAN
OAKS

NORTH
HILLS

PANORAMA
CITY

Van Nuys Blvd.

Burbank Blvd.

5

Mission
San Fernando
Rey de España

5

San Diego Fwy.

405

San Fernando Mission Blvd.

Balboa Blvd.

Sepulveda Dam
Recreation Area

101

Ventura Blvd.

ENCINO

Encino
Res.

TO WESTWOOD AND
SANTA MONICA

White Oak Ave.

118

Reseda Blvd.

San Fernando Valley

San Fernando Valley Fwy.

Devonshire St.

Lassen St.

Plummer St.

Roscoe Blvd.

Saticoy St.

Vanowen Blvd.

Victory Blvd.

Ventura Fwy.

TO CALABASAS

2 miles

3 km

0

0

set Strip restaurant. ⊠ *100 Universal City Plaza, Universal City,* ☎
818/508–9600. ☞ *$36.* ☉ *Daily 9–7; summer 8* AM*–10* PM.

② **Warner Bros. Studios.** Two-hour tours at this major studio center in
Burbank involve a lot of walking, so dress comfortably and casually.
Somewhat technically oriented and centered more on the actual work-
ings of filmmaking than the ones at Universal, tours here vary from
day to day to take advantage of goings-on at the lot. Most tours take
in the back-lot sets, prop construction department, and sound complex. A museum chronicles the studio's film and animation history. Reservations are strongly recommended one week in advance. Children
under 8 are not admitted. Call for special needs. ⊠ *4000 Warner
Blvd., Burbank,* ☎ *818/954–1744.* ☞ *$30.* ☉ *Tours weekdays 9–3
on the hr.*

Pasadena Area

Although now fully absorbed into the general Los Angeles sprawl,
Pasadena is a separate and distinctly defined city. Its varied residential
architecture, augmented by lush landscaping, is among the most spectacular in southern California. Nearby Highland Park has three excellent
museums and San Marino is home to the famous Huntington Library,
Art Collections, and Botanical Gardens.

To reach Pasadena from downtown Los Angeles, drive north on the
Pasadena Freeway (Hwy. 110). From Hollywood use the Glendale
Freeway (Hwy. 2, north), and from the San Fernando Valley use the
Ventura Freeway (Hwy. 134, east), which cuts through Glendale be-
fore arriving in Pasadena.

A Good Tour

*Numbers in the text correspond to numbers in the margin and on the
Pasadena Area, Highland Park, and San Marino map.*

A good place to start a short driving tour of Pasadena is on Orange
Grove Boulevard, a.k.a. Millionaire's Row, where wealthy Easterners
built grand mansions. One example is the **Wrigley Mansion** ①. To get
there, take the Orange Grove exit off the Ventura Freeway (Hwy.
134); turn right at Orange Grove and travel five blocks. From the
Pasadena Freeway (Hwy. 110), stay on the freeway until it ends at Arroyo Parkway. From Arroyo Parkway turn left at California Boulevard
and then right at Orange Grove.

From the Wrigley Mansion, travel north on Orange Grove to Walnut
Street and the **Fenyes Mansion** ②, now headquarters of the Pasadena
Historical Society. Continue on Orange Grove to Arroyo Terrace,
where a left turn will take you into an architectural wonderland.
Greene and Greene, the renowned Pasadena architects, designed all of
the houses on Arroyo Terrace, as well as others in the area. To view
their Craftsman masterpiece, the three-story, shingled **Gamble House** ③,
turn right on Westmoreland Place. Also in this section is the Frank Lloyd
Wright–designed Millard House ("La Miniatura") on Prospect Crescent (from Westmoreland, turn left onto Rosemont Avenue, right on
Prospect Terrace, and right onto Prospect Crescent to No. 645). The
famous **Rose Bowl** ④ is nestled in a gulley just to the west off Arroyo
Boulevard. Leave this area via Rosemont Avenue, driving away from
the hills to the south. From Rosemont, turn right onto Orange Grove
Boulevard. Then, at Colorado Boulevard, turn left. Immediately on the
left is the contemporary, austere **Norton Simon Museum** ⑤. Continue
east on Colorado Boulevard and, after a few blocks, you'll cross the
historic concrete-arched Colorado Street Bridge, built in 1913, rising
160 ft above the Arroyo Seco gorge.

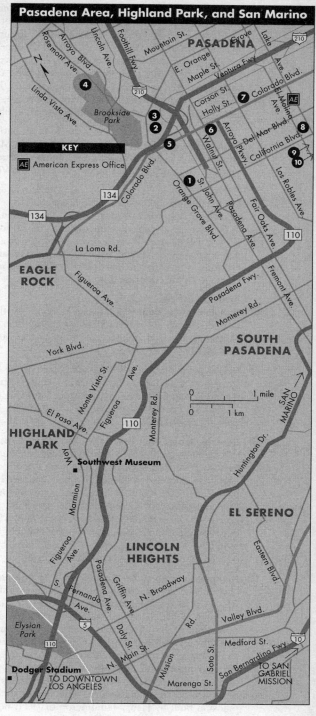

Pasadena Area, Highland Park, and San Marino

KEY

AE American Express Office

After leaving the block-long overpass, you'll enter **Old Town Pasadena** ⑥. You'll want to walk around this section of Pasadena, heading east. For a look at domed Pasadena City Hall, turn left on Fair Oaks Avenue, then right on Holly Street. Garfield Avenue will bring you back to Colorado. The next intersection is Los Robles Avenue. One-half block north on Los Robles is the **Pacific Asia Museum** ⑦. Back on Colorado, head three blocks east to El Molino Avenue. Turn right past the **Pasadena Playhouse** (✉ 39 S. El Molino Avenue, ☎ 626/356–PLAY) and, if you have youngsters, continue along four blocks to **Kidspace** ⑧.

From this point it's a short drive south on El Molino to California Boulevard, where a left turn will take you into San Marino and the **Huntington Library, Art Collections, and Botanical Gardens** ⑨ (follow the signs). Also in this area is the historic **El Molino Viejo** ⑩.

TIMING

Get a late-morning or early afternoon start to see the important architectural sights on this tour, saving Old Pasadena for last. It has one of the best evening street scenes in southern California. You'll want to allow a half day for the entire driving tour. A stop at the Gamble House may take an hour, leaving plenty of time for an afternoon visit to the Norton Simon Museum. Set aside an entire day for the Huntington Library, Art Collections, and Botanical Gardens.

Sights to See

⑩ **El Molino Viejo.** Built in 1816 as a grist mill for the San Gabriel Mission, this is one of the last remaining examples in southern California of Spanish Mission architecture. ✉ *1120 Old Mill Rd., San Marino,* ☎ *626/449–5458.* ⌦ *Free.* ☉ *Tues.–Sun. 1–4.*

❷ **Fenyes Mansion.** The 1905 mansion, one of the Pasadena Historical Museums, still has its original furniture and paintings on the main and second floors. Basement exhibits trace Pasadena's history. ✉ *470 W. Walnut St., Pasadena,* ☎ *626/577–1660.* ⌦ *$4.* ☉ *Thurs.–Sun. 1–4, 1-hr docent-led tour.*

★ ❸ **Gamble House.** Built by Charles and Henry Greene in 1908, this is a spectacular example of Craftsman-style bungalow architecture. To wealthy Easterners such as the Gambles (as in Procter & Gamble), this type of vacation home seemed informal compared with their mansions back home. Check out the hand craftsmanship, including a teak staircase and cabinetry, Greene-designed furniture, and an Emil Lange glass door. To see more Greene and Greene homes in the neighborhood, buy a self-guided tour map in the Gamble House's bookstore. ✉ *4 Westmoreland Pl., Pasadena,* ☎ *626/793–3334.* ⌦ *$5.* ☉ *Thurs.–Sun. noon–3, 1-hr tour every 15–20 min.*

★ ❾ **Huntington Library, Art Collections, and Botanical Gardens.** If you have time for only one stop in the Pasadena area, it should be San Marino, where railroad tycoon Henry E. Huntington built his hilltop home in the early 1900s. Since then, this institution has established a reputation as one of the most extraordinary cultural complexes in the world. The library contains more than 600,000 books and some 300 manuscripts, including such treasures as a Gutenberg Bible, the Ellesmere manuscript of Chaucer's *Canterbury Tales,* George Washington's genealogy in his own handwriting, and first editions by Ben Franklin and Shakespeare. The Huntington Gallery, housed in the original Georgian mansion built by Henry Huntington in 1911, holds a world-famous collection of British paintings, including the original *Blue Boy* by Gainsborough, *Pinkie,* a companion piece by Thomas Lawrence, and the monumental *Sarah Siddons as the Tragic Muse* by Joshua Reynolds.

American paintings and decorative arts are housed in the Virginia Steele Scott Gallery of American Art.

An awesome 150-acre garden, formerly the grounds of the estate, the Huntington Gardens now include a 12-acre Desert Garden featuring the world's largest group of mature cacti and other succulents, arranged by continent. The Japanese Garden holds traditional Japanese plants, stone ornaments, a drum bridge, a Japanese house, a bonsai court, and a Zen rock garden. Besides these gardens, there are collections of azaleas and 1,500 varieties of camellias, the world's largest public collection. The 3-acre rose garden is displayed chronologically, so the development leading to today's strains of roses can be observed. On the grounds is the charming **Rose Tea Garden Room,** where traditional high tea is served. A 1¼-hour guided tour of the gardens is led by docents at posted times, and inexpensive, self-guided tour leaflets are available in the entrance pavilion. ⊠ *1151 Oxford Rd., San Marino,* ☎ *626/405–2100; recorded information 626/405–2141.* ☞ *$8.50, free 1st Thurs. of month.* ☉ *Tues.–Fri. noon–4:30; weekends 10:30–4:30; June–Aug., Tues.–Sun. 10:30–4:30.*

🖐 ❽ **Kidspace.** At this children's museum housed in the gymnasium of an elementary school, kids can direct a television or radio station; dress up in the real uniforms of a firefighter, astronaut, or football player; or play in the sand of an indoor beach. "Critter Caverns" beckons with its large tree house and secret tunnels for exploring insect life firsthand. ⊠ *390 S. El Molino Ave., Pasadena,* ☎ *626/449–9143.* ☞ *$5.* ☉ *Sept.– July 1, Tues. 1:30–5, Wed.–Fri. 1–5, Sat. 10–5, Sun. 1–5; hrs vary during school vacations.*

OFF THE
BEATEN PATH

MISSION SAN GABRIEL ARCHANGEL – In 1771 Father Junípero Serra dedicated this mission to the great archangel and messenger from God, St. Gabriel. As the founders approached the mission site, they were confronted by Native Americans. In the heat of battle, one of the padres revealed the canvas painting *Our Lady of Sorrows,* which so impressed the Indians that they laid down their bows and arrows. Within the next 50 years, the San Gabriel Archangel became the wealthiest of all California missions. In 1833 the Mexican government confiscated the mission and it began to decline. In 1855 the U.S. government returned the mission to the church, but by this time the Franciscans had departed. In 1908 the Claretian Missionaries took charge, and much care and respect has since been poured into the mission. Today, Mission San Gabriel Archangel's adobe walls preserve an era of history, and the magnificent cemetery stands witness to the many people who lived here. ⊠ *428 S. Mission Dr., San Gabriel,* ☎ *626/457–3048.* ☞ *$4.* ☉ *Daily 9–4:30.*

★ ❺ **Norton Simon Museum.** Familiar to television viewers of the Rose Parade, this sleek, modern building makes a stunning background for the passing floats. In 1974 Simon reorganized the failing Pasadena Art Institute and assembled one of the world's finest collections, richest in its Rembrandts, Goyas, Picassos, and, most of all, Degas. This is one of the only two U.S. institutions to hold the complete set of the artist's model bronzes (the other is the Metropolitan Museum of Art, in New York). There are also several Rodin sculptures dotted throughout the museum. Rembrandt's development can be traced in three oils—*The Bearded Man in the Wide Brimmed Hat, Self Portrait,* and *Titus.* The most dramatic Goyas are two oils—*St. Jerome in Penitence* and the *Portrait of Dona Francisca Vicenta Chollet y Caballero.* Picasso's renowned *Woman with a Book* highlights a comprehensive collection of his paintings, drawings, and sculptures. The museum's collections of Impressionist and Cubist work is extensive, and the Asia collection is one of the country's best. Early Renaissance, Baroque, and Rococo artwork are additional specialties. A magical Tiepolo ceiling highlights the Rococo period. A Frank Gehry–designed sculpture garden with a teahouse is the latest addition. ⊠ *411 W. Colorado Blvd., Pasadena,* ☎ *626/449–6840.* ☺ *$4.* ☼ *Thurs.–Sun. noon–6.*

⑥ Old Town Pasadena. Once the victim of decay, the area was revitalized in the 1990s as a blend of restored 19th-century brick buildings with a yuppie overlay. Cafés and restaurants are now plentiful and varied. Old Town's shopping-mall mix of retailers includes Pottery Barn, Banana Republic, and Z Galerie, as well as specialty bookstores and boutiques. In the evenings and on weekends, streets are packed with people. The 12-block historic district is anchored along Colorado Boulevard, between Pasadena Avenue and Arroyo Parkway. West of Old Town, Colorado Boulevard rises onto the **Colorado Street Bridge,** a raised section of roadway on graceful arches. On New Year's Day throngs of people line Colorado Boulevard to watch the Rose Parade.

NEED A BREAK? Walk down to Fair Oaks Avenue to the **Market City Cafe** (⊠ 33 S. Fair Oaks Ave., ☎ 626/568–0203), which you'll recognize by the life-size black-and-white cow in the window. Imaginative Italian fare is served both indoors and alfresco.

⑦ Pacific Asia Museum. Designed in the style of a Chinese imperial palace with a central garden, this building is devoted entirely to the arts and culture of Asia and the Pacific Islands. ⊠ *46 N. Los Robles Ave.,* ☎ *626/449–2742.* ☺ *$5, free 3rd Sat. of month.* ☼ *Wed.–Sun. 10–5.*

④ Rose Bowl. With an enormous rose, the city of Pasadena's logo, tattooed onto its exterior, it's hard to miss this 100,000-seat stadium, host of many Super Bowls and home to the UCLA Bruins. The facility is closed except during games and special events such as the monthly Rose Bowl Swap Meet. Held the second Sunday of the month, it is considered the granddaddy of West Coast flea markets. ⊠ *Rosemont Ave., Pasadena,* ☎ *626/577–3100.* ☼ *Flea market, 2nd Sunday of month, 9–5.*

OFF THE BEATEN PATH **SOUTHWEST MUSEUM –** Readily spotted from the Pasadena Freeway (Highway 110), this huge Mission Revival building stands halfway up Mt. Washington. Inside is an extensive collection of Native American art and artifacts, with special emphasis on the people of the Plains, Northwest coast, Southwest coast, and California. The basket collection is outstanding. ⊠ *234 Museum Dr., off Ave. 43 exit, Highland Park,* ☎ *323/ 221–2163.* ☺ *$5.* ☼ *Tues.–Sun. 10–5.*

① Wrigley Mansion. The chewing gum magnate, William Wrigley, purchased this white Italian Renaissance–style house in 1914. The mansion is now the headquarters for the Tournament of Roses Association. The gardens, with some 1,500 varieties of roses, are open daily. ⊠ *391 S. Orange Grove Blvd., Pasadena,* ☎ *626/449–4100.* ☼ *House tours Feb.–Aug., Thurs. 2–4; gardens, daily sunrise–sunset.*

Long Beach, San Pedro, and Palos Verdes

Long Beach, wholly separate from the city of Los Angeles, began as a seaside resort in the 19th century. During the early part of the 20th century, an oil boom brought Midwesterners and Dust Bowlers in search of a better life. Bust followed boom and the city eventually took on a somewhat raw, neglected tone. A long-term redevelopment program begun in the '70s has done much to brighten the city's image. Across the Vincent Thomas Bridge from Long Beach is San Pedro, L.A's working harbor, and the hilly Palos Verdes Peninsula, a gentrified community of expensive estates.

A Good Tour

Numbers in the text correspond to numbers in the margin and on the Long Beach map.

A single drive around these three South Bay towns would cover more than 100 mi, so it's best to approach the area on two separate tours.

Begin a tour of Long Beach at what is still the city's most famous attraction, the Art Deco ship the **Queen Mary** ①. Take the Queens Way Bridge back across the bay to the **Long Beach Aquarium of the Pacific** ②. From here, stops along Shoreline Drive at **Shoreline Aquatic Park** ③ or the waterfront shopping center **Shoreline Village** ④ afford the best views of the harbor and the Long Beach skyline. At Ocean Boulevard, Shoreline Drive turns into Alamitos Avenue. Continue on Alamitos to the corner of 7th Street for two museums: the **Museum of Latin American Art** ⑦ and the **Oceanic Art Museum Gallery** ⑧. Return to Ocean Boulevard, and turn east. Just past the commercial district lie the **Long Beach Museum of Art** ⑥ and grand old homes dating from the early 20th century. From Ocean Boulevard, turn onto Livingston Drive and then 2nd Street to drive through Belmont Shores before arriving at Alamitos Bay and **Naples** ⑤, a picturesque enclave of canals and marinas, and the place to take a gondola ride.

For an overview of Palos Verdes and San Pedro, begin at the **South Coast Botanic Garden,** on Crenshaw Boulevard 1 mi south of the Pacific Coast Highway (exit from I–405 at Crenshaw Boulevard and head west). Continue west on Crenshaw Boulevard to Crest Road. Turn right on Crest and follow it to Hawthorne Boulevard. Turn left at Hawthorne, and left again at Palos Verdes Drive. Less than a mile farther on your right you'll see Point Vicente Lighthouse, a good spot to watch for whales, and, another 2 mi away, on your left, you'll see the all-glass **Wayfarers Chapel.** Continue south and you'll hit San Pedro and Los Angeles Harbor. Follow the signs to Cabrillo Beach, where you'll find the stark-white building that houses the **Cabrillo Marine Aquarium.**

TIMING

Guided tours of the *Queen Mary* last an hour; the Long Beach Aquarium of the Pacific could occupy most of a morning or an afternoon. Set aside about 90 minutes for a combined visit to the Museum of Latin American Art and the Oceanic Art Museum Gallery and 90 minutes for a separate stop at the Long Beach Museum of Art. If you've planned in advance, you could end the day with a sunset gondola cruise on the canals in Naples. In Palos Verdes, the South Coast Botanic Garden could occupy you for a couple of hours. The Wayfarers Chapel, less than 20 minutes from the garden, is a half-hour stopover. If you have kids in tow, expect to stay a couple of hours at San Pedro's Cabrillo Marine Aquarium, longer if you join one of the tidepool walks. Factor in 10 or 15 minutes of driving time between attractions.

Sights to See

Cabrillo Marine Aquarium. This gem of a small museum is dedicated to the marine life that flourishes off the southern California coast. A modern Frank Gehry–designed building right on the beach houses 35 saltwater tanks. Don't miss the shark tank, the whale and dolphin room, and the see-through tidal tank that enables you to see the long view of a wave. ✉ *3720 Stephen White Dr., San Pedro,* ☎ *310/548–7562.*

Suggested donation $2, parking $6.50. ⊙ *Tues.–Fri. noon–5, week-ends 10–5.*

② **Long Beach Aquarium of the Pacific.** A full-scale model of a blue whale, the largest living creature in the Pacific and on the planet, is suspended above the Great Hall, the entrance to this new aquarium. Seventeen major exhibit tanks and 30 smaller focus tanks contain some 10,000 live marine animals—including seals and sea lions—that inhabit the Pacific Ocean and its environment. You'll also learn about conservation problems such as pollution, endangered coral reefs, and overharvesting. ⊠ *100 Aquarium Way, Long Beach,* ☎ *562/590–3100.* *$13.95.* ⊙ *Daily 10–6.*

⑥ **Long Beach Museum of Art.** The museum celebrates its 50th anniversary in 2000 by expanding into a new pavilion next door to its present home, a 1912 historic oceanfront mansion. That means more room for its permanent collection, which focuses on European and American art. The museum is renowned for its video art collection, one of the largest in the world. ⊠ *2300 E. Ocean Blvd., Long Beach,* ☎ *562/439–2119.* *$2.* ⊙ *Wed.–Sun. 10–5, Fri. 10–8.*

⑦ **Museum of Latin American Art (MOLAA).** The only museum in the country dedicated to contemporary art of Mexico and Central and South America moved into a converted skating rink in 1996, with just two small galleries. Two years later, MOLAA practically exploded onto the art scene when it debuted its renovation of 10,000 square ft of additional gallery space with a spectacular show of Oaxacan artist Laura Hernandez. ⊠ *628 Alamitos Ave., Long Beach,* ☎ *562/437–1689.* *$5.* ⊙ *Tues.–Sat. 11:30–7:30, Sun. noon–6.*

⑤ **Naples.** Arthur Parsons, the developer who came up with the Naples canal idea, learned from the mistakes and bad luck that did in those in Venice, just up the coast, and built the canals to take full advantage of the tidal flow that would keep them clean. Actually three small islands in man-made Alamitos Bay, Naples is best experienced on foot. Park near Bay Shore Avenue and 2nd Street and walk across the bridge, where you can meander around the quaint streets with Italian names. This well-restored neighborhood has eclectic architecture: vintage Victorians, Craftsman bungalows, and Mission Revivals. You may spy a real gondola or two on the canals. You can hire them for a ride, but not on the spur of the moment. **Gondola Getaway** (5437 E. Ocean Blvd., Long Beach, ☎ 562/433–9595) offers one-hour rides, usually touted for romantic couples, although their gondolas can accommodate groups of up to 14 people, and serve bread, salami, and cheese—you bring the wine. Reservations are essential at least one week in advance. Rides cost $55 per couple, $10 each additional person, and run from 11 AM to 11 PM.

❽ Oceanic Art Museum Gallery. Traditional and authentic indigenous art from the islands of Micronesia has become very rare. In 1994, in an effort to preserve the islands' art, the Robert Gumbiner Foundation established the Ethnic Art Institute of Micronesia (EAIM) on the island of Yap to revitalize and re-create indigenous arts and crafts. Through research and the use of historic photographs and drawings, a guild of native master artisans and apprentices re-creates traditional Micronesian works of art. The museum exhibits from its own small collection of Oceanic art and presents changing exhibits drawn from private collections and other museums. ⊠ *694 Alamitos Ave., Long Beach,* ☎ *562/432–4477.* ◻ *Free.* ☉ *Thurs.–Sat. 11–5.*

★ ❶ Queen Mary. Be sure to get at least a glimpse of this huge passenger ship, now sitting snugly in Long Beach Harbor. The 80,000-ton *Queen Mary* was launched in 1934, a floating treasure of Art Deco splendor. It took a crew of 1,100 to minister to the needs of its 1,900 demanding passengers. The former first-class passenger quarters are now a hotel. Allow a half day to explore this most luxurious of luxury liners, admiring the extensive wood paneling, the gleaming nickel- and silver-plated handrails, and the hand-cut glass. Tours of the ship are available, and guests are invited to browse the 12 decks and walk around the bridge, staterooms, officers' quarters, and engine rooms. There are several restaurants and shops on board, a gallery of the ship's original art, and even a wedding chapel. Stay late for fireworks Friday, Saturday, and Sunday nights in the summer. ⊠ *Pier J, Long Beach,* ☎ *562/435–3511.* ◻ *$13, guided 1-hr tour $7 extra.* ☉ *Tours daily 10–4:30, later in summer.*

❸ Shoreline Aquatic Park. Set literally in the middle of Long Beach Harbor is this much-sought-after resting place for RVers. Kite flyers love the winds here, and casual passersby can enjoy a short walk, where the modern skyline, quaint Shoreline Village, the *Queen Mary,* and the ocean all vie for attention. ⊠ *E. Shoreline Dr.*

❹ Shoreline Village. This stretch of 24 gift shops and four restaurants between downtown Long Beach and the *Queen Mary* is a good place for a stroll, day or evening. This is also the place to hop aboard the "AquaBus" water taxi (◻ $1), which travels between major harbor attractions, including the aquarium and the *Queen Mary.* ⊠ *Shoreline Dr. and Shoreline Village Rd., Long Beach.,* ☎ *562/435–2668.* ☉ *May–Sept., daily 10–10; Oct.–Apr., daily 10–9.*

★ South Coast Botanic Garden. This Rancho Palos Verdes botanical garden began life ignominiously—as a garbage dump-cum-landfill. With the intensive ministerings of the experts from the L.A. County Arboreta

Department, the dump soon sprouted lush gardens, with all the plants eventually organized into color groups. Self-guided walking tours take visitors past flower and herb gardens, rare cacti, and a lake with ducks. The Water-Wise Garden showcases alternatives to grass lawns in the parched southern California climate. Picnicking is limited to a lawn area outside the gates. ⊠ *26300 S. Crenshaw Blvd., Rancho Palos Verdes,* ☎ *310/544–6815.* ⌑ *$5.* ☉ *Daily 9–5.*

Wayfarers Chapel. Architect Lloyd Wright, son of Frank Lloyd Wright, designed this modern glass church in 1949 to blend in with an encircling redwood forest. The redwoods are gone, but another forest has taken their place, lush with ferns and azaleas, adding up to a breathtaking combination of ocean, vegetation, and an architectural wonder. This "natural church" is a popular wedding site, so avoid visiting on weekends. ⊠ *5755 Palos Verdes Dr. S., Rancho Palos Verdes,* ☎ *310/377–1650.* ☉ *Daily 7–5.*

DINING

By Bill Stern

L.A.'s restaurants reflect both the city's well-deserved reputation for culinary innovation and its rich ethnic cornucopia. Los Angeles is home not only to many of the country's best-known chefs—Wolfgang Puck, Joachim Splichal, Michel Richard—but also to many unheralded chefs who delight Angelenos daily with the cuisines of their native Shanghai, Oaxaca, Tuscany, and elsewhere.

CATEGORY	COST*
$$$$	over $50
$$$	$30–$50
$$	$20–$30
$	under $20
*per person for a three-course meal, excluding drinks, service, and 8¼% tax	

Beverly Hills, Century City, Hollywood, and West Hollywood

Beverly Hills

AMERICAN

$$–$$$ ✕ **Grill on the Alley.** This fashionable place for power lunching features tasty, simple American fare, including chicken potpies, crab cakes, creamy Cobb salad, and homemade rice pudding, as well as high-quality steaks and seafood. ⊠ *9560 Dayton Way,* ☎ *310/276–0615. Reservations essential. AE, DC, MC, V. No lunch Sun. Valet parking evenings.*

CONTEMPORARY

$$–$$$$ ✕ **The Dining Room at the Regent Beverly Wilshire.** Business people
★ and area residents use this formal but comfortable room for elegant breakfasts, lunches, and dinners. Grilled swordfish with barbecued shrimp sometimes appears on the prix-fixe lunch menu, which generally runs about $28. The dinner menu may include warm fig-and-wild-mushroom salad and Maine lobster with mascarpone-and-potato gnocchi. A la carte choices are also available. ⊠ *9500 Wilshire Blvd.,* ☎ *310/275–5200. Jacket required. AE, D, DC, MC, V. No lunch or dinner Sun. Valet parking.*

$$–$$$$ ✕ **Spago Beverly Hills.** Wolfgang Puck has done it again. The chef who helped define California cuisine at his original Sunset Strip venue now wows celebrity and business circles in a smart Beverly Hills location designed by his wife, Barbara Lazaroff. The restaurant centers around

an outdoor courtyard, from which diners can glimpse the large open kitchen. The menu changes daily offering such starters as white-bean and duck-confit soup and warm crayfish salad with mustard potatoes. Entrées have ranged from wild striped bass with celery-root puree to roasted Cantonese duck with persimmons, pomegranate, and ginger. Also worth trying are Puck's Austrian "childhood favorites," such as *Kärntner Käsenudeln* (cheese ravioli) with hazelnut butter and his renowned pizzas. This Spago attracts as many of Hollywood's who's who as the original does. ⊠ *176 N. Cañon Dr.,* ☎ *310/385–0880. Reservations essential. AE, D, DC, MC, V. No lunch Sun.*

$$–$$$ ✕ **Nouveau Café Blanc.** Chef-owner Tommy Harase has made his
★ modern yet warm and unpretentious restaurant one of Beverly Hills' unexpected treats—especially when lunchtime entrées such as sautéed salmon with basil vinaigrette, or lobster ravioli with *vin blanc* cream sauce cost as little as $10. Equally good-value four- and five-course prix-fixe dinners, $38 and $48, may feature exquisite sautéed foie gras with corn chowder, seared jumbo scallops stuffed with Sevruga caviar, and roasted venison with juniper-berry sauce. Service is both gracious and unintrusive. ⊠ *9777 Little Santa Monica Blvd.,* ☎ *310/888–0108. Reservations essential. AE, D, MC, V. Closed Sun. and Mon.*

CHINESE

$$ ✕ **The Mandarin.** The Mandarin serves Szechuan and Chinese country dishes in a serene, traditional Chinese setting, with roomy bamboo armchairs, soft Chinese music, and linens and crystal. Specialties include minced chicken wrapped in lettuce leaves, scallion pancakes, Singapore noodles, and Beijing duck (order ahead of time). ⊠ *430 N. Camden Dr.,* ☎ *310/859–0926. Reservations essential. AE, DC, MC, V. No lunch weekends. Valet parking evenings.*

DELI

$$–$$$ ✕ **Barney Greengrass.** This *haute* deli on the fifth floor of Barneys has
★ an appropriately high-class aesthetic: limestone floors, mahogany furniture, and a wall of windows. You can savor everything from $99 beluga caviar to a $6.75 peanut butter–and–jelly sandwich. But the specialties are flawless smoked salmon, sturgeon, and whitefish flown in fresh from New York. This deli keeps store hours, closing Thursday at 8, Sunday at 6, and every other day at 7. ⊠ *Barneys, 9570 Wilshire Blvd., Beverly Hills,* ☎ *310/777–5877. AE, MC, V. Valet parking.*

$ ✕ **Nate 'n' Al's.** A famous gathering place for Hollywood comedians and Beverly Hills shoppers, Nate 'n' Al's has regulars bantering with their favorite waitresses who serve first-rate matzo-ball soup, lox and scrambled eggs, cheese blintzes, potato pancakes, and deli sandwiches. ⊠ *414 N. Beverly Dr.,* ☎ *310/274–0101. Reservations not accepted. AE, MC, V. Free parking.*

FRENCH

$$–$$$ ✕ **Bistro K.** Seated outside in an ivy-trellised brick courtyard, with a fountain softly gurgling in the background and a glamorous French waitress taking your order, you'll feel far from urban L.A. Look for steamed mussels in a ginger and lemongrass broth; seared swordfish with lemon, garlic, and spinach; and roast beef in burgundy sauce with pommes frîtes. ⊠ *267 S. Beverly Dr.,* ☎ *310/276–1558. AE, DC, MC, V. No lunch weekends. Valet parking evenings.*

ITALIAN

$$ ✕ **Da Pasquale.** An affordable meal is hard to find here in the land of Gucci and Bijan, which is one reason to visit Da Pasquale. An even better reason is the pizza topped with ingredients like fresh tomato, garlic, and basil or three cheeses and prosciutto. Standards such as antipasti, pastas, and roast chicken are also good. ⊠ *9749 Little Santa*

Beverly Hills, Century City, Hollywood, and West Hollywood Dining

Monica Blvd., ☏ *310/859–3884. AE, MC, V. Closed Sun. No lunch Sat. Free parking after 6* PM.

$$–$$$ ✕ **ObaChine.** Wolfgang Puck and Barbara Lazaroff strike again: this time with pan-Asian food for the Beverly Hills crowd in a loft space with a hammered-copper bar and tables of mahogany and etched glass. Interesting dishes include savory crab *shui mai* (dumplings), Cambodian-style shrimp crepes, and sizzling whole catfish with ginger-ponzu sauce (made with Japanese radishes and citrus juices). ✉ 242 *N. Beverly Dr.,* ☏ *310/274–4440. AE, MC, V. No lunch Sun. Valet parking.*

Century City

$–$$ ✕ **Dive!** A Steven Spielberg creation, this place is as much a theme park as it is a restaurant. Water gurgles through porthole windows, fish swim by on giant screens, and every now and then red lights flash and the whole place makes a simulated submarine dive. Submarine sandwiches, the specialty, include a Portobello mushroom–red bell pepper–arugula variation. ✉ *10250 Santa Monica Blvd.,* ☏ *310/788–3483. AE, D, DC, MC, V. Valet parking or free self-parking.*

$$–$$$ ✕ **Lunaria.** Bernard Jacoupy, who made Bernard's one of the '80s best restaurants, has done it again at this jazz-friendly bistro. The sunny flavors of tomatoes, fennel, and good fresh fish dominate the Provençal menu. There's also an oyster bar. Roomy wicker armchairs and large tables fill the dining room, warmed by watercolors painted by Jacoupy's grandfather. After 8:30 (9:30 on weekends), a wall slides open to reveal the stage and the evening's featured jazz group. ✉ *10351 Santa Monica Blvd.,* ☏ *310/282–8870. AE, DC, MC, V. Closed Sun. No lunch Sat., no dinner Mon. Valet parking.*

$$–$$$ ✕ **Harry's Bar & American Grill.** The dark wood–paneled maritime decor and the selection of dishes—paper-thin carpaccio, *grigliata mista di pesce* (mixed seafood grill), and tagliatellini con *luganega* (sausage)—are intended to evoke Harry's Bar in Venice, but the check will be far lower than in Italy. ✉ *2020 Ave. of the Stars,* ☏ *310/277–2333. Reservations essential. AE, DC, MC. No lunch weekends. Valet parking.*

Hollywood

$$ ✕ **Hollywood Hills Coffee Shop.** Despite the modest name, this little café often has surprisingly good food. Breakfast promises classics such as huevos rancheros, cheese blintzes, and even a whole grilled salmon trout, its reddish flesh set off by eggs and salsa. For dinner, there are vegetarian choices as well as fish and meat. ✉ *6145 Franklin Ave.,* ☏ *323/467–7678. Reservations not accepted. MC, V.*

$–$$ ✕ **Hollywood Canteen.** In the heart of working Hollywood, near soundstages, recording studios, and lighting companies, this handsome "diner" functions as a canteen for executives, actors, and technicians, who come here for simple but upscale grub: organic field-green salads, burgers, risotto with asparagus and shrimp, and various soups. ✉ *1006 Seward St.,* ☏ *323/465–0961. AE, MC, V. Closed Sun. No lunch Sat. Valet parking.*

$ ✕ **Gumbo Pot.** This outdoor Cajun/Creole café in the Farmers Market serves a mean smoky and spicy gumbo rich with shrimp and chicken. It's also the place for *muffulettas* (hero sandwiches), jambalaya, and *beignets* (fried dough dusted with powdered sugar). ⊠ *Farmers Market, 6333 W. 3rd St.,* ☎ *323/933–0358. Reservations not accepted. MC, V.*

CONTEMPORARY

$$$$ ✕ **Patina.** The exterior of Joachim Splichal's flagship restaurant is so
★ understated that it's easy to miss, and the interior is a study in spare elegance. Generally considered one of the best restaurants in Los Angeles, this is the wellspring from which the various Pinot bistros have sprung. Among the mainstays are a corn blini filled with fennel-marinated salmon and crème fraîche, and scallops wrapped in potato slices with brown-butter vinaigrette. ⊠ *5955 Melrose Ave.,* ☎ *323/467–1108. Reservations essential. AE, D, DC, MC, V. No lunch Wed.–Mon. Valet parking.*

$$$–$$$$ ✕ **Citrus.** Chef Michel Richard has opened restaurants elsewhere, but
★ Citrus has remained his hottest ticket, especially within the entertainment industry. Lunch begins on the light side, with starters such as artichoke terrine or ahi tuna carpaccio, followed by sautéed Chilean sea bass with black chanterelle crust or chicken ravioli with Parmesan sauce. The dinner menu features crab cakes with tomato-mustard sauce. ⊠ *6703 Melrose Ave.,* ☎ *323/857–0034. Reservations essential. AE, MC, V. No lunch weekends. Valet parking.*

$$–$$$ ✕ **Pinot Hollywood.** This link in the chain of glamorous bistros Joachim "Patina" Splichal has laid out across the city occupies a walled compound almost next door to Paramount Studios. Lunch entrées, which range from $13 to $18, include poached-salmon salad with tomato vinaigrette, papardelle with braised lamb, and grilled albacore tuna with shrimp pot stickers. For dinner you might find fresh grilled sardines à la Provençal or parsnip gnocchi with lobster and veal shank and caramelized root vegetables. ⊠ *1448 N. Gower St.,* ☎ *323/461–8800. Reservations essential. AE, D, DC, MC, V. No lunch Sat. Closed Sun. Valet parking.*

FRENCH

$–$$$ **Les Deux Cafés.** This handsomely refitted 1904 house with a hidden dining terrace and an even more intimate herb garden is unexpectedly set in a parking lot behind a barbed-wire-topped wall. Chef David Winn appeals to easily bored tastes with inventions such as lobster-and-tabbouleh salad, and a salad of beets, spinach, and horseradish. He also turns out a splendid skate sautéed in brown butter. ⊠ *1683 Las Palmas Ave.,* ☎ *213/465–0509. Reservations essential. AE, MC, V. Closed Sun. No lunch Sat. Valet parking.*

INDIAN

$ ✕ **East India Grill.** With its combination of high-tech sheet metal decor and low-tech tandoori oven this popular café serves traditional, zesty Indian food with a California edge. Traditional dishes such as greencoconut curries, *makhani tikka masalas* (tomato-based curries), and *sagwalas* (spinach dishes) are just as well prepared as the more imaginative, California-influenced novelties like mango ribs and garlic-basil nan. ⊠ *345 N. La Brea Ave.,* ☎ *323/936–8844. AE, MC, V. Free garage parking.*

JAPANESE

$$ ✕ **Ita-Cho.** Specializing in *koryori-ya,* the Japanese pub cuisine that features delicately cooked dishes, the small dining room also serves flawless sashimi (but no sushi). Also try the tender pork simmered in sake and soy for two days, lightly fried tofu cubes in soy-ginger-scallion sauce, and yellowtail braised with teriyaki. ⊠ *6775 Santa Monica Blvd.,* ☎ *323/871–0236. Reservations essential. AE, MC, V. Closed Sun. Valet parking.*

MEXICAN

$-$$ ✕ **El Cholo.** The progenitor of a chain, this landmark south of Holly-
★ wood has been packing them in since the '20s. L.A.-Mex standards are
served—chicken enchiladas, *carnitas* (shredded fried pork), and, from
July through October, green-corn tamales. Portions are large and prices
reasonable. ✉ *1121 S. Western Ave.,* ☎ *323/734–2773. AE, DC, MC,
V. Valet and meter parking.*

RUSSIAN

$-$$ ✕ **Uzbekistan.** Brightly colored murals lend a fittingly folksy air to this
restaurant, which serves a mix of Russian and Central Asian cuisine.
Start with any of the meat dumplings and go on to eggplant sautéed
with tomatoes and garlic or a fragrant stir fry of beef, noodles, and
vegetables perfumed with cumin. ✉ *7077 Sunset Blvd.,* ☎ *323/464–
3663. MC, V.*

SOUL

$ ✕ **Roscoe's House of Chicken 'n' Waffles.** The name of this casual eatery
doesn't sound all that appetizing, considering the strange combination
of foods mentioned, but don't be fooled: this is *the* place for real
down-home Southern cooking. ✉ *1514 N. Gower St.,* ☎ *323/466–
9329. Reservations not accepted. AE, D, DC, MC, V.*

THAI

$-$$ ✕ **Chan Dara.** A rock 'n' roll and showbiz crowd frequents this casual
eatery, which occupies an old Spanish house in a block of doctors' offices near Paramount Pictures. Try any of the noodle dishes, especially
those with crab and shrimp. ✉ *310 N. Larchmont Blvd.,* ☎ *323/467–
1052. AE, D, DC, MC, V. No lunch weekends.*

Los Feliz/Silver Lake

CARIBBEAN

$-$$$ ✕ **Cha Cha Cha.** Because it's off the beaten path, Cha Cha Cha attracts
a discerning, eclectic crowd. It's hip yet not pretentious or overly
trendy. The giant map pinpoints the restaurant's Caribbean influences.
Standard options are Jamaican jerk chicken, fried plantain chips, pork
chops with apricot salsa, and assorted flans. Cha Cha Cha is open daily
for breakfast, lunch, and dinner. ✉ *656 N. Virgil Ave.,* ☎ *323/664–
7723. AE, D, DC, MC, V. Valet parking.*

ECLECTIC

$$ ✕ **Paio.** This new little restaurant has put Silver Lake, a mixed gay and
straight, upwardly mobile neighborhood, on the culinary map. Chef
Alisa Reynolds combines traditional appetizers like white bean soup
with Asian-influenced inventions such as deep-fried salmon wontons.
Her entrées include roasted quail and fried barbecued chicken. Bringing your own wine helps keep the tab down. ✉ *2520 Hyperion Ave.,*
☎ *323/953–1973. AE, MC, V. Closed Sun. and Mon. No lunch. Free
parking.*

ITALIAN

$$ ✕ **Trattoria Farfalla.** This reliable, brick-walled trattoria brought Los
Feliz out of the spaghetti-and-meatballs mode in the '80s and has re-
mained a favorite ever since. Regulars tend to order the Caesar salad
on a pizza-crust bed; roasted herbed free-range chicken; and pasta *alla
Norma* (studded with rich, smoky eggplant). ✉ *1978 N. Hillhurst Ave.,*
☎ *323/661–7365. AE, DC, MC, V. No lunch weekends. Street park-
ing.*

West Hollywood

AMERICAN/CASUAL

$ ✕ **Ed's Coffee Shop.** The coffee shop of choice for decorators and clients from the nearby Pacific Design Center, Ed's serves delicious omelets, huevos rancheros, egg salad, stuffed peppers, meat loaf, and homemade pies. ⊠ *460 N. Robertson Blvd.,* ☎ *310/659–8625. Reservations not accepted. No credit cards. Closed weekends. No dinner.*

$ ✕ **Swingers.** Everyone from powerlunchers to Doc Marten–clad posers takes to this all-day, late-night coffee shop, so be prepared for a wait. Eat at sidewalk tables or inside the pseudo-diner on the ground floor of the no-frills Beverly-Laurel Hotel. Loud alternative music plays to the Gen-X crowd, and a casual menu—breakfast burritos, hamburgers, and chicken breast sandwiches on fresh French bread—goes easy on your pocketbook. ⊠ *8020 Beverly Blvd.,* ☎ *323/653–5858. AE, D, MC, V.*

CONTEMPORARY

$$$–$$$$ ✕ **Campanile.** Mark Peel and Nancy Silverton (also the force behind
★ the adjacent La Brea Bakery) blend robust Mediterranean flavors with those of homey Americana. Among the entrées are bourride of snapper and Manila clams, and pork loin with sweet potatoes and turnip greens. You'll also find some of the best desserts anywhere—try the apple puff pastry with spiced nuts and sabayon. Don't miss weekend brunch on the enclosed patio with a vintage fountain. ⊠ *624 S. La Brea Ave.,* ☎ *323/938–1447. Reservations essential. AE, D, DC, MC, V. No dinner Sun. Valet parking.*

$$$–$$$$ ✕ **Fenix.** You'll find abundant Art Deco splendor at the Argyle Hotel's culinary outpost on the Sunset Strip. The bi-level dining room–bar, accented in dark purple and brushed gold, has plush banquettes, a grand piano, and a romantic city view. Chef Brandon Boudet starts you off with the likes of goat cheese, beets, and walnuts in a phyllo pastry purse and then moves on to tandoori-spiced Chilean sea bass or braised lamb shank with polenta. ⊠ *8358 Sunset Blvd.,* ☎ *323/848–6677. Reservations essential. AE, D, DC, MC, V. Valet parking.*

$$–$$$ ✕ **Boxer.** This small, chic restaurant continues to satisfy its faithful following under its new chef, Phillip Du Bois, who presents seasonal menus. Because there is no wine license, you can buy your own bottle from the owner's well-stocked wine shop next door or bring your own for a modest $6 corkage fee. ⊠ *7615 Beverly Blvd.,* ☎ *323/932–6178. AE, MC, V. Closed Sun. Valet parking.*

$$–$$$ ✕ **Jozu.** The Japanese name, which means *excellent,* and Japanese-theme decor hint at the bias of executive chef Suzanne Tracht's Cal-Asian menu. Start with crisp Sonoma quail with tangerine glaze or deep-fried Ipswich clams. As an entrée, you might try roasted Chilean sea bass with ponzu sauce and cabbage salad. ⊠ *8360 Melrose Ave.,* ☎ *323/655–5600. AE, DC, MC, V. No lunch. Valet parking.*

$$–$$$ ✕ **Lucques.** This historic brick building, once silent-film star Harold
★ Lloyd's carriage house, has been attractively transformed into a restaurant that's been an instant hit with the younger well-heeled set. And the cooking—by Suzanne Goin, formerly of Campanile—is smart, too: consider Moroccan squash soup with crème fraîche followed by seared scallops with fennel and saffron. ⊠ *8474 Melrose Ave.,* ☎ *323/655–6277. Reservations essential. AE, D, DC, MC, V. Closed Mon. No lunch. Valet parking.*

$$–$$$ ✕ **Spago Hollywood.** This is the restaurant that propelled chef-owner Wolfgang Puck into the international culinary spotlight in the early 1980s. Make reservations far in advance to sample tempura Maryland soft-shell crabs, venison with black cherry–port wine sauce, and grilled Alaskan salmon with lemongrass. ⊠ *1114 Horn Ave.,* ☎ *310/652–*

4025. *Reservations essential. D, DC, MC, V. Closed Mon. No lunch. Valet parking.*

DELI

$ ✕ **Canter's.** This granddaddy of Los Angeles delicatessens (it opened in 1928) pickles its own corned-beef pastrami and has its own in-house bakery. Next door is the Kibitz Room, where there's live music every night. ⊠ *419 N. Fairfax Ave.,* ☎ *323/651–2030. Reservations not accepted. MC, V. Parking in lot.*

FRENCH

$$$$ ✕ **L'Orangerie.** Elegant French Mediterranean cuisine is served in this
★   rococo dining room, complete with white flower arrangements and oils depicting European castles. Specialties include coddled eggs served in the shell and topped with caviar, duck with foie gras, rack of lamb for two, and a rich apple tart accompanied by a jug of double cream. ⊠ *903 N. La Cienega Blvd.,* ☎ *310/652–9770. Reservations essential. AE, D, DC, MC, V. Closed Mon. No lunch. Valet parking.*

$$$–$$$$ ✕ **Le Dôme.** This fancy show- and music-biz bistro mixes French country dishes and hearty American fare: escargots Burgundy-style (served with garlic, shallots, and parsley) and coq au vin appeal to Francophiles, while center-cut pork chops and grilled Sonoma lamb chops satisfy patriots. The look is art deco and the crowd—men in ponytails and pressed jeans—looks as if it favors the music business. ⊠ *8720 Sunset Blvd.,* ☎ *310/659–6919. Reservations essential. AE, MC, V. Closed Sun. No lunch Sat. Valet parking.*

$$–$$$ ✕ **Mimosa.** Chef Jean-Pierre Bosc's menu is country French with a Provençal bent. There's Lyonnaise salad, a *tarte flambée alsacienne* (a pizzalike wood-fired onion tart), and hearty chicken terrine with onion marmalade. Standout entrées are bouillabaisse and caramelized pork chops with horseradish and lentils. ⊠ *8009 Beverly Blvd.,* ☎ *323/655–8895. AE, MC, V. Closed Sun. No lunch Sat. Valet parking.*

ITALIAN

$$ ✕ **Ca'Brea.** Chef Antonio Tommasi turns out lamb chops with black-
★   truffle and mustard sauce, whole boneless chicken marinated and grilled with herbs, and a very popular osso buco. Starters make the meal—try baked goat cheese wrapped in pancetta and served atop a Popeye-size mound of spinach. ⊠ *346 S. La Brea Ave.,* ☎ *323/938–2863. AE, D, DC, MC, V. Closed Sun. No lunch weekends.*

$$ ✕ **Locanda Veneta.** This upmarket Italian trattoria has an open kitchen that cooks up specialties such as flattened grilled chicken, veal chops, lobster ravioli with saffron sauce, and an unusual apple tart with polenta crust and caramel sauce. ⊠ *8638 W. 3rd St.,* ☎ *310/274–1893. Reservations essential. AE, D, DC, MC, V. Closed Sun. No lunch Sat. Valet parking.*

$ ✕ **Tavola Calda.** This low-tech Italian favorite draws a budget-watching crowd, with many entrées priced under $10. Best bets on the limited menu are unusual pizzas, like the cheeseless vegetarian pie, and the seafood and porcini risottos. ⊠ *7371 Melrose Ave.,* ☎ *323/658–6340. AE, DC, MC, V. Valet parking.*

JAPANESE

$$$–$$$$ ✕ **Matsuhisa.** Cutting-edge Pacific Rim cuisine is pushed to new lim-
★   its at this modest-looking yet high-profile Japanese bistro. Chef Nobu Matsuhisa creatively infuses his dishes with flavors encountered during his sojourn in Peru. Consider his caviar-capped tuna stuffed with black truffles, and the sea urchin wrapped in a *shiso* leaf. Tempuras are lighter than usual, and the sushi is fresh and authentic. ⊠ *129 N. La Cienega Blvd.,* ☎ *310/659–9639. Reservations essential. AE, DC, MC, V. Valet parking.*

SOUTHWESTERN

$–$$ ✕ **Authentic Cafe.** The Gen-X crowd can't get enough of the Santa Fe salad, wood-grilled chicken with mole, chicken casserole with cornbread crust, and excellent vegetarian dishes. You'll have to wait at peak hours. Breakfast is served on weekends. ✉ *7605 Beverly Blvd.,* ☎ *323/ 939–4626. Reservations not accepted. MC, V.*

SPANISH

$$–$$$ ✕ **Cava.** This two-level tapas bar and restaurant is in the Beverly Plaza Hotel. The artsy dining room is a bit noisy but lots of fun. You can graze on tapas—baked artichoke topped with bread crumbs and tomato, or a fluffy potato omelet served with crème fraîche. Those with bigger appetites can try a paella or aged New York steak with a traditional Argentine steak sauce. Wash it all down with a glass or three of sangria. ✉ *8384 W. 3rd St.,* ☎ *323/658–8898. AE, D, DC, MC, V. Valet parking.*

STEAK

$$$–$$$$ ✕ **Arnie Morton's of Chicago.** In addition to a 24-ounce porterhouse, a New York strip, and a double-cut filet mignon, there are giant veal and lamb chops, thick cuts of prime rib, swordfish steaks, and Maine lobsters at market prices. ✉ *435 S. La Cienega Blvd.,* ☎ *310/246–1501. AE, DC, MC, V. No lunch.*

$$$–$$$$ ✕ **The Palm.** All the New York elements are present at this West Coast replay of the famous Manhattan steak house—mahogany booths, tin ceilings, boisterous atmosphere, and New York–style waiters rushing you through your cheesecake (flown in from the Bronx). This is where you'll find the biggest and best lobster, good steaks, prime rib, chops, great French-fried onion rings, and paper-thin potato slices. ✉ *9001 Santa Monica Blvd.,* ☎ *310/550–8811. AE, DC, MC, V. Reservations essential. No lunch weekends. Valet parking.*

THAI

$–$$ ✕ **Tommy Tang's.** A lot of people-watching goes on at this Melrose Avenue grazing ground. Portions are on the small side but decidedly innovative. Try crisp duck marinated in honey-ginger sauce, pan-seared sea scallops, or the spinach salad tossed with grilled chicken. ✉ *7313 Melrose Ave.,* ☎ *323/937–5733. AE, DC, MC, V. Valet parking.*

VIETNAMESE

$$–$$$ ✕ **Le Colonial.** Like the original Le Colonial in Manhattan, this is a bi-level restaurant with an opulent bar upstairs, and below, a seductive dining room serving dishes such as roasted chicken with lemongrass; fried spring rolls packed with pork, mushrooms, and shrimp; and shredded chicken and cabbage doused in lime juice. ✉ *8783 Beverly Blvd.,* ☎ *310/289–0660. AE, DC, MC, V. No lunch weekends. Valet parking.*

Coastal and Western Los Angeles

Bel-Air

CONTEMPORARY

$$$–$$$$ ✕ **Hotel Bel-Air.** Nestled in the midst of luxuriant Beverly Glen, the restaurant in the Hotel Bel-Air spills out into a romantic country garden with gurgling fountains and a swan lake. Chef Gary Clauson charms diners with such seasonal appetizers as pan-seared foie gras with rhubarb–star anise compote and a roasted beet–and–goat cheese gâteau, which may be followed by Angus beef with Stilton or pan-roasted sea bass with fennel. The Hotel Bel-Air hosts one of the best high teas in town. ✉ *701 Stone Canyon Rd.,* ☎ *310/472–1211. Reservations essential. Jacket and tie. AE, DC, MC, V. Valet parking.*

410

Dining

Bombay Cafe, **12**
Border Grill, **15**
Broadway Deli, **19**
Chinois on Main, **27**
Drago, **13**
Encounter, **38**
Gladstone's 4 Fish, **2**
Granita, **1**
Hotel Bel-Air, **6**
JiRaffe, **14**
JR Seafood, **10**
La Serenata Gourmet, **26**
Lavande, **21**
Ocean Avenue Seafood, **22**
Tra di Noi, **3**
U-Zen, **11**
Valentino, **23**
Vincenti, **4**

Lodging

Barnabey's Hotel, **34**
Belle Blue Inn, **24**
Best Western Ocean View Hotel, **18**
Best Western Royal Palace Inn & Suites, **29**
Century Wilshire Hotel, **8**
Furama Hotel Los Angeles, **36**
Holiday Inn LAX, **39**
Hotel Bel-Air, **6**
Hotel Carmel, **20**
Hotel del Capri, **9**
Hotel Oceana, **16**
Loews Santa Monica Beach Hotel, **21**
Marina Beach Marriott, **30**
Marina International Hotel and Bungalows, **32**
Marina Pacific Hotel & Suites, **28**
Miramar Sheraton, **17**
Ritz-Carlton, Marina del Rey, **31**
Shutters on the Beach, **25**
Summerfield Suites, **33**
Summit Hotel Bel Air, **5**
Westin LAX, **35**
Westwood Marquis Hotel and Gardens, **7**
Wyndham Hotel at Los Angeles Airport, **37**

Coastal Los Angeles Dining and Lodging

LAX

FUSION

$$–$$$ ✕ **Encounter.** In 1961 one of Los Angeles' first modern icons—the Theme Building with its 135-ft-high parabolic steel arches—opened in the very center of Los Angeles International Airport. With vistas from the ocean to the mountains, it now houses Encounter, whose intergalactic atmosphere includes a crater-shape bar. On the menu are a grilled breast of chicken with Gorgonzola and prosciutto, and horseradish-crusted salmon. Be sure to book ahead if you want one of the window tables. Locals come for the food, not for a flight. ⊠ *209 World Way,* ☎ *310/ 215–5151. AE, MC, V.*

Malibu

CONTEMPORARY

$$$–$$$$ ✕ **Granita.** Wolfgang Puck's famed Granita is a glamourous—some call
★ it garish—fantasy world of handmade tiles embedded with seashells, blown-glass lighting fixtures, and etched-glass panels with wavy edges. Chef Jennifer Naylor's menu favors seafood, including polenta crepes with Maine lobster and bigeye tuna with spicy miso glaze. She has also prepared sautéed foie gras with spiced Asian pears and roasted Cantonese duck with a pomegranate-plum glaze. Brunch is served on weekends. ⊠ *23725 W. Malibu Rd.,* ☎ *310/456–0488. Reservations essential. D, DC, MC, V. No lunch weekdays.*

ITALIAN

$$–$$$ ✕ **Tra di Noi.** Regular customers, film celebrities, and non-showbiz folk turn up here, but it's also a great place to bring kids. Nothing fancy on the menu, just hearty lasagna, freshly made pasta, mushroom and veal dishes, and fresh salads. An Italian buffet is laid out for Sunday brunch. ⊠ *3835 Cross Creek Rd.,* ☎ *310/456–0169. AE, MC, V.*

Pacific Palisades

AMERICAN/CASUAL

$$$–$$$$ ✕ **Gladstone's 4 Fish.** Gladstone's is one of the most popular restaurants along the southern California coast. The food is notable mostly for its size: giant bowls of crab chowder, mounds of steamed clams, heaps of barbecued ribs, and the famous mile-high chocolate cake, which can easily feed a small regiment. The real reason to visit Gladstone's is the glorious vista of sea, sky, and beach. ⊠ *17300 Pacific Coast Hwy., at Sunset Blvd.,* ☎ *310/454–3474. AE, D, DC, MC, V. Valet parking.*

Santa Monica

AMERICAN/CASUAL

$–$$ ✕ **Broadway Deli.** This joint venture of Michel Richard and Bruce
★ Marder is a cross between a European brasserie and an upscale diner. Whatever you feel like eating, you'll probably find it on the menu—a platter of assorted smoked fish, Caesar salad, shepherd's pie, or broiled salmon with creamed spinach. ⊠ *1457 3rd St. Promenade,* ☎ *310/ 451–0616. Reservations not accepted. AE, MC, V. Valet parking weekends and evenings.*

CONTEMPORARY

$$$–$$$$ ✕ **Chinois on Main.** A once-revolutionary outpost in Wolfgang Puck's
★ repertoire, this is still one of L.A.'s most crowded restaurants—and one of the noisiest. Puck's wife and partner, Barbara Lazaroff, designed the jazzy interior, which is just as loud as the clientele. The happy marriage of Asian and French cuisines yields seasonal dishes such as grilled Mongolian lamb chops with cilantro vinaigrette and wok-fried vegetables, and Cantonese duck with fresh plum sauce. ⊠ *2709 Main St.,* ☎ *310/392–9025. Reservations essential. AE, D, DC, MC, V. No lunch Sat.–Tues. Valet parking.*

$$$–$$$$ ✕ **Lavande.** Chef Alain Giraud, who was previously at Citrus, conjures up robust Provençal cuisine: crayfish tartlets, classic fish soup Provençal with garlic croutons and rouille, and roasted Chilean sea bass with artichokes. For dessert, the vacherin cheese with lavender ice cream and strawberries is a must. ⊠ *Loews Santa Monica Beach Hotel, 1700 Ocean Ave.,* ☎ *310/576–3181. AE, D, DC, MC, V. No dinner Sun. Valet parking.*

$$–$$$ ✕ **JiRaffe.** The menu at this wood-panel restaurant is as tasteful as the decor. Inventive pastas, such as butternut squash agnolotti with brown-butter sage sauce and squash chips, are an excellent way to kick off a meal of roasted Chilean sea bass with a ragout of salsify, chanterelles, and pearl onions; or roasted rack of lamb with truffled potato gnocchi. ⊠ *502 Santa Monica Blvd.,* ☎ *310/917–6671. Reservations essential. AE, DC, MC, V. Closed Mon. No lunch weekends. Valet parking.*

ITALIAN

$$–$$$$ ✕ **Valentino.** Rated among the nation's best Italian restaurants, Valentino
★   is also generally considered to have the best wine list outside Western Europe. Try the carpaccio with arugula and shaved Parmesan, spaghetti with garlic and *bottarga* (tuna roe), and lamb shank with saffron risotto. Don't miss the daily specials. ⊠ *3115 Pico Blvd.,* ☎ *310/829–4313. Reservations essential. AE, DC, MC, V. Closed Sun. No lunch Sat.–Thurs. Valet parking.*

$$$ ✕ **Drago.** Celestino Drago's home-style fare, though pricey, is carefully
★   prepared and attentively served in stark designer surroundings. Sample pappardelle with pheasant ragout, squid-ink risotto, or ostrich breast with red-cherry sauce. ⊠ *2628 Wilshire Blvd.,* ☎ *310/828–1585. AE, DC, MC, V. No lunch weekends. Valet parking.*

MEXICAN

$$ ✕ **Border Grill.** Hipsters love this loud, trendy eating hall designed by
★   minimalist architect Josh Schweitzer and owned by the talented team of Mary Sue Milliken and Susan Feniger. It's perhaps the most eclectic Mexican restaurant in L.A., with a menu ranging from Yucatán grilled-fish tacos to vinegar-and-pepper-grilled turkey to daily seviche specials. ⊠ *1445 4th St.,* ☎ *310/451–1655. AE, D, DC, MC, V. No lunch Mon.*

SEAFOOD

$$–$$$$ ✕ **Ocean Avenue Seafood.** This cavernous restaurant isn't right on the water, but the Pacific is just across the street—ask for a table by the window for an ocean view. Popular dishes include cioppino, a fish stew made with Dungeness crab, clams, mussels, and prawns; and Chilean sea bass marinated in a sake *kasu* sauce (an intoxicating mixture of sake, soy sauce, white wine, and rice wine vinegar). ⊠ *1401 Ocean Ave.,* ☎ *310/394–5669. AE, DC, MC, V. Valet parking.*

West Los Angeles

CHINESE

$–$$ ✕ **JR Seafood.** Westsiders who once had to drive to Monterey Beach to get a good plate of shrimp in spicy salt have made this place a huge hit. The Hong Kong–style restaurant serves all the Chinese seafood-house standards—seafood soup, rock cod in garlic sauce, kung-pao scallops—that are so plentiful in the San Gabriel Valley but so scarce in these parts. The service can be slow, but as long as the shrimp keeps coming, no one seems to mind. ⊠ *11901 Santa Monica Blvd.,* ☎ *310/268–2463. MC, V. Free parking.*

INDIAN

$–$$ ✕ **Bombay Cafe.** Head to this lively minimall café for high-quality Indian street food. Regulars swear by the chili-laden lamb frankies (sausages), various chutneys, *sev puri* (little wafers topped with onions, potatoes, and chutneys), and other vibrant small dishes. ✉ *12113 Santa Monica Blvd.,* ☎ *310/820–2070. MC, V. Closed Mon. No lunch weekends.*

ITALIAN

$$$ **Vincenti.** This spot has quickly become one of the Westside's hottest
★ culinary destinations. A big, open kitchen is the heart of this handsome, white-tile restaurant, and revolving on its mammoth rotisserie are the savory meats for which chef Gino Angelini is known. This is authentic Northern Italian cooking as seen through an adept modern sensibility. ✉ *11930 San Vicente Blvd.,* ☎ *310/207–0127. Reservations essential. AE, MC, V. Closed Sun. and Mon. No lunch Sat. or Tues.–Thurs. Valet parking.*

JAPANESE

$–$$ ✕ **U-Zen.** This highly regarded Japanese café serves fresh sushi and sashimi, a good selection of sakes, and pub food such as fried spicy tofu and salmon-skin salad. ✉ *11951 Santa Monica Blvd.,* ☎ *310/477–1390. Reservations not accepted. MC, V. No lunch weekends. Self parking.*

MEXICAN

$–$$ ✕ **La Serenata Gourmet.** Crowding in this handsome Westside branch
★ of the East Los Angeles original can be uncomfortable, but the restaurant scores points for its flavorful Mexican cuisine. Moles and pork dishes are delicious, but seafood is the real star. ✉ *10924 W. Pico Blvd.,* ☎ *310/441–9667. Reservations not accepted. AE, D, MC, V. Valet parking.*

Downtown

AMERICAN/CASUAL

$$–$$$ ✕ **Water Grill.** This somewhat noisy brasserie is always packed with well-dressed attorneys, brokers, and other downtown business folk who are joined in the evenings by theater and concert goers. The oyster bar alone is worth a trip. Avoid the pastas and complicated dishes and stick with fresh seafood. ✉ *544 S. Grand Ave.,* ☎ *213/891–0900. Reservations essential. AE, DC, MC, V. No lunch weekends. Valet parking next door.*

$ ✕ **Philippe's the Original.** This downtown landmark near Union Sta-
★ tion and Chinatown has been serving its famous French dip sandwich (four kinds of meat on a freshly baked roll) since 1908. The home cooking includes hearty breakfasts, potato salad, sandwiches, salads, and an enormous pie selection brought in fresh daily from a nearby bakery. The best bargain: a cup of java for only 10¢. ✉ *1001 N. Alameda St.,* ☎ *213/628–3781. Reservations not accepted. No credit cards.*

CONTEMPORARY

$$$–$$$$ ✕ **Checkers.** In the rear of the elegant Wyndham Checkers Hotel, this is one of downtown's best business restaurants. Chef Tony Hodges prepares contemporary American food with Asian influences: lobster, dandelion, and curly endive salad; seared sea bass with rice-shrimp dumpling; and grilled lamb chops in a pumpkin-seed crust have been among the tempting options. ✉ *535 S. Grand Ave.,* ☎ *213/624–0000. Reservations essential. AE, DC, MC, V. Valet parking.*

414

Downtown Los Angeles Dining and Lodging

Dining
Café Pinot, **5**
Checkers, **6**
Cicada, **9**
Ciudad, **4**
Nicola, **1**
Philippe's the
Original, **18**
Traxx, **17**
Water Grill, **8**
Yang Chow, **19**

Lodging
Figueroa Hotel
and Convention
Center, **12**
Hotel
Inter-Continental
Los Angeles, **14**
Hyatt Regency Los
Angeles, **11**
Inn at 657, **10**
The InnTowne, **13**

Kawada Hotel, **15**
Los Angeles Marriott
Downtown, **3**
New Otani Hotel
and Garden, **16**
Regal Biltmore
Hotel, **7**
Westin Bonaventure
Hotel & Suites, **2**
Wyndham Checkers
Hotel, **6**

$$–$$$ ✕ **Traxx.** Union Station is the setting for meals with Asian, Italian, and Californian influences. The menu has included ahi tuna Napoleon with crispy wontons and wasabi caviar; grilled lamb with arugula and red onions; and grilled salmon with olive tapenade. The smartly modern interior space vaguely resembles an old-fashioned dining car. You can also dine on the terrace, which extends out into the station's dramatic concourse, with its 50-ft-high vaulted ceiling, or on a landscaped patio. ✉ *Union Station, 800 N. Alameda St.,* ☎ *213/625–1999. AE, D, MC, V. Closed Sun. No lunch Sat. Valet parking or pay parking lot.*

CHINESE

$–$$$ ✕ **Yang Chow.** This longtime Chinatown favorite is known for its slippery shrimp (crisp, juicy, sweet, hot, and sour all at once), fiery Szechuan dumplings, dried-fried string beans, and panfried dumplings. ✉ *379 N. Broadway,* ☎ *213/625–0811. Reservations essential. AE, MC, V. Valet parking.*

ECLECTIC

$$–$$$ ✕ **Nicola.** Chef Manny Diaz's cooking is mainly Mediterranean with Asian accents, plus the savory spark of Mexico. Start with vegetable spring rolls with tangerine-sweet-and-sour sauce or oysters sautéed on spinach and go on to panfried rice noodles with Peking duck or chicken mole on cilantro rice. ✉ *Sanwa Bank Bldg., 601 S. Figueroa St.,* ☎ *213/485–0927; kiosk, 213/485–0354. AE, D, DC, MC, V. Closed weekends. No dinner weekdays. Valet parking.*

FRENCH

$$–$$$ ✕ **Café Pinot.** Joachim and Christine Splichal, proprietors of Patina and
★ a growing number of Pinot bistros, have succeeded with this warm, convivial restaurant housed in a contemporary pavilion in the garden of the Los Angeles Central Library. If the weather's fine, you can eat outside on the terrace under one of the old olive trees. The menu is rooted in traditional French bistro standards, but it also delivers some low-fat dishes, fresh fish, and a few worthy pastas. ✉ *700 W. 5th St.,* ☎ *213/239–6500. Reservations essential. DC, MC, V. No lunch weekends. Self and valet parking.*

ITALIAN

$$–$$$ ✕ **Cicada.** Cicada occupies the ground floor of a 1928 architectural landmark, the Art Deco Oviatt Building. Modern Italian best describes the menu: risotto-crusted oysters, spinach and ricotta ravioli, sautéed Chilean sea bass with a roasted pepper beurre blanc, and grilled rib eye steak with a Barolo reduction sauce. ✉ *617 S. Olive St.,* ☎ *323/ 655–5559. Reservations essential. AE, DC, MC, V. Closed Sun. No lunch Sat.*

LATIN

$$–$$$ ✕ **Ciudad.** Mary Sue Milliken and Susan Feniger—whose fame began with City Cafe and City Restaurant and continues with the Border Grill in Santa Monica—have invented a new wave of flavorful Central- and South American–inspired cooking. Among the *entradas* (starters), imagine the tastes of *pasteles boriqua* (green plantain tamales jazzed with pork, olives, and raisins) or *arepas* (corn cakes served with cumin-perfumed merguez sausage) with Catalan chile-and-almond-based romesco sauce. *Platos principales* (main courses) range from lamb shank with baby artichokes to chicken roasted Cuban-style with sweet garlic. ✉ *445 S. Figueroa St.,* ☎ *213/486–5171. AE, MC, V. Valet and nonvalet parking.*

Pasadena, Glendale, San Gabriel Valley

Glendale

CONTEMPORARY

$$–$$$ ✕ **Cinnabar.** Glendale's revitalized downtown has plenty of major department stores and movie complexes, but few distinguished restaurants. Enter Cinnabar, a hip, contemporary dining room occupying the double-height ground floor of an early 1930s Art Deco commercial building. Try the charbroiled ostrich tenderloin, spicy lemongrass bouillabaisse, and roasted halibut with kale and asparagus. ✉ *933 S. Brand Blvd., Glendale,* ☎ *818/551–1155. D, DC, MC, V. Closed Mon. No lunch weekends.*

MEXICAN

$–$$ ✕ **La Cabañita.** This is as far from the rice and beans routine as you
★ can get. Savor the thick handmade tortillas wrapped around *picadillo* (ground beef with raisins, almonds, and cinnamon) or on top of a ramekin of roasted mild poblano chilis with sour cream and black beans, then go on to *chuletas* (tender pork) in a delicate pasilla chili sauce. ✉ *3447 N. Verdugo Rd., Glendale,* ☎ *818/957–2711. AE, MC, V.*

Pasadena

CONTEMPORARY

$$$ ✕ **Derek's.** This casually elegant restaurant brought Pasadena into the '90s with its smart Asian-tinged cuisine. Dinner might start with seared foie gras with caramelized mango followed by osso buco with braised vegetables. The mostly dressy crowd dines inside or on the patio. ✉ *181–185 E. Glenarm St., Pasadena,* ☎ *626/799–5252. AE, D, MC, V. Closed Sun. and Mon. No lunch Sat.*

$$ ✕ **Shiro.** Hideo Yamashiro made quite a splash when he first began
★ serving sizzling whole catfish with a tangy soy-citrus-ponzu sauce. The dish has shown up on other menus, but Yamashiro's is still the best. For a sweet conclusion, try the warm souffléed lemon pudding. ✉ *1505 Mission St., Pasadena,* ☎ *626/799–4774. Reservations essential. AE, DC, MC, V. Closed Mon. No lunch.*

CHINESE

$$–$$$ ✕ **Yujean Kang's Gourmet Chinese Cuisine.** Forget any and all pre-
★ conceived notions of what Chinese food should look and taste like. Kang's cuisine is nouvelle-Chinese. Start with tender slices of veal on a bed of enoki mushrooms, topped with a tangle of quick-fried shoestring yams; or sea bass with kumquats and passion-fruit sauce. Finish with poached plums or watermelon ice under a mantle of white chocolate. ✉ *67 N. Raymond Ave., Pasadena,* ☎ *626/585–0855. AE, D, DC, MC, V.*

ECLECTIC

$$–$$$ ✕ **Parkway Grill.** The setting of this well-respected restaurant is all-American—brick walls, wood floors, a carved-wood bar, lots of greenery, and a khaki-clad wait staff. The always-interesting dishes incorporate all kinds of influences, from Italian to Mexican to Chinese. ✉ *510 S. Arroyo Pkwy., Pasadena,* ☎ *626/795–1001. Reservations essential. AE, DC, MC, V. No lunch weekends. Valet parking.*

FRENCH

$$$ ✕ **Bistro 45.** As stylish and sophisticated as any Westside hot spot, Bistro 45 blends rustic French cooking—cassoulet, bouillabaisse, caramelized apple tarts—with more modern and fanciful California hybrids, like seared ahi tuna with black and white sesame crust. ✉ *45 S. Mentor Ave., Pasadena,* ☎ *626/795–2478. Reservations essential. AE, MC, V. Closed Mon., except for wine-maker dinner 4th Mon. of month. No lunch weekends. Valet parking.*

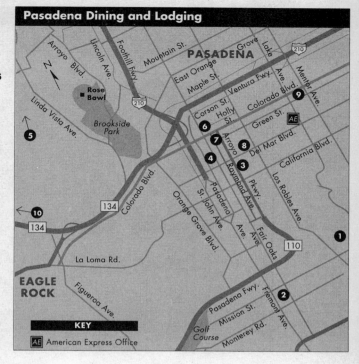

INDIAN

$–$$ ✕ **All India Cafe.** In addition to meat curries and tikkas, there are many
vegetarian selections at this authentic Indian restaurant. The prices are
as palatable as the meals: a full lunch costs less than $6 and the com-
bination dinners are also a good value. ✉ *39 Fair Oaks Ave., Pasadena,*
☎ *626/440–0309. Reservations recommended on weekends. AE, MC,*
V. City parking garage across the street.

THAI

$–$$ ✕ **Saladang.** Although it's a bit off the beaten track—several blocks
south of Old Pasadena—its reasonably priced spinach and duck salad,
seafood soup, rice noodles with basil and bean sprouts, and beef
panang have ensured Saladang a lively following. ✉ *363 S. Fair Oaks*
Blvd., Pasadena, ☎ *626/793–8123. Reservations essential. AE, DC,*
MC, V. Free parking in lot.

San Fernando Valley

Calabasas

CONTEMPORARY

$$$–$$$$ ✕ **Saddle Peak Lodge.** When you've had enough big-city attitude,
★ head for this paradisical retreat in the Santa Monica Mountains. What
was once allegedly a bordello is now a restaurant oozing with Ralph
Lauren–style rugged romance and hunting trophies. The food is a per-
fect match for the upscale lodge setting: updated American classics with
an emphasis on game. ✉ *419 Cold Canyon Rd., Calabasas,* ☎ *818/*
222–3888. Reservations essential on weekends. AE, MC, V. Closed
Mon.–Tues. No lunch, except Sun. brunch. Valet and self parking.

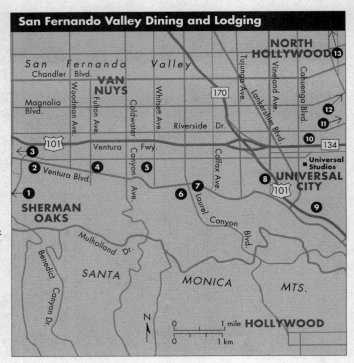

San Fernando Valley Dining and Lodging

North Hollywood

ITALIAN

$–$$ ✕ **Ca' del Sole.** This studio-area establishment draws showbiz and non-
★ showbiz types in search of such classics as sautéed fresh rock shrimp
in a spicy garlic-tomato sauce; citrus-marinated chicken wings braised
with Italian bacon, rosemary, and sage; and linguine with scallops and
Manila clams. ⊠ *4100 Cahuenga Blvd.,* ☎ *818/985–4669. Reservations essential on weekends. AE, DC, MC, V. No lunch Sat. Valet parking.*

Sherman Oaks

CONTEMPORARY

$$–$$$ ✕ **JoeJoe's.** This is American cooking for the next century. Try grilled
shiitakes with smoked mozzarella, seared scallops with apple wood–
smoked bacon, and pistachio-crusted halibut. End with the zippy
lemon tart. ⊠ *13355 Ventura Blvd.,* ☎ *818/990–8280. Reservations
essential. AE, MC, V. Closed Mon. Valet parking.*

$$ ✕ **Cafe Bizou.** This is *the* place for fine California-French bistro fare
★ at bargain prices. Entrée sauces are classic, soups are rich, and com-
binations are creative. If it's on the menu, order the homemade ravi-
oli appetizer, stuffed with lobster and salmon purée. Those who bring
their own bottle pay a mere $2 corkage fee. ⊠ *14016 Ventura Blvd.,*
☎ *818/788–3536. Reservations essential. AE, MC, V. Valet parking.*

ITALIAN

$$$–$$$$ ✕ **Posto.** Owner Piero Selvaggio—of Santa Monica's Valentino—has
brought his modern Italian cuisine to the Valley and made this one of
the most prestigious restaurants in the area. Start with fried crab and
potato chips or roasted rabbit and beets, then continue with pumpkin
risotto with a roasted quail, or chicken and asparagus in marsala

sauce. ⊠ *14928 Ventura Blvd.,* ☎ *818/784–4400. AE, D, DC, MC, V. Closed Sun. No lunch Sat.*

Studio City

DELI

$ ✕ **Art's Delicatessen.** One of the best Jewish-style delicatessens in the
★ city, this mecca serves mammoth corned beef and pastrami sandwiches.
Matzo-ball soup and sweet-and-sour cabbage soup are specialties, and
there is good chopped chicken liver. ⊠ *12224 Ventura Blvd.,* ☎ *818/
762–1221. Reservations not accepted. AE, D, DC, MC, V.*

FRENCH

$$$ ✕ **Perroche.** It's worth going out of your way to eat at this still-young
neighborhood favorite. Refreshing two- and three-course lunches, $13
and $16 respectively, can begin with house-smoked trout or an airy
parfait of chicken livers. Entrées include a grilled swordfish sandwich
and a potato and onion tortilla. On the dinner menu you might also
find rosemary-baked salmon and a roasted pork chop with green cab-
bage and pumpkin chutney. ⊠ *1929 Ventura Blvd.,* ☎ *818/766–1179.
AE, MC, V. Closed Sun. No lunch Sat. Valet parking.*

Toluca Lake

AMERICAN

$ ✕ **Paty's.** Near NBC, Warner Bros., and the Disney Studio, this homey
coffee shop is a reliable, affordable place. Breakfasts include plump
omelets and homemade biscuits. For lunch or dinner there are hearty,
comforting dishes like roast turkey and beef stew. If you're in a hurry,
call ahead with your order and the restaurant will deliver directly to
your car. ⊠ *10001 Riverside Dr.,* ☎ *818/761–9126. Reservations not
accepted. AE, DC, MC, V.*

LODGING

Revised and
updated by
Lisa
Oppenheimer

Whether you're going high-style or budget, select a hotel room for lo-
cation as well as ambience, amenities, and price. Prices for Los Ange-
les hotels run the gamut from bargain basement to sky high. Tax rates
for the area will add 9%–14% to your bill depending on where in Los
Angeles you stay. Because you will need a car no matter where you stay,
parking is another expense to consider. A few hotels have free park-
ing, but most charge for the privilege. Some resorts have valet park-
ing only.

Hotels listed below are organized according to their location, then by
price category.

CATEGORY	COST*
$$$$	over $175
$$$	$120–$175
$$	$80–$120
$	under $80
All prices are for a standard double room, excluding 14% occupancy tax.	

Downtown

$$$$ 🏨 **Hotel Inter-Continental Los Angeles.** Service here is top-notch. Rooms
in the residential-style building are your basic business contemporary,
although floor-to-ceiling windows add a dash of excitement. Little extras include separate bath and shower stalls (in most rooms) and TV
sound in the bathrooms. ⊠ *251 S. Olive St., 90012,* ☎ *213/617–3300
or 800/442–5251,* 𝖥𝖠𝖷 *213/617–3399. 433 rooms, 18 suites. Restaurant, bar, in-room data ports, minibars, no-smoking floors, room ser-*

vice, pool, exercise room, piano, laundry service and dry cleaning, concierge, concierge floor, business services, meeting rooms, parking (fee). AE, D, DC, MC, V.

$$$$ 🏨 **Hyatt Regency Los Angeles.** Windows with dramatic city views jazz up the mahogany- and cherry-wood–filled rooms at this hotel near the Music Center. If you're here to work, ask for the Business Plan, available on floors above the 18th—you'll have access to laptop computers and fax machines. ⊠ 711 S. Hope St., 90017, ☎ 213/683–1234 or 800/233–1234, FAX 213/629–3230. 485 rooms, 41 suites. 2 restaurants, 2 bars, in-room data ports, no-smoking floors, room service, exercise room, laundry service and dry cleaning, concierge, concierge floor, business services, meeting rooms, parking (fee). AE, D, DC, MC, V.

$$$$ 🏨 **Los Angeles Marriott Downtown.** The 14-story building near the First Interstate World Trade Center and the Pacific Stock Exchange changed its name last year from the Sheraton Grande when bought by Marriott. The hotel is still a nice place to check in for business. Guest rooms are oversize, with marble baths and wall-to-wall windows with city views. The extensive business center provides secretarial services. Guests have complimentary use of a fitness center one block away. Complimentary limo service is provided within a 5-mi radius. ⊠ 333 S. Figueroa St., 90071, ☎ 213/617–1133 or 800/228–9290, FAX 213/613–0291. 469 rooms. 3 restaurants, 2 bars, in-room data ports, in-room safes, minibars, no-smoking floors, room service, pool, 4 cinemas, piano, laundry service and dry cleaning, concierge, business services, meeting rooms, parking (fee). AE, D, DC, MC, V.

$$$$ 🏨 **New Otani Hotel and Garden.** "Japanese Experience" rooms at the
★ New Otani have tatami mats instead of beds, extra-deep bathtubs, and shoji screens on windows. You can also have tea and shiatsu massage in the comfort of your own otherwise somewhat plain American-style room. The cuisine in all three of the hotel's restaurants is authentically Japanese, although American fare is also served. ⊠ 120 S. Los Angeles St., 90012, ☎ 213/629–1200, 800/273–2294 in CA, 800/421–8795 elsewhere in the U.S. and Canada, FAX 213/622–0980. 434 rooms, 18 suites. 3 restaurants, 3 bars, in-room safes, minibars, no-smoking rooms, refrigerators, room service, sauna, health club, laundry service and dry cleaning, concierge, business services, meeting rooms, car rental, parking (fee). AE, D, DC, MC, V.

$$$$ 🏨 **Regal Biltmore Hotel.** The Spanish–Italian Renaissance building has rooms you can sink into (flowing draperies, French-style armoires, and overstuffed chairs), making even one night feel like a great escape. Afternoons and evenings, soak up some atmosphere in the beautifully restored Rendezvous Court. A complimentary shuttle travels within a 3-mi radius of the hotel. ⊠ 506 S. Grand Ave., 90071, ☎ 213/624–1011 or 800/245–8673, FAX 213/612–1545. 683 rooms, 100 suites. 3 restaurants, 3 bars, 2 cafés, some in-room data ports, in-room safes, minibars, no-smoking floors, room service, indoor pool, hot tub, spa, health club, laundry service and dry cleaning, concierge, concierge floor, business services, meeting rooms, car rental, parking (fee). AE, D, DC, MC, V.

$$$$ 🏨 **Westin Bonaventure Hotel & Suites.** You can't miss this hotel's image on the downtown L.A. skyline: Its five cylindrical towers are tall (35 stories) and mirrored. Inside is a futuristic lobby with fountains, an indoor lake, and lots of activity. Accommodations, with new furniture and updated decor, are on the small side, but floor-to-ceiling glass windows provide terrific views of the city to the south and east, the mountains to the north, and the ocean to the west. ⊠ 404 S. Figueroa St., 90071, ☎ 213/624–1000 or 800/937–8461, FAX 213/612–4800. 1,354 rooms, 135 suites. 17 restaurants, 5 bars, some in-room data *ports, minibars, no-smoking floors, room service, pool, beauty salon, health club, laundry service and dry cleaning, concierge, business services, meeting rooms, travel services, car rental, parking (fee). AE, D, DC, MC, V.*

$$$$ 🏨 **Wyndham Checkers Hotel.** Opened as the Mayflower Hotel in
★ 1927, Checkers has more character than most downtown hotels, with a lobby full of fine antique furniture, and rooms with oversize beds and upholstered easy chairs. Enjoy afternoon tea in the wood-paneled library. The hotel's highly regarded restaurant, Checkers, is one of downtown's best business restaurants. There's complimentary car service mornings within a 2-mi radius, but the financial district is within walking distance. ⊠ *535 S. Grand Ave., 90071,* ☎ *213/624–0000 or 800/996–3426,* FAX *213/626–9906. 188 rooms, 9 suites. Restaurant, bar, in-room data ports, minibars, no-smoking floors, room service, pool, hot tub, spa, exercise room, library, laundry service and dry cleaning, concierge, business services, meeting rooms, parking (fee). AE, D, DC, MC, V.*

$$$ 🏨 **Inn at 657.** Apartment-size suites at this small bed-and-breakfast–
★ style inn near the University of Southern California have down comforters on the beds, Oriental silks on the walls, and huge dining tables. Homey touches include full kitchens with microwave, and private room entrances off the garden. Room rates include local phone calls. ⊠ *657 W. 23rd St., 90007,* ☎ *213/741–2200 or 800/347–7512. 5 suites. In-room data ports, kitchenettes, no-smoking suites, refrigerators, in-room VCRs, hot tub, laundry service, business services, free parking. Full breakfast. No credit cards.*

$$ 🏨 **Figueroa Hotel and Convention Center.** The Spanish feel of this 12-story hotel built in 1926 is accented by terra-cotta–color rooms, hand-painted furniture, wrought-iron beds, and, in many rooms, ceiling fans. ⊠ *939 S. Figueroa St., 90015,* ☎ *213/627–8971 or 800/421–9092,* FAX *213/689–0305. 285 rooms, 2 suites. 2 restaurants, 2 bars, café, in-room data ports, some refrigerators, pool, hot tub, coin laundry, dry cleaning, concierge, car rental, free parking. AE, DC, MC, V.*

$$ 🏨 **Kawada Hotel.** This eclectic three-story redbrick hotel near the Music Center and local government buildings has European flair. Immaculate guest rooms are on the small side, but come with two phones and a wet bar. A complimentary shuttle traverses the downtown area. ⊠ *200 S. Hill St., 90012,* ☎ *213/621–4455 or 800/752–9232,* FAX *213/687–4455. 115 rooms, 1 suite. Restaurant, bar, deli, kitchenettes, no-smoking rooms, refrigerators, room service, in-room VCRs, coin laundry, laundry service and dry cleaning, concierge, business services, meeting rooms, parking (fee). AE, D, DC, MC, V.*

$ 🏨 **The InnTowne.** This modern three-story hotel just one-and-a-half blocks from the convention center has large rooms with beige-and-white or gray-and-white color schemes. Palm trees and a small garden surround the swimming pool. ⊠ *913 S. Figueroa St., 90015,* ☎ *213/628–2222 or 800/457–8520,* FAX *213/687–0566. 168 rooms, 2 suites. Bar, coffee shop, pool, coin laundry, dry cleaning, meeting room, car rental, free parking. AE, D, DC, MC, V.*

Beverly Hills, Century City, Hollywood, and West Hollywood

Beverly Hills and Vicinity

$$$$ 🏨 **Beverly Hills Hotel.** Celebrities favor the bungalows that have all of
★ life's little necessities: wood-burning fireplaces, period furniture, and even (in some cases) grand pianos. Standard rooms are characteristically decadent, with original artwork, butler-service buttons, walk-in closets, and huge marble bathrooms. All rooms are soundproofed and

have stereos with CD players and personal fax machines. Some have kitchenettes. Twelve acres of landscaped (and carpeted) walkways make for prime strolling grounds if you can bear to leave your room. The fabled Polo Lounge remains a Hollywood meeting place. ⊠ *9641 Sunset Blvd., 90210,* ☎ *310/276–2251 or 800/283–8885,* FAX *310/887– 2887. 203 rooms, 21 bungalows. 4 restaurants, bar, in-room data ports, in-room safes, no-smoking rooms, room service, pool, barber- shop, beauty salon, hot tub, massage, 2 tennis courts, exercise room, jogging, piano, laundry service and dry cleaning, concierge, parking (fee). AE, DC, MC, V.*

$$$$ 🏨 **Beverly Hilton.** With an imposing white exterior, and glass- and mar- ble-filled public areas, the Beverly Hilton is owner Merv Griffin's mix of glitz and luxury. Guest rooms are spacious and tasteful. Service here is extra-helpful. The hotel provides complimentary transportation within a 3-mi radius for exploring Beverly Hills and nearby Century City. ⊠ *9876 Wilshire Blvd., 90210,* ☎ *310/274–7777 or 800/445– 8667,* FAX *310/285–1313. 581 rooms, 42 suites. 2 restaurants, coffee shop, lobby lounge, in-room data ports, minibars, no-smoking floors, refrigerators, room service, pool, massage, exercise room, shops, laun- dry service and dry cleaning, concierge, business services, meeting rooms, travel services, car rental, parking (fee). AE, D, DC, MC, V.*

$$$$ 🏨 **Four Seasons Hotel Los Angeles at Beverly Hills.** With an employee-
★   to-guest ratio greater than one to one, the Four Seasons takes exem- plary care of its guests. Extra touches include everything from complimentary cellular phones to limo service every 15 minutes to Rodeo Drive shops. Impeccable guest rooms are eclectic and bright with VCRs, CD players, and bathroom TVs. Suites have French doors and balconies. ⊠ *300 S. Doheny Dr., 90048,* ☎ *310/273–2222 or 800/ 332–3442,* FAX *310/859–3824. 179 rooms, 106 suites. Restaurant, café, bar, in-room data ports, minibars, no-smoking floors, room ser- vice, pool, hot tub, exercise room, laundry service and dry cleaning, concierge, business services, meeting rooms, car rental, free parking and parking (fee). AE, DC, MC, V.*

$$$$ 🏨 **Hotel Nikko.** Rooms and suites at this high-tech hotel have fax ma- chines and bedside gizmos that control in-room lighting, temperature, TV, VCR, and CD player. Management thoughtfully tends to even the smallest needs: weary travelers get to sit, rather than stand, through the check-in process, and nonvalet parking is free. ⊠ *465 S. La Cienega Blvd., 90048,* ☎ *310/247–0400 or 800/645–5687,* FAX *310/247–0315. 297 rooms, 10 suites. Restaurant, bar, in-room data ports, minibars, no-smoking floors, room service, pool, massage, sauna, exercise room, laundry service and dry cleaning, concierge, business services, meet- ing rooms, free parking, parking (fee). AE, D, DC, MC, V.*

$$$$ 🏨 **L'Ermitage Beverly Hills.** There's a sophisticated city feel to this Bev- erly Hills charmer. The smallish hotel just off Rodeo Drive has spa- cious, uncluttered rooms with lavish baths, silk bedding, walk-in closets, and French doors that open to views of either the city or the mountains. The rooftop pool has drop-dead views and poolside cabanas. ⊠ *9291 Burton Way, 90210,* ☎ *310/278–3344 or 800/800–2113,* FAX *310/278–8247. 111 rooms, 13 suites. 2 restaurants, 2 bars, in-room data ports, minibars, no-smoking floors, room service, pool, massage, steam room, exercise room, laundry service and dry cleaning, concierge, business services, meeting rooms, parking (fee). AE, D, DC, MC, V.*

$$$$ 🏨 **Peninsula Beverly Hills.** The interior of this grand, French Renais-
★   sance–style hotel feels a world removed from the bustle on Little Santa Monica Boulevard. Rooms resemble luxury apartments, with antiques and marble floors. Some suites in the two-story villas have whirlpool tubs, terraces, fireplaces, and CD players. The fifth-floor pool, look- ing out at the Hollywood Hills, is a gem of a place to relax. Other frivoli-

ties include an on-site Bijan store and a courtesy Rolls-Royce for Beverly Hills shopping. ⊠ *9882 Little Santa Monica Blvd., 90212,* ☎ *310/ 551–2888 or 800/462–7899,* FAX *310/788–2319. 196 rooms, 32 suites. 2 restaurants, bar, in-room data ports, in-room safes, minibars, no-smoking floors, room service, in-room VCRs, lap pool, spa, health club, shops, concierge, business services, parking (fee). AE, D, DC, MC, V.*

$$$$ ⊡ **Radisson Beverly Pavilion Hotel.** This eight-floor boutique hotel is in prime shopping territory, within blocks of Rodeo Drive. Guest rooms and executive suites have private balconies; some also have refrigerators. The Radisson's frequent rate specials make it an economical alternative to some of the neighborhood's pricier establishments. ⊠ *9360 Wilshire Blvd., 90212,* ☎ *310/273–1400 or 800/441–5050,* FAX *310/859–8551. 100 rooms, 10 suites. Restaurant, bar, no-smoking floors, in-room data ports, refrigerators, room service, pool, laundry service and dry cleaning, concierge, business services, meeting rooms, parking (fee). AE, D, DC, MC, V.*

$$$$ ⊡ **Regent Beverly Wilshire.** A Four Seasons Hotel since 1993, the Regent offers the franchise's plush accommodations as well as its exemplary service. A refurbishment fluffed up rooms in the older (1928) Wilshire wing of this landmark Italian Renaissance–style hotel, as well as overhauled and upgraded the contemporary accommodations in the hotel's Beverly wing. Throughout the hotel, beds are so comfortable that guests have been known to ask where they can buy the mattresses. Personal services include fresh strawberries and cream and bottled water delivered to your room upon arrival. Guests can enjoy leisure time at the expanded pool area that includes open-air cabanas. ⊠ *9500 Wilshire Blvd., 90212,* ☎ *310/275–5200, 800/427–4354 in CA, 800/421–4354 elsewhere in the U.S.,* FAX *310/274–2851. 393 rooms, 118 suites. 2 restaurants, bar, lobby lounge, in-room data ports, in-room safes, minibars, no-smoking floors, room service, pool, beauty salon, spa, health club, piano, laundry service and dry cleaning, concierge, business services, meeting rooms, parking (fee). AE, DC, MC, V.*

$$$$ ⊡ **Renaissance Beverly Hills.** The former Beverly Prescott Hotel changed its name to Renaissance in July 1998, thus hooking it up with the Marriott group and the company's reward programs. Much of the decor at this 12-story hotel remains the same, however, with a semi-enclosed patio and a tall atrium giving the place an open, airy feel. Stylish, spacious guest rooms are done in warm salmon and caramel tones; all have private balconies, fax machines, stereo/CD players, irons, hair dryers, and coffeemakers. ⊠ *1224 S. Beverwil Dr., 90035,* ☎ *310/277–2800 or 800/421–3212,* FAX *310/203–9537. 137 rooms, 18 suites. Restaurant, bar, in-room data ports, minibars, no-smoking rooms, room service, in-room VCRs, pool, exercise room, laundry service and dry cleaning, concierge, concierge floor, business services, meeting rooms, parking (fee). AE, D, DC, MC, V.*

$$$–$$$$ ⊡ **Beverly Hills Plaza Hotel.** A black-and-white lobby has overstuffed sofas and lots of plants. Suites have an airy feel, with white color schemes and plenty of glass; and each has a kitchen. Accommodations come equipped with bathrobes, hair dryers, in-room movies, and Nintendo. ⊠ *10300 Wilshire Blvd., 90024,* ☎ *310/275–5575,* FAX *310/278–3325. 116 suites. Restaurant, bar, in-room safes, kitchenettes, minibars, pool, exercise room, laundry service and dry cleaning, concierge, business services, parking (fee). AE, D, DC, MC, V.*

$$–$$$$ ⊡ **Carlyle Inn.** Wine and cheese on weekday afternoons and in-room extras such as bathrobes and hair dryers make this four-story inn a good choice. In a safe neighborhood close to Restaurant Row, Century City, and Beverly Hills, a complimentary shuttle runs within a 5-mi radius. A sundeck and hot tub are added bonuses. ⊠ *1119 S. Robertson*

Blvd., 90035, ☎ *310/275–4445 or 800/322–7595,* ᶠᴬˣ *310/859–0496.*
32 rooms. In-room data ports, minibars, no-smoking rooms, in-room
VCRs, hot tub, exercise room, laundry service and dry cleaning, busi-
ness services, parking (fee). Full breakfast. AE, D, DC, MC, V.

$$$ 🏨 **Avalon.** From the remains of the old Beverly Carlton hotel (once
the preferred living quarters of Marilyn Monroe) comes Avalon, a rein-
vented Beverly Hills boutique hotel mercifully priced for the nonfamous-
and-fortunate crowd. Visitors to the three-building property will find
good-size rooms with kicky decor. The downside may be the view, or
lack thereof, as many rooms face the backs of other buildings (although
some look out over the pool). ⊠ *9400 W. Olympic Blvd., 90212,* ☎
310/277–5221 or 800/535–4715, ᶠᴬˣ *310/277–4928. 78 rooms, 10 suites.*
Restaurant, bar, no-smoking rooms, refrigerators, room service, in-room
VCRs, pool, exercise room, coin laundry, laundry service and dry
cleaning, concierge, business services, meeting rooms, parking (fee). AE,
DC, MC, V.

$$$ 🏨 **Beverly Hills Inn.** The 50-room Inn has gotten raves for supplying
★ Beverly Hills luxury at a more palatable cost than some of the more
mammoth hotels. Rooms at this gem surround a courtyard with pool.
Each has a refrigerator, and some have French doors leading to an outdoor sitting area. In addition to complimentary breakfast delivered to
your door each morning, cheese and fresh fruit are served every evening,
and dried fruits are left instead of mints at nightly turndown. Reserve
well in advance. ⊠ *125 S. Spalding Dr., 90212,* ☎ *310/278–0303 or*
800/463–4466, ᶠᴬˣ *310/278–1728. 46 rooms, 4 suites. Bar, in-room*
data ports, no-smoking floor, refrigerator, pool, sauna, exercise room,
laundry service and dry cleaning, concierge, business services, meet-
ing room, free parking. Continental breakfast. AE, DC, MC, V.

$$–$$$ 🏨 **Beverly Terrace Hotel.** Rooms are basic (except for the leopard-print
bedspreads), and bathrooms have shower stalls, not tubs, but the price
is right at this hotel on the fringes of Beverly Hills and West Hollywood. On the corner of Santa Monica Boulevard, the hotel is close to
the Sunset Strip and the heart of West Hollywood. ⊠ *469 N. Doheny*
Dr., 90210, ☎ *310/274–8141,* ᶠᴬˣ *310/385–1998. 39 rooms. Restau-*
rant, some refrigerators, pool, free parking. Continental breakfast.
AE, D, DC, MC, V.

$$ 🏨 **Crescent Hotel.** The small, European-style Crescent Hotel serves com-
plimentary snacks and fresh fruit all day long. Standard rooms are on
the spartan side, but unexpected touches such as original paintings on
the walls and clothes hangers that double as art spice up the mood.
Junior suites are a bit expensive considering that the only features that
distinguish them from the standard rooms are large-screen TVs and
tubs. ⊠ *403 N. Crescent Dr., 90210,* ☎ *310/247–0505 or 800/451–*
1566, ᶠᴬˣ *310/247–9053. 39 rooms, 2 suites. No-smoking rooms, some*
refrigerators, free parking. Continental breakfast. AE, D, DC, MC, V.

Century City

$$$$ 🏨 **Park Hyatt.** Rooms at this elegant luxury hotel are big and com-
fortable. Nice touches include high tea in the lobby and complimen-
tary limousine service within Century City and Beverly Hills. ⊠ *2151*
Ave. of the Stars, 90067, ☎ *310/277–1234 or 800/233–1234,* ᶠᴬˣ *310/*
785–9240. 367 rooms, 189 suites. Restaurant, 2 bars, in-room data
ports, minibars, no-smoking rooms, 24-hour room service, indoor
and outdoor pools, hot tub, massage, sauna, steam room, spa, health
club, piano, laundry service and dry cleaning, concierge, business ser-
vices, meeting rooms, parking (fee). AE, D, DC, MC, V.

$$$ 🏨 **Century City Courtyard by Marriott.** Near the Century City business
complex, this Marriott is well situated and nicely priced. Room ameni-
ties include hair dryers, coffeemakers, irons and boards, and Nin-

tendo. A complimentary shuttle zips guests to businesses, shopping, dining, and entertainment options within a 3-mi radius. ⊠ *10320 W. Olympic Blvd., 90064,* ☎ *310/556–2777 or 800/321–2211,* 𝐅𝐀𝐗 *310/ 203–0563. 134 rooms. Restaurant, bar, minibars, in-room data ports, room service, no-smoking floors, no-smoking rooms, exercise room, laundry service and dry cleaning, business services, concierge, car rental, parking (fee). AE, D, DC, MC, V.*

West Hollywood

$$$$ 🏨 **The Argyle.** You can't miss the gunmetal-gray, pink, and burgundy
  ★   Art Deco facade. Rooms are also deco; marble bathrooms have black-and-white fixtures. Though small, each accommodation has a separate living room with fax machine, two-line speakerphones, and plenty of plants. ⊠ *8358 Sunset Blvd., 90069,* ☎ *323/654–7100 or 800/225– 2637,* 𝐅𝐀𝐗 *323/654–9287. 20 rooms, 44 suites. Restaurant, bar, in-room data ports, in-room safes, minibars, no-smoking floors, room service, in-room VCRs, pool, sauna, exercise room, laundry service and dry cleaning, concierge, business services, meeting rooms, parking (fee). AE, D, DC, MC, V.*

$$$$ 🏨 **Hyatt West Hollywood on Sunset Boulevard.** Its proximity to L.A.'s clubs of the moment makes this Hyatt popular with music-industry types. Rooms that face the boulevard have balconies; those facing the hills do not. Some rooms have aquariums, and all have a deco feel. The view from the rooftop pool is extraordinary—you can practically see inside some of the Hollywood Hills dwellings. ⊠ *8401 Sunset Blvd., 90069,* ☎ *323/656–1234 or 800/233–1234,* 𝐅𝐀𝐗 *323/650–7024. 262 rooms, 21 suites. Restaurant, bar, in-room data ports, no-smoking floors, room service, pool, laundry service and dry cleaning, business services, meeting rooms, parking (fee). AE, D, DC, MC, V.*

$$$$ 🏨 **Le Parc Hotel.** Suites in this modern low rise have sunken living rooms with fireplaces and private balconies; other little extras include microwaves, coffeemakers, stereos with CD players, Nintendo, bathrobes, and slippers. The hotel is on a tree-lined residential street close to CBS Television City and the Pacific Design Center. ⊠ *733 N.W. Knoll Dr., 90069,* ☎ *310/855–8888 or 800/578–4837,* 𝐅𝐀𝐗 *310/659–8508. 154 suites. Restaurant, kitchenettes, in-room data ports, minibars, no-smoking floors, in-room VCRs, pool, hot tub, sauna, tennis court, basketball, health club, coin laundry, laundry and dry cleaning services, concierge, business services, meeting rooms, parking (fee). AE, D, DC, MC, V.*

$$$$ 🏨 **Mondrian.** Mod apartment-size accommodations at this hip Ian
  ★   Schrager property have floor-to-ceiling windows, slipcovered sofas, and marble coffee tables; many have kitchens. Suave touches include scented candles, flowers, wool lap blankets, and vintage movie magazines in each room. At 5 PM the lobby lights are dimmed, candles are lit, and a carpet of light creates visual magic. Meander over to the Sky Bar, where patrons (many celebrities) pay exorbitant prices for the right to drink cocktails out of plastic cups by a pool. ⊠ *8440 Sunset Blvd., 90069,* ☎ *323/650–8999 or 800/525–8029,* 𝐅𝐀𝐗 *323/650–5215. 53 rooms, 185 suites. Restaurant, 2 bars, outdoor café, in-room data ports, kitchenettes, no-smoking rooms, refrigerators, room service, pool, massage, sauna, spa, steam room, health club, laundry service and dry cleaning, concierge, business services, meeting rooms, parking (fee). AE, D, DC, MC, V.*

$$$$ 🏨 **Summerfield Suites Hotel.** Suites here are basic, almost dormlike, but frequent specials make them a good value. Each suite has a private balcony, sleeper sofa (in addition to beds), a gas fireplace, separate vanities, and microwave; most have kitchens as well. The hotel is steps from Santa Monica Boulevard, close to the Sunset Strip and La

Cienega Boulevard's Restaurant Row. ✉ *1000 Westmount Dr., 90069,* ☎ *310/657–7400 or 800/833–4353,* ℻ *310/854–6744. 109 suites. Breakfast room, in-room data ports, no-smoking suites, refrigerators, in-room VCRs, pool, exercise room, coin laundry, laundry service and dry cleaning, meeting room, parking (fee). Continental breakfast. AE, D, DC, MC, V.*

$$$$ 🖬 **Wyndham Bel Age Hotel.** There's a residential feel to this all-suites
★ hotel near the Sunset Strip. All rooms have private terraces. South-facing rooms look out over the Los Angeles skyline, and on a clear day you can see as far as the Pacific. The hotel caters to the entertainment industry, so keep an eye out for celebs. ✉ *1020 N. San Vicente Blvd., 90069,* ☎ *310/854–1111 or 800/996–3426,* ℻ *310/854–0926. 200 suites. 2 restaurants, bar, in-room data ports, no-smoking floors, room service, pool, beauty salon, exercise room, laundry service and dry cleaning, concierge, meeting rooms, parking (fee). AE, D, DC, MC, V.*

$$$ 🖬 **Ramada West Hollywood.** Though part of a chain, this hotel in a largely gay West Hollywood neighborhood has plenty of character. Flashy deco rooms have bright upholstered furniture and ultracomfortable beds, and the bi-level loft suites with kitchenettes are an excellent value. ✉ *8585 Santa Monica Blvd., 90069,* ☎ *310/652–6400 or 800/845–8585,* ℻ *310/652–4207. 135 rooms, 40 suites. Restaurant, bar, in-room data ports, no-smoking floors, room service, refrigerators, pool, coin laundry, dry cleaning and laundry service, concierge, parking (fee). AE, D, DC, MC, V.*

Hollywood and Vicinity

$$$$ 🖬 **Chateau Marmont Hotel.** You'll know this hotel the minute you see
★ it. The exterior is every bit the French castle the name suggests. Entertainment-industry moguls love the hotel's opulent suites, cottages, bungalows, and penthouses. Though the 1920s feel is authentic, some may find the decor looks dated rather than antique. Rooms in the cottages have Frank Lloyd Wright–inspired fabrics; the 1956 bungalows are more contemporary. Not all rooms are air-conditioned, but the non-AC variety can be cooled with portable units available by request. An on-call beauty therapist, masseur, private trainers, and airport meet-and-greeters are all at your beck and call. ✉ *8221 Sunset Blvd., 90046,* ☎ *323/656–1010 or 800/242–8328,* ℻ *323/655–5311. 10 rooms, 53 suites. Restaurant, bar, in-room data ports, in-room safes, minibars, no-smoking rooms, room service, in-room VCRs, pool, massage, exercise room, laundry service and dry cleaning, concierge, business services, parking (fee). AE, DC, MC, V.*

$$$–$$$$ 🖬 **Radisson Wilshire Plaza Hotel.** Guests here will find oak desks, upholstered furniture, and floor-to-ceiling windows offering magnificent views of Hollywood or downtown. The hotel has a small exercise room, but guests also have use of a nearby health club. ✉ *3515 Wilshire Blvd., 90010,* ☎ *213/381–7411 or 800/333–3333,* ℻ *213/386–7379. 380 rooms, 13 suites. 2 restaurants, bar, café, in-room data ports, minibars, no-smoking floor, room service, pool, barbershop, exercise room, laundry service and dry cleaning, concierge, business services, meeting rooms, parking (fee). AE, D, DC, MC, V.*

$$$ 🖬 **Clarion Hotel Hollywood Roosevelt.** The hotel was the site of the original Academy Awards. The Hollywood legacy lives on in the little museum on the second floor and in the 40 suites, which have themes such as Gable and Lombard or Shirley Temple. The Hollywood Walk of Fame, Mann's Chinese Theatre, and the Hollywood Entertainment Museum are all within walking distance, but the neighborhood isn't the best. ✉ *7000 Hollywood Blvd., 90028,* ☎ *323/466–7000 or 800/950–7667,* ℻ *323/462–8056. 320 rooms, 39 suites. Restaurant, bar, lobby lounge, no-smoking floors, room service, pool, hot tub, exer-*

cise room, laundry service and dry cleaning, concierge, business services, meeting rooms, parking (fee). AE, D, DC, MC, V.

$–$$$ 🏨 **Magic Hotel.** This is a great place for college kids and young people on vacation. There's a nice pool, which some rooms overlook. Larger rooms have kitchens with eating areas. The hotel is close to the Hollywood Walk of Fame. ✉ *7025 Franklin Ave., 90028,* 🕾 *323/851–0800 or 800/741–4915,* 𝗙𝗔𝗫 *323/851–4926. 10 rooms, 30 suites. No-smoking rooms, refrigerator, pool, coin laundry, free parking. AE, D, DC, MC, V.*

$ 🏨 **Banana Bungalow Hotel and International Hostel.** International travelers (the hostel is open only to those heading in or out of the country—show a passport and ticket) will find good value at this friendly hostel on 6.8 acres in the Hollywood Hills. Dorm rooms have bunk beds and are equipped with lockers. ✉ *2775 Cahuenga Blvd. W, 90068,* 🕾 *323/851–1129 or 800/446–7835,* 𝗙𝗔𝗫 *323/851–1569. 22 dorm rooms, 10 private rooms. Restaurant, some fans, no-smoking rooms, pool, exercise room, billiards, recreation room, theater, coin laundry, travel services, airport shuttle, car rental, free parking. MC, V.*

$ 🏨 **Highland Gardens Hotel.** Most studios and standard rooms here have kitchens with vinyl chairs and Formica tables. Basic but spacious sleeping areas have either two queen-size beds, or a king bed with a queen-size sleeper sofa. The hotel is just blocks from the Walk of Fame and a few minutes' drive to the Sunset Strip. ✉ *7047 Franklin Ave., 90028,* 🕾 *323/850–0536 or 800/404–5472,* 𝗙𝗔𝗫 *323/850–1712. 70 rooms, 48 suites. Kitchenettes, pool, no-smoking rooms, refrigerators, free parking. AE, MC, V.*

Coastal and Western Los Angeles

Bel-Air

$$$$ 🏨 **Hotel Bel-Air.** Locals swear by this luxury treasure tucked in a
★ wooded canyon. Bungalow-style country French rooms feel like fine homes with extras such as a stereo with CD player, thick terry bathrobes, and slippers. Six of the suites have private outdoor Jacuzzis; most rooms have wood-burning fireplaces. For the quietest accommodations, ask for a room in either the far north or far south sections. ✉ *701 Stone Canyon Rd., 90077,* 🕾 *310/472–1211 or 800/648–4097,* 𝗙𝗔𝗫 *310/476–5890. 52 rooms, 40 suites. Restaurant, bar, in-room data ports, in-room safes, minibars, no-smoking rooms, room service, in-room VCRs, pool, health club, laundry service and dry cleaning, concierge, business services, meeting rooms, parking (fee). AE, DC, MC, V.*

$$$$ 🏨 **Summit Hotel Bel-Air.** Although the Summit Hotel caters primarily to business travelers, its proximity to the Getty Center has also made it popular with museum visitors. Transportation to the Center can be secured upon demand and will run $5 for the round trip. The low-rise building has sleek, modern guest rooms, with patios and terraces overlooking 8 acres of gardens. ✉ *11461 Sunset Blvd., 90049,* 🕾 *310/476–6571 or 800/468–3541,* 𝗙𝗔𝗫 *310/476–1371. 161 rooms, 8 suites. Restaurant, bar, in-room data ports, minibars, no-smoking floors, room service, pool, massage, spa, tennis court, exercise room, laundry service and dry cleaning, concierge, business services, meeting rooms, parking (fee). AE, D, DC, MC, V.*

LAX

$$$$ 🏨 **Summerfield Suites.** This all-suite hotel is ideal for guests who want
★ to spread out and for families. One- and two-bedroom suites are extra large, with bedrooms as well as sleeper sofas in the living room. Guests can either cook in their kitchens (standard in all suites), or make use of one of the gas grills outside. There are plenty of restaurants within

walking distance. ⊠ *810 S. Douglas Ave., El Segundo 90245,* ☎ *310/725–0100 or 800/833–4353,* FAX *310/725–0900. 122 suites. Breakfast room, in-room data ports, no-smoking rooms, pool, hot tub, basketball, exercise room, coin laundry, laundry service and dry cleaning, business services, meeting rooms, free parking. Continental breakfast. AE, D, DC, MC, V.*

$$$ 🏨 **Holiday Inn LAX.** This 12-story international-style hotel appeals to families as well as businesspeople. Refrigerators can be rented. ⊠ *9901 La Cienega Blvd., Los Angeles 90045,* ☎ *310/649–5151 or 800/624–0025,* FAX *310/670–3619. 401 rooms, 1 suite. Restaurant, bar, in-room data ports, pool, exercise room, video games, coin laundry, airport shuttle, parking (fee). AE, D, DC, MC, V.*

$$$ 🏨 **Westin LAX.** This is a great place to stay if you want to be pampered
★   but also need to be close to the airport. Rooms and suites are spacious; many suites have private outdoor hot tubs. ⊠ *5400 W. Century Blvd., Los Angeles 90045,* ☎ *310/216–5858 or 800/937–8461,* FAX *310/670–1948. 723 rooms, 42 suites. Restaurant, bar, in-room data ports, minibars, no-smoking floors, refrigerators, pool, hot tub, sauna, exercise room, laundry service and dry cleaning, business services, meeting rooms, airport shuttle, car rental, parking (fee). AE, D, DC, MC, V.*

$$$ 🏨 **Wyndham Hotel at Los Angeles Airport.** You'll get to your plane in a hurry from this hotel that bills itself as the closest to LAX. Guest rooms are on the small side but have plenty of perks, such as fax machines, voice mail, direct-dial phones, and movies. ⊠ *6225 W. Century Blvd., Los Angeles 90045,* ☎ *310/670–9000 or 800/996–3426,* FAX *310/670–8110. 591 rooms, 12 suites. 2 restaurants, bar, in-room data ports, minibars, no-smoking floors, refrigerators, pool, hot tub, sauna, exercise room, laundry service and dry cleaning, concierge, business services, meeting rooms, parking (fee). AE, D, DC, MC, V.*

$$ 🏨 **Furama Hotel Los Angeles.** In a quiet residential area, the Furama is convenient to jogging paths, tennis, and golf. Rooms all have views of either the pool, the airport, or, if you're high enough up in the tower, the ocean. A shuttle service goes to LAX (about a mile away), Marina del Rey, Venice Beach, and the Santa Monica Mall. ⊠ *8601 Lincoln Blvd., Los Angeles 90045,* ☎ *310/670–8111 or 800/225–8126,* FAX *310/337–1883. 760 rooms, 6 suites. Restaurant, bar, no-smoking floors, room service, pool, hot tub, 2 exercise rooms, laundry service and dry cleaning, concierge, business services, meeting rooms, airport shuttle, parking (fee). AE, D, DC, MC, V.*

Manhattan Beach

$$$ 🏨 **Barnabey's Hotel.** Modeled after a 19th-century English inn, Barn-
★   abey's has tidy rooms with lace curtains, antique furniture, flowered wallpaper, and vintage books. Added luxuries such as a heated towel rack in the bathrooms, down comforters on the beds, and video games are all set to make you relax. Doggie and kitty snacks are available for the hotel's four-legged guests. ⊠ *3501 Sepulveda Blvd. (at Rosecrans Ave.), 90266,* ☎ *310/545–8466 or 800/552–5285,* FAX *310/545–8621. 120 rooms. Restaurant, pub, in-room data ports, no-smoking rooms, pool, hot tub, bicycles, nightclub, laundry service and dry cleaning, business services, meeting rooms, airport shuttle, car rental, parking (fee). Full breakfast. AE, D, DC, MC, V.*

Marina del Rey

$$$$ 🏨 **Marina Beach Marriott.** This Mediterranean-style, nine-story high-
★   rise has a high-tech design softened by pastel tones and accents of brass and marble. There's a gazebo on the patio, and some rooms have water views—ask for upper-floor rooms that face the marina. ⊠ *4100 Admiralty Way, 90292,* ☎ *310/301–3000 or 800/228–9290,* FAX *310/448–4870. 371 rooms, 18 suites. Restaurant, bar, in-room data ports,*

no-smoking floors, some refrigerators, room service, pool, exercise room, laundry service and dry cleaning, concierge, business services, meeting rooms, car rental, parking (fee). AE, D, DC, MC, V.

$$$$ ★ ⊡ **Ritz-Carlton, Marina del Rey.** This European-style hotel occupies a patch of prime real estate right on the docks of the marina, affording panoramic views of the Pacific. Traditionally styled rooms have French doors, marble baths, and honor bars; there's also twice-daily maid service and 24-hour room service. ⊠ *4375 Admiralty Way, 90292,* ☏ *310/ 823–1700 or 800/241–3333,* ℻ *310/823–2403. 306 rooms, 12 suites. 2 restaurants, lobby lounge, in-room safes, minibars, no-smoking floors, room service, pool, hot tub, massage, spa, tennis court, basketball, health club, bicycles, laundry service and dry cleaning, concierge, business services, meeting rooms, parking (fee). AE, D, DC, MC, V.*

$$$ ⊡ **Marina International Hotel & Bungalows.** White shutters on each window and private balconies overlooking the flower-filled courtyard evoke a European village–like feel. Large rooms have contemporary decor and French doors; some rooms have partial views of the water. The split-level bungalows are huge. Across from a sandy beach within the marina, the hotel is a good choice for families with children. ⊠ *4200 Admiralty Way, 90292,* ☏ *310/301–2000 or 800/529–2525,* ℻ *310/301–6687. 110 rooms, 25 bungalows. Restaurant, bar, in-room data ports, minibars, room service, pool, hot tub, health club, laundry service and dry cleaning, concierge, business services, meeting rooms, airport shuttle, free parking. AE, DC, MC, V.*

Santa Monica

$$$$ ⊡ **Hotel Oceana.** Thoughtful touches at this all-suite hotel across the street from the ocean include desks large enough for a computer (which the concierge will bring upon request) and refrigerators stocked with goodies such as Wolfgang Puck frozen dinners. For those who prefer the real thing, the hotel provides room service via the nearby Wolfgang Puck Café. Some suites have ocean-view patios. ⊠ *849 Ocean Ave., 90403,* ☏ *310/393–0486 or 800/777–0758,* ℻ *310/458–1182. 63 suites. Bar, in-room data ports, kitchenettes, no-smoking rooms, refrigerators, room service, pool, spa, exercise room, coin laundry, laundry service and dry cleaning, concierge, business services, parking (fee). Continental breakfast. AE, D, DC, MC, V.*

$$$$ ⊡ **Loews Santa Monica Beach Hotel.** Proximity to the beach is the selling point of the Loews: the sand's just outside the door. Most of the airy, attractive rooms have spectacular views of the Pacific Ocean; some have balconies. ⊠ *1700 Ocean Ave., 90401,* ☏ *310/458–6700 or 800/ 235–6397,* ℻ *310/458–6761. 350 rooms, 24 suites. 2 restaurants, café, bar, in-room data ports, minibars, no-smoking floors, room service, indoor-outdoor pool, beauty salon, hot tub, massage, sauna, spa, steam room, health club, beach, windsurfing, baby-sitting, children's programs (ages 5–12), laundry service and dry cleaning, concierge, business services, meeting rooms, travel services, car rental, parking (fee). AE, D, DC, MC, V.*

$$$$ ⊡ **Miramar Sheraton.** Central for shopping and sunning, the Miramar nevertheless feels like a secluded island resort. There's a bit of Old Hollywood to this 1889 mansion, particularly in the lavish bungalows stocked with huge whirlpool tubs, stereos with CD, and bathroom speakers. Rooms in the 10-story tower have spectacular ocean views. There are also residential-style rooms in the historic wing. ⊠ *101 Wilshire Blvd., 90401,* ☏ *310/576–7777 or 800/325–3535,* ℻ *310/458–7912. 213 rooms, 55 suites, 32 bungalows. 2 restaurants, bar, in-room data ports, in-room safes, minibars, no-smoking floors, pool, beauty salon, spa, health club, piano, laundry service and dry cleaning, concierge,*

business services, meeting rooms, travel services, car rental, parking (fee). AE, D, DC, MC, V.

$$$$ 🏨 **Shutters On The Beach.** You might forget you're only minutes from
★ the city if you stay at Los Angeles's only hotel sitting directly on the
sand. Spacious rooms have sliding shutter doors that open onto tiny
balconies, and deep whirlpool tubs from which, in some rooms, you
can gaze at the ocean. Suites have fireplaces, and all accommodations
have beds with luxurious Frette linens. ⊠ 1 Pico Blvd., 90405, ☎ 310/
458–0030 or 800/334–9000, ℻ 310/458–4589. 186 rooms, 12 suites.
2 restaurants, bar, lobby lounge, in-room data ports, in-room safes,
minibars, no-smoking floors, room service, in-room VCRs, pool, hot
tub, sauna, spa, health club, beach, mountain bikes, laundry service
and dry cleaning, concierge, business services, meeting rooms, parking (fee). AE, D, DC, MC, V.

$$$–$$$$ 🏨 **Belle Blue Inn.** This small hotel with lots of charm has a prime lo-
★ cation along the Pacific and well within walking distance to many of
Santa Monica's shopping areas and eateries. Unusually large rooms feel
like quarters at a private guest house, with light colors and hardwood
floors completing the beachy feel. ⊠ 1670 Ocean Ave., 90401, ☎ 310/
393–2363 or 800/537–8483, ℻ 310/393–1063. 13 rooms, 13 suites.
Beach access, free parking. AE, DC, MC, V.

$$–$$$$ 🏨 **Best Western Ocean View Hotel.** You'll find attractive low-season
rates here considering the prime real estate across the street from the
ocean. During the summer high season, however, the highest ocean-
view room rate seems high, particularly for a hotel without a pool. Guest
rooms are small but comfortable. ⊠ 1447 Ocean Ave., 90401, ☎ 310/
458–4888 or 800/542–4888, ℻ 310/458–0848. 72 rooms. In-room
data ports, no-smoking floors, some refrigerators, laundry service and
dry cleaning, business services, parking (fee). AE, D, DC, MC, V.

$$–$$$ 🏨 **Hotel Carmel.** Price and location are the calling cards of this hotel.
Basic rooms are spacious, and some have ocean views. You can stroll
to the Third Street Promenade or to the beach. Make reservations months
ahead. ⊠ 201 Broadway, 90401, ☎ 310/451–2469 or 800/445–8695,
℻ 310/393–4180. 96 rooms, 8 suites. In-room data ports, laundry service and dry cleaning, parking (fee). Continental breakfast. AE, D, DC,
MC, V.

Venice

$ 🏨 **Marina Pacific Hotel & Suites.** The price is right at this hotel that
faces the Pacific and one of the world's most vibrant boardwalks. It's
nestled among Venice's art galleries, shops, and offbeat restaurants. The
marina is nearby, giving guests easy access to ocean swimming and roller
skating along the strand. ⊠ 1697 Pacific Ave. 90291, ☎ 310/399–7770
or 800/421–8151, ℻ 310/452–5479. 57 rooms, 35 suites. Restaurant,
laundry service, meeting rooms, free parking. AE, D, DC, MC, V.

Westwood

$$$–$$$$ 🏨 **Westwood Marquis Hotel and Gardens.** This all-suite hotel near UCLA
is a favorite of corporate and entertainment types. One-, two-, or
three-bedroom suites have living rooms and dining areas; many have
views of Bel-Air, Beverly Hills, or Century City. The lovely pool is a
nice place to relax. Complimentary transportation takes you within a
5-mi radius. ⊠ 930 Hilgard Ave., 90024, ☎ 310/208–8765 or 800/421–
2317, ℻ 310/824–0355. 258 suites. 2 restaurants, bar, café, in-room
data ports, minibars, no-smoking floors, refrigerators, room service, 2
pools, exercise room, laundry service and dry cleaning, concierge, busi-
ness services, meeting rooms, parking (fee). AE, D, DC, MC, V.

$$–$$$ 🏨 **Hotel Del Capri.** Despite the modest motel sign, you're just as likely
to see Jaguars in the parking lot here as Jettas. Midway between Bev-
erly Hills and Westwood, the small hotel has traditional rooms, many

with kitchenettes. Most rooms have whirlpool tubs, and VCRs can be rented for a small fee. Ask about discounts for those in the arts. ⊠ *10587 Wilshire Blvd., 90024,* ☎ *310/474–3511 or 800/444–6835,* FAX *310/470– 9999. 34 rooms, 45 suites. No-smoking rooms, some refrigerators, pool, coin laundry, laundry service and dry cleaning, business services, meeting rooms, free parking. Continental breakfast. AE, DC, MC, V.*

West Los Angeles

$$ 🏨 **Century Wilshire Hotel.** This homey, English-style hotel, within walking distance of UCLA and Westwood Village, is a favorite among the European crowd. Quaint reminders of the hotel's former life as an apartment building abound. There are milk-delivery traps at the bottom of the room doors, and many of the small, well-kept rooms have full kitchens. ⊠ *10776 Wilshire Blvd., 90024,* ☎ *310/474–4506 or 800/421–7223,* FAX *310/474–2535. 41 rooms, 58 suites. Breakfast room, no-smoking rooms, pool, baby-sitting, laundry service and dry cleaning, travel services, car rental, free parking. Continental breakfast. AE, D, DC, MC, V.*

$ 🏨 **Best Western Royal Palace Inn & Suites.** Low prices and convenient facilities make this Best Western a good deal. Contemporary rooms have microwaves and coffeemakers and Continental breakfast is provided daily. ⊠ *2528 S. Sepulveda Blvd. 90064,* ☎ *310/477–9066 or 800/ 251–3888,* FAX *310/478–4133. 23 rooms, 32 suites. Refrigerators, pool, hot tub, sauna, exercise room, billiards, coin laundry, meeting room, free parking. Continental breakfast. AE, D, DC, MC, V.*

San Fernando Valley

Burbank

$$$–$$$$ 🏨 **Anabelle Hotel.** This classic hotel has traditionally furnished rooms and amenities such as bathrobes and room service. Those doing studio business will like the convenient location: a straight-shot mile from NBC and 3 mi from Warner Bros. ⊠ *2011 W. Olive Ave., Burbank 91506,* ☎ *818/845–7800 or 800/782–4373,* FAX *818/845–0054. 47 rooms, 6 suites. Restaurant, lobby lounge, in-room data ports, no-smoking rooms, refrigerators, room service, pool, exercise room, coin laundry, laundry service and dry cleaning, airport shuttle (Burbank), free parking. AE, DC, MC, V.*

$$$ 🏨 **Hilton Burbank Airport & Convention Center.** Across the street from the Burbank Airport, this contemporary Hilton is geared toward business travelers. Guest rooms have coffeemakers, irons and boards, hair dryers, and in-room movies. Ask for a room with a mountain view. ⊠ *2500 Hollywood Way, 91505,* ☎ *818/843–6000 or 800/468–3576,* FAX *818/842–9720. 486 rooms, 77 suites. Restaurant, bar, in-room data ports, no-smoking floors, room service, 2 pools, outdoor hot tub, sauna, 2 exercise rooms, coin laundry, laundry service and dry cleaning, concierge, convention center, airport shuttle, parking (fee). AE, D, DC, MC, V.*

North Hollywood

$$$ 🏨 **Beverly Garland's Holiday Inn Universal Studios.** There's a country-club atmosphere to this lodgelike hotel in two separate buildings near Universal Studios. Rooms have distressed furniture and muted color schemes. Private balconies and patios overlook the Sierra Madre and Santa Monica mountains. The hotel is next to the Hollywood Freeway, which can be noisy. Ask for a room facing Vineland Avenue. ⊠ *4222 Vineland Ave., 91602,* ☎ *818/980–8000 or 800/238–3759,* FAX *818/766–5230. 246 rooms, 12 suites. Restaurant, bar, no-smoking rooms, room service, pool, sauna, tennis, laundry service and dry* *cleaning, meeting rooms, airport shuttle (Burbank), free parking. AE, D, DC, MC, V.*

Sherman Oaks

$$$ ⊞ **Radisson Valley Center Hotel Los Angeles.** Standard accommodations here are bolstered by the hotel's excellent service. The hotel is conveniently located at the intersection of I–405 and Highway 101, in the Sherman Oaks business district, close to the Fashion Square Mall and excellent restaurants. ⊠ *15433 Ventura Blvd., 91403, ☎ 818/981–5400 or 800/333–3333, FAX 818/981–3175. 188 rooms, 12 suites. Restaurant, bar, in-room data ports, no-smoking floors, room service, pool, beauty salon, hot tub, exercise room, laundry service and dry cleaning, concierge, business services, meeting rooms, car rental, parking (fee). Continental breakfast. AE, D, DC, MC, V.*

Studio City

$$$ ⊞ **Sportsmen's Lodge.** A low-slung, English country–style structure, this hotel is surrounded by waterfalls, a swan-filled lagoon, and a gazebo. The pool area and lush garden make you forget you're near a city. Although service may not be everything you've dreamed of, the accommodations are comfortable and convenient. ⊠ *12825 Ventura Blvd., 91604, ☎ 818/769–4700 or 800/821–8511, FAX 213/877–3898. 191 rooms. 3 restaurants, bar, some in-room data ports, no-smoking floors, room service, pool, barbershop, beauty salon, hot tub, exercise room, coin laundry, laundry service and dry cleaning, travel services, airport shuttle, car rental, free parking. AE, D, DC, MC, V.*

Universal City

$$$$ ⊞ **Sheraton Universal.** With a bit of glitz and lots of comforts, the Sheraton Universal has become a favorite among those visiting Universal Studios. Literally on the back lot of the famed movie studio and theme park, the hotel has warm, stylish rooms with floor-to-ceiling windows from which to gaze at some remarkable Hollywood views. Complimentary transportation takes you to Universal Studios, but you could just as easily walk. ⊠ *333 Universal Terrace Pkwy., 91608, ☎ 818/980–1212 or 800/325–3535, FAX 818/509–4980. 442 rooms, 25 suites. 2 restaurants, bar, in-room data ports, in-room safes, minibars, no-smoking floors, room service, pool, hot tub, exercise room, laundry service and dry cleaning, concierge, business services, meeting rooms, car rental, parking (fee). AE, D, DC, MC, V.*

San Gabriel Valley

Pasadena

$$$$ ⊞ **Ritz-Carlton Huntington Hotel.** The main building of this 1906 land-
★   mark hotel is a Mediterranean-style structure that blends in seamlessly with the lavish houses of the surrounding San Marino neighborhood. Past the intimate lobby and the central courtyard, a wood-paneled grand lounge has a sweeping view of Los Angeles in the distance. Traditionally styled guest rooms are handsome, if a bit small for the high price. The Grill, the more formal of the two dining rooms, is rated among the top restaurants in the world. ⊠ *1401 S. Oak Knoll Ave., 91106, ☎ 626/568–3900 or 800/241–3333, FAX 626/585–1842. 387 rooms, 31 suites. 2 restaurants, bar, in-room data ports, in-room safes, minibars, no-smoking buildings, room service, in-room VCRs, pool, beauty salon, hot tub, mineral baths, spa, tennis court, health club, baby-sitting, laundry service and dry cleaning, concierge, business services, meeting rooms, travel services, car rental, parking (fee). AE, D, DC, MC, V.*

NIGHTLIFE AND THE ARTS

Revised and
updated by
Lina Lecaro

Most bars, clubs, and bistros in this fast-paced city have a shelf life shorter than the miniskirts on Melrose. Hollywood, the locus of L.A. nightlife, is without question the place to start your search. You can't help but stumble into a happening joint if you cruise the streets long enough. L.A. is one of the best cities in the country in which to catch soon-to-be-famous rock bands or check out jazz, blues, and classical acts. Culture vultures will find plenty going on in this hustling, bustling city, from ballet to film to theater.

For the most complete listing of weekly events, consult the current issue of *Los Angeles* magazine. The Calendar section of the *Los Angeles Times* also lists a wide survey of arts events, as do the more alternative publications, the *L.A. Weekly* and the *New Times Los Angeles* (both free). For a telephone report on current music, theater, dance, film, and special events, plus a discount ticket source, call 213/688–2787. Most tickets can be purchased by phone (with a credit card) from **Ticketmaster** (☎ 213/365–3500), **TeleCharge** (☎ 800/762–7666), **Good Time Tickets** (☎ 323/464–7383), **Tickets L.A.** (☎ 323/660–8587), or **Murray's Tickets** (☎ 323/234–0123). Half-price tickets to many shows are available at **Times Tix** (✉ 8500 Beverly Blvd., ☎ 310/659–3678), on the 7th floor of Beverly Center. Tickets must be purchased in person, cash only, and availability is never guaranteed.

The Arts

Call the **Arts Line** (☎ 213/688–2787) for information about cultural events.

Concerts

MAJOR CONCERT HALLS

Part of the Los Angeles Music Center and—with the Hollywood Bowl—the center of L.A.'s classical music scene, the 3,200-seat **Dorothy Chandler Pavilion** (✉ 135 N. Grand Ave., ☎ 213/972–7211) is the home of the Los Angeles Philharmonic. The L.A. Opera presents classics from September through June.

In Griffith Park, the open-air auditorium known as the **Greek Theater** (✉ 2700 N. Vermont Ave., ☎ 323/665–1927), presents big-name performers in its mainly pop-rock-jazz schedule from June through October.

Ever since it opened in 1920, in a park surrounded by mountains, trees, and gardens, the **Hollywood Bowl** (✉ 2301 Highland Ave., ☎ 323/850–2000 or 323/851–3588) has been one of the world's largest and most atmospheric outdoor amphitheaters. Its season runs from early July through mid-September. The L.A. Philharmonic spends its summer season here. There are performances daily except Monday (and some Sundays); the program ranges from jazz to pop to classical. Concert goers usually arrive early, bringing or buying picnic suppers. There are plenty of picnic tables, and box-seat subscribers can reserve a table right in their own box. Restaurant dining is available on the grounds (☎ 323/850–2000 or 323/851–3588); reserve ahead. Be sure to bring a sweater—it gets chilly here in the evening. You might also bring or rent a cushion, as the seats are made of wood. A convenient way to enjoy the Hollywood Bowl experience without the hassle of parking is to take one of the Park-and-Ride buses, which leave from various locations around town; call the Bowl for information.

The **Shrine Auditorium** (✉ 665 W. Jefferson Blvd., ☎ 213/749–5123)
was built in 1926 as Al Malaikah Temple. Touring companies from
all over the world appear in this one-of-a-kind, 6,200-seat theater, as
do higher-profile televised awards shows such as the American Music
Awards and the Grammys. The Los Angeles Opera Theatre and a
broad spectrum of other musical performers comes to the **Wilshire Ebell
Theater** (✉ 4401 W. 8th St., ☎ 323/939–1128), erected in 1924. The
Wiltern Theater (✉ 3790 Wilshire Blvd., ☎ 213/380–5005 or 213/388–
1400), a green terra-cotta, Art Deco masterpiece built in 1930 is home
to the Los Angeles Opera Theater and a venue for pop, rock, jazz, and
dance performances.

Dance

Cal State L.A.'s Dance Department (✉ 5151 State University Dr., ☎
323/343–5124) presents several prominent dance events each year—
including the Dance Fair in March and Dance Kaleidoscope in July—
at Luckman Theater. **Shrine Auditorium** (✉ 665 W. Jefferson Blvd., ☎
213/749–5123) hosts touring dance companies, such as the Kirov, the
Bolshoi, and the American Ballet Theater. **UCLA Center for the Arts** (✉
405 N. Hilgard Ave., ☎ 310/825–2101) welcomes visiting companies,
such as Martha Graham, Paul Taylor, and the Hubbard Street Dance
Company.

Film

ART HOUSES

The 14-screen **Cineplex** (✉ Beverly Center, 8522 Beverly Blvd., 8th floor,
West Hollywood, ☎ 310/652–7760) shows foreign films as well as first-
run features. The multiscreen **Los Feliz Theater** (✉ 1822 N. Vermont
Ave., Los Feliz, ☎ 323/664–2169) features hip, indie flicks of the moment. **Melnitz Hall** (✉ 405 Hilgard Ave., Westwood, ☎ 310/825–
2345) is UCLA's main film theater; here you'll find the old, the avant-
garde, and the neglected. Film festivals, Hollywood classics, documentaries, and notable foreign films are the fare at the **New Beverly
Cinema** (✉ 7165 Beverly Blvd., West L.A., ☎ 323/938–4038). **Nuart**
(✉ 11272 Santa Monica Blvd., West L.A., ☎ 310/478–6379) is the
best-kept of L.A.'s revival houses. The **American Cinematèque Independent Film Series** (✉ 6712 Hollywood Blvd., Hollywood, ☎ 323/
466–3456) screens rare vintage and current independent films in its
outlandish Egyptian Theater. New films by independent filmmakers and
foreign films are the usual fare at the **Royal Theatre** (✉ 11523 Santa
Monica Blvd., Santa Monica, ☎ 310/478–1041). Rare 16mm film noir
clips are screened from Thursday through Sunday at **Tales** (✉ 667 S.
La Brea Ave., Mid-Wilshire, ☎ 323/933–2640), an unusual espresso
bar and bookstore that's a must for old-movie buffs.

MOVIE PALACES

Mann's Chinese Theater (✉ 6925 Hollywood Blvd., Hollywood, ☎
323/464–8111) is perhaps the world's best-known theater, with gala
premieres and three movie screens. The futuristic, geodesic **Pacific Cin-
erama Dome** (✉ 6360 Sunset Blvd., Hollywood, ☎ 323/466–3401)
was the first theater in the United States designed specifically for Cin-
erama. The gigantic screen and multitrack sound system create an unparalleled cinematic experience. Across the street from Mann's Chinese
Theater is the Art Deco **Pacific's El Capitan** (✉ 6838 Hollywood Blvd.,
Hollywood, ☎ 323/467–7674), where first-run features and Disney
animation debuts. At the intersection of Hollywood and Sunset boulevards, the 70-year-old **Vista Theater** (✉ 4473 Sunset Dr., Los Feliz, ☎
323/660–6639) was once Bard's Hollywood Theater, where both moving pictures and vaudeville played.

Television

Audiences Unlimited (✉ 100 Universal City Plaza, Bldg. 153, Universal City, 91608, ☎ 8l8/506–0043) helps fill seats for television programs (and sometimes theater events). There's no charge, but tickets are distributed on a first-come, first-served basis. Shows that may be taping or filming include *Frasier, Third Rock from the Sun,* and *The Drew Carey Show.* Tickets can be picked up at Fox Television Center (✉ 5746 Sunset Blvd., Van Ness Ave. entrance), open weekdays from 8:30 to 6. You must be 16 or older to attend a taping. For a schedule, send a self-addressed, stamped envelope to Audiences Unlimited a few weeks prior to your visit.

Theater

MAJOR THEATERS

Geffen Playhouse (✉ 10886 Le Conte Ave., Westwood, ☎ 310/208–6500 or 310/208–5454), an acoustically superior, 498-seat theater showcases new plays in the summer—primarily musicals and comedies. The 1,038-seat **James A. Doolittle Theatre** (✉ 1615 N. Vine St., Hollywood, ☎ 323/462–6666; 213/365–3500 Ticketmaster) presents new plays, dramas, comedies, and musicals year-round.

In addition to theater performances, lectures, and children's programs, free summer concerts and performances take place at the **John Anson Ford Amphitheater** (✉ 2580 Cahuenga Blvd. E, Hollywood, ☎ 323/461–3673), an outdoor venue in the Hollywood Hills.

There are three theaters in the big downtown complex known as **Music Center** (✉ 135 N. Grand Ave., ☎ 213/972–7211): The **Ahmanson The-atre** presents both classics and new plays; the 3,200-seat **Dorothy Chandler Pavilion** (☞ *above*) shows a smattering of plays in between performances of the L.A. Philharmonic, L.A. Master Chorale, and L.A. Opera; and the 760-seat **Mark Taper Forum** (☎ 213/972–7211) presents new works that often go on to Broadway, such as *Angels in America* and *Master Class.*

Pantages (✉ 6233 Hollywood Blvd., Hollywood, ☎ 323/468–1700; 213/365–3500 Ticketmaster) is a splendid example of high-style Hollywood Art Deco, offering large-scale Broadway musicals such as *Phantom of the Opera.* The **Shubert Theater** (✉ 2020 Avenue of the Stars, Century City, ☎ 310/201–1500) hosts major theatrical productions like *Rent* and *Ragtime.* The 1,900-seat, Art Deco **Wilshire The-ater** (✉ 8440 Wilshire Blvd., Beverly Hills, ☎ 323/468–1716; 323/468–1799; 213/365–3500 Ticketmaster) presents Broadway musicals and occasional concerts.

SMALLER THEATERS

The founders of **Actor's Gang Theater** (✉ 6209 Santa Monica Blvd., Hollywood, ☎ 213/465–0566) include film star Tim Robbins. At the **Bob Baker Marionette Theater** (✉ 1345 W. 1st St., at Glendale Blvd., Downtown, ☎ 213/250–9995) kids sit on a carpeted floor and get a close-up view of the intricate puppets. Shows take place Tuesday through Friday at 10:30 AM, and weekends at 2:30. Reservations are required. Musicals, revivals, and avant-garde improv pieces are performed at the **Cast Theater** (✉ 804 N. El Centro, Hollywood, ☎ 323/462–0265). Excellent original musicals and new dramas are the specialties at the **Coast Playhouse** (✉ 8325 Santa Monica Blvd., West Hollywood, ☎ 323/650–8507).

East West Players (✉ 120 Judge John Aiso St., Little Tokyo, ☎ 213/625–7000) is a well-respected small theater company dedicated to the Asian-American voice. The **Fountain Theater** (✉ 5060 Fountain Ave., Hollywood, ☎ 323/663–1525) is a venue for original American dramas and flamenco dance concerts. The community-oriented **Japan America Theater** (⊠ 244 S. San Pedro St., Downtown, ☎ 213/680–3700) hosts local theater groups, dance troupes, and the L.A. Chamber Orchestra, plus numerous children's theater groups.

The **Morgan-Wixon Theatre** (⊠ 2627 Pico Blvd., Santa Monica, ☎ 310/828–7519) presents varied children's fare. The **Santa Monica Playhouse** (⊠ 1211 4th St., Santa Monica, ☎ 310/394–9779) is worth visiting for its cozy atmosphere, as well as its high-quality comedies, dramas, and children's programs. Many highly inventive productions have been hosted in the 99-seat **Skylight Theater** (⊠ 1816½ N. Vermont Ave., Los Feliz, ☎ 323/666–2202). Angelenos crowd into the **Theatre/Theater** (⊠ 1715 Cahuenga Blvd., Hollywood, ☎ 323/871–0210) to view original works by local authors and international playwrights.

Nightlife

Despite the high energy level of the L.A. nightlife crowd, don't expect to be partying until dawn—this is still an early-to-bed city. Liquor laws require that bars stop serving alcohol at 2 AM. By this time, with the exception of a few after-hours venues and coffeehouses, most clubs have closed for the night.

Nighttime diversions on the Sunset Strip run the gamut from comedy clubs and hard-rock spots to cocktail lounges and restaurants with piano bars. There's a good mix of nightlife in the Mid-Wilshire area, which encompasses the area west of the Harbor Freeway (I–110), east of La Cienega Boulevard, south of Beverly Boulevard, and north of the Santa Monica (I–10) Freeway. Local beer bars abound in Westwood. Downtown Los Angeles has a small contingent of artsy performance spaces and galleries, and a handful of clubs and movie palaces. Some of Los Angeles's best jazz clubs, discos, and comedy clubs are scattered throughout the San Fernando and San Gabriel valleys. In West Hollywood, Santa Monica Boulevard is the heart of the gay-and-lesbian club and coffeehouse scene.

Bars

BEL-AIR AND BEVERLY HILLS

There's serene musical entertainment every night (either a pianist or a vocalist) at the romantically secluded **Hotel Bel-Air** (⊠ 701 Stone Canyon Rd., Bel-Air, ☎ 310/472–1211). A quaint bar with an immense wine selection, **La Scala** (⊠ 410 N. Canon Dr., Beverly Hills, ☎ 310/275–0579) fills with celebrities nightly. Behind the oak bar and brass rail at **R. J.'s** (⊠ 252 N. Beverly Dr., Beverly Hills, ☎ 310/274–3474 or 310/274–7427) are 800 bottles stacked to the ceiling. Plush sofas and high tables set the atmosphere at the elegant piano bar of the **Regent Beverly Wilshire** (⊠ 9500 Wilshire Blvd., Beverly Hills, ☎ 310/275–5200).

CENTURY CITY

Harper's Bar and Grill (⊠ 2040 Ave. of the Stars, ☎ 310/553–1855) is a central place to meet friends for cocktails before a show at the Shubert Theater.

DOWNTOWN

Downtown's loft-dwelling elite frequent **Boyd Street** (⊠ 410 Boyd St., ☎ 213/617–2491), a downtown bar-restaurant with a streamlined '80s motif. In the Biltmore Hotel, the sleek **Grand Avenue Sports Bar** (⊠ 506 S. Grand Ave., ☎ 213/612–1595) serves pricey drinks late into the night. Atop the 32-story Transamerica Building, **The Tower** (⊠ 1150 S. Olive St., ☎ 213/746–1554) is an elegant cocktail bar and restaurant with an unbeatable view.

For a pick-me-up margarita, stop by the kitschy **El Coyote** (✉ 7312 Beverly Blvd., ☎ 323/939–7766) restaurant-bar. The old Hollywood restaurant and watering hole **Formosa** (✉ 7156 Santa Monica Blvd., West Hollywood, ☎ 323/850–9050) was featured in *L.A. Confidential,* though it's long been a favorite of both hipsters and old-timers. Don't be fooled by the seedy, minimall location of **Lava Lounge** (✉ 1533 N. La Brea Ave., ☎ 323/876–6612): inside you'll find groovy, neo-tiki decor (bamboo and faux-lava walls) and wall-to-wall scenesters.

Film-studio moguls and movie extras flock to **Musso and Franks** (✉ 6667 Hollywood Blvd., ☎ 323/467–5123). The unmarked, nondescript exterior of **3 Of Clubs** (✉ 1123 N. Vine St., ☎ 323/462–1123) hardly prepares you for the plush environment within. This dressy bar is a prime location to scout out L.A.'s young and restless. Meet at **Yamashiro's** (✉ 1999 N. Sycamore Ave., ☎ 323/466–5125) for cocktails at sunset on the terrace.

An unassuming '40s-style bar that's been rediscovered by a happening '90s crowd thanks to the film *Swingers,* **Dresden Room** (✉ 1760 N. Vermont Ave., Los Feliz, ☎ 323/665–4294) started the whole lounge revival. The Chinese motif at the trendy **Good Luck Bar** (✉ 1514 Hillhurst Ave., Los Feliz, ☎ 323/666–3524) makes you feel as if you just stepped onto the set of a Hong Kong action movie. Locals gobble bratwurst and knock back steins at **Lowenbrau Keller** (✉ 3211 Beverly Blvd., Silver Lake, ☎ 213/382–5723). **Tiki Ti** (✉ 4427 W. Sunset Blvd., Silver Lake, ☎ 323/669–9381) serves some of the city's best tropical rum drinks in an intimately cozy simulated Tahitian hut.

Ex-cinematographer Burt Hixon collected tropical-drink recipes on his South Seas forays. Here, at **The Warehouse** (✉ 4499 Admiralty Way, ☎ 310/823–5451), he whips up a sinfully rich piña colada.

Both après-work business types and Gen-Xers frequent **HMS Bounty** (✉ 3357 Wilshire Blvd., ☎ 213/385–7275), an elegant old watering hole in the historic Gaylord apartment building. One of L.A.'s most frequented Irish pubs, **Tom Bergin's** (✉ 840 S. Fairfax Ave., ☎ 323/936–7151) is plastered with Day-Glo shamrocks bearing the names of the masses of regular patrons who have passed through its door.

Beckham Place (✉ 77 W. Walnut St., ☎ 626/796–3399), a fancy "Olde English" pub, is known for its huge drinks and free roast-beef sandwiches at Happy Hour. With two pool tables, a nautical motif, and very reasonable prices, **The Colorado Bar** (✉ 2640 E. Colorado Blvd., ☎ 626/449–3485) is a divey refuge for art students, Gen-Xers, and aging barflies. In Pasadena's Old Town, **Market City Cafe** (✉ 33 S. Fair Oaks Ave., ☎ 626/568–0203) draws a crowd at lunchtime and in the early evening. A young collegiate crowd frequents **Q's** (✉ 99 E. Colorado Blvd., ☎ 626/405–9777), an upscale bar and pool hall in the middle of Old Town. With brass fixtures, an oversize fireplace, and a marble-topped bar, the **Ritz-Carlton Huntington Hotel** (✉ 1401 S. Oak Knoll Ave., ☎ 626/568–3900) is a genteel setting for nighttime drinks.

Residuals (✉ 11042 Ventura Blvd., Studio City, ☎ 818/761–8301) is so named because actors who present a residual check for less than a dollar can trade it for a free drink. The lounge at **Sportsmen's Lodge** (✉ 12833 Ventura Blvd., Sherman Oaks, ☎ 818/984–0202) has a tranquil setting with brooks and swan-filled ponds. **Sagebrush Cantina** (✉ 23527 Calabasas Rd., Calabasas, ☎ 818/222–6062), an indoor-outdoor saloon next to a Mexican restaurant, is the Valley's version of the Via Veneto café scene. Motorcycle hippies mix comfortably with computer moguls and showbiz folk, including a platoon of stunt people.

SANTA MONICA
Chez Jay (✉ 1657 Ocean Ave., ☎ 310/395–1741), a shack of a saloon near Santa Monica Pier, has endured for more than 30 years. Named for its 360-degree bar, **The Circle** (✉ 2926 Main St., ☎ 310/392–4898) is the Santa Monica dive to survive Main Street's trendy makeover. **Gotham Hall** (✉ 1431 3rd St. Promenade, ☎ 310/394–8865) is designed like something off the set of Batman. From motorcycles to carriages, something old has been glued or nailed to every square inch of **Oar House** (✉ 2941 Main St., ☎ 310/396–4725). **The Room S.M.** (✉ 1323 Santa Monica Blvd., ☎ 310/458–0707), is a dark and friendly everyman's hangout with stiff drinks and relaxing sounds ranging from Aretha Franklin to Frank Sinatra.

VENICE
Abstract art decorates the walls of **Hal's Bar & Grill** (✉ Abbott Kinney Blvd., ☎ 310/396–3105), a regular haunt of local well-to-do professionals. The very upscale **Rebecca's** (✉ 2025 Pacific Ave., ☎ 310/306–6266) is worth checking out for the outrageous and playful Frank Gehry interior alone.

WEST HOLLYWOOD
A mahogany bar and art nouveau mirrors make **Barefoot** (✉ 8722 W. 3rd St., ☎ 310/276–6223) a swanky place to drink expertly mixed martinis. A hetero bastion in an ultragay neighborhood, **J. Sloane's** (✉ 8623 Melrose Ave., ☎ 310/659–0250) is a sawdust-on-the-floor, football-on-the-tube, frat house kind-of-place. The circular bar at **Le Dôme** (✉ 8720 W. Sunset Blvd., ☎ 310/659–6919) draws the likes of Rod Stewart and Richard Gere. Patrons (many celebrities) must either have a Mondrian room key, screen credit, or a model's body to enter **Sky Bar** (✉ 8440 Sunset Blvd., ☎ 323/650–8999), the poolside bar at the Hotel Mondrian. The bar at the **Sunset Marquis** (✉ 1200 N. Alta Loma Rd., ☎ 310/657–1333) is a convenient watering hole for many visiting celebs.

WESTSIDE
There's a good assortment of Mexican beers at **Acapulco** (✉ 1109 Glendon Ave., Westwood, ☎ 310/208–3884), a convivial Mexican restaurant and bar that's big with the college crowd. "Cocktail Nation" has finally arrived on the Westside. **Liquid Kitty** (✉ 11780 W. Pico Blvd., West L.A., ☎ 310/473–3707) has a hip clientele and cool (occasionally live) music.

Cabaret, Performance, and Variety
The Cinegrill (✉ Clarion Hotel Hollywood Roosevelt, 7000 Hollywood Blvd., Hollywood, ☎ 323/466–7000) is well worth a visit, if not to hear top-tier jazz performers, then just to admire all the Hollywood artifacts lining the lobby of the landmark hotel that houses the club.

Glaxa Studios (✉ 3707 Sunset Blvd., Silver Lake, ☎ 323/663–5295) is a bohemian café-arts venue presenting music, poetry, and performance with an emphasis on the literate, the avant-garde, and the offbeat. Hours and cover (for shows only) vary.

Westside Bohemians come to **Highways** (✉ 1651 18th St., Santa Monica, ☎ 310/453–1755) to hear and see avant-garde spoken-word and performance artists. Reservations are recommended.

Drag queens strut their stuff at **Luna Park** (✉ 665 Robertson Blvd., West Hollywood, ☎ 310/652–0611), an eclectic venue serving fine American cuisine and showcasing an international mix of music.

At **Queen Mary** (✉ 12449 Ventura Blvd., Studio City, ☎ 818/506–5619), female impersonators vamp it up as Diana Ross and Barbra Streisand.

Coffeehouses

Amid the murals and neon of Downtown's artsy loft district, **Bloom's General Store** (✉ 714 3rd St., Downtown, ☎ 213/687–6571) sells cigars, candy, and videos, and is also connected to a soul-food restaurant and art gallery.

Half tiki, half sci-fi, with hand-painted tabletops, tiny **Cacao** (✉ 11609 Santa Monica Blvd., West L.A., ☎ 310/473–7283) is an aesthetic gem.

At **Cyber Java** (✉ 1029 Abbott Kinney Blvd., Venice, ☎ 310/581–1300) you can log onto the Internet while enjoying coffee and snacks. There's also a cozy patio with a tiny sculpture garden.

Valley poets, artists, and hipsters hang out at **Eagle's** (✉ 5231 Lankershim Blvd., North Hollywood, ☎ 818/760–4212), a laid-back café with occasional live music and spoken-word readings.

Highland Grounds (✉ 742 Highland Ave., Hollywood, ☎ 323/466–1507) is one of L.A.'s oldest coffeehouses and features a tasty breakfast and lunch menu, nightly live entertainment, and one of the best cups of coffee in the city.

Comedy

Los Angeles's premier comedy showcase, **Comedy Store** (✉ 8433 Sunset Blvd., West Hollywood, ☎ 323/656–6225) has been going strong for more than a decade.

Groundlings Theatre (✉ 7307 Melrose Ave., Hollywood, ☎ 323/934–9700) is considered a breeding ground for Saturday Night Live performers, with original skits, music, and improv.

Dance Clubs

A dressed-to-impress crowd frequents **The Century Club** (✉ 10131 Constellation Blvd., Century City, ☎ 310/553–6000), where dance grooves range from Latin to hip hop to electronic.

The **Coconut Club** (☎ 310/274–7777) has big-band music, DJs, and a classic supper-club menu. The club takes over the Grand Ballroom of the Beverly Hilton Hotel on Friday and Saturday nights.

If you're nostalgic for the 1960s, stop by the tourist-friendly **Crush Bar** (✉ 1743 Cahuenga Ave., Hollywood, ☎ 323/463–9017), open Friday and Saturday evenings.

Garden of Eden (✉ 7080 Hollywood Blvd., Hollywood, ☎ 323/465–3336) is an exotically decorated space hosting four nights of dancing for a trendy, youngish crowd. Music leans toward electronic and funk.

Big on the swing era, the high-energy **Moonlight Tango Cafe** (✉ 13730 Ventura Blvd., Sherman Oaks, ☎ 818/788–2000) gets moving in the wee hours, when a conga line inevitably takes shape on the dance floor.

Every night of the week, a different promoter takes over **The Ruby** (✉ 7070 Hollywood Blvd., Hollywood, ☎ 323/467–7070), a popular three-room dance venue on the ground floor of a Hollywood office building. You might find anything from house and hip-hop to trance and techno, plus occasional live music.

Gay and Lesbian Clubs

Gays and straights mingle easily at **Akbar** (✉ 4356 Sunset Blvd., Silver Lake, ☎ 323/665–6810), a dark, cozy watering hole with one of the best jukeboxes in town.

Axis (✉ 652 N. La Peer Dr., West Hollywood, ☎ 310/659–0471) and **Love Lounge** (✉ 657 N. Robertson Blvd., West Hollywood, ☎ 310/659–0472) share one site but have different entrances and schedule different events. Some nights are for lesbians and some are for gay men, and there are frequent theme parties. The music runs the gamut: new wave, hi-NRG, tribal, rock, and Latin house. Both clubs are open Wednesday through Saturday; Love Lounge also opens its doors for Tuesday-night drag shows.

An ethnically mixed gay and straight crowd flocks to **Circus Disco and Arena** (✉ 6655 Santa Monica Blvd., Hollywood, ☎ 323/462–1291), two huge side-by-side discos with techno and rock music, as well as a full bar and patio.

With live music and drag shows, **Club 7969** (✉ 7969 Santa Monica Blvd., West Hollywood, ☎ 323/654–0280) caters to gay, lesbian, and mixed crowds depending on the night. There's a large dance floor and a super sound system.

L.A.'s more glamorous lesbians show up for parties sponsored by **Girl Bar** (☎ 323/460–2531). Call the information line for locations.

Jewel's Catch One (✉ 4067 W. Pico Blvd., Mid-Wilshire, ☎ 323/734–8849) attracts gays and straights, blacks and whites, and everyone in between. Its late hours—3 AM weeknights, 4 AM weekends—and its underground vibe make it a prime destination for the serious dance fanatic.

A friendly, publike lesbian bar with a pool table, **The Palms** (✉ 8572 Santa Monica Blvd., West Hollywood, ☎ 310/652–6188) has DJ dancing six nights a week and live bands on Sunday. One-dollar drinks draw a crowd Wednesday nights, and Sunday's beer bust is a lively affair.

Rage (✉ 8911 Santa Monica Blvd., West Hollywood, ☎ 310/652–7055) is a longtime favorite of the "gym boy" set.

Jazz

The eclectic entertainment at the **Atlas Bar & Grill** (✉ 3760 Wilshire Blvd., Mid-Wilshire, ☎ 213/380–8400) includes torch singers as well as Latin and jazz bands. The snazzy supper club is inside the historic Wiltern building.

Crowds squeeze in like sardines to hear powerhouse jazz and blues at the tiny **Baked Potato** (✉ 3787 Cahuenga Blvd. W, North Hollywood, ☎ 818/980–1615).

Big-name acts and innovators play at **Catalina Bar and Grill** (✉ 1640 N. Cahuenga Blvd., Hollywood, ☎ 323/466–2210), a top Hollywood jazz spot. Continental cuisine is served.

You can hear exceptional jazz performers at **Club Brasserie** (✉ Wyndham Bel Age Hotel, 1020 N. San Vicente Blvd., West Hollywood, ☎ 213/854–1111) from Thursday through Saturday. Impressionist paintings on the wall compete with the expansive city view. Best of all, there's no cover.

In the Crenshaw District's Leimert Park arts enclave, **Fifth Street Dick's Coffee Company** (✉ 3347½ W. 43rd Pl., Crenshaw District, ☎ 323/296–3970) is a great spot for coffee and traditional jazz.

Come to **Jazz Bakery** (✉ 3221 Hutchison, Culver City, ☎ 310/271–9039), inside the former Helms Bakery, for coffee, desserts, and a nice selection of world-class jazz. The $17–$20 admission (no credit cards) includes refreshments.

Owned by comedy star Marla Gibbs of *The Jeffersons* and 227, **Marla's Memory Lane Supper Club** (✉ 2323 W. Martin Luther King Jr. Blvd., Crenshaw District, ☎ 323/294–8430) pops with blues, jazz, and easy listening.

Live Music

Alligator Lounge (✉ 3321 Pico Blvd., Santa Monica, ☎ 310/449–1844) books various musical acts and serves Cajun cuisine Friday through Monday.

One of L.A.'s oldest rock dives, **Al's Bar** (✉ 305 S. Hewitt St., downtown, ☎ 213/625–9703) is still going strong.

Blue Saloon (✉ 4657 Lankershim Blvd., North Hollywood, ☎ 818/766–4644) is a friendly club with rock and roll, blues, country, and rockabilly.

At **Coconut Teaszer** (✉ 8117 Sunset Blvd., West Hollywood, ☎ 323/654–4773) you can dance to live music—raw rock at its best—for lively fun.

The Conga Room (✉ 5364 Sunset Blvd., Mid-Wilshire, ☎ 323/938–1696) owned by Latin stars Jennifer Lopez, Jimmy Smits, and Paul Rodriguez (among others), features top-notch Latin and salsa groups.

Put on the ritz at **The Derby** (✉ 4500 Los Feliz Blvd., Los Feliz, ☎ 323/663–8979), a spacious, elegant club. There's live music nightly—swing, jazz, surf, and rock.

Dark, cozy, mysterious—everything a rock-and-roll dive should be—**Dragonfly** (✉ 6510 Santa Monica Blvd., Hollywood, ☎ 323/466–6111) plays an edgy mix of live and dance music.

The gloriously restored Art Deco **El Rey Theater** (✉ 5515 Wilshire Blvd., Mid-Wilshire, ☎ 323/936–4790) showcases top-name bands, and the city's premier goth club, known as Coven 13.

Chandeliers and hubcaps decorate **The Garage** (✉ 4519 Santa Monica Blvd., Silver Lake, ☎ 213/683–3447), a rock dive with some of the best in local and alternative bands.

At the longtime music industry hangout known as **Ghengis Cohen Cantina** (✉ 740 N. Fairfax Ave., Hollywood, ☎ 323/653–0640), you can hear up-and-coming talent in a refreshingly mellow format. A plus is the restaurant's updated Chinese cuisine.

Dan Aykroyd and Jim Belushi own the **House of Blues** (✉ 8430 Sunset Blvd., West Hollywood, ☎ 323/650–1451), home to popular jazz, rock, and blues performers. Past players have included Etta James, Lou Rawls, Joe Cocker, Cheap Trick, and the Commodores. Some shows are presented cabaret style, including dinner. Every Sunday there's a gospel brunch.

Jack's Sugar Shack (✉ 1707 N. Vine St., Hollywood, ☎ 323/466–7005) features big-name alternative rock, surf, blues, rockabilly, Cajun, and country performers in cartoony, Polynesian-style surroundings.

The Key Club (✉ 9039 Sunset Blvd., West Hollywood, ☎ 310/786–1712) is a flashy, multitier Sunset Strip rock club featuring current bands before 11PM and dancing with guest DJs afterward.

Rap music and reggae are served up along with fine Jamaican food at **Kingston 12** (✉ 814 Broadway, Santa Monica, ☎ 310/451–4423), open Thursday through Sunday.

Vintage LPs hang from the ceiling at **The Mint** (✉ 6010 Pico Blvd., Mid-Wilshire, ☎ 323/954–9630), which features some of the best in blues, jazz, rockabilly, and bluegrass.

McCabe's Guitar Shop (✉ 3101 Pico Blvd., Santa Monica, ☎ 310/828–4497; 310/828–4403 concert information) is retro central. Folk, acoustic rock, bluegrass, and soul concerts are featured on weekend nights, with coffee, herbal tea, and homemade sweets served during intermission.

One of the best concert venues in town, **The Palace** (✉ 1735 N. Vine St., Hollywood, ☎ 323/462–3000) is a multilevel Art Deco building with lively entertainment, a fabulous sound system, laser lights, two dance floors, four bars, and a full bar and dining room on the top-level patio. Patrons dress to kill. Friday nights are packed.

The Roxy (✉ 9009 Sunset Blvd., West Hollywood, ☎ 310/276–2222) is a Sunset Strip fixture, featuring local and touring alternative, country, blues, and rockabilly bands.

The hottest bands of tomorrow perform at **Spaceland** (✉ 1717 Silver Lake Blvd., Silver Lake, ☎ 213/413–4442), a tacky former disco that's ground zero of the burgeoning, ultratrendy Silver Lake scene.

The Troubadour (✉ 9081 Santa Monica Blvd., West Hollywood, ☎ 310/276–6168) has weathered the test of time since the '60s, when it first opened as a folk-music club. Once a focal point for the now-moribund L.A. Heavy Metal scene, the old-timer has caught its second wind by booking hot alternative rock acts.

Actor Johnny Depp is part-owner of the **Viper Room** (✉ 8852 Sunset Blvd., West Hollywood, ☎ 310/358–1880), a hangout for musicians and movie stars. There's a different theme every night.

Whiskey A Go Go (✉ 8901 Sunset Blvd., West Hollywood, ☎ 310/652–4202) is the most famous rock-and-roll club on the Sunset Strip, with up-and-coming alternative, very hard rock, and punk bands.

OUTDOOR ACTIVITIES AND SPORTS

Updated by
Lina Lecaro

Transplants to Los Angeles know they've become acclimated when they go to a movie on a beautiful, sunny day. For those who can't stay inside on a beautiful day—of which there are many—Los Angeles supports a range of activities for every level of athlete.

Beaches

From downtown, the easiest way to hit the coast is by taking the Santa Monica Freeway (I–10) due west. Once you reach the end of the freeway, I–10 runs into the famous Highway 1, better known as the Pacific Coast Highway, or PCH. Other routes from the downtown area include Pico, Olympic, Santa Monica, Sunset, and Wilshire boulevards. The MTA bus line runs every 20 minutes to and from the beaches along each of these streets.

Los Angeles County beaches (and state beaches operated by the county) have lifeguards. Public parking is usually available, though fees can often be as much as $8; in some areas, it's possible to find free street parking. Generally, the northernmost beaches are best for surfing, hiking, and fishing, and the wider and sandier southern beaches are better for tanning and relaxing. Almost all are great for swimming, but beware:

pollution in Santa Monica Bay sometimes approaches dangerous levels, particularly after storms. Call 310/457–9701 for beach conditions in Malibu, 310/578–0478 for Santa Monica, and 310/379–8471 for Manhattan and Redondo beaches.

The following beaches are listed in north–south order:

Leo Carrillo State Beach. On the very edge of Ventura County, this narrow beach is better for exploring than swimming or sunning. On your own or with a ranger, venture down at low tide to examine the tide pools among the rocks. Sequit Point creates secret coves, sea tunnels, and boulders on which you can perch and fish. The crowd is a mix of hippie canyon residents, semiprofessional surfers, and families. Picturesque campgrounds are set back from the beach. ⊠ *35000 PCH, Malibu,* ☎ *818/880–0350; 800/444–7275 (camping reservations). Parking, lifeguard (summer), rest rooms, showers, fire pits.*

Robert H. Meyer Memorial State Beach. Perhaps Malibu's most beautiful coastal area, this state beach is made up of three separate minibeaches: El Pescador, La Piedra, and El Matador—all with the same spectacular view. Scramble down the steps to the rocky coves where nude sunbathing appears unofficially to be sanctioned. The huge, craggy boulders that make this beach private and lovely also make it somewhat dangerous. Watch the tide and don't get trapped between the boulders when it comes in. ⊠ *32350, 32700, and 32900 PCH, Malibu,* ☎ *310/457–1324. Parking, rest rooms.*

Zuma Beach Park. Two miles of white sand usually littered with tanning teenagers, this is a great beach for swimming and socializing. It's also a favorite of families with small children. The surf is rough but inconsistent. ⊠ *30050 PCH, Malibu,* ☎ *310/457–9891. Parking, lifeguard (year-round), rest rooms, showers, food concessions, playground, volleyball.*

Malibu Lagoon State Beach/Surfrider Beach. Steady, 3- to 5-ft waves make this beach, just north of the dilapidated and currently closed Malibu Pier, a popular surfing location. Water runoff from Malibu Canyon forms a natural lagoon that's a sanctuary for 250 species of birds. Unfortunately, the lagoon is often polluted and algae-filled, and the debris tends to spill over into the surf. Take a walk on one of the nature trails. ⊠ *23200 block of PCH, Malibu,* ☎ *818/880–0350. Parking, lifeguard (year-round), rest rooms, picnicking, visitor center.*

Topanga State Beach. The beginning of miles of solid public beach, Topanga has good surfing at the western end. Close to a busy section of the PCH and rather narrow, Topanga is not as serene as other beaches, with hordes of teenagers zipping over Topanga Canyon Boulevard from the Valley. ⊠ *18700 block of PCH, Malibu,* ☎ *310/394–3266. Parking, lifeguard (year-round), rest rooms, food concessions.*

Will Rogers State Beach. A dozen volleyball nets, gymnastics equipment, and playground equipment for kids make this clean, sandy, 3-mi beach a favorite of families and young singles. It also has a sizable gay and lesbian following. Surf is even and gentle, but the beach has the dubious distinction of being one of the area's most polluted—beware after a storm. ⊠ *15100 PCH, 2 mi north of Santa Monica pier, Pacific Palisades,* ☎ *310/394–3266. Parking, lifeguard, rest rooms.*

Santa Monica State Beach. The first beach you'll hit after the Santa Monica Freeway (I–10) runs into the PCH, this is one of L.A.'s best-known beaches. Be prepared for a mob scene on summer weekends, when parking becomes an expensive ordeal. The pier has an amusement park with a roller coaster, Ferris wheel, antique carousel, arcade, and food. For a memorable view, climb up the stairway over the PCH to Palisades Park. ⊠ *1642 Promenade, PCH at California Incline, Santa Monica,* ☎ *310/394–3266. Parking, lifeguard (year-round), rest rooms, showers.*

Venice City Beach. The surf and sands of Venice are fine, but the main attraction here is the boardwalk scene: a mile and a half of T-shirt shops, pizza stands, and tattoo parlors. Wander along the path and watch as musicians, magicians, fortune tellers, and dancers compete for your spare change. Around 18th Avenue, look for "Muscle Beach," a big cage where bodybuilders pump iron. For bike rentals try **Venice Pier Bike Shop** (⊠ 21 Washington Blvd., ☎ 310/301–4011); Skatey's (⊠ 102 Washington Blvd., ☎ 310/823–7971) is a good bet for skates. Whatever you do, hold on to your wallet. ⊠ *West of Pacific Ave., Venice,* ☎ *310/ 394–3266. Parking, rest rooms, showers, food concessions.*

Manhattan Beach. Rows of volleyball courts on a wide, sandy strip make this the preferred destination of muscled, tanned young professionals. ⊠ *West of Strand, Manhattan Beach,* ☎ *310/372–2166. Parking, lifeguard (year-round), rest rooms, showers, food concessions, volleyball.*

Redondo Beach. The Redondo Beach Pier marks the starting point of this wide, sandy, busy beach, which continues south for about 2 mi along a heavily developed shoreline community. There are plenty of activities here. Restaurants and shops flourish along the pier; excursion boats and privately owned craft depart from launching ramps; and a reef formed by a sunken ship creates prime fishing and snorkeling conditions. Rock and jazz concerts take place at the pier every summer. ⊠ *Foot of Torrance Blvd., Redondo Beach,* ☎ *310/372–2166. Parking, lifeguard, rest rooms, showers, food concessions, volleyball.*

Parks and Playgrounds

Parks

In the **Angeles National Forest,** above Pasadena, you can drive to the top of Mt. Wilson for spectacular views of Los Angeles. The **Chilao Visitors Center,** 13 mi north of Mt. Wilson, has exhibits about the forest, and trails for nature walks. The main park in the city of Los Angeles is the 4,000-acre **Griffith Park. Hancock Park** is most notable for the La Brea Tar Pits. Outdoorspeople cherish the canyons, waterfalls, lake, and more than 30 mi of trails at **Malibu Creek State Park,** at the summit of Malibu Canyon Road. **Will Rogers State Historic Park** in Pacific Palisades is ideal for children, with broad lawns, walking trails, and even polo games on weekends in summer (☎ 310/454–8212 for polo information).

Playgrounds

Santa Monica's **Douglas Park** (⊠ 1155 Chelsea Ave.) has a busy playground at the quiet end of the park, with street parking only a few feet away. **Griffith Park** (⊠ 4730 Crystal Springs Dr.) has a small playground near the carousel; there's another one across from the Griffith Park Boulevard entrance, and one more just past the golf course.

Participant Sports

For information about tennis courts, hiking and biking trails, and anything else sports-related, call the **City of Los Angeles Department of Recreation and Parks** (☎ 213/485–5515) or the **Los Angeles County Department of Parks and Recreation** (☎ 213/738–2961).

Bicycling

The most famous bike path in the city, and definitely the most beautiful, can be found on the **Pacific Ocean beach,** a 22-mi route from Temescal Canyon down to Redondo Beach. You can park at one of the many lots along the Pacific Coast Highway (be prepared to pay a high fee). Rent bikes at one of many rental shops along the bike path, including **Rental on the Beach** (✉ 2100 Ocean Front Walk, ☎ 310/ 821–9338), which has several additional locations on the path in Venice. Rates are $5 per hour or $18 a day.

Griffith Park (✉ Entrance at Crystal Springs Dr. and Los Feliz Blvd.) has a tree-lined bike route with several options ranging from easy to hard. Stay on Crystal Springs Drive for an easier ride; turn left up Griffith Park Drive for a tougher ride that rewards with great views. For rentals, try **The Annex** (✉ 3157 Los Feliz Blvd., ☎ 323/661–6665), which charges $15 per day. Call the **M.T.A.** (☎ 213/626–4455) for a map of more bike trails.

Many of the areas mentioned in Hiking (☞ *below*) have mountain-biking paths.

Fishing

Shore fishing and surf casting are excellent on many of the beaches, and pier fishing is popular because no license is necessary to fish off public piers. The **Santa Monica** and **Redondo Beach piers** all have nearby bait-and-tackle shops.

Marina del Rey Sport Fishing (✉ Dock 52, Fiji Way, ☎ 310/822–3625) runs excursions for $20 per half day. **Redondo Sport Fishing Company** (✉ 233 N. Harbor Dr., ☎ 310/372–2111) has half-day charters starting at $22 per person. Both companies run whale-watching excursions in winter.

Golf

The Parks and Recreation Department lists seven public 18-hole courses in Los Angeles. **Rancho Park Golf Course** (✉ 10460 W. Pico Blvd., ☎ 310/838–7373) is one of the most heavily played links in the country. It's a beautifully designed course, but the towering pines present an obstacle for those who slice or hook.

Several good public courses are in the San Fernando Valley. The **Balboa and Encino Golf courses** (✉ 16821 Burbank Blvd., Encino, ☎ 818/ 995–1170) are next to each other. The **Woodley Lakes Golf Course** (✉ 6331 Woodley Ave., Van Nuys, ☎ 818/780–6886) is flat as a board and has hardly any trees.

Griffith Park has two splendid 18-hole courses along with a challenging nine-hole course. **Harding Municipal Golf Course** and **Wilson Municipal Golf Course** (✉ 4730 Crystal Springs Dr. for both, ☎ 323/663– 2555) are about 1½ mi inside the park entrance at Riverside Drive and Los Feliz Boulevard. Bridle paths surround the outer fairways, and the San Gabriel Mountains make a scenic background. The nine-hole **Roosevelt Municipal Golf Course** (✉ 2650 N. Vermont Ave., ☎ 323/ 665–2011) can be reached through the park's Vermont Avenue entrance.

Health Clubs

There are dozens of health-club chains in the city; some sell daily or weekly memberships. Two that do are **Bodies in Motion** (✉ 1950 Century Park E, Century City, ☎ 310/836–8000), with a full range of aerobics classes including aerobic boxing and kickboxing classes, and **24 Hour Fitness** (☎ 800/204–2400), with eight locations in the Los Angeles area. Both charge $10 per day.

Hiking

For further information on hiking locations and scheduled outings in Los Angeles, contact the **Sierra Club** (⊠ 3345 Wilshire Blvd., Suite 508, Los Angeles, 90010, ☎ 213/387–4287).

One of the best places to begin is **Griffith Park**; pick up a map from the ranger station (⊠ 4730 Crystal Springs Dr.). Many of the paths in the park are not shaded and can be quite steep. A short hike from Canyon Drive, at the southwest end of the park, takes you to **Bronson Caves.** Begin at the Observatory for a 3-mi round-trip hike to the top of **Mt. Hollywood.**

Head west for ocean views. At **Topanga State Park,** miles of trails wind high in the Santa Monica Mountains. **Will Rogers Historic State Park,** off Sunset Boulevard in Pacific Palisades, abuts Topanga and has a splendid nature trail. A 2-mi hike from Rogers' historic home takes you to a stunning ocean-to-downtown view atop Inspiration Point.

Horseback Riding

More than 50 mi of beautiful bridle trails are open to the public in the Griffith Park area. **Griffith Park Horse Rentals** (⊠ 480 Riverside Dr., Burbank, ☎ 818/840–8401) has a going rate of $15 per hour plus a $15 deposit. **Sunset Ranch** (⊠ 3400 Beachwood Dr., Hollywood, ☎ 323/469–5450) rents horses for $15 an hour, plus a $10 deposit. A Friday-evening package includes a trail ride over the hill into Burbank, where riders tie up their horses and dine at a Mexican restaurant. The package costs $35, not including the cost of dinner.

Ice-Skating

Rinks are all over the city, generally charging about $8 for admission and skate rental. In the Valley, there's the **Pickwick Ice Center** (⊠ 1001 Riverside Dr., Burbank, ☎ 818/846–0032). In Pasadena, try the **Ice Skating Center** (⊠ 310 E. Green St., ☎ 626/578–0800).

In-Line and Roller-Skating

For Rollerblades, **Boardwalk Skates** (⊠ 201½ Ocean Front Walk, Venice, ☎ 310/450–6634) charges $4 an hour or $12 for the day. **Skatey's** (⊠ 102 Washington St., Venice, ☎ 310/823–7971) charges $5 per hour or $10 per day.

For indoor skating, head to **Moonlight Rollerway** (⊠ 5110 San Fernando Rd., Glendale, ☎ 818/241–3630) or **Skateland** (⊠ 18140 Parthenia St., Northridge, ☎ 818/885–1491).

Jogging

San Vicente Boulevard in Santa Monica has a wide grassy median that splits the street for several picturesque miles. The reservoir at **Lake Hollywood,** just east of Cahuenga Boulevard in the Hollywood Hills, is encircled by a 3.3-mi asphalt path with a view of the Hollywood sign. Within hilly **Griffith Park** are thousands of acres' worth of hilly paths and challenging terrain. **Circle Drive,** around the perimeter of UCLA in Westwood, provides a 2½-mi run through academia.

Tennis

Many public parks have courts that require an hourly fee. **Lincoln Park** (⊠ Lincoln and Wilshire Blvds., Santa Monica), **Westwood Park** (⊠ 1375 Veteran Ave., West L.A.), and **Barrington Recreational Center** (⊠ Barrington Ave., south of Sunset Blvd., West L.A.) all have well-maintained courts with lights. **Griffith Park** has three sets of lighted courts: one at Riverside Drive just south of Los Feliz Boulevard; another just north of the Vermont Avenue entrance; and one more at the intersection of Griffith Park and Crystal Springs drives. For a complete list of public courts, contact the **L.A. Department of Recreation and Parks** (☎ 213/485–5515).

Water Sports

BOATING AND KAYAKING
Action Water Sports (✉ 4144 Lincoln Blvd., Marina del Rey, ☎ 310/306–9539) rents single kayaks for $35 and doubles for $45 per day.

SCUBA DIVING AND SNORKELING
Diving and snorkeling off Leo Carrillo State Beach, Catalina, and the Channel Islands is considered some of the best on the Pacific coast. Dive shops, such as **New England Divers** (✉ 2936 Clark Ave., Long Beach, ☎ 562/421–8939) and **Dive 'n Surf** (✉ 504 N. Broadway, Redondo Beach, ☎ 310/372–8423), will provide you with everything you need for your voyage beneath the waves.

SURFING
The surfing culture began here, and the area remains a destination for pros from afar. Novices should beware of rocks and undertows. **Malibu Ocean Sports** (✉ 22935 PCH, Malibu, ☎ 310/456–6302) gives lessons and rents boards.

Spectator Sports

The best source for tickets to all sporting events is **Ticketmaster** (☎ 714/740–2000). Some of the major sports venues in the area are **Edison Field** (✉ 2000 Gene Autry Way, ☎ 714/940–2000), the **Great Western Forum** (✉ 3900 W. Manchester Blvd., Inglewood, ☎ 310/419–3100), **L.A. Sports Arena** (☎ 213/748–6136), **L.A. Memorial Coliseum** (✉ 3939 S. Figueroa St., Downtown, ☎ 213/748–6131), and **Arrowhead Pond** (✉ 2695 E. Katella Ave., Anaheim, ☎ 714/704–2500).

The newest addition to the sports scene is the 20,000-seat **STAPLES Center** (✉ S. Figueroa St., Downtown, ☎ 213/624–3100). Set to open in October 1999, it will be the new home of basketball's Los Angeles Lakers and Clippers, hockey's L.A. Kings, and an arena football league.

Baseball
The **Dodgers** take on their National League rivals at the ever-popular Dodger Stadium (✉ 1000 Elysian Park Ave., exit off I–110, Pasadena Fwy., ☎ 323/224–1400 for ticket information). The **Anaheim Angels** continue their quest for the pennant in the American League West. For Angels ticket information, contact **Anaheim Stadium** (☎ 714/663–9000).

Basketball
COLLEGE
The **University of Southern California** (☎ 213/740–8480) plays at the L.A. Sports Arena, and the Bruins of the **University of California at Los Angeles** (☎ 310/825–8699 athletic department; 310/825–2101 tickets) play at Pauley Pavilion on the UCLA campus.

PROFESSIONAL
The **Los Angeles Lakers** (☎ 310/419–3182) have enjoyed great seasons since the arrivals of superstar center Shaquille O'Neal and young star Kobe Bryant in 1996. Their home court is the Forum. L.A.'s "other" team, the much-maligned **Clippers** (☎ 213/748–8000) make their home at the L.A. Sports Arena; tickets are generally cheaper and easier to get than those for Lakers games. New to the pro basketball scene in L.A. is the all-female **Los Angeles Sparks** (☎ 310/419–3193).

Football
The **Anaheim Piranhas** (☎ 714/475–0838) play arena football at the Arrowhead Pond in Anaheim. The **USC Trojans'** (☎ 213/740–8480)

home turf is the Coliseum. The **UCLA Bruins** (☎ 310/825–2101) pack 'em in at the Rose Bowl. Each season, the two teams face off in one of college football's oldest and most exciting rivalries.

Golf

The hot golf ticket in town each February is the PGA **Nissan Open** (☎ 800/752–6736), played in Pacific Palisades at the Riviera Country Club.

Hockey

The National Hockey League's **L.A. Kings** (☎ 310/673–6003) put their show on ice at the Forum. Disney's **Mighty Ducks** (☎ 714/704–2701) push the puck at the Pond in Anaheim.

Horse Racing

Santa Anita Race Track (✉ Huntington Dr. and Colorado Pl., Arcadia, ☎ 626/574–7223) is the dominant site for exciting Thoroughbred racing. Expect the best racing in the world, from October to mid-November and late December to late April.

The track next to the Forum in Inglewood in **Hollywood Park** (✉ Century Blvd. and Prairie Ave., ☎ 310/419–1500) is another favorite racing venue. It's open from early November to late December and from late April to mid-July.

Soccer

The **Los Angeles Galaxy** (☎ 888/657–5425) professional soccer team plays from March through September at the Rose Bowl in Pasadena.

Tennis

The **Infiniti Open** (☎ 310/824–1010), held in summer at UCLA, attracts top-seeded pro players.

SHOPPING

Updated by
Cynthia
LaFavre Yorks

Most stores in Los Angeles are open from 10 to 6, although many stay open until 9 or later, particularly those on Melrose Avenue and in Santa Monica. Melrose shops, on the whole, don't get moving until 11 AM. In most areas, shops are open for at least a few hours on Sunday. Most stores accept credit cards; traveler's checks are also often allowed with proper identification. Check the *Los Angeles Times* or *L.A. Weekly* for sales.

Beverly Hills Vicinity

Shopping in Beverly Hills centers mainly around the three-block stretch of **Rodeo Drive,** between Santa Monica and Wilshire boulevards, and the streets surrounding it.

SHOPPING CENTERS AND MALLS

The **Beverly Center** (✉ 8500 Beverly Blvd., ☎ 310/854–0070), bound by Beverly, La Cienega, and San Vicente boulevards and 3rd Street, covers more than 7 acres and contains some 200 stores. The **Rodeo Collection** (✉ 421 N. Rodeo Dr., ☎ 310/276–9600), between Brighton Way and Santa Monica Boulevard, is one of several European-style shopping enclaves in Beverly Hills. **Two Rodeo Drive** (✉ 2 Rodeo Dr., at Wilshire Blvd., ☎ 310/247–7040), a.k.a. Via Rodeo, is a collection of glossy retail shops housed on a private cobblestone street.

DEPARTMENT STORES

Barneys New York (✉ 9570 Wilshire Blvd., ☎ 310/276–4400) is a favorite among young hipsters who come to look at cutting-edge (and pricey) designer clothing. **Neiman-Marcus** (✉ 9700 Wilshire Blvd., ☎ 310/550–5900) has a spectacular selection of women's fashions and

Finally, a travel companion that doesn't snore on the plane or eat all your peanuts.

MCI WORLDCOM   *WorldPhone®*

123 456 7891 2345
J.D. SMITH

When traveling, your MCI WorldCom Card is the best way to keep in touch. Our operators speak your language, so they'll be able to connect you back home—no matter where your travels take you. Plus, your MCI WorldCom Card is easy to use, and even earns you frequent flyer miles every time you use it. When you add in our great rates, you get something even more valuable: peace-of-mind. So go ahead. Travel the world. MCI WorldCom just brought it a whole lot closer.

You can even sign up today at www.mci.com/worldphone or ask your operator to make a collect call to 1-410-314-2938.

EASY TO CALL WORLDWIDE

1 **Just dial the WorldPhone access number of the country you're calling from.**
2 **Dial or give the operator your MCI WorldCom Card number.**
3 **Dial or give the number you're calling.**

Australia ◆	
To call using OPTUS	1-800-551-111
To call using TELSTRA	1-800-881-100
Bahamas/Bermuda	1-800-888-8000
British Virgin Islands	1-800-888-8000
Costa Rica ◆	0-800-012-2222
Denmark	8001-0022
Norway ◆	800 -19912
India	000-127
For collect access	000-126
United States/Canada	1-800-888-8000

For your complete WorldPhone calling guide, dial the WorldPhone access number for the country you're in and ask the operator for Customer Service. In the U.S. call 1-800-431-5402.

◆ Public phones may require deposit of coin or phone card for dial tone.

EARN FREQUENT FLYER MILES

AmericanAirlines
A*Advantage*®

Continental Airlines
OnePass

▲ Delta Air Lines
SkyMiles·

▬ MILEAGE PLUS.
United Airlines

U·S AIRWAYS
DIVIDEND MILES

MCI WorldCom, its logo and the names of the products referred to herein are proprietary marks of MCI WorldCom, Inc. All airline names and logos are proprietary marks of the respective airlines. All airline program rules and conditions apply.

MCI *WORLDCOM*

Fodor's

Distinctive guides packed with up-to-date expert advice and smart choices for every type of traveler.

Fodor's. For the world of ways you travel.

accessories. **Robinsons-May** (✉ 9900 Wilshire Blvd., ☎ 310/275–5464) has seen better days but is still a reliable source for simple necessities like panty hose or lipstick. **Saks Fifth Avenue** (✉ 9600 Wilshire Blvd., ☎ 310/275–4211) is one of the best accessory, shoe, and fragrance resources in town.

CHILDREN'S CLOTHING

Oilily (✉ 9520 Brighton Way, ☎ 310/859–9145) is filled with wonderfully whimsical clothing and gifts for children, infants, and even their moms. **Tartine et Chocolat** (✉ 316 N. Beverly Dr., ☎ 310/786–7882) features au courant French wearables and accessories for newborns up to kids' size 16.

HOME ACCESSORIES AND GIFTS

Del Mano Gallery (✉ 11981 San Vicente Blvd., Brentwood, ☎ 310/476–8508) houses the work of some of the country's best contemporary artists working in a variety of mediums. **Pratesi** (✉ 9024 Burton Way, ☎ 310/274–7661) is a luxurious linen emporium. **Tesoro** (✉ 401 N. Canon Dr., ☎ 310/273–9890) features unusual dishware and art objects.

JEWELRY

Cartier (✉ 370 N. Rodeo Dr., ☎ 310/275–4272; ✉ 220 N. Rodeo Dr., ☎ 310/275–5155) carries all manner of luxury gifts and jewelry. **Harry Winston** (✉ 371 N. Rodeo Dr., ☎ 310/271–8554) is the preferred destination for many celebrities looking for Oscar-night jewels. **Tiffany & Co.** (✉ 210 N. Rodeo Dr., ☎ 310/273–8880), the famous name in fine jewelry, silver, and more, packages each purchase in a signature blue Tiffany box. **Van Cleef & Arpels** (✉ 300 N. Rodeo Dr., ☎ 310/276–1161) sells extravagant baubles and fine jewelry.

MEN'S FASHIONS

Battaglia (✉ 306 N. Rodeo Dr., ☎ 310/276–7184) features accessories, shoes, and elegant Italian fashions for men who aren't afraid to dress up. **Bernini** (✉ 326 N. Rodeo Dr., ☎ 310/246–1121) specializes in contemporary Italian designer fashions. **Bijan** (✉ 420 N. Rodeo Dr., ☎ 310/273–6544) is a store shrouded in exclusivity and some say pretention; shopping is by appointment only.

WOMEN'S FASHIONS

BCBG Max Azria (✉ 201C N. Rodeo Dr., ☎ 310/278–3263) is the designer line of the moment on the West Coast. The tiny boutique carries hip, affordable sportswear. **Chanel** (✉ 400 N. Rodeo Dr., ☎ 310/278–5500) houses two floors of ultra-elegant fashions and cosmetics. **Harari** (✉ 9646 Brighton Way, ☎ 310/859–1131) is a favorite haunt of shoppers looking for distinctive, forward-looking fashions and accessories that are less about labels than looks. **Prada** (✉ 9521 Brighton Way, ☎ 310/276–8889) is a must for ladies who crave the signature bags, as well as the sleek, postmodern sportswear.

WOMEN'S AND MEN'S FASHIONS

Emporio Armani Boutique (✉ 9533 Brighton Way, ☎ 310/271–7790) houses three levels of this famous Italian designer's architecturally inspired sportswear, as well as elegant home and fashion accessories, and perfumes. **Gianfranco Ferre** (✉ 2 Rodeo Dr., ☎ 310/273–6311) carries high-quality sportswear and dress apparel for men and women. **Gianni Versace** (✉ 421 N. Rodeo Dr., ☎ 310/205–3921), part of the Rodeo Collection, is the resource for the trendsetting Italian designs. **Shauna Stein** (✉ Beverly Center, 8500 Beverly Blvd., ☎ 310/652–5511) is a distinctive destination for female fans of Eurochic. Labels such as Dolce & Gabanna, Moschino, and Jean-Paul Gaultier beckon shoppers more concerned with panache than price. **Traffic** (✉ Beverly Center, 8500 Beverly Blvd., ☎ 310/659–4313), for men, and **Traffic Studio** (✉ Beverly Center, 8500 Beverly Blvd. ☎ 310/659–3438), for women, are adjoining boutiques featuring men's and women's sportswear and dress apparel by such names as Hugo Boss, Donna Karan, and Alexander McQueen.

Century City Area
Century City is L.A.'s errand central, where entertainment executives and industry types do their serious shopping.

SHOPPING MALLS
Century City Shopping Center & Marketplace (✉ 10250 Santa Monica Blvd., ☎ 310/277–3898), set among gleaming, tall office buildings on what used to be Twentieth Century Fox film studios' back lot, is an open-air mall with an excellent roster of shops, including Macy's and Bloomingdale's.

BOOKSTORES
Brentano's (✉ Century City Shopping Center, 10250 Santa Monica Blvd., ☎ 310/785–0204) is the champagne of bookstores. Well-known authors often do book signings here.

TOYS
Allied Model Trains (✉ 4411 S. Sepulveda Blvd., ☎ 310/313–9353) feels like a huge train museum, with dozens of working train sets toot-tooting around the store.

Downtown
SHOPPING CENTERS
The **Citadel Factory Stores** (✉ 5675 East Telegraph Rd., off I–5, Commerce, ☎ 323/888–1220), on the historic landmark site of the former Uniroyal Tire factory, carry the latest in off-price fashions from famous names such as Joan & David, Ann Taylor, and Betsey Johnson.

BOOKSTORES
KOMA Bookstore (✉ 1764 N. Vermont Ave., ☎ 323/665–0956) sells unorthodox magazines and books.

GIFTS
Gonzales Candle Shop (✉ W14 Olvera St., ☎ 213/625–8771), inside the historic Sepulveda House, lets you soak up the colorful atmosphere of Olvera Street. Since 1929 the artisans here have supplied shoppers with everything from novelty candles to gothic and religious candles, both large and small. **Museum of Contemporary Art Store** (✉ MOCA, 250 S. Grand Ave., ☎ 213/621–1710) sells art posters, books, tableware, children's toys, and jewelry by local and international artists.

Melrose Avenue Vicinity
This bohemian shopping street is a great place to pick up everything from inexpensive trinkets and used clothing to pricey Americana antiques. It's had its ups and downs as a retail area, but with the recent opening of the Miu Miu, Liza Bruce, and Betsey Johnson stores, it looks like Melrose is headed for another turnaround.

ANTIQUES
J. F. Chen Antiques (✉ 8414 Melrose Ave., ☎ 323/655–6310) specializes in ancient Asian pieces. **Licorne** (✉ 8432 Melrose Pl., ☎ 323/852–4765) sells fine 17th-century furnishings.

BOOKSTORES AND MUSIC STORES
Aron's Records (✉ 1150 N. Highland Ave., ☎ 323/469–4700) has an excellent selection of vinyl as well as the latest CD releases. **Book Soup**

(✉ 8818 Sunset Blvd., ☎ 310/659–3110), one of L.A.'s most prominent literary bookstores, is a frequent book-signing venue for authors.

FURNITURE AND HOME ACCESSORIES

Freehand (✉ 8413 W. 3rd St., ☎ 323/655–2607) is an aesthetically pleasing gallery showcasing contemporary American crafts, clothing, and jewelry, mostly by California artists. **Golyester** (✉ 136 S. La Brea Ave., ☎ 323/931–1339) sells funky used clothes and home furnishings. **Zipper** (✉ 8316 W. 3rd St., ☎ 323/951–0620) focuses on design trends from the 1930s to the 1990s.

TOYS AND GAMES

Hollywood Magic Shop (✉ 6614 Hollywood Blvd., ☎ 323/464–5610), a Tinseltown institution, sells costumes year-round and has a wide selection of tricks for beginners and experts.

VINTAGE CLOTHING

Wasteland (✉ 7428 Melrose Ave., ☎ 323/653–3028) carries the kind of retro clothing you might see on Winona Ryder and her celeb contemporaries. The store sells new clothing as well, at reasonable prices.

WOMEN'S FASHIONS AND ACCESSORIES

shu uemura (✉ 8606 Melrose Ave., ☎ 800/743-8205) is the makeup emporium choice for celebrity artists and their clients. The store is especially known for their sable Japanese makeup brushes. **Tyler Trafficante** (✉ 7290 Beverly Blvd., ☎ 323/931–9678) carries designer Richard Tyler's exquisitely tailored, albeit pricey, women's sportswear and evening wear.

WOMEN'S AND MEN'S FASHIONS

Maxfield (✉ 8825 Melrose Ave., ☎ 310/274–8800) is the supplier of choice for celebs and costumers responsible for dressing some of the more fashionable shows on television. **Miu Miu** (✉ 8025 Melrose Ave., ☎ 323/651–0073) could change the face of Melrose shopping. Expect nothing less from the most whimsical extension of the Prada line. This 5,000-square-ft store, with large red hanging partitions and red-lined stainless steel cubes, is the second Miu Miu outlet in the country but the only one to sell men's fashions as well as women's. **Swell Store** (✉ 126 N. La Brea Ave., ☎ 323/937–2096) is a vogue place for shoes, plus men's and women's clothing and accessories.

Santa Monica

Less frenetic and status-conscious than Beverly Hills, Santa Monica is an ideal place for a leisurely shopping stroll. On Wednesday, some of the streets in Santa Monica are blocked off for the weekly farmers market, where parking is next to impossible.

SHOPPING CENTERS AND STREETS

3rd Street Promenade is a pedestrian-only street lined with boutiques, movie theaters, clubs, pubs, and restaurants. Mainstream and funky boutiques line **Main Street,** which leads from southern Santa Monica to Venice. **Montana Avenue** is a pedestrian street surrounded by quaint residential cottages and bungalows. Many of the best shops are between 9th and 17th streets. **Santa Monica Place** (✉ Colorado Ave. and 2nd St.) is a three-story enclosed mall with department stores and chains and a few unusual L.A. stores.

GIFTS, TOYS, AND MEMORABILIA

Imagine (✉ 927 Montana Ave., ☎ 310/395–9553) carries custom-designed furniture and bedding as well as a large assortment of European wooden toys and gifts. **Star Wares on Main** (✉ 23 Main St., ☎ 310/399–0224) sells authentic and duplicate costumes from films and memorabilia from Loretta Swit, Liz Taylor, and other celebs.

HOME ACCESSORIES AND FURNITURE
Brenda Cain (⌂ 1211-A Montana Ave., ☎ 310/395–1559) sells antique jewelry and home accessories, but the hot ticket here is the amazing array of Arts and Crafts pottery. **Brenda Himmel Stationery** (⌂ 1126 Montana Ave., ☎ 310/395–2437) is known for its fine stationery, but antiques, frames, photo albums, and books are additional reasons to shop at this boutique.

WOMEN'S FASHIONS AND ACCESSORIES
Moondance Jewelry Gallery (⌂ 1530 Montana Ave., ☎ 310/395–5516) carries the unique jewelry of 70-odd artists. **Weathervane** (⌂ 1209 Montana Ave., ☎ 310/393–5344) has a friendly staff and fine European women's designer collections.

WOMEN'S AND MEN'S FASHIONS
ABS Clothing (⌂ 1533 Montana Ave., ☎ 310/393–8770) sells contemporary sportswear designed in L.A. **A/X Armani Exchange** (⌂ 2940 Main St., ☎ 310/396–8799) markets the coveted Giorgio Armani label to the masses via T-shirts as well as other sportswear for women and men.

San Fernando and San Gabriel Valleys

Ventura Boulevard is the lifeblood of Valley shopping, which is more renowned for shopping malls than any other neighborhood in L.A.

SHOPPING MALLS
Glendale Galleria (⌂ 2148 Central Blvd., Glendale, ☎ 818/240–9481) has a Nordstrom, Macy's, and assorted specialty stores. **Media City Center** (⌂ 201 E. Magnolia Blvd., Burbank, ☎ 818/566–8617) houses a beautiful Macy's as well as Mervyn's and Sears. **The Promenade** (⌂ 6100 Topanga Canyon Blvd., Woodland Hills, ☎ 818/884–7090), at the northern edge of the Valley, has a 24-hour hot line announcing daily bargains. Within the mall are Macy's and a separate Macy's Men's Store.

ANTIQUES, HOME ACCESSORIES, AND GIFTS
Cranberry House (⌂ 12318 Ventura Blvd., Studio City, ☎ 818/506–8945) is an expansive shopping cooperative covering half a city block with 140 kiosks run by L.A.'s leading antiques dealers. **Imagine That!** (⌂ 13335 Ventura Blvd., Sherman Oaks, ☎ 818/784–8215) is a fun-filled emporium of toys, gifts, decorative accessories, and aromatherapy products for adults and children of all ages.

SIDE TRIPS FROM LOS ANGELES

Big Bear and Lake Arrowhead, both two or three hours away in the San Bernardino mountains, are rustic resorts with beautiful lakes, crisp air, and snowy winters. Catalina Island, an hour's boat ride off the coast, is the Greek isle of the West Coast, with crystal blue waters, a gentle climate, and a friendly, small-town feeling. For those curious about California's Spanish heritage, Riverside, an hour southeast of L.A., retains much of its colonial legacy, including the famed Mission Inn and a number of important museums. For approximate costs of dining and lodging establishments, *see* the price charts, *above*.

Lake Arrowhead and Big Bear Lake

Big Bear comes alive in winter with downhill ski and snowboard resorts, cross-country trails, lodges, and an active village. Summer draws crowds to Lake Arrowhead, known for its cool mountain air, trail-threaded woods, and brilliant lake. The Rim of the World Scenic Byway, which connects with Lake Arrowhead and Big Bear Lake, is a magnificent drive.

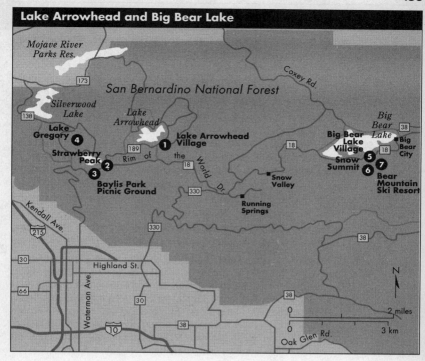

Lake Arrowhead and Big Bear Lake

Numbers in the margin correspond to points of interest on the Lake Arrowhead and Big Bear Lake map.

Lake Arrowhead

90 mi from Los Angeles, I–10 east to I–215 north to Hwy. 30 east (mountain resorts turnoff) to Hwy. 18 (Waterman Ave.), then Hwy. 138 north to Hwy. 173 (Lake Arrowhead turnoff); follow signs from there.

1 **Lake Arrowhead Village** is an alpine community with offices, shops, outlet stores, and eateries that descend the hill to the lake. You can take a scenic 45-minute cruise on the *Arrowhead Queen,* operated daily by LeRoy Sports (☎ 909/336–6992) from the waterfront marina. Tickets are first-come, first-serve and cost $10. Call ahead for departure times. The **Lake Arrowhead Children's Museum** (⊠ lower level of village, ☎ 909/336–1332, above) has plenty to entertain pint-size explorers, including hands-on exhibits, a climbing maze, and a puppet stage.

2 Past the town of Rim Forest, follow Bear Springs Road 2 mi north to the fire lookout tower at **Strawberry Peak.** Brave the steep stairway to the tower, and you'll be treated to a magnificent view and a lesson on fire-spotting by the lookout staff.

3 If you're up for a barbecue in a wooded setting, visit **Baylis Park Picnic Ground,** farther east on Highway 18.

4 **Lake Gregory,** at the ridge of Crestline, was formed by a dam constructed in 1938. Because the water temperature in summer is seldom very cold, this is the best swimming lake in the mountains. It's open in summer only, and there's a nominal charge to swim. Fishing is permitted, there are water slides, and you can rent rowboats at Lake Gregory Village.

Dining and Lodging

$$$ ✕ **Casual Elegance.** The menu changes weekly at this intimate house with a fireplace. The steaks and seafood are first-rate. ⊠ *26848 Hwy. 189, Agua Fria,* ☎ *909/337–8932. AE, D, DC, MC, V.*

$$$–$$$$ ⊡ **Lake Arrowhead Resort.** This lakeside lodge has an Old World feeling reminiscent of the Alps. Guests have access to the attached Village Bay Club and Spa for a $5 daily fee. ⊠ *27984 Hwy. 189, Lake Arrowhead Village, 92352,* ☎ *909/336–1511 or 800/800–6792,* ℻ *909/336–1378. 177 rooms, 4 suites. Restaurant, coffee shop, lobby lounge, pool, health club, beach. AE, D, DC, MC, V.*

$$–$$$ ⊡ **Carriage House Bed & Breakfast.** Down comforters and lake views add to the charm of this New England–style bed-and-breakfast. ⊠ *472 Emerald Dr., Lake Arrowhead Village 92352,* ☎ *909/336–1400 or 800/526–5070,* ℻ *909/336–6092. 3 rooms. AE, MC, V. Full breakfast.*

Big Bear Lake

110 mi from Los Angeles, I–10 east to I–215 north to Hwy. 30 east; Hwy. 330 north to Hwy. 18 east; chains are sometimes needed in winter.

❺ You'll spot an occasional chaletlike building in **Big Bear Lake,** an alpine- and Western-mountain-style town on the lake's south shore. The paddle-wheeler *Big Bear Queen* (☎ 909/866–3218) departs daily from Big Bear Marina, from May through October, for 90-minute scenic tours of the lake; the cost is $9.50. Fishing-boat and equipment rentals are available from several lakeside marinas, including Pine Knot Landing (☎ 909/866–2628). **Big Bear City,** at the east end of the lake, has more restaurants, motels, and a small airport.

❻ Southeast of Big Bear Village is **Snow Summit,** one of the area's top ski resorts. It has an 8,200-ft peak and 31 trails, along with two high-speed quads and nine other lifts. Summit has more advanced runs than nearby ski resorts and usually has the best snow. Trails are open to mountain bikers in summer. ⊠ *880 Summit Blvd., off Big Bear Blvd.,* ☎ *909/866–5766; 888/786–6481 for snow reports.*

❼ **Bear Mountain Ski Resort,** also southeast of Big Bear Lake Village, has 11 chairlifts and 35 trails. Bear Mountain is best for intermediate skiers. On busy winter weekends and holidays, reserve tickets before heading to the mountain. ⊠ *43101 Goldmine Dr., off Moonridge Rd.,* ☎ *909/585–2519, 800/BEARMTN for snow reports.*

Dining and Lodging

$$–$$$ ✕ **The Iron Squirrel.** Hearty French fare such as veal Normandie (veal scallopini sautéed with apples, calvados, and cream) and duck à l'orange (roasted duckling with a Grand Marnier sauce) are two specialties at this country French–style restaurant, but you'll also find a big selection of fresh fish and grilled meats on the menu. ⊠ *646 Pine Knot Blvd., Big Bear Lake,* ☎ *909/866–9121. AE, MC, V.*

$$–$$$ ✕ **Madlon's.** Inside this gingerbread-style cottage you'll be treated to sophisticated home cooking: lamb chops with Gorgonzola butter, cream of jalapeño soup, or perhaps a fillet with béarnaise sauce. Reservations are essential on weekends. ⊠ *829 W. Big Bear Blvd., Big Bear City,* ☎ *909/585–3762. D, MC, V.*

$$$–$$$$ ⊡ **Apples Bed & Breakfast Inn.** Despite its location on a busy road to
★ the ski lifts, the Apples Inn feels remote and peaceful, thanks to the surrounding pine trees. The colorful rooms have working gas fireplaces. ⊠ *42430 Moonridge Rd., Big Bear Lake 92315,* ☎ *909/866–0903. 12 rooms. Hot tubs in 4 rooms. AE, D, MC, V. Full breakfast.*

$$-$$$$ ⊡ **Holiday Inn Big Bear Chateau.** Two minutes from the lake, Big Bear's grandest hotel resembles a mountain château in the European tradition. ⊠ *42200 Moonridge Rd., Big Bear Lake 92315,* ☎ *909/866–6666 or 800/232–7466,* FAX *909/866–8988. 77 rooms, 3 suites. Restaurant, lobby lounge, pool, exercise room. AE, D, DC, MC, V.*

$$-$$$ ⊡ **Northwoods Resort.** Northwoods is a giant log cabin with all the amenities of a resort. The lobby resembles a 1930s hunting lodge, with canoes, antlers, fishing poles, and a grand stone fireplace. Rooms are large but cozy; some have fireplaces and whirlpool tubs. Ski packages are available. ⊠ *40650 Village Dr., Big Bear Lake 92315,* ☎ *909/866–3121 or 800/866–3121,* FAX *909/878–2122. 140 rooms, 8 suites. Restaurant, pool, outdoor hot tub, sauna, exercise room. AE, D, DC, MC, V.*

$-$$$ ⊡ **Robinhood Inn.** Across the street from the Pine Knot Marina, this family-oriented motel has affordable rooms, most with fireplaces and some with whirlpool tubs or minikitchens. All accommodations face a courtyard with an outdoor whirlpool. ⊠ *40797 Lakeview Dr., Big Bear Lake 92315,* ☎ *909/866–4643 or 800/990–9956,* FAX *909/866–4645. 17 rooms, 4 suites. Restaurant, outdoor hot tub. AE, MC, V.*

Lake Arrowhead and Big Bear Lake Essentials

LODGING RESERVATIONS

Most lodgings require a two-night stay on weekends. **Lake Arrowhead Communities Chamber of Commerce** (☞ *below*) has information on camping and lodging. **Big Bear Lake Resort Association** (⊠ Box 1936, Big Bear Lake 92315, ☎ 909/866–7000) will help with lodging arrangements.

VISITOR INFORMATION

Big Bear Chamber of Commerce (⊠ Box 2860, 630 Bartlett Rd., Big Bear Lake 92315, ☎ 909/866–4607). **Lake Arrowhead Communities Chamber of Commerce** (⊠ Box 219, 28200 Hwy. 189, Bldg. F, Suite 290, Lake Arrowhead 92352, ☎ 909/337–3715).

Catalina Island

Just 22 mi across the sea from the L.A. coastline, Catalina has virtually unspoiled mountains, canyons, coves, and beaches. Best of all, it gives you a glimpse of what undeveloped southern California once looked like.

Summer, weekends, and holidays, Catalina crawls with thousands of L.A.-area boaters. Although Catalina is not known for wide, sandy beaches, sunbathing and water sports are big draws. Divers and snorkelers come for the exceptionally clear water surrounding the island. The main town of Avalon is a charming, old-fashioned beach community.

Cruise ships sail into Avalon twice a week and smaller boats shuttle between Avalon and Two Harbors, a small isthmus cove on the island's western end. You can also take bus excursions beyond Avalon. Roads are limited and nonresident vehicles prohibited, so hiking (by permit only) is the only other means of exploring.

In 1975 the Santa Catalina Island Conservancy, a nonprofit foundation, acquired about 86% of the island to help preserve the area's natural resources. These days the conservancy is restoring the rugged interior country with plantings of native grasses and trees. Bus or van tours take you to this interior.

Catalina can be seen in a day, but several inviting hotels make it worth extending your stay for one or more nights. A short itinerary might

Catalina Island

include breakfast along the boardwalk, a tour of the interior, a snorkeling excursion at Casino Point, and dinner in Avalon.

Avalon

1- to 2-hr ferry ride from Long Beach; 15-min helicopter ride from Long Beach or San Pedro.

Avalon, Catalina's only real town, extends from the shore of its natural harbor to the surrounding hillsides. Most activity is centered along the boardwalk of Crescent Avenue, and most sights are easily reached on foot. Private cars are restricted and rental cars aren't allowed, but taxis, trams, and shuttles can take you anywhere you need to go. Bicycles and golf carts can also be rented. Permits for hiking the interior of the island are available free from the Santa Catalina Island Conservancy.

A walk along **Crescent Avenue** is a nice way to begin a tour of the town. Vivid art deco tiles adorn the avenue's fountains and planters. Head to the **Green Pleasure Pier,** at the center of Crescent Avenue. Stand with your back to the harbor and you'll be in a good position to survey the sights. At the top of the hill on your left you'll spot the Inn at Mt. Ada, now a top-of-the-line B&B but once a getaway estate built by William Wrigley, Jr., for his wife. On the pier you'll find the Catalina Island Visitor's Bureau, snack stands, the Harbor Patrol, and scads of squawking seagulls.

On the northwest point of Avalon Bay (looking to your right from Green Pleasure Pier), is the majestic landmark **Casino.** This circular white structure is considered one of the finest examples of Art Deco architecture anywhere. Its Spanish-inspired floors and murals show off brilliant blue and green Catalina tiles. "Casino" is the Italian word for "gathering place" and in this case has nothing to do with gambling. Casino life revolves around the magnificent ballroom: the same big-band dances that made the Casino famous in the 1930s and '40s still take place on holiday weekends. Call 310/510–1520 for tickets to the New Year's Eve dance, a hugely popular event that sells out well in advance. **Daytime tours** (☎ 310/510–8687) of the establishment, lasting about 55 minutes, cost $8.50. You can also visit the **Catalina Island Museum,** in the lower level of the Casino, which investigates 7,000 years of island history; or stop at the **Casino Art Gallery,** which displays works of local artists. First-run movies are screened at the **Avalon Theatre,** noteworthy for its 1929 theater pipe organ. ⊠ *1 Casino Way,* ☎ *310/510–2414 for museum; 310/510–0808 for art gallery; 310/510–0179 for Avalon Theatre.* ☞ *Museum $1.50, art gallery free.* ☉ *Museum Easter–Jan., daily 10:30–4; Jan.–Easter, Fri.–Wed. 10:30–4; art gallery Fri.–Tues. 10:30–4.*

In front of the Casino, snorkelers and divers explore the crystal-clear waters of the **Casino Point Underwater Park,** where moray eels, bat rays, spiny lobsters, and other sea animals cruise around kelp forests and along the sandy bottom. The area is protected from boats and other watercraft. Snorkeling equipment can be rented on and near the pier. **Lover's Cove,** east of the boat landing, is also good for snorkeling.

Two miles south of the bay via Avalon Canyon Road is the **Wrigley Memorial and Botanical Garden,** where you'll find plants native to southern California, including several that grow only on Catalina Island. The Wrigley family commissioned the garden as well as the monument, which has a grand staircase and a Spanish mausoleum inlaid with colorful Catalina tile. Tram service between the memorial and Avalon is available daily between 8 AM and 5 PM during summer, and less regularly in winter. ⊠ *Avalon Canyon Rd.,* ☎ *310/510–2288.* 🎫 *$3.* ☉ *Daily 8–5.*

Walk through the residential hills of Avalon and you'll see interesting architecture like the **Wolfe House,** on Chimes Tower Road, built in 1928 by Rudolf Schindler. Its terraced frame is carefully set into a steep site, affording extraordinary views. The house is a private residence, but you can get a good view of it from the path below and from the street. Across the street the **Zane Grey Estate** (☎ 310/510–0966 or 800/ 378–3256) has been transformed into a rustic hotel. ⊠ *124 Chimes Tower Rd.*

Dining and Lodging

$$–$$$ ✕ **Cafe Prego.** This Italian waterfront restaurant specializes in pasta, seafood, and steak. Reserve ahead, or be prepared for a long wait. ⊠ *603 Crescent Ave.,* ☎ *310/510–1218. AE, D, DC, MC, V.*

$$–$$$ ✕ **Channel House.** A longtime Avalon family owns this restaurant, serv-
★   ing dishes such as Catalina swordfish, coq au vin, and pepper steak with a Continental flair. ⊠ *205 Crescent Ave.,* ☎ *310/510–1617. AE, D, MC, V.*

$$–$$$ ✕ **Rick's Cafe.** On the second floor of the Hotel Vista del Mar, Rick's has a bird's-eye view of the bay. Specialties are local seafood, top sir-loin, and pasta. ⊠ *417 Crescent Ave.,* ☎ *310/510–0333. AE, MC, V. No lunch.*

$$$$ 🛏 **Inn on Mt. Ada.** Occupying the onetime Wrigley mansion, the is-land's most exclusive hotel has all the comforts of a millionaire's home at millionaire's prices. All meals, beverages, snacks, and use of a golf cart are complimentary. The six bedrooms are traditional and elegant. The hilltop view of the Pacific is spectacular. ⊠ *398 Wrigley Rd., 90704,* ☎ *310/510–2030 or 800/608–7669,* 𝖥𝖠𝖷 *310/510–2237. 6 rooms. MC, V. FAP.*

$$$–$$$$ 🛏 **Pavilion Lodge.** Across the street from the beach, this popular motel has simple, spacious rooms. There's a large, grassy courtyard in the center of the complex. ⊠ *513 Crescent Ave., 90704,* ☎ *800/851–0217. 73 rooms. AE, D, DC, MC, V. CP.*

$$–$$$$ 🛏 **Hotel Metropole and Market Place.** This romantic hotel could eas-ily be in the heart of New Orleans' French Quarter. Some guest rooms have balconies overlooking a flower-filled courtyard of restaurants and shops; others have ocean views. ⊠ *205 Crescent Ave., 90704,* ☎ *310/ 510–1884 or 800/541–8528. 42 rooms, 6 suites. AE, MC, V. CP.*

$$–$$$ 🛏 **Hotel Vista del Mar.** Contemporary rooms full of rattan furniture and greenery open onto a skylighted atrium. Some rooms have fire-places, whirlpool tubs, and wet bars. Two larger rooms have ocean views. ⊠ *417 Crescent Ave., 90704,* ☎ *310/510–1452 or 800/601–3836,* 𝖥𝖠𝖷 *310/510–2917. 15 rooms. AE, D, MC, V. CP.*

Nightlife

Warm summer afternoons bring loads of party goers to Catalina's many happy-hour bars, where festivities continue late into the night. **El Galleon** (⊠ 411 Crescent Ave., ☎ 310/510–1188) has microbrews and karaoke. At **Luau Larry's** (⊠ 509 Crescent Ave., ☎ 310/510–1919), you can drink your cocktail with an oyster shooter while wearing a calypso hat.

Two Harbors

45- to 60-min ferry ride (summer only) or 90-min bus ride from Avalon; 3-hr ferry ride (summer only) from Los Angeles.

This fairly primitive resort toward the western end of the island has long been a summer boating destination. The area is named for its two harbors, which are separated by a ½-mi-wide isthmus. Two Harbors recalls the days before tourism became the island's major industry. This side of the island is less tame, with abundant wildlife. Activities here include swimming, diving, boating, hiking, mountain biking, beach-combing, kayaking, and sportfishing.

Lodging

Tiny Two Harbors has limited overnight accommodations, including a few campgrounds. All reservations are made through the **visitor services** office (✉ Box 5086, Two Harbors 90704, ☎ 310/510–0303), which you'll see when you arrive.

Catalina Island Essentials

ARRIVING AND DEPARTING

By Boat: Catalina Cruises (☎ 800/228–2546) departs Long Beach several times daily, taking an hour and 45 minutes to reach Avalon before continuing to Two Harbors. There is no service to Two Harbors in winter. The fare to either destination is $25 round-trip. **Catalina Express** (☎ 310/519–1212 or 800/995–4386) makes an hour-long run from Long Beach or San Pedro to Avalon and a 90-minute run from San Pedro to Two Harbors; round-trip fare from Long Beach and San Pedro is $38. Reservations are advised in summer and on weekends.

Service from Newport Beach is available through **Catalina Passenger Service** (☎ 949/673–5245). Boats leave from Balboa Pavilion at 9 AM, take 75 minutes to reach the island, and cost $36 (reservations advised). Return boats leave Catalina at 4:30 PM.

By Bus: Catalina Safari Shuttle Bus (☎ 310/510–0303 or 800/322–3434) has regular bus service (limited in winter) between Avalon and Two Harbors; the trip takes 90 minutes and costs $18 one-way.

By Helicopter: Island Express (☎ 310/510–2525) flies hourly from San Pedro and Long Beach (8 AM–sunset). The trip takes about 15 minutes and costs $66 one-way, $121 round-trip.

GETTING AROUND

By Bicycle: Bike rentals are widely available in Avalon for about $6 per hour. Look for rental stands on Crescent Avenue and Pebbly Beach Road.

On Foot: The requisite free permits for hikes into the island's interior are available daily from 9 to 5 at the **Santa Catalina Island Conservancy** (✉ 3rd and Claressa Sts., ☎ 310/510–2595) and at **visitor services** in Two Harbors (✉ Box 5086, Two Harbors 90704, ☎ 310/510–0303). No permit is required for shorter hikes, such as the one from Avalon to the Botanical Garden. The Conservancy has maps of the island's east-end hikes, such as Hermit's Gulch trail. If you plan to backpack overnight, you'll need a separate camping permit. The interior is dry and desertlike; bring plenty of water.

By Golf Cart: Golf carts constitute the island's main form of transportation. You can rent them along Avalon's Crescent Avenue and Pebbly Beach Road for about $30 per hour. Try **Island Rentals** (✉ 125 Pebbly Beach Rd., ☎ 310/510–1456).

GUIDED TOURS

Santa Catalina Island Company (☎ 310/510–8687 or 800/322–3434) and **Catalina Adventure Tours** (☎ 310/510–2888) conduct tours of the region.

VISITOR INFORMATION

The **Catalina Island Visitor's Bureau** (✉ Green Pleasure Pier, Box 217, Avalon 90704, ☎ 310/510–1520, FAX 310/510–7606).

LOS ANGELES A TO Z

Arriving and Departing

By Bus
Greyhound Lines (☎ 800/231–2222) serves Los Angeles from many U.S. cities. The terminal is at 1716 East 7th Street, at the corner of Alameda Street.

By Car
Los Angeles is at the western terminus of I–10, a major interstate highway that runs all the way east to Florida. I–15, angling southwest from Las Vegas, swings through the eastern communities around San Bernardino before heading on to San Diego. Interstate 5, which runs north–south through California, leads up to San Francisco and down to San Diego.

By Plane
The major gateway to Los Angeles is **Los Angeles International Airport** (☎ 310/670–3413), commonly called LAX; it is serviced by more than 85 major airlines, including Alaska, America West, American, Continental, Delta, Northwest, Skywest, Southwest, TWA, United, and US Airways. *See* Air Travel *in* Smart Travel Tips for phone numbers.

Long Beach Airport (☎ 562/570–2600), at the southern tip of Los Angeles County, is served by America West, American, and Sunjet International.

Burbank/Glendale/Pasadena Airport (☎ 818/840–8847) serves the San Fernando Valley. Alaska, America West, American, Skywest, Southwest, and United are among the airlines that fly here.

Ontario International Airport (✉ Airport Dr., south from Vineyard Ave. exit of I–10, ☎ 909/937–2700), about 35 mi east of Los Angeles, serves the San Bernardino–Riverside area and is served by Alaska, America West, American, Continental, Delta, Northwest, Skywest, Southwest, TWA, United, and US Air Express.

John Wayne Airport Orange County (☎ 949/252–5006) (☞ Orange County A to Z *in* Chapter 12).

BETWEEN THE AIRPORT AND DOWNTOWN
A taxi ride to downtown from LAX can take as little as 30 minutes, but substantially longer in traffic. Visitors should request the flat fee (about $30) to downtown or choose from the several ground transportation companies that offer set rates.

If you're **driving from LAX to downtown L.A.,** take the San Diego Freeway (I–405) north to the Santa Monica Freeway (I–10) east to the Harbor Freeway (I–110) north until you hit downtown. **To get to Beverly Hills,** take the San Diego Freeway north, exit at Santa Monica Boulevard, and turn right.

From Ontario Airport to downtown L.A., take the Harbor Freeway west to the San Diego Freeway north to the Harbor Freeway south; **to Beverly Hills,** take the Santa Monica Freeway west to the San Diego Freeway north, exit at Santa Monica Boulevard, and turn right.

From Long Beach Airport to downtown L.A., take the San Diego Freeway north to Highway 710 north to the Golden State Freeway (I–5) north. **To Beverly Hills,** take the San Diego Freeway north to the Santa Monica Freeway east, and exit at Century Park. **From the Burbank/Glendale/Pasadena Airport to downtown L.A.,** take the Golden State Freeway to the Harbor Freeway south. From the Burbank air-

Los Angeles Freeways

port **to Beverly Hills,** take the Golden State Freeway south to the Ventura Freeway (Highway 134) west to the Hollywood Freeway (U.S. 101) north to the San Diego Freeway south, and exit at Santa Monica Boulevard.

For directions to downtown and Beverly Hills from **John Wayne Airport,** *see* Orange County A to Z *in* Chapter 12.

SuperShuttle (☎ 310/782–6600 or 323/775–6600) offers direct service between the airport and hotels. The trip to or from downtown hotels costs about $12. The seven-passenger vans operate 24 hours a day. In the airport, call 310/782–6600 or use the SuperShuttle courtesy phone in the luggage area; the van should arrive within 15 minutes. **Shuttle One** (☎ 310/670–6666) provides door-to-door service from LAX to hotels in the Disneyland/Anaheim area. **Airport Bus** (☎ 714/938–8900 or 800/772–5299) provides regular service between LAX and the Pasadena and Anaheim areas.

From Ontario International, ground transportation possibilities include SuperShuttle as well as **Inland Express** (☎ 909/626–6599) and **Southern California Coach** (☎ 714/978–6415). At John Wayne, **Airport Bus** (☎ 800/772–5299) provides ground transportation. **Flyaway Service** (☎ 818/994–5554) offers transportation between LAX and the central San Fernando Valley for $3.50.

MTA (☎ 213/626–4455) has limited airport service to all areas of greater L.A.; bus lines depart from bus docks at the Transit Center attached to parking lot C. Prices vary from $1.35 to $3.10; some routes require transfers. The best line to take to downtown is Bus 42 ($1.35) or the express Bus 439 ($1.85). Both take about 70 minutes.

By Train
Los Angeles can be reached by **Amtrak** (☎ 800/872–7245). Trains terminate at **Union Station** (✉ 800 N. Alameda St.) in downtown Los Angeles.

Getting Around

By Bus
A ride on the **Metropolitan Transit Authority (MTA)** (☎ 213/626–4455) costs $1.35, with 25¢ for each transfer.

DASH (Downtown Area Short Hop) minibuses travel around the downtown area, stopping every two blocks or so. There are six different routes with pickups at five-minute intervals. You pay 25¢ every time you get on. Buses generally run on weekdays between 6 AM and 7 PM and on Saturday between 10 AM and 5 PM; a few downtown weekend routes run on Sunday as well.

By Car
A car is a necessity in Los Angeles. If you plan to drive extensively, consider buying a *Thomas Guide,* which contains detailed maps of the entire county. Despite what you've heard, traffic is not always a major problem, especially if you avoid rush hour (between 7 and 9 AM and 3 and 7 PM). Seat belts must be worn by all passengers at all times. A right turn on red after stopping is permitted unless a sign indicating otherwise is posted. Pedestrians have the right of way.

If your car breaks down on an interstate highway, try to pull over onto the shoulder of the road and either wait for the state police to find you or, if you have other passengers who can wait in the car, walk to the nearest emergency roadside phone and call the state police. If you carry a cellular or car telephone, *55 is the emergency number. When calling for help, note your location according to the small green mileage markers posted along the highway. Other highways are also patrolled but may not have emergency phones or mileage markers.

More than 35 major companies and dozens of local rental companies serve a steady demand for cars at Los Angeles International Airport and various city locations. For a list of the major car-rental companies, *see* Car Rentals *in* Smart Travel Tips.

Parking rules are strictly enforced in Los Angeles; illegally parked cars are ticketed and towed very quickly. Parking is generally available in garages or parking lots; prices vary from 25¢ to $2 per half hour, or a few dollars to $25 per day. In the most heavily trafficked areas, garage rates may be as high as $20 an hour, though prices tend to drop on weekends. Metered parking is also widely available; meter rates vary from 25¢ for 15 minutes in the most heavily trafficked areas to 25¢ for one hour. In some areas, metered parking is free on weekends or on Sunday.

By Limousine

Reputable companies include **Dav-El Livery** (☎ 310/550–0070 or 800/922–0343), **First Class** (☎ 310/676–9771 or 800/400–9771), and **Spectrum Limousine Service** (☎ 800/901–4546).

By Subway

The **Metro Red Line** (☎ 213/626–4455) runs 4½ mi through downtown, from Union Station to MacArthur Park, making five stops. The fare is $1.35.

By Taxi

You probably won't be able to hail a cab on the street. Instead, you should phone one of the many taxi companies. The rate is $1.90 to start and $1.60 per mile. Two reputable companies are **Independent Cab Co.** (☎ 213/385–8294) and **United Independent Taxi** (☎ 323/653–5050).

By Train

The **Metrorail Blue Line** (☎ 213/626–4455) runs daily between 5 AM and 10 PM from downtown Los Angeles (corner of Flower and 7th Streets) to Long Beach (corner of 1st Street and Long Beach Avenue), with 18 stops en route, most of them in Long Beach. The fare is $1.35 one-way.

Contacts and Resources

Emergencies

Ambulance (☎ 911). **Fire** (☎ 911). **Police** (☎ 911).

Most large hospitals in Los Angeles have 24-hour emergency rooms. Two are **Cedar-Sinai Medical Center** (✉ 8700 Beverly Blvd., ☎ 310/855–5000) and **Queen of Angels Hollywood Presbyterian Medical Center** (✉ 1300 N. Vermont Ave., ☎ 213/413–3000).

Guided Tours

Los Angeles is so spread out and has such a wealth of sightseeing possibilities that a tour may prove useful. Reservations must be made in advance. Many hotels can book them for you.

ORIENTATION TOURS

L.A. Tours and Sightseeing (☎ 323/937–3361 or 800/286–8752) has a $42 tour covering various parts of the city, including downtown, Hollywood, and Beverly Hills. The company also operates tours to Disneyland, Universal Studios, Magic Mountain, beaches, and stars' homes. **Starline Tours of Hollywood** (☎ 800/959–3131 or 323/463–

3333) picks up passengers from area hotels as well as around the corner from Mann's Chinese Theater (✉ 6925 Hollywood Blvd.). Universal Studios, Sea World, Knott's Berry Farm, stars' homes, Disneyland, and other attractions are on this company's agenda. Prices range from $29 to $75. **Casablanca Tours** (☎ 323/461–0156 or 800/498–6871) conducts a four-hour insider's look at Hollywood and Beverly Hills. Tours are in minibuses with a maximum of 14 people, and the prices are equivalent to the large bus tours—from $35 to $68.

PERSONAL GUIDES

Elegant Tours for the Discriminating (☎ 310/472–4090) is a personalized sightseeing and shopping service for the Beverly Hills area. Lunch is included. **L.A. Nighthawks** (☎ 310/392–1500) will arrange your nightlife for you. For a hefty price, you'll get a limousine, a guide, and immediate entry into L.A.'s hottest nightspots.

SPECIAL-INTEREST TOURS

LA Today Custom Tours (☎ 310/454–5730) has a wide selection of offbeat tours (costing from $12 to $85), some of which tie in with seasonal and cultural events. Marlene Gordon of **The Next Stage** (☎ 626/577–7880) tours takes from 2 to 200 people by foot, buses, or vans in search of "the real L.A." Popular excursions include Victorian L.A., Notable Women in L.A., and the Insomniac's Tour. **Trolleywood Tours** (☎ 323/469–8184 or 800/782–7287) operates daily tours that take you through downtown Hollywood and by the HOLLYWOOD sign, past star's homes, and through historical parts of town. The cost is $16 to $37 per person, depending on the tour.

WALKING TOURS

The **Los Angeles Conservancy** (☎ 213/623–2489) offers low-cost walking tours of the downtown area. Each Saturday at 10 AM one of several tours leaves from the Olive Street entrance of the Regal Biltmore Hotel. The cost is $5 per person. Make a reservation, because group size is limited.

Late-Night Pharmacies

The **Kaiser Bellflower Pharmacy** (✉ 9400 E. Rosecrans Ave., Bellflower, ☎ 562/461–4213) is open around the clock. Many towns have a Thrifty or Sav-On pharmacy that stays open late.

Visitor Information

Hollywood Visitor Information Center (✉ 6541 Hollywood Blvd., ☎ 213/689–8822). **Los Angeles Convention and Visitors Bureau** (✉ 633 W. 5th St., Suite 6000, 90071, ☎ 213/624–7300 or 800/228–2452).

12 ORANGE COUNTY

No place in southern California evokes the stereotype of California's good life quite the way Orange County does: million-dollar mansions dot the coastline, lush golf courses line beaches and meander through inland hills, and tony convertibles glide down Pacific Coast Highway. But, while visitors and residents are adept at relaxing under swaying palm trees while lounging beachfront, the inland cities are alive with amusement parks, professional sporting events, and dozens of hotels and restaurants, all within minutes of one another.

Updated by
Cindy LaFavre
Yorks

FEW OF THE CITRUS GROVES that gave Orange County its name remain. This region south and east of Los Angeles is now a high-tech business hub where tourism is the number-one industry. Anaheim's theme parks lure hordes of visitors; numerous festivals celebrate the county's culture and relatively brief history; and the area supports fine dining, upscale shopping, and several standout visual and performing arts facilities. With its tropical flowers and palm trees, the stretch of coast between Seal Beach and San Clemente is often called the "American Riviera." Exclusive Newport Beach, artsy Laguna, and the up-and-coming surf town of Huntington Beach are the stars, but lesser-known gems such as Corona del Mar are also worth visiting.

Pleasures and Pastimes

Dining

Italian restaurants and burger joints abound, but you'll also find French, Thai, Scandinavian, Cuban, and other types of cuisine, in every type of setting.

CATEGORY	COST*
$$$$	over $50
$$$	$30–$50
$$	$20–$30
$	under $20

*per person for a three-course meal, excluding drinks, service, and 8¼% tax

Lodging

The prices listed in this chapter are based on summer rates. Prices are often lower in winter, especially near Disneyland, unless there's a convention in Anaheim. Weekend rates are often rock-bottom at business hotels. It's worth calling around to search for bargains.

CATEGORY	COST*
$$$$	over $175
$$$	$120–$175
$$	$80–$120
$	under $80

*All prices are for a standard double room, excluding 14% occupancy tax.

Outdoor Activities and Sports

Water sports rule the coast of Orange County, but other sports don't lag far behind. The sight of people jogging, walking, biking, and blading is nearly inescapable. Wave action along Orange County's coastline ranges from beginner to expert. Surfing is permitted at most beaches year-round (check local newspapers or talk to lifeguards for conditions). The best waves are usually at San Clemente, Newport Beach, and Huntington Beach. Keep a lookout for signs warning of dangerous conditions: undertow, strong currents, and big waves can all be hazardous. Never go in the water when flags with a black circle are flying, and avoid swimming near surfers. Many beaches close just after sunset.

Golf and tennis are two more reasons to visit Orange County. A few public golf courses are listed in this chapter. For more information contact the Southern California Golf Association or the Southern California Public Links Golf Association (☞ Visitor Information *in* Orange County A to Z, *below*). Many hotels have tennis courts, and there are public tennis facilities throughout the county.

For those who wish to enjoy the coastline by bike or on foot, the Santa Ana Riverbed Trail hugs the Santa Ana River for 20½ mi between Pacific Coast Highway (PCH) at Huntington State Beach and Imperial Highway in Yorba Linda. There are entrances, rest rooms, and drinking fountains at all crossings.

Exploring Orange County

Like Los Angeles, Orange County stretches over a large area, lacks a singular focal point, and has limited public transportation. You'll need a car and a sensible game plan to make the most of your visit. If you're headed to Disneyland, you'll probably want to stay in or near Anaheim, organize your activities around the inland-county attractions, and take excursions to the coast.

Numbers in the text correspond to numbers in the margin and on the Orange County map.

Great Itineraries

IF YOU HAVE 1 DAY

You're going to **Disneyland** ①.

IF YOU HAVE 3 DAYS

You're still going to **Disneyland** ① (stay overnight in 🔟 **Anaheim**), but get up early on day two and head to **Laguna Beach,** before the crowds arrive. On day three, visit **Dana Point** or **Huntington Beach,** then either hang out on the sand with a surfboard or head inland to **Costa Mesa,** where you can browse through **South Coast Plaza** ⑫, one of the world's largest retail, entertainment, and dining complexes.

When to Tour Orange County

The sun shines year-round in Orange County, but you can beat the crowds and the heat by visiting during spring and fall. If you're traveling with children, you could easily devote several days to the theme parks—a day or two at the Magic Kingdom, a day at Knott's Berry Farm, and perhaps a day for some of the area's lesser-known diversions.

INLAND ORANGE COUNTY

About a 35-minute drive from downtown Los Angeles on I–5 (also known as the Golden State Freeway) is Anaheim, Orange County's tourist hub, which centers around the big D.

Anaheim

26 mi southeast of Los Angeles, I–5.

The snowcapped Matterhorn, the centerpiece of the Magic Kingdom, dominates Anaheim's skyline and is an enduring reminder of the role Disneyland has played in the growth of Orange County. Disneyland has attracted millions of visitors and thousands of workers, and Anaheim has been their host, becoming Orange County's most populous city and accounting for more than half the county's 40,000 hotel rooms. Anaheim's vast tourism complex also includes Edison International Field, home of the Anaheim Angels baseball team; the Arrowhead Pond, where the Mighty Ducks hockey team plays; and the enormous Anaheim Convention Center.

★ ℭ ❶ **Disneyland** occupies a unique place in the Disney legend, the only one of the four Kingdoms overseen by Walt himself. Mr. Disney's personal stamp has made an imprint that can be felt in the park's genuinely historic feel. There's plenty here that you won't find anywhere else. Sto-

468

Orange County

rybook Land, with its miniature replicas of classic animated Disney scenes, is a Fantasyland favorite. The Matterhorn, the Indiana Jones Adventure, and the new Rocket Rods speed ride are unique to Disneyland.

Start your visit with a stroll along **Main Street,** a romanticized image of small-town America, circa 1900. Trolleys, double-decker buses, and horse-drawn wagons travel up and down a quaint thoroughfare lined with rows of interconnected shops selling everything from Disney products to magic tricks, crystal ware, sports memorabilia, and photo supplies.

Disneyland is divided into themed lands. **Fantasyland,** its entrance marked by Sleeping Beauty Castle, is where you can fly on Peter Pan's Flight, go down the rabbit hole with Alice in Wonderland, take an aerial spin with Dumbo the Flying Elephant, twirl around in giant cups at the Mad Tea Party, bobsled through the Matterhorn, or visit It's a Small World, where Animatron children from 100 countries sing the well-known song.

In **Frontierland** you can take a cruise on the steamboat *Mark Twain* or the sailing ship *Columbia*. Kids of every age enjoy rafting to Tom Sawyer Island for an hour or so of climbing and exploring. Some visitors to **Adventureland** have taken the Jungle Cruise so many times that they know the operators' patter by heart. Special effects and decipherable hieroglyphics entertain guests on line for the Indiana Jones Adventure, a don't-miss thrill ride through the Temple of the Forbidden Eye. Also here are the animated bears of **Critter Country; Splash Mountain,** Disney's steepest, wettest adventure; and the Enchanted Tiki Room.

Tomorrowland has a fictional *Buck Rogers* feel. Ride on the futuristic Astro Orbitor rockets, zip along on the Rocket Rods, ride Space Mountain, or tinker with the toys of tomorrow at Innoventions. The twisting streets of **New Orleans Square** are for shopping and browsing in the company of strolling Dixieland musicians. Also here is the Pirates of the Caribbean ride. The Haunted Mansion, populated by 999 holographic ghosts, is nearby. Theme shops sell hats, Mardi Gras merchandise, and gourmet foods, and the gallery carries original Disney art.

At **Mickey's Toontown** kids can climb up a rope ladder on the *Miss Daisy* (Donald Duck's boat), talk to a mailbox, and walk through Mickey's House to meet Mickey. Here is also where you'll find the Roger Rabbit Car Toon Spin, the largest and most unusual black-light ride in Disneyland history. The Magic Kingdom's crowd-pleasing live-action and special-effects show Fantasmic! features exhilarating music and just about every animated Disney character ever drawn. Daytime and nighttime Main Street parades are often based on the Disney classic of the moment.

During the busy summer season, Disneyland can be mobbed. If possible, visit on a rainy midweek day instead. In summer, try to avoid the hot midday hours. Though most Disney attractions are indoors, you'll be standing in direct sunlight as you wait in lines. Try to arrive early. The box office opens a half hour before the park's scheduled opening time. (On most days, guests of the Disneyland Resort and some Anaheim hotels are admitted before other visitors.) Brochures with maps, available at the entrance, list show and parade times. You can move from one area of Disneyland to another via the Disneyland Railroad. In addition to touring all the "lands," the train travels through the Grand Canyon and a prehistoric jungle.

Characters appear for autographs and photos throughout the day, but you'll probably have to wait in line. Check with a Disneyland employee for information about character stops. You can also meet some of the animated icons at one of the character meals served at the Disneyland or Disneyland Pacific hotels (both open to the public).

Plan meals to avoid peak meal times. If you want to eat at the Blue Bayou restaurant in New Orleans Square, it's best to make reservations as soon as you get to the park. Fast-food spots abound, and healthy snacks such as fruit, pasta, and frozen yogurt are sold at various locations. For a quick lunch on the go, try the Blue Ribbon Bakery's gourmet sandwiches.

You can store belongings and purchases in lockers just off Main Street. Purchases can also be sent to the Package Pickup desk at the front of the park. If you're planning on staying for more than a day or two, ask about the Flex Pass, which gives you five-day admission to Disneyland for roughly the same price as a two-day passport (about $68 at press time). The passes are not sold at the park itself, but you can buy them through travel agents and at most area hotels. Disneyland will expand considerably next year with the opening of its second theme park, the California Adventure. Because of construction detours, your best bet for getting to the park will be to use transportation provided by your hotel. ⊠ *1313 Harbor Blvd.,* ☏ *714/781–4565.* 🎫 *$38.* ◷ *June–mid-Sept., Sun.–Fri. 9 AM–midnight, Sat. 9 AM–1 AM; mid-Sept.– May, weekdays 10–6, Sat. 9–midnight, Sun. 9 AM–10 PM.*

Dining and Lodging

Most Anaheim hotels have complimentary shuttle service to Disneyland, though many are within walking distance.

$$–$$$ ✕ **The Catch/Hop City Blues and Brew.** Across from Anaheim Stadium, this combination of a sports bar and a House of Blues–style dinner-and-entertainment venue draws a crowd at night. The Catch serves hearty portions of steak, seafood, pasta, and salads. The adjacent Hop City steak house serves up live blues along with 14-ounce blackened rib eyes and 20-ounce T-bones. ⊠ *1929–1939 S. State College Blvd.,* ☏ *714/ 634–1829 (The Catch), 714/978–3700 (Hop City). AE, DC, MC, V.*

$$–$$$ ✕ **Mr. Stox.** Oriental rugs, intimate booths, and linen tablecloths create an elegant setting at this family-owned restaurant. Prime rib, mesquite-grilled rack of lamb, and fresh fish specials are excellent; the pasta, bread, and pastries are homemade; and the wine list wins awards. ⊠ *1105 E. Katella Ave.,* ☏ *714/634–2994. AE, D, DC, MC, V. No lunch weekends. Valet parking.*

$$–$$$ ✕ **Thee White House.** Several small dining rooms are set with crisp linens, candles, and flowers in this 1909 mansion. The northern Italian menu includes pasta, veal scalloppini, and a large selection of fresh seafood. A three-course prix-fixe lunch, served weekdays only, costs $16. ⊠ *887 S. Anaheim Blvd.,* ☏ *714/772–1381. AE, DC, MC, V. No lunch weekends.*

$–$$$ ✕ **Luigi's D'Italia.** Despite the simple surroundings—red vinyl booths and plastic checkered tablecloths—Luigi's serves outstanding Italian cuisine: spaghetti marinara, cioppino, and all the classics. Kids will feel at home here. ⊠ *801 S. State College Blvd.,* ☏ *714/490–0990. AE, MC, V.*

$$ ✕ **Yamabuki.** Part of the Disneyland Pacific Hotel complex, this stylish Japanese restaurant serves traditional dishes and has a full sushi bar. The plum-wine ice cream is a treat. ⊠ *Disneyland Pacific Hotel, 1717 S. West St.,* ☏ *714/956–6755. AE, DC, MC, V. No lunch weekends.*

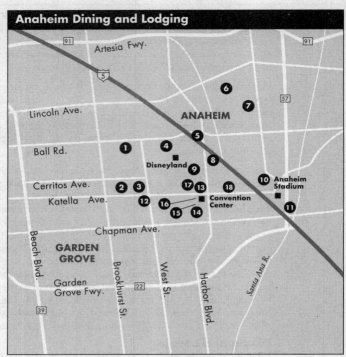

Anaheim Dining and Lodging

$$$–$$$$ 🏨 **Anaheim Hilton and Towers.** Next to the Anaheim Convention Center, this busy Hilton is the largest hotel in southern California: it even has its own post office, as well as shops, restaurants, and cocktail lounges. A shuttle runs to Disneyland, or you can walk the few blocks. Special summer children's programs include a lending desk with games, toys, and books. There's a $10 fee to use the health club. ✉ *777 Convention Way, 92802,* ☎ *714/750–4321 or 800/445–8667,* FAX *714/740–4460. 1,576 rooms, 95 suites. 4 restaurants, 2 lounges, nosmoking floors, room service, pool, beauty salon, hot tub, massage, sauna, health club, piano, children's programs (under 12), laundry service and dry cleaning, concierge, business services, meeting rooms, travel services, airport shuttle, car rental, parking (fee). AE, D, DC, MC, V.*

$$$–$$$$ 🏨 **Anaheim Marriott.** Rooms at this busy convention hotel are well equipped for business travelers, with desks, two phones, and data ports. Some rooms have balconies, and accommodations on the north side have good views of Disneyland's summer fireworks shows. Discounted weekend and Disneyland packages are available. ✉ *700 W. Convention Way, 92802,* ☎ *714/750–8000 or 800/228–9290,* FAX *714/750–9100. 1,033 rooms, 52 suites. 2 restaurants, 2 lounges, in-room data ports, in-room safes, no-smoking floors, room service, 2 pools, 2 hot tubs, health club, piano, coin laundry, laundry service and dry cleaning, concierge, concierge floor, meeting rooms, car rental, parking (fee). AE, D, DC, MC, V.*

$$$–$$$$ 🏨 **Disneyland Hotel.** Disney products are for sale everywhere at this
★ resort with a kitschy, 1950s charm. At Goofy's Kitchen, kids can dine with their favorite Disney characters. Rooms in the Bonita tower overlook the Fantasy Waters, a fountain that's illuminated at night. On most days, guests staying at the hotel are admitted to the park before the

gates open to the general public. Room-and-ticket packages are available. ⊠ *1150 W. Cerritos Ave., 92802,* ☎ *714/778–6600,* FAX *714/956–6561. 1,074 rooms, 62 suites. 4 restaurants, 3 bars, in-room data ports, in-room safes, minibars, refrigerators, room service, 3 pools, hot tub, exercise room, beach, laundry service and dry cleaning, concierge, concierge floor, business services, travel services, airport shuttle, car rental, parking (fee). AE, D, DC, MC, V.*

$$$–$$$$ 🏨 **Disneyland Pacific Hotel.** The newest addition to the Disneyland hotel empire has many of the same Disney touches as the Disneyland Hotel, but the atmosphere is a bit quieter and more ordinary. From here you can walk to Disneyland (a feat that will become easier once construction slows down) or pick up a shuttle or monorail. Start the day with the Minnie and Friends character breakfast, or visit with Mary Poppins in her parlor at the Practically Perfect Tea. ⊠ *1717 S. West St., 92802,* ☎ *714/999–0990,* FAX *714/956–6582. 488 rooms, 14 suites. 2 restaurants, 2 lounges, patisserie, no-smoking rooms, room service, pool, hot tub, exercise room, laundry service and dry cleaning, concierge, concierge floor, parking (fee). AE, D, DC, MC, V.*

$$$ 🏨 **Sheraton Anaheim Hotel.** If you're hoping to escape the commer-
★ cial atmosphere of the hotels surrounding Disneyland, consider this sprawling replica of a Tudor castle. In the flowers-and-plants-filled lobby you're welcome to sit by the grand fireplace, watching fish swim around in a pond. Rooms are sizable, and some first-floor rooms open onto interior gardens and pool area. A Disneyland shuttle is available. ⊠ *1015 W. Ball Rd., 92802,* ☎ *714/778–1700 or 800/325–3535,* FAX *714/535–3889. 447 rooms, 42 suites. Restaurant, bar, deli, some in-room data ports, in-room safes, no-smoking rooms, room service, pool, outdoor hot tub, health club, coin laundry, laundry service and dry cleaning, concierge, concierge floor, meeting rooms, free parking. AE, D, DC, MC, V.*

$$–$$$ 🏨 **Holiday Inn Anaheim at the Park.** Families frequent this Mediter-
ranean-style hotel. Complimentary shuttle service takes guests to popular nearby attractions, including Disneyland, Knott's Berry Farm, the Movieland Wax Museum, Medieval Times, and the Main Place and Anaheim Plaza shopping areas. ⊠ *1221 S. Harbor Blvd., 92805,* ☎ *714/758–0900 or 800/545–7275,* FAX *714/533–1804. 252 rooms, 2 suites. Restaurant, bar, in-room data ports, no-smoking floors, room service, pool, outdoor hot tub, meeting rooms, free parking. AE, D, DC, MC, V.*

$$–$$$ 🏨 **Radisson Maingate.** Some rooms at this friendly hotel have pull-out sofas as well as beds. Regular shuttles zip you to Disneyland or Knott's Berry Farm. ⊠ *1850 S. Harbor Blvd., 92802,* ☎ *714/750–2801 or 800/624–6855,* FAX *714/971–4754. 314 rooms. Restaurant, in-room data ports, bar, no-smoking floors, room service, pool, coin laundry, laundry service and dry cleaning, concierge, meeting rooms, free parking. AE, D, DC, MC, V.*

$–$$$ 🏨 **Candy Cane Inn.** One of the Disneyland area's first hotels (deeds
★ were executed Christmas Eve, hence the name) the Candy Cane has spacious, basic rooms. Deluxe rooms have refrigerators and coffeemakers. A free Disneyland shuttle runs every half hour. ⊠ *1747 S. Harbor Blvd., 92802,* ☎ *714/774–5284 or 800/345–7057,* FAX *714/772–5462 or 714/772–1305. 172 rooms. No-smoking rooms, some refrigerators, pool, wading pool, outdoor hot tub, coin laundry, laundry service and dry cleaning, free parking. Continental breakfast. AE, D, DC, MC, V.*

$–$$$ 🏨 **Desert Palm Inn and Suites.** This hotel midway between Disneyland and the convention center is a great value, with $109 one-bedroom suites that can accommodate the whole family. All rooms, including the standard variety, have microwaves and refrigerators. A light Continental breakfast (coffee, juice, and Danish) is included daily. ⊠ *631 W. Katella*

Ave., 92802, ☎ *714/535–1133 or 800/635–5423,* FAX *714/491–7409. 50 rooms, 50 suites. In-room data ports, no-smoking rooms, refrigerators, pool, outdoor hot tub, sauna, coin laundry, laundry service and dry cleaning, free parking. Continental breakfast. AE, D, DC, MC, V.*

$$ 🏨 **Best Western Stovall's Inn.** Nice touches at this well-kept motel include a topiary garden, a free shuttle to Disneyland, and Nintendo and movie rentals. Ask about discounts if you're staying several nights. ✉ *1110 W. Katella Ave., 92802,* ☎ *714/778–1880 or 800/854–8175,* FAX *714/778–3805. 290 rooms. Coffee bar, bar, no-smoking rooms, room service, 2 pools, outdoor hot tub, coin laundry, laundry service and dry cleaning, meeting rooms, free parking. AE, D, DC, MC, V.*

$$ 🏨 **Four Points Hotel by Sheraton.** Even in hotel-filled Anaheim, it's hard to miss the shiny, new, upmarket Sheraton. It's just a block from the Convention Center and a few blocks from Disney. Contemporary rooms have a hint of Asian flair, all with microwaves and refrigerators. This is an entirely smoke-free establishment. ✉ *515 W. Katella Ave., 92802,* ☎ *714/991–6868 or 888/543–7878,* FAX *714/991–6565. 104 rooms, 1 suite. Restaurant, bar, in-room data ports, in-room safes, no-smoking floors, refrigerators, room service, in-room VCRs, pool, hot tub, exercise room, video games, coin laundry, laundry service and dry cleaning, business services, meeting rooms, free parking. AE, D, DC, MC, V.*

$$ 🏨 **Ramada Inn Conestoga at Disneyland.** Pint-size cowboys will love this Old West–style hotel with swinging saloon doors and a *Bonanza*-style lobby. The restaurants look like saloons, and there's a nice pool area for relaxing. A complimentary shuttle heads to Disneyland every hour. ✉ *1240 S. Walnut Ave., 92802,* ☎ *714/535–0300 or 800/824–5459,* FAX *714/491–8953. 229 rooms, 23 suites. Restaurant, bar, in-room data ports, no-smoking rooms, room service, pool, outdoor hot tub, laundry service and dry cleaning, meeting rooms, free parking. AE, D, DC, MC, V.*

$–$$ 🏨 **Anaheim Fairfield Inn by Marriott.** This hotel provides friendly, detail-oriented service and spacious rooms, most with sleeper sofas as well as beds. Across the street from Disneyland, the hotel runs a free shuttle service to the park. A nearby restaurant provides room service, but kids usually prefer the McDonald's Happy Meals delivered right to your room. ✉ *1460 S. Harbor Blvd., 92802,* ☎ *714/772–6777 or 800/228–2800,* FAX *714/999–1727. 467 rooms. Restaurant, no-smoking floors, refrigerators, room service, pool, outdoor hot tub, travel services, meeting room, free parking. AE, D, DC, MC, V.*

$ 🏨 **Alpine Motel.** With a lobby that looks like a snow-covered lodge, this convenient hotel is just steps from Disneyland and the convention center. Two-room suites are a great value, even during the busy summer season. ✉ *715 W. Katella Ave., 92802,* ☎ *714/535–2186 or 800/772–4422,* FAX *714/535–3714. 41 rooms, 8 suites. No-smoking rooms, pool, coin laundry, laundry service and dry cleaning, free parking. Continental breakfast. AE, D, DC, MC, V.*

Outdoor Activities and Sports

Pro baseball's **Anaheim Angels** play at Edison International Field (✉ 2000 Gene Autry Way, ☎ 714/634–2000). The National Hockey League's **Mighty Ducks of Anaheim** play at Arrowhead Pond (✉ 2695 E. Katella Ave., ☎ 714/740–2000). There are six public tennis courts at **Pearson Park** (✉ 400 N. Harbour Blvd.); call the **Parks and Recreation Department** (☎ 714/765–5191) for details.

Buena Park

25 mi south of Los Angeles, I–5.

A humble farmer in Buena Park created the boysenberry by mixing red raspberries, blackberries, and loganberries. Now on his land is Knott's Berry Farm, a major amusement park.

★ ⟳ ② **Knott's Berry Farm** got its start in 1934, when Cordelia Knott began serving chicken dinners on her wedding china to supplement her family's income. Or so the story goes. The dinners and her boysenberry pies proved more profitable than husband Walter's berry farm, so the two moved first into the restaurant business and then into the entertainment business. Their park is now a 150-acre complex with 100-plus rides and attractions, 60 food concessions and restaurants, and 60 shops.

GhostRider was Orange County's first wooden roller coaster. Traveling 56 mph at its fastest and reaching 118 ft at its highest, the coaster is riddled with sudden dips and curves. Your next stop might be **Ghost Town,** whose authentic old buildings have been relocated from their original mining-town sites. You can stroll down the street, stop and chat with the blacksmith, pan for gold, crack open a geode, ride in an authentic 1880s passenger train, or take the Gold Mine ride and descend into a replica of a working gold mine. A real treasure here is the antique Dentzel carousel.

Camp Snoopy is a miniature High Sierra wonderland where Snoopy and his friends from the "Peanuts" comic strip hang out. Nearby is **Big Foot Rapids,** where you can ride white water in an inner tube and commune with the native peoples of the Northwest coast in the spooky Mystery Lodge. For more water thrills, check out the dolphin and sea lion shows in the Pacific Pavilion at **The Boardwalk,** which houses several attractions including rides such as the **Boomerang** roller coaster; **Kingdom of the Dinosaurs,** a *Jurassic Park*–like thrill ride; and **Montezooma's Revenge,** a roller coaster that goes from 0 to 55 mph in less than five seconds. **Jaguar!** simulates the motions of a cat stalking its prey, twisting, spiraling, and speeding up and slowing down as it takes guests on its stomach-dropping course. **Wind Jammer** is the country's first outdoor dual-action roller coaster, with two cars racing simultaneously through twists and turns at top speed. Shows are scheduled in the Good Time Theater throughout the day. ⊠ *8039 Beach Blvd., between La Palma Ave. and Crescent St.,* ☏ *714/220–5200.* ⌑ *$36.* ⊙ *June–mid-Sept., daily 9 AM–midnight; mid-Sept.–May, weekdays 10–6, Sat. 10–10, Sun. 10–7; closed during inclement weather.*

③ More than 75 years of movie magic are immortalized at the **Movieland Wax Museum,** which holds several hundred wax sculptures of Hollywood's stars and American political figures, including Michael Jackson, John Wayne, Marilyn Monroe, and George Burns. You can buy a combination ticket for $16.90 that also allows you admission to the so-so Ripley's Believe It or Not, across the street. ⊠ *7711 Beach Blvd., between La Palma and Orangethorpe Aves.,* ☏ *714/522–1155.* ⌑ *$12.95.* ⊙ *Daily 9–7.*

Dining and Lodging

$ ✕ **Mrs. Knott's Chicken Dinner Restaurant.** The restaurant, at the park's entrance, still serves all-American crispy fried chicken, along with tangy cole slaw and Mrs. Knott's signature chilled cherry-rhubarb compote. Long lines on weekends may not be worth your valuable time. It's open for breakfast, lunch, and dinner and, on Sunday afternoon, for brunch. ✉ *Knott's Berry Farm, 8039 Beach Blvd.,* ☎ *714/220–5080. AE, D, DC, MC, V.*

$$ 🏨 **Buena Park Hotel and Convention Center.** Rooms have a modern, muted feel, with light-color oak and cherry furniture and earth-tone fabrics. The hotel, within easy walking distance of Knott's Berry Farm, provides complimentary shuttle service to Disneyland. Ask about Family Value Vacation packages, which include admission to one of the parks. ✉ *7675 Crescent Ave., 90620,* ☎ *714/995–1111 or 800/854–8792,* FAX *714/828–8590. 320 rooms, 28 suites. 2 restaurants, bar, pool, hot tub, concierge floor. AE, D, DC, MC, V.*

Yorba Linda, La Habra, and Brea

7–12 mi north of Anaheim, Hwy. 57.

Clustered together just north of Anaheim, Yorba Linda, La Habra, and Brea are quiet suburban towns characterized by lush parks and family-oriented shopping centers. Yorba Linda's main claim to fame is the

④   **Richard Nixon Presidential Library and Birthplace,** final resting place of the 37th president and his wife, Pat. Exhibits illustrate the checkered career of Nixon, from heralded leader of the free world to beleaguered resignee. Visitors can listen to the so-called smoking-gun tape from the Watergate days, among other recorded material. Also here are Pat Nixon's tranquil rose garden and the small farmhouse where Richard Nixon was born in 1913. ✉ *18001 Yorba Linda Blvd., at Imperial Hwy., Yorba Linda,* ☎ *714/993–3393.* 🎫 *$4.* ☉ *Mon.–Sat. 10–5, Sun. 1–5.*

🐾 ⑤   The **Children's Museum at La Habra** is housed in a 1923-vintage Union Pacific railroad depot, with old railroad cars resting nearby. Children can climb behind the wheel of Buster the Bus, a retired transit bus; "dig up" bones in the huge Dinosaur Dig sandbox; or pretend they're early settlers fishing, camping, and exploring caves. ✉ *301 S. Euclid St., La Habra,* ☎ *562/905–9793.* 🎫 *$4.* ☉ *Mon.–Sat. 10–5, Sun. 1–5.*

Dining

$$$–$$$$ ✕ **La Vie en Rose.** It's worth the detour to Brea to sample the stylishly
★   presented traditional French cuisine served in this reproduction Norman farmhouse, complete with a large turret. There's seafood, lamb, veal, and for dessert, a silky crème brûlée and a Grand Marnier soufflé. ✉ *240 S. State College Blvd. (across from Brea mall),* ☎ *714/529–8333. AE, MC, V. Closed Sun.*

Garden Grove and Orange

South of Anaheim, I–5 to Hwy. 22.

Around the intersection of Glassell Street and Chapman Avenue is Orange
⑥   Plaza (or Orange Circle, as locals call it), the heart of **Old Towne Orange.** One of the few historic towns in Orange County, this area is a must-stop for antiques browsers and architecture aficionados. Locals take great pride in their many California Craftsman–style cottages.

⑦   In Garden Grove the main attraction is the **Crystal Cathedral,** the domain of television evangelist Robert Schuller. Designed by Philip Johnson, the sparkling glass structure resembles a four-pointed star, with more than 10,000 panes of glass covering a weblike steel truss to form transparent walls. ✉ *12141 Lewis St. (take I–5 to Chapman Ave. W), Garden Grove,* ☎ *714/971–4013.* 🎫 *Donation requested for tours. Tickets for pageants are $20–$30.* ☉ *Guided tours Mon.–Sat. 9–3:30; call for schedule. Sunday services at 9:30, 11, and 1 (in Spanish).*

Dining

$$–$$$$ ✕ **Citrus City Grill.** Innovative cuisine and striking decor combining history and modernity characterize one of the best restaurants in the county. The citrus theme plays out in everything from the art on the walls to the orange-chocolate crème brûlée. Don't miss the ahi poke salad (tuna on wonton strips). ✉ *122 N. Glassell St., Orange,* ☎ *714/ 639–9600. AE, DC, MC, V. Closed Sun. and Mon. No lunch Sat.*

Santa Ana

12 mi south of Anaheim, I–5 to Hwy. 55.

🖐 ❽ The main attraction in Santa Ana, the county seat, is the **Bowers Museum of Cultural Art.** Permanent exhibits include sculpture, costumes, and artifacts from Oceania; sculpture from west and central Africa; Pacific Northwest wood carvings; dazzling beadwork of the Plains cultures; and still-life paintings. The interactive exhibits at the **Bowers Kidseum,** adjacent to the main facility, are geared toward kids ages 6–12. ✉ *2002 N. Main St., off I–5,* ☎ *714/567–3600.* 🖼 *$6.* ☉ *Tues.–Sun. 10–4, Thurs. 10–9.*

Dining

$$$–$$$$ ✕ **Gustaf Anders/Back Pocket.** At this cool, Scandinavian restaurant,
★ you'll find top-notch grilled gravlax, and a wonderful filet of beef prepared with Stilton cheese, a red-wine sauce, and creamed morel mushrooms. Next door is the more casual, less expensive Gustaf Anders' Back Pocket, with equally excellent food. ✉ *South Coast Plaza Village, 1651 Sunflower Ave.,* ☎ *714/668–1737. AE, DC, MC, V. No lunch Sun. at Back Pocket.*

$–$$ ✕ **Topaz.** Inside the Bowers Museum, this unique ethnic eatery touts a Zuni Indian influence in its regular menu as well as specials. Dine alfresco or inside the funky main dining room and watch the "chef theater" where the spicy, imaginative dishes are prepared. ✉ *2002 N. Main St.,* ☎ *714/835–2002. AE, D, DC, MC, V. No lunch Tues., Thurs.– Sat.*

Irvine

6 mi south of Santa Ana, Hwy. 55 to I–405; 12 mi south of Anaheim, I–5.

Irvine, with its tree-lined streets, uniformly manicured lawns, and pristine parks, may feel surreal to urban visitors. It's ranked in several national surveys as America's safest city. The master-planned community has top-notch schools, a university and a community college, plus dozens of shopping centers, and a network of well-lit walking and biking paths.

❾ Some of the Californian impressionist paintings on display at the small yet intriguing **Irvine Museum** depict the state's rural landscape in the years before freeways and housing developments. The paintings, which are displayed on the 12th floor of the cylindrical marble-and-glass Tower 17 building, were assembled by Joan Irvine Smith, granddaughter of James Irvine, who once owned one-quarter of what is now Orange County. ✉ *18881 Von Karman Ave., at Martin St.,* ☎ *949/476–2565.* 🖼 *Free.* ☉ *Tues.–Sat. 11–5.*

❿ The mind-boggling 32-acre **Entertainment Center at Irvine Spectrum** contains a huge, 21-theater cinema complex (with a six-story IMAX 3-D theater), several lively restaurants and cafés, shops, and a virtual-reality experience set inside the NASCAR Silicon Motor Speedway. ✉

Exit Irvine Center Dr. at intersection of I–405, I–5, and Hwy. 133, ☎
949/450–4900 for film listings.

⓫ Wild Rivers Water Park has more than 40 rides and attractions, including
a wave pool, a few daring slides, a river inner-tube ride, and several
cafés and shops. ⊠ *8770 Irvine Center Dr., off I–405,* ☎ *949/768–
9453.* ⊞ *$21.99.* ☉ *Mid-May–Sept.; call for hrs.*

Dining and Lodging

$$-$$$$ ✕ **Bistango.** A sleek, postmodern, art-filled bistro serves first-rate
American cuisine with a European flair: salads, seafood, pasta, Mediter-
ranean pizzas, and grilled ahi tuna. An attractive group comes to savor
the food, listen to live jazz, and mingle with their well-dressed peers.
⊠ *19100 Von Karman Ave.,* ☎ *949/752–5222. AE, D, DC, MC, V.
Valet parking.*

$$-$$$ ✕ **Prego.** Reminiscent of a Tuscan villa, this is a much larger version
★   of the Beverly Hills Prego, with soft lighting, golden walls, and an out-
door patio. Try the spit-roasted meats and chicken, charcoal-grilled fresh
fish, or pizzas from the oak-burning oven. ⊠ *18420 Von Karman Ave.,*
☎ *949/553–1333. AE, DC, MC, V. No lunch weekends. Valet park-
ing.*

$-$$$ ✕ **Sam Woo.** From fresh- and saltwater tanks comes seafood cooked
to order at this formal Chinese restaurant. Whole fish is presented table-
side. ⊠ *15333 Culver Dr., Suite 720,* ☎ *949/262–0688. AE, MC, V.*

$-$$ ✕ **Kitima Thai Cuisine.** Orange County's best Thai restaurant is a fa-
vorite with the business-lunch crowd. The names may be gimmicky—
Rock-and-Roll Shrimp Salad, Rambo Chicken (sautéed with green
chilis and sweet basil)—but fresh ingredients are used in every dish.
⊠ *2010 Main St., Suite 170,* ☎ *949/261–2929. AE, D, DC, MC, V.
Closed Sun.*

$$$-$$$$ ▦ **Irvine Marriott.** Towering over Koll Business Center, the Marriott
offers a convenient location and amenities designed to appeal to busi-
ness travelers. The hotel has an intimate feel, owing in part to the con-
vivial lobby with love seats and evening entertainment (usually a jazz
pianist). Weekend discounts and packages are usually available, and
there's a courtesy van to South Coast Plaza and the airport. ⊠ *18000
Von Karman Ave., 92715,* ☎ *949/553–0100 or 800/228–9290,* ⅢX *949/
261–7059. 484 rooms, 8 suites. 2 restaurants, coffee bar, sushi bar, in-
door-outdoor pool, hot tub, 4 tennis courts, health club, concierge floors,
business services, airport shuttle. AE, D, DC, MC, V.*

$$-$$$$ ▦ **Atrium Hotel.** Across the street from John Wayne Airport and near
most area offices, this garden-style hotel caters to business travelers.
Rooms have large work areas, coffeemakers, and two phones, and most
offer private balconies overlooking either the pool or gardens. ⊠
18700 MacArthur Blvd., 92612, ☎ *949/833–2770 or 800/854–3012,*
ⅢX *949/757–1228. 214 rooms. Restaurant, bar, pool, health club, car
rental. AE, D, DC, MC, V.*

$$$ ▦ **Hyatt Regency Irvine.** The sleek, ultramodern rooms here offer
practical amenities such as coffeemakers, irons, and hair dryers. Spe-
cial golf packages at nearby Tustin Ranch and Pelican Hills are avail-
able, and a complimentary shuttle runs to local shopping centers.
Rates are lower on weekends. ⊠ *17900 Jamboree Rd., 92714,* ☎ *949/
975–1234 or 800/233–1234,* ⅢX *949/852–1574. 536 rooms, 20 suites.
2 restaurants, 2 bars, pool, 4 tennis courts, health club, bicycles, con-
cierge, business services. AE, D, DC, MC, V.*

Nightlife

Irvine Improv (⊠ 4255 Campus Dr., ☎ 949/854–5455) is a comedy
club that's open from Wednesday through Sunday nights. The **Irvine
Meadows Amphitheater** (⊠ 8808 Irvine Center Dr., ☎ 949/855–4515

or 949/855–6111), a 15,000-seat open-air venue, presents musical events from May through October.

Costa Mesa

6 mi northeast of Irvine, I–405 to Bristol St.

★ ⑫ Costa Mesa's most famous landmark, **South Coast Plaza** is an immense retail, entertainment, and dining complex consisting of two enclosed shopping areas and an open-air collection of boutiques. The Plaza rivals Rodeo Drive in its number of top international designers' shops—Gucci, Armani, Christian Dior, Hermes, Versace, and Prada, to name just a few—along with standard upscale shops such as J. Crew, Ralph Lauren, Calvin Klein, Liz Claiborne, and F. A. O. Schwarz. A free shuttle transports the Plaza's 20 million annual visitors between sections. ⊠ *3333 S. Bristol St., off I–405,* ☎ *714/435–2000.* ☼ *Weekdays 10–9, Sat. 10–7, Sun. 11–6:30.*

⑬ The **Orange County Performing Arts Center** (⊠ 600 Town Center Dr., east of Bristol St., ☎ 714/556–2787) contains a 3,000-seat facility for opera, ballet, symphony, and musicals. Richard Lippold's enormous *Firebird,* a triangular-shape sculpture of polished metal surfaces that resembles a bird taking flight, extends outward from the glass-enclosed lobby. Within walking distance of the center is the **California Scenario** (⊠ 611 Anton Blvd.), a 1½-acre sculpture garden designed by Isamu Noguchi.

Dining and Lodging

$$–$$$ ✕ **Diva.** Ideal for patrons of the South Coast Repertory Theater and ★ the Performing Arts Center, Diva offers unexpected combinations of ingredients presented in ways almost too pretty to eat. Entrées such as salmon with wilted greens and blackberry vinegar, or grilled veal chops with hazelnut butter are heartwarmingly good. ⊠ *600 Anton Blvd.,* ☎ *714/754–0600. AE, D, DC, MC, V. No lunch weekends.*

$$–$$$ ✕ **Habana Restaurant and Bar.** Habana blends an Old World flavor with a hip '90s flair. The Cuban and Caribbean specialties are as flavorful as the setting is cool. Chocolate lovers can't miss the Café Cubano—chocolate mousse topped with chocolate whipped cream and rum sauce. With entertainment six nights a week this restaurant is fast becoming a popular nightspot. ⊠ *2930 Bristol St.,* ☎ *714/556–0176. AE, D, DC, MC, V.*

$$–$$$ ✕ **Pinot Provence.** The county's hottest new French dining spot showcases the innovative cuisine of chef Joachim Splichal (of L.A.'s Patina). Discover the wildly imaginative mix of fresh California ingredients and traditional Provençal cooking. The well-heeled meet in the main dining room amid 18th-century antiques to be seen (and unfortunately heard), so many prefer the more intimate patio dining. ⊠ *686 Anton Blvd.,* ☎ *714/444–5900. Reservations essential. AE, D, DC, MC, V.*

$–$$$ ✕ **Bangkok IV.** Despite its shopping-mall location, this restaurant's stark ★ white-and-black interior, with striking flower arrangements on every table, defies conventional mall dining. The *pla dung,* steamed catfish with a chili-garlic-lemongrass sauce, is exceptional. ⊠ *Across from South Coast Plaza, 3333 Bear St.,* ☎ *714/540–7661. AE, D, DC, MC, V.*

$–$$ ✕ **Memphis Soul Café and Bar.** The gumbo here is the best in the county, ★ and the pork chops are a work of art. ⊠ *2920 Bristol St.,* ☎ *714/432–7685. AE, DC, MC, V.*

$$$–$$$$ 🏠 **Country Side Inn and Suites.** Here you'll get close to the bed-and-breakfast experience with rooms and common areas that look more like Mom's house than a hotel. The Queen Anne–style rooms, with a vaguely European feel, are homey and inviting. ⊠ *325 Bristol St., 92626,* ☎ *714/549–0300 or 800/322–9992,* FAX *714/662–0828. 150 rooms,*

150 suites. Restaurant, bar, 2 pools, 2 hot tubs, exercise room, business center. Full breakfast. AE, D, DC, MC, V.

$$$–$$$$ ⚏ **Westin South Coast Plaza.** This downtown high-rise adjoins the South Coast complex, making it convenient for shoppers and businesspeople. ⊠ *686 Anton Blvd., 92626,* ☎ *714/540–2500 or 800/228–3000,* ℻ *714/662–6695. 373 rooms, 17 suites. Restaurant, lobby lounge, pool, 2 tennis courts. AE, D, DC, MC, V.*

$$–$$$ ⚏ **Doubletree Hotel.** Near John Wayne Airport, this modern, spacious hotel has a glittering atrium lobby with glass elevators. ⊠ *3050 Bristol St., 92626,* ☎ *714/540–7000,* ℻ *714/540–9176. 484 rooms, 10 suites. 2 restaurants, lobby lounge, pool, beauty salon, hot tub, health club. AE, D, DC, MC, V.*

Nightlife and the Arts

Orange County Performing Arts Center (⊠ 600 Town Center Dr., ☎ 714/556–2787) presents major touring companies, among them the American Ballet Theater and the Los Angeles Philharmonic Orchestra. **South Coast Repertory Theater** (⊠ 655 Town Center Dr., ☎ 714/708–5555) is a Tony award–winning theater presenting new and traditional works on two stages.

THE COAST

Running along the Orange County coastline is the scenic Pacific Coast Highway (Highway 1, known locally as PCH). It's well worth the effort to take this route instead of the freeways. Pull over on PCH and a public beach is often just steps away.

Huntington Beach

25 mi west of Anaheim, Hwy. 57 south to Hwy. 22 West to I–405.

Once a sleepy residential town with little more than a string of rugged surf shops, Huntington Beach is slowly transforming into a resort destination. The town's appeal is its broad white-sand beaches with often-towering waves. A lively pier, a large shopping pavilion on Main Street, and the luxurious Waterfront Hilton beckon various locals and visitors.

⓮ **Huntington Pier** stretches 1,800 ft out to sea, well past the powerful waves that made Huntington Beach America's "Surf City." At the end of the pier sits **Ruby's** (☎ 714/969–7829), part of a California chain of '40s-style burger-centered eateries. The **Pierside Pavilion,** across Pacific Coast Highway from the pier, contains shops, restaurants, bars
⓯ with live music, and a theater complex. Just up Main Street, the **International Surfing Museum** (⊠ 411 Olive Ave., ☎ 714/960–3483), open from Wednesday through Sunday between noon and 5 (⚏ $2), pays tribute to the sport's greats with the Surfing Hall of Fame.

Huntington City Beach stretches for 3 mi from the pier area. The beach is most crowded around the pier. Amateur and professional surfers brave the waves daily on its north side. Continuing north, **Huntington State Beach** (☎ 714/536–1454) parallels Pacific Coast Highway. On the state and city beaches there are changing rooms, concessions, lifeguards (except in winter), and ample parking. The state beach also has barbecue pits and RV campsites. At the northern section of the city, **Bolsa Chica State Beach** (☎ 714/846–3460) has barbecue pits and is usually less crowded than its southern neighbors.

★ ⓰ **Bolsa Chica Ecological Reserve** beckons wildlife lovers and bird-watchers with an 1,180-acre salt marsh that is home to 315 species of birds, including great blue herons, snowy and great egrets, and common loons. Throughout the reserve are trails for bird-watching. ✉ *Entrance at Warner Ave. and PCH, opposite Bolsa Chica State Beach,* ☎ *714/897-7003.* 🅿 *Free parking.* ☉ *Daily dawn–sunset.*

Dining and Lodging

$–$$$ ✕ **Baci.** Romantic or kitschy, depending on your style, Baci nevertheless serves dependable Italian food. Among the best dishes are carpaccio with shrimp, tortellini soup, and cannoli for dessert. ✉ *18748 Beach Blvd.,* ☎ *714/965–1194. AE, D, DC, MC, V.*

$–$$ ✕ **Louise's Trattoria.** The local branch of this Italian chain is across the street from the Huntington Beach pier. The chicken marsala and fettuccine with sun-dried tomatoes in a chardonnay-cream sauce hit the spot, and the pizzas are stellar. ✉ *300 PCH,* ☎ *714/960–0996. AE, D, DC, MC, V.*

$ ✕ **Alice's Breakfast in the Park.** Tranquillity is the buzzword at this wooden brunch house nestled among Huntington Park's eucalyptus trees near Huntington Lake. There's seating on the outdoor patio, from which children can feed the ducks, and a small, indoor dining room with flowers and antiques. Be sure to try Alice's "outrageous cinnamon roll." ✉ *6622 Lakeview, off Edwards St.,* ☎ *714/848–0690. No credit cards. No dinner.*

$ ✕ **Wahoo's Fish Taco.** Mahimahi- and wahoo-filled tacos are the specialty of this casual, incredibly popular restaurant. ✉ *120 Main St.,* ☎ *714/536–2050. MC, V.*

$$$–$$$$ 🏨 **Waterfront Hilton.** Rising 12 stories above the surf, this Mediterranean-style resort occupies a spot on 8½ mi of white-sand beach. All rooms have private lanais, many with panoramic ocean views. ✉ *21100 PCH, 92648,* ☎ *714/960–7873 or 800/822–7873,* 🖷 *714/960–2642. 258 rooms, 32 suites. 2 restaurants, bar, pool, hot tub, 2 tennis courts, exercise room, children's programs (ages 5–12; summer only), concierge floor. AE, DC, MC, V.*

Outdoor Activities and Sports

BICYCLING

Team Bicycle Rentals (✉ 8464 Indianapolis Ave., ☎ 714/969–5480) rents touring and other bicycles. **Edison Community Center** (✉ 21377 Magnolia Ave., ☎ 714/960–8870) and the **Murdy Community Center** (✉ 7000 Norma Dr., ☎ 714/960–8895) both have tennis courts available on a first-come, first-served basis in the daytime. Both accept reservations for play after 5 PM at a charge of $2 an hour.

Shopping

Jack's (✉ 101 Main St., ☎ 714/536–4516) and **Huntington Beach Surf and Sport** (✉ 300 PCH, at Main St., ☎ 714/841–4000) carry the latest styles in beachwear and surfing equipment.

Newport Beach

6 mi south of Huntington Beach, Hwy. 1.

Newport Beach has two distinct personalities. It's best known for its island-dotted yacht harbor and wealthy residents. And then there's inland Newport Beach, southwest of John Wayne Airport, a business and commercial hub lined with shopping centers and a clutch of high-rise office buildings and hotels.

★ ⓱ **Newport Harbor,** which shelters nearly 10,000 small boats, may seduce even those who don't own a yacht. Exploring the charming avenues and surrounding alleys can be great fun. To see Newport Harbor from the water, take a one-hour gondola cruise operated by the Gondola Company of Newport (✉ 3400 Via Oporto, Suite 102B, ☎ 949/675–1212). It costs $60 for two.

Within Newport Harbor are eight small islands, including Balboa and
Lido. The houses lining the shore may seem modest, but this is some
of the most expensive real estate in the world.

Newport Pier, which juts out into the ocean near 20th Street, is the
heart of Newport's beach community. On the pier you can go fishing
or grab a burger and shake at **Ruby's** (☎ 949/675–7829). Street parking is difficult at the pier, so grab the first space you find and be prepared to walk. A stroll along West Ocean Front reveals much of the
town's character. On weekday mornings, head for the beach near the
pier, where fishermen hawk their predawn catches. On weekends the
walk is alive with kids of all ages on in-line skates, skateboards, and
bikes dodging pedestrians and whizzing past fast-food joints, swimsuit shops, and bars.

⑱ Newport's best beaches are on **Balboa Peninsula,** whose many jetties
pave the way to ideal swimming areas. The **Balboa Pavilion,** on the
bay side of the Balboa Peninsula, was built in 1905 as a bath- and
boathouse. Today it houses a restaurant and shops and is a departure
point for harbor and whale-watching cruises. Look for it on Main Street,
off Balboa Boulevard. Adjacent to the pavilion is the three-car ferry
that connects the peninsula to Balboa Island.

⑲ The **Orange County Museum of Art** has gathered an esteemed collection of Abstract Expressionist paintings and cutting-edge contemporary works by California artists. ⊠ *850 San Clemente Dr.,* ☎ *949/759–
1122.* 🎟 *$5.* ☉ *Tues.–Sun. 11–5.*

Dining and Lodging

$$$–$$$$ ✕ **Aubergine.** The husband-and-wife team who run this restaurant (he
★ mans the kitchen and she handles the dining room) have set new stan-
dards for fine cuisine in Orange County. The six-course prix-fixe menu
(with an exceptional wine list) is unforgettable. You can also order à
la carte. Classic French dishes are prepared with a modern flair. ⊠ *508
29th St.,* ☎ *949/723–4150. Reservations essential. AE, MC, V. Closed
Sun.–Mon. No lunch.*

$$$–$$$$ ✕ **The Ritz.** Indeed, this is one of the ritziest restaurants in southern
California, complete with black-leather booths, polished-brass trim,
and the requisite attitude. Don't pass up the "carousel" appetizer—
cured gravlax, prawns, Dungeness crab legs, Maine lobster tails, goose
liver pâté, fillet of smoked trout, Parma prosciutto, filet mignon tartare,
and marinated herring, all served on a lazy Susan. ⊠ *880 Newport
Center Dr.,* ☎ *949/720–1800. Reservations essential. AE, DC, MC,
V. No lunch weekends.*

$$–$$$$ ✕ **Twin Palms.** The area's most beautiful people congregate under the
tentlike atmosphere at this haute eatery. Pasta, chicken, pizza, fish spe-
cials, and salads are all on the creative menu in this sister property to
the original Twin Palms in Pasadena. ⊠ *630 Newport Center Dr.,* ☎
949/721–8288. AE, DC, MC, V. Valet parking.

$–$$ ✕ **El Torito Grill.** The tortilla soup is to die for, as is the carne asada.
★ Just-baked tortillas with fresh salsa replace the usual chip basket. The
bar serves hand-shaken margaritas and 80 brands of tequila. ⊠ *Fashion Island, 951 Newport Center Dr.,* ☎ *949/640–2875. AE, D, DC,
MC, V.*

$–$$ ✕ **P. F. Chang's China Bistro.** The tasty Cal-Chinese food at this trendy
chain restaurant includes Mongolian spicy beef and Chang's chicken,
stir-fried in a sweet-and-spicy Szechuan sauce. Almost every table has
an ocean view. ⊠ *Fashion Island, 1145 Newport Center Dr.,* ☎ *949/
759–9007. Reservations not accepted. AE, MC, V.*

$$$$ ★ 🏨 **Four Seasons Hotel.** A stylish hotel in an ultrachic neighborhood, the Four Seasons caters to luxury seekers by offering weekend golf packages (in conjunction with the nearby Pelican Hill golf course), and the use of extensive fitness facilities. Guest rooms have outstanding views, private bars, and original artwork on the walls. Kids are given special treatment: balloons, cookies and milk, game books, and more. ⊠ 690 *Newport Center Dr., 92660,* ☎ *949/759–0808 or 800/332–3442,* FAX *949/759–0568. 285 rooms, 93 suites. 2 restaurants, bar, pool, beauty salon, massage, sauna, 2 tennis courts, health club, mountain bikes, concierge, business services. AE, D, DC, MC, V.*

$$$$ 🏨 **Sutton Place Hotel.** An eye-catching ziggurat design is the trademark of this ultramodern hotel in Koll Center. Despite its futuristic exterior, the inside reflects a traditional elegance with tasteful beige and burgundy accents. Many of the spacious rooms have canopy beds. ⊠ *4500 MacArthur Blvd., 92660,* ☎ *949/476–2001 or 800/243–4141,* FAX *949/476–0153. 435 rooms, 215 suites. 2 restaurants, 2 bars, in-room data ports, minibars, refrigerators, pool, spa, 2 tennis courts, health club, bicycles, concierge, business services, airport shuttle. AE, D, DC, MC, V.*

$$$–$$$$ 🏨 **Newport Beach Marriott Hotel and Tennis Club.** Popular with the international set, this hotel overlooking Newport Harbor features a distinctive fountain surrounded by a plant-filled atrium. Rooms are in one of two towers; all have balconies or patios that look out onto lush gardens or the Pacific. ⊠ *900 Newport Center Dr., 92660,* ☎ *949/640–4000 or 800/228–9290,* FAX *949/640–5055. 577 rooms, 6 suites. Restaurant, bar, 2 pools, sauna, 8 tennis courts, health club, concierge, business services. AE, D, DC, MC, V.*

$$–$$$ 🏨 **Sheraton Newport Beach.** Bamboo trees and palms in the lobby add to the tropical feel of this hotel 5 mi from the beach. Vibrant teals, mauves, and peaches make up the guest-room color scheme. The hotel is convenient to John Wayne Airport. ⊠ *4545 MacArthur Blvd., 92660,* ☎ *949/833–0570 or 800/325–3535,* FAX *949/833–3927. 340 rooms, 4 suites. Restaurant, bar, pool, 2 tennis courts, exercise room. AE, D, DC, MC, V.*

Nightlife

The **Cannery** (⊠ 3010 Lafayette Ave., ☎ 949/675–5777) is a packed seaside restaurant and bar with karaoke and live entertainment. **Tibbie's Music Hall** (⊠ 4647 MacArthur Blvd., ☎ 949/252–0834) is a small dinner theater that's open weekends only. Book in advance, since there's sometimes up to a month wait for reservations.

Outdoor Activities and Sports

BOAT RENTAL

You can rent kayaks ($10 an hour), sailboats ($25 an hour), small motorboats ($30 an hour), cocktail boats ($45 an hour), and ocean boats ($65–$80 an hour) at **Balboa Boat Rentals** (⊠ 510 E. Edgewater Ave., ☎ 949/673–7200). You must have a driver's license, and some knowledge of boating is helpful. Rented boats are not allowed out of the bay.

BOAT TOURS

A fun way to take in the scenery of Newport's harbor is on the two-hour **Cannery Restaurant weekend brunch cruise** (⊠ 3010 Lafayette Ave., ☎ 949/675–5777). Cruises cost $31, and they depart at 10 AM and 1:30 PM. **Catalina Passenger Service** (⊠ 400 Main St., ☎ 949/673–5245) at the Balboa Pavilion operates sightseeing tours ($6 to $8) and, during the winter, whale-watching cruises ($14). **Hornblower Dining Yachts** (⊠ 2431 W. Coast Hwy., ☎ 949/646–0155) books 2½-hour Saturday dinner cruises with dancing for $59.95; Sunday brunch cruises are $39.95. Reservations are required.

Newport Beach Golf Course (✉ 3100 Irvine Ave., ☎ 949/852–8681), an 18-hole, par-59 course, is lighted for nighttime play. Greens fees range from $14 to $18 for 18-hole play; hand carts rent for $2. Reservations are accepted up to one week in advance, but walk-ups are accommodated when possible. **Pelican Hill Golf Club** (✉ 22651 Pelican Hill Rd. S, ☎ 949/640–0238) has two 18-hole courses (par 70 and 71). Greens fees range from $150 to $210 and include the mandatory cart.

In addition to a complete tackle shop, **Davey's Locker** (✉ Balboa Pavilion, 400 Main St., ☎ 949/673–1434) operates sportfishing trips starting at $25, as well as private charters and whale-watching trips.

The River Jetties in northern Newport are good for beginners. The Wedge, farther south, is famous for its steep, punishing shore break.

Call the **recreation department** (☎ 949/644–3151) for information about use of the courts in seven locations throughout Orange County, where play is free and first-come, first-served. Reservations are required at the **Newport Beach Marriott Hotel and Tennis Club** (✉ 900 Newport Center Dr., ☎ 949/640–4000) for $10 per person all day for guests and $15 per person all day for nonguests.

Shopping

The outdoor **Fashion Island** features stellar ocean views for alfresco shopping and dining at several restaurants and stores, including Bloomingdale's, Robinsons-May, Neiman-Marcus, and Macy's, as well as upscale boutiques. ✉ *Newport Center Dr., between Jamboree and MacArthur Blvds., off PCH,* ☎ *949/721–2022.*

Corona del Mar

2 mi south of Newport Beach, Hwy. 1.

A small jewel on the Pacific Coast, Corona del Mar has exceptional beaches that some say resemble their majestic northern California counterparts. **Corona del Mar Beach** (☎ 949/644–3044) is actually made up of two beaches, Little Corona and Big Corona, separated by a cliff. Facilities include fire pits, volleyball courts, food stands, rest rooms, and parking. Two colorful reefs (and the fact that it's off-limits to boats) make Corona del Mar great for snorkeling and for beachcombers who prefer privacy.

Midway between Corona del Mar and Laguna, on the inland side of Pacific Coast Highway, **Crystal Cove State Park** (☎ 949/494–3539) is a hidden treasure: a 3½-mi stretch of unspoiled beach with some of the best tide pooling in southern California. You can see starfish, crabs, and other sea life on the rocks. The park's 2,400 acres of backcountry are ideal for hiking, horseback riding, and mountain biking. Docents lead nature walks on most weekend mornings. Parking costs $6 per car.

The town of Corona del Mar stretches only a few blocks along Pacific Coast Highway, but some of the toniest stores in the county line the route.

㉒ **Sherman Library and Gardens,** a botanical garden and library specializing in the history of the Pacific Southwest, provides a diversion from sun and sand. You can wander among cactus gardens, rose gardens, a wheelchair-height touch-and-smell garden, and a tropical conservatory. ⊠ *2647 PCH,* ☎ *949/673–2261.* ⊠ *$3, free Mon.* ☉ *Daily 10:30–4.*

Dining

$$–$$$$ ✕ **The Bungalow.** Specializing in prime steaks and seafood, this Craftsman-style restaurant is known for its lobster with wild rice. The younger local moneyed set packs the place. ⊠ *2441 E. Coast Hwy.,* ☎ *949/673–6585. AE, MC, V. No lunch.*

$–$$$ ✕ **Bandera.** Pork cutlets, barbecued salmon, and New Orleans–style jambalaya are a few of the American regional specials you'll find at this popular, wood-paneled eatery. ⊠ *3201 E. Coast Hwy.,* ☎ *949/673–3524. Reservations not accepted. AE, DC, MC, V. No lunch.*

$ ✕ **C'est Si Bonne.** This tiny French café serves delightful breakfasts and fresh, hearty pâté-and-cheese plates as well as interesting sandwiches at lunch. For those not lucky enough to secure a table, there's takeout. ⊠ *3444 E. Coast Hwy.,* ☎ *949/675–0994. AE, D, DC, MC, V. No dinner.*

Laguna Beach

★ *10 mi south of Newport Beach on Hwy. 1; 60 mi south of Los Angeles, I–5 south to Hwy. 133, which turns into Laguna Canyon Rd.*

Traditionally a haven of conservative wealth, Laguna Beach attracted the beat, hip, and far-out during the 1950s and '60s (along with what has grown to be Orange County's most visible gay community). Art galleries dot the village streets, which can be unbearably congested in the summer. The surrounding canyons and hills provide a beautiful backdrop to the beachfront village. A 1993 fire, which destroyed more than 300 homes in the hillsides surrounding Laguna Beach, miraculously left the village untouched.

The town's main street, Pacific Coast Highway, is referred to as either South Coast or North Coast Highway, depending on the address. All along the highway and side streets such as Forest or Ocean avenues, you'll find dozens of eclectic fine-art and crafts galleries, clothing boutiques, and jewelry shops.

At the **Pageant of the Masters** (☎ 949/494–1145 or 800/487–3378), Laguna's most impressive event and part of the city's annual Festival of Arts, live models and carefully orchestrated backgrounds are arranged in striking mimicry of classical and contemporary paintings. The festival usually takes place in July and August.

㉑ The **Laguna Art Museum** displays American art, with an emphasis on California artists and works. ⊠ *307 Cliff Dr.,* ☎ *949/494–6531.* ⊠ *$5.* ☉ *Tues.–Sun. 11–5.*

Laguna Beach's **Main Beach Park,** at the end of Broadway at South Coast Highway, has sand volleyball, two basketball half-courts, children's play equipment, picnic areas, rest rooms, showers, and street parking. The colorful crowd ranges from authentic hippies to beach volleyball champs to resident celebrities such as Bette Midler.

Aliso Beach County Park (☎ 949/661–7013) in south Laguna is a recreation area with a fishing pier, a playground, fire pits, parking, food stands, and rest rooms.

Woods Cove, off South Coast Highway at Diamond Street, is especially quiet during the week. Big rock formations hide lurking crabs. As you climb the steps to leave, you can see an English-style mansion that was once the home of Bette Davis.

Dining and Lodging

$$$-$$$$ ✕ **Five Feet.** Others have attempted to mimic this restaurant's inno-
  ★   vative blend of Chinese and French cooking styles, but Five Feet re-
       mains the leader. Among the standout dishes: cheese wontons with
       raspberry coulis, fish in a garlic black-bean sauce, and rabbit with foie
       gras and wild mushrooms. ⊠ *328 Glenneyre St.,* ☎ *949/497–4955.*
       AE, D, DC, MC, V. No lunch.

$$$ ✕ **Sorrento Grille.** High ceilings and two walls of floor-to-ceiling win-
       dows create an illusion of space at this narrow restaurant on a quiet
       side street downtown. Mesquite steaks, seafood, and pastas predom-
       inate on the contemporary menu. ⊠ *370 Glenneyre St.,* ☎ *949/494–*
       8686. AE, DC, MC, V. No lunch.

$$-$$$ ✕ **Odessa.** Fans of this hip spot favor the potato-crusted sea bass and
       the sesame-crusted ahi, just two of the eclectic dishes with a Southern
       accent. In the romantic, dimly lit space, you may not notice the celebri-
       ties at the next table—or the stylish crowd heading upstairs to the night-
       club. ⊠ *680 S. Coast Hwy.,* ☎ *949/376–8792. Reservations essential.*
       AE, D, DC, MC, V. No lunch. Valet parking.

$$-$$$ ✕ **Ti Amo.** A romantic setting and creative Mediterranean cuisine have
       earned this place acclaim. Try the seared tuna with a sesame-seed crust
       or farfalle with smoked chicken and creamy bell pepper sauce. To max-
       imize romance, request a table in the enclosed garden in back. ⊠
       31727 S. Coast Hwy., ☎ *949/499–5350. AE, D, DC, MC, V. No lunch.*

$-$$ ✕ **Tortilla Flats.** This hacienda-style restaurant with a fireplace has a
       wide selection of Mexican tequilas and beers, and a quiet upstairs bar.
       Sunday brunch is a lively affair. ⊠ *1740 S. Coast Hwy.,* ☎ *949/494–*
       6588. AE, MC, V.

$ ✕ **Café Zinc.** Laguna Beach cognoscenti gather at the tiny counter and
       plant-filled patio of this vegetarian breakfast-and-lunch café. Oatmeal
       is sprinkled with berries, poached eggs are dusted with herbs, and the
       orange juice is fresh-squeezed. For lunch, try a sampler plate, with var-
       ious salads like spicy Thai pasta, and asparagus salad with orange peel
       and capers, or one of the gourmet pizzettes. ⊠ *350 Ocean Ave.,* ☎
       949/494–6302. No credit cards. No dinner.

$$$$ ▥ **Surf and Sand Hotel.** Laguna's largest hotel is right on the beach,
  ★   a rarity in environmentally conscious California. Tastefully decorated
       rooms have an appropriately beachlike feel, with soft sand colors,
       bleached-wood shutters, and private balconies. ⊠ *1555 S. Coast Hwy.,*
       92651, ☎ *949/497–4477 or 800/524–8621,* 𝔽𝔸𝕏 *949/494–2897. 164*
       rooms, 15 suites. Restaurant, bar, pool, health club, beach, concierge.
       AE, D, DC, MC, V.

$$-$$$$ ▥ **Eiler's Inn.** A light-filled courtyard with a fountain is the focal point
  ★   of this quaint bed-and-breakfast. Every room is unique, full of antiques
       and travelers' journals for you to fill in. Afternoon wine and cheese is
       served in the courtyard or in the cozy reading room, where you'll find
       the inn's only TV and phone. ⊠ *741 S. Coast Hwy., 92651,* ☎ *949/*
       494–3004, 𝔽𝔸𝕏 *949/497–2215. 12 rooms. Full breakfast. AE, D, MC,*
       V.

$$-$$$$ ▥ **Hotel Laguna.** The oldest hotel in Laguna (opened in 1890) has man-
       icured gardens, a private beach, and an ideal location downtown.
       Four rooms have canopy beds and reproduction Victorian furnishings.
       Others have whitewashed furniture and pastel bedspreads and curtains
       (none has air-conditioning). ⊠ *425 S. Coast Hwy., 92651,* ☎ *949/494–*
       1151 or 800/524–2927, 𝔽𝔸𝕏 *949/497–2163. 63 rooms. 2 restaurants,*
       bar, beach. Continental breakfast. AE, D, DC, MC, V.

$$-$$$$ ▥ **Inn at Laguna Beach.** On a bluff overlooking the ocean, the inn has
       a Mediterranean feel, with terra-cotta tiles and exotic flowers all over
       the grounds. Most guest rooms have views; those on the coastal level
       border Laguna's oceanfront cliffs. ⊠ *211 N. Coast Hwy., 92651,* ☎

949/497–9722 or 800/544–4479, FAX 949/497–9972. *70 rooms. In-room VCRs, minibars, refrigerators, pool. AE, D, DC, MC, V.*

$–$$$$ ⬚ **Coast Inn.** Gay men and some lesbians have been staying at the Coast Inn for more than three decades. Some rooms are standard motel-style; others are larger, with private decks and fireplaces. ✉ *1401 S. Coast Hwy.,* ☎ *949/494–7588 or 800/653–2697,* FAX *949/494–1735. 23 rooms. Restaurant, bar. AE, D, DC, MC, V.*

Nightlife

The **Boom Boom Room** (✉ Coast Inn, 1401 S. Coast Hwy., ☎ 949/ 494–7588) is Laguna Beach's most popular gay club. The **Sandpiper** (✉ 1183 S. Coast Hwy., ☎ 949/494–4694), a hole-in-the-wall dancing joint, attracts an eclectic crowd. Laguna's **White House** (✉ 340 S. Coast Hwy., ☎ 949/494–8088), a chic club on the main strip, has nightly entertainment and dancing.

Outdoor Activities and Sports

BICYCLING

Mountain bikes can be rented at **Rainbow Bicycles** (✉ 485 N. Coast Hwy., ☎ 949/494–5806).

GOLF

Aliso Creek Golf Course (✉ 31106 S. Coast Hwy., ☎ 949/499–1919) is a scenic nine-hole facility with a putting green. Greens fees range from $17 to $25. Reservations are taken up to a week in advance.

TENNIS

Six metered courts can be found at **Laguna Beach High School.** Two courts are available at the **Irvine Bowl.** Six courts are available at **Alta Laguna Park** on a first-come, first-served basis. **Moulton Meadows** has two courts. For more information, call the **City of Laguna Beach Recreation Department** (☎ 949/497–0716).

WATER SPORTS

Because its entire beach area is a marine preserve, Laguna Beach is ideal for snorkelers. Scuba divers should head to the Marine Life Refuge area, which runs from Seal Rock to Diver's Cove.

Shopping

Forest and Ocean avenues are full of art galleries and fine jewelry and clothing boutiques. The **Art Center Gallery** (✉ 266 Forest Ave., ☎ 949/ 376–7596) exhibits the works of local artists. **Georgeo's Art Glass and Jewelry** (✉ 269 Forest Ave., ☎ 949/497–0907) has a large selection of etched-glass bowls, vases, and fine jewelry.

Dana Point

10 mi south of Laguna Beach, Hwy. 1.

Dana Point's claim to fame is its small-boat marina tucked into a dramatic natural harbor and surrounded by high bluffs. In late February, a whale festival features concerts, films, sports competitions, and a weekend street fair. **Dana Point Harbor** was first described more than 100 years ago by its namesake Richard Henry Dana in his book *Two Years Before the Mast.*

Inside Dana Point Harbor, **Swim Beach** has a fishing pier, barbecues, food stands, parking, rest rooms, and showers. At the south end of Dana Point, **Doheny State Park** (☎ 949/496–6171) is one of southern California's top surfing destinations. Here you'll also find five indoor tanks and an interpretive center devoted to the wildlife of the Doheny Marine Refuge. There are also food stands and shops, picnic facilities, volleyball courts, and a pier for fishing. Camping is permitted, though there are no RV hookups.

🐾 ㉒ Two indoor tanks at the **Orange County Marine Institute** contain touchable sea creatures, as well as the complete skeleton of a gray whale. Anchored near the institute is *The Pilgrim,* a full-size replica of the square-rigged vessel on which Richard Henry Dana sailed. You can tour the boat Sunday from 10 to 2:30. Weekend cruises are also available. You can arrange to go whale-watching from January through March, or to explore regional tide pools year-round. ⊠ *24200 Dana Point Harbor Dr.,* ☎ *949/496–2274.* ☞ *Donation requested.* ☉ *Weekends 10–4:30.*

Dining and Lodging

$–$$$ ✕ **Luciana's.** This intimate Italian restaurant is a real find, especially for couples seeking a romantic evening. Dining rooms are small, dressed with crisp white linens and warmed by two fireplaces inside and yet another fireplace on the patio. Try the linguine with clams, prawns, calamari, and green-lip mussels in a light tomato sauce, or veal medallions with haricot verts and oven-dried tomatoes. ⊠ *24312 Del Prado Ave.,* ☎ *949/661–6500. AE, DC, MC, V. No lunch.*

$ ✕ **Proud Mary's.** On a terrace overlooking the fishing boats and pleasure craft in Dana Point Harbor, Proud Mary's serves the best burgers and sandwiches in southern Orange County. Steaks, chicken, and other American standards are served at lunchtime, and you can order breakfast all day. ⊠ *34689 Golden Lantern St.,* ☎ *949/493–5853. AE, D, MC, V. No dinner.*

$$$$ ✕🏨 **Ritz-Carlton, Laguna Niguel.** An unrivaled setting on the edge of
★   the Pacific combined with the hallmark Ritz-Carlton service have earned this grand hotel worldwide recognition. An imposing marble-columned entryway is surrounded by landscaped grounds. The overall impression is that of a Mediterranean country villa. Rooms have marble bathrooms and private balconies with ocean or pool views. In the formal Dining Room (men must wear jackets) chef Yvon Goetz's French-Mediterranean prix-fixe menu includes items such as the seared Hudson Valley foie gras with caramelized rhubarb in a green peppercorn essence. The Dining Room is open for dinner only, and reservations are essential. ⊠ *1 Ritz-Carlton Dr., 92629,* ☎ *949/240–2000 or 800/241–3333,* ℻ *949/240–0829. 332 rooms, 31 suites. 3 restaurants, lobby lounge, 2 pools, beauty salon, massage, 4 tennis courts, health club, concierge. AE, D, DC, MC, V.*

$$$–$$$$ 🏨 **Blue Lantern Inn.** Combining New England–style architecture with
★   a southern California setting, this white clapboard B&B rests on a bluff, overlooking the harbor and ocean. A fire warms the intimate, inviting living area. The French country–style guest rooms also have fireplaces, as well as soda-filled refrigerators and whirlpool tubs. The top-floor tower suite has a 180° ocean view. ⊠ *34343 St. of the Blue Lantern, 92629,* ☎ *949/661–1304,* ℻ *949/496–1483. 29 rooms. Exercise room, concierge. AE, DC, MC, V. Full breakfast.*

$$$–$$$$ 🏨 **Marriott's Laguna Cliffs Resort.** Formerly known as the Dana Point Resort, this whitewashed hillside hotel looks straight out of Cape Cod, except that its views are of the Pacific, not the Atlantic. On Sunday evenings in summer, the Capistrano Valley Symphony performs on the resort's landscaped grounds. ⊠ *25135 Park Lantern, 92629,* ☎ *949/661–5000 or 800/533–9748,* ℻ *949/661–5358. 332 rooms, 18 suites. Restaurant, bar, lobby lounge, 2 pools, 2 outdoor hot tubs, basketball, croquet, health club, volleyball. AE, D, DC, MC, V.*

Outdoor Activities and Sports

Rental stands for surfboards, Windsurfers, small powerboats, and sailboats can be found near most of the piers. **Embarcadero Marina** (✉ 34512 Embarcadero Pl., ☎ 949/496–6177) has powerboats and sailboats for rent near the launching ramp at Dana Point Harbor. **Hobie Sports** (✉ 24825 Del Prado, ☎ 949/496–2366) rents surfboards and Boogie boards. **Dana Wharf Sportfishing** (✉ 34675 Golden Lantern St., ☎ 949/496–5794) runs charters and whale-watching excursions (from early December to late March).

San Juan Capistrano

5 mi north of Dana Point, Hwy. 74; 60 mi north of San Diego, I–5.

Quaint San Juan Capistrano, one of the few noteworthy historical districts in southern California, is best known for its Mission. It is here that the swallows migrating each year from their winter haven in Argentina arrive. St. Joseph's Day, March 19, launches a week of festivities. After summering in the arches of the old stone church, the swallows head home on St. John's Day, October 23.

★ ㉓ **Mission San Juan Capistrano,** founded in 1776 by Father Junípero Serra, was the major Roman Catholic outpost between Los Angeles and San Diego. Though the original Great Stone Church is permanently supported by scaffolding, many of the mission's adobe buildings have been preserved to illustrate mission life, with exhibits of an olive millstone, tallow ovens, tanning vats, metalworking furnaces, and padres' living quarters. The bougainvillea-covered Serra Chapel is believed to be the oldest building standing in California. Mass takes place daily at 7 AM in the chapel and 8:30 in the new church. ✉ *Camino Capistrano and Ortega Hwy.,* ☎ *949/248–2049.* 🎟 *$5.* ☉ *Daily 8:30–5.*

㉔ Near Mission San Juan Capistrano is the **San Juan Capistrano Library,** a postmodern structure erected in 1983. Michael Graves combined a classical design with the style of the mission to striking effect. ✉ *31495 El Camino Real,* ☎ *949/493–1752.* ☉ *Mon.–Wed. 10–8, Thurs. 10–6, Sat. 10–5, Sun. noon–5.*

Dining

$$–$$$ ★ ✕ **Cedar Creek Inn.** Equally suitable for family meals and romantic getaway dinners, the inn has a children's menu as well as a secluded outdoor patio with a roaring fireplace for couples dining alone. The contemporary American menu features crowd-pleasers like ahi burgers, rack of lamb, and herb-crusted halibut. ✉ *26860 Ortega Hwy.,* ☎ *949/240–2229. AE, MC, V.*

$$–$$$ ★ ✕ **L'Hirondelle.** Roast duck, rabbit, and many Belgian dishes are on the menu at this French and Belgian restaurant. ✉ *31631 Camino Capistrano,* ☎ *949/661–0425. AE, MC, V. Closed Mon. No lunch Tues.*

$–$$ ✕ **The Ramos House Cafe.** This quaint outdoor café serves beautifully presented breakfasts in an intimate cobblestone patio setting. Dinners, served monthly only during a full moon, are more elaborate, five-course adventures. ✉ *31752 Los Rios St.,* ☎ *949/443–1342. AE, D, DC, MC, V. Closed Mon.*

Nightlife

Coach House (✉ 33157 Camino Capistrano, ☎ 949/496–8930), a roomy, casual club with long tables and a dark wood bar, draws crowds of varying ages for entertainment from hip, new bands to mellow acoustic guitar to comedy acts.

OFF THE
BEATEN PATH
SAN CLEMENTE – Ten miles south of Dana Point on Pacific Coast Highway, San Clemente has 20 square mi of prime bicycling terrain. Camp Pendleton, the country's largest Marine Corps base, welcomes cyclists to use some of its roads. Surfers favor **San Clemente State Beach** (☎ 949/492–3156), which has camping facilities, RV hookups, and fire rings. San Onofre State Beach, just south of San Clemente, is another surfing destination. Below the bluffs are 3½ mi of sandy beach, where you can swim, fish, and watch wildlife.

ORANGE COUNTY A TO Z

Arriving and Departing

By Bus
The **Los Angeles MTA** (☎ 213/626–4455) has limited service to Orange County. From downtown, Bus 460 goes to Knott's Berry Farm and Disneyland. **Greyhound** (☎ 714/999–1256) serves Anaheim and Santa Ana.

By Car
The San Diego Freeway (I–405) and the Santa Ana Freeway (I–5) run north–south through Orange County. South of Laguna I–405 merges into I–5 (called the San Diego Freeway south from this point). Do your best to avoid freeways during rush hours (6–9 AM and 3:30–6 PM), when they can back up for miles.

By Plane
The county's main facility is **John Wayne Airport Orange County** (✉ MacArthur Blvd. at I–405, ☎ 949/252–5252), in Santa Ana. It is served by Alaska, America West, American, Continental, Delta, Northwest, Reno Air, Southwest, TWA, United, and US Airways, as well as other commuter airlines. *See* Air Travel *in* Smart Travel Tips A to Z for airline phone numbers.

Los Angeles International Airport, known as LAX, is only 35 mi west of Anaheim. **Ontario International Airport** is just northwest of Riverside, 30 mi north of Anaheim. **Long Beach Airport** is about 20 minutes by bus from Anaheim.

BETWEEN THE AIRPORTS AND HOTELS
Airport Bus (☎ 800/772–5299), a shuttle service, carries passengers from John Wayne and LAX to Anaheim and Buena Park. The fare from John Wayne to Anaheim is $10, from LAX to Anaheim $14.

Prime Time Airport Shuttle (☎ 800/262–7433) provides door-to-door service from Orange County hotels to LAX and the San Pedro cruise terminal. The fare is $35 per person and up, depending on your point of pickup. It's $9 a pop for each additional passenger from area Anaheim hotels to LAX.

SuperShuttle (☎ 714/517–6600) provides 24-hour door-to-door service from all the airports to all points in Orange County. The fare to the Disneyland area is $10 per person from John Wayne, $34 from Ontario, $13 from LAX, and $33 from Long Beach Airport.

By Train
Amtrak (☎ 800/872–7245) makes several daily stops in Orange County: at Fullerton, Anaheim, Santa Ana, Irvine, San Juan Capistrano, and San Clemente.

Metrolink (☎ 714/808–5465) is a weekday commuter train that runs to and from Los Angeles and Orange County, starting as far south as

Oceanside and stopping in San Juan Capistrano, Irvine, Santa Ana, Orange, Anaheim, and Fullerton.

Getting Around

By Bus

The **Orange County Transportation Authority** (OCTA, ☎ 714/636–7433) will take you virtually anywhere in the county, but it will take time. OCTA buses go from Knott's Berry Farm and Disneyland to Huntington Beach and Newport Beach. Bus 1 travels along the coast. There is also an express bus to Los Angeles.

By Car

Highways 55 and 91 head west to the ocean and east into the mountains: take Highway 91 to Garden Grove and inland points (Buena Park, Anaheim). Highway 55 leads to Newport Beach. Pacific Coast Highway (Highway 1) allows easy access to beach communities and is the most scenic route.

Contacts and Resources

Emergencies

Ambulance (☎ 911). **Fire** (☎ 911). **Police** (☎ 911).

Anaheim Medical Center (✉ 1111 W. La Palma Ave., Anaheim, ☎ 714/774–1450). **Western Medical Center** (✉ 1025 S. Anaheim Blvd., Anaheim, ☎ 714/533–6220). **Hoag Memorial Presbyterian Hospital** (✉ 1 Hoag Dr., Newport Beach, ☎ 949/645–8600). **South Coast Medical Center** (✉ 31872 PCH, Laguna Beach, ☎ 949/499–1311). **Children's Hospital of Orange County** (✉ 455 S. Main St., Orange, ☎ 714/997–3000).

Guided Tours

Pacific Coast Gray Line Tours (☎ 714/978–8855) provides guided tours from Orange County hotels to Disneyland, Knott's Berry Farm, Universal Studios Hollywood, Six Flags Magic Mountain, the San Diego Zoo, Sea World, Catalina Island, and the Long Beach Aquarium. They also offer a Los Angeles by Night tour.

Visitor Information

Anaheim-Orange County Visitor and Convention Bureau (✉ Anaheim Convention Center, 800 W. Katella Ave., 92802, ☎ 714/999–8999). **Southern California Golf Association** (☎ 818/980–3630). **Southern California Public Links Golf Association** (☎ 714/994–4747).

13 SAN DIEGO

Exploring San Diego is an endless adventure. To visitors the city and county may seem like a conglomeration of theme parks: Old Town and the Gaslamp Quarter, historically oriented; the wharf area, a maritime playground; La Jolla, a throwback to southern California elegance; Balboa Park, a convergence of the town's cerebral and action-oriented personae. There are, of course, real theme parks—Sea World and the San Diego Zoo—but the great outdoors, in the form of forests, landscaped urban areas, and sandy beaches, is the biggest of them all.

SAN DIEGO IS A BIG CITY with a small-town feel. San Diego County covers a vast area, extending from the coast to mile-high mountains to a point near sea level in the desert, but central San Diego is delightfully urban and accessible.

San Diego is strongly defined by its relationship to the ocean—to some degree by default. During the latter half of the 19th century the town was banking on a rail link to the east. A building boom in the 1880s was largely based on the assumption that San Diego would become the western terminus of the Santa Fe Railway. The link was completed in 1885, but it proved unsuccessful for a variety of reasons, including the placement of the line through Temecula Canyon, where 30 mi of track were washed out repeatedly in winter rainstorms.

Instead, San Diego's future was sealed in 1908, when President Theodore Roosevelt's Great White Fleet stopped here on a world tour to demonstrate U.S. naval strength. The U.S. Navy, impressed during that visit by the city's excellent harbor and temperate climate, decided to build a destroyer base on San Diego Bay in the 1920s. The newly developing aircraft industry soon followed (Charles Lindbergh's plane *Spirit of St. Louis* was built here). Through the years San Diego's economy became largely dependent on the military and its attendant enterprises, which provided jobs as well as a demand for local goods and services by those stationed here.

The city conducts most of its financial business in a single neighborhood, the downtown district fronting San Diego Bay, in this way resembling New York more than Los Angeles. San Diego has set some of its most prestigious scientific facilities on the water—Scripps Institution of Oceanography, as well as the Salk Institute.

San Diego also has the ocean to thank for its near-perfect weather. An almost perpetual high-pressure system from the North Pacific is responsible for the city's sunshine and dry air. Moderating breezes off the sea (caused by the water warming and cooling more slowly than the land) keep the summers relatively cool and the winters warm and help clear the air of pollution. In the late spring and early summer the difference between the earth and water temperatures generates coastal fogs.

EXPLORING SAN DIEGO

By Edie Jarolim

San Diego is more a chain of separate communities than a cohesive city. Many of the major attractions are separated by some distance from one another. The streets are fun for getting an up-close look at how San Diegans live, but true southern Californians use the freeways, which crisscross the county in a sensible fashion. If you are going to drive around San Diego, study your maps before you hit the road. If you stick with public transportation, plan on taking your time. The San Diego Trolley has expanded into Mission Valley; a commuter line called the Coaster runs from Oceanside into downtown; and the bus system covers almost all the county—but making the connections necessary to see the various sights is time-consuming.

Great Itineraries

IF YOU HAVE 3 DAYS

Head over to the San Diego Zoo in Balboa Park on the morning of your first day. It would be easy to spend your entire visit to the park here—and if you're traveling with kids, you may have little choice in the matter—but it would be a shame to miss El Prado and its rows of

Exploring San Diego

Torrey Pines
City Beach

University of
California
at San Diego

La Jolla

Torrey

Pines

Ardath Rd.

La Jolla Blvd

PACIFIC
BEACH

MISSION
BEACH

OCEAN
BEACH

POINT
LOMA

Mira Mesa Blvd.

MIRAMAR

Miramar

MIRAMAR
NAVAL AIR
STATION

Clairemont   Mesa   Blvd.

Balboa   Ave.

Aero Dr.

Mission Bay

Mission Bay

LINDA
VISTA

Sea World

Old Town

San Diego River

Adams Ave.

University

Balboa Park

San Diego
International
Airport

N. Harbor Dr.

North Island

U.S. NAVAL
AIR STATION

Coronado
Beach

Central San Diego

DOWNTOWN

Imperial

Nationa

San Diego Bay

PACIFIC OCEAN

0   4 miles

0   6 km

Silver Strand
State Beach

Silver Strand Beach Blvd.

architecturally interesting museums, a five-minute drive south of the zoo on Park Boulevard. Start your second day downtown at Seaport Village. After browsing the shops catch a ferry from the Broadway Pier to Coronado. From Coronado's Ferry Landing Marketplace board a bus going down Orange Avenue to tour the town's Victorian extravaganza, the Hotel Del Coronado. Back in San Diego after lunch, stroll north on the Embarcadero to Ash Street. If you've returned from Coronado early enough, you can view the Maritime Museum. On the third morning, visit La Jolla. Have lunch before heading to the Gaslamp Quarter.

IF YOU HAVE 5 DAYS
Follow the three-day itinerary above, and begin your fourth day with a morning visit to Cabrillo National Monument. Have lunch at one of the seafood restaurants on Scott Street, and then head over to Old Town (take Rosecrans Street north to San Diego Avenue) to see portions of San Diego's earliest history brought to life. If the daily schedule lists low tide for the afternoon, reverse the order to catch the tide pools at Cabrillo. En route to North County stop off at Torrey Pines State Park. If you're not going to Legoland, take Interstate 5 north to Del Mar for lunch, shopping, and sea views. A visit to Mission San Luis Rey, slightly inland from Oceanside on Highway 76, will infuse some history and culture into the tour.

Balboa Park

Overlooking downtown and the Pacific Ocean, 1,200-acre Balboa Park is home to most of San Diego's museums and the world-famous San Diego Zoo. Many of the park's Spanish Colonial Revival buildings were intended to be temporary structures, housing exhibits for the Panama–California International Exposition of 1915, which celebrated the opening of the Panama Canal. Fortunately, city leaders realized the buildings' value and incorporated them in their plans for Balboa Park's acreage, which had been set aside by the city founders in 1868. In an attempt to unify and beautify the museum complex, many of the buildings on El Prado are undergoing restoration to recapture their 1935–36 look.

The Laurel Street Bridge, also known as Cabrillo Bridge, is the park's official gateway. Parking near Balboa Park's museums is no small accomplishment, especially on sunny summer days, when lots fill up quickly. If you're driving in via the Laurel Street Bridge, the first parking area you'll come to is off the Prado to the left, going toward Pan American Plaza. Free trams that depart from the large lot on the east side of the park at Presidents Way provide an alternative way to get back to your car or bus. Trams run about every 8 to 10 minutes from 9:30–4 daily.

Two Good Walks
Numbers in the text correspond to numbers in the margin and on the Balboa Park map.

Enter via Cabrillo Bridge through the West Gate, which depicts the Panama Canal's linkage of the Atlantic and Pacific oceans. Park south of the **Alcazar Garden** ①. It's a short stretch north across El Prado to the landmark **California Building,** modeled on a cathedral in Mexico and now home to the **San Diego Museum of Man** ②. Look up to see busts and statues of heroes of the early days of the state. Next door is the **Simon Edison Centre for the Performing Arts** ③, which adjoins the sculpture garden of the **San Diego Museum of Art** ④, an ornate

Plateresque-style structure built to resemble the 17th-century University of Salamanca in Spain.

Continuing east you'll come to the **Timken Museum of Art** ⑤, the **Botanical Building** ⑥, and the Spanish Colonial Revival–style **Casa del Prado,** where the San Diego Floral Association has its offices and a gift shop. At the end of the row is the **San Diego Natural History Museum** ⑦. Detour a block north to visit the **Spanish Village Art Center** ⑧. If you were to continue north, you would come to the **carousel** ⑨, the **miniature railroad** ⑩, and, finally, the entrance to the **San Diego Zoo** ⑪.

Return to the natural history museum and cross Plaza de Balboa—its large central fountain is a popular meeting spot—to reach the **Reuben H. Fleet Science Center** ⑫. (Beyond the parking lot to the south lies the **Centro Cultural de la Raza** ⑬.) You're now on the opposite side of the Prado and heading west. You'll next pass **Casa de Balboa** ⑭, home to the historical society and model-railroad and photography museums. Next door in the newly reconstructed **House of Hospitality** ⑮ is the **Balboa Park Visitors Center.** Across the Plaza de Panama, the **House of Charm** ⑯, a recent Franciscan Mission–style addition that blends well with older park architecture, is home to a folk art museum and a gallery for San Diego artists. Your starting point, the Alcazar Garden, is west of the House of Charm.

Another option is to walk south from the Plaza de Panama, which doubles as a parking lot. As most of the buildings along El Prado were created for the 1915 exposition, the majority of those along this route date to the 1935 fair, when the architecture of the Maya and native peoples of the Southwest was highlighted. The first building you'll pass is the **Japanese Friendship Garden** ⑰. Next comes the ornate, crown-like **Spreckels Organ Pavilion** ⑱. The round seating area forms the base, with the stage as its diadem. The road forks here. Veer to the left to reach the **House of Pacific Relations** ⑲, a Spanish mission–style cluster of cottages and one of the few structures on this route built for the earlier exposition. Another is the Balboa Park Club, which you'll pass next. Now used for park receptions and banquets, the building resembles a mission church. Step inside to see the huge mural. Continue on beyond the Palisades Building, which hosts the Marie Hitchcock Puppet Theater, to reach the **San Diego Automotive Museum** ⑳, appropriately housed in the building that served as the Palace of Transportation in the 1935–36 exposition.

The road loops back at the spaceshiplike **San Diego Aerospace Museum and International Aerospace Hall of Fame** ㉑. As you head north again you'll notice the Starlight Bowl on your right. It sits in the flight path to San Diego International Airport. During the live musicals presented in the summer on its outdoor stage, actors freeze in their places when planes roar overhead. Next comes perhaps the most impressive structure on this tour, the **Federal Building,** the new home of the **San Diego Hall of Champions** ㉒. Its main entrance was modeled after the Palace of Governors in the ancient Mayan city of Uxmal, Mexico. You'll be back at the Spreckels Organ Pavilion after this, having walked a total of a little less than a mile.

TIMING

You'll want to devote an entire day to the expanding zoo. Though some of the park's museums are open on Monday, most are open Tuesday–Sunday 10–4. During the summer a number have extended hours. Phone ahead to ask. On Tuesday the museums have free admission on a rotating basis. Call the Balboa Park Visitors Center (☞ House of Hospitality, *below*) for a schedule. An alternating variety of free architectural, historical, and nature tours depart from the Botanical Building every Saturday at 10, while park ranger–led tours start out from the visitors center at noon on Wednesday and 11 on Sunday. Free concerts take place Sunday afternoons and summer Monday evenings at the Spreckels Organ Pavilion, and the House of Pacific Relations hosts Sunday afternoon folk-dance performances.

Sights to See

❶ Alcazar Garden. The gardens surrounding the Alcazar Castle in Seville, Spain, were the model for the landscaping here. The flower beds are ever-changing horticultural exhibits, with bright orange and yellow poppies blooming in the spring and deep rust and crimson chrysanthemums appearing in the fall. The park's horticulturists have been working in recent years to restore it to its 1935 appearance. It's off El Prado, next to the San Diego Art Institute and across from the Museum of Man.

❻ Botanical Building. The graceful redwood-lathed structure built for the 1915 exposition houses more than 500 types of tropical and subtropical plants. Ceiling-high tree ferns shade fragile orchids and feathery bamboo. There are benches beside miniature waterfalls for resting in the shade. The lily pond, filled with giant koi fish and blooming water lilies, is popular with photographers. ⊠ *1550 El Prado,* ☎ *619/239–0512.* ☞ *Free.* ☉ *Fri.–Wed. 10–4.*

❾ Carousel. Riders on this antique merry-go-round stretch from their seats to grab the brass rings suspended an arm's-length away and earn a free ride. Hand-carved in 1910, the bobbing animals include zebras, giraffes, and dragons. Real horsehair was used for the tails. ⊠ *1889 Zoo Pl. (behind zoo parking lot).* ☞ *$1.25.* ☉ *Daily 11–5:30 during extended summer vacation; during school yr, only school holidays and weekends.*

❿ Casa de Balboa. This building on El Prado's southeast corner houses three museums: the Museum of Photographic Arts, the San Diego Historical Society, and the San Diego Model Railroad Museum. *See* individual museum descriptions, *below.* ⊠ *1649 El Prado.*

❽ Centro Cultural de la Raza. An old water tower was converted into this center for Mexican, Native American, and Chicano arts. Attractions include a gallery, a theater, and a permanent collection of mural art, a fine example of which may be seen on the tower's exterior. ⊠ *2004 Park Blvd.,* ☎ *619/235–6135.* ☞ *Free.* ☉ *Thurs.–Sun. noon–5.*

⓰ House of Charm. Two formerly far-flung museums found homes in this structure, built in Franciscan Mission–style to fit in with the older El Prado structures: the main branch of the Mingei International Museum of Folk Art moved here in 1996, followed by the San Diego Art Institute in 1997. (*See* individual museum listings, *below.*)

⓯ House of Hospitality. At the reconstructed home of the **Balboa Park Visitors Center** you can pick up schedules and route maps for the free trams that operate around the park. You can also purchase the Passport to Balboa Park, which affords entry to 12 museums for $21; it's worthwhile if you want to visit more than a few and aren't entitled to the discounts that most give to children, senior citizens, and military personnel. In addition, you can pick up a flyer that details the free park tours that depart from here and from the Botanical Building (or call ☎ *619/235–1122* for a schedule). ⊠ *1549 El Prado,* ☎ *619/239–0512.* ☉ *Daily 9–4.*

⓳ House of Pacific Relations. This is not really a house but a cluster of red-tile-roof, stucco cottages representing some 30 foreign countries. And the word "pacific" refers not to the ocean—most of the nations represented are European, not Asian—but to the goal of maintaining

Balboa Park

Alcazar Garden, **1**

Botanical Building, **6**

Carousel, **9**

Casa de Balboa, **14**

Centro Cultural
de la Raza, **13**

House of Charm, **16**

House of
Hospitality, **15**

House of Pacific
Relations, **19**

Japanese Friendship
Garden, **17**

Mingei International
Museum of Folk
Art, **16**

Miniature
Railroad, **10**

Museum of
Photographic Arts, **14**

Reuben H. Fleet
Science Center, **12**

San Diego Aerospace
Museum and
International
Aerospace Hall of
Fame, **21**

San Diego Art
Institute, **16**

San Diego
Automotive
Museum, **20**

San Diego Hall of
Champions, **22**

San Diego Historical
Society, **14**

San Diego Model
Railroad Museum, **14**

San Diego Museum
of Art, **4**

San Diego Museum
of Man, **2**

San Diego Natural
History Museum, **7**

San Diego Zoo, **11**

Simon Edison Centre
for the Performing
Arts, **3**

Spanish Village Art
Center, **8**

Spreckels Organ
Pavilion, **18**

Timken Museum
of Art, **5**

peace. Across the road from the cottages but not affiliated with them, the Spanish colonial–style **United Nations Building** is home to the United Nations Association's International Gift Shop, open daily. ✉ *2160 Pan American Rd. W,* ☎ *619/234–0739.* 🎟 *Free.* ☉ *Sun. 12:30–4:30; hrs may vary with season.*

⑰ Japanese Friendship Garden. A koi pond with a cascading water wall, a 60-ft-high wisteria arbor, a large activity center, and a tea room are all new additions to the park's lovely Eastern-style garden, designed to inspire contemplation. You can wander the peaceful paths and meditate in the traditional stone-and-sand garden. ✉ *2215 Pan American Rd. E,* ☎ *619/232–2780.* 🎟 *$2.* ☉ *Fri.–Sun. and Tues. 10–4.*

The Marston House. The residence of businessman George W. Marston (1850–1946), a San Diego pioneer and philanthropist who financed the architectural landscaping of Balboa Park, was visited by President Teddy Roosevelt and Booker T. Washington, among other prominent people. The 5-acre grounds are landscaped in the English Romantic tradition as interpreted in California. ✉ *3525 7th Ave.,* ☎ *619/298–3142.* 🎟 *$5.* ☉ *Fri.–Sun. 10–4:30 (last tour at 3:45).*

★ ⑯ Mingei International Museum of Folk Art. All ages will enjoy the colorful and creative exhibits of toys, pottery, textiles, costumes, and gadgets from around the globe at the Mingei. You'll find everything from antique American carousel horses to the latest in Japanese ceramics in the light-filled museum. ✉ *1439 El Prado,* ☎ *619/239–0003.* 🎟 *$5.* ☉ *Tues.–Sun. 10–4.*

⑩ Miniature railroad. Adjacent to the zoo parking lot, a pint-size, 48-passenger train runs a ½-mi loop through eucalyptus groves. The engine is a small-scale version of the General Motors F-3 locomotive. ✉ *2885 Zoo Pl.,* ☎ *619/239–4748.* 🎟 *$1.25.* ☉ *Weekends and school holidays 11–4:30, daily during school summer break.*

⑭ Museum of Photographic Arts. World-renowned photographers such as Ansel Adams, Imogen Cunningham, Henri Cartier-Bresson, and Edward Weston are represented in the museum's permanent collection, complemented by interesting contemporary shows. The museum is expanding into the space once occupied by next-door neighbor the San Diego Hall of Champions (☞ *below*). ✉ *Casa de Balboa, 1649 El Prado,* ☎ *619/239–5262.* 🎟 *$4.* ☉ *Daily 10–5; closed some holidays and for installations.*

★ ⑫ Reuben H. Fleet Science Center. Children and adults alike enjoy the Fleet Center's clever interactive exhibits that teach scientific principles. The IMAX Dome Theater screens exhilarating nature and science films shot to make viewers feel as though they're part of an expedition. A planetarium show takes over the theater on the first Wednesday of every month. ✉ *1875 El Prado,* ☎ *619/238–1233; 619/232–6866 for advance tickets.* 🎟 *Science Center, $4; Science Center and IMAX Theater or Science Center and Simulator, $8; Science Center, IMAX Theater, and Simulator, $11; Planetarium show, $5.* ☉ *Mon.–Tues. 9:30–6, Wed.–Sun. 9:30–9 (hrs change seasonally; call ahead).*

㉑ San Diego Aerospace Museum and International Aerospace Hall of Fame. Every available inch of space in the rotunda is filled with exhibits about aviation and aerospace pioneers, including examples of enemy planes during the world wars. A collection of real and replicated aircraft fills the central courtyard. ✉ *2001 Pan American Plaza,* ☎ *619/234–8291.* 🎟 *$6, active military personnel free.* ☉ *Daily 10–4:30.*

⑯ San Diego Art Institute. Outside juries decide which works created by members of the Art Institute will be displayed in rotating shows, which change every five or six weeks. Painting, sculpture, watercolor—everything except crafts—are represented. ⊠ *House of Charm, 1439 El Prado,* ☎ *619/236–0011.* ≌ *$3.* ☉ *Tues.–Sat. 10–4, Sun. noon–4.*

㉑ San Diego Automotive Museum. The museum maintains a core collection of vintage motorcycles and cars, ranging from an 1886 Benz to a De Lorean, as well as a series of rotating exhibits from collections around the world. ⊠ *2080 Pan American Plaza,* ☎ *619/231–2886.* ≌ *$6.* ☉ *Daily 10–4:30.*

㉒ San Diego Hall of Champions. Reopened in June 1999 in a new, larger home, this museum celebrates local jock heroes via a vast collection of memorabilia, uniforms, paintings, photographs, and computer and video displays. ⊠ *Federal Bldg., 2131 Pan American Rd.,* ☎ *619/234– 2544.* ≌ *$3.* ☉ *Daily 10–4:30.*

⑭ San Diego Historical Society. The San Diego Historical Society maintains its research library in the Casa de Balboa's basement and organizes shows on the first floor. Permanent and rotating exhibits survey local urban history after 1850, when California became part of the United States. The museum has a 100-seat theater for public lectures, workshops, and educational programs. A gift shop sells books and amusing historical posters. ⊠ *Casa de Balboa, 1649 El Prado,* ☎ *619/232– 6203.* ≌ *$5.* ☉ *Tues.–Sun. 10–4:30.*

⑭ San Diego Model Railroad Museum. When the six model-train exhibits are in operation, you'll hear the sounds of chugging engines, screeching brakes, and shrill whistles. If you come on Tuesday and Friday evenings, 7:30–11, there's no admission charge to watch the model-train layouts being created. ⊠ *Casa de Balboa, 1649 El Prado,* ☎ *619/696–0199.* ≌ *$3.* ☉ *Tues.–Fri. 11–4, weekends 11–5.*

★ **④ San Diego Museum of Art.** Known primarily for its Spanish Baroque and Renaissance paintings, including works by El Greco, Goya, Rubens, and van Ruisdael, San Diego's most comprehensive art museum also has strong holdings of Southeast Asian art, Indian miniatures, and contemporary California paintings. The Baldwin M. Baldwin wing displays more than 100 pieces by Toulouse-Lautrec. ⊠ *Casa de Balboa, 1450 El Prado,* ☎ *619/232–7931.* ≌ *$7 Tues.–Thurs., $8 Fri.–Sun.* ☉ *Tues.–Sun. 10–4:30.*

② San Diego Museum of Man. Exhibits at this highly respected anthropological museum focus on Southwestern, Mexican, and South American cultures. Carved monuments from the Mayan city of Quirigua in Guatemala, cast from the originals in 1914, are particularly impressive. Among the museum's more recent additions is a hands-on Children's Discovery Center. ⊠ *California Bldg., 1350 El Prado,* ☎ *619/ 239–2001.* ≌ *$4.* ☉ *Daily 10–4:30.*

⑦ San Diego Natural History Museum. The museum focuses on the plants and animals of southern California and Mexico. It frequently schedules free guided nature walks on the weekends, as well as films and lectures throughout the week. ⊠ *1788 El Prado,* ☎ *619/232–3821.* ≌ *$6.* ☉ *Daily 9:30–4:30.*

★ **⑪ San Diego Zoo.** Balboa Park's—and perhaps the city's—most famous attraction is its 100-acre zoo. Nearly 4,000 animals of some 800 diverse species roam in expertly crafted habitats that spread down into, around, and above the natural canyons. Exploring the zoo fully requires the stamina of a healthy hiker, but open-air trams that run throughout the day allow visitors to see 80% of the exhibits on the 3-mi tour. The Kangaroo bus tours include the same informed and amusing narrations as the others but for a few dollars more they let you get on and off as you like at eight different stops. The Skyfari ride, which soars 170 ft above the ground, gives a good overview of the zoo's layout and, on clear days, a panorama of the park, downtown San Diego, the bay, and the ocean, far past the Coronado Bridge.

Still, the zoo is at its best when you wander the paths that climb through the huge, enclosed **Scripps Aviary,** where brightly colored tropical birds swoop between branches just inches from your face. **Gorilla Tropics,** beside the aviary, is among the zoo's latest ventures into bioclimatic zone exhibits, where animals live in enclosed environments modeled on their native habitats.

The simulated Asian rain forest, **Tiger River,** has 10 exhibits with more than 35 species of animals. Here you'll see tigers, Malayan tapirs, and Argus pheasants among the collection of exotic trees and plants. At the popular **Polar Bear Plunge,** where you can watch the featured animals take a chilly dive, Siberian reindeer, white foxes, and other Arctic creatures are separated from their predatory neighbors by a series of camouflaged moats. But these and other zoo locals are being overshadowed by the hoopla surrounding two glamorous overseas visitors: Shi Shi and Bai Yun, a pair of giant pandas on loan for 12 years from the People's Republic of China. Because the pandas are here for conservation research purposes, there's a chance that they won't be on display when you visit. ✉ *2920 Zoo Dr.,* ☎ *619/234–3153.* 🎟 *$16 includes zoo, Children's Zoo, and animal shows; $23 includes above, plus 35-min guided bus tour and Skyfari ride; Kangaroo bus tour $9 additional ($4 additional for purchasers of $23 deluxe package); zoo free for children under 12 in Oct. and for all on Founder's Day (1st Mon. in Oct.); $35.15 pass good for admission to zoo and San Diego Wild Animal Park within 5 days. AE, D, MC, V.* ☉ *Fall–spring, daily 9–4 (visitors may remain until 5); summer, daily 9–9 (visitors may remain until 10); Children's Zoo and Skyfari ride close earlier.*

③ Simon Edison Centre for the Performing Arts. Even if you're not attending a play, the complex, comprising the Cassius Carter Centre Stage, the Lowell Davies Festival Theatre, and the Old Globe Theatre, is a pleasant place to relax between museum visits. The theaters, done in a California version of Tudor style, sit between the Sculpture Garden of the San Diego Museum of Art and the California Tower. ✉ *1363 Old Globe Way,* ☎ *619/239–2255 or 619/234–5623.*

⑧ Spanish Village Art Center. Glassblowers, enamel workers, woodcarvers, sculptors, painters, jewelers, photographers, and other artists rent space in the 35 little red-tile-roof studio-galleries. The artists give demonstrations of their work on a rotating basis. ✉ *1770 Village Pl.,* ☎ *619/233–9050.* 🎟 *Free.* ☉ *Daily 11–4.*

⑱ Spreckels Organ Pavilion. The 2,000-seat pavilion, dedicated in 1915 by sugar magnates John D. and Adolph B. Spreckels, holds the 4,445-pipe Spreckels Organ, believed to be the largest outdoor pipe organ in the world. You can hear this impressive instrument at one of the year-round, 2 PM Sunday concerts. At Christmastime the park's Christmas tree and life-size Nativity display turn the pavilion into a seasonal wonderland. ✉ *2211 Pan American Rd. E,* ☎ *619/702–8138.*

⑤ Timken Museum of Art. This modern structure is made of travertine marble imported from Italy. The small museum houses a selection of minor works by major European and American artists as well as a superb collection of Russian icons. ✉ *1500 El Prado,* ☎ *619/239–5548.* 🎟 *Free.* ☉ *Oct.–Aug., Tues.–Sat. 10–4:30, Sun. 1:30–4:30.*

Downtown

Thanks to a redevelopment effort started in the late 1970s, elegant hotels, upscale condominium complexes, and trendy cafés now attract newcomers and natives to a newly developed city center that has retained an outdoor character. The Martin Luther King Jr. Promenade project put 14 acres of greenery along Harbor Drive from Seaport Village to the convention center, and landscaped the railroad right-of-way from the Santa Fe depot to 8th Avenue. The San Diego Convention Center will double its size to about 1.75 million square ft by fall 2001. A few blocks inland, the hugely successful Horton Plaza shopping center led the way for the hotels, restaurants, shopping centers, and housing developments that are now rising on every square inch of available space in downtown San Diego. The newest downtown project, the 26-block Ballpark District, scheduled to be completed in 2002, will include a new 42,000-seat baseball stadium for the San Diego Padres; a sports-related retail complex; 850 hotel rooms; and several new apartment and condominium complexes.

There are reasonably priced ($3–$6 per day) parking lots along Harbor Drive, Pacific Highway, and lower Broadway and Market Street. The price of many downtown parking meters is $1 per hour, with a maximum stay of two hours.

Two Good Walks

Numbers in the text correspond to numbers in the margin and on the Central San Diego map.

Two distinct areas may be explored on foot. Those who want to stay near the water might start a walk of the **Embarcadero** ① at the foot of Ash Street on Harbor Drive, where the *Berkeley,* headquarters of the **Maritime Museum** ②, is moored. A cement pathway runs south from the *Star of India* along the waterfront to the pastel B Street Pier. Another two blocks south on Harbor Drive brings you to the foot of Broadway and the Broadway Pier, where you can catch the ferry to Coronado. Continue south past Tuna Harbor to **Seaport Village** ③. Six blocks north of Seaport Village on Kettner Boulevard is the **Transit Center** ④; you'll see the mosaic-domed Santa Fe Depot and the tracks for the Trolley to the Mexican border out front. Right next door is the downtown branch of the **Museum of Contemporary Art, San Diego** ⑤.

A tour of the working heart of downtown might begin at the corner of 1st Avenue and Broadway, near Spreckels Theater, a grand old stage that presents pop concerts and touring plays these days. A block east and across the street sits the historic **U. S. Grant Hotel** ⑥. If you cross Broadway, you'll be able to enter **Horton Plaza** ⑦, San Diego's favorite retail playland. Fourth Avenue, the eastern boundary of Horton Plaza, doubles as the western boundary of the 16-block **Gaslamp Quarter** ⑧. Head south to Island Avenue and the William Heath Davis House, where you can get a touring map of the district.

TIMING

The above walks take about an hour each, though there's enough to do in downtown San Diego to keep you busy for at least two days— or three if you really like to shop or if you decide to take a side trip to Coronado or Tijuana. For a guided tour of the Gaslamp Quarter, plan to visit the area on Saturday.

Sights to See

❶ Embarcadero. The bustle along Harbor Drive's waterfront walkway comes less these days from the activities of tuna and other fishing folk, but it remains the nautical soul of San Diego. People here still make a

Central San Diego

DOWNTOWN

TO
OLD TOWN,
QUALCOMM STADIUM

Cedar St.

County Center/
Little Italy Station

Beech St.

Ash St.

Hotel
Circle

Presidio
Hills Park

OLD
TOWN

San Diego Ave.

Pacific Hwy.

Diego
International
Airport

Linda Vista Rd.

Rd.

Juan St.

N. Harbor Dr.

Pacific Hwy.

Kettner Blvd.

India St.

Columbia St.

State St.

Union St.

Front St.

First Ave.

Second Ave.

Third Ave.

Fourth Ave.

Fifth Ave.

Cedar St.

Beech St.

A St.

B St.

A St.

B St.

C St.

C St.

Civic Center
Trolley Station

B St. Pier

Broadway Pier

Coronado
Ferry Terminal

Columbia St.
Station

Broadway

Broadway

AE

E St.

F St.

G St.

Tuna
Harbor

State St.

Union St.

F St.

First Ave.

E St.

G St.

Fourth Ave.

Fifth Ave.

TROLLEY LINE

Seaport Trolley
Station

Children's
Museum

Harbor Dr.

Market St.

Market Pl.

Island Ave.

Second Ave.

William Heath
Davis House

Harbor Dr.

Convention Center
West Station

J St.

Embarcadero
Marina Park
North
South

San Diego
Convention
Center

Imperial Ave.

Harbor Dr.

25th St.

32nd St.

3rd St.

National Ave.

Main St.

San Diego-
Coronado
Bay Bridge

Orange Ave.

Pomona Ave.

NATIONAL
CITY

Coronado
Beach

CORONADO

Silver Strand Blvd.

N

0   1 mile
0   1 km

living from the sea. Seafood restaurants line the piers, as do sea vessels of every variety.

On the north end of the Embarcadero, at Ash Street, you'll find the Maritime Museum (☞ *below*). South of it, the **B Street Pier** is used by ships from major cruise lines as both a port of call and a departure point. The cavernous pier building has a cruise-information center and a small, cool bar and gift shop.

Day-trippers getting ready to set sail gather at the **Broadway Pier,** also known as the excursion pier. Tickets for the harbor tours and whale-watching trips are sold here.

The **San Diego Convention Center,** on Harbor Drive between 1st and 5th avenues, was designed by Arthur Erickson. The backdrop of blue sky and sea complements the building's nautical lines. The center often holds trade shows that are open to the public, and tours of the building are available.

⑧ Gaslamp Quarter. The 16-block national historic district centered between 4th and 5th avenues from Broadway to Market Street contains most of San Diego's Victorian-style commercial buildings from the late 1800s, when Market Street was the center of early downtown. As the move for downtown redevelopment emerged, there was talk of destroying the buildings in the quarter, bulldozing them, and starting from scratch. History buffs, developers, architects, and artists formed the Gaslamp Quarter Council in 1974. Bent on preserving the district, they gathered funds from the government and private benefactors and began cleaning up the quarter, restoring the finest old buildings, and attracting businesses and the public back to the heart of New Town. Their efforts have paid off. Former flophouses have become choice office buildings, and the area is dotted with shops and restaurants.

The **William Heath Davis House** (✉ 410 Island Ave., at 4th Ave., ☎ 619/233–4692), one of the first residences in town, now serves as the information center for the Gaslamp Quarter. Davis was a San Franciscan whose ill-fated attempt to develop the waterfront area preceded the more successful one of Alonzo Horton. Docents give tours ($2) of the house during museum hours, which, theoretically, are weekdays from 10–2, Saturday from 10–4, and Sunday from noon–4. The place is staffed solely by volunteers, so be sure to phone ahead. Two-hour walking tours of the historic district leave from the house on Saturday at 11. The cost for these or a self-guided audio tour (phone ahead to reserve a headset) is $5. The museum also has a detailed map of the district.

The Victorian **Horton Grand Hotel** (✉ 311 Island Ave.) was created in the mid-1980s by joining together two historic hotels, the Kahle Saddlery and the Grand Hotel, built in the boom days of the 1880s. The two hotels were dismantled and reconstructed on a new site, about four blocks from their original locations. A small Chinese Museum serves as a tribute to the surrounding Chinatown district, a collection of modest structures that once housed Chinese laborers and their families.

The section of G Street between 6th and 9th avenues has become a haven for galleries. Stop in one of them to pick up a map of the downtown arts district. For information about openings and other events in the district, call the **Gaslamp Quarter Association** (☎ 619/233–5227).

★ ⑦ Horton Plaza. Downtown's centerpiece is the shopping, dining, and entertainment mall that fronts Broadway and G Street from 1st to 4th avenues and covers more than six city blocks. Horton Plaza is far from what one would imagine a shopping center—or city center—to be. A collage of pastels with elaborate, colorful tile work on benches and stairways, cloth banners waving in the air, and modern sculptures marking the entrances, Horton Plaza rises in uneven, staggered levels to six floors. Great views of downtown from the harbor to Balboa Park and beyond can be had here. The **International Visitor Information Center**, operated in the complex by the San Diego Convention and Visitors Bureau, is the best resource for information on the city.

➋ **Maritime Museum.** With a collection of three restored ships that may be toured for one admission price, the museum affords a glimpse of San Diego during its heyday as a commercial seaport. Its headquarters are the *Berkeley*, an 1898 ferryboat moored at the foot of Ash Street. The most interesting of the museum's ships is the *Star of India*, a windjammer built in 1863. The ship's high wooden masts and white sails flapping in the wind have been a harbor landmark since 1927. ⊠ *1306 N. Harbor Dr.,* ☎ *619/234–9153.* ☜ *$5.* ☉ *Daily 9–8.*

➎ **Museum of Contemporary Art, San Diego.** The downtown branch of the city's modern art museum, which opened in 1993 while the main facility in La Jolla was undergoing renovation, has taken on its own personality. Its postmodern, cutting-edge exhibitions are perfectly complemented by the steel-and-glass transportation complex of which it's a part. Four small galleries in the two-story building host rotating shows, some from the permanent collection in the La Jolla branch, others loaned from far-flung international museums. ⊠ *1001 Kettner Blvd.,* ☎ *619/ 234–1001.* ☜ *$2; free 1st Tues. and Sun. of month.* ☉ *Tues.–Sat. 10– 5, Sun. noon–5.*

★ ➌ **Seaport Village.** A wise developer saw the potential in the stretch of prime waterfront that spreads out across 14 acres and connects the harbor with the hotel towers and the convention center. You can browse through a kite store, a rubber-stamp emporium, and a shop devoted to left-handed people. Nosh to your heart's delight on everything from fast Greek, Mexican, and Italian fare to seafood in nautical-style indoor restaurants. Seaport Village's shops are open daily 10–9 (10–10 in summer); a few eateries open early for breakfast, and many have extended nighttime hours, especially in summer.

☾ I. D. Looff crafted the hand-carved, hand-painted steeds on the **Broadway Flying Horses Carousel** for the Coney Island amusement park in 1890. The ride was moved from its next home, Salisbury Beach in Massachusetts, and faithfully restored for Seaport Village's West Plaza; tickets are $1. Strolling clowns, mimes, musicians, and magicians are also on hand throughout the village to entertain kids. ☎ *619/235–4014; 619/235–4013 for events hot line.*

➍ **Transit Center.** The Mission Revival–style **Santa Fe Depot**, which replaced the original 1887 station on this site, serves Amtrak and Coaster passengers. A booth at the graceful, tile-domed depot has bus schedules, maps, and tourist brochures. Formerly an easily spotted area landmark, it's now overshadowed by **1 America Plaza** across the street. At the base of this 34-story office tower, designed by architect Helmut Jahn, is a center that links the train, trolley, and city bus systems. ⊠ *Broadway and Kettner Blvd.*

➏ **U. S. Grant Hotel.** Far more formal than most other hotels in San Diego, the doyenne of downtown lodgings has a marble lobby, gleaming chandeliers, attentive doormen, and other touches that hark back to the more gracious era when it was built (1910). Funded in part by the son of the president for whom it was named, the hotel was extremely opulent; 350 rooms of 437 had private baths, highly unusual for that time. ✉ *326 Broadway.*

Coronado

Although it's actually an isthmus, easily reached from the mainland if you head north from Imperial Beach, Coronado has always seemed like an island—and is often referred to as such. North Island Naval Air Station was established in 1911 on Coronado's north end, across from Point Loma, and was the site of Charles Lindbergh's departure on the transcontinental flight that preceded his famous transatlantic voyage. The streets of Coronado are wide, quiet, and friendly, with lots of neighborhood parks.

Coronado is visible from downtown and Point Loma and accessible via the San Diego–Coronado Bridge. There is a $1 toll for crossing the bridge into Coronado. Until the bridge was completed in 1969, visitors and residents relied on the Coronado Ferry, which ran across the harbor from downtown. When the bridge was opened, the ferry closed down, much to the chagrin of those who were fond of traveling at a leisurely pace. In 1987 the ferry returned. You can board the ferry, operated by **San Diego Harbor Excursion** (☎ 619/234–4111; 800/442–7847 in CA), at downtown San Diego's Embarcadero from the Broadway Pier at Broadway and Harbor Drive. You'll arrive at the Ferry Landing Marketplace. Boats depart every hour on the hour from the Embarcadero and every hour on the half hour from Coronado, Sunday through Thursday from 9 AM to 9:30 PM, Friday and Saturday until 10:30 PM; the fare is $2 each way, 50¢ extra for bicycles.

San Diego's Metropolitan Transit System runs an inexpensive (50¢) shuttle bus, No. 904, around the island. Pick it up where you disembark the ferry and ride it out as far as the Silver Strand State Beach. Buses start leaving from the ferry landing at 9:30 AM and run (after 10:30) every half hour on the half hour until 5:30 PM.

A Good Tour
Numbers in the text correspond to numbers in the margin and on the Central San Diego map.

Hop on the ferry at the Embarcadero. When you get to Coronado, explore the shops at the **Ferry Landing Marketplace** ⑨ and from there rent a bicycle or catch the shuttle bus that runs down **Orange Avenue** ⑩, Coronado's main tourist drag. You might stop in at the tourist information office and pick up a map, or disembark the bus at an appealing spot and keep strolling along the boutiques-filled promenade until you reach the **Hotel Del Coronado** ⑪ at the end of Orange Avenue. Right across the street from the Del is the **Glorietta Bay Inn** ⑫, another of the island's outstanding early structures. A bit northwest of the hotel is the **Coronado Beach Historical Museum** ⑬. If you've brought your swimsuit, you might continue on to **Silver Strand State Beach** ⑭—just past the Hotel Del, Orange Avenue turns into Silver Strand Boulevard, which soon becomes Highway 75.

TIMING
A leisurely stroll through Coronado takes an hour or so, more if you shop or walk along the beach. If you're a history buff, you might want to visit on Thursday or Saturday, when you can combine the tour of Coronado's historic homes that departs from the Glorietta Bay Inn at 11 AM with a visit to the Coronado Beach Historical Museum, open Wednesday through Sunday afternoons. The last shuttle to the Ferry Landing Marketplace leaves from the Loews Coronado Bay Resort at 5:57.

Sights to See

⑬ Coronado Beach Historical Museum. An East Coast family built this Cape Cod–style cottage in 1898. The restored building now houses a museum that celebrates the island's history with photographs and displays of its formative events and major sites. ⊠ *1126 Loma Ave.,* ☎ *619/435–7242.* ☞ *Free; donations accepted.* ☉ *Wed.–Sat. 10–4, Sun. noon–4.*

⑨ Ferry Landing Marketplace. The aptly named point of disembarkation for the ferry, this collection of shops is actually a new development on an old site. Its buildings resemble the gingerbread domes of the Hotel Del Coronado, long the area's main attraction. ⊠ *1201 1st St. at B Ave.,* ☎ *619/435–8895.*

⑫ Glorietta Bay Inn. The former residence of John Spreckels, the original owner of North Island and the property on which the Hotel Del Coronado stands, is now a popular hotel. On Tuesday, Thursday, and Saturday mornings at 11, it's the departure point for a fun and informative 1½-hour walking tour of a few of the area's 86 officially designated historical homes. The tour focuses on the Glorietta Bay Inn and the Hotel Del Coronado across the street. ⊠ *1630 Glorietta Blvd.,* ☎ *619/435–5892; 619/435–5993 for tour information.* ☞ *$6 for historical tour.*

★ ⑪ Hotel Del Coronado. The island's most prominent landmark, selected as a national historic landmark in 1977, the Del, as natives call it, has a colorful history, integrally connected with that of Coronado itself. Historic photos from the Del's early days line the lower-level corridors. Broad steps lead up to the main lobby, with grand oak pillars and ceiling, which in turn opens out onto a central courtyard and gazebo. To the right is the cavernous **Crown Room,** whose arched ceiling of notched sugar pine was constructed without nails. A lavish Sunday brunch is served here from 9–2. The **Grand Ballroom** overlooks the ocean and a long white beach. ⊠ *1500 Orange Ave.,* ☎ *619/435–6611.* ☞ *$15 for guided tour.* ☉ *1-hr guided tours (from lobby) Mon.–Sat. 11 and 1, Sun. 3.*

⑩ Orange Avenue. It's easy to imagine you're on a street in Cape Cod when you stroll along this thoroughfare, Coronado's version of a downtown. The clapboard houses, small restaurants, and boutiques—selling everything from upscale clothing to surfboards—are in some ways more characteristic of New England than they are of California. But the East Coast illusion tends to dissipate quickly when you catch sight of one of the avenue's many citrus trees—or realize it's February and the sun is warming your face. Just off Orange Avenue, the Coronado Visitors Bureau (⊠ 1047 B Ave., ☎ 619/437–8788 or 800/622–8300) is open weekdays 9–5, Sat. 10–5, and Sun. 11–4 year-round.

⑭ Silver Strand State Beach. The stretch of sand that runs along Silver Strand Boulevard from the Hotel Del Coronado to Imperial Beach dispels the illusion that Coronado is an island. The clean beach is a perfect family gathering spot, with rest rooms and lifeguards.

Harbor Island, Point Loma, and Shelter Island

Point Loma curves around the San Diego Bay west of downtown and the airport, protecting the center city from the Pacific's tides and waves. Although military installations are based here and some main streets are cluttered with motels and fast-food shacks, Point Loma is an old and wealthy enclave of stately family homes. Its bay-side shores front huge estates, with sailboats and yachts packed tightly in private marinas. Nearby Harbor and Shelter islands, both created out of sand dredged from the San Diego Bay in the second half of this century, have become tourist hubs, their high-rise hotels, seafood restaurants, and boat-rental centers looking as solid as those anywhere else in the city.

A Good Tour

Numbers in the text correspond to numbers in the margin and on the Central San Diego map.

Take Catalina Drive all the way south to the tip of Point Loma to reach **Cabrillo National Monument** ⑮; you'll be retracing the steps of the earliest European explorers if you use this as a jumping-off point for a tour. North of the monument, as you head back into the neighborhoods of Point Loma, you'll see the white headstones of **Fort Rosecrans National Cemetery** ⑯. Continue north on Catalina Boulevard to Hill Street and turn left to reach the dramatic **Sunset Cliffs** ⑰, at the western side of Point Loma near Ocean Beach. Return to Catalina Boulevard and backtrack south for a few blocks to find Canon Street, which leads toward the peninsula's eastern (bay) side. Almost at the shore you'll see **Scott Street** ⑱, the main commercial drag of Point Loma. Scott Street is bisected by Shelter Island Drive, which leads to **Shelter Island** ⑲, a most impressive product of landfill. For another example of what can be done with tons of material dredged from a bay, go back up Shelter Island Drive, turn right on Rosecrans Street, and make another right on North Harbor Drive to get to **Harbor Island** ⑳.

TIMING

If you're interested in seeing the tidal pools at Cabrillo National Monument, you'll need to call ahead to find out when low tide will occur. Scott Street, with its Point Loma Seafoods, is a good place to find yourself at lunchtime, and Sunset Cliffs Park is where you might want to be when the daylight starts to wane. This drive takes about an hour if you stop briefly at each sight, but you'll want to devote at least an hour to Cabrillo National Monument.

Sights to See

★ ⑮ **Cabrillo National Monument.** This 144-acre preserve marks the site of the first European visit to San Diego, made by Portuguese explorer Juan Rodríguez Cabrillo (circa 1498–1543)—his real name was João Rodrigues Cabrilho, but it was later Hispanicized. The **visitor center** presents films and lectures about Cabrillo's voyage, the sea-level tidal pools, and the gray whales migrating offshore. The center has a shop with books about nature, San Diego, and the sea. Exploring the grounds consumes time and calories. Bring a picnic and rest on a bench overlooking the sailboats. A **statue of Cabrillo** overlooks downtown from the next windy promontory, where visitors gather to admire the stunning panorama over the bay, from the snowcapped San Bernardino Mountains, 130 mi north, to the hills surrounding Tijuana to the south.

The western and southern cliffs of Cabrillo National Monument are prime whale-watching territory. A sheltered viewing station has a tape-recorded lecture describing the great gray whales' migration from the Bering and Chukchi seas near Alaska to Baja, and high-powered telescopes help you focus on the whales' water spouts. The whales are visible on clear days in January and February, mostly in early morning. More accessible sea creatures can be seen in the **tidal pools** (☉ 9–4:30) at the foot of the monument's western cliffs. Drive north from the visitor center to the first road on the left, which winds down to the coast guard station and the shore. When the tide is low you can walk on the rocks around saltwater pools filled with starfish, crabs, anemones, octopuses, and hundreds of other sea creatures and plants. ✉ *1800*

Cabrillo Memorial Dr., ☎ *619/557–5450.* ◻ *$5 per car, $2 per person entering on foot or by bicycle; free for Golden Age, Golden Access, and Golden Eagle passport holders, and children under 17.* ◷ *Park daily 9–5:15 (call for later summer hrs, which vary).*

⓰ **Fort Rosecrans National Cemetery.** Many of those laid to rest at this place were killed in battles that predate California's statehood. Perhaps the most impressive structure in the cemetery is the 75-ft granite obelisk called the Bennington Monument, which commemorates the 66 crew members who died in a boiler explosion and fire on board the *USS Bennington* in 1905. ☎ *619/553–2084.* ◷ *Weekdays 7–5, weekends 9–5.*

⓴ **Harbor Island.** In 1961 a 1½-mi-long peninsula was created adjacent to San Diego International Airport out of 12 million cubic yards of sand and mud dredged from San Diego Bay. Restaurants and high-rise hotels now line the inner shores of Harbor Island.

⓲ **Scott Street.** Running along Point Loma's waterfront from Shelter Island to the Marine Corps Recruiting Center on Harbor Drive, this thoroughfare is lined with deep-sea fishing charters and whale-watching boats. It's a good spot from which to watch fishermen (and women) haul marlin, tuna, and puny mackerel off their boats.

⓳ **Shelter Island.** Actually a peninsula, this is the center of San Diego's yacht-building industry, and boats in every stage of construction are visible in the yacht yards. A long sidewalk runs from the landscaped lawns of the **San Diego Yacht Club** (tucked down Anchorage Street off Shelter Island Drive), past boat brokerages to the hotels and marinas, which line the inner shore, facing Point Loma. Within walking distance is the huge Friendship Bell, given to San Diegans by the people of Yokohama, Japan, in 1960.

⓱ **Sunset Cliffs.** As their name suggests, the 60-ft-high bluffs on the western side of Point Loma south of Ocean Beach are a perfect place to watch the sun descend over the sea. To view the tidal pools along the shore, you can descend a staircase off Sunset Cliffs Boulevard at the foot of Laredo Street.

La Jolla

La Jollans have long considered their village to be the Monte Carlo of California, and with good cause. Its coastline curves into natural coves backed by verdant hillsides and covered with homes worth millions. Though La Jolla is considered part of San Diego, it has its own postal zone and a coveted sense of class. It's gotten far more plebeian these days, but old-monied residents still mingle here with visiting film stars and royalty who frequent established hotels and private clubs. Development and construction have radically altered the once serene and private character of the village, but it has gained a cosmopolitan air that makes it a popular vacation resort. Prospect Street and Girard Avenue, the village's main drags, are lined with expensive shops and office buildings.

A Good Tour
Numbers in the text correspond to numbers in the margin and on the La Jolla map.

At the intersection of La Jolla Boulevard and Nautilus Street, turn toward the sea to reach **Windansea Beach** ①, one of the best surfing spots in town. **Mount Soledad** ②, about 1½-mi east on Nautilus Street, is La Jolla's highest spot. In the village itself you'll find the town's cultural center, the **Museum of Contemporary Art, San Diego** ③, on the less trafficked southern end of Prospect. A bit farther north, at the intersection of Prospect and Girard Avenue, sits the pretty-in-pink **La Valencia Hotel** ④. The hotel looks out onto the village's great natural attraction, **La Jolla Cove** ⑤, which can be accessed from Coast Boulevard, one block to the west. Past the far northern point of the cove, a trail leads down to **La Jolla Caves** ⑥. The beaches along La Jolla Shores Drive north of the caves are some of the finest in the San Diego area, with long stretches allotted to surfers or swimmers. Nearby is the campus of the Scripps Institution of Oceanography. The institution's **Stephen Birch Aquarium-Museum** ⑦ is inland a bit. La Jolla Shores Drive eventually curves onto Torrey Pines Road, off which you'll soon glimpse the world-famous **Salk Institute** ⑧, designed by Louis I. Kahn. The same road that leads to the institute ends at the cliffs used as the **Torrey Pines Glider Port** ⑨. The hard-to-reach stretch of sand at the foot of the cliffs is officially named **Torrey Pines City Park Beach** ⑩, but locals call it Black's Beach. At the intersection of Torrey Pines Road and Genesee Avenue you'll come to the northern entrance of the huge campus of the **University of California at San Diego** ⑪ and, a bit farther north, to the stretch of wilderness that marks the end of what most locals consider San Diego proper, **Torrey Pines State Beach and Reserve** ⑫.

TIMING

This tour makes for a leisurely day, though it can be driven in about a couple of hours, including stops to take in the views and explore the village of La Jolla. The Museum of Contemporary Art is closed Monday, and guided tours of the Salk Institute are offered Tuesday through Thursday only.

Sights to See

⑥ **La Jolla Caves.** It's a walk down 145 sometimes slippery steps to Sunny Jim Cave, the largest of the grottoes in La Jolla Cove. For many years the caves were entered via the La Jolla Cave and Shell Shop, but in 1998 the shop moved to Seaport Village and the cave entrance came under the aegis of the Cave Store, a throwback to the 1902 shop that served as the underground portal. ⊠ *1325 Cave St.,* ☎ *619/459–0746.* ✄ *$2.* ☉ *Daily 9 am until dark.*

★ ⑤ **La Jolla Cove.** The wooded spread that looks out over a shimmering blue inlet is what first attracted everyone to La Jolla, from Native Americans to the glitterati. It is the village's enduring cachet. You'll find the cove—as locals always refer to it, as though it were the only one in San Diego—beyond where Girard Avenue dead-ends into Coast Boulevard, marked by towering palms that line a promenade where people strolling in drop-dead designer duds are as common as Frisbee throwers.

An underwater preserve at the north end of La Jolla Cove makes the adjoining beach the most popular one in the area. On summer days, when the water visibility reaches 20 ft deep or so, the sea seems to disappear under the mass of bodies floating face down, snorkels poking up out of the water. The **Children's Pool,** at the south end of the park, is aptly named for its curving beach and shallow waters, protected by a seawall from strong currents and waves. Walk through **Ellen Browning Scripps Park,** past the groves of twisted junipers to the cliff's edge. Perhaps one of the open-air shelters overlooking the sea will be free, and you can spread your picnic out on a table and enjoy the scenery.

④ **La Valencia Hotel.** The art deco–style La Valencia, which has operated as a luxury hotel since 1928, has long been a gathering spot for Hollywood celebrities. The hotel's grand lobby has floor-to-ceiling win-

La Jolla

PACIFIC OCEAN

N
0   1 mile
0   1 km

S21

N. Torrey Pines Rd.

Genesee Ave.

Torrey Pines Rd.

La Jolla Village Dr.

↑ TO
GOLDEN
TRIANGLE

Gilman Dr.

5

La Jolla
Shores

La Jolla Shores Dr.

Point La Jolla

Shell
Beach   AE

Children's
Pool

Prospect St.

Torrey Pines

Virginia Way

Torrey Pines Rd.

Ardath Rd.

Marine
St. Beach

La Jolla Blvd.

Pearl St.

Girard Ave.

La Jolla
Country
Club

Nautilus St.

KEY

AE American Express Office

La Jolla Caves, **6**
La Jolla Cove, **5**
La Valencia Hotel, **4**
Mount Soledad, **2**
Museum of
Contemporary Art,
San Diego, **3**
Salk Institute, **8**
Stephen Birch
Aquarium-
Museum, **7**

Torrey Pines City
Park Beach, **10**
Torrey Pines Glider
Port, **9**
Torrey Pines State
Beach and
Reserve, **12**
University of
California at San
Diego, **11**
Windansea Beach, **1**

dows overlooking La Jolla Cove. ⊠ *1132 Prospect St.,* ☎ *619/454–0771.*

❷ Mount Soledad. La Jolla's highest spot can be reached by taking Nautilus Street all the way east. The top of the mountain is an excellent vantage point from which to get a sense of San Diego's geography: looking down from here you can see the coast from the county's northern border to the south far beyond downtown.

★ **❸ Museum of Contemporary Art, San Diego.** The permanent collection of post-1950s art naturally has a strong representation of California artists but also includes examples of every major art movement of the past half-century. ⊠ *700 Prospect St.,* ☎ *619/454–3541.* 🎫 *$4; free 1st Tues. and Sun. of month.* ☉ *Tues. and Thurs.–Sat. 10–5, Wed. 10–8, Sun. noon–5.*

❽ Salk Institute. The world-famous biological-research facility founded by polio vaccine inventor Jonas Salk sits on 26 cliff-top acres in La Jolla. A foot-wide "Stream of Life" flows through the center of a travertine marble courtyard between the buildings. The courtyard and stream of water were inspired by architect Louis Barragán. ⊠ *10010 N. Torrey Pines Rd.,* ☎ *619/453–4100.* 🎫 *Free.* ☉ *Grounds 7–6; guided architecture tours Tues.–Thurs. at 11 and noon.*

❼ Stephen Birch Aquarium-Museum. The largest oceanographic exhibit in the United States, a program of the Scripps Institution of Oceanography, sits at the end of a signed drive leading off North Torrey Pines Road just south of La Jolla Village Drive. More than 30 huge tanks are filled with colorful saltwater fish, and a 70,000-gallon tank simulates a La Jolla kelp forest. Besides the fish themselves, attractions include a simulated submarine ride. ⊠ *2300 Expedition Way,* ☎ *619/534–3474.* 🎫 *$7.50, active military free, parking $3.* ☉ *Daily 9–5.*

❿ Torrey Pines City Park Beach. Black's Beach—as locals call it—is one of the most beautiful and secluded stretches of sand in San Diego, backed by cliffs whose colors change with the angle of the sun. There are no rest rooms, showers, or snack shops. Although nudity is now prohibited by law, many people still shed their suits whenever the authorities are out of sight.

❾ Torrey Pines Glider Port. On days when the winds are just right, gliders line the cliffs, waiting for the perfect gust to carry them into the sky. If you're coming via the freeway, take the Genesee Avenue exit west from Interstate 5 and follow the signs when you approach the coast.

⓬ Torrey Pines State Beach and Reserve. *Pinus torreyana,* the rarest native pine tree in the United States, enjoys a 1,750-acre sanctuary at the northern edge of La Jolla. About 6,000 of these unusual trees, some as tall as 60 ft, grow on the cliffs here. The park is one of only two places where the torrey pine grows naturally. The reserve has several hiking trails leading to the cliffs, 300 ft above the ocean. **Los Penasquitos Lagoon** at the north end of the reserve is one of the many natural estuaries that flow inland between Del Mar and Oceanside. It's a good place to watch shorebirds. Volunteers lead guided nature walks at 11:30 and 1:30 on most weekends. ⊠ *N. Torrey Pines Rd. (also known as Old Hwy. 101). Exit I–5 onto Carmel Valley Rd. going west, then turn left (south) on Old Hwy. 101,* ☎ *619/755–2063.* 🎫 *Parking $4 (two large parking lots on both sides of Los Penasquitos Lagoon; another up the hill by park visitor center).* ☉ *Daily 8–sunset.*

⓫ University of California at San Diego. The campus of San Diego's most prestigious university spreads over canyons and eucalyptus groves, where students and faculty jog, bike, and rollerblade to class. Look for the postmodern Geisel Library (named for longtime La Jolla residents "Dr. Seuss" and his wife), which resembles a large spaceship. *Exit I–5 onto La Jolla Village Dr. going west; take the Gilman Dr. off-ramp to the right and continue on to the information kiosk at the campus entrance,* ☎ *619/534–4414 for campus tour information.* ☉ *Campus tours Sun. at 2 from the South Gilman Information Pavilion; reserve before 3 Fri.*

❶ **Windansea Beach.** Fans of pop satirist Tom Wolfe may recall *The Pump House Gang,* which pokes fun at the southern California surfing culture. Wolfe drew many of his barbs from observations he made at Windansea, the surfing beach west of La Jolla Boulevard near Nautilus Street. The wave action here is said to be as good as that in Hawaii.

Mission Bay and Sea World

The 4,600-acre Mission Bay aquatic park is San Diego's monument to sports and fitness. Admission to its 27 mi of bay-shore beaches and 17 mi of ocean frontage is free.

A Good Tour
Numbers in the text correspond to numbers in the margin and on the Mission Bay map.

If you're coming from Interstate 5, the **Visitors Information Center** ① is near the end of the Clairemont Drive–East Mission Bay Drive exit (you'll see the prominent sign). At the point where East Mission Bay Drive turns into Sea World Drive you can detour left to **Fiesta Island** ②, popular with jet skiers and speedboat racers. Continue around the curve to the west to reach **Sea World San Diego** ③, the area's best-known attraction. You'll next come to Ingraham Street, the central north–south drag through the bay. If you take it north, you'll shortly spot Vacation Road, which leads into the focal point of this part of the bay, the waterskiing mecca of **Vacation Isle** ④. At Ingraham, Sea World Drive turns into Sunset Cliffs Boulevard and intersects with West Mission Bay Drive. Past this intersection, Quivira Way leads west toward **Hospitality Point** ⑤, where there are nice, quiet places to have a picnic.

If, instead, you continue west on West Mission Bay Drive, just before it meets Mission Boulevard, you'll come to the Bahia Resort Hotel, where you can catch the *Bahia Belle* ⑥ for a cruise around the bay. Ventura Cove, opposite the Bahia Hotel, is another good spot to unpack your cooler. Almost immediately south of where West Mission Bay Drive turns into Mission Boulevard is the resurrected **Belmont Park** ⑦.

TIMING
It would take less than an hour to drive this tour. You may not find a visit to Sea World fulfilling unless you spend at least a half day; a full day is recommended. The park is open daily, but not all its attractions are open year-round.

Sights to See
❻ *Bahia Belle.* At the dock of the Bahia Resort Hotel, on the eastern shores of West Mission Bay Drive, you can board a restored stern-wheeler for a sunset cruise of the bay. Owned and operated by the hotel, the boat is free for guests of the Bahia or its sister hotel, the Catamaran. The *Bahia Belle* also stops at the San Diego Paradise Point Resort to pick up passengers. ✉ *998 W. Mission Bay Dr.,* ☎ *619/488–0551.* 🎟 *$6 for unlimited cruising (9:30 PM or later, cruisers must be at least 21).* ☉ *Oct.–Nov. and Jan.–June, Fri.–Sat. 7:30 PM–1:30 AM, departures every hr on the ½ hr; July–Sept., Wed.–Sun. on same schedule.*

Mission Bay

❼ Belmont Park. The once-abandoned amusement park between the bay and Mission Beach boardwalk is now a shopping, dining, and recreation mecca. Twinkling lights outline the refurbished **roller coaster** on which screaming thrill-seekers ride. Created as the Giant Dipper in 1925, this is one of the few old-time roller coasters left in the United States. It's listed on the National Register of Historic Places. **The Plunge,** an indoor swimming pool, also opened in 1925 as the largest—60 by 125 ft—saltwater pool in the world. It's had fresh water since 1951. ✉ *3146 Mission Blvd.,* ☎ *619/491–2988 for recorded park information; 619/488–3110 for pool.* ☉ *Park opens at 11 daily.*

❷ Fiesta Island. The most undeveloped area of Mission Bay Park is popular with bird-watchers (there's a large protected nesting site for the California tern at the northern tip of the island) as well as with dog owners—it's the only place in the park where their pets can run free. Jet skiers and speedboat racers come here, too.

❺ Hospitality Point. Enjoy lunch in this pretty, secluded spot, with a view of sailboats and yachts entering the open sea. At the entrance to Hospitality Point, the Mission Bay Park Headquarters supplies area maps and other recreational information. ✉ *2581 Quivira Ct.,* ☎ *619/221–8901.* ☉ *9–5 weekdays, closed city holidays.*

❸ Sea World San Diego. One of the world's largest marine-life amusement parks is spread over 100 tropically landscaped bay-front acres, where a cool breeze always seems to rise from the water. The traditional favorite exhibit at Sea World is the **Shamu show,** with killer whales entertaining the crowds, but dolphins, sea lions, and otters at other shows also delight audiences. **Shamu Backstage** lets guests watch trainers interact with the killer whales behind the scenes—and even help feed them on occasion. At another popular exhibit, the **Penguin Encounter,** a moving sidewalk passes through a glass-enclosed Arctic environment, in which hundreds of emperor penguins slide over glaciers into icy waters. The penguins like it cold, so consider bringing a light sweater along for this one. Youngsters are especially fond of the **Shark Encounter**, where you come face-to-face with a variety of species of the predators. The hands-on **California Tide Pool** exhibit gives visitors a chance to explore San Diego's indigenous marine life with a guide well versed in the habits of these creatures. At **Forbidden Reef** you can feed bat rays and come nose-to-nose with creepy moray eels. Visitors to **Rocky Point Preserve** can interact with bottlenose dolphins, and Alaskan sea otters that were brought here after being rescued from the 1989 *Exxon Valdez* oil spill. **Wild Arctic** starts out with a simulated helicopter ride to a research post at the North Pole. Beluga whales, walruses, harbor seals, and polar bears can be viewed in areas designed to look like the wrecked hulls of two 19th-century sailing ships. The newest attraction, **Manatee Rescue** lets you watch the gentle-giant marine mammals cavorting in a 215,000-gallon tank. In addition, various **freshwater** and **saltwater aquariums** hold underwater creatures from around the world. ✉ *1720 South Shores Rd., near the west end of I–8,* ☎ *619/226–3815; 619/226–3901 for recorded information.* ✉ *$38; parking $6 cars, $3 motorcycles, $8 RVs and campers; 90-min behind-the-scenes walking tours $8 additional. D, MC, V.* ⊙ *Daily 10–dusk; extended hrs during summer; call ahead for park hrs.*

❹ Vacation Isle. Ingraham Street bisects this Mission Bay island, which provides two distinct experiences for visitors. The west side is taken up by the San Diego Paradise Point Resort, but you don't have to be a guest to enjoy the hotel's lushly landscaped grounds and bay-front restaurants. The water-ski clubs congregate at **Ski Beach** on the east side of the island, where there's a parking lot as well as picnic areas and rest rooms.

❶ Visitors Information Center. In addition to being an excellent resource for San Diego tourists—you can have hotel or motel reservations made for you here, and pick up discount coupons along with maps and other guides—the center is also a gathering spot for runners, walkers, and exercisers. It's the place to get a list of rules for playing in the water at Mission Bay Park, or a self-guided tour map of the park's environmental resources, including the Northern Wildlife Preserve. There's a small gift shop. ✉ *2688 E. Mission Bay Dr.,* ☎ *619/276–8200.* ⊙ *Mon.–Sat. 9–5 (until 6 in summer), Sun. 9:30–4:30 (until 5:30 in summer).*

Old Town

Although Old Town is often credited as being the first European settlement in southern California, the true beginnings took place overlooking Old Town from atop Presidio Park, where Father Junípero Serra established the first of California's missions, San Diego de Alcalá, in 1769. In 1774 the hilltop was declared a Royal Presidio, or fortress, and the mission was moved 6 mi west to the San Diego River.

On San Diego Avenue, the district's main drag, art galleries and expensive gift shops are interspersed with tacky curio shops, restaurants, and open-air stands selling inexpensive Mexican pottery, jewelry, and blankets. The Old Town Esplanade between Harney and Conde streets is the best of several mall-like affairs constructed in mock Mexican-plaza style. Shops and restaurants also line Juan and Congress streets. Ten bus lines stop here, as do the Trolley and the Coaster commuter rail line.

A Good Tour

Numbers in the text correspond to numbers in the margin and on the Old Town San Diego map.

Visit the information center at Seeley Stable, just off Old Town Plaza, to orient yourself to the various sights in **Old Town San Diego State Historic Park** ①. When you've had enough history, cross north on the west side of the plaza to **Bazaar del Mundo** ②, where you can shop or enjoy some nachos on the terrace of a Mexican restaurant. Walk down San Diego Avenue, which flanks the south side of Old Town's historic plaza, east to Harney Street and the **Thomas Whaley Museum** ③. Then continue east 2½ blocks on San Diego Avenue beyond Arista Street to the **El Campo Santo** ④ cemetery. **Heritage Park** ⑤ is perched on a hill above Juan Street, north of the museum and cemetery. Drive west on Juan Street and north on Taylor Street to Presidio Drive, which will lead you up the hill on which **Presidio Park** ⑥ and the **Junípero Serra Museum** ⑦ sit.

TIMING

If possible, avoid coming here on weekends as the parking lots are even fuller than usual when San Diegans are off work (this won't be a problem if you take the San Diego Trolley). It takes about two hours to walk through Old Town. If you drive to Presidio Park, allot another hour to explore the grounds and museum.

Sights to See

❷ **Bazaar del Mundo.** North of San Diego's Old Town Plaza lies the area's unofficial center, built to represent a colonial Mexican square. The central courtyard is always in blossom, with magenta bougainvillea, scarlet hibiscus, and irises, poppies, and petunias in season. Ballet Folklorico and flamenco dancers perform on weekend afternoons, and the bazaar frequently hosts arts-and-crafts exhibits and Mexican festivals. Colorful shops specializing in Latin American crafts and unusual gift items border the square. Although many of the shops here have high-quality wares, prices can be considerably higher than those at shops on the other side of Old Town Plaza. ⊠ *2754 Calhoun St.,* ☎ *619/ 296–3161.* ⊙ *Shops daily 10–9.*

❹ **El Campo Santo.** The old adobe-walled cemetery established in 1849 was the burial place for many members of Old Town's founding families, as well as for some gamblers and bandits who passed through town until 1880. ⊠ *North side of San Diego Ave. S, between Arista and Ampudia Sts.*

❺ **Heritage Park.** Save Our Heritage Organization moved and restored a number of San Diego's important Victorian buildings—they're now the focus of this 7.8-acre park, up the Juan Street hill near Harney Street. Among them is southern California's first synagogue, a one-room Classic Revival–style structure built in 1889 for Congregation Beth Israel. The most interesting of the six former residences might be the Sherman Gilbert House, which has a widow's walk and intricate carving on its decorative trim. ⊠ *2455 Heritage Park Row (park office),* ☎ *619/694–3049.*

❼ **Junípero Serra Museum.** The original Spanish presidio and California's first mission were perched atop the 160-ft hill overlooking Mission Valley. It's now the domain of a museum devoted to the history of the Spanish and Mexican periods. Built in 1929, the museum houses an interesting collection of artifacts from San Diego's earliest days. ⊠ *2727 Presidio Dr.,* ☎ *619/297–3258.* ⊡ *$5.* ⊙ *Fri.–Sun. 10–4.*

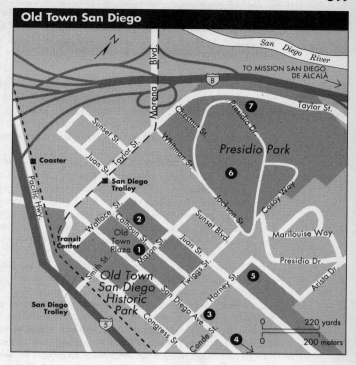

Old Town San Diego

★ **❶** **Old Town San Diego State Historic Park.** The six square blocks on the site of San Diego's original pueblo are the heart of Old Town. Most of the 20 historic buildings preserved or re-created by the park cluster around **Old Town Plaza,** bounded by Wallace Street on the west, Calhoun Street on the north, Mason Street on the east, and San Diego Avenue on the south; you can see the presidio from behind the cannon by the flagpole. The plaza is a pleasant place for resting and regrouping as you plan your tour of the park and watch other visitors stroll by. San Diego Avenue is closed to traffic here. The tour map available at Seeley Stable gives details about all of the historic houses on the plaza and in its vicinity. The noncommercial houses are open to visitors daily 10–5 (winter hours, which start in November, are shorter); none charge admission, though donations are appreciated.

The **Robinson-Rose House** was the original commercial center of old San Diego, housing railroad offices, law offices, and the first newspaper press. For many years it served as the park's visitor center and administrative center. It now hosts a model of Old Town as it looked in 1872, as well as various historic exhibits. On Mason Street, at the corner of Calhoun Street, **La Casa de Bandini** is one of the prettiest haciendas in San Diego. **Seeley Stable** (⌧ 2630 Calhoun St., ☎ 619/220–5427), next door, became San Diego's stagecoach stop in 1867 and was the transportation hub of Old Town until near the turn of the century, when trains became the favored mode of travel. The stable now houses a collection of horse-drawn vehicles, some so elaborate that you can see where the term "carriage trade" came from.

❻ **Presidio Park.** The rolling hillsides of the 40-acre green space overlooking Old Town from the north end of Taylor Street are popular with picnickers. It's a nice walk to the summit from Old Town if you're in good shape and wearing the right shoes—it should take about a half hour.

You can also drive to the top of the park via Presidio Drive, off Taylor Street, and then wander around on foot. At the end of Mason Street, veer left on Jackson Street to reach the **Presidio Ruins**, where adobe walls and a bastion have been built above the foundations of the original fortress and chapel.

❸ **Thomas Whaley Museum.** Among the historical artifacts here is one of the six life masks that exist of Abraham Lincoln. The place is perhaps most famed for the ghosts that are said to inhabit it. ⊠ *2482 San Diego Ave.,* ☎ *619/298–2482.* ⚏ *$4.* ⊙ *Daily 10–4:30 in spring and summer; closed Tues. in fall and winter; shorter winter hrs (call ahead).*

OFF THE
BEATEN PATH
MISSION SAN DIEGO DE ALCALÁ – Mission San Diego de Alcalá, the first of a chain of 21 missions stretching northward along the California coast, was established by Father Junípero Serra in 1769 on Presidio Hill, and moved to its present location in 1774. There was no greater security from enemy attack here: Padre Luis Jayme, California's first Christian martyr, was clubbed to death by Native Americans in 1775. The present church is the fifth to be built on the site; it was reconstructed in 1931 following the outlines of the 1813 church. It's 150 ft long but only 35 ft wide because, without easy means of joining beams, the mission buildings were only as wide as the trees that served as their ceiling supports. Father Jayme is buried in the mission sanctuary. A small museum named for him documents the history of the mission, exhibiting tools and artifacts from the early days. From the peaceful palm-bedecked gardens out back you can gaze at the 46-ft-high *campanario*, the mission's most distinctive feature. One of its five bells was cast in 1822. ⊠ *10818 San Diego Mission Rd. (from I–15, take Friars Rd. east and Rancho Mission Rd. south),* ☎ *619/281–8449.* ⚏ *$2.* ⊙ *Daily 9–5.*

DINING

By Kathryn
Shevelow
A stroll down 5th Avenue will provide ample evidence of San Diego's love affair with Italian cuisine, echoed in other parts of the city. But the cooking of Spain and France, as well as the various cuisines of Latin America, Asia, the Middle East—and even the United States—are also well represented. San Diego is an informal city. The advised attire at most of the restaurants listed below is casual.

CATEGORY	COST*
$$$$	over $50
$$$	$30–$50
$$	$20–$30
$	under $20

per person for a three-course meal, excluding drinks, service, and 7¾% sales tax

American

Uptown

$–$$$ ✕ **Montanas American Grill.** One of Hillcrest's most popular restaurants serves hearty California-American food in a sleek, trendy setting. Stick with the least complicated dishes, such as the barbecued meats, chicken, and salmon. The appetizer duck cakes are tasty and rich. Wash down your barbecue with one of the interesting microbrews on tap. ⊠ *1421 University Ave.,* ☎ *619/297–0722,* ℻ *619/296–9669. AE, DC, MC, V. No lunch weekends.*

$ ✕ **Hob Nob Hill.** This comforting restaurant is still under the same ownership and management as it was when it started in 1944. With its dark wood booths and patterned carpets, Hob Nob Hill seems suspended in the '50s, but you don't need to be a nostalgia buff to appreciate the bargain-priced American home cooking. Reservations are suggested for Sunday breakfast. ⊠ 2271 1st Ave., ☎ 619/239–8176. AE, D, MC, V.

American/Casual

Beaches

$–$$ ✕ **The Mission Cafe and Coffeehouse.** This comfy, laid-back Mission Beach café serves whimsical cuisine that it dubs "Chino-Latino." All menu items may be made vegetarian. The café serves good beer on tap, specialty coffee drinks, and shakes and smoothies. ⊠ 3795 Mission Blvd., ☎ 619/488–9060; North Park branch: 2801 University Ave., ☎ 619/220–8992. AE, MC, V.

Uptown

$–$$ ✕ **Crest Cafe.** Often jammed with locals, this Hillcrest institution specializes in good renditions of basic American café food, served from breakfast to late-night dinner. You can't go wrong with old favorites such as pancakes, burgers, onion rings, salads, and the homemade desserts. ⊠ 425 Robinson Ave., ☎ 619/295–2510. Reservations not accepted. AE, D, DC, MC, V.

Belgian

Beaches

$$–$$$ ✕ **Belgian Lion.** Discerning diners come here for exquisite Belgian
★ food. One of the signature dishes is the cassoulet, a rich stew of white beans, sausage, and duck that makes you feel protected from the elements (even in San Diego, where there aren't that many elements). An impressive selection of carefully chosen wines complements the food. ⊠ 2265 Bacon St., Ocean Beach, ☎ 619/223–2700. Reservations essential. AE, D, DC, MC, V. Closed Sun.–Wed. No lunch.

Cajun and Creole

Downtown

$–$$ ✕ **Bayou Bar and Grill.** Ceiling fans, dark-green wainscoting, and light-pink walls help create a New Orleans atmosphere for spicy Cajun and Creole specialties. Come here on Sunday for a hearty brunch. ⊠ 329 Market St., ☎ 619/696–8747, ℻ 619/696–6667. AE, D, DC, MC, V.

Chinese

Downtown

$–$$$ ✕ **Panda Inn.** One of the better Chinese restaurants in town, this dining room at the top of Horton Plaza serves subtly seasoned Mandarin and Szechuan dishes in an elegant setting that feels far removed from the rush of commerce below. ⊠ 506 Horton Plaza, ☎ 619/233–7800. AE, D, DC, MC, V.

Contemporary

Downtown

$$–$$$ ✕ **Dobson's.** Although the small, two-tier building suggests an earlier
★ era, there's nothing outdated about the cuisine. The predominantly California wine list is excellent. ⊠ 956 Broadway Circle, ☎ 619/231–6771, ℻ 619/696–0861. AE, DC, MC, V. Closed Sun. No lunch Sat.

522

San Diego Dining

DOWNTOWN

⑲ ⑳ ㉑ ㉒ ㉓ ㉔

TO
OLD TOWN,
QUALCOMM STADIUM

Cedar St.

Cedar St.

■ County Center/
Little Italy
Trolley Station

Beech St.

Beech St.

Ash St.

A St.

A St.

⑱

B St.

B St.

Fifth Ave.
Trolley Station

⑰

B St.
Pier

C St.

C St.

N. Harbor Dr.

Pacific Hwy.

Kettner Blvd.

India St.

Columbia St.

State St.

Union St.

Front St.

First Ave.

Second Ave.

Third Ave.

Fourth Ave.

Fifth Ave.

**LINDA
VISTA**

Amtrak/Transfer
Station ■

Broadway

Broadway

AE

E St.

E St.

㉝

㉛

Vista

㉕

F St.

F St.

㉞

㉖

State St.

Union St.

㉟

First Ave.

Horton
Plaza ■

㊱

㊲

Friars

San Diego R.

G St.

G St.

Fifth Ave.

㉜

Seaport Village
Trolley Station

Second Ave.

㊳

㉘

Market St.

Fourth Ave.

㉙

Island Ave.

㊵

Ft. Stockton
Dr.

㉚

Market Pl.

㊴

Convention
Center West
Station

J St.

㊶

㉗

■ Seaport Village

K St.

Hwy.

Harbor Dr.

Balboa Park

6th Ave.

94

Broadway

94

Market St.

47th St.

Imperial Ave.

National Ave.

Harbor Dr.

75

San Diego-
Coronado Bay
Bridge

Orange Ave.

National City Blvd.

Highland Ave.

8th St.

805

18th St.

**NATIONAL
CITY**

*Coronado
Beach*

Silver Strand Blvd.

San Diego Bay

La Jolla

$$$-$$$$ ✕ **The Marine Room.** The menu has gotten a face-lift at this venerable La Jolla Shores institution, where diners can gaze at the ocean and, if they're lucky, watch the grunion run or the waves beat against the glass. Even if the ocean isn't producing any special effects, the Marine Room offers genteel beachfront dining-and-dancing and creative (though some will think *too* creative) contemporary cuisine. ⊠ *2000 Spindrift Dr.,* ☎ *619/459–7222. AE, D, DC, MC, V.*

$$$-$$$$ ✕ **Top O' the Cove.** Although glitzier newcomers now rival this once peerless La Jolla institution, the elegant but comfortable Top O' the Cove still receives high marks from San Diego diners for the romantic ocean view from its cottage windows and its fine contemporary European–American cuisine. The service is attentive but not overbearing, and the award-winning wine list is enormous. ⊠ *1216 Prospect St.,* ☎ *619/454–7779,* FAX *619/454–3783. AE, DC, MC, V.*

$$-$$$ ✕ **Cafe Japengo.** One of the most stylish dining rooms in town, this Pacific Rim spot serves Asian-inspired cuisine with many North and South American touches. You can also order very fresh sushi from your table or from a seat at the sushi bar. ⊠ *Aventine Center, 8960 University Center La.,* ☎ *619/450–3355,* FAX *619/552–6064. AE, D, DC, MC, V. No lunch weekends.*

$$-$$$ ✕ **Roppongi.** A hit from the moment its doors opened, this newcomer
★   to the La Jolla dining scene offers global cuisine with strong Asian notes. The contemporary dining room, with a row of comfortable booths lining a wall, is lovely, done in wood tones and accented with Asian statuary. The menu invites you to choose among a range of imaginative Euro-Asian tapas that you may order as appetizers or combine to make a full meal. ⊠ *875 Prospect St.,* ☎ *619/551–5252,* FAX *619/551–5252. AE, D, DC, MC, V.*

$-$$$ ✕ **Brockton Villa Restaurant.** This informal restaurant in a restored historic beach cottage overlooks La Jolla Cove and the ocean. Come for breakfast or lunch to take advantage of the fabulous daytime view. The extensive menu has something for everyone, and there's a good range of coffee drinks. You'll have to fight the crowds on sunny weekends. ⊠ *1235 Coast Blvd.,* ☎ *619/454–7393. AE, D, MC, V. No dinner Mon.*

Uptown

$$-$$$ ✕ **California Cuisine.** The menu in this minimalist-chic dining room is
★   consistently innovative. You can count on whatever you order to be carefully prepared and elegantly presented. The staff is knowledgeable and attentive, the wine list is good, and the baked desserts and sorbets are mighty tempting. Heat lamps make the garden patio a romantic year-round option. ⊠ *1027 University Ave.,* ☎ *619/543–0790,* FAX *619/543–0106. AE, D, DC, MC, V. Closed Mon. No lunch weekends.*

Deli

La Jolla

$-$$$ ✕ **SamSon's.** About as close as you'll come to a real Jewish deli in coastal San Diego, SamSon's boasts a vast menu and serves enormous portions. ⊠ *8861 Villa La Jolla Dr.,* ☎ *619/455–1462. AE, D, DC, MC, V.*

French

La Jolla

$$$-$$$$ ✕ **Tapenade.** French cuisine is making a comeback in San Diego, and
★   it has shed some weight in the process. Tapenade takes its inspiration from the South of France. The cuisine matches the unpretentious, light, and airy room. Very fresh ingredients, a delicate touch with sauces, and an emphasis on seafood make this a winner. The tables can

be cramped, however, and the service does not rise to the level of the cooking. ⊠ *7612 Fay Ave., between Kline and Pearl,* ☎ *619/551–7500,* FAX *619/551–9913. AE, D, DC, MC, V. Closed Mon.*

$$–$$$ ✕ **Cindy Black's.** This quietly chic restaurant in La Jolla's Bird Rock neighborhood serves modern interpretations of French cuisine, offering subtle, stylishly presented dishes, often with a Mediterranean touch. The menu changes seasonally. ⊠ *5721 La Jolla Blvd.,* ☎ *619/ 456–6299,* FAX *619/456–0433. AE, D, DC, MC, V. Closed Mon. No lunch.*

Uptown

$$–$$$ ✕ **Laurel.** This acclaimed restaurant celebrates the cooking of southern France and the Mediterranean. Its culinary philosophy is straightforward: the best fresh ingredients prepared simply, but with flair. The wine list is renowned. ⊠ *505 Laurel St., at 5th Ave.,* ☎ *619/239–2222. AE, D, DC, MC, V. No lunch.*

Greek

Downtown

$–$$$ ✕ **Athens Market.** This cheerful eatery bustles with downtown office workers and members of San Diego's small but active Greek community. Greek music and belly dancers add to the festive atmosphere on weekend evenings. ⊠ *109 W. F St.,* ☎ *619/234–1955,* FAX *619/236– 1951. AE, D, DC, MC, V. No lunch weekends.*

Indian

Mission Valley

$ ✕ **KC's Tandoor.** KC's Tandoor defies expectations by serving genuine and tasty Indian food. The tandoori chicken is flavorful, the nan bread is rich and chewy, and the curries are appealing. Hearty appetites will find a bargain in the all-you-can-eat Sunday buffet brunch. ⊠ *Friars Mission Center, 5608 Mission Center Rd.,* ☎ *619/497–0751. MC, V.*

Uptown

$–$$$ ✕ **Bombay Exotic Cuisine of India.** This elegant Indian restaurant serves dishes that are perhaps too Americanized for some aficionados, who should firmly inform the waiter that they are serious about spiciness, but no one can deny the loveliness of their presentation. The chef's generous hand with raw and cooked vegetables gives each course a colorful freshness reminiscent of California cuisine, though the flavors definitely hail from India. ⊠ *Hillcrest Center, 3975 Fifth Ave., Suite 100,* ☎ *619/298–3155,* FAX *619/297–6969. AE, D, DC, MC, V.*

$–$$ ✕ **Maharajah.** Indian-food lovers who are searching for un-Americanized flavors and a menu that features southern and northern Indian dishes will find happy dining and great prices at this Hillcrest restaurant. ⊠ *1220 Cleveland Ave., No. M113,* ☎ *619/543–1163. AE, D, DC, MC, V. Closed Mon.*

Italian

Downtown

$$–$$$ ✕ **Bella Luna.** This small restaurant whose owner hails from the island of Capri has developed a loyal following among diners who prefer good cuisine to being seen. The service is gracious and attentive. The menu includes dishes from all over Italy. ⊠ *748 5th Ave.,* ☎ *619/239–3222.* FAX *619/239–1202. AE, MC, V. No lunch weekends.*

$$–$$$ ✕ **Fio's.** Glitzy young singles mingle with staid business-suit types in this lively Gaslamp Quarter restaurant. Contemporary variations on traditional northern Italian cuisine are served in a high-ceiling, brick-

and-wood dining room overlooking the 5th Avenue street scene. ✉ *801 5th Ave.*, ☎ *619/234–3467*, ☏ *619/234–5431. AE, D, DC, MC, V. No lunch.*

$$–$$$ ✕ **Trattoria Mamma Anna.** The owners' native Sicilian cuisine shows up on the menu, but the fare ventures into the rest of Italy as well. Portions are generous. This is one of the few good 5th Avenue restaurants open on weekends for lunch as well as dinner. ✉ *644 5th Ave.*, ☎ *619/235–8144.* ☏ *619/235–6213. AE, D, DC, MC, V.*

La Jolla

$–$$$ ✕ **Piatti Ristorante.** On weekends this trattoria is filled to overflow-
★   ing with singles and local families. A wood-burning oven turns out fla-
           vorful pizzas. The weekday lunch menu includes elaborate salads and
           delicious *panini* (sandwiches); brunch is served weekends. A fountain
           splashes softly on the tree-shaded patio, where heat lamps allow din-
           ers to sit even on chilly evenings. ✉ *2182 Avenida de la Playa*, ☎ *619/454–1589*, ☏ *619/454–1799. AE, DC, MC, V.*

Japanese

Beaches

$–$$ ✕ **Sushi Ota.** Feast here on San Diego's best sushi. For the cautious,
★   Sushi Ota offers the cooked as well as the raw. ✉ *4529 Mission Bay Dr.*, ☎ *619/270–5670. Reservations essential. AE, D, MC, V. No lunch Sat.–Mon.*

Downtown

$–$$$ ✕ **Taka.** If downtown dining starts to seem oppressively Eurocentric, take refuge behind a platter of sushi in this attractive 5th Avenue alternative. You could make a meal by starting with sushi and then ordering from the large selection of cold and hot appetizers. The entrée menu mixes Japanese standards such as salmon teriyaki with an occasional European selection, such as the good seafood linguine. ✉ *555 5th Ave.*, ☎ *619/338–0555*, ☏ *619/232–6902. No lunch.*

Latin American

Old Town

$–$$ ✕ **Berta's Latin American Restaurant.** A San Diego rarity—and a surprise in a section of town where the food leans toward the safe and touristy—Berta's serves wonderful Latin American dishes. The wine list showcases good Chilean wines, and the food manages to be tasty and health-conscious at the same time. ✉ *3928 Twiggs St.*, ☎ *619/295–2343. AE, MC, V.*

Mexican

Beaches

$–$$ ✕ **Palenque.** A welcome alternative to the standard Sonoran-style café, this family-run restaurant in Pacific Beach serves regional Mexican dishes. Seating is in comfortable round-back leather chairs; in warm weather you can dine on a small deck in front. ✉ *1653 Garnet Ave., Pacific Beach*, ☎ *619/272–7816. AE, D, DC, MC, V. No lunch Mon.*

Mission Valley

$–$$ ✕ **El Tecolote.** The long-established El Tecolote (The Owl) does a good job with the usual taco-burrito fare, but come here also to sample Mexican specialties—the enchiladas in mole, the chicken breast with poblana or ancho chili sauce, or the rich "Aztec layered cake" (tortillas stacked with cheese, chilies, enchilada sauce, guacamole, and sour cream). ✉ *6110 Friars Rd. W*, ☎ *619/295–2087*, ☏ *619/295–7788. AE, D, DC, MC, V. No lunch Sun.*

Uptown

$ ✕ **Chilango's Mexico City Grill.** Proof positive that good things come in small packages is this tiny but cheerful storefront restaurant. The burritos and *tortas* (sandwiches) are like no others in the city. This much-loved restaurant, which opens at 9 AM Friday–Sunday, quickly fills to overflowing in the evening, so consider coming in off-hours or ordering takeout. ✉ *142 University Ave.,* ☎ *619/294–8646,* ℻ *619/294–8803. No credit cards.*

Seafood

Downtown

$$$–$$$$ ✕ **Anthony's Star of the Sea Room.** The flagship of Anthony's local
★ fleet of seafood restaurants ensconces its patrons in a formal dining room whose vaguely marine '60s decor got a much-needed face-lift early in 1999. The menu changes seasonally, but expect to find contemporary preparations of fresh seafood. The patio takes full advantage of the choice waterfront location of one of San Diego's premier seafood restaurants. ✉ *1360 N. Harbor Dr.,* ☎ *619/232–7408. AE, D, DC, MC, V. No lunch.*

$$–$$$$ ✕ **Blue Point Coastal Cuisine.** High ceilings, gleaming woodwork, and expansive windows give this seafood establishment an urbane air. Blue Point situates its cuisine firmly on the Pacific Rim, incorporating Asian accents and south-of-the-border flavors. Go for the appetizers and seafood entrées here. The pasta dishes are disappointing. ✉ *565 5th Ave.,* ☎ *619/233–6623. AE, D, DC, MC, V. No lunch.*

$$–$$$$ ✕ **Sally's.** The dining room is très chic postmodern, and similarly stylish is the cuisine: pan-Mediterranean with a light French accent. Seafood is the star here, although the menu has something for carnivores and vegetarians, as well. Outdoor dining is available. ✉ *Hyatt Regency San Diego, 1 Market Pl.,* ☎ *619/687–6080,* ℻ *619/687–6078. AE, D, DC, MC, V.*

$–$$$$ ✕ **The Fish Market.** Diners at this informal restaurant may choose from a large variety of fresh mesquite-grilled fish. The view is stunning: enormous plate-glass windows look directly out onto the harbor. This is one of those rare places where families with young children can feel comfortable without sacrificing their taste buds. There's a little sushi bar, too. A more formal restaurant upstairs, the Top of the Market ($24–$100), is expensive but worth the splurge. Or economize by visiting for lunch or Sunday brunch. ✉ *750 N. Harbor Dr.,* ☎ *619/232–3474 for the Fish Market; 619/234–4867 for the Top of the Market. No reservations downstairs. AE, D, DC, MC, V.*

La Jolla

$$$ ✕ **George's at the Cove.** The elegant main dining room, with a wall-
★ length window overlooking La Jolla Cove, is renowned for its daily fresh seafood specials and its fine preparations of beef and lamb. For more informal dining and a sweeping view of the coast try the rooftop Ocean Terrace (or order from its menu in the second-story bar). Wonderful for breakfast, lunch, or brunch on a fine day, but also serving dinner, the Terrace does not take reservations. ✉ *1250 Prospect St.,* ☎ *619/454–4244,* ℻ *619/454–5458. Reservations essential for main dining room on weekends. AE, D, DC, MC, V.*

Old Town

$$–$$$ ✕ **Cafe Pacifica.** The airy Cafe Pacifica serves eclectic contemporary cuisine with an emphasis on seafood. Fresh fish is grilled with your choice of savory sauces. Other good bets include the griddle-fried mustard catfish, the seared ahi tuna, and the grilled lamb chops. Cafe Pacifica's wine list has received kudos from *Wine Spectator* magazine. ✉

2414 San Diego Ave., ☎ *619/291–6666. AE, D, DC, MC, V. No lunch.*

Spanish

Downtown

$$–$$$ ✕ **La Gran Tapa.** Dark-wood tables and a black-and-white checkered floor give this established restaurant a particularly urban air. Come here for a meal of the small Spanish dishes called tapas. Take advantage of the opportunity to try a good Spanish wine. ⊠ *611 B St.,* ☎ *619/234–8272,* 𝔽𝔸𝕏 *619/231–8272. AE, MC, V. Closed Sun. No lunch Sat.*

Thai

Uptown

$–$$ ✕ **Taste of Thai.** Usually packed with value-minded diners, this modest café seats you at close quarters but compensates by serving yummy Thai and vegetarian cuisine at reasonable prices. ⊠ *527 University Ave.,* ☎ *619/291–7525. AE, D, DC, MC, V.*

$ ✕ **Saffron.** Formerly a take-out restaurant specializing in spit-roasted chicken served with a choice of sauces, Saffron recently added a noodle house. Now you can choose among an impressive array of Thai and Vietnamese noodle dishes, including soups that are satisfying for lunch and dinner. There's limited outdoor seating as well. This is an ideal place to pick up a meal to take to Mission Bay or the beach. ⊠ *3737 India St. (from downtown, take I–5 to Washington St. exit),* ☎ *619/574–7737. Reservations not accepted. MC, V.*

LODGING

By Sharon K. Gillenwater and Edie Jarolim

Updated by Arian E. Collins

San Diego is spread out, so the first thing to consider when selecting lodging is location. If you choose one of the many hotels with a waterfront location and extensive outdoor sports facilities, you need never leave the premises. But if you plan to sightsee, take into account a hotel's proximity to the attractions you most want to visit. In general, price need not be a major factor in your decision. Even the most expensive areas have some reasonably priced rooms.

The **Bed & Breakfast Guild of San Diego** (☎ 619/523–1300) lists a number of high-quality member inns. The **Bed & Breakfast Directory for San Diego** (⊠ Box 3292, 92163, ☎ 619/297–3130 or 800/619–7666) covers San Diego County.

CATEGORY	COST*
$$$$	over $175
$$$	$120–$175
$$	$80–$120
$	under $80

*for a double room in high (summer) season, excluding 10½% San Diego room tax

Coronado

$$$$ 🏨 **Coronado Island Marriott Resort.** Flamingos greet you at the entrance
★   to this 16-acre landscaped resort, formerly Le Meridien. Large rooms and suites in low-slung buildings are done in a cheerful California-country French fashion, with colorful Impressionist prints; all rooms have separate showers and tubs and come with plush robes. The spa facilities are top-notch, as is the award-winning Marius restaurant, which serves innovative French Provençale cuisine. ⊠ *2000 2nd St., 92118,* ☎ *619/435–3000; 800/543–4300 for central reservations;* 𝔽𝔸𝕏 *619/*

435–3032. 265 rooms, 7 suites, 28 villa units. 2 restaurants, bar, in-room data ports, room service, 3 pools, barbershop, beauty salon, 2 outdoor hot tubs, massage, sauna, spa, 6 tennis courts, aerobics, health club, beach, snorkeling, windsurfing, bicycles, pro shop, shops, children's programs, laundry service, concierge, business services, convention center, meeting rooms, parking (fee). AE, D, DC, MC, V.

$$$$ ⊞ **Loews Coronado Bay Resort.** You can park your boat at the 80-slip marina of this elegant resort set on a secluded 15-acre peninsula on the Silver Strand. Rooms are formally but tastefully decorated, and all have furnished balconies with views of water—either bay, ocean, or marina. The hotel lounge has nightly entertainment. The Azzura Point restaurant specializes in Pacific seafood. ⊠ *4000 Coronado Bay Rd., 92118,* ☎ *619/424–4000 or 800/815–6397,* ℻ *619/424–4400. 403 rooms, 37 suites. 3 restaurants, 3 bars, deli, in-room data ports, room service, 3 pools, barbershop, beauty salon, 3 hot tubs, 5 tennis courts, health club, marina, beach, windsurfing, boating, jet skiing, waterskiing, bicycles, pro shop, children's programs, laundry service, concierge, business services, convention center, meeting rooms, parking (fee). AE, D, DC, MC, V.*

$$$–$$$$ ⊞ **Hotel Del Coronado.** "The Del" is a social and historic landmark. The rooms and suites in the ornate 1888 building are charmingly quirky. Some have sleeping areas that seem smaller than the baths. Other rooms are downright palatial; two are even said to come with a resident ghost. More standardized room sizes are available in the newer high-rise. Air-conditioning is available only in the newer building. Robes, irons, ironing boards, and hair dryers are included in every room. There are separate men's and women's health facilities. Past guests of the hotel have included U.S. presidents and members of European royalty. ⊠ *1500 Orange Ave., 92118,* ☎ *619/435–6611 for hotel; 619/ 522–8000, 800/468–3533 for reservations;* ℻ *619/522–8262. 692 rooms. 3 restaurants, 4 bars, deli, in-room data ports, room service, 2 pools, barbershop, beauty salon, outdoor hot tub, massage, sauna, steam room, 6 tennis courts, exercise room, beach, bicycles, shops, video games, concierge, business services, convention center, meeting rooms, parking (fee). AE, D, DC, MC, V.*

$$–$$$$ ⊞ **Glorietta Bay Inn.** The main building of this property—across the street from the Hotel Del, adjacent to the Coronado harbor, and near many restaurants and shops—was built in 1908 for sugar baron John D. Spreckels, who once owned much of downtown San Diego. Rooms in this Edwardian-style mansion and in the newer motel-style buildings are attractively furnished. The well-appointed inn is much smaller than the Hotel Del Coronado; its clients experience a quieter and less expensive stay. Tours ($6) of the island's historical buildings depart from the inn's lobby three mornings a week. Some rooms have kitchenettes, patios, and balconies. Complimentary Continental breakfast is offered. ⊠ *1630 Glorietta Blvd., 92118,* ☎ *619/435–3101 or 800/283– 9383,* ℻ *619/435–6182. 100 rooms. In-room data ports, refrigerators, pool, outdoor hot tub, spa, concierge, bicycles, coin laundry, business services, free parking. AE, D, DC, MC, V.*

Downtown

$$$$ ⊞ **Hyatt Regency San Diego.** This high-rise adjacent to Seaport Vil-
★   lage successfully combines old-world opulence with California airiness. Palm trees pose next to ornate tapestry couches in the light-filled lobby, and all of the British Regency–style guest rooms have views of the water. The hotel's proximity to the convention center attracts a large business trade. The 40th-floor lounge has 360-degree sunset views. ⊠ *1 Market Pl., 92101,* ☎ *619/232–1234; 800/233–1234 for central reser-*

San Diego Lodging

vations; ☎ *619/233–6464. 820 rooms, 55 suites and Regency Club rooms. 2 restaurants, 2 bars, in-room data ports, room service, pool, outdoor hot tub, sauna, steam room, 4 tennis courts, health club, boating, bicycles, shops, laundry service, business services, meeting rooms, parking (fee). AE, D, DC, MC, V.*

$$$$ ⊞ **San Diego Marriott Hotel and Marina.** This twin-tower high-rise next to the San Diego Convention Center has everything a business traveler could want, not to mention a superb view of the bay and city from the upper floors. A major site for conventions, the complex can be hectic and impersonal but has such intriguing features as lagoon-style pools nestled between cascading waterfalls. Vacationers will appreciate the location right on the San Diego Bay boardwalk. ⊠ *333 W. Harbor Dr., 92101,* ☎ *619/234–1500; 800/228–9290 for central reservations;* ☎ *619/234–8678. 1,300 rooms, 54 suites. 3 restaurants, 3 bars, in-room data ports, room service, 2 pools, barbershop, beauty salon, outdoor hot tub, sauna, 6 tennis courts, aerobics, basketball, health club, jogging, shops, recreation room, coin laundry, concierge, business services, meeting rooms, car rental, parking (fee). AE, D, DC, MC, V.*

$$$$ **San Diego Marriott Suites Downtown.** This 15-story hotel is near the financial district and Balboa Park. It's too far inland to have good views of the harbor, but it has an interesting view of parts of downtown. It's ideal for those in town on business. All rooms have modem connections, wet bars, coffeemakers, and cable TV. ⊠ *701 A St., 92101,* ☎ *619/696–9800 or 800/228–9290,* ☎ *619/696–1555. 264 suites. Restaurant, bar, in-room data ports, indoor heated pool, hot tub, sauna, exercise room, concierge, meeting rooms, business services, airport shuttle, valet parking. AE, D, DC, MC, V.*

$$$$ ⊞ **U. S. Grant Hotel.** This San Diego classic built in 1910 by the grandson of President Ulysses S. Grant sits across the street from Horton Plaza. Crystal chandeliers and polished marble floors in the lobby and Queen Anne–style mahogany furnishings in the stately and spacious rooms recall a more gracious era when such dignitaries as President Franklin D. Roosevelt and Charles Lindbergh stayed here. High-power business types still gather at the hotel's clubby Grant Grill, and English high tea is served in the lobby from 2–6. ⊠ *326 Broadway, 92101,* ☎ *619/232–3121 or 800/237–5029,* ☎ *619/232–3626. 220 rooms, 60 suites. Restaurant, 2 bars, café, room service, exercise room, shops, concierge, business services, airport shuttle, parking (fee). AE, D, DC, MC, V.*

$$$$ ⊞ **Westgate Hotel.** A nondescript, modern high-rise across from Hor-
★   ton Plaza hides what must be the most opulent hotel in San Diego. The lobby, modeled after the anteroom at Versailles, has hand-cut Baccarat chandeliers. Rooms are individually furnished with antiques, Italian marble counters, and bath fixtures with 24-karat-gold overlays. From the ninth floor up the views of the harbor and city are breathtaking. Afternoon high tea is served in the lobby to the accompaniment of piano music. ⊠ *1055 Second Ave., 92101,* ☎ *619/238–1818 or 800/221–3802; 800/522–1564 in CA;* ☎ *619/557–3737. 223 rooms. 2 restaurants, bar, deli, in-room data ports, room service, barbershop, exercise room, bicycles, concierge, business services, meeting rooms, airport shuttle, parking (fee). AE, D, DC, MC, V.*

$$$–$$$$ ⊞ **Embassy Suites San Diego Bay.** It's a short walk to the convention center, the Embarcadero, and Seaport Village from one of downtown's most popular hotels. The front door of each spacious suite opens out onto the 12-story atrium. The contemporary decor is pleasant, and the views from rooms facing the harbor are spectacular. Business travelers will find it easy to set up shop here. Families can make good use of the in-room refrigerators, microwaves, and separate sleeping areas. A cooked-to-order breakfast and afternoon cocktails are complimen-

tary, as are airport transfers. ✉ *601 Pacific Hwy., 92101,* ☎ *619/239–2400; 800/362–2779 for central reservations;* ⊠ *619/239–1520. 337 suites. Restaurant, bar, pool, barbershop, beauty salon, sauna, health club, bicycles, shops, coin laundry, business services, meeting rooms, airport shuttle, parking (fee). AE, D, DC, MC, V.*

$$$–$$$$ 🏨 **Horton Grand Hotel.** A Victorian confection in the heart of the historic Gaslamp Quarter, the Horton Grand comprises two 1880s hotels moved brick by brick from nearby locations and fit together. Its delightfully retro rooms are furnished with period antiques, ceiling fans, and gas-burning fireplaces. The choicest rooms overlook a garden courtyard that twinkles with miniature lights each night. The hotel is a charmer, but service can be erratic. ✉ *311 Island Ave., 92101,* ☎ *619/544–1886 or 800/542–1886,* ⊠ *619/239–3823. 105 rooms, 24 suites. Restaurant, bar, business services, meeting rooms, airport shuttle, parking (fee). AE, D, DC, MC, V.*

$$$–$$$$ 🏨 **Westin Hotel San Diego–Horton Plaza.** Although it is fronted by a startling lighted blue obelisk, this high-rise is all understated marble and brass. The spacious rooms are in pastels of coral blue and pale orange. With its prime downtown location, the hotel attracts many business travelers. The lobby lounge is packed every night with local financiers and weary shoppers from the adjacent Horton Plaza. ✉ *910 Broadway Circle, 92101,* ☎ *619/239–2200,* ☎ ⊠ *619/557–3737. 450 rooms, 14 suites. 2 restaurants, bar, in-room data ports, pool, indoor hot tub, 2 tennis courts, health club, basketball, business services, meeting rooms, parking (fee). AE, D, DC, MC, V.*

$$$–$$$$ 🏨 **Wyndham Emerald Plaza Hotel.** This property's office and conference facilities draw many business travelers. Still, the Wyndham is also fine for vacationers who want to be near downtown shopping and restaurants. Many of the upper-floor accommodations have panoramic views. The bland, beige-dominated standard rooms are not overly large. The health club is quite good. ✉ *400 W. Broadway, 92101,* ☎ *619/239–4500 or 800/996–3426,* ⊠ *619/239–4527. 416 rooms, 20 suites. Restaurant, bar, in-room data ports, pool, outdoor hot tub, sauna, steam room, health club, shops, concierge, business services, meeting rooms, parking (fee). AE, D, DC, MC, V.*

$$–$$$$ 🏨 **Balboa Park Inn.** Directly across the street from Balboa Park, this all-suites B&B is housed in four Spanish colonial–style 1915 residences connected by courtyards. Prices are reasonable for the romantic one- and two-bedroom suites. Each has a different flavor, including contemporary versions of Italian, French, Spanish, or early Californian; some have fireplaces, wet bars, whirlpool tubs, patios, and kitchens with microwaves. All rooms have coffeemakers and minirefrigerators. Continental breakfast is complimentary. ✉ *3402 Park Blvd., 92103,* ☎ *619/298–0823 or 800/938–8181,* ⊠ *619/294–8070. 26 suites. AE, D, DC, MC, V.*

$$–$$$ 🏨 **Holiday Inn on the Bay.** On the Embarcadero and overlooking San Diego Bay, this twin high-rise hotel is convenient for vacationers and business travelers. Rooms are unsurprising but spacious and comfortable, and views from the balconies are hard to beat. The hotel is very close to the airport and Amtrak station. ✉ *1355 N. Harbor Dr., 92101,* ☎ *619/232–3861; 800/877–8920 for central reservations;* ⊠ *619/232–4924. 600 rooms, 17 suites. Restaurant, bar, in-room data ports, pool, exercise room, shops, coin laundry, meeting rooms, airport shuttle, parking (fee). AE, D, DC, MC, V.*

$–$$$ 🏨 **Gaslamp Plaza Suites.** Listed on the National Registry of Historic Places, this 11-story structure a block from Horton Plaza was built in 1913 as San Diego's first "skyscraper." Elegant public areas have old marble, brass, and mosaics. Guests can enjoy the view and a complimentary Continental breakfast on the rooftop terrace. Book ahead if you're visiting in high season. ✉ *520 E St., 92101,* ☎ *619/232–9500 or 800/874–8770,* ℻ *619/238–9945. 52 suites. Restaurant, bar, parking (fee). AE, D, DC, MC, V.*

$$ ⊞ **Clarion Hotel Bay View.** Two blocks from the Gaslamp Quarter and close to the San Diego Convention Center, this is a good hotel for budget conventioneers who want to be close to shopping, nightlife, and restaurants. All rooms have coffeemakers and safes. The two-room suites have wet bars, and you can request microwaves, minirefrigerators, and video players for added fees. A Trolley station is two blocks away. ✉ *660 K St., 92101,* ☎ *619/696–0234 or 800/252–7466,* ℻ *619/231–8199. 264 rooms, 48 suites. Restaurant, bar, pool, in-room data ports, hot tub, sauna, exercise room, video games, coin laundry, concierge, meeting rooms, airport shuttle, parking (fee). AE, D, DC, MC, V.*

$$ ⊞ **Radisson Hotel–Harbor View.** This 16-story hotel dwarfs most buildings in the area, providing many rooms great views of San Diego Bay and the downtown skyline. The hotel is surrounded by two-story Victorian homes, making it seem very out of place. Although the hotel has its own restaurant, try the eateries and coffeehouses of the Little Italy community nearby. ✉ *1648 Front St., 92101,* ☎ *619/239–6800 or 800/ 333–3333,* ℻ *619/238–9461. 333 rooms. Restaurant, bar, pool, hot tub, sauna, exercise room, business services, meeting rooms. AE, D, DC, MC, V.*

$$ ⊞ **Ramada Inn & Suites–Downtown.** Formerly the St. James Hotel, this historic 1913 building's 12 stories made it the tallest building in the city when it was built. The hotel is one of several boutique hotels sprouting up downtown using older buildings that have been thoroughly renovated. At the north end of the Gaslamp Quarter, the hotel is close to the area's many restaurants, nightclubs, and shops, but away from the hustle and bustle on Fourth and Fifth avenues. ✉ *830 Sixth Ave., 92101,* ☎ *619/431–8877 or 800/664–4400,* ℻ *619/231–8307. 82 rooms, 17 suites. Restaurant, massage, exercise room. AE, D, DC, MC, V.*

$–$$ ⊞ **Rodeway Inn.** On one of downtown's quieter streets, this Cortez Hill property is clean, comfortable, and nicely decorated. Continental breakfast is complimentary. The hotel is near Balboa Park, the zoo, and freeways. ✉ *833 Ash St., 92101,* ☎ *619/239–2285; 800/228–2000 for central reservations; 800/522–1528 in CA;* ℻ *619/235–6951. 45 rooms. In-room data ports, hot tub, sauna, coin laundry, business services, meeting rooms, free parking. AE, D, DC, MC, V.*

$ ⊞ **Super 8 Bayview.** This motel's location is less noisy than those of other low-cost establishments. The accommodations are nondescript but clean, and some have refrigerators. Continental breakfast is complimentary. ✉ *1835 Columbia St., 92101,* ☎ *619/544–0164 or 800/ 537–9902,* ℻ *619/237–9940. 101 rooms. Pool, coin laundry, airport shuttle, free parking. AE, DC, MC, V.*

Harbor Island, Shelter Island, and Point Loma

$$$–$$$$ ⊞ **Sheraton San Diego Hotel & Marina.** Of this property's two highrises, the smaller, more intimate West Tower has larger rooms with separate areas suitable for business entertaining. The East Tower has better sports facilities. Rooms throughout are California-style. Views from the upper floors of both sections are superb, but because the West Tower is closer to the water it has fine outlooks from the lower floors, too. ✉ *1380 Harbor Island Dr., 92101,* ☎ *619/291–2900; 800/325– 3535 for central reservations;* ℻ *619/692–2337. 1,053 rooms. 2 restaurants, 2 bars, deli, patisserie, in-room data ports, room service, 3 pools, wading pool, 2 outdoor hot tubs, massage, 4 tennis courts, health club, jogging, beach, boating, bicycles, pro shop, airport shuttle, parking (fee). AE, D, DC, MC, V.*

$$–$$$$ ⊡ **Bay Club Hotel & Marina.** Rooms in this appealing low-rise Shelter Island property are large, light, and furnished with rattan tables and chairs and Polynesian tapestries; all have refrigerators and views of either the bay or the marina from outside terraces. A buffet breakfast and limo service to and from the airport or Amtrak station are included in the room rate. ⊠ *2131 Shelter Island Dr., 92106,* ☎ *619/224–8888 or 800/672–0800,* FAX *619/225–1604. 95 rooms, 10 suites. Restaurant, bar, room service, pool, outdoor hot tub, exercise room, concierge, business services, meeting rooms, free parking. AE, D, DC, MC, V.*

$$–$$$$ ⊡ **Kona Kai Continental Plaza Resort and Marina.** Though the Kona Kai name may suggest a Polynesian theme, this 11-acre property has been refurbished in a mixture of Mexican and Mediterranean styles. The spacious and light-filled lobby, with its Mayan sculptures and terra-cotta tiles, opens onto a lush esplanade that overlooks the hotel's marina. The rooms are well-appointed, if a bit small, and most look out onto either the marina or San Diego Bay. ⊠ *1551 Shelter Island Dr., 92106,* ☎ *619/221–8000 or 800/566–2524,* FAX *619/221–5953. 168 rooms, 38 suites. Restaurant, bar, room service, 2 pools, 2 hot tubs, 2 saunas, 2 tennis courts, jogging, health club, volleyball, beach, airport shuttle, free parking. AE, D, DC, MC, V.*

$$–$$$ ⊡ **Best Western Island Palms Hotel & Marina.** This waterfront inn with an airy skylighted lobby is a good choice if you have a boat to dock. The adjacent marina has guest slips. Both harbor- and marina-view rooms are available. Standard accommodations are fairly small. If you're traveling with family or more than one friend, the two-bedroom suites with kitchens are a good deal. ⊠ *2051 Shelter Island Dr., 92106,* ☎ *619/222–0561 or 800/922–2336,* FAX *619/222–9760. 68 rooms, 29 suites. Restaurant, bar, in-room data ports, pool, outdoor hot tub, business services, meeting rooms, free parking. AE, D, DC, MC, V.*

$$–$$$ ⊡ **Humphrey's Half Moon Inn.** This sprawling South Seas–style resort has grassy open areas with palm trees and tiki torches. Rooms, some with kitchens and some with harbor or marine views, have modern furnishings. Locals throng to Humphrey's, the on-premises seafood restaurant, and to the jazz lounge. The hotel also hosts outdoor jazz and pop concerts June–October. ⊠ *2303 Shelter Island Dr., 92106,* ☎ *619/224–3411; 800/345–9995 for reservations;* FAX *619/224–3478. 128 rooms, 54 suites. Restaurant, bar, in-room data ports, room service, pool, hot tub, putting green, croquet, Ping-Pong, boating, bicycles, coin laundry, business services, meeting rooms, airport shuttle, free parking. AE, D, DC, MC, V.*

$$–$$$ ⊡ **Travelodge Hotel–Harbor Island.** Lodgers here get the views and amenities of more expensive hotels for less, with such perks as in-room coffeemakers and free local phone calls. Those staying on the two executive floors also get a free buffet breakfast. The public areas and guest rooms are bright and airy. ⊠ *1960 Harbor Island Dr., 92101,* ☎ *619/291–6700; 800/578–7878 for central reservations;* FAX *619/293–0694. 201 rooms, 6 suites. Restaurant, bar, in-room data ports, pool, outdoor hot tub, exercise room, jogging, shops, laundry service, meeting rooms, airport shuttle, free parking. AE, D, DC, MC, V.*

$–$$ ⊡ **Best Western Posada Inn.** Many of the rooms at this comfortable if plain inn have harbor views. Some rooms have microwaves, minirefrigerators, and video players. Point Loma's seafood restaurants are within walking distance. Weekly rates, package plans, and senior discounts are available. Continental breakfast is included. ⊠ *5005 N. Harbor Dr., 92106,* ☎ *619/224–3254 or 800/231–3811,* FAX *619/224–2186. 112 rooms. In-room data ports, pool, outdoor hot tub, exercise room, laundry service, meeting rooms, airport shuttle, free parking. AE, D, DC, MC, V.*

$–$$ ☷ **Ramada Limited Suites Point Loma.** Renovations make this motel nicer than its next-door neighbor the Outrigger, but there are no kitchen units. The location is convenient, though on a busy street, and the rooms with bay views are quite a deal. Continental breakfast is complimentary. There is a heated pool, a bay-view bar with billiards, and a free shuttle to area attractions. ✉ *1403 Rosecrans St., 92106,* ☎ *619/225–9461,* 🖷 *619/225–1163. 86 rooms. Bar, breakfast room, pool, meeting rooms, airport shuttle, free parking. AE, D, DC, MC, V.*

$ ☷ **Travelodge Point Loma.** You'll get the same view here as at the higher-priced hotels—for far less money. There are fewer amenities and the neighborhood isn't as serene, but the rooms—all with coffeemakers—are adequate and clean. ✉ *5102 N. Harbor Dr., 92106,* ☎ *619/223–8171; 800/578–7878 for central reservations;* 🖷 *619/222–7330. 45 rooms. Pool, free parking. AE, D, DC, MC, V.*

Hotel Circle, Mission Valley, and Old Town

$$–$$$$ ☷ **Heritage Park Bed & Breakfast Inn.** The beautifully restored mansions in Old Town's Heritage Park include this romantic 1889 Queen Anne–style inn. Rooms range from smallish to ample, and most are bright and cheery. A two-bedroom suite is decorated with period antiques, and there is also a minisuite. A full breakfast and afternoon tea are included. Transportation is available to area attractions and the Amtrak station. ✉ *2470 Heritage Park Row, 92110,* ☎ *619/299–6832 or 800/995–2470,* 🖷 *619/299–9465. 10 rooms, 2 suites. In-room data ports, airport shuttle. AE, MC, V.*

$$$ ☷ **Best Western Hacienda Hotel Old Town.** Pretty and white, with balconies and Spanish-tile roofs, the Hacienda is in a quiet part of Old Town, away from the freeway and the main retail bustle. The layout is somewhat confusing, and accommodations are not large enough to earn the "suite" label the hotel gives them, but they're decorated in tasteful Southwestern style and equipped with microwaves, coffeemakers, minirefrigerators, clock radios, and video players. ✉ *4041 Harney St., 92110,* ☎ *619/298–4707 or 800/888–1991,* 🖷 *619/298–4771. 168 rooms. Restaurant, bar, pool, outdoor hot tub, exercise room, coin laundry, concierge, meeting rooms, airport shuttle, free parking. AE, D, DC, MC, V.*

$$$ ☷ **Best Western Hanalei Hotel.** As its name suggests, the theme of this friendly Hotel Circle property is Hawaiian: palm trees, waterfalls, koi ponds, and tiki torches abound. Rooms are decorated in tropical prints. What used to be a golf course next door has been restored as a bird sanctuary. Free transportation is provided to local malls and Old Town. ✉ *2270 Hotel Circle N, 92108,* ☎ *619/297–1101 or 800/882–0858,* 🖷 *619/297–6049. 416 rooms. 2 restaurants, bar, in-room data ports, pool, hot tub, exercise room, meeting rooms. AE, D, DC, MC, V.*

$$$ ☷ **San Diego Marriott Mission Valley.** This high-rise sits in the middle of the San Diego River valley near Qualcomm Stadium and the Rio Vista Plaza shopping center, minutes from the Mission Valley and Fashion Valley malls. A San Diego Trolley station is across the street. The hotel is well equipped for business travelers, but the Marriott also caters to vacationers with comfortable rooms and individual balconies, a friendly staff, and free transportation to the malls. ✉ *8757 Rio San Diego Dr., 92108,* ☎ *619/692–3800; 800/228–9290 for central reservations;* 🖷 *619/692–0769. 347 rooms, 6 suites. Restaurant, sports bar, in-room data ports, room service, heated pool, outdoor hot tub, sauna, tennis court, exercise room, nightclub, coin laundry, business services, airport shuttle, free parking. AE, D, DC, MC, V.*

$$$ 🏨 **San Diego Mission Valley Hilton.** Directly fronting Interstate 8, this property has soundproof rooms decorated in a colorful contemporary style. The stylish public areas and lush greenery in the back will make you forget the hotel's proximity to the freeway. Although geared toward business travelers—the hotel has a business center and guests are allowed complimentary use of a personal computer—children stay free. ⊠ *901 Camino del Rio S, 92108,* ☎ *619/543–9000, 800/733– 2332, or 800/445–8667,* FAX *619/543–9358. 342 rooms, 8 suites. 2 restaurants, 2 bars, in-room data ports, pool, outdoor hot tub, exercise room, free parking. AE, D, DC, MC, V.*

$$–$$$ 🏨 **Doubletree Hotel San Diego Mission Valley.** Near Fashion Valley Shopping Center and adjacent to the Hazard Center—which has a seven-screen movie theater, four major restaurants, a food pavilion, and more than 20 shops—the Doubletree is also convenient to Highway 163 and Interstate 8. A San Diego Trolley station is within walking distance. Public areas are light-filled and comfortable, well suited to this hotel's large business clientele. ⊠ *7450 Hazard Center Dr., 92108,* ☎ *619/297–5466; 800/547–8010 for central reservations;* FAX *619/ 297–5499. 294 rooms, 6 suites. Restaurant, 2 bars, in-room data ports, room service, 2 pools, outdoor hot tub, sauna, 2 tennis courts, shops, nightclub, business services, meeting rooms, airport shuttle, free parking. AE, D, DC, MC, V.*

$$ 🏨 **Holiday Inn Hotel & Suites Old Town.** The hacienda-style hotel has Spanish colonial–style fountains, courtyards, and painted tiles, and Southwestern decor in the rooms. Breakfast, cocktail reception, and transfers to the airport, bus, and Amtrak station are all complimentary. Business-class rooms have modem lines and other amenities. ⊠ *2435 Jefferson St., 92110,* ☎ *619/260–8500,* FAX *619/297–2078. 182 rooms, 17 suites. Restaurant, pool, outdoor hot tub, exercise room, meeting rooms, airport shuttle, free parking. AE, D, DC, MC, V.*

$–$$ 🏨 **Days Inn–Hotel Circle.** Rooms in this large complex are par for a chain motel but have the bonus of Nintendo for the kids and irons and ironing boards; some units also have kitchenettes. Airport, Amtrak, zoo, and Sea World shuttles are provided. ⊠ *543 Hotel Circle S, 92108,* ☎ *619/297–8800; 800/227–4743 on weekdays 8–4:30; 800/ 325–2525 for central reservations;* FAX *619/298–6029. 280 rooms. Restaurant, refrigerators, pool, outdoor hot tub, barbershop, beauty salon, coin laundry, meeting rooms, airport shuttle, free parking. AE, D, DC, MC, V.*

$–$$ 🏨 **Vacation Inn–Old Town/San Diego.** This cheerful property throws
★ in such perks as garage parking, Continental breakfast, and afternoon snacks. You'll find modern conveniences—coffeemakers, microwave ovens, and refrigerators—but rustic colors and reproduction furnishings lend rooms an old-country-inn feel. Guests will appreciate the proximity to Old Town attractions and restaurants, along with the heated pool off the shaded courtyard. ⊠ *3900 Old Town Ave., 92110,* ☎ *619/299– 7400 or 800/451–9846,* FAX *619/299–1619. 125 rooms. In-room data ports, refrigerators, pool, outdoor hot tub, coin laundry, business services, meeting rooms, airport shuttle, free parking. AE, D, DC, MC, V.*

La Jolla

$$$$ 🏨 **La Valencia.** This pink Spanish-Mediterranean confection drew film
★ stars down from Hollywood in the 1930s and '40s for its setting and views of La Jolla Cove. Many rooms have a genteel European look, with antique pieces and rich-color rugs. The personal attention provided by the staff, as well as in-room features such as plush robes and grand bathrooms, make the stay even more pleasurable. All rooms have wet bars, coffeemakers, safes, and video players. ⊠ *1132 Prospect St.,*

92037, ☎ 619/454–0771 or 800/451–0772, FAX 619/456–3921. 88
rooms, 12 suites. 3 restaurants, bar, pool, outdoor hot tub, health club,
shuffleboard, business services, meeting rooms, parking (fee). AE, D,
DC, MC, V.

$$$$ 🏨 **Sea Lodge.** Palms, fountains, red-tile roofs, and Mexican tile work
lend a Spanish flavor to this low-lying compound on La Jolla Shores
beach. Rooms, a few with kitchenettes, have rattan furniture and flo-
ral-print bedspreads; all have hair dryers, coffeemakers, irons, and
wooden balconies that overlook lush landscaping and the sea. ⊠ 8110
Camino del Oro, 92037, ☎ 619/459–8271 or 800/237–5211, FAX 619/
456–9346. 128 rooms. Restaurant, bar, in-room data ports, room service, pool, outdoor hot tub, sauna, 2 tennis courts, exercise room, Ping-
Pong, beach, coin laundry, business services, meeting rooms, free
parking. AE, D, DC, MC, V.

$$$$ 🏨 **Sheraton Grande Torrey Pines.** The low-rise, high-class Sheraton
★ Grande blends discreetly into the Torrey Pines cliff top, looking almost
insignificant until you step inside the luxurious lobby and gaze through
native and subtropical foliage at the Pacific Ocean and the 18th hole
of the Torrey Pines Municipal Golf Course. Amenities include complimentary butler service and free town-car service to La Jolla and Del
Mar. The oversize accommodations are simple but elegant; most have
balconies or terraces. In addition to easy access to the golf course, guests
also have privileges ($7.50) next door at the fine health club–sports
center at the Scripps Clinic. ⊠ 10950 N. Torrey Pines Rd., 92037, ☎
619/558–1500; 800/325–3535 for central reservations; FAX 619/450–
4584. 392 rooms, 17 suites. Restaurant, 2 bars, in-room data ports,
in-room safes, minibars, room service, pool, outdoor hot tub, sauna,
putting green, 2 tennis courts, aerobics, croquet, exercise room, volleyball, bicycles, concierge, business services, meeting rooms, parking
(fee). AE, D, DC, MC, V.

$$$–$$$$ 🏨 **Colonial Inn.** A tastefully restored Victorian-era building, this is the
oldest hotel in La Jolla. In keeping with the period, rooms are formal
(some could use new carpets and furniture coverings). Ocean views cost
more than village views. The inn is on one of La Jolla's main thor-
oughfares, near boutiques, restaurants, and La Jolla Cove. Minire-
frigerators are provided in some rooms. ⊠ 910 Prospect St., 92037,
☎ 619/454–2181; 800/832–5525; 800/826–1278 in CA, FAX 619/454–
5679. 75 rooms. Restaurant, bar, pool, business services, meeting
rooms, parking (fee). AE, DC, MC, V.

$$$–$$$$ 🏨 **Hyatt Regency La Jolla.** The Hyatt is in the Golden Triangle area,
★ about 10 minutes from the beach and the village of La Jolla. The post-
modern design elements of architect Michael Graves' striking lobby
continue in the spacious rooms, where warm cherry-wood furnishings
contrast with austere gray closets. Fluffy down comforters and cushy
chairs and couches make you feel right at home. Business travelers will
appreciate the endless array of office and in-room services. The hotel's
four trendy restaurants include Cafe Japengo. Rates are lower here on
weekends. ⊠ Aventine Center, 3777 La Jolla Village Dr., 92122, ☎
619/552–1234; 800/233–1234 for central reservations; FAX 619/552–
6066. 400 rooms, 25 suites. 4 restaurants, bar, pool, outdoor hot tub,
beauty salon, massage, 2 tennis courts, aerobics, basketball, health club,
jogging, business services, meeting rooms, parking (fee). AE, D, DC,
MC, V.

$$–$$$$ 🏨 **Bed & Breakfast Inn at La Jolla.** Noted architect Irving Gill designed
this B&B in a quiet section of La Jolla across the street from the Mu-
seum of Contemporary Art and one block from the beach. Rooms are
of various sizes and styles but all are pretty. Nice touches include complimentary full breakfast, fresh fruit, sherry, and terry robes. ⊠ 7753

Draper Ave., 92037, ☎ *619/456–2066 or 800/582–2466,* FAX *619/456–1510. 16 rooms, 15 with bath. MC, V.*

$$-$$$$ 🏨 **Holiday Inn Express–La Jolla.** Many rooms at this modest property in the southern section of La Jolla are remarkably large, with huge closets; some have kitchenettes, and three suites have separate eat-in kitchens. The decor is nothing to write home about, but this is a good value for families who want to stay in La Jolla and still have a few dollars left over for shopping and dining. Continental breakfast is included. ✉ *6705 La Jolla Blvd., 92037,* ☎ *619/454–7101 or 800/451–0358,* FAX *619/454–6957. 51 rooms, 10 suites. Pool, outdoor hot tub, billiards, coin laundry, meeting rooms, free parking. AE, D, DC, MC, V.*

$$-$$$$ 🏨 **La Jolla Cove Suites.** It may lack the charm of some of the older properties of this exclusive area, but this motel with studios and suites (some with spacious oceanfront balconies) gives its guests the same first-class views of La Jolla Cove at much lower rates. Snorkelers and divers can take advantage of lockers and outdoor showers. Continental breakfast is served in the sunroom. The free underground lot is also a bonus in a section of town where a parking spot is a prime commodity. ✉ *1155 S. Coast Blvd., 92037,* ☎ *619/459–2621 or 800/248–2683,* FAX *619/454–3522. 96 rooms. Kitchenettes, pool, hot tub, putting green, coin laundry, business services, meeting rooms, free parking. AE, D, DC, MC, V.*

$$-$$$$ 🏨 **Prospect Park Inn.** One block from the beach and near some of the
★ best shops and restaurants, this European-style inn with a delightful staff sits in a prime spot in La Jolla Village. Many rooms (some with kitchenettes) have sweeping ocean views from their balconies. An upstairs sundeck with fantastic views is a great spot to enjoy the delicious complimentary Continental breakfast. There is no smoking on the premises. ✉ *1110 Prospect St., 92037,* ☎ *619/454–0133 or 800/433–1609,* FAX *619/454–2056. 20 rooms, 2 suites. In-room data ports, business services, free parking. AE, D, DC, MC, V.*

$$-$$$$ 🏨 **Scripps Inn.** You'd be wise to make reservations well in advance for this small, quiet inn tucked away on Coast Boulevard. Its popularity with repeat visitors ensures that it is booked year-round. Lower weekly and monthly rates (not available in summer) make it attractive to long-term guests. All accommodations have ocean views and in-room safes, and some have fireplaces, coffeemakers, microwaves, and refrigerators. Continental breakfast is served in the lobby. ✉ *555 S. Coast Blvd., 92037,* ☎ *619/454–3391,* FAX *619/456–0389. 13 rooms. AE, D, MC, V.*

Mission Bay and the Beaches

$$$$ 🏨 **Pacific Terrace Inn.** This terrific hotel, overlooking the beach, offers great ocean views from most rooms. It's a perfect place for those who love to watch sunsets over the Pacific. Private balconies (or patios), minirefrigerators, coffeemakers, and safes come with every room. Some rooms have spas, kitchenettes, and video players. Continental breakfast is complimentary. ✉ *610 Diamond St., 92109,* ☎ *619/581–3500 or 800/344–3370. 73 rooms, 8 suites. Pool, outdoor hot tub, coin laundry, meeting rooms, free parking. AE, D, DC, MC, V.*

$$$-$$$$ 🏨 **Catamaran Resort Hotel.** Resident birds are often poised on a perch
★ in the lush lobby of this appealing hotel, set on Mission Bay in Pacific Beach. The grounds are similarly tropical, and tiki torches light the way for guests staying at one of the six two-story buildings or the 14-story high-rise. The room decor echoes the Polynesian theme. ✉ *3999 Mission Blvd., 92109,* ☎ *619/488–1081 or 800/288–0770; 800/233–8172 in Canada;* FAX *619/488–1387 for reservations; 619/488–1619 for front desk. 313 rooms. Restaurant, 2 bars, in-room data ports, pool,*

outdoor hot tub, exercise room, boating, bicycles, nightclub, meeting rooms, parking (fee). AE, D, DC, MC, V.

$$$–$$$$ 🖭 **Hyatt Islandia.** Its location in appealing Mission Bay Park is one of the many pluses of this property, which has rooms in several low-level, lanai-style units, as well as marina suites and rooms in a high-rise building. Many of the modern accommodations overlook the hotel's gardens and koi fish pond; others have dramatic views of the bay area. This hotel is famous for its lavish Sunday champagne brunch. ✉ *1441 Quivira Rd., 92109,* ☎ *619/224–1234; 800/233–1234 for central reservations;* 𝔽𝔸𝕏 *619/224–0348. 346 rooms, 76 suites. 2 restaurants, bar, in-room data ports, pool, outdoor hot tub, exercise room, boating, fishing, laundry service, meeting rooms, free parking. AE, D, DC, MC, V.*

$$$–$$$$ 🖭 **San Diego Hilton Beach & Tennis Resort.** Trees, Japanese bridges, and ponds surround the bungalow accommodations at this deluxe resort. Rooms and suites in the high-rise building have views of Mission Bay Park. Most of the well-appointed rooms have wet bars, minirefrigerators, coffeemakers, spacious bathrooms, and patios or terraces. ✉ *1775 E. Mission Bay Dr., 92109,* ☎ *619/276–4010; 800/445–8667 for central reservations;* 𝔽𝔸𝕏 *619/275–7991. 337 rooms, 20 suites. 3 restaurants, bar, in-room data ports, pool, wading pool, 2 hot tubs, spa, 4 putting greens, 5 tennis courts, exercise room, boating, bicycles, playground, meeting rooms, car rental, free parking. AE, D, DC, MC, V.*

$$$–$$$$ 🖭 **San Diego Paradise Point Resort.** The landscape at this 44-acre resort is so beautiful that it's been the setting for a number of movies, and it provides a wide range of recreational activities as well as access to a marina. Bright fabrics and plush carpets make for a cheery ambience. Unfortunately, the walls here are motel-thin. All rooms have minirefrigerators, private patios, and coffeemakers, and a number have kitchens. ✉ *1404 W. Vacation Rd., 92109,* ☎ *619/274–4630 or 800/344–2626,* 𝔽𝔸𝕏 *619/581–5929. 462 cottages. 3 restaurants, 2 bars, room service, 5 pools, outdoor hot tub, sauna, 18-hole putting golf course, 6 tennis courts, croquet, exercise room, jogging, volleyball, boating, bicycles, free parking. AE, D, DC, MC, V.*

$$–$$$$ 🖭 **Crystal Pier Motel.** A landmark since the 1930s, this place is no longer the bargain it once was, nor does it have the amenities of the other properties in its price category. Call four to six weeks in advance for reservations. The minimum stay permitted is three nights from mid-June through mid-September, two nights the rest of the year. ✉ *4500 Ocean Blvd., 92109,* ☎ *619/483–6983 or 800/748–5894,* 𝔽𝔸𝕏 *619/483–6811. 29 cottages. Kitchenettes, free parking. D, MC, V.*

$$$ 🖭 **Bahia Resort Hotel.** This huge complex on a 14-acre peninsula in Mission Bay Park has furnished studios and suites with kitchens; many have wood-beam ceilings and tropical decor. The hotel's *Bahia Belle* cruises Mission Bay at sunset and also has a Blues Cruise on Saturday night and live entertainment on Friday night. Rates are reasonable for a place so well located—within walking distance of the ocean—and with so many amenities, including use of the facilities at its sister hotel, the nearby Catamaran. ✉ *998 W. Mission Bay Dr., 92109,* ☎ *619/ 488–0551 or 800/288–0770; 800/233–8172 in Canada;* 𝔽𝔸𝕏 *619/488– 7055; 619/488–1387 for reservations. 321 rooms. Restaurant, 2 bars, pool, outdoor hot tub, 2 tennis courts, bicycles, rollerblading, meeting rooms, free parking. AE, D, DC, MC, V.*

$$–$$$ 🖭 **Best Western Blue Sea Lodge.** Many of the rooms at this Pacific Beach low rise have balconies and ocean views; some have kitchenettes. A shopping center with restaurants and boutiques is nearby. ✉ *707 Pacific Beach Dr., 92109,* ☎ *619/488–4700 or 800/258–3732,* 𝔽𝔸𝕏 *619/*

488–7276. *100 rooms. In-room safes, pool, outdoor hot tub. AE, D, DC, MC, V.*

$$–$$$ ⊞ **Pacific Shores Inn.** One of the better motels in the Mission Bay area, this property is less than a half-block from the beach. Rooms, some of them spacious, are decorated in a simple contemporary style. Kitchen units with multiple beds are available at reasonable rates. Continental breakfast is included, and all rooms have minirefrigerators. ⊠ *4802 Mission Blvd., 92109,* ☎ *619/483–6300 or 800/826–0715,* FAX *619/483–9276. 55 rooms. Refrigerators, pool, coin laundry, free parking. AE, D, DC, MC, V.*

$–$$$ ⊞ **Dana Inn & Marina.** This hotel with an adjoining marina is a bargain. Rooms are in bright pastels, and the lobby includes a fun aquarium. High ceilings in the second-floor rooms give a welcome sense of space, and some even have a view of the inn's marina. ⊠ *1710 W. Mission Bay Dr., 92109,* ☎ *619/222–6440 or 800/445–3339,* FAX *619/222–5916. 196 rooms. Restaurant, bar, room service, pool, outdoor hot tub, 2 tennis courts, Ping-Pong, shuffleboard, boating, bicycles, coin laundry, business services, airport and Amtrak shuttle, free parking. AE, D, DC, MC, V.*

$–$$ ⊞ **Surfer Motor Lodge.** This four-story building is right on the beach and directly behind a shopping center with restaurants and boutiques. Rooms are plain, but those on the upper floors have good views. ⊠ *711 Pacific Beach Dr., 92109,* ☎ *619/483–7070 or 800/787–3373,* FAX *619/274–1670. 52 rooms. Restaurant, pool, bicycles, free parking. AE, DC, MC, V.*

$ ⊞ **Mission Bay Motel.** A half-block from the beach and right on the local main street, this motel has modest units, some with kitchenettes. Great restaurants and nightlife are within walking distance, but you may find the area a bit noisy. ⊠ *4221 Mission Blvd., 92109,* ☎ *619/483–6440. 50 rooms. Pool, free parking. D, MC, V.*

$ ⊞ **Ocean Manor Apartment Hotel.** This Sunset Cliffs hotel rents units by the day (three-day minimum for ones with kitchens), week, or month in winter. Reserve well in advance. The comfortable studios and one- and two-bedroom suites are furnished plainly in the style of the 1950s. ⊠ *1370 Sunset Cliffs Blvd., 92107,* ☎ *619/222–7901; 619/224–1379 for guest calls. 25 units. Pool, Ping-Pong, shuffleboard, free parking. MC, V.*

Hostels

$ ⊞ **Banana Bungalow San Diego.** Literally a few feet from the beach, this hostel's location is its greatest asset. Continental breakfast is complimentary and served on the sundeck. ⊠ *707 Reed Ave., 92109,* ☎ *619/273–3060 or 800/546–7835.*

$ ⊞ **Grand Pacific International Hostel.** Ideally located near restaurants,
★ shopping, and nightspots, the Grand Pacific is bright and clean. There are 60 beds, and five private rooms. Group and weekly rates are available. Continental breakfast is complimentary. ⊠ *726 Fifth Ave., 92101,* ☎ *619/232–3100 or 800/438–8622.*

$ ⊞ **HI–Elliott International Hostel–Point Loma.** This hostel is in a large converted house, in a much quieter area. It isn't very close to any of San Diego's attractions or nightlife, but there's a bus stop nearby. Special events are scheduled weekly. The hostel has a large kitchen, a large patio, a coin laundry, and a TV room. ⊠ *3790 Udall St., 92107,* ☎ *619/223–4778. MC, V.*

$ ⊞ **HI–The Metropolitan Hostel–Downtown San Diego.** This hostel in the
★ Gaslamp Quarter has new and modern furnishings and facilities. There are 150 beds, and most rooms are dorm-style with four bunks each.

⊠ *521 Market St., 92101,* ☎ *619/525–1531; 800/909–4776 code #43,* 𝔽𝔸𝕏 *619/338–0129. MC, V.*

$ 🖵 **Ocean Beach International Backpackers Hostel.** This converted 1920s hotel is two blocks from the beach and offers free use of used surfboards and boogie boards. There are 100 beds. Private rooms with private baths are available. Continental breakfast is complimentary, and dinner is free on Tuesday and Friday. Weekly rates are available. ⊠ *4961 Newport Ave., 92107,* ☎ *619/223–7873 or 800/339–7263,* 𝔽𝔸𝕏 *619/223–7881. MC, V.*

NIGHTLIFE AND THE ARTS

By Dan Janeck

Updated by
Kate Deely

Check the *Reader,* a free weekly, for band information or *San Diego* magazine's "Restaurant & Nightlife Guide" for the full slate of after-dark possibilities.

Nightlife

California law prohibits the sale of alcoholic beverages after 2 AM. Last call is usually at about 1:40. You must be 21 to purchase and consume alcohol, and most places will insist on identification. Bars, nightclubs, and restaurants are smoke-free by law.

Bars and Nightclubs

Bitter End (⊠ 770 5th Ave., Gaslamp Quarter, ☎ 619/338–9300) is a sophisticated martini bar, a hip dance club, and a private lounge where you can kick up your feet. **Blue Tattoo** (⊠ 835 5th Ave., Gaslamp Quarter, ☎ 619/238–7191) is a popular destination for young professionals, who often wait in long lines to get in. A strict dress code is enforced (no jeans, T-shirts, hats, sweatshirts, or tennis shoes) on Friday and Saturday nights. **Cannibal Bar** (⊠ 3999 Mission Blvd., Pacific Beach, ☎ 619/488–1081) customers devour the oldies, contemporary jazz, blues, and swing music performed by local bands. Because of its beach location, this tropical-theme nightclub in the Catamaran Resort Hotel attracts locals and visitors of all ages. **Club 66** (⊠ 901 5th Ave., downtown, ☎ 619/234–4166), under the restaurant Dakota's, takes the old Route 66 as its inspiration, with stainless-steel decor and gas-station memorabilia. The DJ plays disco, high energy, and Top 40.

E Street Alley (⊠ 919 4th Ave., downtown, ☎ 619/231–9200) is a treat for the senses. The Blue Room, with its scattered plush couches and pool tables, serves up live jazz on Thursday and blues the rest of the week. Club E is a smartly designed, spacious dance club with a DJ spinning Top 40 tunes. Chino's is an exquisite restaurant featuring American cuisine with a Southeast Asian flair. Noise from the waterfront **Hurricane's Bar and Grill** (⊠ 3105 Ocean Front Walk, Mission Beach, ☎ 619/488–1780) carries all the way to the breaking waves as talented rock bands perform nightly for a lively crowd. **Jimmy Love's** (⊠ 672 5th Ave., Gaslamp Quarter, ☎ 619/595–0123) combines a dance club, a sports bar, and a restaurant all into one venue. Expect lines.

Moose McGillycuddy's (⊠ 1165 Garnet Ave., Pacific Beach, ☎ 619/274–2323; ⊠ 535 5th Ave., Gaslamp Quarter, ☎ 619/702–5595), a major pick-up palace, is also a great place to go with friends or hang out with the locals. **O'Hungrys** (⊠ 2547 San Diego Ave., Old Town, ☎ 619/298–0133) is famous for its yard-long beers and sing-alongs. **Pacific Beach Bar & Grill** (⊠ 860 Garnet Ave., Pacific Beach, ☎ 619/272–4745), a block away from the beach, is a popular nightspot with a huge outdoor patio. There is plenty to see and do, from billiards and satellite TV sports to an interactive trivia game.

Coffeehouses

Brockton Villa Restaurant (✉ 1235 Coast Blvd., La Jolla, ☎ 619/454–7393), a palatial café overlooking La Jolla Cove, has indoor and outdoor seating, as well as scrumptious desserts and coffee drinks. It closes at 10. **Café Crema** (✉ 1001 Garnet Ave., Pacific Beach, ☎ 619/273–3558) is a meeting spot for the pre- and post-bar crowd. **Euphoria** (✉ 1045 University Ave., Hillcrest, ☎ 619/295–1769) has a Gen-X feel and is a great place to meet friends before dinner or barhopping. For many people it's an alternative to the bars.

Pannikin (✉ 7468 Girard Ave., La Jolla, ☎ 619/454–5453) is a bright coffeehouse, with indoor and outdoor seating, that draws a regular crowd but also tends to draw folks who've been shopping and sightseeing in La Jolla's village. **The Study** (✉ 401-A University Ave., Hillcrest, ☎ 619/296–4847) attracts those who value seclusion—private conversation or study is made easier with the cubicle-like seating areas. **The Living Room** (✉ 1050 Rosecrans St., Point Loma, ☎ 619/296–0616), is near the end of the charming neighborhood community of Point Loma. It's a great place to catch a caffeine buzz before walking along Shelter Island.

Comedy and Cabaret

Comedy Store South (✉ 916 Pearl St., La Jolla, ☎ 619/454–9176), like its sister establishment in Hollywood, hosts some of the best national touring and local talent. **Tidbits** (✉ 3838 5th Ave., Hillcrest, ☎ 619/543–0300) showcases the best of southern California's female impersonators in hilarious nightly cabaret and comedy "tidbits," with charity benefit shows on Sunday.

Country-Western

In Cahoots (✉ 5373 Mission Center Rd., Mission Valley, ☎ 619/291–8635), with its great sound system, large dance floor, and occasional big-name performers, is the destination of choice for cowgirls, cowboys, and city slickers alike. Free dance lessons are given every day except Wednesday, when seasoned two-steppers strut their stuff. Happy hour seven days a week is one of this bar's many lures. **Zoo Country** (✉ 1340 Broadway, El Cajon, ☎ 619/442–9900) attracts herds of line-dancin', two-steppin' cowpersons. There is live music Friday through Sunday and a DJ nightly. Free dance lessons are given Friday, Saturday, and Sunday.

Dance Clubs

Buffalo Joe's (✉ 600 5th Ave., downtown, ☎ 619/236–1616) may sound like a cowboy stop, but it's probably one of the best locales in the Gaslamp Quarter for a rocking dance floor. It's a common stop for bachelorette parties. **Johnny M's 801 Crabhouse Courtyard Club** (✉ 801 4th St., Gaslamp Quarter, ☎ 619/233–1131) patrons get down and boogie to '70s and '80s dance music at this huge disco. A blues room is open Wednesday, Friday, and Saturday from 10 PM to 1:30 AM. **Live Wire** (✉ 2103 El Cajon Blvd., North Park, ☎ 619/291–7450), an underground twentysomething hole-in-the-wall, has plenty of character. There are usually more tattoos and pierced body parts than people.

Olé Madrid (✉ 751 5th Ave., Gaslamp Quarter, ☎ 619/557–0146) is not for the meek or mild. Celebrated DJs spin deep house grooves and tribal rhythms in the basement. Between songs, sip a tangy sangria. **Pourhouse** (✉ 528 F St., downtown, ☎ 619/232–7687) is a beer and boogie bar with lots of microbrews on tap and various bands on stage. **Sevilla** (✉ 555 4th Ave., Gaslamp Quarter, ☎ 619/233–5979) provides a little bit of Brazil with a tapas bar and salsa dancing. **Supper Club A-Go-Go** (✉ 322 5th Ave., Gaslamp Quarter, ☎ 619/235–4646) offers a swinging good time in a 1940s motif. There is a special smoking section on an outside patio.

Gay and Lesbian

Bourbon Street (✉ 4612 Park Blvd., University Heights, ☎ 619/291–0173), resembling its New Orleans namesake with relaxing surroundings and courtyard, is a piano bar with live entertainment nightly. **Brass Rail** (✉ 3796 5th Ave., Hillcrest, ☎ 619/298–2233), a fixture since the early '60s, is the oldest gay bar in San Diego. The club hosts dancing nightly and go-go boys on weekends. **The Flame** (✉ 3780 Park Blvd., Hillcrest, ☎ 619/295–4163), a San Diego institution, is a friendly dance club that caters to lesbians most of the week. On Tuesday the DJ spins for the popular Boys' Night. **Flicks** (✉ 1017 University Ave., Hillcrest, ☎ 619/297–2056), one of few local video bars, plays music and comedy videos on four big screens. Drink specials and video formats vary each night. **Numbers** (✉ 3811 Park Blvd., North Park, ☎ 619/294–9005) has a giant-screen TV, six pool tables, darts, and daily drink specials. **Rich's** (✉ 1051 University Ave., Hillcrest, ☎ 619/295–2195), a popular dance club, has nightly male revues.

Jazz

Croce's (✉ 802 5th Ave., Gaslamp Quarter, ☎ 619/233–4355), the intimate jazz cave of restaurateur Ingrid Croce (singer-songwriter Jim Croce's widow), books superb acoustic-jazz musicians. Next door, Croce's Top Hat puts on live R&B nightly from 9 to 2. A. J. Croce, son of Jim and Ingrid, often headlines at both clubs. **Elario's** (✉ 7955 La Jolla Shores Dr., La Jolla, ☎ 619/459–0541), perched on the top floor of the Summer House Inn, delivers an ocean view and a lineup of internationally acclaimed jazz musicians. **Humphrey's by the Bay** (✉ 2241 Shelter Island Dr., Shelter Island, ☎ 619/523–1010 for concert information), surrounded by water, is the summer stomping grounds for musical legends such as Harry Belafonte and Three Dog Night.

Piano Bars/Mellow

Hotel Del Coronado (✉ 1500 Orange Ave., Coronado, ☎ 619/435–6611) has piano music in its Crown Room and Palm Court. The Ocean Terrace Lounge has live bands nightly from 9 to 1. **Inn at the Park** (✉ 3167 5th Ave., Hillcrest, ☎ 619/296–0057) is tucked away in a hotel of the same name. It makes for a nice stop after a day in Balboa Park. **Top O' the Cove** (✉ 1216 Prospect St., La Jolla, ☎ 619/454–7779) pianists play show tunes and standards from the '40s to the '80s at this magnificent Continental restaurant. **Westgate Hotel** (✉ 1055 2nd Ave., downtown, ☎ 619/238–1818), one of the most elegant settings in San Diego, has piano music in the Plaza Bar.

Rock, Pop, Folk, Reggae, and Blues

Belly Up Tavern (✉ 143 S. Cedros Ave., Solana Beach, ☎ 619/481–9022), an eclectic live-concert venue in converted Quonset huts, hosts critically acclaimed artists who play everything from reggae and folk to—well, you name it. The Belly Up attracts people of all ages. Sunday nights are usually cover-free and spotlight local R&B artists. **Bodie's** (✉ 528 F St., Gaslamp Quarter, ☎ 619/236–8988) presents the best rock and blues bands in San Diego, as well as up-and-coming bands from out of town. **Brick by Brick** (✉ 1130 Buenos Ave., Bay Park, near Mission Bay, ☎ 619/275–5483) is always abuzz with the music of San Diego's top alternative and experimental rock groups. **Winston's Beach Club** (✉ 1921 Bacon St., Ocean Beach, ☎ 619/222–6822), a bowling alley turned rock club, hosts local bands, reggae groups, and occasionally '60s rockers bands. The crowd, mostly locals, can get rowdy. There is also a location in east San Diego.

Singles Bars

Barefoot Bar and Grill (✉ San Diego Princess Resort, 1404 W. Vacation Rd., ☎ 619/274–4630), a beachfront bar, attracts flocks of singles, especially on spring and summer Sunday nights. Live music and happy-hour specials fill the joint up early, making for long latecomer lines. **Dick's Last Resort** (✉ 345 4th Ave., downtown, ☎ 619/231–9100) is not for Emily Post adherents. The surly wait staff and abrasive service are part of the gimmick. The rudeness notwithstanding, fun-loving party people pile into this barnlike restaurant and bar. Dick's has live music and one of the most extensive beer lists in San Diego. **Jose's** (✉ 1037 Prospect St., La Jolla, ☎ 619/454–7655) is a hit with yuppies from La Jolla and other neighboring beach communities. This small but clean hole-in-the-wall's lack of space gives suave singles an excuse to get up close and personal. **U. S. Grant Hotel** (✉ 326 Broadway, downtown, ☎ 619/232–3121) is the classiest spot in town for meeting fellow travelers while relaxing with a Scotch or a martini at the mahogany bar. The best local Latin, jazz, and blues bands alternate appearances. It's definitely for the over-30 business set.

The Arts

Half-price tickets to most theater, music, and dance events can be bought on the day of performance at **Times Arts Tix** (✉ Horton Plaza, ☎ 619/497–5000). Only cash is accepted. Advance full-price tickets may also be purchased. Visa and MasterCard holders may buy tickets for many scheduled performances through **Ticketmaster** (☎ 619/220–8497).

Dance

California Ballet Company (☎ 619/560–5676 or 619/560–6741) performs high-quality contemporary and traditional works, from story ballets to Balanchine, September–May. The *Nutcracker* is staged annually at the **Civic Theatre** (✉ 202 C St., downtown).

Music

La Jolla Chamber Music Society (☎ 619/459–3724) presents internationally acclaimed chamber ensembles, orchestras, and soloists at Sherwood Auditorium and the Civic Theatre. **San Diego Chamber Orchestra** (☎ 760/753–6402), a 35-member ensemble, performs once a month, October–April. **San Diego Opera** (✉ Civic Theatre, 202 C St., downtown, ☎ 619/236–6510 then 00 for operator) draws international artists. Its season of five operas runs January–April. **Spreckels Organ Pavilion** (✉ Balboa Park, ☎ 619/702–8138) holds a giant outdoor pipe organ dedicated in 1915 by sugar magnate Adolph Spreckels. Robert Plimpton performs on most Sunday afternoons and on most Monday evenings in summer. Local military bands, gospel groups, and barbershop quartets also perform here on summer evenings. **Spreckels Theatre** (✉ 121 Broadway, ☎ 619/235–0494), a designated-landmark theater erected more than 80 years ago, hosts musical events—everything from mostly Mozart to small rock concerts. Ballets and theatrical productions are also held here.

Theater

California Center for the Arts (✉ 340 N. Escondido, ☎ 760/738–4100) presents mainstream theatrical productions such as *Grease* and *The Odd Couple*. **Coronado Playhouse** (✉ 1775 Strand Way, Coronado, ☎ 619/435–4856), a cabaret-type theater near the Hotel Del Coronado, stages regular dramatic and musical performances. Friday and Saturday dinner packages are available. **Diversionary Theatre** (✉ 4545 Park Blvd., University Heights, ☎ 619/220–0097) is San Diego's premier gay and lesbian company. **Gaslamp Quarter Theatre Com-**

pany (⊠ Hahn Cosmopolitan Theatre, 444 4th Ave., downtown, ☎ 619/234–9583) stages comedies, dramas, mysteries, and musicals at a 250-seat venue.

La Jolla Playhouse (⊠ Mandell Weiss Center for the Performing Arts, University of California at San Diego, 2910 La Jolla Village Dr., ☎ 619/550–1010) crafts exciting and innovative productions, from May through November. **La Jolla Stage Company** (⊠ Parker Auditorium, 750 Nautilus St., La Jolla, ☎ 619/459–7773) presents lavish productions of Broadway favorites and popular comedies year-round on the La Jolla High School campus. **Old Globe Theatre** (⊠ Simon Edison Centre for the Performing Arts, Balboa Park, 1363 Old Globe Way, ☎ 619/239–2255) is the oldest professional theater in California, performing classics, contemporary dramas, and experimental works. It produces the famous summer Shakespeare Festival at the Old Globe and its sister theaters, the Cassius Carter Centre Stage and the Lowell Davies Festival Theatre.

San Diego Comic Opera Company (⊠ Casa del Prado Theatre, Balboa Park, ☎ 619/231–5714) presents four different productions of Gilbert and Sullivan and similar works from October through July. **Starlight Musical Theatre** (⊠ Starlight Bowl, Balboa Park, ☎ 619/544–7827 during season), a local summertime favorite, is a series of musicals performed in an outdoor amphitheater from mid-June through early September. Because of the theater's proximity to the airport, actors are often forced to freeze mid-scene while a plane flies over. **The Theatre in Old Town** (⊠ 4040 Twiggs St., Old Town, ☎ 619/688–2494) presents punchy revues and occasional classics. Shows like *Forbidden Broadway, Ruthless, Gilligan's Island,* and *Forbidden Hollywood* have made this a popular place. **Welk Resort Theatre** (⊠ 8860 Lawrence Welk Dr., Escondido, ☎ 760/749–3448 or 800/932–9355), a famed dinner theater about a 45-minute drive northeast of downtown, puts on polished Broadway-style productions.

OUTDOOR ACTIVITIES AND SPORTS

Updated by
Kate Deely

People in this outdoors-oriented community recreate more than spectate. It's hard not to, with the variety of choices available, from boccie and ballooning to golf, surfing, sailing, and volleyball, plus the constant sunshine.

Beaches

San Diego's beaches are among its greatest natural attractions. In some places the shorefront is wide and sandy; in others it's narrow and rocky or backed by impressive sandstone cliffs. The beaches below are listed from south to north.

Coronado

Silver Strand State Beach. This quiet Coronado beach is ideal for families. The water is relatively calm, lifeguards and rangers are on duty year-round, and there are places to rollerblade or ride bikes. Four parking lots provide room for more than 1,500 cars. Sites at a campground ($12–$16 per night) for self-contained RVs are available on a first-come, first-served basis. Stays are limited to seven nights. *From San Diego–Coronado Bay Bridge, turn left onto Orange Ave., which becomes Hwy. 75, and follow signs,* ☎ *619/435–5184.* 🅿 *Parking $4, but not always collected Labor Day–Feb.*

Coronado Beach. With the famous Hotel Del Coronado as a backdrop, this stretch of sandy beach is one of San Diego County's largest and most picturesque. It's perfect for sunbathing or games of Frisbee. Parking can be difficult on the busiest days. There are plenty of rest rooms and service facilities, as well as fire rings. *From the bridge, turn left on Orange Ave. and follow signs.*

Point Loma

Sunset Cliffs. Beneath the jagged cliffs on the west side of the Point Loma peninsula is one of the more secluded beaches in the area. It's popular with surfers and locals. At the south end of the peninsula, near Cabrillo Point, tidal pools teeming with small sea creatures are revealed at low tide. There are no facilities. *Take I–8 west to Sunset Cliffs Blvd. and head west.*

San Diego

Ocean Beach. Much of this mile-long beach is a haven for volleyball players, sunbathers, and swimmers. The area around the municipal pier at the south end is a hangout for surfers and transients. The pier itself is open to the public for fishing and walking and has a restaurant at the middle. The beach is south of the channel entrance to Mission Bay. You'll find food vendors and fire rings. Limited parking is available. Swimmers should beware of unusually vicious rip currents here. *Take I–8 west to Sunset Cliffs Blvd. and head west. Turn right on Santa Monica Ave.*

Mission Beach. San Diego's most popular beach draws huge crowds on hot summer days. The 2-mi-long continuous stretch extends from the north entrance of Mission Bay to Pacific Beach. A narrow boardwalk paralleling the beach is popular with walkers, runners, roller skaters, bladers, and bicyclists. Surfers, swimmers, and volleyball players congregate at the south end. Parking can be a challenge, but there are plenty of rest rooms and restaurants in the area. *Exit I–5 at Garnet Ave. and head west to Mission Blvd. Turn south and look for parking.*

Pacific Beach/North Pacific Beach. The boardwalk turns into a sidewalk here, but there are still bike paths and picnic tables along the beachfront. Pacific Beach runs from the north end of Mission Beach to Crystal Pier. North Pacific Beach extends from the pier north. There are designated surfing areas, and fire rings are available. On-street parking is your best bet, or you can try the big lot at Belmont Park near the south end. *Exit I–5 at Garnet Ave. and head west to Mission Blvd. Turn north and look for parking.*

La Jolla

Tourmaline Surfing Park. This is one of the area's most popular beaches for surfing and sailboarding year-round. There is a 175-space parking lot at the foot of Tourmaline Street, but it's normally filled to capacity by midday. *Take Mission Blvd. north (it turns into La Jolla Blvd.) and turn west on Tourmaline St.*

Children's Pool. In addition to panoramic views of ocean and coastline, this shallow lagoon, protected by a seawall, has small waves and no riptide. The pool is popular with scuba divers who explore the offshore reef when the surf is low. It's also a good place to watch marine mammals—seals and sea lions frequent the cove. *Follow La Jolla Blvd. north. When it forks, take the left, then turn right onto Coast Blvd.*

Shell Beach. North of Children's Pool is a small cove, accessible by stairs, with a relatively secluded beach. The exposed rocks off the coast have been designated a protected habitat for sea lions. Watch them sun themselves and frolic in the water. *Continue along Coast Blvd. north from Children's Pool.*

La Jolla Cove. This is one of the prettiest spots in the world. A palm-lined park sits on top of cliffs formed by the incessant pounding of the waves. At low tide the tidal pools and cliff caves provide a destination for explorers. Divers and snorkelers can explore the underwater delights of the San Diego–La Jolla Underwater Ecological Reserve. The cove is also a favorite of rough-water swimmers for whom buoys mark distances. *Follow Coast Blvd. north to signs, or take the La Jolla Village Dr. exit from I–5, head west to Torrey Pines Rd., turn left, and drive down hill to Girard Ave. Turn right and follow signs.*

La Jolla Shores. On summer holidays all access routes are usually closed to one of San Diego's most popular beaches. The lures here are a wide sandy beach and the most gentle wave action in San Diego. A concrete boardwalk parallels the beach. Arrive early to get a parking spot in the lot at the foot of Calle Frescota. *From I–5 take La Jolla Village Dr. west and turn left onto La Jolla Shores Dr. Head west to Camino del Oro or Vallecitos St. Turn right.*

Black's Beach. The powerful waves at this beach, officially known as Torrey Pines City Park Beach, attract surfers, and its relative isolation appeals to nudist nature lovers (though by law nudity is prohibited). There are no lifeguards on duty, and strong ebb tides are common. Only experienced swimmers should take the plunge. The cliffs are dangerous to climb and should be avoided. *Take Genesee Ave. west from I–5 and follow signs to Glider Port; easier access, via a paved path, available on La Jolla Farms Rd., but parking limited to 2 hrs.*

Del Mar
Del Mar Beach. Parking can be a problem on nice summer days, but access is relatively easy. The portions of Del Mar south of 15th Street are lined with cliffs and are rarely crowded. Leashed dogs are permitted on most sections of Del Mar Beach year-round. *Take the Via de la Valle exit from I–5 west to Old Hwy. 101 (also known as Camino del Mar in Del Mar) and turn left.*

Torrey Pines State Beach/Reserve. One of San Diego's best beaches contains 1,700 acres of bluffs, bird-filled marshes, and sandy shoreline. A network of trails leads through rare pine trees to the coast below. The large parking lot is rarely full. Lifeguards are on duty weekends (weather permitting) from Easter until Memorial Day, daily from then until Labor Day, and again on weekends through September. *Take the Carmel Valley Rd. exit west from I–5,* ☎ *619/755–2063.* 🅿 *Parking $4.*

Cardiff-by-the-Sea
Cardiff State Beach. This beach begins at the parking lot immediately north of the cliffs at Solana Beach. A reef break draws surfers, though this area otherwise is not particularly appealing. *From I–5 turn west on Lomas Santa Fe Dr. to S21 (Old Hwy. 101) and turn right.* ☎ *760/753–5091.* 🅿 *Parking $4.*

San Elijo State Beach. There are campsites (☎ 800/444–7275 for reservations) atop a scenic bluff at this park, which also has a store and shower facilities plus beach access for swimmers and surfers. Sites run $17–$23. *From I–5 turn west on Lomas Santa Fe Dr. to S21 (Old Hwy. 101) and turn right.* ☎ *760/753–5091.* 🅿 *Parking $4.*

Encinitas
Sea Cliff Roadside Park. Palms and the golden domes of the nearby Self Realization Fellowship earned this picturesque beach its local nickname, Swami's. The beach is also a top surfing spot. The only access is by a long stairway leading down from the cliff-top park. *Fol-*

low S21 (Old Hwy. 101) north from Cardiff, or exit I–5 at Encinitas Blvd., go west to S21, and turn left.

Moonlight Beach. Large parking areas and a wide range of facilities make this beach, tucked into a break in the cliffs, a pleasant stop. *Take the Encinitas Blvd. exit from I–5 and head west until you hit the Moonlight parking lot.*

Participant Sports

Ballooning

Enjoy the views of the Pacific Ocean, the mountains, and the coastline south to Mexico and north to San Clemente from a hot-air balloon at sunrise or sunset. The conditions are perfect: necessary winds and wide-open spaces. Ballooning companies operating in the San Diego area include **California Dreamin'** (⊠ 162 S. Rancho Santa Fe Rd., Suite F10, Encinitas, ☎ 760/438–3344 or 800/373–3359), and **Skysurfer Balloon Company** (⊠ 1221 Camino del Mar, Del Mar, ☎ 619/481–6800; 800/660–6809 in CA).

Bicycling

On any given summer day Highway S21 from La Jolla to Oceanside looks like a freeway for cyclists. Never straying more than a quarter-mile from the beach, it is easily the most popular and scenic bike route around. San Diego also has a **velodrome** (☎ 619/296–3345) in Balboa Park. **Bicycle Barn** in Pacific Beach (⊠ 746 Emerald St., ☎ 619/581–3665) and **Hamel's Action Sports Center** in Mission Beach (⊠ 704 Ventura Pl., ☎ 619/488–5050) are among the places that rent bikes.

Diving

Enthusiasts the world over flock to San Diego to skin dive and scuba dive off La Jolla and Point Loma. At La Jolla Cove you'll find the **San Diego–La Jolla Underwater Ecological Park.** Farther north, off the south end of Black's Beach, the rim of **Scripps Canyon** lies in about 60 ft of water. The canyon plummets to more than 900 ft in some sections. Another popular diving spot is **Sunset Cliffs** in Point Loma, where the sea life and flora are relatively close to shore. Strong rip currents make it an area best enjoyed by experienced divers. It is illegal to take any wildlife from the ecological preserves in La Jolla or near Cabrillo Point. Spearfishing requires a license (available at most dive stores), and it is illegal to take out-of-season lobster and game fish.

Diving equipment and boat trips can be arranged through **San Diego Divers Supply** (⊠ 4004 Sports Arena Blvd., ☎ 619/224–3439) and (⊠ 1084 Broadway, Chula Vista, ☎ 619/420–5441), and **Ocean Enterprises Scuba Diving** (⊠ 7710 Balboa Ave., ☎ 619/565–6054). For recorded diving information, contact the **San Diego City Lifeguards Office** (☎ 619/221–8884).

Fishing

The Pacific Ocean is full of corbina, croaker, and halibut. No license is required to fish from a public pier, such as the Ocean Beach pier. A fishing license from the state **Department of Fish and Game** (⊠ 4949 Viewridge Ave., San Diego 92123, ☎ 619/467–4201), available at most bait-and-tackle stores, is required for fishing from the shoreline. Children under 15 do not need a license.

Several companies conduct half-day, full-day, or multiday fishing expeditions in search of marlin, tuna, and other deep-water fish. **Fisherman's Landing** in Point Loma (⊠ 2838 Garrison St., ☎ 619/221–8500); **H & M Sportfishing Landings** in Point Loma (⊠ 2803 Emerson St., ☎ 619/222–1144); and **Seaforth Boat Rentals** in West Mission Bay (⊠

1641 Quivira Rd., ☎ 619/223–1681) are among the companies operating from San Diego.

Fitness

Most major hotels have full health clubs, with at least weight machines, stationary bicycles, and spas. Several hotels with elaborate spas offer one-day spa-and-fitness programs for nonguests.

The Spa at the Coronado Island Marriott Resort (⊠ 2000 2nd St., Coronado, ☎ 619/435–3000) has pampering packages that include the use of fitness facilities and admission to exercise classes. **Frog's Athletic & Racquet Club** (⊠ 901 Hotel Circle S, ☎ 619/291–3500) has a weight room, saunas, and tennis and racquetball courts. The **24 Hour Fitness Centers** in the area (⊠ 5885 Rancho Mission Rd., ☎ 619/281–5543; ⊠ 3675 Midway Dr., ☎ 619/224–2902; ⊠ 4405 La Jolla Village Dr., ☎ 619/457–3930) welcome nonmembers for a small fee.

Golf

Most public courses in the area provide a list of fees for all San Diego courses. The greens fee is included for each course. Carts (in some cases mandatory), instruction, and other costs are additional.

COURSES

Coronado Municipal Golf Course (⊠ 2000 Visalia Row, Coronado, ☎ 619/435–3121) has 18 holes, a driving range, equipment rentals, and a snack bar. Views of San Diego Bay and the Coronado Bridge from the back nine holes on this good walking course make it popular—but rather difficult to get on. Greens fee: $20–$30.

Mission Bay Golf Center (⊠ 2702 N. Mission Bay Dr., ☎ 619/490–3370) has 18 holes, a driving range, equipment rentals, and a restaurant. A not-very-challenging executive (par 3 and 4) course, Mission Bay is lit for night play. Greens fee: $14–$16.50.

Torrey Pines Municipal Golf Course in La Jolla (⊠ 11480 N. Torrey Pines Rd., ☎ 619/452–3226) has 36 holes, a driving range, and equipment rentals. One of the best public golf courses in the United States, Torrey Pines has views of the Pacific from every hole and is sufficiently challenging to host the Buick Invitational in February. Greens fee: $45–$50.

RESORTS

Aviara Golf Club (⊠ 7447 Batiquitos Dr., Carlsbad, ☎ 760/929–0077) has 18 holes (designed by Arnold Palmer), a driving range, equipment rentals, and views of the protected adjacent Batiquitos Lagoon and the Pacific Ocean. Greens fee: $105–$125.

La Costa Resort and Spa (⊠ Costa del Mar Rd., Carlsbad, ☎ 760/438–9111 or 800/854–5000) has two 18-hole PGA-rated courses, a driving range, a clubhouse, equipment rentals, a golf school, and a pro shop. One of the premier golf resorts in southern California, La Costa hosts the Mercedes Championships in January. Greens fee: $130–$170.

Rancho Bernardo Inn and Country Club (⊠ 17550 Bernardo Oaks Dr., Rancho Bernardo, ☎ 619/675–8470, ext. 1) has 45 holes on site, a driving range, equipment rentals, and a restaurant. Guests can play three other golf courses at company-operated resorts: Mount Woodson, Temecula Creek, and Twin Oaks. Ken Blanchard's Golf University of San Diego is based here. Rancho Bernardo Inn lays out one of the best Sunday brunches in the county. Greens fee: $65–$80.

Hiking and Nature Trails

Guided hikes are conducted regularly through Los Penasquitos Canyon Preserve and the Torrey Pines State Reserve (☞ La Jolla *above*), the

San Dieguito River Valley Regional Open Space (✉ 21 mi north of San Diego on I–5 to Lomas Santa Fe Dr., east 1 mi to Sun Valley Rd., north into park, ☎ 619/235–5440), and the **Tijuana Estuary** (☎ 619/575–3613). **Mission Trails Regional Parks** (✉ 1 Father Junípero Serra Tr., 92119, ☎ 619/668–3275), which encompasses nearly 6,000 acres of mountains, wooded hillsides, lakes, and riparian streams, is only 8 mi northeast of downtown.

Jet Skiing

Waveless Mission Bay and the small **Snug Harbor Marina** (☎ 760/434–3089), east of the intersection of Tamarack Avenue and Interstate 5 in Carlsbad, are favorite spots. Jet skis can be launched from most beaches, although they need to be ridden beyond surf lines, and some beaches have special regulations governing their use. **California Water Sports** (☎ 760/434–3089) has information about equipment rentals and purchases. **Seaforth Boat Rentals** (☎ 619/223–1681) rents jet skis for use in the South Bay Marina in Coronado, and they are also available at Snug Harbor in Carlsbad.

Jogging

From downtown, the most popular run is along the Embarcadero, which stretches around the bay. There are uncongested sidewalks all through the area. The alternative for downtown visitors is to head east to Balboa Park, where trails snake through the canyons. Mission Bay is renowned among joggers for its wide sidewalks and basically flat landscape. Trails head west around Fiesta Island from Mission Bay, providing distance as well as a scenic route. Del Mar has the finest running trails along the bluff. Park your car near 15th Street and run south along the cliffs for a gorgeous view of the ocean.

Surfing

If you're a beginner, consider paddling in the waves off Mission Beach, Pacific Beach, Tourmaline, La Jolla Shores, Del Mar, or Oceanside. More experienced surfers usually head for Sunset Cliffs, the La Jolla reef breaks, Black's Beach, or Sea Cliff Roadside Park in Encinitas. *See* Beaches, *above,* for descriptions. **Kahuna Bob's Surf School** (☎ 760/721–7700) conducts two-hour lessons seven days a week; all equipment is supplied. Many local surf shops rent boards, including **Star Surfing Company** (☎ 619/273–7827) in Pacific Beach.

Swimming

The most spectacular pool in town is Belmont Park's 58-yard-long **Plunge** (✉ 3115 Ocean Front Walk, ☎ 619/488–3110) in Mission Beach.

Tennis

Most of the more than 1,300 courts around the county are in private clubs, but a few are public. The **Balboa Tennis Club at Morley Field** (☎ 619/295–9278) in Balboa Park has 25 courts, 19 of which are lighted. Nonmembers can make reservations after paying a $4 fee. Heaviest usage is 9 AM–11 AM and after 5 PM; at other times you can usually arrive and begin playing. The **La Jolla Tennis Club** (✉ 7632 Draper Ave., ☎ 619/454–9950) has nine free public courts near downtown La Jolla; five are lighted. The 12 lighted courts at the privately owned **Peninsula Tennis Club** (✉ Robb Field, ☎ 619/226–3407) in Ocean Beach are available to the public for a $3 day-use fee.

Waterskiing

Mission Bay is one of the most popular waterskiing areas in southern California. It is best to get out early, when the water is smooth and the crowds are thin. Boats and equipment can be rented from **Seaforth Boat Rentals** (✉ 1641 Quivira Rd., near Mission Bay, ☎ 619/223–1681). The private **San Diego and Mission Bay Boat and Ski Club** (✉ 2606

N. Mission Bay Dr., ☎ 619/270–0840) operates a slalom course and
ski jump in Mission Bay's Hidden Anchorage. Permission from the club
or the Mission Bay Harbor Patrol (☎ 619/221–8985) is required.

Windsurfing

Also known as sailboarding, windsurfing is a sport best practiced on
smooth waters, such as Mission Bay or the Snug Harbor Marina at
the intersection of Interstate 5 and Tamarack Avenue in Carlsbad.
Rentals and instruction are available at the **Bahia Resort Hotel** (✉ 998
W. Mission Bay Dr., ☎ 619/488–0551), and at the **Catamaran Resort
Hotel** (✉ 3999 Mission Blvd., ☎ 619/488–1081).

Spectator Sports

Qualcomm Stadium (✉ 9449 Friars Rd., ☎ 619/525–8282) is at the
intersection of Interstates 15 and 8. To get to the **San Diego Sports Arena**
(✉ 3500 Sports Arena Blvd., ☎ 619/224–4171), take the Rosecrans
exit off Interstate 5 and turn right onto Sports Arena Boulevard.

Baseball

The **San Diego Padres** (☎ 619/280–4636) of the National League West
play at Qualcomm Stadium from April through October.

Football

The **San Diego Chargers** (☎ 619/280–2121) of the National Football
League fill Qualcomm Stadium from August through December. Games
with AFC West rivals the Oakland Raiders and Denver Broncos are
particularly intense. The **San Diego State University Aztecs** compete in
the Western Athletic Conference. The biggest game of the year is always a showdown with Brigham Young University.

Golf

The La Costa Resort and Spa (☎ 760/438–9111) hosts the prestigious
Mercedes Championships in January, featuring the winners of the pre-
vious year's tournaments. The **Buick Invitational** brings the pros to the
Torrey Pines Municipal Golf Course in February (☎ 619/452–3226).

Horse Racing

The annual summer meeting of the **Del Mar Thoroughbred Club** (☎ 619/
755–1141) on the Del Mar Fairgrounds attracts the best horses and
jockeys in the country. Racing begins in July and continues through
early September, every day except Tuesday. You can also bet on races
at tracks throughout California, shown on TV via satellite (☎ 619/
755–1167). Take Interstate 5 north to the Via de la Valle exit.

SHOPPING

By Bobbi Zane
Coronado

Orange Avenue, in the center of town, has six blocks of ritzy boutiques
and galleries. The elegant **Hotel Del Coronado** (✉ 1500 Orange Ave.)
houses 26 exclusive specialty shops on its Galleria level. **Ferry Landing Marketplace** (✉ 1201 1st St., at B Ave.), with a great view of the
San Diego skyline across the bay, is a delightful place to stroll and shop.
It has 26 boutiques and shops plus a Tuesday afternoon **Farmers Market** where you can pick up some of the wonderful fruits and vegetables grown in the area.

Downtown

Horton Plaza, bordered by Broadway, 1st Avenue, G Street, and 4th
Avenue, anchoring one side of the Gaslamp Quarter and within walking distance of most downtown hotels, is an open-air visual delight accented by pastel-painted walls, original neon signs, and flag-draped
facades. The multilevel shopping, dining, and entertainment complex

has department stores, including **Macy's** (☎ 619/231–4747) and **Nord-strom** (☎ 619/239–1700), fast-food counters, classy restaurants, the Lyceum Theater, and cinemas.

Victorian buildings and renovated warehouses in the historic **Gaslamp Quarter** along 4th and 5th avenues house art galleries, antiques, and specialty shops.

Golden Triangle

University Towne Centre (⊠ La Jolla Village Dr. between I–5 and I–805, ☎ 858/546–8858), a handy outdoor mall several miles east of La Jolla, has 160 specialty shops, department stores, cinemas, and restaurants, plus an **Ice Chalet** (☎ 858/452–9110) skating rink.

Kensington, Hillcrest, and North Park

Though their boundaries blur, each of these three established neighborhoods north and northeast of downtown contains a distinct urban village with shops, cafés, and entertainment venues.

More than 20 dealers in the **Adams Avenue** area of Kensington sell everything from postcards and kitchen utensils to cut glass and porcelain.

Gay and funky **Hillcrest,** north of Balboa Park, is home to many gift, book, and music stores. **International Male** (⊠ 3964 5th Ave., ☎ 619/294–8600) sells contemporary men's fashions at reasonable prices. **Obelisk** (⊠ 1029 University Ave., ☎ 619/297–4171), in a busy area between gay bars and a coffeehouse, stocks a bounty of gay and lesbian literature, cards, and gifts. Don't miss **Babette Schwartz** (⊠ 421 University Ave., ☎ 619/220–7048), a zany pop-culture store. The **Uptown District,** an open-air shopping center on University Avenue, includes several furniture, gift, and specialty shops.

Retro rules in North Park. Nostalgia shops along **Park Boulevard** and **University Avenue at 30th Street** carry clothing, accessories, furnishings, wigs, and bric-a-brac of the 1920s–'60s. **Auntie Helen's** (⊠ 4028 30th St., ☎ 619/584–8438), a nonprofit thrift emporium, sells heirlooms, collectibles, seasonal items, furniture, and brand-name clothing. Proceeds provide medical equipment, clothing, and laundry service to people with AIDS.

La Jolla

Familiar mall shops such as Victoria's Secret and Ann Taylor have found their way into spots along once-exclusive Prospect Street, but you'll find plenty of chic boutiques along side streets such as Girard and Drury. Shopping hours vary widely in La Jolla, so it's wise to call specific stores in advance. The **Green Dragon Colony** (⊠ Prospect St., near Ivanhoe St.), La Jolla's historic shopping area, dates back to 1895, when the first structure was built by Anna Held, who was governess for Ulysses S. Grant Jr. Perched on a bluff overlooking La Jolla Cove, the Green Dragon and adjacent **Coast Walk Plaza** contain 22 shops and three restaurants.

Mission Valley/Hotel Circle

The Mission Valley/Hotel Circle area, northeast of downtown near Interstate 8 and Highway 163, has four major shopping centers. **Fashion Valley Center** (⊠ 452 Fashion Valley), **Hazard Center** (⊠ 7676 Hazard Center Dr.), **Mission Valley Center** (⊠ 1640 Camino del Rio N), and **Rio Vista Shopping Center** (⊠ Rio San Diego Dr., Stadium Way exit off I–8) contain hundreds of shops, as well as restaurants, cinemas, and branches of almost every San Diego department store.

Old Town

North of downtown, off Interstate 5, the colorful Old Town historic district recalls a Mexican marketplace. Adobe architecture, flower-filled plazas, fountains, and courtyards decorate the shopping areas of **Bazaar del Mundo, La Esplanade,** and **Old Town Mercado,** where you'll find international goods, toys, souvenirs, and arts and crafts.

Seaport Village

Northwest of the convention center, **Seaport Village** (⊠ West Harbor Dr., at Kettner Blvd.) is a waterfront complex of shops and restaurants.

SIDE TRIP TO THE SAN DIEGO NORTH COAST

By Bobbi Zane   San Diego proper has more open space than most cities its size, but even its residents like to repair occasionally to the less-congested (though rapidly growing) North County and Anza-Borrego Desert. North County attractions continue to multiply following the 1999 opening of the Legoland California theme park.

Numbers in the margin correspond to points of interest on the San Diego North County map.

Del Mar

23 mi north of downtown San Diego on I–5, 9 mi north of La Jolla on S21.

Del Mar is best known for its racetrack, chic shopping strip, celebrity visitors, and wide beaches. Along with its collection of shops, **Del Mar Plaza** (⊠ 15th St., at S21—a.k.a. Camino del Mar) also contains outstanding restaurants and landscaped plazas and gardens with Pacific views. Del Mar has become headquarters for romantic hot-air-balloon excursions. The late afternoon is the best time to spot the colorful balloons as they float over the hills and coastline.

Access to Del Mar's beaches is from the streets that run east–west off Coast Boulevard. Summer evening concerts take place at **Seagrove Park** (⊠ 15th St., west end), a small stretch of grass overlooking the ocean.

❶ The **Del Mar Fairgrounds** is home to the **Del Mar Thoroughbred Club** (⊠ 2260 Jimmy Durante Blvd., ☎ 858/755–1141). The racing season here (usually July–September, Wednesday–Monday, post time 2 PM) is one of the most fashionable in California. Del Mar Fairgrounds hosts more than 100 different events each year, including the San Diego County Fair. *Head west at I–5's Via de la Valle Rd. exit,* ☎ 858/793–5555.

☺ **Freeflight,** a small exotic-bird training aviary adjacent to the Del Mar Fairgrounds, is open to the public. Visitors are allowed to handle the birds—a guaranteed child pleaser. ⊠ *2132 Jimmy Durante Blvd.,* ☎ *858/481–3148.* ☐ *$1.* ☉ *Daily 10–4.*

Dining and Lodging

$$–$$$ ✕ **Cilantros.** Seafood enchiladas, shark fajitas, and spit-roasted chicken with a mild chili sauce are among the subtly spiced Southwestern-style dishes served at this Del Mar favorite. ⊠ *3702 Via de la Valle,* ☎ *619/259–8777. AE, DC, MC, V.*

$$–$$$ ✕ **Epazote.** The menu changes seasonally at this offspring of Cilantros, serving good Southwestern-style cuisine. The happy-hour appetizers and drinks are a bargain. There's an ocean view from the patio. ⊠ *1555 Camino del Mar, Suite 322,* ☎ *619/259–9966.* ☎ *619/259–0611. AE, DC, MC, V.*

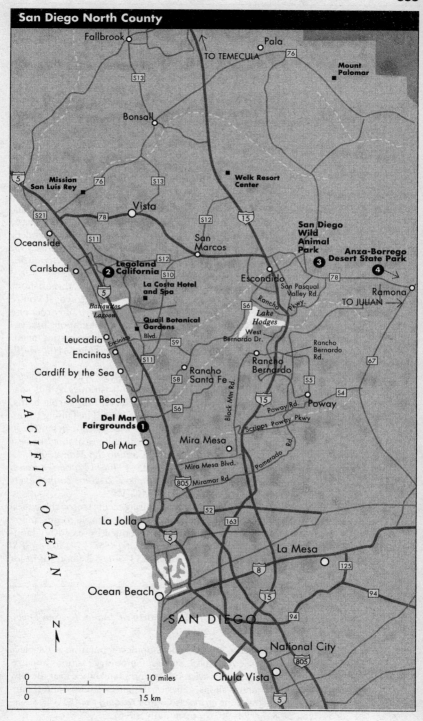

San Diego North County

Fallbrook

Pala

TO TEMECULA

76

Mount
Palomar

S13

Bonsall

5

Mission
San Luis Rey

76

S13

Welk Resort
Center

S21

Vista

78

S12

15

Oceanside

S11

San Diego
Wild
Animal
Park

San
Marcos

Carlsbad

Legoland
California

S12

2

S10

Anza-Borrego
Desert State Park

3

La Costa Hotel
and Spa

Escondido

5

78

4

Ramona

San Pasqual
Valley Rd.

TO JULIAN →

Batiquitos
Lagoon

S6

Rancho

Quail Botanical
Gardens

Blvd.

Lake
Hodges

Leucadia

S9

West
Bernardo Dr.

Rancho
Bernardo
Rd.

Encinitas

S11

67

Cardiff by the Sea

Rancho
Santa Fe

Rancho
Bernardo

S8

S5

Solana Beach

15

S4

S6

Poway Rd.

Poway

Del Mar
Fairgrounds

1

Black Mtn Rd.

Scripps Poway Pkwy

Del Mar

Mira Mesa

Pomerado Rd.

Mira Mesa Blvd.

805

Miramar Rd.

52

PACIFIC OCEAN

La Jolla

163

5

La Mesa

8

125

Ocean Beach

15

94

N

SAN DIEGO

94

National City

805

Chula Vista

5

0   10 miles

0   15 km

$$–$$$ ✕ **The Fish Market.** There's no ocean view at the North County branch of downtown's splashy restaurant, but this eatery remains popular with residents and tourists alike for its simple preparations of very fresh fish. The scene is lively, crowded, and noisy. ⊠ *640 Via De La Valle,* ☎ *619/755–2277.* FAX *619/755–3912. Reservations essential for 8 or more. AE, D, DC, MC, V.*

$–$$$ ✕ **Torrey Pines Cafe.** Locals flock to this reasonably priced sister of the Bird Rock Cafe in La Jolla to enjoy an eclectic menu of home-style cooking. Brunch is served on Sunday. ⊠ *2334 Carmel Valley Rd.,* ☎ *619/259–5878. AE, D, DC, MC, V. No lunch Sat. No dinner Mon.*

$–$$ ✕ **Kitima.** This contemporary restaurant serves an elegant interpretation of Thai cuisine. Sample the quick and cool spring rolls, the rock and roll shrimp salad, and especially the shrimp dish dubbed "the evil prince of a wild jungle." ⊠ *1555 Camino del Mar, Suite 201,* ☎ *619/ 792–7000. AE, D, DC, MC, V.*

$–$$ ✕ **Spices Thai Cafe.** One of the North County's most stylish ethnic restaurants serves beautiful dishes. The traditional pad Thai is a colorful feast, and the seafood selections and salads are also highly recommended. ⊠ *Piazza Carmel Shopping Center, 3810 Valley Centre Dr., Suite 903,* ☎ *619/259–0889;* ⊠ *16441 Bernardo Center Dr., Rancho Bernardo,* ☎ *619/674–4665. AE, D, DC, MC, V.*

$–$$ ✕ **Taste of Thai.** Conveniently located near the racetrack, this offshoot of the popular Hillcrest café continues to please the crowd. If you're seeking an extensive menu of tasty Thai food, come here and order one of the curries, noodle dishes, or vegetable-meat combinations in a variety of sauces. Vegetarians will find much to choose from on this menu. ⊠ *15770 San Andreas Rd. (at the east end of the Flower Hill Mall),* ☎ *619/793–9695. AE, D, DC, MC, V.*

$$$$ ✕⊞ **L'Auberge Del Mar Resort and Spa.** L'Auberge, which occupies a colorful garden setting, is filled with dark-wood antiques. All its spacious rooms have wet bars; many have fireplaces, full marble baths, and private balconies with garden or coastal views. The Dining Room at L'Auberge features contemporary Pacific-Mediterranean cuisine in a casually elegant atmosphere. The dinner specials are among the best culinary bargains in San Diego. ⊠ *1540 Camino del Mar, 92014,* ☎ *858/259–1515 or 800/553–1336,* FAX *858/755–4940. 112 rooms, 8 suites. Restaurant, bar, 2 pools, outdoor hot tub, spa, 2 tennis courts, exercise room, meeting rooms. AE, D, DC, MC, V.*

$$–$$$$ ⊞ **Best Western Stratford Inn of Del Mar.** During racing season this equestrian-theme inn hosts horse owners and jockeys. Ample rooms, many with ocean views or kitchenettes, are surrounded by six lushly landscaped acres. ⊠ *710 Camino del Mar, 92014,* ☎ *858/755–1501 or 888/ 478–7829,* FAX *858/755–4704. 67 rooms, 33 suites. 2 pools, outdoor hot tub. AE, D, DC, MC, V.*

Solana Beach

1 mi north of Del Mar on S21, 25 mi north of downtown San Diego on I–5 to Lomas Santa Fe Dr. west.

Once-quiet Solana Beach is quickly developing a reputation as *the* place to look for antiques, collectibles, and contemporary fashions and artwork. The Cedros Design District, occupying a long block near the new Amtrak station, contains shops, galleries, designers' studios, and restaurants. You can browse the stores at **Cedros Trading Co.** (⊠ 307 S. Cedros Ave., ☎ 858/794–9016), open daily 10–6.

Dining

$$–$$$ ✕ **Pamplemousse Grill.** Justly celebrated as one of North County's best
★ restaurants, the "Grapefruit Grill" offers French country dining California-style. A choice of sauces accompanies succulent grilled meats
and fish, and the main course salads are a feast for the eye as well as
the palate. ⊠ *514 Via de la Valle,* ☎ *619/792–9090. AE, D, DC, MC,
V. No lunch Sat.–Tues.*

$–$$$ ✕ **Parioli Italian Bistro.** This Italian bistro offers fine dining in a plain
but appealing wrapper. In its simple dining room, Parioli serves Ital-
ian dishes graced with an occasional French note. ⊠ *647 Hwy. 101,*
☎ *619/755–2525. AE, DC, MC, V. Closed Mon. No lunch Sun.*

$–$$ ✕ **Fidel's.** One among a cluster of neighborhood Mexican restaurants
in Solana Beach's "barrio Eden Gardens," Fidel's serves good rendi-
tions of traditional south-of-the-border dishes in a casual atmosphere.
The restaurant's outdoor patio draws a lively crowd. There's also a
Fidel's Norte up the coast in Carlsbad. ⊠ *607 Valley Ave.,* ☎ *619/
755–5292;* ⊠ *3003 Carlsbad Blvd.,* ☎ *760/729–0903. MC, V.*

$ ✕ **Zinc Cafe.** Solana Beach's most popular sidewalk café lies at the head
of trendy Cedros Avenue. Sit at one of the outdoor tables and enjoy
the vegetarian breakfast and lunch selections or some truly decadent
desserts. ⊠ *132 S. Cedros Ave.,* ☎ *619/793–5436. No credit cards.
Closes at 5.*

Rancho Santa Fe

*4 mi east of Solana Beach on S8 (Lomas Santa Fe Dr.), 29 mi north of
downtown San Diego on I–5 to S8 east.*

Rancho Santa Fe, east of Interstate 5 on Via de la Valle Road, is horse
country. It's common to see entire families riding the many trails that
crisscross the hillsides. The challenging Rancho Santa Fe Golf Course,
the original site of the Bing Crosby Pro-Am and considered one of the
best courses in southern California, is open only to members of the
Rancho Santa Fe community and guests of the inn.

Dining and Lodging

$$$$ ✕ **Mille Fleurs.** The perennial winner of local and national fine dining
★ awards, this gem of a French auberge remains San Diego County's premiere restaurant. Its setting is as romantic as its light, contemporary
French cuisine is exquisite. The menu changes daily. Mille Fleurs is near
Chino's, the county's foremost vegetable farm, where the chef shops
daily. ⊠ *6009 Paseo Delicias,* ☎ *619/756–3085. Reservations essential. AE, DC, MC, V. No lunch weekends.*

$$$$ ✕🏠 **Rancho Valencia Resort.** One of southern California's hidden
★ treasures has luxurious accommodations in Spanish-style casitas scattered among landscaped grounds. Gardens yield a year-round profusion of flowers. Spacious suites have corner fireplaces that can be seen
from the bed, luxurious Berber carpeting, wet bars, and plantation-
shuttered French doors leading to private patios shaded by market um-
brellas. Rancho Valencia is adjacent to three well-designed golf courses
and is one of the top tennis resorts in the nation. ⊠ *5921 Valencia Circle, 92067,* ☎ *858/756–1123 or 800/548–3664,* 𝙵𝙰𝚇 *858/756–0165. 43
suites. Restaurant, bar, 2 pools, 3 outdoor hot tubs, 18 tennis courts,
croquet, health club, hiking, bicycles. AE, DC, MC, V.*

$$–$$$$ ✕🏠 **Inn at Rancho Santa Fe.** Understated elegance is the theme of this
genteel old resort in the heart of the village. This is the sort of place
where people don their "whites" and play croquet on the lawn Sun-
day afternoons. Most accommodations are in red-tile-roof cottages scat-
tered about the property's parklike 20 acres. Some cottages have two
bedrooms, private patios, fireplaces, and hot tubs. The inn also main-

tains a beach house at Del Mar for guest use and has membership at the exclusive Rancho Santa Fe Golf Club. ⊠ *5951 Linea del Cielo, 92067,* ☎ *858/756–1131 or 800/843–4661,* FAX *858/759–1604. 73 rooms, 19 suites. Dining room, bar, room service, pool, golf privileges, 3 tennis courts, croquet, exercise room, library, meeting rooms. AE, DC, MC, V.*

Carlsbad

6 mi from Encinitas on S21, 36 mi north of downtown San Diego on I–5.

The end of the century marked a turning point for once laid-back Carlsbad, a Bavarian-inspired coastal community that is popular with beachgoers and sun seekers. The 1999 opening of the Legoland California theme park moved much of the visitor appeal inland east of Interstate 5. Carlsbad owes its name and Bavarian look to John Frazier, who lured people to the area a century ago with talk of the healing powers of mineral water bubbling from a coastal well. The water was found to have the same properties as water from the German mineral wells of Karlsbad—hence the name of the new community. Remnants from this era, including the original well and a monument to Frazier, are found at the **Alt Karlsbad Haus** (⊠ 2802A Carlsbad Blvd.).

Development has destroyed many of the lagoons and saltwater marsh wildlife habitats that punctuated the North County coastline, but **Batiquitos Lagoon** has been restored to support fish and bird populations. A local group is developing trails to the best viewing spots around the lagoon. This is a quiet spot for contemplation or a picnic. ⊠ *Batiquitos Dr. south (east of I–5's Poinsettia La. exit),* ☎ *760/943–7583.* ☉ *Tours 1st, 3rd Sat. of month, from 9 to 11.*

☙ ❷ With the March 1999 opening of **Legoland California,** Carlsbad became an instant family destination. Legoland, the centerpiece of a development with golf courses, resort hotels, a winery, and a designer discount shopping mall, offers a full day of entertainment for pint-size visitors and their parents. Kids can climb on and over, operate, manipulate, and explore displays and attractions constructed out of plastic blocks. Included are a nature maze and power tower with an ocean view; a driving school with miniature cars and boats; a waterworks operated by joysticks; and a junior roller coaster. Stage shows and restaurants with kid-friendly buffets are also part of the mix. The admission fee for children between the age of 3 and 16 is $25; there's no charge for children two and under. At press time the park's hours were still subject to change, so call ahead. ⊠ *1 Lego Dr., (exit I–5 at Cannon Rd. and follow signs east ¼ mi),* ☎ *760/918–5346.* ☞ *$32.* ☉ *Daily 10–6.*

Dining and Lodging

$$$$ ✕⊞ **La Costa Hotel and Spa.** Don't expect glitz and glamour at this famous resort. It's surprisingly low-key, with low-slung buildings and vaguely Southwestern contemporary–style rooms. Rooms are unusually large with opulent marble bathrooms; many have garden patios. Although many guests come for La Costa's tranquil setting, the resort has one of the most comprehensive sports programs in the area. There are two PGA championship golf courses and a golf school, plus a large tennis center. The spa is world famous. The complex includes Pisces restaurant, long one of San Diego's top seafood venues. ⊠ *2100 Costa del Mar Rd., 92009,* ☎ *760/438–9111 or 800/854–5000,* FAX *760/931–7569. 397 rooms, 82 suites. 4 restaurants, 2 bars, in-room data ports, room service, 5 pools, beauty salon, spa, 2 18-hole golf courses, 21*

tennis courts, croquet, health club, hiking, jogging, bicycles, confer-
ence center, car rental. AE, D, DC, MC, V.

$$$$ 🔟 **Four Seasons Resort Aviara.** This hilltop resort sitting on 30 acres
★ overlooking Batiquitos Lagoon is the most luxurious in the San Diego
area, featuring typical Four Seasons amenities: acres of gleaming marble corridors, original artwork on the walls, crystal chandeliers, and
enormous flower arrangements in public areas. Rooms, somewhat
smaller than those in nearby luxury resorts, boast every possible
amenity. The resort is home to the Arnold Palmer–designed Aviara Golf
Club, ranked among the top new resort golf courses, and the Aviara
Golf Academy. ✉ *7100 Four Seasons Point, 92009,* ☎ *760/931–6672*
or 800/332–3442, FAX *760/603–6878. 287 rooms, 44 suites. 4 restau-*
rants, bar, 2 pools, beauty salon, spa, 18-hole golf course, 6 tennis courts,
health club, hiking, bicycles, children's programs for ages 4 to 12, meet-
ing rooms, car rental. AE, D, DC, MC, V.

$$$–$$$$ 🔟 **Carlsbad Inn.** Gabled roofs, half-timbered walls, and stone supports
are among the architectural elements of note at this sprawling Euro-
pean-style inn and time-share condominium complex in the heart of
Carlsbad, steps from the beach. Rooms are furnished in old-world fash-
ion, with pencil-post beds and wall sconces. Many have ocean views
and kitchenettes. ✉ *3075 Carlsbad Blvd., 92008,* ☎ *760/434–7020*
or 800/235–3939, FAX *760/729–4853. 61 rooms, 1 suite. Pool, outdoor*
hot tub, sauna, exercise room, bicycles, children's programs, play-
ground, coin laundry, meeting rooms. AE, D, DC, MC, V.

OFF THE **MISSION SAN LUIS REY** — Built by Franciscan friars in 1798 under the
BEATEN PATH direction of Father Fermin Lasuen to help educate and convert local Na-
tive Americans, the well-preserved San Luis Rey was the 18th and
largest of the California missions. The *sala* (parlor), a friar's bedroom, a
weaving room, the kitchen, and a collection of religious art convey
much about early mission life. Retreats are still held here, but a picnic
area, a gift shop, and a museum (which has the most extensive collec-
tion of old Spanish vestments in the United States) are also on the
grounds. Self-guided tours are available. The mission is on Highway 76,
which becomes Mission Avenue inland from S21 (from the ocean, con-
tinue east on Highway 76 about 4 mi, past the Mission Avenue business
district and Interstate 5). ✉ *4050 Mission Ave.,* ☎ *760/757–3651.* 🔟
$4. ☉ *Daily 10–4:30.*

San Diego North Coast Essentials

Arriving and Departing

BY BUS

The San Diego Transit District (☎ 619/233–3004) covers the city of San
Diego up to Del Mar. The **North County Transit District** (☎ 760/743–
6283) serves San Diego County from Del Mar north.

BY CAR

Interstate 5 is the main freeway artery connecting San Diego to Los
Angeles. To the west, running parallel to it, is S21 (known locally, but
not signed, as Old Highway 101, and at points signed as Highway 101
or Coast Highway 101), which never strays too far from the ocean.
Watch the signs, because the road has a different name as it passes
through each community.

BY PLANE

McClellan Palomar Airport (✉ 2198 Palomar Airport Rd., Carlsbad,
☎ 760/431–4646) is a general-aviation airport run by the county of
San Diego and open to the public. American Eagle and United Airlines

operate commuter service between Los Angeles and McClellan Palomar.

BY TRAIN

See Arriving and Departing *in* San Diego A to Z, *below.*

Visitor Information

San Diego North Convention and Visitors Bureau (✉ 720 N. Broadway, Escondido, 92025, ☎ 760/745–4741).

SIDE TRIP TO INLAND NORTH COUNTY

Even though the coast is only a short drive away, the beach communities seem far removed from the quiet lakes of Escondido, the avocado-growing country surrounding Fallbrook, or the vineyards of Temecula, which is just across the Orange County line. Home to missions, San Diego Wild Animal Park, the Welk Resort Center, and innumerable three-generation California families, the inland area of North County is the quiet rural sister to the rest of San Diego County.

Numbers in the margin correspond to points of interest on the San Diego North County map.

Rancho Bernardo

23 mi northeast of downtown San Diego on I-15.

Rancho Bernardo straddles a stretch of Interstate 15 between San Diego and Escondido. Primarily a suburban community, it is the location of the Rancho Bernardo Inn, one of San Diego's most delightful resorts. The town is also the home base of Ken Blanchard's Golf University of San Diego.

Lodging

$$$$ ✕⌂ **Rancho Bernardo Inn.** Truly a gem of a resort secluded amid a well-
★   established residential community, this adobe early California–style inn feels as comfortable and cozy as a slipper. Public areas are a collection of small sitting rooms where Spanish mission–style sofas and chairs invite you to linger with a good book. There are fireplaces everywhere, overstuffed furnishings, and Oriental rugs on tiled floors. The grounds comprise 265 oak-shaded acres including a championship golf course. Service here is exceptional. ✉ *17550 Bernardo Oaks Dr., 92128,* ☎ *858/675–8500 or 800/542–6096,* FAX *858/675–8437. 264 rooms, 10 suites. 2 restaurants, 2 bars, in-room data ports, room service, 2 pools, 8 outdoor hot tubs, sauna, spa, steam room, driving range, 18-hole golf course, putting green, 12 tennis courts, exercise room, volleyball, bicycles, shops, children's programs for ages 5 to 17, concierge, business services, meeting rooms. AE, D, DC, MC, V.*

Escondido

8 mi north of Rancho Bernardo on I-15, 31 mi northeast of downtown San Diego on I-15.

Escondido is a thriving, rapidly expanding residential and commercial city of more than 80,000 people and the center of a variety of attractions.

The **California Center for the Arts,** an entertainment complex with two theaters, an art museum, and a conference center, presents operas, musicals, plays, dance performances, and symphony and chamber-music concerts. The museum's focus is 20th-century California art. ✉ *340*

N. *Escondido Blvd.,* ☎ *box office 760/738–4100, museum 760/839–4120.* 🖅 *Museum $4.* ⊙ *Tues.–Sat. 10–5, Sun. noon–5.*

★ ☺ ❸ **San Diego Wild Animal Park** is an extension of the San Diego Zoo. The 2,200-acre preserve in the San Pasqual Valley is designed to protect endangered species of animals from around the world. Exhibit areas have been carved out of the dry, dusty canyons and mesas to represent the animals' natural habitats—North Africa, South Africa, East Africa, Heart of Africa, Australian Rain Forest, Asian Swamps, and Asian Plains. The best way to see these preserves is on the 50-minute, 5-mi Wgasa Bushline Monorail ride (included in the price of admission). As you pass in front of the large, naturally landscaped enclosures, you'll see animals bounding through prairies and mesas as they would in the wild. More than 3,000 animals of 450 species roam or fly above the expansive grounds. Predators are separated from prey by deep moats, but only the tigers, lions, and cheetahs are kept in isolation. In summer the monorail travels through the park after dark, and sodium-vapor lamps highlight the active animals. ✉ *Take I–15 north to Via Rancho Pkwy. and follow signs (6 mi),* ☎ *760/480–0100.* 🖅 *$19.95, includes all shows and monorail tour; a combination pass ($35.15) grants entry, within 5 days of purchase, to both the San Diego Zoo and the San Diego Wild Animal Park; parking $3. V.* ⊙ *Daily at 9; closing hrs vary with season (call ahead).*

San Pasqual Battlefield State Historic Park and Museum commemorates an important moment in the Mexican-American War. On December 6, 1846, a contingent of Americans, including famous frontier scout Kit Carson, was defeated by a group of Californios (Spanish-Mexican residents of California). ✉ *15808 San Pasqual Valley Rd.,* ☎ *760/489–0076.* 🖅 *Free.* ⊙ *Tues. 10–4, weekends 10–5.*

Dining and Lodging

$$–$$$ ✕ **150 Grand Cafe.** The seasonal menu of this pretty restaurant showcases contemporary California-style dishes prepared with a European flair. It's within walking distance of the California Center for the Arts. ✉ *150 W. Grand Ave.,* ☎ *760/738–6868. AE, DC, MC, V. No lunch Sat. Closed Sun., except certain performance nights (call for information).*

$–$$$ ✕ **Sirino's.** This spot is an excellent choice for dining before attending an event at the nearby California Center for the Arts. The simpler dishes are particularly recommended. The wine list is serious, as are the desserts. ✉ *113 W. Grand Ave.,* ☎ *760/745–3835. AE, D, MC, V. Closed Sun.–Mon. No lunch Sat.*

$$–$$$$ 🏨 **Welk Resort Center.** This resort sprawls over 600 acres of rugged, oak-studded hillside. Built by bandleader Lawrence Welk in the 1960s, the resort includes a hotel, time-share condominiums, and a recreation and entertainment complex. A museum displays Welk memorabilia, a theater presents Broadway-style musicals year-round, and there are many shops on the premises. Hotel rooms, decorated with a Southwestern flair, have golf-course views. ✉ *8860 Lawrence Welk Dr., 92026,* ☎ *760/749–3000 or 800/932–9355,* 🖷 *760/749–6182. 137 rooms, 10 suites. Restaurant, deli, 3 pools, 3 outdoor hot tubs, 2 18-hole golf courses, theater, children's programs, meeting rooms. AE, D, DC, MC, V.*

Inland North County Essentials

Arriving and Departing

BY BUS

North County Transit District (☎ 760/743–6283) routes crisscross the Escondido area.

Escondido sits at the intersection of Highway 78, which heads east from
Oceanside, and I–15, the inland freeway connecting San Diego to
Riverside, which is 30 minutes north of Escondido. Del Dios Highway
winds from Rancho Santa Fe through the hills past Lake Hodges to
Escondido. Highway 76, which connects with I–15 north of Escondido,
veers east to Mount Palomar. Interstate 15 continues north to Fallbrook
and Temecula.

Visitor Information
Escondido Chamber of Commerce (⊠ 720 N. Broadway, 92025, ☎ 760/
745–2125).

SIDE TRIP TO THE BACKCOUNTRY

The Cuyamaca and Laguna mountains to the east of Escondido—
sometimes referred to as the backcountry by county residents—are favorite weekend destinations for hikers, nature lovers, and apple-pie
fanatics. Most of the latter group head to Julian, an historic mining
town that is now better known for apples than for the gold that once
was extracted from its hills. Nearby Cuyamaca Rancho State Park is
full of well-maintained trails and picnic and camping areas.

Julian

62 mi from San Diego (to Julian), east on I–8 and north on Hwy. 79.

Gold was discovered in the Julian area in 1869 and gold-bearing
quartz a year later. More than $15 million worth of gold was taken
from local mines in the 1870s. Today this mountain town retains some
historic false-front buildings from its mining days. When gold and quartz
became scarce the locals turned to growing apples and pears. During
the fall harvest season you can buy fruit, sip cider, eat apple pie, and
shop for antiques and collectibles. But spring is equally enchanting (and
less congested with visitors), as the hillsides explode with wildflowers,
lilacs, and peonies. Artists and craftspeople have long maintained studios in the hillsides surrounding Julian. Their work is frequently on
display in local shops and galleries.

Dining and Lodging

$-$$$ ✕ **Julian Grille.** The menu at this casual restaurant inside a historic home
appeals to a variety of tastes, including vegetarian. Chicken dishes are
popular. ⊠ *2224 Main St.,* ☎ *760/765–0173. AE, MC, V. No dinner
Mon.*

$$$-$$$$ ⌂ **Orchard Hill Country Inn.** Perched on a hill above town, this inn with
★ a sweeping view of the surrounding countryside sets a new standard
for luxury among backcountry accommodations. All rooms are dec-
orated with antiques and handcrafted quilts. ⊠ *Washington St., Ju-
lian 92036,* ☎ *760/765–1700 or 800/716–7242,* FAX *760/765–0290.
10 rooms, 12 suites. Dining room, meeting rooms. AE, MC, V.*

$-$$ ⌂ **Julian Lodge.** This bed-and-breakfast near the center of town is a
replica of a late-19th-century Julian hotel. The rooms and public spaces
are furnished with antiques. ⊠ *4th and C Sts., Julian 92036,* ☎ *760/
765–1420 or 800/542–1420. 23 rooms. AE, D, MC, V.*

The Backcountry Essentials

Arriving and Departing
A loop drive beginning and ending in San Diego is a good way to explore this area. You can take the Sunrise National Scenic Byway High-

way (sometimes icy in winter) from I–8 to Highway 79 and return through Cuyamaca. If you're only going to Julian, take either the Sunrise Highway or Highway 79, and return to San Diego via Highway 78 past Santa Ysabel to Ramona and Highway 67; from here I–8 heads west to downtown.

Visitor Information
Julian Chamber of Commerce (✉ 2129 Main St., 92036, ☎ 760/765–1857).

SIDE TRIP TO THE DESERT

Every spring the stark desert landscape east of the Cuyamaca Mountains explodes with colorful wildflowers. The beauty of this spectacle, as well as the natural quiet and blazing climate, lures many tourists and natives each year to Anza-Borrego Desert State Park, less than a two-hour drive from central San Diego. The desert is best visited from October through May to avoid the extreme summer temperatures. Winter temperatures are comfortable, but nights (and sometimes days) are cold, so bring a warm jacket.

Numbers in the margin correspond to points of interest on the San Diego North County map.

Anza-Borrego Desert State Park

❹ *88 mi from downtown San Diego (to park border due west of Borrego Springs), east on I–8, north on Hwy. 67, east on S4 and Hwy. 78, north on Hwy. 79, and east on S2 and S22.*

Today more than 600,000 acres are included in the Anza-Borrego Desert State Park, making it the largest state park in the contiguous United States. It is also one of the few parks in the country where people can camp anywhere. No campsite is necessary. Follow the trails and pitch a tent wherever you like. Five hundred miles of paved and dirt roads traverse the park, and visitors are required to stay on them so as not to disturb the ecological balance. However, 28,000 acres have been set aside in the eastern part of the desert near Ocotillo Wells for off-road enthusiasts.

Many of the park's sites can be seen from paved roads, but some require driving on dirt roads. Rangers recommend using four-wheel-drive vehicles when traversing dirt roads. Carry the appropriate supplies: shovel and other tools, flares, blankets, and plenty of water. Canyons are susceptible to flash flooding. Inquire about weather conditions before entering. Rangers and displays at an underground **Visitors Information Center** (✉ Palm Canyon Dr., Borrego Springs, ☎ 760/767–5311; 760/767–4684 wildflower hot line; ☉ Oct.–May daily 9–5, June–Sept. weekends and holidays 9–5) can point you in the right direction.

SAN DIEGO A TO Z

Arriving and Departing

By Bus
Greyhound (☎ 619/239–8082 or 800/231–2222) operates buses between the downtown terminal at 120 West Broadway and Los Angeles. Many buses are express or nonstop; others make stops at coastal towns en route.

By Car

Interstate 5 stretches from Canada to the Mexican border and bisects San Diego. Interstate 8 provides access from Yuma, Arizona, and points east. Drivers coming from Nevada and the mountain regions beyond can reach San Diego on I–15.

By Plane

San Diego International Airport (☎ 619/231–2100), about a five-minute drive from downtown, is San Diego's main airport. Carriers serving the city include Aeromexico, Alaska, America West, American, American Eagle, British Airways, Continental, Delta, Northwest, Reno Air, Southwest, TWA, United, and US Airways. *See* Air Travel *in* Smart Travel Tips for airline phone numbers.

BETWEEN THE AIRPORT AND DOWNTOWN

San Diego Metropolitan Transit (☎ 619/233–3004) Route 2 buses leave daily from 5:30 AM to 1 AM. Buses depart from the front of East Terminal's US Airways section and travel along Broadway, downtown. The fare is $1.50 per person.

Cloud 9 Shuttle (☎ 619/278–8877; 800/974–8885 in San Diego) and **San Diego Xpress Airport Shuttle** (☎ 619/220–8454) operate van shuttles that take you directly to your destination, often for less than a cab would cost.

If you have rented a car at the airport, you can take Harbor Drive, at the perimeter of the airport, to downtown, which is 3 mi east. Take Harbor Drive west to reach Shelter Island and Point Loma. Harbor Island is adjacent to the airport. To reach I–5 or I–8, take Harbor Drive west to Nimitz Boulevard, then right on Rosecrans Street. You can reach La Jolla and North County via I–5 North. Interstate 8 East leads to Hotel Circle and Qualcomm Stadium. To reach Mission Bay, continue on Nimitz Boulevard, which intersects with Sunset Cliffs Boulevard. To reach Coronado, take Harbor Drive east through downtown to the San Diego–Coronado Bay Bridge. The taxi fare from the airport to downtown hotels costs from $7 to $9 plus tip.

By Train

Amtrak (☎ 800/872–7245) services downtown San Diego's **Santa Fe Depot** (✉ 1050 Kettner Blvd., ☎ 619/239–9021) with daily trains to and from Los Angeles and Santa Barbara. Amtrak stops in San Diego North County at Solana Beach and Oceanside.

Coaster (☎ 800/COASTER) commuter trains, which run between Oceanside and San Diego, stop at stations in Del Mar, Solana Beach, Encinitas, and Carlsbad.

Getting Around

By Bus

The **San Diego Transit Information Line** (☎ 619/233–3004; in operation from 5:30 AM to 8:30 PM) has details about all routes.

Regional bus companies that service areas outside the city include **ATC Van Co.** (☎ 619/427–5660), for Coronado, the Silver Strand, and Imperial Beach; **Chula Vista Transit** (☎ 619/233–3004), for Chula Vista; **National City Transit** (☎ 619/474–7505), for National City, and **North County Transit District** (☎ 760/722–6283), for the area bound by the ocean, east to Escondido, north to Camp Pendleton, and south to Del Mar.

By Car

A car is essential for San Diego's sprawling freeway system. Avoid the freeways during rush hour when possible. All the major car-rental companies are represented in San Diego. For a list, *see* Car Rentals *in* Smart Travel Tips.

Limousine companies operate airport shuttles and customized tours. Rates vary and are per hour, per mile, or both, with some minimums established. Companies that provide service include **La Jolla Limousines** (☎ 858/459–5891), **Premier Ride** (☎ 619/234–7433), and **Presidential Limousine Service** (☎ 619/291–2820).

By Ferry

The **San Diego–Coronado Ferry** (☎ 619/234–4111) leaves from the Broadway Pier daily, every hour on the hour, 9 AM to 9 PM from Sunday through Thursday, until 10 PM on Friday and Saturday. The fare is $2 each way and 50¢ for each bicycle.

By Taxi

Taxis departing from the airport are subject to regulated fares—all companies charge the same rate (generally $1.80 for the first mile, $1.20 for each additional mile). Fares vary among companies on other routes, including the ride back to the airport. If you call ahead and ask for the flat rate ($7), you'll get it; otherwise, you'll be charged by the mile (which works out to $9 or so).

Cab companies that serve most areas of the city are **Co-op Silver Cabs** (☎ 619/280–5555), **Coronado Cab** (☎ 619/435–6211), **La Jolla Cab** (☎ 858/453–4222), **Orange Cab** (☎ 619/291–3333), and **Yellow Cab** (☎ 619/234–6161).

Contacts and Resources

Emergencies

Ambulance (☎ 911). **Fire** (☎ 911). **Police** (☎ 911).

Major hospitals are **Scripps Mercy Hospital and Medical Center** (⊠ 4077 5th Ave., ☎ 619/294–8111), **Scripps Memorial Hospital** (⊠ 9888 Genesee Ave., La Jolla, ☎ 858/457–4123), **UCSD Medical Center** (⊠ 200 W. Arbor Dr., San Diego, ☎ 619/543–6222), and **Veterans Administration Hospital** (⊠ 3350 La Jolla Village Dr., La Jolla, ☎ 858/552–8585).

Hotel Doctors (☎ 619/275–2663) provides 24-hour medical service to guests at San Diego hotels. The **San Diego County Dental Society** (☎ 619/275–0244) can provide referrals Monday through Friday to those with dental emergencies.

Guided Tours

ORIENTATION TOURS

Gray Line Tours (☎ 619/491–0011; 800/331–5077 outside CA) and **San Diego Mini Tours** (☎ 619/477–8687) operate sightseeing excursions for about $25.

The **Old Town Trolley** (☎ 619/298–8687) travels to almost every attraction and shopping area on open-air trackless trolleys. Drivers double as tour guides. You can take the full two-hour, narrated city tour or get on and off as you please at any of the nine stops. An all-day pass costs $20. The trolley, which leaves every 30 minutes, operates daily 9 to 5 in summer, 9 to 4 in winter.

Free two-hour trolley tours of the downtown redevelopment area, including the Gaslamp Quarter, are hosted by **Centre City Development Corporation Downtown Information Center** (☎ 619/235–2222). Groups of 35 passengers leave from 225 Broadway, Suite 160, downtown, the first and third Saturday of each month at 10 AM. Reservations are necessary.

Two companies operate one- and two-hour harbor cruises. **San Diego Harbor Excursion** (☎ 619/234–4111) and **Hornblower Invader Cruises** (☎ 619/234–8687) boats depart from the Broadway Pier. No reservations are necessary for the voyages, which cost between $12 and $17. Both vessels have snack bars on board. **Classic Sailing Adventures** (☎ 619/224–0800) has morning and afternoon tours of the harbor and San Diego Bay and nighttime in summer cruises for $45 per person.

Visitor Information

International Visitor Information Center (✉ 11 Horton Plaza, at 1st Ave. and F St., ☎ 619/236–1212). **San Diego Convention & Visitors Bureau** (✉ 401 B St., Suite 1400, 92101, ☎ 619/232–3101). **San Diego Visitor Information Center** (✉ 2688 E. Mission Bay Dr., 92109, ☎ 619/276–8200).

14 PALM SPRINGS

The Desert Resorts and Joshua Tree

Palm Springs and its neighbors—Palm Desert, Rancho Mirage, Indian Wells—are among the fastest-growing and wealthiest communities in the nation. The desert lures visitors and residents for the same reasons: striking scenery and the therapeutic benefits of a warm, arid climate. Resort hotel complexes contain championship golf courses, tennis stadiums, and sparkling swimming pools. Lushly landscaped oases, towering palms, natural waterfalls, and hot mineral springs round out the picture.

By Bobbi Zane

THE DESERT AROUND PALM SPRINGS hasn't always been filled with luxury resorts, but various settlers through the years have recognized the region's rich natural attributes. The Agua Caliente Band of Indians discovered the hot springs in the Coachella Valley—the valley in which the desert-resorts area lies—and made use of their healing properties. In the last half of the 19th century, farmers established a date-growing industry at the southern end of the valley. By 1900, word had spread about the manifold health benefits of the area's dry climate, inspiring the gentry of the northern United States to winter under the warm desert sun.

By the time of the Great Depression, Palm Springs had caught Hollywood's eye. It was an ideal hideaway: celebrities could slip into town, play a few sets of tennis, lounge around the pool, attend a party or two, and, unless things got out of hand, remain safely beyond the reach of gossip columnists.

Growth hit the desert in the 1970s. Developers began to construct the world-class golf courses, country clubs, and residential communities that drew celebrities, tycoons, and politicians. Privacy is still the watchword here. Many communities are walled and gate-guarded.

The downside to the region's growth has included urban sprawl and overbuilding (of sometimes less than stellar structures). The city of Palm Springs lost some of its luster as the wealthy moved on to newer, more glamorous communities—Palm Desert, Rancho Mirage, Indian Wells. But Palm Springs has reinvented itself. Formerly exclusive Palm Canyon Drive is a lively avenue with coffeehouses, outdoor cafés and bars, and frequent special events.

You'll still find celebrities in the desert, where streets are named for Bob Hope, Gerald Ford, Dinah Shore, and Frank Sinatra. Hollywood stars, sports personalities, politicians, and other high-profile folks can be spotted at charity events, in restaurants, or on the golf course. Sean Connery, Kevin Costner, Elizabeth Taylor, and Joe Pesci have all swept into town in recent years. The prospect of a brush with glamour, along with the desert's natural beauty, heightens the area's appeal for tourists.

Pleasures and Pastimes

Desert Wildlife

Visitors who want to learn about the natural history of the desert and see some spectacular scenery can explore the terrain at ground level at the Living Desert Wildlife and Botanical Park and Joshua Tree National Park or take in the full panorama at the top of the Palm Springs Aerial Tramway. Exhibits in the Palm Springs Desert Museum (☞ Exploring Palm Springs, *below*) explain it all.

Dining

Long a culinary wasteland, the desert now supports many trendy if not overly adventurous restaurants. Although Italian cuisine remains popular, a new collection of ethnic eateries has sprung up in recent years. Many menus include heart-healthy items for those who are careful about fat and cholesterol. Dining is casual. Many restaurants that were traditionally closed in summer are now opening on a limited basis; hours vary so call in advance.

CATEGORY	COST*
$$$$	over $50
$$$	$30–$50
$$	$20–$30
$	under $20

per person for a three-course meal, excluding drinks, service, and 7¾% tax

Golf

The Palm Springs area has more than 90 golf courses, many of which are familiar to golfing fans as the sites of championship tournaments. You can tee off where the pros play at PGA West, Mission Hills North, and La Quinta, all of which have instructors ready to help you finesse your swing.

Lodging

You can stay in Palm Springs for as little as $40 per night or for more than $1,000. Rates vary widely from summer (low) to winter (high) season. Budget lodgings are most easily found in Palm Springs proper. The city-operated **visitor center** (☎ 800/347–7746) represents 85 properties. Discounts are sometimes given for extended stays. **Palm Springs Desert Resorts** (☎ 800/417–3529) can also make accommodation reservations throughout the area. Condos, apartments, and individual houses may be rented by the day, week, month, or for longer periods. Some hotels, including Marriott's Desert Springs Resort and Spa, have villas for rent.

CATEGORY	COST*
$$$$	over $200
$$$	$125–$200
$$	$75–$125
$	under $75

All prices are for a standard double room, excluding 9%–11% tax.

Nightlife and the Arts

The Fabulous Palm Springs Follies—a vaudeville-style revue starring retired professional performers—is a must-see for most visitors. Arts festivals occur on a regular basis, especially during the winter and spring. Nightlife options include a good jazz bar (Peabody's), a clutch of new "retro" shows and glamour clubs, several dance clubs, and hotel entertainment. The "Desert Guide" from *Palm Springs Life* magazine, available at most hotels and visitor information centers, has nightlife listings, as does the "Weekender" pullout in the Friday edition of the daily *Palm Desert Sun* newspaper. The gay scene is covered in the *Bottom Line*.

Outdoor Sports and Activities

With almost 30,000 pools in the desert region, swimming (or at least hanging out poolside) is a daily ritual. Several hundred courts make playing or watching tennis a serious pursuit. More than 35 mi of bike trails crisscross the Palm Springs area; the terrain here is mostly flat. Indian Canyons, Mount San Jacinto State Park and Wilderness, Living Desert Wildlife and Botanical Park, Joshua Tree National Park, and Big Morongo Canyon Preserve have hiking trails. Avoid outdoor activities midday during the hot season. Take precautions against the sun, and wear a hat any time of the year. Always drink plenty of water to prevent dehydration.

Shopping

More than half the respondents to a recent visitor survey ranked shopping as the "recreation" they enjoyed most, which may be the reason the Palm Springs area has begun to look like one big mall. Boutiques, art galleries, and an ever-growing collection of consignment, estate-sale, and antiques shops make for diverse browsing. El Paseo in Palm Desert has upscale galleries and shops, and Cabazon holds many factory outlets.

Exploring Palm Springs

Some visitors' idea of "exploring" Palm Springs is to navigate the distance from their hotel room to the pool or spa. This has, after all, always been a place for indulging oneself. Most social, sports, shopping, and entertainment scenes revolve around Palm Springs and Palm Desert. Cathedral City and Rancho Mirage are west of Palm Desert (and east of Palm Springs) on Highway 111. Indian Wells, La Quinta, and Indio are all east of Palm Desert on the highway. North of Palm Springs is Desert Hot Springs. As for the region's natural wonders, Joshua Tree National Park and other outdoor attractions are easily visited as day trips from any of the resort towns.

Numbers in the text correspond to numbers in the margin and on the Palm Springs Desert Resorts map.

Great Itineraries

IF YOU HAVE 1 DAY

If you've just slipped into town for the day, focus your activities around Palm Springs. Get an early morning scenic overview by taking the **Palm Springs Aerial Tramway** ① to the top of Mount San Jacinto. In the afternoon, head for **Palm Canyon Drive** ② in Palm Springs, have lunch alfresco at the Blue Coyote Grill, and drop by the **Showbiz Museum** at the Plaza Theater, where you can pick up tickets for an evening performance of the **Fabulous Palm Springs Follies** (better still, make reservations before your visit). In the afternoon, visit **Palm Desert,** the trendiest of the desert cities, for a walk through the canyons and hillsides of the **Living Desert Wildlife and Botanical Park** ⑨ and a pre-show dinner on **El Paseo.**

IF YOU HAVE 3 DAYS

On your first day head to the **Palm Springs Aerial Tramway** ① in the morning and have lunch on **Palm Canyon Drive** ②. Spend the afternoon browsing the Palm Canyon shops, or (unless it's the height of the summer) hiking through the **Indian Canyons** ⑥. On day two take an early morning drive to **Joshua Tree National Park** ⑩, where you can explore the terrain, crawl through the entrance to Hidden Valley, and stop by the Oasis of Mara visitor center. Have a picnic lunch in the park or head back to **El Paseo** in Palm Desert for a midafternoon bite before exploring the chic shopping area. On the third morning take in the **Palm Springs Desert Museum** ④. In the afternoon pamper yourself by partaking of the regimen at either Merv Griffin's Resort Hotel and Givenchy Spa or the Spa Hotel and Casino (☞ Lodging, *below,* for both). Then, appropriately relaxed, take in a performance of the **Fabulous Palm Springs Follies.**

IF YOU HAVE 5 DAYS

Ride the **Palm Springs Aerial Tramway** ① and cruise **Palm Canyon Drive** ② on the first day. Explore the **Living Desert** ⑨ and have lunch and shop on **El Paseo** ⑧ or visit the **Indian Canyons** ⑥. On the third day, visit the **Palm Springs Desert Museum** ④, have lunch, and then spend the afternoon lounging poolside at your hotel or touring **Moorten Botanical Garden** ⑤. Spend the entire fourth day touring **Joshua Tree National Park** ⑩, starting at the West Entrance near Joshua Tree and exiting at the Cottonwood Visitor Center (come back via I–10 unless you want to poke through some of the desert towns along slower

Highway 111). Following all this activity, you'll be ready for a fifth day of total relaxation, perhaps a massage, aromatherapy, and an herbal wrap.

When to Tour Palm Springs

During the "season" (from January through April) the desert weather is at its best, with daytime temperatures ranging between 70° and 90°F. This is the time when you're most likely to see a colorful display of wildflowers and when most of the golf and tennis tournaments take place. Prices soar and accommodations can be difficult to secure at this time without advance reservations. The fall months are nearly as lovely, less crowded, and less expensive. During the summer months daytime temperatures rise to 110°F or higher, though evenings cool to the mid-70s. Some attractions and restaurants close during this period. Hotel prices frequently average 50% less in summer than in winter and early spring.

FROM PALM SPRINGS TO PALM DESERT

The Agua Caliente Band of Cahuilla Indians settled in and around the Coachella Valley about 1,000 years ago. They considered the mineral springs to be sacred, with great curative and restorative powers. The springs became a tourist attraction in 1871 when the tribe built a bathhouse on the site to serve passengers on a pioneer stage route. The Agua Caliente still own about 32,000 acres of desert, 6,700 of which lie within the city limits of Palm Springs.

The desert became a Hollywood hideout in the 1920s, when La Quinta Hotel opened the Coachella Valley's first golf course. But it took a pair of tennis-playing celebrities to put Palm Springs on the map in the 1930s. Actors Charlie Farrell and Ralph Bellamy bought 200 acres of land for $30 an acre and opened the Palm Springs Racquet Club, which soon listed Ginger Rogers, Humphrey Bogart, and Clark Gable among its members. Farrell served as the town's mayor in the '50s.

Joshua Tree, upgraded from "monument" status in the mid-1990s, is beginning to blossom as a national park. Major projects and facilities within the park are still in the future, but it will only be a matter of time before development in the communities around the park occurs. In the meantime, nature, particularly in the form of spring wildflowers, continues to bloom with spectacular regularity. The Cottonwood Springs area is one of the desert's best for wildflower viewing. Carpets of white, yellow, purple, and red flowers stretch as far as the eye can see on the hillsides east of the freeway.

Exploring the Desert

★ ☙ ❶ A trip on the **Palm Springs Aerial Tramway** provides a stunning overview of the desert through the picture windows of rotating gondolas. The 2½-mi ascent brings you to an elevation of 8,516 ft in less than 20 minutes. On clear days, which are common, the view stretches 75 mi from the peak of Mount San Gorgonio to the north to the Salton Sea in the southeast. At the top you'll find several diversions. The Mountain Station has an alpine cafeteria, a cocktail lounge, apparel and gift shops, a theater that screens a 22-minute film on the history of the tramway, and picnic facilities. The tram is a popular attraction, so lines can be long. ✉ 1 Tramway Rd., ☎ 760/325–1391 or 888/515–8726. 🎫 $17.65. ☉ Tram cars depart at least every 30 min from 10 AM weekdays and 8 AM weekends; last car up leaves at 8 PM, last one down 9:45 PM. Closed mid-summer for renovation and maintenance.

Palm Springs Desert Resorts

KEY

AE American Express Office

0 — 4 miles
0 — 6 km

Children's Discovery
Museum of the
Desert, **7**

El Paseo, **8**

Indian Canyons, **6**

Joshua Tree
National Park, **10**

Living Desert Wildlife
and Botanical Park, **9**

Moorten Botanical
Garden, **5**

Palm Canyon Drive, **2**

Palm Springs Aerial
Tramway, **1**

Palm Springs Desert
Museum, **4**

Village Green
Heritage Center, **3**

Mount San Jacinto Wilderness State Park, accessible only by hiking or taking the Palm Springs Aerial Tramway, has 54 mi of hiking trails, and camping and picnic areas. Guided wilderness mule rides are available here during snow-free months. During winter the Nordic Ski Center has cross-country ski equipment for rent. ☎ *909/659–2607 for park information.* ✉ *Free; permits (also free) required for day or overnight wilderness hiking.*

OFF THE
BEATEN PATH

WINDMILLS – Four thousand windmills flutter mightily on the slopes surrounding Palm Springs, generating electricity used by southern California residents. Each windmill stands more than 150 ft high. EV Adventures conducts 1½-hour tours among the turbines. ✉ *20th Ave. north of I-10,* ☎ *760/251–1997.* ✉ *$23.* ☉ *Tours daily 9–3. Reservations recommended.*

❷ A stroll down **Palm Canyon Drive,** which is lined with shops, includes the **Palm Springs Starwalk,** with stars embedded in the sidewalk (à la the Hollywood Walk of Fame). Some of the names you'll recognize (like Lauren Bacall and Liberace); others are local celebs. The tiny but illuminating **Showbiz Museum** (✉ 132 S. Palm Canyon Dr.) documents the area's roots in the entertainment industry. On Thursday night the
★ **Village Fest** fills the section between Tahquitz Canyon Way and Baristo Road with street musicians, a farmers' market, and stalls with food, crafts, art, and antiques.

❸ Three small museums at the **Village Green Heritage Center** (✉ 221 S. Palm Canyon Dr., ☎ 760/323–8297) illustrate pioneer life in Palm Springs. There's a nominal fee for entrance to each. The adjacent **Agua Caliente Cultural Museum,** admission to which is free, is devoted to the culture and history of Cahuilla Indians.

❹ The **Palm Springs Desert Museum** focuses on natural science, the visual arts, and the performing arts. The display on the natural history of the desert is itself worth a visit, and the grounds hold several striking sculpture courts. A modern-art gallery has works by artists such as Alberto Giacometti, Henry Moore, and Helen Frankenthaler. Of interest to movie fans are the exhibits of the late actor William Holden's art collection, and furniture designed and crafted by actor George Montgomery. The Annenberg Theater presents plays, concerts, lectures, operas, and other cultural events. ✉ *101 Museum Dr.,* ☎ *760/325–7186.* ✉ *$7.50; free 1st Fri. of month.* ☉ *Tues.–Sa. 10–5, Sun. noon–5.*

The **Palm Springs Air Museum** showcases several dozen World War II aircraft including a B-17 Flying Fortress bomber, a P-51 Mustang, a Lockheed P-38, and a Grumman TBF Avenger. Guided tours are conducted on weekends at noon and 2 PM. ✉ *745 N. Gene Autry Trail,* ☎ *760/778–6262.* ✉ *$7.50.* ☉ *Daily 10–5.*

❺ Four-acre **Moorten Botanical Garden** nurtures more than 3,000 plant varieties in settings that simulate their original environments. Indian artifacts and rock, crystal, and wood forms are exhibited. ✉ *1701 S. Palm Canyon Dr.,* ☎ *760/327–6555.* ✉ *$2.* ☉ *Mon.–Sat. 9–4:30, Sun. 10–4.*

❻ The **Indian Canyons** hold the ancestral home of the Agua Caliente Band of Cahuilla Indians, who selected them for their lush oases, abundant water, and wildlife. Visitors can see remnants of this life: rock art, house pits and foundations, irrigation ditches, bedrock mortars, pictographs, and stone houses and shelters built atop high cliff walls. Three canyons are open: Palm Canyon, noted for its stand of Washingtonia palms; Murray, home of Peninsula bighorn sheep and a herd of wild ponies;

and Andreas, where a stand of fan palms contrasts with sharp rock formations. The trading post in Palm Canyon has hiking maps, refreshments, Indian art, jewelry, and weavings. ✉ *38-500 S. Palm Canyon Dr.*, ☎ *760/325–5673.* 🖘 *$6.* ⊘ *Daily 8–5, summer 8–6.*

Much of the scenery in exclusive **Rancho Mirage** is behind the walls of gated communities and country clubs. The rich and famous live in celebrity estates or patronize the elegant resorts and fine-dining establishments, and the city's golf courses are the sight of world-class tournaments. The Betty Ford Center, for those recovering from alcohol or drug addiction, is also here.

❼ The **Children's Discovery Museum of the Desert** contains instructive hands-on exhibits for kids—a miniature rock-climbing area, a magnetic sculpture wall, make-it-and-take-it-apart projects, a rope maze, a family center, and an area for toddlers. ✉ *71-701 Gerald Ford Dr., Rancho Mirage,* ☎ *760/321–0602,* 🖘 *$5.* ⊘ *Tues.–Sat. 10–5, Sun. noon–5.*

❽ Some of the best desert people-watching, shopping, and dining can be found along trendy **El Paseo,** west of Highway 111 in Palm Desert (☞ Shopping, *below*).

★ ❾ Come eyeball to eyeball with coyotes, mountain lions, cheetahs, bighorn sheep, golden eagles, warthogs, and owls at the **Living Desert Wildlife and Botanical Park.** Easy to challenging trails traverse desert gardens populated with plants of the Mojave, Colorado, and Sonoran deserts. One exhibit depicts the path of the San Andreas earthquake fault across the valley. During the holidays the park presents Wildlights, an evening light show. Wildlife shows take place daily in Tennity Amphitheater. Shuttle service, strollers, and wheelchairs are available. The park is embarking on an expansion that will ultimately include re-creations of desert life on four continents. The three-acre African Wa TuTu village, opened in 1999, centers around a traditional marketplace. Animals on exhibit include camels, leopards, and hyenas. Children can handle African domestic animals, including goats and guinea fowl, in a petting kraal. ✉ *47-900 Portola Ave. (follow signs west from Hwy. 111), Palm Desert,* ☎ *760/346–5694.* 🖘 *$7.50.* ⊘ *Oct.–mid-June, daily 9–5, mid-June–July and Sept., daily 8–1.*

The **Santa Rosa Mountains National Scenic Area Visitor Center,** operated by the Bureau of Land Management, contains exhibits illustrating the natural history of the desert and is staffed by knowledgeable volunteers. A landscaped garden displays native plants and frames a sweeping view. ✉ *51-500 Hwy. 74, Palm Desert,* ☎ *760/862–9984.* ⊘ *Fri.–Mon. 9–4.*

Most major hotels in the desert that have spas and fitness facilities—Merv Griffin's Resort Hotel and Givenchy Spa in Palm Springs and the Marriott Desert Springs resort in Palm Desert among them—offer day programs for nonguests as well as guests. **Spa du Jour** (✉ 4050B Airport Center, Palm Springs, ☎ 760/864–4150) offers spa regimens ranging from two to six hours and including essential oil and aromatherapy wraps, massages, botanical and enzyme facials, beauty services, and healthy lunches. The **Palms at Palm Springs** (✉ 572 N. Indian Canyon Dr., Palm Springs, ☎ 760/325–1111, ꜰꜰ 760/327–0867) has a one-day spa program that begins with a 6 AM walk. The package includes a choice of 16 classes, the use of exercise equipment, lectures, and individually designed low-calorie meals and snacks. Massage, facials, and wraps are among the treatment options.

Dining

CATHEDRAL CITY

$$–$$$$ ✕ **The Wilde Goose.** Its name notwithstanding, the specialty of the house at the Wilde Goose is duck, served a number of ways. You'll also find steaks, poultry, fish dishes, and extravagant desserts at this romantic restaurant. ⊠ 67-938 E. Palm Canyon Dr., ☎ 760/328–5775. AE, D, DC, MC, V. No lunch.

$$ ✕ **Oceans.** The many repeat customers at this small seafood restaurant tucked in the back of a shopping center testify to the creativity of its chefs and the hospitality of the wait staff. Bouillabaisse and other Continental-style dishes are so fresh you might forget you're dining in the desert. ⊠ Canyon Plaza South, 67-555 E. Palm Canyon Dr., ☎ 760/324–1554. Reservations essential on weekends. AE, D, MC, V. No lunch weekends.

INDIAN WELLS

$$$–$$$$ ✕ **Hamiltons.** Actor/entrepreneur George Hamilton selected celebrity-rich Indian Wells as the home of the second of his new group of show-biz-style restaurants. Part of the Hyatt Grand Champions complex, Hamiltons offers a glamorous mood with Moroccan-inspired decor, tented ceilings, and a private pool. Local critics have raved about the food. Popular dishes include pancetta-wrapped pork loin, braised duck in orange and almonds with couscous, and tri-color linguine with lobster. ⊠ 44-600 Indian Wells Lane, ☎ 760/340–4499. AE, MC, V. No lunch Sun. and Mon. Hrs vary in summer.

LA QUINTA

$$–$$$$
★   ✕ **La Quinta Cliffhouse.** Sweeping mountain views at sunset and the early California ambience of a western movie set draw patrons to this restaurant perched halfway up a hillside. The eclectic menu roams the globe: Caesar salad with grilled chicken, ahi tuna Szechuan style, and, for dessert, Kimo's Hula Pie with house-made macadamia-nut ice cream. ⊠ 78-250 Hwy. 111, ☎ 760/360–5991. Reservations essential. AE, D, DC MC, V. No lunch.

$$–$$$ ✕ **Cunard's Sandbar.** Sturdy steaks, hearty fresh-fish and pasta specials, and reasonable prices lure locals and celebrities to this quiet La Quinta eatery. ⊠ 78-120 Calle Tampico, ☎ 760/564–3660. AE, DC, MC, V. Closed some weekdays off-season. No lunch.

PALM DESERT

$$$–$$$$ ✕ **Augusta.** Artwork fills this showplace, one of the region's most talked-about eateries. Two popular items on the eclectic menu are spit-roasted duck with a cilantro sauce and Chilean sea bass marinated in sake. ⊠ 73-951 El Paseo, ☎ 760/779–9200. Reservations essential in season. AE, DC, MC, V. Closed Aug. No lunch Sun.

$$$–$$$$
★   ✕ **Cuistot.** Chef-owner Bernard Dervieux trained with French culinary star Paul Bocuse, but he's taken a more worldly approach at his own restaurant, tucked into the back of an El Paseo courtyard. Signature dishes include grilled shrimp with spinach linguine, Chinese-style duck in a mango-Madeira-ginger sauce, and rack of lamb with rosemary. ⊠ 73-111 El Paseo, ☎ 760/340–1000. Reservations essential. AE, DC, MC, V. Closed Mon. No lunch Sun.

$$$–$$$$ ✕ **Mayo's.** Bob Mayo presides over a snazzy, retro supper club. There's even a private room dedicated to Hollywood's famed Rat Pack, decorated with larger-than-life-size photos of Frank Sinatra, Sammy Davis, and Dean Martin. The menu offers an updated version of Continental cuisine: pasta, Lake Superior whitefish, and New York steak. ⊠ 73-990 El Paseo, ☎ 760/346–2284. Reservations essential weekends. AE, D, DC, MC, V. Hrs vary in summer.

$$$–$$$$ ✕ **Morton's of Chicago.** Palm Springs residents like their steaks served with style as well as sizzle. Posh, clublike Morton's delivers. A regular slab will cost you about $30 (à la carte), but if only a 48-ounce porterhouse will satisfy, the charge is $62. Ask for a smaller portion and the price will go down slightly. The bar is always busy. Sinatra (and only Sinatra) plays softly in the background. Jackets are requested for men. ⊠ *74-880 Country Club Dr.,* ☎ *760/340–6865. AE, DC, MC, V. No lunch.*

$$$ ✕ **Doug Arango's.** Even the dish of liver and onions receives star treatment at this bistro with colorful sidewalk umbrellas and tomato-red walls. The entrées include American standards and inventive Euro-tinged creations. ⊠ *73-520 El Paseo,* ☎ *760/341–4120. Reservations essential. AE, D, DC, MC, V. Closed Mon. year-round. Closed Sun., no lunch June–mid-Sept.*

$$$ ✕ **Jillian's.** Husband-and-wife team June and Jay Trubee are the stars behind this fancy yet casual restaurant. He tends to the kitchen; she runs the business. Antiques and framed art decorate the three dining rooms, and the nighttime sky provides the ambience in the center courtyard. Try the monumental appetizer called tower of crab (layers of crab, tomatoes, avocados, and brioche), and the main dishes such as salmon baked in parchment and fettuccini with lobster. Save room for the popular Hawaiian cheesecake with macadamia nut crust. Men will feel more comfortable wearing jackets. ⊠ *74-155 El Paseo,* ☎ *760/ 776–8242. Reservations essential. AE, DC, MC, V. Closed 2nd week of June–Sept. No lunch.*

$$–$$$ ✕ **Café des Beaux Arts.** The café brings a little bit of Paris to the desert, with sidewalk dining, colorful flower boxes, and a bistro menu of French and Californian favorites like a hefty bouillabaisse, and the broiled Portobello mushroom with grilled chicken and an artichoke heart, served with a sherry sauce. (Try to stop munching on those flavorful breads.) Leisurely dining is encouraged, which gives you more time to savor the well-chosen French and domestic wines. ⊠ *73-640 El Paseo,* ☎ *760/ 346–0669. AE, DC, MC, V. Closed July–mid-Sept.*

$$–$$$ ✕ **Gila Steaks and Seafood.** Talented chef Fernando Valenzuela (no, not the pitcher) whips up fresh fish, Cajun shrimp, garlic-roasted chicken, certified Angus beef, and other fine dishes at this Palm Springs favorite. The ambience at Gila is casual sleek, and there's a patio for outdoor dining. ⊠ *74-950 Country Club Dr.,* ☎ *760/346–4452. Reservations essential in season. AE, D, DC, MC, V.*

$$–$$$ ✕ **Locanda Toscana.** Celebrities and celebrity-watchers patronize this Tuscan-style restaurant that's known for excellent service, many antipasti choices, and fine soups. Veal, chicken, and fish all receive snazzy preparation. ⊠ *72-695 Hwy. 111, next to Von's,* ☎ *760/776–7500. Reservations essential weekends Nov.–May. AE, D, DC, MC, V. Closed Aug. No lunch.*

$$–$$$ ✕ **Omri and Boni.** Chef Omri Siklai showed the same flair decorating this establishment that he displays nightly in the kitchen preparing an eclectic menu of contemporary Mediterranean dishes. Caesar salads, homemade pastas, chicken and veal dishes—and even ostrich and kangaroo—are prepared with skill and imagination. The restaurant, which is managed by Omri's wife, Boni, is so popular the couple enlarged it three times in four years. ⊠ *73-675 Hwy. 111,* ☎ *760/773–1735. Reservations essential. MC, V. Closed Sun. and July–Sept. No lunch.*

$$–$$$ ✕ **Palomino Euro Bistro.** One of the desert's longtime favorites specializes in grilled and roasted entrées: spit-roasted garlic chicken, oak-fired thin-crust pizza, paella, and oven-roasted prawns. Huge reproductions of famous French Impressionist paintings cover the walls of this active bistro. ⊠ *73-101 Hwy. 111,* ☎ *760/773–9091. AE, D, DC, MC, V. No lunch.*

$$–$$$ ✕ **Ristorante Mamma Gina.** The greatest hits of Florence and Tuscany appear on the menu at this festive, upscale restaurant. The appetizers and salads are superb, but save room for pasta dishes or smartly

crafted chicken, veal, and fish dishes. The wine selection favors Italian and Californian vintages. ✉ *73-705 El Paseo,* ☎ *760/568–9898. Reservations essential in season. AE, DC, MC, V. No lunch. Summer hrs vary.*

$–$$$ ✕ **Bananaz Grill & Bar.** The energy at this large, boisterous eatery is exceedingly convivial. The food is cheap (for the area) and bountiful—husky sandwiches, entrée salads, roast chicken, and a dozen other options. The many TVs and frequent live entertainment will keep you amused while you dine. Bananaz becomes a nightclub after 10 nightly with live music and dancing. ✉ *72-291 Hwy. 111,* ☎ *760/776–4333. AE, D, MC, V.*

$–$$ ✕ **Daily Grill.** A combination upscale coffee shop and bar, the Daily Grill serves good salads (the Niçoise is particularly scrumptious), a fine gazpacho, zesty pasta dishes, and various blue-plate specials. The sidewalk terrace invites people-watching. Sunday brunch is a regular party. ✉ *73-061 El Paseo,* ☎ *760/779–9911. AE, DC, MC, V.*

$ ✕ **McGowan's Irish Inn.** Home-style comfort foods—meat loaf, chicken and dumplings, corned beef and cabbage, and beef stew—get the full Irish treatment at this family-owned restaurant with a full bar and sidewalk dining. The portions are beyond generous, and the service is good natured. ✉ *73-340 Hwy. 111,* ☎ *760/346–6032. MC, V. Closed Sun. June–Sept.*

PALM SPRINGS

$$$–$$$$ ✕ **Le Vallauris.** In a tasteful old home with a beautiful garden, Le Vallauris serves Californian-accented French cuisine—dishes such as grilled veal chop with porcini ravioli and grilled halibut with sun-dried-tomato crust and a lemon sauce. A pianist plays nightly. Sunday brunch is a hit with locals. ✉ *385 W. Tahquitz Canyon Way,* ☎ *760/325–5059. Reservations essential. AE, D, DC, MC, V. Closed Mon.–Tues. July–Aug. No lunch Wed.–Sat. July–Aug.*

$$–$$$ ✕ **Blue Coyote Grill.** Diners sit under blue umbrellas and munch on burritos, tacos, fajitas (or more unusual items, such as Yucatán lamb or orange chicken) at this casual restaurant that has several flower-decked patios in addition to inside dining rooms. Two busy cantinas serve up tasty margaritas to a youngish crowd. ✉ *445 N. Palm Canyon Dr.,* ☎ *760/327–1196. AE, DC, MC, V.*

$$–$$$ ✕ **Otani Garden Restaurant.** Sushi, tempura, and teppan (grilled) specialties are served in a serene garden setting at Otani. An always fresh Sunday brunch buffet includes tempura, stir-fried entrées, salads, sushi, and desserts. ✉ *266 Avenida Caballeros,* ☎ *760/327–6700. AE, D, DC, MC, V. No lunch Sat.*

$$–$$$ ✕ **Palmie.** The humble location in the back of a shopping arcade and
★ the simple decor of Toulouse-Lautrec and other Gallic posters give nary a hint of the subtle creations prepared at this gem of a French restaurant. The two-cheese soufflé is one of several mouthwatering appetizers. Equally impressive are the duck confit and duck fillets dish served with pear slices in red wine, and Palmie's signature entrée, a perfectly crafted fish stew in a thin-yet-rich butter-cream broth. ✉ *Galeria Henry Frank, 276 N. Palm Canyon Dr.,* ☎ *760/320–3375. AE, DC, MC, V. Closed Aug.–mid-Sept. No lunch.*

$$–$$$ ✕ **St. James at the Vineyard.** A multihued interior, an outdoor terrace with street views, and a bubbling modern fountain set a playful mood at this hot spot for dining and sipping smart cocktails. Pastas, chicken dishes, and curries are the menu mainstays. The service can be mildly chaotic on weekend nights in high season. ✉ *265 S. Palm Canyon Dr.,* ☎ *760/320–8041. Reservations essential. AE, D, DC, MC, V.*

$$ ✕ **Edgardo's Cafe Veracruz.** If you're hankering for Mexican dishes that eschew rice and beans and other staples of Sonoran cuisine, head to this high-spirited restaurant where the coastal Mexican fare includes treasured chicken, steak, and seafood recipes of the owner's family. The items for Sunday brunch are zestier than those at most places in the desert. ✉ *494 N. Palm Canyon Dr.,* ☎ *760/320–3558. Reservations essential. AE, D, DC, MC, V.*

$$–$$$ ✕ **Bangkok V.** Fresh flowers always adorn the tables at this attractively decorated Thai restaurant, where the food is prepared with sizzle (literally) and flair. Start with one of the spicy soups, followed by delicate wok-cooked catfish with garlic-cilantro sauce, or any of the curries. Make your level of comfort with spices known, or you may find yourself on fire. ✉ *69-930 Hwy. 111,* ☎ *760/770–9508. AE, D, DC, MC, V.*

$$–$$$ ✕ **Shame on the Moon.** Superior service and high-quality food at reasonable prices have made this restaurant a perennial desert favorite. The kitchen turns out consistently delicious Continental fare like roasted salmon with horseradish crust and calf's liver and onions with a bourbon glaze. The desserts are alluringly decadent. ✉ *69-950 Frank Sinatra Dr.,* ☎ *760/324–5515. Reservations essential. AE, MC, V. No lunch. Closed Aug.*

$$ ✕ **Las Casuelas Nuevas.** Hundreds of diverting artifacts from Guadalajara lend a festive charm to the dining room at this casual Mexican-style restaurant with a 100-seat garden patio. Tamales and shellfish dishes are among the specialties of the house. The margaritas will make you wish you'd brought your cha-cha heels. ✉ *70-050 Hwy. 111,* ☎ *760/328–8844. AE, D, MC, V.*

Lodging

$$$$ ⬚ **Hyatt Grand Champions Resort.** This stark white resort on 34 acres of natural desert hosts the *Newsweek* Champions and State Farm Evert Cup professional tennis tournaments. Suite-style rooms have balconies or terraces, sunken sitting areas, and minibars. The villas here may be the most luxurious accommodations in the desert. Resembling a private residence, each has a secluded garden courtyard with outdoor whirlpool tub, a living room with fireplace, a dining room, and a bedroom. A private butler awaits your commands. The pool area has been transformed into a garden water park surrounded by palms and private cabanas. ✉ *44-600 Indian Wells La., 92210,* ☎ *760/341–1000 or 800/233–1234,* ℻ *760/568–2236. 342 suites, 16 villas. 2 restaurants, bar, 5 pools, beauty salon, 3 outdoor hot tubs, massage, sauna, spa, steam room, driving range, 2 golf courses, putting green, 12 tennis courts, aerobics, health club, bicycles, pro shop, children's programs, laundry service, business services, convention center, meeting rooms. AE, D, DC, MC, V.*

$$$$ ⬚ **Renaissance Esmeralda Resort.** The centerpiece of this luxurious Mediterranean-style resort is an eight-story atrium lobby with a fountain that flows through a rivulet in the floor, into cascading pools, and outside to lakes surrounding the property. Given its size, the hotel has a surprisingly intimate ambience. Spacious guest rooms are decorated in light wood with desert-color accents. They have sitting areas, balconies, refreshment centers, two TV sets, and travertine-marble vanities in the bathrooms. One pool has a sandy beach. Golf and tennis instruction are available. ✉ *44-400 Indian Wells La., 92210,* ☎ *760/773–4444 or 800/408–3571,* ℻ *760/773–9250. 541 rooms, 19 suites. 2 restaurants, bar, snack bar, minibars, 3 pools, wading pool, 2 outdoor hot tubs, massage, sauna, spa, steam room, 2 golf courses, putting green, 4 tennis courts, basketball, health club, volleyball, bicycles, pro shop, coin laundry, concierge, meeting rooms. AE, D, DC, MC, V.*

$$$$ ⊞ **La Quinta Resort and Club.** The desert's oldest resort, opened in 1926,
★ is a lush green oasis. Rooms are in adobe casitas separated by broad
expanses of lawn and in newer two-story units surrounding individual swimming pools and brilliant gardens. Fireplaces, robes, stocked
refrigerators, and fruit-laden orange trees contribute to a discreet and
sparely luxurious atmosphere. A premium is placed on privacy, which
accounts for La Quinta's continuing popularity with Hollywood celebrities. Managed jointly with PGA West, La Quinta arranges access to
some of the desert's most celebrated golf courses. ⊠ *49-499 Eisenhower
Dr., 92253, ☎ 760/564–4111 or 800/598–3828, FAX 760/564–5768.
618 rooms, 22 suites. 5 restaurants, bar, 25 pools, spa, beauty salon,
38 outdoor hot tubs, 4 golf courses, 23 tennis courts, health club, children's programs, concierge, business services. AE, D, DC, MC, V.*

$$$–$$$$ ⊞ **Two Angels Inn.** This bed-and-breakfast occupies a somewhat
startling faux French chateau perched on the banks of a small lake.
Innkeepers Hap and Holly Harris offer luxurious accommodations. All
rooms have fireplaces, patios or balconies, and carefully selected an-
tique or contemporary furnishings. Two have private outdoor hot
tubs. ⊠ *78–120 Caleo Bay, 92253, ☎ 760/564–7332 or 888/226–4546,
FAX 760/564–6356. 11 rooms. Pool, outdoor hot tub. Full breakfast.
AE, D, MC, V.*

$$$$ ⊞ **Marriott's Desert Springs Resort and Spa.** This sprawling business-
and convention-oriented hotel has a dramatic U-shape design. The build-
ing wraps around the desert's largest private lake, into which an in-
door, stair-stepped waterfall flows. Rooms have lake or mountain
views, balconies, and oversize bathrooms. There are long walks from
the lobby to rooms; if driving, request one close to the parking lot. ⊠
*74-855 Country Club Dr., 92260, ☎ 760/341–2211 or 800/331–
3112, FAX 760/341–1872. 833 rooms, 51 suites. 5 restaurants, 2 bars,
snack bar, minibars, 5 pools, barbershop, beauty salon, 3 outdoor hot
tubs, spa, driving range, 2 golf courses, putting green, 20 tennis courts,
basketball, croquet, health club, jogging, volleyball, shops, children's
programs, laundry service, business services, convention center, car rental.
AE, D, DC, MC, V.*

$$–$$$ ⊞ **Tres Palmas Bed and Breakfast.** Enormous windows, high open-beam
ceilings, light wood, and textured peach tile floors lend this contem-
porary inn near El Paseo a bright and spacious feel. The Southwest-
ern decor in common areas and guest rooms (which are functional rather
than luxurious) incorporates old Navajo rugs from the innkeepers' col-
lection. ⊠ *73-135 Tumbleweed La., ☎ 760/773–9858 or 800/770–
9858, FAX 760/776–9159. 4 rooms. Pool, outdoor hot tub. Continen-
tal breakfast. AE, MC, V.*

$$$$ ⊞ **Hyatt Regency Suites.** This hotel's six-story asymmetrical atrium lobby
holds an enormous metal sculpture suspended from the ceiling. One-
and two-bedroom suites have private balconies and two TVs. The
suites in the back have pool and mountain views. There's free under-
ground parking, and guests have golf privileges at Rancho Mirage Coun-
try Club and four other area courses. ⊠ *285 N. Palm Canyon Dr., 92262,
☎ 760/322–9000 or 800/322–6009, FAX 760/325–4027. 192 suites. 3
restaurants, bar, pool, beauty salon, outdoor hot tub, spa, golf privi-
leges, exercise room, concierge, business services, meeting rooms, air-
port shuttle. AE, D, DC, MC, V.*

$$$$ ⊞ **Merv Griffin's Resort Hotel and Givenchy Spa.** Indulgence is the word
★ for this resort modeled after the Givenchy spa in Versailles. The am-
bience is totally French, from the Empire-style decor to the perfectly
manicured rose gardens. Many rooms are one- or two-bedroom suites,

with separate salons, some with private patios and mountain or garden views. Personalized spa services include everything from facials to marine mud wraps to aromatherapy. Restaurant menus emulate those found in Paris; spa cuisine is also offered. ⊠ *4200 E. Palm Canyon Dr., 92264,* ☎ *760/770–5000 or 800/276–5000,* ℻ *760/324–6104. 56 rooms, 37 suites. 2 restaurants, 2 pools, barbershop, beauty salon, spa, golf privileges, 6 tennis courts, health club, jogging, shops, concierge, business services, meeting rooms. AE, D, DC, MC, V.*

$$$$ ⊞ **Palm Springs Hilton Resort and Racquet Club.** The cool, white marble elegance of this plant-filled resort hotel off Palm Canyon Drive makes it a popular choice. Rooms have private balconies. ⊠ *400 E. Tahquitz Canyon Way, 92262,* ☎ *760/320–6868 or 800/522–6900,* ℻ *760/320–2126. 254 rooms, 6 suites. Restaurant, bar, pool, outdoor hot tub, golf privileges, 6 tennis courts, health club, tennis pro shop, video games, children's programs, concierge, business services. AE, D, DC, MC, V.*

$$$$ ⊞ **Sundance Villas.** Two- and three-bedroom duplex homes in this complex are decorated in soft desert colors. All have full kitchens, bathrooms with huge sunken tubs, outdoor pools and hot tubs, and laundry facilities. The villas are away from most desert attractions in a secluded residential area at the north end of Palm Springs. Rates, though high, are for up to six people. ⊠ *303 W. Cabrillo Rd., 92262,* ☎ *760/325–3888 or 800/455–3888,* ℻ *760/323–3029. 19 villas. In-room VCRs, pools, outdoor hot tub, golf privileges, tennis court, concierge. AE, D, DC, MC, V.*

$$$$ ⊞ **Willows Historic Palm Springs Inn.** This luxurious bed-and-break-
★ fast occupies a hillside that's within walking distance of many village attractions. An opulent mansion built in the 1920s, it features natural hardwood and slate floors, stone fireplaces, fresco ceilings, hand-painted tiles, iron balconies, and a 50-ft waterfall that splashes into a pool outside the dining room. Guest rooms are decorated to recall the movies of Hollywood's golden era of the 1930s. ⊠ *412 W. Tahquitz Canyon Way 92262,* ☎ *760/320–0771,* ℻ *760/320–0780. 8 rooms. Pool, outdoor hot tub. Full breakfast. AE, D, DC, MC, V.*

$$$–$$$$ ⊞ **Harlow Hotel.** A resort that caters to a gay clientele, this is ideal for those seeking secluded accommodations in a lush garden setting. Rooms are in hacienda-style buildings surrounding a pool; many have fireplaces, private patios, and unusually large bathrooms. Crimson bougainvillea cascades from the rooftops. Date palms grow on the property, as do fruit-laden orange, tangerine, and grapefruit trees. There's a secluded clothing-optional sunbathing area. The room rates include breakfast and lunch. ⊠ *175 E. El Alameda, 92262,* ☎ *760/323–3977 or 800/223–4073,* ℻ *760/320–1218. 14 rooms, 1 suite. Pool, outdoor hot tub, exercise room. Full breakfast and lunch. AE, D, DC, MC, V.*

$$$–$$$$ ⊞ **Spa Hotel and Casino.** Rooms at this hotel built over the original Agua Caliente springs are decorated in soft desert pinks and blues and light wood furniture. Not trendy or splashy, the Spa, which is owned by the Agua Caliente tribe, appeals to an older crowd that appreciates its soothing waters and downtown location. The hotel's Spa Experience is a sampling of services—sink into a tub filled with naturally hot mineral water, rest in the cool white relaxation room, swim in the outdoor mineral pool, or let the sauna warm your spirits. ⊠ *100 N. Indian Canyon Dr., 92262,* ☎ *760/325–1461 or 800/854–1279,* ℻ *760/ 325–3344. 220 rooms, 10 suites. 2 restaurants, 3 bars, 3 pools, barbershop, beauty salon, 2 outdoor hot tubs, spa, steam room, 18-hole golf course, tennis privileges, shops, casino, concierge, business services, meeting rooms. AE, D, DC, MC, V.*

$$$–$$$$ ⊞ **Wyndham Palm Springs.** The main appeal of this hotel is its location adjacent to the Palm Springs Convention Center. The terra-cotta Spanish-colonial building surrounds the largest swimming pool in

Palm Springs. Rooms are functional rather than glitzy. Because most of the Wyndham's customers are here on business, the atmosphere is more serious than at most desert establishments. ⊠ *888 Tahquitz Canyon Way, 92262,* ☎ *760/322–6000 or 800/822–4200,* FAX *760/322–5351. 252 rooms, 158 suites. Restaurant, bar, pool, wading pool, barbershop, beauty salon, 2 outdoor hot tubs, sauna, golf and tennis privileges, exercise room, shops, business services, convention center. AE, D, DC, MC, V.*

$$–$$$$ ⊞ **Ingleside Inn.** The hacienda-style Ingleside attracts its share of Hollywood personalities, who appreciate the attentive good service and relative seclusion. Many rooms have antiques, fireplaces, whirlpool tubs and steam showers, stocked refrigerators, and private patios. The accommodations in the main building are dark and cool, even in summer. The adjacent Melvyn's Restaurant, which serves Continental and American dishes, is popular locally. ⊠ *200 W. Ramon Rd., 92264,* ☎ *760/325–0046 or 800/772–6655,* FAX *760/325–0710. 30 rooms. Restaurant, bar, outdoor pool, outdoor hot tub, concierge. Continental breakfast. AE, D, DC, MC, V.*

$$–$$$ ⊞ **Casa Cody.** The service is personal and gracious at this Western-style B&B a few steps from the Palm Springs Desert Museum. Spacious studios and one- and two-bedroom suites are furnished simply. Some have fireplaces, and most have kitchens. In 1998, the owners opened an historic adobe on the property dating to 1910. ⊠ *175 S. Cahuilla Rd., 92262,* ☎ *760/320–9346 or 800/231–2639,* FAX *760/325–8610. 14 rooms, 8 suites. 2 pools, outdoor hot tub. Continental breakfast. AE, D, DC, MC, V.*

$$–$$$ ⊞ **Korakia Pensione.** This Moorish-style villa, built in the 1920s by Scottish artist Gordon Coutts, has long been a haven for the creative set. Winston Churchill came here to paint. More recently photographer Annie Leibovitz has enjoyed the villa's scenic mountain view. Inside, rooms are furnished with antiques, handmade furniture, and Oriental rugs; some have fireplaces, and many have kitchens. ⊠ *257 S. Patencio Rd., 92262,* ☎ *760/864–6411. 11 rooms, 9 suites. 2 pools. Continental breakfast. No credit cards. Closed mid-July–mid-Sept.*

$–$$$ ⊞ **Bee Charmer Inn.** This Southwestern-style inn with a red-tile roof and terra-cotta tile floors caters exclusively to women. Spacious rooms surround a pool and tropical courtyard; comfortably but not lavishly decorated in contemporary earth tones, they come with refrigerators and microwaves. Most rooms have wet bars, and one has a whirlpool bath. ⊠ *1600 E. Palm Canyon Dr., 92264,* ☎ *760/778–5883 or 888/321–5699,* FAX *760/416–2200. 13 rooms. Pool. Continental breakfast. AE, D, DC, MC, V.*

$$ ⊞ **Hampton Inn.** This chain motel at the north end of Palm Springs occupies landscaped grounds with views of Mount San Jacinto. Appointments are basic, but there are barbecues for guest use. ⊠ *200 N. Palm Canyon Dr., 92262,* ☎ *760/320–0555 or 800/732–7755,* FAX *760/320–2261. 96 rooms. Pool, outdoor hot tub, business services, meeting rooms. Continental breakfast. AE, D, DC, MC, V.*

$–$$ ⊞ **Howard Johnson Lodge.** This typical motel-style property is popular with tour groups. Ask about special discounts. ⊠ *701 E. Palm Canyon Dr., 92264,* ☎ *760/320–2700 or 800/854–4345,* FAX *760/320–1591. 204 rooms, 1 suite. Pool, 3 outdoor hot tubs, coin laundry, business services. AE, D, DC, MC, V.*

$–$$ ⊞ **Vagabond Inn.** Rooms are smallish at this centrally located motel but they're clean, comfortable, and a good value. ⊠ *1699 S. Palm Canyon Dr., 92264,* ☎ *760/325–7211 or 800/522–1555,* FAX *760/322–9269. 117 rooms, 3 suites. Coffee shop, pool, outdoor hot tub, 2 saunas. AE, D, MC, V.*

$$$$ 🏨 **Rancho Las Palmas Marriott Resort & Spa.** The atmosphere is lux-
★   uriously laid-back at this family-oriented resort on 240 landscaped acres.
A Spanish theme prevails throughout the public areas and guest accommodations. Rooms in a series of two-story buildings are unusually large; all have sitting areas, private balconies or patios, and views
of colorful gardens or well-manicured fairways and greens. A luxury
spa with 26 treatment rooms and a salon opened in early 1999. ⊠ *41-
000 Bob Hope Dr., 92270,* ☎ *760/568–2727 or 800/458–8786,* FAX
*760/568–5845. 450 rooms, 22 suites. 4 restaurants, bar, 2 snack bars,
3 pools, barbershop, beauty salon, 3 outdoor hot tubs, 27-hole golf
course, putting green, 25 tennis courts, health club, jogging, pro shop,
children's programs, playground, concierge, business services, convention center, car rental. AE, D, DC, MC, V.*

$$$$ 🏨 **Ritz-Carlton Rancho Mirage.** This hotel is tucked into a hillside in
★   the Santa Rosa Mountains with sweeping views of the valley below.
The surroundings are elegant, with gleaming marble and brass, original artwork, plush carpeting, and remarkable comfort. All rooms are
spacious and meticulously appointed with antiques, fabric wall coverings, marble bathrooms, and often two phones and two TVs. The
service is impeccable. ⊠ *68-900 Frank Sinatra Dr., 92270,* ☎ *760/321–
8282 or 800/241–3333,* FAX *760/321–6928. 219 rooms, 21 suites. 3
restaurants, bar, pool, barbershop, beauty salon, outdoor hot tub, spa,
golf privileges, 9-hole putting course, 10 tennis courts, basketball, croquet, health club, hiking, volleyball, pro shop, shops, children's programs, concierge, concierge floor, business services, meeting rooms. AE,
D, DC, MC, V.*

$$$$ 🏨 **Westin Mission Hills Resort.** A sprawling Moroccan-style resort on
360 acres, home to the Frank Sinatra Celebrity Golf Tournament, the
Westin is surrounded by fairways and putting greens. Rooms, in two-
story buildings that envelop patios and fountains, have soft desert colors, terra-cotta tile floors, and private patios or balconies. Paths and
creeks meander through the complex, encircling a lagoon-style swimming pool with a several-story water slide. ⊠ *71-333 Dinah Shore Dr.,
92270,* ☎ *760/328–5955 or 800/937–8161,* FAX *760/321–2607. 472
rooms, 40 suites. 2 restaurants, bar, 3 snack bars, 3 pools, beauty salon,
4 outdoor hot tubs, steam room, 2 18-hole golf courses, 7 tennis
courts, aerobics, croquet, health club, shuffleboard, volleyball, recreation room, children's programs. AE, D, DC, MC, V.*

Nightlife and the Arts

BARS AND CLUBS

Bananaz Grill and Bar (⊠ 72–291 Hwy. 111, Palm Desert, ☎ 760/
776–4333) has dancing nightly, live music on Sunday, a billiards room,
and a big-screen TV. **Blue Tattoo** (⊠ 42-250 Bob Hope Dr., Rancho
Mirage, ☎ 760/773–1111) draws a thirty- to fortysomething crowd
ready to party. There's live entertainment and dancing Wednesday
through Sunday. **C. C. Construction Company** (⊠ 67–399 E. Palm
Canyon Dr., Cathedral City, ☎ 760/778–1234), a popular gay club,
has a huge disco that is open from Friday through Sunday and a
smaller dance floor open nightly. **Peabody's Jazz Studio and Coffee
Bar** (⊠ 134 S. Palm Canyon Dr., Palm Springs, ☎ 760/322–1877) attracts everyone from grannies to grungers for live jazz. **Zelda's** (⊠ 169
N. Indian Canyon Dr., Palm Springs, ☎ 760/325–2375) has two
rooms, one featuring techno jazz and another with Top-40 dance
music and a male dance revue.

CASINOS

State law restricts Indian-run casinos from providing the type of action typically seen in Las Vegas, but they do have video slot machines

that pay off with a printed chit redeemable for cash, and various versions of poker, bingo, and lottery-type games. **Casino Morongo** (⊠ Cabazon off-ramp, I–10, west of Palm Springs, ☎ 800/252–4499). **Fantasy Springs Casino** (⊠ Auto Center Dr. off I–10, Indio, ☎ 760/342–5000). **Spa Casino** (⊠ 140 N. Indian Canyon Dr., Palm Springs, ☎ 760/323–5865). **Spotlight 29 Casino** (⊠ 46-200 Harrison Pl., Coachella, ☎ 760/775–5566).

FESTIVALS
The mid-January **Nortel Palm Springs International Film Festival** (☎ 760/322–2930) brings stars and more than 150 feature films from 25 countries, plus panel discussions, short films, and documentaries, to Palm Desert's McCallum Theatre and other venues. The **La Quinta Arts Festival** (☎ 760/564–1244), normally held the third weekend in March, includes some fine work, entertainment, and food.

THEATER
Annenberg Theater (⊠ Palm Springs Desert Museum, 101 Museum Dr., ☎ 760/325–4490) hosts Broadway shows, opera, lectures, Sunday-afternoon chamber concerts, and other events. **Fabulous Palm Springs Follies** (⊠ Plaza Theater, 128 S. Palm Canyon Dr., ☎ 760/327–0225), the hottest ticket in the desert, presents 10 sellout performances each week from November through May. The vaudeville-style revue stars extravagantly costumed, retired (but very much in shape) showgirls, singers, and dancers. Tickets are priced from $30 to $65. **McCallum Theatre** (⊠ 73-000 Fred Waring Dr., Palm Desert, ☎ 760/340–2787), the principal cultural venue in the desert, presents film, classical and popular music, opera, ballet, and theater.

Outdoor Activities and Sports
BICYCLING
Big Horn Bicycles (⊠ 302 N. Palm Canyon, Palm Springs, ☎ 760/325–3367) operates tours to celebrity homes and Indian Canyons and rents bikes. **Mac's Bicycle Rental** (⊠ 70-053 Hwy. 111, Rancho Mirage, ☎ 760/321–9444) will deliver mountain, three-speed, and tandem bikes to area hotels. **Palm Springs Recreation Department** (⊠ 401 S. Pavilion Way, ☎ 760/323–8272) has maps of some city trails.

FAMILY FUN
Camelot Park (⊠ 67-700 E. Palm Canyon Dr., Cathedral City, ☎ 760/770–7522) has miniature golf, bumper boats, batting cages, an arcade, and video games. **Oasis Waterpark** (⊠ 1500 Gene Autry Trail, Palm Springs, ☎ 760/327–0499), open from mid-March through October (weekends only after Labor Day), has 13 water slides, a huge wave pool, an arcade, and other attractions.

FITNESS
Gold's Gym (⊠ 4070 Airport Center Dr., Palm Springs, ☎ 760/322–4653; ⊠ 39-605 Entrepreneur La., Palm Desert, ☎ 760/360–0565).

GOLF
The **Bob Hope Desert Classic** takes place in late January and early February. The **Dinah Shore LPGA Championship** is a March or April event. Palm Springs hosts more than 100 golf tournaments annually. The Palm Springs Desert Resorts Convention and Visitors Bureau **Events Hotline** (☎ 760/770–1992) lists dates and locations.

Desert Princess Country Club & Resort (⊠ 28-555 Landau Blvd., Cathedral City, ☎ 760/322–1655) has an 18-hole, par-72 course and an additional 9 holes. Twenty-one lakes make most of the 27 holes challenging. The greens fees range from $30–$75 for 9 holes, and $45–$120 for 18 holes, depending upon the time of year.

Tahquitz Creek Palm Springs Golf Resort (✉ 1885 Golf Club Dr., Palm Springs, ☎ 760/328–1005) has two 18-hole, par-72 courses and a 50-space driving range. The greens fees, including cart, range from $50–$80, depending on the course and day of the week.

Tommy Jacobs' Bel-Aire Greens Country Club (✉ 1001 S. El Cielo Rd., Palm Springs, ☎ 760/322–6062) is a nine-hole executive course. The greens fee is $19 ($12 for replay).

PGA West (✉ 49-499 Eisenhower Dr., La Quinta, ☎ 760/564–7170) operates two 18-hole, par-72 championship courses and provides instruction and golf clinics. The greens fee ranges from $85 on weekdays in summer to $260 in February and March. The fee includes a mandatory cart.

Westin Mission Hills Resort Golf Club (✉ 71-501 Dinah Shore Dr., Rancho Mirage, ☎ 760/328–3198), an 18-hole, par-70 course designed by Pete Dye, hosts major tournaments and well-known politicians and movie stars. The greens fee is $175 during peak season, including a mandatory cart; off-season promotional packages during the summer are sometimes as low as $50. Gary Player designed the Westin's other links, an 18-hole, par-72 course where the greens fee ranges from $50 to $175 depending on when you play.

POLO

The **Eldorado Polo Club** (✉ 50-950 Madison St., Indio, ☎ 760/342–2223), known as the Winter Polo Capital of the West, is home to world-class polo events. You can pack a picnic and watch practice matches free during the week; there's a $6 per person charge on Sunday.

TENNIS

The *Newsweek* **Champions Cup** and **Evert Cup** professional tennis tournaments (☎ 760/340–3166) are held at the Hyatt Grand Champions Resort in Indian Wells for 10 days in March; they attract top-ranked players.

Demuth Park (✉ 4375 Mesquite Ave., ☎ no phone) has four lighted courts. **Palm Springs Tennis Center** (✉ 1300 E. Baristo Rd., ☎ 760/320–0020) has nine lighted courts—the fees run between $12 and $14. **Ruth Hardy Park** (✉ Tamarisk and Caballeros, ☎ no phone) has eight lighted courts.

Shopping

SHOPPING DISTRICTS

Palm Desert's **El Paseo,** a long, Mediterranean-style avenue with fountains and courtyards, contains French and Italian fashion boutiques, shoe salons, jewelry stores, children's shops, restaurants, a Saks Fifth Avenue branch, and nearly 30 galleries. Stores here are generally open from 10 to 6 Monday through Saturday; some close in summer. **Palm Desert Town Center** is the largest enclosed mall in the desert, with more than 140 specialty shops, major department stores, movie theaters, an ice-skating rink, and restaurants.

Palm Canyon Drive is the main shopping destination in the city of Palm Springs. Its commercial core extends from Alejo Road on the north to Ramon Road on the south. Anchoring the center of the drive is the **Palm Springs Promenade,** with a Saks Fifth Avenue and about 35 boutiques. The Village Fest, along Palm Canyon here on Thursday night, brings out craftspeople, antiques sellers, a farmers market, and entertainment.

Some of the items for sale in the **Heritage Gallery and Antique District,** a collection of consignment and secondhand shops centered in the 700 and 800 blocks of North Palm Canyon Drive in Palm Springs, come from the homes of celebrities and other wealthy residents.

Angel, Archer & Tigre Ltd. Estate Jewelers (73-655 El Paseo, Palm Desert, ☎ 760/341–1122) specializes in diamonds, antique engagement rings, and watches.

Celebrity Seconds (✉ 333 N. Palm Canyon Dr., Palm Springs, ☎ 760/416–2072) sells hot items like Ginger Rogers' private collection of gowns and jewelry, and dresses once worn by Julie Andrews and Elizabeth Taylor.

Classic Consignment Co. (✉ 73-847 El Paseo, Palm Desert, ☎ 760/568–4948) shows Baccarat crystal, barely used contemporary glass and Lucite furnishings, accessories, fine art, and jewelry. Prices match the shop's trendy location.

Estate Sale Co. (✉ 4185 E. Palm Canyon Dr., Palm Springs, ☎ 760/321–7628) is the biggest consignment store in the desert, with a warehouse of furniture, fine art, china and crystal, accessories, jewelry, movie memorabilia, and exercise equipment. Prices are set to keep merchandise moving.

The Village Emporium (✉ 849 N. Palm Canyon Dr., ☎ 760/320–6165) specializes in furniture and accessories from the 1960s and 1970s.

CLOTHING

Caroldean El Paseo/Caroldean Body & Sole (✉ 73-130 El Paseo, Palm Desert, ☎ 760/341–8982) features designer fashions and shoes by Vera Wang, Natalie M, and Brighton.

Nicole Miller Palm Desert (✉ 73-061 El Paseo, Palm Desert, ☎ 760/862–9242) carries a line of signature golf togs, plus funky ties, shirts, dresses, and accessories.

St. John Boutique (✉ 73-061 El Paseo, Palm Desert, ☎ 760/568–5900) offers the latest knit fashions from the famed designer.

DRIED FRUIT

Hadley's Fruit Orchards (✉ 48-190 Seminole Rd., Cabazon, ☎ 909/849–5255) sells dried fruit, nuts, date shakes, and wines.

Oasis Date Gardens (✉ 59-111 Hwy. 111, Thermal, ☎ 760/399–5665) sells shakes and conducts twice-a-day tours that show how dates are pollinated, grown, sorted, stored, and packed for shipping.

Shields Date Gardens (✉ 80-225 Hwy. 111, Indio, ☎ 760/347–0996) presents a continuous slide program on the history of the date and sells shakes.

FACTORY OUTLETS

Desert Hills Factory Stores (✉ 48-650 Seminole Rd., Cabazon, ☎ 909/849–6641) is an outlet center with more than 150 brand-name discount fashion shops, among them Polo, Giorgio Armani, Nike, and Spa Gear.

VINTAGE CLOTHING

Patsy's Clothes Closet (✉ 4121 E. Palm Canyon Dr., Palm Springs, ☎ 760/324–8825) specializes in high-fashion and designer clothing for women and men.

Side Trip to Joshua Tree National Park via Desert Hot Springs

Joshua Tree National Park in the Little San Bernardino Mountains preserves some of the desert's most interesting and beautiful scenery. For visitors it also provides a living example of the rigors of desert life. Highlights of rock formations, historic sites, and unusual plants can be seen in half a day. A more thorough expedition into the backcountry takes a day or more. There are campgrounds within the park, but no other accommodations (a few quaint lodgings can be found in the towns along the northern edge of the park). Desert Hot Springs, Joshua Tree, and Twentynine Palms are among the towns on the northern route to the park—Gene Autry Trail north from Palm Springs to Pierson Boulevard west in Desert Hot Springs to Highway 62. If you aren't going to visit Desert Hot Springs, you can take Interstate 10 northwest from Palm Springs to connect with Highway 62.

Desert Hot Springs

9 mi north of Palm Springs on Gene Autry Trail.

Known for its hot mineral springs, Desert Hot Springs is home to more than 40 spa resorts, ranging from tiny to large and offering a variety of exotic treatments.

LODGING

$$$-$$$$ ⊞ **Two Bunch Palms Resort and Spa.** This gate-guarded resort (you must call for advance reservations) is the most exclusive and romantic resort in the desert. According to legend, gangster Al Capone built the stone-fortress watchtower. The resort is the spa of choice for celebrities who savor the 148° mineral waters, the laid-back atmosphere, and the privacy. Massage styles include Swedish, Japanese, and Native American. The landscaped grounds contain two rock-grotto mineral pools surrounded by palms, secluded picnic areas, meditation benches, and outdoor mud baths. Accommodations range from hotel-style rooms to luxury villas with living rooms, kitchens, private whirlpool tubs, and private patios. ⊠ *67–425 Two Bunch Palms Trail, 92240,* ☎ *760/329–8791 or 800/472–4334,* 𝖥𝖠𝖷 *760/329–1874. 19 rooms, 26 suites. Restaurant, bar, 2 pools, spa, 2 tennis courts, health club, hiking. Continental breakfast. AE, MC, V.*

OFF THE BEATEN PATH

BIG MORONGO CANYON PRESERVE – Once an Indian village and later a cattle ranch, this serene natural oasis contains a year-round stream and waterfalls that support a variety of birds and animals. Cottonwoods and willows line a stream favored by great horned owls and many songbirds. A shaded meadow is a fine place for a picnic, and hiking options include several choice trails. No pets are permitted. ⊠ *East Dr., Morongo Valley,* ☎ *760/363–7190.* 🖭 *Free.* ☉ *Daily 7:30 AM–sunset.*

Joshua Tree

17 mi from Desert Hot Springs, north and east on Hwy. 62.

Primarily a gateway to the national park, the town of Joshua Tree has basic services, a few fast-food outlets, and one lodging of note.

LODGING

$$-$$$ ⊞ **Joshua Tree Inn.** If these walls could talk: this 1950s-style B&B was a motel popular with rock stars in the 1970s and early 1980s. The building's cinder-block construction is still visible, but there's a nice garden and a pool. ⊠ *61259 29 Palms Hwy., 92252,* ☎ *760/366–1188,* 𝖥𝖠𝖷 *760/366–3805. 10 rooms, 2 suites. In-room modem lines, pool. Full breakfast. AE, DC, MC, V.*

Twentynine Palms

11 mi east of Joshua Tree on Hwy. 62, 56 mi from Palm Springs, northwest on I–10 and north and east on Hwy. 62.

Colorful outdoor murals depicting local history are among the ways this onetime liberty town for U.S. Marines is trying to lure visitors headed to Joshua Tree National Park.

LODGING

$–$$$$ ☒ **29 Palms Inn.** The funky 29 Palms, on the Oasis of Mara (☞ Joshua Tree National Park, *below*), comprises a collection of adobe and wood-frame cottages scattered about 70 acres. The contemporary fare at the inn's popular restaurant is more sophisticated than its Western ambience. ⊠ *73950 Inn Ave., 92277,* ☎ *760/367–3505,* FAX *760/367–4425. 15 rooms, 4 suites. Restaurant, pool, hot tub. Continental breakfast. AE, D, DC, MC, V.*

$$–$$$ ☒ **Homestead Inn.** An authentic throwback to the old days in the desert, the Homestead is run by a salt-of-the-earth innkeeper who has a flock of roadrunners as pets. The rooms are comfortable, but not particularly stylish; a couple have their original tile work and fixtures. Three have refrigerators, phones, TV/VCRs, microwaves, and private patios. ⊠ *74153 Two Mile Rd., 92277,* ☎ *760/367–0030,* FAX *760/367–1108. 7 rooms. Full breakfast. No smoking. AE, D, MC, V. Closed early July–Sept.*

$$ ☒ **Roughley Manor.** No expense was spared by the wealthy pioneer who erected the stone mansion occupied by this B&B. A 50-ft-long planked maple floor is the centerpiece of the great room, the carpentry on the walls throughout is intricate, and huge stone fireplaces warm the house on the rare cold night. Original fixtures still gleam in the bathrooms, and the elegant bedrooms are furnished with pencil and canopied beds. An acre or so of gardens shaded by Washingtonia palms surrounds the house. ⊠ *74744 Joe Davis Dr., 92277,* ☎ *760/367–3238,* FAX *760/367–4483. 2 rooms with baths, 5 rooms share 2 baths, 2 suites with baths. Hot tub. Full breakfast. No smoking indoors. AE, MC, V.*

$–$$ ☒ **Best Western Gardens Motel.** This bright complex has smartly furnished rooms, some of which have coffeemakers, refrigerators, and microwaves. ⊠ *71-487 Twentynine Palms Hwy., 92277,* ☎ *760/367–9141,* FAX *760/367–2584. 72 rooms, 12 suites. Pool, hot tub, laundry service. Continental breakfast. AE, D, DC, MC, V.*

Joshua Tree National Park

★ ❿   *61 mi from Palm Springs, northwest on I–10, north and east on Hwy. 62 to the town of Joshua Tree; from here head southeast on Park Blvd. to the park's west entrance or continue east on Hwy. 62 to Twentynine Palms and follow signs to Utah Trail and the north entrance.*

The 794,000-acre Joshua Tree National Park contains complex, ruggedly beautiful scenery. Its mountains of jagged rock, natural cactus gardens, and lush oases shaded by tall fan palms mark the meeting place of the Mojave (high) and Colorado (low) deserts. This is prime hiking, rock climbing, and exploring country, where coyotes, desert pack rats, and exotic plants, such as the creamy white yucca, red-tipped ocotillo, and cholla cactus, reside. Extensive stands of Joshua trees give the park its name. The trees were named by early white settlers who felt their unusual forms resembled the biblical Joshua raising his arms toward heaven.

Portions of the park can be seen in a half-day excursion from desert-resort cities. A full day's driving tour would reveal highlights and allow time for a nature walk or two and stops at many of the 50 wayside exhibits, which provide insight into Joshua Tree's geology and rich vegetation. Some of the park is above 4,000 ft so it can be chilly in winter. There are no services within the park and little water. Visitors are advised to carry a gallon of water per person per day.

Those planning a half-day visit to Joshua Tree National Park should enter through the West Entrance Station off Highway 62 at Joshua Tree and follow the Park Boulevard loop road to the North Entrance Station near Twentynine Palms, backtracking to the resort cities via Highway 62. The stands of Joshua trees along this route are particularly alluring in spring, when the upraised branches support creamy white blossoms. The many piles of rocks in this section are fun to explore and climb.

Those planning to spend a full day in the park can proceed through the west entrance, explore the northern loop, stop at the Oasis Visitor Center, and then take the stunning but winding desert drive southward toward the Cottonwood Springs area, which in springtime has one of the desert's best displays of wildflowers. The Cottonwood Visitor Center has a small museum, picnic tables, water, and a 1-mi interpretive trail to the **Cottonwood Spring Oasis**, which gets very crowded in spring.

The **Oasis Visitor Center** (⊠ Utah Trail, ½ mi south of Hwy. 62) has many free and inexpensive brochures, books, posters, and maps as well as several educational exhibits. Rangers are on hand to answer questions. **Oasis of Mara** (a ½-mi walk from the visitor center), inhabited first by Native Americans and later by prospectors and homesteaders, now provides a home for birds, small mammals, and other wildlife.

A crawl through the big boulders that block **Hidden Valley,** once a cattle rustlers' hideout, reveals a bit of the wild and woolly human history of Joshua Tree. The 1¹⁄₁₀-mi loop trail from Hidden Valley to **Barker Dam** goes past petroglyphs (painted over by a film crew) on the way to a dam built by early ranchers and miners; today the dam collects rainwater and is used by wildlife.

Keys View is the most dramatic overlook in Joshua Tree National Park. At elevation 5,185 ft, the view extends across the desert to Mount San Jacinto and on clear days as far south as the Salton Sea. Sunrise and sunset are magical times, when the light throws rocks and trees into high relief before (or after) bathing the hills in brilliant shades of red, orange, and gold.

Geology Tour Road, recommended for four-wheel-drive vehicles, is a self-guided 18-mi dirt road that winds through some of the park's most fascinating landscape.

At the **Cholla Cactus Gardens,** a huge stand of the legendary "jumping cactus," a short trail interprets the wildlife and plants typical of the Colorado Desert.

If you're entering the park from the south, you'll pass the Cottonwood Visitor Center a few miles after you exit Interstate 10 (head north) east of the town of Mecca. The center has a small museum, picnic tables, water, rest rooms, and a 1-mi interpretative trail to the **Cottonwood Spring Oasis.**

⊠ *Joshua Tree National Park, 74-485 National Park Dr., Twentynine Palms 92277,* ☎ *760/367–5500.* ☞ *$10 per car; $5 for those who arrive by other means.* ☉ *Visitor centers daily 8–4:30, park 24 hrs.*

PALM SPRINGS A TO Z

Arriving and Departing

By Bus
Greyhound (☎ 800/231–2222) provides service to the Palm Springs Depot (✉ 311 N. Indian Canyon Dr., ☎ 760/325–2053).

By Car
Palm Springs is about a two-hour drive east of Los Angeles and a three-hour drive northeast of San Diego. Highway 111 brings you right onto Palm Canyon Drive, the main thoroughfare in Palm Springs and the connecting route to other desert communities. From Los Angeles take the San Bernardino Freeway (I–10) east to Highway 111. From San Diego, I–15 heading north connects with the Pomona Freeway (Highway 60), leading to the San Bernardino Freeway (I–10) east. An alternative, more scenic, good-weather route from San Diego begins east on I–8. Then take Highways 67, 78, and 79 north to Aguanga, where Highway 371 heads east to Highway 74 (Palms to Pines Highway), which joins Highway 111 between Palm Desert and Indian Wells. Desert exits are clearly marked: Highway 111 for Palm Springs, Monterey for Palm Desert, Washington for La Quinta. If you're coming from the Riverside area, you can also take Highway 74 east.

By Plane
Major airlines serving **Palm Springs Regional Airport** (☎ 760/323–8161) include Alaska, American/American Eagle, America West/America West Express, Northwest, United/United Express, and US Airways Express. *See* Air Travel *in* Smart Travel Tips A to Z for airline phone numbers. Most hotels provide service to and from the airport, which is about 2 mi from downtown Palm Springs.

By Train
The **Amtrak** (☎ 800/872–7245) *Sunset Limited,* which runs between Florida and Los Angeles, stops in Palm Springs and Indio.

Getting Around

By Bus
SunBus, operated by the Sunline Transit Agency (☎ 760/343–3451), serves the entire Coachella Valley from Desert Hot Springs to Mecca.

By Car
The desert-resort communities occupy a stretch of about 20 mi between Interstate 10 in the east and Palm Canyon Drive in the west. Although some areas such as Palm Canyon Drive in Palm Springs and El Paseo are walkable, having a car is the best way to get around.

By Taxi
California Cab (☎ 760/772–1793) serves the Coachella Valley and Los Angeles and Ontario International airports. **A Valley Cabousine** (☎ 760/340–5845) serves the Coachella Valley.

Contacts and Resources

Car Rental
Most major car-rental companies are represented in the Palm Springs area (☞ Car Rental *in* Smart Travel Tips A to Z).

Emergencies
Ambulance (☎ 911). **Police** (☎ 911).

Desert Regional Medical Center (☎ 760/323–6511).

Guided Tours

AERIAL TOURS

Fantasy Balloon Flights (☎ 760/398–6322) organizes trips in the Coachella Valley. **Sunrise Balloons** (☎ 800/548–9912) has balloon excursions in the desert.

CELEBRITY TOURS

Palm Springs Celebrity Tours (✉ 4751 E. Palm Canyon Dr., Palm Springs, ☎ 760/770–2700) has hour-long and 2½-hour tours that cover Palm Springs area history, points of interest, and celebrity homes. Prices range from $17 to $20.

DESERT TOURS

Covered Wagon Tours (☎ 760/347–2161) takes visitors on an old-time, two-hour exploration of the desert with a cookout at the end of the journey. **Desert Adventures** (☎ 760/324–5337) takes to the wilds with Jeep tours of Indian canyons, off-road in the Santa Rosa Mountains, and into a mystery canyon. **Desert Safari Guides** (✉ Box 194, Rancho Mirage, ☎ 760/776–6087 or 888/867–2327) leads tours of various lengths through Indian Canyons and conducts nighttime full-moon desert excursions.

Vacation Rentals

McLean Company Rentals (✉ 477 S. Palm Canyon Dr., Palm Springs 92262, ☎ 800/777–4606). **Rental Connection** (✉ 170 E. Palm Canyon Dr., Palm Springs 92263, ☎ 760/320–7336 or 800/462–7256). **Sunrise Co.** (✉ 76-300 Country Club Dr., Palm Desert 92211, ☎ 800/869–1130).

Visitor Information

Palm Springs Desert Resorts (✉ 69-930 Hwy. 111, Suite 201, Rancho Mirage 92270, ☎ 760/770–9000 or 800/967–3767; 760/770–1992 Activities Hotline). **Palm Springs Visitor Information Center** (✉ 2781 N. Palm Canyon Dr., Palm Springs 92262, ☎ 800/347–7746).

15 THE MOJAVE DESERT AND DEATH VALLEY

When most people assemble their "must-see" list of California attractions, the desert isn't often among the top contenders. With its heat and vast, sparsely populated tracts of land, the desert is no Disneyland. But that's precisely why it deserves a closer look. The natural riches here are overwhelming: rolling waves of sand dunes, black cinder cones thrusting up hundreds of feet from a blistered desert floor, riotous sheets of wildflowers, bizarrely shaped Joshua trees basking in the orange glow of a sunset, and an abundant silence that is both dramatic and startling.

THE MOJAVE DESERT begins at the base of the San Bernardino Mountains, northeast of Los Angeles, and extends north 150 mi into the Eureka Valley and east 200 mi to the Colorado River. Death Valley lies north and east of the Mojave, jutting into Nevada near Beatty. The Mojave, with elevations ranging from 3,000 to 5,000 ft above sea level, is known as the High Desert. Death Valley, the Low Desert, drops to almost 300 ft below sea level and contains the lowest spot on land in the Western Hemisphere.

Updated by
Sasha
Abramsky

Because of the vast size of California's deserts, an area about as big as Ohio, and the frequently extreme weather, careful planning is essential. Conveniences, facilities, trails, gas stations, and supermarkets do not lurk around the corner from many desert sights. Be sure to fill your tank before entering Death Valley. Fuel is cheaper on the interstates. Also, check your vehicle's fluids and tire pressure. Shut off your air-conditioning on steep grades to avoid engine overheating.

Believe everything you've ever heard about desert heat. It can be brutal. But during mornings and evenings, particularly in the spring and fall, the temperature ranges from cool and crisp to pleasantly warm and dry. Bring sunglasses, a hat, and sufficient clothing to block the sun's rays or the wind. Reliable maps are a must, as signage is limited and, in some places, nonexistent. Other important accessories include a compass, a cellular phone (though these don't always work in remote areas), extra food and water (three gallons per person per day is recommended, plus additional radiator water). A pair of binoculars can come in handy, and don't forget your camera. You're likely to see things you've never seen before.

Pleasures and Pastimes

Camping
Because vegetation in the desert is sparse, campers are truly one with the elements, including the hot sun. Bring equipment that can handle extreme temperatures. Campgrounds are inexpensive or free. Most sites are primitive.

Dining
The restaurants in Death Valley range from a coffee shop to an upscale Continental restaurant. There are fast-food and chain establishments in Ridgecrest, Victorville, and Barstow, as well as some ethnic eateries. Experienced desert travelers carry an ice chest stocked with food and beverages. Replenish your food stash in the larger towns of Ridgecrest and Barstow, where you'll find a better selection and nontourist prices.

CATEGORY	COST*
$$$$	over $40
$$$	$30–$40
$$	$20–$30
$	under $20
*per person for a three-course meal, excluding drinks, service, and tax	

Hiking
Hiking trails are abundant throughout the desert and meander toward sights that would be missed from the road. Plan your walks for before or after the noonday sun, bring protective clothing, and be wary of tarantulas, snakes, and other potentially hazardous creatures. (If you wear closed shoes and watch where you're walking, these shouldn't

be a problem). Paths through canyons are sometimes partially shielded from the sun and not as hot, so if your time is limited, save these for midday. Some of the best trails are unmarked. Ask locals for directions.

Lodging

Larger towns such as Barstow seem to have a motel on every corner, but there are only three places to sleep indoors in all of Death Valley; the cheapest is in Stovepipe Wells Village. Those preferring quiet nights and an unfettered view of the desert sky and Mosaic Canyon will enjoy Stovepipe. Families with children may prefer the Furnace Creek end of Death Valley, where there's easy access to the visitor center and various sights.

CATEGORY	COST*
$$$$	over $200
$$$	$125–$200
$$	$75–$125
$	under $75
*All prices are for a standard double room, excluding tax.	

Exploring the Desert

The Mojave Desert is a sprawling space, but many of its visitable attractions are conveniently situated on a north–south axis along U.S. 395 and Highway 178. The western Mojave region has Ridgecrest (on U.S. 395) as its major northern hub and Victorville (on I–15) as its southern one. If you plan to stop overnight en route to Death Valley, both Ridgecrest and Lone Pine have tourist services and accommodations, as do Barstow and Baker on I–15. The bulk of the eastern Mojave lies between the parallel routes of I–15 and I–40. Barstow, at the junction of the two interstates, is the region's western hub. Needles, at the intersection of I–40 and U.S. 95, has the most services on the eastern side. You may spot fossils at some of the archaeological sites in the desert. Leave any fossils you find where they are; it's against the law to remove them.

Numbers in the text correspond to numbers in the margin and on the Mojave Desert and Death Valley maps.

Great Itineraries

IF YOU HAVE 3 DAYS

Well-preserved Randsburg, part of the **Rand Mining District** ②, is a good starting point from either San Francisco or Los Angeles. Pack a picnic lunch and drive through colorful **Red Rock Canyon State Park** ③ and take a walk among the volcanic rock formations of **Fossil Falls** ④ before moving on to 🔢 **Ridgecrest** ⑤ for a stop at the Maturango Museum. Have dinner and spend the night in Ridgecrest. The following day, see the surreal **Trona Pinnacles** ⑥, and then continue on to the 🔢 **Furnace Creek** ⑪ visitor center before catching awe-inspiring perspectives of the Death Valley region from **Artists Palette** ⑭, **Zabriskie Point** ⑮, and **Dante's View** ⑯. Return home on the third day after stopping at the **Harmony Borax Works** ⑩, where the famed 20-mule teams once toiled, and hiking through **Golden Canyon** ⑫.

IF YOU HAVE 6 OR 7 DAYS

If you're already in southern California, head to the **Western Mojave Desert,** touring the **Rand Mining District** ②, **Red Rock Canyon** ③, and **Fossil Falls** ④ before stopping in 🔢 **Ridgecrest** ⑤ to dine and lodge. (If you're coming from northern California, visit Fossil Falls first and stop briefly at the Maturango Museum in Ridgecrest before driving to Red Rock Canyon and the Rand Mining District.) On your second day, visit the **Bureau of Land Management Regional Wild Horse and Burro Cor-**

rals on the way to the **Trona Pinnacles** ⑥ and Death Valley's ⌂ **Stovepipe Wells Village** ⑦. (If you're visiting on a spring or fall weekend, make advance arrangements at the Maturango Museum to tour the **Petroglyph Canyons** on day two.) On the third morning, stroll through **Mosaic Canyon** before driving north to spend a full day at **Scotty's Castle** ⑧ and **Ubehebe Crater** ⑨. Loop back toward ⌂ **Furnace Creek** ⑪ and stop in at the visitor center in the late afternoon. If you're in the area on a performance day, zip down to Death Valley Junction to see the 7:45 PM show at **Marta Becket's Amargosa Opera House** ⑱. On day four, hike through **Golden Canyon** ⑫ and drive to **Badwater** ⑬ before returning via **Artists Palette** ⑭. Visit the lookout at **Zabriskie Point** ⑮ and walk along **Dante's View** ⑯ before driving south to ⌂ **Baker** ⑲. Use Baker as your fifth-day base. Drive along Kelbaker Road to the **Kelso Dunes** ⑳ and visit the **Mitchell Caverns** in **Providence Mountains State Recreation Area** ㉑. If time and road conditions permit, drive through **Afton Canyon** ㉒ before staying overnight in ⌂ **Barstow** ㉓. On day six, hike around the **Rainbow Basin National Natural Landmark** ㉔ and tour the **Calico Early Man Archeological Site** ㉖ (open from Wednesday through Sunday; the last tour starts at 3:30). On day seven, especially if you have kids, visit **Calico Ghost Town** ㉕ before leaving the desert.

When to Tour the Mojave Desert and Death Valley

Spring and fall are the best seasons to tour the desert. Winters are generally mild, but summers can be brutal. If you're on a budget, keep in mind that room rates drop as the temperatures rise. Early morning is the best time to visit sights and avoid crowds, but some museums and visitor centers don't open until 10. If you schedule your town arrivals for late afternoon, you can drop by the visitor centers just before closing hours to line up an itinerary for the next day. It's best to visit the Rand Mining District on the weekend or, if you must come during the week, in the afternoon, when some of the antiques shops open up. Plan indoor activities for midday during hot months. Because relatively few people visit the desert, many attractions have limited hours of access: Petroglyph Canyon tours are given on weekends only during fall and spring, the Calico Early Man Archeological Site does not offer tours Monday and Tuesday, and so on.

THE WESTERN MOJAVE

The prime western Mojave attractions are along or near U.S. 395 or Highways 14 and 178. The key sights after the San Andreas Fault are listed clockwise, heading north and west from Randsburg, looping around eastward to the Trona Pinnacles.

❶ The infamous **San Andreas Fault** traverses the desert near Cajon Pass, a few miles south of I–15's U.S. 395 exit. If you're driving from Los Angeles, it's an apocalyptic way to start a desert trip.

Rand Mining District

❷ *137 mi northeast of Los Angeles, I–10 to I–15 to U.S. 395; 360 mi southeast of San Francisco, I–80 to I–580 to I–5 to Hwy. 178 to Hwy. 14 to U.S. 395.*

The towns of Randsburg, Red Mountain, and Johannesburg make up the Rand Mining District. **Randsburg** first boomed with the discovery of gold in the Rand Mountains in 1895 and, along with the neighboring settlements, grew to support the successful Yellow Aster Mine. Rich tungsten ore, used in World War I to make steel alloy, was discovered in 1907, and silver was found in 1919. Randsburg is one of the few

Mojave Desert

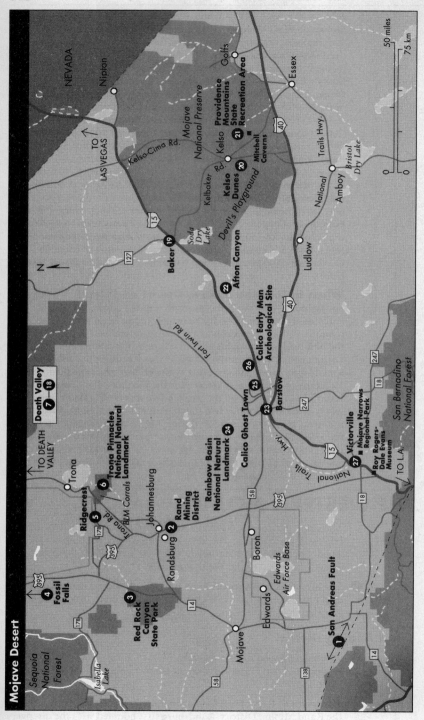

gold-rush-era communities not to have become a ghost town; the former city jail is among the original buildings still standing. The small **Desert Museum** (✉ 161 Butte Ave., ☎ no phone) exhibits old mining paraphernalia and historic photos. Staffed by volunteers, it's open only on weekends and holidays, usually from late morning until midafternoon. **The Randsburg General Store** (✉ 35 Butte Ave., ☎ 760/374–2418) serves as the town's informal visitor center, selling maps and rockhounding guides. It's open daily, unlike most of the town's dozen antiques shops, which tend to be shuttered during the week (though sometimes they open in the afternoon).

Johannesburg was founded as a slightly upmarket suburb of the rough gold-mining town of Randsburg. These days it's very ghostly, the spirits dwelling in the stunning Old West **cemetery** in the hills above town. It's one of the region's great hidden treasures.

Dining and Lodging

$ ✕ **Randsburg Opera House Café.** A very small diner in a very small town, this old wooden café is the meeting place for locals. Standard breakfast fare and a skimpy selection of burgers and sandwiches are about it here, but the staff is friendly. The only other option in town is the saloon opposite the general store. ✉ *26741 Butte Ave., Randsburg* ☎ *760/374–1037. No credit cards. No dinner.*

$ 🏠 **The Cottage Hotel.** An unexpectedly civilized lodging in rough-and-tumble Randsburg, this B&B resulted from a painstaking makeover of the boom-time hotel for which it was named. You enter through an antiques shop to rooms done in Victorian style but with TVs and modern bathrooms. Two rooms have balconies. A back garden and a cedar-lined room with a hot tub are bonuses. The housekeeping cottage next door has a kitchen; breakfast isn't included for its occupants as it is for the B&B guests. ✉ *130 Butte Ave., Randsburg, 93554,* ☎ *760/374–2285 or 888/268–4622, FAX 760/374–2132. 4 rooms, 1 cottage. Hot tub, meeting room. Full breakfast. AE, D, MC, V.*

$ 🏠 **HI-Death Valley Hostel.** You don't need a reservation at this basic ranch-style hostel. There are separate dorm-style quarters for men and women, a kitchen (fresh food is available for purchase), a dining area, and a common room with many books on the desert. You can rent a bicycle, or sign up for one of many free tours of the region. Manager Michelle Mowey is a great desert character who loves to take her young charges on tours of the surrounding wilderness. ✉ *301 Hwy. 395, Box 277, Johannesburg, 93528,* ☎ *FAX 760/374–2323. 2 dorm rooms, 1 private room, shared baths. No credit cards.*

$ 🏠 **Old Owl Inn.** This onetime whorehouse sits off Highway 395, surrounded by old mines. The antiques shop attached to it still has a "Girl Wanted" sign on one wall and the keys to the brothel cubicles on another. In these tamer times, Lynn and Jeannie Walker run the inn as a two-cabin bed-and-breakfast. The larger cabin, made of the original wood used by the old owner, can hold up to seven people. The smaller is slightly optimistically named the Honeymoon Cottage. Both have small, functional bathrooms. Jeannie's grandfather came to the area in 1910 to dig for gold, and today she's a terrific font of information on the area. Ask her to point out unmarked trails into the hills. ✉ *701 Hwy. 395, Red Mountain 93558,* ☎ *760/374–2235 or 888/653–6954, FAX 760/374–2354. 2 cabins. D, MC, V.*

Red Rock Canyon State Park

❸ *17 mi west of U.S. 395 via Red Rock–Randsburg Rd.*

A feast for the eyes with its layers of pink, white, red, rust, and brown rocks, **Red Rock Canyon State Park** is a region of fascinating biological diversity—the ecosystems of the Sierra Nevada, the Mojave Desert, and the Basin Range all converge here. Entering the park from the south, you'll pass through a steep-walled gorge and come to a wide bowl tinted pink by what was once hot volcanic ash. The human history of this area goes back 20,000 years to the canyon dwellers known as the Old People; Mojave Indians roamed the land for centuries. Gold-rush fever hit the region in the 1800s. You can still see remains of mining operations in the countryside. In the 20th century, Hollywood invaded the canyon, which has been seen in westerns, TV shows, ads, and music videos. Its greatest claim to fame is as a backdrop in Steven Spielberg's *Jurassic Park.* ⊠ *Ranger station: Abbott Dr. off Hwy. 14,* ☎ *805/942–0662.* 🎫 *$5 (day use).* ⊙ *Year-round; visitor center weekends only.*

Camping

🏕 **Red Rock Canyon State Park.** The park's campground is in the colorful cliff region of the southern El Paso Mountains, which offer many hiking options. ⊠ *Off Hwy. 14, 30 mi southwest of Ridgecrest,* ☎ *805/942–0662 for reservations. 50 sites. Fire pits, pit toilets, water.* 🎫 *$10, $1 additional for dogs.* ⊙ *Year-round.*

En Route   Heading north from Red Rock Canyon on U.S. 395 toward Fossil Falls you'll pass **Little Lake,** a good place to view migrating waterfowl in the spring and fall—ducks, geese, perhaps even pelicans. The area north of the lake is often covered with wildflowers. As you pass the lake, a red cinder cone known as **Red Hill** comes into view. The hill, a small volcano that was last active about 10,000 years ago, is now being mined.

Fossil Falls

❹ *Off U.S. 395, 20 mi north of U.S. 395/Hwy. 14 junction.*

The stark, roughly hewn, mostly black basalt rocks at **Fossil Falls** (⊠ Cinder Cone Rd., ½ mi east of U.S. 395) are the result of volcanic eruptions in the western Mojave region about 20,000 years ago. The fossils at Fossil Falls are the falls themselves—their sources dried up centuries ago. The only time you'll see water is when it's raining. A study in shape and texture, the falls drop off an impressive distance along a channel cut by the Owens River through hardened lava flows. A brief hike leads to the bottom of the formation; Native Americans camped along the streams here. South of the falls, the Owens River cut the huge valley between the Sierra Nevada range to the west and the Coso Range to the east. There's a very primitive **campsite** amid the boulders.

Ridgecrest

❺ *35 mi north of Randsburg, U.S. 395 to Hwy. 178.*

Ridgecrest, with stores and dining and lodging options, is a good base for exploring the northwestern Mojave.

The **Maturango Museum,** which also serves as a visitor information center, has pamphlets and books about the northern Mojave and Death Valley—the sights, history, flora, and fauna. Small but informative exhibits detail the natural and cultural history of the northern Mojave. The museum runs wildflower tours in March and April. ⊠ *100 E. Las Flores Ave., at China Lake Blvd., 93555,* ☎ *760/375–6900,* FAX *760/375–0479.* 🎫 *$2; $5 for wildflower tour.* ⊙ *Daily 10–5.*

On weekends in the spring and fall, the Maturango Museum arranges
★   the only tours to the **Petroglyph Canyons,** among the desert's most amazing spectacles. (Call several months ahead; space is limited on these full-day excursions.) The two canyons, commonly called Big and Lit-

tle Petroglyph, are in the Coso mountain range on the million-acre U.S. Naval Weapons Center at China Lake, which allows only limited access. Each of the canyons holds a superlative concentration of rock art, the largest of its kind in the Northern Hemisphere. Thousands of images of animals and humans are scratched or pecked into the shiny desert varnish—oxidized minerals—that coats the canyon's dark basaltic rocks. The age of these well-preserved glyphs remains a matter of debate. ☎ 760/375–6900. ☞ *$20, children under 10 not admitted; $40 for less regular extended trips for photographers and others who want to see sunrise and sunset in the Little Petroglyph Canyon.* ⊘ *Tours Mar.– June and Sept. or Oct.–1st weekend in Dec.*

OFF THE BEATEN PATH

BUREAU OF LAND MANAGEMENT REGIONAL WILD HORSE AND BURRO CORRALS – Animals gathered from public lands throughout the Southwest are fed and prepared for adoption here. It's OK to feed the animals, so bring along an apple or a carrot to share with the horses (the burros are usually too wild to approach). ⊠ *3 mi east of Ridgecrest via Hwy. 178 (make a right turn as the road reaches the top of the rise),* ☎ *760/446– 6064 to arrange tours.* ☞ *Free.* ⊘ *Weekdays 7:30–4.*

⑥ **Trona Pinnacles National Natural Landmark** is not easy to reach. The best road to the area can be impassable after a rainstorm. But it's worth the effort, especially to sci-fi buffs, who will recognize the pinnacles from the film *Star Trek V.* These fantastic looking formations of calcium carbonate, known as tufa, were formed underwater along fault lines in the bed of what is now Searles Dry Lake—first as hollow tubes, then as mounds, and finally as the spires visible today. A ½-mi trail winds around this surreal landscape of more than 500 spires, some of them rising as high as 140 ft. Wear sturdy shoes—tufa cuts like coral. ⊠ *From the Trona–Red Mountain Rd., take Hwy. 178 east for 8 mi. Or, from its junction with U.S. 395, take Hwy. 178 for 29 mi to dirt intersection; turn southeast and go ½ mi to a fork. Continue south via right fork, cross railroad tracks, and drive onward 5 mi.*

The tiny town of Inyokern boasts the small outdoor **United States Aerospace Museum.** Old military fighters and transport planes are on display behind fencing. The locale, surrounded by mountains, is glorious in daylight. ⊠ *Hwy. 178, just west of Inyokern.* ☞ *Free.*

Dining and Lodging

$–$$ ✕ **Santa Fe Grill.** The many Hollywood crews that film in the Ridge-

★ crest area might explain the presence of this unexpectedly hip and health-conscious New Mexican–style eatery in what is by and large a conservative military town. Hot tortillas, made on the premises, come to the table with a wonderful salsa, its distinctive smoky taste derived from fire-grilled chilies. Beans (not refried) and a sweet corn cake accompany most of the entrées. Specialties include seafood enchiladas and chicken fajitas. ⊠ *901 N. Heritage Dr.,* ☎ *760/446–5404. AE, D, MC, V.*

$–$$ ✕🏠 **Heritage Inn.** All the rooms here have refrigerators and microwaves. The well-appointed, though somewhat bland, facility is geared toward commercial travelers, but the staff is equally attentive to tourists' concerns. A sister property nearby is an all-suites hotel. The inn's Farris Restaurant, with a Continental menu, is a favorite fine-dining spot of locals. ⊠ *1050 N. Norma St.,* ☎ *760/446–7951 or 800/ 843–0693,* 𝖥𝖠𝖷 *760/446–2884. 125 rooms. Restaurant, bar, refrigerators, pool, hot tub, coin laundry, business services, meeting rooms. AE, D, DC, MC, V.*

$–$$ 🎦 **Carriage Inn.** This large, well-kept hotel caters both to visitors to the nearby military base and to travelers. Rooms are large and tastefully decorated. The poolside cabanas have a homier feel. A mister sends spray up to cool off sunbathers during the hot summer months. ⊠ *901 N. China Lake Blvd., 93555,* ☎ *760/446–7910 or 800/772–8527,* 🗚 *760/446–6408. 158 rooms, 2 suites, 2 cabanas. 2 restaurants, bar, refrigerators, pool, hot tubs, sauna, exercise room, meeting rooms. AE, D, DC, MC, V.*

$ 🎦 **The BevLen Bed & Breakfast.** A central location, country-cute rooms, and outgoing hosts—the retired couple Bev and Len de Geus—make this B&B an appealing stop. The place is especially good for single guests, as the rates are low and only one of the three rooms is really large enough for two people. ⊠ *809 N. Sanders St., 93555,* ☎ *760/375–1988 or 800/375–1989,* 🗚 *760/375–6871. 3 rooms. AE, D, MC, V.*

DEATH VALLEY

The topography of Death Valley is a lesson in geology. Two hundred million years ago seas covered the area, depositing layers of sediment and fossils. Between 35 million and 5 million years ago faults in the Earth's crust and volcanic activity pushed and folded the ground, causing mountain ranges to rise and the valley floor to drop. The valley was then filled periodically by lakes, which eroded the surrounding rocks into fantastic formations and deposited the salts that now cover the floor of the basin. The area has 14 square mi of sand dunes, 200 square mi of crusty salt flats, 11,000-ft mountains, hills, and canyons of many colors. There are more than 1,000 species of plants and trees—21 of which are unique to the valley, such as the yellow Panamint daisy and the blue-flowered Death Valley sage.

With more than 3.3 million acres, **Death Valley National Park** is the largest national park outside Alaska—and certainly the most uncomfortable at times. But seeing nature at its most extreme is precisely what attracts many people, especially Europeans. There are more visitors to Death Valley in July and August than in December and January. Distances can be deceiving: some sights appear in clusters, but others require extensive travel. The trip from Death Valley Junction to Scotty's Castle, for example, can take a half day. The entrance fee ($10 per vehicle), collected at the park's entrance stations and at the Visitor Center at Furnace Creek (☞ *below*), is valid for seven consecutive days.

Stovepipe Wells Village

❼   *102 mi northeast of Ridgecrest, Hwy. 178 to Hwy. 190.*

Stovepipe Wells Village was the first resort in Death Valley. The tiny town, which dates back to 1926, takes its name from the stovepipe that early prospectors left to indicate they'd found water. The area contains a motel, a restaurant, a grocery store, a landing strip, and campgrounds.

The polished, multicolor, partly marble walls of **Mosaic Canyon** are extremely narrow in spots. A reasonably easy ¾-mi hike yields the flavor of the area, but, if weather permits, it's rewarding to continue farther into the canyon for a few more miles. ⊠ *Off Hwy. 190, on 3 mi gravel road immediately southwest of Stovepipe Wells Village.*

Dining, Lodging, and Camping

$–$$ ✕🎦 **Stovepipe Wells Village.** An aircraft landing strip is an unusual touch for a motel, as is a heated mineral pool, but everything else here is pretty standard. Still, this is the best lodging bargain inside the park,

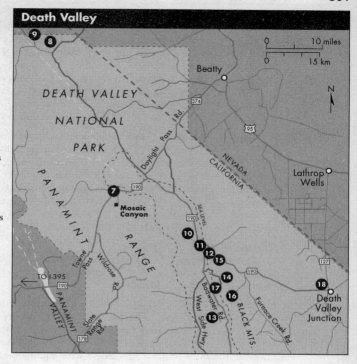

with pleasant rooms at a reasonable rate. The Old West–style Toll Road restaurant serves up all-you-can-eat buffets in summer and à la carte American menus the rest of the year. The adjoining Badwater Saloon provides the park's only nightlife outside that in Furnace Creek. ⊠ *Hwy. 190, Death Valley National Park 92328,* ☎ *760/786–2387,* FAX *760/ 786–2389. 83 rooms. Restaurant, bar, pool, coin laundry. AE, D, MC, V.*

⚠ **Mahogany Flat.** If you've got a four-wheel-drive vehicle and want to scale the park's highest mountain, you might want to sleep at one of the few shaded spots in Death Valley, located at a cool 8,133 ft. A 7-mi (one-way) trail leads from the campground to the summit of Telescope Peak (11,049 ft), but if you don't want to go the distance, many shorter strolls in this wooded high-country area afford terrific valley views. ⊠ *Off Wildrose Rd., south of Charcoal Kilns. 10 sites. Pit toilets, no water.* ☎ *Free.* ☉ *Mar.–Nov.*

En Route   Visible from Highway 190 heading east past Stovepipe Wells are **sand dunes** that cover a 14-square-mi field. The sand that forms the hills is actually minute pieces of quartz and other rock.

Scotty's Castle Area

44 mi north of Stovepipe Wells Village; head east on Hwy. 190, then north at signs for castle.

⑧ Scotty's Castle is an odd apparition rising out of a canyon. This Moorish mansion, begun in 1924 and never completed, takes its name from Walter Scott, better known as Death Valley Scotty. An ex-cowboy, prospector, and performer in Buffalo Bill's Wild West Show, Scotty always told people the castle was his, financed by gold from a secret mine. In reality, there was no mine. The house belonged to a Chicago millionaire named Albert Johnson (advised by doctors to spend time in a warm, dry climate) whom Scott had finagled into investing in the fictitious mine. The house functioned for a while as a hotel—guests included Bette Davis and Norman Rockwell—and contains works of art, imported carpets, handmade European furniture, and a tremendous pipe organ. Costumed rangers re-create life at the castle circa 1939. Fifty-minute tours are conducted frequently, but waits of up to two hours are possible. Try to arrive for the first tour of the day, which will guarantee short lines following a traffic-free drive through desert country. ☎ 760/786–2392. ☞ $8. ☉ Daily 8–6; tours until 5.

❾ The impressive **Ubehebe Crater,** 500 ft deep and ½ mi across, is the result of violent underground steam and gas explosions about 3,000 years ago; its volcanic ash spreads out over most of the area, and the cinders are as thick as 150 ft near the crater's rim. You'll get some superb views of the valley from here, and you can take a fairly easy hike around the west side of the rim to Little Hebe Crater, one of a smaller cluster of craters to the south and west. It's always windy on this rise 8 mi northwest of Scotty's Castle, so hold on to your hat.

Camping

⚠ **Mesquite Springs.** There are tent and RV spaces here, some of them shaded. ⊠ 2 mi south of Scotty's Castle. 30 sites. Flush toilets, stoves or fireplaces, water. ☞ $10. ☉ Year-round.

En Route On Highway 190, south of its junction with Scotty's Castle Road and 14 mi north of the town of Furnace Creek, is a 1-mi gravel road that leads to the ½-mi **Salt Creek Nature Trail.** The trail, a boardwalk circuit, loops through a spring-fed wash. The nearby hills are brown and gray, but the floor of the wash is alive with aquatic plants like pickerelweed and salt grass. The trail is the best place for bird-watching in Death Valley. You might see ravens, common snipes, killdeer, or great blue herons.

Furnace Creek Area

54 mi south of Scotty's Castle, 25 mi southeast of Stovepipe Wells Village on Hwy. 90.

❿ The renowned mule teams hauled borax from the **Harmony Borax Works** to the railroad town of Mojave, 165 mi away. Those teams were a sight to behold: 20 mules hitched up to two massive wagons, each carrying a load of 10 tons of borax through the burning desert. The teams plied the route between 1884 and 1907, when the railroad finally arrived in Zabriskie. The Borax Museum, 2 mi south of the borax works, houses original mining machinery and historical displays in a building that once served as a boardinghouse for miners; the adjacent structure is the original mule-team barn. ⊠ Harmony Borax Works Rd., west off Hwy. 190.

⓫ **Furnace Creek** is a center of activity amid the sprawling quiet of Death Valley. Covered with tropical landscaping, it has jogging and bicycle paths, golf, tennis, horseback riding, a general store, and, rare for these parts, dining options. The Furnace Creek Ranch (☞ Dining and Lodging, below) operates most of the above, plus guided carriage rides and hay rides for guests and nonguests. The rides traverse trails with views of the surrounding mountains, where multicolor volcanic rock and alluvial fans form a background for date palms and other vegetation.

Trail maps, brochures, and books and exhibits on the desert can be found at the **Visitor Center at Furnace Creek.** ⊠ Hwy. 190, ☎ 760/786–2331. ☉ Daily 8–6.

⑫ **Golden Canyon** is named for the glowing color of its walls. A mild hike into this spacious landform affords some spectacular views of yellow and orange rock. Farther up the canyon, you'll encounter a colorful formation called Red Cathedral. ⊠ *Badwater Rd., 3 mi south from Furnace Creek; turn left into parking lot.*

⑬ Reaching **Badwater,** you'll see a shallow pool, containing mostly sodium chloride, saltier than the sea, lying almost lifeless against an expanse of desolate salt flats—a sharp contrast to the expansive canyons and elevation not too far away. Here's the legend: one of the early surveyors saw that his mule wouldn't drink from the pool and noted "badwater" on his map. Badwater is the lowest spot on land in the Western Hemisphere—282 ft below sea level—and also one of the hottest. ⊠ *Badwater Rd., 19 mi south of Visitor Center at Furnace Creek.*

★ ⑭ The **Artists Palette,** named for the brilliant array of pigments created by volcanic deposits, is one of the most magnificent sights in Death Valley. Artists Drive, the approach to the area, is one-way heading north off Badwater Road, so if you're visiting Badwater it's more efficient to come here on the way back. The drive winds through foothills composed of colorful sedimentary and volcanic rocks. ⊠ *8 mi north of Badwater, Badwater Rd. to Artists Dr.; 10 mi south of Furnace Creek, Hwy. 190 to Badwater Rd. to Artists Dr.*

⑮ **Zabriskie Point** is one of Death Valley National Park's most scenic spots. Not particularly high—only about 710 ft—it overlooks a striking badlands panorama with wrinkled, multicolor hills. Film buffs of a certain vintage may recognize it—or at least its name—from the film *Zabriskie Point* by the Italian director Michelangelo Antonioni. ⊠ *Hwy. 190, 5 mi south of Furnace Creek.*

OFF THE
BEATEN PATH

TWENTY MULE TEAM CANYON – The thrills in this colorful canyon are more than just natural. At times along the loop road off Highway 190 the soft rock walls reach high on both sides, making it seem like you're on an amusement-park ride. Remains of prospectors' tunnels are visible here, along with some brilliant rock formations. ⊠ *Twenty Mule Team Rd. off Hwy. 190, 1½ mi south of Zabriskie Point. Trailers not permitted.*

★ ⑯ **Dante's View** is more than 5,000 ft up in the Black Mountains. In the dry desert air you can see most of the 110 mi the valley stretches across. The oasis of Furnace Creek is a green spot to the north. The view up and down is equally astounding: the tiny blackish patch far below is Badwater, at 282 ft below sea level the lowest point on land in the Western Hemisphere; on the western horizon is Mt. Whitney, at 14,494 ft the highest spot in the contiguous United States. ⊠ *Dante's View Rd. off Hwy. 190, 21 mi south of Zabriskie Point.*

⑰ At **Devil's Golf Course** thousands of miniature salt pinnacles, carved into surreal shapes by the desert wind, dot the landscape. The salt was pushed up to the surface by pressures created as underground salt and water-bearing gravel crystallized. Nothing grows on this barren landscape. ⊠ *Badwater Rd., 13 mi south of Visitor Center at Furnace Creek. Turn right onto dirt road and drive 1 mi.*

Dining, Lodging, and Camping

$$–$$$ ✗ **Inn Dining Room.** White stucco walls, lace tablecloths, two fireplaces, and windows with views of the Panamint Mountains make for a visual and culinary mirage at this restaurant. The upscale menu may include seared ahi tuna and fire-roasted corn chowder as starters. Seasonally changing main courses might include sesame-crusted salmon or medallions of veal. A few vegetarian entrées are usually prepared

as well. ⊠ *Furnace Creek Inn Resort, Hwy. 190,* ☎ *760/786–2345, ext. 150. AE, D, DC, MC, V.*

$$$–$$$$ 🏨 **Furnace Creek Inn Resort.** This historic stone structure is something of a desert oasis. The creek meanders through beautifully landscaped gardens, and the pool here is spring-fed. All the rooms have views; about half have balconies. Rates drop considerably during the summer. The restaurant serves high tea during the afternoon. At night, diners aren't permitted to wear jeans. ⊠ *Hwy. 190, Box 1, Death Valley National Park 92328,* ☎ *760/786–2361,* 📠 *760/786–2423. 290 rooms. Restaurant, bar, pool, 4 tennis courts, meeting rooms. AE, D, DC, MC, V.*

$$–$$$ 🏨 **Furnace Creek Ranch.** The ranch was originally crew headquarters for a borax company, the activities of which the on-site Borax Museum details. Four two-story buildings adjacent to the golf course have motel-type rooms that are good for families. The general store sells supplies and gifts. ⊠ *Hwy. 190, Box 1, Death Valley National Park 92328,* ☎ *760/786–2345,* 📠 *760/786–9945. 224 rooms. Restaurant, bar, coffee shop, pool, 18-hole golf course, 2 tennis courts, horseback riding Oct.–May, meeting rooms. AE, D, DC, MC, V.*

🏕 **Furnace Creek.** This campground, 196 ft below sea level, has RV and tent sites (some shaded) and tables. Pay showers, a laundry, and a swimming pool are at nearby Furnace Creek Ranch (☞ *above*). Reservations are accepted for stays between mid-October and mid-April; at other times sites are available on a first-come, first-served basis. ⊠ *Adjacent to Visitor Center at Furnace Creek,* ☎ *760/786–2331; 800/365–2267 for reservations. 136 sites. Fireplaces, flush and pit toilets, disposal station, water.* 🎫 *$16.* ☉ *Year-round.*

🏕 **Texas Spring.** Open only from October through May, this campsite south of the Visitor Center at Furnace Creek has good facilities and is a few dollars cheaper than the main campground. ⊠ *Just off Badwater Rd., south of the Visitor Center.* ☎ *800/365–2267. 92 sites. Fireplaces, flush toilets, disposal station, water.* 🎫 *$12.* ☉ *Open Oct.–May.*

Death Valley Junction

30 mi south of Furnace Creek, 25 mi south of Zabriskie Point on Hwy. 190.

⑱ **Marta Becket's Amargosa Opera House** is an unexpected pleasure in an unlikely place. Marta Becket is an artist and dancer from New York who first saw the town of Amargosa while on tour in 1964. Three years later she came back and on impulse decided to buy a boarded-up theater amid a complex of run-down Spanish colonial buildings. The population is still in single digits (cats outnumber people here), but it swells when cars, motor homes, and buses roll in to catch her blend of classical ballet, mime, and 19th-century melodrama. To compensate for the sparse crowds in the early days, Becket painted herself an audience, turning the walls and ceiling of the theater into a trompe l'oeil masterpiece. Now she often performs to sell-out crowds (call ahead to reserve a seat). After the show you can meet her in the adjacent art gallery, where she sells her paintings and autographs her posters and books. There's also an ice cream parlor and a deli in the complex. ⊠ *Hwy. 127,* ☎ *760/852–4441. Call ahead for reservations.* 🎫 *$10.* ☉ *Performances Nov., Feb., Mar., and Apr., Sat. and Mon. 7:45 PM; Oct., Dec., Jan., and May (through Mother's Day weekend), Sat. only.*

$ ✕🏨 **Opera House Hotel.** Adjoining the theater is a quaint, 1920s-style adobe bungalow structure. A long row of rooms—with walls exhibiting murals of antique furniture and clothes and lamps topped with frilly velvet shades—is available for opera guests. ⊠ *Hwy. 127,* ☎ *760/ 852–4441,* ℻ *760/852–4138. 14 rooms. MC, V.*

THE EASTERN MOJAVE

The eastern Mojave is a sharp contrast to Death Valley, with welcome sights of vegetation and somewhat cooler temperatures. Much of this land is untended, so precautions are necessary when driving the many back roads, where towns and services are few and far between.

Baker

⑲ *84 mi south of Death Valley Junction on Hwy. 127.*

The small town of Baker, unappealing except as a rest stop, lies between the east and west Mojave areas and Death Valley National Park. You can't miss the city's 134-ft thermometer, the height of which commemorates the corresponding U.S. temperature record in degrees Fahrenheit, which was set in Death Valley on July 10, 1913.

The thermometer is also a landmark for the National Park Service's **Mojave Desert Information Center** (☎ 760/733–4040). Baker offers only minimal provisions. There are a few restaurants, most of them fast-food outlets, one general store—as the site of the most Lotto jackpot winners in the state of California it tends to be popular—three motels, and several gas stations.

Dining and Lodging

$ ✕ **Bun Boy.** It doesn't have as much character inside as its 1926 facade promises, but Bun Boy does serve up primo diner food in a clean, comfortable setting. All the classics are represented—burgers, hot dogs, Reuben sandwiches, and more. The dessert specialty is strawberry pie. *I–15 at State Rd. 177,* ☎ *760/733–4363. AE, D, DC, MC, V.*

$ ☲ **Wills Fargo Motel.** Two of Baker's three motels are owned by the same person and they're just down the road from each other, so there's no difference in rates or location. This one, however, has rooms with marginally more character, as well as a pool and a grassy lawn out front. *I–15 at State Rd. 177, Box 130, 92309,* ☎ *760/733–4477,* ℻ *760/ 733–4680. 30 rooms. Pool. AE, D, DC, MC, V.*

Mojave National Preserve

The 1.4 million acres set aside in 1994 as the Mojave National Preserve don't conform to the standard image of the desert, encompassing as they do a surprising variety of plant and animal life at elevations up to nearly 8,000 ft. There's a good deal of evidence of human habitation as well, including abandoned army posts and the vestiges of towns that grew up around the area's mines and ranches. The town of Cima still has a small functioning store. But as you enter the preserve from the north, passing beautiful red-black cinder cones, you'll encounter
⑳ stereotypical desert terrain in the **Kelso Dunes** (Kelbaker Rd.; 42 mi south of Baker, 7 mi north of Kelso), perfect, pristine slopes of gold-white sand. They cover 70 square mi, often at heights of 500 to 600 ft, and can be reached in an easy ½-mi walk from where you leave your car. When you reach the top of one of the dunes, kick a little bit of sand down the lee side and find out why they say the sand "sings." In the town of Kelso a Mission Revival depot dating from 1925 is one of the few of its kind still standing.

㉑ The National Park Service administers most of the preserve, but **Providence Mountains State Recreation Area** is under the jurisdiction of the

California Department of Parks. The visitor center, elevation 4,300 ft, has views of mountain peaks, dunes, buttes, crags, and desert valleys. The nearby **Mitchell Caverns Natural Preserve** provides the rare opportunity to see all three types of cave formations—dripstone, flowstone, and erratics—in one place. The year-round 65°F temperature provides a break from the heat. ⊠ *Essex Rd., 16 mi north of I–40,* ☎ *760/928–2586.* ⊡ *$6.* ⊙ *Guided tours of caves Sept.–June, weekdays 1:30, weekends 10, 1:30, and 3; July–Aug., weekends only. Tours depart from the visitor center.*

Camping

⚠ **Hole-in-the-Wall Campground.** At a cool 4,500 ft above sea level and backed by sculptured volcanic rock formations, this is a fine place to spend a quiet night and to begin a hike during the day. The area was named by Bob Hollimon, a member of the Butch Cassidy gang, because it reminded him of his former hideout in Wyoming. There's a visitor center nearby. ⊠ *Black Canyon Rd. south of Kelso (for reservations write Mojave National Preserve, 222 E. Main St., Ste. 202, Barstow 92311),* ☎ *760/733–4040 or 760/255–8801 (weekdays). 35 campsites for motor homes and trailers, 2 walk-in tent sites.* ⊡ *$10. Fire rings, pit toilets, disposal station, potable water (in limited supply). No credit cards.* ⊙ *Year-round.*

Afton Canyon

㉒   *27 mi southwest of Baker, I–15 to Afton Canyon Rd.*

Because of its colorful, steep walls, **Afton Canyon** is often called the Grand Canyon of the Mojave. Afton was carved over many thousands of years by the rushing waters of the Mojave River, which makes one of its few aboveground appearances here. And where you find water in the desert you'll find trees, grasses, and wildlife. The canyon has been popular for a long time; Indians and later white settlers following the Mojave Trail from the Colorado River to the Pacific Ocean set up camp here, near the welcome presence of water. The dirt road that leads here is ungraded in spots, so this is best visited via all-terrain vehicle. Check with the Mojave Desert Information Center in Baker (☞ *above*) regarding road conditions before you head in. ⊠ *Take Afton turnoff and follow dirt road about 3 mi southwest.*

Camping

⚠ **Afton Canyon Campground.** The camping here is at elevation 1,408 ft, in a wildlife area where the Mojave River surfaces. High-desert scenic cliffs and a mesquite thicket surround the campground. ⊠ *Afton Canyon Rd. off I–15,* ☎ *760/252—6060. 22 sites. Fire rings, pit toilets, potable water (in limited supply).* ⊡ *$6 (reservations not accepted).* ⊙ *Year-round.*

Barstow Area

㉓   *63 mi southwest of Baker on I–15.*

Barstow was established in 1886 when a subsidiary of the Atchison, Topeka, and Santa Fe Railway began construction of a depot and hotel here. Outlet stores and modern chain restaurants and motels abound, though old-time neon signs light up Barstow's main street, which is part of Historic Route 66. The **California Welcome Center** (⊠ 2796 Tanger Way, ☎ 760/253–4813) has exhibits about desert ecology, wildflowers, wildlife, and other features of the desert environment.

★ ㉔ **Rainbow Basin National Natural Landmark** looks as if it could be on Mars, perhaps because so many science-fiction movies depicting the red planet have been filmed here. The sense of upheaval is palpable; huge slabs of red, orange, white, and green stone tilt at crazy angles like ships about to capsize. At points along the 6-mi drive, it is easy to imagine you are alone in the world, hidden among the colorful badlands that give the basin its name. Hike the many washes, and you'll probably see the fossilized remains of creatures that roamed the basin from 16 million to 12 million years ago: mastodons, large and small camels, rhinos, dog-bears, birds, and insects. ⊠ *8 mi north of Barstow (take Fort Irwin Rd. 5 mi north to Fossil Bed Rd., a graded dirt road, and head west 3 mi),* ☎ *760/252–6000.*

🐾 ㉕   What's now **Calico Ghost Town** became a wild and wealthy mining town after a rich deposit of silver was found around 1881. In 1886, after more than $85 million worth of silver, gold, and other precious metals were harvested from the multicolor "calico" hills, the price of silver fell and the town slipped into decline. Frank "Borax" Smith helped revive Calico in 1889 when he started mining the unglamorous but profitable mineral borax, but that boom had gone bust by the dawn of the 20th century. Many of the buildings here are authentic, but it's a theme-park version of the 1880s you get strolling the wooden sidewalks of Main Street, browsing through western shops, roaming the tunnels of Maggie's Mine, and taking a ride on the Calico–Odessa Railroad. Festivals in March, May, October, and November promote Calico's Wild West theme. ⊠ *Ghost Town Rd., 3 mi north of I-15,* ☎ *760/254–2122.* 🎫 *$6.* ☉ *Daily 8–sunset, shops 9–5.*

★ ㉖   If you're at all curious about life 200,000 years ago, the **Calico Early Man Archeological Site** is a must-see. Nearly 12,000 tools—scrapers, cutting tools, choppers, hand picks, stone saws, and the like—have been excavated from the site since 1964. Prior to the site's discovery, many archaeologists believed the first humans came to North America "only" 10,000 to 20,000 years ago. Dr. Louis Leakey, the noted archaeologist, was so impressed with the findings that he became the Calico Project director in 1963, serving until his death in 1972; his old camp is now a visitor center and museum. The earliest known Americans fashioned the artifacts buried in the walls and floors of the excavated pits. The only way in is by guided tour (call ahead; scheduled tours sometimes don't take place). ⊠ *15 mi northeast of Barstow, I-15 to Minneola Rd. north for 3 mi,* ☎ *760/252–6000.* 🎫 *Small donation suggested.* ☉ *Guided tours of dig Wed.–Thurs. 1:30 and 3:30, Fri.–Sun. 9–3:30.*

Dining, Lodging, and Camping

$ ✕ **Carlos & Toto's.** If you've tired of chain restaurants and food from your cooler, head for this touch of Mexico. Locally famous for its fajitas, the restaurant is open daily and lays out a Sunday buffet brunch from 9:30 to 2. ⊠ *901 W. Main St.,* ☎ *760/256–7513. AE, D, MC, V.*

$–$$ 🏨 **Holiday Inn.** This large property has more facilities than the many other hotels that line Main Street, so it tends to attract business travelers. It's slightly more expensive than the others, but worth it if you want the highest level of comfort Barstow has to offer. ⊠ *1511 E. Main St.,* ☎ *760/256–5673,* 𝖥𝖠𝖷 *760/256–5917. 148 rooms. Restaurant, pool, hot tub, laundry service, meeting rooms. AE, D, DC, MC, V.*

  🏕 **Calico Ghost Town Regional Park.** In addition to the campsites here there are cabins ($28) and bunkhouse accommodations ($5 per person, with a 12-person minimum). ⊠ *Ghost Town Rd., 3 mi north of I-15, east from Barstow,* ☎ *760/254–2122 or 800/862–2542 for reservations. 250 sites. Electric hookups, fire rings, flush toilets, showers,* *hot and cold water.* ☞ *$18 per night for tent camping, $22 for full RV hook-ups; 2-night minimum during festival weekends.* ⊘ *Year-round.*

Victorville

㉗ *34 mi southwest of Barstow on I–15.*

At the southwest corner of the Mojave is the sprawling town of Victorville, home of the Roy Rogers–Dale Evans Museum.

Mojave Narrows Regional Park makes use of one of the few spots where the Mojave River flows aboveground. The park has 87 camping units, hot showers, secluded picnic areas, and two lakes, surrounded by cottonwoods and cattails. You'll find fishing, rowboat rentals, a bait shop, equestrian paths, and a trail for visitors with disabilities. ✉ *18000 Yates Rd.,* ☎ *760/245–2226.* ☞ *$5 per vehicle; dry camping $10, camping with utilities $15.* ⊘ *Daily 7:30–sunset.*

The **Roy Rogers–Dale Evans Museum** draws old-timers and cowboy kitsch fans, who come to see the personal and professional memorabilia of its namesake stars and their friends on the Western film circuit. Everything from glittering costumes and custom cars to cereal box promotions testifies to just how successful they all once were. Animal-rights activists will probably want to stay away: exhibits include safari trophies—stuffed exotic cats and other animals shot by Roy and sometimes Dale. Even Trigger and Buttermilk have been preserved, though they apparently died of natural causes. ✉ *15650 Seneca Rd. (take Roy Rogers Dr. exit off I–15, then left on Civic Dr.),* ☎ *760/243–4547.* ☞ *$8.* ⊘ *Daily 9–5.*

Lodging

$ 🏨 **Best Western Green Tree Inn.** This member of the chain sits off I–15, a few blocks from the Roy Rogers–Dale Evans Museum. Many of the rooms are suite-size and have refrigerators and microwaves, making the inn a good choice for families. The decor is no-nonsense but clean. Prime rib is a mainstay of the on-site restaurant, which prepares a weekday luncheon buffet. ✉ *14173 Green Tree Blvd., 92392,* ☎ *760/245–3461 or 800/528–1234,* 🖷 *760/245–7745. 168 rooms. Restaurant, bar, coffee shop, pool, hot tub, shuffleboard, meeting rooms. AE, D, DC, MC, V.*

THE MOJAVE DESERT AND DEATH VALLEY A TO Z

Arriving and Departing

By Bus

Greyhound (☎ 800/231–2222) serves Baker, Barstow, Ridgecrest, and Victorville, but traveling by bus to the Mojave Desert is neither convenient nor inexpensive. There is no scheduled bus service to Death Valley National Park.

By Car

Much of the desert can be seen from the comfort of an air-conditioned car. Don't despair if you are without air-conditioning—just avoid the middle of the day and the middle of the summer, good advice for all desert travel.

The Mojave is shaped like a giant *L*, with one leg north and the other east. To travel north through the Mojave, take I–10 east out of Los

Angeles to I–15 north and (just past Cajon Pass), pick up U.S. 395, which runs north through Victor Valley, Boron, the Rand Mining District, and China Lake. To travel east, continue on I–15 to Barstow. From Barstow you can take I–40, which passes through the mountainous areas of San Bernardino County, whisks by the Providence mountains, and enters Arizona at Needles. The more northerly option is I–15, which passes near Devil's Playground and the Kelso Sand Dunes, and then veers northeast toward Las Vegas.

To avoid Cajon Pass, elevation 4,250 ft, take I–210 north of Los Angeles and continue north on Highway 14. Head east 67 mi on Highway 58 to the town of Barstow and pick up I–15 there. Continue east on I–15 to Highway 127, a very scenic route north through the Mojave to Death Valley.

Death Valley can be entered from the southeast or the west. From the southeast, take Highway 127 north from I–15 and then link up with Highway 178, which travels west into the valley and then cuts north toward Badwater before meeting up with Highway 190 at Furnace Creek. To enter from the west, exit U.S. 395 at either Highway 190 or 178.

By Plane
Inyokern Airport (✉ Inyokern Rd./Hwy. 178, 9 mi west of Ridgecrest, ☎ 760/377–5844) is served by United Express (☎ 800/241–6522) from Los Angeles. It takes about the same amount of time to drive from **McCarran International Airport** (☎ 702/261–5733) in Las Vegas (which is served by many more airlines) to Furnace Creek in Death Valley National Park as it does from Inyokern.

Getting Around

See Arriving and Departing, *above.*

Contacts and Resources

Camping
The Mojave Desert and Death Valley have about two dozen campgrounds in various desert settings. For further information the following booklets are useful: *High Desert Recreation Resource Guide,* from the Mojave Chamber of Commerce; *San Bernardino County Regional Parks,* from the Regional Parks Department; and *California Desert Camping,* from the Bureau of Land Management. *See* Visitor Information, *below,* for addresses and phone numbers.

Emergencies
Ambulance (☎ 911). **Fire** (☎ 911). **Police** (☎ 911).

BLM Rangers (☎ 760/255–8700). **Community Hospital** (✉ Barstow, ☎ 760/256–1761). **San Bernardino County Sheriff** (☎ 760/256–1796 for Barstow, 760/733–4448 for Baker).

Guided Tours
Fred Harvey Tours (✉ Furnace Creek Inn, Box 1, Death Valley National Park 92328 (☎ 760/786–2345, ext. 222). **Nature Conservancy** (✉ Box 188, Thousand Palms, 92276, ☎ 760/343–1234). **Sierra Club** (✉ 3345 Wilshire Blvd., Suite 508, Los Angeles 90010, ☎ 213/387–4287).

Visitor Information
Bureau of Land Management (✉ California Desert District Office, 6221 Box Springs Blvd., Riverside 92507, ☎ 909/697–5200). **California Desert Information Center** (✉ 831 Barstow Rd., Barstow 92311, ☎

760/252–6060). **Mojave Chamber of Commerce** (✉ 15836 Sierra Hwy., Mojave 93591, ☎ 805/824–2481). **National Park Service** (✉ Visitor Center at Furnace Creek, 92328, ☎ 760/786–3211). **Ridgecrest Area Convention and Visitors Bureau** (✉ 100 W. California Ave., Ridgecrest 93555, ☎ 760/375–8202 or 800/847–4830). **San Bernardino County Regional Parks Department** (✉ 777 E. Rialto Ave., San Bernardino 92415, ☎ 909/387–2594).

16 BACKGROUND AND ESSENTIALS

Books and Videos

Smart Travel Tips A to Z

O   R

Crescent
City

Yreka

Redwood
National
Park   Klamath

KLAMATH
NATIONAL
FOREST

Mt.
Shasta

97

Mt. Shasta

89

3

101

Arcata

Eureka

Fortuna

Shasta Lake

Redding

44

36

TRINITY
NATIONAL
FOREST

Ed R.

101

Red Bluff

Garberville

Leggett

MENDOCINO
NATIONAL
FOREST

99

5

Sacramento Valley

1   101

Fort Bragg   Willits

Mendocino

20

128   Ukiah

Boonville   253

Clear
Lake

Point Arena

101

505

WINE

COUNTRY

Santa Rosa   29   Vacaville

Napa

Petaluma   Fairfield

Novato

680

Point Reyes
National
Seashore   Berkeley   Cor

SAN FRANCISCO   Oaklan

San Mateo

1

Sunnyvale

PACIFIC   OCEAN

N

0   50 miles
0   75 km

Santa Cruz

Southern California

PACIFIC OCEAN

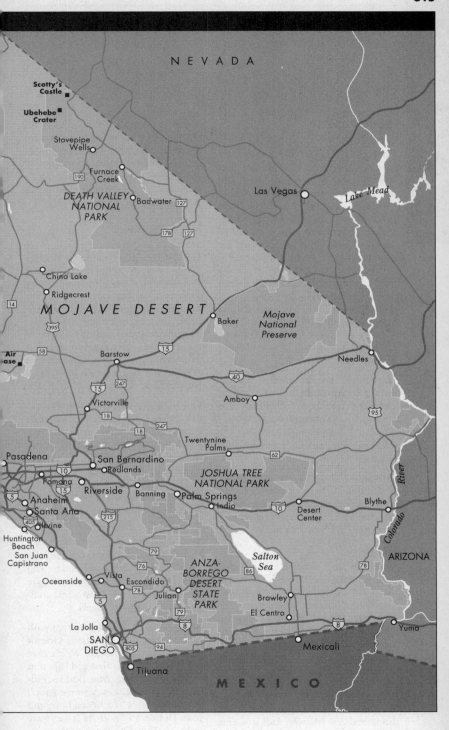

BOOKS AND VIDEOS

San Francisco

BOOKS

Many novels are set in San Francisco, but none come better than *The Maltese Falcon,* by Dashiell Hammett, the founder of the hard-boiled school of detective fiction. *The Barbary Coast: An Informal History of the San Francisco Underworld,* published in 1933 and still in print, is Herbert Asbury's searing look at life in what really was a wicked city before the turn of the century. Another standout is Vikram Seth's *Golden Gate,* a novel in verse about life in San Francisco and Marin County in the early '80s. Others are John Gregory Dunne's *The Red White and Blue* and Alice Adams's *Rich Rewards.*

Two books that are filled with interesting background information on the city are Richard H. Dillon's *San Francisco: Adventurers and Visionaries* and *San Francisco: As It Is, As It Was,* by Paul C. Johnson and Richard Reinhardt.

Armistead Maupin's soap-opera-style *Tales of the City* stories are set in San Francisco; they were made into a successful 1993 PBS series; a sequel screened on Showtime in 1998.

VIDEOS

San Francisco, starring Clark Gable and Jeanette MacDonald, re-creates the 1906 earthquake with outstanding special effects. In *Escape from Alcatraz,* Clint Eastwood plays the prisoner who allegedly escaped from the famous jail on a rock in the San Francisco Bay. *The Times of Harvey Milk,* about San Francisco's first openly gay elected official, won the Academy Award for best documentary feature in 1984. Alfred Hitchcock immortalized Mission Dolores and the Golden Gate Bridge in *Vertigo,* the eerie story of a detective with a fear of heights, starring Jimmy Stewart

and Kim Novak. A few other noteworthy films shot in San Francisco are *Dark Passage,* with Humphrey Bogart; the 1978 remake of *Invasion of the Body Snatchers;* and the 1993 comedy *Mrs. Doubtfire,* starring Robin Williams.

Los Angeles

BOOKS

Los Angeles: The Enormous Village, 1781–1981, by John D. Weaver, and *Los Angeles: Biography of a City,* by John and LaRee Caughey, will give you a fine background in how Los Angeles came to be the city it is today. The unique social and cultural life of the whole southern California area is explored in *Southern California: An Island on the Land,* by Carey McWilliams.

One of the most outstanding features of Los Angeles is its architecture. *Los Angeles: The Architecture of Four Ecologies,* by Reyner Banham, relates the physical environment to the architecture. *Architecture in Los Angeles: A Compleat Guide,* by David Gebhard and Robert Winter, is exactly what the title promises and is very useful.

Two controversial books by Mike Davis, *Ecology of Fear: Los Angeles and the Imagination of Disaster* and *City of Quartz: Excavating the Future in Los Angeles,* offer historical analyses of the City of Angels.

Many novels have been written with Los Angeles as the setting. One of the very best, Nathanael West's *Day of the Locust,* was first published in 1939 but still rings true. Budd Schulberg's *What Makes Sammy Run?,* Evelyn Waugh's *The Loved One,* and Joan Didion's *Play It As It Lays* are unforgettable. Other novels that give a sense of contemporary life in Los Angeles are *Sex and Rage,* by Eve

Books and Videos

Babitz, and *Less Than Zero,* by Bret Easton Ellis. Raymond Chandler and Ross Macdonald have written many suspense novels with a Los Angeles background.

VIDEOS AND TV

Day of the Locust and *Play It As It Lays* were made into two of the grimmer cinematic looks at life in Los Angeles. Billy Wilder's *Sunset Boulevard* is a classic portrait of a faded star and her attempt to recapture past glory. Roman Polanski's *Chinatown,* arguably one of the best American films ever made, is a fictional account of the wheeling and dealing that helped make L.A. what it is today. Southern California's varied urban and rural landscapes are used to great effect (as is an all-star cast that includes Ethel Merman and Spencer Tracy) in Stanley Kramer's manic *It's a Mad, Mad, Mad, Mad World.*

San Diego

BOOKS

There is no better way to establish the mood for your visit to Old Town San Diego than by reading Helen Hunt Jackson's 19th-century romantic novel, *Ramona,* a steady seller for decades and still in print. The Casa de Estudillo in Old Town has been known for many years as Ramona's Marriage Place because of its close resemblance to the house described in the novel. Richard Henry Dana Jr.'s *Two Years Before the Mast* (1869), based on the author's experiences as a merchant sailor, provides a masculine perspective on early San Diego history.

Other novels with a San Diego setting include Raymond Chandler's mystery about the waterfront, *Playback;* Wade Miller's mystery, *On Easy Street;* Eric Higgs's gothic thriller, *A Happy Man;* Tom Wolfe's satire of the La Jolla surfing scene, *The Pump House Gang;* and David Zielinski's modern-day story, *A Genuine Monster.*

VIDEOS AND TV

Filmmakers have taken advantage of San Diego's diverse and amiable climate since the dawn of cinema. Westerns, comedy-westerns, and tales of the sea were early staples: *Cupid in Chaps, The Sagebrush Phrenologist* (how's that for a title?), the 1914 version of *The Virginian,* and Lon Chaney's *Tell It to the Marines* were among the silent films shot in the area. Easy-to-capture outdoor locales have lured many productions south from Hollywood over the years, including the following military-oriented talkies, all or part of which were shot in San Diego: James Cagney's *Here Comes the Navy* (1934), Errol Flynn's *Dive Bomber* (1941), John Wayne's *The Sands of Iwo Jima* (1949), Ronald Reagan's *Hellcats of the Navy* (1956, costarring Nancy Davis, the future First Lady), Rock Hudson's *Ice Station Zebra* (1967), Tom Cruise's *Top Gun* (1986), Sean Connery's *Hunt for Red October,* Charlie Sheen's *Navy Seals* (1990), and Danny Glover's *Flight of the Intruder* (1991).

In a lighter military vein, the famous talking mule hit the high seas in *Francis Joins the Navy* (1955), in which a very young Clint Eastwood has a bit part. The Tom Hanks–Darryl Hannah hit *Splash* (1984), *Spaceballs* (1987), *Wayne's World II* (1993), and *Mr. Wrong* (1996) are more recent comedies with scenes filmed here. Billy Wilder's *Some Like It Hot*—starring Marilyn Monroe, Jack Lemmon, and Tony Curtis—takes place at the Hotel Del Coronado (standing in for a Miami resort).

The amusingly low-budget *Attack of the Killer Tomatoes* (1976) makes good use of local scenery. The producers must have liked what they found in town as they returned for three sequels: *Return of the Killer Tomatoes* (1988), *Killer Tomatoes Strike Back* (1990), and—proving just how versatile the region is as a film location—*Killer Tomatoes Go to France* (1991). Unlike many films in which San Diego itself doesn't figure in the plot, the screen version of Helen Hunt Jackson's novel *Ramona* (1936), starring Loretta Young as the title character, incorporated historical settings or replicas.

Television producers zip south for series and made-for-TV movies all the time. The alteration of San Diego's skyline in the 1980s was partially documented on the hit show *Simon & Simon.* San Diego is virtually awash in syndicated productions: *Silk Stalkings, Baywatch, High Tide,* and *Renegade* are among the shows that have been shot here. Reality and cop shows love the area, too: *Unsolved Mysteries, Rescue 911, America's Missing Children, Totally Hidden Video, America's Most Wanted,* and *America's Funniest People* have all taped in San Diego, making it one of the most-seen—yet often uncredited—locales in movie and video land.

Around the State

BOOKS

John Steinbeck immortalized the Monterey-Salinas area in numerous books, including *Cannery Row* and *East of Eden.* Joan Didion captured the heat—solar, political, and otherwise—of the Sacramento Delta area in *Run River.* Mark Twain's *Roughing It* and Bret Harte's *The Luck of Roaring Camp* evoke life during the Gold Rush. For a window on the past and present of the Central Valley, see *Highway 99: A Literary Journey Through California's Great Central Valley,* edited by Stan Yogi.

VIDEOS AND TV

Steinbeck's *East of Eden* was a hit film starring James Dean and later a television movie. Buster Keaton's masterpiece *Steamboat Bill, Jr.* was shot in Sacramento. The exteriors in Alfred Hitchcock's *Shadow of a Doubt* were shot in Santa Rosa, and his ultra-creepy *The Birds* was shot in Bodega Bay, along the North Coast. *Shack Out on 101* is a loopy 1950s beware-the-Commies caper also set on the California coast.

Erich von Stroheim used a number of northern California locations for his films: *Greed* takes place in San Francisco but includes excursions to Oakland and other points in the East Bay. Carmel is one of the locations for his *Foolish Wives.* The various Star Trek movies and Michelangelo Antonioni's *Zabriskie Point* are among the features that have made use of the eastern desert region. Initial footage of Sam Peckinpah's western *Ride the High Country* was shot in the Sierra Nevada mountains before his studio yanked him back to southern California, where he blended the original shots with ones of the Santa Monica Mountains and the Hollywood Hills.

ESSENTIAL INFORMATION

AIR TRAVEL

BOOKING YOUR FLIGHT

When you book **look for nonstop flights** and **remember that "direct" flights stop at least once.** Try to avoid connecting flights, which require a change of plane.

CARRIERS

➤ MAJOR AIRLINES: **Air Canada** (☎ 800/776–3000). **Alaska** (☎ 800/426–0333). **America West** (☎ 800/235–9292). **American** (☎ 800/433–7300). **British Airways** (☎ 800/247–9297). **Cathay Pacific** (☎ 800/233–2742). **Continental** (☎ 800/231–0856). **Delta** (☎ 800/221-1212). **Japan Air Lines** (☎ 800/525–3663). **Northwest/KLM** (☎ 800/225–2525). **Qantas** (☎ 800/227–4500). **Southwest** (☎ 800/435–9792). **TWA** (☎ 800/892–4141). **United** (☎ 800/241–6522). **US Airways** (☎ 800/428–4322).

➤ SMALLER AIRLINES: **American Trans Air** (☎ 800/435–9282). **Midwest Express** (☎ 800/452–2022). **Mountain Air** (☎ 562/595–1011 or 800/788–4247). **Reno Air** (☎ 800/736–6247). **Skywest** (☎ 800/453–9417).

➤ FROM THE U.K.: **American** (☎ 0345/789–789). **British Airways** (☎ 0345/222–111). **Delta** (☎ 0800/414–767). **United** (☎ 0800/888–555). **Virgin Atlantic** (☎ 01293/747–747).

CHECK-IN & BOARDING

Assuming that not everyone with a ticket will show up, airlines routinely overbook planes. When that happens, airlines ask for volunteers to give up their seats. In return these volunteers usually get a certificate for a free flight and are rebooked on the next flight out. If there are not enough volunteers, the airline must choose who will be denied boarding. The first to get bumped are passengers who checked in late and those flying on discounted tickets, so **get to the gate and check in as early as possible,** especially during peak periods.

Always **bring a government-issued photo ID to the airport.** You may be asked to show it before you are allowed to check in.

CUTTING COSTS

The least-expensive airfares to California must usually be purchased in advance and are non-refundable. It's smart to **call a number of airlines, and when you are quoted a good price, book it on the spot**—the same fare may not be available the next day. Always **check different routings** and look into using different airports. Travel agents, especially low-fare specialists (☞ Discounts & Deals, *below*), are helpful.

Consolidators are another good source. They buy tickets for scheduled international flights at reduced rates from the airlines, then sell them at prices that beat the best fare available directly from the airlines, usually without restrictions. Sometimes you can even get your money back if you need to return the ticket. Carefully read the fine print detailing penalties for changes and cancellations, and **confirm your consolidator reservation with the airline.**

When you **fly as a courier** you trade your checked-luggage space for a ticket deeply subsidized by a courier service. There are restrictions on when you can book and how long you can stay.

➤ CONSOLIDATORS: **Cheap Tickets** (☎ 800/377–1000). **Discount Airline Ticket Service** (☎ 800/576–1600). **Unitravel** (☎ 800/325–2222). **Up & Away Travel** (☎ 212/889–2345). **World Travel Network** (☎ 800/409–6753).

ENJOYING THE FLIGHT

For more legroom **request an emergency-aisle seat.** Don't sit in the row in front of the emergency aisle or in front of a bulkhead, where seats may not recline. If you have dietary concerns, **ask for special meals when booking.** These can be vegetarian, low-cholesterol, or kosher, for example. On long flights, try to maintain a normal routine, to help fight jetlag. At night **get some sleep.** By day **eat light meals, drink water** (not alcohol), and **move around the cabin** to stretch your legs.

FLYING TIMES

Flying time is roughly five hours from New York and four hours from Chicago. Flying between San Francisco and Los Angeles takes one hour.

HOW TO COMPLAIN

If your baggage goes astray or your flight goes awry, complain right away. Most carriers require that you **file a claim immediately.**

➤ AIRLINE COMPLAINTS: U.S. Department of Transportation **Aviation Consumer Protection Division** (✉ C-75, Room 4107, Washington, DC 20590, ☎ 202/366–2220). Federal Aviation Administration Consumer Hotline (☎ 800/322–7873).

AIRPORTS

Major gateways to California are **Los Angeles International Airport (LAX), San Francisco International Airport (SFO),** and **San Diego International Airport (SAN).**

➤ AIRPORT INFORMATION: **Los Angeles International Airport** (☎ 310/646–5252). **San Diego International Airport** (☎ 619/231–2100). **San Francisco International Airport** (☎ 650/761–0800).

BIKE TRAVEL

There are beautiful places to bike throughout California. For each part of the state, please see the specific chapter.

BIKES IN FLIGHT

Most airlines accommodate bikes as luggage, provided they are dismantled and boxed. For bike boxes, often free at bike shops, you'll pay about $5 (at least $100 for bike bags) from airlines. International travelers can sometimes substitute a bike for a piece of checked luggage at no charge;

otherwise, the cost is about $100. Domestic and Canadian airlines charge $25–$50.

BUS TRAVEL

➤ BUS INFORMATION: **Greyhound** (☎ 800/231–2222).

CAMERAS & PHOTOGRAPHY

The pounding surf, glorious mountains, towering trees, and sparkling beaches—not to mention the cities, towns, deserts, and countryside in between—make California a photographer's dream destination. Bring lots of film to capture the special moments of your trip.

EQUIPMENT PRECAUTIONS

Always **keep your film and tape out of the sun.** Carry an extra supply of batteries, and **be prepared to turn on your camera or camcorder** to prove to security personnel that the device is real. Always **ask for hand inspection of film,** which becomes clouded after successive exposures to airport X-ray machines, and **keep videotapes away from metal detectors.**

➤ PHOTO HELP: **Kodak Information Center** (☎ 800/242–2424). *Kodak Guide to Shooting Great Travel Pictures,* available in bookstores or from Fodor's Travel Publications (☎ 800/533–6478; $16.50 plus $4 shipping).

CAR RENTAL

Rates in Los Angeles begin at around $29 a day and $125 a week. This does not include tax on car rentals, which is 8¼%. In San Diego, rates for an economy car with unlimited mileage begin around $23 a day and $137 a week. This does not include tax on car rentals, which is 7¾%. In San Francisco, rates begin around $38 a day and $138 a week. This does not include tax on car rentals, which is 8¼%.

➤ MAJOR AGENCIES: **Alamo** (☎ 800/327–9633; 0181/759–6200 in the U.K.). **Avis** (☎ 800/331–1212; 800/879–2847 in Canada; 02/9353–9000 in Australia; 09/525–1982 in New Zealand). **Budget** (☎ 800/527–0700; 0144/227–6266 in the U.K.). **Dollar** (☎ 800/800–4000; 0181/897–0811 in the U.K., where it is known as

Eurodollar; 02/9223–1444 in Australia). **Hertz** (☎ 800/654–3131; 800/263–0600 in Canada; 0181/897–2072 in the U.K.; 02/9669–2444 in Australia; 03/358–6777 in New Zealand). **National InterRent** (☎ 800/227–7368; 0345/222525 in the U.K., where it is known as Europcar InterRent).

CUTTING COSTS

When pricing cars, **ask about the location of the rental lot.** Some off-airport locations offer lower rates, and their lots are only minutes from the terminal via complimentary shuttle. To get the best deal **book through a travel agent who will shop around.** Also **price local car-rental companies,** although the service and maintenance may not be as good as those of a major player. Remember to ask about required deposits, cancellation penalties, and drop-off charges if you're planning to pick up the car in one city and leave it in another. If you're traveling during a holiday period, also make sure that a confirmed reservation guarantees you a car.

Do **look into wholesalers,** companies that do not own fleets but rent in bulk from those that do and often offer better rates than traditional car-rental operations.

➤ WHOLESALERS: **Auto Europe** (☎ 207/842–2000 or 800/223–5555, FAX 800/235–6321).

INSURANCE

When driving a rented car you are generally responsible for any damage to or loss of the vehicle as well as for any property damage or personal injury that you may cause. Before you rent see what coverage your personal auto-insurance policy and credit cards already provide.

For about $15 to $20 per day, rental companies sell protection, known as a collision- or loss-damage waiver (CDW or LDW), that eliminates your liability for damage to the car. Some states, including California, have capped the price of the CDW and LDW. In most states you don't need a CDW if you have personal auto insurance or other liability insurance. However, **make sure you have enough coverage to pay for the car.** If you do not have auto insurance or an umbrella policy that covers damage to third parties, purchasing liability insurance and a CDW or LDW is highly recommended.

REQUIREMENTS & RESTRICTIONS

In California you must be 21 to rent a car, and rates may be higher if you're under 25. You'll pay extra for child seats (about $3 per day), which are compulsory for children under five, and for additional drivers (about $2 per day). Non-U.S. residents will need a reservation voucher, a passport, a driver's license, and a travel policy that covers each driver, in order to pick up a car.

SURCHARGES

Before you pick up a car in one city and leave it in another **ask about drop-off charges or one-way service fees,** which can be substantial. Note, too, that some rental agencies charge extra if you return the car before the time specified in your contract. To avoid a hefty refueling fee **fill the tank just before you turn in the car,** but be aware that gas stations near the rental outlet may overcharge.

CAR TRAVEL

Three major highways—Interstate 5 (I–5), U.S. 101, and Highway 1—run north-south through the state. The main routes into the state from the east are I–15 and I–10 in southern California and I–80 in northern California.

AUTO CLUBS

➤ IN AUSTRALIA: **Australian Automobile Association** (☎ 02/6247–7311).

➤ IN CANADA: **Canadian Automobile Association** (CAA, ☎ 613/247–0117).

➤ IN NEW ZEALAND: **New Zealand Automobile Association** (☎ 09/377–4660).

➤ IN THE U.K.: **Automobile Association** (AA, ☎ 0990/500–600). **Royal Automobile Club** (RAC, ☎ 0990/722–722 for membership; 0345/121–345 for insurance).

➤ IN THE U.S.: **American Automobile Association** (☎ 800/564–6222).

EMERGENCIES

Dial 911 to report accidents on the road and to reach police, the California Highway Patrol, or fire department.

GASOLINE

Prices vary widely depending on location, oil company, and whether you buy full-serve or self-serve gasoline. Prices on the West Coast also tend to be higher than in the Midwest. At press time, regular unleaded gasoline at self-serve stations cost about $1.25 a gallon.

ROAD CONDITIONS

Avoid major urban highways during rush hour. Some of the smaller routes over the mountain ranges are prone to flash flooding—drivers should check road conditions before heading into stormy weather. During snowy weather, tire chains are required in many mountain areas. When the rains are severe, coastal Highway 1 can quickly become a slippery nightmare, buffeted by strong winds and obstructed by falling debris from the cliffs above. When the weather is particularly bad, Highway 1 may be closed.

➤ ROAD CONDITIONS: **Statewide hotline** (☎ 800/427–7623). **Northern California updates** (☎ 916/445–7623). **Southern California updates** (☎ 213/628–7623).

ROAD MAPS

You can buy detailed maps in bookstores and gas stations and at some grocery and drug stores. The various California branches of the American Automobile Association (☞ *above*) have state and local maps that are free to members.

RULES OF THE ROAD

The speed limit on many rural highways is 70 mph, 75 mph on some. In the cities, freeway speed limits are between 55 and 65 mph. Many city routes have commuter lanes, but the operating rules vary from city to city: in San Francisco, for example, you need three people in a car to use these lanes, in Los Angeles only two.

Seat belts are required at all times. Tickets can be given for failing to comply. Small children must be in child safety seats. Unless otherwise indicated, right turns are allowed on red lights after you've come to a full stop, and left turns onto adjoining one-way streets are allowed on red lights after you've come to a full stop. Drivers stopped by the police who have a blood-alcohol level higher than 0.08 are subject to arrest.

CHILDREN IN CALIFORNIA

California is made to order for traveling with children: kids love Disneyland, the San Diego Zoo, the Monterey Aquarium, the San Francisco cable cars, the city-owned gold mine in Placerville, and the caverns at Lake Shasta.

If you are renting a car don't forget to **arrange for a car seat** when you reserve.

➤ LOCAL INFORMATION: Consult Fodor's lively by-parents, for-parents **Where Should We Take the Kids? California** (available in bookstores, or ☎ 800/533–6478); $17.

FLYING

If your children are two or older **ask about children's airfares.** As a general rule, infants under two not occupying a seat fly at greatly reduced fares or even for free.

Experts agree that it's a good idea to use safety seats aloft for children weighing less than 40 pounds. Airlines set their own policies: U.S. carriers usually require that the child be ticketed, even if he or she is young enough to ride free, since the seats must be strapped into regular seats. Do **check your airline's policy about using safety seats during takeoff and landing.** And since safety seats are not allowed just everywhere in the plane, get your seat assignments early.

When reserving, **request children's meals or a freestanding bassinet** if you need them. But note that bulkhead seats, where you must sit to use the bassinet, may lack an overhead bin or storage space on the floor.

LODGING

Most hotels in California allow children under a certain age to stay in their parents' room at no extra charge, but others charge for them as extra adults; be sure to **find out the cutoff age for children's discounts.**

SIGHTS & ATTRACTIONS

Places that are especially good for children are indicated by a rubber duckie icon in the margin.

CONSUMER PROTECTION

Whenever shopping or buying travel services in California, **pay with a major credit card** so you can cancel payment or get reimbursed if there's a problem. If you're doing business with a particular company for the first time, **contact your local Better Business Bureau and the attorney general's offices** in your state and the company's home state, as well. Have any complaints been filed? Finally, if you're buying a package or tour, always **consider travel insurance** that includes default coverage (☞ Insurance, *below*).

➤ LOCAL BBBs: **Council of Better Business Bureaus** (✉ 4200 Wilson Blvd., Suite 800, Arlington, VA 22203, ☎ 703/276–0100, ℻ 703/525–8277).

CUSTOMS & DUTIES

When shopping, **keep receipts** for all purchases. Upon reentering the country, **be ready to show customs officials what you've bought.** If you feel a duty is incorrect or object to the way your clearance was handled, note the inspector's badge number and ask to see a supervisor. If the problem isn't resolved, write to the appropriate authorities, beginning with the port director at your point of entry.

IN AUSTRALIA

Australia residents who are 18 or older may bring home $A400 worth of souvenirs and gifts (including jewelry), 250 cigarettes or 250 grams of tobacco, and 1,125 ml of alcohol (including wine, beer, and spirits). Residents under 18 may bring back $A200 worth of goods. Prohibited items include meat products. Seeds, plants, and fruits need to be declared upon arrival.

➤ INFORMATION: **Australian Customs Service** (Regional Director, ✉ Box 8, Sydney, NSW 2001, ☎ 02/9213–2000, ℻ 02/9213–4000).

IN CANADA

Canadian residents who have been out of Canada for at least seven days may bring home C$500 worth of goods duty-free. If you've been away less than seven days but more than 48 hours, the duty-free allowance drops to C$200; if your trip lasts 24–48 hours, the allowance is C$50. You may not pool allowances with family members. Goods claimed under the C$500 exemption may follow you by mail; those claimed under the lesser exemptions must accompany you. Alcohol and tobacco products may be included in the seven-day and 48-hour exemptions but not in the 24-hour exemption. If you meet the age requirements of the province or territory through which you reenter Canada, you may bring in, duty-free, 1.14 liters (40 imperial ounces) of wine or liquor *or* 24 12-ounce cans or bottles of beer or ale. If you are 16 or older you may bring in, duty-free, 200 cigarettes and 50 cigars. Check ahead of time with Revenue Canada or the Department of Agriculture for policies regarding meat products, seeds, plants, and fruits.

You may send an unlimited number of gifts worth up to C$60 each duty-free to Canada. Label the package UNSOLICITED GIFT—VALUE UNDER $60. Alcohol and tobacco are excluded.

➤ INFORMATION: **Revenue Canada** (✉ 2265 St. Laurent Blvd. S, Ottawa, Ontario K1G 4K3, ☎ 613/993–0534; 800/461–9999 in Canada).

IN NEW ZEALAND

Homeward-bound residents 17 or older may bring back $700 worth of souvenirs and gifts. Your duty-free allowance also includes 4.5 liters of wine or beer; one 1,125-milliliter bottle of spirits; and either 200 cigarettes, 250 grams of tobacco, 50 cigars, or a combination of the three up to 250 grams. Prohibited items include meat products, seeds, plants, and fruits.

➤ INFORMATION: **New Zealand Customs** (Custom House, ✉ 50 Anzac Ave., Box 29, Auckland, New Zealand, ☎ 09/359–6655, ℻ 09/359–6732).

IN THE U.K.

➤ INFORMATION: **HM Customs and Excise** (✉ Dorset House, Stamford St., Bromley Kent BR1 1XX, ☎ 0171/202–4227).

IN THE U.S.

Non-U.S. residents ages 21 and older may import into the United States 200 cigarettes or 50 cigars or 2 kilograms of tobacco, 1 liter of alcohol, and gifts worth $100. Meat products, seeds, plants, and fruits are prohibited.

➤ INFORMATION: **U.S. Customs Service** (inquiries, ✉ 1300 Pennsylvania Ave. NW, Washington, DC 20229, ☎ 202/927–6724; complaints, ✉ Office of Regulations and Rulings, 1300 Pennsylvania Ave. NW, Washington, DC 20229; registration of equipment, ✉ Resource Management, 1300 Pennsylvania Ave. NW, Washington, DC 20229, ☎ 202/927–0540).

DINING

California has led the pack in bringing natural and organic foods to the forefront of American cooking. The Asian and Latin influence in California cooking is also strong. Wherever you go, you're likely to find fresh local ingredients and produce being used.

The restaurants we list are the cream of the crop in each price category. Properties indicated by an ✕🏠 are lodging establishments whose restaurant warrants a special trip.

RESERVATIONS & DRESS

Reservations are always a good idea: we mention them only when they're essential or are not accepted. Book as far ahead as you can, and reconfirm as soon as you arrive. We mention dress only when men are required to wear a jacket or a jacket and tie.

WINE, BEER & SPIRITS

If you like wine, no trip to California can be complete without trying a few of the local vintages. Throughout the state, but especially in the famed regions of Napa and Sonoma Valleys, you'll find wineries to visit with tours and tasting rooms available. In the Far North, beer lovers will want to

stop at the Sierra Nevada Brewing Company.

DISABILITIES & ACCESSIBILITY

California is a national leader in making attractions and facilities accessible to people with disabilities. State laws provide special privileges, such as license plates allowing special parking spaces, unlimited parking in time-limited spaces, and free parking in metered spaces. Insignia from other states are honored.

LODGING

When discussing accessibility with an operator or reservations agent **ask hard questions.** Are there any stairs, inside *or* out? Are there grab bars next to the toilet *and* in the shower/tub? How wide is the doorway to the room? To the bathroom? For the most extensive facilities meeting the latest legal specifications **opt for newer accommodations.**

➤ COMPLAINTS: **Disability Rights Section** (✉ U.S. Department of Justice, Civil Rights Division, Box 66738, Washington, DC 20035-6738, ☎ 202/514–0301; 800/514–0301; 202/514–0301 TTY; 800/514–0301 TTY; 🖷 202/307–1198) for general complaints. **Aviation Consumer Protection Division** (☞ Air Travel, *above*) for airline-related problems. **Civil Rights Office** (✉ U.S. Department of Transportation, Departmental Office of Civil Rights, S-30, 400 7th St. SW, Room 10215, Washington, DC 20590, ☎ 202/366–4648, 🖷 202/366–9371) for problems with surface transportation.

TRAVEL AGENCIES

In the United States, although the Americans with Disabilities Act requires that travel firms serve the needs of all travelers, some agencies specialize in working with people with disabilities.

➤ TRAVELERS WITH MOBILITY PROBLEMS: **Access Adventures** (✉ 206 Chestnut Ridge Rd., Rochester, NY 14624, ☎ 716/889–9096), run by a former physical-rehabilitation counselor. **Accessible Vans of the Rockies, Activity and Travel Agency** (✉ 2040 W. Hamilton Pl., Sheridan, CO 80110, ☎ 303/806–5047 or 888/

837–0065, FAX 303/781–2329). **Care-Vacations** (✉ 5-5110 50th Ave., Leduc, Alberta T9E 6V4, ☎ 780/986–6404 or 780/986–8332) has group tours and is especially helpful with cruise vacations. **Flying Wheels Travel** (✉ 143 W. Bridge St., Box 382, Owatonna, MN 55060, ☎ 507/451–5005 or 800/535–6790, FAX 507/451–1685). **Hinsdale Travel Service** (✉ 201 E. Ogden Ave., Suite 100, Hinsdale, IL 60521, ☎ 630/325–1335).

➤ TRAVELERS WITH DEVELOPMENTAL DISABILITIES: **New Directions** (✉ 5276 Hollister Ave., Suite 207, Santa Barbara, CA 93111, ☎ 805/967–2841 or 888/967–2841, FAX 805/964–7344).

DISCOUNTS & DEALS

Be a smart shopper and **compare all your options** before making decisions. A plane ticket bought with a promotional coupon from travel clubs, coupon books, and direct-mail offers may not be cheaper than the least expensive fare from a discount ticket agency. And always keep in mind that what you get is just as important as what you save.

DISCOUNT RESERVATIONS

To save money **look into discount-reservations services** with toll-free numbers, which use their buying power to get a better price on hotels, airline tickets, even car rentals. When booking a room, always **call the hotel's local toll-free number** (if one is available) rather than the central reservations number—you'll often get a better price. Always ask about special packages or corporate rates.

➤ AIRLINE TICKETS: ☎ **800/FLY–4–LESS.** ☎ **800/FLY–ASAP.**

➤ HOTEL ROOMS: **Accommodations Express** (☎ 800/444–7666). **Central Reservation Service (CRS)** (☎ 800/548–3311). **Hotel Reservations Network** (☎ 800/964–6835). **Players Express Vacations** (☎ 800/458–6161). **Quickbook** (☎ 800/789–9887). **Room Finders USA** (☎ 800/473–7829). **RMC Travel** (☎ 800/245–5738). **Steigenberger Reservation Service** (☎ 800/223–5652).

PACKAGE DEALS

Don't confuse packages and guided tours. When you buy a package, you travel on your own, just as though you had planned the trip yourself. Fly/drive packages, which combine airfare and car rental, are often a good deal.

ELECTRICITY

Many overseas visitors will need to bring adapters to convert their personal appliances to the U.S. standard: AC, 110 volts/60 cycles, with a plug of two flat pins set parallel to one another.

GAY & LESBIAN TRAVEL

San Francisco, Los Angeles, West Hollywood, San Diego, and Palm Springs are among the California cities with visible lesbian and gay communities.

LOCAL INFORMATION

Many California cities large and small have lesbian and gay publications available in sidewalk racks and at bars and other social spaces; most have extensive events and information listings.

➤ LOCAL PAPERS: **Bay Area Reporter** (✉ 395 9th St., San Francisco 94103, ☎ 415/861–5019). **Bottom Line** (✉ 1243 N. Gene Autry Trail, Suite 121, Palm Springs 92262, ☎ 760/323–0552). **Edge** (✉ 6434 Santa Monica Blvd., Los Angeles 90038, ☎ 323/962–6994). **Uptown Publications** (✉ 911 Normal St., San Diego, 92103, ☎ 619/299–6397). **Mom Guess What Newspaper** (✉ 1725 L St., Sacramento 95814, ☎ 916/441–6397).

➤ SWITCHBOARDS AND HOT LINES: **Gay and Lesbian Community Services Center** (✉ 1 625 N. Schrader Blvd., Los Angeles 90028, ☎ 323/993–7400). **Lambda Community Center** (✉ 9 920 20th St., Sacramento 95814, ☎ 916/442–0185). **Lesbian and Gay Men's Community Center** (✉ 3916 Normal St., San Diego 92103, ☎ 619/692–4297). **Pacific Center Lesbian, Gay and Bisexual Switchboard** (☎ 510/841–6224).

➤ GAY- AND LESBIAN-FRIENDLY TRAVEL AGENCIES: **Different Roads Travel** (✉ 8383 Wilshire Blvd., Suite 902, Beverly Hills, CA 90211, ☎ 323/651–5557 or 800/429–8747, FAX 323/651–3678). **Kennedy Travel** (✉ 314 Jericho Turnpike, Floral Park, NY

11001, ☎ 516/352–4888 or 800/
237–7433, FAX 516/354–8849). **Now
Voyager** (✉ 4406 18th St., San Francisco, CA 94114, ☎ 415/626–1169
or 800/255–6951, FAX 415/626–8626).
Yellowbrick Road (✉ 1500 W. Bal-
moral Ave., Chicago, IL 60640, ☎
773/561–1800 or 800/642–2488, FAX
773/561–4497). **Skylink Travel and
Tour** (✉ 1006 Mendocino Ave.,
Santa Rosa, CA 95401, ☎ 707/546–
9888 or 800/225–5759, FAX 707/546–
9891), serving lesbian travelers.

HOLIDAYS

Major national holidays include New
Year's Day (Jan. 1); Martin Luther
King, Jr., Day (3rd Mon. in Jan.);
President's Day (3rd Mon. in Feb.);
Memorial Day (last Mon. in May);
Independence Day (July 4); Labor
Day (1st Mon. in Sept.); Thanksgiv-
ing Day (4th Thurs. in Nov.); Christ-
mas Eve and Christmas Day (Dec. 24
and 25); and New Year's Eve (Dec.
31).

INSURANCE

The most useful travel insurance plan
is a comprehensive policy that includes coverage for trip cancellation
and interruption, default, trip delay,
and medical expenses (with a waiver
for preexisting conditions).

Without insurance you will lose all or
most of your money if you cancel
your trip, regardless of the reason.
Default insurance covers you if your
tour operator, airline, or cruise line
goes out of business. Trip-delay
covers expenses that arise because of
bad weather or mechanical delays.
Study the fine print when comparing
policies.

British and Australian citizens need
extra medical coverage when traveling overseas.

Always **buy travel policies directly
from the insurance company**; if you
buy it from a cruise line, airline, or
tour operator that goes out of business you probably will not be covered
for the agency or operator's default, a
major risk. Before you make any
purchase **review your existing health
and home-owner's policies** to find
what they cover away from home.

➤ TRAVEL INSURERS: In the U.S. **Ac-
cess America** (✉ 6600 W. Broad St.,
Richmond, VA 23230, ☎ 804/285–
3300 or 800/284–8300), **Travel
Guard International** (✉ 1145 Clark
St., Stevens Point, WI 54481, ☎ 715/
345–0505 or 800/826–1300). In
Canada **Voyager Insurance** (✉ 44
Peel Center Dr., Brampton, Ontario
L6T 4M8, ☎ 905/791–8700; 800/
668–4342 in Canada).

➤ INSURANCE INFORMATION: In the
U.K. the **Association of British Insurers** (✉ 51–55 Gresham St., London
EC2V 7HQ, ☎ 0171/600–3333, FAX
0171/696–8999). In Australia the
Insurance Council of Australia (☎
03/9614–1077, FAX 03/9614–7924).

LODGING

The lodgings we list are the cream of
the crop in each price category. We
always list the facilities that are
available—but we don't specify
whether they cost extra: when pricing
accommodations, always ask what's
included and what costs extra. Properties indicated by an ✗▢ are lodging establishments whose restaurant
warrants a special trip.

Assume that hotels operate on the
European Plan (EP, with no meals)
unless we specify that they use the
Continental Plan (CP, with a Continental breakfast daily), Modified
American Plan (MAP, with breakfast
and dinner daily), or the Full American Plan (FAP, with all meals).

APARTMENT & VILLA RENTALS

If you want a home base that's roomy
enough for a family and comes with
cooking facilities **consider a furnished
rental.** These can save you money,
especially if you're traveling with a
group. Home-exchange directories
sometimes list rentals as well as
exchanges.

➤ INTERNATIONAL AGENTS: **Europa-
Let/Tropical Inn-Let** (✉ 92 N. Main
St., Ashland, OR 97520, ☎ 541/482–
5806 or 800/462–4486, FAX 541/482–
0660). **Hometours International** (✉
Box 11503, Knoxville, TN 37939, ☎
423/690–8484 or 800/367–4668).
Interhome (✉ 1990 N.E. 163rd St.,
Suite 110, Miami Beach, FL 33162,
☎ 305/940–2299 or 800/882–6864,
FAX 305/940–2911). **Rent-a-Home**

International (✉ 7200 34th Ave. NW, Seattle, WA 98117, ☎ 206/789–9377, FAX 206/789–9379). **Vacation Home Rentals Worldwide** (✉ 235 Kensington Ave., Norwood, NJ 07648, ☎ 201/767–9393 or 800/633–3284, FAX 201/767–5510). **Hideaways International** (✉ 767 Islington St., Portsmouth, NH 03801, ☎ 603/430–4433 or 800/843–4433, FAX 603/430–4444; membership $99).

CAMPING

➤ INFORMATION: **California Travel Parks Association** (✉ Box 5648, Auburn, CA 95604, ☎ 530/823–1076, FAX 530/823–6331).

➤ RESERVATIONS: **National Parks** (☎ 800/365–2267). **State Parks** (☎ 800/444–7275).

HOME EXCHANGES

If you would like to exchange your home for someone else's **join a home-exchange organization,** which will send you its updated listings of available exchanges for a year and will include your own listing in at least one of them. It's up to you to make specific arrangements.

➤ EXCHANGE CLUBS: **HomeLink International** (✉ Box 650, Key West, FL 33041, ☎ 305/294–7766 or 800/638–3841, FAX 305/294–1448; $88 per year). **Intervac U.S.** (✉ Box 590504, San Francisco, CA 94159, ☎ 800/756–4663, FAX 415/435–7440; $83 per year).

HOSTELS

No matter what your age you can **save on lodging costs by staying at hostels.** In some 5,000 locations in more than 70 countries around the world, Hostelling International (HI), the umbrella group for a number of national youth-hostel associations, offers single-sex, dorm-style beds and, at many hostels, couples rooms and family accommodations. Membership in any HI national hostel association, open to travelers of all ages, allows you to stay in HI-affiliated hostels at member rates (one-year membership is about $25 for adults; hostels run about $10–$25 per night). Members also have priority if the hostel is full; they're eligible for discounts around the world, even on rail and bus travel in some countries.

➤ ORGANIZATIONS: **Australian Youth Hostel Association** (✉ 10 Mallett St., Camperdown, NSW 2050, ☎ 02/9565–1699, FAX 02/9565–1325). **Hostelling International—American Youth Hostels** (✉ 733 15th St. NW, Suite 840, Washington, DC 20005, ☎ 202/783–6161, FAX 202/783–6171). **Hostelling International—Canada** (✉ 400–205 Catherine St., Ottawa, Ontario K2P 1C3, ☎ 613/237–7884, FAX 613/237–7868). **Youth Hostel Association of England and Wales** (✉ Trevelyan House, 8 St. Stephen's Hill, St. Albans, Hertfordshire AL1 2DY, ☎ 01727/855215 or 01727/845047, FAX 01727/844126). **Youth Hostels Association of New Zealand** (✉ Box 436, Christchurch, New Zealand, ☎ 03/379–9970, FAX 03/365–4476). Membership in the U.S. $25, in Canada C$26.75, in the U.K. £9.30, in Australia $44, in New Zealand $24.

HOTELS

Most major hotel chains are represented in California. All hotels listed have private bath unless otherwise noted.

➤ TOLL-FREE NUMBERS: **Adam's Mark** (☎ 800/444/2326). **Best Western** (☎ 800/528–1234). **Choice** (☎ 800/221–2222). **Clarion** (☎ 800/252–7466). **Colony** (☎ 800/777–1700). **Comfort** (☎ 800/228–5150). **Days Inn** (☎ 800/325–2525). **Doubletree and Red Lion Hotels** (☎ 800/222–8733). **Embassy Suites** (☎ 800/362–2779). **Fairfield Inn** (☎ 800/228–2800). **Forte** (☎ 800/225–5843). **Four Seasons** (☎ 800/332–3442). **Hilton** (☎ 800/445–8667). **Holiday Inn** (☎ 800/465–4329). **Howard Johnson** (☎ 800/654–4656). **Hyatt Hotels & Resorts** (☎ 800/233–1234). **Inter-Continental** (☎ 800/327–0200). **La Quinta** (☎ 800/531–5900). **Marriott** (☎ 800/228–9290). **Le Meridien** (☎ 800/543–4300). **Nikko Hotels International** (☎ 800/645–5687). **Omni** (☎ 800/843–6664). **Quality Inn** (☎ 800/228–5151). **Radisson** (☎ 800/333–3333). **Ramada** (☎ 800/228–2828). **Renaissance Hotels & Resorts** (☎ 800/468–3571). **Ritz-Carlton** (☎ 800/241–3333). **Sheraton** (☎ 800/325–3535). **Sleep Inn** (☎ 800/221–2222). **Westin Hotels & Resorts** (☎

800/228–3000). **Wyndham Hotels & Resorts** (☎ 800/822-4200).

MONEY MATTERS

Los Angeles and San Francisco tend to be expensive cities to visit, and rates at coastal and desert resorts are nearly comparable. Hotel rates average from $150 to $200 a night (though you can find less expensive places), and three-course meals at even moderately trendy restaurants often cost from $30 to $50 per person. Costs in the Gold Country, the Far North, and the Mojave Desert/Death Valley region are considerably less—many fine Gold Country B&Bs charge around $100 a night, and some motels in the Far North and the Mojave charge from $50 to $70. Prices throughout this guide are given for adults. Substantially reduced fees are almost always available for children, students, and senior citizens. For information on taxes, *see* Taxes, *below*.

ATMS

ATMs are readily available throughout California. If you're going to very remote areas of the mountains or deserts, take some extra cash with you or find out ahead of time if you can pay your way with credit cards.

CREDIT CARDS

Throughout this guide, the following abbreviations are used: **AE**, American Express; **D**, Discover; **DC**, Diner's Club; **MC**, Master Card; and **V**, Visa.

➤ REPORTING LOST CARDS: To report lost or stolen credit cards: **American Express** (☎ 800/327–2177); **Discover Card** (☎ 800/347–2683); **Diners Club** (☎ 800/234–6377); **Mastercard** (☎ 800/307–7309); and **Visa** (☎ 800/847–2911).

NATIONAL PARKS

Look into discount passes to save money on park entrance fees. The Golden Eagle Pass ($50) gets you and your companions free admission to all parks for one year. (Camping and parking are extra.) Both the Golden Age Passport ($10), for those 62 and older, and the Golden Access Passport (free), for travelers with disabilities, entitle holders to free entry to all national parks, plus 50% off fees for the use of many park facilities and services. You must show proof of age and of U.S. citizenship or permanent residency (such as a U.S. passport, driver's license, or birth certificate) and, if requesting Golden Access, proof of disability. All three passes are available at all national park entrances where entrance fees are charged. Golden Eagle and Golden Access passes are also available by mail.

➤ PASSES BY MAIL: **National Park Service** (⊠ National Capitol Area Office, 1100 Ohio Dr. SW, Washington, DC 20242, ☎ 202/208–4747).

STATE PARKS

➤ INFORMATION: **California State Park System** (⊠ Dept. of Parks and Recreation, Box 942896 Sacramento 94296, ☎ 916/653–6995).

OUTDOORS & SPORTS

California is an outdoors-lover's paradise—scale high peaks, hike through sequoia groves, fish, bike, sail, dive, ski, golf. Whatever sport you love, you can do it in California. See the individual regional chapters for more information.

FISHING

You'll need a license to fish in California. State residents pay $27.05 ($4.25 for senior citizens and those on limited income), but nonresidents are charged $73.50 for a one-year license, or $27.05 for a 10-day license. Both residents and nonresidents can purchase a one-day license for $9.70.

➤ INFORMATION: **Department of Fish and Game** (⊠ 3 211 S St., Sacramento 95816, ☎ 916/227–2244 or 916/227–2242).

PACKING

When packing for a California vacation, **prepare for changes in temperature.** Take along sweaters, jackets, and clothes for layering as your best insurance for coping with variations in temperature. Include shorts or cool cottons unless you are packing for a midwinter ski trip. Always tuck in a bathing suit; many lodgings have a pools, spas, and saunas. Casual dressing is a hallmark of the California lifestyle, but in the evening men will need a jacket and tie at some good restaurants, and women will be more comfortable in something dressier than sightseeing garb. Bear in mind that **San Francisco and other coastal towns can be chilly** at any time of the year, especially in summer, when the fog is apt to descend and stay.

In your carry-on luggage **bring an extra pair of eyeglasses or contact lenses** and **enough of any medication you take** to last the entire trip. You may also want your doctor to write a spare prescription using the drug's generic name, since brand names may vary from country to country. In luggage to be checked, **never pack prescription drugs or valuables.** To avoid customs delays, carry medications in their original packaging. And don't forget to copy down and carry addresses of offices that handle refunds of lost traveler's checks.

CHECKING LUGGAGE

How many carry-on bags you can bring with you is up to the airline. Most allow two, but not always, so make sure that everything you carry aboard will fit under your seat, and get to the gate early. Note that if you have a seat at the back of the plane, you'll probably board first, while the overhead bins are still empty.

If you are flying internationally, note that baggage allowances may be determined not by piece but by weight—generally 88 pounds (40 kilograms) in first class, 66 pounds (30 kilograms) in business class, and 44 pounds (20 kilograms) in economy.

Airline liability for baggage is limited to $1,250 per person on flights within the United States. On international flights it amounts to $9.07 per pound or $20 per kilogram for checked baggage (roughly $640 per 70-pound bag) and $400 per passenger for unchecked baggage. You can buy additional coverage at check-in for about $10 per $1,000 of coverage, but it excludes a rather extensive list of items, shown on your airline ticket.

Before departure **itemize your bags' contents** and their worth, and label the bags with your name, address, and phone number. (If you use your home address, cover it so that potential thieves can't see it readily.) Inside each bag **pack a copy of your itinerary.** At check-in **make sure that each bag is correctly tagged** with the destination airport's three-letter code. If your bags arrive damaged or fail to arrive at all, file a written report with the airline before leaving the airport.

PASSPORTS & VISAS

➤ U.K. CITIZENS: U.S. Embassy Visa Information Line (☎ 01891/200–290; calls cost 49p per minute, 39p per minute cheap rate) for U.S. visa information. **U.S. Embassy Visa Branch** (✉ 5 Upper Grosvenor Sq., London W1A 1AE) for U.S. visa information; send a self-addressed, stamped envelope. Write the **U.S. Consulate General** (✉ Queen's House, Queen St., Belfast BTI 6EO) if you live in Northern Ireland. Write the **Office of Australia Affairs** (✉ 59th fl., MLC Centre, 19-29 Martin Pl., Sydney NSW 2000) if you live in Australia. Write the **Office of New Zealand Affairs** (✉ 29 Fitzherbert Terr., Thorndon, Wellington) if you live in New Zealand.

PASSPORT OFFICES

The best time to apply for a passport or to renew is during the fall and winter. Before any trip, check your passport's expiration date, and, if necessary, renew it as soon as possible.

➤ AUSTRALIAN CITIZENS: **Australian Passport Office** (☎ 131–232).

➤ NEW ZEALAND CITIZENS: **New Zealand Passport Office** (☎ 04/494–0700 for information on how to apply; 04/474–8000 or 0800/225–050 in New Zealand for information on applications already submitted).

➤ U.K. CITIZENS: **London Passport Office** (☎ 0990/210–410) for fees and documentation requirements and to request an emergency passport.

SENIOR-CITIZEN TRAVEL

To qualify for age-related discounts **mention your senior-citizen status up front** when booking hotel reservations (not when checking out) and before you're seated in restaurants (not when paying the bill). When renting a car ask about promotional car-rental discounts, which can be cheaper than senior-citizen rates.

➤ EDUCATIONAL PROGRAMS: **Elderhostel** (✉ 75 Federal St., 3rd fl., Boston, MA 02110, ☎ 877/426–8056, FAX 877/426–2166).

STUDENTS IN CALIFORNIA

➤ STUDENT IDs & SERVICES: **Council on International Educational Exchange** (CIEE, ✉ 205 E. 42nd St., 14th fl., New York, NY 10017, ☎ 212/822–2600 or 888/268–6245, FAX 212/822–2699) for mail orders only, in the U.S. **Travel Cuts** (✉ 187 College St., Toronto, Ontario M5T 1P7, ☎ 416/979–2406 or 800/667–2887) in Canada.

TELEPHONES

CREDIT-CARD CALLS

U.S. telephone credit cards are not like the magnetic cards used in some European countries, which pay for calls in advance; they simply represent an account that lets you charge a call to your home or business phone. On any phone, you can make a credit-card call by punching in your individual account number or by telling the operator that number. Certain specially marked pay phones (usually found in airports, hotel lobbies, and so on) can be used only for credit-card calls. To get a credit card, contact your long-distance telephone carrier, such as AT&T, MCI, or Sprint.

AREA CODES

The insatiable appetite of Californians for faxes, cellular phones, and other telephonic gadgets has led to numerous changes in area codes. Areas in both southern California and northern California where new area codes were added just a few years ago will be receiving still more area codes—the 619, 310, 415, and 408 codes will split again in 1999 or 2000. For more details, visit Pacific Bell's Web site dedicated to the topic at www.pacbell.com/about-pb/area-codes.

DIRECTORY & OPERATOR INFORMATION

For assistance from an operator, dial "0". To find out a telephone number within the same area code you're calling from, dial 411; in a few places it is necessary to dial 555–1212. If you want to charge a long-distance call to the person you're calling, you can call collect by dialing "0" instead of "1" before the 10-digit number, and an operator will come on the line to assist you (the party you're calling, however, has the right to refuse the call).

INTERNATIONAL CALLS

International calls can be direct-dialed from most phones; dial 011, followed by the country code and then the local number (the front pages of many local telephone directories include a list of overseas country codes). To have an operator assist you, dial 0 and ask for the overseas operator. The country code for Australia is 61; New Zealand, 64; and the United Kingdom, 44. To reach Canada, dial 1 + area code + number.

LONG-DISTANCE CALLS

Competitive long-distance carriers make calling within the United States relatively convenient and let you avoid hotel surcharges. By dialing an 800 number, you can get connected to the long-distance company of your choice.

➤ LONG-DISTANCE CARRIERS: **AT&T** (☎ 800/225–5288). **MCI** (☎ 800/888–8000). **Sprint** (☎ 800/366–2255).

PUBLIC PHONES

Instructions for pay telephones should be posted on the phone, but generally you insert your coins—35¢ for most local calls—in a slot and wait for the steady hum of a dial tone before dialing the number you wish to reach. If you dial a long-distance number, the operator will come on the line and tell you how much more money you must insert for your call to go through.

TIPPING

At restaurants, a 15% tip is standard for waiters; up to 20% may be expected at more expensive establishments. The same goes for taxi drivers, bartenders, and hairdressers. Coat-check operators usually expect $1; bellhops and porters should get 50¢

to $1 per bag; hotel maids in upscale hotels should get about $1 per day of your stay. On package tours, conductors and drivers usually get $10 per day from the group as a whole; check whether this has already been figured into your cost. For local sightseeing tours, you may individually tip the driver-guide $1 if he or she has been helpful or informative. Ushers in theaters do not expect tips.

TOURS & PACKAGES

On a prepackaged tour or independent vacation everything is prearranged so you'll spend less time planning—and often get it all at a good price.

BOOKING WITH AN AGENT

Travel agents are excellent resources. But it's a good idea to collect brochures from several agencies because some agents' suggestions may be influenced by relationships with tour and package firms that reward them for volume sales. If you have a special interest **find an agent with expertise in that area**; ASTA (☞ Travel Agencies, *below*) has a database of specialists worldwide.

Make sure your travel agent knows the accommodations and other services of the place they're recommending. Ask about the hotel's location, room size, beds, and whether it has a pool, room service, or programs for children, if you care about these. Has your agent been there in person or sent others whom you can contact?

Do some homework on your own, too: Local tourism boards can provide information about lesser-known and small-niche operators, some of which may sell only direct.

BUYER BEWARE

Each year consumers are stranded or lose their money when tour operators—even large ones with excellent reputations—go out of business. So **check out the operator.** Ask several travel agents about its reputation, and try to **book with a company that has a consumer-protection program.** (Look for information in the company's brochure.) In the United States, members of the National Tour Association and United States Tour Operators Association are required to set aside funds to cover your payments and travel arrangements in case the company defaults. It's also a good idea to choose a company that participates in the American Society of Travel Agent's Tour Operator Program (TOP); ASTA will act as mediator in any disputes between you and your tour operator.

Remember that the more your package or tour includes the better you can predict the ultimate cost of your vacation. Make sure you know exactly what is covered, and **beware of hidden costs.** Are taxes, tips, and transfers included? Entertainment and excursions? These can add up.

➤ Tour-Operator Recommendations: **American Society of Travel Agents** (☞ Travel Agencies, *below*). **National Tour Association** (NTA, ✉ 546 E. Main St., Lexington, KY 40508, ☎ 606/226–4444 or 800/682–8886). **United States Tour Operators Association** (USTOA, ✉ 342 Madison Ave., Suite 1522, New York, NY 10173, ☎ 212/599–6599 or 800/468–7862, FAX 212/599–6744).

GROUP TOURS

Among companies that sell tours to California, the following are nationally known, have a proven reputation, and offer plenty of options. The classifications used below represent different price categories, and you'll probably encounter these terms when talking to a travel agent or tour operator. The key difference is usually in accommodations, which run from budget to better, and better-yet to best.

➤ Deluxe: **Globus** (☎ 303/797–2800 or 800/221–0090). **Maupintour** (☎ 913/843–1211 or 800/255–4266). **Tauck Tours** ☎ 203/226–6911 or 800/468–2825).

➤ First Class: **Brendan Tours** (☎ 818/785–9696 or 800/421–8446). **Caravan Tours** (☎ 312/321–9800 or 800/227–2826). **Collette Tours** (☎ 401/728–3805 or 800/340–5158). **Gadabout Tours** (☎ 760/325–5556 or 800/952–5068). **Mayflower Tours** (☎ 708/960–3430 or 800/323–7064). **Trafalgar Tours** (☎ 212/689–8977 or 800/854–0103).

➤ BUDGET: **Cosmos** (☎ 303/797–2800 or 800/221–0090).

PACKAGES

Like group tours, independent vacation packages are available from major tour operators and airlines. The companies listed below offer vacation packages in a broad price range.

➤ AIR/HOTEL: **American Airlines Vacations** (☎ 800/321–2121). **Continental Vacations** (☎ 800/634–5555). **Delta Vacations** (☎ 800/872–7786, FAX 954/357–4687). **United Vacations** (☎ 800/328–6877). **US Airways Vacations** (☎ 800/455–0123).

➤ CUSTOM PACKAGES: **Amtrak Vacations** (☎ 800/321–8684).

➤ FLY/DRIVE: **American Airlines Vacations** (☎ 800/321–2121). . **Continental Vacations** (☎ 800/634–5555) **United Vacations** (☎ 800/328–6877).

➤ HOTEL ONLY: **Globetrotters** (☎ 800/333–1234).

THEME TRIPS

➤ ADVENTURE: **Access to Adventure** (☎ 530/469–3322 or 800/552–6284). **American Wilderness Experience** (☎ 303/444–2622 or 800/444–0099). **Mountain Travel-Sobek** (☎ 510/527–8100 or 888/687–6235). **Tahoe Trips & Trails** (☎ 530/583–4506 or 800/581–4453).

➤ BICYCLING: **Backroads** (☎ 510/527–1555 or 800/462–2848). **Imagine Tours** (☎ 530/758–8782 or 888/592–8687).

➤ FISHING: **Fishing International** (☎ 707/539–3366 or 800/950–4242). **Rod & Reel Adventures** (☎ 209/785–0444).

➤ LEARNING: **Naturequest** (☎ 949/499–9561 or 800/369–3033). **Oceanic Society Expeditions** (☎ 415/441–1106 or 800/326–7491). **Smithsonian Study Tours and Seminars** (☎ 202/357–4700).

➤ RIVER RAFTING: **Access to Adventure** (☞ Adventure, *above*). **James Henry River Tours** (☎ 415/868–1836 or 800/786–1830). **OARS** (☎ 209/736–4677 or 800/346–6277). White-

water **Voyages** (☎ 510/222–5994 or 800/488–7238).

➤ TENNIS: **Championship Tennis Tours** (☎ 602/990–8760 or 800/468–3664).➤ TRAIL RUNNING: **Backroads** (☞ Bicycling, *above*).

➤ WALKING/HIKING: **American Wilderness Experience**(☞ Adventure, *above*). **Backroads** (☞ Bicycling, *above*).

➤ YACHT CHARTERS: **Five Star Charters** (☎ 415/332–7187 or 800/762–6287).

TRAIN TRAVEL

Amtrak's *California Zephyr* train from Chicago via Denver terminates in Oakland. The *Coast Starlight* train travels between southern California and the state of Washington. The *Sunset Limited* heads west from Florida through New Orleans and Texas to Los Angeles.

➤ TRAIN INFORMATION: **Amtrak** (☎ 800/872–7245).

TRAVEL AGENCIES

A good travel agent puts your needs first. Look for an agency that has been in business at least five years, emphasizes customer service, and has someone on staff who specializes in your destination. In addition **make sure the agency belongs to a professional trade organization.** The American Society of Travel Agents (ASTA), with 27,000 agents in some 170 countries, is the largest and most influential in the field. Operating under the motto "Integrity in Travel," it maintains and enforces a strict code of ethics and will step in to help mediate any agent-client disputes if necessary. ASTA also maintains a Web site that includes a directory of agents. (Note that if a travel agency is also acting as your tour operator, *see* Buyer Beware *in* Tours & Packages, *above*.)

➤ LOCAL AGENT REFERRALS: **American Society of Travel Agents** (ASTA, ☎ 800/965–2782 24-hr hot line, FAX 703/684–8319). **Association of British Travel Agents** (✉ 55–57 Newman St., London W1P 4AH, ☎ 0171/637–2444, FAX 0171/637–0713). **Association of Canadian Travel Agents** (✉ 1729 Bank St., Suite 201,

Ottawa, Ontario K1V 7Z5, ☎ 613/
521–0474, FAX 613/521–0805). **Australian Federation of Travel Agents**
(✉ Level 3, 309 Pitt St., Sydney 2000,
☎ 02/9264–3299, FAX 02/9264–
1085). **Travel Agents' Association of
New Zealand** (✉ Box 1888, Wellington 10033, ☎ 04/499–0104, FAX 04/
499–0786).

VISITOR INFORMATION

For general information about California, contact the state tourism
office; for the numbers of regional
and city visitors bureaus and chambers of commerce, see the A to Z
sections at the end of Chapters 2 to
16.

➤ STATEWIDE INFORMATION: **California Division of Tourism** (✉ 801 K
St., Suite 1600, Sacramento, CA
95814, ☎ 916/322–2881 or 800/
862–2543, FAX 916/322–3402 or 916/
322–0501).

➤ IN THE U.K.: **California Tourist
Office** (✉ ABC California, Box 35,
Abingdon, Oxfordshire OX14 4TB,
☎ 0891/200–278, FAX 0171/242–
2838). Calls cost 50p per minute peak
rate or 45p per minute cheap rate.
Brochures can be obtained by sending
to the above address a cheque for £3
made to ABC California.

WEB SITES

Do **check out the World Wide Web**
when you're planning. You'll find
everything from up-to-date weather
forecasts to virtual tours of famous
cities. Fodor's Web site, www.fodors.
com, is a great place to start your online travels. For more information
specifically on California, visit the
following sites.

GENERAL INFORMATION

The **California Division of Tourism
web site** has travel tips, events calen-
dars, and other resources, and the site
will link you—via the Regions icon—
to the web sites of city and regional
tourism offices and attractions.
www.gocalif.ca.gov/

THE GREAT OUTDOORS

The no-frills site of the **California
Department of Fish and Game** provides information on fishing and
hunting zones, licenses, and schedules. www.dfg.ca.gov/

The **California Parks Department** site
has the lowdown on state-run parks
and other recreational areas.
cal-parks.ca.gov/

A must-visit for outdoors and adventure travel enthusiasts, the **Great
Outdoor Recreation Page** is arranged
into three easily navigated categories:
attractions, activities, and locations.
www.gorp.com/

DAILIES

The **Los Angeles Times** is the state's
largest newspaper. www.latimes.com/

NEWSWEEKLIES

The state's newsweeklies are a great
source of up-to-the-minute arts and
entertainment information, from
what shows are on the boards to
who's playing the clubs.

L.A. Weekly maintains a hip site with
lively features and and insiders'
guides to dining, the arts, and
nightlife in the L.A. metro area.
www.laweekly.com/

The smart features on **MetroActive,**
the online version of *San Jose Metro*,
include guides to nightlife, the arts,
dining, and entertainment in the San
Francisco Bay Area, including Silicon
Valley and Santa Cruz.
www.sanjosemetro.com/

The site of the **San Diego Reader** isn't
visually impressive, but it provides a
thorough guide to what's happening
in San Diego. www.sdreader.com/

For Tales of the City, or simply for
good entertainment and dining information, check out the **San Francisco
Bay Guardian.**
www.sfbayguardian.com/

The colorful and easy-to-navigate
web site of **SF Weekly** has the lowdown on the San Francisco Bay Area.
www.sfweekly.com/

WINERIES

The site of the **Wine Institute,** which is
based in San Francisco, provides
events listings and detailed information about the California wine industry and has links to the home pages of
regional wine associations.
www.wineinstitute.org/

WHEN TO GO

Any time of the year is the right time to go to California. There won't be skiable snow in the mountains between Easter and Thanksgiving. There will usually be rain in December, January, and February in the lowlands. It will be much too hot to enjoy Palm Springs or Death Valley in the summer. But San Francisco, Los Angeles, and San Diego are delightful year-round; the Wine Country's seasonal variables are enticing; and the coastal areas are almost always cool.

CLIMATE

The climate varies amazingly in California, not only over distances of several hundred miles but occasionally within an hour's drive. A foggy, cool August day in San Francisco makes you grateful for a sweater, tweed jacket, or light wool coat. Head north 50 mi to the Napa Valley to check out the Wine Country and you'll probably wear shirt sleeves and thin cottons.

Daytime and nighttime temperatures may also swing widely apart. Take Sacramento, a city that is at sea level but in California's Central Valley. In the summer, afternoons can be very warm, in the 90s and occasionally over 100°. But the nights cool down, often dropping 40°.

It's hard to generalize much about the weather in this varied state. Rain comes in the winter, with snow at higher elevations. Summers are dry everywhere. As a rule, compared to the coastal areas, which are cool year-round, inland regions are warmer in summer and cooler in winter. As you climb into the mountains, there are more distinct variations with the seasons: Winter brings snow, autumn is crisp, spring is variable, and summer is clear and warm.

➤ FORECASTS: **Weather Channel Connection** (☎ 900/932–8437), 95¢ per minute from a Touch-Tone phone.

The following are average daily maximum and minimum temperatures for the major California cities.

Climate in California

LOS ANGELES

Jan.	64F	18C	May	72F	22C	Sept.	81F	27C
	44	7		53	12		60	16
Feb.	64F	18C	June	76F	24C	Oct.	76F	24C
	46	8		57	14		55	13
Mar.	66F	19C	July	81F	27C	Nov.	71F	22C
	48	9		60	16		48	9
Apr.	70F	21C	Aug.	82F	28C	Dec.	66F	19C
	51	11		62	17		46	8

SAN DIEGO

Jan.	62F	17C	May	66F	19C	Sept.	73F	23C
	46	8		55	13		62	17
Feb.	62F	17C	June	69F	21C	Oct.	71F	22C
	48	9		59	15		57	14
Mar.	64F	18C	July	73F	23C	Nov.	69F	21C
	50	10		62	17		51	11
Apr.	66F	19C	Aug.	73F	23C	Dec.	64F	18C
	53	12		64	18		48	9

SAN FRANCISCO

Jan.	55F	13C	May	66F	19C	Sept.	73F	23C
	41	5		48	9		51	11
Feb.	59F	15C	June	69F	21C	Oct.	69F	21C
	42	6		51	11		50	10
Mar.	60F	16C	July	69F	21C	Nov.	64F	18C
	44	7		51	11		44	7
Apr.	62F	17C	Aug.	69F	21C	Dec.	57F	14C
	46	8		53	12		42	6

FESTIVALS AND SEASONAL EVENTS

➤ JANUARY: Palo Alto's annual **East-West Shrine All-Star Football Classic** (☎ 415/661–0291) is America's oldest all-star sports event. In Pasadena, the annual **Tournament of Roses Parade and Football Game** (☎ 626/449–7673) takes place on New Year's Day, with lavish flower-decked floats, marching bands, and equestrian teams, followed by the Rose Bowl game.

➤ FEBRUARY: The legendary **AT&T Pebble Beach National Pro-Am** golf tournament (☎ 831/649–1533) begins in late January and ends in early February. San Francisco's Chinatown is the scene of parades and noisy fireworks, all part of a several-day **Chinese New Year Celebration** (☎ 415/982–3000). Los Angeles also has a **Chinese New Year Parade** (☎ 213/617–0396). Indio's **Riverside County Fair and National Date Festival** (☎ 800/811–3247) is an exotic event with an Arabian Nights theme; camel and ostrich races, date exhibits, and tastings are among the draws.

➤ MARCH: **Snowfest** in North Lake Tahoe (☎ 530/583–7625) is the largest winter carnival in the West, with skiing, food, fireworks, parades, and live music. The finest female golfers in the world compete for the richest purse on the LPGA circuit at the **Nabisco Dinah Shore Golf Tournament** in Rancho Mirage (☎ 760/324–4546). The **Mendocino/Fort Bragg Whale Festival** (☎ 800/726–2780) includes whale-watching excursions, marine art exhibits, wine and beer tastings, crafts displays, and a chowder contest.

➤ APRIL: The **Cherry Blossom Festival** (☎ 415/563–2313), an elaborate presentation of Japanese culture and customs, winds up with a colorful parade through San Francisco's Japantown. The **Toyota Grand Prix** (☎ 562/436–9953) in Long Beach, the largest street race in North America, draws top competitors from all over the world.➤ MAY: Thousands sign up to run the **San Francisco Examiner Bay to Breakers Race** (☎ 415/777–7770), a 7½-mile route from bay side to ocean side that's a hallowed San Francisco tradition. In-

spired by Mark Twain's story "The Notorious Jumping Frog of Calaveras County," the **Jumping Frog Jubilee** in Angels Camp (☎ 209/736–2561) is for frogs and trainers who take their competition seriously. Sacramento hosts the four-day **Sacramento Jazz Jubilee** (☎ 916/372–5277); the late-May event is the world's largest Dixieland festival, with 125 bands from around the world. In Monterey, the squirmy squid is the main attraction for the Memorial Day weekend **Great Monterey Squid Festival** (☎ 831/649–6544). You'll see squid-cleaning and -cooking demonstrations, taste treats, and enjoy the usual festival fare: entertainment, arts and crafts, and educational exhibits.

➤ JUNE: Starting in late May and running into early June is a national ceramics competition and exhibition called **Feats of Clay** in the Gold Country (☎ 916/645–9713). The **Summer Solstice Ride & Arts Celebration** (☎ 209/223–5145) boosts spirits with bicycle rides, walks, and hands-on arts-and-crafts workshops for adults and children in Plymouth. During the first weekend in June, Pasadena City Hall Plaza hosts the **Chalk It Up Festival.** Artists use the pavement as their canvas to create masterpieces that wash away when festivities have come to a close. There are also musical performances and exotic dining kiosks. The proceeds benefit arts and homeless organizations of the Light-Bringer Project (☎ 626/440–7379). The **Napa Valley Wine Auction** in St. Helena features open houses, a wine tasting, and an auction. Preregistration by fax in early March is required (☎ 707/942–9775, FAX 707/942–0171). During the latter part of June, Ojai hosts a noted outdoor **classical music festival** (☎ 805/646–2094).

➤ JULY: During the **Carmel Bach Festival,** the works of Johann Sebastian Bach and 18th-century contemporaries are performed for three weeks; events include concerts, recitals, and seminars (☎ 831/624–1521). During the last full weekend in July, Gilroy, the self-styled Garlic Capital of the World, celebrates its smelly but delicious product with the **Gilroy Garlic Festival** (☎ 408/842–

1625), featuring such unusual concoctions as garlic ice cream.

➤ AUGUST: The **Cabrillo Music Festival** in Santa Cruz (☎ 831/426–6966), one of the longest-running contemporary orchestral festivals, brings in American and other composers for two weeks in early August. The **California State Fair** (☎ 916/263–3000) showcases the state's agricultural side, with high-tech exhibits, a rodeo, horse racing, a carnival, and big-name entertainment. It runs 18 days from August to Labor Day in Sacramento. Santa Barbara's **Old Spanish Days' Fiesta** (☎ 805/962–8101) is the nation's largest all-equestrian parade, featuring riders on horses and horses pulling 19th-century carriages. The citywide celebration includes two parades, two Mexican marketplaces, free variety shows with costumed dancers and singers, a carnival, and a rodeo.

➤ SEPTEMBER: In Guerneville, jazz fans and musicians jam at Johnson's Beach for the **Russian River Jazz Festival** (☎ 707/869–3940). The **San Francisco Blues Festival** (☎ 415/826–6837) is held at Fort Mason in late September. The **Los Angeles County Fair** in Pomona (☎ 909/623–3111) is the largest county fair in the world. It hosts entertainment, exhibits, livestock, horse racing, food, and more.

➤ OCTOBER: The **Grand National Rodeo, Horse, and Stock Show** (☎ 415/469–6057) at San Francisco's Cow Palace is a 10-day, world-class competition straddling the end of October and the beginning of November. In Carmel, speakers and poets gather for readings on the beach, seminars, a banquet, and a book signing at the **Pismo Beach Clam Festival** on the Central Coast. Restaurants along Pomeroy Avenue engage in a competition for the best clam chowder. The **Tor House Poetry Festival** (☎ 831/624–1813) honors the late poet Robinson Jeffers, an area resident for many years.

➤ NOVEMBER: The **Death Valley '49er Encampment,** at Furnace Creek, commemorates the historic crossing of Death Valley in 1849, with a fiddlers' contest and an art show (☎ 760/786–2331). Pasadena's **Doo Dah Parade,** a fun-filled spoof of the annual Rose Parade, features the Lounge Lizards, who dress as reptiles and lip-synch to Frank Sinatra favorites, and West Hollywood cheerleaders in drag (☎ 626/440–7379).

➤ DECEMBER: For the **Newport Harbor Christmas Boat Parade** in Newport Beach (☎ 714/729–4400), more than 200 festooned boats glide through the harbor nightly December 17–23. In Columbia in early December, the **Miner's Christmas Celebration** features costumed carolers and children's piñatas. Related events include a Victorian Christmas feast at the City Hotel, lamplight tours, and **Las Posados Nativity Procession** (☎ 209/536–1672). The internationally acclaimed **El Teatro Campesino** (☎ 831/623–2444) annually stages its nativity play *La Virgen Del Tepeyac* in the Mission San Juan Bautista.

INDEX

NOTES

NOTES

L@@king
© FOR A
great place to go?

We know just the place. In fact, it attracts more than 125,000 visitors a day, making it one of the world's most popular travel destinations. It's previewtravel.com, the Web's comprehensive resource for travelers. It gives you access to over 500 airlines, 25,000 hotels, rental cars, cruises, vacation packages and support from travel experts 24 hours a day. Plus great information from Fodor's travel guides and travelers just like you. All of which makes previewtravel.com quite a find.

Preview Travel has everything you need to plan & book your next trip.

**air, car & hotel
reservations**

**vacation packages
& cruises**

**destination planning
& travel tips**

**24-hour
customer service**

previewtravel.com

preview
travel℠

aol keyword: previewtravel
www.previewtravel.com

FODOR'S CALIFORNIA

EDITOR: Jennifer Levitsky Kasoff

Editorial Contributors: Lotus Abrams, Sasha Abramsky, Christopher Baty, Herb Benham, Jeffrey Boswell, Deke Castleman, Arian Collins, Kate Deely, Stephen Dolainski, Caroline Haberfeld, Lisa Hamilton, Edie Jarolim, Lina Lecaro, Denise M. Leto, Tim Lohnes, Daniel Mangin, Amy McConnell, Andy Moore, Clark Norton, Marty Olmstead, Lisa Oppenheimer, Kathryn Shevelow, Sharon Silva, Bill Stern, Cynthia LaFavre Yorks, Bobbi Zane

Editorial Production: Nicole Revere

Maps: David Lindroth, *cartographer*; Robert Blake, Steven K. Amsterdam, *map editors*

Design: Fabrizio La Rocca, *creative director*; Guido Caroti, *art director*

Cover Design: Pentagram

Picture Editor: Jolie Novak

Photo Researcher: Melanie Marin

Production/Manufacturing: Robert B. Shields

ISBN 0-679-00343-6

ISSN 0192-9925

SPECIAL SALES
Fodor's Travel Publications are available at special discounts for bulk purchases for sales promotions or premiums. Special editions, including personalized covers, excerpts of existing guides, and corporate imprints, can be created in large quantities for special needs. For more information, contact your local bookseller or write to Special Markets, Fodor's Travel Publications, 201 East 50th Street, New York, NY 10022. Inquiries from Canada should be directed to your local Canadian bookseller or sent to Random House of Canada, Ltd., Marketing Department, 2775 Matheson Boulevard East, Mississauga, Ontario L4W 4P7. Inquiries from the United Kingdom should be sent to Fodor's Travel Publications, 20 Vauxhall Bridge Road, London SW1V 2SA, England.

PRINTED IN THE UNITED STATES OF AMERICA
10 9 8 7 6 5 4 3 2 1

IMPORTANT TIP
Although all prices, opening times, and other details in this book are based on information supplied to us at press time, changes occur all the time in the travel world, and Fodor's cannot accept responsibility for facts that become outdated or for inadvertent errors or omissions. So **always confirm information when it matters,** especially if you're making a detour to visit a specific place.

PHOTOGRAPHY
Corbis: *Darrell Gulin*, cover (Yosemite).

Amargosa Opera House, Inc.: *Tony Scodwell, 24B.*

CalTour: *Robert Holmes, 2 top left, 2 top right, 2 bottom right, 3 top right, 3 bottom left, 6C, 7A, 7C, 8B, 10A, 14A, 14B, 21B, 21C, 27B, 30C, 30F, 30H. John Poimiroo, 12C.*

Château du Sureau, *30E.*

©Disney Enterprises, *20B.*

Hearst San Simeon State Historical Monument: *Ellis-Sawyer, 17B.*

Robert Holmes, *7B, 8C, 9D, 13A, 15A, 15B, 23D.*

Hotel Bel-Air, *30G.*

The Image Bank: *Alan Becker, 24A. Luis Castañeda, 28C. Gary Cralle, 9F. Macduff Everton, 17A. Grant V. Faint, 19E, 26A, 32. Tracy Frankel, 1. Larry Dale Gordon, 19D. GK & Vikki Hart, 10B. Eddie Hironaka, 18–19A. Jeff Hunter, 30I. R. Johnson, 25F. Tom Mareschal, 16A. Michael Melford, 8 bottom. Piecework Productions, 6A, 9E, 11C, 12B, 16C, 25E. Andrea Pistolesi, 11E, 29D. Charles C. Place, 19F, 23B. Steve Proehl, 16D. Harald Sund, 6B, 25D. Joseph Van Os, 16B. Ulf E. Wallin, 24C. Stephen Wilkes, 8A, 18B, 20A.*

Kimpton Group: *Fred Licht, 3 bottom right, 30J.*

Lake Tahoe Visitors Authority, *13B.*

La Quinta Resort & Club, *23C.*

James Lemass, *11D, 21A.*

Montrio Restaurant: *Russell Levin Photography, 30B.*

Northstar-at-Tahoe, *2 bottom center.*

The Ritz-Carlton, Laguna Niguel, *30D.*

Robert Ordway, *13C.*

Palm Springs Tourism, *3 top left, 22A.*

San Diego Convention & Visitors Bureau: *James Blank, 29E. Bob Yarbrough, 2 bottom left.*

Santa Barbara Mission, *30A.*

Universal Studios, *18C.*

Nik Wheeler, *4–5, 12A, 15 bottom, 20C.*

ABOUT OUR WRITERS

EVERY Y2K TRIP is a significant trip. So if there was ever a time you needed excellent travel information, it's now. Acutely aware of that fact, we've pulled out all stops in preparing Fodor's California 2000. To help you zero in on what to see in California, we've gathered some great color photos of the key sights in every region. To show you how to put it all together, we've created great itineraries and neighborhood walks. And to direct you to the places that are truly worth your time and money in this important year, we've rallied the team of endearingly picky know-it-alls we're pleased to call our writers. Having seen all corners of the regions they cover for us, they're real experts. If you knew them, you'd poll them for tips yourself.

Sasha Abramsky, a freelance journalist for numerous publications, took on two very different regions this year: the beautiful Central Coast and the haunting Mojave Desert and Death Valley. A frequent visitor to California whose relatives live in the southern part of the state, he enjoyed the chance to explore the coast and the desert.

Herb Benham has lived in the San Joaquin Valley 34 of his 44 years. He has been a columnist for the *Bakersfield Californian* for the last 12 years. His father was a cotton and almond farmer, so Herb got to know the Valley from the ground up.

Deke Castleman, who updated the Lake Tahoe chapter, grew up in New York and Boston but fled the East Coast for the wide-open spaces of the American West. He discovered the region's many wonders while engaged in a variety of occupations—door-to-door vacuum-cleaner salesman in central California, tour guide at Alaska's Denali National Park, and locksmith on Lake Tahoe's north shore.

Tim Lohnes took a break from playing croquet by the lake in Oakland to update the Far North chapter. Highlights from the travel were constant rainy days and the lack of snake sightings.

Andy Moore was born across the street from Disney Studios near downtown Burbank. His childhood included many family vacations throughout the Golden State, including gold-panning expeditions with his grandfather, memories he relived while updating the Sacramento and the Gold Country chapter. Andy, a 20-year San Francisco resident, also updated the Lodging section of the San Francisco chapter.

Clark Norton, author of Fodor's *Where Do We Take the Kids? California,* updated the Monterey Bay and Sierra National Parks chapters. The recipient of several major travel-writing awards, Clark has written about traveling with children for *Parenting, Family Fun, California Travel Ideas, Baby Talk,* and the *San Francisco Examiner.*

Marty Olmstead, who updated the North Coast and Wine Country chapters, writes a column about the Wine Country for the *Marin Independent Journal.* She lives in Sonoma County.

Bobbi Zane, who updated the Palm Springs chapter, has been visiting the region since her grandfather, a Hollywood producer, took her on weekend getaways to La Quinta Resort. She is a frequent Fodor's contributor. With her husband, Gregg, she publishes *Yellow Brick Road,* a newsletter about bed-and-breakfast inns.

We would also like to thank the many writers involved with the San Francisco, Los Angeles, Orange County, and San Diego chapters.

Don't Forget to Write

We love feedback—positive and negative—and follow up on all suggestions. So contact the California editor at editors@fodors.com or c/o Fodor's, 201 East 50th Street, New York, New York 10022. Have a wonderful trip!

Karen Cure

Karen Cure
Editorial Director